CURRENT LAW STATUTES ANNOTATED
1992

VOLUME ONE

AUSTRALIA
The Law Book Company
Brisbane ● Sydney ● Melbourne ● Perth

CANADA
Carswell
Ottawa ● Toronto ● Calgary ● Montreal ● Vancouver

Agents:
Steimatzky's Agency Ltd., Tel Aviv;
N. M. Tripathi (Private) Ltd., Bombay;
Eastern Law House (Private) Ltd., Calcutta;
M.P.P. House, Bangalore;
Universal Book Traders, Delhi;
Aditya Books, Delhi;
MacMillan Shuppan KK, Tokyo;
Pakistan Law House, Karachi

CURRENT LAW

STATUTES

ANNOTATED

1992

VOLUME ONE

SWEET & MAXWELL EDITORIAL TEAM
SARAH ANDREWS
CAROLINE EADIE
BARBARA GRANDAGE
PHILIPPA JOHNSON
SOPHIE LOWE
BETHAN OWEN
ROSANNA ROTHERY
CLARE TURNER
HELEN WAUCHOPE

W. GREEN EDITORIAL TEAM
ELANOR BOWER
ALISON GAY
PETER NICHOLSON
IAN YOUNG

LONDON

SWEET & MAXWELL

EDINBURGH

W. GREEN

1992

Published by
SWEET & MAXWELL LIMITED
of South Quay Plaza, 183 Marsh Wall, London E14 9FT
Typeset by MFK Typesetting Ltd., Hitchin, Herts.
Printed in Great Britain
by The Bath Press,
Bath, Avon.

ISBN This Volume only : 0 421 48650 3
As a set   : 0 421 48690 2

CONTENTS

Chronological Table . . . . *page* v

Index of Short Titles vii

CHRONOLOGICAL TABLE

VOLUME ONE

VOLUME ONE

- *c.*1. Consolidated Fund Act 1992
- 2. Stamp Duty (Temporary Provisions) Act 1992
- 3. Severn Bridges Act 1992
- 4. Social Security Contributions and Benefits Act 1992
- 5. Social Security Administration Act 1992
- 6. Social Security (Consequential Provisions) Act 1992
- 7. Social Security Contributions and Benefits (Northern Ireland) Act 1992
- 8. Social Security Administration (Northern Ireland) Act 1992
- 9. Social Security (Consequential Provisions) (Northern Ireland) Act 1992

INDEX OF SHORT TITLES

STATUTES 1992

(References are to chapter numbers of 1992)

Consolidated Fund Act 1992	1
Severn Bridges Act 1992	3
Social Security Administration Act 1992	5
Social Security Administration (Northern Ireland) Act 1992	8
Social Security (Consequential Provisions) Act 1992	6
Social Security (Consequential Provisions) (Northern Ireland) Act 1992	9
Social Security Contributions and Benefits Act 1992	4
Social Security Contributions and Benefits (Northern Ireland) Act 1992	7
Stamp Duty (Temporary Provisions) Act 1992	2

CONSOLIDATED FUND ACT 1992

(1992 c. 1)

An Act to apply certain sums out of the Consolidated Fund to the service of the years ending on 31st March 1992 and 1993.   [13th February 1992]

PARLIAMENTARY DEBATES
Hansard, H.C. Vol. 203, col. 998; H.L. Vol. 535, col. 843.

INTRODUCTION
This Act provides for the application of £450,000,000 from the Consolidated Fund for the year ending March 31, 1992, and for the application of £1,000 for the year ending March 31, 1992.

Issue out of the Consolidated Fund for the year ending 31st March 1992

1. The Treasury may issue out of the Consolidated Fund of the United Kingdom and apply towards making good the supply granted to Her Majesty for the service of the year ending on 31st March 1992 the sum of £450,000,000.

Issue out of the Consolidated Fund for the year ending 31st March 1993

2. The Treasury may issue out of the Consolidated Fund of the United Kingdom and apply towards making good the supply granted to Her Majesty for the service of the year ending on 31st March 1993 the sum of £1,000.

Short title

3. This Act may be cited as the Consolidated Fund Act 1992.

INDEX

References are to section numbers

CITATION, 3

ISSUES OUT OF CONSOLIDATED FUND,
   year ending March 31, 1992, 1
   year ending March 31, 1993, 2

STAMP DUTY (TEMPORARY PROVISIONS) ACT 1992

(1992 c. 2)

An Act to make provision conferring temporary relief from stamp duty and provision for payments by the Commissioners of Inland Revenue in respect of instruments already stamped.   [13th February 1992]

PARLIAMENTARY DEBATES
Hansard, H.C. Vol. 202, col. 117; H.L. Vol. 535, col. 682.

INTRODUCTION
This Act provides for temporary relief from stamp duty by altering the Finance Act 1963, s.55 and the Finance Act (Northern Ireland) 1963, s.4. The Act is retrospective in effect, being deemed to have come into force on January 16, 1992 and provision is made for the repayment of moneys paid in respect of duty which would not now be chargeable.

Temporary relief from stamp duty

1.—(1) In relation to instruments to which this section applies, section 55 of the Finance Act 1963 (rate of stamp duty on conveyance or transfer on sale) and section 4 of the Finance Act (Northern Ireland) 1963 (equivalent provision for Northern Ireland) shall have effect as if—

    (a) each reference to £30,000 in subsection (1) of each of those sections were to £250,000, and

    (b) the reference to £300 in subsection (2) of each of those sections were to £2,500.

(2) This section applies to—

    (a) instruments executed on or after 20th December 1991 and before 16th January 1992 and not stamped before 16th January 1992;

    (b) instruments executed on or after 16th January 1992 and before 20th August 1992.

(3) For the purposes of section 14(4) of the Stamp Act 1891 (instruments not to be given in evidence etc. unless stamped in accordance with the law in force at the time of first execution) the law in force at the time of execution of an instrument falling within subsection (2)(a) above shall be deemed to be that as varied in accordance with subsection (1) above.

(4) This section shall be deemed to have come into force on 16th January 1992.

Payments in respect of stamped instruments

2.—(1) This section applies where—

    (a) the Commissioners are satisfied in the case of an instrument that it was executed on or after 20th December 1991 and before 16th January 1992 and stamped before 16th January 1992,

    (b) the Commissioners are satisfied that stamp duty was chargeable in respect of the instrument and that, had it not been stamped before 16th January 1992, no stamp duty would have been chargeable in respect of it or less stamp duty would have been chargeable than was in fact chargeable,

    (c) a claim is made under this section before the expiry of the period of one year beginning with the day on which the instrument was executed, and

    (d) such other conditions (if any) as the Commissioners may determine are satisfied.

(2) In such a case the Commissioners shall pay to such person as the Commissioners consider appropriate an amount equal to the duty which would not have been chargeable.

(3) Conditions under subsection (1)(d) above may relate to the production of the instrument, to its being stamped so as to indicate that it has been produced under this section, or to other matters.

(4) For the purposes of section 10 of the Exchequer and Audit Departments Act 1866 (Commissioners to deduct repayments from gross revenues) any amount paid under this section shall be treated as a repayment.

Citation and construction

3.—(1) This Act may be cited as the Stamp Duty (Temporary Provisions) Act 1992.

(2) This Act shall be construed as one with the Stamp Act 1891.

INDEX

References are to section numbers

CITATION, 3(1)
CONSIDERATION,
    £30,000 limit raised to £250,000, 1(1)(a)
    £300 limit raised to £2,500, 1(1)(b)
CONSTRUCTION, 3(2)

DATES OF EXECUTION OF INSTRUMENTS,
    between January 16, 1992 and August 20,
        1992, 1(2)(b)
    between December 20, 1991 and January
        16, 1992, 1(2)(a)

EFFECTIVE DATE, 1(4)
EVIDENTIAL REQUIREMENTS, 1(3)

REPAYMENT CLAIMS FOR STAMPED INSTRUMENTS,
    2

UNSTAMPED INSTRUMENTS, 1(2)(a)

SEVERN BRIDGES ACT 1992

(1992 c. 3)

ARRANGEMENT OF SECTIONS

PART I

CONSTRUCTION OF NEW SEVERN BRIDGE

SECT.
1. Construction of new bridge and other works.
2. Acquisition and occupation of land.
3. Authorised works: supplementary.

PART II

OPERATION OF SEVERN BRIDGES

Introductory

4. Concession agreement.

Tolls

5. Power of Secretary of State to levy tolls.
6. Exercise of power to levy tolls by concessionaire.
7. Early end of tolling by Secretary of State.
8. Vehicles subject to tolls.
9. Level of tolls.
10. Level of tolls: supplementary.
11. Two-way tolling.
12. Temporary suspension of tolls.
13. Pre-payment of tolls.
14. Payment regulations and offences.

Management of bridges etc.

15. Exercise of relevant functions by concessionaire.
16. Delegation of relevant functions.
17. Grant to concessionaire of interests in land.
18. Avon County Council bridge staff.
19. Termination of concession agreement.
20. Termination: supplementary.

Regulation of traffic etc.

21. Prevention of obstruction.
22. Special traffic restrictions.
23. Appointed persons.
24. Prevention of damage etc.
25. Use of cycleway or footway.

Financial matters

26. Recovery of tolls and charges.
27. Accounts provided by concessionaire.
28. Accounts of Secretary of State.

PART III

MISCELLANEOUS AND GENERAL

Interference with river Severn

29. Works affecting river Severn.
30. Dredging etc.

31. Protection of new bridge.

Miscellaneous

32. Toll plaza areas and vehicle pounds.
33. Consent of National Rivers Authority etc.
34. Rates.
35. Planning permission.

General

36. Offences by bodies corporate.
37. Orders and regulations.
38. Financial provisions.
39. Interpretation.
40. Repeals.
41. Short title.
42. Commencement.

SCHEDULES:
    Schedule 1—Scheduled works.
        Part I—The scheduled works.
        Part II—Supplementary.
    Schedule 2—Acquisition and occupation of land.
        Part I—Acquisition of land outside limits of deviation.
        Part II—Acquisition: supplementary.
        Part III—Temporary occupation of land.
        Part IV—Correction of deposited plans.
    Schedule 3—Authorised works: supplementary.
    Schedule 4—Early end of tolling by Secretary of State.
    Schedule 5—Repeals.

An Act to provide for the construction of a new bridge over the Severn Estuary between England and Wales and roads leading to the new bridge and associated works; to make provision for the levying of tolls in respect of use of the existing Severn bridge and the new bridge; to make other provision for and in connection with the operation of the bridges; and for connected purposes.   [13th February 1992]

PARLIAMENTARY DEBATES
   Hansard, H.C. Vol. 194, col. 270; Vol. 203, col. 1000; H.L. Vol. 531, col. 1038; Vol. 533, col. 219; Vol. 534, col. 730; Vol. 535, col. 240.
   The Bill was discussed in Select Committee between March 12 and May 22, 1991 and in Standing Committee D between June 11 and 18, 1991.

INTRODUCTION
   This Act provides for the construction of a second tolled bridge over the Severn Estuary between Avon and Gwent, together with a new toll plaza and connecting roads to the M4 and M5. Provision is also made for a common financial and tolling régime for both bridges and the Secretary of State is authorised to make agreements with a private concessionaire to maintain the bridges and levy tolls for a maximum of 30 years.
   The cost of constructing the roads connecting the bridge to the M4 and M5 is estimated at £148m for England and £45m for Wales.
   The cost of the new bridge and the deficit on the existing bridge at the start of tolling by the new concessionaire will be met by the concessionaire, as will the cost of maintaining and regulating the bridges and toll plaza areas (while he has the right to levy tolls) and after, by the Secretary of State.

PART I

CONSTRUCTION OF NEW SEVERN BRIDGE

Construction of new bridge and other works
   1.—(1) The Secretary of State may construct the works specified in Part I

of Schedule 1 to this Act ("the scheduled works"), being works for the construction of a new bridge over the Severn Estuary between England and Wales and roads leading to the new bridge and associated works.

(2) Subject to Part II of that Schedule (supplementary provisions relating to the scheduled works, including provisions permitting deviation from the deposited plans and the deposited sections), the scheduled works shall be constructed in the lines or situations shown on those plans and in accordance with the levels shown on those sections.

Acquisition and occupation of land

2.—(1) The Secretary of State is authorised by this section to acquire compulsorily—

    (a) so much of the land shown on the deposited plans within the limits of deviation for the scheduled works as may be required for or in connection with the works authorised by this Act,

    (b) so much of the land specified in columns (1) and (2) in Part I of Schedule 2 to this Act, and shown on the deposited plans within the limits of land to be acquired, as may be required for the purpose specified in relation to the land in column (3) in that Part of that Schedule, and

    (c) so much of the land in the Community of Rogiet in the Borough of Monmouth shown numbered 34, 49, 50, 55, 56, 57 and 59 on the deposited plans as may be required for the relocation of the rifle range in the Community of Caldicot in that Borough in consequence of the acquisition of the land numbered 2 and 2a on those plans.

(2) Nothing in this section authorises the Secretary of State to acquire compulsorily any of the land in the City of Bristol shown numbered 25, 41 or 42 on the deposited plans.

(3) Part I of the Compulsory Purchase Act 1965 (except section 4 and paragraph 3(3) of Schedule 3), in so far as it is not inconsistent with the provisions of this Act, shall apply to the acquisition of land under this section—

    (a) as it applies to a compulsory purchase to which Schedule 1 to the Acquisition of Land Act 1981 applies, and

    (b) as if this Act were a compulsory purchase order under that Act.

(4) A notice to treat under Part I of the Compulsory Purchase Act 1965 for the purpose of acquiring land under this section shall not be served after 31st December 1995.

(5) The Lands Clauses Consolidation Act 1845 shall not apply to the acquisition of land under this section.

(6) Schedule 2 to this Act (supplementary provisions as to land acquisition, temporary occupation of land etc.) shall have effect.

Authorised works: supplementary

3. Schedule 3 to this Act (provision relating to highways in connection with the works authorised by this Act) shall have effect.

PART II

OPERATION OF SEVERN BRIDGES

Introductory

Concession agreement

4.—(1) Where (either before or after the passing of this Act) the Secretary of State enters into an agreement with a person for the construction by that person of the new bridge (whether or not together with any other of the scheduled works), the agreement may also provide—

(a) for the power to levy tolls in respect of use of the bridges which is conferred on the Secretary of State by section 5 below to be exercisable by that person in accordance with section 6 below, and

(b) for all relevant functions, or so many of them as may be specified in the agreement, to be exercisable by that person in accordance with section 15 below.

(2) In this Act—

(a) "the concessionaire" means the person with whom the Secretary of State enters into an agreement making the provision mentioned in subsection (1) above, and

(b) "concession agreement" means an agreement making the provision mentioned in subsection (1) above (together with any agreement supplementing it).

(3) In this Act "relevant functions" means functions of the Secretary of State—

(a) with respect to the maintenance and improvement of, or other dealing with—

(i) the bridges or the highways carried by them, or

(ii) the toll plaza areas or the highways within them,

(b) with respect to any land which may be acquired by the Secretary of State in exercise of any of his powers under Part XII of the Highways Act 1980 in relation to any highway or other area within paragraph (a) above, and

(c) under sections 29 and 30 below,

other than the power to levy tolls.

Tolls

Power of Secretary of State to levy tolls

5.—(1) Tolls may be levied by the Secretary of State in respect of vehicles using either of the bridges.

(2) Subject to section 11 below, tolls may only be levied in respect of vehicles travelling from east to west.

(3) The power to levy tolls shall commence—

(a) with the appointed day, as respects vehicles using the existing bridge, and

(b) with the day on which the new bridge is first open for public use, as respects vehicles using that bridge.

(4) The power to levy tolls shall terminate at the end of the period of 35 years beginning with the appointed day.

(5) The Secretary of State may appoint any person to collect tolls as his agent.

(6) A local authority may enter into an agreement with the Secretary of State (on such terms and subject to such conditions, as to payment or otherwise, as they consider appropriate) to perform such services and provide such facilities as may be specified in the agreement in connection with the collection of tolls; and a local authority may perform services and provide facilities in accordance with such an agreement.

(7) No agreement entered into under section 17(1) of the Severn Bridge Tolls Act 1965 (agreement between Secretary of State and local authority for performance of services and provision of facilities in connection with tolling) shall have effect on or after the appointed day.

Exercise of power to levy tolls by concessionaire

6.—(1) Where a concession agreement is subsisting on the appointed day, the power to levy tolls conferred on the Secretary of State by section 5 above shall be exercisable by the concessionaire (instead of by the Secretary of State) during the concession period.

(2) The power shall be exercised by the concessionaire in accordance with the concession agreement.

(3) In this Act "the concession period" means the period—

(a) beginning with the appointed day, and

(b) ending at the time specified in subsection (4) below.

(4) The time referred to in subsection (3)(b) above is the earliest of—

(a) the end of the period of 30 years beginning with the appointed day,

(b) any time determined under subsection (5) below as that at which the right of the concessionaire to exercise the power to levy tolls is to end, and

(c) any earlier time at which, in accordance with the concession agreement, that right is to end.

(5) Where it appears to the Secretary of State that the revenue requirement has been met on a day, the right of the concessionaire to exercise the power to levy tolls shall end at such time after that day as the Secretary of State may determine.

(6) The time determined under subsection (5) above shall not be later than the end of the period of 120 days beginning with the day mentioned in that subsection; but (subject to that) the determination under that subsection shall be made in accordance with the concession agreement.

(7) For the purposes of this section—

(a) the revenue requirement is met on a day if the aggregate amount of toll income received by the concessionaire on or before that day is equal to or greater than the amount which he is entitled to receive in accordance with the concession agreement, and

(b) "toll income" means tolls and sums received in lieu of tolls which, in accordance with the concession agreement, are to be treated for the purposes of this section in the same way as tolls.

(8) Subject to the concession agreement—

(a) in exercising the power to levy tolls in accordance with this section the concessionaire shall not be regarded for any purpose as acting as the agent of the Secretary of State, and

(b) in accordance with paragraph (a) above, tolls levied by the concessionaire shall be payable to him and be his property.

(9) The concessionaire may appoint any person to collect tolls as his agent.

(10) A local authority may enter into an agreement with the concessionaire (on such terms and subject to such conditions, as to payment or otherwise, as they consider appropriate) to perform such services and provide such facilities as may be specified in the agreement in connection with the collection of tolls; and a local authority may perform services and provide facilities in accordance with such an agreement.

Early end of tolling by Secretary of State

7.—(1) Where it appears to the Secretary of State that the funding requirement is met on a day on which the power to levy tolls is being exercised by him, no tolls shall be levied by him after that day.

(2) For the purposes of this section the funding requirement is met on a day if the aggregate of the receipts mentioned in paragraph 1 of Schedule 4 to this Act before that day is equal to or greater than the amount required before that day for the purposes specified in paragraph 2 of that Schedule.

Vehicles subject to tolls

8.—(1) Tolls may be levied in respect of the following descriptions of vehicles (and no others)—

(a) motor cars and motor caravans (category 1 vehicles),

(b) small goods vehicles and small buses (category 2 vehicles), and

(c) other goods vehicles and buses (category 3 vehicles);

and where a vehicle would otherwise fall within more than one category it shall be taken for the purposes of this Act to fall only within that with the lower or lowest number.

(2) In this section—

"motor car" has the meaning given by section 185 of the Road Traffic Act 1988,

"motor caravan" means a motor vehicle constructed or adapted for the carriage of passengers and their effects which contains, as permanently installed equipment, the facilities which are reasonably necessary for enabling the vehicle to provide mobile living accommodation for its users,

"goods vehicle" means a motor vehicle constructed or adapted for use for the carriage or haulage of goods or burden of any description, and

"bus" means a motor vehicle constructed or adapted to carry more than eight passengers.

(3) For the purposes of this section—

(a) a small goods vehicle is a goods vehicle which has an operating weight for the purposes of section 138 of the Road Traffic Regulation Act 1984 not exceeding 3,500 kilograms, and

(b) a small bus is a bus constructed or adapted to carry not more than sixteen passengers.

(4) The Secretary of State may by order make such amendments of subsections (2) and (3) above as he considers necessary or expedient.

(5) Tolls may not be levied in respect of—

(a) a vehicle being used in the discharge of the functions of a fire authority under the Fire Services Acts 1947 to 1959,

(b) a vehicle being used for police purposes,

(c) a vehicle exempt from duty under the Vehicles (Excise) Act 1971 by virtue of section 7(4) of that Act (civil defence vehicles),

(d) a vehicle exempt from duty under the Vehicles (Excise) Act 1971 under—

(i) section 4(1)(c) of that Act (ambulances),

(ii) section 4(1)(kb) of that Act (vehicles other than ambulances used by recognised bodies for the carriage of disabled persons), or

(iii) section 7(2) of that Act (vehicles of certain persons in receipt of disability living allowance and certain other disabled persons),

(e) a vehicle being driven by a disabled person, or being used for the carriage of one or more disabled persons, which displays a current disabled person's badge issued under—

(i) section 21 of the Chronically Sick and Disabled Persons Act 1970, or

(ii) section 14 of the Chronically Sick and Disabled Persons (Northern Ireland) Act 1978,

(f) a vehicle being used in connection with—

(i) the collection of tolls, or

(ii) the inspection, maintenance, improvement or renewal of, or other dealing with, either of the bridges or toll plaza areas or any of the highways carried by the bridges, within the toll plaza areas or connecting the new toll plaza area and the new bridge (or any structure, works or apparatus on, under or over any of those highways),

(g) a vehicle which, having broken down on either of the bridges while travelling in one direction, is travelling in the opposite direction otherwise than under its own power, or

(h) a vehicle of a description specified in an order made by the Secretary of State as a description of vehicle in respect of which tolls may not be levied.

Level of tolls

9.—(1) Subject to section 11(3) below, the toll leviable in respect of a vehicle of a category shall be that fixed for the time being in respect of vehicles of that category by an order made by the Secretary of State under subsection (2) below.

(2) The Secretary of State shall—

(a) before the appointed day make an order to come into force on that day, and

(b) in each month of December beginning after that day make an order to come into force at the beginning of the year commencing immediately after the end of that month.

(3) Subject to the following provisions of this section and sections 10 and 11 below, the amount of the toll to be fixed by an order under subsection (2) above in respect of each of the categories of vehicles specified in section 8(1) above shall be—

(a) in the case of an order under paragraph (a) of subsection (2) above, the amount specified in the table below with respect to the category for the year in which the appointed day falls, as adjusted in accordance with subsection (4) below, and

(b) in the case of an order under paragraph (b) of that subsection, the amount so specified for the year at the beginning of which the order is to come into force, as so adjusted.

TABLE

Category of vehicle	1992	1993	1994	1995 and each subsequent year
1	£2.35	£2.51	£2.68	£2.85
2	£4.70	£5.02	£5.35	£5.71
3	£7.05	£7.52	£8.03	£8.56

(4) The adjustment in the amounts specified in the table in subsection (3) above which is referred to in that subsection is an adjustment by the same percentage as the percentage difference between the retail prices index for March 1989 and the retail prices index for the month of September immediately preceding the making of the order.

(5) Where a change in any amount specified in the provisions of the concession agreement corresponding to the table in subsection (3) above is made in response to the occurrence of any of the particular circumstances in which the agreement authorises the making of such a change, the Secretary of State may by order provide for the same change to be made in that table.

(6) An amount which falls in accordance with subsections (3) to (5) above to be fixed by an order under subsection (2) above—

(a) if it is neither a multiple of ten pence nor an amount which on division by ten produces a remainder of five pence, shall be rounded to the nearest ten pence, and

(b) if it is an amount which on division by ten produces a remainder of five pence, shall be increased by five pence.

Level of tolls: supplementary

10.—(1) Subject to subsection (2) below—

(a) an order under paragraph (a) of subsection (2) of section 9 above may fix tolls at an amount less than that arrived at in accordance with that section, and

(b) where the amount of a toll which, in accordance with that section, falls to be fixed by an order under paragraph (b) of that subsection in respect of a category of vehicles exceeds that in force under the last order made under that subsection, the new order may fix an amount which does not implement the increase or implements it only in part.

(2) If it appears to the Secretary of State that at the time when an order under section 9(2) above is to come into force the power to levy tolls will be exercisable by the concessionaire, the order shall not fix tolls in accordance with subsection (1) above except with the concessionaire's consent.

(3) Subject to subsection (4) below, the references in section 9(4) above to the retail prices index are references to the general index of retail prices (for all items) published by the Central Statistical Office of the Chancellor of the Exchequer.

(4) If that index is not published for any month those references are references to any other index, or substitute for an index, for that month which the Secretary of State may by order prescribe; and in determining which index or substitute to prescribe the Secretary of State shall have regard to any relevant provisions of the concession agreement.

Two-way tolling

11.—(1) The Secretary of State may by order provide for tolls to be leviable in respect of vehicles travelling from west to east (as well as in respect of vehicles travelling from east to west).

(2) Where at the time of the making of an order under subsection (2) of section 9 above it appears to the Secretary of State that on its coming into force tolls will be leviable in respect of vehicles travelling from west to east (as well as vehicles travelling from east to west), the amount of the tolls to be fixed by the order shall be determined as if the amounts specified in the table in subsection (3) of that section were one-half of the amounts actually so specified.

(3) Where an order under subsection (1) above comes into force on a day which is neither the appointed day nor the first day of a year, the toll leviable in respect of a vehicle of a category on and after the day on which it comes into force until the end of the year in which that day falls shall be that fixed in respect of vehicles of that category by that order.

(4) The amounts of the tolls to be fixed by such an order—
(a) subject to paragraph (b) below, shall be determined as they would have been for the purposes of the order fixing the amounts of the tolls leviable immediately before it comes into force ("the current order") in accordance with subsection (2) above, and
(b) where it revokes an earlier order providing for the levying of tolls in respect of vehicles travelling from west to east (as well as in respect of vehicles travelling from east to west), shall be determined as they would have been determined for the purposes of the current order but for that subsection.

Temporary suspension of tolls

12.—(1) Tolls may be suspended—
(a) by the concessionaire for any period during which the power of the Secretary of State to levy tolls is exercisable by him, and
(b) by the Secretary of State for any other period.
(2) A suspension under this section may relate—
(a) to all vehicles,
(b) only to vehicles using the existing bridge or only to vehicles using the new bridge, or
(c) (when there is in force an order under section 11(1) above providing for tolls to be leviable in respect of vehicles travelling from west to east as well as in respect of vehicles travelling from east to west) only to vehicles travelling in one direction.

Pre-payment of tolls

13.—(1) The Secretary of State, or (if the power to levy tolls is exercisable by the concessionaire) the concessionaire, may enter into agreements under which persons make payments in advance, on such terms as may be agreed, with respect to tolls for use of the bridges by them, by other persons or by any vehicles.

(2) Agreements may relate to use on an agreed number of occasions or during an agreed period.

(3) Prepaid vouchers issued in accordance with an order under section 2(3) of the Severn Bridge Tolls Act 1965 shall not be valid on or after the appointed day; but where—

(a) any such vouchers have not been used before that day, and

(b) the person to whom they were issued makes an application to the Secretary of State within such period beginning with the appointed day as the Secretary of State may direct,

the Secretary of State may make to him in respect of the unused vouchers a payment of such amount as the Secretary of State considers appropriate.

Payment regulations and offences

14.—(1) The Secretary of State may by regulations—

(a) designate places within the toll plaza areas at which tolls (other than tolls with respect to which a pre-payment has been made) are to be paid,

(b) make provision as to the persons by whom, and the manner in which, such tolls are to be paid,

(c) make provision for securing that vehicles in respect of which tolls are leviable do not use either of the bridges without payment of the tolls, and

(d) make provision for preventing a vehicle which, having used one of the bridges, has arrived at the place at which a toll is payable in respect of it from proceeding beyond that place without the toll having been paid.

(2) Regulations made under this section shall provide for a notice, specifying—

(a) the categories of vehicles in respect of which tolls are leviable,

(b) the amount of the tolls in respect of each category, and

(c) other provisions in accordance with which tolls are leviable,

to be displayed at each place designated in accordance with subsection (1)(a) above.

(3) Regulations under this section may include provisions modifying the general provisions of the regulations in the case of vehicles in relation to which a pre-payment of tolls has been made.

(4) A person who without reasonable excuse—

(a) refuses or fails to pay a toll for which he is liable, or

(b) attempts to evade payment of such a toll,

shall be guilty of an offence and liable on summary conviction to a fine not exceeding level 3 on the standard scale.

(5) A person who contravenes or fails to comply with a provision of regulations under this section shall be guilty of an offence and liable on summary conviction to a fine not exceeding level 3 on the standard scale.

Management of bridges etc.

Exercise of relevant functions by concessionaire

15.—(1) Where a concession agreement is subsisting on the appointed day, all relevant functions, or so many of them as are specified in the concession agreement, shall be exercisable by the concessionaire (instead of by the Secretary of State) during the concession period.

(2) The functions concerned shall be exercised by the concessionaire in accordance with the concession agreement.

(3) In exercising a function in accordance with this section the concessionaire shall not be regarded for any purpose as acting as the agent of the Secretary of State.

(4) The concessionaire may enter into and carry into effect agreements with any person for any purpose connected with the exercise of any relevant function.

(5) Nothing in this section or in the concession agreement shall prevent the Secretary of State from exercising a relevant function if he considers that it is in the public interest for him to do so.

(6) Where a concession agreement is subsisting on the appointed day, no agreement made before that day under section 6 of the Highways Act 1980 (agreement between Secretary of State and council for delegation of functions to council) shall have effect on or after that day in so far as it relates to—

(a) the existing bridge or the highway carried by it, or

(b) the existing toll plaza area or the highway within it.

Delegation of relevant functions

16.—(1) The Secretary of State may by an agreement under this section delegate any relevant function which is not for the time being exercisable by the concessionaire to any person (other than a council to which it may be delegated under section 6(1) of the Highways Act 1980).

(2) Functions delegated by an agreement under this section shall be exercised in accordance with such conditions as the Secretary of State may attach to the delegation; and the delegation shall end in accordance with the agreement.

(3) In exercising a function delegated by an agreement under this section the person to whom it is delegated shall act as agent for the Secretary of State.

(4) A person to whom a relevant function is delegated by an agreement under this section may enter into and carry into effect agreements with any person for any purpose connected with the exercise of the function.

(5) Nothing in this section or in an agreement made under it shall prevent the Secretary of State from exercising a relevant function if he considers that it is in the public interest for him to do so.

(6) Where a function may be delegated by an agreement under this section to a person other than a council to which subsection (1) of section 6 of the Highways Act 1980 applies, the function may also be delegated to such a council in accordance with that subsection (if it could not be apart from this subsection).

Grant to concessionaire of interests in land

17.—(1) The Secretary of State may grant to the concessionaire a lease or other interest in or right over any land if it appears to the Secretary of State expedient to do so for the purpose of or in connection with the exercise by the concessionaire of the functions conferred or imposed on him under the concession agreement or under or by virtue of this Act.

(2) No enactment or rule of law regulating the rights and obligations of landlords and tenants shall prejudice the operation of an agreement between the Secretary of State and the concessionaire as to the terms on which land which is the subject of a lease granted in pursuance of this section is to be provided for his use.

(3) Accordingly, no such enactment or rule of law shall apply in relation to the rights and obligations of the parties to a lease granted in pursuance of this section—

   (a) so as to exclude or in any respect modify any of the rights and obligations of those parties under the terms of the lease, whether with respect to the termination of the tenancy or any other matter,

   (b) so as to confer or impose on either party a right or obligation arising out of or connected with anything done or omitted on or in relation to land which is the subject of the lease, in addition to such a right or obligation provided for by the terms of the lease, or

   (c) so as to restrict the enforcement (whether by action for damages or otherwise) by either party to the lease of an obligation of the other party under the lease.

Avon County Council bridge staff

18.—(1) Where a concession agreement is subsisting on the appointed day, there shall be treated as made by Avon County Council to the concessionaire on that day a transfer of an undertaking, to which the Transfer of Undertakings (Protection of Employment) Regulations 1981 shall apply, in which all the persons specified in subsection (2) below are employed.

(2) The persons referred to in subsection (1) above are persons who—

   (a) immediately before the appointed day are employed by Avon County Council in connection with the collection of tolls under the Severn Bridge Tolls Act 1965 or the maintenance or improvement of, or other dealing with—

      (i) the existing bridge or the highway carried by it, or

      (ii) the existing toll plaza area or the highway within it, and

   (b) are designated, or of a description of persons designated, by an order made by the Secretary of State.

(3) Where by reason of the application to a person of the Transfer of Undertakings (Protection of Employment) Regulations 1981 by virtue of subsection (1) above the person ceases to be employed by Avon County Council he shall not be treated for any purpose as having been made redundant.

(4) Subsection (5) below has effect in relation to a pension to which paragraph 1 of Schedule 3 to the Pensions (Increase) Act 1971 (local government pensions) applies if the latest services in respect of which it is payable are services rendered at any time before the appointed day in connection with—

   (a) the collection of tolls under the Severn Bridge Tolls Act 1965, or

   (b) the maintenance or improvement of, or other dealing with—

      (i) the existing bridge or the highway carried by it, or

      (ii) the existing toll plaza area or the highway within it.

(5) For the purposes of sub-paragraph (2) of that paragraph (funding of pension increases after transfer of functions), nothing occurring immediately before, on or at any time after the appointed day by reason of the operation of any provision of this Act or of the Highways Act 1980 shall be taken to amount to a transfer from Avon County Council to another authority of the function in connection with which the latest services were rendered.

Termination of concession agreement

19.—(1) Where the concession agreement terminates, there shall be transferred to the Secretary of State under this subsection all property, rights and liabilities of the concessionaire which, in accordance with the concession agreement, fall to be so transferred in the circumstances (not including any rights or liabilities relating to any person's employment).

(2) There shall also be treated as made by the concessionaire to the Secretary of State on the termination a transfer of an undertaking, to which the Transfer of Undertakings (Protection of Employment) Regulations 1981 shall apply, in which all the persons specified in subsection (3) below are employed.

(3) The persons referred to in subsection (2) above are persons—

(a) who immediately before the termination are employed by the concessionaire in connection with the collection of tolls or the exercise of relevant functions, and

(b) whose only or main place of work in that employment immediately before the termination is at the bridges or toll plaza areas.

(4) All rights and liabilities of the concessionaire under any agreement or arrangement for the payment of pensions, allowances or gratuities to or in respect of—

(a) persons to whom subsection (2) above applies, or

(b) persons specified in subsection (5) below,

shall be transferred to the Secretary of State under this subsection on the termination.

(5) The persons referred to in subsection (4)(b) above are persons—

(a) who have ceased to be employed by the concessionaire before the termination but immediately before so ceasing were employed by him in connection with the collection of tolls or the exercise of relevant functions, and

(b) whose only or main place of work in that employment was at the bridges or toll plaza areas.

(6) All property, rights and liabilities transferred under or by virtue of this section shall vest in the Secretary of State.

Termination: supplementary

20.—(1) Property vested in the Secretary of State under section 19 above shall vest free from any security to which it was subject immediately before the termination.

(2) Where before the termination possession of such property has been taken by a person in pursuance of legal process or distress, the Secretary of State may recover that property from any person in possession of it without being required, as a condition of doing so, to meet a liability in respect of which that process or distress was issued or levied.

(3) Subsection (1) above shall not affect a liability secured by a security from which such property is released by virtue of that subsection; and subsection (2) above shall not affect a liability in respect of which the process or distress was issued or levied.

(4) Where a liability which, if it had subsisted immediately before the termination, would have fallen to be transferred to the Secretary of State under or by virtue of section 19 above has been discharged before termination, nothing in the Insolvency Act 1986 shall—

(a) affect the validity of anything done by the concessionaire or by any other person in discharging that liability,

(b) authorise a court to make an order affecting the property of, or imposing an obligation on, any person in consequence of or in connection with the receipt by that person or by any other person of a payment made, property transferred or other benefit provided by the concessionaire or by any other person in discharging that liability, or

(c) be treated as giving rise to a trust affecting money or property so transferred.

(5) Subject to subsection (1) above, property vested in the Secretary of State under section 19 above shall be held by him subject to all covenants,

conditions and restrictions subject to which the property was held by the concessionaire.

(6) A dispute between the Secretary of State and the concessionaire as to the property, rights or liabilities transferred under or by virtue of section 19 above shall be determined in accordance with the concession agreement.

(7) A dispute between the Secretary of State and any person other than the concessionaire as to any such matter shall be determined by arbitration; and the arbitration shall be conducted by a single arbitrator agreed between the parties or, in default of agreement, appointed on the application of either party (after notice in writing to the other) by the President of the Law Society.

(8) Subject to the concession agreement and to subsection (1) above, all agreements and other transactions entered into or effected by the concessionaire and subsisting immediately before the termination, in so far as they relate to property, rights or liabilities transferred to the Secretary of State under or by virtue of section 19 above, shall have effect with the substitution of the Secretary of State for the concessionaire.

(9) Accordingly—

(a) such an agreement or transaction may be enforced by or against the Secretary of State, and

(b) references to the concessionaire in an agreement (whether or not in writing) and in a deed, bond, instrument or other document, so far as relating to property, rights or liabilities so transferred, shall be taken after the termination as referring to the Secretary of State.

(10) Subject to the concession agreement, all legal and other proceedings begun before the termination and relating to property, rights or liabilities transferred to the Secretary of State under or by virtue of section 19 above, other than proceedings for enforcing a security from which such property is released by virtue of subsection (1) above, may be carried on with the substitution of the Secretary of State for the concessionaire; and such proceedings may be amended in such manner as may be necessary for that purpose.

(11) In this section "security" means a mortgage, charge, lien or other security.

Regulation of traffic etc.

Prevention of obstruction

21.—(1) For the purpose of preventing obstruction of the roads carried by the bridges and the roads within the toll plaza areas, the Secretary of State may by regulations—

(a) prohibit vehicles from stopping or remaining at rest in prescribed places on those roads, except in prescribed circumstances,

(b) require any person in charge of a vehicle which is at rest by reason of breakdown in a prescribed place on any of those roads to take prescribed steps for reporting that fact and the position and circumstances in which the vehicle is at rest,

(c) prohibit any person, other than a constable or an appointed person—

(i) from carrying out, or attempting to carry out, a repair, adjustment or refuelling of such a vehicle except with permission expressly given by a constable or an appointed person, and

(ii) from moving, or attempting to move, such a vehicle from the position in which it is at rest,

(d) prohibit appointed persons from carrying out, or attempting to carry out, a repair, adjustment or refuelling of such a vehicle except in prescribed circumstances,

(e) empower a constable or an appointed person to remove from its position to a prescribed area a vehicle which is for the time being at rest in a prescribed place on any of the roads to which the regulations relate—

    (i) in contravention of the regulations,

    (ii) by reason of breakdown,

    (iii) without any person being in charge of it, or

    (iv) with the person in charge of it not being present in or on it,

  (f) in the case of a vehicle which is so removed or which at the request of the person in charge of it is repaired, adjusted or refuelled (instead of being removed) by an appointed person, require the prescribed person to pay a charge of an amount to be determined in accordance with such scales and other provisions as may be prescribed—

    (i) where the power to levy tolls is for the time being exercisable by the concessionaire, to him, and

    (ii) otherwise, to the Secretary of State, and

  (g) prohibit a person from obstructing any action taken by a constable or an appointed person for the purpose of removing a vehicle in accordance with the regulations.

(2) A person who contravenes or fails to comply with a provision of regulations under this section shall be guilty of an offence and liable on summary conviction to a fine not exceeding level 3 on the standard scale.

(3) Subject to subsection (4) below, this section and regulations under it shall have effect in relation to—

  (a) vehicles belonging to, or used for the purposes of, a Minister of the Crown or government department, and

  (b) things done, or omitted to be done, in connection with such vehicles by persons in the public service of the Crown,

as they have effect in relation to other vehicles and persons.

(4) Regulations under this section may provide that, in their application in relation to—

  (a) vehicles belonging to the Crown and used for naval, military or air force purposes, or

  (b) vehicles used for the purposes of such a body, contingent or detachment of the forces of any country as is a visiting force for the purposes of any of the provisions of the Visiting Forces Act 1952, or used for the purposes of any headquarters or organisation designated by an Order in Council under section 1 of the International Headquarters and Defence Organisations Act 1964,

the regulations shall have effect subject to such modifications as may be prescribed.

(5) In this section—

"breakdown", in relation to a vehicle, includes mechanical defect, lack of fuel, oil or water required for the vehicle, and any other circumstances in which a person in charge of the vehicle could not immediately, safely and without damage to the vehicle or its accessories, drive it under its own power away from the roads to which regulations under this section relate, and

"prescribed" means prescribed by regulations under this section.

(6) No arrangements made under section 12(1) of the Severn Bridge Tolls Act 1965 (arrangements between Secretary of State and another person for operation of vehicle removal service) shall have effect on or after the appointed day.

Special traffic restrictions

22.—(1) In relation to the roads carried by the bridges and the roads within the toll plaza areas, the power conferred by subsection (2) of section 14 of the Road Traffic Regulation Act 1984 (temporary prohibition or restriction of traffic on roads) shall be exercisable by a constable or an appointed person (as well as by the Secretary of State as traffic authority).

(2) Where that power is exercised by virtue of subsection (1) above, it may be exercised either by notice or by such other means as the constable or appointed person considers appropriate for communicating the prohibition or restriction to persons affected by it; and subsections (4) and (7) of that section shall apply in relation to a communication made by such other means as they apply in relation to a notice under subsection (2) of that section.

(3) In relation to the roads carried by the bridges and the roads within the toll plaza areas, the power conferred by section 17 of the Road Traffic Regulation Act 1984 (traffic regulation on special roads) shall include power, by regulations made under that section, to prohibit, or to empower appointed persons to prohibit, the use of the roads by—

(a) a particular vehicle, or
(b) vehicles of a particular description,

either generally, in particular circumstances, or unless particular requirements imposed by or under the regulations are complied with.

Appointed persons

23.—(1) In this Act "appointed person" means—

(a) where the power to levy tolls is for the time being exercisable by the concessionaire, a person appointed by him, and
(b) otherwise, a person appointed by the Secretary of State.

(2) Appointments under subsection (1)(a) above shall be subject to the approval of the Secretary of State.

(3) An appointed person may not act as such unless wearing a uniform of a description approved by the Secretary of State.

(4) A local authority may enter into an agreement with the concessionaire or the Secretary of State (on such terms and subject to such conditions, as to payment or otherwise, as they consider appropriate) in pursuance of which employees of the authority are to be appointed persons; and a local authority may provide employees (and associated services and facilities) in accordance with such an agreement.

Prevention of damage etc.

24.—(1) The Secretary of State may by regulations impose such prohibitions and restrictions as he may consider necessary for preventing—

(a) injury to persons on the roads carried by the bridges or the roads within the toll plaza areas,
(b) damage to, and other interference with, the bridges and toll plazas, those roads and structures, works and apparatus on, under or over those roads or used in connection with the regulation of traffic on those roads or with the collection of tolls,
(c) removal, defacing or obscuring of notices and signs placed on or near the bridges or toll plazas or those roads, or on such structures, works or apparatus, in connection with the regulation of traffic on those roads or with the collection of tolls.

(2) A person who contravenes or fails to comply with a provision of regulations under this section shall be guilty of an offence and liable on summary conviction to a fine not exceeding level 3 on the standard scale.

Use of cycleway or footway

25.—(1) The Secretary of State may by regulations make provision authorising and regulating the use of the cycleway or footway by vehicles which are exempt from tolls under section 8(5)(f) above and by other vehicles in the case of an accident or emergency.

(2) In subsection (1) above—

"the cycleway" means the part of the road carried by the existing bridge which is provided for the use of traffic of Classes VII, X and XI (as specified in Schedule 4 to the Highways Act 1980), and

"the footway" means the part of that road which is provided for the use of pedestrians and other traffic of Class IX (as specified in that Schedule).

Financial matters

Recovery of tolls and charges

26. Where tolls or charges payable under or by virtue of this Part of this Act remain unpaid after they have become due for payment, the person to whom they are payable may recover from the person liable to pay them the amount of the tolls or charges together with a reasonable sum to cover administrative expenses.

Accounts provided by concessionaire

27. The Secretary of State shall lay before Parliament copies of accounts and reports on accounts which are provided to him by the concessionaire in pursuance of the concession agreement.

Accounts of Secretary of State

28.—(1) The Secretary of State shall prepare a statement of accounts in respect of—

(a) the period beginning immediately after the period covered by the last statement of accounts prepared under section 21 of the Severn Bridge Tolls Act 1965 and ending immediately before the appointed day, and

(b) each financial year falling within the period beginning with the appointed day and ending with the last day on which tolls may be levied (or, where part only of a financial year falls within that period, the part which so falls).

(2) A statement of accounts prepared under this section—

(a) shall be in such form and contain such particulars, compiled in such manner, as the Treasury may from time to time direct, and

(b) shall be sent by the Secretary of State to the Comptroller and Auditor General.

(3) A statement of accounts prepared under subsection (1)(b) above shall be sent to the Comptroller and Auditor General not later than the end of the month of November following the end of the financial year to which it relates.

(4) The Comptroller and Auditor General shall examine and certify a statement sent to him under this section and shall lay copies of it, together with his report on it, before Parliament.

PART III

MISCELLANEOUS AND GENERAL

Interference with river Severn

Works affecting river Severn

29.—(1) For the purpose of, or in connection with, the construction, maintenance or improvement of the new bridge, the Secretary of State may—

(a) temporarily interfere with the river Severn and, at any point in the river within the limits of land to be acquired, construct and maintain such temporary structures, and do such works, as he may consider necessary or expedient,

(b) temporarily moor or anchor barges or other vessels or craft in the river, or

(c) temporarily close the river, or a part of it, to navigation.

(2) The power conferred by subsection (1) above shall not be exercised in relation to any part of the river which is—

    (a) outside the limits within which the Gloucester Harbour Trustees have authority at the passing of this Act, or

    (b) upstream of the relevant inward limit.

(3) The Gloucester Harbour Trustees shall be consulted before the power conferred by subsection (1) above is exercised.

(4) The power conferred by subsection (1)(c) above shall be exercised in a way which secures—

    (a) that no more of the river is closed to navigation at any time than is at that time necessary in the circumstances, and

    (b) that, if complete closure of the river to navigation becomes necessary, all reasonable steps are taken to secure that the minimum obstruction, delay or interference is caused to vessels or craft which may be using or intending to use the river.

(5) No liability in respect of any loss suffered, or costs or expenses sustained, as a direct or indirect result of the exercise of the power conferred by subsection (1) above shall be incurred by the person by whom the power is exercised.

Dredging etc.

30.—(1) For the purpose of the construction, maintenance or improvement of the new bridge, the Secretary of State may deepen, widen, dredge, scour, cleanse, alter or improve the bed of the river Severn or blast any rock in it.

(2) The power conferred by subsection (1) above shall not be exercised in relation to any part of the river which is—

    (a) outside the limits within which the Gloucester Harbour Trustees have authority at the passing of this Act, or

    (b) upstream of the relevant inward limit.

(3) The Secretary of State shall not exercise the power conferred by subsection (1) above—

    (a) within the area bounded by planes passing vertically along the length of lines drawn forty metres laterally distant from the longitudinal centre line of the Severn Tunnel, or

    (b) by blasting within the area bounded by planes passing vertically along the length of lines drawn one hundred metres laterally distant from that centre line,

without the consent of the British Railways Board; and where the Secretary of State requests the consent of the Board for the purposes of this subsection it shall not be unreasonably withheld or delayed.

(4) The Secretary of State may use, appropriate or sell or otherwise dispose of anything removed in exercise of the power conferred by subsection (1) above.

Protection of new bridge

31.—(1) The Secretary of State may make regulations for the purpose of protecting the new bridge (both during construction and once it is completed) from damage which may be caused to it by vessels or craft using the river Severn.

(2) Regulations under this section shall not be made so as to apply to the use of any part of the river which is—

    (a) outside the limits within which the Gloucester Harbour Trustees have authority at the passing of this Act, or

(b) upstream of the relevant inward limit.

(3) Before making regulations under this section the Secretary of State shall consult the Gloucester Harbour Trustees.

(4) Without prejudice to the generality of the power conferred by sub-section (1) above, regulations under this section may—

(a) prohibit vessels or craft of descriptions prescribed by the regulations from passing under the new bridge,

(b) prohibit vessels or craft of other descriptions so prescribed from passing under the new bridge without the consent of the Secretary of State, and

(c) provide for the granting of such consent subject to conditions which appear to the Secretary of State to be appropriate.

(5) A person who contravenes or fails to comply with a provision of regulations under this section, or a condition imposed under such a provision, shall be guilty of an offence and liable—

(a) on conviction on indictment, to a fine, or

(b) on summary conviction, to a fine not exceeding the statutory maximum.

Miscellaneous

Toll plaza areas and vehicle pounds

32.—(1) The Secretary of State may—

(a) maintain, improve and extend the toll plaza areas by carrying out such works as may be expedient for the purpose of or in connection with the collection of tolls, and

(b) provide, maintain and improve areas for accommodating vehicles removed in accordance with regulations under section 21(1)(e) above.

(2) Any work done or to be done in pursuance of the power conferred by subsection (1) above—

(a) if it is done or to be done by virtue of paragraph (a), shall be treated as an improvement of a special road under Part V of the Highways Act 1980, and

(b) if it is done or to be done by virtue of paragraph (b), shall be treated as the provision, maintenance or improvement of a service station for use in connection with a special road;

and section 239(3) and (4)(c) of that Act (power to acquire land) shall apply accordingly.

Consent of National Rivers Authority etc.

33.—(1) The Secretary of State shall not use or interfere with any watercourse (including the banks of a watercourse), or any drainage or other works, vested in or under the control of the National Rivers Authority or any other drainage body within the meaning of the Land Drainage Act 1991 in the exercise of any of the powers conferred by this Act without the consent of the National Rivers Authority or that body.

(2) A consent required for the purposes of subsection (1) above shall not be unreasonably withheld; and if any question arises whether the withholding of consent is unreasonable either party may require it to be referred to an arbitrator to be appointed, in default of agreement, by the President of the Institution of Civil Engineers.

Rates

34. The bridges and the premises situated within the toll plaza areas shall be exempt from non-domestic rating.

Planning permission

35. The carrying out on any land of works required or permitted to be carried out by the concession agreement shall not be taken for the purposes of the Town and Country Planning Act 1990 to involve development of the land.

General

Offences by bodies corporate

36.—(1) Where a body corporate is guilty of an offence under this Act and the offence is proved to have been committed with the consent or connivance of, or to be attributable to neglect on the part of, a director, manager, secretary or other similar officer of the body corporate or a person who was purporting to act in such a capacity, he (as well as the body corporate) shall be guilty of that offence and liable to be proceeded against and punished accordingly.

(2) Where the affairs of a body corporate are managed by its members, subsection (1) above shall apply in relation to the acts and defaults of a member in connection with his functions of management as if he were a director of the body corporate.

Orders and regulations

37.—(1) Any power conferred by this Act to make an order or regulations shall be exercisable by statutory instrument.

(2) A statutory instrument containing an order under subsection (5) of section 9 above which substitutes a higher amount for an amount which would otherwise be specified in the table in subsection (3) of that section shall not be made unless a draft of it has been laid before Parliament and approved by a resolution of each House.

(3) A statutory instrument containing—

(a) an order under section 8(4) or (5)(h), 10(4), 11(1) or 18(2)(b) above,

(b) an order under section 9(5) above to which subsection (2) above does not apply, or

(c) regulations under section 14, 21, 24, 25 or 31 above,

shall be subject to annulment in pursuance of a resolution of either House of Parliament.

(4) If it appears to the Secretary of State that at the time when an order under section 8(4) or (5)(h) or 11(1) above is to come into force the power to levy tolls will be exercisable by the concessionaire, the order shall not be made except with the concessionaire's consent.

(5) Regulations under this Act may make different provision for different cases or classes of case to which they apply.

Financial provisions

38.—(1) There shall be paid out of money provided by Parliament—

(a) expenditure of the Secretary of State under this Act, and

(b) increases attributable to this Act in the sums payable out of such money under any other enactment.

(2) Sums received by the Secretary of State under or by virtue of this Act shall be paid into the Consolidated Fund.

Interpretation

39.—(1) In this Act, except where the context otherwise requires—

"the appointed day" means such day as the Secretary of State may by order appoint,

"appointed person" has the meaning given by section 23(1),

"the bridges" means the existing bridge and the new bridge,

"bridleway" has the same meaning as in the Highways Act 1980,

"concession agreement" has the meaning given by section 4(2)(b),

"the concessionaire" has the meaning given by section 4(2)(a),

"the concession period" has the meaning given by section 6,

"cycle track" has the same meaning as in the Highways Act 1980,

"the deposited plans" and "the deposited sections" mean respectively the plans and sections deposited in November 1990 in connection with the Severn Bridges Bill in the office of the Clerk of the Parliaments and the Private Bill Office of the House of Commons,

"exercise" includes performance and related expressions shall be construed accordingly,

"the existing bridge" means the bridges and viaduct shown as the existing bridge on the explanatory map,

"the existing toll plaza area" means the area shown as such on the explanatory map (including extensions to it),

"the explanatory map" means the map marked "Existing bridge and toll plaza area" deposited in November 1990 in connection with the Severn Bridges Bill in the office of the Clerk of the Parliaments and the Private Bill Office of the House of Commons,

"footpath" has the same meaning as in the Highways Act 1980,

"functions" includes powers, duties and obligations,

"highway" has the same meaning it has for the purposes of the Highways Act 1980,

"the limits of deviation" mean the limits of deviation which are shown on the deposited plans,

"the limits of land for temporary occupation" means the limits of land of which temporary possession may be taken which are so shown,

"the limits of land to be acquired" means the limits of land to be acquired which are so shown,

"local authority" means a district council or a county council,

"maintenance" includes repair and related expressions shall be construed accordingly,

"modifications" includes omissions, additions and alterations and related expressions shall be construed accordingly,

"the new bridge" means the bridge mentioned in section 1(1) (Work No. 3),

"the new toll plaza area" means so much of Work No. 2 as lies within the area marked as such on the deposited plans (including extensions to it),

"owner" has the same meaning as in the Acquisition of Land Act 1981,

"relevant functions" has the meaning given by section 4(3),

"the relevant inward limit" means an imaginary straight line drawn from east to west through the Inward Rocks on the western bank of the river Severn at Ordnance Survey National Grid reference ST 56895 95270,

"retail prices index" shall be construed in accordance with section 10(3) and (4),

"the scheduled works" shall be construed in accordance with section 1(1),

"special road" has the same meaning as in the Highways Act 1980,

"toll" means a toll leviable under this Act,

"the toll plaza areas" means the existing toll plaza area and the new toll plaza area, and

"trunk road" has the same meaning as in the Highways Act 1980.

(2) In this Act—

(a) a reference to a highway or any other place identified by letters and numbers or a real name is a reference to the highway or place shown as such on the deposited plans,

(b) a reference to a work identified by a number (or a number and a letter) is a reference to the scheduled work of that number (or number and letter),

(c) references to specified distances shall be construed as if the words "or thereabouts" were inserted after each such distance, and

(d) distances between points on a highway shall be measured along the centre line of the highway.

Repeals

40. The enactments specified in Schedule 5 to this Act are repealed to the extent specified in the third column of that Schedule.

Short title

41. This Act may be cited as the Severn Bridges Act 1992.

Commencement

42.—(1) Sections 16, 22(1) and (2), 34 and 40 above shall not come into force until the appointed day.

(2) No regulations made under section 21, 24 or 25 above, or by virtue of section 22(3) above, shall come into force before the appointed day.

(3) Regulations made under section 5, 7, 9 or 18(3), or by virtue of section 8(3), of the Severn Bridge Tolls Act 1965 and in force immediately before the appointed day shall (unless revoked) have effect on and after that day, with any necessary modifications, as if made (respectively) under section 14, 21(1), 24 or 21(4), or by virtue of section 22(3), of this Act.

SCHEDULES

Section 1   SCHEDULE 1

Scheduled Works

Part I

The Scheduled Works

In the Borough of Monmouth (Community of Magor with Undy) in the County of Gwent—

Work No. 1—A widening (1,400 metres in length) of the M4 commencing at a point 40 metres east of the edge of the eastern overbridge of Magor Interchange and terminating at a point 300 metres east of the edge of Undy/Knollbury overbridge.

Work No. 1A—Realignment (320 metres in length) of the eastbound on slip road of Magor Interchange commencing at a point 65 metres north-east of the edge of the eastern overbridge of the Interchange and terminating at a point 110 metres west of St. Bride's Brook culvert.

Work No. 1B—Realignment (340 metres in length) of the westbound off slip road of Magor Interchange commencing at a point 65 metres south-east of the edge of the eastern overbridge of the Interchange and terminating at a point 100 metres west of St. Bride's Brook culvert.

In the Borough of Monmouth (Communities of Magor with Undy, Rogiet and Caldicot) in the County of Gwent—

Work No. 2—A new road comprising dual carriageways (6,010 metres in length) commencing at the termination of Work No. 1 and terminating at a point 230 metres east of the point at which Nedern Brook passes through the Severn Estuary sea defences, including a new bridge over the westbound slip road onto the M4 (Work No. 2B), a bridge over the B4245 Caldicot Road, a bridge over the railway tracks of the British Railways Board, the provision of a toll plaza, the realignment of the sea defences and maintenance accesses.

In the Borough of Monmouth (Communities of Magor with Undy and Rogiet) in the County of Gwent—

Work No. 2A—A diversion (620 metres in length) of the M4 eastbound carriageway commencing at a point 15 metres east of Rockfield underbridge and terminating at a point 280 metres west of Bencroft Lane underbridge.

Work No. 2B—A diversion (1,355 metres in length) of the M4 westbound carriageway commencing at a point 190 metres west of Rockfield underbridge and terminating at a point 230 metres east of Bencroft Lane underbridge, including a bridge carrying that diversion over Bencroft Lane.

In the Borough of Monmouth (Communities of Caldicot and Portskewett) in the County of Gwent and in the District of Northavon (Parish of Pilning and Severn Beach) in the County of Avon—

Work No. 3—A fixed bridge with approach viaducts carrying a new road (5,190 metres in length) comprising dual carriageways, commencing at the termination of Work No. 2 and terminating at a point 60 metres east of the Binn Wall and 140 metres north of the Severn Tunnel Air Shaft, including supporting piers and protection for shipping in the Severn Estuary and reconstruction of the sea defences.

In the District of Northavon (Parishes of Pilning and Severn Beach and Olveston) in the County of Avon—

Work No. 4—A new road comprising dual carriageways (6,690 metres in length) commencing at the termination of Work No. 3 and terminating at a point on the M4, 160 metres south-east of Moor Lane, including bridges carrying the road over the interchange (Work No. 4A) and the Pill, an extension of the Tockington Mill Rhine culvert and Moor Lane underbridge and emergency accesses.

In the District of Northavon (Parish of Pilning and Severn Beach) in the County of Avon—

Work No. 4A—An interchange (1,030 metres in length) commencing at a point 140 metres west of the termination of Work No. 3 and terminating at a point 80 metres west of Redwick Road comprising a roundabout and slip roads connecting with Works Nos. 4 and 5.

In the District of Northavon (Parish of Olveston) in the County of Avon—

Work No. 4B—Realignment (300 metres in length) of the M4 eastbound carriageway, commencing at a point 210 metres north-west of Hardy Lane overbridge and terminating at a point 80 metres south-east of that overbridge, including emergency access.

Work No. 4C—A diversion (1,300 metres in length) of the M4 westbound carriageway commencing at a point 85 metres north-west of Catherine Hill overbridge and terminating at a point 15 metres north-west of Moor Lane underbridge, including emergency access and a bridge carrying that diversion over Work No. 4.

In the District of Northavon (Parishes of Pilning and Severn Beach and Almondsbury) and City of Bristol in the County of Avon—

Work No. 5—A new road comprising dual carriageways (8,020 metres in length) commencing by a junction with Work No. 4A at a point 500 metres east of the commencement of that work and terminating at a point 450 metres south-west of Lawrence Weston Road, including a bridge under the railway track of the British Railways Board at Hallen.

In the City of Bristol in the County of Avon—

Work No. 6—A new link road (1,930 metres in length) commencing at the termination of Work No. 5 and terminating on the M5 at a point 450 metres south-west of the M5 spur overbridge, including bridges carrying the road over the M5, the diversion of the northbound on slip road (Work No. 6E) and an access track.

Work No. 6A—A new slip road (430 metres in length) commencing by a junction with Work No. 6 at a point 950 metres from the commencement of that work and terminating on the M5 spur at a point 110 metres east of the M5 spur overbridge.

Work No. 6B—A new link road (870 metres in length) commencing at the termination of Work No. 5 and terminating on the M5 at a point 340 metres north-east of the M5 spur overbridge, including bridges carrying the road over the diversion of the northbound on slip road (Work No. 6E) and an access track.

Work No. 6C—A new link road (1,800 metres in length) commencing by a junction with Work No. 5 at a point 100 metres south of Lawrence Weston Road and terminating at a point on the M5 spur 280 metres west of the M5 spur overbridge, including a bridge over an access track.

Work No. 6D—A diversion (850 metres in length) of the M5 southbound off slip road of Lawrence Weston interchange commencing by a junction with the M5 at a point 100 metres south-west of Lawrence Weston Road overbridge and terminating by a junction with Work No. 6 at a point 600 metres south of the commencement of that work, including a bridge over an access track.

Work No. 6E—A diversion (960 metres in length) of the M5 northbound on slip road of Lawrence Weston interchange commencing by a junction with the M5 at a point 180

metres south of Lawrence Weston Road overbridge and terminating by a junction
with Work No. 6C at a point 1,000 metres south of the commencement of that work,
including a bridge over an access track.

In the Borough of Monmouth (Community of Rogiet) in the County of Gwent—

    Work No. 7—A diversion (500 metres in length) of Station Road and track CRF16
commencing at a point 480 metres north of the junction of that track and track CRF15
and terminating at a point 5 metres north of that junction, including a bridge over
Work No. 2 and accesses to the toll plaza (part of Work No. 2).

    Work No. 7A—A diversion (680 metres in length) of track CRF15 commencing at a point
400 metres north of the junction of that track and track CRF16 and terminating at a
point 530 metres north-east of that junction.

In the Borough of Monmouth (Community of Caldicot) in the County of Gwent—

    Work No. 8—A diversion (870 metres in length) of footpath FP19 commencing at the
junction of footpath FP19 and the sewage works access track and terminating by a
junction with footpath FP6 at a point 370 metres east of the junction of Back Ditch and
Summerway Reen, including a footbridge carrying the diversion over Work No. 2.

    Work No. 9—A new road (350 metres in length) commencing at the junction of Symonds-
cliff Way and Pill Row and terminating at the Severn Estuary sea defences at a point
150 metres east of the point at which Nedern Brook passes through those defences,
including the realignment of the junction of Symondscliff Way and Pill Row and a
level crossing over the tracks of the British Railways Board.

In the Borough of Monmouth (Communities of Mathern and Portskewett) in the County of
Gwent—

    Work No. 9A—A diversion (330 metres in length) of the A48 commencing at a point 390
metres west of the junction of that road and the B4245 and terminating at a point 80
metres west of that junction, including a roundabout.

In the Borough of Monmouth (Community of Portskewett) in the County of Gwent—

    Work No. 9B—A diversion (370 metres in length) of the B4245 commencing by a junction
with Work No. 9A at a point 170 metres west of the junction of that road and the A48
and terminating at a point 410 metres south-west of that junction.

In the Borough of Monmouth (Communities of Mathern and Portskewett) in the County of
Gwent—

    Work No. 9C—A diversion (200 metres in length) of the R140 commencing by a junction
with Work No. 9B at a point 165 metres south-west of the junction of that road and the
B4245 and terminating at a point 45 metres south-east of that junction.

In the Borough of Monmouth (Community of Portskewett) in the County of Gwent—

    Work No. 9D—An improvement (130 metres in length) of the B4245 commencing at a
point 240 metres west of the access to Severn Farm and terminating at a point 110
metres west of that access.

    Work No. 9E—An improvement (320 metres in length) of the B4245 commencing at a
point 160 metres north-east of Mount Ballan crossroad and terminating at a point 160
metres south-west of that crossroad.

    Work No. 9F—A diversion (100 metres in length) of the R139 commencing at a point 110
metres north-west of the junction of that road with the B4245 and terminating by a
junction with Work No. 9E at a point 140 metres from the commencement of that
work.

    Work No. 9G—A diversion (120 metres in length) of the R139 commencing at a point 130
metres south-east of the junction of that road with the B4245 and terminating by a
junction with Work No. 9E at a point 190 metres from the commencement of that
work.

    Work No. 9H—An improvement (280 metres in length) of Caldicot Road commencing at a
point 200 metres west of the junction of that road and Symondscliff Way and
terminating at a point 80 metres east of that junction, including an improvement of
that junction.

In the District of Northavon (Parish of Pilning and Severn Beach) in the County of Avon—

    Work No. 10—A new access track (130 metres in length) commencing at the Binn Wall at a
point 130 metres north of the junction of Shaft Road and the Binn Wall and terminating at that junction.

    Work No. 11—A diversion (420 metres in length) of the B4064 New Passage Road/
Redwick Road commencing at a point 50 metres south-east of the sewage works
entrance and terminating at a point 390 metres south-east of that entrance by a
junction with Work No. 18, including a bridge carrying the diversion over Work No. 4.

    Work No. 12—A diversion (1,070 metres in length) of the A403 Severn Road commencing
at a point 450 metres north of the access to Southworthy Farm and terminating at a
point 610 metres south-west of that access, including a bridge carrying the diversion
over Work No. 4.

In the district of Northavon (Parishes of Pilning and Severn Beach and Olveston) in the County of Avon—

    Work No. 13—A diversion (520 metres in length) of the B4055 Northwick Road and Redham Lane commencing at a point 35 metres south-west of the entrance to Laurel Farm and terminating in Redham Lane at a point 140 metres north-west of the junction of footpath FP30 and bridleway BW31.

    Work No. 13A—A diversion (300 metres in length) of the B4055 Northwick Road commencing at a point 170 metres north-east of the junction of Northwick Road and Redham Lane and terminating by a junction with Work No. 13 at a point 230 metres from the commencement of that work, including a bridge carrying the diversion over Work No. 4.

    Work No. 14—A diversion (370 metres in length) of bridleway BW8 commencing at a point 290 metres north of its junction with Redham Lane and terminating at that junction, including a bridge carrying the diversion over Work No. 4.

In the District of Northavon (Parish of Olveston) in the County of Avon—

    Work No. 15—A diversion (440 metres in length) of Holm Lane commencing at a point 590 metres north-west of its junction with Redham Lane and terminating at a point 160 metres north-west of that junction, including a bridge carrying the diversion over Work No. 4.

    Work No. 16—A diversion (600 metres in length) of Greenditch Street and Awkley Lane commencing in Greenditch Street at a point 360 metres west of its junction with Awkley Lane and terminating in Awkley Lane at a point 370 metres south of that junction.

    Work No. 16A—A diversion (260 metres in length) of Greenditch Street commencing at a point 30 metres east of the junction of Greenditch Street and Awkley Lane and terminating by a junction with Work No. 16 at a point 220 metres from the commencement of that work, including a bridge carrying the diversion over Work No. 4.

    Work No. 17—A diversion (620 metres in length) of Hardy Lane commencing at a point 240 metres north-east of the north abutment of the M4 overbridge in Hardy Lane and terminating at a point 320 metres south-west of the south abutment of that overbridge, including a replacement bridge carrying the diversion over Works Nos. 4 and 4B and a bridge carrying the diversion over Work No. 4C.

In the District of Northavon (Parish of Pilning and Severn Beach) in the County of Avon—

    Work No. 18—A diversion (1,070 metres in length) of Green Lane commencing at a point 50 metres east of the junction of Beach Road and Beach Avenue and terminating on Redwick Road at a point 540 metres south-east of the sewage works entrance, including a bridge carrying the diversion over Work No. 5.

    Work No. 18A—A diversion (180 metres in length) of Shaft Road commencing at a point 110 metres north-west of its junction with Green Lane and terminating by a junction with Work No. 18 at a point 60 metres from the commencement of that work.

    Work No. 19—A footpath (350 metres in length) commencing in Church Road at a point 140 metres west of its junction with the A403 Severn Road and terminating in Church Road at a point 150 metres east of its junction with Little Green Lane, including a footbridge carrying the footpath over Work No. 5.

    Work No. 20—A diversion (750 metres in length) of the A403 Severn Road commencing at a point 30 metres north-east of its junction with Church Road and terminating at a point 720 metres south-west of that junction, including a bridge carrying the diversion over Work No. 5.

    Work No. 21—A new track (430 metres in length) commencing at a point 365 metres north-west of the junction of footpath FP61 and footpath FP59 and terminating on footpath FP58 at a point 420 metres south-west of the junction of that footpath and footpath FP59, including a bridge carrying the track over Work No. 5.

In the District of Northavon (Parishes of Pilning and Severn Beach and Almondsbury) in the County of Avon—

    Work No. 22—A diversion of Farm Lane and a new road (980 metres in length) commencing at a point 240 metres south-east of its junction with Impool Rhine and terminating by a junction with Central Avenue at a point 190 metres west of the east end of that road, including a bridge carrying the diversion over Work No. 5.

In the District of Northavon (Parish of Pilning and Severn Beach) in the County of Avon—

    Work No. 22A—A diversion (200 metres in length) of Farm Lane commencing at a point 330 metres north-west of its junction with Impool Rhine and terminating by a junction with Work No. 22 at a point 420 metres from the commencement of that work.

In the District of Northavon (Parish of Almondsbury) and City of Bristol in the County of Avon—

    Work No. 23—A diversion (750 metres in length) of Severn Road, Hallen commencing at a point 320 metres south-east of the junction of that road and the access road to the gas works and terminating at a point 430 metres north-west of that junction, including a diversion (part) of bridleway BW101 (Minor's Lane) and a bridge carrying the diversions over Work No. 5.

Work No. 23A—A diversion (part) (340 metres in length) of bridleway BW101 (Minor's Lane) commencing at a point 160 metres south-east of its junction with the access road to the gas works and terminating at the junction of Severn Road, Hallen and that access road.

Work No. 23B—A diversion (part) (360 metres in length) of bridleway BW101 (Minor's Lane) commencing at its junction with the access road to the gas works and terminating at a point 120 metres north-west of the junction of Severn Road, Hallen and that access road.

In the City of Bristol in the County of Avon—

Work No. 24—A diversion (370 metres in length) of Moorhouse Lane commencing at a point 360 metres south-east of the bridge carrying the railway over Moorhouse Lane and terminating at a point 10 metres east of that bridge, including a bridge carrying the diversion over Work No. 5.

Work No. 25—A footpath and cycle track (110 metres in length) commencing in Lawrence Weston Road at a point 130 metres south-east of the entrance to Poplar Farm and terminating at a point 20 metres south-east of that entrance, including a subway carrying the footpath and cycle track under Work No. 5.

Work No. 26—A diversion (1,060 metres in length) of Kings Weston Lane commencing at a point 65 metres south-east of its junction with Campbell Farm Drive and terminating at a point 65 metres south-east of its junction with Ballast Lane, including bridges carrying the diversion over the M5 and Works Nos. 6, 6B, 6C and 6E.

In the Borough of Monmouth (Communities of Caldicot and Portskewett) in the County of Gwent—

Work No. 27—A cofferdam (1,205 metres in length) commencing at the Severn Estuary sea defences at a point 60 metres east of the point at which Nedern Brook passes through those defences and terminating in the Severn Estuary at a point 1,205 metres east of its commencement, including modifications to a drainage outfall.

In the District of Northavon (Parish of Pilning and Severn Beach) in the County of Avon—

Work No. 28—An access causeway (2,380 metres in length) commencing in the Severn Estuary at a point on the eastern edge of The Shoots navigation channel 510 metres south-west of the Severn Tunnel and terminating on the Binn Wall at a point 190 metres north of the Severn Tunnel Air Shaft.

Work No. 29—A jetty (185 metres in length) commencing on the Binn Wall at a point 200 metres north of the Severn Tunnel Air Shaft and terminating in the Severn Estuary at a point 185 metres west of its commencement.

Work No. 30—A jetty (155 metres in length) commencing on the Binn Wall at a point 300 metres north of the Severn Tunnel Air Shaft and terminating in the Severn Estuary at a point 155 metres west of its commencement.

Work No. 31—A surface water drain and outfall (210 metres in length) commencing 15 metres south-west of New Passage Road at a point 340 metres north-west of the sewage works entrance and terminating in The Pill at a point 20 metres south-east of the tide lock.

Part II

Supplementary

1.—(1) The Secretary of State may carry out such works as may be necessary or expedient for the purposes of, in connection with or in consequence of the construction of the scheduled works including, in particular—

(a) landscaping and drainage works,

(b) works involving the alteration of the position of mains and cables, and

(c) works consisting of the provision of new means of access to premises affected by the scheduled works.

(2) Sub-paragraph (1) above—

(a) shall not authorise the carrying out of works outside the limits of land to be acquired, and

(b) shall authorise the carrying out of works outside the limits of deviation for the scheduled works only if the works are carried out on land specified in columns (1) and (2) in Part I of Schedule 2 to this Act for the purpose specified in relation to the land in column (3) in that Part of that Schedule.

2. In constructing the scheduled works the Secretary of State may—

(a) deviate laterally from the lines or situations shown on the deposited plans within the limits of deviation for those works, and

(b) deviate vertically from the levels shown on the deposited sections—
      (i) to any extent not exceeding three metres upwards, or
      (ii) subject to paragraph 3 below, to any extent downwards.

3.—(1) In constructing the new bridge the Secretary of State shall provide headway of not less than 37·7 metres above the prescribed level over a clear central span of at least 415 metres.

(2) In sub-paragraph (1) above "the prescribed level" means 6·8 metres above ordnance datum (Newlyn).

4. The British Railways Board may, subject to such requirements as the Secretary of State may from time to time lay down, provide, maintain and operate at or near the level crossing forming part of Work No. 9 such barriers, lights, traffic signs and automatic or other devices and appliances as may be approved by the Secretary of State.

Section 2

SCHEDULE 2

ACQUISITION AND OCCUPATION OF LAND

PART I

ACQUISITION OF LAND OUTSIDE LIMITS OF DEVIATION

(1) *Area*	(2) *Number of land shown on deposited plans*	(3) *Purpose for which land may be acquired*
Borough of Monmouth Community of Rogiet	16a, 17a, 18a and 19a	Access (including a temporary bridge over the railway), provision of services and drainage
	26a, 27a, 30a, 51, 52, 53, 54 and 58	Access for drainage work along West Pill Reen and at West Pill
	34a	Access to severed land
Borough of Monmouth Community of Caldicot	2a, 3a and 15a	Drainage outfall and access to Back Ditch and Severn Estuary sea defences
	38a, 39a and 44a	Marine operations, construction and access
	42	Preservation of woodlands for landscaping
Borough of Monmouth Community of Portskewett	1	Preservation of woodlands for landscaping
	2a	Marine operations, construction and access
District of Northavon Parish of Pilning and Severn Beach	1a, 2a, 39a and 40a	Marine operations, construction and access
	21	Footpath
	58 and 59	Footpath
	68a	Service diversion
	98 and 100	Access to severed land
District of Northavon Parish of Almondsbury	1a	Access to severed land
	3a, 4a, 5a, 7a and 8a	Service diversions
	13a	Footpath
City of Bristol	2a and 5	Footpath
	13a and 43	Footpath and cycle track
	27, 28 and 29	Footpath
	31	Playing field

PART II

ACQUISITION: SUPPLEMENTARY

Acquisition of rights

1.—(1) The Secretary of State may under section 2 of this Act acquire easements or other rights in or over land by creating them as well as acquiring easements or other rights already in existence.

(2) In relation to the compulsory acquisition of a right by virtue of sub-paragraph (1) above the provisions of the Highways Act 1980 specified in sub-paragraph (3) below shall apply—

(a) as if references to such a compulsory acquisition were included in references to the compulsory acquisition of a right by virtue of section 250 of that Act, and

(b) as if such an acquisition were made by a compulsory purchase order made in the exercise of highway land acquisition powers.

(3) The provisions of the Highways Act 1980 referred to in sub-paragraph (2) above are—

(a) section 250(4) and (5) and Part II of Schedule 19 (adaptations of Compulsory Purchase Act 1965 and the enactments relating to compensation for compulsory purchase),

(b) section 251 (rights acquired to be binding on successive owners of the land), and

(c) section 252 (power of landowners affected by rights acquisition to compel acquisition of whole interest).

Subsoil and under-surface

2. The Secretary of State may under section 2 of this Act acquire so much of the subsoil and under-surface of land as is required as mentioned in that section without being required to acquire an interest in any other part of it.

Mines and minerals

3.—(1) Parts II and III of Schedule 2 to the Acquisition of Land Act 1981 (exception of mines and minerals from compulsory purchase and regulation of the working of mines and minerals underlying an authorised undertaking) shall apply in relation to land within the limits of land to be acquired as if it were comprised in a compulsory purchase order providing for the incorporation with the order of those Parts of that Schedule.

(2) For the purposes of Part III of that Schedule as it applies by virtue of sub-paragraph (1) above, paragraph 1(3) of that Schedule (meaning of underlying) shall have effect as if the prescribed distance in relation to any mines or minerals lying under land near any of the works authorised by this Act were the greater of—

(a) such lateral distance from those works on every side as is equal at every point along those works to one-half of the depth of the mines or minerals below the natural surface of the ground at that point, and

(b) 40 metres.

Private rights of way

4.—(1) All private rights of way over land which may be acquired compulsorily under section 2 of this Act shall be extinguished on the acquisition of the land, whether compulsorily or by agreement, or on the entry on the land in pursuance of section 11(1) of the Compulsory Purchase Act 1965, as applied by section 2 of this Act, whichever is the sooner.

(2) A person who suffers loss by the extinguishment of a right under this paragraph shall be entitled to compensation to be determined, in case of dispute, under and in accordance with Part I of the Land Compensation Act 1961.

Compensation

5. Section 4 of the Acquisition of Land Act 1981 (assessment of compensation where unnecessary work undertaken to obtain compensation) shall have effect in relation to a compulsory acquisition under section 2 of this Act as if it were a compulsory purchase to which that Act applies.

6. Where land is or rights in or over land are compulsorily acquired under section 2 of this Act, section 261 of the Highways Act 1980 (benefit to be taken into account in assessing compensation) shall have effect as if the acquisition were one in relation to which that section has effect.

PART III

TEMPORARY OCCUPATION OF LAND

7.—(1) Subject to the provisions of this paragraph, the Secretary of State may, in connection with the construction of—

(a) the scheduled works specified in column (1) of the following table, or

(b) any works which are necessary or expedient for the purposes of, in connection with or in consequence of those works, enter upon and take temporary possession of the land in the areas specified in columns (2) and (3) of that table for such purposes as are specified in column (4) of that table and may, for such purposes, remove buildings on that land and provide means of access to that land.

TABLE

(1) Works Nos.	(2) Area	(3) Number of land shown on deposited plans	(4) Purpose for which temporary possession may be taken
1, 1A and 1B	Borough of Monmouth Community of Magor with Undy	4t, 5t, 6t, 7t and 10t	Construction access
1, 1B, 2, 2A, 2B, 7, 7A and 8	Borough of Monmouth Community of Rogiet	3t, 6 and 10	Construction access
2, 2A, 2B, 7, 7A and 8	Borough of Monmouth Community of Rogiet	11, 12, 13 and 14	Construction access and regrading of land prior to return to agriculture
2, 2A, 2B, 7, 7A and 8	Borough of Monmouth Community of Rogiet	21 and 22	Construction access
2	Borough of Monmouth Community of Rogiet	35, 36, 37, 38, 39 and 40	Temporary service diversions
2, 3, 9 and 27	Borough of Monmouth Community of Caldicot	14, 15, 16, 17, 18, 19, 20, 21 and 31t	Construction and manufacturing site and access and surface water drainage outfalls
3, 10, 28, 29, 30 and 31	District of Northavon Parish of Pilning and Severn Beach	2t and 76	Construction and manufacturing site and access
4, 4B, 4C, 13, 13A, 14, 15, 16, 16A and 17	District of Northavon Parish of Olveston	43t	Construction access
5	District of Northavon Parish of Almondsbury	1t, 12, 19 and 20	Temporary service diversions

(2) Not less than 28 days before entering upon and taking temporary possession of land under this paragraph the Secretary of State shall give notice to the owners and occupiers of the land.

(3) The Secretary of State shall not, without the agreement of the owners and occupiers of the land, remain in possession of land under this paragraph after a period of one year from the completion of the work specified in relation to that land in column (1) of the table in sub-paragraph (1) above.

(4) All private rights of way over land of which the Secretary of State takes temporary possession under this paragraph shall be suspended and unenforceable for so long as the Secretary of State remains in lawful possession of the land.

(5) Before giving up possession of land of which temporary possession has been taken under this paragraph, the Secretary of State shall remove all temporary works and restore the land to the reasonable satisfaction of the owners and occupiers of the land; but the Secretary of State shall not be required to replace a building removed by him under this paragraph.

(6) The Secretary of State shall pay compensation to—

(a) the owners and occupiers of land of which temporary possession is taken under this paragraph for loss or damage resulting from the exercise of the powers conferred by this paragraph in relation to that land, and

(b) a person who suffers loss or damage by reason of the suspension of a right under this paragraph.

(7) Nothing in this paragraph shall affect any liability to pay compensation under section 10(2) of the Compulsory Purchase Act 1965, as applied by section 2 of this Act, or under any other enactment, in respect of loss or damage arising from the execution of any works, other than loss or damage for which compensation is payable under sub-paragraph (6) above.

(8) A dispute as to a person's entitlement to compensation under sub-paragraph (6) above, or as to the amount of the compensation, shall be determined under and in accordance with Part I of the Land Compensation Act 1961.

PART IV

CORRECTION OF DEPOSITED PLANS

8.—(1) If the deposited plans or the book of reference to those plans are inaccurate in their description of any land, or in their statement or description of the ownership or occupation of any land, the Secretary of State, after giving not less than ten days' notice to the owner and occupier of the land in question, may apply to two justices having jurisdiction in the place where the land is situated for the correction of the plans or book of reference.

(2) If on such an application it appears to the justices that the misstatement or wrong description arose from mistake or inadvertence, the justices shall certify accordingly and shall in their certificate state in what respect a matter is misstated or wrongly described.

(3) The certificate shall be deposited in the office of the Clerk of the Parliaments and a copy of it in the Private Bill Office of the House of Commons and at the principal offices of Avon County Council, Gwent County Council, Bristol City Council, Northavon District Council and Monmouth Borough Council; and the deposited plans or the book of reference shall be deemed to be corrected according to the certificate and it shall be lawful for the Secretary of State, in accordance with the certificate, to proceed under this Act as if the deposited plans or the book of reference had always been in the corrected form.

(4) A person with whom a copy of the certificate is deposited under this paragraph shall keep it with the documents to which it relates.

(5) In this paragraph "book of reference" means the book deposited in November 1990 in connection with the Severn Bridges Bill in the office of the Clerk of the Parliaments and the Private Bill Office of the House of Commons.

Section 3	SCHEDULE 3

AUTHORISED WORKS: SUPPLEMENTARY

Stopping up of highways

1.—(1) Subject to the provisions of this paragraph, the Secretary of State may, in connection with the construction of the works authorised by this Act, stop up—

(a) each of the highways or parts of highways specified, by reference to the letters and numbers shown on the deposited plans, in columns (1) and (2) of the following table, and

(b) any other bridleways or footpaths within the limits of deviation for the scheduled works.

(2) On his doing so, all rights of way over or along the highway or part so stopped up shall be extinguished.

(3) An existing highway or part of a highway specified in columns (1) and (2) of Part II of the following table shall not be stopped up under this paragraph until the Secretary of State is satisfied that the new highway to be substituted for it, which is specified in relation to it by reference to the letters shown on the deposited plans or by reference to scheduled works in column (3) of that Part of the table, has been completed and is open for public use.

TABLE

PART I

HIGHWAYS TO BE STOPPED UP

(1) *Area*	(2) *Length of highway to be stopped up*
County of Gwent Borough of Monmouth Community of Caldicot	Footpath FP5 from B2 to B5

(1) Area	(2) Length of highway to be stopped up
County of Avon District of Northavon Parish of Olveston	Bridleway BW11 from K1 to K2 Footpath FP9 from L1 to L2 Footpath FP12 from M1 to M2 Awkley Lane from P1 to P2
Parish of Pilning and Severn Beach	Footpath FP46 from N1 to N2
Parish of Almondsbury	Vimpennys Lane from A1 to A2

PART II

HIGHWAYS TO BE STOPPED UP AND NEW HIGHWAYS SUBSTITUTED FOR THEM

(1) Area	(2) Highway or part to be stopped up	(3) New highway to be substituted for it
County of Gwent Borough of Monmouth Community of Magor with Undy	Track CRF30 from A1 to A2	Track from A1 to A3
Communities of Magor with Undy and Rogiet	M4 eastbound carriageway from B1 to B2	Work No. 2A
	M4 westbound carriageway from C1 to C2	Work No. 2B
Community of Rogiet	Station Road and Track CRF16 from A1 to A2	Work No. 7
	Track CRF15 from B1 to B2	Works Nos. 7 and 7A
Community of Caldicot	Footpath FP19 from A1 to A2	Work No. 8
	Footpath FP6 from B1 to B2 and footpath FP3 from B2 to B3	Footpath from B1 to B4
	Footpath FP2 from B3 to B6	Work No. 9
Communities of Mathern and Portskewett	A48 from A1 to A2	Work No. 9A
	B4245 from B1 to B2 to B3 and R140 from B2 to B4	Works Nos. 9A, 9B and 9C
Community of Portskewett	R139 from C1 to C2	Works Nos. 9E, 9F and 9G
County of Avon District of Northavon Parish of Pilning and Severn Beach	B4064 New Passage Road/ Redwick Road from A1 to A2	Works Nos. 11 and 18
	Footpath FP9 from B3 to B4	Work No. 11
	Footpath FP10 from B1 to B2	Footpath from B1 to B3 and Work No. 11
	Footpath FP13 from C1 to C2 and from C3 to C4	Footpath from C1 to C5 to C6 to C7 to C8, Work No. 12 and footpath from C9 to C4
	A403 Severn Road from D1 to D2	Work No. 12
Parishes of Pilning and Severn Beach and Olveston	B4055 Northwick Road from E1 to E2	Works Nos. 13 and 13A
	Redham Lane from F1 to F2	Works Nos. 13 and 13A

(1) *Area*	(2) *Highway or part to be stopped up*	(3) *New highway to be substituted for it*
Parish of Olveston	Footpath FP10 from A1 to A2	Footpath from A1 to A3 and Work No. 14
	Bridleway BW8 from B1 to B2	Work No. 14
	Holm Lane from C1 to C2	Work No. 15
	Footpath FP19 from D1 to D2 and footpath FP20 from D1 to D3	Footpath from D2 to D3
	Greenditch Street from E1 to E2	Works Nos. 16 and 16A
	Awkley Lane from F1 to F2	Works Nos. 16 and 16A
	Footpath FP21 from G1 to G2	Footpath from G1 to G3 to G4 and Works Nos. 16 and 16A
	Footpath FP28 from O1 to O2 and footpath FP62 from O2 to O3	Footpath from O1 to O3
	Bridleway (unnumbered) from R1 to R2	Bridleway from R1 to R3
	Hardy Lane from H1 to H2	Work No. 17
	M4 westbound carriageway from J1 to J2	Work No. 4C
Parish of Pilning and Severn Beach	Shaft Road from G1 to G2	Works Nos. 18 and 18A
	Green Lane from H1 to H2	Works Nos. 11 and 18
	Footpath FP15 from V1 to V2	Works Nos. 11 and 18
	Footpath FP28 from J1 to J2	Footpath from J1 to J3 to J4
	Church Road from K1 to K2	Footpath from K1 to K3 and Work No. 19
	A403 Severn Road from L1 to L2	Work No. 20
	Footpath FP49 from M1 to M2	Footpath from M1 to M3, Work No. 20 and footpath from M4 to M2
	Footpath FP48 from P1 to P2	Footpath from N1 to P1
	Footpath FP58 from Q1 to Q2	Work No. 21
Parishes of Pilning and Severn Beach and Almondsbury	Footpath FP61 from R1 to R2 to R3 to R4 to R5, footpath FP60 from R3 to R6 and footpath FP62 from R2 to R7	Footpath from R1 to R7 to R8 to R9 and Works Nos. 22 and 22A
	Farm Lane from S1 to S2	Works Nos. 22 and 22A
Parish of Almondsbury and City of Bristol	Bridleway BW101 Minor's Lane from B1 to B2	Works Nos. 23A, 23 and 23B
City of Bristol	Severn Road Hallen from A1 to A2	Work No. 23
	Footpath FP556 from B1 to B2	Footpath from B2 to B3
	Footpath FP555 from C1 to C2	Footpath from C1 to C3, Work No. 23 and footpath from B3 to B2 to C4

(1) Area	(2) Highway or part to be stopped up	(3) New highway to be substituted for it
	Footpath FP553 from D1 to D2	Footpath from D1 to C1 to C3, Work No. 23, footpath from B3 to B2 to C4, footpath FP555 and footpath from C2 to D2
	Moorhouse Lane from E1 to E2	Work No. 24
	Footpath FP4 from F1 to F2	Footpath from F2 to F3
	Lawrence Weston Road from G1 to G2	Footpath and cycle track from G1 to G3 and Work No. 25
	Kings Weston Lane from H1 to H2	Work No. 26
	M5 southbound off slip road of Lawrence Weston interchange from J1 to J2	Works Nos. 6, 6A and 6D
	M5 northbound on slip road of Lawrence Weston interchange from K1 to K2	Works Nos. 6C and 6E

(4) No part of a highway shall be stopped up under this paragraph unless the condition specified in sub-paragraph (5) below is satisfied in relation to all land abutting on any side of that part of the highway.

(5) The condition referred to in sub-paragraph (4) above is that—

(a) the Secretary of State is in possession of the land, or

(b) there is no right of access to the land from the part of the highway concerned, or

(c) the Secretary of State is satisfied that there is reasonably convenient access to the land otherwise than from the part of the highway concerned, or

(d) the owners and occupiers of the land have agreed to the stopping up.

(6) A person who suffers loss by the extinguishment of a private right under this paragraph shall be entitled to compensation to be determined, in case of dispute, under and in accordance with Part I of the Land Compensation Act 1961.

Temporary interference with highways

2.—(1) The Secretary of State may, for the purpose of constructing the works authorised by this Act, temporarily stop up, open, break up or interfere with, or alter or divert, the whole or a part of a highway within—

(a) the limits of deviation for the scheduled works,

(b) the limits of land to be acquired, or

(c) the limits of land for temporary occupation,

and may carry out all necessary works for, or in connection with, doing so.

(2) The Secretary of State shall provide reasonable access for all persons, with or without vehicles, going to or returning from premises abutting on a highway affected by the exercise of the powers conferred by this paragraph if there would otherwise be no such access.

Provision of new trunk and special roads

3.—(1) On the day on which this Act is passed the new highways forming or forming part of Works Nos. 2, 2A, 2B, 3, 4, 4A, 4C, 5, 6, 6A, 6B, 6C, 6D and 6E shall become trunk roads and special roads for the exclusive use of traffic of Classes I and II of the classes of traffic specified in Schedule 4 to the Highways Act 1980.

(2) The highways which become special roads by virtue of sub-paragraph (1) above shall be treated as provided by the Secretary of State (by means of the construction of new highways under section 24(1) of the Highways Act 1980) under a scheme made by him under section 16 of that Act—

(a) prescribing the route of those roads as the route for the special roads to be provided under the scheme,

(b) prescribing both the classes of traffic specified in that sub-paragraph, and

(c) specifying the day on which this Act is passed as the date on which the roads become trunk roads.

Trunk and special road improvements

4. Works Nos. 1, 1A, 1B and 4B shall be treated as improvements of the M4 and its slip roads carried out under Part V of the Highways Act 1980.

Other highway works

5.—(1) Works Nos. 7, 7A, 8, 9, 9A, 9B, 9C, 9D, 9E, 9F, 9G, 9H, 11, 12, 13, 13A, 14, 15, 16, 16A, 17, 18, 18A, 19, 20, 21, 22, 22A, 23, 23A, 23B, 24, 25 and 26 and the stopping up of highways in pursuance of this Schedule shall be treated as authorised by an order made by the Secretary of State under section 18 of the Highways Act 1980 in relation to the roads to which paragraphs 3 and 4 above apply.

(2) The new highways forming or forming part of the works referred to in sub-paragraph (1) above shall be treated as new highways authorised to be constructed by the order so referred to.

(3) The provisions of Schedule 1 to this Act and this Schedule relating to a work or operation which is treated by this paragraph as authorised by the order referred to in sub-paragraph (1) above shall be treated for the purposes of the Highways Act 1980 as provisions of the order.

(4) The order referred to in sub-paragraph (1) above shall be deemed to include provision preserving (subject to section 21 of the Highways Act 1980) the rights of any persons who are statutory undertakers for the purposes of that Act in respect of any apparatus of theirs which is under, in, on, over, along or across a highway immediately before it is stopped up in pursuance of this Schedule.

6.—(1) The Secretary of State may determine in the case of a highway to which paragraph 5(2) above applies that the highway is to be a footpath, a cycle track, a bridleway or an all purpose road.

(2) In sub-paragraph (1) above "all purpose road" means a highway (other than a cycle track) over which the public right of way includes a right of way for the passage of vehicles.

(3) The Secretary of State may classify a highway to which paragraph 5(2) above applies in any manner in which, and for any purposes for which, he can classify highways under subsection (3) of section 12 of the Highways Act 1980; and on the date of its transfer under sub-paragraph (4) below a highway classified under this sub-paragraph shall become a highway classified in the manner and for the purposes in question as if so classified under that subsection.

(4) On the date certified by the Secretary of State as the date on which a highway to which paragraph 5(2) above applies is open for public use—

(a) if it is in England, it shall be transferred to Avon County Council, and

(b) if it is in Wales, it shall be transferred to Gwent County Council.

Section 7   SCHEDULE 4

EARLY END OF TOLLING BY SECRETARY OF STATE

Receipts

1.—(1) The receipts referred to in section 7 of this Act are relevant receipts and assumed interest receipts.

(2) In this Schedule "relevant receipts" means—

(a) tolls collected by or on behalf of the Secretary of State,

(b) other sums received by the Secretary of State—

    (i) under or by virtue of this Act, or

    (ii) in connection with the exercise of relevant functions by him or on his behalf,

(c) capital sums and interest paid to the Secretary of State by the concessionaire in accordance with the concession agreement in respect of the existing deficit,

(d) any sums received by the Secretary of State in consequence of or in connection with the termination of the concession agreement or in pursuance of a right transferred to him under or by virtue of section 19 of this Act on the termination, and

(e) any other receipts of the Secretary of State which he may specify as relevant receipts.

(3) In this Schedule "assumed interest receipts" means interest assumed to accrue on any daily surplus of relevant receipts over the amounts treated as applied for the purposes mentioned in paragraph 2 below.

Purposes

2. The purposes referred to in section 7 of this Act and this Schedule are—
(a) meeting with interest the existing deficit,
(b) reimbursement with interest of any expenditure properly chargeable to capital account and incurred by the Secretary of State in respect of—
  (i) the construction of the new bridge or the toll plaza forming part of Work No. 2, or
  (ii) the making safe, dismantling or reconstruction of that bridge or toll plaza if partly constructed otherwise than at the expense of the Secretary of State,
(c) reimbursement with interest of all expenditure (not falling within sub-paragraph (b) above) properly chargeable to capital account and incurred by the Secretary of State in making (whether to the concessionaire or to any other person) any payment in consequence of or in connection with the termination of, or otherwise under, the concession agreement,
(d) reimbursement with interest of any expenditure properly chargeable to capital account and incurred by the Secretary of State—
  (i) under or by virtue of this Act, or
  (ii) in connection with the exercise of relevant functions by him or on his behalf,
  before the end of the period during which tolls may be levied,
(e) meeting all expenditure (including administrative expenses) properly chargeable to revenue account and so incurred,
(f) making any provision which the Secretary of State may consider appropriate for defraying the expenditure properly chargeable to revenue account and likely to be incurred by the Secretary of State as mentioned in sub-paragraph (d)(i) and (ii) above after the end of the period during which tolls may be levied,
(g) making such provision as in the opinion of the Secretary of State is required for making payments to or in respect of persons employed by him or by a person appointed to collect tolls as his agent whose contracts of employment are terminated in consequence of tolls ceasing to be leviable,
(h) making such provision as in the opinion of the Secretary of State is equivalent to that which would be required—
  (i) for keeping the bridges and toll plaza areas insured against damage not amounting to complete destruction throughout the period during which tolls may be levied,
  (ii) for insuring against liabilities arising in that period from the Secretary of State's ownership or occupation of the bridges and toll plaza areas, or from anything done or omitted in the course of the exercise by or on behalf of the Secretary of State of relevant functions or the power to levy tolls,
  if the bridges and toll plaza areas were owned and maintained, and those functions were exercisable, by a commercial undertaking,
(i) meeting any other expenditure (not falling within any of the preceding sub-paragraphs) which is incurred by the Secretary of State in consequence of this Act and which is specified by him as falling within this paragraph,
(j) making provision for interest assumed to be due on any daily deficiency of relevant receipts as against the amounts treated as applied for the purposes mentioned in this paragraph, and
(k) meeting with interest the aggregate of any annual deficiencies of relevant receipts and assumed interest receipts as against the amounts treated as applied for any of the purposes mentioned in the preceding sub-paragraphs.

Supplementary

3. For the purpose of determining the amount of relevant receipts and assumed interest receipts or the amounts from time to time required for the purposes mentioned in paragraph 2 above, such assumptions shall be followed by the Secretary of State as to—
(a) the manner in which those receipts are to be treated as applied for those purposes,
(b) the times at which payments would be made in respect of expenditure, interest and other amounts referred to in any sub-paragraph of that paragraph, and
(c) the amounts of such payments,
as the Treasury may direct; and such a direction may require different assumptions to be followed in relation to different times and in relation to, or to interest on, different expenditure or other amounts referred to in any sub-paragraph of that paragraph.

4. A reference in this Schedule to interest is a reference to interest at such rate as may be determined to be appropriate in accordance with directions given by the Treasury; and different rates may be so determined in relation to—
(a) different times,

    (b) different descriptions of relevant receipts, and

    (c) different sub-paragraphs of paragraph 2 above, and different expenditure or other amounts referred to in any of those sub-paragraphs.

    5. In this Schedule "the existing deficit" means the amount shown in the statement of accounts prepared under section 28(1)(a) of this Act as the amount of the debt to the Consolidated Fund immediately before the appointed day, adjusted if necessary to take account of any amounts so shown as stores or owed by debtors, or as due to creditors.

Section 40   SCHEDULE 5

REPEALS

Chapter	Short title	Extent of repeal
1965 c. 24.	The Severn Bridge Tolls Act 1965.	The whole Act.
1980 c. 66.	The Highways Act 1980.	In Schedule 24, paragraph 14.

INDEX

References are to section numbers

ACQUISITION OF LAND, 2
  compensation, Sched. 2, Pt. II, paras. 5–6
  compulsory powers, 2(3)
  easements, Sched. 2, Pt. II, para. 1
  Land Clauses Act 1845 inapplicable, 2(5)
  mines and minerals, Sched. 2, Pt. II, para. 3
  notices to treat, cut-off date, 2(4)
  outside limits of deviation, 2(1)(b), Sched. 2, Pt. I
  private rights of way, Sched. 2, Pt. II, para. 4
  relocation of Caldicot rifle range, 2(1)(c)
  subsoil and under surface, Sched. 2, Pt. II, para. 2
  supplementary provisions as to, 2(6), Sched. 2
  within limits of deviation, 2(1)(a)
AVON COUNTY COUNCIL,
  staff presently employed, 18

BRISTOL,
  land not to be acquired, 2(2)

CALDICOT RIFLE RANGE, 2(1)(c)
CITATION, 41
COMMENCEMENT, 42
CONCESSION AGREEMENT, 4
  accounts and reports, 27
  exercise of management functions, 15
  existing bridge staff employed by Avon County Council, 18
  interests in land granted to concessionaire, 17
  power to levy tolls, 6
  termination, 19–20
CONSTRUCTION OF NEW BRIDGE, 1–3
  concession agreement, 4
  protection of, 31
  Secretary of State's powers, 1(1)
  Town and Country Planning Act 1990, not development under, 35

FINANCIAL MATTERS,
  accounting assumptions, Sched. 4, paras. 3–5
  accounts and reports,
    of concessionaire, 27
    of Secretary of State, 27
  receipts and expenditure, 38
  unpaid tolls, 26

GLOUCESTER HARBOUR TRUSTEES, 29(2)–(3)

HIGHWAYS,
  special roads,
    improvements, Sched. 3, para. 4
    provision of, Sched. 3, para. 3
    traffic regulations, 32(2)
  stopping up, 3, Sched. 3
  temporary interference with, Sched. 3, para. 2
  trunk roads,
    improvements, Sched. 3, para. 4
    provision of new, Sched. 3, para. 3
  works, generally, Sched. 3, para. 5

INTERPRETATION, 39

LOCAL AUTHORITIES,
  Avon County Council existing staff, 18
  employees as appointed persons, 23(4)
  services in connection with tolls, 5(6)–(7), 6(10)

MANAGEMENT, 15–20
  delegation of functions to concessionaire, 16
  interests in land granted to concessionaire, 17
  on termination of concession agreement, 19–20
  staff employed by Avon County Council, 18
  under concession agreement, 15

NOTICES TO TREAT, 2(4)

OFFENCES,
  bodies corporate, by, 36
  prevention of damage, 24(2)
  river traffic regulations, 31(5)
  road traffic regulations, 21(2)
  tolls, 14(4)–(5)
OPERATION OF BRIDGES, *see* CONCESSION AGREEMENT; FINANCIAL MATTERS; MANAGEMENT; TOLLS; TRAFFIC MANAGEMENT
ORDERS AND REGULATIONS, 37

PLANS,
  construction in accordance with, 1(2)
  correction of, Sched. 2, Pt. IV
  deviation from, Sched. 1, Pt. II, 1(2)

PLAZA AREAS, *see* TOLLS
PROTECTION OF NEW BRIDGE, 31

REPEALS, 40, Sched. 5
ROGIET, 2(1)(c)

SCHEDULED WORKS, 1(1), Sched. 1
SEVERN RIVER,
  dredging, 30
  interference with river, 29
  regulation of traffic, 31(4)–(5)

TEMPORARY OCCUPATION OF LAND, 2(6), Sched.
  2, Pt. III
TOLLS,
  direction of travel, 5(2)
    two-way, 11
  early end of, 7
    provisions as to, Sched. 4
  funding requirement, 7
  level of, 9
    supplementary provisions, 10
  local authority services, 5(6)–(7), 6(10)
  notices to be displayed, 14(2)
  offences, 14(4)–(5)
  payment regulations, 14
  plaza areas,
    designation, 14(1)(a)
    maintenance of, 32(1)
    rating exemption, 34

TOLLS—*cont.*
  power to levy, 5(1)
    appointment of agent, 5(5)
    commencement, 5(3)
    concession agreement, under, 6
    termination, 5(4)
  pre-payment, 13, 14(3)
  suspension of, 12
  unpaid, recovery of, 26
  vehicles affected, 8
TRAFFIC REGULATION,
  appointed persons, 23
  breakdowns and repairs, 21(1)(b)–(e)
    breakdown defined, 21(5)
  Crown immunity, 21(3)–(4)
  cycleways, 25
  footways, 25
  obstruction, prevention of, 21
  offences, 21(2)
  prevention of damage, 24
  removal of vehicles, 21(1)(e)–(g), 21(6)
    accommodation pounds, 32(2)
  special restrictions, 22
  special roads, 32(2)

VEHICLES,
  categories subject to tolls, 8
  See also TRAFFIC REGULATION

WATERCOURSES,
  interference with, 33

SOCIAL SECURITY CONTRIBUTIONS AND BENEFITS ACT 1992*

(1992 c. 4)

ARRANGEMENT OF SECTIONS

PART I

CONTRIBUTIONS

Preliminary

SECT.
1. Outline of contributory system.
2. Categories of earners.
3. "Earnings" and "earner".
4. Payments treated as remuneration and earnings.

Class 1 contributions

5. Earnings limits for Class 1 contributions.
6. Liability for Class 1 contributions.
7. "Secondary contributor".
8. Calculation of primary Class 1 contributions.
9. Calculation of secondary Class 1 contributions.

Class 1A contributions

10. Class 1A contributions.

Class 2 contributions

11. Liability for Class 2 contributions.
12. Late paid Class 2 contributions.

Class 3 contributions

13. Class 3 contributions.
14. Restriction on right to pay Class 3 contributions.

Class 4 contributions

15. Class 4 contributions recoverable under the Income Tax Acts.
16. Application of Income Tax Acts and destination of Class 4 contributions.
17. Exceptions, deferment and incidental matters relating to Class 4 contributions.
18. Class 4 contributions recoverable under regulations.

General

19. General power to regulate liability for contributions.

PART II

CONTRIBUTORY BENEFITS

Preliminary

20. Descriptions of contributory benefits.
21. Contribution conditions.
22. Earnings factors.
23. Provisions supplemental to sections 21 and 22.
24. Records of earnings and calculation of earnings factors in absence of records.

Unemployment benefit

25. Unemployment benefit.
26. Duration of unemployment benefit.

---

* Annotations by N.J. Wikeley, M.A. (Cantab.), Barrister, Lecturer in Law, University of Birmingham.

27. Interruption of employment in connection with trade dispute.
28. Unemployment benefit—other disqualifications etc.
29. Exemptions from disqualification for unemployment benefit.
30. Abatement of unemployment benefit on account of payments of occupational or personal pension.

Sickness benefit

31. Sickness benefit.
32. Sickness benefit—disqualifications etc.

Invalidity benefits

33. Invalidity pension.
34. Invalidity allowance.

Maternity

35. State maternity allowance.

Benefits for widows and widowers

36. Widow's payment.
37. Widowed mother's allowance.
38. Widow's pension.
39. Rate of widowed mother's allowance and widow's pension.
40. Invalidity pension for widows.
41. Invalidity pension for widowers.
42. Entitlement to invalidity pension on termination of employment after period of entitlement to disability working allowance.

Retirement pensions (Categories A and B)

43. Persons entitled to more than one retirement pension.
44. Category A retirement pension.
45. The additional pension in a Category A retirement pension.
46. Modifications of section 45 for calculating the additional pension in certain benefits.
47. Increase of Category A retirement pension for invalidity.
48. Use of former spouse's contributions.
49. Category B retirement pension for women.
50. Rate of Category B retirement pension for women.
51. Category B retirement pension for widowers.
52. Special provision for surviving spouses.
53. Special provision for married women.
54. Category A and Category B retirement pensions: supplemental provisions.
55. Increase of retirement pension where entitlement is deferred.

Child's special allowance

56. Child's special allowance—existing beneficiaries.

Provisions relating to unemployment benefit, sickness benefit and invalidity benefit

57. Determination of days for which benefit is payable.
58. Incapacity for work: work as councillor to be disregarded.

Invalidity benefit—disqualifications etc.

59. Invalidity benefit—disqualifications etc.

Complete or partial failure to satisfy contribution conditions

60. Complete or partial failure to satisfy contribution conditions.
61. Exclusion of increase of benefit for failure to satisfy contribution condition.

Graduated retirement benefit

62. Graduated retirement benefit.

Part III

Non-Contributory Benefits

63. Descriptions of non-contributory benefits.

Attendance allowance

64. Entitlement.
65. Period and rate of allowance.
66. Attendance allowance for the terminally ill.
67. Exclusions by regulation.

Severe disablement allowance

68. Entitlement and rate.
69. Severe disablement allowance: age related addition.

Invalid care allowance

70. Invalid care allowance.

Disability living allowance

71. Disability living allowance.
72. The care component.
73. The mobility component.
74. Mobility component for certain persons eligible for invalid carriages.
75. Persons 65 or over.
76. Disability living allowance—supplementary.

Guardian's allowance

77. Guardian's allowance.

Benefits for the aged

78. Category C and Category D retirement pensions and other benefits for the aged.
79. Age addition.

Part IV

Increases for Dependants

Child dependants

80. Beneficiary's dependent children.
81. Restrictions on increase—child not living with beneficiary etc.

Adult dependants

82. Short-term benefit: increase for adult dependants.
83. Pension increase (wife).
84. Pension increase (husband).
85. Pension increase (person with care of children).
86. Increase of woman's invalidity pension (husband).
87. Rate of increase where associated retirement pension is attributable to reduced contributions.
88. Pension increases to be in respect of only one adult dependant.

Miscellaneous

89. Earnings to include occupational and personal pensions for purposes of provisions relating to increases of benefits in respect of child or adult dependants.
90. Beneficiaries under sections 68 and 70.
91. Effect of trade disputes on entitlement to increases.
92. Dependency increases: continuation of awards in cases of fluctuating earnings.
93. Dependency increases on termination of employment after period of entitlement to disability working allowance.

PART V

BENEFIT FOR INDUSTRIAL INJURIES

General provisions

94. Right to industrial injuries benefit.
95. Relevant employments.
96. Persons treated as employers for certain purposes.
97. Accidents in course of illegal employments.
98. Earner acting in breach of regulations, etc.
99. Earner travelling in employer's transport.
100. Accidents happening while meeting emergency.
101. Accident caused by another's misconduct etc.

Sickness benefit

102. Sickness benefit in respect of industrial injury.

Disablement pension

103. Disablement pension.
104. Increase where constant attendance needed.
105. Increase for exceptionally severe disablement.

Other benefits and increases

106. Benefits and increases subject to qualifications as to time.

Successive accidents

107. Adjustments for successive accidents.

Prescribed industrial diseases etc.

108. Benefit in respect of prescribed industrial diseases, etc.
109. General provisions relating to benefit under section 108.
110. Respiratory diseases.

Old cases

111. Workmen's compensation etc.

PART VI

MISCELLANEOUS PROVISIONS RELATING TO PARTS I TO V

Earnings

112. Certain sums to be earnings.

Disqualification and suspension

113. General provisions as to disqualification and suspension.

Persons maintaining dependants etc.

114. Persons maintaining dependants, etc.

Special cases

115. Crown employment—Parts I to VI.
116. Her Majesty's forces.
117. Mariners, airmen, etc.
118. Married women and widows.
119. Persons outside Great Britain.
120. Employment at sea (continental shelf operations).
121. Treatment of certain marriages.

Interpretation

122. Interpretation of Parts I to VI and supplementary provisions.

Part VII

Income-Related Benefits

General

123. Income-related benefits.

Income support

124. Income support.
125. Severe hardship cases.
126. Trade disputes.
127. Effect of return to work.

Family credit

128. Family credit.

Disability working allowance

129. Disability working allowance.

Housing benefit

130. Housing benefit.

Community charge benefits

131. Community charge benefits.
132. Couples.
133. Polygamous marriages.

General

134. Exclusions from benefit.
135. The applicable amount.
136. Income and capital.
137. Interpretation of Part VII and supplementary provisions.

Part VIII

The Social Fund

138. Payments out of the social fund.
139. Awards by social fund officers.
140. Principles of determination.

Part IX

Child Benefit

141. Child benefit.
142. Meaning of "child".
143. Meaning of "person responsible for child".
144. Exclusions and priority.
145. Rate of child benefit.
146. Persons outside Great Britain.
147. Interpretation of Part IX and supplementary provisions.

Part X

Christmas bonus for pensioners

148. Entitlement of pensioners to Christmas bonus.
149. Provisions supplementary to section 148.
150. Interpretation of Part X.

PART XI

STATUTORY SICK PAY

Employer's Liability

151. Employer's liability.

The qualifying conditions

152. Period of incapacity for work.
153. Period of entitlement.
154. Qualifying days.

Limitations on entitlement, etc.

155. Limitations on entitlement.
156. Notification of incapacity for work.

Rate of payment, etc.

157. Rate of payment.
158. Recovery by employers of amounts paid by way of statutory sick pay.
159. Power to substitute provisions for s.158(2).

Miscellaneous

160. Relationship with benefits and other payments, etc.
161. Crown employment—Part XI.
162. Special classes of persons.
163. Interpretation of Part XI and supplementary provisions.

PART XII

STATUTORY MATERNITY PAY

164. Statutory maternity pay—entitlement and liability to pay.
165. The maternity pay period.
166. Rates of payment.
167. Recovery of amounts paid by way of statutory maternity pay.
168. Relationship with benefits and other payments etc.
169. Crown employment—Part XII.
170. Special classes of persons.
171. Interpretation of Part XII and supplementary provisions.

PART XIII

GENERAL

Interpretation

172. Application of Act in relation to territorial waters.
173. Age.
174. References to Acts.

Subordinate legislation

175. Regulations, orders and schemes.
176. Parliamentary control.

Short title, commencement and extent

177. Short title, commencement and extent.

SCHEDULES:
   Schedule 1—Supplementary provisions relating to contributions of Classes 1, 1A, 2 and 3.
   Schedule 2—Levy of Class 4 contributions with income tax.

Schedule 3—Contribution conditions for entitlement to benefit.
    Part I—The conditions.
    Part II—Satisfaction of conditions in early years of contribution.
Schedule 4—Rates of benefits, etc.
    Part I—Contributory periodical benefits.
    Part II—Widow's payment.
    Part III—Non-contributory periodical benefits.
    Part IV—Increases for dependants.
    Part V—Rates of industrial injuries benefit.
Schedule 5—Increase of pension where entitlement is deferred.
Schedule 6—Assessment of extent of disablement.
Schedule 7—Industrial injuries benefits.
    Part I—Unemployability supplement.
    Part II—Disablement gratuity.
    Part III—Increase of disablement pension during hospital treatment.
    Part IV—Reduced earnings allowance.
    Part V—Retirement allowance.
    Part VI—Industrial death benefit.
Schedule 8—Industrial injuries and diseases (Old Cases).
    Part I—Workmen's compensation and industrial diseases benefit in respect of employment before 5th July 1948.
    Part II—Regulations providing for benefit.
    Part III—Interpretation.
Schedule 9—Exclusions from entitlement to child benefit.
Schedule 10—Priority between persons entitled to child benefit.
Schedule 11—Circumstances in which periods of entitlement to statutory sick pay do not arise.
Schedule 12—Relationship of statutory sick pay with benefits and other payments, etc.
Schedule 13—Relationship of statutory maternity pay with benefits and other payments etc.

An Act to consolidate certain enactments relating to social security contributions and benefits with amendments to give effect to recommendations of the Law Commission and the Scottish Law Commission.

[13th February 1992]

PARLIAMENTARY DEBATES
Hansard, H.L. Vol. 534, col. 1480.
The Bill was discussed in Joint Committee on November 27 and December 4, 1991.

INTRODUCTION AND GENERAL NOTE

The consolidation of social security law has long been overdue. The Social Security Contributions and Benefits Act 1992 is one of three statutes which seeks to achieve this objective so far as Great Britain is concerned. This Act deals with the contributions on which certain benefits depend, and the primary legislation governing individual benefits. The Social Security Administration Act 1992 covers such matters as claims for and payments of benefit, adjudication, appeals, enforcement and uprating. The Social Security (Consequential Provisions) Act 1992 contains repeals and consequential and transitional provisions arising out of the other two Acts. The Social Security Act 1975 is repealed in its entirety, as are the Child Benefit Act 1975 and the Social Security (Contributions) Acts of 1981, 1982 and 1991. There are substantial repeals of the Social Security Acts 1979, 1980, 1985, 1986, 1988, 1989 and 1990. Three further Acts deal with Northern Ireland (see General Note to s.177). The Law Commission and the Scottish Law Commission's report on the consolidating legislation was published in November 1991 (Cm 1726).

There is a presumption that Parliament, in enacting consolidating legislation, does not intend to alter the existing law. Furthermore, in interpreting a consolidating Act, reference should only be made to legislative antecedents if the words are unclear (*Farrell* v. *Alexander* [1977] A.C. 59; see also *Morton* v. *Chief Adjudication Officer* [1988] I.R.L.R. 444 on the construction of consolidating regulations). Decisions of the Social Security Commissioners and the courts on the earlier provisions will still be precedents. Some of the most important authorities are mentioned in these annotations, but, for a full analysis of this complex area of law, reference should be made to the latest annual edition of *Bonner, Mesher, Findlay and Ward* or *Rowland* as appropriate (see below). This is especially important given the frequent changes to regulations.

Commencement

The Act came into force on July 1, 1992, subject to the modifications contained in the Social Security (Consequential Provisions) Act 1992, Sched. 4 (s.177(4)).

Abbreviations

AO	:	adjudication officer
Bonner	:	*Non-Means Tested Benefits: The Legislation*, by D. Bonner, I. Hooker and R. White
DLADWAA 1991	:	Disability Living Allowance and Disability Working Allowance Act 1991
DSS	:	Department of Social Security
Findlay and Ward	:	*CPAG's Housing Benefit and Community Charge Legislation*, by L. Findlay and M. Ward
ICTA	:	Income and Corporation Taxes Act 1988
Lewis	:	*Compensation for Industrial Injury* (1987)
Mesher	:	*CPAG's Income Related Benefits: The Legislation*, by J. Mesher
Ogus and Barendt	:	*The Law of Social Security* (3rd ed., 1988)
Rowland	:	*Medical and Disability Appeal Tribunals: The Legislation*, by M. Rowland
SERPS	:	State earnings-related pension scheme
SSA 1975	:	Social Security Act 1975
SSA 1986	:	Social Security Act 1986
SSA 1988	:	Social Security Act 1988
SSA 1989	:	Social Security Act 1989
SSA 1990	:	Social Security Act 1990
SSAA 1992	:	Social Security Administration Act 1992
SS(CP)A 1992	:	Social Security (Consequential Provisions) Act 1992
SSHBA 1982	:	Social Security and Housing Benefits Act 1982
SSPA 1975	:	Social Security Pensions Act 1975
SSPA 1991	:	Statutory Sick Pay Act 1991
SSAT	:	social security appeal tribunal
The Way Ahead	:	*The Way Ahead: Benefits for Disabled People* (Cm 917, 1990)
Williams	:	*National Insurance Contributions, Statutory Sick Pay and Statutory Maternity Pay* (1987, looseleaf)

Part I

Contributions

Preliminary

Outline of contributory system

1.—(1) The funds required—

(a) for paying such benefits under this Act as are payable out of the National Insurance Fund and not out of other public money; and

(b) for the making of payments under section 162 of the Administration Act towards the cost of the National Health Service,

shall be provided by means of contributions payable to the Secretary of State by earners, employers and others, together with the additions under subsection (5) below.

(2) Contributions under this Part of this Act shall be of the following five classes—

(a) Class 1, earnings-related, payable under section 6 below, being—

(i) primary Class 1 contributions from employed earners; and

(ii) secondary Class 1 contributions from employers and other persons paying earnings;

(b) Class 1A, payable under section 10 below in respect of cars made available for private use and car fuel by persons liable to pay secondary Class 1 contributions and certain other persons;

(c) Class 2, flat-rate, payable weekly under section 11 below by self-employed earners;

(d) Class 3, payable under section 13 below by earners and others voluntarily with a view to providing entitlement to benefit, or making up entitlement; and

(e) Class 4, payable under section 15 below in respect of the profits or gains of a trade, profession or vocation, or under section 18 below in respect of equivalent earnings.

(3) The amounts and rates of contributions in this Part of this Act and the other figures in it which affect the liability of contributors shall—

(a) be subject to regulations under sections 19(4) and 116 to 120 below; and

(b) to the extent provided for by Part IX of the Administration Act be subject to alteration by orders made by the Secretary of State from year to year under that Part,

and the provisions of this Part of this Act are subject to the provisions of Part III of the Pensions Act (contracting-out—reduced rates of contributions).

(4) Schedule 1 to this Act—

(a) shall have effect with respect to the computation, collection and recovery of contributions of Classes 1, 1A, 2 and 3, and otherwise with respect to contributions of those classes; and

(b) shall also, to the extent provided by regulations made under section 18 below, have effect with respect to the computation, collection and recovery of Class 4 contributions, and otherwise with respect to such contributions, where under that section provision is made for contributions of that class to be recovered by the Secretary of State and not by the Inland Revenue.

(5) For each financial year there shall, by way of addition to contributions, be paid out of money provided by Parliament, in such manner and at such times as the Treasury may determine, amounts the total of which for any such year is equal to the aggregate of all statutory sick pay and statutory maternity pay recovered by employers and others in that year, as estimated by the Government Actuary or the Deputy Government Actuary.

(6) No person shall—

(a) be liable to pay Class 1, Class 1A or Class 2 contributions unless he fulfils prescribed conditions as to residence or presence in Great Britain;

(b) be entitled to pay Class 3 contributions unless he fulfils such conditions; or

(c) be entitled to pay Class 1, Class 1A or Class 2 contributions other than those which he is liable to pay, except so far as he is permitted by regulations to pay them.

DEFINITIONS

"the Administration Act": s.174.
"benefit": s.122(1).
"earner": ss.3(1) and 122(1).
"employed earner": ss.2(1) and 122(1).
"Great Britain": s.172.
"Inland Revenue": s.122(1).
"the Pensions Act": s.174.
"prescribe": s.122(1).
"self-employed earner": ss.2(1) and 122(1).

GENERAL NOTE

The basic structure of the National Insurance scheme was established in its present form as from April 6, 1975. Since then it has been subject to frequent amendment (see Report by the

Government Actuary, *National Insurance Fund Long-Term Financial Estimates* (H.C. 582, Session 1989–90)). The National Insurance Fund is used principally to pay contributory benefits, but allocations are also made to the National Health Service (subs. (1)(b)). The cost of providing industrial injuries benefits, statutory sick pay and statutory maternity pay was transferred from the National Insurance Fund to general taxation by SSA 1990, s.16. In the case of the latter two benefits this actually operates by way of a transfer of the appropriate sums from the Consolidated Fund to the National Insurance Fund (subs. (5)). The Redundancy Fund was merged with the National Insurance Fund by the Employment Act 1990, s.13.

The finances of the National Insurance Fund (excluding investment income) are derived from two sources: insured persons (either employees or self-employed persons) and employers (subs. (1)). The Exchequer contribution was abolished by SSA 1989, s.3. On the administration of the Fund, see SSAA 1992, Pt. XII.

There are now five classes of contributions (subs. (2)):

Class 1: earnings-related contributions by employed earners (primary Class 1 contributions) and their employers (secondary Class 1 contributions): ss.5–9.

Class 1A: graduated contributions by employers in respect of cars and fuel provided to directors and certain employees where private use is allowed: s.10.

Class 2: flat-rate contributions from self-employed earners: ss.11 and 12.

Class 3: voluntary flat-rate contributions by earners and others: ss.13 and 14.

Class 4: contributions from self-employed earners payable on profits or gains: ss.15–18.

The National Insurance Fund is financed on a pay-as-you-go basis with the contribution rates set from year to year so as to generate the income required to meet current expenditure on benefits and administration costs (subs. (3)).

Regulations made under subs. (3) also enable special provision to be made for married women and widows, members of H.M. forces, mariners and airmen, etc., persons outside Great Britain and those employed at sea.

Further detailed provision is made in Sched. 1 and in the Social Security (Contributions) Regulations 1979 (S.I. 1979 No. 591).

Categories of earners

2.—(1) In this Part of this Act and Parts II to V below—

(a) "employed earner" means a person who is gainfully employed in Great Britain either under a contract of service, or in an office (including elective office) with emoluments chargeable to income tax under Schedule E; and

(b) "self-employed earner" means a person who is gainfully employed in Great Britain otherwise than in employed earner's employment (whether or not he is also employed in such employment).

(2) Regulations may provide—

(a) for employment of any prescribed description to be disregarded in relation to liability for contributions otherwise arising from employment of that description;

(b) for a person in employment of any prescribed description to be treated, for the purposes of this Act, as falling within one or other of the categories of earner defined in subsection (1) above, notwithstanding that he would not fall within that category apart from the regulations.

(3) Where a person is to be treated by reference to any employment of his as an employed earner, then he is to be so treated for all purposes of this Act; and references throughout this Act to employed earner's employment shall be construed accordingly.

(4) Subsections (1) to (3) above are subject to the provision made by section 95 below as to the employments which are to be treated, for the purposes of industrial injuries benefit, as employed earner's employments.

(5) For the purposes of this Act, a person shall be treated as a self-employed earner as respects any week during any part of which he is such an earner (without prejudice to his being also treated as an employed earner as respects that week by reference to any other employment of his).

DEFINITIONS
  "contract of service": s.122(1).

"earner": ss.3(1) and 122(1).
"employed earner": subs. (1).
"employment": s.122(1).
"Great Britain": s.172.
"industrial injuries benefit": s.122(1).
"self-employed earner": s.122(1).
"week": s.122(1).

GENERAL NOTE
This section seeks to define the concepts of an "employed earner" and a "self-employed earner". This is primarily important for ascertaining an individual's liability to pay contributions in any given class.

Subs. (1)
The distinction between an employed earner and a self-employed earner is fundamental to the National Insurance scheme. Employed earners are liable to pay Class 1 contributions and may qualify for all contributory benefits. Self-employed earners are liable to pay Class 2 contributions (and those for Class 4 where profits or gains exceed the relevant threshold) and are eligible for all contributory benefits except unemployment benefit (s.21(2)). The decision on classification of an individual's working status is one for the Secretary of State, not the usual independent statutory adjudicating authorities. A question of law arising from such a decision may be referred for final determination to the High Court (or the Court of Session in Scotland): SSAA 1992, ss.17 and 18.

Employed earner. There are two types of employed earners: those *gainfully employed* under a *contract of service*, and those *gainfully employed* in an *office* with emoluments chargeable to income tax under Schedule E. Each of these three terms merits separate treatment.

Gainfully employed. Earlier legislation used the concept of being "gainfully occupied". The significance of the change in terminology in 1975 is not entirely clear, but it appears that the meaning of the phrase remains substantially unchanged. In the context of the definition of employed earner the term is probably otiose. It may, however, have some significance in the definition of self-employed earner, as a self-employed earner who has recently become "gainfully employed" may voluntarily contribute even if not currently liable to contribute. See further *Vandyk* v. *Minister of Pensions and National Insurance* [1955] 1 Q.B. 29.

Contract of service. The distinction between a contract of service and a contract for services is much litigated in various spheres of law. The definition of contract of service proffered by s.122(1) is only of very limited assistance, and so guidance must be sought from the case law. The preferred view of the courts today, in determining whether a contractual relationship is properly characterised as a contract of service or for services, is that account must be taken of a whole range of factors, no one of which is conclusive. Furthermore, the significance of any one factor may vary as it may have different weight attached to it in different cases. This is sometimes known as the "multiple factors" test (*Ready Mixed Concrete South East* v. *Minister of Pensions and National Insurance* [1968] 2 Q.B. 497).

Relevant considerations will usually include: closeness of supervision of work, powers of appointment and dismissal, form of remuneration, duration of contract, responsibility for equipment, place of work, mutuality of obligations and discretion as to hours of work. Sometimes the courts resort to the "economic reality" test, which appears to be shorthand for the multiple factors test, *i.e.* "is the worker in business on his or her own account ?" (see *Lee Ting Sang* v. *Chung Chi-Keung* [1990] A.C. 374).

The extensive case law in this area includes: *Whittaker* v. *Minister of Pensions and National Insurance* [1967] 1 Q.B. 156, *Argent* v. *Minister of Social Security* [1968] 1 W.L.R. 1749, *Willy Scheidegger Swiss Typewriting School (London)* v. *Minister of Social Security* (1968) 5 K.I.R. 65, *Market Investigations* v. *Minister of Social Security* [1969] 2 Q.B. 173, *Global Plant* v. *Secretary of State for Health and Social Security* [1971] 3 All E.R. 385, *Ferguson* v. *Dawson (John) and Partners (Contractors)* [1976] 1 W.L.R. 346, *B.S.M. (1257)* v. *Secretary of State for Social Services* [1978] I.C.R. 894, *Young & Woods* v. *West* [1980] I.R.L.R. 201, *Midland Sinfonia Concert Society* v. *Secretary of State for Social Services* [1981] I.C.R. 454, *Warner Holidays* v. *Secretary of State for Social Services* [1983] I.C.R. 440, *O'Kelly* v. *Trust House Forte* [1984] Q.B. 90, *Narich Pty.* v. *Commissioner of Pay-Roll Tax* [1984] I.C.R. 286, *Nethermere (St. Neots)* v. *Taverner* [1984] I.C.R. 612, *Singh (Santokh)* v. *Guru Nanak Gurdwara* [1990] I.C.R. 309, *R.* v. *Lord Chancellor's Department,* ex p. *Nangle* [1991] I.C.R. 743.

Office. This alternative basis for categorisation as an employed earner was introduced in 1973 in order to simplify the collection of contributions by correlating Class 1 contributors with

Schedule E taxpayers. On the meaning of office-holder, see *Edwards (Inspector of Taxes)* v. *Clinch* [1982] A.C. 845.

Self-employed earner. This negatively framed formulation defines self-employed earners as all those persons who are gainfully employed (see above) in Great Britain otherwise than under a contract of service or in an office (including elective office) with emoluments chargeable to income tax under Schedule E (s.2(1)). Persons will be regarded as self-employed for Class 2 purposes if they are self-employed for any part of a week, even just one day (subs. (5)).

Further provision in connection with self-employed earners is made by the Social Security (Categorisation of Earners) Regulations 1978 (S.I. 1978 No. 1689): for a detailed analysis see Williams.

Subs. (2)

This enables the Secretary of State to shift particular groups of earners from one class of contributors to another by provisions in regulations. This power has been extensively used: see Social Security (Categorisation of Earners) Regulations 1978 (S.I. 1978 No. 1689). Some employments are treated as Class 1 occupations (*e.g.* office cleaners, certain part-time lecturers, teachers and instructors, etc.) where they might otherwise be characterised as falling within Class 2. Other forms of employment are disregarded, *i.e.* excluded from Classes 1 or 2 (*e.g.* self-employment, where it is not the person's ordinary occupation).

Subs. (4)

The concept of "employed earner's employment" is modified in certain respects for the purposes of industrial injuries benefits by virtue of s.95: see further Social Security (Employed Earners' Employments for Industrial Injuries Purposes) Regulations 1975 (S.I. 1975 No. 467).

"Earnings" and "earner"

3.—(1) In this Part of this Act and Parts II to V below—
(a) "earnings" includes any remuneration or profit derived from an employment; and
(b) "earner" shall be construed accordingly.
(2) For the purposes of this Part of this Act and of Parts II to V below other than those of Schedule 8—
(a) the amount of a person's earnings for any period; or
(b) the amount of his earnings to be treated as comprised in any payment made to him or for his benefit,
shall be calculated or estimated in such manner and on such basis as may be prescribed.
(3) Regulations made for the purposes of subsection (2) above may prescribe that payments of a particular class or description made or falling to be made to or by a person shall, to such extent as may be prescribed, be disregarded or, as the case may be, be deducted from the amount of that person's earnings.

DEFINITIONS
"earner": subs. (1).
"earnings": subs. (1).
"employment": s.122(1).
"prescribe": s.122(1).

GENERAL NOTE
The concept of "earnings" is important in two ways in the social security scheme. First, it is relevant for calculating the appropriate level of National Insurance contributions. Secondly, it is necessary in order to determine entitlement to certain benefits (*e.g.* for increases of benefit for dependants). In either case the starting-point under this section is that earnings are computed on the basis of the individual's gross remuneration from his or her employment(s) (subs. (1)). "Employment" itself is defined as "any trade, business, profession, office or vocation" (s.122(1)).

The underlying distinction is between income which is derived from an employment in this broad sense, and payments which the individual receives in some other capacity. Thus earnings include any payments received in connection with an employment. These include directors' fees, even if the duties involved are very limited (*R(G) 14/56*), and allowances paid to councillors (*R(P) 2/76*). Genuinely *ex-gratia* payments do not constitute earnings (*R(P) 4/67*), but further income from the same source may be regarded as earnings, especially where it has been the subject of income tax relief (*R(P) 1/69*). Income received by an individual as a shareholder does not count as earnings (*R(P) 22/64*). The same principle would apply to other investment income.

The calculation of earnings is based on the sums which the individual is entitled to receive in respect of a given period, not those actually received (*R(P) 5/53*). On the calculation of earnings from self-employment, see *R(U) 3/88*.

Further provision on the calculation of earnings is made by s.4. The concept of earnings is also modified by the Social Security Benefit (Computation of Earnings) Regulations 1978 (S.I. 1978 No. 1698), made under subs. (2). These provide for certain permissible deductions from earnings (*e.g.* expenses incurred in connection with employment and National Insurance contributions, but not income tax). The regulations also allow for certain disregards (*e.g.* the value of meals provided at the place of work) and deal with situations in which earnings cannot be immediately ascertained.

Payments treated as remuneration and earnings

4.—(1) For the purposes of section 3 above there shall be treated as remuneration derived from employed earner's employment—
  (a) any sum paid to or for the benefit of a person in satisfaction (whether in whole or in part) of any entitlement of that person to—
      (i) statutory sick pay; or
      (ii) statutory maternity pay; and
  (b) any sickness payment made—
      (i) to or for the benefit of the employed earner; and
      (ii) in accordance with arrangements under which the person who is the secondary contributor in relation to the employment concerned has made, or remains liable to make, payments towards the provision of that sickness payment.

(2) Where the funds for making sickness payments under arrangements of the kind mentioned in paragraph (b) of subsection (1) above are attributable in part to contributions to those funds made by the employed earner, regulations may make provision for disregarding, for the purposes of that subsection, the prescribed part of any sum paid as a result of the arrangements.

(3) For the purposes of subsections (1) and (2) above "sickness payment" means any payment made in respect of absence from work due to incapacity for work, within the meaning of section 57 below.

(4) For the purposes of section 3 above there shall be treated as remuneration derived from an employed earner's employment any sum paid to or for the benefit of an employed earner which is chargeable to tax by virtue of section 313 of the Income and Corporation Taxes Act 1988 (taxation of consideration for certain restrictive undertakings) otherwise than by virtue of subsection (4) of that section.

(5) For the purposes of section 3 above regulations may make provision for treating as remuneration derived from an employed earner's employment any payment made by a body corporate to or for the benefit of any of its directors where that payment would, when made, not be earnings for the purposes of this Act.

Definitions
  "employed earner": ss.2(1) and 122(1).
  "employment": s.122(1).
  "prescribe": s.122(1).
  "sickness payment": subs. (3).

General Note
  Further to the general definition in s.3, earnings include statutory maternity pay and both statutory and contractual sick pay (subs. (1)). Earnings also include payments on termination of

certain employments which represent consideration for entering into restrictive undertakings chargeable to income tax under ICTA 1988, s.313 (subs. (4)). This allows Class 1 contributions to be levied on such payments.

Class 1 contributions

Earnings limits for Class 1 contributions

5.—(1) For the purposes of this Act there shall for every tax year be—
(a) a lower earnings limit for Class 1 contributions, being the level of weekly earnings at which employed earners become liable for such, contributions in respect of the earnings from their employments; and
(b) an upper earnings limit for Class 1 contributions, being the maximum amount of weekly earnings in respect of which primary Class 1 contributions are payable;

and those limits shall be the amounts specified for that year by regulations made in accordance with subsections (2) and (3) below.

(2) The amount specified as the lower earnings limit for any tax year shall be an amount equal to or not more than 99p less than—
(a) the sum which at the beginning of that year is specified in section 44(4) below as the weekly rate of the basic pension in a Category A retirement pension; or
(b) that sum as increased by any Act or order passed or made before the beginning of that year and taking effect before 6th May in that year.

(3) The amount specified as the upper earnings limit for any tax year shall be an amount which either—
(a) is equal to 7 times the sum by reference to which the lower earnings limit for that year is specified in accordance with subsection (2) above; or
(b) exceeds or falls short of 7 times that sum by an amount not exceeding half that sum.

DEFINITIONS
"earnings": ss.3(1) and 122(1).
"employed earner": ss.2(1) and 122(1).
"employment": s.122(1).
"lower earnings limit": subs. (1)(a).
"upper earnings limit": subs. (1)(b).
"tax year": s.122(1).

GENERAL NOTE
Class 1 contributions (and those for other classes) are paid on the basis of the tax year (*e.g.* April 6, 1992–April 5, 1993: s.122(1)). For the purpose of Class 1 contributions, weekly lower and upper earnings limits are laid down for each tax year (subs. (1)). The lower earnings limit represents a threshold for contributions to the National Insurance scheme. It was originally set under the Social Security Act 1973 at a figure approximately equal to one-quarter of national average male industrial earnings (Williams, *Social Security Taxation* (1982), p. 90). The upper earnings limit represents a ceiling in that currently employees do not pay contributions on income in excess of that prescribed maximum. The lower earnings limit for any tax year must be set at a level equivalent to (or not more than 99p less than) the standard Category A retirement pension (subs. (2)). The upper earnings limit for any tax year must be set at a level which is between 6½ and 7½ times the lower earnings limit (subs. (3)). For further details on liability for Class 1 contributions, see ss.6–9.

Liability for Class 1 contributions

6.—(1) Where in any tax week earnings are paid to or for the benefit of an earner in respect of any one employment of his which is employed earner's employment and—
(a) he is over the age of 16; and
(b) the amount paid is equal to or exceeds the current lower earnings limit

for Class 1 contributions (or the prescribed equivalent in the case of earners paid otherwise than weekly),

a primary and a secondary Class 1 contribution shall be payable in accordance with this section and sections 8 and 9 below.

(2) Except as may be prescribed, no primary Class 1 contribution shall be payable in respect of earnings paid to or for the benefit of an employed earner after he attains pensionable age, but without prejudice to any liability to pay secondary Class 1 contributions in respect of any such earnings.

(3) The primary and secondary Class 1 contributions referred to in subsection (1) above are payable as follows—

(a) the primary contribution shall be the liability of the earner; and

(b) the secondary contribution shall be the liability of the secondary contributor;

but nothing in this subsection shall prejudice the provisions of paragraph 3 of Schedule 1 to this Act relating to the manner in which the earner's liability falls to be discharged.

(4) Except as provided by this Act, the primary and secondary Class 1 contributions in respect of earnings paid to or for the benefit of an earner in respect of any one employment of his shall be payable without regard to any other such payment of earnings in respect of any other employment of his.

(5) Regulations may provide for reducing primary or secondary Class 1 contributions which are payable in respect of persons to whom section 81 of the Employment Protection (Consolidation) Act 1978 (redundancy payments) does not apply by virtue of section 144(2) or 149 of that Act.

(6) The power conferred by subsection (1) above to prescribe an equivalent of the lower earnings limit includes power to prescribe an amount which exceeds, by not more than £1.00, the amount which is the arithmetical equivalent of that limit.

DEFINITIONS

"current": s.122(1).
"earner": ss.3(1) and 122(1).
"earnings": ss.3(1) and 122(1).
"employed earner": ss.2(1) and 122(1).
"employment": s.122(1).
"lower earnings limit": ss.5(1)(a) and 122(1).
"pensionable age": s.122(1).
"prescribe": s.122(1).
"secondary contributor": s.7(1).
"tax week": s.122(1).

GENERAL NOTE

Liability to pay Class 1 contributions only arises where an employed earner is aged 16 or over (but under pensionable age: subs. (2)) and has earnings in excess of the current lower earnings limit (subs. (1)). Where these conditions are met, the employed earner is liable to pay primary Class 1 contributions (subs. (3) and s.8) and the employer (technically the "secondary contributor": see s.7) is responsible for secondary Class 1 contributions (subs. (3) and s.9). Where earners are paid otherwise than weekly, regulations detail equivalent figures for the lower and upper earnings limits (see also subs. (6)).

In practice the employer is responsible for the collection and payment over of contributions (Sched. 1, para. 3). Although an employed earner who has attained pensionable age is not liable for primary Class 1 contributions, the employer must pay secondary Class 1 contributions (subs. (2)).

Where a person has two or more employed earner's employments (or offices), for which there are separate secondary contributors, a liability arises to pay Class 1 contributions in respect of each employment, irrespective of the existence of the other employment(s) (subs. (4)). There are, however, rules which mitigate the overpayment of contributions in cases of multiple employments: see Social Security (Contributions) Regulations 1979 (S.I. 1979 No. 591), regs. 10–13 and 48–49, and DSS Leaflet NP28.

Reduced contributions may be payable where there is a special redundancy scheme in operation (subs. (5)).

"Secondary contributor"

7.—(1) For the purposes of this Act, the "secondary contributor" in relation to any payment of earnings to or for the benefit of an employed earner, is—

(a) in the case of an earner employed under a contract of service, his employer;

(b) in the case of an earner employed in an office with emoluments, either—

(i) such person as may be prescribed in relation to that office; or

(ii) if no person is prescribed, the government department, public authority or body of persons responsible for paying the emoluments of the office;

but this subsection is subject to subsection (2) below.

(2) In relation to employed earners who—

(a) are paid earnings in a tax week by more than one person in respect of different employments; or

(b) work under the general control or management of a person other than their immediate employer,

and in relation to any other case for which it appears to the Secretary of State that such provision is needed, regulations may provide that the prescribed person is to be treated as the secondary contributor in respect of earnings paid to or for the benefit of an earner.

DEFINITIONS

"contract of service": s.122(1).
"earner": ss.3(1) and 122(1).
"earnings": ss.3(1) and 122(1).
"employed earner": ss.2(1) and 122(1).
"employment": s.122(1).
"prescribe": s.122(1).
"secondary contributor": s.7(1).
"tax week": s.122(1).

GENERAL NOTE

This section defines the secondary contributor for the purposes of liability to pay secondary Class 1 contributions. In the usual case, where the earner is an employee, the secondary contributor is the employer (subs. (1)(a)). Where the earner is employed in an office with emoluments, the bodies detailed in subs. (1)(b) will be liable as secondary contributors.

Where the employee has multiple employments, or works under the control or management of a person other than his or her immediate employer (*e.g.* for an agency), the Secretary of State has the power to transfer liability to another prescribed person (subs. (2)). The Secretary of State may also exercise this power more generally wherever it appears "that such provision is needed". See further Social Security (Categorisation of Earners) Regulations 1978 (S.I. 1978 No. 1689), Sched. 3.

Calculation of primary Class 1 contributions

8.—(1) Where a primary Class 1 contribution is payable, the amount of that contribution shall be the aggregate of—

(a) the initial primary percentage of so much of the earner's earnings paid in the tax week, in respect of the employment in question, as does not exceed the current lower earnings limit; and

(b) the main primary percentage of so much of those earnings as exceeds that limit but does not exceed the current upper earnings limit;

but this subsection is subject to regulations under section 6(5) above and sections 116 to 120 below and to section 27 of the Pensions Act (contracted-out rates).

(2) For the purposes of this Act the primary percentages shall be as follows—

(a) the initial primary percentage shall be 2 per cent.; and

(b) the main primary percentage shall be 9 per cent.;
but the rates of those primary percentages are subject to alteration under sections 143 and 145 of the Administration Act.

(3) In the case of earners paid otherwise than weekly, any reference in subsection (1) above to the current upper, or (as the case may be) lower, earnings limit shall be taken as a reference to the prescribed equivalent of that limit.

(4) The power conferred by subsection (3) above to prescribe an equivalent of a limit includes power to prescribe an amount which exceeds, by not more than £1.00, the amount which is the arithmetical equivalent of that limit.

DEFINITIONS
   "the Administration Act": s.174.
   "earner": ss.3(1) and 122(1).
   "earnings": ss.3(1) and 122(1).
   "employment": s.122(1).
   "lower earnings limit": s.5(1)(a).
   "the Pensions Act": s.174.
   "prescribe": s.122(1).
   "upper earnings limit": s.5(1)(b).
   "tax week": s.122(1).

GENERAL NOTE
   The basis of calculating primary Class 1 contributions has undergone a number of changes in recent years. Under the original scheme, employed earners with earnings above the lower earnings limit paid contributions at a set rate on all their earnings up to the upper earnings limit. In 1985 the contribution rates were graduated (five, seven and nine per cent. respectively) for those with earnings between three different brackets. This was thought to create a disincentive effect, and so in 1989 a new structure was introduced, now embodied in subss. (1) and (2). As before, the lower earnings limit represents the threshold for entry to the National Insurance scheme. Primary Class 1 contributions are then payable on the basis of two per cent. of earnings up to that level (the "initial primary percentage") and nine per cent. on the remainder up to the upper earnings limit. These rates may be altered by the Secretary of State in accordance with ss.143 and 145 of the SSAA 1992.
   As before, special rates apply to those who have opted out of SERPS (SSPA 1975, s.27). This group pays the same initial primary percentage but pays two per cent. less than that due from contracted-in employees on earnings between the lower and upper earnings limits.

Calculation of secondary Class 1 contributions

   9.—(1) Where a secondary Class 1 contribution is payable, the amount of that contribution shall be the appropriate secondary percentage of the earnings paid in the week in respect of the employment in question.

   (2) For the purposes of subsection (1) above, the "appropriate secondary percentage", in relation to the earner's earnings, is the percentage specified in subsection (3) below as appropriate to the secondary earnings bracket (or the prescribed equivalent in the case of earners paid otherwise than weekly) into which those earnings fall.

   (3) The secondary earnings brackets and the percentages appropriate to them shall be as set out below—

	Weekly earnings	*Appropriate percentage*
Bracket 1	Current lower earnings limit to £89.99	4.6 per cent.
Bracket 2	£90.00 to £134.99	6.6 per cent.
Bracket 3	£135.00 to £189.99	8.6 per cent.
Bracket 4	£190.00 or more	10.4 per cent.

   (4) Subsections (1) and (3) above are subject as mentioned below, that is to say—

(a) subsection (1) is subject to section 27 of the Pensions Act and to regulations under section 6(5) above and sections 116 to 120 below;

(b) subsection (3) is subject to any order under Part IX of the Administration Act (alteration of contributions and earnings brackets).

(5) The power conferred by subsection (2) above to prescribe an equivalent of a bracket includes power to prescribe an amount which exceeds, by not more than £1.00, the amount which is the arithmetical equivalent of that bracket.

DEFINITIONS
"the Administration Act": s.174.
"appropriate secondary percentage": subs. (2).
"current": s.122(1).
"earner": ss.3(1) and 122(1).
"earnings": ss.3(1) and 122(1).
"employment": s.122(1).
"lower earnings limit": s.5(1)(a).
"the Pensions Act": s.174.
"prescribe": s.122(1).
"week": s.122(1).

GENERAL NOTE
This section sets out the basis for calculating secondary Class 1 contributions, *i.e.* those contributions paid by employers and other secondary contributors (s.7). The progressive bands of contribution rates introduced in 1985 have been retained for secondary Class 1 contributions, unlike for those paid by employed earners (see General Note to s.8). Accordingly there is no liability for secondary Class 1 contributions where earnings are below the lower earnings limit. For earnings above that level, contributions are computed on the basis of a percentage of all earnings, according to the relevant band (subs. (3)). The number of these brackets may be altered by order by the Secretary of State (SSAA 1992, s.146). Secondary Class 1 contributions are payable on earnings above the upper earnings limit, unlike the present position for employed earners' contributions. A reduction of 3.8 per cent. on earnings between the lower and upper earnings limits applies for contracted-out employees (SSPA 1975, s.27(2)).

Class 1A contributions

Class 1A contributions

10.—(1) Where—

(a) for any tax year an amount in respect of a car is by virtue of section 157 of the Income and Corporation Taxes Act 1988 chargeable on an earner to income tax under Schedule E; and

(b) the employment by reason of which the car is made available is employed earner's employment,

a Class 1A contribution shall be payable for that tax year, in accordance with this section, in respect of the earner and car in question.

(2) The Class 1A contribution referred to in subsection (1) above is payable by—

(a) the person who is liable to pay the secondary Class 1 contribution relating to the last (or only) relevant payment of earnings in the tax year in relation to which there is a liability to pay such a contribution; or

(b) if no such contribution is payable in relation to a relevant payment of earnings in the tax year, the person who would be liable but for section 6(1)(b) above to pay a secondary Class 1 contribution relating to the last (or only) relevant payment of earnings in the tax year.

(3) A payment of earnings is a "relevant payment of earnings" for the purposes of subsection (2) above if it is made to or for the benefit of the earner in respect of the employment by reason of which the car is made available.

(4) The amount of the Class 1A contribution referred to in subsection (1) above shall be—

(a) the Class 1A percentage of the cash equivalent of the benefit of the car to the earner in the tax year; or

(b) where for the tax year an amount in respect of fuel for the car is by virtue of section 158 of the Income and Corporation Taxes Act 1988 also chargeable on the earner to income tax under Schedule E, the aggregate of—

   (i) the Class 1A percentage of the cash equivalent of the benefit of the fuel to the earner in the tax year; and

   (ii) the amount mentioned in paragraph (a) above,

the cash equivalents of the benefit of a car or fuel being ascertained, subject to the provisions of this section, in accordance with section 157 or, as the case may be, 158 of the Income and Corporation Taxes Act 1988 and Schedule 6 to that Act.

(5) In subsection (4) above "the Class 1A percentage" means a percentage rate equal to the percentage rate for secondary Class 1 contributions specified in section 9(3) above as appropriate for the highest secondary earnings bracket for the tax year in question.

(6) In calculating for the purposes of subsection (4) above the cash equivalent of the benefit of a car or fuel—

(a) the car shall not be treated as being unavailable on a day by virtue of paragraph 2(2)(b) of Schedule 6 to the Income and Corporation Taxes Act 1988 for the purposes of section 158(5) of that Act or paragraph 2(2), 3(2) or 5(2) of that Schedule, unless the person liable to pay the contribution has information to show that the condition specified in paragraph 2(2)(b) is satisfied as regards that day;

(b) the use of the car for the earner's business travel shall be taken—

   (i) for the purposes of section 158(5) of that Act and sub-paragraph (1) of paragraph 3 of that Schedule to have amounted to less than 18,000 miles (or such lower figure as is applicable by virtue of sub-paragraph (2) of that paragraph); and

   (ii) for the purposes of sub-paragraph (1) of paragraph 5 of that Schedule to have amounted to not more than 2,500 miles (or such lower figure as is applicable by virtue of sub-paragraph (2) of that paragraph),

unless in either case the person liable to pay the contribution has information to show the contrary; and

(c) for the purposes of paragraph 5(3) of that Schedule, the car shall be treated as not having been the car used to the greatest extent for the employee's business travel, unless the person liable to pay the contribution has information to show the contrary.

(7) Regulations may make such amendments of this section as appear to the Secretary of State to be necessary or expedient in consequence of any alteration to section 157 or 158 of the Income and Corporation Taxes Act 1988 or Schedule 6 to that Act.

(8) A person shall be liable to pay different Class 1A contributions in respect of different earners, different cars and different tax years.

(9) Regulations may provide—

(a) for persons to be excepted in prescribed circumstances from liability to pay Class 1A contributions;

(b) for reducing Class 1A contributions in prescribed circumstances.

DEFINITIONS
"Class 1A percentage": subs. (5).
"earner": ss.3(1) and 122(1).
"earnings": ss.3(1) and 122(1).
"employed earner": ss.2(1) and 122(1).

"employment": s.122(1).
"prescribe": s.122(1).
"secondary earnings bracket": s.9(3).
"relevant payment of earnings": subs. (3).
"tax year": s.122(1).

GENERAL NOTE

Class 1A contributions were introduced by the Social Security (Contributions) Act 1991 and became payable from April 6, 1991. Class 1A contributions must be paid by the employer in respect of any car provided for directors or employees (or for members of their families or households) by reason of their employment if the car is also available for private use. Contributions must also be paid on fuel provided for private use in that car. Contributions are calculated on the basis of 10.4 per cent. (subs. (5)) of the appropriate scale charge (*i.e.* the car/fuel cash equivalent).

The directors or employees concerned must be in employed earner's employment and must be liable under s.157 of ICTA 1988 on the scale charge value of the car (and, where appropriate, under s.158 for private fuel). The employer's liability applies to cars and fuel made available to directors irrespective of their earnings (subject to certain exceptions) but only to employees with emoluments of £8,500 or more a year (including taxable benefits and expenses).

So far as payments (*e.g.* by petrol vouchers or petrol charge cards) by employers to employees to cover their private motoring costs are concerned, it has been held that both primary and secondary Class 1 contributions are payable (*R.* v. *Secretary of State for Social Security,* ex p. *Overdrive Credit Card* [1991] 1 W.L.R. 635).

Class 2 contributions

Liability for Class 2 contributions

11.—(1) Every self-employed earner who is over the age of 16 shall be liable to pay Class 2 contributions at the rate of £5.35 a week, subject to the provisions of this section and sections 12 and 19(4)(b) below.

(2) No Class 2 contributions shall be payable by an earner in respect of any period after he attains pensionable age.

(3) Regulations may make provision so that an earner is liable for a weekly rate of Class 2 contributions higher than that specified in subsection (1) above where—

(a) in respect of any employment of his, he is treated by regulations under section 2(2)(b) above as being a self-employed earner; and

(b) in any period or periods he has earnings from that employment and—

(i) those earnings are such that (disregarding their amount) he would be liable for Class 1 contributions in respect of them if he were not so treated in respect of the employment, and

(ii) no Class 4 contribution is payable in respect of the earnings by virtue of regulations under section 18(1) below.

(4) Regulations may provide for an earner otherwise liable for Class 2 contributions in respect of employment as a self-employed earner to be excepted from the liability in respect of any period in which his earnings from such employment are, or are treated by regulations as being, less than £3,030 a tax year.

(5) Regulations made for the purposes of subsection (4) above shall not except a person from liability to pay contributions otherwise than on his own application, but may provide for so excepting a person with effect from any date not earlier than 13 weeks before the date on which his application was made.

DEFINITIONS

"earner": ss.3(1) and 122(1).
"earnings": ss.3(1) and 122(1).
"employment": s.122(1).
"pensionable age": s.122(1).
"self-employed earner": ss.2(1) and 122(1).
"tax year": s.122(1).

GENERAL NOTE

Class 2 contributions are paid by the self-employed. Class 2 contributions give rise to entitlement to all contributory benefits except unemployment benefit (s.21(2)). Contributors must be over 16 years and under pensionable age (subss. (1) and (2)). Modifications are laid down in the Social Security (Contributions) Regulations 1979 (S.I. 1979 No. 591), Pt. III. Class 2 contributions are assessed on a weekly flat-rate basis (subs. (1)), with special rates for share fishermen and volunteer development workers overseas (who, unlike usual Class 2 contributors, qualify for unemployment benefit).

Self-employed people may be excepted from liability to pay Class 2 contributions on the grounds of low earnings, the threshold being £3,030 for 1992–93 (subs. (4)). Certificates of exception can only be backdated up to 13 weeks before the date of application (subs. (5)), although the regulations now provide for repayment of contributions (Social Security (Contributions) Regulations 1979 (S.I. 1979 No. 591), reg. 26A). Payment is also excused on the grounds of inability to earn (reg. 23). Contributions may still be made voluntarily. Where self-employed earnings exceed a higher threshold (at present £6,120), an additional liability to pay Class 4 contributions arises (ss.15–18).

The weekly contribution rate (subs. (1)) and low earnings threshold (subs. (4)) are both liable to annual review under SSAA 1992, s.141.

Late paid Class 2 contributions

12.—(1) This section applies to any Class 2 contribution paid in respect of a week falling within a tax year ("the contribution year") earlier than the tax year in which it is paid ("the payment year").

(2) Subject to subsections (3) to (5) below, the amount of a contribution to which this section applies shall be the amount which the earner would have had to pay if he had paid the contribution in the contribution year.

(3) Subject to subsections (4) to (6) below, in any case where—

(a) the earner pays an ordinary contribution to which this section applies after the end of the tax year immediately following the contribution year; and

(b) the weekly rate of ordinary contributions for the week in respect of which the contribution was payable in the contribution year differs from the weekly rate applicable at the time of payment in the payment year,

the amount of the contribution shall be computed by reference to the highest weekly rate of ordinary contributions in the period beginning with the week in respect of which the contribution is paid and ending with the day on which it is paid.

(4) The Secretary of State may by regulations direct that subsection (3) above shall have effect in relation to a higher-rate contribution to which this section applies subject to such modifications as may be prescribed.

(5) Subject to subsection (6) below, for the purposes of proceedings in any court relating to an earner's failure to pay Class 2 contributions, the amount of each contribution which he is to be treated as having failed to pay is the amount which he would have paid in accordance with subsections (1) to (3) above or regulations under subsection (6) below if he had paid that contribution on the date on which the proceedings commenced.

(6) The Secretary of State may by regulations provide that the amount of any contribution which, apart from the regulations, would fall to be computed in accordance with subsection (3) or (5) above shall instead be computed by reference to a tax year not earlier than the contribution year but earlier—

(a) in a case falling within subsection (3) above, than the payment year; and

(b) in a case falling within subsection (5) above, than the tax year in which the proceedings commenced.

(7) For the purposes of this section—

(a) proceedings in the High Court or a county court commence when an action commences; and

(b) proceedings under section 114 of the Administration Act (offences relating to contributions) commence when an information is laid.

(8) In this section—

"ordinary contribution" means a contribution under section 11(1) above; and

"higher-rate contribution" means a contribution under regulations made under section 11(3) above.

DEFINITIONS

"the Administration Act": s.174.
"contribution year": subs. (1).
"earner": ss.3(1) and 122(1).
"higher-rate contribution": s.122(1).
"ordinary contribution": s.122(1).
"payment year": subs. (1).
"prescribe": s.122(1).
"tax year": s.122(1).
"week": s.122(1).

GENERAL NOTE

This section concerns the late payment of Class 2 contributions. Class 2 contributions should technically be paid in the week in which they fall due. They may still count for benefit purposes if paid later providing that they are paid within six years of the end of the tax year in which they were due.

Class 3 contributions

Class 3 contributions

13.—(1) Regulations shall provide for earners and others, if over the age of 16, to be entitled if they so wish, but subject to any prescribed conditions, to pay Class 3 contributions; and, subject to the following provisions of this section, the amount of a Class 3 contribution shall be £5.25.

(2) Payment of Class 3 contributions shall be allowed only with a view to enabling the contributor to satisfy contribution conditions of entitlement to benefit by acquiring the requisite earnings factor for the purposes described in section 22 below.

(3) Regulations may provide for Class 3 contributions, although paid in one tax year, to be appropriated in prescribed circumstances to the earnings factor of another tax year.

(4) The amount of a Class 3 contribution in respect of a tax year earlier than the tax year in which it is paid shall be the same as if it had been paid in the earlier year and in respect of that year, unless it falls to be calculated in accordance with subsection (6) below or regulations under subsection (7) below.

(5) In this section—

"the payment year" means the tax year in which a contribution is paid; and

"the contribution year" means the earlier year mentioned in subsection (4) above.

(6) Subject to subsection (7) below, in any case where—

(a) a Class 3 contribution is paid after the end of the next tax year but one following the contribution year; and

(b) the amount of a Class 3 contribution applicable had the contribution been paid in the contribution year differs from the amount of a Class 3 contribution applicable at the time of payment in the payment year,

the amount of the contribution shall be computed by reference to the highest of those two amounts and of any other amount of a Class 3 contribution in the intervening period.

(7) The Secretary of State may by regulations provide that the amount of a contribution which apart from the regulations would fall to be computed in

accordance with subsection (6) above shall instead be computed by reference to the amount of a Class 3 contribution for a tax year earlier than the payment year but not earlier than the contribution year.

DEFINITIONS
"benefit": s.122(1).
"contribution year": subs. (5).
"earner": s.122(1).
"earnings factor": s.22(1).
"payment year": subs. (5).
"prescribe": s.122(1).
"tax year": s.122(1).

GENERAL NOTE
Class 3 contributions are entirely voluntary. They may be paid by people contributing in Class 1 or 2, but with deficiencies in their contribution records, or by persons who are outside the labour market. Payment of Class 3 contributions only gives rise to entitlement to widows' benefits and Category A and B retirement pensions (s.21(2)). Class 3 contributions are not payable if the individual's earnings factor in the given year is otherwise sufficient to meet the second contribution condition for these benefits (s.14). The contribution required is a weekly flat-rate sum, just less than the Class 2 contribution, and is reviewed annually (SSAA 1992, s.141).

Further provision is made by the Social Security (Contributions) Regulations 1979 (S.I. 1979 No. 591), Pt. III.

Restriction on right to pay Class 3 contributions

14.—(1) No person shall be entitled to pay a Class 3 contribution in respect of any tax year if his earnings factor, or the aggregate of his earnings factors, for that year derived—

(a) in the case of 1987–88 or any subsequent year, from earnings upon which Class 1 contributions have been paid or treated as paid or from Class 2 contributions actually paid; or

(b) in the case of any earlier year, from contributions actually paid,

is equal to or exceeds the qualifying earnings factor for that year; and regulations may provide for precluding the payment of Class 3 contributions in other cases.

(2) Regulations may provide for the repayment of Class 3 contributions that have been paid in cases where their payment was precluded by, or by regulations made under, subsection (1) above.

(3) Contributions repayable by virtue of regulations under subsection (2) above shall, for the purpose of determining the contributor's entitlement to any benefit, be treated as not having been paid (but nothing in this subsection shall be taken to imply that any other repayable contributions are to be treated for the purposes of benefit as having been paid).

DEFINITIONS
"benefit": s.122(1).
"earnings": ss.3(1) and 122(1).
"earnings factor": s.22(1).
"qualifying earnings factor": s.122(1).
"tax year": s.122(1).

GENERAL NOTE
See General Note to s.13.

Class 4 contributions

Class 4 contributions recoverable under the Income Tax Acts

15.—(1) Class 4 contributions shall be payable for any tax year in respect of all annual profits or gains which—

(a) are immediately derived from the carrying on or exercise of one or more trades, professions or vocations, and

(b) are profits or gains chargeable to income tax under Case I or Case II of Schedule D for the year of assessment corresponding to that tax year.

(2) Class 4 contributions in respect of profits or gains shall be payable—

(a) in the same manner as any income tax which is, or would be, chargeable in respect of those profits or gains (whether or not income tax in fact falls to be paid), and

(b) by the person on whom the income tax is (or would be) charged,

in accordance with assessments made from time to time under the Income Tax Acts.

(3) A Class 4 contribution for any tax year shall be an amount equal to 6.3 per cent. of so much of the profits or gains referred to in subsection (1) above (as computed in accordance with Schedule 2 to this Act) as exceeds £6,120 and does not exceed £21,060.

(4) The reference in subsection (1) above to profits or gains chargeable to income tax under Case I or Case II of Schedule D shall be taken to include a reference to profits or gains consisting of a payment of enterprise allowance chargeable to income tax under Case VI of Schedule D by virtue of section 127(2) of the Income and Corporation Taxes Act 1988.

(5) For the purposes of this section the year of assessment which corresponds to a tax year is the year of assessment (within the meaning of the Tax Acts) which consists of the same period as that tax year.

DEFINITIONS
  "Income Tax Acts": Interpretation Act 1978, s.5 and Sched. 1.
  "tax year": s.122(1).

GENERAL NOTE
  Class 4 contributions are earnings-related payments by the self-employed. Liability for Class 4 contributions is largely coincident with liability under Sched. D of the Income Tax Acts (but see s.17) and is levied at the rate of 6.3 per cent. of profits and gains between an upper and lower limit (subs. (3)). These limits are reviewed annually (SSAA 1992, s.141). Where an individual is liable to pay both Class 1 and 4 contributions, the total is limited to the maximum liability under one class only. For this and further provisions, see the Social Security (Contributions) Regulations 1979 (S.I. 1979 No. 591), Pt. VII.

Application of Income Tax Acts and destination of Class 4 contributions

16.—(1) All the provisions of the Income Tax Acts, including in particular—

(a) provisions as to assessment, collection, repayment and recovery, and

(b) the provisions of Part X of the Taxes Management Act 1970 (penalties),

shall, with the necessary modifications, apply in relation to Class 4 contributions under this Act and the Northern Ireland Contributions and Benefits Act as if those contributions were income tax chargeable under Case I or Case II of Schedule D.

(2) Subsection (1) above is subject to any provision made by or under—

(a) sections 17(3) and (4) and 18 below;

(b) sections 17(3) and (4) and 18 of the Northern Ireland Contributions and Benefits Act; and

(c) Schedule 2 to this Act.

(3) Schedule 2 to this Act has effect for the application or modification, in relation to Class 4 contributions under this Act and the Northern Ireland Contributions and Benefits Act, of certain provisions of the Income Tax Acts, and the exclusion of other provisions, and generally with respect to the contributions.

(4) The Inland Revenue shall, at such times and in such manner as the Treasury may direct, account to the Secretary of State for, and pay to him—

(a) the sums estimated by the Inland Revenue (in the manner so directed) to have been collected by them as Class 4 contributions under section 15 above and section 15 of the Northern Ireland Contributions and Benefits Act; and

(b) so much of any interest recovered by the Inland Revenue by virtue of paragraph 6 of Schedule 2 to this Act as remains after the deduction by them of any administrative costs attributable to its recovery.

(5) So much of any money received by the Secretary of State under subsection (4) above as is estimated by him, in accordance with any directions of the Treasury, to represent Class 4 contributions collected, or interest in respect of such contributions recovered, from persons in Northern Ireland shall be paid over by him to the Northern Ireland Department.

DEFINITIONS
"Income Tax Acts": Interpretation Act 1978, s.5 and Sched. 1.
"Inland Revenue": s.122(1).
"Northern Ireland Contributions and Benefits Act": s.174.
"Northern Ireland Department": s.122(1).

GENERAL NOTE
This section applies the provisions of the Income Tax Acts as to the assessment, collection, repayment and recovery of taxes, etc., to Class 4 contributions. These powers are subject to provision made under regulations (subs. (2); see ss.17 and 18) and in Sched. 2 (subs. (3)).

Exceptions, deferment and incidental matters relating to Class 4 contributions

17.—(1) The Secretary of State may by regulations made with the concurrence of the Inland Revenue provide—

(a) for excepting persons from liability to pay Class 4 contributions in accordance with sections 15 and 16(1) to (3) above; or

(b) for deferring any person's liability,

and may certify from time to time to the Inland Revenue the persons who are excepted from liability, or whose liability is to be deferred, and who accordingly are not required (except in accordance with the regulations) to be assessed for contributions.

(2) Exception from liability, or deferment, under subsection (1) above may, in particular, be by reference—

(a) to a person otherwise liable for contributions being under a prescribed age at the beginning of a tax year;

(b) to a person having attained pensionable age;

(c) to a person being in receipt of earnings in respect of which primary Class 1 contributions are, or may be, payable; or

(d) to a person not satisfying prescribed conditions as to residence or presence in the United Kingdom.

(3) Regulations may provide for any incidental matters arising out of the payment of any Class 4 contributions recovered by the Inland Revenue, including in particular the return, in whole or in part, of such contributions in cases where—

(a) payment has been made in error; or

(b) repayment ought for any other reason to be made.

(4) Regulations may provide for any matters arising out of the deferment of liability for Class 4 contributions under subsection (1) above, including in particular provision for the amount of a person's profits or gains (as computed in accordance with Schedule 2 to this Act) to be certified by the Inland Revenue to the Secretary of State and the person liable.

(5) No such certificate as is referred to in subsection (4) above shall relate to a person's profits or gains so far as they exceed the higher of the two money sums for the time being specified in section 15(3) above.

(6) Any regulations under subsection (3) or (4) above must be made with the concurrence of the Inland Revenue.

DEFINITIONS
"earnings": s.122(1).
"Inland Revenue": s.122(1).
"pensionable age": s.122(1).
"prescribe": s.122(1).
"primary Class 1 contributions": s.6(3).
"tax year": s.122(1).
"United Kingdom": s.172.

GENERAL NOTE
    This section enables the Secretary of State to make regulations excluding certain groups from liability for Class 4 contributions. This allows for some differences between assessment for Class 4 contributions and under Sched. D for income tax purposes. For example, liability for Class 4 contributions is confined to persons aged 16 or over but under pensionable age (subs. (2)): see further the Social Security (Contributions) Regulations 1979 (S.I. 1979 No. 591), Pt. VII.

Class 4 contributions recoverable under regulations

18.—(1) Provision may be made by regulations so that where—
(a) an earner, in respect of any one or more employments of his, is treated by regulations under section 2(2)(b) above as being self-employed; and
(b) in any tax year he has earnings from any such employment (one or more) which fall within paragraph (b)(i) of subsection (3) of section 11 above but is not liable for a higher weekly rate of Class 2 contributions by virtue of regulations under that subsection; and
(c) the total of those earnings exceeds £6,120,
he is to be liable, in respect of those earnings, to pay a Class 4 contribution of an amount equal to 6.3 per cent. of so much of the total as exceeds £6,120 and does not exceed £21,060.

(2) It shall be for the Secretary of State, and not the Inland Revenue, to recover Class 4 contributions payable by virtue of regulations under this section and generally to be responsible for the relevant administration; and, in relation to contributions so payable, regulations may—
(a) apply any of the provisions of Schedule 1 to this Act (except a provision conferring power to make regulations); and
(b) make any such provision as may be made by regulations under that Schedule, except paragraph 6.

DEFINITIONS
"earner": s.122(1).
"earnings": s.122(1).
"employment": s.122(1).
"Inland Revenue": s.122(1).
"tax year": s.122(1).

GENERAL NOTE
    Where persons have earnings chargeable to income tax under Sched. E, but are also paying Class 2 contributions, they are subject to the same liability to pay Class 4 contributions as other

self-employed earners. Liability is deferred until the end of the relevant tax year and collection is the responsibility of the Secretary of State, not the Inland Revenue.

General

General power to regulate liability for contributions

19.—(1) Regulations may provide either generally or in relation to—

(a) any prescribed category of earners; or

(b) earners in any prescribed category of employments,

that their liability in a particular tax year in respect of contributions of prescribed classes is not to exceed such maximum amount or amounts as may be prescribed.

(2) Regulations made for the purposes of subsection (1) above may provide—

(a) for an earner whose liability is subject to a maximum prescribed under that subsection to be liable in the first instance for the full amount of any contributions due from him apart from the regulations, or to be relieved from liability for such contributions in prescribed circumstances and to the prescribed extent; and

(b) for contributions paid in excess of any such maximum to be repaid at such times, and in accordance with such conditions, as may be prescribed.

(3) Regulations may provide, in relation to earners otherwise liable for contributions of any class, for excepting them from the liability for such periods, and in such circumstances, as may be prescribed.

(4) As respects any woman who was married or a widow on 6th April 1977 (the date of the coming into force of the repeal of the old provisions that primary Class 1 contributions might be paid at a reduced rate and Class 2 contributions need not be paid by a married woman or a widow) regulations shall provide—

(a) for enabling her to elect that her liability in respect of primary Class 1 contributions shall be a liability to contribute at such reduced rate as may be prescribed; and

(b) either for enabling her to elect that her liability in respect of Class 2 contributions shall be a liability to contribute at such reduced rate as may be prescribed or for enabling her to elect that she shall be under no liability to pay such contributions; and

(c) for enabling her to revoke any such election.

(5) Regulations under subsection (4) above may—

(a) provide for the making or revocation of any election under the regulations to be subject to prescribed exceptions and conditions;

(b) preclude a person who has made such an election from paying Class 3 contributions while the election has effect;

(c) provide for treating an election made or revoked for the purpose of any provision of the regulations as made or revoked also for the purpose of any other provision of the regulations;

(d) provide for treating an election made in accordance with regulations under section 130(2) of the 1975 Act as made for the purpose of regulations under subsection (4) above.

(6) Regulations may provide for earnings factors to be derived, for such purposes as may be prescribed, as follows, that is to say—

(a) in the case of earnings factors for 1987–88 or any subsequent tax year—

(i) from earnings upon which primary Class 1 contributions are paid at a reduced rate by virtue of regulations under subsection (4) above; or

(ii) from Class 2 contributions paid at a reduced rate by virtue of such regulations; and

   (b) in the case of earnings factors for any earlier tax year, from contributions which are paid at a reduced rate by virtue of regulations under subsection (4) above;

and if provision is made for a person to have earnings factors so derived for the purpose of establishing entitlement to any benefit, the regulations may, in relation to that person, vary or add to the requirements for entitlement to that benefit.

<small>DEFINITIONS</small>
  "the 1975 Act": s.172.
  "benefit": s.122(1).
  "earner": s.122(1).
  "earnings factor": s.22(1).
  "employment": s.122(1).
  "prescribe": s.122(1).
  "tax year": s.122(1).

<small>GENERAL NOTE</small>
  This is a general regulation-making provision. See further the Social Security (Contributions) Regulations 1979 (S.I. 1979 No. 591).

PART II

CONTRIBUTORY BENEFITS

Preliminary

Descriptions of contributory benefits

20.—(1) Contributory benefits under this Part of this Act are of the following descriptions, namely—
  (a) unemployment benefit (with increase for adult and, where the beneficiary is over pensionable age, child dependants);
  (b) sickness benefit (with increase for adult and, where the beneficiary is over pensionable age, child dependants);
  (c) invalidity benefit, comprising—
      (i) invalidity pension under section 33, 40 or 41 below (with increase for adult and child dependants);
      (ii) invalidity allowance;
  (d) maternity allowance (with increase for adult dependants);
  (e) widow's benefit, comprising—
      (i) widow's payment;
      (ii) widowed mother's allowance (with increase for child dependants);
      (iii) widow's pension;
  (f) retirement pensions of the following categories—
      (i) Category A, payable to a person by virtue of his own contributions (with increase for adult and child dependants); and
      (ii) Category B, payable to a woman by virtue of her husband's contributions or payable to a man by virtue of his late wife's contributions (with increase for child dependants);
  (g) for existing beneficiaries only, child's special allowance.
  (2) In this Act—
    "long-term benefit" means—
      (a) an invalidity pension under section 33, 40 or 41 below;
      (b) a widowed mother's allowance;
      (c) a widow's pension; and
      (d) a Category A or Category B retirement pension; and
    "short-term benefit" means—

(a) unemployment benefit;
(b) sickness benefit; and
(c) maternity allowance.

(3) The provisions of this Part of this Act are subject to the provisions of Part III of the Pensions Act (contracting-out—reduced rates of benefit).

DEFINITIONS
"the Pensions Act": s.174.
"beneficiary": s.122(1).
"benefit": s.122(1).
"child": s.122(1).
"long-term benefit": subs. (2).
"pensionable age": s.122(1).
"the Pensions Act": s.174.
"short-term benefit": subs. (2).

GENERAL NOTE
Subsection (1) simply sets out the contributory benefits payable under Pt. II of the Act, while subs. (2) is a definition provision. Subsection (3) had no immediate statutory forerunner but is a drafting measure to draw attention to the inter-relationship with Pt. III of the SSPA 1975.

Contribution conditions

21.—(1) Entitlement to any of the benefits specified in section 20(1) above, other than invalidity benefit, depends on contribution conditions being satisfied (either by the claimant or by some other person, according to the particular benefit).

(2) The class or classes of contribution which, for the purposes of subsection (1) above, are relevant in relation to each of those benefits are as follows—

Short-term benefit

Unemployment benefit	Class 1
Sickness benefit	Class 1 or 2
Maternity allowance	Class 1 or 2

Other benefits

Widow's payment	Class 1, 2 or 3
Widowed mother's allowance	Class 1, 2 or 3
Widow's pension	Class 1, 2 or 3
Category A retirement pension	Class 1, 2 or 3
Category B retirement pension	Class 1, 2 or 3
Child's special allowance	Class 1, 2 or 3

(3) The relevant contribution conditions in relation to the benefits specified in subsection (2) above are those specified in Part I of Schedule 3 to this Act.

(4) Part II of Schedule 3 to this Act shall have effect as to the satisfaction of contribution conditions for benefit, other than maternity allowance, in certain cases where a claim for a short-term benefit or a widow's payment is, or has on a previous occasion been, made in the first or second year after that in which the contributor concerned first became liable for primary Class 1 or Class 2 contributions.

(5) In subsection (4) above and Schedule 3 to this Act—
(a) "the contributor concerned", for the purposes of any contribution condition, means the person by whom the condition is to be satisfied;

(b) "a relevant class", in relation to any benefit, means a class of contributions specified in relation to that benefit in subsection (2) above;

(c) "the earnings factor"—

(i) where the year in question is 1987–88 or any subsequent tax year, means, in relation to a person, the aggregate of his earnings factors derived from all his earnings upon which primary Class 1 contributions have been paid or treated as paid and from his Class 2 and Class 3 contributions; and

(ii) where the year in question is any earlier tax year, means, in relation to a person's contributions of any class or classes, the aggregate of his earnings factors derived from all those contributions;

(d) except in the expression "benefit year", "year" means a tax year.

(6) In this Part of this Act "benefit year" means a period—

(a) beginning with the first Sunday in January in any calendar year, and

(b) ending with the Saturday immediately preceding the first Sunday in January in the following calendar year;

but for any prescribed purposes of this Part of this Act "benefit year" may by regulations be made to mean such other period (whether or not a period of 12 months) as may be specified in the regulations.

Definitions

"a relevant class": subs. (5).
"benefit year": subs. (6).
"benefit": s.122(1).
"contributor concerned": subs. (5).
"earnings factor": subs. (5).
"prescribe": s.122(1).
"short-term benefit": s.20(2).
"year": subs. (5).

General Note

This section details those benefits to which entitlement may arise by virtue of contributions of the various classes. Under subs. (2) only persons who have paid Class 1 contributions can qualify for unemployment benefit. Exceptions to this principle are made by regulations for share fishermen and volunteer development workers (Social Security (Contributions) Regulations 1979 (S.I. 1979 No. 591), regs. 98 and 123A–F). Class 2 contributions confer title to any contributory benefit except unemployment benefit. Voluntary Class 3 contributions only enable a person to qualify for widow's benefits and Category A or B retirement pensions (child's special allowance is preserved only for existing beneficiaries: s.56). The specific contribution conditions required for each benefit are listed in Pt. I of Sched. 3. Class 4 contributions give rise to no benefit entitlement.

Earnings factors

22.—(1) A person shall, for the purposes specified in subsection (2) below, be treated as having annual earnings factors derived—

(a) in the case of 1987–88 or any subsequent tax year, from those of his earnings upon which primary Class 1 contributions have been paid or treated as paid and from Class 2 and Class 3 contributions; and

(b) in the case of any earlier tax year, from his contributions of any of Classes 1, 2 and 3;

but subject to the following provisions of this section and those of section 23 below.

(2) The purposes referred to in subsection (1) above are those of—

(a) establishing, by reference to the satisfaction of contribution conditions, entitlement to any benefit specified in section 20(1) above, other than maternity allowance; and

(b) calculating the additional pension in the rate of a long-term benefit.

(3) Separate earnings factors may be derived for 1987–88 and subsequent tax years—

(a) from earnings upon which primary Class 1 contributions have been paid or treated as paid;

(b) from earnings which have been credited;

(c) from contributions of different classes paid or credited in the same tax year;

(d) by any combination of the methods mentioned in paragraphs (a) to (c) above,

and may be derived for any earlier tax year from contributions of different classes paid or credited in the same tax year, and from contributions which have actually been paid, as opposed to those not paid but credited.

(4) Subject to regulations under section 19(4) to (6) above, no earnings factor shall be derived—

(a) for 1987–88 or any subsequent tax year, from earnings upon which primary Class 1 contributions are paid at the reduced rate, or

(b) for any earlier tax year, from primary Class 1 contributions paid at the reduced rate or from secondary Class 1 contributions.

(5) Regulations may provide for crediting—

(a) for 1987–88 or any subsequent tax year, earnings or Class 2 or Class 3 contributions, or

(b) for any earlier tax year, contributions of any class,

for the purpose of bringing a person's earnings factor for that tax year to a figure which will enable him to satisfy contribution conditions of entitlement to any prescribed description of benefit (whether his own entitlement or another person's).

(6) Regulations may impose limits with respect to the earnings factors which a person may have or be treated as having in respect of any one tax year.

(7) The power to amend regulations made before 30th March 1977 (the passing of the Social Security (Miscellaneous Provisions) Act 1977) under subsection (5) above may be so exercised as to restrict the circumstances in which and the purposes for which a person is entitled to credits in respect of weeks before the coming into force of the amending regulations; but not so as to affect any benefit for a period before the coming into force of the amending regulations if it was claimed before 18th March 1977.

DEFINITIONS
"benefit": s.122(1).
"earnings": s.122(1).
"earnings factor": s.21(5).
"long-term benefit": s.20(2).
"prescribe": s.122(1).
"tax year": s.122(1).
"week": s.122(1).

GENERAL NOTE
This section (together with s.23) lays down the basic framework for computing earnings factors. Earnings factors are used to calculate whether the contribution conditions set out in Sched. 3 have been met for contributory benefits (except maternity allowance). They are also significant in calculating the additional pension under SERPS (subs. (2)). In the case of Class 1 contributions, the earnings factor is the amount of earnings upon which contributions have been paid (s.23(3)(a)). For Class 2 or Class 3 contributions, the earnings factor is the lower earnings limit for Class 1 multiplied by the number of contributions made in the relevant tax year (s.23(3)). For further details, see Social Security (Earnings Factor) Regulations 1975 (S.I. 1975 No. 468).

Provisions supplemental to sections 21 and 22

23.—(1) Earnings factors derived as mentioned in section 22(1)(a) above, including earnings factors as increased by any order under section 148 of the Administration Act—

(a) shall be expressed, subject to subsection (2) below, as whole numbers of pounds; and

(b) shall be made ascertainable from tables or rules to be drawn up by the Secretary of State and embodied in regulations.

(2) Subsection (1) above does not require earnings factors in respect of the tax year 1978–79 or any subsequent tax year which have been revalued for the purpose of calculating guaranteed minimum pensions under the Pensions Act to be expressed as whole numbers of pounds.

(3) The tables and rules referred to in subsection (1) above shall be drawn up so that, in general—

(a) in respect of the tax year 1987–88 and any subsequent tax year, the amount of earnings upon which primary Class 1 contributions have been paid or treated as paid gives rise, subject to subsection (4) below, to an earnings factor for that year equal or approximating to the amount of those earnings; and

(b) any number of Class 2 or Class 3 contributions in respect of a tax year gives rise to an earnings factor for that tax year equal or approximating to that year's lower earnings limit for Class 1 contributions multiplied by the number of contributions.

(4) The Secretary of State may by regulations make such modifications of subsection (3)(a) above as appear to him to be appropriate in consequence of section 8(2) above.

DEFINITIONS
   "the Administration Act": s.174.
   "earnings": s.122(1).
   "earnings factor": s.22(1).
   "lower earnings limit": s.5(1)(a).
   "the Pensions Act": s.174.
   "tax year": s.122(1).

GENERAL NOTE
   See General Note to s.22. The legislative history of subs. (4) is dealt with by the Law Commissions (Cm 1726, 1991), para. 1.

Records of earnings and calculation of earnings factors in absence of records

24.—(1) Regulations may provide for requiring persons to maintain, in such form and manner as may be prescribed, records of such earnings paid by them as are relevant for the purpose of calculating earnings factors, and to retain such records for so long as may be prescribed.

(2) Where the Secretary of State is satisfied that records of earnings relevant for the purpose of calculating a person's earnings factors for the tax year 1987–88 or any subsequent tax year have not been maintained or retained or are otherwise unobtainable, then, for the purpose of determining those earnings factors, he may—

(a) compute, in such manner as he thinks fit, an amount which shall be regarded as the amount of that person's earnings on which primary Class 1 contributions have been paid or treated as paid; or

(b) take the amount of those earnings to be such sum as he may specify in the particular case.

DEFINITIONS
   "earnings": s.122(1).
   "earnings factor": s.22(1).
   "prescribe": s.122(1).
   "tax year": s.122(1).

GENERAL NOTE
   Subsection (1) enables the Secretary of State to make regulations requiring employers to keep records of earnings for the purpose of calculating earnings factors. Subsection (2)

empowers the Secretary of State to calculate earnings factors in the absence of proper records, so as to protect the potential benefit entitlement of employees.

Unemployment benefit

Unemployment benefit

25.—(1) Subject to the provisions of this section, a person who satisfies any of the three conditions of subsection (2) below shall be entitled to unemployment benefit in respect of any day of unemployment which forms part of a period of interruption of employment.

(2) The conditions of this subsection are that—

(a) the person is under pensionable age on the day in question and satisfies the contribution conditions specified for unemployment benefit in Schedule 3, Part I, paragraph 1; or

(b) on that day the person—

(i) is over pensionable age, but not more than 5 years over that age, and

(ii) would be entitled to a Category A retirement pension if his entitlement had not been deferred or if he had not made an election under section 54(1) below; or

(c) on that day the person—

(i) is over pensionable age, but not more than 5 years over that age; and

(ii) would be entitled to a Category B retirement pension by virtue of the contributions of his deceased spouse, but for any such deferment or election.

(3) A person shall not be entitled to unemployment benefit for the first 3 days of any period of interruption of employment.

(4) In the case of a person entitled under paragraph (a) of subsection (2) above unemployment benefit shall be payable at the weekly rate specified in Schedule 4, Part I, paragraph 1.

(5) In the case of any person over pensionable age who is entitled under paragraph (b) or (c) of subsection (2) above, unemployment benefit shall be payable at the weekly rate at which the retirement pension referred to in the applicable paragraph of that subsection would have been payable; but in determining that rate for the purposes of this subsection any increase specified in subsection (6) below shall be disregarded.

(6) The increases to be disregarded for the purposes of subsection (5) above are the following—

(a) any increase (for invalidity) under section 47(1) below;

(b) any increase (for married women) under section 53(2) below or (for deferred retirement) under Schedule 5 to this Act;

(c) any increase (for dependants) under section 80, 83 or 85 below; and

(d) any increase (for Category A or Category B pensioners) under section 150 of the Administration Act (annual up-rating).

(7) The amount payable by way of benefit under this section for any day of unemployment shall be one sixth of the appropriate weekly rate.

DEFINITIONS
   "the Administration Act": s.174.
   "deferred": s.122(1).
   "entitled": s.122(1).
   "pensionable age": s.122(1).
   "period of interruption of employment": s.57(1)(d).

GENERAL NOTE
   This section deals with the basic conditions of entitlement to unemployment benefit. Benefit is payable in respect of "any day of unemployment which forms part of a period of interruption of employment" (subs. (1)). The preliminary requirements are that the claimant has met the

contribution conditions in Sched. 3, and is either under pensionable age or is no more than five years over pensionable age and has deferred entitlement to a contributory retirement pension.

The first question then to be determined is whether the claimant is indeed unemployed. Under the Social Security (Unemployment, Sickness, and Invalidity Benefit) Regulations 1983 (S.I. 1983 No. 1598), benefit is not payable where the claimant is "engaged in any employment" (reg. 7(1)(g)). On the broad meaning of employment, see s.122(1). The underlying principle is that a person is unemployed if he or she is not engaged in an activity from which it is intended to derive remuneration or profit. The concept of being in employment is thus wider than simply working under a contract of service: see Ogus and Barendt, pp.67–71.

The second issue to be decided is whether the day for which benefit is claimed is indeed a "day of unemployment". There is no single definition of this term to be found in the Act or the regulations. Rather, it is a technical construct, the meaning of which must be derived from various provisions in the Act (see s.57), the regulations (see especially reg. 7) and the case law. For a full analysis, see Bonner.

Thirdly, the day of unemployment must be part of a "period of interruption of employment"; in determining this account must be taken of the linking rules (s.57(1)(d)). Finally, reference must also be made to the requirement that the claimant is capable of work, available for employment and actively seeking such employment (s.57(1)(a)) and that there is no disqualification by virtue of involvement in a trade dispute (s.27) or "voluntary" unemployment (s.28).

Unemployment benefit is not payable for the first three "waiting days" of a period of interruption of employment (subs. (3)). It is paid at a flat rate, which may be supplemented by an increase for a dependent spouse. The daily rate is one-sixth of the weekly rate (subs. (7)) as Sundays (or appropriate substituted days) do not count for these purposes (s.57(1)(e)).

Special rules apply to men aged 65–70, and women aged 60–65, who have not retired, but who would have been entitled to a Category A or Category B retirement pension if they had retired. They are paid at the current rate of the appropriate pension (subs. (5) disregarding the increases mentioned in subs. (6)). These special rules are potentially discriminatory as contrary to Art. 4 of the E.C. Directive on Equal Treatment 79/7: see *Secretary of State for Social Security* v. *Thomas* [1991] 2 W.L.R. 886 and also Webb (1992) 55 M.L.R. 393.

Duration of unemployment benefit

26.—(1) A person who, in respect of any period of interruption of employment, has been entitled to unemployment benefit for 312 days shall not thereafter be entitled to that benefit for any day of unemployment (whether in the same or a subsequent period of interruption of employment) unless before that day he has requalified for benefit.

(2) A person who has exhausted his right to unemployment benefit requalifies for it on the next occasion when, having again been in employment as an employed earner, he makes a claim for that benefit in circumstances such that the requalification conditions are satisfied with respect to each of at least 13 weeks in the period of 26 weeks immediately preceding—

(a) the day on which the claim is made, or

(b) if he would not requalify by reference to that day, his first day of unemployment since he was last in employment as an employed earner.

(3) For the purposes of subsection (2) above the requalification conditions are satisfied with respect to any week if—

(a) the person in question has been in employment as an employed earner in that week;

(b) he has worked in such employment for at least 16 hours in that week; and

(c) the week begins after the last day for which he was entitled to unemployment benefit.

(4) Subsection (2) above shall have effect in prescribed cases with the substitution for the reference to 26 weeks of a reference to such longer period as may be prescribed.

(5) Where a person requalifies for unemployment benefit, subsection (1) above shall again apply to him but, in a case where the period of interruption of employment in which he exhausted his right to that benefit continues after

his requalification, as if the part before and the part after his requalification were distinct periods of interruption of employment.

(6) Regulations may provide for a person who would be entitled to unemployment benefit but for the operation of any provision of this Act or of regulations disentitling him to it or disqualifying him for it to be treated as if entitled to it for the purposes of this section.

DEFINITIONS
  "claim": s.122(1).
  "employed earner": s.122(1).
  "employment": s.122(1).
  "entitled": s.122(1).
  "period of interruption of employment": s.57(1)(d).
  "prescribe": s.122(1).
  "week": s.122(1).

GENERAL NOTE
  Under subs. (1) the right to unemployment benefit is exhausted after the claimant has been entitled for 312 days in any one period of interruption of employment (in effect one year, subject to the linking rule and allowing for the disregard of Sundays or alternate days: s.57(1)(e)). A person can requalify for unemployment benefit after the 312 days if he or she has been in employment as an employed earner for at least 13 weeks within the 26 weeks immediately before reclaiming, and in each of those weeks has been employed for at least 16 hours (subss. (2) and (3)). See *R(U)* 3/82 and *R(U)* 5/88. Exceptions are prescribed for the purposes of the 13 weeks in 26 weeks rule: Social Security (Unemployment, Sickness, and Invalidity Benefit) Regulations 1983 (S.I. 1983 No. 1598), reg. 6A, on which see Bonner.
  Once a person has requalified for benefit, entitlement runs for a further maximum duration of 312 days in any period of interruption of employment (subs. (5)). Subsection (6) enables rules to be made preventing claimants from extending their entitlement to benefit by manipulating the rules relating to periods of interruption of employment. See further Ogus and Barendt, p. 125 and regs. 16 and 28.

Interruption of employment in connection with trade dispute

27.—(1) Subject to the following provisions of this section—

(a) an employed earner who has lost employment as an employed earner by reason of a stoppage of work due to a trade dispute at his place of employment is disqualified for receiving unemployment benefit for any day during the stoppage unless he proves that he is not directly interested in the dispute; and

(b) an employed earner who has withdrawn his labour in furtherance of a trade dispute, but does not fall within paragraph (a) above, is disqualified for receiving unemployment benefit for any day on which his labour remains withdrawn.

(2) A person disqualified under subsection (1)(a) above for receiving unemployment benefit shall cease to be so disqualified if he proves that during the stoppage—

(a) he has become bona fide employed elsewhere; or

(b) his employment has been terminated by reason of redundancy within the meaning of section 81(2) of the Employment Protection (Consolidation) Act 1978; or

(c) he has bona fide resumed employment with his employer but has subsequently left for a reason other than the trade dispute.

(3) In this Act—

(a) "place of employment" in relation to any person, means the factory, workshop, farm or other premises or place at which he was employed, so however that, where separate branches of work which are commonly carried on as separate businesses in separate premises or at separate places are in any case carried on in separate departments on the same premises or at the same place, each of those departments shall for the purposes of this paragraph be deemed to be a separate factory or workshop or farm or separate premises or a separate place, as the case may be;

(b) "trade dispute" means any dispute between employers and employees, or between employees and employees, which is connected with the employment or non-employment or the terms of employment or the conditions of employment of any persons, whether employees in the employment of the employer with whom the dispute arises, or not.

DEFINITIONS

"employed earner": s.122(1).
"employment": s.122(1).
"place of employment": subs. (3)(a).
"trade dispute": subs. (3)(b).

GENERAL NOTE

Claimants are disqualified from unemployment benefit if they have lost their employment by reason of a stoppage of work due to a trade dispute at their place of employment (subs. (1)(a)). There are exceptions to this rule (see proviso to subs. (1)(a) and subs. (2)). Alternatively, even if a claimant is not debarred by virtue of subs. (1)(a), disqualification will ensue under subs. (1)(b) where the person's labour has been withdrawn in furtherance of a trade dispute.

Subs. (1)(a)

In order for a claimant to be disqualified under this head, the adjudication officer must show on the balance of probabilities that (1) there is a trade dispute (subs. (3)(b)); (2) at the claimant's place of employment (subs. (3)(a)); (3) resulting in a stoppage of work; and (4) as a result of that stoppage the claimant lost employment (*R(U) 17/52*).

Stoppage of work. A stoppage of work means "a situation in which operations are being stopped or hindered otherwise than to a negligible extent" (*R(U) 1/87*). It must be "in the nature of a strike or lock-out, that is to say it must be a move in a contest between an employer and his employees, the object of which is that employment shall be resumed on certain conditions" (*R(U) 17/52*).

In principle the disqualification lasts as long as the stoppage (not the trade dispute) is in existence. The disqualification will end earlier if the stoppage is no longer part of the trade dispute (*R(U) 1/65*) or has ended for some other reason (*R(U) 15/80*).

Claimants may also be able to invoke the proviso that they are not directly interested in the trade dispute. In practice this will be very difficult as in essence claimants have to demonstrate that they have nothing to gain, either financially or in terms of their conditions of employment, from the outcome of the dispute (*Presho* v. *Department of Health and Social Security (Insurance Officer)* [1984] A.C. 310 and *Cartlidge* v. *Chief Adjudication Officer* [1986] Q.B. 360). The direct interest may terminate if the employer effects a genuine severance of all relations with the employees in question (*R(U) 1/87*); dismissal as a tactical gambit in a dispute would not be sufficient.

A claimant may moreover be able to escape the impact of the disqualification by relying upon one of the grounds detailed in subs. (2).

Lost employment by reason of... The claimant need not be an active participant in strike action; under subs. (1)(a) it is sufficient that he or she has "lost employment... by reason of a stoppage of work", *i.e.* the disqualification covers people who are laid off or unable to go to work because of picketing. Furthermore, once a claimant has lost some days due to this cause, the disqualification applies for the duration of the stoppage (*Cartlidge* v. *Chief Adjudication Officer* [1986] Q.B. 360, and see above: but note subs. (2)).

Subs. (1)(b)

This head of disqualification was introduced in 1986. It is essentially a catch-all provision to disbar strikers who might escape disqualification through a lacuna in subs. (1)(a). The only requirement is that the individual has withdrawn his or her labour in furtherance of a trade dispute. There is no need for a stoppage of work or for the trade dispute to be at the claimant's place of employment. The disqualification applies for so long as the person's labour is withdrawn.

Subs. (2)

These special grounds enable claimants to escape any disqualification imposed under subs. (1)(a) (but not under subs. (1)(b)).

Bona fide employed elsewhere. The onus is on the claimant to show that the employment elsewhere which has subsequently ceased was genuine and taken up for an honest motive (*R(U) 39/56, R(U) 6/74*).

His employment has been terminated. This deals with the perceived injustice in *Cartlidge* v. *Chief Adjudication Officer* [1986] Q.B. 360, in which a miner under notice of redundancy, who had sought to work out his notice, was disqualified under the trade dispute rule because the stoppage of work continued after his employment had ended.

Bona fide resumed employment. This provision, similarly inspired by *Cartlidge*, is designed as an escape clause for claimants who have withdrawn their labour, then returned to work, and later still left for some other reason (*e.g.* a resignation on grounds of ill-health).

Subs. (3)

Place of employment. Under subs. (1)(a) the trade dispute must be at the claimant's place of employment. The essence of this convoluted definition is that it may be open to the claimant to show that the trade dispute is taking place in a separate department which fulfils the criteria set out. See further *R(U) 4/58, R(U) 4/62, R(U) 1/70* and *CU 66/1986* (discussed in Bonner).

Trade dispute. This broad definition, which is relevant to disqualification under both subs. (1)(a) and (1)(b), covers official and unofficial strikes, lock-outs and demarcation disputes. It is therefore wider than the current definition used for the purposes of conferring immunity in tort for strike action. The dispute must have reached "a certain stage of contention" before it may be regarded as a trade dispute (*R(U) 21/59*).

Unemployment benefit—other disqualifications etc.

28.—(1) Subject to section 29 below a person shall be disqualified for receiving unemployment benefit for such period not exceeding 26 weeks as may be determined in accordance with Part II of the Administration Act if—

(a) he has lost his employment as an employed earner through his misconduct, or has voluntarily left such employment without just cause;

(b) after a situation in any employment has been properly notified to him as vacant or about to become vacant, he has without good cause refused or failed to apply for that situation or refused to accept that situation when offered to him;

(c) he has without good cause neglected to avail himself of a reasonable opportunity of employment;

(d) he has without good cause refused or failed to carry out any official recommendations given to him with a view to assisting him to find employment, being recommendations which were reasonable having regard to his circumstances and to the means of obtaining that employment usually adopted in the district in which he resides;

(e) he has lost his place on an approved training scheme through his misconduct, or has voluntarily left such a place without good cause;

(f) after a place on an approved training scheme has been properly notified to him as vacant or about to become vacant, he has without good cause refused or failed to apply for that place or refused to accept that place when offered to him; or

(g) he has without good cause neglected to avail himself of a reasonable opportunity of a place on an approved training scheme.

(2) The Secretary of State may by order substitute a shorter period for the period for the time being mentioned in subsection (1) above.

(3) Regulations may also provide for imposing, in the case of any prescribed category of persons—

(a) additional conditions with respect to the receipt of unemployment benefit; and

(b) restrictions on the rate and duration of unemployment benefit,

if, having regard to special circumstances, it appears to the Secretary of State necessary to do so for the purpose of preventing inequalities, or injustice to the general body of employed earners, or of earners generally, as the case may be.

(4) For the purposes of this section a person who has been dismissed by his employer by reason of redundancy within the meaning of section 81(2) of the

Employment Protection (Consolidation) Act 1978 after volunteering or agreeing so to be dismissed shall not be deemed to have left his employment voluntarily.

(5) For the purposes of subsection (1) above regulations may—

(a) prescribe matters which are or are not to be taken into account in determining whether a person does or does not have good cause for any act or omission; or

(b) prescribe circumstances in which a person is or is not to be regarded as having or not having good cause for any act or omission;

but, subject to any such regulations, in determining for the purposes of that subsection whether a person does or does not have good cause for any act or omission, there shall be disregarded any matter relating to the level of remuneration in the employment in question.

(6) For the purposes of this section—

(a) "properly notified", in subsection (1)(b) and (f) above, means notified by the Secretary of State, a local education authority or some other recognised agency, or by or on behalf of an employer;

(b) "official recommendations", in subsection (1)(d) above, means recommendations in writing made by an officer of a local education authority or the Secretary of State;

(c) "approved training scheme", in subsection (1)(e), (f) and (g) above, means a scheme under which persons—

(i) are trained for employment; or

(ii) acquire work-experience for the purpose of becoming or keeping fit for entry to or return to regular employment,

and which is approved by the Secretary of State for the purposes of this section;

(d) "local education authority", in relation to Scotland, means an education authority, that is to say, a regional or islands council; and

(e) "week" means any period of 7 days.

DEFINITIONS

"the Administration Act": s.174.
"approved training scheme": subs. (6)(c).
"earner": s.122(1).
"employed earner": s.122(1).
"employment": s.122(1).
"local education authority": subs. (6)(d).
"official recommendations": subs. (6)(b).
"prescribe": s.122(1).
"properly notified": subs. (6)(a).
"week": subs. (6)(e).

GENERAL NOTE

This important section provides for claimants to be disqualified from unemployment benefit in cases of "voluntary" unemployment. In practice by far the most common ground for disqualification is under subs. (1)(a), which is concerned with the manner in which the claimant lost his or her previous job. Far fewer disqualifications are imposed on the grounds concerned with the claimant's subsequent behaviour and job-search activity while unemployed, or with conduct in connection with training schemes (subs. (1)(b)–(g)).

The length of the period of disqualification may be as little as one day or as much as 26 weeks (subs. (1)). On the way in which this discretion should be exercised, see *R(U) 8/74* and *R(U) 4/87*. The underlying purpose of the rule is said to be to protect the National Insurance Fund against unwarranted claims (*CU 190/50*).

All these heads of disqualification are subject to s.29, which provides for certain exemptions in connection with refusals of offers of employment. In practice this means that the proviso "subject to s.29 below" has no application to subs. (1)(e)–(g), which concerns training schemes.

Subs. (1)(a)

This provision contains two quite distinct grounds for disqualification: loss of job through misconduct and voluntarily leaving without just cause.

Misconduct. This has been defined as "conduct which is causally but not necessarily directly connected with the employment, and having regard to the relationship of employer and employee and the rights and duties of both, can fairly be described as blameworthy, reprehensible and wrong" (*R(U) 2/77*). In *R(U) 7/57* the test was formulated as follows: was the claimant's conduct such as would cause a reasonable employer to dispense with the employee's services on the ground that, having regard to the conduct in question, he or she was not a fit person to hold that position?

Misconduct need not be deliberate, but only more serious forms of negligence will amount to such behaviour (*R(U) 8/57*). The misconduct need not occur at work, but where it occurs outside working hours there must still be some nexus with the job (*e.g.* a lorry driver losing his licence whilst driving his own car: *R(U) 7/57*, but see *R(U) 1/71*).

The onus of establishing misconduct lies on the adjudication officer (*R(U) 2/60*). On the relevance of other legal proceedings, see *R(U) 10/54* (criminal court) and *R(U) 2/74* (industrial tribunal).

Voluntarily left. Three conditions must be satisfied before disqualification can be imposed on this ground. First, the claimant must have left the employment in question. Secondly, the leaving must have been voluntary. Thirdly, it must have been without just cause (see below). The onus is on the adjudication officer to establish both that the claimant left the employment and that this was voluntary (*R(U) 20/64*). Although most cases under this head involve resignation, the concept also covers losing a job through absenteeism and, exceptionally, cases of dismissal prompted by the claimant's actions (*R(U) 16/52*). Taking early retirement can amount to voluntarily leaving employment (*Crewe v. Anderson (National Insurance Officer), sub nom. Crewe v. Social Security Commissioner* [1982] 1 W.L.R. 1209, but see *R(U) 3/81* and subs. (4)).

Without just cause. Whereas "good cause", as it applies to subs. (1)(b)–(g), is now regulated by statute, the concept of "just cause" is defined by reference to case law. According to *Crewe v. Anderson (National Insurance Officer), sub nom. Crewe v. Social Security Commissioner* [1982] 1 W.L.R. 1209, the issue is not what is in the claimant's interests or even in the broader public interest. Rather, "just cause" means that the interests of the claimant and those of other contributors to the National Insurance Fund need to be balanced. Just cause has been found to exist where claimants have left jobs because of grievances at work or where personal or domestic circumstances have made it impossible for them to continue. See further *R(U) 4/87* and Bonner for a full discussion of the case law.

Subs. (1)(b)

This applies the sanction to claimants who refuse to apply for, or fail to apply for, or refuse to accept a vacancy when offered to them. Until 1989 there was a requirement that the employment in question be "suitable". Although this has now disappeared, there is still a "good cause" proviso. Good cause, however, is determined solely in accordance with statute (subs. (5) and Social Security (Unemployment, Sickness, and Invalidity Benefit) Regulations 1983 (S.I. 1983 No. 1598), reg. 12E). See further Bonner. On "properly notified", see subs. (6)(a).

Subs. (1)(c)

There is a degree of overlap between this head of disqualification and that in subs. (1)(b). Until 1989 there was a requirement that the opportunity of employment be "suitable". Although this has now disappeared, there is the "good cause" proviso. For relevant pre-amendment case law, see *R(U) 28/55* and *R(U) 5/71*.

Subs. (1)(d)

The concept of "good cause" here has the same meaning as in the parallel provisions in this section. On "official recommendations", see subs. (6)(b).

Subs. (1)(e)–(g)

These provisions, introduced in 1989, are intended to apply the same grounds of disqualification in respect of a claimant losing a place on an approved training scheme, and associated forms of behaviour, as relate to the employment grounds in subs. (1)(a)–(c). The only difference is that subs. (1)(a) applies the sanction in cases of leaving employment "without just cause", whereas subs. (1)(e) only applies where the claimant has left an approved training scheme (on which see subs. (6)(c)) "without good cause". In principle "just cause" may be more difficult to establish than "good cause" (*Crewe v. Anderson (National Insurance Officer), sub nom. Crewe v. Social Security Commissioner* [1982] 1 W.L.R. 1209), but whereas the principles governing just cause are purely a matter of case law, good cause is now determined solely in accordance with statute (subs. (5) and Social Security (Unemployment, Sickness, and Invalidity Benefit) Regulations 1983 (S.I. 1983 No. 1598), reg. 12E). On the inapplicability of the proviso relating to s.29, see the General Note above.

Subs. (4)

This provision, implemented in 1985, is unfortunately drafted. Its purpose is to ensure that individuals who volunteer for (or agree to) redundancy should not face disqualification for voluntarily leaving without just cause. Technically the operative words should read "after volunteering or agreeing so to be dismissed shall be deemed not to have left his employment voluntarily". In order to rely on this escape clause, the claimant must be dismissed *and* the reason for dismissal must be redundancy within the meaning of the employment protection legislation. Difficulties may arise in showing that the claimant has actually been dismissed, rather than having agreed a consensual termination of the contract of employment (*Birch* v. *University of Liverpool* [1985] I.C.R. 470). See further the Rosyth Dockyard cases, *CSU/33/88*, *CSU/34/88* and *CSU/21/90*.

Subs. (5)

See Social Security (Unemployment, Sickness, and Invalidity Benefit) Regulations 1983 (S.I. 1983 No. 1598), reg. 12E.

Exemptions from disqualification for unemployment benefit

29.—(1) Nothing in section 28 above or in regulations under that section shall be taken to disqualify a person for receiving unemployment benefit by reason only of his refusal—

  (a) to seek or accept employment in a situation which is vacant in consequence of a stoppage of work due to a trade dispute; or

  (b) to seek or accept during the permitted period any employment other than employment in his usual occupation at a level of remuneration not lower than he is accustomed to receive.

(2) Regulations shall make provision for the purpose of enabling any person of a prescribed description to accept any employed earner's employment without being disqualified under—

  (a) subsection (1)(a) of section 28 above, so far as it relates to a person who voluntarily leaves such employment without just cause, or

  (b) subsection (1)(c) of that section,

should he leave that employment voluntarily and without just cause at any time after the end of the sixth week, but not later than the end of the twelfth week, of a trial period.

(3) In this section—

"permitted period", in relation to any person, means such period, whether expired or not, as may be determined in accordance with regulations by an adjudication officer on the submission of the question whether that person is disqualified under section 28 above for receiving unemployment benefit; and any such regulations may prescribe—

    (a) the day on which any such period shall be regarded as having commenced in any case;

    (b) the shortest and longest periods which may be so determined in any case; and

    (c) criteria to which the adjudication officer is to have regard in determining the permitted period in any case; and

"trial period" means a period of 12 weeks beginning with the commencement of the employment in question; but regulations may—

    (a) make provision for the purpose of determining the day on which a person's employment is to be regarded as commencing; and

    (b) provide that, for the purpose of determining the time at which the sixth or twelfth week of a trial period ends, prescribed periods may be disregarded in prescribed circumstances.

DEFINITIONS

"employed earner": s.122(1).

"employment": s.122(1).

"permitted period": subs. (3).

"prescribe": s.122(1).
"trade dispute": s.27(3)(b).
"trial period": subs. (3).
"week": s.122(1).

GENERAL NOTE
This section has two purposes. First, subs. (1) provides a degree of relief from the disqualification provisions in s.28. Claimants are not subject to the sanction if they refuse to seek or accept employment which has become available as a result of a stoppage of work due to a trade dispute. Equally, disqualification may not be imposed where claimants decline work other than their normal employment during the permitted period which is paid at a lower rate than they are accustomed to receive.

Permitted period. See subs. (3) and Social Security (Unemployment, Sickness, and Invalidity Benefit) Regulations 1983 (S.I. 1983 No. 1598), reg. 12F.

Secondly, subs. (2) suspends the operation of the disqualification rule for certain claimants. Those who meet the conditions laid down in Social Security (Unemployment, Sickness, and Invalidity Benefit) Regulations 1983 (S.I. 1983 No. 1598), reg. 12G are not liable to disqualification even though they voluntarily leave a job without just cause provided that they leave between the end of the sixth week and the end of a twelfth week of a trial period (subs. (3)). The intention is to act as an incentive to unemployed claimants to take up opportunities where they may be unsure as to whether the job is right for them.

Abatement of unemployment benefit on account of payments of occupational or personal pension

30.—(1) If payments by way of occupational or personal pension which in the aggregate exceed the maximum sum are made for any week to a person who has attained the age of 55, the rate of any unemployment benefit to which apart from this section he is entitled for that week shall be reduced by 10 pence for each 10 pence of the excess; and in this subsection "the maximum sum" means such sum not less than £35 as is prescribed.

(2) Where a reduction in the rate of unemployment benefit payable to a person falls to be made under this section the reduction shall be made, so far as is necessary—

   (a) initially against so much of the benefit as falls to be paid by virtue of section 25(4) or (5) above or of regulations under section 60 below;

   (b) then against any increase in the benefit payable under section 82 below; and

   (c) finally against any increase in the benefit payable under section 80 below.

(3) Regulations may provide—

   (a) for such sums as are specified in or determined under the regulations to be disregarded for the purposes of this section;

   (b) for securing that no reduction in pursuance of subsection (1) above is made in the unemployment benefit for any day before the day which in pursuance of the regulations is treated as that on which relevant payments by way of occupational or personal pension begin;

   (c) for this section to apply, in cases where—

      (i) a lump sum is paid to a person in connection with a former employment of his or arrangements are made for a lump sum to be so paid; or

      (ii) benefits of any description are made available to a person in connection with a former employment of his or arrangements are made for them to be made so available; or

      (iii) payments by way of occupational or personal pension to a person are assigned, reduced or postponed or are made otherwise than weekly,

as if there were made to the person such weekly payments by way of occupational or personal pension as are specified in or determined under the regulations;

(d) for the method of determining whether payments by way of occupational or personal pension are made to a person for any week and the
amount of any such payments which are so made;

(e) for section 26(1) above and section 57(1) below to have effect, in
relation to a person whose rate of unemployment benefit is reduced
by virtue of this section, with such modifications as are prescribed.

(4) In this section—

"employer" means—

(a) in relation to an employment under a contract of service,
the employer under the contract;

(b) in relation to an employment in an office with emoluments, the person responsible for paying the emoluments;

"employment" means an employment under a contract of service or in
an office with emoluments;

"modifications" includes additions, omissions and amendments;

and the reference in subsection (1) above to unemployment benefit includes
any increase of the benefit on account of dependants.

DEFINITIONS
"employer": subs. (4).
"employment": subs. (4).
"entitled": s.122(1).
"maximum sum": subs. (1).
"modifications": subs. (4).
"payments by way of occupational or personal pension": s.122(1).
"prescribe": s.122(1).
"week": s.122(1).

GENERAL NOTE
This section introduces a significant element of means-testing into unemployment benefit for
those approaching retirement age. Where the claimant is 55 or over, and has an occupational or
personal pension which exceeds £35 per week, unemployment benefit is reduced by 10 pence
for every 10 pence that the pension exceeds the threshold. The £35 limit has remained
unchanged since this rule was first enacted in 1980. A Tribunal of Commissioners has held that,
notwithstanding that more men are likely to be affected by it than women, this provision is not
in breach of the E.C. Directive on Equal Treatment 79/7 (*R(U) 10/88*).

Payments by way of occupational or personal pension. The definition in s.122(1) is very wide:
see *R(U) 4/85* and *R(U) 1/89*. Broadly, the statutory definition covers all periodical payments
made in connection with the ending of an employment from money provided wholly or partly by
the employer, or from money provided under legislation, or from specified types of pension
scheme. However, sums paid in respect of redundancy and not part of an occupational pension
scheme are disregarded (Social Security (Unemployment, Sickness, and Invalidity Benefit)
Regulations 1983 (S.I. 1983 No. 1598), reg. 25), as are lump sums paid instead of periodical
payments (*R(U) 5/85*; but see also reg. 27). Where no benefit is received for a given day because
of the operation of this section, the day still counts as a day of unemployment for the purposes of
the rule limiting entitlement to 312 days (reg. 28).

Sickness benefit

Sickness benefit

31.—(1) Subject to the provisions of this section, a person who satisfies
any of the three conditions of subsection (2) below shall be entitled to
sickness benefit in respect of any day of incapacity for work which forms part
of a period of interruption of employment.

(2) The conditions of this subsection are that—

(a) the person is under pensionable age on the day in question and
satisfies the contribution conditions specified for sickness benefit in
Schedule 3, Part I, paragraph 2; or

(b) on that day the person—

(i) is over pensionable age, but not more than 5 years over that
age; and

(ii) would be entitled to a Category A retirement pension if his entitlement had not been deferred or if he had not made an election under section 54(1) below; or

(c) on that day the person—

(i) is over pensionable age, but not more than 5 years over that age; and

(ii) would be entitled to a Category B retirement pension by virtue of the contributions of his deceased spouse, but for any such deferment or election.

(3) Subsection (1) above is subject to the provision made by section 102 below in relation to entitlement to sickness benefit in cases of industrial injury.

(4) A person shall not be entitled to sickness benefit for the first 3 days of any period of interruption of employment.

(5) In the case of a person entitled under paragraph (a) of subsection (2) above (including a person entitled by virtue of that paragraph and section 102 below) sickness benefit shall be payable at the weekly rate specified in Schedule 4, Part I, paragraph 2.

(6) In the case of any person over pensionable age who is entitled under paragraph (b) or (c) of subsection (2) above, sickness benefit shall be payable at the weekly rate at which the retirement pension referred to in the applicable paragraph of that subsection would have been payable; but in determining that rate for the purposes of this subsection any increase specified in subsection (7) below shall be disregarded.

(7) The increases to be disregarded for the purposes of subsection (6) above are the following—

(a) any increase (for married women) under section 53(2) below or (for deferred retirement) under Schedule 5 to this Act;

(b) any increase (for dependants) under section 80, 83 or 85 below; and

(c) any increase (for Category A or Category B pensioners) under section 150 of the Administration Act (annual up-rating).

(8) The amount payable by way of benefit under this section for any day of incapacity for work shall be one-sixth of the appropriate weekly rate.

DEFINITIONS

"the Administration Act": s.174.
"day of incapacity for work": ss.57(1)(a) and 122(1).
"deferred": s.122(1).
"entitled": s.122(1).
"pensionable age": s.122(1).
"period of interruption of employment": s.57(1)(d).

GENERAL NOTE

Sickness benefit is now a residual benefit for claimants who do not qualify for statutory sick pay (under Pt. XI) for some reason. The structure of this section is very similar to s.25 governing unemployment benefit (previously both benefits were dealt with together in SSA 1975, s.14). Benefit is payable for any day of incapacity for work (see ss.57(1)(a)(ii) and 122(1)) which forms part of a period of interruption of employment (see General Note to s.25). The conditions set out in subs. (2) are the same as for unemployment benefit. Where the contribution conditions are not satisfied, sickness benefit is still payable where the claimant has become incapable of work due to an industrial accident or disease (subs. (3) and s.102).

As with unemployment benefit, there are three waiting days (subs. (4)) and the daily rate is one-sixth of the weekly rate (subs. (8)). The special rules as regards the rate of benefit for those who are over pensionable age but within five years of that age also apply (subs. (6)), although the invalidity increase in respect of Category A retirement pensions is not disregarded (subs. (7); compare s.25(6)(a)). See the General Note to s.25 on possible E.C. implications of these rules in so far as they are discriminatory. See also s.32 on the disqualification provisions.

Sickness benefit—disqualifications etc.

32.—(1) Regulations may provide for disqualifying a person for receiving sickness benefit for such period not exceeding 6 weeks as may be determined in accordance with Part II of the Administration Act if—

    (a) he has become incapable of work through his own misconduct; or

    (b) he fails without good cause to attend for, or to submit himself to, such medical or other examination or treatment as may be required in accordance with the regulations, or to observe any prescribed rules of behaviour.

(2) Regulations may also provide for imposing, in the case of any prescribed category of persons—

    (a) additional conditions with respect to the receipt of sickness benefit; and

    (b) restrictions on the rate and duration of sickness benefit,

if, having regard to special circumstances, it appears to the Secretary of State necessary to do so for the purpose of preventing inequalities, or injustice to the general body of employed earners, or of earners generally, as the case may be.

(3) For the purposes of this section "week" means any period of 7 days.

<small>DEFINITIONS</small>
    "the Administration Act": s.174.
    "earner": s.122(1).
    "employed earner": s.122(1).
    "medical examination": s.122(1).
    "medical treatment": s.122(1).
    "prescribe": s.122(1).
    "week": subs. (3).

<small>GENERAL NOTE</small>
    This section allows regulations to be made disqualifying claimants from receiving sickness benefit for up to six weeks (not 26 weeks, as with unemployment benefit). The purpose of these rules has been described as threefold: to protect the National Insurance Fund against fraudulent claims, to exclude those who are incapacitated through their own deliberate misconduct, and to reinforce the machinery for the control and administration of the scheme (Ogus and Barendt, p. 156). See further Social Security (Unemployment, Sickness and Invalidity Benefit) Regulations 1983 (S.I. 1983 No. 1598), reg. 17 and commentary in Bonner. Section 59 is a parallel enabling provision for invalidity benefit. There are no equivalent provisions governing statutory sick pay.

Invalidity benefits

Invalidity pension

    33.—(1) Where in respect of any period of interruption of employment a person has been entitled to sickness benefit for 168 days (including, in the case of a woman, any day for which she was entitled to a maternity allowance) then—

    (a) he shall cease to be entitled to that benefit for any subsequent day of incapacity for work falling within that period; and

    (b) he shall be entitled to an invalidity pension under this section for any day of incapacity for work in that period for which, by virtue only of paragraph (a) above, he is not entitled to sickness benefit if on that day either—

        (i) he is under pensionable age, or

        (ii) being over that age but not more than 5 years over it he satisfies either of the conditions of subsection (2) below;

and any day in the first 3 days of a period of interruption of employment which was a day of incapacity for work shall be treated for the purposes of this subsection as a day on which he was so entitled.

(2) The conditions of this subsection are that on that day—

    (a) the person would be entitled to a Category A retirement pension if his entitlement had not been deferred or if he had not made an election under section 54(1) below; or

(b) the person would be entitled to a Category B retirement pension by virtue of the contributions of his deceased spouse, but for any such deferment or election.

(3) Except as provided by subsection (4) below, the weekly rate of an invalidity pension under this section shall for any period of interruption of employment be determined in accordance with the provisions of sections 44 and 45 below as they apply in the case of a Category A retirement pension, but—

(a) with the modification provided by section 46(1) below, and

(b) with the substitution for section 44(7) below of the following—

"(7) In the application of this section for the purpose of determining the weekly rate of a person's invalidity pension for any period of interruption of employment—

(a) "relevant year" means any tax year, being neither earlier than the tax year 1978–79 nor later than the tax year 1990–91, in the period which—

(i) begins with the tax year in which the invalidity pensioner attained the age of 16; and

(ii) ends with the tax year immediately preceding the tax year which includes or included the first day of entitlement to the pension in respect of that period of interruption of employment; and

(b) "final relevant year" means the last tax year which is a relevant year in relation to the invalidity pensioner.".

(4) In the case of a person (over pensionable age) who is entitled to an invalidity pension under this section under paragraph (a) or (b) of subsection (2) above, the pension shall be payable at the weekly rate at which the retirement pension referred to in the applicable paragraph of that subsection would have been payable, apart from any increase to be disregarded by virtue of subsection (5) below.

(5) The increases to be disregarded for the purposes of subsection (4) above are the following—

(a) if he is also entitled to an invalidity allowance, any increase under section 47(1) or 50(2) below;

(b) any increase (for married women) under section 53(2) below or (for deferred entitlement) under Schedule 5 to this Act;

(c) any increase (for dependants) under section 80, 83 or 85 below; and

(d) any increase (for Category A or Category B pensioners) under section 150 of the Administration Act.

(6) The amount payable by way of an invalidity pension under this section shall for any day of incapacity for work be one sixth of the appropriate weekly rate.

(7) Where—

(a) a person who is engaged and normally engaged in remunerative work ceases to be so engaged; and

(b) he is entitled to a disability working allowance for the week in which there falls the last day on which he is so engaged; and

(c) he qualified for a disability working allowance for that week by virtue of an invalidity pension under this section having been payable to him; and

(d) the first relevant day after he ceases to be engaged as mentioned in paragraph (a) above is for him a day of incapacity for work and falls not later than the end of the period of 2 years beginning with the last day for which he was entitled to such a pension,

any day since that day which fell within a week for which he was entitled to a disability working allowance shall be treated for the purposes of any claim for such a pension for a period commencing after he ceases to be engaged as mentioned in paragraph (a) above as having been a day of incapacity for work.

(8) Any day other than a Sunday or a day prescribed under section 57(1)(e) below is a relevant day for the purposes of subsection (7) above.

(9) Regulations may make provision in relation to entitlement to invalidity pension under this section—

(a) corresponding to that made by or under section 102 below in relation to sickness benefit for persons who have attained pensionable age;

(b) restricting entitlement to invalidity pension under this section in cases where in respect of one or more of the 168 days mentioned in subsection (1) above the person claiming invalidity pension (whether or not he has attained pensionable age) would not have been entitled to sickness benefit but for the provision so made.

(10) The Secretary of State may by regulations provide that, for the purpose of entitlement to invalidity pension under this section, such days as may be prescribed, in respect of which a person is or has been entitled to statutory sick pay, shall be days in respect of which he is deemed to be or to have been entitled to sickness benefit.

(11) A person under pensionable age who is deemed in accordance with regulations under subsection (10) above to have been entitled to sickness benefit for the whole or any part of a period of 168 days such as is mentioned in subsection (1) above shall not be entitled to invalidity pension under this section unless he would have satisfied the contribution conditions for sickness benefit had he claimed that benefit on the first of those days.

DEFINITIONS

"the Administration Act": s.174.
"day of incapacity of work": ss.57(1)(a) and 122(1).
"deferred": s.122(1).
"entitled": s.122(1).
"final relevant year": subs. (3).
"pensionable age": s.122(1).
"period of interruption of employment": s.57(1)(d).
"prescribe": s.122(1).
"relevant year": subs. (3).
"tax year": s.122(1).

GENERAL NOTE

Invalidity benefit is a contributory benefit for people incapable of work whose incapacity extends beyond the maximum period of entitlement to statutory sick pay or sickness benefit (*i.e.* 168 days, or 28 weeks). It consists of an invalidity pension, governed by this section, and, where appropriate, an invalidity allowance (s.34). Invalidity pension is payable to claimants under pensionable age and to those not more than five years above that age (subs. (1)). This raises the question as to whether there is a breach of E.C. Directive 79/7 on Equal Treatment. According to Advocate General Tesauro in *R.* v. *Secretary of State for Social Security*, ex p. *Smithson* [1992] 1 C.M.L.R. 1601, the automatic discontinuance of invalidity pension five years after reaching pensionable age, inasmuch as it is linked to different retirement ages, is not a necessary consequence of the different ages at which entitlement to an old age pension arises. It is not therefore covered by the exception in Art. 7(1)(a) of the Directive. The E.C.J. itself did not deal with this issue, deciding the case on other grounds.

The day of claim must be a day of incapacity for work which falls within the same period of interruption of employment as that in which the maximum entitlement to sickness benefit (or maternity allowance) ended. Where a claimant has been in receipt of statutory sick pay, this requirement is deemed to be met (subs. (10)). There are special rules for widows so far as the qualifying period is concerned (s.40).

For claimants under pensionable age invalidity pension is essentially paid at the same rate as a Category A retirement pension (subs. (3)). Claimants who are over pensionable age have to meet the extra condition specified in subs. (2) and are paid at the appropriate rate equivalent to a category A or B retirement pension, excluding the specified increases (subss. (4) and (5)). As with unemployment benefit and sickness benefit, the daily rate is one-sixth of the weekly rate (subs. (6)). For the disqualification rules, see s.59.

As a general rule, claimants who leave invalidity benefit are exempt from the 28-week qualifying rule if they re-claim within eight weeks of the end of their earlier claim (s.57). The period under this linking rule is extended to two years for those in receipt of disability working allowance (subs. (7)).

Invalidity allowance

34.—(1) If a person is more than 5 years below pensionable age on the qualifying date in any period of interruption of employment then, subject to the following provisions of this section, in respect of every day of that period in respect of which he is entitled to an invalidity pension, he shall also be entitled to an invalidity allowance at the appropriate weekly rate specified in Schedule 4, Part I, paragraph 3.

(2) In this section "the qualifying date" means the first day in the period of interruption of employment in question (whether that day falls before the coming into force of this section or later) which is a day of incapacity for work or such earlier day as may be prescribed.

(3) An invalidity allowance shall be payable—

(a) at the higher rate specified in Schedule 4, Part I, paragraph 3, if—

    (i) the qualifying date fell before 5th July 1948; or

    (ii) on the qualifying date the beneficiary was under the age of 35;
or

    (iii) on the qualifying date the beneficiary was under the age of 40 and had not attained pensionable age before 6th April 1979;

(b) at the middle rate so specified if paragraph (a) above does not apply and either—

    (i) on the qualifying date the beneficiary was under the age of 45;
or

    (ii) on the qualifying date the beneficiary was under the age of 50 and had not attained pensionable age before 6th April 1979;

(c) at the lower rate so specified if paragraphs (a) and (b) above do not apply, and on the qualifying date the beneficiary was a man under the age of 60 or a woman under the age of 55.

(4) Where for any period the weekly rate of the invalidity pension to which the beneficiary is entitled includes an additional pension such as is mentioned in section 44(3)(b) below, for that period the relevant amount shall be deducted from the appropriate weekly rate of invalidity allowance and he shall be entitled to invalidity allowance only if there is a balance after the deduction and, if there is such a balance, at a weekly rate equal to it.

(5) In this section "the relevant amount" means an amount equal to the additional pension reduced by the amount of any reduction in the weekly rate of the invalidity pension made by virtue of section 29 of the Pensions Act.

(6) In this section references to an additional pension are references to that pension after any increase under section 52(3) below but without any increase under paragraphs 1 and 2 of Schedule 5 to this Act.

(7) The amount payable by way of invalidity allowance shall for any day of incapacity for work be one sixth of the appropriate weekly rate or, where subsection (4) above applies, of the weekly rate payable under that subsection.

DEFINITIONS
    "beneficiary": s.122(1).
    "day of incapacity for work": ss.57(1)(a) and 122(1).
    "entitled": s.122(1).
    "pensionable age": s.122(1).
    "the Pensions Act": s.174.
    "period of interruption of employment": s.57(1)(d).
    "qualifying date": subs. (2).
    "relevant amount": subs. (5).

GENERAL NOTE
Invalidity allowance is paid as a supplement to invalidity benefit for men who are aged under 60 and women under 55 on the first day of incapacity for work in a period of interruption of employment. The rate of benefit depends on the individual's age: the highest rate is payable to those under 40, the middle rate to those aged between 40 and 49, and the lower rate for men aged 50–60 and women aged 50–54 (subs. (3)). The discrimination against women aged 55–59 would appear to be unlawful under Art. 4 of E.C. Directive 79/7 (see *Thomas* v. *Chief Adjudication Officer and Secretary of State for Social Security*; *Cooze* v. *Same*; *Beard* v. *Same*; *Murphy* v. *Same*; *Morley* v. *Same* [1991] 2 W.L.R. 886 and the General Note to s.25).

Amounts received by way of earnings-related components or guaranteed minimum pension are deducted from the allowance (subss. (4)–(6)).

Maternity

State maternity allowance

35.—(1) A woman shall be entitled to a maternity allowance at the weekly rate specified in Schedule 4, Part I, paragraph 4, if—

(a) she has become pregnant and has reached, or been confined before reaching, the commencement of the 11th week before the expected week of confinement; and

(b) she has been engaged in employment as an employed or self-employed earner for at least 26 weeks in the 52 weeks immediately preceding the 14th week before the expected week of confinement; and

(c) she satisfies the contribution condition for a maternity allowance specified in Schedule 3, Part I, paragraph 3; and

(d) she is not entitled to statutory maternity pay for the same week in respect of the same pregnancy.

(2) Subject to the following provisions of this section, a maternity allowance shall be payable for the period ("the maternity allowance period") which, if she were entitled to statutory maternity pay, would be the maternity pay period under section 165 below.

(3) Regulations may provide—

(a) for disqualifying a woman for receiving a maternity allowance if—

(i) during the maternity allowance period she does any work in employment as an employed or self-employed earner, or fails without good cause to observe any prescribed rules of behaviour; or

(ii) at any time before she is confined she fails without good cause to attend for, or submit herself to, any medical examination required in accordance with the regulations;

(b) that this section and Schedule 3, Part I, paragraph 3 shall have effect subject to prescribed modifications in relation to cases in which a woman has been confined and—

(i) has not made a claim for a maternity allowance in expectation of that confinement (other than a claim which has been disallowed); or

(ii) has made a claim for a maternity allowance in expectation of that confinement (other than a claim which has been disallowed), but she was confined more than 11 weeks before the expected week of confinement.

(4) A woman who has become entitled to a maternity allowance shall cease to be entitled to it if she dies before the beginning of the maternity allowance period; and if she dies after the beginning, but before the end, of that period, the allowance shall not be payable for any week subsequent to that in which she dies.

(5) Where for any purpose of this Part of this Act or of regulations it is necessary to calculate the daily rate of a maternity allowance—

(a) Sunday or such other day in each week as may be prescribed shall be disregarded; and

(b) the amount payable by way of that allowance for any other day shall be taken as one sixth of the weekly rate of the allowance.

(6) In this section "confinement" means—

(a) labour resulting in the issue of a living child, or

(b) labour after 28 weeks of pregnancy resulting in the issue of a child whether alive or dead,

and "confined" shall be construed accordingly; and where a woman's labour begun on one day results in the issue of a child on another day she shall be taken to be confined on the day of the issue of the child or, if labour results in the issue of twins or a greater number of children, she shall be taken to be confined on the day of the issue of the last of them.

(7) The fact that the mother of a child is being paid maternity allowance shall not be taken into consideration by any court in deciding whether to order payment of expenses incidental to the birth of the child.

DEFINITIONS

"claim": s.122(1).
"confined": subs. (6).
"confinement": subs. (6).
"employed earner": s.122(1).
"employment": s.122(1).
"entitled": s.122(1).
"maternity allowance period": subs. (2).
"prescribe": s.122(1).
"self-employed earner": s.122(1).
"week": s.122(1).

GENERAL NOTE

The state maternity allowance is a residual contributory benefit and replaced the old maternity allowance. Most women workers will be entitled to statutory maternity pay (under Pt. XII) in the event of pregnancy. Entitlement to statutory maternity pay and state maternity allowance are mutually exclusive (subs. (1)(d)). State maternity allowance is payable to women who do not qualify for statutory maternity pay, e.g. because they are self-employed or fail to meet the continuous employment test for that benefit.

There are four main conditions for entitlement to state maternity allowance. The claimant must:

(1) satisfy the contribution condition (subs. (1)(c); see Sched. 3, Pt. I, para. 3);

(2) have been employed for at least 26 weeks in the 52 weeks ending before the 14th week before the expected week of confinement (subs. (1)(b));

(3) either be expecting a child within the next 11 weeks or have recently given birth (subs. (1)(a); and see R(G) 4/56 and R(G) 12/59); and

(4) not be working (see also the regulations below).

Like statutory maternity pay, state maternity allowance is payable for 18 weeks, commencing not earlier than the eleventh week before the expected week of confinement (subs. (2)).

The Social Security (Maternity Allowance) Regulations 1987 (S.I. 1987 No. 416), made under subs. (3), provide for certain disqualifications for benefit and for modifications of the maternity allowance period.

Benefits for widows and widowers

Widow's payment

36.—(1) A woman who has been widowed shall be entitled to a widow's payment of the amount specified in Schedule 4, Part II if—

(a) she was under pensionable age at the time when her late husband died, or he was then not entitled to a Category A retirement pension under section 44 below; and

(b) her late husband satisfied the contribution condition for a widow's payment specified in Schedule 3, Part I, paragraph 4.

(2) The payment shall not be payable to a widow if she and a man to whom she is not married are living together as husband and wife at the time of her husband's death.

(3) A widow's payment is payable only in cases where the husband dies on or after 11th April 1988 (the coming into force of section 36(1) of the 1986 Act, which introduced the widow's payment by making provision corresponding to this section).

DEFINITIONS

"the 1986 Act": s.174.
"entitled": s.122(1).
"late husband": s.122(1).
"pensionable age": s.122(1).

GENERAL NOTE

The widow's payment is a lump-sum payment which replaced the widow's allowance (a weekly benefit paid for the first six months of widowhood) from April 1988. Under subs. (1) this benefit is only payable if the widow was under pensionable age when her husband died (or if he was not entitled to a Category A retirement pension) and if her husband satisfied the contribution conditions (or died as a result of an industrial accident or disease: s.60(2)). No benefit is payable where the widow is cohabiting with another man at the time of her husband's death (subs. (2); see also the General Note to s.38).

Widowed mother's allowance

37.—(1) A woman who has been widowed shall be entitled to a widowed mother's allowance at the rate determined in accordance with section 39 below if her late husband satisfied the contribution conditions for a widowed mother's allowance specified in Schedule 3, Part I, paragraph 5 and either—
  (a) the woman is entitled to child benefit in respect of a child falling within subsection (2) below; or
  (b) the woman is pregnant by her late husband; or
  (c) if the woman and her late husband were residing together immediately before the time of his death, the woman is pregnant as the result of being artificially inseminated before that time with the semen of some person other than her husband, or as the result of the placing in her before that time of an embryo, of an egg in the process of fertilisation, or of sperm and eggs.
(2) A child falls within this subsection if one of the conditions specified in section 81(2) below is for the time being satisfied with respect to the child and the child is either—
  (a) a son or daughter of the woman and her late husband; or
  (b) a child in respect of whom her late husband was immediately before his death entitled to child benefit; or
  (c) if the woman and her late husband were residing together immediately before his death, a child in respect of whom she was then entitled to child benefit.
(3) The widow shall not be entitled to the allowance for any period after she remarries, but, subject to that, she shall continue to be entitled to it for any period throughout which she satisfies the requirements of subsection (1)(a), (b) or (c) above.
(4) A widowed mother's allowance shall not be payable—
  (a) for any period falling before the day on which the widow's entitlement is to be regarded as commencing for that purpose by virtue of section 5(1)(k) of the Administration Act; or
  (b) for any period during which she and a man to whom she is not married are living together as husband and wife.

DEFINITIONS

"the Administration Act": s.174.

"child": s.122(1).
"entitled": s.122(1).
"late husband": s.122(1).

GENERAL NOTE
Widowed mother's allowance is a weekly benefit for which two conditions have to be satisfied. First, the widow's late husband must have met the contribution conditions (or have died as a result of an industrial accident or disease: s.60(2)). Secondly, the widow must be receiving child benefit for a child falling within subs. (2), or be pregnant with her husband's child, or pregnant by A.I.D. (so long as she was residing with her husband immediately before his death). Widowed mother's allowance ends on remarriage and is suspended during any period of cohabitation (subss. (3) and (4); see General Note to s.38). Once it ceases (*e.g.* because child benefit is no longer payable for any child), a widow's pension may be payable under s.38.

Widow's pension

38.—(1) A woman who has been widowed shall be entitled to a widow's pension at the rate determined in accordance with section 39 below if her late husband satisfied the contribution conditions for a widow's pension specified in Schedule 3, Part I, paragraph 5 and either—

(a) she was, at the husband's death, over the age of 45 but under the age of 65; or

(b) she ceased to be entitled to a widowed mother's allowance at a time when she was over the age of 45 but under the age of 65.

(2) The widow shall not be entitled to the pension for any period after she remarries, but, subject to that, she shall continue to be entitled to it until she attains the age of 65.

(3) A widow's pension shall not be payable—

(a) for any period falling before the day on which the widow's entitlement is to be regarded as commencing for that purpose by virtue of section 5(1)(k) of the Administration Act;

(b) for any period for which she is entitled to a widowed mother's allowance; or

(c) for any period during which she and a man to whom she is not married are living together as husband and wife.

(4) In the case of a widow whose late husband died before 11th April 1988 and who either—

(a) was over the age of 40 but under the age of 55 at the time of her husband's death; or

(b) is over the age of 40 but under the age of 55 at the time when she ceases to be entitled to a widowed mother's allowance,

subsection (1) above shall have effect as if for "45" there were substituted "40".

DEFINITIONS
"the Administration Act": s.174.
"entitled": s.122(1).
"late husband": s.122(1).

GENERAL NOTE
The widow's pension is a weekly benefit payable to widows aged under 65 who are not entitled to widowed mother's allowance (s.37) and whose late husbands satisfied the contributions requirement (or whose death was due to an industrial accident or disease: s.60(2)). Finally, if the husband died on or after April 11, 1988, the widow must have been over 45 but under 65 at the time of his death or when she was no longer eligible for widowed mother's allowance (subs. (1)). Alternatively, where the husband died before April 11, 1988 the widow need only have been over 40 but under 65 on either of these dates (subs. (4)). The basic rate of benefit is the same as the Category A retirement pension, but is reduced if the claimant was under 55 at the relevant date, or 50 where the bereavement was before April 11, 1988 (s.39(4)–(6)).

It is fundamental to widowhood that (a) there was a valid marriage in existence at the time of the husband's death, and (b) that the husband is in fact dead. So far as (a) is concerned, this is usually evidenced by production of a copy of the marriage certificate. Difficulties may arise in connection with Scottish marriages, which may be proved by "cohabitation with habit and repute" (*R(G) 2/82, R(G) 5/83* and *R(G) 4/84*), or with foreign marriages (*R(G) 2/71*): see Bonner. Marriage may be brought to an end by decree absolute of divorce or nullity, although a void marriage has no legal effect at any time.

As regards (b), this is again usually evidenced by production of a copy of the relevant certificate. See SSAA 1992, s.3, in cases where death is difficult to establish, and Bonner for discussion of the position where the husband is presumed dead. Where the widow is herself responsible for her late husband's death, the provisions of the Forfeiture Act 1982 apply.

Entitlement to widow's pension terminates on remarriage or on her attaining the age of 65 (subs. (2)). Benefit is suspended so long as the widow is living with another man as husband and wife. For analysis of this expression, see annotations to s.137. The principles governing the same term in the context of income support (formerly supplementary benefit) apply equally to widow's benefits (*R(SB) 17/81* and *R(G) 3/81*).

Rate of widowed mother's allowance and widow's pension

39.—(1) The weekly rate of—

(a) a widowed mother's allowance,

(b) a widow's pension,

shall be determined in accordance with the provisions of sections 44 and 45 below as they apply in the case of a Category A retirement pension, but subject, in particular, to the following provisions of this section and section 46(2) below.

(2) In the application of sections 44 and 45 below by virtue of subsection (1) above—

(a) where the woman's husband was over pensionable age when he died, references in those sections to the pensioner shall be taken as references to the husband, and

(b) where the husband was under pensionable age when he died, references in those sections to the pensioner and the tax year in which he attained pensionable age shall be taken as references to the husband and the tax year in which he died.

(3) In the case of a woman whose husband dies after 5th April 2000, the additional pension falling to be calculated under sections 44 and 45 below by virtue of subsection (1) above shall (before making any reduction required by subsection (4) below) be one half of the amount which it would be apart from this subsection.

(4) Where a widow's pension is payable to a woman who was under the age of 55 at the time when the applicable qualifying condition was fulfilled, the weekly rate of the pension shall be reduced by 7 per cent. of what it would be apart from this subsection multiplied by the number of years by which her age at that time was less than 55 (any fraction of a year being counted as a year).

(5) For the purposes of subsection (4) above, the time when the applicable qualifying condition was fulfilled is the time when the woman's late husband died or, as the case may be, the time when she ceased to be entitled to a widowed mother's allowance.

(6) In the case of a widow whose late husband died before 11th April 1988 and who either—

(a) was over the age of 40 but under the age of 55 at the time of her husband's death; or

(b) is over the age of 40 but under the age of 55 at the time when she ceases to be entitled to a widowed mother's allowance,

subsection (4) above shall have effect as if for "55" there were substituted "50", in both places where it occurs.

DEFINITIONS
"entitled": s.122(1).

"late husband": s.122(1).
"pensionable age": s.122(1).
"tax year": s.122(1).

GENERAL NOTE
This section deals with the rate at which the weekly benefits under ss.37 and 38 are payable. Essentially both benefits are paid at the same rate as the Category A retirement pension. The widow's pension is reduced in the case of younger widows (subss. (4)–(6); see General Note to s.38). Claimants widowed after April 5, 2000 will be entitled to only half the increase under SERPS as is payable in relation to deaths before that date (subs. (3)).

Invalidity pension for widows

40.—(1) Subject to subsection (2) below, this section applies to a woman who—

(a) on her late husband's death is not entitled to a widowed mother's allowance or subsequently ceases to be entitled to such an allowance; and

(b) is incapable of work at the time when he dies or when she subsequently ceases to be so entitled; and

(c) either—

(i) would have been entitled to a widow's pension if she had been over the age of 45 when her husband died or when she ceased to be entitled to a widowed mother's allowance; or

(ii) is entitled to such a pension with a reduction under section 39(4) above.

(2) This section does not apply to a woman unless—

(a) her husband died after 5th April 1979; or

(b) she ceased to be entitled to a widowed mother's allowance after that date (whenever her husband died).

(3) Subject to subsection (7) below, a woman to whom this section applies shall be entitled to an invalidity pension under this section for any day of incapacity for work which—

(a) falls in a period of interruption of employment that began before the time when her late husband died or she subsequently ceased to be entitled to a widowed mother's allowance; and

(b) is after that time and after the first 168 days of incapacity for work in that period.

(4) An invalidity pension under this section shall be payable at the higher of—

(a) the weekly rate which would apply if the pension were payable under section 33 above; or

(b) the weekly rate specified in subsection (5) below.

(5) The weekly rate referred to in subsection (4)(b) above is—

(a) if the woman is not entitled to a widow's pension, a weekly rate equal to that of the widow's pension to which she would have been entitled if she had been over the age of 55 when her husband died; and

(b) if she is entitled to a widow's pension with a reduction under section 39(4) above, a weekly rate equal to the difference between the weekly rate of that pension and what it would have been without the reduction,

but, in calculating the weekly rate of a widow's pension for the purposes of paragraph (a) above, or the weekly rate of a widow's pension without reduction, for the purposes of paragraph (b) above, any additional pension by virtue of section 44(3) below as it applies for the purposes of section 39 above shall be determined without reference to any surpluses in her late husband's earnings factors for tax years after 1990–91.

(6) For the purpose of calculating the rate of an invalidity pension for a woman to whom this section applies by virtue of subsection (1)(c)(ii) above, subsections (4) and (5) above shall have effect with such modifications as are prescribed.

(7) A woman shall not be entitled to an invalidity pension under this section if she is over pensionable age and is entitled to a Category A or Category B retirement pension; but if she has attained pensionable age, and the period of interruption of employment mentioned in subsection (3)(a) above did not terminate earlier than the day before she attained that age—

   (a) she shall, if not otherwise entitled to a Category A retirement pension, be entitled to such a pension; and
   (b) the weekly rate of the Category A retirement pension to which she is entitled (whether by virtue of paragraph (a) above or otherwise) shall be determined in the prescribed manner.

(8) No invalidity pension shall be payable under section 33 above for any day of incapacity for which an invalidity pension is payable under this section.

(9) In subsection (6) above "modifications" includes additions, omissions and amendments.

DEFINITIONS
   "day of incapacity for work": ss.57(1)(a) and 122(1).
   "entitled": s.122(1).
   "late husband": s.122(1).
   "modifications": subs. (9).
   "pensionable age": s.122(1).
   "period of interruption of employment": s.57(1)(d).
   "prescribe": s.122(1).
   "tax year": s.122(1).

GENERAL NOTE
   A widow who falls within subss. (1) and (2) may claim invalidity benefit after 168 days of incapacity even though she does not satisfy the normal requirement of receipt of statutory sick pay or sickness benefit during this period (subs. (3)). The additional component is calculated on the basis of her own contributions or those of her late husband, whichever is the more favourable to her (subs. (4)). The same principle applies to widowers (s.41(3)).

Invalidity pension for widowers

   41.—(1) This section applies to a man whose wife has died on or after 6th April 1979 and who either—
   (a) was incapable of work at the time when she died; or
   (b) becomes incapable of work within the prescribed period after that time.

(2) Subject to subsection (7) below, a man to whom this section applies shall be entitled to an invalidity pension under this section for any day of incapacity for work which—
   (a) falls in a period of interruption of employment that began before the time when his wife died or within the prescribed period after that time; and
   (b) is after that time and after the first 168 days of incapacity for work in that period.

(3) An invalidity pension under this section shall be payable at the higher of—
   (a) the weekly rate which would apply if the pension were payable under section 33 above; or
   (b) the weekly rate specified in subsection (4) below.

(4) The weekly rate mentioned in subsection (3)(b) above is a rate determined in accordance with the provisions of sections 44 and 45 below as they apply in the case of a Category A retirement pension, but subject, in particular, to subsections (5) and (6) and section 46(2) below.

(5) In the application of sections 44 and 45 below by virtue of subsection (4) above—
   (a) where the man's wife was over pensionable age when she died,

references in those sections to the pensioner shall be taken as references to the wife; and

  (b) where the man's wife was under pensionable age when she died, references in those sections to the pensioner and the tax year in which he attained pensionable age shall be taken as references to the wife and the tax year in which she died; and

  (c) any additional pension shall be determined without reference to any surpluses in her earnings factors for tax years after 1990–91.

(6) In the case of a widower whose wife dies after 5th April 2000, the additional pension falling to be calculated under sections 44 and 45 below by virtue of subsection (4) above shall be one half of the amount which it would be apart from this subsection.

(7) A man shall not be entitled to an invalidity pension under this section if he is over pensionable age and is entitled to a Category A or Category B retirement pension; but if he has attained pensionable age, and the period of interruption of employment mentioned in subsection (2)(a) above did not terminate earlier than the day before he attained that age—

  (a) he shall, if not otherwise entitled to a Category A retirement pension and also not entitled to a Category B retirement pension by virtue of section 51 below, be entitled to a Category A retirement pension; and

  (b) the weekly rate of the Category A retirement pension to which he is entitled (whether by virtue of paragraph (a) above or otherwise) shall be determined in the prescribed manner.

(8) No invalidity pension shall be payable under section 33 above for any day of incapacity for which an invalidity pension is payable under this section.

DEFINITIONS
  "day of incapacity for work": ss.57(1)(a) and 122(1).
  "earnings factor": s.22(1).
  "entitled": s.122(1).
  "pensionable age": s.122(1).
  "period of interruption of employment": s.57(1)(d).
  "prescribe": s.122(1).
  "tax year": s.122(1).

GENERAL NOTE
  The contributory benefits scheme has no special benefits for widowers. This section provides one concession in that a man who falls within subs. (1) is entitled to an invalidity pension, based on either his own contributions or those of his late wife, whichever produces the higher rate.

Entitlement to invalidity pension on termination of employment after period of entitlement to disability working allowance

42.—(1) Where—

  (a) a person who is engaged and normally engaged in remunerative work ceases to be so engaged; and

  (b) he is entitled to a disability working allowance for the week in which there falls the last day on which he is so engaged; and

  (c) he qualified for a disability working allowance for that week by virtue of an invalidity pension under section 40 or 41 above having been payable to him; and

  (d) the first relevant day after he ceases to be engaged as mentioned in paragraph (a) above is a day on which he is incapable of work and falls not later than the end of the period of two years beginning with the last day for which he was entitled to such a pension,

any day since that day which fell within a week for which he was entitled to a disability working allowance shall be treated for the purposes of any claim for such a pension for a period commencing after he ceases to be engaged as mentioned in paragraph (a) above as having been a day on which he was incapable of work.

(2) Any day other than a Sunday or a day prescribed under section 57(1)(e) below is a relevant day for the purposes of this section.

DEFINITIONS
 "entitled": s.122(1).
 "prescribe": s.122(1).

GENERAL NOTE
 This is an analogous provision to the linking rule under s.33(7) but in relation to claims for invalidity pension by people over pensionable age.

Retirement pensions (Categories A and B)

Persons entitled to more than one retirement pension

43.—(1) A person shall not be entitled for the same period to more than one retirement pension under this Part of this Act except as provided by subsection (2) below.

(2) A person who, apart from subsection (1) above, would be entitled for the same period to both—

 (a) a Category A or a Category B retirement pension under this Part; and

 (b) a Category C or a Category D retirement pension under Part III below,

shall be entitled to both of those pensions for that period, subject to any adjustment of them in pursuance of regulations under section 73 of the Administration Act.

(3) A person who, apart from subsection (1) above, would be entitled—

 (a) to both a Category A and a Category B retirement pension under this Part for the same period, or

 (b) to both a Category C and a Category D retirement pension under Part III below for the same period,

may from time to time give notice in writing to the Secretary of State specifying which of the pensions referred to in paragraph (a) or, as the case may be, paragraph (b) above he wishes to receive.

(4) If a person gives such a notice, the pension so specified shall be the one to which he is entitled in respect of any week commencing after the date of the notice.

(5) If no such notice is given, the person shall be entitled to whichever of the pensions is from time to time the most favourable to him (whether it is the pension which he claimed or not).

DEFINITIONS
 "the Administration Act": s.174.
 "entitled": s.122(1).
 "week": s.122(1).

GENERAL NOTE
 There are four types of retirement pension:
 Category A: paid on the basis of the claimant's own contribution record (s.44).
 Category B: paid to married women on the basis of their husband's contribution record and also to certain widows and widowers on the basis of their deceased spouse's contributions (ss.49–51).
 Category C: paid to those who were already over pensionable age on July 5, 1948, or whose husband was then over that age (s.78).
 Category D: paid to those aged over 80 years of age who do not qualify for another retirement pension (s.78).
 The general rule, not surprisingly, is that a claimant is not entitled to more than one retirement pension at a time (subs. (1)). A special rule operates in the cases mentioned in subss. (2) and (3).

Category A retirement pension

44.—(1) A person shall be entitled to a Category A retirement pension if—

(a) he is over pensionable age; and

(b) he satisfies the contribution conditions for a Category A retirement pension specified in Schedule 3, Part I, paragraph 5;

and, subject to the provisions of this Act, he shall become so entitled on the day on which he attains pensionable age and his entitlement shall continue throughout his life.

(2) A Category A retirement pension shall not be payable in respect of any period falling before the day on which the pensioner's entitlement is to be regarded as commencing for that purpose by virtue of section 5(1)(k) of the Administration Act.

(3) A Category A retirement pension shall consist of—

(a) a basic pension payable at a weekly rate; and

(b) an additional pension payable where there are one or more surpluses in the pensioner's earnings factors for the relevant years.

(4) The weekly rate of the basic pension shall be £54.15 except that, so far as the sum is relevant for the purpose of calculating the rate of sickness benefit under section 31(6) above, it shall be £51.95.

(5) For the purposes of this section and section 45 below—

(a) there is a surplus in the pensioner's earnings factor for a relevant year if that factor exceeds the qualifying earnings factor for the final relevant year; and

(b) the amount of the surplus is the amount of that excess;

and for the purposes of paragraph (a) above the pensioner's earnings factor for any relevant year shall be taken to be that factor as increased by the last order under section 148 of the Administration Act to come into force before the end of the final relevant year.

(6) Any reference in this section or section 45 below to the pensioner's earnings factor for any relevant year is a reference—

(a) where the relevant year is 1987–88 or any subsequent tax year, to the aggregate of—

(i) his earnings factors derived from earnings upon which primary Class 1 contributions were paid or treated as paid in respect of that year, and

(ii) his earnings factors derived from Class 2 and Class 3 contributions actually paid in respect of it; and

(b) where the relevant year is an earlier tax year, to the aggregate of his earnings factors derived from contributions actually paid by him in respect of that year.

(7) In this section—

(a) "relevant year" means 1978–79 or any subsequent tax year in the period between—

(i) (inclusive) the tax year in which the pensioner attained the age of 16, and

(ii) (exclusive) the tax year in which he attained pensionable age;

(b) "final relevant year" means the last tax year which is a relevant year in relation to the pensioner.

(8) For the purposes of this section any order under section 21 of the Pensions Act (which made provision corresponding to section 148 of the Administration Act) shall be treated as an order under section 148 (but without prejudice to sections 16 and 17 of the Interpretation Act 1978).

DEFINITIONS

"additional pension": s.45(1).

"the Administration Act": s.174.

"earnings": s.122(1).

"earnings factor": s.22(1).
"entitled": s.122(1).
"final relevant year": subs. (7)(b).
"pensionable age": s.122(1).
"the Pensions Act": s.174.
"qualifying earnings factor": s.122(1).
"relevant year": subs. (7)(a).
"tax year": s.122(1).

GENERAL NOTE

The Category A retirement pension is the standard old-age pension. The two eligibility conditions are that the claimant has reached pensionable age and has satisfied the necessary contribution requirements (subs. (1)). The retirement condition and the earnings rule were abolished by SSA 1989, so a pension may be drawn when the above two conditions are met, irrespective of whether the claimant intends to remain in regular employment. Reduced rate pensions are payable where the claimant has an incomplete contributions record (Social Security (Widow's Benefit and Retirement Pensions) Regulations 1979 (S.I. 1979 No. 642), reg. 6).

The weekly Category A retirement pension consists of a flat-rate basic component and an earnings-related additional component (subs. (3)). Subsections (4)–(6) and s.45 deal with the calculation of this benefit. A Category A pension may be increased by the age addition of 25p per week for claimants over 80 (s.79), a higher pension by deferring entitlement (s.55), a graduated retirement benefit based on earnings between 1961 and 1975 (s.62) and, in certain cases, invalidity allowance (s.47). The Christmas bonus (s.148) is also payable.

Subs. (1)

The difference in pensionable ages for men and women (s.122(1)) is permitted by Art. 7 of E.C. Directive 79/7 (*R(P) 3/90*).

Subs. (6)

Note the transitory modification in SS(CP)A 1992, Sched. 4, paras. 2 and 3.

The additional pension in a Category A retirement pension

45.—(1) The weekly rate of the additional pension in a Category A retirement pension in any case where the pensioner attained pensionable age in a tax year before 6th April 1999 shall be the weekly equivalent of $1\frac{1}{4}$ per cent. of the amount of the surpluses mentioned in section 44(3)(b) above.

(2) The weekly rate of the additional pension in a Category A retirement pension in any case where the pensioner attained pensionable age in a tax year after 5th April 1999 shall be—

   (a) in relation to any surpluses in the pensioner's earnings factors for the tax years in the period beginning with 1978–79 and ending with 1987–88, the weekly equivalent of 25/N per cent. of the amount of those surpluses; and

   (b) in relation to any surpluses in the pensioner's earnings factors in a tax year after 1987–88, the weekly equivalent of the relevant percentage of the amount of those surpluses.

(3) In subsection (2)(b) above, "relevant percentage" means—

   (a) 20/N per cent., where the pensioner attained pensionable age in 2009–10 or any subsequent tax year;

   (b) (20 + X)/N per cent., where the pensioner attained pensionable age in a tax year falling within the period commencing with 1999–2000 and ending with 2008–09.

(4) In this section—

   (a) X = 0.5 for each tax year by which the tax year in which the pensioner attained pensionable age precedes 2009–10; and

   (b) N = the number of tax years in the pensioner's working life which fall after 5th April 1978;

but paragraph (b) above is subject, in particular, to subsection (5) and, where applicable, section 46 below.

(5) Regulations may direct that in prescribed cases or classes of cases any tax year shall be disregarded for the purpose of calculating N under subsection (4)(b) above, if it is a tax year after 5th April 1978 in which the pensioner—

(a) was credited with contributions or earnings under this Act by virtue of regulations under section 22(5) above, or

(b) was precluded from regular employment by responsibilities at home, or

(c) in prescribed circumstances, would have been treated as falling within paragraph (a) or (b) above,

but not so as to reduce the number of years below 20.

(6) For the purposes of subsections (1) and (2) above, the weekly equivalent of the amount of any surpluses shall be calculated by dividing that amount by 52 and rounding the result to the nearest whole penny, taking any 1/2p as nearest to the next whole penny.

(7) Where the amount falling to be rounded under subsection (6) above is a sum less than 1/2p, the amount calculated under that subsection shall be taken to be zero, notwithstanding any other provision of this Act or the Administration Act.

(8) The sums which are the weekly rate of the additional pension in a Category A retirement pension are subject to alteration by orders made by the Secretary of State under section 150 of the Administration Act.

DEFINITIONS
"the Administration Act": s.174.
"earnings factor": s.22(1).
"pensionable age": s.122(1).
"prescribe": s.122(1).
"relevant percentage": subs. (3).
"tax year": s.122(1).

GENERAL NOTE
This details the method of calculation for the additional pension under s.44(3)(b), but subject to the modifications under s.46.

Modifications of section 45 for calculating the additional pension in certain benefits

46.—(1) For the purpose of determining the additional pension falling to be calculated under section 45 above by virtue of section 33(3) above, the following definition shall be substituted for the definition of "N" in section 45(4)(b) above—

"N = the number of tax years which begin after 5th April 1978 and end before the first day of entitlement to the additional pension in the period of interruption of employment in which that day falls, except that if—

(i) in a case where the person entitled to the pension is a man, that number would be greater than 49; or

(ii) in a case where the person so entitled is a woman, that number would be greater than 44,

N = 49 or 44, as the case may be".

(2) For the purpose of determining the additional pension falling to be calculated under section 45 above by virtue of section 39(1) or 41(4) above or section 50(3) below in a case where the deceased spouse died under pensionable age, the following definition shall be substituted for the definition of "N" in section 45(4)(b) above—

"N = the number of tax years which begin after 5th April 1978 and end before the date when the entitlement to the additional pension commences, except that if—

   (i) in a case where the deceased spouse was a man, that
number would be greater than 49, or
   (ii) in a case where the deceased spouse was a woman, that
number would be greater than 44,
N = 49 or 44, as the case may be".

DEFINITIONS
 "additional pension": s.45(1).
 "pensionable age": s.122(1).
 "period of interruption of employment": s.57(1)(d).
 "tax year": s.122(1).

GENERAL NOTE
 See General Note to s.45.

Increase of Category A retirement pension for invalidity

47.—(1) Subject to section 61 below, the weekly rate of a Category A
retirement pension shall be increased if the pensioner was entitled to an
invalidity allowance in respect of—
 (a) any day falling within the period of 8 weeks ending immediately
  before the day on which he attains pensionable age; or
 (b) the last day before the beginning of that period;
and the increase shall, subject to subsection (2) below, be of an amount
equal to the appropriate weekly rate of the invalidity allowance on that day.
 (2) Where for any period the weekly rate of a Category A retirement
pension includes an additional pension, for that period the relevant amount
shall be deducted from the amount that would otherwise be the increase
under subsection (1) above and the pensioner shall be entitled to an increase
under that subsection only if there is a balance remaining after that deduction and, if there is such a balance, of an amount equal to it.
 (3) In subsection (2) above the "relevant amount" means an amount equal
to the additional pension, reduced by the amount of any reduction in the
weekly rate of the Category A retirement pension made by virtue of section
29 of the Pensions Act.
 (4) In this section any reference to an additional pension is a reference to
that pension after any increase under section 52(3) below but without any
increase under paragraphs 1 and 2 of Schedule 5 to this Act.
 (5) In ascertaining for the purposes of subsection (1) above the rate of a
pensioner's invalidity allowance, regard shall be had to the rates in force
from time to time.
 (6) Regulations may provide that subsection (1) above shall have effect as
if for the reference to 8 weeks there were substituted a reference to a larger
number of weeks specified in the regulations.

DEFINITIONS
 "entitled": s.122(1).
 "pensionable age": s.122(1).
 "the Pensions Act": s.174.
 "relevant amount": subs. (3).
 "week": s.122(1).

GENERAL NOTE
 A claimant in receipt of invalidity allowance (s.34) in the period immediately before attaining
pensionable age may keep that benefit as a supplement to a Category A retirement pension. If
the claimant is also entitled to an increased pension by virtue of SERPS (or its equivalent if
contracted-out), such an increase is set against the invalidity allowance and only the balance
becomes payable. This section is subject to s.61, which excludes increases of benefit where
there has been a failure to satisfy a contribution condition.

Use of former spouse's contributions

48.—(1) Where a person—
(a) has been married, and
(b) in respect of the tax year in which the marriage terminated or any previous tax year, does not with his own contributions satisfy the contribution conditions for a Category A retirement pension,
then, for the purpose of enabling him to satisfy those conditions (but only in respect of any claim for a Category A retirement pension), the contributions of his former spouse may to the prescribed extent be treated as if they were his own contributions.

(2) Subsection (1) above shall not apply in relation to any person who attained pensionable age before 6th April 1979 if the termination of his marriage also occurred before that date.

(3) Where a person has been married more than once this section applies only to the last marriage and the references to his marriage and his former spouse shall be construed accordingly.

DEFINITIONS
"pensionable age": s.122(1).
"prescribe": s.122(1).
"tax year": s.122(1).

GENERAL NOTE
A widow or widower who has not attained pensionable age before his or her spouse died, and who has not remarried before that age, can rely on that deceased spouse's contributions record. See further Social Security (Widow's Benefit and Retirement Pensions) Regulations 1979 (S.I. 1979 No. 642), reg. 8 and Sched. 1.

Category B retirement pension for women

49.—(1) A woman who is or has been married, and has attained pensionable age, shall be entitled to a Category B retirement pension by virtue of the contributions of her husband; and the cases in which a woman is so entitled are those specified in subsections (2) to (5) below.

(2) The first case of entitlement is where the woman is married to that husband at the time when she attains pensionable age and—
(a) he also has attained pensionable age and has become entitled to a Category A retirement pension; and
(b) he satisfies the relevant contribution conditions.

(3) The second case of entitlement is where the woman marries after attaining pensionable age and—
(a) her husband has also attained pensionable age and has become entitled to a Category A retirement pension; and
(b) he satisfies the relevant contribution conditions.

(4) The third case of entitlement is where the woman's husband is dead and his death was after she attained pensionable age, and—
(a) she was married to him when he died; and
(b) before his death he satisfied the relevant contribution conditions.

(5) The fourth case of entitlement is where the woman's husband is dead and his death was before she attained pensionable age, and—
(a) she was a widow immediately before attaining pensionable age and is entitled (or is treated by regulations as entitled) to a widow's pension; and
(b) she became entitled to the pension in consequence of the husband's death.

(6) The relevant contribution conditions for the purposes of the first, second and third cases of entitlement are those specified in Schedule 3, Part I, paragraph 5.

(7) Subject to the provisions of this Act, a woman's entitlement to a Category B retirement pension shall commence on the day on which the conditions of entitlement become satisfied in her case and shall continue throughout her life.

(8) A woman's Category B retirement pension shall not be payable for any period falling before the day on which the pensioner's entitlement is to be regarded as commencing for that purpose by virtue of section 5(1)(k) of the Administration Act.

DEFINITIONS
  "the Administration Act": s.174.
  "entitled": s.122(1).
  "pensionable age": s.122(1).

GENERAL NOTE
  A married woman or widow can claim a Category B retirement pension on the basis of her husband's contributions record, provided that she has attained pensionable age, in any of the circumstances set out in subss. (2)–(5). A Category B pension may be supplemented by the age addition of 25p per week for claimants over 80 (s.79), a higher pension by deferring entitlement (s.55) and the Christmas bonus (s.148).

Rate of Category B retirement pension for women

50.—(1) A woman's Category B retirement pension—
  (a) in the first and second cases of entitlement under section 49 above, shall—
      (i) during any period in which the husband is alive, be payable at the weekly rate specified in Schedule 4, Part I, paragraph 5, and
      (ii) during any period after he is dead, be payable at a weekly rate ascertained in accordance with subsection (3) below;
  (b) in the third case of entitlement under that section, shall be payable at a weekly rate ascertained in accordance with subsection (3) below; and
  (c) in the fourth case of entitlement under that section, shall be payable at the same weekly rate as her widow's pension.
(2) In any case where—
  (a) a woman would, apart from section 43(1) above, be entitled both to a Category A and to a Category B retirement pension, and
  (b) subsection (1) of section 47 above would apply for the increase of the Category A retirement pension,
that subsection shall be taken as applying also for the increase of the Category B retirement pension, subject to reduction or extinguishment of the increase by the application of section 47(2) above or section 29B(2) of the Pensions Act.
(3) The weekly rate referred to in paragraphs (a)(ii) and (b) of subsection (1) above for a woman's Category B retirement pension shall be determined in accordance with the provisions of sections 44 and 45 above as they apply in the case of a Category A retirement pension, but subject, in particular—
  (a) to section 46(2) above; and
  (b) to subsections (4) and (5) below.
(4) In the application of sections 44 and 45 above by virtue of subsection (3) above—
  (a) references in those sections to the pensioner shall be taken as references to the husband, and
  (b) where, in the third case of entitlement under section 49 above, the husband was under pensionable age when he died, references in those sections to the pensioner and the tax year in which he attained pensionable age shall be taken as references to the husband and the tax year in which he died.

(5) In the case of a widow whose husband dies after 5th April 2000, the additional pension falling to be calculated under sections 44 and 45 above by virtue of subsection (3) above shall be one half of the amount which it would be apart from this subsection.

DEFINITIONS
"additional pension": s.45(1).
"entitled": s.122(1).
"pensionable age": s.122(1).
"the Pensions Act": s.174.
"tax year": s.122(1).

GENERAL NOTE
This section deals with the method of calculating the rate of a Category B retirement pension. The additional pension will be reduced to half that of her husband if he dies after April 5, 2000 (subs. (5)).

Category B retirement pension for widowers

51.—(1) A man shall be entitled to a Category B retirement pension if—
(a) he has had a wife and she has died on or after 6th April 1979, and he was married to her when she died; and
(b) they were both over pensionable age when she died; and
(c) before her death she satisfied the contribution conditions for a Category A retirement pension in Schedule 3, Part I, paragraph 5.

(2) The weekly rate of a man's Category B retirement pension under this section shall, subject to subsection (3) below, be determined in accordance with the provisions of sections 44 and 45 above as they apply in the case of a Category A retirement pension, taking references in those sections to the pensioner as references to the wife.

(3) In the case of a widower whose wife dies after 5th April 2000, the additional pension falling to be calculated under sections 44 and 45 above by virtue of subsection (2) above shall be one half of the amount which it would be apart from this subsection.

(4) Subject to the provisions of this Act, a man shall become entitled to a Category B retirement pension on the day on which the conditions of entitlement become satisfied in his case and his entitlement shall continue throughout his life.

DEFINITIONS
"additional pension": s.45(1).
"entitled": s.122(1).
"pensionable age": s.122(1).

GENERAL NOTE
The SSPA 1975 extended entitlement to a Category B retirement pension to a widower whose wife died on or after April 6, 1979, provided that they were both over pensionable age when she died and that before her death she satisfied the contribution conditions for a Category A retirement pension. As under s.50, widowers will only receive half of their partners' additional pension if the latter die after April 5, 2000 (subs. (3)). Unlike widows, a widower cannot qualify for a Category B pension if his wife died before he reached pensionable age.

Special provision for surviving spouses

52.—(1) This section has effect where, apart from section 43(1) above, a person would be entitled both—
(a) to a Category A retirement pension; and
(b) to a Category B retirement pension—
(i) under section 49 above by virtue of the contributions of a husband who has died; or
(ii) under section 51 above.

(2) If by reason of a deficiency of contributions the basic pension in the Category A retirement pension falls short of the full amount, that basic pension shall be increased by the lesser of—

(a) the amount of the shortfall, or

(b) the amount of the basic pension in the rate of the Category B retirement pension,

"full amount" meaning for this purpose the sum specified in section 44(4) above as the weekly rate of the basic pension in a Category A retirement pension.

(3) If the additional pension in the Category A retirement pension falls short of the prescribed maximum, that additional pension shall be increased by the lesser of—

(a) the amount of the shortfall, or

(b) the amount of the additional pension in the Category B retirement pension.

(4) This section does not apply in any case where the death of the wife or husband, as the case may be, occurred before 6th April 1979 and the surviving spouse had attained pensionable age before that date.

DEFINITIONS

"additional pension": s.45(1).
"entitled": s.122(1).
"full amount": subs. (2).
"pensionable age": s.122(1).

GENERAL NOTE

This section applies where a person's spouse died on or after April 6, 1979, and they themselves had not attained pensionable age before that date. If their own contribution record does not entitle them to a full Category A retirement pension, a "composite" pension is payable using all or part of the Category B pension entitlement to raise the Category A pension to the full basic pension rate (subs. (2)). The same principle applies to the additional earnings-related element (subs. (3)).

Special provision for married women

53.—(1) This section has effect where, apart from section 43(1) above, a married woman would be entitled both—

(a) to a Category A retirement pension; and

(b) to a Category B retirement pension by virtue of the contributions of her husband.

(2) If by reason of a deficiency of contributions the basic pension in the Category A retirement pension falls short of the weekly rate specified in Schedule 4, Part I, paragraph 5, that basic pension shall be increased by the lesser of—

(a) the amount of the shortfall, or

(b) the amount of the weekly rate of the Category B retirement pension.

(3) This section does not apply in any case where both the husband and wife attained pensionable age before 6th April 1979.

DEFINITIONS

"entitled": s.122(1).
"pensionable age": s.122(1).

GENERAL NOTE

This section enables a married woman to add a husband's pension rights to her own in order to obtain a composite Category A retirement pension. This option is not open to divorced women.

Category A and Category B retirement pensions: supplemental provisions

54.—(1) Regulations may provide that in the case of a person of any prescribed description who—

(a) has become entitled to a Category A or Category B retirement pension but is, in the case of a woman, under the age of 65 or, in the case of a man, under the age of 70; and

(b) elects in such manner and in accordance with such conditions as may be prescribed that the regulations shall apply in his case,

this Part of this Act shall have effect as if that person had not become entitled to such a retirement pension.

(2) Regulations under subsection (1) above may make such modifications of the provisions of this Part of this Act, or of those of Part II of the Administration Act as those provisions apply in a case where a person makes an election under the regulations, as may appear to the Secretary of State necessary or expedient.

(3) Where a husband and wife have both become entitled to retirement pensions and—

(a) the husband's pension is Category A; and

(b) the wife's pension is—

(i) Category B by virtue of that husband's contributions, or

(ii) Category A with an increase under section 53(2) above by virtue of that husband's contributions,

the husband shall not be entitled to make an election in accordance with regulations made under subsection (1) above without the consent of the wife, unless that consent is unreasonably withheld.

(4) In any case where—

(a) a person claims a Category A or Category B retirement pension; and

(b) the date specified in the claim as the date on which entitlement to the pension is to commence falls after the date when the claim was made,

such a pension may be awarded as from the date so specified but, if so awarded, shall be conditional on the person's not ceasing to be entitled to the pension in consequence of any election under subsection (1) above.

DEFINITIONS
"the Administration Act": s.174.
"entitled": s.122(1).
"prescribe": s.122(1).

GENERAL NOTE
This section enables a retirement pensioner under 65 (for a woman) or 70 (for a man) to "de-retire" by notifying the authorities in the prescribed manner (subs. (1)). Such a decision may be cancelled at any time, although it is not possible to "de-retire" a second time thereafter (Social Security (Widow's Benefit and Retirement Pensions) Regulations 1979 (S.I. 1979 No. 642), reg. 2). This facility is also subject to the wife's consent (unless unreasonably withheld) where she is entitled to a Category B retirement pension based on his contributions or a "composite" Category A pension based in part on such contributions (subs. (3)).

On the potentially discriminatory nature of the "de-retiring" rules, see *R.* v. *Secretary of State for Social Security,* ex p. *Smithson* [1992] 1 C.M.L.R. 1601 (see General Note to s.33).

Increase of retirement pension where entitlement is deferred

55.—(1) Where a person's entitlement to a Category A or Category B retirement pension is deferred, Schedule 5 to this Act shall have effect for increasing the rate of his pension.

(2) For the purposes of this Act a person's entitlement to a Category A or Category B retirement pension is "deferred" if and so long as he does not become entitled to that pension by reason only—

(a) that he has not satisfied the conditions of section 1 of the Administration Act (entitlement to benefit dependent on claim); or

(b) that, in the case of a woman's Category B retirement pension by virtue of her husband's contributions, her husband has not satisfied those conditions with respect to his Category A retirement pension;

and, in relation to any such pension, "period of deferment" shall be construed accordingly.

"the Administration Act": s.174.
"deferred": subs. (2).
"period of deferment": subs. (2).

GENERAL NOTE
This section introduces Sched. 5 which provides for the deferment of retirement. During the first five years after attaining pensionable age, claimants are able to defer entitlement to a Category A or B retirement pension. This gives rise to a higher rate of benefit once the pension is actually taken up. See Ogus and Barendt, pp. 222–224.

Child's special allowance

Child's special allowance—existing beneficiaries

56.—(1) Subject to the provisions of this Act (and in particular to those of section 81 below), a woman whose marriage has been terminated by divorce shall be entitled to a child's special allowance at the weekly rate specified in Schedule 4, Part I, paragraph 6, if—
  (a) the husband of that marriage is dead and satisfied the contribution condition for a child's special allowance specified in Schedule 3, Part I, paragraph 6; and
  (b) she is entitled to child benefit in respect of a child and either—
        (i) she was so entitled immediately before that husband's death; or
        (ii) in such circumstances as may be prescribed, he was then so entitled; and
  (c) either—
        (i) that husband had before his death been contributing at not less than the prescribed weekly rate to the cost of providing for that child; or
        (ii) at the date of that husband's death she was entitled, under an order of a court, trust or agreement which she has taken reasonable steps to enforce, to receive (whether from that husband or from another person) payments in respect of that child at not less than that rate provided or procured by that husband.
  (2) A child's special allowance shall not be payable to a woman—
  (a) for any period after her remarriage; or
  (b) for any period during which she and a man to whom she is not married are living together as husband and wife.
  (3) Where, apart from this subsection, a person is entitled to receive, in respect of a particular child, payment of an amount by way of a child's special allowance, that amount shall not be payable unless one of the conditions specified in subsection (4) below is satisfied.
  (4) Those conditions are—
  (a) that the beneficiary would be treated for the purposes of Part IX of this Act as having the child living with him; or
  (b) that the requisite contributions are being made to the cost of providing for the child.
  (5) The condition specified in subsection (4)(b) above is to be treated as satisfied if, but only if—
  (a) such contributions are being made at a weekly rate not less than the amount referred to in subsection (3) above—
        (i) by the beneficiary; or
        (ii) where the beneficiary is one of two spouses residing together, by them together; and

(b) except in prescribed cases, the contributions are over and above those required for the purpose of satisfying section 143(1)(b) below.

(6) A child's special allowance shall not be payable for any period after 5th April 1987 except to a woman who immediately before 6th April 1987—

(a) satisfied the conditions set out in paragraphs (a) to (c) of subsection (1) above; and

(b) was not barred from payment of the allowance for either of the reasons mentioned in subsection (2) above,

and who has so continued since 6th April 1987.

DEFINITIONS
    "beneficiary": s.122(1).
    "child": s.122(1).
    "entitled": s.122(1).
    "prescribe": s.122(1).

GENERAL NOTE
    The child's special allowance was designed to provide a degree of assistance to a woman who failed to qualify for a widowed mother's allowance (see now s.37) because she was divorced from her former husband before he died. The child's special allowance was abolished as from April 6, 1987, by SSA 1986, s.40, except for existing beneficiaries. Such entitlement ceases where the claimant is no longer entitled to child benefit for the child, or remarries or lives with a man as husband and wife (subs. (6)). For a full analysis, see Ogus and Barendt (2nd ed., pp. 236–239).

Provisions relating to unemployment benefit, sickness benefit and invalidity benefit

Determination of days for which benefit is payable

57.—(1) For the purposes of any provisions of this Act relating to unemployment benefit, sickness benefit or invalidity benefit—

(a) subject to the provisions of this Act, a day shall not be treated in relation to any person—

   (i) as a day of unemployment unless on that day he is capable of work and he is, or is deemed in accordance with regulations to be, available to be employed in employed earner's employment and that day falls in a week in which he is, or is deemed in accordance with regulations to be, actively seeking such employment; or

   (ii) as a day of incapacity for work unless on that day he is, or is deemed in accordance with regulations to be, incapable of work by reason of some specific disease or bodily or mental disablement,

   ("work", in this paragraph, meaning work which the person can reasonably be expected to do);

(b) where a person is an employed earner and his employment as such has not been terminated, then in any week a day on which in the normal course that person would not work in that employment or in any other employed earner's employment shall not be treated as a day of unemployment unless each other day in that week (other than the day referred to in paragraph (e) below) on which in the normal course he would so work is a day of interruption of employment;

(c) "day of interruption of employment" means a day which is a day of unemployment or of incapacity for work;

(d) the following periods, namely—

   (i) any two days of unemployment, whether consecutive or not, within a period of six consecutive days,

   (ii) any four or more consecutive days of incapacity for work,

   shall be treated as a period of interruption of employment, and any two such periods not separated by a period of more than eight weeks ("week" for this purpose meaning any period of seven days) shall be treated as one period of interruption of employment;

(e) Sunday or such other day in each week as may be prescribed shall not be treated as a day of unemployment or of incapacity for work and shall be disregarded in computing any period of consecutive days.

(2) Any day which falls within the maternity allowance period (as defined in section 35(2) above) shall be treated for the purposes of any provision of this Act relating to unemployment benefit, sickness benefit or invalidity benefit as a day of incapacity for work unless the woman is disqualified for receiving a maternity allowance in respect of that day by virtue of regulations under section 35(3)(a) above.

(3) Regulations may—

(a) make provision (subject to subsections (1) and (2) above) as to the days which are or are not to be treated for the purposes of unemployment benefit, sickness benefit and invalidity benefit as days of unemployment or of incapacity for work;

(b) make provision with respect to—

(i) steps which a person is required to take in any week if he is to be regarded as actively seeking employed earner's employment in that week;

(ii) the meaning of "week" in subsection (1)(a)(i) above or in any other provision relating to a person's actively seeking employed earner's employment;

(c) prescribe respective circumstances in which, for the purposes of subsection (1)(b) above—

(i) employment which has not been terminated may be treated as if it had been terminated; or

(ii) a day which falls in a period when an employed earner's employment is suspended but does not fall to be so treated and which, apart from the regulations, would not fall to be treated as a day of interruption of employment may be treated as such a day.

(4) Where it has been determined that a person is to be deemed in accordance with regulations to be available for employment in employed earner's employment in respect of any day, the question of his actual availability for such employment in respect of that day may be subsequently determined on a review of the determination as to his deemed availability.

(5) Where it has been determined that a person is to be deemed in accordance with regulations to be actively seeking employed earner's employment in any week, the question of his actually doing so in that week may be subsequently determined on a review of the determination as to his deemed doing so.

(6) If regulations under paragraph (a) of subsection (3) above provide that for the purposes of unemployment benefit days falling in a post-employment period are not to be treated in relation to a person as days of unemployment, then, for the purpose of determining that period, the regulations may, in particular, make provision—

(a) for calculating or estimating the amount or value of any payment made, or goods or services provided, to or for that person by his employer;

(b) for calculating or estimating that person's level of earnings in the employment in question during any period or for treating him as having such a level of earnings as may be prescribed; and

(c) for calculating or estimating the amount or value of any other sum which falls to be taken into account under the regulations.

(7) In subsection (6) above "post-employment period" means a period following the termination of a person's employment and falling to be determined in accordance with the regulations by reference to the amount or value of payments made, or goods or services provided, to or for the person

by his employer at the time of, or within a prescribed period before or after, the termination of the employment.

(8) Subsections (1) and (3) above shall, on and after such day as the Secretary of State may by order appoint, have effect—

(a) with the substitution for paragraph (b) of subsection (1) of the following paragraph—

"(b) where a person is an employed earner and his employment as such has not been terminated but has been suspended by the employer, a day shall not be treated in relation to that person as a day of unemployment unless it is the 7th or a later day in a continuous period of days on which that suspension has lasted, there being disregarded for the purposes of determining the first six days of the period (but for no other purpose)—

(i) Sunday or such other day in each week as may have been prescribed under paragraph (e) of this subsection,

(ii) any day of recognised or customary holiday in connection with the suspended employment,

(iii) such other day or days as may be prescribed;"; and

(b) with the substitution for paragraph (c) of subsection (3) of the following paragraph—

"(c) prescribe respective circumstances in which for the purposes of subsection (1)(b) above an employed earner's employment may be treated—

(i) as having been or, as the case may be, as not having been terminated, or

(ii) as having been or, as the case may be, as not having been suspended.".

(9) The Secretary of State may by regulations provide—

(a) that paragraph (d) of subsection (1) above shall have effect as if for the reference to eight weeks there were substituted a reference to a larger number of weeks specified in the regulations; and

(b) that sub-paragraph (ii) of that paragraph shall have effect in such cases as may be specified in the regulations, as if—

(i) the period of four days mentioned there were such lesser period as may be specified; and

(ii) the word "consecutive" were omitted.

(10) Regulations under subsection (9)(b) above may be made to have effect from such date, not earlier than 14th September 1980, as may be specified in the regulations.

DEFINITIONS

"day of incapacity for work": subs. (1)(a)(ii).
"day of interruption of employment": subs. (1)(c).
"earnings": s.122(1).
"employed earner": s.122(1).
"employment": s.122(1).
"period of interruption of employment": subs. (1)(d).
"post-employment period": subs. (7).
"prescribe": s.122(1).
"week": subs. (1)(d) and s.122(1).
"work": subs. (1)(a).

GENERAL NOTE

It would have been more helpful if this section could have been placed immediately after ss.25–34. It lays down some basic principles as to the days for which unemployment benefit, sickness benefit and invalidity benefit are payable. The key provisions are contained in subs. (1). The rest of the section consists of consequential or enabling provisions.

So far as unemployment benefit is concerned, to qualify as a day of unemployment (*e.g.* for the purpose of s.25(1)) the claimant must on that day be capable of work, be available to be employed in employed earner's employment and be actively seeking such employment (subs.

(1)(a)(i)). Days of incapacity for work for the purpose of sickness and invalidity benefits are dealt with by subs. (1)(a)(ii).

Subs. (1)(a)(i)

Day of unemployment. There is no comprehensive statutory definition of this concept. See General Note to s.25.

Capable of work. This requirement makes it clear that those unable to work through ill health are not entitled to unemployment benefit.

Available to be employed. The law requires that the claimant be available for employed earner's employment. This does not mean that a job has to be shown to be available to the claimant (*R(U) 44/53*). Availability for part-time work may suffice (*CU/109/48(KL)*), but not for self-employed work only (*R(U) 14/51*). "Work" means work that the person can reasonably be expected to do.

Availability may be either actual or deemed. Actual availability is determined in accordance with Commissioners' case law and the Social Security (Unemployment, Sickness, and Invalidity Benefit) Regulations 1983 (S.I. 1983 No. 1598), reg. 7B. In *R(U) 5/80* it was said that availability "means being available in an active, positive sense, that is by making oneself available. Availability implies some active step by the person concerned to draw attention to his availability: it is not a passive state in which a person may be said to be available provided he is sought out and his location is ascertained".

The case law demonstrates that two further conditions have to be met in order for the claimant to be available for employment. First, there must be a reasonable prospect of the claimant finding employment on his stated terms of the type for which he holds himself out as available (leaving aside any wider issues as to the impact of an economic recession). See *R(U) 12/52, R(U) 44/53* and reg. 7B. Secondly, the claimant must be willing and able to accept employment (*R(U) 1/53, R(U) 1/85* and *R(U) 2/90*). See Bonner for detailed analysis of both conditions. On deemed availability, see regs. 9–14.

Actively seeking such employment. Since October 1988, as well as being available for employment, claimants must be actively seeking such employment. As with availability, claimants may be actively seeking work or be deemed to be so doing. The detailed provisions are set out in regs. 12B–D (see Bonner).

Subs. (1)(a)(ii)

Day of incapacity for work. The concept of a day of incapacity for work is fundamental to entitlement to sickness benefit, statutory sick pay, invalidity benefit, severe disablement allowance and invalidity pensions for widows or widowers. A claimant is incapable of work if he or she is suffering from a disease or bodily or mental disablement such that he or she is incapable of doing any work which it would be reasonable to expect such a person to do. Some claimants who are able to work may be deemed to be incapable of work (*e.g.* Social Security (Unemployment, Sickness, and Invalidity Benefit) Regulations 1983 (S.I. 1983 No. 1598), reg. 3). See further Ogus and Barendt, pp. 149–56, and Bonner.

See also subs. (2), deeming days within the maternity allowance period (s.35(2)) as days of incapacity for work for the purposes of unemployment benefit, sickness benefit or invalidity benefit (unless the claimant is disqualified).

Subs. (1)(b)

This is the basis for the so-called normal idle day rule, under which a claimant is not entitled to unemployment benefit for a day on which he or she would not have worked in any event. The rule is inapplicable where the claimant's employment has been terminated, where there is no recognised or customary working week or where the claimant does not regularly work for the same number of days each week. In practice it is not used as widely as the full extent normal rule (reg. 7(1)(e)), but it may be applicable in situations where workers have been temporarily put on short time. See further Social Security (Unemployment, Sickness, and Invalidity Benefit) Regulations 1983 (S.I. 1983 No. 1598), reg. 19.

Subs. (1)(d)

A day of unemployment for the purposes of entitlement to unemployment benefit must form part of a period of interruption of employment (s.25(1)). The same principle applies to days of incapacity for work so far as incapacity benefits are concerned (*e.g.* s.31(1)). This paragraph embodies the "continuity" and "linking" rules: see Bonner.

Subs. (1)(e)

See Social Security (Unemployment, Sickness, and Invalidity Benefit) Regulations 1983 (S.I. 1983 No. 1598), reg. 4 and *R(S) 3/88*.

Subs. (2)
 See the note to subs. (1)(a)(ii).

Subs. (3)
 See Social Security (Unemployment, Sickness, and Invalidity Benefit) Regulations 1983 (S.I. 1983 No. 1598).

Subs. (4)
 Where a query has arisen over a claimant's availability for work, he or she is deemed to be so available until such time as a decision on the matter is taken (Social Security (Unemployment, Sickness, and Invalidity Benefit) Regulations 1983 (S.I. 1983 No. 1598), reg. 12A). This section enables the claimants' actual availability to be determined subsequently on review.

Subs. (5)
 This is an analogous provision to subs. (4) but in relation to the "actively seeking work" requirement.

Subs. (6)
 This is an enabling power which elaborates on that contained in subs. (3)(a). It provides the authority for the regulations disentitling claimants from receiving unemployment benefit for a period after they have received a payment in connection with the termination of their previous employment. See Social Security (Unemployment, Sickness, and Invalidity Benefit) Regulations 1983 (S.I. 1983 No. 1598), reg. 7(1)(d) and (6).

Subs. (8)
 No order was ever made bringing into force the predecessor to this provision, but Social Security (Unemployment, Sickness, and Invalidity Benefit) Regulations 1983 (S.I. 1983 No. 1598), regs. 6, 7(1)(h) and 19 borrow the concepts used in subs. (8)(a).

Incapacity for work: work as councillor to be disregarded

58.—(1) In determining for the purposes of any of the provisions of this Part of this Act which relate to sickness benefit or invalidity benefit whether any day is to be treated as a day of incapacity for work in relation to a person, there shall be disregarded any work which that person has undertaken, or is capable of undertaking, as a councillor.

(2) Where the net amount of councillor's allowance to which a person is entitled in respect of any week exceeds the permitted earnings limit, an amount equal to the excess shall be deducted from the amount of any sickness benefit or invalidity benefit to which he is entitled in respect of that week, and only the balance remaining (if any) shall be payable.

(3) In determining whether a person satisfies the conditions of entitlement for any such benefit, he shall be treated as having been incapable of work on any day which falls in the pre-commencement period and which—

(a) would have been treated as a day on which he was so incapable, were there disregarded any work which he undertook (or was capable of undertaking) as a councillor; but

(b) would not have been so treated apart from this subsection.

(4) In this section—

"councillor" means—

(a) in relation to England and Wales, a member of a London borough council, a county council, a district council, a parish or community council, the Common Council of the City of London or the Council of the Isles of Scilly; and

(b) in relation to Scotland, a member of a regional, islands or district council;

"councillor's allowance" means an allowance under or by virtue of—

(a) section 173 or 177 of the Local Government Act 1972, or a scheme made by virtue of section 18 of the Local Government and Housing Act 1989, other than such an allowance as is mentioned in section 173(4) of that Act of 1972; or

(b) section 49 of the Local Government (Scotland) Act 1973 or a scheme made by virtue of section 18 of the Local Government and Housing Act 1989;

and where any such allowance is paid otherwise than weekly, an amount calculated or estimated in accordance with regulations shall be regarded as the weekly amount of the allowance;

"net amount", in relation to any councillor's allowance to which a person is entitled, means the aggregate amount of the councillor's allowance or allowances to which he is entitled for the week in question, reduced by the amount of any expenses incurred by him in that week in connection with his membership of the council or councils in question;

"permitted earnings limit" means the amount specified in regulation 3(3) of the Social Security (Unemployment, Sickness and Invalidity Benefit) Regulations 1983;

"pre-commencement period" means the period beginning with 11th May 1987 and ending immediately before 9th October 1989 (the coming into force of paragraph 2 of Schedule 8 to the Social Security Act 1989 which made provision corresponding to the provision made by this section).

(5) Any reference in this section to the work which a person undertakes, or is capable of undertaking, as a councillor shall be taken to include a reference to any work which he undertakes, or is capable of undertaking, as a member of any of the bodies referred to in—

(a) section 177(1) of the Local Government Act 1972; or
(b) section 49(1) or (1A) of the Local Government (Scotland) Act 1973, of which he is a member by virtue of his being a councillor.

DEFINITIONS
"councillor": subs. (4).
"councillor's allowance": subs. (4).
"day of incapacity for work": s.122(1).
"net amount": subs. (4).
"permitted earnings limit": subs. (4).
"pre-commencement period": subs. (4).
"week": s.122(1).

GENERAL NOTE
Entitlement to sickness benefit (ss.31–32) and invalidity benefit (ss.33–34) is dependent upon proof of incapacity for work. The therapeutic earnings rule (Social Security (Unemployment, Sickness and Invalidity Benefit) Regulations 1983 (S.I. 1983 No. 1598), reg. 3(3))—here described as the "permitted earnings limit" (subs. (4))—provides a limited exception to this requirement. For this purpose attendance allowances paid to local government councillors are counted as earnings (*R(S) 3/86* and *R(S) 6/86*).

This section, which originally appeared as SSA 1989, Sched. 8, para. 2, provides that work undertaken by councillors is to be disregarded in assessing incapacity for work (subs. (1)). Furthermore, the earnings rule is modified so that benefit is withdrawn on a tapered basis. Accordingly, incapacity benefits are reduced only in so far as the attendance allowance exceeds the permitted earnings limit (subs. (2)). This relaxation is backdated to the period starting with May 11, 1987 (subs. (3)).

Invalidity benefit—disqualifications etc.

Invalidity benefit—disqualifications etc.

59.—(1) Regulations may provide for disqualifying a person for receiving invalidity benefit for such period not exceeding six weeks as may be determined in accordance with Part II of the Administration Act if—

(a) he has become incapable of work through his own misconduct; or
(b) he fails without good cause to attend for, or to submit himself to, such medical or other examination or treatment as may be required in

accordance with the regulations, or to observe any prescribed rules of behaviour.

(2) Regulations may also provide for imposing, in the case of any prescribed category of persons—

(a) additional conditions with respect to the receipt of invalidity benefit; and

(b) restrictions on the rate and duration of invalidity benefit,

if, having regard to special circumstances, it appears to the Secretary of State necessary to do so for the purpose of preventing inequalities, or injustice to the general body of employed earners, or of earners generally, as the case may be.

(3) For the purposes of this section "week" means any period of seven days.

DEFINITIONS
"the Administration Act": s.174.
"earner": s.122(1).
"employed earner": s.122(1).
"medical examination": s.122(1).
"medical treatment": s.122(1).
"prescribe": s.122(1).
"week": subs. (3).

GENERAL NOTE
See the General Note to s.32, the parallel provision in relation to sickness benefit. It is not obvious why this section could not have been located immediately after those relating to the substantive conditions for invalidity benefit (ss.33 and 34).

Complete or partial failure to satisfy contribution conditions

Complete or partial failure to satisfy contribution conditions

60.—(1) Subject to the provisions of this section, regulations may provide for persons to be entitled to any of the following benefits, namely—

(a) a widowed mother's allowance,
(b) a widow's pension,
(c) a Category A retirement pension,
(d) a Category B retirement pension,

in cases where the first contribution condition specified in relation to that benefit in paragraph 5 of Schedule 3 to this Act is satisfied and the second contribution condition so specified is not.

(2) Subject to subsection (8) below, in any case where—

(a) an employed earner who is married dies as a result of—

(i) a personal injury of a kind mentioned in section 94(1) below, or

(ii) a disease or injury such as is mentioned in section 108(1) below, and

(b) the contribution conditions are not wholly satisfied in respect of him, those conditions shall be taken to be satisfied for the purposes of his widow's entitlement to any of the benefits specified in subsection (3) below.

(3) The benefits referred to in subsection (2) above are the following—

(a) a widow's payment;
(b) a widowed mother's allowance;
(c) a widow's pension;
(d) a Category B retirement pension payable to a woman which is payable to her at the same rate as her widow's pension or which falls within section 49(4) above.

(4) Subject to subsections (6) and (7) below, regulations under subsection (1) above shall provide for benefit payable by virtue of any such regulations to be payable at a rate, or to be of an amount, less than that which would be

applicable under this Part of this Act had both of the relevant contribution conditions been fully satisfied.

(5) Subject to subsections (6) and (7) below, the rate or amount prescribed by regulations under subsection (1) above may vary with the extent to which the relevant contribution conditions are satisfied (and may be nil).

(6) The amount prescribed by regulations under subsection (1) above for any increase of benefit in respect of a child shall, subject to subsection (7) below, be the same as if both of the relevant contribution conditions had been fully satisfied.

(7) Regulations may provide that where—

(a) a person is entitled by virtue of subsection (1) above to a Category A or Category B retirement pension consisting only of the additional pension with no basic pension, and

(b) that retirement pension, and any graduated retirement benefit to which he may be entitled, together amount to less than the prescribed rate,

that person's entitlement as respects that retirement pension shall be satisfied either altogether or for a prescribed period by the making of a single payment of the prescribed amount.

(8) Subsection (2) above only has effect where the employed earner's death occurred on or after 11th April 1988.

DEFINITIONS
  "child": s.122(1).
  "employed earner": s.122(1).
  "entitled": s.122(1).
  "prescribe": s.174.

GENERAL NOTE
  This section provides for a reduced rate of benefit of certain long-term benefits where the second contribution condition has only been partially satisfied. Regulations made under the predecessor to subs. (1) specify that the basic component is calculated according to the proportion of reckonable years (*i.e.* years in which the qualifying earnings factor has been attained) to the number of years prescribed for the particular benefit concerned (see Social Security (Widow's Benefit and Retirement Pensions) Regulations 1979 (S.I. 1979 No. 642), reg. 6). The second contribution condition must have been met in at least 25 per cent. of the years in question. Increases for adult dependants are subject to the same reduction but increases for child dependants are unaffected (subs. (6)).

  Widows whose husbands died as a result of an industrial accident or disease on or after April 11, 1988 are deemed to have met the contribution conditions for widows' benefits and the Category B retirement pension (subss. (2) and (3)). This is the only form in which the industrial preference continues for women widowed on or after that date.

Exclusion of increase of benefit for failure to satisfy contribution condition

  61.—(1) A Category A or Category B retirement pension which is payable by virtue of section 60(1) above and a widowed mother's allowance which is so payable shall not be increased under section 47(1) above or under Part IV below on account of a child or an adult if the pension or allowance contains no basic pension in consequence of a failure to satisfy a contribution condition.

(2) Where a person is entitled—

(a) to unemployment benefit at a rate determined under section 25(5) above; or

(b) to sickness benefit at a rate determined under section 31(6) above; or

(c) to an invalidity pension under section 33 above at a rate determined under section 33(4) above,

and the retirement pension by reference to which the rate of the benefit or invalidity pension is determined—

  (i) would have been payable only by virtue of section 60 above; and

(ii) would, in consequence of a failure to satisfy a contribution condition, have contained no basic pension,

the benefit or invalidity pension shall not be increased under section 47(1) above or under Part IV below on account of a child or an adult.

DEFINITIONS
"child": s.122(1).

GENERAL NOTE
See General Note to s.47.

Graduated retirement benefit

Graduated retirement benefit

62.—(1) So long as sections 36 and 37 of the National Insurance Act 1965 (graduated retirement benefit) continue in force by virtue of regulations made under Schedule 3 to the Social Security (Consequential Provisions) Act 1975 or under Schedule 3 to the Consequential Provisions Act, regulations may make provision—

(a) for replacing section 36(4) of the National Insurance Act 1965 (increase of graduated retirement benefit in cases of deferred retirement) with provisions corresponding to those of paragraphs 1 to 3 of Schedule 5 to this Act;

(b) for extending section 37 of that Act (increase of woman's retirement pension by reference to her late husband's graduated retirement benefit) to men and their late wives.

(2) This section is without prejudice to any power to modify the said sections 36 and 37 conferred by Schedule 3 to the Consequential Provisions Act.

DEFINITIONS
"the Consequential Provisions Act": s.174.
"late husband": s.122(1).

GENERAL NOTE
Graduated retirement benefit is payable to all those who paid graduated Class 1 National Insurance contributions between April 1961 and April 1975 in addition to the standard flat-rate contributions. See Social Security (Graduated Retirement Benefit) (No. 2) Regulations 1978 (S.I. 1978 No. 393).

PART III

NON-CONTRIBUTORY BENEFITS

Descriptions of non-contributory benefits

63. Non-contributory benefits under this Part of this Act are of the following descriptions, namely—

(a) attendance allowance;

(b) severe disablement allowance (with age related addition and increase for adult and child dependants);

(c) invalid care allowance (with increase for adult and child dependants);

(d) disability living allowance;

(e) guardian's allowance;

(f) retirement pensions of the following categories—

(i) Category C, payable to certain persons who were over pensionable age on 5th July 1948 and their wives and widows (with increase for adult and child dependants), and

(ii) Category D, payable to persons over the age of 80;

(g) age addition payable, in the case of persons over the age of 80, by way of increase of a retirement pension of any category or of some other pension or allowance from the Secretary of State.

DEFINITIONS
"child": s.122(1).
"pensionable age": s.122(1).

GENERAL NOTE

This lists the various non-contributory benefits. Mobility allowance, which appeared in the predecessor to this section (SSA 1975, s.34, as amended), was abolished by the DLADWAA 1991 as it was superseded by the mobility component of disability living allowance (s.73 below).

Attendance allowance

Entitlement

64.—(1) A person shall be entitled to an attendance allowance if he is aged 65 or over, he is not entitled to the care component of a disability living allowance and he satisfies either—
  (a) the condition specified in subsection (2) below ("the day attendance condition"), or
  (b) the condition specified in subsection (3) below ("the night attendance condition"),
and prescribed conditions as to residence and presence in Great Britain.

(2) A person satisfies the day attendance condition if he is so severely disabled physically or mentally that, by day, he requires from another person either—
  (a) frequent attention throughout the day in connection with his bodily functions, or
  (b) continual supervision throughout the day in order to avoid substantial danger to himself or others.

(3) A person satisfies the night attendance condition if he is so severely disabled physically or mentally that, at night,—
  (a) he requires from another person prolonged or repeated attention in connection with his bodily functions, or
  (b) in order to avoid substantial danger to himself or others he requires another person to be awake for a prolonged period or at frequent intervals for the purpose of watching over him.

DEFINITIONS
"entitled": s.122(1).
"Great Britain": s.172.
"prescribe": s.122(1).

GENERAL NOTE

As a result of amendments made by the DLADWAA 1991, attendance allowance is now a benefit for elderly people whose care needs arise too late in life for them to be entitled to disability living allowance (DLA; see ss.72 and 75). The attendance allowance provisions are less generous than those for DLA in that there is no third lower tier of attendance allowance and claimants have to wait six months (rather than three) before payment begins (s.65). This form of attendance allowance is known as AA65+. For the special review and appeals procedure, see SSAA 1992, ss.30–35.

Subs. (1)

The qualifying conditions for the receipt of attendance allowance were modified in two respects by the DLADWAA 1991. The first change was of a technical nature to clarify that a claimant must satisfy prescribed criteria as to both residence *and* presence in Great Britain. See Social Security (Attendance Allowance) Regulations 1991 (S.I. 1991 No. 2740), reg. 2. The decision of the European Court of Justice in *Case 356/89, Newton* v. *Chief Adjudication Officer* [1992] 1 C.M.L.R. 149 implied by analogy that such conditions could not disentitle a British worker in receipt of attendance allowance who goes to live in another Member State (but see now the reservation discussed in the annotations to s.71(6)).

Secondly, and more importantly, attendance allowance is now restricted to those claimants who are aged 65 or over and are not entitled to the care component of DLA (s.72). People with disabilities who qualify for DLA before they reach 65 will continue to receive the new benefit after that age, provided they continue to satisfy the qualifying conditions. People who fulfil the care criteria only after attaining the age of 65 are only eligible for attendance allowance (*i.e.* AA65+).

Subs. (2)

So severely disabled physically or mentally... This relates to a condition of body or mind that is capable of medical definition. It is not meant to cover anti-social behaviour which is not related to serious mental illness (*R(A) 2/92*).

Subs. (2)(a)

Frequent attention. This means, according to Lord Denning M.R.'s rather unhelpful explanation, "several times—not once or twice" (*R.* v. *National Insurance Commissioner,* ex p. *Secretary of State for Social Services* [1981] 1 W.L.R. 1017 at p. 1022, C.A.—the *Packer* case).

Throughout the day. Commissioners' decisions have stressed the importance of looking at the overall pattern of care needs (*R(A) 2/74*). The attention must therefore be required "at intervals spread over the day" (*CA/281/1989*).

In connection with his bodily functions. Lord Denning M.R., in a much-cited passage in the *Packer* case, defined "bodily functions" as including:

"breathing, hearing, seeing, eating, drinking, walking, sitting, sleeping, getting in and out of bed, dressing, undressing, eliminating waste products—and the like—all of which an ordinary person—who is not suffering from any disability—does for himself. But they do not include cooking, shopping or any of the other things which a wife or daughter does as part of her domestic duties: or generally which one of the household normally does for the rest of the family" (p. 1022).

Subsequently the House of Lords has held that the phrase "bodily functions" is a restricted and precise one, narrower than "bodily needs" (*Woodling* v. *Secretary of State for Social Services* [1984] 1 W.L.R. 348 at p. 352, *per* Lord Bridge).

Somewhat more problematic has been the requirement that the attention be "in connection with" the claimant's bodily functions. Lord Denning M.R. gave the following guidance in the *Packer* case:

"I would hold that ordinary domestic duties such as shopping, cooking meals, making tea or coffee, laying the table or the tray, carrying it into the room, making the bed or filling the hot water bottle, do not qualify as 'attention... in connection with [the] bodily functions' of the disabled person. But that duties that are out of the ordinary—doing for the disabled person what a normal person would do for himself—such as cutting up food, lifting the cup to the mouth, helping to dress or undress or at the toilet—all do qualify as 'attention... in connection with [the] bodily functions of the disabled person'" (p. 1022).

Lord Bridge, approving dicta of Dunn L.J. in *Packer's* case, held in rather more abstract terms that the phrase "connotes a high degree of personal intimacy between the person giving and the person receiving the attention" (*Woodling* v. *Secretary of State for Social Services*, *supra*, at p. 352).

The test is ultimately therefore one of proximity and remoteness, and it is difficult to resolve such issues at the borderline. It would appear to be an error of law to hold that an activity which is an "ordinary" household duty (*e.g.* cooking or washing clothes or bedding) is necessarily not in connection with the claimant's bodily functions. In *R(A) 1/87* (where the carer had to prepare and control a very specialised diet for a child suffering from phenylketonuria (PKU)) it was held that the preparation of food could be part of the attention required in connection with the disabled person's bodily functions. See also *R(A) 1/91*.

Subs. (2)(b)

Continual supervision throughout the day in order to avoid substantial danger to himself or others. A Tribunal of Commissioners has held that this alternative requirement for the day condition involves four elements (*R(A) 1/83*). First, the claimant's medical condition must be such that there is a substantial danger to himself or to someone else. This is ultimately a question of fact and should not be construed too narrowly (*R(A) 1/73, R(A) 2/91*). Secondly, that danger must not be too remote a possibility. Thus the remoteness of the risk should be weighed against the seriousness of the consequences should the risk actually arise (*R(A) 2/89, R(A) 3/89* and *R(A) 6/89*). Thirdly, supervision by another person must be required in order to avoid the danger. It must be needed in order to effect a real reduction in the risk of harm, not in order to eliminate all substantial danger: *R(A) 3/92.* Supervision is, however, a more passive concept than attention, and covers being in a position to intervene if necessary in an emergency (*R(A) 6/72* and *Moran* v. *Secretary of State for Social Services*, reported as Appendix to *R(A) 1/88*). Fourthly, the supervision must be "continual". The "characteristic nature of supervision is overseeing or watching over considered with reference to its frequency or regularity of occurrence" (*R(A) 2/75*). In *Moran* the Court of Appeal held that the relative frequency or infrequency of attacks is immaterial to the question of whether supervision is continual, so long as the risk of substantial danger is not so remote a possibility that it ought reasonably to be disregarded. A need for periodic supervision is therefore insufficient (*Devlin* v. *Secretary of State for Social Services* (1991) S.L.T. 815).

Subs. (3)

Prolonged or repeated attention. Official guidance issued by the former Attendance Allowance Board (AAB) stated that:

"The Board accept as prolonged that attention which reasonably, in the light of medical expertise, can be claimed to last for 20 minutes or more. Repeated attention is attention which is needed on more than one occasion during the same night, not necessarily for the same purpose each time" (DHSS/AAB, *Handbook for Delegated Medical Practitioners* (1988), HMSO, p. 27).

This suggests that a smaller amount of care will be needed to satisfy the night-time criteria for the middle rate than will be required during the day for the lower rate.

In connection with his bodily functions. See annotations to subs. (2)(a) above.

He requires another person to be awake for a prolonged period or at frequent intervals for the purpose of watching over him. Originally the wording of this condition was identical to the parallel day condition. The Court of Appeal in *Moran* (see above) held that such continual supervision could be provided at night where the carer was asleep nearby, ready to be summoned if need be. The formulation of the alternative night condition was amended by SSA 1988, s.1, such that the claimant now needs the carer "to be awake for a prolonged period or at frequent intervals for the purpose of watching over him". It was explained at the time that the amendment was designed to "restore the law to what it was believed to be by emphasising that for the night time condition to be satisfied active supervision was envisaged—a wakeful and watchful presence" (*per* Mr J. Moore, *Hansard*, H.C. Vol. 121, col. 661, November 2, 1987).

Period and rate of allowance

65.—(1) Subject to the following provisions of this Act, the period for which a person is entitled to an attendance allowance shall be—

    (a) a period throughout which he has satisfied or is likely to satisfy the day or the night attendance condition or both; and

    (b) a period preceded immediately, or within such period as may be prescribed, by one of not less than six months throughout which he satisfied, or is likely to satisfy, one or both of those conditions.

(2) For the purposes of subsection (1) above a person who suffers from renal failure and is undergoing such form of treatment as may be prescribed shall, in such circumstances as may be prescribed, be deemed to satisfy or to be likely to satisfy the day or the night attendance condition or both.

(3) The weekly rate of the attendance allowance payable to a person for any period shall be the higher rate specified in Schedule 4, Part III, paragraph 1, if both as regards that period and as regards the period of six months mentioned in subsection (1)(b) above he has satisfied or is likely to satisfy both the day and the night attendance conditions, and shall be the lower rate in any other case.

(4) A person shall not be entitled to an attendance allowance for any period preceding the date on which he makes or is treated as making a claim for it.

(5) Notwithstanding anything in subsection (4) above, provision may be made by regulations for a person to be entitled to an attendance allowance for a period preceding the date on which he makes or is treated as making a claim for it if such an allowance has previously been paid to or in respect of him.

(6) Except in so far as regulations otherwise provide and subject to section 66(1) below—

    (a) a claim for an attendance allowance may be made during the period of six months immediately preceding the period for which the person to whom the claim relates is entitled to the allowance; and

(b) an award may be made in pursuance of a claim so made, subject to the condition that, throughout that period of six months, that person satisfies—

(i) both the day and the night attendance conditions, or

(ii) if the award is at the lower rate, one of those conditions.

DEFINITIONS
"claim": s.122(1).
"entitled": s.122(1).
"prescribe": s.122(1).

GENERAL NOTE
A claimant for attendance allowance must have satisfied either or both of the conditions specified in s.64 for a period of six months before the claim (subs. (1)). It is possible to make a claim in anticipation of satisfying that requirement (subs. (6)). Awards are made for a fixed number of years (in which case a renewal claim may be made on expiry) or for life. There is no upper age limit to attendance allowance. The higher rate of attendance allowance is payable if both the day and night attendance conditions are met; otherwise the lower rate applies (subs. (3)).

Special provision is made in the Social Security (Attendance Allowance) Regulations 1991 (S.I. 1991 No. 2740) for claimants on dialysis (subs. (2) and reg. 5).

Attendance allowance for the terminally ill

66.—(1) If a terminally ill person makes a claim expressly on the ground that he is such a person, then—

(a) he shall be taken—

(i) to satisfy, or to be likely to satisfy, both the day attendance condition and the night attendance condition for the remainder of his life, beginning with the date of the claim or, if later, the first date on which he is terminally ill; and

(ii) to have satisfied those conditions for the period of six months immediately preceding that date (so however that no allowance shall be payable by virtue of this sub-paragraph for any period preceding that date); and

(b) the period for which he is entitled to attendance allowance shall be the remainder of the person's life, beginning with that date.

(2) For the purposes of subsection (1) above—

(a) a person is "terminally ill" at any time if at that time he suffers from a progressive disease and his death in consequence of that disease can reasonably be expected within six months; and

(b) where a person purports to make a claim for an attendance allowance by virtue of that subsection on behalf of another, that other shall be regarded as making the claim, notwithstanding that it is made without his knowledge or authority.

DEFINITIONS
"claim": s.122(1).
"terminally ill": subs. (2).

GENERAL NOTE
Claimants who are terminally ill are treated as special cases and are granted automatic entitlement to the higher rate of attendance allowance for the remainder of their life. Subsection (1) deems the terminally ill to be satisfying both the day and night attendance conditions for the relevant period (including the six-month qualifying period). The definition of "terminally ill" (subs. (2)(b)) is somewhat problematic (see Bonner and Rowland). In practice the great majority of claims on this basis are successful. Even if death does not follow within six months or so, as a matter of practice claims are only reconsidered by the Benefits Agency Medical Service once a period of 15 months has elapsed.

Exclusions by regulation

67.—(1) Regulations may provide that, in such circumstances, and for such purposes as may be prescribed, a person who is, or is treated under the regulations as, undergoing treatment for renal failure in a hospital or other similar institution otherwise than as an in-patient shall be deemed not to satisfy or to be unlikely to satisfy the day attendance condition or the night attendance condition, or both of them.

(2) Regulations may provide that an attendance allowance shall not be payable in respect of a person for any period when he is a person for whom accommodation is provided—

(a) in pursuance—
(i) of Part III of the National Assistance Act 1948; or
(ii) of paragraph 2 of Schedule 8 to the National Health Service Act 1977; or
(iii) of Part IV of the Social Work (Scotland) Act 1968; or
(iv) of section 7 of the Mental Health (Scotland) Act 1984; or

(b) in circumstances in which the cost is, or may be, borne wholly or partly out of public or local funds, in pursuance of those enactments or of any other enactment relating to persons under disability.

DEFINITIONS
"prescribe": s.122(1).

GENERAL NOTE
Special provision is made under subs. (1) for claimants receiving renal dialysis (Social Security (Attendance Allowance) Regulations 1991 (S.I. 1991 No. 2740), reg. 5). Various categories of claimant who receive state subsidy for their accommodation are excluded from entitlement to attendance allowance by virtue of subs. (2) (regs. 6–8).

Severe disablement allowance

Entitlement and rate

68.—(1) Subject to the provisions of this section, a person shall be entitled to a severe disablement allowance for any day ("the relevant day") if he satisfies—

(a) the conditions specified in subsection (2) below; or
(b) the conditions specified in subsection (3) below.

(2) The conditions mentioned in subsection (1)(a) above are that—
(a) on the relevant day he is incapable of work; and
(b) he has been incapable of work for a period of not less than 196 consecutive days—
(i) beginning not later than the day on which he attained the age of 20; and
(ii) ending immediately before the relevant day.

(3) The conditions mentioned in subsection (1)(b) above are that—
(a) on the relevant day he is both incapable of work and disabled; and
(b) he has been both incapable of work and disabled for a period of not less than 196 consecutive days ending immediately before the relevant day.

(4) A person shall not be entitled to a severe disablement allowance if—
(a) he is under the age of 16; or
(b) he is receiving full-time education; or
(c) he does not satisfy the prescribed conditions—
(i) as to residence in Great Britain; or
(ii) as to presence there; or
(d) he has attained pensionable age and—
(i) was not entitled to a severe disablement allowance immediately before he attained that age; and

(ii) is not treated by regulations as having been so entitled immediately before he attained that age.

(5) A person shall not be entitled to a severe disablement allowance for any day which as between him and his employer falls within a period of entitlement for the purposes of statutory sick pay.

(6) A person is disabled for the purposes of this section if he suffers from loss of physical or mental faculty such that the extent of the resulting disablement assessed in accordance with Schedule 6 to this Act amounts to not less than 80 per cent.

(7) A severe disablement allowance shall be paid at the weekly rate specified in Schedule 4, Part III, paragraph 2.

(8) The amount of severe disablement allowance payable for any relevant day shall be one sixth of the weekly rate referred to in subsection (7) above.

(9) In any case where—

(a) a severe disablement allowance is payable to a woman in respect of one or more relevant days in a week; and

(b) an amount of statutory maternity pay becomes payable to her on any day in that week,

the amount of the severe disablement allowance (including any increase for a child or adult dependant under section 90(a) below) so payable shall be reduced by the amount of the statutory maternity pay, and only the balance (if any) shall be payable.

(10) Where—

(a) a person who is engaged and normally engaged in remunerative work ceases to be so engaged; and

(b) he is entitled to a disability working allowance for the week in which there falls the last day on which he is so engaged; and

(c) he qualified for a disability working allowance for that week by virtue of a severe disablement allowance having been payable to him; and

(d) the first day after he ceases to be engaged as mentioned in paragraph (a) above is a day on which he is incapable of work and falls not later than the end of the period of two years beginning with the last day for which he was entitled to a severe disablement allowance,

any day since that day which fell within a week for which he was entitled to a disability working allowance shall be treated for the purposes of any claim for a severe disablement allowance for a period commencing after he ceases to be engaged as mentioned in paragraph (a) above as having been a day on which he was both incapable of work and disabled.

(11) Regulations—

(a) may direct that persons who—

(i) have attained retiring age; and

(ii) were entitled to a severe disablement allowance immediately before they attained that age,

shall continue to be so entitled notwithstanding that they do not satisfy the conditions specified in subsection (2) or (3) above;

(b) may direct—

(i) that persons who have previously been entitled to a severe disablement allowance shall be entitled to such an allowance notwithstanding that they do not satisfy the conditions specified in subsection (2)(b) or (3)(b) above;

(ii) that subsections (2)(b) and (3)(b) above shall have effect in relation to such persons subject to such modifications as may be specified in the regulations;

(c) may prescribe the circumstances in which a person is or is not to be treated—

(i) as incapable of work; or

(ii) as receiving full-time education;

(d) may provide that, where the net amount of councillor's allowance (within the meaning of section 58 above) to which a person is entitled in respect of any week exceeds a prescribed sum, then, except in prescribed cases, an amount equal to the excess shall be deducted from the amount of any severe disablement allowance to which he is entitled in respect of that week, and only the balance remaining (if any) shall be payable; and

(e) may provide for disqualifying a person from receiving a severe disablement allowance for such period not exceeding six weeks as may be determined in accordance with the Administration Act if—

(i) he has become incapable of work through his own misconduct; or

(ii) he fails without good cause to attend for, or to submit himself to, such medical or other examination or treatment as may be required in accordance with the regulations, or to observe any prescribed rules of behaviour.

(12) In determining whether a person satisfies the conditions specified in subsection (2)(b) and (3)(b) above he shall be treated as having been incapable of work on any day which falls in the pre-commencement period and which—

(a) would have been treated as a day on which he was so incapable, were there disregarded any work which he undertook (or was capable of undertaking) as a councillor, but

(b) would not have been treated apart from this subsection.

(13) In this section—

"councillor" and "pre-commencement period" have the meanings assigned to them by section 58(4) above;

"retiring age" means 70 in the case of a man and 65 in the case of a woman,

and section 58(5) above has effect for the purposes of subsection (12) above as it has effect for the purposes of section 58 above.

DEFINITIONS

"the Administration Act": s.174.
"child": s.122(1).
"councillor": subs. (13).
"councillor's allowance": s.58(4).
"entitled": s.122(1).
"Great Britain": s.172.
"medical examination": s.122(1).
"medical treatment": s.122(1).
"pensionable age": s.122(1).
"pre-commencement period": subs. (13).
"prescribe": s.122(1).
"relevant day": subs. (1).
"retiring age": subs. (13).
"week": s.122(1).

GENERAL NOTE

Severe disablement allowance (SDA) is a non-contributory benefit paid to people who have been incapable of work and have satisfied an extra condition of severe disability for a continuous period of 196 days (28 weeks). SDA replaced the non-contributory invalidity pension in 1984. It is paid at a lower rate than the contributory invalidity benefit but may be supplemented by age-related additions (s.69).

All SDA claimants must be incapable of work and have been so for 196 days immediately before the date of claim. Claimants must then satisfy any one of three separate further conditions:

(1) *Incapacity when young.* The claimant must show that the 196 days of incapacity began on or before his or her twentieth birthday (subs. (2)). There is a special concession which allows young people to work for no more than 182 days without losing entitlement to benefit under this route (Social Security (Severe Disablement Allowance) Regulations 1984 (S.I. 1984 No. 1303),

reg. 7(3)). Those who take advantage of this facility need not satisfy the disablement test under subs. (3).

(2) *The severely disabled.* Any claimant under pensionable age may qualify for SDA by showing that he or she is 80 per cent. disabled or more (subs. (3) and (6)). The assessment criteria used under the industrial injuries scheme apply in this context. Individuals with certain types of disability are deemed to meet the 80 per cent. threshold without the need for a medical examination (reg. 10).

(3) *Prior entitlement to SDA.* Transitional rules apply to those formerly entitled to the non-contributory invalidity pension (reg. 20). The E.C.J. has held that these provisions contravene Art. 4(1) of E.C. Directive 79/7: *Johnson* v. *Chief Adjudication Officer* (Case C–31/90) [1992] 2 All E.R. 705.

Finally, claimants must not be excluded by virtue of subss. (4) or (5). The rules of entitlement as to residence and presence are elaborated upon in regulations. The exclusion of persons of pensionable age has been found to be contrary to E.C. Directive 79/7 (*Thomas* v. *Chief Adjudication Officer and Secretary of State for Social Security*; *Cooze* v. *Same*; *Beard* v. *Same*; *Murphy* v. *Same*; *Morley* v. *Same* [1991] 2 W.L.R. 886).

Severe disablement allowance: age related addition

69.—(1) If a person was under the age of 60 on the day on which he qualified for severe disablement allowance, the weekly rate of his severe disablement allowance shall be increased by an age related addition at whichever of the weekly rates specified in the second column of paragraph 3 of Part III of Schedule 4 to this Act is applicable in his case, that is to say—

(a) the higher rate, if he was under the age of 40 on the day on which he qualified for severe disablement allowance;

(b) the middle rate, if he was between the ages of 40 and 50 on that day; or

(c) the lower rate, if he was between the ages of 50 and 60 on that day.

(2) Subject to subsection (4) below, for the purposes of this section the day on which a person qualified for severe disablement allowance is his first day of incapacity for work in the period of not less than 196 consecutive days mentioned in section 68(2)(b) or (3)(b) above, as the case may be, which preceded the first day in his current period of entitlement.

(3) For the purposes of this section, a person's "current period of entitlement" is a current period—

(a) which consists of one or more consecutive days on which he is or has been entitled to a severe disablement allowance; and

(b) which begins immediately after the last period of one or more consecutive days for which he was not entitled to such an allowance.

(4) Regulations—

(a) may prescribe cases where a person is to be treated for the purposes of this section as having qualified for severe disablement allowance on a prescribed day earlier than the day ascertained in accordance with subsection (2) above;

(b) may provide for days which are not days of incapacity for work in relation to a person to be treated as days of incapacity for work for the purpose of determining under this section the day on which he qualified for severe disablement allowance; and

(c) may make provision for disregarding prescribed days in computing any period of consecutive days for the purposes of subsection (3) above.

DEFINITIONS
"current period of entitlement": subs. (3).
"day of incapacity for work": s.122(1).
"prescribe": s.122(1).

GENERAL NOTE
The basic rate of severe disablement allowance is less than that for invalidity benefit. SSA 1990 (s.2) introduced age-related additions for SDA (set at the same levels as the invalidity allowance rates) to help narrow this gap. The higher rate is payable to claimants who are below the age of 40 on the first day of the 196-day qualifying period. A middle rate is payable to those who are aged 40–49 on qualifying, and a lower rate for those aged 50–59. This reform followed

the proposals set out in *The Way Ahead* which were designed to assist those disabled early in life.

Invalid care allowance

Invalid care allowance

70.—(1) A person shall be entitled to an invalid care allowance for any day on which he is engaged in caring for a severely disabled person if—

(a) he is regularly and substantially engaged in caring for that person;

(b) he is not gainfully employed; and

(c) the severely disabled person is either such relative of his as may be prescribed or a person of any such other description as may be prescribed.

(2) In this section, "severely disabled person" means a person in respect of whom there is payable either an attendance allowance or a disability living allowance by virtue of entitlement to the care component at the highest or middle rate or such other payment out of public funds on account of his need for attendance as may be prescribed.

(3) A person shall not be entitled to an allowance under this section if he is under the age of 16 or receiving full-time education.

(4) A person shall not be entitled to an allowance under this section unless he satisfies prescribed conditions as to residence or presence in Great Britain.

(5) Subject to subsection (6) below, a person who has attained pensionable age shall not be entitled to an allowance under this section unless he was so entitled (or is treated by regulations as having been so entitled) immediately before attaining that age.

(6) Regulations may make provision whereby a person who has attained retiring age, and was entitled to an allowance under this section immediately before attaining that age, continues to be so entitled notwithstanding that he is not caring for a severely disabled person or no longer satisfies the requirements of subsection (1)(a) or (b) above.

(7) No person shall be entitled for the same day to more than one allowance under this section; and where, apart from this subsection, two or more persons would be entitled for the same day to such an allowance in respect of the same severely disabled person, one of them only shall be entitled and that shall be such one of them—

(a) as they may jointly elect in the prescribed manner, or

(b) as may, in default of such an election, be determined by the Secretary of State in his discretion.

(8) Regulations may prescribe the circumstances in which a person is or is not to be treated for the purposes of this section as engaged, or regularly and substantially engaged, in caring for a severely disabled person, as gainfully employed or as receiving full-time education.

(9) An invalid care allowance shall be payable at the weekly rate specified in Schedule 4, Part III, paragraph 4.

(10) In this section "retiring age" means 70 in the case of a man and 65 in the case of a woman.

DEFINITIONS

"entitled": s.122(1).

"pensionable age": s.122(1).

"prescribe": s.122(1).

"relative": s.122(1).

"retiring age": subs. (10).

"severely disabled person": subs. (2).

GENERAL NOTE

Invalid care allowance (ICA) is a non-contributory benefit payable to those who provide regular and substantial care for a person who receives attendance allowance, the care component of disability living allowance at the higher or middle rate or (as prescribed by the Social Security (Invalid Care Allowance) Regulations 1976 (S.I. 1976 No. 409), reg. 3) constant attendance allowance in respect of industrial or war disablement (subs. (2)). Claimants under the age of 16 (subs. (3)) and over pensionable age are not eligible for ICA (subs. (5), but see *Thomas* v. *Chief Adjudication Officer and Secretary of State for Social Security*; *Cooze* v. *Same*; *Beard* v. *Same*; *Murphy* v. *Same*; *Morley* v. *Same* [1991] 2 W.L.R. 886), but those in receipt of ICA before reaching pensionable age may retain their entitlement.

Subs. (1)

Regularly and substantially engaged. Although subs. (1) refers to ICA as a daily benefit, reg. 4 establishes a threshold of at least 35 hours of care a week (subject to a concession where there is a temporary break in caring).

Not gainfully employed. Claimants are regarded as not being in gainful employment if they earn no more than a weekly limit set by reg. 8 (£40 for 1992/93). ICA is not, therefore, restricted to those who give up paid work completely to look after an invalid.

The disabled person is either such relative. No distinction is made in the regulations between invalids who are related or not to the carer (reg. 6).

Subs. (3)

Receiving full-time education. This concept is defined as a course involving attendance of 21 hours or more a week (reg. 5, substituted by S.I. 1992 No. 470). The former restriction on married women and those cohabiting was repealed following the decision of the E.C.J. in *Drake* v. *Chief Adjudication Officer (No. 150/85)* [1987] Q.B. 166.

Subs. (4)

Residence or presence. See reg. 9, which as a general rule requires the claimant to be present and ordinarily resident in Great Britain.

Subs. (7)

ICA is only payable in respect of the care provided for one invalid. There is no provision for entitlement where the carer looks after two individuals, neither of whom is entitled to one of the prescribed benefits, but whose care needs together amount to more than 35 hours a week.

Disability living allowance

Disability living allowance

71.—(1) Disability living allowance shall consist of a care component and a mobility component.

(2) A person's entitlement to a disability living allowance may be an entitlement to either component or to both of them.

(3) A person may be awarded either component for a fixed period or for life, but if his award of a disability living allowance consists of both components, he may not be awarded the components for different fixed periods.

(4) The weekly rate of a person's disability living allowance for a week for which he has only been awarded one component is the appropriate weekly rate for that component as determined in accordance with this Act or regulations under it.

(5) The weekly rate of a person's disability living allowance for a week for which he has been awarded both components is the aggregate of the appropriate weekly rates for the two components as so determined.

(6) A person shall not be entitled to a disability living allowance unless he satisfies prescribed conditions as to residence and presence in Great Britain.

DEFINITIONS
"entitled": s.122(1).
"Great Britain": s.172.
"week": s.122(1).

GENERAL NOTE
Disability living allowance (DLA) was created by merging attendance allowance and mobility allowance and by extending their coverage to include people with less severe disabilities.

These changes came into effect in April 1992 under the DLADWAA 1991. DLA is a composite benefit with three possible rates for the care component (as against two for attendance allowance) and two rates for the mobility component (as against one for the former mobility allowance). Attendance allowance is preserved only for claimants who are aged 65 or more when they qualify for the first time under the care criteria (see ss.64–67), while mobility allowance has been abolished.

The highest and middle rates of the care component are equivalent to the two rates of attendance allowance. The higher of the two rates for the mobility component is equivalent to the old mobility allowance (MobA). The new lower rate of the care component was designed for "people who need help with self-care during the day but less frequently than those who currently qualify for AA" (*The Way Ahead*, para. 4.12). The lower rate of the mobility component is for "people who are not independently mobile and who do not otherwise fulfil the current criteria for MobA" (para. 4.13). DLA is therefore something of a misnomer in that it fails to provide assistance with the many other extra living costs faced by disabled people.

Sections 71–76 set out the basic framework for DLA. Matters of detail are dealt with in the Social Security (Disability Living Allowance) Regulations 1991 (S.I. 1991 No. 2890). DLA has been designed so far as possible to enable self-assessment in claiming benefit. For the special review and appeals procedure, see SSAA 1992, ss.30–35. Advice in relation to DLA is offered to the Secretary of State by the Disability Living Allowance Advisory Board (SSAA 1992, s.175).

Subs. (2)

Consequently there are 11 different rates of payment for DLA, ranging from the lowest rate of just one component to the top rate of both components.

Subs. (3)

A DLA component may be awarded for a fixed period or for life. If a claimant is entitled to both components of the new benefit, they may not be awarded for different fixed periods. This means that a claimant with care and mobility needs will find one award shortened to align it with the other, unless one of the awards is for life. The rationale for this is partly in claimants' interests by minimising the need for repeated assessment and adjudication but also partly for reasons of administrative convenience.

Subs. (6)

The residence and presence criteria for DLA are dealt with in regulations. The claimant must be ordinarily resident in Great Britain, present in Great Britain for an aggregate of not less than 26 weeks in the 12 months preceding the date of claim and present in Great Britain throughout the claim. The residence and presence conditions apply to terminally ill claimants for the care component, who are otherwise excused from the retrospective and prospective qualifying periods under s.72(2) below (see s.72(5)).

These rules are necessarily subject to the relevant E.C. legislation, and in particular Reg. 1408/71. In *Newton* v. *Chief Adjudication Officer* [1992] 1 C.M.L.R. 149 the European Court of Justice held that mobility allowance could not be withdrawn from a British national who had been awarded benefit but then moved to live in France. As from May 1, 1992, however, various income-related and non-contributory benefits (including mobility allowance and disability living allowance) have become non-exportable: see Reg. 1408/71, art. 10a and Annex IIa, inserted by Reg. 1247/92.

The care component

72.—(1) Subject to the provisions of this Act, a person shall be entitled to the care component of a disability living allowance for any period throughout which—

(a) he is so severely disabled physically or mentally that—

    (i) he requires in connection with his bodily functions attention from another person for a significant portion of the day (whether during a single period or a number of periods); or

    (ii) he cannot prepare a cooked main meal for himself if he has the ingredients; or

(b) he is so severely disabled physically or mentally that, by day, he requires from another person—

    (i) frequent attention throughout the day in connection with his bodily functions; or

    (ii) continual supervision throughout the day in order to avoid substantial danger to himself or others; or

(c) he is so severely disabled physically or mentally that, at night,—
  (i) he requires from another person prolonged or repeated attention in connection with his bodily functions; or
  (ii) in order to avoid substantial danger to himself or others he
  requires another person to be awake for a prolonged period or at
  frequent intervals for the purpose of watching over him.
(2) Subject to the following provisions of this section, a person shall not be
entitled to the care component of a disability living allowance unless—
  (a) throughout—
    (i) the period of three months immediately preceding the date on
    which the award of that component would begin; or
    (ii) such other period of three months as may be prescribed,
  he has satisfied or is likely to satisfy one or other of the conditions
  mentioned in subsection (1)(a) to (c) above; and
  (b) he is likely to continue to satisfy one or other of those conditions
  throughout—
    (i) the period of six months beginning with that date; or
    (ii) (if his death is expected within the period of six months
    beginning with that date) the period so beginning and ending with
    his death.
(3) Three weekly rates of the care component shall be prescribed.
(4) The weekly rate of the care component payable to a person for each
week in the period for which he is awarded that component shall be—
  (a) the highest rate, if he falls within subsection (2) above by virtue of
  having satisfied or being likely to satisfy both the conditions mentioned in subsection (1)(b) and (c) above throughout both the period
  mentioned in paragraph (a) of subsection (2) above and that mentioned in paragraph (b) of that subsection;
  (b) the middle rate, if he falls within that subsection by virtue of having
  satisfied or being likely to satisfy one or other of those conditions
  throughout both those periods; and
  (c) the lowest rate in any other case.
(5) For the purposes of this section, a person who is terminally ill, as
defined in section 66(2) above, and makes a claim expressly on the ground
that he is such a person, shall be taken—
  (a) to have satisfied the conditions mentioned in subsection (1)(b) and (c)
  above for the period of three months immediately preceding the date
  of the claim, or, if later, the first date on which he is terminally ill (so
  however that the care component shall not be payable by virtue of this
  paragraph for any period preceding that date); and
  (b) to satisfy or to be likely to satisfy those conditions for the remainder of
  his life beginning with that date.
(6) For the purposes of this section in its application to a person for any
period in which he is under the age of 16—
  (a) sub-paragraph (ii) of subsection (1)(a) above shall be omitted; and
  (b) neither the condition mentioned in sub-paragraph (i) of that paragraph nor any of the conditions mentioned in subsection (1)(b) and
  (c) above shall be taken to be satisfied unless—
    (i) he has requirements of a description mentioned in subsection
    (1)(a), (b) or (c) above substantially in excess of the normal
    requirements of persons of his age; or
    (ii) he has substantial requirements of any such description which
    younger persons in normal physical and mental health may also
    have but which persons of his age and in normal physical and
    mental health would not have.
(7) Subject to subsections (5) and (6) above, circumstances may be
prescribed in which a person is to be taken to satisfy or not to satisfy such of
the conditions mentioned in subsection (1)(a) to (c) above as may be
prescribed.

(8) Regulations may provide that a person shall not be paid any amount in respect of a disability living allowance which is attributable to entitlement to the care component for a period when he is a person for whom accommodation is provided—

(a) in pursuance—

(i) of Part III of the National Assistance Act 1948 or paragraph 2 of Schedule 8 to the National Health Service Act 1977; or

(ii) of Part IV of the Social Work (Scotland) Act 1968 or section 7 of the Mental Health (Scotland) Act 1984; or

(b) in circumstances in which the cost is, or may be, borne wholly or partly out of public or local funds, in pursuance of those enactments or of any other enactment relating to persons under disability or to young persons or to education or training.

DEFINITIONS

"claim": s.122(1).
"entitled": s.122(1).
"prescribe": s.122(1).

GENERAL NOTE

This section deals with entitlement to and payment of the care component of disability living allowance. Three separate criteria for the award of the care component of DLA are specified. A claimant who only meets either of the conditions set out in subs. (1)(a) will receive the lowest rate of care component (subs. (4)(c)). A claimant who meets the criteria in either subs. (1)(b) or (c) will qualify for the middle rate of this component (subs. (4)(b)), whilst a claimant who satisfies both of the conditions in subss. (1)(b) and (c) will be awarded the highest rate (subs. (4)(a)).

Subs. (1)(a)

This condition is the basis for the lowest rate of the care component. It is therefore designed for people whose care needs would not be regarded as severe enough for them to qualify under the rules for attendance allowance. It comprises two quite distinct and alternative tests:

(i) He requires in connection with his bodily functions.... The first limb of the day condition for DLA (subs. (1)(b)(i)) is only satisfied if the claimant requires "frequent attention throughout the day in connection with his bodily functions". The wording of this subsection is intended to enable people who need a lower level of care to qualify for DLA, so long as it is required "for a significant portion of the day (whether during a single period or a number of periods)". The Government envisaged "'significant portion' being interpreted as an hour or thereabouts. For example, this route will help people who need help getting in and out of bed or a bath, or people who require assistance in administering courses of injections or medicines" (*per* Lord Henley, *Hansard*, H.L. Vol. 526, col. 884, February 26, 1991). For discussion of the meaning of "in connection with his bodily functions", see annotations to s.64(2)(a) above.

(ii) He cannot prepare a cooked main meal for himself.... This condition is purely hypothetical and is to be determined in accordance with the principle of self-assessment.

Subs. (1)(b)

The wording of these alternative heads of entitlement is identical in all material respects to the day condition for attendance allowance (s.64(2) above) and so the case law on that provision will remain relevant.

Subs. (1)(c)

The wording of these alternative heads of entitlement is identical in all material respects to the night condition for attendance allowance (s.64(3) above) and so the case law on that provision will remain relevant.

Subs. (2)

In addition to meeting the care criteria specified in subs. (1), claimants for the care component must also satisfy the qualifying period conditions laid down in this subsection (except those who are terminally ill: see subs. (5)). These conditions, which apply equally to the mobility component (see s.73(9)), are a compromise between the previous requirements for attendance allowance and mobility allowance.

Subs. (3)

The three weekly rates of the care component are specified in regulations. The top and middle rates are equivalent to the two rates of attendance allowance, whilst the third and lower rate was introduced in April 1992.

Subs. (4)

This subsection details the level of care component to be awarded in any given case: see General Note.

Subs. (5)

This makes special provision for claimants who are terminally ill. A person is terminally ill if "he suffers from a progressive disease and his death in consequence of that disease can reasonably be expected within six months" (s.66(2), on which see commentary in Bonner and Rowland). People who meet this criterion are deemed to satisfy the qualifying period. People who are terminally ill must still satisfy the residence and presence conditions prescribed under s.71(6) above.

Subs. (6)

As with the original form of attendance allowance, special rules apply where the disabled person is a child. Children aged under 16 will only qualify for the lower rate of care component if they satisfy the test in subs. (1)(a)(i) above, the abstract cooking test in subs. (1)(a)(ii) being inappropriate. Furthermore, with regard to both the test in subs. (1)(a)(i) and those under subs. (1)(b) and (c), the additional condition detailed in subs. (6)(b) must be met. This formulation emphasises that disabled children should not be denied benefit merely because they have substantial care or attention needs which may be shared by younger but physically and mentally healthy children.

Subs. (7)

This is an enabling provision permitting regulations to specify circumstances in which a person is deemed to satisfy or not to satisfy the care criteria in subs. (1) above. Special rules are made under this power for claimants on renal dialysis.

Subs. (8)

This enabling provision allows the payment of benefit to be restricted where people are being cared for in residential accommodation which is paid for out of public funds. Under the regulations the care component ceases to be payable once the claimant has been in such accommodation (or has been in hospital) for 28 days. Different rules apply to the mobility component; see further s.73(14).

The mobility component

73.—(1) Subject to the provisions of this Act, a person shall be entitled to the mobility component of a disability living allowance for any period in which he is over the age of five and throughout which—

(a) he is suffering from physical disablement such that he is either unable to walk or virtually unable to do so; or

(b) he falls within subsection (2) below; or

(c) he falls within subsection (3) below; or

(d) he is able to walk but is so severely disabled physically or mentally that, disregarding any ability he may have to use routes which are familiar to him on his own, he cannot take advantage of the faculty out of doors without guidance or supervision from another person most of the time.

(2) A person falls within this subsection if—

(a) he is both blind and deaf; and

(b) he satisfies such other conditions as may be prescribed.

(3) A person falls within this subsection if—

(a) he is severely mentally impaired; and

(b) he displays severe behavioural problems; and

(c) he satisfies both the conditions mentioned in section 72(1)(b) and (c) above.

(4) For the purposes of this section in its application to a person for any period in which he is under the age of 16, the condition mentioned in subsection (1)(d) above shall not be taken to be satisfied unless—

    (a) he requires substantially more guidance or supervision from another person than persons of his age in normal physical and mental health would require; or

    (b) persons of his age in normal physical and mental health would not require such guidance or supervision.

  (5) Subject to subsection (4) above, circumstances may be prescribed in which a person is to be taken to satisfy or not to satisfy a condition mentioned in subsection (1)(a) or (d) or subsection (2)(a) above.

  (6) Regulations shall specify the cases which fall within subsection (3)(a) and (b) above.

  (7) A person who is to be taken for the purposes of section 72 above to satisfy or not to satisfy a condition mentioned in subsection (1)(b) or (c) of that section is to be taken to satisfy or not to satisfy it for the purposes of subsection (3)(c) above.

  (8) A person shall not be entitled to the mobility component for a period unless during most of that period his condition will be such as permits him from time to time to benefit from enhanced facilities for locomotion.

  (9) A person shall not be entitled to the mobility component of a disability living allowance unless—

    (a) throughout—

        (i) the period of three months immediately preceding the date on which the award of the component would begin; or

        (ii) such other period of three months as may be prescribed,

    he has satisfied or is likely to satisfy one or other of the conditions mentioned in subsection (1) above; and

    (b) he is likely to continue to satisfy one or other of those conditions throughout—

        (i) the period of six months beginning with that date; or

        (ii) (if his death is expected within the period of six months beginning with that date) the period so beginning and ending with his death.

  (10) Two weekly rates of the mobility component shall be prescribed.

  (11) The weekly rate of the mobility component payable to a person for each week in the period for which he is awarded that component shall be—

    (a) the higher rate, if he falls within subsection (9) above by virtue of having satisfied or being likely to satisfy one or other of the conditions mentioned in subsection (1)(a), (b) and (c) above throughout both the period mentioned in paragraph (a) of subsection (9) above and that mentioned in paragraph (b) of that subsection; and

    (b) the lower rate in any other case.

  (12) For the purposes of this section in its application to a person who is terminally ill, as defined in section 66(2) above, and who makes a claim expressly on the ground that he is such a person—

    (a) subsection (9)(a) above shall be omitted; and

    (b) subsection (11)(a) above shall have effect as if for the words from "both" to "subsection," in the fourth place where it occurs, there were substituted the words "the period mentioned in subsection (9)(b) above".

  (13) Regulations may prescribe cases in which a person who has the use—

    (a) of an invalid carriage or other vehicle provided by the Secretary of State under section 5(2)(a) of the National Health Service Act 1977 and Schedule 2 to that Act or under section 46 of the National Health Service (Scotland) Act 1978 or provided under Article 30(1) of the Health and Personal Social Services (Northern Ireland) Order 1972; or

    (b) of any prescribed description of appliance supplied under the enactments relating to the National Health Service being such an appliance as is primarily designed to afford a means of personal and independent locomotion out of doors, is not to be paid any amount attributable to entitlement to the mobility component or is to be paid disability living allowance at a reduced rate in so far as it is attributable to that component.

(14) A payment to or in respect of any person which is attributable to his entitlement to the mobility component, and the right to receive such a payment, shall (except in prescribed circumstances and for prescribed purposes) be disregarded in applying any enactment or instrument under which regard is to be had to a person's means.

DEFINITIONS
  "entitled": s.122(1).
  "prescribe": s.122(1).
  "week": s.122(1).

GENERAL NOTE
  This section specifies the criteria for the award of the mobility component. Two conditions must be satisfied under subs. (1): the age condition and the mobility condition. So far as age is concerned, the mobility component is not payable to children aged under five (in contrast, there is no lower age limit for the care component, subject to the initial qualifying period). Claims made by children aged five or over must also satisfy the additional condition laid down in subs. (4). At the other end of the age spectrum, initial claims for the mobility component are generally not possible by people over 65 (see s.75).
  The claimant must then meet one of the four mobility conditions set out in subs. (1)(a)–(d), as elaborated upon by subs. (2) and (3). Criteria (a) and (b) replicate tests which were used for the former mobility allowance and, together with condition (c), give rise to entitlement to the higher rate of the mobility component. The fourth condition only qualifies the claimant for the lower rate.

Subs. (1)
  (a) He is suffering from physical disablement such that he is either unable to walk or virtually unable to do so. This formula adopted is elaborated upon in the Social Security (Disability Living Allowance) Regulations 1991 (S.I. 1991 No. 2890), reg. 12. The crucial point is that the inability to walk must result from a physical rather than a psychological cause (*Lees* v. *Secretary of State for Social Services* [1985] A.C. 930, and *Harrison* v. *Secretary of State for Social Services*, reported as appendix to *R(M) 1/88*). *Lees* demonstrates that an individual will be not "unable to walk"—and so will be ineligible for mobility allowance—if he can put one foot in front of another without the assistance of a third party, even though guidance may be required. This type of case may now fall within subs. (1)(b)–(d) below.
  The meaning of "virtually unable to walk" is a question of law (*R(M) 1/78*). The base point is a total inability to walk, but this is extended to take in people who can technically walk but only to an insignificant extent. An inability to walk to the shops or to the bus stop and so lead a normal life is not sufficient to ground entitlement: *R(M) 3/78, R(M) 1/91*.
  (b) He falls within subsection (2) below. Special provision for the deaf-blind to claim mobility allowance was made as from April 1990. Under the regulations this is defined as 100 per cent. sight loss and at least 80 per cent. hearing loss.
  (c) He falls within subsection (3) below. The decision of the House of Lords in *Lees* made it very difficult for claimants with behavioural problems to claim mobility allowance. A Tribunal of three Commissioners ruled that the essential question in such cases was "whether the claimant *could* not walk, as distinct from *would* not walk" (*R(M) 3/86(T)*, para. 8). In that case it was held that claims were possible where the disabled person's condition was such that he behaved erratically, sometimes running off and sometimes stopping completely. The formula set out in subs. (3) first appeared in the DLADWAA 1991 and was designed to extend the higher rate of the mobility component to a group of some 8,000 to 9,000 people who suffer from severe mental handicap and severe behavioural problems.
  (d) He is able to walk but is so severely disabled physically or mentally.... This head of entitlement was introduced by the DLADWAA 1991 and is entirely hypothetical. It was designed so that "a person who can go by himself to the local corner shop because he is familiar with the journey but needs help to go anywhere else should receive benefit" (*per* Lord Henley, *Hansard*, H.L. Vol. 526, col. 1578, March 7, 1991). Where the claimant is a person aged under 16, the additional condition set out in subs. (4) must be satisfied.

Subs. (3)
  (a) He is severely mentally impaired. The regulations define this as where a person suffers "from a state of arrested development or incomplete physical development of the brain, which

includes severe impairment of intelligence and social functioning" (Social Security (Disability Living Allowance) Regulations 1991 (S.I. 1991 No. 2890), reg. 12(5)).

(b) *He displays severe behavioural problems.* The regulations define this as where a person exhibits disruptive behaviour which is (i) extreme, (ii) regularly requires another person to intervene and physically restrain him in order to prevent him causing physical injury to himself or another, or damage to property, and (iii) is so unpredictable that he requires another person to be present and watching over him whenever he is awake (reg. 12(6)).

Entitlement only arises if the claimant also satisfies both the day and night conditions for the care component. See further Rowland.

Subs. (4)

This is analogous to the additional condition for children aged under 16 in relation to the care component (s.72(6) above). It does not apply to the first three mobility conditions set out in subs. (1)(a)–(c).

Subs. (5)

This enables regulations to prescribe the circumstances in which a person is to be taken to satisfy or not to satisfy the various mobility conditions specified. These include provision for people who have had both legs amputated to be awarded the mobility component automatically.

Subs. (7)

This means, for example, that a person who is terminally ill and is thereby deemed to meet the care criteria in s.72 above is regarded as also satisfying those conditions for the purpose of qualifying for mobility allowance under subs. (3)(c).

Subs. (8)

This excludes from entitlement people whom it is unsafe to move at all and persons so severely mentally handicapped that a high degree of supervision and restraint is needed to prevent them from injuring themselves or a third party (*R(M) 2/83*).

Subs. (9)

See annotations to s.72(2) above which applies the same tests to the care component.

Subs. (10)

Regulations set out the two rates for the mobility component. The higher rate is equivalent to the old mobility allowance whilst the lower rate will be available to those who meet the conditions specified in subs. (1)(d) above.

Subs. (11)

This subsection specifies the level of mobility component to be awarded. Claimants who meet any of the criteria in subs. (1)(a)–(c) above throughout the qualifying period mentioned in subs. (9) are entitled to the higher rate. People who only qualify under subs. (1)(d) receive the lower rate. Recipients of the lower rate are not exempt from vehicle excise duty, unlike claimants on the higher rate (Vehicles (Excise) Act 1971, s.7(2), as amended).

Subs. (12)

As with the care component, claimants who are terminally ill are exempted from the prior qualifying period. They must still satisfy the residence and presence conditions prescribed under s.71(6) above.

Subs. (13)

This enables regulations to be made to avoid duplicate provision by ensuring that the mobility component is not payable, or is payable at a reduced rate, to people who have the use of such an invalid vehicle.

Subs. (14)

The mobility component of DLA, unlike the care component (see s.72(8)), is generally to be disregarded in any means-testing.

Mobility component for certain persons eligible for invalid carriages

74.—(1) Regulations may provide for the issue, variation and cancellation of certificates in respect of prescribed categories of persons to whom this section applies; and a person in respect of whom such a certificate is issued shall, during any period while the certificate is in force, be deemed for the purposes of section 73 above to satisfy the condition mentioned in subsection (1)(a) of that section and to fall within paragraphs (a) and (b) of subsection (9) by virtue of having satisfied or being likely to satisfy that condition throughout both the periods mentioned in those paragraphs.

(2) This section applies to any person whom the Secretary of State considers—

(a) was on 1st January 1976 in possession of an invalid carriage or other vehicle provided in pursuance of section 33 of the Health Services and Public Health Act 1968 (which related to vehicles for persons suffering from physical defect or disability) or receiving payments in pursuance of subsection (3) of that section; or

(b) had at that date, or at a later date specified by the Secretary of State, made an application which the Secretary of State approved for such a carriage or vehicle or for such payments; or

(c) was, both at some time during a prescribed period before that date and at some time during a prescribed period after that date, in possession of such a carriage or vehicle or receiving such payments; or

(d) would have been, by virtue of any of the preceding paragraphs, a person to whom this section applies but for some error or delay for which in the opinion of the Secretary of State the person was not responsible and which was brought to the attention of the Secretary of State within the period of one year beginning with 30th March 1977 (the date of the passing of the Social Security (Miscellaneous Provisions) Act 1977, section 13 of which made provision corresponding to the provision made by this section).

DEFINITIONS
"prescribe": s.122(1).

GENERAL NOTE
Regulations made under this section enable people who have a small car or tricycle under the pre-1976 Invalid Vehicle Scheme to transfer automatically to the mobility component of DLA as and when they give up use of such a vehicle.

Persons 65 or over

75.—(1) Except to the extent to which regulations provide otherwise, no person shall be entitled to either component of a disability living allowance for any period after he attains the age of 65 otherwise than by virtue of an award made before he attains that age.

(2) Regulations may provide in relation to persons who are entitled to a component of a disability living allowance by virtue of subsection (1) above that any provision of this Act which relates to disability living allowance, other than section 74 above, so far as it so relates, and any provision of the Administration Act which is relevant to disability living allowance—

(a) shall have effect subject to modifications, additions or amendments; or

(b) shall not have effect.

DEFINITIONS
"the Administration Act": s.174.
"entitled": s.122(1).

GENERAL NOTE
This section restricts the entitlement to DLA of people aged 65 or over to those who have already been receiving the benefit before that age. In doing so it follows the pattern of mobility allowance. There is, however, no upper limit to receipt of DLA.

Subs. (1)
   The basic rule is that claimants whose disabilities start on or after their 65th birthday are not eligible for DLA. Thus a person who, after attaining the age of 65, for the first time satisfies the test for the middle or higher rate of the care component is only eligible for attendance allowance (see s.64 above). A person who, after reaching 65, qualifies for the first time for what would be the lower rate of the care component or either rate of the mobility component is not eligible for benefit at all. People who qualify for DLA before the age of 65 are still entitled, provided that they make a claim before they reach 66 (as with mobility allowance: see *R(M) 3/89*). More generally, claimants already in receipt of DLA before the age of 65 will continue to be eligible after that age, assuming the other criteria are still satisfied.

Subs. (2)
   Regulations made under this provision ensure that people receiving disability living allowance are not treated differently from other claimants if their circumstances change after they reach the age of 65.

Disability living allowance—supplementary

   76.—(1) Subject to subsection (2) below, a person shall not be entitled to disability living allowance for any period preceding the date on which a claim for it is made or treated as made by him or on his behalf.
   (2) Notwithstanding anything in subsection (1) above, provision may be made by regulations for a person to be entitled to a component of a disability living allowance for a period preceding the date on which a claim for such an allowance is made or treated as made by him or on his behalf if he has previously been entitled to that component.
   (3) For the purposes of sections 72(5) and 73(12) above where—
      (a) a person purports to make a claim for a disability living allowance on behalf of another; and
      (b) the claim is made expressly on the ground that the person on whose behalf it purports to be made is terminally ill,
that person shall be regarded as making the claim notwithstanding that it is made without his knowledge or authority.

DEFINITIONS
   "claim": s.122(1).
   "entitled": s.122(1).

GENERAL NOTE

Subs. (1)
   Entitlement to DLA cannot be backdated, subject to the narrow exception in subs. (2). There is, therefore, no provision for "good cause" to enable backdating of claims, unlike with claims for industrial injuries benefits, invalidity benefit, severe disablement allowance and other benefits.
   Or treated as made. This a useful relaxation of an otherwise harsh rule. Under the regulations the date of claim for a claim form which is received within six weeks of a request for a form is the date of receipt of such a request.

Subs. (2)
   This allows regulations to be made ensuring that there are no gaps in entitlement where repeat claims are delayed.

Subs. (3)
   This follows the special provision for claims on behalf of the terminally ill for attendance allowance (s.66(2)(b) above).

Guardian's allowance

Guardian's allowance

77.—(1) A person shall be entitled to a guardian's allowance in respect of a child if—

(a) he is entitled to child benefit in respect of that child, and

(b) the circumstances are any of those specified in subsection (2) below;

but this subsection is subject, in particular, to section 81 below.

(2) The circumstances referred to in subsection (1)(b) above are—

(a) that both of the child's parents are dead; or

(b) that one of the child's parents is dead and the person claiming a guardian's allowance shows that he was at the date of the death unaware of, and has failed after all reasonable efforts to discover, the whereabouts of the other parent; or

(c) that one of the child's parents is dead and the other is in prison.

(3) There shall be no entitlement to a guardian's allowance in respect of a child unless at least one of the child's parents satisfies, or immediately before his death satisfied, such conditions as may be prescribed as to nationality, residence, place of birth or other matters.

(4) Where, apart from this subsection, a person is entitled to receive, in respect of a particular child, payment of an amount by way of a guardian's allowance, that amount shall not be payable unless one of the conditions specified in subsection (5) below is satisfied.

(5) Those conditions are—

(a) that the beneficiary would be treated for the purposes of Part IX of this Act as having the child living with him; or

(b) that the requisite contributions are being made to the cost of providing for the child.

(6) The condition specified in subsection (5)(b) above is to be treated as satisfied if, but only if—

(a) such contributions are being made at a weekly rate not less than the amount referred to in subsection (4) above—

(i) by the beneficiary; or

(ii) where the beneficiary is one of two spouses residing together, by them together; and

(b) except in prescribed cases, the contributions are over and above those required for the purpose of satisfying section 143(1)(b) below.

(7) A guardian's allowance in respect of a child shall be payable at the weekly rate specified in Schedule 4, Part III, paragraph 5.

(8) Regulations—

(a) may modify subsection (2) or (3) above in relation to cases in which a child has been adopted or is illegitimate, or the marriage of a child's parents has been terminated by divorce;

(b) shall prescribe the circumstances in which a person is to be treated for the purposes of this section as being in prison (by reference to his undergoing a sentence of imprisonment for life or of a prescribed minimum duration, or to his being in legal custody in prescribed circumstances); and

(c) may, for cases where entitlement to a guardian's allowance is established by reference to a person being in prison, provide—

(i) for requiring him to pay to the National Insurance Fund sums paid by way of a guardian's allowance;

(ii) for suspending payment of an allowance where a conviction, sentence or order of a court is subject to appeal, and for matters arising from the decision of an appeal;

(iii) for reducing the rate of an allowance in cases where the person in prison contributes to the cost of providing for the child.

(9) Where a husband and wife are residing together and, apart from this subsection, they would each be entitled to a guardian's allowance in respect of the same child, only the wife shall be entitled, but payment may be made either to her or to him unless she elects in the prescribed manner that payment is not to be made to him.

(10) Subject to subsection (11) below, no person shall be entitled to a guardian's allowance in respect of a child of which he or she is the parent.

(11) Where a person—

(a) has adopted a child; and

(b) was entitled to guardian's allowance in respect of the child immediately before the adoption,

subsection (10) above shall not terminate his entitlement.

DEFINITIONS

"beneficiary": s.122(1).
"child": s.122(1).
"entitled": s.122(1).
"prescribe": s.122(1).

GENERAL NOTE

Guardian's allowance (GA) is a benefit paid to those who are looking after children who are orphans (although in certain cases only one parent need be dead). The claimant does not have to be the child's guardian in any formal sense (*e.g.* as appointed under the Children Act 1989, s.5).

Subs. (1)

The claimant must be entitled to child benefit for the child for whom the allowance is claimed. This emphasises the need for something approximating a parent-child relationship. Note also the further requirements relating to the claimant laid down in subss. (5) and (6).

Subs. (2)

The first basis of entitlement is the conventional meaning of orphanhood. It is not possible to be awarded GA merely because both parents are missing, however diligent the claimant's enquiries have been. The second and third situations cover cases where one parent is dead and the other parent is missing or in prison. The presumption of death after seven years' absence may be relied upon for GA claims (*R(G) 11/52(T)*).

The onus under subs. (2)(b) is on the claimant to show that "all reasonable efforts" have been made to discover the whereabouts of the missing parent, *i.e.* "efforts that would be reasonably expected to be made by a person who wanted to find [that] person" (*R(G) 2/83*). Commissioners in Northern Ireland appear to have taken a markedly more generous approach to the interpretation of this provision than those in Great Britain (see Bonner).

Regulations define being "in prison" as serving a sentence of imprisonment of five years or more (including life sentences) or being detained at Her Majesty's pleasure (Social Security (Guardian's Allowance) Regulations 1975 (S.I. 1975 No. 515), reg. 5). This has been held not to cover cases of detention under the Mental Health Act 1983 (*R(G) 4/65, R(G) 2/80*). These heads of entitlement are modified for certain special cases by regulations made under subs. (8) below.

Subs. (3)

One of the child's parents must either have been born in the United Kingdom or at the date of death of the parent whose death gave rise to the claim have been present in Great Britain for at least 52 weeks in any period of two years after attaining the age of 16 (reg. 6).

Subss. (5) and (6)

No GA is payable unless the claimant has the child living with him or her for the purposes of child benefit or contributes to the child's maintenance at a weekly rate which is at least equivalent to GA over and above any contribution being made to qualify for child benefit.

Subs. (8)

Where a child has been adopted, the adopters count as the parents (reg. 2). It is therefore possible if the adoptive parents die for the natural parents to become entitled to GA (*Secretary of State for Social Services* v. *Smith* [1983] 1 W.L.R. 1110). Adoptive parents may continue to receive GA if they were entitled to it immediately before the adoption (subs. (11)).

Where a child's parents were not married to each other at the time of his or her birth, GA is payable after the death of the mother only, unless paternity had been found by a court or otherwise admitted or established (reg. 3).

Where the child's parents were divorced, and one parent has died and the other did not have custody of the child (and was neither maintaining the child nor liable to do so under a court order), then a claimant other than the surviving parent is eligible for GA (reg. 4).

Subs. (10)

Step-parents do not count as parents. Thus a step-parent is not debarred from receiving GA under subs. (10), nor does the existence of a step-parent disentitle a person looking after the child.

Benefits for the aged

Category C and Category D retirement pensions and other benefits for the aged

78.—(1) A person who was over pensionable age on 5th July 1948 and who satisfies such conditions as may be prescribed shall be entitled to a Category C retirement pension at the appropriate weekly rate.

(2) If a woman whose husband is entitled to a Category C retirement pension—

(a) is over pensionable age; and

(b) satisfies such other conditions as may be prescribed,

she shall be entitled to a Category C retirement pension at the appropriate weekly rate.

(3) A person who is over the age of 80 and satisfies such conditions as may be prescribed shall be entitled to a Category D retirement pension at the appropriate weekly rate if—

(a) he is not entitled to a Category A, Category B or Category C retirement pension; or

(b) he is entitled to such a pension, but it is payable at a weekly rate which, disregarding those elements specified in subsection (4) below, is less than the appropriate weekly rate.

(4) The elements referred to in subsection (3)(b) above are—

(a) any additional pension;

(b) any increase so far as attributable to—

(i) any additional pension, or

(ii) any increase in a guaranteed minimum pension;

(c) any graduated retirement benefit; and

(d) any increase (for dependants) under section 80, 83 or 85 below.

(5) The appropriate weekly rate of a Category C retirement pension—

(a) shall be the lower rate specified in Schedule 4, Part III, paragraph 6, where—

(i) the pensioner is a married woman, and

(ii) she has not, at any time since she became entitled to her pension, ceased to be a married woman; and

(b) shall be the higher rate so specified in any other case.

(6) The appropriate weekly rate of a Category D retirement pension shall be that specified in Schedule 4, Part III, paragraph 7.

(7) Entitlement to a Category C or Category D retirement pension shall continue throughout the pensioner's life.

(8) A Category C or Category D retirement pension shall not be payable for any period falling before the date on which the pensioner's entitlement is to be regarded as commencing for that purpose by virtue of section 5(1)(k) of the Administration Act.

(9) Regulations may provide for the payment—

(a) to a widow whose husband was over pensionable age on 5th July 1948; or
(b) to a woman whose marriage to a husband who was over pensionable age on that date was terminated otherwise than by his death,

of a Category C retirement pension or of benefit corresponding to a widow's pension or a widowed mother's allowance; and any such retirement pension or any such benefit shall be at the prescribed rate.

DEFINITIONS
"additional pension": s.45(1).
"the Administration Act": s.174.
"entitled": s.122(1).
"graduated retirement benefit": s.62.
"pensionable age": s.122(1).
"prescribe": s.122(1).

GENERAL NOTE
The Category C non-contributory retirement pension was introduced in 1970. Initially it applied to persons who were excluded from the National Insurance scheme because they were over pensionable age on July 5, 1948. This is obviously a rapidly diminishing group. The Category C retirement pension also applies to certain dependants of such people. In 1971 the Category D non-contributory pension was brought in. This is available to persons who are aged 80 or over, satisfy the residence tests and either fail to qualify for a contributory retirement pension or qualify for one at a lower rate than the Category C pension. There were only some 32,000 non-contributory retirement pensions in payment in September 1990 (*Social Security Statistics 1991*, p. 108).

Age addition

79.—(1) A person who is over the age of 80 and entitled to a retirement pension of any category shall be entitled to an increase of the pension, to be known as "age addition".

(2) Where a person is in receipt of a pension or allowance payable by the Secretary of State by virtue of any prescribed enactment or instrument (whether passed or made before or after this Act) and—

(a) he is over the age of 80; and
(b) he fulfils such other conditions as may be prescribed,

he shall be entitled to an increase of that pension or allowance, also known as age addition.

(3) Age addition shall be payable for the life of the person entitled, at the weekly rate specified in Schedule 4, Part III, paragraph 8.

DEFINITIONS
"entitled": s.122(1).
"prescribe": s.122(1).

GENERAL NOTE
All retirement pensions are increased by an extra 25p a week if the recipient is aged 80 or over. The age addition also applies to certain other benefits prescribed under subs. (2). This addition is paid automatically and so does not need a separate claim. The value of the age addition has not been uprated since its introduction in 1971.

PART IV

INCREASES FOR DEPENDANTS

Child dependants

Beneficiary's dependent children

80.—(1) Subject to section 61 above and to the following provisions of this Part of this Act, the weekly rate of any benefit to which this subsection applies shall, for any period for which the beneficiary is entitled to child benefit in respect of a child or children, be increased in respect of that child, or each respectively of those children, by the amount specified in relation to the benefit in question in Schedule 4, Part IV, column (2).

(2) Subsection (1) above applies to—

(a) unemployment benefit where the beneficiary is over pensionable age;

(b) sickness benefit where the beneficiary is over pensionable age;

(c) invalidity pension; and

(d) Category A, Category B or Category C retirement pension.

(3) In any case where—

(a) a beneficiary is one of two persons who are—

(i) spouses residing together; or

(ii) an unmarried couple; and

(b) the other person had earnings in any week,

the beneficiary's right to payment of increases for the following week under subsection (1) above shall be determined in accordance with subsection (4) below.

(4) No such increase shall be payable—

(a) in respect of the first child where the earnings were £115 or more; and

(b) in respect of a further child for each complete £15 by which the earnings exceeded £115.

(5) Subject to section 81 below, the weekly rate of a widowed mother's allowance payable by virtue of subsection (1)(a) of section 37 above shall be increased for any period in respect of the child or, if more than one, each respectively of the children falling within subsection (2)(a), (b) or (c) of that section in respect of whom she is for the time being entitled to child benefit by the amount specified in relation to that allowance in Schedule 4, Part IV, column (2).

(6) Subject to section 81 below, the weekly rate of a child's special allowance shall, for any period for which the beneficiary is entitled to child benefit in respect of two or more children with respect to whom the conditions specified in section 56(1)(b) and (c) above are satisfied, be increased in respect of each respectively of those children other than the elder or eldest by the amount specified in relation to that allowance in Schedule 4, Part IV, column (2).

(7) In this section—

"unmarried couple" means a man and a woman who are not married to each other but are living together as husband and wife; and

"week" means such period of seven days as may be prescribed for the purposes of this section.

DEFINITIONS

"beneficiary": s.122(1).

"benefit": s.122(1).

"child": s.122(1).

"child benefit": s.141.

"earnings": s.122(1).

"entitled": s.122(1).

"pensionable age": s.122(1).

"unmarried couple": subs. (7).

"week": subs. (7).

GENERAL NOTE

Where any of the benefits listed in subs. (2) are payable, they may be supplemented by increases for child dependants. Three criteria need to be met in such cases.

First, the claimant must be entitled to child benefit in respect of the child(ren) in question (see Pt. IX). These rules are modified in certain respects by the Social Security Benefit (Dependency) Regulations 1977 (S.I. 1977 No. 343), regs. 4A and 4B.

Secondly, the child(ren) must be living with the claimant or the claimant must contribute to the cost of their keeping at a weekly rate of not less than the amount of the increase, over and above any amount received by way of child benefit (s.81).

Thirdly, the increase is not payable where either the claimant or partner earns more than the amount specified in subs. (4). "Earnings" include occupational or personal pensions (s.89(1)).

Subsections (5) and (6) contain special rules in relation to widowed mother's allowance and child's special allowance.

Restrictions on increase—child not living with beneficiary etc.

81.—(1) Where, apart from this subsection, a person is entitled to receive, in respect of a particular child, payment of an amount by way of an increase under section 80 above of any benefit, that amount shall not be payable unless one of the conditions specified in subsection (2) below is satisfied.

(2) Those conditions are—

(a) that the beneficiary would be treated for the purposes of Part IX of this Act as having the child living with him; or

(b) that the requisite contributions are being made to the cost of providing for the child.

(3) The condition specified in subsection (2)(b) above is to be treated as satisfied if, but only if—

(a) such contributions are being made at a weekly rate not less than the amount referred to in subsection (1) above—

(i) by the beneficiary; or

(ii) where the beneficiary is one of two spouses residing together, by them together; and

(b) except in prescribed cases, the contributions are over and above those required for the purpose of satisfying section 143(1)(b) below.

DEFINITIONS

"beneficiary": s.122(1).
"benefit": s.122(1).
"child": s.122(1).
"entitled": s.122(1).
"prescribe": s.122(1).

GENERAL NOTE

See General Note to s.80 and *R(U) 14/62*.

Adult dependants

Short-term benefit: increase for adult dependants

82.—(1) Subject to section 61 above and section 87 below, the weekly rate of unemployment benefit or sickness benefit shall be increased by the amount specified in relation to the benefit in question in Schedule 4, Part IV, column (3), for any period during which—

(a) the beneficiary is—

(i) residing with his wife, or

(ii) contributing to the maintenance of his wife at a weekly rate not less than that amount; and

(b) his wife does not have weekly earnings which exceed that amount.

(2) Subject, in particular, to subsection (5) and section 87 below, the weekly rate—

(a) of unemployment benefit or sickness benefit in the case of a beneficiary not entitled to an increase under subsection (1) above, and

(b) of a maternity allowance in any case,

shall be increased by the amount specified in relation to the benefit in question in Schedule 4, Part IV, column (3) ("the amount of the relevant increase") for any period to which this subsection applies by virtue of subsection (3) or (4) below.

(3) Subsection (2) above applies by virtue of this subsection to any period during which—
(a) the beneficiary's husband does not have weekly earnings which exceed the amount of the relevant increase, and
(b) either she and her husband are residing together or she is contributing to his maintenance at a weekly rate not less than that amount.
(4) Subsection (2) above applies by virtue of this subsection to any period during which a person—
(a) who is neither the spouse of the beneficiary nor a child, and
(b) in respect of whom such further conditions as may be prescribed are fulfilled,
has the care of a child or children in respect of whom the beneficiary is entitled to child benefit.
(5) A beneficiary shall not under subsection (2) above be entitled for the same period to an increase of benefit in respect of more than one person.

DEFINITIONS
"amount of the relevant increase": subs. (2).
"beneficiary": s.122(1).
"child": s.122(1).
"earnings": s.122(1).
"prescribe": s.122(1).

GENERAL NOTE
This section enables increases to be paid for adult dependants to supplement unemployment benefit, sickness benefit or maternity allowance. A claimant is entitled to such an increase for a spouse where two conditions are satisfied. First, the husband and wife must be residing together or (where separated) the claimant is paying weekly maintenance at a level at least equal to the increase (subss. (1)(a) and (3)(a)). Secondly, the spouse's weekly earnings must not exceed the amount of the increase (subss. (1)(b) and (3)(a)). "Earnings" include occupational or personal pensions (s.89(1)). Increases are alternatively payable where some other adult is looking after a child or children (subs. (4)).

Subs. (1)
Wife. The marriage must be one which is recognised in the United Kingdom and subsisting at the time of the event giving rise to the claim for benefit. Cohabitees are excluded (*R(S) 6/89*). For detailed analysis, see Bonner.
Residing with. See Social Security Benefit (Persons Residing Together) Regulations 1977 (S.I. 1977 No. 956), *R(P) 1/90* and Ogus and Barendt, pp. 343–5.

Pension increase (wife)

83.—(1) This section applies to—
(a) a Category A or Category C retirement pension;
(b) an invalidity pension under section 33 or 41 above.
(2) Subject to subsection (3) below, the weekly rate of a pension to which this section applies, when payable to a man, shall be increased by the amount specified in relation to the pension in Schedule 4, Part IV, column (3)—
(a) for any period during which the pensioner is residing with his wife; or
(b) for any period during which the pensioner is contributing to the maintenance of his wife at a weekly rate not less than that amount, and his wife does not have weekly earnings which exceed that amount.
(3) Regulations may provide that for any period during which the pensioner is residing with his wife and his wife has earnings—
(a) the increase of benefit under this section shall be subject to a reduction in respect of the wife's earnings; or
(b) there shall be no increase of benefit under this section.

DEFINITIONS
"earnings": s.122(1).

GENERAL NOTE
This section provides for a married man to receive an increase for his wife in the case of the benefits mentioned in subs. (1). The conditions are either that they are residing together and she is earning no more than the amount of the increase (Social Security (Dependency) Regulations 1977 (S.I. 1977 No. 343), reg. 8) or that they are residing apart but he is contributing to her maintenance at a weekly rate not less than the amount of the increase. "Earnings" include occupational or personal pensions (s.89(1)). On the meaning of "wife" and "residing with", see General Note to s.82. Only one such addition is payable (s.88).

Pension increase (husband)

84.—(1) Where a Category A retirement pension is payable to a woman for any period—

(a) which began immediately upon the termination of a period for which the pensioner was entitled to an increase in unemployment benefit, sickness benefit or invalidity pension by virtue of section 82(3) above or 86(1) below, and

(b) during which the requirements of either paragraph (a) or (b) of subsection (2) below are satisfied (without interruption),

then the weekly rate of the pensioner's Category A retirement pension shall be increased by the amount specified in relation to that pension in Schedule 4, Part IV, column (3) ("the specified amount").

(2) The requirements referred to in subsection (1)(b) above are—

(a) that the pensioner is residing with her husband;

(b) that the pensioner is contributing to the maintenance of her husband at a weekly rate not less than the specified amount, and her husband does not have weekly earnings which exceed that amount.

(3) Regulations may provide that for any period during which the pensioner is residing with her husband and her husband has earnings—

(a) the increase of benefit under this section shall be subject to a reduction in respect of the husband's earnings; or

(b) there shall be no increase of benefit under this section.

DEFINITIONS
"earnings": s.122(1).
"entitled": s.122(1).
"specified amount": subs. (1).

GENERAL NOTE
This provision enables a wife to receive an addition for her husband as an increase to her Category A retirement pension on similar terms to those under s.83 for a man. Only one such addition is payable (s.88).

An extra requirement is laid down by subs. (1): the woman must become entitled to that pension immediately after being entitled to an increase for the husband to one of those benefits specified in subs. (1)(a). Although apparently discriminatory, the validity of this rule was upheld in *R(P) 3/88*. This decision may itself now be open to challenge in the light of the Court of Appeal's decision in *Thomas* v. *Chief Adjudication Officer and Secretary of State for Social Security*; *Cooze* v. *Same*; *Beard* v. *Same*; *Murphy* v. *Same*; *Morley* v. *Same* [1991] 2 W.L.R. 886.

Pension increase (person with care of children)

85.—(1) This section applies to—

(a) a Category A retirement pension;

(b) a Category C retirement pension payable by virtue of section 78(1) above;

(c) an invalidity pension under section 33, 40 or 41 above.

(2) Subject to the following provisions, the weekly rate of a pension to which this section applies shall be increased by the amount specified in relation to that pension in Schedule 4, Part IV, column (3) for any period during which a person who is neither the spouse of the pensioner nor a child has the care of a child or children in respect of whom the pensioner is entitled to child benefit.

(3) Subsection (2) above does not apply if the pensioner is a man whose wife is entitled to a Category B retirement pension, or to a Category C retirement pension by virtue of section 78(2) above or in such other cases as may be prescribed.

(4) Regulations may, in a case within subsection (2) above in which the person there referred to is residing with the pensioner and fulfils such further conditions as may be prescribed, authorise an increase of benefit under this section, but subject, taking account of the earnings of the person residing with the pensioner, other than such of that person's earnings as may be prescribed, to provisions comparable to those that may be made by virtue of section 83(3) above.

DEFINITIONS
  "benefit": s.122(1).
  "child": s.122(1).
  "entitled": s.122(1).
  "earnings": s.122(1).
  "prescribe": s.122(1).

GENERAL NOTE
  This section provides for an increase in the benefits listed in subs. (1) for a person caring for the claimant's child(ren). The claimant must be entitled to child benefit (subs. (2)), or treated as so entitled (Social Security Benefit (Dependency) Regulations 1977 (S.I. 1977 No. 343), regs. 4A and 4B). For further conditions see Social Security (Dependency) Regulations 1977 (S.I. 1977 No. 343), regs. 8 and 10. "Earnings" include occupational or personal pensions (s.89(1)). Only one such addition is payable (s.88).

Increase of woman's invalidity pension (husband)

86.—(1) Subject to section 87 below, the weekly rate of an invalidity pension payable to a woman shall be increased by the amount specified in relation to an invalidity pension in Schedule 4, Part IV, column (3) for any period during which either—
  (a) the pensioner and her husband are residing together and he does not have earnings at a weekly rate in excess of the amount specified in Schedule 4, Part I, paragraph 1; or
  (b) they are not residing together, he does not have earnings at a weekly rate in excess of the amount specified in relation to an invalidity pension in Schedule 4, Part IV, column (3) and she is contributing to his maintenance at a weekly rate not less than the amount so specified.

(2) Regulations may provide that—
  (a) the increase of benefit under this section shall be subject to a reduction in respect of the husband's earnings; or
  (b) there shall be no increase of benefit under this section.

DEFINITIONS
  "earnings": s.122(1).

GENERAL NOTE
  A married woman may be entitled to an increase in invalidity pension for her husband on the same terms as under s.83(2). "Earnings" include occupational or personal pensions (s.89(1)). Only one such addition is payable (s.88).

Rate of increase where associated retirement pension is attributable to reduced contributions

87.—(1) Where a person—
  (a) is entitled—
      (i) to unemployment benefit by virtue of section 25(2)(b) or (c) above, or

(ii) to sickness benefit by virtue of section 31(2)(b) or (c) above, or

(iii) to an invalidity pension by virtue of section 33(2) above; and

(b) would have been entitled only by virtue of section 60(1) above to the retirement pension by reference to which the rate of that benefit or invalidity pension is determined,

the amount of any increase of the benefit or invalidity pension attributable to sections 82 to 86 above shall not be determined in accordance with those sections but shall be determined in accordance with regulations.

(2) The regulations shall not provide for any such increase in a case where the retirement pension by reference to which the rate of the said benefit or invalidity pension is determined—

(a) would have been payable only by virtue of section 60 above; and

(b) would, in consequence of a failure to satisfy a contribution condition, have contained no basic pension.

DEFINITIONS
"entitled": s.122(1).

GENERAL NOTE
Where a person is entitled to one of the benefits listed in subs. (1), the amount of any increase in that benefit in respect of an adult dependant is to be determined according to regulations. See Social Security (Dependency) Regulations 1977 (S.I. 1977 No. 343), reg. 13.

Pension increases to be in respect of only one adult dependant

88. A pensioner shall not under sections 83 to 86 above be entitled for the same period to an increase of benefit in respect of more than one person.

DEFINITIONS
"benefit": s.122(1).
"entitled": s.122(1).

Miscellaneous

Earnings to include occupational and personal pensions for purposes of provisions relating to increases of benefits in respect of child or adult dependants

89.—(1) Except as may be prescribed, in section 80 and sections 82 to 86 above any reference to earnings includes a reference to payments by way of occupational or personal pension.

(2) For the purposes of the provisions mentioned in subsection (1) above, the Secretary of State may by regulations provide, in relation to cases where payments by way of occupational or personal pension are made otherwise than weekly, that any necessary apportionment of the payments shall be made in such manner and on such basis as may be prescribed.

DEFINITIONS
"earnings": s.122(1).
"payments by way of occupational or personal pension": s.122(1).
"prescribe": s.122(1).

GENERAL NOTE
See *R(U) 1/89* on civil service pensions.

Beneficiaries under sections 68 and 70

90. The weekly rates—

(a) of a severe disablement allowance, and

(b) of an invalid care allowance,

shall, in such circumstances as may be prescribed, be increased for child or adult dependants by the appropriate amount specified in relation to the allowance in question in Schedule 4, Part IV.

DEFINITIONS
  "child": s.122(1).
  "prescribe": s.122(1).

GENERAL NOTE
  This section enables increases to be paid for child and adult dependants to supplement severe disablement allowance and invalid care allowance. See Social Security (Dependency) Regulations 1977 (S.I. 1977 No. 343), reg. 12.

Effect of trade disputes on entitlement to increases

91.—(1) A beneficiary shall not be entitled—
  (a) to an increase in any benefit under sections 82 to 88 above; or
  (b) to an increase in benefit for an adult dependant by virtue of regulations under section 90 above,
if the person in respect of whom he would be entitled to the increase falls within subsection (2) below.
  (2) A person falls within this subsection if—
  (a) he is disqualified under section 27 above for receiving unemployment benefit; or
  (b) he would be so disqualified if he were otherwise entitled to that benefit.

DEFINITIONS
  "beneficiary": s.122(1).
  "entitled": s.122(1).

GENERAL NOTE
  This provision, first introduced in 1986, disentitles claimants from receiving dependants' increases where they have been disqualified from unemployment benefit under s.27 or would have been so disqualified had they claimed that benefit.

Dependency increases: continuation of awards in cases of fluctuating earnings

92.—(1) Where a beneficiary—
  (a) has been awarded an increase of benefit under this Part of this Act, but
  (b) ceases to be entitled to the increase by reason only that the weekly earnings of some other person ("the relevant earner") exceed the amount of the increase or, as the case may be, some specified amount,
then, if and so long as the beneficiary would have continued to be entitled to the increase, disregarding any such excess of earnings, the award shall continue in force but the increase shall not be payable for any week if the earnings relevant to that week exceed the amount of the increase or, as the case may be, the specified amount.
  (2) In this section the earnings which are relevant to any week are those earnings of the relevant earner which, apart from this section, would be taken into account in determining whether the beneficiary is entitled to the increase in question for that week.

DEFINITIONS
  "beneficiary": s.122(1).
  "earnings": s.122(1).
  "entitled": s.122(1).
  "relevant earner": subs. (1).
  "week": s.122(1).

GENERAL NOTE

The purpose of this infelicitously drafted section is to ensure that once a dependency increase is awarded, it will not end merely because the relevant person's income has exceeded the specified amount. It is a technical provision which ensures that a repeat claim does not become necessary every time earnings fall below the earnings limit.

Dependency increases on termination of employment after period of entitlement to disability working allowance

93. Where—

(a) a person becomes entitled to an invalidity pension or a severe disablement allowance by virtue of section 33(7), 42 or 68(10) above; and

(b) when he was last entitled to that pension or allowance, it was increased in respect of a dependant by virtue of—

(i) regulation 8(6) of the Social Security Benefit (Dependency) Regulations 1977;

(ii) regulation 2 of the Social Security (Savings for Existing Beneficiaries) Regulations 1984;

(iii) regulation 3 of the Social Security Benefit (Dependency) Amendment Regulations 1984; or

(iv) regulation 4 of the Social Security Benefit (Dependency and Computation of Earnings) Amendment Regulations 1989,

for the purpose of determining whether his pension or allowance should be increased by virtue of that regulation for any period beginning with the day on which he again becomes entitled to his pension or allowance, the increase in respect of that dependant shall be treated as having been payable to him on each day between the last day on which his pension or allowance was previously payable and the day on which he again becomes entitled to it.

DEFINITIONS

"entitled": s.122(1).

GENERAL NOTE

This section is concerned with disability working allowance recipients who have to leave work and go back on to invalidity benefit or severe disablement allowance under the two-year linking rule. In such cases their benefit will be calculated in the same way as before, including any increases for dependants.

PART V

BENEFIT FOR INDUSTRIAL INJURIES

General provisions

Right to industrial injuries benefit

94.—(1) Industrial injuries benefit shall be payable where an employed earner suffers personal injury caused after 4th July 1948 by accident arising out of and in the course of his employment, being employed earner's employment.

(2) Industrial injuries benefit consists of the following benefits—

(a) disablement benefit payable in accordance with sections 103 to 105 below, paragraphs 2 and 3 of Schedule 7 below and Parts II and III of that Schedule;

(b) reduced earnings allowance payable in accordance with Part IV;

(c) retirement allowance payable in accordance with Part V; and

(d) industrial death benefit, payable in accordance with Part VI.

(3) For the purposes of industrial injuries benefit an accident arising in the course of an employed earner's employment shall be taken, in the absence of evidence to the contrary, also to have arisen out of that employment.

(4) Regulations may make provision as to the day which, in the case of night workers and other special cases, is to be treated for the purposes of industrial injuries benefit as the day of the accident.

(5) Subject to sections 117, 119 and 120 below, industrial injuries benefit shall not be payable in respect of an accident happening while the earner is outside Great Britain.

(6) In the following provisions of this Part of this Act "work" in the contexts "incapable of work" and "incapacity for work" means work which the person in question can be reasonably expected to do.

DEFINITIONS
"earner": s.122(1).
"employed earner": s.122(1).
"employed earner's employment": s.95(1).
"Great Britain": s.172.
"industrial injuries benefit": subs. (2) and s.122(1).
"work": subs. (6).

GENERAL NOTE
The industrial injuries scheme today is radically different from that established in 1948. All the important changes have taken place since 1980. Since the abolition of industrial injury benefit (1982), industrial death benefit (1988) and reduced earnings allowance and retirement allowance (1990), the principal benefit under the scheme has been disablement benefit (s.103). The list of benefits contained in subs. (2) is therefore potentially misleading, as those mentioned in subs. (2)(b)–(d) are only payable where the accident or the onset of the disease occurred before October 1, 1990 (reduced earnings allowance and retirement allowance) or the relevant death occurred before April 11, 1988 (industrial death benefit): see s.106. The principal adjudication provisions are contained in SSAA 1992, ss.44–50.

Subs. (1)
The definition of entitlement to industrial injuries benefit contained in subs. (1) has been the subject of a wealth of case law. There are four basic elements:
    (a) the claimant must be "an employed earner... in employed earner's employment";
    (b) the claimant must suffer "personal injury";
    (c) the personal injury must be "caused after 4 July 1948 by accident"; and
    (d) the accident must arise "out of and in the course of his employment".
An employed earner... in employed earner's employment. The self-employed are hence excluded. See further s.95.
Suffers personal injury. This means some "hurt to body or mind" (*Jones* v. *Secretary of State for Social Services*; *Hudson* v. *Same* [1972] A.C. 944 at 1020, *per* Lord Simon). A temporary strain is unlikely to be sufficient; there must be some discernible physiological worsening of the claimant's condition (*R(I) 19/60, R(I) 1/76*). See further Lewis, pp. 43–45.
Caused after 4th July 1948 by accident. This apparently straightforward formulation has given rise to much litigation. There are two difficult areas of interpretation, relating to the meaning of "accident" and "caused by".
Accident. The standard definition of accident is "an unlooked-for mishap or an untoward event which is neither expected nor designed" (*Fenton* v. *J. Thorley & Co.* [1903] A.C. 443 at 448, *per* Lord Macnaghten). The incident may still be an accident if deliberately caused by a third party (*Trim Joint District School Board* v. *Kelly* [1914] A.C. 667).
The distinction between accident and process is especially problematic: "There must come a time when the indefinite number of so-called accidents and the length of time over which they occur take away the element of accident and substitute that of process" (*Roberts* v. *Dorothea Slate Quarries* [1948] 2 All E.R. 201, *per* Lord Porter). The significance of this is that an injury caused by an accident gives rise to entitlement to benefit, whereas one caused by a process does not, unless the resultant condition is scheduled as a prescribed disease (s.108). At times this has led to some very fine if not arbitrary distinctions. For example, in *R(I) 43/61* digital neuritis caused by less than three days' use of scissors was held to be due to an accident, while in *R(I) 19/56* osteoarthritis of the fingers caused by three days of stitching was found to be the cumulative result of a process. For a recent controversial illustration, see *R(I) 6/91* (asthma brought on by passive smoking held on special facts to be a series of accidents).
Difficulties may also arise where the injury sustained is alleged to be the accident for the purposes of entitlement to benefit: see *R(I) 11/80* and *R(I) 6/82*. See further Bonner and Lewis, pp. 38–43.

Caused by. The onus is on the claimant to establish that the accident caused the injury (*R(I) 14/51*). The claimant must also show that but for the accident the injury would not have occurred, and that the accident is an effective cause of the injury. See Lewis, pp. 45–49.

Arising out of and in the course of his employment. This expression dates back to the Workmen's Compensation Act 1897. The underlying intention is to restrict the industrial injuries scheme to injuries which may be regarded as work-related and to exclude those which are the result of the ordinary risks of life (*e.g. R(I) 62/53*). As a general rule a claimant will establish a prima facie case if he can show that the accident occurred at his normal place of work and during his normal hours of work. Inevitably the application of this principle to individual cases has caused considerable difficulty.

Authoritative guidance on the meaning of this phrase has been given in *Nancollas* v. *Insurance Officer* [1985] 2 All E.R. 833, and (albeit in a different context) *Smith* v. *Stages* [1989] A.C. 928. For recent Commissioners' decisions, see *R(I) 1/88* and *R(I) 1/91* and, for a full analysis of this difficult area, Ogus and Barendt, pp. 261–78, Lewis, pp. 50–89 and Bonner.

Note that the concept of work-related accidents is extended by the deeming provisions in ss.98–101 (especially s.99, concerning earners sustaining accidents while travelling in their employer's transport).

Subs. (3)
This presumption is of limited value as the claimant must still prove that the accident occurred in the course of the employment and there must be no evidence to the contrary.

Subs. (5)
As a general principle industrial injuries benefit is not payable in respect of accidents occurring outside Great Britain. The statute contains special provisions for mariners, airmen and those employed on the continental shelf (ss.117 and 119–120). Accidents occurring abroad may also give rise to benefit under the Social Security Benefit (Persons Abroad) Regulations 1975 (S.I. 1975 No. 563). Where the accident occurs in another member state of the European Community the claimant may be able to rely on E.C. Regs. 1408/71 and 574/72. In respect of other states there may be special provision in the relevant reciprocal convention on social security.

Relevant employments

95.—(1) In section 94 above, this section and sections 98 to 109 below "employed earner's employment" shall be taken to include any employment by virtue of which a person is, or is treated by regulations as being for the purposes of industrial injuries benefit, an employed earner.

(2) Regulations may provide that any prescribed employment shall not be treated for the purposes of industrial injuries benefit as employed earner's employment notwithstanding that it would be so treated apart from the regulations.

(3) For the purposes of the provisions of this Act mentioned in subsection (1) above an employment shall be an employed earner's employment in relation to an accident if (and only if) it is, or is treated by regulations as being, such an employment when the accident occurs.

(4) Any reference in the industrial injuries and diseases provisions to an "employed earner" or "employed earner's employment" is to be construed in relation to any time before 6th April 1975, as a reference respectively to an "insured person" or "insurable employment" within the meaning of the provisions relating to industrial injuries and diseases which were in force at that time.

(5) In subsection (4) above "the industrial injuries and diseases provisions" means—
(a) this section and sections 96 to 110 below;
(b) any other provisions of this Act so far as they relate to those sections; and
(c) any provisions of the Administration Act so far as they so relate.

DEFINITIONS
"the Administration Act": s.174.
"employed earner": subs. (4) and s.122(1).

"employed earner's employment": subss. (1) and (4).
"employment": s.122(1).
"industrial injuries and diseases provisions": subs. (5).
"industrial injuries benefit": s.122(1).
"prescribe": s.122(1).

<small>GENERAL NOTE</small>
This section enables the Secretary of State by regulation to extend or exclude certain categories of earners for the purposes of the scheme (see also s.2(4)). See Social Security (Employed Earners' Employments for Industrial Injuries Purposes) Regulations 1975 (S.I. 1975 No. 467). Decisions as to whether a claimant is or was employed in employed earner's employment are for the Secretary of State, not the independent statutory authorities (SSAA 1992, s.17(1)(d)). There is therefore no right of appeal to a SSAT.

Persons treated as employers for certain purposes

96. In relation to—
(a) a person who is an employed earner for the purposes of this Part of this Act otherwise than by virtue of a contract of service or apprenticeship; or
(b) any other employed earner—
    (i) who is employed for the purpose of any game or recreation and is engaged or paid through a club; or
    (ii) in whose case it appears to the Secretary of State there is special difficulty in the application of all or any of the provisions of this Part of this Act relating to employers,
regulations may provide for a prescribed person to be treated in respect of industrial injuries benefit and its administration as the earner's employer.

<small>DEFINITIONS</small>
"contract of service": s.122(1).
"employed earner": s.122(1).
"industrial injuries benefit": s.122(1).
"prescribe": s.122(1).

<small>GENERAL NOTE</small>
See Social Security (Employed Earners' Employments for Industrial Injuries Purposes) Regulations 1975 (S.I. 1975 No. 467).

Accidents in course of illegal employments

97.—(1) Subsection (2) below has effect in any case where—
(a) a claim is made for industrial injuries benefit in respect of an accident, or of a prescribed disease or injury; or
(b) an application is made under section 44 of the Administration Act for a declaration that an accident was an industrial accident, or for a corresponding declaration as to a prescribed disease or injury.
(2) The Secretary of State may direct that the relevant employment shall, in relation to that accident, disease or injury, be treated as having been employed earner's employment notwithstanding that by reason of a contravention of, or non-compliance with, some provision contained in or having effect under an enactment passed for the protection of employed persons or any class of employed persons, either—
(a) the contract purporting to govern the employment was void; or
(b) the employed person was not lawfully employed in the relevant employment at the time when, or in the place where, the accident happened or the disease or injury was contracted or received.
(3) In subsection (2) above "relevant employment" means—
(a) in relation to an accident, the employment out of and in the course of which the accident arises; and
(b) in relation to a prescribed disease or injury, the employment to the nature of which the disease or injury is due.

DEFINITIONS
"the Administration Act": s.174.
"employed earner": s.122(1).
"employment": s.122(1).
"industrial injuries benefit": s.122(1).
"relevant employment": subs. (3).

GENERAL NOTE
This section enables the Secretary of State to direct that a particular employment is covered by the industrial injuries scheme, notwithstanding that the employment is illegal or the contract of service void. This could provide some protection for children who are illegally employed (Lewis, p. 33).

Earner acting in breach of regulations, etc.

98. An accident shall be taken to arise out of and in the course of an employed earner's employment, notwithstanding that he is at the time of the accident acting in contravention of any statutory or other regulations applicable to his employment, or of any orders given by or on behalf of his employer, or that he is acting without instructions from his employer, if—
  (a) the accident would have been taken so to have arisen had the act not been done in contravention of any such regulations or orders, or without such instructions, as the case may be; and
  (b) the act is done for the purposes of and in connection with the employer's trade or business.

DEFINITIONS
"employed earner's employment": s.95(1).
"employment": s.122(1).
"trade or business": s.122(1).

GENERAL NOTE
As a general principle an employee who is injured while acting in contravention of regulations or orders has not suffered an accident which arises out of and in the course of the employment. This principle is modified by this section, which deems certain accidents to be attributable to the employment if two conditions are satisfied. It is always necessary in such cases to consider as a preliminary issue whether the claim can succeed under the general principles relating to s.94(1) (*CI 210/50*).

The section requires first that the accident would have met the statutory test under s.94(1) had the employee not been acting against or without authority. Secondly, the act done without such authority must have been performed for the purposes of and in connection with the employer's trade or business.

In cases where the injured employee was doing something which was the duty of another employee, whose duties were not interchangeable with those of the victim, it may be impossible to rely on this deeming provision (*R(I) 12/61, R(I) 1/66*). See further Lewis, pp. 70–73.

Earner travelling in employer's transport

99.—(1) An accident happening while an employed earner is, with the express or implied permission of his employer, travelling as a passenger by any vehicle to or from his place of work shall, notwithstanding that he is under no obligation to his employer to travel by that vehicle, be taken to arise out of and in the course of his employment if—
  (a) the accident would have been taken so to have arisen had he been under such an obligation; and
  (b) at the time of the accident, the vehicle—
        (i) is being operated by or on behalf of his employer or some other person by whom it is provided in pursuance of arrangements made with his employer; and
        (ii) is not being operated in the ordinary course of a public transport service.
  (2) In this section references to a vehicle include a ship, vessel, hovercraft or aircraft.

    "employed earner": s.122(1).
    "vehicle": subs. (2).

GENERAL NOTE
    Accidents which occur while travelling have given rise to a considerable body of case law in the industrial injuries scheme. The starting point is that travel to or from the claimant's usual place of work is normally outside the scope of the employment. This section provides an exception to this principle so far as a narrow class of commuting accidents are concerned. Journeys to and from work are deemed to arise out of and in the course of the claimant's employment provided that:
    (a) the claimant is travelling as a passenger to or from his or her place of work;
    (b) the vehicle is operated by or on behalf of the employer or provided by some third party under an arrangement with the employer;
    (c) the claimant has the employer's permission to travel by the vehicle;
    (d) the vehicle is not being operated in the ordinary course of a public transport service; and
    (e) the accident would have qualified under s.94 had the claimant been under an obligation to travel in the vehicle.
    See further Lewis (pp. 80–2).

Accidents happening while meeting emergency

100. An accident happening to an employed earner in or about any premises at which he is for the time being employed for the purposes of his employer's trade or business shall be taken to arise out of and in the course of his employment if it happens while he is taking steps, on an actual or supposed emergency at those premises, to rescue, succour or protect persons who are, or are thought to be or possibly to be, injured or imperilled, or to avert or minimise serious damage to property.

DEFINITIONS
    "employed earner": s.122(1).
    "employment": s.122(1).
    "trade or business": s.122(1).

GENERAL NOTE
    As a general principle, irrespective of this section, most employees injured whilst acting in an emergency will qualify for industrial injuries benefits. Case law establishes that an employee may claim where he or she acts in response to an emergency in a manner which is reasonable, in the employer's interests and reasonably incidental to the employment. These conditions have historically been construed in a broad fashion: see *R(I) 46/60* and the discussion in Lewis, pp. 67–69.
    In the relatively unusual case where the claimant is unable to rely upon the general principles outlined above, recourse may be had to this section. It is wider than the general principles in that the employee need not be acting in the employer's interests (*e.g. R(I) 6/63,* where a milkman was injured while trying to rescue children trapped in a bungalow on fire). It is narrower, however, in that the emergency must be "in or about" premises connected with the employment.

Accident caused by another's misconduct etc.

101. An accident happening after 19th December 1961 shall be treated for the purposes of industrial injuries benefit, where it would not apart from this section be so treated, as arising out of an employed earner's employment if—
    (a) the accident arises in the course of the employment; and
    (b) the accident either is caused—
              (i) by another person's misconduct, skylarking or negligence, or
              (ii) by steps taken in consequence of any such misconduct, skylarking or negligence, or
              (iii) by the behaviour or presence of an animal (including a bird, fish or insect),

or is caused by or consists in the employed earner being struck by any object or by lightning; and

(c) the employed earner did not directly or indirectly induce or contribute to the happening of the accident by his conduct outside the employment or by any act not incidental to the employment.

DEFINITIONS

"industrial injuries benefit": s.122(1).
"employed earner": s.122(1).
"employed earner's employment": s.95(1).

GENERAL NOTE

This provision was first introduced in 1961 to reverse the effect of *R. v. National Insurance (Industrial Injuries) Commissioner,* ex p. *Richardson* [1958] 1 W.L.R. 851. In that case the Divisional Court had held that a bus conductor, who was the subject of what appeared to be an indiscriminate attack by a gang of youths, could not claim under the industrial injuries scheme as his position was no different from that of any other member of the public. The section effectively deems various accidents at work to be arising out of insured employment. There is no obvious common thread between the situations detailed in subs. (b).

There has been little reported case law on this provision. See, however, *R(I) 3/67* and the discussion in Lewis, pp. 86–88.

Sickness benefit

Sickness benefit in respect of industrial injury

102.—(1) In any case where—

(a) an employed earner is incapable of work as a result of a personal injury of a kind mentioned in section 94(1) above; and

(b) the contribution conditions are not satisfied in respect of him,

those conditions shall be taken to be satisfied for the purposes of paragraph (a) or, as the case may be, paragraph (b) of section 31(2) above.

(2) In the case of a person who—

(a) is entitled, by virtue of this section, to sickness benefit under subsection (2)(b) of section 31 above, and

(b) is not also entitled to sickness benefit under subsection (2)(c) of that section,

the weekly rate at which sickness benefit is payable shall be determined in accordance with regulations.

(3) In subsection (1) above "contribution conditions" means—

(a) in the case of a person who is under pensionable age, the contribution conditions specified for sickness benefit in Schedule 3, Part I, paragraph 2; and

(b) in the case of a person who has attained pensionable age but who is not for the time being entitled to a Category A or Category B retirement pension, the contribution conditions for a Category A retirement pension specified in Schedule 3, Part I, paragraph 5.

DEFINITIONS

"contribution conditions": subs. (3).
"employed earner": s.122(1).
"pensionable age": s.122(1).
"work": s.94(6).

GENERAL NOTE

This section was introduced as a result of the abolition of short-term industrial injury benefit in 1982. It deems industrial injury claimants to have satisfied the contribution conditions for sickness benefit. This protects the few industrial accident victims who would otherwise have failed to qualify for this incapacity benefit.

Disablement pension

Disablement pension

103.—(1) Subject to the provisions of this section, an employed earner shall be entitled to disablement pension if he suffers as the result of the relevant accident from loss of physical or mental faculty such that the assessed extent of the resulting disablement amounts to not less than 14 per cent. or, on a claim made before 1st October 1986, 20 per cent.

(2) In the determination of the extent of an employed earner's disablement for the purposes of this section there may be added to the percentage of the disablement resulting from the relevant accident the assessed percentage of any present disablement of his—

(a) which resulted from any other accident after 4th July 1948 arising out of and in the course of his employment, being employed earner's employment, and

(b) in respect of which a disablement gratuity was not paid to him after a final assessment of his disablement,

(as well as any percentage which may be so added in accordance with regulations under subsection (2) of section 109 below made by virtue of subsection (4)(b) of that section).

(3) Subject to subsection (4) below, where the assessment of disablement is a percentage between 20 and 100 which is not a multiple of 10, it shall be treated—

(a) if it is a multiple of 5, as being the next higher percentage which is a multiple of 10, and

(b) if it is not a multiple of 5, as being the nearest percentage which is a multiple of 10,

and where the assessment of disablement on a claim made on or after 1st October 1986 is less than 20 per cent., but not less than 14 per cent., it shall be treated as 20 per cent.

(4) Where subsection (2) above applies, subsection (3) above shall have effect in relation to the aggregate percentage and not in relation to any percentage forming part of the aggregate.

(5) In this Part of this Act "assessed", in relation to the extent of any disablement, means assessed in accordance with Schedule 6 to this Act; and for the purposes of that Schedule there shall be taken to be no relevant loss of faculty when the extent of the resulting disablement, if so assessed, would not amount to 1 per cent.

(6) A person shall not be entitled to a disablement pension until after the expiry of the period of 90 days (disregarding Sundays) beginning with the day of the relevant accident.

(7) Subject to subsection (8) below, where disablement pension is payable for a period, it shall be paid at the appropriate weekly rate specified in Schedule 4, Part V, paragraph 1.

(8) Where the period referred to in subsection (7) above is limited by reference to a definite date, the pension shall cease on the death of the beneficiary before that date.

DEFINITIONS

"assessed": subs. (6).
"beneficiary": s.122(1).
"employed earner": s.122(1).
"employed earner's employment": s.95(1).
"employment": s.122(1).
"loss of physical faculty": s.122(1).

GENERAL NOTE

Disablement pension, or disablement benefit as it is more commonly known, is now the most important feature of the industrial injuries scheme. There are three conditions of entitlement:

(1) the claimant must suffer from a loss of physical or mental faculty, as a result of one or more industrial accidents or prescribed diseases or injuries;

(2) the resultant disablement must be assessed as being at least 14 per cent. (except for pneumoconiosis, byssinosis and diffuse mesothelioma: see General Note to s.110);

(3) 90 days (excluding Sundays, *i.e.* 15 weeks) must have passed since the date of the accident or the onset of the prescribed disease or injury.

The claimant must of course also be an employed earner (so excluding the self-employed), but there is no need to establish any contribution conditions.

Condition (2) was introduced as from October 1, 1986 (subs. (1)). Before that date disablement benefit was paid in respect of any injury or disease where the level of disablement was assessed at one per cent. Under the old rules any assessment of less than 20 per cent. led to the payment of a lump sum disablement gratuity rather than a pension. Since 1986 assessments of between 14 and 19 per cent. have been paid at the 20 per cent. rate (subs. (3)). There is also an administrative practice of making assessments in steps of 10 per cent., so the special respiratory conditions mentioned above will attract a 10 per cent. award as a minimum (awards for mesothelioma, a fatal cancer, are customarily much higher). Guidance as to the assessment of disablement is contained in Sched. 6 (subs. (5)); see also the tariff in Sched. 2 to the Social Security (General Benefit) Regulations 1982 (S.I. 1982 No. 1408).

Historically, disablement benefit was capable of being supplemented by one or more of various special increases. Constant attendance allowance and exceptionally severe disablement allowance (ss.104 and 105) are still available, but unemployability supplement and hospital treatment allowance (s.106 and Sched. 7) were abolished as from April 6, 1987, except for existing claimants. Special hardship allowance, to compensate for lower earnings, was a supplement to disablement benefit until it was replaced in 1986 by reduced earnings allowance, a benefit in its own right. This latter benefit has itself since been abolished, with savings for those already entitled (s.106 and Sched. 7).

Increase where constant attendance needed

104.—(1) Where a disablement pension is payable in respect of an assessment of 100 per cent., then, if as the result of the relevant loss of faculty the beneficiary requires constant attendance, the weekly rate of the pension shall be increased by an amount, not exceeding the appropriate amount specified in Schedule 4, Part V, paragraph 2 determined in accordance with regulations by reference to the extent and nature of the attendance required by the beneficiary.

(2) An increase of pension under this section shall be payable for such period as may be determined at the time it is granted, but may be renewed from time to time.

(3) The Secretary of State may by regulations direct that any provision of sections 64 to 67 above shall have effect, with or without modifications, in relation to increases of pension under this section.

(4) In subsection (3) above, "modifications" includes additions and omissions.

DEFINITIONS
"beneficiary": s.122(1).
"modifications": subs. (4).

GENERAL NOTE
Constant attendance allowance is payable where a claimant is entitled to an ordinary industrial disablement pension based on a degree of disablement assessed at 100 per cent. and, because of the relevant loss of faculty, requires constant attendance. The criteria governing the different rates of constant attendance allowance are set out in the Social Security (General Benefit) Regulations 1982 (S.I. 1982 No. 1408), reg. 19. See further Lewis, pp. 159–161 and 250–251. Decisions on entitlement to constant attendance allowance are for the Secretary of State and not the independent statutory adjudicating authorities (Social Security (Adjudication) Regulations 1986 (S.I. 1986 No. 2218), reg. 19(1)(a)), so there is no right of appeal to a SSAT.

Increase for exceptionally severe disablement

105.—(1) Where a disablement pension is payable to a person—
(a) who is or, but for having received medical or other treatment as an

in-patient in a hospital or similar institution, would be entitled to an increase of the weekly rate of the pension under section 104 above, and the weekly rate of the increase exceeds the amount specified in Schedule 4, Part V, paragraph 2(a); and

(b) his need for constant attendance of an extent and nature qualifying him for such an increase at a weekly rate in excess of that amount is likely to be permanent,

the weekly rate of the pension shall, in addition to any increase under section 104 above, be further increased by the amount specified in Schedule 4, Part V, paragraph 3.

(2) An increase under this section shall be payable for such period as may be determined at the time it is granted, but may be renewed from time to time.

DEFINITIONS
"medical treatment": s.122(1).

GENERAL NOTE
Exceptionally severe disablement allowance is a further addition to disablement benefit payable to claimants who are entitled to the higher rate of constant attendance allowance (or would be if they were not in hospital) and whose need for such attendance is likely to be permanent. As with constant attendance allowance (s.104), decisions on entitlement are taken on behalf of the Secretary of State so there is no right of appeal.

Other benefits and increases

Benefits and increases subject to qualifications as to time

106. Schedule 7 to this Act shall have effect in relation—
(a) to unemployability supplement;
(b) to disablement gratuity;
(c) to increases of disablement pension during hospital treatment;
(d) to reduced earnings allowance;
(e) to retirement allowance; and
(f) to industrial death benefit,
for all of which the qualifications include special qualifications as to time.

GENERAL NOTE
This section introduces Sched. 7, which contains various savings provisions for benefits under the industrial injuries scheme which have been abolished in recent years for new claimants. The key dates for the benefits in question are as follows:
(a) unemployability supplement: April 6, 1987;
(b) disablement gratuity: October 1, 1986;
(c) increases to disablement pension during hospital treatment: April 6, 1987;
(d) reduced earnings allowance: October 1, 1990;
(e) retirement allowance: October 1, 1990;
(f) industrial death benefit: April 11, 1988.
On the consolidation of legislation relating to industrial death benefit, see the report of the Law Commissions (Cm 1726, 1991), para. 16.

Successive accidents

Adjustments for successive accidents

107.—(1) Where a person suffers two or more successive accidents arising out of and in the course of his employed earner's employment—
(a) he shall not for the same period be entitled (apart from any increase of benefit mentioned in subsection (2) below) to receive industrial injuries benefit by way of two or more disablement pensions at an aggregate weekly rate exceeding the appropriate amount specified in Schedule 4, Part V, paragraph 4; and

(b) regulations may provide for adjusting—
    (i) disablement benefit, or the conditions for the receipt of that benefit, in any case where he has received or may be entitled to a disablement gratuity;
    (ii) any increase of benefit mentioned in subsection (2) below, or the conditions for its receipt.

(2) The increases of benefit referred to in subsection (1) above are those under the following provisions of this Act—
    section 104,
    section 105,
    paragraph 2, 4 or 6 of Schedule 7.

DEFINITIONS
"employed earner": s.122(1).
"employed earner's employment": s.95(1).

GENERAL NOTE
As a general principle a claimant who has the misfortune to suffer from disablement caused by two successive accidents (or diseases) is entitled to an assessment based on the aggregate of the respective degrees of disablement. The aggregate amount cannot exceed the weekly amount payable in respect of 100 per cent. disablement (subs. (1)(a)). See also Security (General Benefit) Regulations 1982 (S.I. 1982 No. 1408), regs. 38 and 39.

Prescribed industrial diseases etc.

Benefit in respect of prescribed industrial diseases, etc.

108.—(1) Industrial injuries benefits shall, in respect of a person who has been in employed earner's employment, be payable in accordance with this section and sections 109 and 110 below in respect of—
(a) any prescribed disease, or
(b) any prescribed personal injury (other than an injury caused by accident arising out of and in the course of his employment),
which is a disease or injury due to the nature of that employment and which developed after 4th July 1948.

(2) A disease or injury may be prescribed in relation to any employed earners if the Secretary of State is satisfied that—
(a) it ought to be treated, having regard to its causes and incidence and any other relevant considerations, as a risk of their occupations and not as a risk common to all persons; and
(b) it is such that, in the absence of special circumstances, the attribution of particular cases to the nature of the employment can be established or presumed with reasonable certainty.

(3) Regulations prescribing any disease or injury for those purposes may provide that a person who developed the disease or injury on or at any time after a date specified in the regulations (being a date before the regulations came into force but not before 5th July 1948) shall be treated, subject to any prescribed modifications of this section or section 109 or 110 below, as if the regulations had been in force when he developed the disease or injury.

(4) Provision may be made by regulations for determining—
(a) the time at which a person is to be treated as having developed any prescribed disease or injury; and
(b) the circumstances in which such a disease or injury is, where the person in question has previously suffered from it, to be treated as having recrudesced or as having been contracted or received afresh.

(5) Notwithstanding any other provision of this Act, the power conferred by subsection (4)(a) above includes power to provide that the time at which a person shall be treated as having developed a prescribed disease or injury shall be the date on which he first makes a claim which results in the payment

of benefit by virtue of this section or section 110 below in respect of that disease or injury.

(6) Nothing in this section or in section 109 or 110 below affects the right of any person to benefit in respect of a disease which is a personal injury by accident within the meaning of this Part of this Act, except that a person shall not be entitled to benefit in respect of a disease as being an injury by accident arising out of and in the course of any employment if at the time of the accident the disease is in relation to him a prescribed disease by virtue of the occupation in which he is engaged in that employment.

DEFINITIONS
"benefit": s.122(1).
"employed earner": s.122(1).
"employed earner's employment": s.95(1).
"employment": s.122(1).
"industrial injuries benefit": s.122(1).
"prescribe": s.122(1).

GENERAL NOTE
The concept of a prescribed disease dates back to the Workmen's Compensation Act 1906. The system of prescribed diseases enables benefit to be paid to individuals who suffer from defined occupational hazards. As such, it provides a degree of flexibility which avoids the difficult problems of "accident" or "process" (see annotations to s.94). The list of currently prescribed diseases and injuries is contained in Sched. 1 to the Social Security (Industrial Injuries) (Prescribed Diseases) Regulations 1985 (S.I. 1985 No. 967).

The issue as to whether a particular condition should be prescribed for the purposes of the industrial injuries scheme is normally referred to the Industrial Injuries Advisory Council (IIAC), constituted under SSAA 1992 (s.171 and Sched. 6). IIAC has a specialist Research Working Group to examine such matters and to keep diseases as yet unprescribed under review. The traditionally cautious approach of IIAC in deciding whether the prescription test (subs. (2)) has been satisfied in the case of any given condition has been the subject of criticism (Lewis, pp. 92–7).

Special adjudication arrangements apply in cases of industrial disease: see SSAA 1992, s.62.

General provisions relating to benefit under section 108

109.—(1) Subject to the power to make different provision by regulations, and to the following provisions of this section and section 110 below—

(a) the benefit payable under section 108 above in respect of a prescribed disease or injury, and

(b) the conditions for receipt of benefit,

shall be the same as in the case of personal injury by accident arising out of and in the course of employment.

(2) In relation to prescribed diseases and injuries, regulations may provide—

(a) for modifying any provisions contained in this Act or the Administration Act which relate to disablement benefit or reduced earnings allowance or their administration; and

(b) for adapting references in this Act and that Act to accidents,

and for the purposes of this subsection the provisions of the Administration Act which relate to the administration of disablement benefit or reduced earnings allowance shall be taken to include section 1 and any provision which relates to the administration of both the benefit in question and other benefits.

(3) Without prejudice to the generality of subsection (2) above, regulations under that subsection may in particular include provision—

(a) for presuming any prescribed disease or injury—

(i) to be due, unless the contrary is proved, to the nature of a person's employment where he was employed in any prescribed occupation at the time when, or within a prescribed period or for a prescribed length of time (whether continuous or not) before, he developed the disease or injury,

　　(ii) not to be due to the nature of a person's employment unless he was employed in some prescribed occupation at the time when, or within a prescribed period or for a prescribed length of time (whether continuous or not) before, he developed the disease or injury;

(b) for such matters as appear to the Secretary of State to be incidental to or consequential on provisions included in the regulations by virtue of subsection (2) and paragraph (a) above.

(4) Regulations under subsection (2) above may also provide—

(a) that, in the determination of the extent of an employed earner's disablement resulting from a prescribed disease or injury, the appropriate percentage may be added to the percentage of that disablement; and

(b) that, in the determination of the extent of an employed earner's disablement for the purposes of section 103 above, the appropriate percentage may be added to the percentage of disablement resulting from the relevant accident.

(5) In subsection (4)(a) above "the appropriate percentage" means the assessed percentage of any present disablement of the earner which resulted—

(a) from any accident after 4th July 1948 arising out of and in the course of his employment, being employed earner's employment, or

(b) from any other prescribed disease or injury due to the nature of that employment and developed after 4th July 1948,

and in respect of which a disablement gratuity was not paid to him after a final assessment of his disablement.

(6) In subsection (4)(b) above "the appropriate percentage" means the assessed percentage of any present disablement of the earner—

(a) which resulted from any prescribed disease or injury due to the nature of his employment and developed after 4th July 1948, and

(b) in respect of which a disablement gratuity was not paid to him after a final assessment of his disablement.

(7) Where regulations under subsection (2) above—

(a) make provision such as is mentioned in subsection (4) above, and

(b) also make provision corresponding to that in section 103(3) above,

they may also make provision to the effect that those corresponding provisions shall have effect in relation to the aggregate percentage and not in relation to any percentage forming part of the aggregate.

DEFINITIONS
　　"the Administration Act": s.174.
　　"appropriate percentage": subss. (5) and (6).
　　"benefit": s.122(1).
　　"employed earner": s.122(1).
　　"employment": s.122(1).
　　"prescribe": s.122(1).

GENERAL NOTE
　　See further the Social Security (Industrial Injuries) (Prescribed Diseases) Regulations 1985 (S.I. 1985 No. 967).

Respiratory diseases

　　110.—(1) As respects pneumoconiosis, regulations may further provide that, where a person is found to be suffering from pneumoconiosis accompanied by tuberculosis, the effects of the tuberculosis shall be treated for the purposes of this section and sections 108 and 109 above as if they were effects of the pneumoconiosis.

(2) Subsection (1) above shall have effect as if after "tuberculosis" (in both places) there were inserted "emphysema or chronic bronchitis", but only in relation to a person the extent of whose disablement resulting from pneumoconiosis, or from pneumoconiosis accompanied by tuberculosis, would (if his physical condition were otherwise normal) be assessed at not less than 50 per cent.

(3) A person found to be suffering from pneumoconiosis shall be treated for the purposes of this Act as suffering from a loss of faculty such that the assessed extent of the resulting disablement amounts to not less than 1 per cent.

(4) In respect of byssinosis, a person shall not (unless regulations otherwise provide) be entitled to disablement benefit unless he is found to be suffering, as the result of byssinosis, from loss of faculty which is likely to be permanent.

DEFINITIONS
"pneumoconiosis": s.122(1).

GENERAL NOTE
This section makes special provision for certain respiratory diseases. Regulations made under subs. (1) enable the effects of tuberculosis to be taken into account where it accompanies pneumoconiosis (see Social Security (Industrial Injuries) (Prescribed Diseases) Regulations 1985 (S.I. 1985 No. 967), reg. 21). The same principle apples to emphysema or chronic bronchitis, provided that the assessment attributable to pneumoconiosis (with or without tuberculosis) is at least 50 per cent. (subs. (2) and reg. 22).

Some claimants with pneumoconiosis may also benefit from the rule in subs. (3) that where the condition is diagnosed there must be an assessment of at least one per cent. (This could occur where pneumoconiosis is diagnosed in the absence of any present respiratory disablement). The non-statutory administrative practice of making assessments in steps of 10 per cent. means that a pneumoconiosis sufferer is guaranteed an assessment of at least 10 per cent. Awards in respect of pneumoconiosis (which includes asbestosis: s.122(1)) are not subject to the 14 per cent. thréshold (reg. 20).

The qualification for byssinosis in subs. (4) has been disapplied by regulations (reg. 20(2)).

Old cases

Workmen's compensation etc.

111. Schedule 8 to this Act shall have effect—
(a) to continue workmen's compensation;
(b) to enable schemes—
    (i) to supplement workmen's compensation; and
    (ii) to provide for the payment of allowances or other benefits for industrial diseases in respect of employment before 5th July 1948; and
(c) to enable regulations to confer rights to other payments in respect of such employment.

DEFINITIONS
"employment": s.122(1).

GENERAL NOTE
This section, introducing Sched. 8, is a saving provision. Schedule 8 itself re-enacts the relevant sections of the Industrial Injuries (Old Cases) Act 1975 (which itself consolidated earlier legislation). The Schedule provides for benefits to be paid out of the National Insurance Fund in respect of accidents which happened as a result of (or diseases caused by) employment before July 5, 1948. Regulations have established two schemes to deal with such cases: the Workmen's Compensation (Supplementation) Scheme (S.I. 1982 No. 1489) and the Pneumoconiosis, Byssinosis and Miscellaneous Diseases Benefit Scheme (S.I. 1983 No. 136). On administrative arrangements, see SSAA 1992, s.185 and Sched. 9.

PART VI

MISCELLANEOUS PROVISIONS RELATING TO PARTS I TO V

Earnings

Certain sums to be earnings

112.—(1) Regulations may provide—
(a) that any employment protection entitlement shall be deemed for the purposes of Parts I to V of this Act to be earnings payable by and to such persons as are prescribed and to be so payable in respect of such periods as are prescribed; and
(b) that those periods shall, so far as they are not periods of employment, be deemed for those purposes to be periods of employment.

(2) In subsection (1) above "employment protection entitlement" means—
(a) any sum, or a prescribed part of any sum, mentioned in subsection (3) below; and
(b) prescribed amounts which the regulations provide are to be treated as related to any of those sums.

(3) The sums referred to in subsection (2) above are the following—
(a) a sum payable in respect of arrears of pay in pursuance of an order for reinstatement or re-engagement under the Employment Protection (Consolidation) Act 1978;
(b) a sum payable by way of pay in pursuance of an order under that Act for the continuation of a contract of employment;
(c) a sum payable by way of remuneration in pursuance of a protective award under the Employment Protection Act 1975.

DEFINITIONS
"earnings": s.122(1).
"employment": s.122(1).
"employment protection entitlement": subs. (2).
"prescribe": s.122(1).

GENERAL NOTE
See Social Security (Contributions) (Employment Protection) Regulations 1977 (S.I. 1977 No. 622).

Disqualification and suspension

General provisions as to disqualification and suspension

113.—(1) Except where regulations otherwise provide, a person shall be disqualified for receiving any benefit under Parts II to V of this Act, and an increase of such benefit shall not be payable in respect of any person as the beneficiary's wife or husband, for any period during which the person—
(a) is absent from Great Britain; or
(b) is undergoing imprisonment or detention in legal custody.

(2) Regulations may provide for suspending payment of such benefit to a person during any period in which he is undergoing medical or other treatment as an in-patient in a hospital or similar institution.

(3) Regulations may provide for a person who would be entitled to any such benefit but for the operation of any provision of this Act or the Administration Act to be treated as if entitled to it for the purposes of any rights or obligations (whether his own or another's) which depend on his entitlement, other than the right to payment of the benefit.

DEFINITIONS
"the Administration Act": s.174.

"beneficiary": s.122(1).
"benefit": s.122(1).
"entitled": s.122(1).
"Great Britain": s.172.
"medical treatment": s.122(1).

GENERAL NOTE
This section provides the authority for the disqualification or suspension of claimants from receiving benefit under Pts. II to V in the specified instances.

Subs. (1)
Is absent from Great Britain. The test for absence is simply whether the person is "not physically present" in England, Scotland or Wales (*R(U) 16/62*). Presence at any time in the past is not necessary. This basic principle as to disqualification is subject to the Social Security Benefit (Persons Abroad) Regulations 1975 (S.I. 1975 No. 563), on which see *R*. v. *Social Security Commissioner,* ex p. *Akbar* [1992] C.O.D. 245. The position is also complicated by the existence of a considerable body of European Community law and of a large number of reciprocal conventions (see Bonner).
Is undergoing imprisonment or detention in legal custody. The imprisonment must be imposed by a court exercising criminal jurisdiction (*R(S) 8/79*), so imprisonment for non-payment of maintenance does not of itself disqualify a claimant from receiving benefit. Further provision, including certain exceptions, is made in the Social Security (General Benefit) Regulations 1982 (S.I. 1982 No. 1408), regs. 2 and 3.

Persons maintaining dependants etc.

Persons maintaining dependants, etc.

114.—(1) Regulations may provide for determining the circumstances in which a person is or is not to be taken, for the purposes of Parts II to V of this Act—
  (a) to be wholly or mainly, or to a substantial extent, maintaining, or to be contributing at any weekly rate to the maintenance of, another person; or
  (b) to be, or have been, contributing at any weekly rate to the cost of providing for a child.

(2) Regulations under this section may provide, for the purposes of the provisions relating to an increase of benefit under Parts II to V of this Act in respect of a wife or other adult dependant, that where—
  (a) a person is partly maintained by each of two or more beneficiaries, each of whom would be entitled to such an increase in respect of that person if he were wholly or mainly maintaining that person, and
  (b) the contributions made by those two or more beneficiaries towards the maintenance of that person amount in the aggregate to sums which would, if they had been contributed by one of those beneficiaries, have been sufficient to satisfy the requirements of regulations under this section,
that person shall be taken to be wholly or mainly maintained by such of those beneficiaries as may be prescribed.

(3) Regulations may provide for any such sum or sums paid by a person by way of contribution towards either or both of the following, that is to say—
  (a) the maintenance of his or her spouse, and
  (b) the cost of providing for one or more children,
to be treated for the purposes of any of the provisions of this Act specified in subsection (4) below as such contributions, of such respective amounts equal in the aggregate to the said sum or sums, in respect of such persons, as may be determined in accordance with the regulations so as to secure as large a payment as possible by way of benefit in respect of the dependants.

(4) The provisions in question are sections 56, 81 to 84, 86 and paragraphs 5 and 6 of Schedule 7 to this Act.

DEFINITIONS
  "beneficiary": s.122(1).
  "benefit": s.122(1).
  "child": s.122(1).
  "prescribe": s.122(1).

GENERAL NOTE
  See Social Security Benefit (Dependency) Regulations 1977 (S.I. 1977 No. 343).

Special cases

Crown employment—Parts I to VI

115.—(1) Subject to the provisions of this section, Parts I to V and this Part of this Act apply to persons employed by or under the Crown in like manner as if they were employed by a private person.

(2) Subsection (1) above does not apply to persons serving as members of Her Majesty's forces in their capacity as such.

(3) Employment as a member of Her Majesty's forces and any other prescribed employment under the Crown are not, and are not to be treated as, employed earner's employment for any of the purposes of Part V of this Act.

(4) The references to Parts I to V of this Act in this section and sections 116, 117, 119, 120 and 121 below do not include references to section 111 above.

DEFINITIONS
  "employed earner": s.122(1).
  "employed earner's employment": s.95(1).
  "employment": s.122(1).
  "prescribe": s.122(1).

GENERAL NOTE
  Crown employees are in principle in the same position as ordinary employees so far as the National Insurance scheme is concerned, but there are special rules governing members of HM forces (see s.116).

Her Majesty's forces

116.—(1) Subject to section 115(2) and (3) above and to this section, a person who is serving as a member of Her Majesty's forces shall, while he is so serving, be treated as an employed earner, in respect of his membership of those forces, for the purposes—

(a) of Parts I to V and this Part of this Act; and

(b) of any provision of the Administration Act in its application to him as an employed earner.

(2) The Secretary of State may make regulations modifying Parts I to V and this Part of this Act, and any provision of Part II of the Administration Act which replaces provisions of Part III of the 1975 Act, in such manner as he thinks proper, in their application to persons who are or have been members of Her Majesty's forces; and regulations under this section may in particular provide—

(a) in the case of persons who are employed earners in respect of their membership of those forces, for reducing the rate of the contributions payable in respect of their employment and for determining—

(i) the amounts payable on account of those contributions by the Secretary of State and the time and manner of payment, and

(ii) the deductions (if any) to be made on account of those contributions from the pay of those persons;

(b) for preventing a person who is discharged from Her Majesty's forces at his own request from being thereby disqualified for receiving unemployment benefit on the ground that he has voluntarily left his employment without just cause.

(3) For the purposes of Parts I to V and this Part of this Act, Her Majesty's forces shall be taken to consist of such establishments and organisations as may be prescribed, being establishments and organisations in which persons serve under the control of the Defence Council.

DEFINITIONS
"the Administration Act": s.174.
"employed earner": s.122(1).
"Her Majesty's forces": subs. (3).

GENERAL NOTE
See, *e.g.* Social Security (Benefit) (Members of the Forces) Regulations 1975 (S.I. 1975 No. 493) and Social Security (Contributions) Regulations 1979 (S.I. 1979 No. 591), Pt. VIII, Case E.

Mariners, airmen, etc.

117.—(1) The Secretary of State may make regulations modifying provisions of Parts I to V and this Part of this Act, and any provision of Part II of the Administration Act which replaces provisions of Part III of the 1975 Act, in such manner as he thinks proper, in their application to persons who are or have been, or are to be, employed on board any ship, vessel, hovercraft or aircraft.

(2) Regulations under subsection (1) above may in particular provide—

(a) for any such provision to apply to such persons, notwithstanding that it would not otherwise apply;

(b) for excepting such persons from the application of any such provision where they neither are domiciled nor have a place of residence in any part of Great Britain;

(c) for requiring the payment of secondary Class 1 contributions in respect of such persons, whether or not they are (within the meaning of Part I of this Act) employed earners;

(d) for the taking of evidence, for the purposes of any claim to benefit, in a country or territory outside Great Britain, by a British consular official or such other person as may be prescribed;

(e) for enabling persons who are or have been so employed to authorise the payment of the whole or any part of any benefit to which they are or may become entitled to such of their dependants as may be prescribed.

DEFINITIONS
"the 1975 Act": s.174.
"the Administration Act": s.174.
"employed earner": s.122(1).
"entitled": s.122(1).
"Great Britain": s.172.
"prescribe": s.122(1).

GENERAL NOTE
See, *e.g.* Social Security (Airmen's Benefits) Regulations 1975 (S.I. 1975 No. 494), Social Security (Mariners' Benefits) Regulations 1975 (S.I. 1975 No. 529) and Social Security (Contributions) Regulations 1979 (S.I. 1979 No. 591), Pt. VIII, Cases A and C.

Married women and widows

118. The Secretary of State may make regulations modifying any of the following provisions of this Act, namely—

(a) Part I;

(b) Part II (except section 60); and

(c) Parts III and IV,

in such manner as he thinks proper, in their application to women who are or have been married.

GENERAL NOTE
Historically, married women have been subject to differential treatment under the social security system. Until April 1977 married women and widows could elect to pay National Insurance contributions at a reduced rate (with lesser entitlements). Such an election may be revoked, but, once lost, the right to pay reduced contributions cannot be reclaimed. The details are set out in the Social Security (Contributions) Regulations 1979 (S.I. 1979 No. 591), Pt. VIII, Case D (on which see Williams). The impact of European Community law has narrowed the range of situations in which differential treatment is still permissible.

Persons outside Great Britain

119. The Secretary of State may make regulations modifying Parts I to V of this Act, and any provision of Part II of the Administration Act which replaces provisions of Part III of the 1975 Act, in such manner as he thinks proper, in their application to persons who are or have been outside Great Britain at any prescribed time or in any prescribed circumstances.

DEFINITIONS
"the 1975 Act": s.174.
"the Administration Act": s.174.
"Great Britain": s.172.
"prescribe": s.122(1).

GENERAL NOTE
See, *e.g.* Social Security Benefit (Persons Abroad) Regulations 1975 (S.I. 1975 No. 563) and Social Security (Contributions) Regulations 1979 (S.I. 1979 No. 591), Pt. VIII, Case F.

Employment at sea (continental shelf operations)

120.—(1) The Secretary of State may make regulations modifying Parts I to V and this Part of this Act, and any provision of Part II of the Administration Act which replaces provisions of Part III of the 1975 Act, in such manner as he thinks proper, in their application to persons in any prescribed employment (whether under a contract of service or not) in connection with continental shelf operations.

(2) "Continental shelf operations" means any activities which, if paragraphs (a) and (d) of subsection (6) of section 23 of the Oil and Gas (Enterprise) Act 1982 (application of civil law to certain offshore activities) were omitted, would nevertheless fall within subsection (2) of that section.

(3) In particular (but without prejudice to the generality of subsection (1) above), the regulations may provide for any prescribed provision of Parts I to V and this Part of this Act to apply to any such person notwithstanding that he does not fall within the description of an employed or self-employed earner, or does not fulfil the conditions prescribed under section 1(6) above as to residence or presence in Great Britain.

DEFINITIONS
"the 1975 Act": s.174.
"the Administration Act": s.174.
"continental shelf operations": subs. (2).
"contract of service": s.122(1).
"employed earner": s.122(1).
"employment ": s.122(1).
"prescribe": s.122(1).
"self-employed earner": s.122(1).

GENERAL NOTE
See, *e.g.* Social Security Benefit (Persons Abroad) Regulations 1975 (S.I. 1975 No. 563) and Social Security (Contributions) Regulations 1979 (S.I. 1979 No. 591), Pt. VIII, Case B.

Treatment of certain marriages

121.—(1) Regulations may provide—

(a) for a voidable marriage which has been annulled, whether before or after the date when the regulations come into force, to be treated for the purposes of the provisions to which this subsection applies as if it had been a valid marriage which was terminated by divorce at the date of annulment;

(b) as to the circumstances in which, for the purposes of the enactments to which this section applies—

　　(i) a marriage celebrated under a law which permits polygamy; or

　　(ii) any marriage during the subsistence of which a party to it is at any time married to more than one person.

is to be treated as having, or not having, the consequences of a marriage celebrated under a law which does not permit polygamy.

(2) Subsection (1) above applies—

(a) to any enactment contained in Parts I to V or this Part of this Act; and

(b) to regulations under any such enactment.

GENERAL NOTE
See Ogus and Barendt, pp. 351–3.

Interpretation

Interpretation of Parts I to VI and supplementary provisions

122.—(1) In Parts I to V above and this Part of this Act, unless the context otherwise requires—

"beneficiary", in relation to any benefit, means the person entitled to that benefit;

"benefit" means—

　　(a) benefit under Parts II to V of this Act other than Old Cases payments;

　　(b) as respects any period before 1st July 1992 but not before 6th April 1975, benefit under Part II of the 1975 Act; or

　　(c) as respects any period before 6th April 1975, benefit under—

　　　(i) the National Insurance Act 1946 or 1965; or

　　　(ii) the National Insurance (Industrial Injuries) Act 1946 or 1965;

"child" means a person under the age of 19 who would be treated as a child for the purposes of Part IX of this Act or such other person under that age as may be prescribed;

"claim" is to be construed in accordance with "claimant";

"claimant", in relation to benefit other than industrial injuries benefit, means a person who has claimed benefit;

"claimant", in relation to industrial injuries benefit, means a person who has claimed industrial injuries benefit;

"contract of service" means any contract of service or apprenticeship whether written or oral and whether express or implied;

"current", in relation to the lower and upper earnings limits under section 5(1) above, means for the time being in force;

"day of incapacity for work" and "day of interruption of employment" have the meanings assigned to them by section 57 above;

"deferred" and "period of deferment" have the meanings assigned to them by section 55 above;

"earner" and "earnings" are to be construed in accordance with sections 3, 4 and 112 above;

"employed earner" has the meaning assigned to it by section 2 above;

"employment" includes any trade, business, profession, office or vocation and "employed" has a corresponding meaning;

"entitled", in relation to any benefit, is to be construed in accordance with—

(a) the provisions specifically relating to that benefit;

(b) in the case of a benefit specified in section 20(1) above, section 21 above; and

(c) sections 1 to 3 and 68 of the Administration Act;

"industrial injuries benefit" means benefit under Part V of this Act, other than under Schedule 8;

"initial primary percentage" is to be construed in accordance with section 8(1) and (2) above and as referring to the percentage rate from time to time specified in section 8(2)(a) above as the initial primary percentage;

"the Inland Revenue" means the Commissioners of Inland Revenue;

"late husband", in relation to a woman who has been more than once married, means her last husband;

"long-term benefit" has the meaning assigned to it by section 20(2) above;

"loss of physical faculty" includes disfigurement whether or not accompanied by any loss of physical faculty;

"lower earnings limit" and "upper earnings limit" are to be construed in accordance with section 5(1) above and references to the lower or upper earnings limit of a tax year are to whatever is (or was) for that year the limit in force under that subsection;

"main primary percentage" is to be construed in accordance with section 8(1) and (2) above and as referring to the percentage rate from time to time specified in section 8(2)(b) above as the main primary percentage;

"medical examination" includes bacteriological and radiographical tests and similar investigations, and "medically examined" has a corresponding meaning;

"medical treatment" means medical, surgical or rehabilitative treatment (including any course or diet or other regimen), and references to a person receiving or submitting himself to medical treatment are to be construed accordingly;

"the Northern Ireland Department" means the Department of Health and Social Services for Northern Ireland;

"Old Cases payments" means payments under Part I or II of Schedule 8 to this Act;

"payments by way of occupational or personal pension" means, in relation to a person, periodical payments which, in connection with the coming to an end of an employment of his, fall to be made to him—

(a) out of money provided wholly or partly by the employer or under arrangements made by the employer; or

(b) out of money provided under an enactment or instrument having the force of law in any part of the United Kingdom or elsewhere; or

(c) under a personal pension scheme as defined in section 84(1) of the 1986 Act; or

(d) under a contract or trust scheme approved under Chapter III of Part XIV of the Income and Corporation Taxes Act 1988; or

(e) under a personal pension scheme approved under Chapter IV of that Part of that Act,

and such other payments as are prescribed;

"pensionable age" means—

(a) the age of 65, in the case of a man; and

(b) the age of 60, in the case of a woman;

"pneumoconiosis" means fibrosis of the lungs due to silica dust, asbestos dust, or other dust, and includes the condition of the lungs known as dust-reticulation;

"prescribe" means prescribe by regulations;

"primary percentage" is to be construed in accordance with section 8(1) and (2) above;

"qualifying earnings factor" means an earnings factor equal to the lower earnings limit for the tax year in question multiplied by 52;

"relative" includes a person who is a relative by marriage;

"relevant accident" means the accident in respect of which industrial injuries benefit is claimed or payable;

"relevant injury" means the injury in respect of which industrial injuries benefit is claimed or payable;

"relevant loss of faculty" means—

(a) in relation to severe disablement allowance, the loss of faculty which results in the disablement; or

(b) in relation to industrial injuries benefit, the loss of faculty resulting from the relevant injury;

"self-employed earner" has the meaning assigned to it by section 2 above;

"short-term benefit" has the meaning assigned to it by section 20(2) above;

"tax week" means one of the successive periods in a tax year beginning with the first day of that year and every seventh day thereafter, the last day of a tax year (or, in the case of a tax year ending in a leap year, the last two days) to be treated accordingly as a separate tax week;

"tax year" means the 12 months beginning with 6th April in any year, the expression "1978–79" meaning the tax year beginning with 6th April 1978, and any correspondingly framed reference to a pair of successive years being construed as a reference to the tax year beginning with 6th April in the earlier of them;

"trade or business" includes, in relation to a public or local authority, the exercise and performance of the powers and duties of that authority;

"trade union" means an association of employed earners;

"week", except in relation to disability working allowance, means a period of seven days beginning with Sunday.

(2) Regulations may make provision modifying the meaning of "employment" for the purposes of any provision of Parts I to V and this Part of this Act.

(3) Provision may be made by regulations as to the circumstances in which a person is to be treated as residing or not residing with another person for any of the purposes of Parts I to V and this Part of this Act and as to the circumstances in which persons are to be treated for any of those purposes as residing or not residing together.

(4) A person who is residing with his spouse shall be treated for the purposes of Parts I to V and this Part of this Act as entitled to any child benefit to which his spouse is entitled.

(5) Regulations may, for the purposes of any provision of those Parts under which the right to any benefit or increase of benefit depends on a person being or having been entitled to child benefit, make provision whereby a person is to be treated as if he were or had been so entitled or as if he were not or had not been so entitled.

(6) For the purposes of Parts I to V and this Part of this Act a person is "permanently incapable of self-support" if (but only if) he is incapable of

supporting himself by reason of physical or mental infirmity and is likely to remain so incapable for the remainder of his life.

DEFINITIONS
"the 1975 Act": s.174.
"the 1986 Act": s.174.
"the Administration Act": s.174.
"permanently incapable of self-support": subs. (6).

GENERAL NOTE

Subs. (6)
Permanently incapable of self-support. This term appears to be relevant solely in the context of industrial death benefit, which itself is only payable in respect of deaths before April 11, 1988 (see s.106). See, for example, Sched. 7, Pt. VI, paras. 16(2)(c) and 17(1)(b).

PART VII

INCOME-RELATED BENEFITS

General

Income-related benefits

123.—(1) Prescribed schemes shall provide for the following benefits (in this Act referred to as "income-related benefits")—

(a) income support;
(b) family credit;
(c) disability working allowance;
(d) housing benefit; and
(e) community charge benefits.

(2) The Secretary of State shall make copies of schemes prescribed under subsection (1)(a), (b) or (c) above available for public inspection at local offices of the Department of Social Security at all reasonable hours without payment.

(3) Every authority granting housing benefit—

(a) shall take such steps as appear to them appropriate for the purposes of securing that persons who may be entitled to housing benefit from the authority become aware that they may be entitled to it; and
(b) shall make copies of the housing benefit scheme, with any modifications adopted by them under the Administration Act, available for public inspection at their principal office at all reasonable hours without payment.

(4) Each charging authority shall take such steps as appear to it appropriate for the purpose of securing that any person who may be entitled to a community charge benefit as regards a personal or collective community charge of the authority becomes aware that he may be entitled to it.

(5) Each levying authority shall take such steps as appear to it appropriate for the purpose of securing that any person who may be entitled to a community charge benefit in respect of a personal community charge payable to the authority becomes aware that he may be entitled to it.

(6) Each charging authority and each levying authority shall make copies of the community charge benefits scheme, with any modifications adopted by it under the Administration Act, available for public inspection at its principal office at all reasonable hours without payment.

DEFINITIONS
"the Administration Act": s.174.
"charging authority": s.137(1).
"income-related benefits": subs. (1).

"levying authority": s.137(1).
"prescribes": s.137(1).

<small>GENERAL NOTE</small>
   This section sets out the income-related or means-tested benefits (subs. (1)). It also imposes a duty on the Secretary of State to make available for inspection copies of the rules relating to the income support, family credit and disability working allowance schemes at DSS local offices. Such a facility must be available at all reasonable hours and free of charge (subs. (2)). An analogous duty is imposed on the relevant local government bodies in respect of the housing benefit and community charge benefit schemes (subss. (3)(b) and (6)). The local authorities are also under an obligation to take such steps as appear to them appropriate for the purpose of securing that persons who may be entitled to housing benefit or community charge benefit become aware that they are so entitled (subss. (3)(a), (4) and (5)). No parallel duty is imposed on the Secretary of State to publicise the principal schemes listed in subs. (1)(a)–(c).

Income support

Income support

   124.—(1) A person in Great Britain is entitled to income support if—
   (a) he is of or over the age of 18 or, in prescribed circumstances and for a prescribed period, of or over the age of 16 or he is a person to whom section 125(1) below applies;
   (b) he has no income or his income does not exceed the applicable amount;
   (c) he is not engaged in remunerative work and, if he is a member of a married or unmarried couple, the other member is not so engaged; and
   (d) except in such circumstances as may be prescribed—
      (i) he is available for, and actively seeking, employment;
      (ii) he is not receiving relevant education.
   (2) In subsection (1)(a) above "period" includes—
   (a) a period of a determinate length;
   (b) a period defined by reference to the happening of a future event; and
   (c) a period of a determinate length but subject to earlier determination upon the happening of a future event.
   (3) Circumstances may be prescribed in which a person must not only satisfy the condition specified in subsection (1)(d)(i) above but also be registered in the prescribed manner for employment.
   (4) Subject to subsection (5) below, where a person is entitled to income support, then—
   (a) if he has no income, the amount shall be the applicable amount; and
   (b) if he has income, the amount shall be the difference between his income and the applicable amount.
   (5) Where a person is entitled to income support for a period to which this subsection applies, the amount payable for that period shall be calculated in such manner as may be prescribed.
   (6) Subsection (5) above applies—
   (a) to a period of less than a week which is the whole period for which income support is payable; and
   (b) to any other period of less than a week for which it is payable.

<small>DEFINITIONS</small>
   "Great Britain": s.172.
   "married couple": s.137(1).
   "period": subs. (2).
   "prescribed": s.137(1).
   "unmarried couple": s.137(1).

GENERAL NOTE

This section establishes the framework for entitlement to income support. The basic conditions are laid down in subs. (1) and amplified by the Income Support (General) Regulations 1987 (S.I. 1987 No. 1967). See further Mesher.

As a general rule income support is only payable to persons who have reached the age of 18. Some 16- and 17-year-olds may qualify for benefit by either of two routes. Some may be eligible by virtue of falling into one of the categories prescribed under subs. (1)(a), while others may be awarded benefit on the basis that otherwise they will suffer severe hardship (s.125). Decisions in the first category are made by adjudication officers (with a right of appeal to a SSAT) while decisions under s.125 are made by the Secretary of State (with no right of appeal).

Subsection (1)(b) sets out the income means-test (see further subs. (4)). There is also a capital limit (currently £8,000) laid down in regulations under s.134(1). In addition, claimants (or their partners) must not be engaged in remunerative work (defined as 16 hours a week or more from April 7, 1992: Income Support (General) Amendment No. 4 Regulations 1991 (S.I. 1991 No. 1559)). Unless excepted by regulations, they must also be available for and actively seeking employment and not receiving relevant education. See further Mesher.

The rate of income support is calculated in accordance with the appropriate applicable amount. Where the claimant has no income, the applicable amount is paid. Where the claimant has some income, this is set against the applicable amount and the balance represents the benefit payable (subs. (5)). Subsections (5) and (6) enable regulations to deal with entitlement to income support for part weeks.

The interrelationship between income support and maintenance is dealt with by SSAA 1992, Pt. V (ss.105–109).

Severe hardship cases

125.—(1) If it appears to the Secretary of State—

(a) that a person of or over the age of 16 but under the age of 18 is not entitled to income support; and

(b) that severe hardship will result to that person unless income support is paid to him,

the Secretary of State may direct that this subsection shall apply to him.

(2) Any such direction may specify a period for which subsection (1) above is to apply to the person to whom the direction relates.

(3) The person to whom such a direction relates shall be treated in accordance with it, but if at any time it appears to the Secretary of State that there has been a change of circumstances as a result of which failure to receive income support need no longer result in severe hardship to him, he may revoke the direction.

(4) The Secretary of State may also revoke the direction if—

(a) he is satisfied that it was given in ignorance of some material fact or was based on a mistake as to some material fact; and

(b) he considers that but for his ignorance or mistake he would not have determined that failure to receive income support would result in severe hardship.

(5) In this section "period" includes—

(a) a period of a determinate length;

(b) a period defined by reference to the happening of a future event; and

(c) a period of a determinate length but subject to earlier determination upon the happening of a future event.

DEFINITIONS

"period": subs. (5).

GENERAL NOTE

As a general rule entitlement to income support does not arise until a person attains the age of 18 (s.124(1)(a)). This section, however, enables some 16- and 17-year-olds to qualify for benefit. This is only possible where both (i) the individual in question does not fall into one of the special categories of 16- and 17-year-olds prescribed in regulations under s.124(1)(a) and (ii) severe hardship will result unless income support is paid. Decisions on awards of benefit under this section are made in the name of the Secretary of State, rather than by an adjudication officer. There is therefore no right of appeal to a SSAT. Even if both subs. (1)(a) and (b) are satisfied, the Secretary of State retains a discretion as to whether to make an award. Awards may be for a fixed period or until the happening of some future event and may be revoked if there is a change in circumstances (subss. (2)–(5)).

Trade disputes

126.—(1) This section applies to a person, other than a child or a person of a prescribed description—

(a) who is disqualified under section 27 above for receiving unemployment benefit; or

(b) who would be so disqualified if otherwise entitled to that benefit,

except during any period shown by the person to be a period of incapacity for work by reason of disease or bodily or mental disablement or to be within the maternity period.

(2) In subsection (1) above "the maternity period" means the period commencing at the beginning of the 6th week before the expected week of confinement and ending at the end of the 7th week after the week in which confinement takes place.

(3) For the purpose of calculating income support—

(a) so long as this section applies to a person who is not a member of a family, the applicable amount shall be disregarded;

(b) so long as it applies to a person who is a member of a family but is not a member of a married or unmarried couple, the portion of the applicable amount which is included in respect of him shall be disregarded;

(c) so long as it applies to one of the members of a married or unmarried couple—

(i) if the applicable amount consists only of an amount in respect of them, it shall be reduced to one half; and

(ii) if it includes other amounts, the portion of it which is included in respect of them shall be reduced to one-half and any further portion of it which is included in respect of the member of the couple to whom this section applies shall be disregarded;

(d) so long as it applies to both the members of a married or unmarried couple—

(i) if neither of them is responsible for a child or person of a prescribed description who is a member of the same household, the applicable amount shall be disregarded; and

(ii) in any other case, the portion of the applicable amount which is included in respect of them and any further portion of it which is included in respect of either of them shall be disregarded.

(4) Where a reduction under subsection (3)(c) above would not produce a sum which is a multiple of 5p, the reduction shall be to the nearest lower sum which is such a multiple.

(5) Where this section applies to a person for any period, then, except so far as regulations provide otherwise—

(a) in calculating the entitlement to income support of that person or a member of his family the following shall be treated as his income and shall not be disregarded—

(i) any payment which he or a member of his family receives or is entitled to obtain by reason of the person to whom this section applies being without employment for that period; and

(ii) without prejudice to the generality of sub-paragraph (i) above, any amount which becomes or would on an application duly made become available to him in that period by way of repayment of income tax deducted from his emoluments in pursuance of section 203 of the Income and Corporation Taxes Act 1988 (PAYE); and

(b) any payment by way of income support for that period or any part of it which apart from this paragraph would be made to him, or to a person whose applicable amount is aggregated with his—

(i) shall not be made if the weekly rate of payment is equal to or less than the relevant sum; or

(ii) if it is more than the relevant sum, shall be at a weekly rate equal to the difference.

(6) In respect of any period less than a week, subsection (5) above shall have effect subject to such modifications as may be prescribed.

(7) Subject to subsection (8) below, "the relevant sum" for the purposes of subsection (5) above shall be £22.50.

(8) If an order under section 150 of the Administration Act (annual up-rating) has the effect of increasing payments of income support, from the time when the order comes into force there shall be substituted, in subsection (5)(b) above, for the references to the sum for the time being mentioned in it references to a sum arrived at by—

(a) increasing that sum by the percentage by which the personal allowance under paragraph 1(1) of Part I of Schedule 2 to the Income Support (General) Regulations 1987 for a single person aged not less than 25 has been increased by the order; and

(b) if the sum as so increased is not a multiple of 50p, disregarding the remainder if it is 25p and, if it is not, rounding it up or down to the nearest 50p,

and the order shall state the substituted sum.

DEFINITIONS
"the Administration Act": s.174.
"child": s.137(1).
"family": s.137(1).
"married couple": s.137(1).
"maternity period": subs. (2).
"prescribed": s.137(1).
"relevant sum": subs. (7).
"unmarried couple": s.137(1).

GENERAL NOTE
  This section lays down the rules relating to income support where the claimant is disqualified for unemployment benefit under s.27 (or would be so disqualified if otherwise entitled) by reason of involvement in a trade dispute. The section only comes into play once the s.27 question has been determined. The income support trade dispute rule does not apply if the claimant is incapable of work or within the maternity period (proviso to subs. (1)).
  The two principal modifications to income support entitlement where this section applies relate to the calculation of the relevant applicable amount (subs. (3)) and to the assessment of the claimant's income (subs. (5)). In particular, the applicable amounts to which claimants are entitled are much reduced. Furthermore, claimants caught by the operation of this rule are assumed to receive the "relevant sum" by way of strike pay, irrespective of whether the person is on strike (as opposed to locked-out or laid off), is a member of a union or whether their union offers strike pay. For 1992/93 the "relevant sum" is £22.50 per week. See further Mesher.

Effect of return to work

127. If a person returns to work with the same employer after a period during which section 126 above applies to him, and whether or not his return is before the end of any stoppage of work in relation to which he is or would be disqualified for receiving unemployment benefit—

(a) that section shall cease to apply to him at the commencement of the day on which he returns to work; and

(b) until the end of the period of 15 days beginning with that day, section 124(1) above shall have effect in relation to him as if the following paragraph were substituted for paragraph (c)—

"(c) in the case of a member of a married or unmarried couple; the other member is not engaged in remunerative work; and"; and

(c) any sum paid by way of income support for that period of 15 days to him or, where he is a member of a married or unmarried couple, to the other member of that couple, shall be recoverable in accordance with the regulations from the person to whom it was paid or from any prescribed person or, where the person to whom it was paid is a member of a married or unmarried couple, from the other member of the couple.

DEFINITIONS
"married couple": s.137(1).
"prescribed": s.137(1).
"unmarried couple": s.137(1).

GENERAL NOTE
This section enables income support to be paid for the first 15 days following a return to work after a trade dispute. In such cases benefit would otherwise be precluded by virtue of s.124(1)(c).

Family credit

Family credit

128.—(1) Subject to regulations under section 5(1)(a) of the Administration Act, a person in Great Britain is entitled to family credit if, when the claim for it is made or is treated as made—
(a) his income—
(i) does not exceed the amount which is the applicable amount at such date as may be prescribed; or
(ii) exceeds it, but only by such an amount that there is an amount remaining if the deduction for which subsection (2)(b) below provides is made;
(b) he or, if he is a member of a married or unmarried couple, he or the other member of the couple, is engaged and normally engaged in remunerative work;
(c) except in such circumstances as may be prescribed, neither he nor any member of his family is entitled to a disability working allowance; and
(d) he or, if he is a member of a married or unmarried couple, he or the other member, is responsible for a member of the same household who is a child or a person of a prescribed description.
(2) Where a person is entitled to family credit, then—
(a) if his income does not exceed the amount which is the applicable amount at the date prescribed under subsection (1)(a)(i) above, the amount of the family credit shall be the amount which is the appropriate maximum family credit in his case; and
(b) if his income exceeds the amount which is the applicable amount at that date, the amount of the family credit shall be what remains after the deduction from the appropriate maximum family credit of a prescribed percentage of the excess of his income over the applicable amount.
(3) Family credit shall be payable for a period of 26 weeks or such other period as may be prescribed and, subject to regulations, an award of family credit and the rate at which it is payable shall not be affected by any change of circumstances during that period or by any order under section 150 of the Administration Act.
(4) Regulations may provide that an award of family credit shall terminate—
(a) if a person who was a member of the family at the date of the claim becomes a member of another family and some member of that family is entitled to family credit; or
(b) if income support or a disability working allowance becomes payable

in respect of a person who was a member of the family at the date of the claim for family credit.

(5) Regulations shall prescribe the manner in which the appropriate maximum family credit is to be determined in any case.

(6) The provisions of this Act relating to family credit apply in relation to persons employed by or under the Crown as they apply in relation to persons employed otherwise than by or under the Crown.

DEFINITIONS
"the Administration Act": s.174.
"child": s.137(1).
"family": s.137(1).
"Great Britain": s.172.
"married couple": s.137(1).
"prescribed": s.137(1).
"unmarried couple": s.137(1).

GENERAL NOTE
This section establishes the framework for entitlement to family credit. The basic conditions are laid down in subs. (1) and amplified by the Family Credit (General) Regulations 1987 (S.I. 1987 No. 1973). See further Mesher.

Family credit is payable to single claimants or couples who are responsible for a child or children (subs. (1)(d)). Claimants (or their partners) must also be engaged and normally engaged in remunerative work (the threshold for which is 16 hours per week from April 7, 1992: Family Credit (General) Amendment Regulations 1991 (S.I. 1991 No. 1520)).

As with the other income-related benefits, determination of the rate of benefit in any given case depends on the relationship between the claimant's income and his or her applicable amount. Maximum family credit is payable where the claimant's income (as aggregated with the rest of his or her family) does not exceed the relevant applicable amount (subs. (1)(a)(i) and (2)(a)). Where income exceeds the applicable amount, the maximum family credit payable is reduced by a percentage of the excess (currently 70 per cent.) (subss. (1)(a)(ii) and (2)(b)). There is also a capital limit (at present £8,000) laid down in regulations under s.134(1).

Once an award of family credit is made, it will run for 26 weeks, regardless of any uprating orders issued during that time or (as a general rule) any changes in circumstances (subs. (3)). Subsection (4) enables regulations to be made preventing duplication of awards of family credit or where a member of the family starts to receive income support or disability working allowance.

Disability working allowance

Disability working allowance

129.—(1) A person in Great Britain who has attained the age of 16 and qualifies under subsection (2) below is entitled to a disability working allowance if, when the claim for it is made or is treated as made—
  (a) he is engaged and normally engaged in remunerative work;
  (b) he has a physical or mental disability which puts him at a disadvantage in getting a job;
  (c) his income—
        (i) does not exceed the amount which is the applicable amount at such date as may be prescribed; or
        (ii) exceeds it, but only by such an amount that there is an amount remaining if the deduction for which subsection (5)(b) below provides is made; and
  (d) except in such circumstances as may be prescribed, neither he nor, if he has a family, any member of it, is entitled to family credit.

(2) Subject to subsection (4) below, a person qualifies under this subsection if—
  (a) for one or more of the 56 days immediately preceding the date when the claim for a disability working allowance is made or is treated as made there was payable to him one or more of the following—

  (i) an invalidity pension under section 33, 40 or 41 above;
  (ii) a severe disablement allowance;
  (iii) income support, housing benefit or community charge benefit,

or a corresponding benefit under any enactment having effect in Northern Ireland;

(b) when the claim for a disability working allowance is made or is treated as made, there is payable to him one or more of the following—

  (i) an attendance allowance;
  (ii) a disability living allowance;
  (iii) an increase of disablement pension under section 104 above;
  (iv) an analogous pension increase under a war pension scheme or an industrial injuries scheme,

or a corresponding benefit under any enactment having effect in Northern Ireland; or

(c) when the claim for a disability working allowance is made or is treated as made, he has an invalid carriage or other vehicle provided by the Secretary of State under section 5(2)(a) of the National Health Service Act 1977 and Schedule 2 to that Act or under section 46 of the National Health Service (Scotland) Act 1978 or provided under Article 30(1) of the Health and Personal Social Services (Northern Ireland) Order 1972.

(3) For the purposes of subsection (1) above a person has a disability which puts him at a disadvantage in getting a job only if he satisfies prescribed conditions or prescribed circumstances exist in relation to him.

(4) If the only benefit mentioned in paragraph (a) of subsection (2) above which is payable to a person as there mentioned is—

(a) a benefit mentioned in sub-paragraph (iii) of that paragraph; or
(b) a corresponding benefit under any enactment having effect in Northern Ireland,

he only qualifies under that subsection in prescribed circumstances.

(5) Where a person is entitled to a disability working allowance, then—

(a) if his income does not exceed the amount which is the applicable amount at the date prescribed under subsection (1)(c)(i) above, the amount of the disability working allowance shall be the amount which is the appropriate maximum disability working allowance in his case; and

(b) if his income exceeds that amount, the amount of the disability working allowance shall be what remains after the deduction from the appropriate maximum disability working allowance of a prescribed percentage of the excess of his income over that amount.

(6) A disability working allowance shall be payable for a period of 26 weeks or such other period as may be prescribed and, subject to regulations, an award of a disability working allowance and the rate at which it is payable shall not be affected by any change of circumstances during that period or by any order under section 150 of the Administration Act.

(7) Regulations may provide that an award of a disability working allowance to a person shall terminate if—

(a) a disability working allowance becomes payable in respect of some other person who was a member of his family at the date of his claim for a disability working allowance; or

(b) income support or family credit becomes payable in respect of a person who was a member of the family at that date.

(8) Regulations shall prescribe the manner in which the appropriate maximum disability working allowance is to be determined in any case.

(9) The provisions of this Act relating to disability working allowance apply in relation to persons employed by or under the Crown as they apply in relation to persons employed otherwise than by or under the Crown.

DEFINITIONS
"the Administration Act": s.174.
"family": s.137(1).
"Great Britain": s.172.
"industrial injuries scheme": s.137(1).
"prescribed": s.137(1).
"war pension scheme": s.137(1).

GENERAL NOTE
Disability working allowance was introduced by the DLADWAA 1991 and first became payable in April 1992. It was devised to tackle a long-standing weakness of the British social security scheme, namely the absence of any partial incapacity benefit. The main income replacement benefit for people who are incapable of work is invalidity benefit, a contributory benefit paid under s.34 above. Invalidity benefit is payable only to people who are incapable of all work, although claimants may engage in therapeutic work and earn up to £40.50 per week (at 1992–93 rates) without losing benefit (Social Security (Unemployment, Sickness and Invalidity Benefit) Regulations 1983 (S.I. 1983 No. 1598), reg. 3). *The Way Ahead* announced a new benefit, disability employment credit, designed along the same lines as family credit as a work incentive benefit, except that it would be available to single disabled people and couples without children. This would be for disabled people who were only partially incapable for work and would involve a tapered withdrawal of benefit as income increased. The DLADWAA 1991 retitled this benefit disability working allowance (DWA).

DWA was designed to be cost-neutral in the long term. As is inevitable with a means-tested benefit, not all eligible claimants will be better off on DWA (although most will be). A relatively small group of people will be worse off if they take a low-paid job supplemented by DWA. This consists of some claimants with mortgages and others with children whose total income takes them just above income support levels with consequential loss of free school meals. Invalidity benefit claimants will be worse off if they have a large extra pension or other income or capital, or a partner in work, or if they are taking advantage of the therapeutic earnings rule.

The basic conditions for entitlement to DWA are set out in subs. (1) as amplified by the Disability Working Allowance (General) Regulations 1991 (S.I. 1991 No. 2887). They are closely modelled on those for family credit. Where a person has a choice between claiming either of these benefits, DWA will generally be the better option as it includes an amount equivalent to a single person's income support disability premium. However, recipients of DWA are not automatically exempt from prescription charges and charges for dental and optical services. Nor does DWA act as a passport for reimbursement of fares to hospital. These exemptions do apply to family credit claimants. DWA claimants may still qualify under the low income scheme operated by the DSS (National Health Service (Travelling Expenses and Remission of Charges) Regulations 1988 (S.I. 1988 No. 551)).

A further and important condition of eligibility is that the claimant satisfies the qualifying benefits criterion in the subs. (2). This means that many people partially capable of work are not eligible for DWA because they do not qualify for one of these passporting benefits.

For rules governing initial and repeat claims, see SSAA 1992, s.11, and for the special review and appeals procedure, see ss.30–35. See generally Rowland.

Subs. (1)
This subsection specifies the conditions of entitlement to DWA and is closely modelled on the analogous provision for family credit (s.128). The preliminary conditions are that the claimant is in Great Britain, is aged 16 years or more and meets the qualifying criteria set out in subs. (2) below. The four main conditions are then:

(a) He is engaged and normally engaged in remunerative work. This is defined by regulations as 16 hours a week, which also represents the starting point for most employment protection rights. Disabled people working fewer than 16 hours a week will still be able to claim income support with the higher rate of disregard and some claimants may be eligible to take advantage of the therapeutic earnings rule in relation to invalidity benefit or severe disablement allowance.

The fact that this condition is expressed in the present tense means that disabled people are not able to make a claim in advance of starting work, which may act as a disincentive. Assurances have been given that such claims are to be given the highest priority, the aim being to clear the vast majority within five days (*per* Mr N. Scott, Standing Committee E, col. 190, January 17, 1991).

(b) He has a physical or mental disability which puts him at a disadvantage in getting a job. This concept is defined in regulations made under subs. (3) below. This condition is in addition to the qualifying benefits condition under subs. (2) which acts to passport the claimant to DWA.

(c) His income.... The claimant's income must not exceed the prescribed applicable amount, or may exceed it only by such an amount that there is an amount remaining after the application of the income taper prescribed under s.129(5)(b). Where income does not exceed the applicable amount, the maximum level of DWA will be awarded, depending on the composition of the family. Where income exceeds the applicable amount, benefit will be reduced by a proportion of the claimant's income above the applicable amount. There is also a capital limit (currently £16,000) laid down in regulations under s.134(1).

(d) Except in such circumstances as may be prescribed. Neither the claimant nor a member of their family must be entitled to family credit.

Subs. (2)

This subsection defines the qualifying benefit criterion for entitlement to DWA. The claimant must satisfy one of the conditions set out in subs. (2)(a)–(c). The advantage of this extra condition is that it makes the traditional medical examination for incapacity benefits unnecessary, and hence has permitted the streamlining of the adjudication arrangements. As with DLA, there is an emphasis on self-assessment in claiming. The chief disadvantage is that many disabled people are not eligible for DWA because they do not qualify for one of the benefits listed in this subsection.

Subs. (2)(a)

This means that, in at least one of the eight weeks immediately before the date of claim, invalidity benefit, severe disablement allowance, income support, housing benefit, or community charge benefit must have been payable to the claimant. The choice of eight weeks rather than any longer period is directly related to the linking rule for incapacity benefits. Extra conditions so far as those in receipt of the last three benefits are specified in regulations made under subs. (4) below. These provide that the claimant must qualify for the disability premium for one of these benefits.

Subs. (2)(b)

This provides a second route to qualifying: at the point of claim attendance allowance, DLA, constant attendance allowance or an analogous pension increase under a war pension or industrial injuries scheme must be payable to the claimant. In subs. (2)(b)(ii) the words "a mobility allowance under section 37A of the 1975 Act" should be substituted in respect of claims made (or treated as made) before the first day for which disability living allowance became payable (April 6, 1992): see SS(CP)A 1992, Sched. 4, para. 21.

Subs. (2)(c)

The third and final possible qualifying condition is that the claimant has an invalid carriage or other vehicle (instead of the mobility component to DLA).

Subs. (3)

This enabling provision allows the Secretary of State to prescribe in regulations the circumstances in which a person meets the condition set out in subs. (1)(b) above. The Disability Working Allowance (General) Regulations (S.I. 1991 No. 2887) list a range of relevant physical and mental disabilities.

Subs. (4)

See annotations to subs. (2)(a) above.

Subs. (5)

This specifies the method for calculating DWA and follows the parallel provision for family credit (s.128(2)).

Subs. (6)

This provides that DWA is to be awarded for a fixed period of 26 weeks. Subject to exceptions to be prescribed, the award is not affected by changes in the claimant's circumstances or any uprating order under SSAA 1991, s.150. The same rules govern the family credit scheme.

Housing benefit

Housing benefit

130.—(1) A person is entitled to housing benefit if—

(a) he is liable to make payments in respect of a dwelling in Great Britain which he occupies as his home;

(b) there is an appropriate maximum housing benefit in his case; and

(c) either—

(i) he has no income or his income does not exceed the applicable amount; or

(ii) his income exceeds that amount, but only by so much that there is an amount remaining if the deduction for which subsection (3)(b) below provides is made.

(2) In subsection (1) above "payments in respect of a dwelling" means such payments as may be prescribed, but the power to prescribe payments does not include power to prescribe mortgage payments or, in relation to Scotland, payments under heritable securities.

(3) Where a person is entitled to housing benefit, then—

(a) if he has no income or his income does not exceed the applicable amount, the amount of the housing benefit shall be the amount which is the appropriate maximum housing benefit in his case; and

(b) if his income exceeds the applicable amount, the amount of the housing benefit shall be what remains after the deduction from the appropriate maximum housing benefit of prescribed percentages of the excess of his income over the applicable amount.

(4) Regulations shall prescribe the manner in which the appropriate maximum housing benefit is to be determined in any case.

(5) Regulations under subsection (4) above may provide for benefit to be limited by reference to determinations made by rent officers in exercise of functions conferred under section 121 of the Housing Act 1988 or section 70 of the Housing (Scotland) Act 1988.

DEFINITIONS

"dwelling": s.137(1).
"Great Britain": s.172.
"payments in respect of a dwelling": subs. (2).
"prescribed": s.137(1).

GENERAL NOTE

This section establishes the framework for entitlement to housing benefit, which is administered by local authorities and not the DSS. The basic conditions are laid down in subs. (1) and amplified by the Housing Benefit (General) Regulations 1987 (S.I. 1987 No. 1971): see Findlay and Ward. As with the other income-related benefits, determination of the rate of benefit in any given case depends on the relationship between the claimant's income and his or her applicable amount. Individuals who have no income, or income not in excess of the applicable amount, receive the maximum housing benefit appropriate to their situation (subss. (1)(c)(i) and (3)(a)). Claimants with more income than their applicable amount receive a proportion of their maximum entitlement after the application of a taper (subss. (1)(c)(ii) and (3)(b)). There is also a capital limit (currently £16,000) laid down in regulations under s.134(1).

Housing benefit is payable in respect of prescribed categories of payments in respect of dwellings, but not for mortgage payments (subs. (2)). Assistance with mortgage payments is only available under the income support scheme (Income Support (General) Regulations 1987 (S.I. 1987 No. 1967), Sched. 3).

Financial and administrative arrangements for housing benefit are provided for by SSAA 1992, Pt. VIII (ss.134–137).

Community charge benefits

Community charge benefits

131.—(1) A person is entitled to a community charge benefit in respect of a particular day falling after 31st March 1990 if each of the three conditions set out in subsections (3) to (6) below is fulfilled.

(2) A community charge benefit—

(a) shall not be allowed to a person in respect of any day falling before the day on which his entitlement is to be regarded as commencing for that purpose by virtue of paragraph (1) of section 6(1) of the Administration Act; but

(b) may be allowed to him in respect of not more than six days immediately following the day on which his period of entitlement would otherwise come to an end, if his entitlement is to be regarded by virtue of that paragraph as not having ended for that purpose.

(3) In relation to England and Wales, the first condition is that—

(a) for the day the person concerned is shown, in a charging authority's community charges register, as subject to a personal community charge of the authority and is not there shown as undertaking a full-time course of education on the day, or

(b) the day consists of or falls within a contribution period in respect of which the person concerned is liable to pay an amount under section 9 of the 1988 Act (collective community charge contributions).

(4) In relation to Scotland, the first condition is that—

(a) in respect of the day the person concerned is shown, in a community charges register, as being liable to pay the personal community charge and is not there shown as undertaking a full-time course of education or nursing education on the day, or

(b) the day consists of or falls within a contribution period in respect of which the person concerned is liable to pay a collective community charge contribution under section 11(11) of the 1987 Act.

(5) The second condition is that there is an appropriate maximum community charge benefit in the case of the person concerned.

(6) The third condition is that—

(a) the day falls within a week in respect of which the person concerned has no income,

(b) the day falls within a week in respect of which his income does not exceed the applicable amount, or

(c) neither paragraph (a) nor paragraph (b) above is fulfilled in his case but amount A exceeds amount B.

(7) As regards a person—

(a) amount A is the appropriate maximum community charge benefit in his case, and

(b) amount B is a prescribed percentage of the difference between his income in respect of the week in which the day falls and the applicable amount.

(8) In respect of the same day, a person shall be entitled to a separate community charge benefit in respect of each charge or contribution period concerned (if more than one).

(9) But regulations may provide that if—

(a) a person would (apart from the regulations) be entitled, in respect of the same day, to separate community charge benefits, and

(b) the circumstances are such as are prescribed,

he shall not be entitled to such one of the benefits as may be identified in accordance with prescribed rules.

(10) Where a person is entitled to a community charge benefit in respect of a day, and subsection (6)(a) or (b) above applies, the amount to which he is entitled shall be the amount which is the appropriate maximum community charge benefit in his case.

(11) Where a person is entitled to a community charge benefit in respect of a day, and subsection (6)(c) above applies, the amount to which he is entitled shall be found by deducting amount B from amount A, where

"amount A" and "amount B" have the meanings given by subsection (7) above.

(12) Regulations shall prescribe the manner in which the appropriate maximum community charge benefit is to be determined in any case.

Definitions
   "the 1987 Act": s.137(1).
   "the 1988 Act": s.137(1).
   "the Administration Act": s.174.
   "charging authority": s.137(1).
   "contribution period": s.137(1).
   "prescribed": s.137(1).
   "week": s.137(1).

General Note
   This section establishes the framework for entitlement to community charge benefits. The detailed rules for benefit entitlement are set out in the Community Charge Benefits (General) Regulations 1989 (S.I. 1989 No. 1321): see Findlay and Ward. Benefit is only payable to individuals in respect of their personal community charge liability (subss. (3) and (4)). There is therefore no entitlement in respect of the standard community charge payable for second homes. Persons in full-time education (or, in Scotland, in nursing education) are not eligible for benefit as they are liable for only 20 per cent. of the personal charge (subss. (3)(a) and (4)(a)). Subsections (3)(b) and (4)(b) deal with persons who are liable to contribute to a collective community charge contribution by virtue of being in "short-stay" accommodation. The impact of these rules is different in England and Wales as compared with Scotland (see Findlay and Ward). Subsections (5)–(7) are parallel provisions to those in s.130(1)(b) and (c). There is also a capital limit (currently £16,000) laid down in regulations under s.134(1). Further statutory provision is made in respect of couples and polygamous marriages by ss.132 and 133.
   Financial and administrative arrangements for community charge benefit are provided for by SSAA 1992, Pt. VIII (ss.138–140).

Couples

   132.—(1) As regards any case where a person is a member of a married or unmarried couple throughout a particular day, regulations may make such provision as the Secretary of State sees fit as to—
   (a) the entitlement of the person to a community charge benefit in respect of the day, and
   (b) the amount to which he is entitled.
   (2) Nothing in subsections (3) to (8) below shall prejudice the generality of subsection (1) above.
   (3) The regulations may provide that prescribed provisions shall apply instead of prescribed provisions of this Part of this Act, or that prescribed provisions of this Part of this Act shall not apply or shall apply subject to prescribed amendments or adaptations.
   (4) The regulations may provide that, for the purpose of calculating in the case of the person concerned the matters mentioned in subsection (5) below, prescribed amounts relating to the person and his partner are to be aggregated and the aggregate is to be apportioned.
   (5) The matters are income, capital, the applicable amount, and the appropriate maximum community charge benefit.
   (6) The regulations may—
   (a) amend section 139(6) of the Administration Act so as to allow for disregarding the whole or part of any pension payable to the partner of the person concerned in determining the latter's income;
   (b) amend section 139(7) of that Act accordingly.
   (7) The regulations may contain different provision as to the following different cases—
   (a) cases where the first condition is fulfilled on the day concerned by the person concerned but not by his partner;

(b) cases where the first condition is fulfilled on the day concerned by the person concerned and by his partner.

(8) The regulations may include such supplementary, incidental or consequential provisions as appear to the Secretary of State to be necessary or expedient.

(9) In this section—

(a) references to a person's partner are to the other member of the couple concerned, and

(b) references to the first condition are to the condition mentioned in section 131(3) or (4) above (as the case may be).

DEFINITIONS
  "the Administration Act": s.174.
  "first condition": subs. (9)(b).
  "married couple": s.137(1).
  "partner": subs. (9)(a).
  "prescribed": s.137(1).
  "unmarried couple": s.137(1).

GENERAL NOTE

This section empowers the Secretary of State to make regulations dealing with the entitlement to community charge benefit of persons who are members of a married or unmarried couple. Such regulations may also deal with the amount of such benefit to which they are entitled. Subsections (3)–(8) merely elaborate the broad enabling power in subs. (1). See further Findlay and Ward.

The position as regards polygamous marriages is dealt with by s.133.

Polygamous marriages

133.—(1) This section applies to any case where—

(a) throughout a particular day a person (the person in question) is a husband or wife by virtue of a marriage entered into under a law which permits polygamy; and

(b) either party to the marriage has for the time being any spouse additional to the other party.

(2) For the purposes of section 132 above neither party to the marriage shall be taken to be a member of a couple on the day.

(3) Regulations under this section may make such provision as the Secretary of State sees fit as to—

(a) the entitlement of the person in question to a community charge benefit in respect of the day, and

(b) the amount to which he is entitled.

(4) Without prejudice to the generality of subsection (3) above the regulations may include provision equivalent to that included under section 132 above subject to any modifications the Secretary of State sees fit.

DEFINITIONS
  "the person in question": subs. (1)(a).

GENERAL NOTE

This makes parallel provision for members of polygamous marriages to that made for monogamously married and unmarried couples by s.132.

General

Exclusions from benefit

134.—(1) No person shall be entitled to an income-related benefit if his capital or a prescribed part of it exceeds the prescribed amount.

(2) Except in prescribed circumstances the entitlement of one member of a family to any one income-related benefit excludes entitlement to that benefit for any other member for the same period.

(3) Subsection (2) above does not prevent different members of the same family becoming entitled to different community charge benefits by virtue of their fulfilling the conditions in respect of different charges or of different contribution periods.

(4) Where the amount of any income-related benefit would be less than a prescribed amount, it shall not be payable except in prescribed circumstances.

DEFINITIONS
    "family": s.137(1).
    "income-related benefit": s.123(1).
    "prescribed": s.137(1).

GENERAL NOTE
    The actual maximum capital limits (subs. (1)) for the income-related benefits are laid down in regulations. For 1992/93 they are £8,000 (income support and family credit) and £16,000 (disability working allowance, housing benefit and community charge benefit). Generally, where one member of a family receives a benefit listed in s.123(1), other members of the family are precluded from receiving the same benefit for the same period (subs. (2)). An exception is made in the case of community charge benefits (subs. (3)), as individual family members are separately liable for the community charge. Subsection (4) allows for regulations to specify that *de minimis* entitlements to benefit are not to be payable (*e.g.* less than 50p per week in the case of family credit: Social Security (Claims and Payments) Regulations 1987 (S.I. 1987 No. 1968), reg. 27(2)).

The applicable amount

135.—(1) The applicable amount, in relation to any income-related benefit, shall be such amount or the aggregate of such amounts as may be prescribed in relation to that benefit.

(2) The power to prescribe applicable amounts conferred by subsection (1) above includes power to prescribe nil as an applicable amount.

(3) In prescribing, for the purposes of income support, amounts under subsection (1) above in respect of accommodation in any area for qualifying persons in cases where prescribed conditions are fulfilled, the Secretary of State shall take into account information provided by local authorities or other prescribed bodies or persons with respect to the amounts which they have agreed to pay for the provision of accommodation in relevant premises in that area.

(4) In subsection (3) above—
    "accommodation" includes any board or care;
    "local authority"—
        (a) in relation to areas in England and Wales, has the same meaning as it has in Part III of the National Assistance Act 1948; and
        (b) in relation to areas in Scotland, has the meaning given by section 1(2) of the Social Work (Scotland) Act 1968;
    "qualifying person" means any person who falls within—
        (a) subsection (1) of section 26A of the National Assistance Act 1948 (which is inserted by the National Health Service and Community Care Act 1990 and relates to persons ordinarily resident in residential care or nursing homes immediately before the commencement of that section); or
        (b) subsection (1) of section 86A of the Social Work (Scotland) Act 1968 (the corresponding provision for Scotland),
    or who would fall within either of those subsections apart from any regulations under subsection (3) of the section in question;
    "relevant premises"—

(a) in relation to areas in England and Wales, has the meaning given by section 26A(2) of the National Assistance Act 1948; and

(b) in relation to areas in Scotland, has the meaning given by section 86A(2) of the Social Work (Scotland) Act 1968.

(5) In relation to income support, housing benefit and any community charge benefit, the applicable amount for a severely disabled person shall include an amount in respect of his being a severely disabled person.

(6) Regulations may specify circumstances in which persons are to be treated as being or as not being severely disabled.

DEFINITIONS
"accommodation": subs. (4).
"income-related benefit": s.123(1).
"local authority": subs. (4).
"prescribed": s.137(1).
"qualifying person": subs. (4).
"relevant premises": subs. (4).

GENERAL NOTE

Subss. (1) and (2)
The applicable amount is a crucial factor in determining the rate of entitlement to an income-related benefit (see, *e.g.* s.124(4)). The applicable amounts are laid down in regulations and uprated each year. See, *e.g.* Income Support (General) Regulations 1987 (S.I. 1987 No. 1967), Pt. IV and Sched. 2.

Subss. (3) and (4)
These provisions, first enacted by SSA 1990, s.9, are concerned with the Government's changes in community care. When those reforms are implemented (in April 1993) new residents in residential care and nursing homes will receive financial support from local authorities, who will negotiate prices and contracts with care suppliers. Existing residents will still be supported by income support, so the weekly limits set out in Sched. 4 of the Income Support (General) Regulations 1987 (S.I. 1987 No. 1967) will remain important. Subsection (3) requires the Secretary of State to take into account information supplied by local authorities about price levels. There is no statutory obligation to maintain the income support limits in line with market prices.
Note the transitory modification in SS(CP)A 1992, Sched. 4, para. 4.

Subss. (5) and (6)
These provisions, originally inserted in the SSA 1986 by the House of Lords against the wishes of the Government, were the subject of the controversial decision in *Chief Adjudication Officer and Secretary of State for Social Security* v. *Foster* [1992] 1 Q.B. 31. The majority of the Court of Appeal (Lord Donaldson M.R. dissenting) held that the conditions laid down for the receipt of the severe disability premium for income support (Income Support (General) Regulations 1987 (S.I. 1987 No. 1967), Sched. 2, para. 13) were *intra vires* these provisions in as much as they entitled the Secretary of State to specify requirements extraneous to the individual's disability (*e.g.* the presence of a non-dependant in the claimant's household). The Court of Appeal also held unanimously that a Social Security Commissioner (and therefore a SSAT or an AO) had no power to determine the *vires* of such regulations. An appeal in this case is expected to be heard by the House of Lords in October 1992.

Income and capital

136.—(1) Where a person claiming an income-related benefit is a member of a family, the income and capital of any member of that family shall, except in prescribed circumstances, be treated as the income and capital of that person.

(2) Regulations may provide that capital not exceeding the amount prescribed under section 134(1) above but exceeding a prescribed lower amount shall be treated, to a prescribed extent, as if it were income of a prescribed amount.

(3) Income and capital shall be calculated or estimated in such manner as may be prescribed.

(4) A person's income in respect of a week shall be calculated in accordance with prescribed rules; and the rules may provide for the calculation to be made by reference to an average over a period (which need not include the week concerned).

(5) Circumstances may be prescribed in which—

(a) a person is treated as possessing capital or income which he does not possess;

(b) capital or income which a person does possess is to be disregarded;

(c) income is to be treated as capital;

(d) capital is to be treated as income.

DEFINITIONS
"family": s.137(1).
"income-related benefit": s.123(1).
"prescribed": s.137(1).

GENERAL NOTE

The general rule for income-related benefits is that income and capital resources belonging to family members are aggregated (subs. (1)). The principal exceptions prescribed under the regulations relate to children and young persons. Subsection (2) enables regulations to provide that capital between the lower limit (£3,000 for 1992/93) and the appropriate maximum limit (£8,000 or £16,000: see General Note to s.134) shall be assumed to generate a certain tariff income. Subsections (3)–(5) give the Secretary of State sweeping powers to prescribe how resources are to be calculated, including the remarkable powers to deem income to be capital and vice versa (subs. (5)(c) and (d)).

Interpretation of Part VII and supplementary provisions

137.—(1) In this Part of this Act, unless the context otherwise requires—

"charging authority" has the same meaning as in the 1988 Act;

"child" means a person under the age of 16;

"contribution period", in relation to England and Wales, has the same meaning as in section 9 of the 1988 Act;

"contribution period", in relation to Scotland, means a continuous period of residence in any premises (which falls in a chargeable financial year) in respect of each day of which a person is liable to pay a collective community charge contribution under section 11(11) of the 1987 Act;

"dwelling" means any residential accommodation, whether or not consisting of the whole or part of a building and whether or not comprising separate and self-contained premises;

"family" means—

(a) a married or unmarried couple;

(b) a married or unmarried couple and a member of the same household for whom one of them is or both are responsible and who is a child or a person of a prescribed description;

(c) except in prescribed circumstances, a person who is not a member of a married or unmarried couple and a member of the same household for whom that person is responsible and who is a child or a person of a prescribed description;

"industrial injuries scheme" means a scheme made under Schedule 8 to this Act or section 159 of the 1975 Act or under the Old Cases Act;

"levying authority" has the same meaning as in the 1987 Act;

"married couple" means a man and woman who are married to each other and are members of the same household;

"the 1987 Act" means the Abolition of Domestic Rates Etc. (Scotland) Act 1987;

"the 1988 Act" means the Local Government Finance Act 1988;

"prescribed" means specified in or determined in accordance with regulations;

"unmarried couple" means a man and woman who are not married to each other but are living together as husband and wife otherwise than in prescribed circumstances;

"war pension scheme" means a scheme under which war pensions (as defined in section 25 of the Social Security Act 1989) are provided;

"week", in relation to community charge benefits, means a period of seven days beginning with a Monday.

(2) Regulations may make provision for the purposes of this Part of this Act—

(a) as to circumstances in which a person is to be treated as being or not being in Great Britain;

(b) continuing a person's entitlement to benefit during periods of temporary absence from Great Britain;

(c) as to what is or is not to be treated as remunerative work or as employment;

(d) as to circumstances in which a person is or is not to be treated as—
  (i) engaged or normally engaged in remunerative work;
  (ii) available for employment; or
  (iii) actively seeking employment;

(e) as to what is or is not to be treated as relevant education;

(f) as to circumstances in which a person is or is not to be treated as receiving relevant education;

(g) specifying the descriptions of pension increases under war pension schemes or industrial injuries schemes that are analogous to the benefits mentioned in section 129(2)(b)(i) to (iii) above;

(h) as to circumstances in which a person is or is not to be treated as occupying a dwelling as his home;

(i) for treating any person who is liable to make payments in respect of a dwelling as if he were not so liable;

(j) for treating any person who is not liable to make payments in respect of a dwelling as if he were so liable;

(k) for treating as included in a dwelling any land used for the purposes of the dwelling;

(l) as to circumstances in which persons are to be treated as being or not being members of the same household;

(m) as to circumstances in which one person is to be treated as responsible or not responsible for another.

DEFINITIONS
"the 1975 Act": s.174.
"Great Britain": s.172.
"the Old Cases Act": s.174.

GENERAL NOTE
This section includes a number of important definitions for the purposes of the income-related benefits.

Charging authority. This is defined by s.144(1) of the Local Government Finance Act 1988 as a district council, London borough council, the Common Council and the Council of the Isles of Scilly.

Child. Although the age of majority is 18, a child is defined as a person under the age of 16. See also the definition of young person in Income Support (General) Regulations 1987 (S.I. 1987 No. 1967), reg. 14.

Dwelling. See also, in the context of housing benefit, Housing Benefit (General) Regulations 1987 (S.I. 1987 No. 1971), reg. 2(4).

Family. This means, in other words, married and unmarried couples, with or without a child or children, and single claimants with a child or children. As to the test of membership of a household and children, see, *e.g. England* v. *Secretary of State for Social Services* (1982) 3 F.L.R. 222. There are deeming rules in the various sets of regulations.

Levying authority. This is defined by Sched. 2, para. 1 of the Abolition of Domestic Rates Etc. (Scotland) Act 1987 as a regional or islands council.

Married couple. The key point of this definition is the concept of household. It is quite possible to have more than one household in any one house: see *R(SB) 4/83* and matrimonial cases such as *Fuller* v. *Fuller* [1973] 1 W.L.R. 730.

Unmarried couple. The concept of living together as husband and wife (sometimes known as the cohabitation rule) gives rise to some of the most difficult issues which SSATs have to determine. The rule is important in two main types of case. First, in relation to the income-related benefits, resources are aggregated within a family unit, and the applicable amount for a couple is less than twice that for a single claimant. Secondly, widow's benefits (ss.36–38) are not payable so long as a widow is living together with a man as husband and wife. The same principles should apply as between income support and widow's benefits (*R(SB) 17/81* and *R(G) 3/81*) and between the income-related benefits themselves (*R.* v. *Penwith District Council Housing Benefits Review Board,* ex p. *Menear* (1992) 24 H.L.R. 114).

According to *R(G) 3/71,* three main factors have to be considered in determining whether a man and woman are living together as husband and wife: "(1) their relationship in relation to sex; (2) their relationship in relation to money; (3) their general relationship. Although all three are as a rule relevant, no single one of them is necessarily conclusive". These factors were amplified in the *Supplementary Benefit Handbook* (1984, DHSS), and an earlier version of these official guidelines was approved in *Crake* v. *Supplementary Benefits Commission; Butterworth* v. *Same* [1982] 1 All E.R. 498. These six pointers have remained the basis of decision-making by AOs and SSATs in this area. The factors are: (1) members of the same household; (2) stability; (3) financial support; (4) sexual relationship; (5) children; and (6) public acknowledgment.

It is not necessary that all six aspects are found to exist in any given situation. For example, a couple may be regarded as living together as husband and wife even though they have no children and keep their own names, bank accounts, etc. However, the parties must in any event be living in the same household. This concept is in itself by no means unproblematic (see *R(SB) 30/83, R(SB) 8/85* and *R(SB) 19/85*).

The other factors to be considered are equally not without difficulty. For example, in deciding whether there is a stable relationship, time is not the only matter to be considered. The true nature of the relationship must also be explored, as the parties may have a stable relationship as landlady and lodger, or as two members of the opposite sex living together for mutual support, rather than specifically as husband and wife. See *Butterworth* v. *SBC (supra)*, *Robson* v. *Secretary of State for Social Services* (1982) 3 F.L.R. 232, *Kaur* v. *Secretary of State for Social Services* (1982) 3 F.L.R. 237, *R(SB) 17/81* and *R(SB) 35/85*. For a detailed analysis, see the annotations in Mesher under this provision and in Bonner in respect of s.38.

PART VIII

THE SOCIAL FUND

Payments out of the social fund

138.—(1) Payments may be made out of the social fund, in accordance with this Part of this Act—

    (a) of prescribed amounts, whether in respect of prescribed items or otherwise, to meet, in prescribed circumstances, maternity expenses and funeral expenses; and

    (b) to meet other needs in accordance with directions given or guidance issued by the Secretary of State.

(2) Payments may also be made out of that fund, in accordance with this Part of this Act, of a prescribed amount or a number of prescribed amounts to prescribed descriptions of persons, in prescribed circumstances to meet expenses for heating which appear to the Secretary of State to have been or to be likely to be incurred in cold weather.

(3) The power to make a payment out of the social fund such as is mentioned in subsection (1)(b) above may be exercised by making a payment to a third party with a view to the third party providing, or arranging for the provision of, goods or services for the applicant.

(4) In this section "prescribed" means specified in or determined in accordance with regulations.

DEFINITIONS
   "prescribed": subs. (4).

GENERAL NOTE

The introduction of the social fund in April 1988 was one of the most controversial aspects of the reform of the social security scheme instigated by the Fowler Review. The previous system of regulation-based single payments and urgent needs payments was abandoned when income support superseded supplementary benefit. In its place the social fund was established to provide loans and grants to those unable to finance certain purchases or costs out of the ordinary weekly rate of benefit. On the financial arrangements for the social fund, see SSAA 1992, ss.167-9.

The social fund falls into two distinct parts. First, there is a regulation-based system of payments for maternity, funeral and cold-weather payments (subs. (1)(a) and (2)). These payments are akin to single payments under the pre-1988 scheme in that entitlement is a matter of right once the conditions in the regulations have been satisfied. Decisions under this part of the social fund are made by AOs and can be challenged on appeal before a SSAT. There is a further right of appeal (with leave and on a point of law only) in the ordinary way to a Social Security Commissioner.

The bulk of social fund payments fall into the second category: the discretionary part of the social fund. These take the form of budgeting loans, crisis loans and community care grants (subs. (1)(b) and the *Social Fund Manual*). On the necessity for applications for such payments to be in the prescribed form, see SSAA 1992, s.12. Social fund officers, and not adjudication officers, decide whether to grant applications for discretionary payments from the social fund. In reaching their decisions, social fund officers must have regard to all the circumstances of the case and in particular the factors listed in s.140(1). Furthermore, social fund officers must follow the Secretary of State's directions and must take account of any guidance issued by him (s.140(2)). In particular, the discretionary part of the social fund is subject to budgetary control (s.140(3)). Social fund officers' decisions cannot be appealed to a SSAT; instead there is the opportunity for an internal review to be carried out. If the applicant remains dissatisfied, a further review may be conducted by a social fund inspector: see SSAA 1992, s.66. The only recourse to the courts is by way of judicial review.

Subs. (1)(a)

The regulation-based part of the social fund is not subject to any budgetary limit. Decisions are made by AOs with the normal right of appeal to a SSAT. Details of entitlement are provided in the Social Fund Maternity and Funeral Expenses (General) Regulations 1987 (S.I. 1987 No. 481), on which see Mesher. Note also that non-discretionary payments may also be made for cold-weather costs (subs. (2)).

Subs. (1)(b)

This subsection empowers the Secretary of State to issue directions and guidance in connection with the discretionary part of the social fund. The ambit of this provision was considered in *R. v. Secretary of State for Social Services*, ex p. *Stitt; R. v. Social Security Fund Inspector*, ex p. *Sherwin; R. v. Same*, ex p. *Roberts* [1991] C.O.D. 68 and in *R. v. Secretary of State for Social Services*, ex p. *Stitt; R. v. Same*, ex p. *Healey; R. v. Social Fund Inspector*, ex p. *Ellison, The Times*, December 31, 1991. In ex p. *Stitt* both the Divisional Court and the Court of Appeal held that a direction excluding community care grants from the social fund for domestic assistance were validly made. The Divisional Court and Purchas L.J. in the Court of Appeal concluded that such directions could be made in exercise of the Secretary of State's control and management functions (see now SSAA 1992, s.167(2)). Butler-Sloss L.J. and Sir Patrick Connor held that the power arose under what is now s.138(1)(b) and s.140(2). All the members of the Court of Appeal expressed their surprise at the breadth of the powers granted to the Secretary of State.

Following this decision, the Court of Appeal in ex p. *Healey* held that it was not irrational for the Secretary of State to exclude from payment from the social fund needs which, on social grounds, are as worthy as those which are eligible for payment. This principle applies even where such needs cannot be met elsewhere in the public sector, since social considerations are immaterial to the lawfulness of the decision to exclude a given need.

Subs. (2)

As with payments made from the social fund under subs. (1)(a) above, cold-weather payments are not subject to budgetary control. Decisions are made by AOs with the normal right of appeal to a SSAT. Details of entitlement are provided in the Social Fund Cold Weather Payments (General) Regulations 1988 (S.I. 1988 No. 1724), on which see Mesher.

Subs. (3)

This power is only appropriate in special cases, as indicated in the *Social Fund Manual*.

Awards by social fund officers

139.—(1) The questions whether a payment such as is mentioned in section 138(1)(b) above is to be awarded and how much it is to be shall be determined by a social fund officer.

(2) A social fund officer may determine that an award shall be payable in specified instalments at specified times.

(3) A social fund officer may determine that an award is to be repayable.

(4) An award that is to be repayable shall be repayable upon such terms and conditions as before the award is paid the Secretary of State notifies to the person by or on behalf of whom the application for it was made.

(5) Payment of an award shall be made to the applicant unless the social fund officer determines otherwise.

DEFINITIONS
"social fund officer": SSAA 1992, s.64(1).

GENERAL NOTE
The Secretary of State's directions and guidance as to how social fund officers should exercise their functions under this section are contained in the *Social Fund Manual*. See also Mesher.

Principles of determination

140.—(1) In determining whether to make an award to the applicant or the amount or value to be awarded a social fund officer shall have regard, subject to subsection (2) below, to all the circumstances of the case and, in particular—

(a) the nature, extent and urgency of the need;

(b) the existence of resources from which the need may be met;

(c) the possibility that some other person or body may wholly or partly meet it;

(d) where the payment is repayable, the likelihood of repayment and the time within which repayment is likely;

(e) any relevant allocation under section 168(1) to (4) of the Administration Act.

(2) A social fund officer shall determine any question in accordance with any general directions issued by the Secretary of State and in determining any question shall take account of any general guidance issued by him.

(3) Without prejudice to the generality of subsection (2) above, the Secretary of State may issue directions under that subsection for the purpose of securing that a social fund officer or group of social fund officers shall not in any specified period make awards of any specified description which in the aggregate exceed the amount, or a specified portion of the amount, allocated to that officer or group of officers under section 168(1) to (4) of the Administration Act for payments under awards of that description in that period.

(4) Without prejudice to the generality of subsection (2) above, the power to issue general directions conferred on the Secretary of State by that subsection includes power to direct—

(a) that in circumstances specified in the direction a social fund officer shall not determine an application and, without prejudice to the generality of this paragraph, that a social fund officer shall not determine an application which is made before the end of a specified period after the making of an application by the same person for a payment such as is mentioned in section 138(1)(b) above to meet the same need and without there having been any relevant change of circumstances since the previous application;

(b) that for a category of need specified in the direction a social fund officer shall not award less than an amount specified in the direction;

    (c) that for a category of need specified in the direction a social fund officer shall not award more than an amount so specified;

    (d) that payments to meet a category of need specified in the direction shall in all cases or in no case be made by instalments;

    (e) that payments to meet a category of need specified in the direction shall in all cases or in no case be repayable; and

    (f) that a payment such as is mentioned in section 138(1)(b) above shall only be awarded to a person if either—

        (i) he is in receipt of a benefit which is specified in the direction and the circumstances are such as are so specified; or

        (ii) in a case where the conditions specified in sub-paragraph (i) above are not satisfied, the circumstances are such as are specified in the direction,

and the power to issue general guidance conferred on him by that subsection includes power to give social fund officers guidance as to any matter to which directions under that subsection may relate.

(5) In determining a question a social fund officer shall take account (subject to any directions or guidance issued by the Secretary of State under this section) of any guidance issued by the social fund officer nominated for his area under section 64 of the Administration Act.

DEFINITIONS
    "the Administration Act": s.174.
    "social fund officer": SSAA 1992, s.64(1).

GENERAL NOTE
    Social fund officers, in deciding whether to grant an application, must consider all the circumstances of the case and especially the five factors listed in subs. (1). Their apparent discretion under subs. (1) is severely constrained by subs. (2), which requires officers to follow directions and to take into account guidance issued by the Secretary of State (see *Social Fund Manual*). The crucial distinction is that directions are mandatory (assuming they are *intra vires*) whereas guidance is not. The state of the budget is merely one factor amongst several under subs. (1), but directions issued under subs. (3) give it a higher status. Subsection (3) was inserted in SSA 1986 by SSA 1990 in order to overturn the effect of the Divisional Court's ruling in *R.* v. *Social Fund Inspector and Secretary of State for Social Security,* ex p. *Roberts, The Times,* February 23, 1990 (affirmed on other grounds in *R.* v. *Secretary of State for Social Services,* ex p. *Stitt* [1991] C.O.D. 68) that the original guidance in the *Social Fund Manual* on budgets was unlawful.

PART IX

CHILD BENEFIT

Child benefit

141. A person who is responsible for one or more children in any week shall be entitled, subject to the provisions of this Part of this Act, to a benefit (to be known as "child benefit") for that week in respect of the child or each of the children for whom he is responsible.

DEFINITIONS
    "child": s.142(1).
    "responsible for": s.143(1).
    "week": s.147(1).

GENERAL NOTE
    Child benefit was introduced by the Child Benefit Act 1975. The new benefit, which in part replaced family allowances, came into operation between 1977 and 1980 as children's tax allowances were phased out. During the 1980s the real value of child benefit declined to the extent that there were serious doubts as to the Government's commitment to this universal benefit (Brown, *Child Benefit: Investing in the Future* (1988)). These concerns were mollified by the decision to uprate child benefit in 1991.

Entitlement to child benefit turns on two principal issues. These are (1) whether the child is one in respect of whom benefit is payable (s.142), and (2) whether the claimant is a person who is "responsible for" the child or children (s.143). On the necessity for an application for benefit, see SSAA 1992, s.13.

Meaning of "child"

142.—(1) For the purposes of this Part of this Act a person shall be treated as a child for any week in which—
   (a) he is under the age of 16; or
   (b) he is under the age of 18 and not receiving full-time education and prescribed conditions are satisfied in relation to him; or
   (c) he is under the age of 19 and receiving full-time education either by attendance at a recognised educational establishment or, if the education is recognised by the Secretary of State, elsewhere.

(2) The Secretary of State may recognise education provided otherwise than at a recognised educational establishment for a person who, in the opinion of the Secretary of State, could reasonably be expected to attend such an establishment only if the Secretary of State is satisfied that education was being so provided for that person immediately before he attained the age of 16.

(3) Regulations may prescribe the circumstances in which education is or is not to be treated for the purposes of this Part of this Act as full-time.

(4) In determining for the purposes of paragraph (c) of subsection (1) above whether a person is receiving full-time education as mentioned in that paragraph, no account shall be taken of such interruptions as may be prescribed.

(5) Regulations may provide that a person who in any week ceases to fall within subsection (1) above shall be treated as continuing to do so for a prescribed period; but no person shall by virtue of any such regulations be treated as continuing to fall within that subsection for any week after that in which he attains the age of 19.

DEFINITIONS
   "child": subs. (1).
   "prescribed": s.147(1).
   "recognised educational establishment": s.147(1).
   "week": s.147(1).

GENERAL NOTE
The starting point for the statutory meaning of "child" in the context of child benefit is subs. (1). This provides for a normal age-limit of 16, but in certain cases the upper age-limit is raised to 18 or 19. This general rule is then modified by the Child Benefit (General) Regulations 1976 (S.I. 1976 No. 965).

For example, children who have just left school and are under 19 are deemed to be in full-time education for a specified period, subject to certain exceptions (reg. 7). Child benefit entitlement therefore continues for this period, and may be extended if the young person is under 18 and satisfies further conditions, *e.g.* as to registration as to availability for work or youth training, etc. (reg. 7D). The continuation of child benefit during this "extension period" reflects the withdrawal of income support entitlement from most 16- and 17-year-olds in their own right. Child benefit may also be payable to children under 19 who are in "full-time education". This concept is defined in great detail in regs. 5 and 6. For a full analysis, see Bonner.

Meaning of "person responsible for child"

143.—(1) For the purposes of this Part of this Act a person shall be treated as responsible for a child in any week if—
   (a) he has the child living with him in that week; or
   (b) he is contributing to the cost of providing for the child at a weekly rate which is not less than the weekly rate of child benefit payable in respect of the child for that week.

(2) Where a person has had a child living with him at some time before a particular week he shall be treated for the purposes of this section as having the child living with him in that week notwithstanding their absence from one another unless, in the 16 weeks preceding that week, they were absent from one another for more than 56 days not counting any day which is to be disregarded under subsection (3) below.

(3) Subject to subsection (4) below, a day of absence shall be disregarded for the purposes of subsection (2) above if it is due solely to the child's—

(a) receiving full-time education by attendance at a recognised educational establishment;

(b) undergoing medical or other treatment as an in-patient in a hospital or similar institution; or

(c) being, in such circumstances as may be prescribed, in residential accommodation pursuant to arrangements made under—

(i) section 21 of the National Assistance Act 1948;

(ii) the Children Act 1989; or

(iii) the Social Work (Scotland) Act 1968.

(4) The number of days that may be disregarded by virtue of subsection (3)(b) or (c) above in the case of any child shall not exceed such number as may be prescribed unless the person claiming to be responsible for the child regularly incurs expenditure in respect of the child.

(5) Regulations may prescribe the circumstances in which a person is or is not to be treated—

(a) as contributing to the cost of providing for a child as required by subsection (1)(b) above; or

(b) as regularly incurring expenditure in respect of a child as required by subsection (4) above;

and such regulations may in particular make provision whereby a contribution made or expenditure incurred by two or more persons is to be treated as made or incurred by one of them or whereby a contribution made or expenditure incurred by one of two spouses residing together is to be treated as made or incurred by the other.

DEFINITIONS

"child": s.142(1).

"prescribed": s.147(1).

"recognised educational establishment": s.147(1).

"week": s.147(1).

GENERAL NOTE

Entitlement to child benefit is not based on the blood tie between parent and child. Instead, child benefit is payable to a person who is "responsible for" the child. This is defined by subs. (1) as either a person with whom the child is living or a person who is contributing to the child's maintenance by an amount which is at least as much as the appropriate rate of weekly child benefit. Where more than one person is responsible for the child, priorities are determined by s.144(3) and Sched. 10.

Subs. (1)

He has the child living with him .... This concept was discussed in *R(F) 2/79* by Commissioner Hallett, who held that "living with" is not synonymous with "residing together". In determining whether the child lives with the claimant all the relevant evidence must be considered, including such factors as who has *de facto* care and control of the children and where they regard home as being (see also *R(F) 2/81*). Note that certain temporary absences may be disregarded for these purposes by virtue of subss. (2)–(4) and reg. 4.

He is contributing to the cost of providing for the child .... The alternative (and in practice much rarer) route to qualifying for child benefit is where the claimant contributes to the child's upkeep at the level of at least the current rate of child benefit. For guidance see *R(F) 8/61* and *R(F) 9/61*.

Subs. (3)(c)

Note the transitory modification in SS(CP)A 1992, Sched. 4, para. 5.

Exclusions and priority

144.—(1) Regulations may provide that child benefit shall not be payable by virtue—

    (a) of paragraph (b) of section 142(1) above and regulations made under that paragraph; or

    (b) of paragraph (c) of that subsection,

in such cases as may be prescribed.

    (2) Schedule 9 to this Act shall have effect for excluding entitlement to child benefit in other cases.

    (3) Where, apart from this subsection, two or more persons would be entitled to child benefit in respect of the same child for the same week, one of them only shall be entitled; and the question which of them is entitled shall be determined in accordance with Schedule 10 to this Act.

DEFINITIONS

    "child": s.142(1).
    "prescribed": s.147(1).
    "week": s.147(1).

GENERAL NOTE

    Schedule 9, introduced by subs. (2), excludes entitlement to child benefit in certain circumstances. These situations are essentially where (1) the child has been in prison, detained in custody or in the care of a local authority for more than 8 weeks; (2) the child is aged 16 or more but under 19 and is receiving full-time employment because of some office or employment held (*e.g.* apprentices); (3) the child is married; or (4) the United Kingdom income of the claimant (or spouse) is exempt from tax under various provisions. These rules are subject to the provisions of the Child Benefit (General) Regulations 1976 (S.I. 1976 No. 965): see Bonner.

    Schedule 10, introduced by subs. (3), deals with the position where more than one person is regarded as being responsible for the child under s.143. Priority is accorded in the first instance to the person with whom the child is living. The order of priority is then wife (where residing with husband), parent, mother (where residing with father but not married to him) and, as between others, the individual agreed amongst the claimants. Failing such agreement the Secretary of State may nominate the recipient.

Rate of child benefit

145.—(1) Child benefit shall be payable at such weekly rate as may be prescribed.

    (2) Different rates may be prescribed in relation to different cases, whether by reference to the age of the child in respect of whom the benefit is payable or otherwise.

    (3) The power to prescribe different rates under subsection (2) above shall be exercised so as to bring different rates into force on such day as the Secretary of State may by order specify.

    (4) No rate prescribed in place of a rate previously in force shall be lower than the rate that it replaces.

    (5) Regulations under this section shall be made by the Secretary of State in conjunction with the Treasury.

    (6) An order under subsection (3) above may be varied or revoked at any time before the date specified thereby.

    (7) An order under that subsection shall be laid before Parliament after being made.

DEFINITIONS

    "child": s.142(1).
    "parent": s.147(3).
    "prescribed": s.147(1).

GENERAL NOTE

    Since April 1991 child benefit has been paid at an enhanced rate for the first or only child in the family. In October 1991 the basic rate of child benefit was increased for the first time since April 1987.

Persons outside Great Britain

146.—(1) Regulations may modify the provisions of this Part of this Act in their application to persons who are or have been outside Great Britain at any prescribed time or in any prescribed circumstances.

(2) Subject to any regulations under subsection (1) above, no child benefit shall be payable in respect of a child for any week unless—

(a) he is in Great Britain in that week; and

(b) either he or at least one of his parents has been in Great Britain for more than 182 days in the 52 weeks preceding that week.

(3) Subject to any regulations under subsection (1) above, no person shall be entitled to child benefit for any week unless—

(a) he is in Great Britain in that week; and

(b) he has been in Great Britain for more than 182 days in the 52 weeks preceding that week.

DEFINITIONS
"child": s.142(1).
"Great Britain": s.172.
"prescribed": s.147(1).
"week": s.147(1).

GENERAL NOTE
This section lays down two general rules relating to entitlement to child benefit. First, the child in question must be in Great Britain for the relevant week and either the child or the parent must have been in Great Britain for more than 182 days in the previous 52 weeks (subs. (2); see *R(F) 1/88*). Secondly, the person claiming child benefit must be in Great Britain for that week and for 182 days out of the previous 52 weeks. These rules are subject to the qualifications contained in the Child Benefit (Residence and Persons Abroad) Regulations 1976 (S.I. 1976 No. 963).

Interpretation of Part IX and supplementary provisions

147.—(1) In this Part of this Act—

"prescribed" means prescribed by regulations;

"recognised educational establishment" means an establishment recognised by the Secretary of State as being, or as comparable to, a university, college or school;

"voluntary organisation" means a body, other than a public or local authority, the activities of which are carried on otherwise than for profit; and

"week" means a period of seven days beginning with a Monday.

(2) Subject to any provision made by regulations, references in this Part of this Act to any condition being satisfied or any facts existing in a week shall be construed as references to the condition being satisfied or the facts existing at the beginning of that week.

(3) References in this Part of this Act to a parent, father or mother of a child shall be construed as including references to a step-parent, step-father or step-mother.

(4) Regulations may prescribe the circumstances in which persons are or are not to be treated for the purposes of this Part of this Act as residing together.

(5) Regulations may make provision as to the circumstances in which—

(a) a marriage celebrated under a law which permits polygamy; or

(b) a marriage during the subsistence of which a party to it is at any time married to more than one person,

is to be treated for the purposes of this Part of this Act as having, or not having, the consequences of a marriage celebrated under a law which does not permit polygamy.

(6) Nothing in this Part of this Act shall be construed as conferring a right to child benefit on any body corporate; but regulations may confer such a

right on voluntary organisations and for that purpose may make such modifications as the Secretary of State thinks fit—
  (a) of any provision of this Part of this Act; or
  (b) of any provision of the Administration Act relating to child benefit.

DEFINITIONS
  "the Administration Act": s.174.

GENERAL NOTE
  The meaning of "week" (subs. (1)) was considered by the Commissioners in *R(F) 1/82(T)*. The principal Regulations made under this section are the Child Benefit (General) Regulations 1976 (S.I. 1976 No. 965), on which see Bonner.

PART X

CHRISTMAS BONUS FOR PENSIONERS

Entitlement of pensioners to Christmas bonus

148.—(1) Any person who in any year—
  (a) is present or ordinarily resident in the United Kingdom or any other member State at any time during the relevant week; and
  (b) is entitled to a payment of a qualifying benefit in respect of a period which includes a day in that week or is to be treated as entitled to a payment of a qualifying benefit in respect of such a period,
shall, subject to the following provisions of this Part of this Act and to section 1 of the Administration Act, be entitled to payment under this subsection in respect of that year.
  (2) Subject to the following provisions of this Part of this Act, any person who is a member of a couple and is entitled to a payment under subsection (1) above in respect of a year shall also be entitled to payment under this subsection in respect of that year if—
  (a) both members have attained pensionable age not later than the end of the relevant week; and
  (b) the other member satisfies the condition mentioned in subsection (1)(a) above; and
  (c) either—
        (i) he is entitled or treated as entitled, in respect of the other member, to an increase in the payment of the qualifying benefit; or
        (ii) the only qualifying benefit to which he is entitled is income support.
  (3) A payment under subsection (1) or (2) above—
  (a) is to be made by the Secretary of State; and
  (b) is to be of £10 or such larger sum as the Secretary of State may by order specify.
  (4) Where the only qualifying benefit to which a person is entitled is income support, he shall not be entitled to a payment under subsection (1) above unless he has attained pensionable age not later than the end of the relevant week.
  (5) Only one sum shall be payable in respect of any person.

DEFINITIONS
  "the Administration Act": s.174.
  "couple": s.150(3).
  "pensionable age": s.150(1).
  "qualifying benefit": s.150(1).
  "the relevant week": s.150(4).
  "United Kingdom": ss.149(1) and 172.

GENERAL NOTE
  The Christmas bonus was introduced in 1972. As Ogus and Barendt note, "in social policy

terms, it serves little obvious purpose except that of courting political popularity" (p. 372). The amount payable (£10: subs. (3)) has not changed since 1972. The qualifying benefits are set out in s.150(1). On the determination of questions, see SSAA 1992, s.67.

Provisions supplementary to section 148

149.—(1) For the purposes of section 148 above the Channel Islands, the Isle of Man and Gibraltar shall be treated as though they were part of the United Kingdom.

(2) A person shall be treated for the purposes of section 148(1)(b) above as entitled to a payment of a qualifying benefit if he would be so entitled—

(a) in the case of a qualifying benefit other than income support, but for the fact that he or, if he is a member of a couple, the other member is entitled to receive some other payment out of public funds;

(b) in the case of income support, but for the fact that his income or, if he is a member of a couple, the income of the other member was exceptionally of an amount which resulted in his having ceased to be entitled to income support.

(3) A person shall be treated for the purposes of section 148(2)(c)(i) above as entitled in respect of the other member of the couple to an increase in a payment of a qualifying benefit if he would be so entitled—

(a) but for the fact that he or the other member is entitled to receive some other payment out of public funds;

(b) but for the operation of any provision of section 83(2) or (3) above or paragraph 6(4) of Schedule 7 to this Act or any regulations made under paragraph 6(3) of that Schedule whereby entitlement to benefit is affected by the amount of a person's earnings in a given period.

(4) For the purposes of section 148 above a person shall be taken not to be entitled to a payment of a war disablement pension unless not later than the end of the relevant week he has attained the age of 70 in the case of a man or 65 in the case of a woman.

(5) A sum payable under section 148 above shall not be treated as benefit for the purposes of any enactment or instrument under which entitlement to the relevant qualifying benefit arises or is to be treated as arising.

(6) A payment and the right to receive a payment—

(a) under section 148 above or any enactment corresponding to it in Northern Ireland; or

(b) under regulations relating to widows which are made by the Secretary of State under any enactment relating to police and which contain a statement that the regulations provide for payments corresponding to payments under that section,

shall be disregarded for all purposes of income tax and for the purposes of any enactment or instrument under which regard is had to a person's means.

DEFINITIONS
"United Kingdom": subs. (1) and s.172.

Interpretation of Part X

150.—(1) In this Part of this Act "qualifying benefit" means—

(a) a retirement pension;
(b) an invalidity pension;
(c) a widowed mother's allowance or widow's pension;
(d) a severe disablement allowance;
(e) an invalid care allowance;
(f) industrial death benefit;
(g) an attendance allowance;
(h) an unemployability supplement or allowance;
(i) a war disablement pension;
(j) a war widow's pension;

(k) income support.

(2) In this Part of this Act—

"attendance allowance" means—

(a) an attendance allowance;

(b) a disability living allowance;

(c) an increase of disablement pension under section 104 or 105 above;

(d) a payment under regulations made in exercise of the powers in section 159(3)(b) of the 1975 Act or paragraph 7(2) of Schedule 8 to this Act;

(e) an increase of allowance under Article 8 of the Pneumoconiosis, Byssinosis and Miscellaneous Diseases Benefit Scheme 1983 (constant attendance allowance for certain persons to whom that Scheme applies) or under the corresponding provision of any Scheme which may replace that Scheme;

(f) an allowance in respect of constant attendance on account of disablement for which a person is in receipt of war disablement pension, including an allowance in respect of exceptionally severe disablement;

"pensionable age" means—

(a) in the case of a man, the age of 65;

(b) in the case of a woman, the age of 60;

"retirement pension" includes graduated retirement benefit, if paid periodically;

"unemployability supplement or allowance" means—

(a) an unemployability supplement payable under Part I of Schedule 7 to this Act; or

(b) any corresponding allowance payable—

(i) by virtue of paragraph 6(4)(a) of Schedule 8 to this Act;

(ii) by way of supplement to retired pay or pension exempt from income tax under section 315(1) of the Income and Corporation Taxes Act 1988;

(iii) under the Personal Injuries (Emergency Provisions) Act 1939; or

(iv) by way of supplement to retired pay or pension under the Polish Resettlement Act 1947;

"war disablement pension" means—

(a) any retired pay, pension or allowance granted in respect of disablement under powers conferred by or under the Air Force (Constitution) Act 1917, the Personal Injuries (Emergency Provisions) Act 1939, the Pensions (Navy, Army, Air Force and Mercantile Marine) Act 1939, the Polish Resettlement Act 1947, or Part VII or section 151 of the Reserve Forces Act 1980;

(b) without prejudice to paragraph (a) of this definition, any retired pay or pension to which subsection (1) of section 315 of the Income and Corporation Taxes Act 1988 applies;

"war widow's pension" means any widow's pension or allowance granted in respect of a death due to service or war injury and payable by virtue of any enactment mentioned in paragraph (a) of the preceding definition or a pension or allowance for a widow granted under any scheme mentioned in subsection (2)(e) of the said section 315;

and each of the following expressions, namely "attendance allowance", "unemployability supplement or allowance", "war disablement pension" and "war widow's pension", includes any payment which the Secretary of State accepts as being analogous to it.

(3) References in this Part of this Act to a "couple" are references to a married or unmarried couple; and for this purpose "married couple" and

"unmarried couple" are to be construed in accordance with Part VII of this Act and any regulations made under it.

(4) In this Part of this Act "the relevant week", in relation to any year, means the week beginning with the first Monday in December or such other week as may be specified in an order made by the Secretary of State.

DEFINITIONS
"the 1975 Act": s.174.
"attendance allowance": subs. (2).
"couple": subs. (3).
"married couple": subs. (3).
"pensionable age": subs. (2).
"relevant week": subs. (4).
"retirement pension": subs. (2).
"unemployability supplement or allowance": subs. (2).
"unmarried couple": subs. (3).
"war disablement pension": subs. (2).
"war widow's pension": subs. (2).

PART XI

STATUTORY SICK PAY

Employer's liability

Employer's liability

151.—(1) Where an employee has a day of incapacity for work in relation to his contract of service with an employer, that employer shall, if the conditions set out in sections 152 to 154 below are satisfied, be liable to make him, in accordance with the following provisions of this Part of this Act, a payment (to be known as "statutory sick pay") in respect of that day.

(2) Any agreement shall be void to the extent that it purports—

(a) to exclude, limit or otherwise modify any provision of this Part of this Act, or

(b) to require an employee to contribute (whether directly or indirectly) towards any costs incurred by his employer under this Part of this Act.

(3) For the avoidance of doubt, any agreement between an employer and an employee authorising any deductions from statutory sick pay which the employer is liable to pay to the employee in respect of any period shall not be void by virtue of subsection (2)(a) above if the employer—

(a) is authorised by that or another agreement to make the same deductions from any contractual remuneration which he is liable to pay in respect of the same period, or

(b) would be so authorised if he were liable to pay contractual remuneration in respect of that period.

(4) For the purposes of this Part of this Act a day shall not be treated as a day of incapacity for work in relation to any contract of service unless on that day the employee concerned is, or is deemed in accordance with regulations to be, incapable by reason of some specific disease or bodily or mental disablement of doing work which he can reasonably be expected to do under that contract.

(5) In any case where an employee has more than one contract of service with the same employer the provisions of this Part of this Act shall, except in such cases as may be prescribed and subject to the following provisions of this Part of this Act, have effect as if the employer were a different employer in relation to each contract of service.

(6) Circumstances may be prescribed in which, notwithstanding the provisions of subsections (1) to (5) above, the liability to make payments of statutory sick pay is to be a liability of the Secretary of State.

GENERAL NOTE
Statutory sick pay was brought in by the SSHBA 1982 and supersedes sickness benefit so far as most employees are concerned. It is administered by employers although disputes may be referred to the normal social security adjudication machinery. As originally implemented, employers received 100 per cent. reimbursement for payments under the scheme. This was reduced under the SSPA 1991 to an 80 per cent. refund for all bar small employers (see s.158).

As a preliminary issue, the claimant must be an employee (subs. (1) and Statutory Sick Pay (General) Regulations 1982 (S.I. 1982 No. 894), reg. 17). Furthermore, in order for a claimant to qualify for statutory sick pay, the day in question must (1) form part of a period of incapacity for work (s.152); (2) fall within a period of entitlement (s.153); and (3) be a qualifying day (s.154).

Limitations on entitlement appear in s.155, while s.156 deals with notification of incapacity for work. Section 157 concerns rates of payment and ss.158 and 159 provide for refunds to employers of payments. The duties of employees and employers in respect of statutory sick pay are prescribed under SSAA 1992, ss.14 and 130 respectively.

The qualifying conditions

Period of incapacity for work

152.—(1) The first condition is that the day in question forms part of a period of incapacity for work.

(2) In this Part of this Act "period of incapacity for work" means any period of four or more consecutive days, each of which is a day of incapacity for work in relation to the contract of service in question.

(3) Any two periods of incapacity for work which are separated by a period of not more than eight weeks shall be treated as a single period of incapacity for work.

(4) The Secretary of State may by regulations direct that a larger number of weeks specified in the regulations shall be substituted for the number of weeks for the time being specified in subsection (3) above.

(5) No day of the week shall be disregarded in calculating any period of consecutive days for the purposes of this section.

(6) A day may be a day of incapacity for work in relation to a contract of service, and so form part of a period of incapacity for work, notwithstanding that—

(a) it falls before the making of the contract or after the contract expires or is brought to an end; or

(b) it is not a day on which the employee concerned would be required by that contract to be available for work.

GENERAL NOTE
The first condition for entitlement to statutory sick pay is that the day in question falls within a period of incapacity for work. This means a period of four or more consecutive days of incapacity, whether or not they are normally working days (subss. (2) and (5)). A linking rule operates by virtue of subs. (3), so that any two periods separated by not more than eight weeks

can be aggregated as one period of incapacity for work, so avoiding a duplication of the three "waiting days" (s.155(1)).

Period of entitlement

153.—(1) The second condition is that the day in question falls within a period which is, as between the employee and his employer, a period of entitlement.

(2) For the purposes of this Part of this Act a period of entitlement, as between an employee and his employer, is a period beginning with the commencement of a period of incapacity for work and ending with which-ever of the following first occurs—

(a) the termination of that period of incapacity for work;

(b) the day on which the employee reaches, as against the employer concerned, his maximum entitlement to statutory sick pay (deter-mined in accordance with section 155 below);

(c) the day on which the employee's contract of service with the employer concerned expires or is brought to an end;

(d) in the case of an employee who is, or has been, pregnant the day immediately preceding the beginning of the disqualifying period.

(3) Schedule 11 to this Act has effect for the purpose of specifying circumstances in which a period of entitlement does not arise in relation to a particular period of incapacity for work.

(4) A period of entitlement as between an employee and an employer of his may also be, or form part of, a period of entitlement as between him and another employer of his.

(5) The Secretary of State may by regulations—

(a) specify circumstances in which, for the purpose of determining whether an employee's maximum entitlement to statutory sick pay has been reached in a period of entitlement as between him and an employer of his, days falling within a previous period of entitlement as between the employee and any person who is or has in the past been an employer of his are to be counted; and

(b) direct that in prescribed circumstances an employer shall provide a person who is about to leave his employment, or who has been employed by him in the past, with a statement in the prescribed form containing such information as may be prescribed in relation to any entitlement of the employee to statutory sick pay.

(6) Regulations may provide, in relation to prescribed cases, for a period of entitlement to end otherwise than in accordance with subsection (2) above.

(7) In a case where the employee's contract of service first takes effect on a day which falls within a period of incapacity for work, the period of entitle-ment begins with that day.

(8) In a case where the employee's contract of service first takes effect between two periods of incapacity for work which by virtue of section 152(3) above are treated as one, the period of entitlement begins with the first day of the second of those periods.

(9) In any case where, otherwise than by virtue of section 6(1)(b) above, an employee's earnings under a contract of service in respect of the day on which the contract takes effect do not attract a liability to pay secondary Class 1 contributions, subsections (7) and (8) above shall have effect as if for any reference to the contract first taking effect there were substituted a reference to the first day in respect of which the employee's earnings attract such a liability.

(10) Regulations shall make provision as to an employer's liability under this Part of this Act to pay statutory sick pay to an employee in any case where the employer's contract of service with that employee has been

brought to an end by the employer solely, or mainly, for the purpose of avoiding liability for statutory sick pay.

(11) Subsection (2)(d) above does not apply in relation to an employee who has been pregnant if her pregnancy terminated, before the beginning of the disqualifying period, otherwise than by confinement.

(12) In this section—

"confinement" is to be construed in accordance with section 171(1) below;

"disqualifying period" means—

(a) in relation to a woman entitled to statutory maternity pay, the maternity pay period; and

(b) in relation to a woman entitled to maternity allowance, the maternity allowance period;

"maternity allowance period" has the meaning assigned to it by section 35(2) above, and

"maternity pay period" has the meaning assigned to it by section 165(1) below.

DEFINITIONS
"confinement": subs. (12).
"disqualifying period": subs. (12).
"contract of service": s.163(1).
"employee": s.163(1).
"employer": s.163(1).
"maternity allowance period": subs. (12).
"maternity pay period": subs. (12).
"period of entitlement": subs. (2).
"period of incapacity for work": s.152(2).
"prescribed": s.163(1).

GENERAL NOTE
The claimant's period of entitlement generally begins with the period of incapacity for work (but see special rules in subss. (7)–(9)) and ends on the occurrence of any of the events listed in subs. (2) or under regulations, *e.g.* Statutory Sick Pay (General) Regulations 1982 (S.I. 1982 No. 894), reg. 3. The maximum period of entitlement is 28 weeks.

Subsection (3) introduces Sched. 11, which in turn sets out various circumstances in which employees are precluded from claiming statutory sick pay (*e.g.* where they are earning less than the National Insurance lower earnings limit currently in force); see further Bonner.

Qualifying days

154.—(1) The third condition is that the day in question is a qualifying day.

(2) The days which are for the purposes of this Part of this Act to be qualifying days as between an employee and an employer of his (that is to say, those days of the week on which he is required by his contract of service with that employer to be available for work or which are chosen to reflect the terms of that contract) shall be such day or days as may, subject to regulations, be agreed between the employee and his employer or, failing such agreement, determined in accordance with regulations.

(3) In any case where qualifying days are determined by agreement between an employee and his employer there shall, in each week (beginning with Sunday), be at least one qualifying day.

(4) A day which is a qualifying day as between an employee and an employer of his may also be a qualifying day as between him and another employer of his.

DEFINITIONS
"contract of service": s.163(1).
"employee": s.163(1).
"employer": s.163(1).
"week": s.163(1).

In essence a qualifying day is a day on which the employee is required to be available for work. Employers and employees are granted a degree of flexibility by subs. (2) to agree which days count as qualifying days (but note subs. (3)). Further provision is made by the Statutory Sick Pay (General) Regulations 1982 (S.I. 1982 No. 894), reg. 5.

Subs. (2)
Required by his contract of service. This means, namely, not days where an employee is merely "asked" to work overtime: *R(SSP) 1/82.*

Limitations on entitlement, etc.

Limitations on entitlement

155.—(1) Statutory sick pay shall not be payable for the first three qualifying days in any period of entitlement.

(2) An employee shall not be entitled, as against any one employer, to an aggregate amount of statutory sick pay in respect of any one period of entitlement which exceeds his maximum entitlement.

(3) The maximum entitlement as against any one employer is reached on the day on which the amount to which the employee has become entitled by way of statutory sick pay during the period of entitlement in question first reaches or passes the entitlement limit.

(4) The entitlement limit is an amount equal to 28 times the appropriate weekly rate set out in section 157 below.

(5) Regulations may make provision for calculating the entitlement limit in any case where an employee's entitlement to statutory sick pay is calculated by reference to different weekly rates in the same period of entitlement.

DEFINITIONS
"employee": s.163(1).
"employer": s.163(1).
"period of entitlement": s.153(2).
"qualifying day": s.154.

GENERAL NOTE
As with unemployment benefit and sickness benefit, no statutory sick pay is payable for the first three qualifying days or "waiting days" (subs. (1)). An employee's maximum entitlement is determined in accordance with subss. (2)–(4) and amounts to 28 weeks.

Notification of incapacity for work

156.—(1) Regulations shall prescribe the manner in which, and the time within which, notice of any day of incapacity for work is to be given by or on behalf of an employee to his employer.

(2) An employer who would, apart from this section, be liable to pay an amount of statutory sick pay to an employee in respect of a qualifying day (the "day in question") shall be entitled to withhold payment of that amount if—

(a) the day in question is one in respect of which he has not been duly notified in accordance with regulations under subsection (1) above; or

(b) he has not been so notified in respect of any of the first three qualifying days in a period of entitlement (a "waiting day") and the day in question is the first qualifying day in that period of entitlement in respect of which the employer is not entitled to withhold payment—
(i) by virtue of paragraph (a) above; or
(ii) in respect of an earlier waiting day by virtue of this paragraph.

(3) Where an employer withholds any amount of statutory sick pay under this section—

(a) the period of entitlement in question shall not be affected; and

(b) for the purposes of calculating his maximum entitlement in accordance with section 155 above the employee shall not be taken to have become entitled to the amount so withheld.

DEFINITIONS

"employee": s.163(1).
"employer": s.163(1).
"period of entitlement": s.153(2).
"qualifying day": s.154.
"waiting day": subs. (2)(b).

GENERAL NOTE

This section is amplified by the Statutory Sick Pay (General) Regulations 1982 (S.I. 1982 No. 894), reg. 7. Where the employer has not been duly notified of the day of incapacity for work, statutory sick pay may be withheld (subs. (2)), but such days do not affect the period of entitlement; nor do they count towards the employee's maximum entitlement (subs. (3)).

Rates of payment, etc.

Rates of payment

157.—(1) Statutory sick pay shall be payable by an employer at the weekly rate of—

(a) £52.50, in a case where the employee's normal weekly earnings under his contract of service with that employer are not less than £190; or

(b) £45.30, in any other case.

(2) The Secretary of State may by order—

(a) substitute alternative provisions for the paragraphs of subsection (1) above; and

(b) make such consequential amendments as appear to him to be required of any provision contained in this Part of this Act.

(3) The amount of statutory sick pay payable by any one employer in respect of any day shall be the weekly rate applicable on that day divided by the number of days which are, in the week (beginning with Sunday) in which that day falls, qualifying days as between that employer and the employee concerned.

DEFINITIONS

"contract of service": s.163(1).
"earnings": Statutory Sick Pay (General) Regulations 1982 (S.I. 1982 No. 894), reg. 17.
"employee": s.163(1).
"employer": s.163(1).
"normal weekly earnings": s.163(2) and Statutory Sick Pay (General) Regulations 1982 (S.I. 1987 No. 894), reg. 19.
"qualifying day": s.154.
"week": s.163(1).

GENERAL NOTE

There are two rates of statutory sick pay, the higher rate being payable where the employee's normal weekly earnings exceed a prescribed amount. Unlike sickness benefit, statutory sick pay has never had to be uprated in line with inflation. In 1990 employees became eligible for the higher rate if they earned £125 per week or more; this threshold was raised to £185 in 1991, and to £190 for 1992. The higher rate itself has not been uprated since April 1990.

The concepts of "earnings" and "normal weekly earnings" are defined in the Statutory Sick Pay (General) Regulations 1982 (S.I. 1982 No. 894).

Recovery by employers of amounts paid by way of statutory sick pay

158.—(1) Regulations shall make provision—

(a) entitling, except in prescribed circumstances, any employer who has made one or more payments of statutory sick pay in a prescribed period to recover an amount equal to the sum of—

(i) the aggregate of such of those payments as qualify for small employers' relief; and

(ii) an amount equal to 80 per cent. of the aggregate of such of those payments as do not so qualify,

by making one or more deductions from his contributions payments; and

(b) for the payment, in prescribed circumstances, by or on behalf of the Secretary of State of sums to employers who are unable so to recover the whole, or any part, of the amounts which they are entitled to recover by virtue of paragraph (a) above.

(2) For the purposes of this section, a payment of statutory sick pay which an employer is liable to make to an employee for any day which forms part of a period of incapacity for work qualifies for small employers' relief if—

(a) on that day the employer is a small employer who has been liable to pay statutory sick pay in respect of that employee for earlier days forming part of that period of incapacity for work; and

(b) the aggregate amount of those payments exceeds the entitlement threshold, that is to say, an amount equal to $W \times R$, where—

W is a prescribed number of weeks; and

R is the appropriate weekly rate set out in section 157 above;

and regulations may make provision for calculating the entitlement threshold in any case where the employee's entitlement to statutory sick pay is calculated by reference to different weekly rates in the same period of incapacity for work.

(3) For the purposes of this section, "small employer" shall have the meaning assigned to it by regulations, and, without prejudice to the generality of the foregoing, any such regulations—

(a) may define that expression by reference to the amount of an employer's contributions payments for any prescribed period; and

(b) if they do so, may in that connection make provision for the amount of those payments for that prescribed period—

(i) to be determined without regard to any deductions that may be made from them under this section or under any other enactment or instrument; and

(ii) in prescribed circumstances, to be adjusted, estimated or otherwise attributed to him by reference to their amount in any other prescribed period.

(4) In this section "contributions payments", in relation to an employer, means any payments which the employer is required, by or under any enactment, to make in discharge of any liability in respect of primary or secondary Class 1 contributions.

(5) Regulations under this section may, in particular,—

(a) provide for any deduction made in accordance with the regulations to be disregarded for prescribed purposes; and

(b) provide for the rounding up or down of any fraction of a penny which would otherwise result from calculating the amount which an employer is entitled to recover for any period by virtue of subsection (1)(a) above.

(6) Where, in accordance with any provision of regulations made under this section, an amount has been deducted from an employer's contributions payments, the amount so deducted shall (except in such cases as may be prescribed) be treated for the purposes of any provision made by or under any enactment in relation to primary or secondary Class 1 contributions as having been—

(a) paid (on such date as may be determined in accordance with the regulations); and

(b) received by the Secretary of State,
towards discharging the liability mentioned in subsection (4) above.

(7) Any day of incapacity for work falling before 6th April 1991 shall be left out of account for the purposes of subsection (2) above.

DEFINITIONS
"contributions payments": subs. (4).
"employee": s.163(1).
"employer": s.163(1).
"period of incapacity for work": s.152(2).
"prescribed": s.163(1).
"small employer": subs. (3).
"week": s.163(1).

GENERAL NOTE
Statutory sick pay is indirectly financed by social security contributions, in that employer's payments are offset against their contributions liability under arrangements made under this section. Originally this offset represented 100 per cent. of the cost of statutory sick pay payments, but reimbursement was reduced to 80 per cent. by the SSPA 1991. Small employers continue to receive 100 per cent. reimbursement (subs. (1)(a)(i) and (2); but see also s.159). A small employer is defined (for 1992/93) as one who pays (or is liable to pay) £16,000 or less in gross national insurance contributions in the relevant tax year (Statutory Sick Pay (Small Employers' Relief) Amendment Regulations 1992 (S.I. 1992 No. 797)). The SSPA 1991 also abolished the compensatory sum previously paid to employers to cover administrative costs and contributions paid during periods of statutory sick pay.

Power to substitute provisions for s.158(2)

159.—(1) If the Secretary of State by order so provides for any tax year, the following subsections shall have effect for that tax year in substitution for section 158(2) above—

"(2A) For the purposes of this section, a payment of statutory sick pay which an employer is liable to make to an employee for any day in a tax year qualifies for small employers' relief if—

(a) on that day the employer is a small employer who has been liable to make payments of statutory sick pay for earlier days in that tax year in respect of any employees of his; and

(b) the aggregate of any such payments for those earlier days exceeds a prescribed sum.

(2B) In any case where—

(a) an employer is liable to make two or more payments of statutory sick pay for the same day in a tax year; and

(b) by virtue of the condition in subsection (2A)(b) above, none of those payments would qualify for small employers' relief; but

(c) that condition would have been fulfilled in relation to a proportion of the aggregate amount of those payments, had he been liable—

(i) to pay as statutory sick pay for an earlier day in that tax year, instead of for the day in question, the smallest part of that aggregate that would enable that condition to be fulfilled; and

(ii) to pay the remainder as statutory sick pay for the day in question,

he shall be treated for the purposes of subsection (2A) above as if he had been liable to make payments of statutory sick pay as mentioned in paragraph (c) above instead of as mentioned in paragraph (a) above.

(2C) If, in a case not falling within subsection (2B) above—

(a) an employer is liable to make a single payment of statutory sick pay for a day in a tax year; and

(b) by virtue of the condition in subsection (2A)(b) above, that payment would not qualify for small employers' relief; but

(c) that condition would have been fulfilled in relation to a proportion of that payment, had he been liable—

(i) to pay as statutory sick pay for an earlier day in that tax year, instead of for the day in question, the smallest part of that payment that would enable that condition to be fulfilled; and

(ii) to pay the remainder as statutory sick pay for the day in question,

he shall be treated for the purposes of subsection (2A) above as if he had been liable to make payments of statutory sick pay as mentioned in paragraph (c) above instead of the payment mentioned in paragraph (a) above.".

(2) Without prejudice to section 175(4) below, the Secretary of State may by regulations make such transitional or consequential provision or savings as he considers necessary or expedient in connection with the coming into force of an order under subsection (1) above or the expiry or revocation of any such order and the consequent revival of section 158(2) above.

DEFINITIONS
"employee": s.163(1).
"employer": s.163(1).
"prescribed": s.163(1).
"small employer": s.158(3).

GENERAL NOTE
This provides for an alternative basis for small employers' relief under s.158(2).

Miscellaneous

Relationship with benefits and other payments, etc.

160. Schedule 12 to this Act has effect with respect to the relationship between statutory sick pay and certain benefits and payments.

GENERAL NOTE
This section introduces Sched. 12, which provides that no day of incapacity (whether or not it is also a qualifying day) within a period of entitlement to statutory sick pay can count as part of a period of interruption of employment. Consequently there can be no entitlement to sickness benefit in such a case.

Crown employment—Part XI

161.—(1) Subject to subsection (2) below, the provisions of this Part of this Act apply in relation to persons employed by or under the Crown as they apply in relation to persons employed otherwise than by or under the Crown.

(2) The provisions of this Part of this Act do not apply in relation to persons serving as members of Her Majesty's forces, in their capacity as such.

(3) For the purposes of this section Her Majesty's forces shall be taken to consist of such establishments and organisations as may be prescribed, being establishments and organisations in which persons serve under the control of the Defence Council.

GENERAL NOTE
Employees of the Crown are eligible for statutory sick pay unless they are members of H.M. forces (an exception which does not apply to statutory maternity pay: see s.169).

Special classes of persons

162.—(1) The Secretary of State may make regulations modifying this Part of this Act in such manner as he thinks proper in their application to any person who is, has been or is to be—

(a) employed on board any ship, vessel, hovercraft or aircraft;
(b) outside Great Britain at any prescribed time or in any prescribed circumstances; or
(c) in prescribed employment in connection with continental shelf operations, as defined in section 120(2) above.
(2) Regulations under subsection (1) above may in particular provide—
(a) for any provision of this Part of this Act to apply to any such person, notwithstanding that it would not otherwise apply;
(b) for any such provision not to apply to any such person, notwithstanding that it would otherwise apply;
(c) for excepting any such person from the application of any such provision where he neither is domiciled nor has a place of residence in any part of Great Britain;
(d) for the taking of evidence, for the purposes of the determination of any question arising under any such provision, in a country or territory outside Great Britain, by a British consular official or such other person as may be determined in accordance with the regulations.

DEFINITIONS
"Great Britain": s.172.
"prescribed": s.163(1).

GENERAL NOTE

Subs. 2(d)
On the drafting of this provision, see the Law Commission's report (Cm 1726, 1991), para. 4.

Interpretation of Part XI and supplementary provisions
163.—(1) In this Part of this Act—
"contract of service" (except in paragraph (a) of the definition below of "employee") includes any arrangement providing for the terms of appointment of an employee;
"employee" means a person who is—
　　(a) gainfully employed in Great Britain either under a contract of service or in an office (including elective office) with emoluments chargeable to income tax under Schedule E; and
　　(b) over the age of 16;
　　but subject to regulations, which may provide for cases where any such person is not to be treated as an employee for the purposes of this Part of this Act and for cases where any person who would not otherwise be an employee for those purposes is to be treated as an employee for those purposes;
"employer", in relation to an employee and a contract of service of his, means a person who under section 6 above is, or but for subsection (1)(b) of that section would be, liable to pay secondary Class 1 contribution in relation to any earnings of the employee under the contract;
"period of entitlement" has the meaning given by section 153 above;
"period of incapacity for work" has the meaning given by section 152 above;
"period of interruption of employment" has the same meaning as it has in the provisions of this Act relating to unemployment benefit, sickness benefit and invalidity benefit by virtue of section 57(1)(d) above;
"prescribed" means prescribed by regulations;
"qualifying day" has the meaning given by section 154 above;
"week" means any period of seven days.
(2) For the purposes of this Part of this Act an employee's normal weekly earnings shall, subject to subsection (4) below, be taken to be the average

weekly earnings which in the relevant period have been paid to him or paid for his benefit under his contract of service with the employer in question.

(3) For the purposes of subsection (2) above, the expressions "earnings" and "relevant period" shall have the meaning given to them by regulations.

(4) In such cases as may be prescribed an employee's normal weekly earnings shall be calculated in accordance with regulations.

(5) Without prejudice to any other power to make regulations under this Part of this Act, regulations may specify cases in which, for the purposes of this Part of this Act or such of its provisions as may be prescribed—

(a) two or more employers are to be treated as one;

(b) two or more contracts of service in respect of which the same person is an employee are to be treated as one.

(6) Where, in consequence of the establishment of one or more National Health Service trusts under Part I of the National Health Service and Community Care Act 1990 or the National Health Service (Scotland) Act 1978, a person's contract of employment is treated by a scheme under that Part or Act as divided so as to constitute two or more contracts, regulations may make provision enabling him to elect for all of those contracts to be treated as one contract for the purposes of this Part of this Act or of such provisions of this Part of this Act as may be prescribed; and any such regulations may prescribe—

(a) the conditions that must be satisfied if a person is to be entitled to make such an election;

(b) the manner in which, and the time within which, such an election is to be made;

(c) the persons to whom, and the manner in which, notice of such an election is to be given;

(d) the information which a person who makes such an election is to provide, and the persons to whom, and the time within which, he is to provide it;

(e) the time for which such an election is to have effect;

(f) which one of the person's employers under the two or more contracts is to be regarded for the purposes of statutory sick pay as his employer under the one contract;

and the powers conferred by this subsection are without prejudice to any other power to make regulations under this Part of this Act.

(7) Regulations may provide for periods of work which begin on one day and finish on the following day to be treated, for the purposes of this Part of this Act, as falling solely within one or other of those days.

DEFINITIONS
"Great Britain": s.172.

GENERAL NOTE
See further the Statutory Sick Pay (General) Regulations 1982 (S.I. 1982 No. 894).

PART XII

STATUTORY MATERNITY PAY

Statutory maternity pay—entitlement and liability to pay

164.—(1) Where a woman who is or has been an employee satisfies the conditions set out in this section, she shall be entitled, in accordance with the following provisions of this Part of this Act, to payments to be known as "statutory maternity pay".

(2) The conditions mentioned in subsection (1) above are—

(a) that she has been in employed earner's employment with an employer for a continuous period of at least 26 weeks ending with the week immediately preceding the 14th week before the expected week of confinement but has ceased to work for him, wholly or partly because of pregnancy or confinement;

    (b) that her normal weekly earnings for the period of eight weeks ending with the week immediately preceding the 14th week before the expected week of confinement are not less than the lower earnings limit in force under section 5(1)(a) above immediately before the commencement of the 14th week before the expected week of confinement; and

    (c) that she has become pregnant and has reached, or been confined before reaching, the commencement of the 11th week before the expected week of confinement.

(3) The liability to make payments of statutory maternity pay to a woman is a liability of any person of whom she has been an employee as mentioned in subsection (2)(a) above.

(4) Except in such cases as may be prescribed, a woman shall be entitled to payments of statutory maternity pay only if—

    (a) she gives the person who will be liable to pay it notice that she is going to be absent from work with him, wholly or partly because of pregnancy or confinement; and

    (b) the notice is given at least 21 days before her absence from work is due to begin or, if that is not reasonably practicable, as soon as is reasonably practicable.

(5) The notice shall be in writing if the person who is liable to pay the woman statutory maternity pay so requests.

(6) Any agreement shall be void to the extent that it purports—

    (a) to exclude, limit or otherwise modify any provision of this Part of this Act; or

    (b) to require an employee or former employee to contribute (whether directly or indirectly) towards any costs incurred by her employer or former employer under this Part of this Act.

(7) For the avoidance of doubt, any agreement between an employer and an employee authorising any deductions from statutory maternity pay which the employer is liable to pay to the employee in respect of any period shall not be void by virtue of subsection (6)(a) above if the employer—

    (a) is authorised by that or another agreement to make the same deductions from any contractual remuneration which he is liable to pay in respect of the same period, or

    (b) would be so authorised if he were liable to pay contractual remuneration in respect of that period.

(8) Regulations shall make provision as to a former employer's liability to pay statutory maternity pay to a woman in any case where the former employer's contract of service with her has been brought to an end by the former employer solely, or mainly, for the purpose of avoiding liability for statutory maternity pay.

(9) The Secretary of State may by regulations—

    (a) specify circumstances in which, notwithstanding subsections (1) to (8) above, there is to be no liability to pay statutory maternity pay in respect of a week;

    (b) specify circumstances in which, notwithstanding subsections (1) to (8) above, the liability to make payments of statutory maternity pay is to be a liability of his;

    (c) specify in what circumstances employment is to be treated as continuous for the purposes of this Part of this Act;

    (d) provide that a woman is to be treated as being employed for a continuous period of at least 26 weeks where—

        (i) she has been employed by the same employer for at least 26 weeks under two or more separate contracts of service; and

       (ii) those contracts were not continuous;

    (e) provide that any of the provisions specified in subsection (10) below shall have effect subject to prescribed modifications—

        (i) where a woman has been dismissed from her employment;

        (ii) where a woman is confined before the beginning of the 14th week before the expected week of confinement; and

        (iii) in such other cases as may be prescribed;

    (f) provide for amounts earned by a woman under separate contracts of service with the same employer to be aggregated for the purposes of this Part of this Act; and

    (g) provide that—

        (i) the amount of a woman's earnings for any period, or

        (ii) the amount of her earnings to be treated as comprised in any payment made to her or for her benefit,

shall be calculated or estimated in such manner and on such basis as may be prescribed and that for that purpose payments of a particular class or description made or falling to be made to or by a woman shall, to such extent as may be prescribed, be disregarded or, as the case may be, be deducted from the amount of her earnings.

(10) The provisions mentioned in subsection (9)(e) above are—

    (a) subsection (2)(a) and (b) above; and

    (b) section 166(2), (4) and (5) below.

DEFINITIONS

    "confined": s.171(1).
    "confinement": s.171(1).
    "dismissed": s.171(1).
    "employee": s.171(1).
    "employer": s.171(1).
    "prescribed": s.171(1).
    "week": s.171(1).

GENERAL NOTE

Statutory maternity pay came into being in April 1987. It superseded the maternity pay provisions under the employment protection legislation and effectively replaced maternity allowance for most women employees. Maternity allowance remains in existence for employees who are not entitled to statutory maternity pay (s.35). Statutory maternity pay is analogous to statutory sick pay in that it is administered by employers (subs. (3)) and disputes can be referred to the normal social security adjudication machinery.

An employee is entitled to statutory maternity pay if she satisfies four main conditions:

(1) She has been continuously employed in employed earner's employment for 26 weeks up to and including the fifteenth week (the qualifying week) before the expected week of confinement (subs. (2)(a)). Regulations (see below) provide for certain disregards in calculating this period.

(2) Her average weekly earnings in the eight weeks before the qualifying week exceeded the current lower earnings limit for National Insurance contributions (subs. (2)(b)). Regulations (see below) define earnings and normal weekly earnings. Note, however, that there are no contributions conditions as such.

(3) She is pregnant and has reached (or has been confined by) the 11th week before the expected week of confinement (subs. (2)(c)). Regulations (see below) provide for modifications where a woman has been dismissed by an employer solely or mainly for the purpose of avoiding liability to pay statutory maternity pay.

(4) She gives notice of her absence for pregnancy or confinement at least 21 days before such absence (or, if that is not reasonably practicable, as soon as reasonably practicable) (subs. (4) and (5)). On the interpretation of this requirement, see by analogy *Nu-Swift International* v. *Mallison* [1979] I.C.R. 157.

This basic scheme is modified by regulations made by the Secretary of State under subss. (8) and (9): see Statutory Maternity Pay (General) Regulations 1986 (S.I. 1986 No. 1960). The duties of employees and employers in respect of statutory maternity pay are prescribed under SSAA 1992, ss.15 and 132 respectively.

The maternity pay period

165.—(1) Statutory maternity pay shall be payable, subject to the provisions of this Part of this Act, in respect of each week during a prescribed period ("the maternity pay period") of a duration not exceeding 18 weeks.

(2) Subject to subsections (3) and (7) below, the first week of the maternity pay period shall be the 11th week before the expected week of confinement.

(3) Cases may be prescribed in which the first week of the period is to be a prescribed week later than the 11th week before the expected week of confinement, but not later than the 6th week before the expected week of confinement.

(4) Statutory maternity pay shall not be payable to a woman by a person in respect of any week during any part of which she works under a contract of service with him.

(5) It is immaterial for the purposes of subsection (4) above whether the work referred to in that subsection is work under a contract of service which existed immediately before the maternity pay period or a contract of service which did not so exist.

(6) Except in such cases as may be prescribed, statutory maternity pay shall not be payable to a woman in respect of any week after she has been confined and during any part of which she works for any employer who is not liable to pay her statutory maternity pay.

(7) Regulations may provide that this section shall have effect subject to prescribed modifications in relation—

    (a) to cases in which a woman has been confined before the 11th week before the expected week of confinement; and

    (b) to cases in which—

        (i) a woman is confined during the period beginning with the 11th week, and ending with the 7th week, before the expected week of confinement; and

        (ii) the maternity pay period has not then commenced for her.

DEFINITIONS
    "confinement": s.171(1).
    "employer": s.171(1).
    "maternity pay period": subs. (1).
    "modifications": s.171(1).
    "prescribed": s.171(1).
    "week": s.171(1).

GENERAL NOTE
    Statutory maternity pay is payable for a maximum of 18 weeks (subs. (1)). This "maternity pay period" must begin no earlier than 11 weeks before the expected week of confinement (subs. (2)). The start of this period of 18 weeks' entitlement may be postponed to begin no later than six weeks before the expected week of confinement (subs. (3)). This allows women a degree of flexibility. These rules are modified by Statutory Maternity Pay (General) Regulations 1986 (S.I. 1986 No. 1960), Pt. II, for special cases.

    No statutory maternity pay is payable for any week in which the woman works for an employer liable to pay her this benefit (subss. (4) and (5)). Nor is a woman entitled where she works for another employer after her confinement (subs. (6), but see reg. 8). Further exclusions of entitlement are provided for in the regulations.

Rates of payment

166.—(1) There shall be two rates of statutory maternity pay, in this Act referred to as "the higher rate" and "the lower rate".

(2) The higher rate is a weekly rate equivalent to nine-tenths of a woman's normal weekly earnings for the period of eight weeks immediately preceding the 14th week before the expected week of confinement or the weekly rate prescribed under subsection (3) below, whichever is the higher.

(3) The lower rate is such weekly rate as may be prescribed.

(4) Subject to the following provisions of this section, statutory maternity pay shall be payable at the higher rate to a woman who for a continuous period of at least two years ending with the week immediately preceding the 14th week before the expected week of confinement has been an employee in employed earner's employment of any person liable to pay it to her, and shall be so paid by any such person in respect of the first six weeks in respect of which it is payable.

(5) Statutory maternity pay shall not be payable at the higher rate to a woman whose relations with the person liable to pay it are or were governed by a contract of service which normally involves or involved employment for less than 16 hours weekly unless during a continuous period of at least five years ending with the week immediately preceding the 14th week before the expected week of confinement her contract of service normally involved employment for eight hours or more weekly.

(6) The Secretary of State may by regulations make provision as to when a contract of service is to be treated for the purposes of subsection (5) above as normally involving or having involved employment—

(a) for less than 16 hours weekly; or

(b) for eight hours or more weekly,

or as not normally involving or having involved such employment.

(7) Statutory maternity pay shall be payable to a woman at the lower rate if she is entitled to statutory maternity pay but is not entitled to payment at the higher rate.

(8) If a woman is entitled to statutory maternity pay at the higher rate, she shall be entitled to it at the lower rate in respect of the portion of the maternity pay period after the end of the six week period mentioned in subsection (4) above.

DEFINITIONS
> "confinement": s.171(1).
> "employee": s.171(1).
> "higher rate": subs. (2).
> "lower rate": subs. (3).
> "prescribed": s.171(1).
> "week": s.171(1).

GENERAL NOTE
> There are two rates of statutory maternity pay. The higher rate is 90 per cent. of the average weekly earnings in the eight weeks preceding the qualifying week (subs. (2)). This rate is only payable to women who have been employed by the relevant employer for at least 16 hours a week for a continuous period of two years immediately before the qualifying week (or for at least eight hours a week for the previous five years): subss. (4)–(5). The lower rate is a flat-rate sum payable both to those who do not qualify for the higher rate (subs. (7)) and for the remaining 12 weeks of entitlement for those who qualify for six weeks on the higher rate (subs. (8)).

Recovery of amounts paid by way of statutory maternity pay

167.—(1) Regulations shall make provision—

(a) entitling, except in prescribed circumstances, any person who has made a payment of statutory maternity pay to recover the amount so paid by making one or more deductions from his contributions payments;

(b) for the payment, in prescribed circumstances, by the Secretary of State or by the Commissioners of Inland Revenue on behalf of the Secretary of State, of sums to persons who are unable so to recover the whole, or any part, of any payments of statutory maternity pay which they have made;

(c) giving any person who has made a payment of statutory maternity pay

a right, except in prescribed circumstances, to an amount, determined in such manner as may be prescribed—
      (i) by reference to secondary Class 1 contributions paid in respect of statutory maternity pay; or
      (ii) by reference to secondary Class 1 contributions paid in respect of statutory sick pay; or
      (iii) by reference to the aggregate of secondary Class 1 contributions paid in respect of statutory maternity pay and secondary Class 1 contributions paid in respect of statutory sick pay;
  (d) providing for the recovery, in prescribed circumstances, of the whole or any part of any such amount from contributions payments;
  (e) for the payment in prescribed circumstances, by the Secretary of State or by the Commissioners of Inland Revenue on behalf of the Secretary of State, of the whole or any part of any such amount.
  (2) In this section "contributions payments", in relation to an employer, means any payments which the employer is required, by or under any enactment, to make in discharge of any liability in respect of primary or secondary Class 1 contributions.
  (3) Regulations under subsection (1) above may, in particular, provide for any deduction made in accordance with the regulations to be disregarded for prescribed purposes.
  (4) Where, in accordance with any provision of regulations made under this section, an amount has been deducted from an employer's contributions payments, the amount so deducted shall (except in such cases as may be prescribed) be treated for the purposes of any provision made by or under any enactment in relation to primary or secondary Class 1 contributions as having been—
  (a) paid (on such date as may be determined in accordance with the regulations); and
  (b) received by the Secretary of State,
towards discharging the employer's liability in respect of such contributions.

DEFINITIONS
  "contributions payments": subs. (2).
  "employer": s.171(1).
  "prescribed": s.171(1).

GENERAL NOTE

Subs. (2)
  The inclusion of a specific definition of "contributions payments", equivalent to that for statutory maternity pay (s.158(4)), follows the recommendation of the Law Commissions (Cm 1726, 1991), para. 5.

Relationship with benefits and other payments etc.

  168. Schedule 13 to this Act has effect with respect to the relationship between statutory maternity pay and certain benefits and payments.

GENERAL NOTE
  This section introduces Sched. 13 which provides that as a general principle entitlement to statutory maternity pay precludes any entitlement to maternity allowance, statutory sick pay, sickness benefit or unemployment benefit in respect of the same period.

Crown employment—Part XII

  169. The provisions of this Part of this Act apply in relation to women employed by or under the Crown as they apply in relation to women employed otherwise than by or under the Crown.

GENERAL NOTE
  The exclusion of women members of H.M. forces from receiving statutory maternity pay

was ended by SSA 1990, Sched. 6, para. 25. In this respect statutory maternity pay differs from statutory sick pay (s.161).

Special classes of persons

170.—(1) The Secretary of State may make regulations modifying this Part of this Act in such manner as he thinks proper in their application to any person who is, has been or is to be—

(a) employed on board any ship, vessel, hovercraft or aircraft;

(b) outside Great Britain at any prescribed time or in any prescribed circumstances; or

(c) in prescribed employment in connection with continental shelf operations, as defined in section 120(2) above.

(2) Regulations under subsection (1) above may in particular provide—

(a) for any provision of this Part of this Act to apply to any such person, notwithstanding that it would not otherwise apply;

(b) for any such provision not to apply to any such person, notwithstanding that it would otherwise apply;

(c) for excepting any such person from the application of any such provision where he neither is domiciled nor has a place of residence in any part of Great Britain;

(d) for the taking of evidence, for the purposes of the determination of any question arising under any such provision, in a country or territory outside Great Britain, by a British consular official or such other person as may be determined in accordance with the regulations.

DEFINITIONS
"Great Britain": s.172.

GENERAL NOTE
See further Statutory Maternity Pay (Persons Abroad and Mariners) Regulations 1987 (S.I. 1987 No. 418).

Subs. (2)(d)
See General Note to s.162(2) above.

Interpretation of Part XII and supplementary provisions

171.—(1) In this Part of this Act—

"confinement" means—

(a) labour resulting in the issue of a living child, or

(b) labour after 28 weeks of pregnancy resulting in the issue of a child whether alive or dead,

and "confined" shall be construed accordingly; and where a woman's labour begun on one day results in the issue of a child on another day she shall be taken to be confined on the day of the issue of the child or, if labour results in the issue of twins or a greater number of children, she shall be taken to be confined on the day of the issue of the last of them;

"dismissed" is to be construed in accordance with section 55(2) to (7) of the Employment Protection (Consolidation) Act 1978;

"employee" means a woman who is—

(a) gainfully employed in Great Britain either under a contract of service or in an office (including elective office) with emoluments chargeable to income tax under Schedule E; and

(b) over the age of 16;

but subject to regulations which may provide for cases where any such woman is not to be treated as an employee for the purposes of this Part of this Act and for cases where a woman who would not otherwise be an employee for those purposes is to be treated as an employee for those purposes;

"employer", in relation to a woman who is an employee, means a person who under section 6 above is, or but for subsection (1)(b) of that section would be, liable to pay secondary Class 1 contributions in relation to any of her earnings;

"maternity pay period" has the meaning assigned to it by section 165(1) above;

"modifications" includes additions, omissions and amendments, and related expressions shall be construed accordingly;

"prescribed" means specified in or determined in accordance with regulations;

"week" means a period of seven days beginning with Sunday or such other period as may be prescribed in relation to any particular case or class of cases.

(2) Without prejudice to any other power to make regulations under this Part of this Act, regulations may specify cases in which, for the purposes of this Part of this Act or of such provisions of this Part of this Act as may be prescribed—

(a) two or more employers are to be treated as one;

(b) two or more contracts of service in respect of which the same woman is an employee are to be treated as one.

(3) Where, in consequence of the establishment of one or more National Health Service trusts under Part I of the National Health Service and Community Care Act 1990 or the National Health Service (Scotland) Act 1978, a woman's contract of employment is treated by a scheme under that Part or Act as divided so as to constitute two or more contracts, regulations may make provision enabling her to elect for all of those contracts to be treated as one contract for the purposes of this Part of this Act or of such provisions of this Part of this Act as may be prescribed; and any such regulations may prescribe—

(a) the conditions that must be satisfied if a woman is to be entitled to make such an election;

(b) the manner in which, and the time within which, such an election is to be made;

(c) the persons to whom, and the manner in which notice of such an election is to be given;

(d) the information which a woman who makes such an election is to provide, and the persons to whom, and the time within which, she is to provide it;

(e) the time for which such an election is to have effect;

(f) which one of the woman's employers under the two or more contracts is to be regarded for the purposes of statutory maternity pay as her employer under the one contract;

and the powers conferred by this subsection are without prejudice to any other power to make regulations under this Part of this Act.

(4) For the purposes of this Part of this Act a woman's normal weekly earnings shall, subject to subsection (6) below, be taken to be the average weekly earnings which in the relevant period have been paid to her or paid for her benefit under the contract of service with the employer in question.

(5) For the purposes of subsection (4) above "earnings" and "relevant period" shall have the meanings given to them by regulations.

(6) In such cases as may be prescribed a woman's normal weekly earnings shall be calculated in accordance with regulations.

DEFINITIONS

"Great Britain": s.172.

GENERAL NOTE

See further Statutory Maternity Pay (General) Regulations 1986 (S.I. 1986 No. 1960).

PART XIII

GENERAL

Interpretation

Application of Act in relation to territorial waters

172. In this Act—
(a) any reference to Great Britain includes a reference to the territorial waters of the United Kingdom adjacent to Great Britain;
(b) any reference to the United Kingdom includes a reference to the territorial waters of the United Kingdom.

Age

173. For the purposes of this Act a person—
(a) is over or under a particular age if he has or, as the case may be, has not attained that age; and
(b) is between two particular ages if he has attained the first but not the second;
and in Scotland (as in England and Wales) the time at which a person attains a particular age expressed in years is the commencement of the relevant anniversary of the date of his birth.

References to Acts

174. In this Act—
"the 1975 Act" means the Social Security Act 1975;
"the 1986 Act" means the Social Security Act 1986;
"the Administration Act" means the Social Security Administration Act 1992;
"the Consequential Provisions Act" means the Social Security (Consequential Provisions) Act 1992;
"the Northern Ireland Contributions and Benefits Act" means the Social Security Contributions and Benefits (Northern Ireland) Act 1992;
"the Old Cases Act" means the Industrial Injuries and Diseases (Old Cases) Act 1975; and
"the Pensions Act" means the Social Security Pensions Act 1975.

Subordinate legislation

Regulations, orders and schemes

175.—(1) Subject to section 145(5) above, regulations and orders under this Act shall be made by the Secretary of State.

(2) Powers under this Act to make regulations, orders or schemes shall be exercisable by statutory instrument.

(3) Except in the case of an order under section 145(3) above and in so far as this Act otherwise provides, any power under this Act to make regulations or an order may be exercised—
(a) either in relation to all cases to which the power extends, or in relation to those cases subject to specified exceptions, or in relation to any specified cases or classes of case;
(b) so as to make, as respects the cases in relations to which it is exercised—
(i) the full provision to which the power extends or any less provision (whether by way of exception or otherwise),
(ii) the same provision for all cases in relation to which the power is exercised, or different provision for different cases or different

classes of case or different provision as respects the same case or class of case for different purposes of this Act,

    (iii) any such provision either unconditionally or subject to any specified condition;

and where such a power is expressed to be exercisable for alternative purposes it may be exercised in relation to the same case for any or all of those purposes; and powers to make regulations or an order for the purposes of any one provision of this Act are without prejudice to powers to make regulations or an order for the purposes of any other provision.

(4) Without prejudice to any specific provision in this Act, any power conferred by this Act to make regulations or an order (other than the power conferred in section 145(3) above) includes power to make thereby such incidental, supplementary, consequential or transitional provision as appears to the Secretary of State to be expedient for the purposes of the regulations or order.

(5) Without prejudice to any specific provisions in this Act, a power conferred by any provision of this Act except—

    (a) sections 30, 47(6), 57(9)(a) and 145(3) above and paragraph 3(9) of Schedule 7 to this Act;

    (b) section 122(1) above in relation to the definition of "payments by way of occupational or personal pension"; and

    (c) Part XI,

to make regulations or an order includes power to provide for a person to exercise a discretion in dealing with any matter.

(6) Any power conferred by this Act to make orders or regulations relating to housing benefit or community charge benefits shall include power to make different provisions for different areas.

(7) Any power of the Secretary of State under any provision of this Act, except the provisions mentioned in subsection (5)(a) and (b) above and Part IX, to make any regulations or order, where the power is not expressed to be exercisable with the consent of the Treasury, shall if the Treasury so direct be exercisable only in conjunction with them.

(8) Any power under any of sections 116 to 120 above to modify provisions of this Act or the Administration Act extends also to modifying so much of any other provision of this Act or that Act as re-enacts provisions of the 1975 Act which replaced provisions of the National Insurance (Industrial Injuries) Acts 1965 to 1974.

(9) A power to make regulations under any of sections 116 to 120 above shall be exercisable in relation to any enactment passed after this Act which is directed to be construed as one with this Act; but this subsection applies only so far as a contrary intention is not expressed in the enactment so passed, and is without prejudice to the generality of any such direction.

(10) Any reference in this section or section 176 below to an order or regulations under this Act includes a reference to an order or regulations made under any provision of an enactment passed after this Act and directed to be construed as one with this Act; but this subsection applies only so far as a contrary intention is not expressed in the enactment so passed, and without prejudice to the generality of any such direction.

DEFINITIONS
    "the 1975 Act": s.174.
    "the Administration Act": s.174.

Parliamentary control

    176.—(1) Subject to the provisions of this section, a statutory instrument containing (whether alone or with other provisions)—

    (a) regulations made by virtue of—

        section 11(3);

section 18;
section 19(4) to (6);
section 28(3);
section 32(2);
section 59(2);
section 104(3);
section 117;
section 118;
section 145;
section 158(2) or (3);

(b) regulations prescribing payments for the purposes of the definition of "payments by way of occupational or personal pension" in section 122(1) above;

(c) an order under—
section 28(2);
section 57(8);
section 148(3)(b);
section 157(2);
section 159(1),

shall not be made unless a draft of the instrument has been laid before Parliament and been approved by a resolution of each House.

(2) Subsection (1) above does not apply to a statutory instrument by reason only that it contains—

(a) regulations under section 117 which the instrument states are made for the purpose of making provision consequential on the making of an order under section 141, 143, 145, 146 or 162 of the Administration Act;

(b) regulations under powers conferred by any provision mentioned in paragraph (a) of that subsection (other than section 158(2) or (3)) which are to be made for the purpose of consolidating regulations to be revoked in the instrument;

(c) regulations which, in so far as they are made under powers conferred by any provision mentioned in paragraph (a) of that subsection (other than section 145 or 158(2) or (3)), only replace provisions of previous regulations with new provisions to the same effect.

(3) A statutory instrument—

(a) which contains (whether alone or with other provisions) any order, regulations or scheme made under this Act by the Secretary of State, other than an order under section 145(3) above; and

(b) which is not subject to any requirement that a draft of the instrument shall be laid before and approved by a resolution of each House of Parliament,

shall be subject to annulment in pursuance of a resolution of either House of Parliament.

DEFINITIONS
"the Administration Act": s.174.

Short title, commencement and extent

Short title, commencement and extent

177.—(1) This Act may be cited as the Social Security Contributions and Benefits Act 1992.

(2) This Act is to be read, where appropriate, with the Administration Act and the Consequential Provisions Act.

(3) The enactments consolidated by this Act are repealed, in consequence of the consolidation, by the Consequential Provisions Act.

(4) Except as provided in Schedule 4 to the Consequential Provisions Act, this Act shall come into force on 1st July 1992.

(5) The following provisions extend to Northern Ireland—
    section 16 and Schedule 2;
    section 116(2); and
    this section.

(6) Except as provided by this section, this Act does not extend to Northern Ireland.

DEFINITIONS
    "the Administration Act": s.174.
    "the Consequential Provisions Act": s.174.

GENERAL NOTE

Subss. (4) and (5)
    Provision for Northern Ireland is made by the Social Security Contributions and Benefits (Northern Ireland) Act 1992, the Social Security Administration (Northern Ireland) Act 1992 and the Social Security (Consequential Provisions) (Northern Ireland) Act 1992.

SCHEDULES

Section 1(4)   SCHEDULE 1

SUPPLEMENTARY PROVISIONS RELATING TO CONTRIBUTIONS OF CLASSES 1, 1A, 2 AND 3

Class 1 contributions where earner employed in more than one employment

1.—(1) For the purposes of determining whether Class 1 contributions are payable in respect of earnings paid to an earner in a given week and, if so, the amount of the contributions—
    (a) all earnings paid to him or for his benefit in that week in respect of one or more employed earner's employments under the same employer shall, except as may be provided by regulations, be aggregated and treated as a single payment of earnings in respect of one such employment; and
    (b) earnings paid to him or for his benefit in that week by different persons in respect of different employed earner's employments shall in prescribed circumstances be aggregated and treated as a single payment of earnings in respect of one such employment;
and regulations may provide that the provisions of this sub-paragraph shall have effect in cases prescribed by the regulations as if for any reference to a week there were substituted a reference to a period prescribed by the regulations.

(2) Where earnings in respect of employments which include any contracted-out employment and any employment which is not a contracted-out employment are aggregated under sub-paragraph (1) above and the aggregated earnings are not less than the current lower earnings limit, then, except as may be provided by regulations—
    (a) the amount of the primary Class 1 contribution in respect of the aggregated earnings shall be determined in accordance with sub-paragraph (3) below; and
    (b) the amount of the secondary Class 1 contribution in respect of the aggregated earnings shall be determined in accordance with sub-paragraph (6) below.

(3) The amount of the primary Class 1 contributions shall be the aggregate of the amounts obtained—
    (a) by applying the rates of primary Class 1 contributions that would apply if the aggregated earnings were all attributable to contracted-out employments—
        (i) to the part of the aggregated earnings attributable to any such employments, or
        (ii) if that part exceeds the current upper earnings limit, to so much of that part as does not exceed that limit; and
    (b) if that part is less than that limit, by applying the rate of primary Class 1 contributions that would apply if the aggregated earnings were all attributable to employments which are not contracted-out to so much of the remainder of the aggregated earnings as, when added to that part, does not exceed that limit.

(4) In relation to earners paid otherwise than weekly, any reference in sub-paragraph (2) or (3) above to the lower or upper earnings limit shall be construed as a reference to the prescribed equivalent of that limit.

(5) The power under sub-paragraph (4) above to prescribe an equivalent of a limit includes power to prescribe an amount which exceeds, by not more than £1.00, the amount which is the arithmetical equivalent of that limit.

(6) The amount of the secondary Class 1 contribution shall be the aggregate of the amounts obtained—

(a) by applying the rates of secondary Class 1 contributions that would apply if the aggregated earnings were all attributable to contracted-out employments to the part of the aggregated earnings attributable to any such employments; and

(b) by applying the rate of secondary Class 1 contributions that would apply if the aggregated earnings were all attributable to employments which are not contracted-out to the remainder of the aggregated earnings.

(7) Where any single payment of earnings is made in respect of two or more employed earner's employments under different employers, liability for Class 1 contributions shall be determined by apportioning the payment to such one or more of the employers as may be prescribed, and treating a part apportioned to any employer as a separate payment of earnings by him.

(8) Where earnings are aggregated under sub-paragraph (1)(b) above, liability (if any) for the secondary contribution shall be apportioned, in such manner as may be prescribed, between the secondary contributors concerned.

Earnings not paid at normal intervals

2. Regulations may, for the purposes of Class 1 contributions, make provision as to the intervals at which payments of earnings are to be treated as made.

Method of paying Class 1 contributions

3.—(1) Where earnings are paid to an employed earner and in respect of that payment liability arises for primary and secondary Class 1 contributions, the secondary contributor shall (except in prescribed circumstances), as well as being liable for his own secondary contribution, be liable in the first instance to pay also the earner's primary contribution, on behalf of and to the exclusion of the earner; and for the purposes of this Act and the Administration Act contributions paid by the secondary contributor on behalf of the earner shall be taken to be contributions paid by the earner.

(2) Notwithstanding any contract to the contrary, no secondary contributor shall be entitled—

(a) to make, from earnings paid by him, any deduction in respect of his own or any other person's secondary Class 1 contributions, or

(b) otherwise to recover such contributions from any earner to whom he pays earnings.

(3) A secondary contributor shall be entitled, subject to and in accordance with regulations, to recover from an earner the amount of any primary Class 1 contribution paid or to be paid by him on behalf of the earner; and notwithstanding anything in any enactment, regulations under this sub-paragraph shall provide for recovery to be made by deduction from the earner's earnings, and for it not to be made in any other way.

General provisions as to Class 1 contributions

4. Regulations may, in relation to Class 1 contributions, make provision—

(a) for calculating the amounts payable according to a scale prepared from time to time by the Secretary of State or otherwise adjusting them so as to avoid fractional amounts or otherwise facilitate computation;

(b) for requiring that the liability in respect of a payment made in a tax week, in so far as the liability depends on any conditions as to a person's age or retirement, shall be determined as at the beginning of the week or as at the end of it;

(c) for securing that liability is not avoided or reduced by a person following in the payment of earnings any practice which is abnormal for the employment in respect of which the earnings are paid; and

(d) without prejudice to sub-paragraph (c) above, for enabling the Secretary of State, where he is satisfied as to the existence of any practice in respect of the payment of earnings whereby the incidence of Class 1 contributions is avoided or reduced by means of irregular or unequal payments, to give directions for securing that such contributions are payable as if that practice were not followed.

Class 1A contributions where car made available by reason of more than one employment

5. Regulations may modify section 10 above in relation to cases where a car is made available by reason of two or more employed earner's employment under different employers.

Power to combine collection of contributions with tax

6.—(1) Regulations made with the concurrence of the Inland Revenue may—

(a) provide for Class 1, Class 1A or Class 2 contributions to be paid, accounted for and recovered in like manner as income tax deducted from the emoluments of an office or employment by virtue of regulations under section 203 of the Income and Corporation Taxes Act 1988 (PAYE);

(b) apply or extend with or without modification in relation to such contributions any of the provisions of the Income Tax Acts or of regulations under that section;

(c) make provision for the appropriation of the payments made by any person between his liabilities in respect of income tax and contributions.

(2) Without prejudice to the generality of sub-paragraph (1) above, the provision that may be made by virtue of paragraph (a) of that sub-paragraph includes in relation to Class 1 or Class 1A contributions—

(a) provision for requiring the payment of interest on sums due in respect of Class 1 or Class 1A contributions which are not paid by the due date, for determining the date (being, in the case of Class 1 contributions, not less than 14 days after the end of the tax year in respect of which the sums are due) from which such interest is to be calculated and for enabling the repayment or remission of such interest;

(b) provision for requiring the payment of interest on sums due in respect of Class 1 or Class 1A contributions which fall to be repaid and for determining the date (being not less than one year after the end of the tax year in respect of which the sums are due) from which such interest is to be calculated;

(c) provision for, or in connection with, the imposition and recovery of penalties in relation to any returns required to be made which relate to Class 1 or Class 1A contributions, but subject to sub-paragraph (7) and paragraph 7 below;

and any reference to contributions or income tax in paragraph (b) or (c) of sub-paragraph (1) above shall be construed as including a reference to any interest or penalty in respect of contributions or income tax, as the case may be.

(3) The rate of interest applicable for any purpose of this paragraph shall be the rate from time to time prescribed for that purpose under section 178 of the Finance Act 1989.

(4) Regulations under this paragraph may require the payment of interest on sums due in respect of contributions, notwithstanding that a question arising in relation to the contributions has not been determined under section 17 of the Administration Act by the Secretary of State, except that where—

(a) any such question arises which affects a person's liability for, or the amount of, any such interest, and

(b) either—

(i) that person requires the question to be determined under section 17, or

(ii) a question of law arising in connection with the determination of the question is, or is to be, referred to a court under section 18 of the Administration Act,

the regulations shall not require the payment of any such interest until the question has been determined under section 17 of the Administration Act by the Secretary of State or the reference has been finally disposed of under section 18 of that Act, as the case may be; but, subject to that, this paragraph is without prejudice to sections 17 to 19 of the Administration Act.

(5) The power to make regulations under this paragraph includes power to make such provision as the Secretary of State considers expedient in consequence of any provision made by or under section 158 or 167 above.

(6) Provision made in regulations under this paragraph, by virtue of sub-paragraph (5) above, may in particular require the inclusion—

(a) in returns, certificates and other documents; or

(b) in any other form of record;

which the regulations require to be kept or produced or to which those regulations otherwise apply, of such particulars relating to statutory sick pay, statutory maternity pay or deductions or payments made by virtue of section 167(1) above as may be prescribed by those regulations.

(7) Section 98 of the Taxes Management Act 1970 shall apply in relation to regulations made by virtue of this paragraph as it applies in relation to regulations made under section 203 of the Income and Corporation Taxes Act 1988 (PAYE).

(8) The Inland Revenue shall, at such times and in such manner as the Treasury may direct, account to the Secretary of State for, and pay to him—

(a) the sums estimated by the Inland Revenue, in such manner as may be so directed, to have been received by them as contributions in accordance with regulations made by virtue of this paragraph; and

(b) so much of any interest recovered by the Inland Revenue by virtue of this paragraph as remains after the deduction by them of any administrative costs attributable to its recovery.

Special penalties in the case of certain returns

7.—(1) This paragraph applies where regulations under paragraph 6 above make provision requiring any return which is to be made in accordance with a specified provision of regulations under that paragraph (the "contributions return") to be made—

(a) at the same time as any specified return required to be made in accordance with a provision of regulations made by the Inland Revenue under section 203(2) or 566(1) (sub-contractors) of the Income and Corporation Taxes Act 1988 to which section 98A of the Taxes Management Act 1970 applies (the "tax return"); or

(b) if the circumstances are such that the return mentioned in paragraph (a) above does not fall to be made, at a time defined by reference to the time for making that return, had it fallen to be made;

and, in a case falling within paragraph (b) above, any reference in the following provisions of this paragraph to the tax return shall be construed as a reference to the return there mentioned.

(2) Where this paragraph applies, regulations under paragraph 6 above may provide that section 98A of the Taxes Management Act 1970 (penalties for late, fraudulent or negligent returns) shall apply in relation to any specified provision of regulations in accordance with which the contributions return is required to be made; and where they so provide then, subject to the following provisions of this paragraph—

(a) that section shall apply in relation to the contributions return as it applies in relation to the tax return; and

(b) sections 100 to 100D and 102 to 104 of that Act shall apply in relation to a penalty under section 98A of that Act to which a person is liable by virtue of this sub-paragraph as they apply in relation to any other penalty under that section.

(3) Where a person is liable to a penalty under paragraph (a) of subsection (2) of section 98A of that Act (first twelve months' default) in consequence of a failure in respect of a tax return, he shall not also be liable to a penalty under that paragraph in respect of any failure in respect of the associated contributions return.

(4) In any case where—

(a) a person is liable to a penalty under subsection (2)(b) or (4) of that section (tax-related penalties) in respect of both a tax return and its associated contributions return, and

(b) an officer of the Inland Revenue authorised for the purposes of section 100 of that Act has determined that a penalty is to be imposed under that provision in respect of both returns,

the penalty so imposed shall be a single penalty of an amount not exceeding the limit determined under sub-paragraph (5) below.

(5) The limit mentioned in sub-paragraph (4) above is an amount equal to the sum of—

(a) the maximum penalty that would have been applicable under subsection (2)(b) or (4) of section 98A of that Act (as the case may be) for a penalty in relation to the tax return only; and

(b) the maximum penalty that would have been so applicable in relation to the associated contributions return only.

(6) So much of any single penalty imposed by virtue of sub-paragraph (4) above as is recovered by the Inland Revenue shall, after the deduction of any administrative costs of the Inland Revenue attributable to its recovery, be apportioned between the Inland Revenue and the Secretary of State in the ratio T:C, where—

T is the maximum penalty that could have been imposed under the provision in question in relation to the tax return only; and

C is the maximum penalty that could have been so imposed in relation to the associated contributions return only.

(7) The Inland Revenue shall, at such times and in such manner as the Treasury may direct, account to the Secretary of State for, and pay to him—

(a) the amounts apportioned to him under sub-paragraph (6) above in respect of such penalties as are there mentioned; and

(b) so much of any penalty otherwise imposed by virtue of this paragraph and recovered by the Inland Revenue as remains after the deduction by them of any administrative costs attributable to its recovery.

(8) Sub-paragraphs (6) and (7) above shall have effect notwithstanding any provision which treats a penalty under section 98A of that Act as if it were tax charged in an assessment and due and payable.

(9) In the application of section 98A of that Act by virtue of this paragraph, any reference to a year of assessment shall be construed, in relation to a contributions return, as a reference to the tax year corresponding to that year of assessment.

(10) In the application of section 100D of that Act (court proceedings for penalties in cases of fraud) by virtue of this paragraph—

(a) subsection (2) shall have effect with the omission of the words "Northern Ireland" and paragraph (c); and

(b) subsection (3) shall have effect with the omission of the words from "and any such proceedings instituted in Northern Ireland" onwards.

(11) In the application of section 103 of that Act (time limit for recovery) by virtue of this paragraph—

(a) any reference in subsection (1) to tax shall be taken to include a reference to Class 1 and Class 1A contributions;

(b) any penalty by virtue of sub-paragraph (4) above shall be regarded as a penalty in respect of the tax return in question; and

(c) where, by virtue of subsection (2) (death), subsection (1)(b) does not apply in relation to a penalty under section 98A(2)(b) or (4) of that Act in respect of a tax return, it shall also not apply in relation to a penalty so imposed in respect of the associated contributions return.

(12) A penalty under section 98A of that Act as it applies by virtue of this paragraph may be imposed notwithstanding that a question arising in relation to contributions has not been determined under section 17 of the Administration Act by the Secretary of State, except that where—

(a) any such question arises which affects a person's liability for, or the amount of, the penalty, and

(b) either—

(i) that person requires the question to be determined under section 17, or

(ii) a question of law arising in connection with the determination of the question is, or is to be, referred to a court under section 18 of the Administration Act,

the penalty shall not be imposed until the question has been determined under section 17 of the Administration Act by the Secretary of State or the reference has been finally disposed of under section 18 of that Act, as the case may be; but, subject to that, this paragraph is without prejudice to sections 17 to 19 of the Administration Act.

(13) For the purposes of this paragraph—

(a) "contributions return" and "tax return" shall be construed in accordance with sub-paragraph (1) above; and

(b) a contributions return and a tax return are "associated" if the contributions return is required to be made—

(i) at the same time as the tax return, or

(ii) where sub-paragraph (1)(b) above applies, at a time defined by reference to the time for making the tax return.

General regulation-making powers

8.—(1) Regulations may provide—

(a) for requiring persons to maintain, in such form and manner as may be prescribed, records—

(i) of the earnings paid by them to and in respect of earners, and

(ii) of the contributions paid or payable in respect of earnings so paid,

for the purpose of enabling the incidence of liability for contributions of any class to be determined, and to retain the records for so long as may be prescribed;

(b) for requiring persons to maintain, in such form and manner as may be prescribed, records of such matters as may be prescribed for the purpose of enabling the incidence of liability for Class 1A contributions to be determined, and to retain the records for so long as may be prescribed;

(c) for treating primary Class 1 contributions, when payable on the primary contributor's behalf by the secondary contributor, but not paid, as actually paid where the failure to pay is shown not to have been with the consent or connivance of, or attributable to any negligence on the part of, the primary contributor and, in the case of contributions so treated, for treating them also as paid at a prescribed time or in respect of a prescribed period;

(d) for treating, for the purpose of any entitlement to benefit, contributions paid at or after any prescribed time as paid at some other time (whether earlier or later) or, in the case of contributions paid after the due date for payment, or at such later date as may be prescribed, as not having been paid;

(e) for enabling contributions to be treated as paid in respect of a tax year earlier or later than that in respect of which they were actually paid;

(f) for treating (for the purposes of Class 2 contributions) a week which falls partly in one, and partly in another, tax year as falling wholly within one or the other of those tax years;

(g) for treating contributions of the wrong class, or at the wrong rate, or of the wrong amount, as paid on account of contributions properly payable (notwithstanding section 14 above, in the case of Class 3 contributions) or as paid (wholly or in part) in discharge of a liability for a state scheme premium;

(h) for the repayment, in prescribed cases, of the whole or a prescribed part of any contributions paid by reference to earnings which have become repayable;

(i) for the repayment, in prescribed cases, of a prescribed part of any Class 1A contribution as to which the Secretary of State is satisfied in the light of information of a kind mentioned in section 10(6)(a), (b) or (c) above that has become available to him, that too much has been paid;

(j) for the repayment, on the making of an application in the prescribed manner and within the prescribed time, of Class 2 contributions paid by a person in respect of a period which consists of, or falls within a tax year for which his earnings from employment as a self-employed earner were, or were such as to be treated by regulations under subsection (4) of section 11 above as being, at a lower rate than the one specified in that subsection for that year;

(k) for excepting a person from liability for contributions repaid by virtue of paragraph (j) above, to the extent that he would not have been so excepted by virtue of section 11(4) above;

(l) without prejudice to paragraph (g) above, for enabling—

(i) the whole or part of any payment of secondary Class 1 contributions to be treated as a payment of Class 1A contributions;

(ii) the whole or part of any payment of Class 1A contributions to be treated as a payment of secondary Class 1 contributions or Class 2 contributions;

(iii) the whole or part of any payment of Class 2 contributions to be treated as a payment of secondary Class 1 contributions or Class 1A contributions;

(m) for the return of the whole or any prescribed part of any contributions paid either in error or in such circumstances that, under any provision of Part I of this Act or of regulations, they fall to be repaid;

(n) for treating a person as being an employed earner, notwithstanding that his employment is outside Great Britain;

(o) for treating a person's employment as continuing during periods of holiday, unemployment or incapacity for work and in such other circumstances as may be prescribed;

(p) for requiring persons to apply to the Secretary of State for the allocation of a national insurance number;

(q) for any other matters incidental to the payment, collection or return of contributions.

(2) Regulations made by the Secretary of State under sub-paragraph (1) above providing for the payment of Class 2 or Class 3 contributions (at the option of the persons liable to pay) either—

(a) by means of adhesive stamps; or

(b) by some alternative method, the use of which involves greater expense in administration to the government departments concerned than would be incurred if the contributions were paid by means of such stamps,

may include provision for the payment to the Secretary of State by any person who adopts any alternative method, and for the recovery by the Secretary of State, of the prescribed fees in respect of any difference in the expense in administration.

(3) Where under regulations made by virtue of sub-paragraph (1) above contributions are payable by means of adhesive stamps, the Secretary of State—

(a) may, with the consent of the Treasury, arrange for the preparation and sale of those stamps, and

(b) may by regulations provide for applying, with the necessary modifications as respects those stamps, all or any of the provisions of the Stamp Duties Management Act 1891, section 9 of the Stamp Act 1891 and section 63 of the Post Office Act 1953.

9. Regulations may provide that—

(a) for the purpose of determining whether a contribution is payable in respect of any person, or

(b) for determining the amount or rate of any contribution,

he is to be treated as having attained at the beginning of a week, or as not having attained until the end of a week, any age which he attains during the course of that week.

Deduction of contributions from pension, etc.

10.—(1) Where a person is in receipt of a pension or allowance payable by the Secretary of State by virtue of any prescribed enactment or instrument, the Secretary of State may with the consent of that person pay any contributions (other than Class 1 or Class 4 contributions) payable by him and deduct the amount so paid from the pension or allowance.

(2) Sub-paragraph (1) above shall have effect notwithstanding anything in any Act, Royal Warrant, Order in Council, order or scheme.

Sickness payments counting as remuneration

11.—(1) Regulations may make provision as to the manner in which, and the person through whom, any sickness payment which, by virtue of section 4(1) above, is to be treated as remuneration derived from employed earner's employment is to be made.

(2) In any case where regulations made under sub-paragraph (1) above have the effect of requiring a registered friendly society (within the meaning of the Friendly Societies Act 1974) to make amendments to its rules, the amendments may, notwithstanding any provision of those rules, be made in accordance with the procedure prescribed by regulations made by the Chief Registrar of Friendly Societies for the purposes of this paragraph.

GENERAL NOTE

This Schedule consolidates SSA 1975, Sched. 1 (as amended) and concerns the rules and regulation-making powers governing the computation, collection and recovery of National Insurance contributions under Classes 1, 1A, 2 and 3. It also applies to Class 4 contributions in so far as they are collected by the Secretary of State rather than the Inland Revenue (s.1(4)(b)).

Para. 6
Note the transitory modifications in SS(CP)A 1992, Sched. 4, paras. 6 and 7.

Section 16(3)   SCHEDULE 2

LEVY OF CLASS 4 CONTRIBUTIONS WITH INCOME TAX

Interpretation

1. In this Schedule—
(a) "the Act of 1988" means the Income and Corporation Taxes Act 1988;
(b) "the Act of 1990" means the Capital Allowances Act 1990;
(c) "year" means year of assessment within the meaning of the Act of 1988.

Method of computing profits or gains

2. Subject to the following paragraphs, Class 4 contributions shall be payable in respect of the full amount of all profits or gains of any relevant trade, profession or vocation chargeable to income tax under Case I or II of Schedule D, subject to—
(a) deductions for—
(i) allowances which under section 140(2) of the Act of 1990 fall to be made as a deduction in charging the profits or gains to income tax, and
(ii) any allowance the amount of which falls to be given by way of discharge or repayment of income tax under section 141 of that Act,
where in either case the allowance arises from activities of any relevant trade, profession or vocation; and
(b) additions for any such charges as under section 140(7) of that Act fall to be made for purposes of income tax on the profits or gains.

Reliefs

3.—(1) For the purposes of computing the amount of profits or gains in respect of which Class 4 contributions are payable, relief shall be available under, and in the manner provided by, the following provisions of the Act of 1988—
(a) sections 380 and 381 (set-off of trade losses against general income), but only where loss arises from activities the profits or gains of which would be brought into computation for the purposes of Class 4 contributions;
(b) section 383 (extension of right of set-off to capital allowances);
(c) section 385 (carry-forward of loss against subsequent profits); and
(d) sections 388 and 389 (carry-back of terminal losses).
(2) The following relief provisions of the Act of 1988 shall not apply, that is to say—
(a) Chapter I of Part VII (personal reliefs);
(b) section 353 (relief for payment of interest);
(c) section 387 (carry-forward as losses of amounts to be taxed under section 350);
(d) section 390 (treatment of interest as a loss of purposes of carry-forward or carry-back);
(e) section 617(5) (relief for Class 4 contributions); and

(f) sections 619 and 620 (premiums or other consideration under annuity contracts and trust schemes).

(3) Where in the year 1989–90 or any previous year of assessment for which a person claims and is allowed relief by virtue of sub-paragraph (1) above—

(a) there falls to be made in computing his total income for income tax purposes, or that of his spouse, a deduction in respect of any loss, and

(b) the deduction or part of it falls to be so made from income other than profits or gains of a trade, profession or vocation,

the amount of the deduction made from the other income shall be treated as reducing the person's profits or gains (that is to say the profits or gains of any relevant trade, profession or vocation as computed for the purpose of the charge to Class 4 contributions) for subsequent years (being deducted as far as may be from those of the immediately following year, whether or not he claims or is entitled to claim relief under this paragraph for that year, and, so far as it cannot be so deducted, then from those of the next year, and so on).

(4) Where in the year 1990–1991 or any subsequent year of assessment for which a person claims and is allowed relief by virtue of sub-paragraph (1) above there falls to be made in computing his total income for income tax purposes a deduction in respect of any loss in any relevant trade, profession or vocation—

(a) the amount of the deduction shall, as far as may be, be treated for the purpose of the charge to Class 4 contributions as reducing the person's profits or gains for that year of any relevant trade, profession or vocation, and

(b) any excess shall be treated for that purpose as reducing such profits or gains for subsequent years (being deducted as far as may be from those of the immediately following year, whether or not the person claims or is entitled to claim relief under this paragraph for that year, and, so far as it cannot be so deducted, then from those of the next year, and so on).

(5) Relief shall be allowed, in respect of —

(a) payments under section 348 or 349(1) of the Act of 1988 (annuities and other annual payments, etc.); or

(b) payments under section 353 of that Act (relief for payment of interest), being payments for which relief from income tax is or can be given,

so far as incurred wholly or exclusively for the purposes of any relevant trade, profession or vocation, by way of deduction from or set-off against profits of gains chargeable to Class 4 contributions for the year in which the payments are made; and, in the case of any insufficiency of the profits or gains of that year, the payments shall be carried forward and deducted from or set off against the profits or gains of any subsequent year (being deducted or set off as far as may be from or against the profits or gains of the immediately following year, whether or not relief can be claimed under this paragraph for that year, and so far as it cannot be so deducted, from or against those of the next year, and so on).

Partnerships

4.—(1) Where a trade or profession is carried on by two or more persons jointly, the liability of any one of them in respect of Class 4 contributions shall arise in respect of his share of the profits or gains of that trade or profession (so far as immediately derived by him from carrying it on); and for this purpose his share shall be aggregated with his share of the profits or gains of any other trade, profession or vocation (so far as immediately derived by him from carrying it on or exercising it).

(2) Where sub-paragraph (1) above applies, the Class 4 contributions for which a person is liable in respect of the profits or gains of the trade or profession carried on jointly (aggregated, where appropriate, as mentioned in that sub-paragraph) may either be charged on him separately or (to the extent only that the liability arises in respect of the profits or gains of that partnership) be the subject of a joint assessment to contributions made in the partnership name; and sections 111 to 115 of the Act of 1988 shall apply accordingly, but substituting this paragraph for section 111.

Trustees, etc.

5. In any circumstances in which apart from this paragraph a person would—

(a) under section 72 of the Taxes Management Act 1970 be assessable and chargeable to Class 4 contributions as trustee, guardian, tutor, curator, or committee of an incapacitated person in respect of the profits or gains of a trade, profession or vocation, or

(b) by virtue of section 59 of the Act of 1988 be assessed and charged to such contributions in respect of profits or gains received or receivable by him in the capacity of trustee,

such contributions shall not be payable either by him or by any other person.

Other provisions

6.—(1) Sections 86 and 88(1), (4) and (5)(a) and (b) of the Taxes Management Act 1970 (interest on amounts overdue, and on tax recovered to make good loss due to taxpayer's fault) shall apply in relation to any amount due in respect of Class 4 contributions as they apply in relation to income tax; and section 824 of the Act of 1988 (repayment supplements) shall, with the necessary modifications, apply in relation to Class 4 contributions as it applies in relation to income tax.

(2) The Inland Revenue shall have the same powers under section 1 of the Taxes Management Act 1970 (general functions of care and management) in relation to the remission of interest payable under section 86 or 88 of that Act by virtue of this paragraph as they have in relation to the remission of interest payable under either of those sections on tax.

7. Where an assessment has become final and conclusive for the purposes of income tax for any year, that assessment shall also be final and conclusive for the purposes of computing liability for Class 4 contributions; and no allowance or adjustment of liability, on the ground of diminution of income or loss, shall be taken into account in computing profits or gains chargeable to Class 4 contributions unless that allowance or adjustment has previously been made on an application under the special provisions of the Income Tax Acts relating to it, or falls to be allowed under paragraph 3(5) of this Schedule.

8. The provisions of Part V of the Taxes Management Act 1970 (appeals, etc.) shall apply with the necessary modifications in relation to Class 4 contributions as they apply in relation to income tax, but nothing in the Income Tax Acts shall apply with respect to the determination of any question arising—

  (a) under subsection (1) of section 17 above or subsection (1) of section 17 of the Northern Ireland Contributions and Benefits Act as to whether by regulations under that subsection a person is excepted from liability for Class 4 contributions, or his liability is deferred; or

  (b) under regulations made by virtue of section 17(3) or (4) or 18 above or section 17(3) or (4) or 18 of the Northern Ireland Contributions and Benefits Act.

Husband and wife—1989–90 and previous years of assessment

9.—(1) For the year 1989–90 and previous years of assessment Chapter II of Part VII of the Act of 1988 shall apply for the purposes of Class 4 contributions as it applies for those of income tax; and an application by a husband or wife for separate assessment under section 283 of that Act, and an election by them under section 287 of that Act (separate taxation of wife's earnings) shall operate as respects liability for such contributions as it does for income tax, the wife being liable for Class 4 contributions in respect of her own profits or gains.

(2) Such an application or election as is referred to in sub-paragraph (1) above shall not be made separately for the purposes of Class 4 contributions apart from those of income tax.

(3) Where section 279 of the Act of 1988 applies and there is no separate assessment under section 283 of that Act and no election under section 287 of that Act, the wife's profits and gains are to be computed, for the purposes of Class 4 contributions as if section 279 did not apply, but the contributions shall be assessed on, and recoverable from, the husband.

(4) In this paragraph "year of assessment" has the meaning assigned to it by section 832 of the Act of 1988.

GENERAL NOTE

This Schedule consolidates SSA 1975, Sched. 2 (as amended) and concerns the rules governing the levying of Class 4 National Insurance contributions.

Para. 6

Note the transitory modifications in SS(CP)A 1992, Sched. 4, paras. 8 and 9.

Section 21(3) and (4)   SCHEDULE 3

CONTRIBUTION CONDITIONS FOR ENTITLEMENT TO BENEFIT

PART I

THE CONDITIONS

Unemployment benefit

1.—(1) The contribution conditions for unemployment benefit are the following.

(2) The first condition is that—

(a) the claimant must have actually paid contributions of a relevant class in respect of one of the last two complete years before the beginning of the relevant benefit year, and those contributions must have been paid before the relevant time; and

(b) the earnings factor derived as mentioned in sub-paragraph (4) below must be not less than that year's lower earnings limit multiplied by 25.

(3) The second condition is that—

(a) the claimant must in respect of the last two complete years before the beginning of the relevant benefit year have either paid or been credited with contributions of a relevant class or been credited (in the case of 1987–88 or any subsequent year) with earnings; and

(b) the earnings factor derived as mentioned in sub-paragraph (5) below must be not less in each of those years than the year's lower earnings limit multiplied by 50.

(4) The earnings factor referred to in paragraph (b) of sub-paragraph (2) above is that which is derived—

(a) if the year in question is 1987–88 or any subsequent year, from earnings upon which primary Class 1 contributions have been paid or treated as paid; and

(b) if the year in question is an earlier year, from the contributions paid as mentioned in paragraph (a) of that sub-paragraph.

(5) The earnings factor referred to in paragraph (b) of sub-paragraph (3) above is that which is derived—

(a) if the year in question is 1987–88 or any subsequent year, from earnings upon which primary Class 1 contributions have been paid or treated as paid or from earnings credited; and

(b) if the year in question is an earlier year, from the contributions referred to in paragraph (a) of that sub-paragraph.

(6) For the purposes of these conditions—

(a) "the relevant time" is the day in respect of which benefit is claimed;

(b) "the relevant benefit year" is the benefit year in which there falls the beginning of the period of interruption of employment which includes the relevant time.

Sickness benefit

2.—(1) The contribution conditions for sickness benefit are the following.

(2) The first condition is that—

(a) the claimant must have actually paid contributions of a relevant class in respect of any one year, and those contributions must have been paid before the relevant time; and

(b) the earnings factor derived as mentioned in sub-paragraph (4) below must be not less than that year's lower earnings limit multiplied by 25.

(3) The second condition is that—

(a) the claimant must in respect of the last two complete years before the beginning of the relevant benefit year have either paid or been credited with contributions of a relevant class or been credited (in the case of 1987–88 or any subsequent year) with earnings; and

(b) the earnings factor derived as mentioned in sub-paragraph (5) below must be not less in each of those years than the year's lower earnings limit multiplied by 50.

(4) The earnings factor referred to in paragraph (b) of sub-paragraph (2) above is that which is derived—

(a) if the year in question is 1987–88 or any subsequent year—

    (i) from earnings upon which primary Class 1 contributions have been paid or treated as paid; or

    (ii) from Class 2 contributions; and

(b) if the year in question is an earlier year, from the contributions paid as mentioned in paragraph (a) of that sub-paragraph.

(5) The earnings factor referred to in paragraph (b) of sub-paragraph (3) above is that which is derived—

(a) if the year in question is 1987–88 or any subsequent year—

    (i) from earnings upon which primary Class 1 contributions have been paid or treated as paid or from earnings credited; or

    (ii) from Class 2 contributions; and

(b) if the year in question is an earlier year, from the contributions referred to in paragraph (a) of that sub-paragraph.

(6) For the purposes of these conditions—

(a) "the relevant time" is the day in respect of which benefit is claimed;

(b) "the relevant benefit year" is the benefit year in which there falls the beginning of the period of interruption of employment which includes the relevant time.

Maternity allowance

3.—(1) Subject to sub-paragraph (2) below, the contribution condition for a maternity allowance is—
  (a) that the claimant must, in respect of at least 26 weeks in the 52 weeks immediately preceding the 14th week before the expected week of confinement, have actually paid contributions of a relevant class; and
  (b) in the case of Class 1 contributions, that they were not secondary contributions and were paid otherwise than at the reduced rate.
(2) In the case of a claimant who is or has been paid otherwise than weekly, any week—
  (a) in respect of which she did not pay contributions of a relevant class; but
  (b) for which her earnings were such that, had she been paid weekly, she would have been required to pay primary Class 1 contributions in respect of that week; and
  (c) for which no such election as is mentioned in section 19(4)(a) above was in force in her case,
shall be treated for the purposes of sub-paragraph (1) above as a week in respect of which she actually paid such contributions otherwise than at a reduced rate.
(3) For the purposes of sub-paragraph (2) above, the amount of the claimant's earnings for any week shall be determined in accordance with regulations.

Widow's payment

4.—(1) The contribution condition for a widow's payment is that—
  (a) the contributor concerned must in respect of any one relevant year have actually paid contributions of a relevant class; and
  (b) the earnings factor derived as mentioned in sub-paragraph (2) below must be not less than that year's lower earnings limit multiplied by 25.
(2) The earnings factor referred to in paragraph (b) of sub-paragraph (1) above is that which is derived—
  (a) if the year in question is 1987–88 or any subsequent year, from earnings upon which primary Class 1 contributions have been paid or treated as paid and from Class 2 and Class 3 contributions, or
  (b) if the year in question is an earlier year, from the contributions referred to in paragraph (a) of that sub-paragraph.
(3) For the purposes of this condition a relevant year is any year ending before the date on which the contributor concerned attained pensionable age or died under that age.

Widowed mother's allowance and widow's pension; retirement pensions (Categories A and B)

5.—(1) The contribution conditions for a widowed mother's allowance, a widow's pension or a Category A or Category B retirement pension are the following.
(2) The first condition is that—
  (a) the contributor concerned must in respect of any one relevant year have actually paid contributions of a relevant class; and
  (b) the earnings factor derived—
        (i) if that year is 1987–88 or any subsequent year, from earnings upon which such of those contributions as are primary Class 1 contributions were paid or treated as paid and any Class 2 or Class 3 contributions, or
        (ii) if that year is an earlier year, from the contributions referred to in paragraph (a) above,
      must be not less than the qualifying earnings factor for that year.
(3) The second condition is that—
  (a) the contributor concerned must, in respect of each of not less than the requisite number of years of his working life, have paid or been credited with contributions of a relevant class; and
  (b) in the case of each of those years, the earnings factor derived as mentioned in sub-paragraph (4) below must be not less than the qualifying earnings factor for that year.
(4) For the purposes of paragraph (b) of sub-paragraph (3) above, the earnings factor—
  (a) in the case of 1987–88 or any subsequent year, is that which is derived from—
        (i) any earnings upon which such of the contributions mentioned in paragraph (a) of that sub-paragraph as are primary Class 1 contributions were paid or treated as paid or earnings credited; and
        (ii) any Class 2 or Class 3 contributions for the year; or
  (b) in the case of any earlier year, is that which is derived from the contributions mentioned in paragraph (a) of that sub-paragraph.

(5) For the purposes of the first condition, a relevant year is any year ending before that in which the contributor concerned attained pensionable age or died under that age; and the following table shows the requisite number of years for the purpose of the second condition, by reference to a working life of a given duration—

Duration of working life	*Requisite number of years*
10 years or less	The number of years of the working life, minus 1.
20 years or less (but more than 10)	The number of years of the working life, minus 2.
30 years or less (but more than 20)	The number of years of the working life, minus 3.
40 years or less (but more than 30)	The number of years of the working life, minus 4.
More than 40 years	The number of years of the working life, minus 5.

(6) The first condition shall be taken to be satisfied if the contributor concerned was entitled to an invalidity pension at any time during—
  (a) the year in which he attained pensionable age or died under that age, or
  (b) the year immediately preceding that year.

(7) The second condition shall be taken to be satisfied notwithstanding that paragraphs (a) and (b) of sub-paragraph (3) above are not complied with as respects each of the requisite number of years if—
  (a) those paragraphs are complied with as respects at least half that number of years (or at least 20 of them, if that is less than half); and
  (b) in each of the other years the contributor concerned was, within the meaning of regulations, precluded from regular employment by responsibilities at home.

(8) For the purposes of this paragraph a person's working life is the period between—
  (a) (inclusive) the tax year in which he attained the age of 16; and
  (b) (exclusive) the tax year in which he attained pensionable age or died under that age.

Child's special allowance

6.—(1) The contribution condition for a child's special allowance is that—
  (a) the contributor concerned must in respect of any one relevant year have actually paid contributions of a relevant class; and
  (b) the earnings factor derived from those contributions must be not less than that year's lower earnings limit multiplied by 50.

(2) For the purposes of this condition, a relevant year is any year ending before the date on which the contributor concerned attained pensionable age or died under that age.

Part II

Satisfaction of Conditions in Early Years of Contribution

7.—(1) Sub-paragraph (3) below shall apply where a claim is made for a widow's payment and the last complete year before the beginning of the benefit year in which the relevant time falls was either—
  (a) the year in which the contributor concerned first became liable for primary Class 1 or Class 2 contributions; or
  (b) the year preceding that in which he first became so liable.

(2) The relevant time for the purposes of this paragraph is the date on which the contributor concerned attained pensionable age or died under that age.

(3) For the purposes of satisfaction by the contributor concerned of paragraph (b) of the contribution condition for a widow's payment, all earnings factors falling within sub-paragraph (4) below may be aggregated and that aggregate sum shall be treated as his earnings factor for the last complete year before the beginning of the benefit year in which the relevant time falls.

(4) The earnings factors referred to in sub-paragraph (3) above are—
  (a) the contributor's earnings factors for 1987–88 and each subsequent year derived from the aggregate of his earnings upon which primary Class 1 contributions were paid or treated as paid and from Class 2 contributions actually paid by him before the relevant time; and
  (b) his earnings factors for each earlier year, derived from his contributions of a relevant class actually paid by him before the relevant time.

8. Where a person claims sickness benefit, he shall be taken to satisfy the first contribution condition for the benefit if on a previous claim for any short-term benefit he has satisfied the first contribution condition for that benefit, by virtue of paragraph 8 of Schedule 3 to the 1975 Act, with contributions of a class relevant to sickness benefit.

9. Where a woman claims a widow's payment, the contributor concerned for the purposes of the claim shall be taken to satisfy the contribution condition for the payment if on a claim made in the past for any short-term benefit he has satisfied the first contribution condition for the benefit, by virtue of paragraph 8 of Schedule 3 to the 1975 Act, with contributions of a class relevant to widow's payment.

GENERAL NOTE

This Schedule consolidates SSA 1975, Sched. 3 (as amended) and sets out the contribution conditions for the benefits listed in s.20, the main conditions for which are detailed elsewhere in Pt. II.

SCHEDULE 4

RATES OF BENEFITS, ETC

Note: This Schedule is subject to alteration by orders made by the Secretary of State under Part X of the Administration Act.

PART I

CONTRIBUTORY PERIODICAL BENEFITS

Description of benefit	*Weekly rate*
1. Unemployment benefit.	£43.10.
2. Sickness benefit.	£41.20.
3. Invalidity allowance.	(a) higher rate ... ... £11.55 (b) middle rate ... ... £7.20 (c) lower rate ... ... £3.60 (the appropriate rate being determined in accordance with section 34(3)).
4. Maternity allowance.	£42.25.
5. Category B retirement pension where section 50(1)(a)(i) applies.	£32.55.
6. Child's special allowance.	£10.85.

PART II

WIDOW'S PAYMENT

Widow's payment.	£1,000.00

PART III

NON-CONTRIBUTORY PERIODICAL BENEFITS

Description of benefit	*Weekly rate*
1. Attendance allowance.	(a) higher rate ... ... £43.35 (b) lower rate ... ... £28.95 (the appropriate rate being determined in accordance with section 65(3)).
2. Severe disablement allowance.	£32.55.
3. Age related addition.	(a) higher rate ... ... £11.55 (b) middle rate ... ... £7.20 (c) lower rate ... ... £3.60 (the appropriate rate being determined in accordance with section 69(1)).

4. Invalid care allowance.	£32.55.
5. Guardian's allowance.	£10.85.
6. Category C retirement pension.	(a) lower rate ... ... £19.45 (b) higher rate ... ... £32.55 (the appropriate rate being determined in accordance with section 78(5)).
7. Category D retirement pension.	The higher rate for Category C retirement pensions under paragraph 6 above.
8. Age addition (to a pension of any category, and otherwise under section 79).	£0.25.

PART IV

INCREASES FOR DEPENDANTS

Benefit to which increase applies	Increase for qualifying child	Increase for adult dependant
(1)	(2) £	(3) £
1. Unemployment or sickness benefit—		
(a) unemployment benefit, where the beneficiary is under pensionable age	—	26.60
(b) unemployment benefit, where the beneficiary is over pensionable age	10.85	32.55
(c) sickness benefit, where the beneficiary is under pensionable age	—	25.50
(d) sickness benefit, where the beneficiary is over pensionable age	10.85	31.20
2. Invalidity pension.	10.85	32.55
3. Maternity allowance.	—	25.50
4. Widowed mother's allowance.	10.85	—
5. Category A or B retirement pension.	10.85	32.55
6. Category C retirement pension.	10.85	19.45
7. Child's special allowance.	10.85	—
8. Severe disablement allowance.	10.85	19.45
9. Invalid care allowance.	10.85	19.45

PART V

RATES OF INDUSTRIAL INJURIES BENEFIT

Description of benefit, etc.	*Rate*
1. Disablement pension (weekly rates).	For the several degrees of disablement set out in column (1) of the following Table, the respective amounts in that Table, using— (a) column (2) for any period during which the beneficiary is over the age of 18 or is entitled to an increase of benefit in respect of a child or adult dependant; (b) column (3) for any period during which the beneficiary is not over the age of 18 and not so entitled;

TABLE

Degree of disablement	*Amount*	
(1)	*(2)*	*(3)*
Per cent.	£	£
100	88.40	54.15
90	79.56	48.74
80	70.72	43.32
70	61.88	37.91
60	53.04	32.49
50	44.20	27.08
40	35.36	21.66
30	26.52	16.25
20	17.68	10.83

2. Maximum increase of weekly rate of disablement pension where constant attendance needed.	(a) except in cases of exceptionally severe disablement ... ... £35.40 (b) in any case £70.80
3. Increase of weekly rate of disablement pension (exceptionally severe disablement).	£35.40
4. Maximum of aggregate of weekly benefit payable for successive accidents.	(a) for any period during which the beneficiary is over the age of 18 or is entitled to an increase in benefit in respect of a child or adult dependant ... ... £88.40 (b) for any period during which the beneficiary is not over the age of 18 and not so entitled £54.15
5. Unemployability supplement under paragraph 2 of Schedule 7.	£54.15

6. Increase under paragraph 3 of Schedule 7 of weekly rate of unemployability supplement.	(a) if on the qualifying date the beneficiary was under the age of 35 or if that date fell before 5th July 1948 ... ... £11.55 (b) if head (a) above does not apply and on the qualifying date the beneficiary was under the age of 40 and he had not attained pensionable age before 6th April 1979 ... ... £11.55 (c) if heads (a) and (b) above do not apply and on the qualifying date the beneficiary was under the age of 45 ... ... £7.20 (d) if heads (a), (b) and (c) above do not apply and on the qualifying date the beneficiary was under the age of 50 and had not attained pensionable age before 6th April 1979 ... ... £7.20 (e) in any other case £3.60
7. Increase under paragraph 4 of Schedule 7 of weekly rate of disablement pension.	£10.85
8. Increase under paragraph 6 of Schedule 7 of weekly rate of disablement pension.	£32.55
9. Maximum disablement gratuity under paragraph 9 of Schedule 7.	£5,870.00
10. Widow's pension (weekly rates).	(a) initial rate ... ... £57.65 (b) higher permanent rate ... £54.15 (c) lower permanent rate ... 30 per cent. of the first sum specified in section 44(4) (Category A basic retirement pension) (the appropriate rate being determined in accordance with paragraph 16 of Schedule 7).
11. Widower's pension (weekly rate).	£54.15
12. Weekly rate of allowance in respect of children under paragraph 18 of Schedule 7.	In respect of each qualifying child £10.85

GENERAL NOTE

This Schedule sets out the various rates of benefit. Uprating takes place in April of each year. See further SSAA 1992, ss.150–154.

Section 55   SCHEDULE 5

INCREASE OF PENSION WHERE ENTITLEMENT IS DEFERRED

Increase of pension where pensioner's entitlement is deferred

1. Where a person's entitlement to a Category A or Category B retirement pension is deferred, the rate of his Category A or Category B retirement pension shall be increased by an amount equal to the aggregate of the increments to which he is entitled under paragraph 2 below, but only if that amount is enough to increase the rate of the pension by at least 1 per cent.

2.—(1) Subject to paragraph 3 below, a person is entitled to an increment under this paragraph for each complete incremental period in his period of enhancement.

(2) In this Schedule—

"incremental period" means any period of six days which are treated by regulations as days of increment for the purposes of this Schedule in relation to the person and the pension in question; and "the period of enhancement", in relation to that person and that pension, means the period which—

(a) begins on the same day as the period of deferment in question; and

(b) ends on the same day as that period or, if earlier, on the day before the 5th anniversary of the beginning of that period.

(3) Subject to paragraph 3 below, the amount of the increment for any such incremental period shall be 1/7th per cent. of the weekly rate of the Category A or Category B retirement pension to which that person would have been entitled for the period if his entitlement had not been deferred.

(4) Where an amount is required to be calculated in accordance with the provisions of sub-paragraph (3) above—

(a) the amount so calculated shall be rounded to the nearest penny, taking any 1/2p as nearest to the next whole penny above; and

(b) where the amount so calculated would, apart from this sub-paragraph, be a sum less than 1/2p, that amount shall be taken to be zero, notwithstanding any other provision of this Act, the Pensions Act or the Administration Act.

(5) For the purposes of sub-paragraph (3) above the weekly rate of pension for any period shall be taken—

(a) to include any increase under section 47(1) above and any increase under paragraph 4, 5 or 6 below, but

(b) not to include any increase under section 80, 83 or 85 above or any graduated retirement benefit.

(6) The reference in sub-paragraph (5) above to any increase under subsection (1) of section 47 above shall be taken as a reference to any increase that would take place under that subsection if subsection (2) of that section and section 29B(2) of the Pensions Act were disregarded.

(7) Where one or more orders have come into force under section 150 of the Administration Act during the period of enhancement, the rate for any incremental period shall be determined as if the order or orders had come into force before the beginning of the period of enhancement.

(8) Where a pensioner's rights premium is paid in respect of a person who is, or if his entitlement had not been deferred would be, entitled to a Category A or Category B retirement pension, then, in calculating any increment under this paragraph which falls to be paid to him in respect of such a pension after the date on which the premium is paid there shall be disregarded any guaranteed minimum pension to which the pensioner was entitled in connection with the employment to which the premium relates.

3.—(1) Regulations may provide that sub-paragraphs (1) to (3) of paragraph 2 above shall have effect with such additions, omissions and amendments as are prescribed in relation to a person during whose period of enhancement there has been a change, other than a change made by such an order as is mentioned in sub-paragraph (7) of that paragraph, in the rate of the Category A or Category B retirement pension to which he would have been entitled if his entitlement to the pension had commenced on attaining pensionable age.

(2) Any regulations under this paragraph may make such consequential additions, omissions and amendments in paragraph 8(3) below as the Secretary of State considers are appropriate in consequence of any changes made by virtue of this paragraph in paragraph 2 above.

Increase of pension where pensioner's deceased spouse has deferred entitlement

4.—(1) Subject to sub-paragraph (3) below, where a woman is entitled to a Category A or Category B retirement pension and—

(a) she has had a husband and he has died, and she was married to him when he died; and

(b) the husband either—

(i) was entitled to a Category A or Category B retirement pension with an increase under this Schedule; or

(ii) would have been so entitled if his period of deferment had ended on the day before his death,

the rate of her pension shall be increased by an amount equal to the increase to which he was or would have been entitled under this Schedule apart from paragraph 6.

(2) Subject to sub-paragraph (3) below, where a man is entitled to a Category A or Category B retirement pension and—

(a) he has had a wife and she has died, and he was married to her when she died;

(b) he was over pensionable age when she died; and

(c) the wife either—

(i) was entitled to a Category A or Category B retirement pension with an increase under this Schedule; or

(ii) would have been so entitled if her period of deferment had ended on the day before her death, the rate of his pension shall be increased by an amount equal to the increase to which she was or would have been entitled under this Schedule apart from paragraph 5.

(3) If a married person dies after 5th April 2000, the rate of the retirement pension for that person's widow or widower shall be increased by an amount equivalent to the sum of—

(a) the increase in the basic pension to which the deceased spouse was entitled; and

(b) one-half of the increase in the additional pension.

(4) In any case where—

(a) there is a period between the death of the former spouse and the date on which the surviving spouse becomes entitled to a Category A or Category B retirement pension, and

(b) one or more orders have come into force under section 150 of the Administration Act during that period,

the amount of the increase to which the surviving spouse is entitled under this paragraph shall be determined as if the order or orders had come into force before the beginning of that period.

(5) This paragraph does not apply in any case where the deceased spouse died before 6th April 1979 and the widow or widower attained pensionable age before that date.

5.—(1) Where a woman is entitled to a Category A or Category B retirement pension and—

(a) she has had a husband and he has died, and she was married to him when he died; and

(b) the husband either—

(i) was entitled to a guaranteed minimum pension with an increase under section 35(6) of the Pensions Act, or

(ii) would have been so entitled if he had retired on the date of his death,

the rate of her pension shall be increased by an amount equal to the sum of the amounts set out in sub-paragraph (2) or, as the case may be, (3) below.

(2) Where the husband dies before 6th April 2000, the amounts referred to in sub-paragraph (1) above are the following—

(a) an amount equal to one-half of the increase mentioned in paragraph (b) of that sub-paragraph;

(b) the appropriate amount; and

(c) an amount equal to any increase to which he had been entitled under paragraph 6 below.

(3) Where the husband dies after 5th April 2000, the amounts referred to in sub-paragraph (1) above are the following—

(a) one-half of the appropriate amount after it has been reduced by the amount of any increases under section 37A of the Pensions Act; and

(b) one-half of any increase to which the husband had been entitled under paragraph 6 below.

6.—(1) Where a man is entitled to a Category A or Category B retirement pension and—

(a) he has had a wife and she has died, and he was married to her when she died;

(b) he was over pensionable age when she died; and

(c) the wife either—

(i) was entitled to a guaranteed minimum pension with an increase under section 35(6) of the Pensions Act; or

(ii) would have been so entitled if she had retired on the date of her death,

the rate of his pension shall be increased by an amount equal to the sum of the amounts set out in sub-paragraph (2) or, as the case may be, (3) or (4) below.

(2) Where the wife dies before 6th April 1989, the amounts referred to in sub-paragraph (1) above are the following—

(a) an amount equal to the increase mentioned in paragraph (c) of that sub-paragraph;

(b) the appropriate amount; and

(c) an amount equal to any increase to which she had been entitled under paragraph 5 above.

(3) Where the wife dies after 5th April 1989 but before 6th April 2000, the amounts referred to in sub-paragraph (1) above are the following—

(a) the increase mentioned in paragraph (c) of that sub-paragraph, so far as attributable to employment before 6th April 1988;

(b) one-half of that increase, so far as attributable to employment after 5th April 1988;

(c) the appropriate amount reduced by the amount of any increases under section 37A of the Pensions Act; and

(d) any increase to which she had been entitled under paragraph 5 above.

(4) Where the wife dies after 5th April 2000, the amounts referred to in sub-paragraph (1) above are the following—

(a) one-half of the increase mentioned in paragraph (c) of that sub-paragraph, so far as attributable to employment before 6th April 1988;

(b) one-half of the appropriate amount after it has been reduced by the amount of any increases under section 37A of the Pensions Act; and

(c) one-half of any increase to which she had been entitled under paragraph 5 above.

7.—(1) For the purposes of paragraphs 5 and 6 above, the "appropriate amount" means the greater of—
  (a) the amount by which the deceased person's Category A or Category B retirement pension had been increased under section 150(1)(e) of the Administration Act; or
  (b) the amount by which his Category A or Category B retirement pension would have been so increased had he died immediately before his surviving spouse became entitled to a Category A or Category B retirement pension.
(2) Where an amount is required to be calculated in accordance with the provisions of paragraph 5 or 6 or sub-paragraph (1) above—
  (a) the amount so calculated shall be rounded to the nearest penny, taking any 1/2p as nearest to the next whole penny above; and
  (b) where the amount so calculated would, apart from this sub-paragraph, be a sum less than 1/2p, that amount shall be taken to be zero, notwithstanding any other provision of this Act, the Pensions Act or the Administration Act.

Married women

8.—(1) For the purposes of paragraphs 1 to 3 above in their application to a Category B retirement pension to which a married woman is entitled by virtue of her husband's contributions, a married woman who would have become entitled to such a pension on an earlier day if her husband's entitlement to his Category A retirement pension had not been deferred shall be treated as having (in addition to any other period of enhancement) a period of enhancement which begins on that earlier day and ends on the same day as her husband's period of enhancement.
(2) The reference in sub-paragraph (1) above to the day on which the woman's husband's period of enhancement ends shall, where the marriage is terminated before that day, be construed as a reference to the date on which the marriage is terminated.
(3) In the case of—
  (a) a Category B retirement pension to which a married woman is entitled by virtue of her husband's contributions; or
  (b) a married woman's Category A retirement pension with an increase under section 53(2) above attributable to her husband's contributions,
the reference in paragraph 2(3) above to the pension to which a person would have been entitled if his entitlement had not been deferred shall be construed as a reference to the pension to which she would have been entitled if neither her nor her husband's entitlement to a retirement pension had been deferred.
(4) Paragraph 4(2)(c) above shall not apply to a Category B retirement pension to which the wife was or would have been entitled by virtue of the man's contributions; and where the Category A retirement pension to which the wife was or would have been entitled includes an increase under section 53(2) above attributable to his contributions, the increase to which he is entitled under that paragraph shall be calculated as if there had been no increase under that section.

Uprating

9. The sums which are the increases in the rates of retirement pensions under this Schedule are subject to alteration by order made by the Secretary of State under section 150 of the Administration Act.

GENERAL NOTE
  See General Note to s.55.

Sections 68(6) and 103(5)   SCHEDULE 6

ASSESSMENT OF EXTENT OF DISABLEMENT

General provisions as to method of assessment

1. For the purposes of section 68 or 103 above and Part II of Schedule 7 to this Act, the extent of disablement shall be assessed, by reference to the disabilities incurred by the claimant as a result of the relevant loss of faculty, in accordance with the following general principles—
  (a) except as provided in paragraphs (b) to (d) below, the disabilities to be taken into account shall be all disabilities so incurred (whether or not involving loss of earning power or additional expense) to which the claimant may be expected, having regard to his physical and mental condition at the date of the assessment, to be subject during the period taken into account by the assessment as compared with a person of the same age and sex whose physical and mental condition is normal;

(b) except in the case of an assessment for the purposes of section 68 above, regulations may make provision as to the extent (if any) to which any disabilities are to be taken into account where there are disabilities which, though resulting from the relevant loss of faculty, also result, or without the relevant accident might have been expected to result, from a cause other than the relevant accident;

(c) the assessment shall be made without reference to the particular circumstances of the claimant other than age, sex and physical and mental condition;

(d) the disabilities resulting from such loss of faculty as may be prescribed shall be taken as amounting to 100 per cent. disablement and other disabilities shall be assessed accordingly.

2. Provision may be made by regulations for further defining the principles on which the extent of disablement is to be assessed and such regulations may in particular direct that a prescribed loss of faculty shall be treated as resulting in a prescribed degree of disablement; and, in connection with any such direction, nothing in paragraph 1(c) above prevents the making of different provision, in the case of loss of faculty in or affecting hand or arm, for right-handed and for left-handed persons.

3. Regulations under paragraph 1(d) or 2 above may include provision—

(a) for adjusting or reviewing an assessment made before the date of the coming into force of those regulations;

(b) for any resulting alteration of that assessment to have effect as from that date;

so however that no assessment shall be reduced by virtue of this paragraph.

Severe disablement allowance

4.—(1) In the case of an assessment of any person's disablement for the purposes of section 68 above, the period to be taken into account for any such assessment shall be the period during which that person has suffered and may be expected to continue to suffer from the relevant loss of faculty beginning not later than—

(a) the first claim day, if his entitlement to benefit falls to be determined in accordance with section 68(3)(b) above as modified by regulations under section 68(11)(b);

(b) where his disablement has previously been assessed for the purposes of section 68 above at a percentage which is not less than 80 per cent.—

(i) if the period taken into account for that assessment was or included the period of 196 days ending immediately before the first claim day, the first claim day, or

(ii) if the period so taken into account included any day falling within that period of 196 days, the day immediately following that day or, if there is more than one such day, the last such day;

(c) in any other case, 196 days before the first claim day;

and, in any case, ending not later than the day on which that person attains the age of 65, if a woman, or 70, if a man.

(2) In this paragraph "the first claim day" means the first day in respect of which the person concerned has made the claim in question for a severe disablement allowance.

5.—(1) An assessment of any person's disablement for the purposes of section 68 above shall state the degree of disablement in the form of a percentage and shall specify the period taken into account by the assessment.

(2) For the purposes of any such assessment—

(a) a percentage which is not a whole number shall be rounded to the nearest whole number or, if it falls equally near two whole numbers, shall be rounded up to the higher; and

(b) a percentage between 5 and 100 which is not a multiple of 10 shall be treated, if it is a multiple of 5, as being the next higher percentage which is a multiple of 10 and, in any other case, as being the nearest percentage which is a multiple of 10.

(3) If on the assessment the person's disablement is found to be less than 5 per cent., that degree of disablement shall for the purposes of section 68 above be disregarded and, accordingly, the assessment shall state that he is not disabled.

Disablement benefit

6.—(1) Subject to sub-paragraphs (2) and (3) below, the period to be taken into account by an assessment for the purposes of section 103 above and Part II of Schedule 7 to this Act of the extent of a claimant's disablement shall be the period (beginning not earlier than the end of the period of 90 days referred to in section 103(6) above and in paragraph 9(3) of that Schedule and limited by reference either to the claimant's life or to a definite date) during which the claimant has suffered and may be expected to continue to suffer from the relevant loss of faculty.

(2) If on any assessment the condition of the claimant is not such, having regard to the possibility of changes in that condition (whether predictable or not), as to allow of a final

assessment being made up to the end of the period provided by sub-paragraph (1) above, then, subject to sub-paragraph (3) below—

    (a) a provisional assessment shall be made, taking into account such shorter period only as seems reasonable having regard to his condition and that possibility; and

    (b) on the next assessment the period to be taken into account shall begin with the end of the period taken into account by the provisional assessment.

(3) Where the assessed extent of a claimant's disablement amounts to less than 14 per cent., then, subject to sub-paragraphs (4) and (5) below, that assessment shall be a final assessment and the period to be taken into account by it shall not end before the earliest date on which it seems likely that the extent of the disablement will be less than one per cent.

(4) Sub-paragraph (3) above does not apply in any case where it seems likely that—

    (a) the assessed extent of the disablement will be aggregated with the assessed extent of any present disablement, and

    (b) that aggregate will amount to 14 per cent. or more.

(5) Where the extent of the claimant's disablement is assessed at different percentages for different parts of the period taken into account by the assessment, then—

    (a) sub-paragraph (3) above does not apply in relation to the assessment unless the percentage assessed for the latest part of that period is less than 14 per cent., and

    (b) in any such case that sub-paragraph shall apply only in relation to that part of that period (and subject to sub-paragraph (4) above).

7. An assessment for the purposes of section 103 above and Part II of Schedule 7 to this Act shall—

    (a) state the degree of disablement in the form of a percentage;

    (b) specify the period taken into account by the assessment; and

    (c) where that period is limited by reference to a definite date, specify whether the assessment is provisional or final;

but the percentage and the period shall not be specified more particularly than is necessary for the purpose of determining in accordance with section 103 above and Parts II and IV of Schedule 7 to this Act the claimant's rights as to disablement pension or gratuity and reduced earnings allowance (whether or not a claim has been made).

Special provision as to entitlement to constant attendance allowance, etc.

8.—(1) For the purpose of determining whether a person is entitled—

    (a) to an increase of a disablement pension under section 104 above; or

    (b) to a corresponding increase of any other benefit by virtue of paragraph 6(4)(b) or 7(2)(b) of Schedule 8 to this Act,

regulations may provide for the extent of the person's disablement resulting from the relevant injury or disease to be determined in such manner as may be provided for by the regulations by reference to all disabilities to which that person is subject which result either from the relevant injury or disease or from any other injury or disease in respect of which there fall to be made to the person payments of any of the descriptions listed in sub-paragraph (2) below.

(2) Those payments are—

    (a) payments by way of disablement pension;

    (b) payments by way of benefit under paragraph 4 or 7(1) of Schedule 8 to this Act; or

    (c) payments in such circumstances as may be prescribed by way of such other benefit as may be prescribed (being benefit in connection with any hostilities or with service as a member of Her Majesty's forces or of such other organisation as may be specified in the regulations).

GENERAL NOTE

    This Schedule consolidates SSA 1975, Sched. 8 (as amended) and specifies the rules governing the assessment of disablement for the purposes of severe disablement allowance, disablement benefit and constant attendance allowance. See Lewis, Chap. 5.

Section 106   SCHEDULE 7

INDUSTRIAL INJURIES BENEFITS

PART I

UNEMPLOYABILITY SUPPLEMENT

Availability

1. This Part of this Schedule applies only in relation to persons who were beneficiaries in

receipt of unemployability supplement under section 58 of the 1975 Act immediately before 6th April 1987.

Rate and duration

2.—(1) The weekly rate of a disablement pension shall, if as the result of the relevant loss of faculty the beneficiary is incapable of work and likely to remain so permanently, be increased by the amount specified in Schedule 4, Part V, paragraph 5.

(2) An increase of pension under this paragraph is referred to in this Act as an "unemployability supplement".

(3) For the purposes of this paragraph a person may be treated as being incapable of work and likely to remain so permanently, notwithstanding that the loss of faculty is not such as to prevent him being capable of work, if it is likely to prevent his earnings in a year exceeding a prescribed amount not less than £104.

(4) An unemployability supplement shall be payable for such period as may be determined at the time it is granted, but may be renewed from time to time.

Increase of unemployability supplement

3.—(1) Subject to the following provisions of this paragraph, if on the qualifying date the beneficiary was—

(a) a man under the age of 60, or

(b) a woman under the age of 55,

the weekly rate of unemployability supplement shall be increased by the appropriate amount specified in Schedule 4, Part V, paragraph 6.

(2) Where for any period the beneficiary is entitled to a Category A or Category B retirement pension or an invalidity pension and the weekly rate of the pension includes an additional pension such as is mentioned in section 44(3)(b) above, for that period the relevant amount shall be deducted from the amount that would otherwise be the increase under this paragraph and the beneficiary shall be entitled to an increase only if there is a balance after that deduction and, if there is such a balance, only to an amount equal to it.

(3) In this paragraph "the relevant amount" means an amount equal to the additional pension reduced by the amount of any reduction in the weekly rate of the retirement or invalidity pension made by virtue of section 29 of the Pensions Act.

(4) In this paragraph references to an additional pension are references to that pension after any increase under section 52(3) above but without any increase under paragraphs 1 and 2 of Schedule 5 to this Act.

(5) In this paragraph "the qualifying date" means, subject to sub-paragraphs (6) and (7) below, the beginning of the first week for which the beneficiary qualified for unemployability supplement.

(6) If the incapacity for work in respect of which unemployability supplement is payable forms part of a period of interruption of employment which has continued from a date earlier than the date fixed under sub-paragraph (5) above, the qualifying date means the first day in that period which is a day of incapacity for work, or such earlier day as may be prescribed.

(7) Subject to sub-paragraph (6) above, if there have been two or more periods for which the beneficiary was entitled to unemployability supplement, the qualifying date shall be, in relation to unemployability supplement for a day in any one of those periods, the beginning of the first week of that period.

(8) For the purposes of sub-paragraph (7) above—

(a) a break of more than 8 weeks in entitlement to unemployability supplement means that the periods before and after the break are two different periods; and

(b) a break of 8 weeks or less is to be disregarded.

(9) The Secretary of State may by regulations provide that sub-paragraph (8) above shall have effect as if for the references to 8 weeks there were substituted references to a larger number of weeks specified in the regulations.

(10) In this paragraph "period of interruption of employment" has the same meaning as it has for the purposes of unemployment benefit.

(11) The provisions of this paragraph are subject to section 29C of the Pensions Act (contracting-out and increases of unemployability supplement).

Increase for beneficiary's dependent children

4.—(1) Subject to the provisions of this paragraph and paragraph 5 below, the weekly rate of a disablement pension where the beneficiary is entitled to an unemployability supplement shall be increased for any period during which the beneficiary is entitled to child benefit in respect of a child or children.

(2) The amount of the increase shall be as specified in Schedule 4, Part V, paragraph 7.

(3) In any case where—

(a) a beneficiary is one of two persons who are—

    (i) spouses residing together, or

    (ii) an unmarried couple, and

(b) the other person had earnings in any week,

the beneficiary's right to payment of increases for the following week under this paragraph shall be determined in accordance with sub-paragraph (4) below.

(4) No such increase shall be payable—

(a) in respect of the first child where the earnings were £110 or more; and

(b) in respect of a further child for each complete £14 by which the earnings exceeded £110.

(5) The Secretary of State may by order substitute larger amounts for the amounts for the time being specified in sub-paragraph (4) above.

(6) In this paragraph "week" means such period of 7 days as may be prescribed by regulations made for the purposes of this paragraph.

Additional provisions as to increase under paragraph 4

5.—(1) An increase under paragraph 4 above of any amount in respect of a particular child shall for any period be payable only if during that period one or other of the following conditions is satisfied with respect to the child—

(a) the beneficiary would be treated for the purposes of Part IX of this Act as having the child living with him; or

(b) the requisite contributions are being made to the cost of providing for the child.

(2) The condition specified in paragraph (b) of sub-paragraph (1) above is to be treated as satisfied if, and only if—

(a) such contributions are being made at a weekly rate not less than the amount referred to in that sub-paragraph—

    (i) by the beneficiary, or

    (ii) where the beneficiary is one of two spouses residing together, by them together; and

(b) except in prescribed cases, the contributions are over and above those required for the purposes of satisfying section 143(1)(b) above.

Increase for adult dependants

6.—(1) The weekly rate of a disablement pension where the beneficiary is entitled to an unemployability supplement shall be increased under this paragraph for any period during which—

(a) the beneficiary is—

    (i) residing with his spouse, or

    (ii) contributing to the maintenance of his spouse at the requisite rate; or

(b) a person—

    (i) who is neither the spouse of the beneficiary nor a child, and

    (ii) in relation to whom such further conditions as may be prescribed are fulfilled, has the care of a child or children in respect of whom the beneficiary is entitled to child benefit.

(2) The amount of the increase under this paragraph shall be that specified in Schedule 4, Part V, paragraph 8 and the requisite rate for the purposes of sub-paragraph (1)(a) above is a weekly rate not less than that amount.

(3) Regulations may provide that, for any period during which—

(a) the beneficiary is contributing to the maintenance of his or her spouse at the requisite rate, and

(b) the weekly earnings of the spouse exceed such amount as may be prescribed,

there shall be no increase of benefit under this paragraph.

(4) Regulations may provide that, for any period during which the beneficiary is residing with his or her spouse and the spouse has earnings—

(a) the increase of benefit under this paragraph shall be subject to a reduction in respect of the spouse's earnings; or

(b) there shall be no increase of benefit under this paragraph.

(5) Regulations may, in a case within sub-paragraph (1)(b) above in which the person there referred to is residing with the beneficiary and fulfils such further conditions as may be prescribed, authorise an increase of benefit under this paragraph, but subject, taking account of the earnings of the person residing with the beneficiary, other than such of that person's earnings from employment by the beneficiary as may be prescribed, to provisions comparable to those that may be made by virtue of sub-paragraph (4) above.

(6) Regulations under this paragraph may, in connection with any reduction or extinguishment of an increase of benefit in respect of earnings, prescribe the method of calculating or estimating the earnings.

(7) A beneficiary shall not be entitled to an increase of benefit under this paragraph in respect of more than one person for the same period.

Earnings to include occupational and personal pensions for purposes of disablement pension

7.—(1) Except as may be prescribed, any reference to earnings in paragraph 4 or 6 above includes a reference to payments by way of occupational or personal pension.

(2) For the purposes of those paragraphs, the Secretary of State may by regulations provide, in relation to cases where payments by way of occupational or personal pension are made otherwise than weekly, that any necessary apportionment of the payments shall be made in such manner and on such basis as may be prescribed.

Dependency increases: continuation of awards in cases of fluctuating earnings

8.—(1) Where a beneficiary—
(a) has been awarded an increase of benefit under paragraph 4 or 6 above, but
(b) ceases to be entitled to the increase by reason only that the weekly earnings of some other person ("the relevant earner") exceed the amount of the increase or, as the case may be, some specified amount,

then, if and so long as the beneficiary would have continued to be entitled to the increase, disregarding any such excess of earnings, the award shall continue in force but the increase shall not be payable for any week if the earnings relevant to that week exceed the amount of the increase or, as the case may be, the specified amount.

(2) In this paragraph the earnings which are relevant to any week are those earnings of the relevant earner which, apart from this paragraph, would be taken into account in determining whether the beneficiary is entitled to the increase in question for that week.

Part II

Disablement Gratuity

9.—(1) An employed earner shall be entitled to a disablement gratuity, if—
(a) he made a claim for disablement benefit before 1st October 1986;
(b) he suffered as the result of the relevant accident from loss of physical or mental faculty such that the extent of the resulting disablement assessed in accordance with Schedule 6 to this Act amounts to not less than one per cent.; and
(c) the extent of the disablement is assessed for the period taken into account as amounting to less than 20 per cent.

(2) A disablement gratuity shall be—
(a) of an amount fixed, in accordance with the length of the period and the degree of the disablement, by a prescribed scale, but not in any case exceeding the amount specified in Schedule 4, Part V, paragraph 9; and
(b) payable, if and in such cases as regulations so provide, by instalments.

(3) A person shall not be entitled to disablement gratuity until after the expiry of the period of 90 days (disregarding Sundays) beginning with the day of the relevant accident.

Part III

Increase of Disablement Pension During Hospital Treatment

10.—(1) This Part of this Schedule has effect in relation to a period during which a person is receiving medical treatment as an in-patient in a hospital or similar institution and which—
(a) commenced before 6th April 1987; or
(b) commenced after that date but within a period of 28 days from the end of the period during which he last received an increase of benefit under section 62 of the 1975 Act or this paragraph in respect of such treatment for the relevant injury or loss of faculty.

(2) Where a person is awarded disablement benefit, but the extent of his disablement is assessed for the period taken into account by the assessment at less than 100 per cent., it shall be treated as assessed at 100 per cent. for any part of that period, whether before or after the making of the assessment or the award of benefit, during which he receives, as an in-patient in a hospital or similar institution, medical treatment for the relevant injury or loss of faculty.

(3) Where the extent of the disablement is assessed for that period at less than 20 per cent., sub-paragraph (2) above shall not affect the assessment; but in the case of a disablement

pension payable by virtue of this paragraph to a person awarded a disablement gratuity wholly or partly in respect of the same period, the weekly rate of the pension (after allowing for any increase under Part V of this Act) shall be reduced by the amount prescribed as being the weekly value of his gratuity.

PART IV

REDUCED EARNINGS ALLOWANCE

11.—(1) Subject to the provisions of this paragraph, an employed earner shall be entitled to reduced earnings allowance if—

(a) he is entitled to a disablement pension or would be so entitled if that pension were payable where disablement is assessed at not less than one per cent.; and

(b) as a result of the relevant loss of faculty, he is either—

(i) incapable, and likely to remain permanently incapable, of following his regular occupation; and

(ii) incapable of following employment of an equivalent standard which is suitable in his case,

or is, and has at all times since the end of the period of 90 days referred to in section 103(6) above been, incapable of following that occupation or any such employment;

but a person shall not be entitled to reduced earnings allowance to the extent that the relevant loss of faculty results from an accident happening on or after 1st October 1990 (the day on which section 3 of the Social Security Act 1990 came into force).

(2) A person—

(a) who immediately before that date is entitled to reduced earnings allowance in consequence of the relevant accident; but

(b) who subsequently ceases to be entitled to that allowance for one or more days,

shall not again be entitled to reduced earnings allowance in consequence of that accident; but this sub-paragraph does not prevent the making at any time of a claim for, or an award of, reduced earnings allowance in consequence of that accident for a period which commences not later than the day after that on which the claimant was last entitled to that allowance in consequence of that accident.

(3) For the purposes of sub-paragraph (2) above—

(a) a person who, apart from section 103(6) above, would have been entitled to reduced earnings allowance immediately before 1st October 1990 shall be treated as entitled to that allowance on any day (including a Sunday) on which he would have been entitled to it apart from that provision;

(b) regulations may prescribe other circumstances in which a person is to be treated as entitled, or as having been entitled, to reduced earnings allowance on any prescribed day.

(4) The Secretary of State may by regulations provide that in prescribed circumstances employed earner's employment in which a claimant was engaged when the relevant accident took place but which was not his regular occupation is to be treated as if it had been his regular occupation.

(5) In sub-paragraph (1) above—

(a) references to a person's regular occupation are to be taken as not including any subsidiary occupation, except to the extent that they fall to be treated as including such an occupation by virtue of regulations under sub-paragraph (4) above; and

(b) employment of an equivalent standard is to be taken as not including employment other than employed earner's employment;

and in assessing the standard of remuneration in any employment, including a person's regular occupation, regard is to be had to his reasonable prospect of advancement.

(6) For the purposes of this Part of this Schedule a person's regular occupation is to be treated as extending to and including employment in the capacities to which the persons in that occupation (or a class or description of them to which he belonged at the time of the relevant accident) are in the normal course advanced, and to which, if he had continued to follow that occupation without having suffered the relevant loss of faculty, he would have had at least the normal prospects of advancement; and so long as he is, as a result of the relevant loss of faculty, deprived in whole or in part of those prospects, he is to be treated as incapable of following that occupation.

(7) Regulations may for the purposes of this Part of this Schedule provide that a person is not to be treated as capable of following an occupation or employment merely because of his working thereat during a period of trial or for purposes of rehabilitation or training or in other prescribed circumstances.

(8) Reduced earnings allowance shall be awarded—

(a) for such period as may be determined at the time of the award; and

(b) if at the end of that period the beneficiary submits a fresh claim for the allowance, for such further period, commencing as mentioned in sub-paragraph (2) above, as may be determined.

(9) The award may not be for a period longer than the period to be taken into account under paragraph 4 or 6 of Schedule 6 to this Act.

(10) Reduced earnings allowance shall be payable at a rate determined by reference to the beneficiary's probable standard of remuneration during the period for which it is granted in any employed earner's employments which are suitable in his case and which he is likely to be capable of following as compared with that in the relevant occupation, but in no case at a rate higher than 40 per cent. of the maximum rate of a disablement pension or at a rate such that the aggregate of disablement pension (not including increases in disablement pension under any provision of this Act) and reduced earnings allowance awarded to the beneficiary exceeds 140 per cent. of the maximum rate of a disablement pension.

(11) Sub-paragraph (10) above shall have effect in the case of a person who retired from regular employment before 6th April 1987 with the substitution for "140 per cent." of "100 per cent.".

(12) In sub-paragraph (10) above "the relevant occupation" means—

(a) in relation to a person who is entitled to reduced earnings allowance by virtue of regulations under sub-paragraph (4) above, the occupation in which he was engaged when the relevant accident took place; and

(b) in relation to any other person who is entitled to reduced earnings allowance, his regular occupation within the the meaning of sub-paragraph (1) above.

(13) On any award except the first the probable standard of his remuneration shall be determined in such manner as may be prescribed; and, without prejudice to the generality of this sub-paragraph, regulations may provide in prescribed circumstances for the probable standard of remuneration to be determined by reference—

(a) to the standard determined at the time of the last previous award of reduced earnings allowance; and

(b) to scales or indices of earnings in a particular industry or description of industries or any other data relating to such earnings.

(14) In this paragraph "maximum rate of a disablement pension" means the rate specified in the first entry in column (2) of Schedule 4, Part V, paragraph 1 and does not include increases in disablement pension under any provision of this Act.

Supplementary

12.—(1) A person who on 10th April 1988 or 9th April 1989 satisfies the conditions—

(a) that he has attained pensionable age;

(b) that he has retired from regular employment; and

(c) that he is entitled to reduced earnings allowance,

shall be entitled to that allowance for life.

(2) In the case of any beneficiary who is entitled to reduced earnings allowance by virtue of sub-paragraph (1) above, the allowance shall be payable, subject to any enactment contained in Part V or VI of this Act or in the Administration Act and to any regulations made under any such enactment, at the weekly rate at which it was payable to the beneficiary on the relevant date or would have been payable to him on that date but for any such enactment or regulations.

(3) For the purpose of determining under sub-paragraph (2) above the weekly rate of reduced earnings allowance payable in the case of a qualifying beneficiary, it shall be assumed that the weekly rate at which the allowance was payable to him on the relevant date was—

(a) £25.84, where that date is 10th April 1988, or

(b) £26.96, where that date is 9th April 1989.

(4) In sub-paragraph (3) above "qualifying beneficiary" means a person entitled to reduced earnings allowance by virtue of sub-paragraph (1) above who—

(a) did not attain pensionable age before 6th April 1987, or

(b) did not retire from regular employment before that date,

and who, on the relevant date, was entitled to the allowance at a rate which was restricted under paragraph 11(10) above by reference to 40 per cent. of the maximum rate of disablement pension.

(5) For a beneficiary who is entitled to reduced earnings allowance by virtue of satisfying the conditions in sub-paragraph (1) above on 10th April 1988 the relevant date is that date.

(6) For a beneficiary who is entitled to it by virtue only of satisfying those conditions on 9th April 1989 the relevant date is that date.

PART V

RETIREMENT ALLOWANCE

13.—(1) Subject to the provisions of this Part of this Schedule, a person who—

(a) has attained pensionable age; and

(b) gives up regular employment on or after 10th April 1989; and

(c) was entitled to reduced earnings allowance (by virtue either of one award or of a number of awards) on the day immediately before he gave up such employment,

shall cease to be entitled to reduced earnings allowance as from day on which he gives up regular employment.

(2) If the date before a person ceases under sub-paragraph (1) above to be entitled to reduced earnings allowance he is entitled to the allowance (by virtue either of one award or of a number of awards) at a weekly rate or aggregate weekly rate of not less than £2.00, he shall be entitled to a benefit, to be known as "retirement allowance".

(3) Retirement allowance shall be payable to him (subject to any enactment contained in Part V or VI of this Act or in the Administration Act and to any regulations made under any such enactment) for life.

(4) Subject to sub-paragraph (6) below, the weekly rate of a beneficiary's retirement allowance shall be—

(a) 25 per cent. of the weekly rate at which he was last entitled to reduced earnings allowance; or

(b) 10 per cent. of the maximum rate of a disablement pension,

whichever is the less.

(5) For the purpose of determining under sub-paragraph (4) above the weekly rate of retirement allowance in the case of a beneficiary who—

(a) retires or is deemed to have retired on 10th April 1989, and

(b) on 9th April 1989 was entitled to reduced earnings allowance at a rate which was restricted under paragraph 11(10) above by reference to 40 per cent. of the maximum rate of disablement pension,

it shall be assumed that the weekly rate of reduced earnings allowance to which he was entitled on 9th April 1989 was £26.96.

(6) If the weekly rate of the beneficiary's retirement allowance—

(a) would not be a whole number of pence; and

(b) would exceed the whole number of pence next below it by 1/2p or more,

the beneficiary shall be entitled to retirement allowance at a rate equal to the next higher whole number of pence.

(7) The sums falling to be calculated under sub-paragraph (4) above are subject to alteration by orders made by the Secretary of State under section 150 of the Administration Act.

(8) Regulations may—

(a) make provision with respect to the meaning of "regular employment" for the purposes of this paragraph; and

(b) prescribe circumstances in which, and periods for which, a person is or is not to be regarded for those purposes as having given up such employment.

(9) Regulations under sub-paragraph (8) above may, in particular—

(a) provide for a person to be regarded—

    (i) as having given up regular employment, notwithstanding that he is or intends to be an earner; or

    (ii) as not having given up regular employment, notwithstanding that he has or may have one or more days of interruption of employment; and

(b) prescribe circumstances in which a person is or is not to be regarded as having given up regular employment by reference to—

    (i) the level or frequency of his earnings during a prescribed period; or

    (ii) the number of hours for which he works during a prescribed period calculated in a prescribed manner.

(10) "Day of interruption of employment" has the same meaning for the purposes of this paragraph as it has for the purposes of provisions of this Act relating to unemployment benefit, sickness benefit or invalidity benefit.

(11) In this paragraph "maximum rate of a disablement pension" means the rate specified in the first entry in column (2) of Schedule 4, Part V, paragraph 1 and does not include increases in disablement pension under any provision of this Act.

4–204

PART VI

INDUSTRIAL DEATH BENEFIT

Introductory

14.—(1) This Part of this Schedule only has effect in relation to deaths before 11th April 1988.

(2) In this Part of this Schedule "the deceased" means the person in respect of whose death industrial death benefit is claimed or payable.

Widow's benefit (entitlement)

15.—(1) The widow of the deceased shall be entitled to death benefit if at his death either—

(a) she was residing with him; or

(b) she was receiving or entitled to receive, or would but for the relevant accident have been receiving or entitled to receive, from him periodical payments for her maintenance of not less than the prescribed amount.

(2) In the case of a widow, death benefit shall be a pension commencing from the death of the deceased and payable, at the weekly rate for the time being applicable under paragraph 16 below for life or until she remarries.

(3) A pension under this paragraph shall not be payable for any period during which the beneficiary is living as husband and wife with a man not her husband.

(4) In this paragraph—

(a) references to a widow receiving or being entitled to receive payments from the deceased are only to her receiving or being entitled to receive (whether from him or from another) payments provided or procured by the deceased; and

(b) "entitled" means, in relation to any such payments, entitled under any order of a court, trust or agreement which the widow has taken reasonable steps to enforce.

Widow's benefit (rate)

16.—(1) The weekly rate of a pension payable under paragraph 15 above shall, for the period of 26 weeks next following the deceased's death, be the initial rate specified in Schedule 4, Part V, paragraph 10.

(2) The weekly rate of the pension shall, after the end of that period, be the higher permanent rate specified in that paragraph—

(a) for any period for which the widow is entitled, or is treated by regulations as entitled, to an allowance for children under paragraph 18 below; or

(b) where the widow was over the age of 50 at the deceased's death or was over the age of 40 at the end of the period for which she was entitled to such an allowance; or

(c) where the widow at the deceased's death was permanently incapable of self-support; or

(d) while the widow is pregnant by the deceased.

(3) After the end of the period of 26 weeks referred to in sub-paragraph (1) above, the weekly rate of the pension shall, in any case not within sub-paragraph (2) above, be the lower permanent rate specified in Schedule 4, Part V, paragraph 10.

Widower's benefit (entitlement and rate)

17.—(1) The widower of the deceased shall be entitled to death benefit if at her death he—

(a) was being wholly or mainly maintained by her or would but for the relevant accident have been so maintained; and

(b) was permanently incapable of self-support.

(2) In the case of a widower, death benefit shall be a pension at the weekly rate specified in Schedule 4, Part V, paragraph 11 commencing from the death of the deceased and payable for life.

Children of deceased's family

18.—(1) Subject to paragraph 19 below, where at his death the deceased was entitled to child benefit in respect of a child or children, then, for any period for which—

(a) the widow of the deceased is entitled—

(i) to death benefit (other than a gratuity) under paragraphs 15 and 16 above; and

(ii) to child benefit in respect of that child or one or more of those children; or

(b) such other person as may be prescribed is entitled to child benefit in respect of that child or one or more of those children,

the widow or, as the case may be, the person so prescribed shall be entitled in respect of that child, or in respect of each respectively of those children, to death benefit by way of an allowance at the weekly rate specified in Schedule 4, Part V, paragraph 12.

(2) Paragraph 5 above applies in relation to an allowance under this paragraph as it applies in relation to an increase of benefit under paragraph 4 above.

Limits of entitlement to industrial death benefit in respect of children

19. Where two or more persons satisfy the conditions, in respect of the same death, for receipt of an allowance or allowances under paragraph 18 above for any period—
 (a) not more than one of those persons shall be entitled for that period to such an allowance in respect of the same child;
 (b) where the deceased leaves a widow or widower, then for any period for which she or he is entitled to death benefit as the deceased's widow or widower and satisfies the conditions for receipt of such an allowance in respect of a child, she or he shall be entitled to the allowance in respect of that child;
 (c) subject to sub-paragraph (b) above, regulations may make provision as to the priority in any prescribed circumstances of two or more persons satisfying the said conditions.

Death of person with constant attendance allowance

20.—(1) If a person dies at a time when—
 (a) he is entitled to an increase under section 104 above of a disablement pension and the amount of the increase is not less than the amount which at that time is specified in Schedule 4, Part V, paragraph 2(a); or
 (b) he would have been so entitled but for having received medical or other treatment as an in-patient in a hospital or similar institution,
he is to be regarded for the purposes of entitlement to industrial death benefit as having died as a result of the injury in respect of which the disablement pension was payable.

(2) The reference in sub-paragraph (1) above to an increase under section 104 above includes only a payment by way of increase of a disablement pension, and in particular does not include any payment for constant attendance under paragraph 7(2)(b) of Schedule 8 to this Act.

(3) Sub-paragraph (1) above does not affect death benefit where the death occurred before 26th July 1971.

Pulmonary disease

21.—(1) If a person dies as a result of any pulmonary disease and—
 (a) he was entitled, for a period which includes the date of his death, to disablement pension or gratuity in respect of pneumoconiosis or byssinosis or pneumoconiosis accompanied by tuberculosis; and
 (b) the extent of the disablement in respect of which the benefit was payable was assessed for such a period at not less than 50 per cent.,
then, subject to sub-paragraph (2) below, his death shall be treated, for the purposes of this Part of this Schedule, as having been caused by the disease in respect of which the benefit was payable.

(2) Unless regulations provide otherwise, the requirements of paragraph (b) of sub-paragraph (1) above shall be treated as unsatisfied in a case where, had the physical condition of the deceased at the time of the assessment been normal, apart from the diseases mentioned in paragraph (a) of that sub-paragraph, the extent of the disablement in question would have been assessed at less than 50 per cent.

(3) This paragraph does not affect death benefit where the death occurred before 30th March 1977.

GENERAL NOTE
This Schedule deals with various benefits under the industrial injuries scheme which have been phased out in recent years. See General Note to ss.94 and 106.

Paras. 11 and 12
Note the transitory modifications in SS(CP)A 1992, Sched. 4, paras. 10 and 11.

Section 111   SCHEDULE 8

INDUSTRIAL INJURIES AND DISEASES (OLD CASES)

PART I

WORKMEN'S COMPENSATION AND INDUSTRIAL DISEASES BENEFIT IN RESPECT OF EMPLOYMENT BEFORE 5TH JULY 1948

Continuation of workmen's compensation

1. The Workmen's Compensation Acts and any other enactment specified in Schedule 9 to

the original Industrial Injuries Act which was repealed by section 89 of that Act shall continue to apply to any cases to which, if the 1967 Act had not been passed, they would have applied by virtue of the said section 89, being certain cases where a right to compensation arises or has arisen in respect of employment before 5th July 1948.

Schemes for supplementing workmen's compensation

2.—(1) The Secretary of State may, by scheme made with the consent of the Treasury, provide for conferring a right to allowances on persons who are, or have at any time after 20th March 1951 been, entitled to weekly payments by way of workmen's compensation, other than a person whose entitlement to such payments—

  (a) arose in consequence of an accident happening after 31st December 1923; and
  (b) ceased before 5th July 1956.

(2) Subject to the provisions of this Schedule, the right to such an allowance or to a payment on account of such an allowance shall be subject to such conditions, and the rate of the allowance shall be such, as may be provided by a scheme under sub-paragraph (1) above.

(3) The allowances for the payment of which a scheme under sub-paragraph (1) above may make provision shall be—

  (a) where the relevant accident happened before 1st January 1924, an allowance (in this paragraph referred to as a "basic allowance") in respect of any period such as is mentioned in sub-paragraph (8) below;
  (b) an allowance in respect of any period such as is mentioned in sub-paragraph (8)(a) below (in this paragraph referred to as a "major incapacity allowance");
  (c) subject to sub-paragraphs (4) and (5) below, an allowance in respect of any period such as is mentioned in sub-paragraph (8)(b) below (in this paragraph referred to as a "lesser incapacity allowance");

and a major incapacity allowance or lesser incapacity allowance in respect of any period shall be payable whether or not a basic allowance is also payable in respect of that period.

(4) A lesser incapacity allowance—

  (a) shall not be payable to any person in respect of any period unless there is or may be expected to be (or, but for the cesser at a time after 1st March 1966 of that person's entitlement to workmen's compensation, would or might be expected to have been) payable to that person in respect of that period either a weekly payment by way of basic allowance or a weekly payment by way of workmen's compensation which is not a notional payment;
  (b) except to a person who immediately before 1st March 1966 was receiving an allowance under a scheme made under the Workmen's Compensation (Supplementation) Act 1951, shall not be payable if the relevant accident happened after 31st December 1923 and the claimant's entitlement to workmen's compensation in consequence of it ceased before 1st March 1966.

(5) For the purposes of a lesser incapacity allowance, a weekly payment by way of workmen's compensation shall be treated as a notional payment if awarded or paid for the purpose of safeguarding a potential entitlement to compensation and not related to any existing loss of earnings; and a scheme under sub-paragraph (1) above may provide that—

  (a) in such circumstances or cases as may be specified in the scheme; and
  (b) in particular, in cases where weekly payments by way of such compensation are being paid to a person to whom such payments were not made, or were made at a lower rate, during the period of 12 months immediately preceding such date not earlier than 30th November 1965 as may be specified in the scheme,

a weekly payment by way of such compensation shall be deemed to be a notional payment unless the contrary is proved.

(6) The weekly rate—

  (a) of a basic allowance shall not exceed £2 less the amount of the recipient's workmen's compensation and, in respect of a period such as is mentioned in sub-paragraph (8)(b) below which is a period of partial incapacity only, shall also not exceed the difference between 2/3rds of the amount representing his weekly loss of earnings determined in accordance with a scheme under sub-paragraph (1) above and the amount of his workmen's compensation;
  (b) of a major incapacity allowance shall be the corresponding disablement pension rate;
  (c) of a lesser incapacity allowance shall not exceed £32.55.

(7) Sub-paragraph (6)(b) above shall have effect in relation to any person who has retired, or is treated as having retired, from regular employment, for the purposes of Parts I to VI of this Act, for so long as he continues to be treated as retired for those purposes, as if at the end of the paragraph there were added the words "less the amount of the recipient's workmen's compensation and less the amount of his basic allowance, if any".

(8) The periods referred to in sub-paragraph (3) above are—

(a) any period during which the person claiming or receiving an allowance under this paragraph—

(i) being or having been entitled to his workmen's compensation in respect of any injury or disease other than pneumoconiosis or byssinosis, is as a result of that injury or disease totally incapable of work and likely to remain so incapable for a considerable period; or

(ii) being or having been entitled to his workmen's compensation in respect of pneumoconiosis, is certified under a scheme made under the Workmen's Compensation (Silicosis) Act 1918 (as originally enacted or as extended by the Workmen's Compensation (Silicosis) Act 1924 or under section 47 of the Workmen's Compensation Act 1925 (as originally enacted or as extended by any subsequent enactment), or is determined in accordance with a scheme under sub-paragraph (1) above, to be totally disabled; or

(iii) is, or but for the determination of his right would be, entitled to his workmen's compensation in respect of byssinosis; or

(iv) being or having been entitled to his workmen's compensation in respect of two or more injuries or diseases such as are mentioned in sub-paragraphs (i) to (iii) above, is as the joint result of those injuries or diseases totally incapable of work and likely to remain so incapable for a considerable period;

(b) any period which, not being a period such as is mentioned in paragraph (a) above, is a period of total or partial incapacity for work resulting from the relevant injury or disease.

Provisions supplementary to paragraph 2

3.—(1) For the purposes of paragraph 2 above—

(a) the expressions "relevant accident" and "relevant injury or disease" mean the accident in consequence of which or, as the case may be, the injury or disease in respect of which, an entitlement to weekly payments by way of workmen's compensation arose;

(b) any reference to the happening of an accident shall, in relation to a case of disease, be construed in the same way as for the purposes of the Workmen's Compensation Acts;

(c) a payment—

(i) under the Workmen's Compensation (War Addition) Acts 1917 and 1919; or

(ii) under the Workmen's Compensation (Supplementary Allowances) Act 1940 as amended by the Workmen's Compensation (Temporary Increases) Act 1943,

shall be treated as a weekly payment by way of workmen's compensation.

(2) For the purposes of paragraph 2(1) above, a person shall be deemed to be or have been entitled to weekly payments by way of workmen's compensation at any time if he would be or, as the case may be, have been so entitled at that time if—

(a) the amount of any payment, allowance or benefit received by him otherwise than by way of workmen's compensation; or

(b) where the relevant accident happened before 1st January 1924, either that amount, or the amount he is earning or able to earn in some suitable employment or business, or both those amounts,

were sufficiently reduced.

(3) Subject to sub-paragraph (7) below, for the purpose of the reference in paragraph 2(8)(b) above to a period of total incapacity for work resulting from the relevant injury or disease, a person who is or has been unable to obtain employment shall be treated as subject to such an incapacity if he is treated as being so for the purposes of his workmen's compensation in respect of the relevant injury or disease and in such other circumstances as may be provided by a scheme under paragraph 2 above.

(4) Any reference in paragraph 2 above or this paragraph to the amount of a person's workmen's compensation shall (subject to sub-paragraphs (5) to (7) below) be taken as referring to the amount, if any, of the weekly payments to which for the time being he is, or would but for the determination of his right be, entitled in respect of the relevant injury or disease except that—

(a) where in fixing the amount of those weekly payments under the provisions relating to them regard was had to any payment, allowance or benefit which he might receive during the period of his incapacity from the person liable for the compensation, and the amount is shown to have been reduced in consequence, the amount of those weekly payments shall for the purposes of this sub-paragraph be taken to be the reduced amount so fixed with the addition of the amount of the reduction; and

(b) where the amount of those weekly payments has not been fixed under the said provisions, it shall be fixed for the purposes of this sub-paragraph without regard to any such payment, allowance or benefit.

(5) A scheme under paragraph 2 above may include provision that, in such special circumstances or cases and for such purposes as may be specified in the scheme, any reference in paragraph 2 above or this paragraph to the amount of a person's workmen's compensation shall be taken as referring to such amount as it may be determined in manner provided by the scheme ought reasonably and properly to have been the amount of the weekly payments referred to in sub-paragraph (4) above.

(6) Where a person is, or has at any time after 20th March 1951 been, entitled to payments under the enactments referred to in sub-paragraph (1)(c)(i) or (ii) above but ceased before 21st March 1951 to be entitled to any other weekly payments by way of workmen's compensation in respect of the relevant injury or disease, the amount of his workmen's compensation shall for the purposes of paragraph 2 above be calculated as if he had not ceased to be entitled to such other payments.

(7) A scheme under paragraph 2 above may provide for modifying the operation of sub-paragraphs (3) to (5) above in relation to a person whose workmen's compensation is or was compensation under a contracting-out scheme in such a manner as appears to the Secretary of State to be proper having regard to the provisions of the contracting-out scheme.

Industrial diseases benefit schemes

4.—(1) The Secretary of State may, by schemes made with the consent of the Treasury, provide for the payment of allowances or other benefits—

(a) to persons who, having been employed in Great Britain before 5th July 1948 in any occupation prescribed in relation to a disease to which this paragraph applies, are at the commencement of the scheme, or thereafter become, disabled by that disease;

(b) to any person who, as the joint result of—

(i) a disease to which this paragraph applies in respect of which he is, or has at any time after 4th July 1956 been, entitled to weekly payments by way of an allowance by virtue of paragraph (a) above or by virtue of section 1(1)(a) of the Pneumoconiosis and Byssinosis Benefit Act 1951 or section 5(1)(a) of the Old Cases Act; and

(ii) one or more other diseases or injuries in respect of each of which he is, or has at any such time been, entitled to weekly payments by way either of such an allowance or of workmen's compensation or of an allowance under paragraph 2 above or under the Workmen's Compensation (Supplementation) Act 1951 or section 2 of the Old Cases Act,

is totally incapable of work and likely to remain so incapable for a considerable period;

(c) to the dependants of persons who, having been so employed, died, or have at any time, after 31st December 1949 died, as a result of the disease in question, so however, that in relation to such a disease as is mentioned in sub-paragraph (2)(d) below this paragraph shall have effect as if for the reference to 31st December 1949 there were substituted a reference to 27th July 1967.

(2) The diseases to which this paragraph applies are—

(a) pneumoconiosis;

(b) byssinosis;

(c) any disease in respect of which compensation was payable under the Workmen's Compensation Act 1925 by virtue of section 43 of that Act;

(d) any other disease which is a malignant or potentially malignant neoplasm and is for the time being prescribed for the purposes of Part V of this Act;

but a scheme under this paragraph shall not provide for the payment of benefit in respect of such a disease as is mentioned in paragraph (c) or (d) above unless the Secretary of State is satisfied that the disease is of such a nature that there are likely to be cases where—

(i) a person suffers from it and it is due to the nature of his employment; but

(ii) it does not manifest itself until more than 12 months after he has ceased to be engaged in the employment.

(3) Subject to the provisions of this Schedule, the right to benefit in pursuance of a scheme under this paragraph shall be subject to such conditions as may be provided by the scheme, and the rate or amount of any such benefit shall be such as may be so provided.

(4) A scheme under this paragraph may make provision as to the circumstances in which any benefit payable to a person in pursuance of the scheme may be paid to another person on his behalf.

Restrictions on scope of schemes under paragraph 4

5.—(1) A scheme under paragraph 4 above shall not provide for the payment of benefit to or in respect of a person disabled or dying as a result of a disease to which that paragraph applies—

(a) if he or any other person is or has been entitled to benefit under Part V of this Act in respect of the disablement or death;

(b) if he or any member of his family within the meaning of the Workmen's Compensation Act 1925 has received or is entitled to compensation in respect of the disablement or death under the Workmen's Compensation Acts or by virtue of a scheme made or certified under those Acts or by virtue of any scheme or law in force in any country or territory outside Great Britain providing for compensation in respect of that disease;

(c) if he would have received or would be entitled to such compensation by virtue of any scheme so made or certified under the Workmen's Compensation Acts but for the fact that he was or is entitled to receive compensation in respect of disablement from any other disease or in respect of an injury by accident;

(d) if he or his personal representative or any of his relatives has recovered any sum by way of damages in respect of the disablement or death, whether at common law or under the Fatal Accidents Act 1976 or section 1 of the Law Reform (Miscellaneous Provisions) Act 1934;

(e) if throughout the employment mentioned in paragraph 4(1)(a) above he was employed otherwise than as a workman within the meaning of the Workmen's Compensation Act 1925.

(2) A scheme under paragraph 4 above shall not provide for the payment of benefit to a person disabled as a result of the disease of byssinosis unless it is determined in accordance with the scheme that the disablement is likely to be permanent.

(3) Sub-paragraphs (1) and (2) above shall be without prejudice to any other restrictions which may be imposed by a scheme under paragraph 4 above in respect of the persons to or in respect of whom benefit is payable under the scheme; and those other restrictions shall include restrictions relating to the nature or degree of disablement.

(4) For the avoidance of doubt, the benefits in relation to which restrictions are or may be imposed by virtue of this paragraph shall not include an allowance by virtue of paragraph 4(1)(b) above.

(5) Notwithstanding anything in this paragraph the Pneumoconiosis, Byssinosis and Miscellaneous Diseases Benefit Scheme 1983 and any further scheme under paragraph 4 above may contain any provision which the Secretary of State considers corresponds to a provision which was required by paragraph 2 or authorised by paragraph 3 of Schedule 1 to the Social Security (Miscellaneous Provisions) Act 1977.

Nature and amount of benefit under paragraph 4

6.—(1) The benefit payable to any person in pursuance of a scheme under paragraph 4 above by virtue of sub-paragraph (1)(a) or (b) of that paragraph shall be by way of a weekly allowance.

(2) Subject to the provisions of this Schedule and to any provisions of the scheme for the adjustment of benefit under it by reference to pensions, allowances or other benefits payable out of public funds, the weekly rate—

(a) of an allowance by virtue of paragraph 4(1)(a) above in respect of total disablement shall be the corresponding disablement pension rate;

(b) of an allowance by virtue of paragraph 4(1)(a) above in respect of disablement which is not total shall be £32.55;

(c) of an allowance by virtue of paragraph 4(1)(b) above shall be the corresponding disablement pension rate.

(3) Sub-paragraph (2)(c) above shall have effect in relation to any person who has retired, or is treated as having retired, from regular employment, for the purposes of Parts I to VI above, for so long as he continues to be treated as retired for those purposes, as if at the end of the paragraph there were added the words "less the amount of any weekly payments by way of workmen's compensation payable to the recipient in consequence of any of the diseases or injuries in consequence of which the allowance is payable".

(4) The weekly rate of an allowance such as is mentioned in sub-paragraph (2)(a) or (b) above shall be increased, in such circumstances and subject to such conditions as may be prescribed by the scheme (in accordance, for the purposes of paragraph (b) of this paragraph, with any regulations in force under paragraph 8 of Schedule 6 to this Act)—

(a) in any case, by an amount equal to the unemployability supplement which would be payable under paragraph 2 of Schedule 7 to this Act or, as the case may be, paragraphs 2 and 3 of that Schedule if the person entitled to the allowance were entitled to a disablement pension;

(b) where the person requires constant attendance as the result of the disablement, by an amount equal to any increases which would be payable under section 104 or 105 above if he were entitled to a disablement pension in respect of an assessment of 100 per cent.;

(c) where the person is entitled to child benefit in respect of a child or children, and is in receipt of an allowance which comprises such an increase as is mentioned in paragraph (a) above, by an amount equal to any increase which would be payable under paragraph 4 of Schedule 7 to this Act in respect of that child or those children if he were entitled to disablement pension plus unemployability supplement;

(d) where the person is treated under the provisions of the scheme as residing with his or her spouse or contributing at a weekly rate of not less than the relevant amount towards the maintenance of his or her spouse, by the relevant amount (that is to say, an amount equal to any increase which would be payable under section 82 above in respect of the spouse if the person were entitled to sickness benefit).

(5) Where under this paragraph an allowance comprises such an increase as is mentioned in paragraph (a) of sub-paragraph (4) above, that sub-paragraph shall have effect as if for paragraph (d) there were substituted the following paragraph—

"(d) where the person is treated under the provisions of the scheme as residing with his or her spouse or contributing at a weekly rate of not less than the relevant amount towards the maintenance of his or her spouse, by the relevant amount (that is to say, an amount equal to any increase which would be payable under paragraph 6 of Schedule 7 to this Act in respect of the spouse if the person were entitled to disablement pension plus unemployability supplement).".

(6) The benefit payable in pursuance of such a scheme in respect of the death of any person shall be payable to or for the benefit of such persons as may be prescribed by the scheme (being members of the deceased's family within the meaning of the Workmen's Compensation Act 1925); and subject to the provisions of this Schedule such benefit shall be a capital sum or sums of an amount or aggregate amount not exceeding £300.

PART II

REGULATIONS PROVIDING FOR BENEFIT

7.—(1) This paragraph applies to any person who is or has been at any time after 4th July 1948—

(a) entitled in respect of any injury or disease to weekly payments by way of compensation under the Workmen's Compensation Acts, or under any contracting-out scheme duly certified under those Acts; or

(b) entitled to payments on account of an injury pension under or by virtue of any enactment in respect of an injury received or disease contracted by him before 5th July 1948 or in respect of his retirement in consequence of such an injury or disease.

(2) Regulations may provide—

(a) for conferring on persons to whom this paragraph applies who as a result of the injury or disease in question are, or could for the purpose of the provisions of this Act relating to unemployability supplement and any provisions of the Administration Act, so far as they so relate, be treated as being, incapable of work and likely to remain permanently so incapable—

　(i) the like right to payments under Schedule 7 to this Act by way of unemployability supplement; and

　(ii) the like right to payments under Schedule 7 to this Act in respect of a child or adult dependant,

as if the injury or disease were one in respect of which a disablement pension were for the time being payable;

(b) for conferring on persons to whom this paragraph applies who as a result of the injury or disease in question require constant attendance—

　(i) the like right to payments under this Act in respect of the need for constant attendance; and

　(ii) the like right to an increase for exceptionally severe disablement,

as if the injury or disease were one in respect of which a disablement pension were for the time being payable in respect of an assessment of 100 per cent.;

(c) for applying in relation to payments under this paragraph the provisions of this Act relating to industrial injuries benefit, in so far as those provisions apply in relation to—

　(i) an unemployability supplement;

　(ii) an increase of a disablement pension in respect of a child or adult dependant; or

　(iii) an increase of a disablement pension in respect of the need for constant attendance or exceptionally severe disablement,

(as the case may be) subject to any additions or modifications.

PART III

INTERPRETATION

8.—(1) In this Schedule, except where the context otherwise requires—

"corresponding disablement pension rate" means the weekly rate for the time being of a disablement pension in respect of an assessment of 100 per cent.:

"the 1967 Act" means the Industrial Injuries and Diseases (Old Cases) Act 1967;

"injury pension" includes any pension or similar benefit payable in respect of a person's employment or former employment, being a pension or benefit which would not be payable or would be payable at a less rate but for an injury or disease referable to that employment;

"the original Industrial Injuries Act" means the National Insurance (Industrial Injuries) Act 1946;

"prescribed", in relation to an occupation and a disease to which paragraph 4 above applies, means any occupation in the case of which, by virtue of regulations under section 108 of this Act that disease is prescribed in relation to earners employed in employed earners' employment;

"workmen's compensation" means compensation under any of the Workmen's Compensation Acts or under any contracting-out scheme duly certified under any of those Acts;

"the Workmen's Compensation Acts" means the Workmen's Compensation Acts 1925 to 1945, or the enactments repealed by the Workmen's Compensation Act 1925, or the enactments repealed by the Workmen's Compensation Act 1906.

(2) Without prejudice to sub-paragraph (3) below, in the case of a person who suffers from pneumoconiosis accompanied by tuberculosis, the effects of the tuberculosis may be treated, for the purposes of any scheme under paragraph 2 or 4 above, as if they were effects of the pneumoconiosis.

(3) In the case of a person the extent of whose disablement resulting from pneumoconiosis, or from pneumoconiosis accompanied by tuberculosis, would if his physical condition were otherwise normal, be determined in accordance with a scheme under paragraph 2 or 4 above to be of a gravity comparable to an assessment at not less than 50 per cent., and the pneumoconiosis is accompanied or, as the case may be, further accompanied by emphysema or chronic bronchitis, the effects of the emphysema or chronic bronchitis may be treated for the purposes of any such scheme as if they were effects of the pneumoconiosis.

(4) In sub-paragraph (1) above, in the definition of "prescribed", the reference to regulations shall be construed, in relation to any scheme under paragraph 4 above, as a reference to the regulations in force at the commencement of the scheme or at such time thereafter as may be prescribed by the scheme, whether regulations under section 76 of the 1975 Act, section 56 of the National Insurance (Industrial Injuries) Act 1965 or section 108 above.

(5) For the purposes of this Schedule—

(a) a period shall be treated as considerable if it lasts or can be expected to last for not less than 13 weeks;

(b) a person may be treated as being, as the result of an injury or disease or as the joint result of two or more injuries or diseases, totally incapable of work and likely to remain so incapable for a considerable period notwithstanding that the disability resulting from the injury or disease or, as the case may be, from the injuries or diseases taken together is not such as to prevent him from being capable of work, if it is likely to prevent his earnings (including any remuneration or profit derived from a gainful occupation) exceeding in a year such amount as is for the time being prescribed for purposes of unemployability supplement.

(6) For the purposes of paragraphs 6 and 7 above paragraph 4 of Schedule 3 to the 1986 Act and paragraph 1 of Schedule 7 to this Act shall be deemed not to have been enacted.

GENERAL NOTE
This Schedule consolidates the Industrial Injuries and Diseases (Old Cases) Act 1975 (as amended) and concerns claims in respect of industrial accidents or diseases which occurred before July 5, 1948. See General Note to s.111.

Section 144(2)   SCHEDULE 9

EXCLUSIONS FROM ENTITLEMENT TO CHILD BENEFIT

Children in detention, care, etc.

1. Except where regulations otherwise provide, no person shall be entitled to child benefit in respect of a child for any week if in that week the child—

(a) is undergoing imprisonment or detention in legal custody;

(b) is subject to a supervision requirement made under section 44 of the Social Work

(Scotland) Act 1968 and is residing in a residential establishment within the meaning of that section; or

(c) is in the care of a local authority in such circumstances as may be prescribed.

Employed trainees, etc.

2.—(1) No person shall be entitled to child benefit by virtue of section 142(1)(c) above in respect of a child if the education in question is received by that child by virtue of his employment or of any office held by him.

(2) Regulations may specify the circumstances in which a child is or is not to be treated as receiving education as mentioned in sub-paragraph (1) above.

Married children

3. Except where regulations otherwise provide, no person shall be entitled to child benefit in respect of a child who is married.

Persons exempt from tax

4. Except where regulations otherwise provide, no person shall be entitled to child benefit in respect of a child if either that person or such other person as may be prescribed is exempt from tax under such provisions as may be prescribed.

Children entitled to severe disablement allowance

5. Except where regulations otherwise provide, no person shall be entitled to child benefit in respect of a child for any week in which the child is entitled to a severe disablement allowance.

GENERAL NOTE

This Schedule consolidates Sched. 1 to the Child Benefit Act 1975 (as amended) and specifies various exclusions from entitlement to child benefit. See General Note to s.144.

Section 144(3)   SCHEDULE 10

PRIORITY BETWEEN PERSONS ENTITLED TO CHILD BENEFIT

Person with prior award

1.—(1) Subject to sub-paragraph (2) below, as between a person claiming child benefit in respect of a child for any week and a person to whom child benefit in respect of that child for that week has already been awarded when the claim is made, the latter shall be entitled.

(2) Sub-paragraph (1) above shall not confer any priority where the week to which the claim relates is later than the third week following that in which the claim is made.

Person having child living with him

2. Subject to paragraph 1 above, as between a person entitled for any week by virtue of paragraph (a) of subsection (1) of section 143 above and a person entitled by virtue of paragraph (b) of that subsection the former shall be entitled.

Husband and wife

3. Subject to paragraphs 1 and 2 above, as between a husband and wife residing together the wife shall be entitled.

Parents

4.—(1) Subject to paragraphs 1 to 3 above, as between a person who is and one who is not a parent of the child the parent shall be entitled.

(2) Subject as aforesaid, as between two persons residing together who are parents of the child but not husband and wife, the mother shall be entitled.

Other cases

5. As between persons not falling within paragraphs 1 to 4 above, such one of them shall be entitled as they may jointly elect or, in default of election, as the Secretary of State may in his discretion determine.

Supplementary

6.—(1) Any election under this Schedule shall be made in the prescribed manner.

(2) Regulations may provide for exceptions from and modifications of the provisions of paragraphs 1 to 5 above in relation to such cases as may be prescribed.

GENERAL NOTE
This Schedule consolidates Sched. 2 to the Child Benefit Act 1975 and details the rules governing priority among claimants for child benefit. See General Note to s.144.

Section 153(3)   SCHEDULE 11

CIRCUMSTANCES IN WHICH PERIODS OF ENTITLEMENT TO STATUTORY SICK PAY DO NOT ARISE

1. A period of entitlement does not arise in relation to a particular period of incapacity for work in any of the circumstances set out in paragraph 2 below or in such other circumstances as may be prescribed.
2. The circumstances are that—
   (a) at the relevant date the employee is over pensionable age;
   (b) the employee's contract of service was entered into for a specified period of not more than three months;
   (c) at the relevant date the employee's normal weekly earnings are less than the lower earnings limit then in force under section 5(1)(a) above;
   (d) the employee had—
       (i) in the period of 57 days ending immediately before the relevant date, at least one day which formed part of a period of interruption of employment; and
       (ii) at any time during that period of interruption of employment, an invalidity pension day (whether or not the day referred to in paragraph (i) above);
   (e) in the period of 57 days ending immediately before the relevant date the employee had at least one day on which—
       (i) he was entitled to sickness benefit (or on which he would have been so entitled if he had satisfied the contribution conditions for sickness benefit mentioned in section 31(2)(a) above), or
       (ii) she was entitled to a maternity allowance;
   (f) the employee has done no work for his employer under his contract of service;
   (g) on the relevant date there is, within the meaning of section 27 above, a stoppage of work due to a trade dispute at the employee's place of employment;
   (h) the employee is, or has been, pregnant and the relevant date falls within the disqualifying period (within the meaning of section 153(12) above).
3. In this Schedule "relevant date" means the date on which a period of entitlement would begin in accordance with section 153 above if this Schedule did not prevent it arising.
4.—(1) Paragraph 2(b) above does not apply in any case where—
   (a) at the relevant date the contract of service has become a contract for a period exceeding three months; or
   (b) the contract of service (the "current contract") was preceded by a contract of service entered into by the employee with the same employer (the "previous contract") and—
       (i) the interval between the date on which the previous contract ceased to have effect and that on which the current contract came into force was not more than eight weeks; and
       (ii) the aggregate of the period for which the previous contract had effect and the period specified in the current contract (or, where that period has been extended, the specified period as so extended) exceeds 13 weeks.
   (2) For the purposes of sub-paragraph (1)(b)(ii) above, in any case where the employee entered into more than one contract of service with the same employer before the current contract, any of those contracts which came into effect not more than eight weeks after the date on which an earlier one of them ceased to have effect shall be treated as one with the earlier contract.
5.—(1) In paragraph 2(d) above "invalidity pension day" means a day—
   (a) for which the employee in question was entitled to an invalidity pension, a non-contributory invalidity pension (under section 36 of the 1975 Act) or a severe disablement allowance; or
   (b) for which he was not so entitled but which was the last day of the invalidity pension qualifying period.
   (2) In sub-paragraph (1)(b) above the "invalidity pension qualifying period" means the period mentioned in section 33(1) or, as the case may be, 40(3) or 41(2) above as falling within the period of interruption of employment referred to in whichever of those provisions is applicable.

6. For the purposes of paragraph 2(f) above, if an employee enters into a contract of service which is to take effect not more than eight weeks after the date on which a previous contract of service entered into by him with the same employer ceased to have effect, the two contracts shall be treated as one.

7. Paragraph 2(g) above does not apply in the case of an employee who proves that at no time on or before the relevant date did he have a direct interest in the trade dispute in question.

8. Paragraph 2(h) above does not apply in relation to an employee who has been pregnant if her pregnancy terminated, before the beginning of the disqualifying period, otherwise than by confinement (as defined for the purposes of statutory maternity pay in section 171(1) above).

GENERAL NOTE

This Schedule consolidates SSHBA 1982, Sched. 1, and specifies the situations in which periods of entitlement to statutory sick pay do not arise. See General Note to s.153.

Section 160   SCHEDULE 12

RELATIONSHIP OF STATUTORY SICK PAY WITH BENEFITS AND OTHER PAYMENTS, ETC

The general principle

1. Any day which—
(a) is a day of incapacity for work in relation to any contract of service; and
(b) falls within a period of entitlement (whether or not it is also a qualifying day),
shall not be treated for the purposes of this Act as a day of incapacity for work for the purposes of determining whether a period is a period of interruption of employment.

Contractual remuneration

2.—(1) Subject to sub-paragraphs (2) and (3) below, any entitlement to statutory sick pay shall not affect any right of an employee in relation to remuneration under any contract of service ("contractual remuneration").
(2) Subject to sub-paragraph (3) below—
(a) any contractual remuneration paid to an employee by an employer of his in respect of a day of incapacity for work shall go towards discharging any liability of that employer to pay statutory sick pay to that employee in respect of that day; and
(b) any statutory sick pay paid by an employer to an employee of his in respect of a day of incapacity for work shall go towards discharging any liability of that employer to pay contractual remuneration to that employee in respect of that day.
(3) Regulations may make provision as to payments which are, and those which are not, to be treated as contractual remuneration for the purposes of sub-paragraph (1) or (2) above.

Sickness benefit

3.—(1) This paragraph applies in any case where—
(a) a period of entitlement as between an employee and an employer of his comes to an end; and
(b) the first day immediately following the day on which the period of entitlement came to an end—
    (i) is a day of incapacity for work in relation to that employee; and
    (ii) is not prevented by paragraph 1 above from being treated as a day of incapacity for work for the purposes of determining whether a period is a period of interruption of employment.
(2) In a case to which this paragraph applies, the day of incapacity for work mentioned in sub-paragraph (1)(b) above shall, except in prescribed cases, be or as the case may be form part of a period of interruption of employment notwithstanding section 57(1)(d)(ii) above.
(3) Where each of the first two consecutive days, or the first three consecutive days, following the day on which the period of entitlement came to an end is a day falling within sub-paragraphs (i) and (ii) of sub-paragraph (1)(b) above, sub-paragraph (2) above shall have effect in relation to the second day or, as the case may be, the second and third days, as it has effect in relation to the first day.
(4) Any day which is, by virtue of section 57(1)(e) above to be disregarded in computing any period of consecutive days for the purposes of Part II of this Act shall be disregarded in determining, for the purposes of this paragraph, whether a day is the first day following the end of a period of entitlement or, as the case may be, the second or third consecutive such day.

4.—(1) This paragraph applies in any case where—
(a) a period of entitlement as between an employee and an employer of his comes to an end; and

(b) that employee has a day of incapacity for work which—
    (i) is, or forms part of, a period of interruption of employment; and
    (ii) falls within the period of 57 days immediately following the day on which the period of entitlement came to an end.

(2) In a case to which this paragraph applies, section 31(4) above shall not apply in relation to a day of incapacity for work of a kind mentioned in sub-paragraph (1)(b) above or to any later day in the period of interruption of employment concerned.

Invalidity pension for widows and widowers

5. Paragraph 1 above does not apply for the purpose of determining whether the conditions specified in section 40(3) or 41(2) above are satisfied.

Unemployability supplement

6. Paragraph 1 above does not apply in relation to paragraph 3 of Schedule 7 to this Act and accordingly the references in paragraph 3 of that Schedule to a period of interruption of employment shall be construed as if the provisions re-enacted in this Part of this Act had not been enacted.

GENERAL NOTE
    This Schedule consolidates SSHBA 1982, Sched. 2 and deals with the interrelationship between statutory sick pay and other benefits. See General Note to s.160.

Section 168   SCHEDULE 13

RELATIONSHIP OF STATUTORY MATERNITY PAY WITH BENEFITS AND OTHER PAYMENTS ETC

The general principle

1. Except as may be prescribed, a day which falls within the maternity pay period shall not be treated for the purposes of this Act as a day of unemployment or of incapacity for work for the purpose of determining whether it forms part of a period of interruption of employment.

Invalidity

2.—(1) Regulations may provide that in prescribed circumstances a day which falls within the maternity pay period shall be treated as a day of incapacity for work for the purpose of determining entitlement to an invalidity pension.

(2) Regulations may provide that an amount equal to a woman's statutory maternity pay for a period shall be deducted from invalidity benefit in respect of the same period and a woman shall be entitled to invalidity benefit only if there is a balance after the deduction and, if there is such a balance, at a weekly rate equal to it.

Contractual remuneration

3.—(1) Subject to sub-paragraphs (2) and (3) below, any entitlement to statutory maternity pay shall not affect any right of a woman in relation to remuneration under any contract of service ("contractual remuneration").

(2) Subject to sub-paragraph (3) below—
(a) any contractual remuneration paid to a woman by an employer of hers in respect of a week in the maternity pay period shall go towards discharging any liability of that employer to pay statutory maternity pay to her in respect of that week; and
(b) any statutory maternity pay paid by an employer to a woman who is an employee of his in respect of a week in the maternity pay period shall go towards discharging any liability of that employer to pay contractual remuneration to her in respect of that week.

(3) Regulations may make provision as to payments which are, and those which are not, to be treated as contractual remuneration for the purposes of sub-paragraphs (1) and (2) above.

GENERAL NOTE
    This Schedule consolidates SSA 1986, Sched. 4, paras. 11–12, and deals with the interrelationship between statutory maternity pay and other benefits. See General Note to s.168.

TABLE OF DERIVATIONS

Note:

1. The following abbreviations are used in this Table:—

1975(1) =	Social Security Act 1975 (c.14)
1975(2) =	Social Security Pensions Act 1975 (c.60)
1975(3) =	Child Benefit Act 1975 (c.61)
1975 (Old Cases) =	Industrial Injuries and Diseases (Old Cases) Act 1975 (c.16)
1977 =	Social Security (Miscellaneous Provisions) Act 1977 (c.5)
1978 =	Employment Protection (Consolidation) Act 1978 (c.4)
1979 =	Social Security 1979 (c.18)
1980(1) =	Social Security Act 1980 (c.30)
1980(2) =	Social Security (No. 2) Act 1980 (c.39)
1981(1) =	Social Security (Contributions) Act 1981 (c.1)
1981(2) =	Social Security Act 1981 (c.33)
1982(1) =	Social Security (Contributions) Act 1982 (c.2)
1982(2) =	Social Security and Housing Benefits Act 1982 (c.24)
1983 =	Health and Social Services and Social Security Adjudications Act 1983 (c.41)
1984 =	Health and Social Security Act 1984 (c.48)
1985 =	Social Security Act 1985 (c.53)
1986 =	Social Security Act 1986 (c.50)
1987 =	Social Fund (Maternity and Funeral Expenses) Act 1987 (c.7)
1988(1) =	Social Security Act 1988 (c.7)
1988(2) =	Local Government Finance Act 1988 (c.41)
1989 =	Social Security Act 1989 (c.24)
1990 =	Social Security Act 1990 (c.27)
1991(1) =	Statutory Sick Pay Act 1991 (c.3)
1991(2) =	Disability Living Allowance and Disability Working Allowance Act 1991 (c.21)
1991(3) =	Social Security (Contributions) Act 1991 (c.42)
R followed by a number =	the Law Commission recommendation of that number

2. The Table does not contain any entries in respect of section 66(2) of the Social Security Pensions Act 1975 (c. 60) which provides that, with certain exceptions, that Act and the Social Security Act 1975 (c. 14) shall have effect as if the provisions of the Social Security Pensions Act 1975 were contained in the Social Security Act 1975. The effect is that the general provisions of the Social Security Act 1975 apply to the provisions of the Social Security Pensions Act 1975.

3. Numerous sums specified in this Act are subject to frequent alteration by statutory instrument. There are three relevant statutory instruments in force—

(a) The Social Security (Contributions) (Re-rating) (No. 2) Order 1991 (S.I. 1991/2909), ("the Contributions Order");

(b) The Social Security Benefits (Up-rating) (No. 2) Order 1991 (S.I. 1991/2910), ("the Benefits Order");

(c) The Statutory Sick Pay (Rate of Payment) (No. 2) Order 1991 (S.I. 1991/2911), ("the Sick Pay Order");

The order in which the provisions amended by the Benefits Order are consolidated is not identical with the order in which they appear in the Social Security Act 1975.

4. The Table does not show the effect of transfer of functions orders.

Provision	Derivation
1(1)	1975(1) s.1(1); 1990 s.16(1), (2)
(2)	1975 s.1(2); 1991(3) s.1(2)
(3)	1975(1) s.1(3); 1985 s.29(1), Sch. 5, para. 5
(4)	1975(1) s.1(4); 1991(3) s.2(1)(a)
(5)	1975(1) s.1(4A); 1990 s.16(2); 1991(1) s.1(4)
(6)	1975(1) s.1(6); 1991(3) s.1(3)
2	1975(1) s.2
3(1)	1975(1) s.3(1)
(2), (3)	1975(1) s.3(2), (3)
4(1)	1975(1) s.3(1A); 1982(2) ss.23, 37(1); 1986 s.49, Sch. 4, para. 10
(2), (3)	1975(1) s.3(1B), (1C); 1982(2) s.37(1)
(4)	1975(1) s.3(1D); 1989 s.31(1), Sch. 8, para. 1
(5)	1975(1) s.3(4); 1982(2) s.48(5), Sch. 4, para. 8
5(1)	1975(1) s.4(1); 1975(2) ss.1(1), 65(1), Sch. 4, para. 36(a); 1985 s.7(1)
(2)	1975(2) s.1(2); 1986 s.74(6)
(3)	1975(2) s.1(3)
6(1)	1975(1) s.4(2); Education (School-Leaving Dates) Act 1976 (c.5) s.2(4)
(2)	1975(2) s.4(1); 1984 s.21, Sch. 7, para. 3(a)
(3)	1975(1) s.4(3); 1989 s.26, Sch. 7, para. 2(1)
(4)	1975(1) s.4(2)
(5)	1975(1) s.4(7); 1979 s.14(1); 1985 s.8(1)
(6)	1986 s.74(5)
7	1975(1) s.4(4), (5)
8(1)–(3)	1975(1) s.4(6), (6A), (6B); 1989 s.1(1)
(4)	1986 s.74(5)
9(1)	1975(1) s.4(6C); 1985 s.7(2); 1989 s.26, Sch. 7, para. 2(2)
(2)	1975(1) s.4(6D); 1985 s.7(2)
(3)	1975(1) s.4(6E); 1985 s.7(2); Contributions Order art. 2(2)
(4)	1975(1) s.4(6C), (6E); 1985 s.7(2)
(5)	1986 s.74(5)
10	1975(1) s.4A; 1991(3) s.1(5)
11(1)	1975(1) s.7(1); Education (School-Leaving Dates) Act 1976 (c.5) s.2(4); 1984 s.17(1); Contributions Order art. 3(a)
(2)	1975(2) s.4(2)
(3)	1975(1) s.7(4)
(4)	1975(1) s.7(5) Contributions Order art. 3(b)
(5)	1975(1) s.7(6)
12(1), (2)	1975(1) s.7A(1), (2); 1984 s.17(2)
(3)	1975(1) s.7A(3); 1984 s.17(2); 1989 s.26, Sch. 7, para. 3(b), (c); The Social Security (Contributions and Credits) (Transitional and Consequential Provisions) Regulations 1985 (S.I. 1985/1398) reg. 4(2)
(4)–(8)	1975(1) s.7A(4)–(8); 1984 s.17(2)
13(1)	1975(1) s.8(1); Education (School-Leaving Dates) Act 1976 (c.5) s.2(4); 1984 s.18(1)(a) Contributions Order art. 4
(2)	1975(1) s.8(2)
(3)	1975(1) s.8(2)(a)
(4)	1975(1) s.8(2A); 1984 s.18(1)(b), (3)
(5)	1975(1) s.8(2B); 1984 s.18(3)
(6)	1975(1) s.8(2C); 1984 s.18(3); 1989 s.26, Sch. 7, para. 4; The Social Security (Contributions and Credits) (Transitional and Consequential Provisions) Regulations 1985 (S.I. 1985/1398) reg. 4(3)

Provision	Derivation
(7)	1975(1) s.8(2D); 1984 s.18(3)
14(1)	1975(2) s.5(1); 1986 s.75, Sch. 8, para. 6
(2), (3)	1975(2) s.5(2); 1977 s.1(5)
15(1), (2)	1975(1) s.9(1); 1989 s.26, Sch. 7, para. 5(a), (b)
(3)	1975(1) s.9(2); Social Security (Contributions, Re-rating) Order 1982 (S.I. 1982/1790) art. 5(a) Contributions Order art. 5
(4)	Income and Corporation Taxes Act 1988 (c.1) s.844, Sch. 29, para. 14
(5)	1975(1) s.9(1); 1989 s.26, Sch. 7, para. 5(c)
16(1), (2)	1975(1) s.9(3)
(3)	1975(1) s.9(4)
(4)	1975(1) s.9(5); 1990 s.17(1)
(5)	1975(1) s.9(6); 1990 s.17(2)
17(1), (2)	1975(1) s.9(7), (8)
(3)–(6)	1975(1) s.9(9)
18(1)	1975(1) s.10(1); Social Security (Contributions, Re-rating) Order 1982 (S.I. 1982/1790) art. 5(a) Contributions Order art. 5
(2)	1975(1) s.10(2)
19(1)–(3)	1975(1) s.11
(4), (5)	1975(2) s.3(2), (3)
(6)	1975(2) s.3(4); 1986 s.75, Sch. 8, para. 5
20(1)	1975(1) s.12(1); 1975(2) s.65(1), Sch. 4, para. 37; 1984 s.13, Sch. 5, para. 2(a); 1986 s.86, Sch. 10, para. 63; 1989 s.26, Sch. 7, para. 6
(2) "long term benefit"	1975(1) s.168(1), Sch. 20 "long-term benefit"; 1975(2) s.65(1), Sch. 4, para. 64
"short-term benefit"	1975(1) s.12(2)
(3)	Drafting
21(1), (2)	1975(1) s.13(1); 1986 s.86, Sch. 10, para. 64
(3)	1975(1) s.13(6)
(4)	1975(1) s.13(8); 1986 s.86, Sch. 10, para. 72(b)
(5)	1975(1) s.13(6); 1986 s.75, Sch. 8, para. 2(6)
(6)	1975(1) s.13(7)
22(1), (2)	1975(1) s.13(2); 1975(2) s.65(1), Sch. 4, para. 38(a); 1986 ss.18(1), 75, 86, Sch. 8, para. 2(1), Sch. 10, para. 72
(3)	1975(1) s.13(5); 1986 s.75, Sch. 8, para. 2(4)(c); 1989 s.26, Sch. 7, para. 7
(4)	1975(1) s.13(3); 1975(2) s.65(1), Sch. 4, para. 38(b); 1986 s.75, Sch. 8, para. 2(2)
(5)	1975(1) s.13(4); 1986 s.75, Sch. 8, para. 2(3)
(6)	1975(1) s.13(5AA); 1989 s.4(3)
(7)	1977 s.2
23(1)	1975(1) s.13(5); 1979 s.21(4), Sch. 3, para. 5; 1986 s.75, Sch. 8, para. 2(4)(a); 1988(1) s.9, Sch. 2, para. 1(1)(a)
(2)	1975(1) s.13(5ZA); 1988(1) s.9, Sch. 2, para. 1(1)(b)
(3)	1975(1) s.13(5); 1989 s.4(2)
(4)	1975(1) s.13(5A); 1985 s.29(1), Sch. 5, para. 6(b); R1
24(1)	1975(1) s.13(5B); 1986 s.75, Sch. 8, para. 2(5)
(2)	1975(1) s.13(5C); 1989 s.4(4)
25(1)	1975(1) s.14(1)
(2)	1975(1) s.14(2); 1989 s.7, Sch. 1, para. 4(1)
(3)	1975(1) s.14(3)
(4)	1975(1) s.14(4); 1975(2) s.18(1)

Provision	Derivation
(5), (6)	1975(1) s.14(6); 1975(2) s.65(1), Sch. 4, para. 39(b); 1979 s.21(4), Sch. 3, para. 6; 1986 s. 86, Sch. 10, para. 83
(7)	1975(1) s.14(8)
26(1)	1975(1) s.18(1)
(2)–(4)	1975(1) s.18(2)–(2B); 1989 s.11
(5)	
(6)	1975(1) s18(4); 1986 s.43(1)
27(1), (2)	1975(1) s.19(1), (1A); 1986 s.44(1)
(3)	1975(1) s.19(2)
28(1)	1975(1) s.20(1); Employment Act 1988 (c.19) s.27(2); 1989 s.12(1); Unemployment Benefit (Disqualification Period) Order 1988 (S.I. 1988/487) art. 2
(2)	1975(1) s.20(1A); 1986 s.43(3)(a)
(3)	1975(1) s.20(3)
(4)	1975(1) s.20(3A); 1985 s.10
(5)	1975(1) s.20(4); 1989 s.12(3)
(6)	Education (Scotland) Act 1962 (c.47) s.145 (16); Local Government (Scotland) Act 1973 (c.65) s.129, Sch. 11, para. 12; 1975(1) s.20(5); Employment Act 1988 (c.19) s.27 (3)
29	1975(1) s.20A; 1989 s.12(4)
30(1)	1980(2) s.5(1); 1988(1) s.7(a); 1989 s.9(1)
(2)	1980(2) s.5(1A); 1982(2) s.48(5), Sch. 4, para. 34(2)
(3)	1980(2) s.5(2); 1982(2) s.48(5), Sch. 4, para. 34(3); 1989 s.9(1)
(4) "employer"	1980(2) s.5(3) "employer"
"employment"	1980(2) s.5(3) "employment"
"modifications"	1980(2) s.5(3) "modifications"
31(1)	1975(1) s.14(1)
(2)	1975(1) s.14(2); 1989 s.7, Sch. 1, para. 4(1)
(3)	1975 s.14(2A); 1982(2) s.39(3)
(4)	1975(1) s.14(3)
(5)	1975(1) s.14(4); 1975(2) s.18(1); 1982(2) s.48 (5), Sch. 4, para. 9
(6), (7)	1975(1) s.14(6); 1975(2) s.65(1), Sch. 4, para. 39(b); 1979 s.21(4), Sch. 3, para. 6; 1986 s.86, Sch. 10, para. 83
(8)	1975(1) s.14(8)
32(1), (2)	1975(1) s.20(2), (3)
(3)	1975(1) s.20(5)(d) "week"
33(1)	1975(1) s.15(1); 1989 s.7, Sch. 1, para. 5(1)
(2)	1975(1) s.15(2); 1989 s.7, Sch. 1, para. 5(2)
(3)	1975(1) s.15(3); 1975(2) ss.14, 65(1), Sch. 4, para. 40(b); 1990 s.4(1)
(4), (5)	1975(1) s.15(4); 1975(2) s.65(1), Sch. 4, para. 40(c); 1979 ss.5, 21(4), Sch. 1, para. 1, Sch. 3, para. 7; 1986 s.86, Sch. 10, para. 83
(6)	1975(1) s.15(5)
(7), (8)	1975(1) s.15(5A), (5B); 1991(2) s.9(1)
(9)	1975(1), s.15(6); 1982(2) s.48(5), Sch. 4, para. 10
(10), (11)	1975(1) s.15A(1), (2); 1985 s.18(3)
34(1), (2)	1975(1) s.16(1); 1985 s.9(1)(a)
(3)	1975(1) s.16(2); 1979 s.5, Sch. 1, para. 10(a)
(4)	1975(1) s.16(2B)(a); 1985 s.9(1)(b); 1986 s.18 (1)

Provision	Derivation
(5)	1975(1) s.16(2C)(a); 1985 s.9(1)(b); 1986 s.18 (1)
(6)	1975(1) s.16(2D)(a); 1985 s.9(1)(b); 1986 s.18 (1)
(7)	1975(1) s.16(3); 1985 s.9(1)(c)
35(1)–(3)	1975(1) s.22(1)–(3); 1986 s.49(2), Sch. 4, para. 13
(4)	1975(1) s.22(4A); 1988(1) s.16, Sch. 4, para. 5(b)
(5)	1975(1) s.22(5); 1986 s.49(2), Sch. 4, para. 13
(6)	1975(1) s.22(6); 1986 ss.49(2), 50, Sch. 4, para. 13
(7)	1975(1) s.22(7); 1986 s.49(2), Sch. 4, para. 13
36(1), (2)	1975(1) s.24(1), (2); 1986 s.36(1)
(3)	1975(1) s.24(3); 1989 s.26, Sch. 7, para. 8
37(1)	1975(1) s.25(1); 1975(2) s.65(1), Sch. 4, para. 41; 1975(3) s.21(1), Sch. 4, para. 9(a); Human Fertilisation and Embryology Act 1990 (c.37) s.49, Sch. 4, para. 2
(2)	1975(1) s.25(2); 1975(3) s.21(1), Sch. 4, para. 9(b)
(3), (4)	1975(1) s.25(3), (4); 1989 s.31(1), Sch. 8, para. 4(1)
38(1)	1975(1) s.26(1); 1975(2) s.65(1), Sch. 4, para. 42; 1986 s.36(3)(a)
(2), (3)	1975(1) s.26(3), (4); 1989 s.31(1), Sch. 8, para. 4(2)
(4)	1989 s.6(1)
39(1)	1975(2) s.13(1), (3)
(2)	1975(2) s.13(2)
(3)	1986 s.19(1)(c)
(4), (5)	1975(1) s.26(2); 1986 s.36(3)(b)
(6)	1989 s.6(1)
40(1)	1975(2) s.15(1); 1986 s.86, Sch. 10, para. 70(a)
(2)	1975(2) s.15(1A); 1989 s.26, Sch. 7, para. 20(1)
(3)	1975(2) s.15(2); 1986 s.86, Sch. 10, para. 70(b)
(4)	1975(2) s.15(3)
(5)	1975(2) s.15(4); 1986 s.86, Sch. 10, para. 70(c); 1990 s.4(2)
(6)	1977 s.17(6)
(7)	1975(2) s.15(5); 1977 s.4(4); 1989 s.7, Sch. 1, para. 10(1)
(8)	1975(2) s.15(6)
(9)	1977 s.24(1) "modifications"
41(1)	1975(2) s.16(1); 1979 s.5, Sch. 1, para. 18
(2), (3)	1975(2) s.16(2), (3)
(4), (5)	1975(2) s.16(4); 1990 s.4(3)
(6)	1986 s.19(1)(d)
(7)	1975(2) s.16(5); 1977 s.4(4); 1989 s.7, Sch. 1, para. 10(2)
(8)	1975(2) s.16(6)
42	1975(2) s.16A; 1991(2) s.9(3)
43(1)	1975(1) s.27(6)
(2)	1977 s.4(1); 1979 s.5, Sch. 1, para. 8
(3), (4)	1975(2) s.25(1)
(5)	1975(2) s.25(2)
44(1)	1975(1) s.28(1); 1975(2) s.65(1), Sch. 4, para. 43; 1989 s.31(1), Sch. 8, para. 4(3)

Provision	Derivation
(2)	1975(1) s.28(1A); 1989 s.31(1), Sch. 8, para. 4(4)
(3), (4)	1975(2) s.6(1); 1986 s.18(1); Benefits Order art. 4(2)
(5)	1975(2) s.6(4); 1979 s.21(4), Sch. 3, para. 14
(6)	1975(2) s.6(5); 1986 s.75, Sch. 8, para. 7(1) (a); 1989 s.26, Sch. 7, para. 19
(7)	1975(2) s.6(6)
(8)	Transitional
45(1)	1975(2) s.6(2); 1986 s.18(1), (2)
(2), (3)	1975(2) s.6(2A); 1986 s.18(3)
(4), (5)	1975(2) s.6(2B); 1986 s.18(3)
(6), (7)	1975(2) ss.6(3), 60A; 1979 s.18; 1986 s.18(4)
(8)	Drafting
46(1)	1986 s.18(6)
(2)	1986 s.18(5)
47(1)	1975(1) s.28(7); 1980(2) s.3(3); 1985 s.9(2)(a) ,(b)
(2)	1975(1) s.28(7A)(a); 1985 s.9(2)(c); 1986 s.18 (1)
(3)	1975(1) s.28(7B)(a); 1985 s.9(2)(c); 1986 s.18 (1)
(4)	1975(1) s.28(7C)(a); 1985 s.9(2)(c); 1986 s.18 (1)
(5)	1975(1) s.28(8)
(6)	1980(2) s.3(4)
48(1)	1975(2) s.20(1); 1979 s.5, Sch. 1, para. 5
(2)	1979 s.5, Sch. 1, para. 20
(3)	1975(2) s.20(2)
49(1)	1975(1) s.29(1)
(2), (3)	1975(1) s.29(2), (3); 1989 s.7(3)(a)
(4)	1975(1) s.29(4)
(5)	1975(1) s.29(5)
(6)	1975(1) s.29(6)
(7), (8)	1975(1) s.29(9), (9A); 1989 s.31(1), Sch. 8, para. 4(5)
50(1)	1975(1) s.29(7); 1975(2) s.65(1), Sch. 4, para. 44
(2)	1975(1) s.29(8); 1985 s.9(3)
(3), (4)	1975(2) s.7
(5)	1986 s.19(1)(a)
51(1)	1975(2) s.8(1); 1979 s.5, Sch. 1, paras. 4,14
(2)	1975(2) s.8(2)
(3)	1986 s.19(1)(b)
(4)	1975(2) s.8(3); 1989 s.7, Sch. 1, para. 9(2)
52(1)	1975(2) s.9(1)
(2), (3)	1975(2) s.9(2), (3); 1986 s.18(1)
(4)	1979 s.5, Sch. 1, para. 15
53(1)	1975(2) s.10(1)
(2)	1975(2) s.10(2); 1986 s.18(1)
(3)	1979 s.5, Sch. 1, para. 16
54(1), (2)	1975(1) s.30(3)
(3)	1975(1) s.30(4); 1975(2) s.65(1), Sch. 4, para. 45
(4)	1975(1) s.30(5); 1989 s.7, Sch. 1, para. 2(2)
55	1975(2) s.12; 1989 s.7(4)
56(1), (2)	1975(1) s.31; 1975(3) s.21(1), Sch. 4, para. 10; 1977 s.22(2)
(3), (4)	1975(1) s.43(1); 1975(3) s.21(1), Sch. 4, para. 15(a)

Provision	Derivation
(5)	1975(1) s.43(2); 1975(3) s.21(1), Sch. 4, para. 15(b); 1977 s.22(3)
(6)	1986 s.40
57(1)	1975(1) s.17(1); 1980(2) s.3(1); 1989 s.10(2)
(2)	1975(1) s.22(4); 1986 s.49, Sch. 4, para. 13; 1988(1) s.16, Sch. 4, para. 5(a)
(3)	1975(1) s.17(2); 1989 s.10(3); R2
(4)	1975(1) s.17(2A); 1988(1) s.16, Sch. 4, para. 4
(5)	1975(1) s.17(2B); 1989 s.10(4)
(6), (7)	1975(1) s.17(2C), (2D); 1989 s.31(1), Sch. 8, para. 3
(8)	1975(1) s.17(3)
(9), (10)	1975(1) s.17(4), (5); 1980(2) s.3(4); 1981(2) s.5
58(1)	1989 s.31(1), Sch. 8, para. 2(1)
(2)	1989 s.31(1), Sch. 8, para. 2(2), (6) "incapacity benefit"; 1990 s.21(1), Sch. 6, para. 30(2)
(3)	1989 s.31(1), Sch. 8, para. 2(3)
(4)	1989 s.31(1), Sch. 8, para. 2(6); Local Government and Housing Act 1989 (c.42) s.194, Sch. 11, para. 113; 1990 s.21(1), Sch. 6, para. 30(4)
(5)	1989 s.31(1), Sch. 8, para. 2(7)
59(1), (2)	1975(1) s.20(2), (3)
(3)	1975(1) s.20(5)(d) "week"
60(1)	1975(1) s.33(1), (2)
(2), (3)	1986 s.39, Sch. 3, para. 10; 1988(1) s.2, Sch. 1, para. 5(b)
(4)–(6)	1975(1) s.33(3); 1975(2) s.65(1), Sch. 4, para. 46; 1990 s.21(1), Sch. 6, para. 3(1)
(7)	1975(1) s.33(4); 1975(2) s.19(5); 1986 s.18(1)
(8)	1988(1) s.2, Sch. 1, para. 5(a)
61(1)	1977 s.8(1); 1986 s.18(1); 1990 s.21(1), Sch. 6, para. 3(3)
(2)	1977 s.8(2); 1986 s.18(1); 1990 s.21(1), Sch. 6, para. 3(4)
62(1)	1975(2) s.24(1)(b), (c)
(2)	1975(2) s.24(2)
63	1975(1) s.34; 1984 s.11, Sch. 4, para. 3; 1990 s.2(3); 1991(2) s.1(1)
64	1975(1) s.35(1); 1988(1) s.1(1); 1991(2) s.2(1)
65(1)	1975(1) s.35(2); 1979 s.2(2); 1989 s.31(1), Sch. 8, para. 5(2)
(2)	1975(1) s.35(2A); 1979 s.2(3)
(3)	1975(1) s.35(3); 1991(2) s.4, Sch. 2, para. 3(2)
(4)	1975(1) s.35(4); 1989 s.31(1), Sch. 8, para. 5(3); 1991(2) s.4, Sch. 2, para. 3(3)
(5)	1975(1) s.35(4A); 1980(1) s.2, Sch. 1, para. 8; 1989 s.31(1), Sch. 8, para. 5(4); 1991(2) s.4, Sch. 2, para. 3(3)
(6)	1975(1) s.35(4)(a); 1979 s.2(5); 1989 s.31(1), Sch. 8, para. 5(3); 1990 s.1(2)
66	1975(1) s.35(2B), (2C); 1990 s.1(1); 1991(2) s.4, Sch. 2, para. 3(1)
67(1)	1975(1) s.35(5A); 1979 s.2(6)
(2)	1975(1) s.35(6); National Health Service Act 1977 (c.49) s.129, Sch. 15, para. 63; 1991(2) s.4, Sch. 2, para. 3(4)
68(1)–(4)	1975(1) s.36; 1984 s.11(1)
(5)	1975(1) s.36(4A); 1985 s.21, Sch. 4, para. 3

Provision	Derivation
(6), (7)	1975(1) s.36(5), (6); 1984 s.11(1)
(8), (9)	1975(1) s.36(6A), (6B); 1989 s.31(1), Sch. 8, para. 6
(10)	1975(1) s.36(6C); 1991(2) s.9(2)
(11)	1975(1) s.36(7); 1984 s.11(1); 1989 s.31(1), Sch. 8, para. 2(5); 1990 s.21(1), Sch. 6, para. 30(5)
(12)	1989 s.31(1), Sch. 8, para. 2(4)
(13)	1975(1) s.36(8); 1984 s.11(1); 1989 s.31(1), Sch. 8, para. 2(6) "councillor"; "pre-commencement period", (7)
69	1975(1) s.36A; 1990 s.2(1)
70(1)	1975(1) s.37(1)
(2)	1975(1) s.37(2); 1991(2) s.4, Sch. 2, para. 4
(3)–(5)	1975(1) s.37(3)–(5)
(6)	1975(1) s.37(6); 1989 s.26, Sch. 7, para. 10
(7)–(9)	1975(1) s.37(7)–(9)
(10)	1975(1) s.37(6)
71	1975(1) s.37ZA; 1991(2) s.1(2)
72	1975(1) s.37ZB; 1991(2) s.1(2)
73	1975(1) s.37ZC; 1991(2) s.1(2)
74(1)	1977 s.13(1); 1991(2) s.4, Sch. 2, para. 7
(2)	1977 s.13(3)
75	1975(1) s.37ZD; 1991(2) s.1(2)
76	1975(1) s.37ZE; 1991(2) s.1(2)
77(1)	1975(1) s.38(1); 1975(3) s.21(1), Sch. 4, para. 12(a)
(2), (3)	1975(1) s.38(2), (3)
(4), (5)	1975(1) s.43(1); 1975(3) s.21(1), Sch. 4, para. 15(a)
(6)	1975(1) s.43(2); 1975(3) s.21(1), Sch. 4, para. 15(b); 1977 s.22(3)
(7)	1975(1) s.38(1)
(8)	1975(1) s.38(4)
(9)	1975(1) s.38(5); 1975(3) s.21(1), Sch. 4, para. 12(c)
(10)	1975(1) s.38(6); 1986 s.45(a)
(11)	1975(1) s.38(7); 1986 s.45(b)
78(1), (2)	1975(1) s.39(1)(a), (b)
(3), (4)	1975(1) s.39(1)(c); 1979 s.5, Sch. 1, para. 2; 1986 s.18(1)
(5)	1975(1) s.39(2)
(6)	1975(1) s.39(2A); 1985 s.12(1)(b)
(7), (8)	1975(1) s.39(3), (3A); 1989 s.31(1), Sch. 8, para. 4(6)
(9)	1975(1) s.39(4)
79	1975(1) s.40
80(1)	1975(1) s.41(1); 1975(3) s.21(1), Sch. 4, para. 13
(2)	1975(1) s.41(2); 1984 s.13, Sch. 5, para. 3(a)
(3)	1975(1) s.41(2A); 1984 s.13, Sch. 5, para. 3(c)
(4)	1975(1) s.41(2B); 1984 s.13, Sch. 5, para. 3(c); Benefits Order 1991 art. 11
(5), (6)	1975(1) s.41(4), (5); 1975(3) s.21(1), Sch. 4, para. 13
(7)	1975(1) s.41(2D); 1984 s.13, Sch. 5, para. 3(c)
81(1), (2)	1975(1) s.43(1); 1975(3) s.21(1), Sch. 4, para. 15(a)
(3)	1975(1) s.43(2); 1975(3) s.21(1), Sch. 4, para. 15(b); 1977 s.22(3)

Provision	Derivation
82(1)	1975(1) s.44(1); 1975(3) s.22(1), Sch. 4, para. 16(a); 1980(1) s.21, Sch. 1, para. 5(2); 1988 (1) s.16, Sch. 4, para. 16(a)
(2)	1975(1) s.44(2); 1975(3) s.22(1), Sch. 4, para. 16(a); 1980(1) s.21, Sch. 1, para. 5(2)
(3)	1975(1) s.44(3)(a); 1988(1) s.16, Sch. 4, para. 16(b)
(4)	1975(1) s.44(3)(c); 1975(3) s.22(1), Sch. 4, para. 16(b); 1980(1) s.2, Sch. 1, para. 4(a)
(5)	1975(1) s.44(4)
83(1)	1975(1) s.45(1)
(2)	1975(1) s.45(2); 1975(3) s.21(1), Sch. 4, para. 17; 1988(1) s.16, Sch. 4, para. 7(a)
(3)	1975(1) s.45(2A); 1985 s.13(1)
84(1)	1975(1) s.45A(1); 1984 s.12; 1985 s.13(2)(a)
(2)	1975(1) s.45A(2); 1985 s.13(2)(b); 1988(1) s.16, Sch. 4, para. 8(a)
(3)	1975(1) s.45A(3); 1985 s.13(2)(b)
85(1)	1975(1) s.46(1)
(2)	1975(1) s.46(2); 1975(3) s.21(1), Sch. 4, para. 18; 1980(1) s.2, Sch. 1, para. 4(b)
(3)	1975(1) s.46(3)
(4)	1975(1) s.46(4); 1985 s.13(3)
86(1)	1975(1) s.47(1); 1975(3) s.21(1), Sch. 4, para. 19; 1980(1) s.2, Sch. 1, para. 5(2); 1989 s.31(1), Sch. 8, para. 7(1)
(2)	1975(1) s.47(1A); 1985 s.13(4)(b)
87(1)	1975(1) s.47A(a); 1980(1) s.2, Sch. 1, para. 5(1); 1990 s.21(1), Sch. 6, para. 3(2)
(2)	1975(1) s.47A(b); 1990 s.21(1), Sch. 6, para. 3(2)
88	1975(1) s.48(1)
89	1975(1) s.47B; 1984 s.14(a); 1989 s.9(3)
90	1975(1) s.49; 1984 s.11, Sch. 4, para. 3
91	1975(1) s.49A; 1986 s.44(2)
92	1975(1) s.84A; 1989 s.31, Sch. 8, para. 7(2)
93	1991(2) s.9(5)
94(1)	1975(1) s.50(1); 1986 s.39, Sch. 3, para. 2
(2)	1975(1) s.50(1A); 1988(1) s.16, Sch. 4, para. 11
(3)	1975(1) s.50(3)
(4)	1975(1) s.50(4); 1982(2) s.48(5), Sch. 4, para. 12(2)
(5)	1975(1) s.50(5)
(6)	1975(1) s.50(6); 1982(2) s.48(5), Sch. 4, para. 12(3)
95(1)–(3)	1975(1) s.51
(4), (5)	1977 s.17(3)
96	1975(1) s.157
97	1975(1) s.156
98–101	1975(1) ss.52–55
102(1), (2)	1975(1) s.50A(1), (2); 1982(2) s.39(4)
(3)	1975(1) s.50A(3); 1982(2) s.39(4); 1989 s.7, Sch. 1, para. 8(1)
103(1)	1975(1) s.57(1); 1986 s.39, Sch. 3, para. 3(1)
(2)–(4)	1975(1) s.57(1A)–(1C); 1986 s.39, Sch. 3, para. 3(2)
(5)	1975(1) s.57(3)
(6)	1975(1) s.57(4); 1982(2) s.39(2); 1989 s.26, Sch. 7, para. 12
(7), (8)	1975(1) s.57(6); 1986 s.39, Sch. 3, para. 3(4)

Provision	Derivation
104(1), (2)	1975(1) s.61(1), (2)
(3), (4)	1975(1) s.61(3), (4); 1986 s.39, Sch. 3, para. 6
105	1975(1) s.63
106	Drafting
107(1)	1975(1) s.91(1); 1982(2) s.48(5), Sch. 4, para. 15
(2)	1975(1) s.91(2); R3
108(1)–(4)	1975(1) s.76(1)–(4)
(5)	1975(1) s.76(4A); 1990 s.21(1), Sch. 6, para. 4(1)
(6)	1975(1) s.76(5)
109(1)	1975(1) s.77(1)
(2)	1975(1) s.77(2); 1990 ss.3(7), 21(1), Sch. 6, para. 4(2)
(3)	1975(1) s.77(3)
(4)–(6)	1975(1) s.77(4); 1986 s.39, Sch. 3 para. 13
(7)	1975(1) s.77(5); 1986 s.39, Sch. 3 para. 13
110	1975(1) s.78
111	Drafting
112(1), (2)	1977 s.18(1)
(3)	1977 s.18(2); Employment Protection (Consolidation) Act 1978 (c.44) s.159, Sch. 16, para. 29(d); 1986 s.86, Sch. 10, para. 74
113(1), (2)	1975(1) s.82(5), (6)
(3)	1975(1) s.83; 1985 s.29(1), Sch. 5, para. 8
114(1), (2)	1975(1) s.84(1), (2)
(3)	1975(1) s.84(4); 1985 s.13(6)
(4)	1975(1) s.84(5); 1985 s.13(8); 1986 s.39, Sch. 3, paras. 4, 16
115(1)	1975(1) s.127(1)
(2), (3)	1975(1) s.127(2)
(4)	Drafting
116	1975(1) s.128(1)–(3)
117	1975(1) s.129
118	1975(1) s.130
119	1975(1) s.131
120(1)	1975(1) s.132(1)
(2)	1975(1) s.132(2); Oil and Gas (Enterprise) Act 1982 (c.23) s.37, Sch. 3, para. 21
(3)	1975(1) s.132(3)
121	1975(1) s.162
122(1) "beneficiary"	1975(1) s.168(1), Sch. 20, "beneficiary"
"benefit"	1975(1) s.168(1), Sch. 20, "benefit"
"child"	1975(1) s.168(1), Sch. 20, "child"; 1975(3) s.21(1), Sch. 4, para. 38
"claim"	1975(1) s.168(1), Sch. 20, "claim"
"claimant"	1975(1) s.168(1), Sch. 20, "claimant"
"contract of service"	1975(1) s.168(1), Sch. 20, "contract of service"
"current"	1975(1) s.168(1), Sch. 20, "current"
"day of incapacity for work"; "day of interruption of employment"; "deferred"; "period of deferment"; "earnings"; "earner"; "employed earner"	Drafting
"employment"; "employed"	1975(1) s.168(1), Sch. 20, "employment"; "employed"
"entitled"	1975(1) s.168(1), Sch. 20, "entitled"; 1985 s.29(1), Sch. 5, para. 14; 1990 s.5(2)
"industrial injuries benefit"	1975(1) s.168(1), Sch. 20, "industrial injuries benefit"

Provision	Derivation
"initial primary percentage"	1975(1) s.168(1), Sch. 20, "initial primary percentage"; 1989 s.1(9)
"the Inland Revenue"	1975(1) s.168(1), Sch. 20, "the Inland Revenue"
"late husband"	1975(1) s.168(1), Sch. 20, "late husband"
"long-term benefit"	Drafting
"loss of physical faculty"	1975(1) s.168(1), Sch. 20, "loss of physical faculty"; 1984 s.11, Sch. 4, para. 11(a)
"lower earnings limit", "upper earnings limit"	1975(1) s.168(1), Sch. 20, "lower earnings limit", "upper earnings limit"
"main primary percentage"	1975(1) s.168(1), Sch. 20, "main primary percentage"; 1989 s.1(9)
"medical examination"	1975(1) s.168(1), Sch. 20, "medical examination"
"medical treatment"	1975(1) s.168(1), Sch. 20, "medical treatment"
"the Northern Ireland Department"	1975(1) s.168(1), Sch. 20, "the Northern Ireland Department"
"Old Cases payments"	Drafting
"payments by way of occupational or personal pension"	1975(1) s.168(1), Sch. 20 "payments by way of occupational or personal pension"; 1980(2) s.5(3) "payments by way of occupational or personal pension"; 1984 s.21, Sch. 7, para. 2; 1989 s.9(2), (4)
"pensionable age"	1975(1) ss.27(1), 168(1), Sch. 20, "pensionable age"
"pneumoconiosis"	1975(1) s.168(1), Sch. 20, "pneumoconiosis"
"prescribe"	1975(1) s.168(1), Sch. 20, "prescribe"
"primary percentage"	1975(1) s.168(1), Sch. 20, "primary percentage"; 1989 s.1(9)
"qualifying earnings factor"	1975(1) s.168(1), Sch. 20, "qualifying earnings factor"; am. 1975(2) s.65, Sch. 4, para. 64
"relative"	1975(1) s.168(1), Sch. 20, "relative"
"relevant accident"	1975(1) s.168(1), Sch. 20, "relevant accident"
"relevant injury"	1975(1) s.168(1), Sch. 20, "relevant injury"
"relevant loss of faculty"	1975(1) s.168(1), Sch. 20, "relevant loss of faculty"; 1984 s.11, Sch. 4, para. 11(b)
"self-employed earner"; "short-term benefit"	Drafting
"tax week"	1975(1) s.168(1), Sch. 20, "tax week"
"tax year"	1975(1) s.168(1), Sch. 20, "tax year"; 1990 s.21(1), Sch. 6, para. 11
"trade or business"	1975(1) s.168(1), Sch. 20, "trade or business"
"trade union"	1975(1) s.168(1), Sch. 20, "trade union"
"week"	1975(1) s.168(1), Sch. 20, "week"; 1991(2) s.9(4)
(2)	1975(1) s.168(1), Sch. 20, "employment"; 1989 s.12(5)
(3)	1977 s.22(1)
(4), (5)	1975(1) s.168(1), Sch. 20, "entitled to child benefit"; 1975(3) s.21(1), Sch. 4, para. 38
(6)	1975(1) s.168(1), Sch. 20, "permanently incapable of self support"; 1980(1) s.2, Sch. 1, para. 7
123(1)	1986 s.20(1); 1988(2) s.135, Sch. 10, para. 2(2); 1991(2) s.6(2)
(2)	1986 s.20(2); 1991(2) s.6(3); S.I. 1988/1843 Sch. 3, para. 4(c)
(3)	1986 s.31(4)
(4)–(6)	1986 s.31G(4)–(6); 1988(2) s.135, Sch. 10, para. 6
124(1)	1986 s.20(3); 1988(1) s.4(1); 1989 s.13(1)

Provision	Derivation
(2)	1986 s.20(4N); 1988(1) s.4(2)
(3)	1986 s.20(4)
(4)	1986 s.21(1); 1988(1) s.16, Sch. 4, para. 23(1)
(5), (6)	1986 s.21(1A), (1B); 1988(1) s.16, Sch. 4, para. 23(2)
125(1)–(4)	1986 s.20(4A)–(4D); 1988(1) s.4(2)
(5)	1986 s.20(4N); 1988(1) s.4(2)
126(1)–(4)	1986 s.23(1)–(4)
(5)	1986 s.23(5); Income and Corporation Taxes Act 1988 (c.1) s.844, Sch. 29, para. 32
(6)	1986 s.23(5A); 1988(1) s.16, Sch. 4, para. 24(1)
(7)	1986 s.23(6); 1990 s.21(1), Sch. 6, para. 17(2) Benefits Order art. 16
(8)	1986 s.23(7); 1990 s.21(1), Sch. 6, para. 17(3)
127	1986 s.23A; 1988(1) s.16, Sch. 4, para. 25; 1989 s.31(1), Sch. 8, para. 16
128(1)	1986 s.20(5), (5A); 1988(1) s.3(a); 1991(2) s.8(1)
(2)	1986 s.21(2), (3)
(3)	1986 s.20(6); 1989 s.31(1), Sch. 8, para. 15(1)
(4)	1986 s.20(10); 1991(2) s.8(2)
(5)	1986 s.21(6)(a)
(6)	1986 s.79(3)
129(1)	1986 s.20(6A), (6D); 1991(2) s.6(4)
(2), (3)	1986 s.20(6B), (6C); 1991(2) s.6(4)
(4)	1986 s.20(6E); 1991(2) s.6(4)
(5)	1986 s.21(3A), (3B); 1991(2) s.6(8)
(6)	1986 s.20(6F); 1991(2) s.6(4)
(7)	1986 s.27B(4); 1991(2) s.7(1)
(8)	1986 s.21(6)(aa); 1991(2) s.6(9)
(9)	1986 s.79(3); 1991(2) s.7, Sch. 3, para. 7
130(1), (2)	1986 s.20(7), (8)
(3)	1986 s.21(4), (5)
(4), (5)	1986 s.21(6); Housing (Scotland) Act 1988 (c.43) s.70(3); Housing Act 1988 (c.50) s.121(4)
131(1)	1986 s.20(8A); 1988(2) s.135, Sch. 10, para. 2(3)
(2)	1986 s.20(8AA); 1989 s.31(1), Sch. 8, para. 9(2)
(3)–(9)	1986 s.20(8B)–(8H); 1988(2) s.135, Sch. 10, para. 2(3)
(10), (11)	1986 s.21(5A), (5B); 1988(2) s.135, Sch. 10, para. 3(2)
(12)	1986 s.21(6)(c); 1988(2) s.135, Sch. 10, para. 3(3)
132	1986 s.22A; 1988(2) s.135, Sch. 10, para. 5
133(1)	1986 s.22B(1); 1988(2) s.135, Sch. 10, para. 5; 1989 s.31(1), Sch. 8, para. 9(3)
(2)–(4)	1986 s.22B(2)–(4); 1988(2) s.135, Sch. 10, para. 5
134(1)	1986 s.22(6)
(2)	1986 s.20(9)
(3)	1986 s.20(9A); 1988(2) s.135, Sch. 10, para. 2(4)
(4)	1986 s.21(7)
135(1), (2)	1986 s.22(1), (2)
(3), (4)	1986 s.22(2A), (2B); 1990 s.9
(5)	1986 s.22(3); 1988(2) s.135, Sch. 10, para. 4(2)

Provision	Derivation
(6)	1986 s.22(4)
136(1)	1986 s.22(5)
(2), (3)	1986 s.22(7), (8)
(4)	1986 s.22(8A); 1988(2) s.135, Sch. 10, para. 4(3)
(5)	1988 s.22(9)
137(1) "charging authority"	1986 s.20(11) "charging authority"; 1988(2) s.135, Sch. 10, para. 2(5)
"child"	1986 s.20(11) "child"; 1989 s.5(1)
"contribution period"	1986 s.20(11) "contribution period"; 1988(2) s.135, Sch. 10, para. 2(5)
"dwelling"	1986 s.84(1) "dwelling"
"family"	1986 s.20(11) "family"
"industrial injuries scheme"	1986 s.20(11) "industrial injuries scheme"; 1991(2) s.6(6)(a)
"levying authority"	1986 s.20(11) "levying authority"; 1988(2) s.135, Sch. 10, para. 2(5)
"married couple"	1986 s.20(11) "married couple"
"the 1987 Act", "the 1988 Act"	Drafting
"prescribed"	1986 s.84(1) "prescribed"
"unmarried couple"	1986 s.20(11) "unmarried couple"
"war pension scheme"	1986 s.20(11) "war pension scheme"; 1991(2) s.6(6)(b)
"week"	1986 s.20(11) "week"; 1988(2) s.135, Sch. 10, para. 2(5)
(2)	1986 s.20(12); 1989 s.13(2); 1991(2) s.6(7)
138(1)	1986 s.32(2); 1987 s.1
(2)	1986 s.32(2A); 1988(1) s.11, Sch. 3, para. 2
(3)	1986 s.33(1A); 1988(1) s.11, Sch. 3, para. 10
(4)	1986 s.84(1) "prescribed"
139(1)–(3)	1986 s.33(2)–(4)
(4)	1986 s.33(4A); 1988(1) s.11, Sch. 3, para. 11
(5)	1986 s.33(11)
140(1)	1986 s.33(9); 1988(1) s.11, Sch. 3, para. 12
(2)	1986 s.33(10)
(3)	1986 s.33(10ZA); 1990 s.10(3)
(4)	1986 s.33(10A); 1988(1) s.11, Sch. 3, para. 13; 1990 s.10(4)
(5)	1986 s.32(11); 1988(1) s.11, Sch. 3, para. 7
141	1975(3) s.1(1)
142(1)	1975(3) s.2(1); 1986 s.70(1)(a); 1988(1) s.4(3)
(2), (3)	1975(3) s.2(1A), (1B); 1986 s.70(1)(b)
(4), (5)	1975(3) s.2(2), (3)
143(1), (2)	1975(3), s.3(1), (2)
(3)	1975(3) s.3(3); National Health Service and Community Care Act 1990 (c.19) s.66(1), Sch. 9, para. 15
(4), (5)	1975(3) s.3(4), (5)
144(1), (2)	1975(3) s.4(1); 1988(1), s.4(4)
(3)	1975(3) s.4(2)
145(1)–(4)	1975(3) s.5(1)–(4)
(5)	1975(3) s.22(1)(a)
(6)	1975(3) s.22(8)
(7)	1975(3) s.22(9)
146	1975(3) s.13
147(1) "prescribed"	1975(3) s.24(1) "prescribed"
"recognised educational establishment"	1975(3) s.24(1) "recognised educational establishment"
"voluntary organisation"	1975(3) s.24(1) "voluntary organisation"
"week"	1975(3) s.24(1) "week"
(2)	1975(3) s.24(2)

Provision	Derivation
(3)	1975(3) s.24(3)(b)
(4)	1975(3) s.24(4)
(5)	1975(3) s.9(2)
(6)	1975(3) s.24(5)
148	1986 s.66, Sch. 6, para. 2
149	1986 s.66, Sch. 6, para. 3
150(1)	1986 s.66, Sch. 6, para. 1(1)
(2) "attendance allowance"	1986 s.66, Sch. 6, para. 1(2) "attendance allowance"; 1991(2) s.4, Sch. 2, para. 16
"pensionable age"	1986 s.66, Sch. 6, para. 1(2) "pensionable age"
"retirement pension"	1986 s.66, Sch. 6, para. 1(2) "retirement pension"
"unemployability supplement or allowance"	1986 s.66, Sch. 6, para. 1(2) "unemployability supplement or allowance"; Income and Corporation Taxes Act 1988 (c.1) s.844, Sch. 29, para. 32, Table
"war disablement pension"	1986 s.84(1) "war disablement pension"; Income and Corporation Taxes Act 1988 s.844, Sch. 29, para. 32, Table
"war widow's pension"	1986 s.84(1) "war widow's pension"; Income and Corporation Taxes Act 1988 s.844, Sch. 29, para. 32, Table
(3)	1986 s.66, Sch. 6, para. 1(2) "married couple"; "unmarried couple"
(4)	1986 s.66, Sch. 6, para. 1(3)
151(1), (2)	1982(2) s.1(1), (2)
(3)	1982(2) s.23A(1); 1984 s.21, Sch. 7, para. 8
(4), (5)	1982(2) s.1(3), (4)
(6)	1982(2) s.1(5); 1986 s.68
152(1), (2)	1982(2) s.2(1), (2)
(3)	1982(2) s.2(3); The Statutory Sick Pay (General) Regulations 1982 (S.I. 1982/894) reg. 2A; The Statutory Sick Pay (General) Amendment Regulations 1986 (S.I. 1986/477) reg. 2
(4)	1982(2) s.2(3A); 1985 s.18(4)
(5), (6)	1982(2) s.2(4), (5)
153(1)–(4)	1982(2) s.3(1)–(4)
(5)	1982(2) s.3(4A); 1985 s.18(5)
(6), (7)	1982(2) s.3(5), (6)
(8), (9)	1982(2) s.3(6A), (6B); 1985 s.29(1), Sch. 4, para. 4
(10), (11)	1982(2) s.3(7), (8)
(12)	1982(2) s.3(9); 1986 s.86, Sch. 10, para. 77
154(1)	1982(2) s.4(1)
(2)	1982(2) s.4(2); 1984 s.21, Sch. 7, para. 7
(3), (4)	1982(2) s.4(3), (4)
155(1)–(3)	1982(2) s.5(1)–(3)
(4)	1982(2) s.5(4); 1985 s.18(1)
(5)	1982(2) s.5(5)
156	1982(2) s.6
157(1)	1982(2) s.7(1) Sick Pay Order reg. 2
(2)	1982(2) s.7(1A); 1986 s.67(1); 1990 s.21(1), Sch. 6, para. 15(1)
(3)	1982(2) s.7(2)
158(1)	1982(2) s.9(1); 1991(1) s.1(1)
(2)	1982(2) s.9(1B); 1991(1) s.2(1)
(3)	1982(2) s.9(1D); 1991(1) s.2(1)
(4)	1982(2) s.9(2); 1991(1) s.2(2)
(5)	1982(2) s.9(3)(b), (c); 1991(1) s.1(3)

Provision	*Derivation*
(6)	1982(2) s.9(6)
(7)	1991(1) s.2(5)
159	1982(2) s.9(1C); 1991(1) s.2(1)
160	Drafting
161(1), (2)	1982(2) s.27(1), (2)
(3)	1982(2) s.27(3); 1989 s.26, Sch. 7, para. 23
162	1982(2) s.22; Oil and Gas (Enterprise) Act 1982 (c.23) s.37, Sch. 3, para. 44; R4
163(1) "contract of service"	1982(2) s.26(1) "contract of service"
"employee"	1982(2) s.26(1) "employee"
"employer"	1982(2) s.26(1) "employer"; 1985 s.29(1), Sch. 4, para. 6
"period of entitlement"; "period of incapacity for work"; "period of interruption of employment"	Drafting
"prescribed"	1982(2) s.26(1) "prescribed"
"qualifying day"	Drafting
"week"	1982(2) s.26(1) "week"
(2)	1982(2) s.26(2); 1985 s.29(1), Sch. 4, para. 7
(3)–(5)	1982(2) s.26(3)–(5)
(6)	1982(2) s.26(5A); 1990 s.21(1), Sch. 6, para. 16
(7)	1982(2) s.26(6)
164(1)–(5)	1986 s.46(1)–(5)
(6), (7)	1982(2) s.23A(1); 1984 s.21, Sch. 7, para. 8; 1986 s.46(6)
(8)	1986 s.46(7)
(9)	1986 s.46(8); 1988(1) s.16, Sch. 4, para. 16(1)
(10)	1986 s.46(9); 1988(1) s.16, Sch. 4, para. 16(2)
165(1)–(6)	1986 s.47(1)–(6)
(7)	1986 s.47(7); 1989 s.26, Sch. 7, para. 25
166(1)	1986 s.48(1)
(2)	1986 s.48(2); 1988(1), s.16, Sch. 4, para. 17
(3)–(8)	1986 s.48(3)–(8)
167(1)	1986 s.49, Sch. 4, para. 1
(2)	R5
(3)	1986 s.49, Sch. 4, para. 2
(4)	1986 s.49, Sch. 4, para. 5
168	Drafting
169	1986 s.79(4)
170	1986 s.80; R4
171(1) "confinement"	1986 s.50(1) "confinement"
"dismissed"	1986 s.50(1) "dismissed"
"employee"	1986 s.50(1) "employee"
"employer"	1986 s.50(1) "employer"
"maternity pay period"	Drafting
"modifications"	1986 s.84(1) "modifications"
"prescribed"	1986 s.84(1) "prescribed"
"week"	1986 s.50(1) "week"
(2)	1986 s.50(2)
(3)	1986 s.50(2A); 1990 s.21(1), Sch. 6, para. 22
(4)–(6)	1986 s.50(3)–(5)
172	1982(2) ss.26(7), 44(1)(b), (c), (d), (2)(a), (b); 1986 s.84(4)
173	1975(1), s.168(1), Sch. 20 "age"; 1980(1), s.18; 1980(2) s.5(6); 1991(1) s.3(1)(b)
174	Drafting
175(1)	1975(1) s.168(1), Sch. 20 "regulations"; 1975 (3) s.22(1)(b); 1977 s.24(1) "regulations"; 1980(2) ss.3(4), 5(3) "regulations"; 1982(2) s.47 "regulations"; 1986 s.84(1) "regulations"; 1989 s.30(1) "regulations"

Provision	Derivation
(2)	1975(1) s.166(1); 1975 (Old Cases) ss.4(8), 8(1); 1975(3) s.22(2); 1977 s.24(3); 1980(2) s.7(3); 1982(2) s.45(2); 1986 s.83(1); 1989 s.29(1); 1990 s.21(1), Sch. 6, paras. 8(7), 12
(3)	1975(1) ss.162, 166(2); 1975(3) s.22(6); 1977 s.24(3); 1980(2) s.7(3); 1982(2) s.45(1); 1986 s.83(1); 1989 s.29(1)
(4)	1975(1) s.166(3); 1975(3) s.22(7); 1977 s.24 (3); 1980(2) s.7(3); 1982(2) s.45(1); 1986 s.83(1); 1989 ss.29(1), 31(1), Sch. 8, para. 10(1); R6
(5)	1975(1) s.166(3A); 1975(3) s.22(7A); 1977 s.24(3); 1986 ss.62(1), (2), 83(1); 1989 s.29 (1)
(6)	1986 s.83(2); 1988(2) s.135, Sch. 10, para. 11(2)
(7)	1975(1) s.166(5); 1977 s.24(3); 1982(2) s.45 (1); 1986 s.83(6); 1989 s.29(6); R7
(8)	1975(1) s.166(6)
(9)	1975(1) s.166(7)
(10)	1975(1) s.168(4)
176(1)	1975(1) s.167(1); 1975(2) s.62(1); 1975(3) s.22(3); 1980(2) s.5(4); 1982(2) ss.7(1B), 9(1F); 1986 ss.43(3)(b), 62(3), 67(1), 83(3) (e); 86, Sch. 10, para. 65; 1989 s.9(1); 1990 s.21(1), Sch. 6, paras. 8(2), (3), (5), 15(2); 1991(1) s.2(1); R15
(2)	1975(1) s.167(2); 1975(3) s.22(4); 1990 s.21 (2), Sch. 6, para. 8(1), (3)
(3)	1975(1) s.167(3); 1975 (Old Cases) ss.4(8), 8(1); 1975(3) s.22(5); 1977 s.24(5); 1980(2) s.7(4); 1982(2) s.45(2); 1986 s.83(4); 1989 s.29(3); 1990 s.21(1), Sch. 6, para. 8(1), (3), (4), (6), (7), (9), (12)
177(1)	Short title
(2)	Commencement
(3), (4)	1975(1) ss.9(3), 169(2)
Sch. 1	
para. 1(1)	1975(1) s.1(4), Sch. 1, para. 1(1); 1977 s.1(3)
(2)	1975(1) s.1(4), Sch. 1, para. 1(1A); 1980(1) s.2, Sch. 1, para. 16; 1985 s.29(1), Sch. 5, para. 13(a)
(3), (4)	1975(1) s.1(4), Sch. 1, para. 1(1B), (1C); 1985 s.29(1), Sch. 5, para. 13(b)
(5)	1986 s.74(5)
(6)	1975(1) s.1(4), Sch. 1, para. 1(1D); 1985 s.29 (1), Sch. 5, para. 13(b)
(7), (8)	1975(1) s.1(4), Sch. 1, para. 1(2), (3)
para. 2	1975(1) s.1(4), Sch. 1, para. 2
para. 3(1)	1975(1) s.1(4), Sch. 1, para. 3(1)
(2)	1975(1) s.1(4), Sch. 1, para. 3(2); Criminal Justice Act 1982 (c.48) ss.38, 46, 54; Criminal Procedure (Scotland) Act 1975 (c.21) ss.289F, 289G
(3)	1975(1) s.1(4), Sch. 1, para. 3(3)
para. 4	1975(1) s.1(4), Sch. 1, para. 4; 1977 s.1(4)
para. 5	1975(1) s.1(4), Sch. 1, para. 4A; 1991(3) s.2(2)
para. 6(1)	1975(1) s.1(4), Sch. 1, para. 5(1); 1991(3) s.2(3)(a)
(2)	1975(1) s.1(4), Sch. 1, para. 5(1A); 1990 s.17 (5); 1991(3) s.2(3)(b)

Provision	Derivation
(3), (4)	1975(1) s.1(4), Sch. 1, para. 5(1B), (1C); 1990 s.17(5)
(5)	1982(2) s.9(4); 1986 s.49, Sch. 4, para. 3
(6)	1982(2) s.9(5); 1985 s.19; 1986 s.49, Sch. 4, para. 4
(7)	1975(1) s.1(4), Sch. 1, para. 5(2)
(8)	1975(1) s.1(4), Sch. 1, para. 5(3); 1990 s.17(6)
para. 7(1)–(10)	1975(1) s.1(4), Sch. 1, para. 5A(1)–(10); 1990 s.17(7), Sch. 5
(11)	1975(1) s.1(4), Sch. 1, para. 5A(11); 1990 s.17(7), Sch. 5; 1991(3) s.2(4)
(12), (13)	1975(1) s.1(4), Sch. 1, para. 5A(12), (13); 1990 s.17(7), Sch. 5
para. 8(1)(a)	1975(1) s.1(4), Sch. 1, para. 6(1)(a)
(b)	1975(1) s.1(4), Sch. 1, para. 6(1)(aa); 1991(3) s.2(5)(a)
(c)–(f)	1975(1) s.1(4), Sch. 1, para. 6(1)(b)–(e)
(g)	1975(1) s.1(4), Sch. 1, para. 6(1)(f); 1975(2) s.65(1), Sch. 4, para. 61
(h)	1975(1) s.1(4), Sch. 1, para. 6(1)(gg); 1989 s.2
(i)	1975(1) s.1(4), Sch. 1, para. 6(1)(ggg); 1991 (3) s.2(5)(c)
(j), (k)	1975(1) s.1(4), Sch. 1, para. 6(1)(gh), (gj); 1990 s.21(1), Sch. 6, para. 9
(l)	1975(1) s.1(4), Sch. 1, para. 6(1)(g); 1991(3) s.2(5)(b)
(m)	1975(1) s.1(4), Sch. 1, para. 6(1)(h); 1986 s.86, Sch. 10, para. 10
(n)–(q)	1975(1) s.1(4), Sch. 1, para. 6(1)(j)–(m)
(2), (3)	1975(1) s.1(4), Sch. 1, para. 6(2), (3)
paras. 9, 10	1975(1) s.1(4), Sch. 1, paras. 7,8
para. 11	1975(1) s.1(4), Sch. 1, para. 9; 1982(2) s.37(2)
Sch. 2	
para. 1	Drafting
para. 2	1975(1) s.9(4), Sch. 2, para. 2; Capital Allowances Act 1990 (c.1) s.164, Sch. 1, para. 2
para. 3(1), (2)	1975(1) s.9(4), Sch. 2, para. 3(1), (2); Income and Corporation Taxes Act 1988 s.844, Sch. 29, para. 32, Table
(3)	1975(1) s.9(4), Sch. 2, para. 3(3)
(4)	1975(1) s.9(4), Sch. 2, para. 3(3); Finance Act 1988 (c.39) s.35, Sch.3, para. 31
(5)	1975(1) s.9(4), Sch. 2, para. 3(4); Income and Corporation Taxes Act 1988 s.844, Sch. 29, para. 32, Table
paras. 4, 5	1975(1) s.9(4), Sch. 2, paras. 5, 6; Income and Corporation Taxes Act 1988 s.844, Sch. 29, para. 32, Table
para. 6(1)	1975(1) s.9(4), Sch. 2, para. 7(1); Income and Corporation Taxes Act 1988, s.844, Sch. 29, para. 32, Table; 1990 s.17(8)
(2)	1975(1) s.9(4), Sch. 2, para. 7(2); 1990 s.17(9)
paras. 7, 8	1975(1) s.9(4), Sch. 2, paras. 8, 9
para. 9	1975(1) s.9(4), Sch. 2, para. 4; Income and Corporation Taxes Act 1988 s.844, Sch. 29, para. 32, Table; Finance Act 1988 (c.39) s.145, Sch. 14, Part VIII and Note 6
Sch. 3	
para. 1(1)	1975(1) s.13(6), Sch. 3, para. 1(1)
(2)	1975(1) s.13(6), Sch. 3, para. 1(2); 1986 s.75, Sch. 8, para. 3(1); 1988(1) s.6(2)(a)

Provision	Derivation
(3)	1975(1) s.13(6), Sch. 3, para. 1(3); 1986 s.75, Sch. 8, para. 3(2), (3); 1988(1) s.6(2)(b)
(4)	1975(1) s.13(6), Sch. 3, para. 1(2)(b)(i); 1986 s.75, Sch. 8, para. 3(1)
(5)	1975(1) s.13(6), Sch. 3, para. 1(3)(b)(i); 1986 s.75, Sch. 8, para. 3(3)
(6)	1975(1) s.13(6), Sch. 1, para. 1(4)
para. 2(1)	1975(1) s.13(6), Sch. 3, para. 1(1)
(2)	1975(1) s.13(6), Sch. 3, para. 1(2); 1986 s.75, Sch. 8, para. 3(1); 1988(1) s.6(2)(a)
(3)	1975(1) s.13(6), Sch. 3, para. 1(3); 1986 s.75, Sch. 8, para. 3(2), (3); 1988(1) s.6(2)(b)
(4)	1975(1) s.13(6), Sch. 3, para. 1(2)(b)(ii); 1986 s.75, Sch. 8, para. 3(1)
(5)	1975(1) s.13(6), Sch. 3, para. 1(3)(b)(ii); 1986 s.75, Sch. 8, para. 3(3)
(6)	1975(1) s.13(6), Sch. 1, para. 1(4)
para. 3(1)	1975(1) s.13(6), Sch. 3, para. 3(1); 1986 s.49, Sch. 4, para. 14; 1990 s.21(1), Sch. 6, para. 10(1)
(2), (3)	1975(1) s.13(6), Sch. 3, para. 3(2), (3); 1990 s.21(1), Sch. 6, para. 10(2)
para. 4(1), (2)	1975(1) s.13(6), Sch. 3, para. 4(1); 1986 ss.75, 86, Sch. 8, para. 3(4), Sch. 10, para. 66(a)
(3)	1975(1) s.13(6), Sch. 3, para. 4(2)
para. 5(1)	1975(1) s.13(6), Sch. 3, para. 5(1)
(2)	1975(1) s.13(6), Sch. 3, para. 5(2); 1975(2) s.19(2); 1986 s.75 Sch. 8, para. 3(5)
(3), (4)	1975(1) s.13(6), Sch. 3, para. 5(3); 1986 s.75, Sch. 8, para. 3(6)
(5), (6)	1975(1) s.13(6), Sch. 3, para. 5(4), (5)
(7)	1975(1) s.13(6), Sch. 3, para. 5(6); 1979 s.5, Sch. 1, para. 3
(8)	1975(1) s.27(2)
para. 6	1975(1) s.31(6), Sch. 3, para. 6
para. 7(1)	1975(1) s.13(8), Sch. 3, para. 8(1); 1989 s.26, Sch. 7, para. 16
(2)	1975(1) s.13(8), Sch. 3, para. 8(2); 1986 s.86, Sch. 10, para. 66(b)
(3), (4)	1975(1) s.13(8), Sch. 3, para. 8(3); 1979 s.21 (4), Sch. 3, para. 10; 1986 ss.75, 86, Sch. 8, para. 3(7), Sch. 10, para. 66(b)
para. 8	1975(1) s.13(8), Sch. 3, para. 10
para. 9	1975(1) s.13(8), Sch. 3, para. 13; 1986 s.86, Sch. 10, para. 66(c)
Sch. 4	
Part I	
para. 1	1975(1) s.14, Sch. 4, Part I, para. 1(a); Benefits Order art. 3(2), (3), Sch. 1
para. 2	1975(1) s.14, Sch. 4, Part I, para. 1(b); Benefits Order art. 3(2), (3), Sch. 1
para. 3	1975(1) s.16, Sch. 4, Part I, para. 3; Benefits Order art. 3(2), (3), Sch. 1
para. 4	1975(1) s.22, Sch. 4, Part I, para. 4; Benefits Order art. 3(2), (3), Sch. 1
para. 5	1975(1) s.29(7), Sch. 4, Part I, para. 9; 1975 (2), s.65(1), Sch. 4, para. 62; Benefits Order art. 3(2), (3), Sch. 1
para. 6	1975(1) s.31, Sch. 4, Part I, para. 10; Benefits Order art. 3(2), (3), Sch. 1
Part II	1975(1) s.24, Sch. 4, Part IA; 1986 s.36(2)

Provision	Derivation
Part III	
para. 1	1975(1) s.35, Sch. 4, Part III, para. 1; Benefits Order art. 3(2), (3), Sch. 1
para. 2	1975(1) s.36, Sch. 4, Part III, para. 2; 1984 s.11, Sch. 4, para. 3; Benefits Order art. 3(2), (3), Sch. 1
para. 3	1975(1) s.36A, Sch. 4, Part III, para. 2A; 1990 s.2(2); Benefits Order art. 3(2), (3), Sch. 1
para. 4	1975(1) s.37, Sch. 4, Part III, para. 3; Benefits Order art. 3(2), (3), Sch. 1
para. 5	1975(1) s.38, Sch. 4, Part III, para. 4; Benefits Order art. 3(2), (3), Sch. 1
para. 6	1975(1) s.39, Sch. 4, Part III, para. 5; Benefits Order art. 3(2), (3), Sch. 1
para. 7	1975(1) s.39, Sch. 4, Part III, para. 5A; 1985 s.12(2); Benefits Order art. 3(2), (3), Sch. 1
para. 8	1975(1) s.40, Sch. 4, Part III, para. 6
Part IV	
col.(1)	1975(1) ss.41–49, Sch. 4, Part IV, col.(1); 1984 s.11, Sch. 4, para. 3; Benefits Order art. 3(2), (3), Sch. 1
col.(2)	1975 ss.41–49, Sch. 4, Part IV, col.(2); Benefits Order art. 3(2), (3), Sch. 1
col.(3)	1975(1) ss.41–49, Sch. 4, Part IV, col.(3); Benefits Order art. 3(2), (3), Sch. 1
Part V	
para. 1	1975(1) s.57(6), Sch. 4, Part V, para. 3; Benefits Order art. 3(2), (3), Sch. 1
para. 2	1975(1) s.61, Sch. 4, Part V, para. 7; Benefits Order art. 3(2), (3), Sch. 1
para. 3	1975(1) s.63, Sch. 4, Part V, para. 8; Benefits Order art. 3(2), (3), Sch. 1
para. 4	1975(1) s.91, Sch. 4, Part V, para. 16; Benefits Order art. 3(2), (3), Sch. 1
para. 5	1975(1) s.58, Sch. 4, Part V, para. 4; Benefits Order art. 3(2), (3), Sch. 1
para. 6	1975(1) s.59, Sch. 4, Part V, para. 5; 1979 s.5, Sch. 1, para. 13; Benefits Order art. 3(2), (3), Sch. 1
para. 7	1975(1) s.64, Sch. 4, Part V, para. 10; Benefits Order art. 3(2), (3), Sch. 1
para. 8	1975(1) s.66(2), Sch. 4, Part V, para. 12; Benefits Order art. 3(2), (3), Sch. 1
para. 9	1975(1) s.57(5), Sch. 4, Part V, para. 2; Benefits Order art. 3(2), (3), Sch. 1
para. 10	1975(1) s.68, Sch. 4, Part V, para. 13; 1975(2) s.65(1), Sch. 4, para. 63; Benefits Order art. 3(2), (3), Sch. 1
para. 11	1975(1) s.69, Sch. 4, Part V, para. 14; Benefits Order art. 3(2), (3), Sch. 1
para. 12	1975(1) s.70, Sch. 4, Part V, para. 15; Benefits Order art. 3(2), (3), Sch. 1
Sch. 5	
para. 1	1975(2) s.12, Sch. 1, para. 1; 1989 s.7, Sch. 1, para. 3(1)
para. 2(1)	1975(2) s.12, Sch. 1, para. 2(1); 1989 s.7, Sch. 1, para. 3(2)
(2)	1975(2) s.12, Sch. 1, para. 2(2); 1989 s.7, Sch. 1, para. 3(3)
(3)	1975(2) s.12, Sch. 1, para. 2(3); 1977 s.3(1)(b); 1989 s.7, Sch. 1, para. 3(4)

Provision	Derivation
(4)	1975(2) s.60A; 1979 s.18
(5)	1975(2) s.12, Sch. 1, para. 2(4); 1977 s.3(1) (c); 1980(1) s.3(11)
(6)	1975(2) s.12, Sch. 1, para. 2(4A); 1985 s.9(5)
(7)	1975(2) s.12, Sch. 1, paras. 2(5); 1986 s.86, Sch. 10, para. 95(a); 1989 s.7, Sch. 1, para. 3(5)
(8)	1975(2) s.12, Sch. 1, para. 2(6); 1977 s.3(1) (d); 1989 s.7, Sch. 1, para. 3(6)
para. 3	1975(2) s.12, Sch. 1, para. 3; 1977 s.3(1)(e); 1989 s.7, Sch. 1, para. 3(7)
para. 4(1)	1975(2) s.12, Sch. 1, para. 4(1); 1979 s.21(4), Sch. 3, para. 23; 1986 s.19(2)(a); 1989 s.7, Sch. 1, para. 3(8)
(2)	1975(2) s.12, Sch. 1, para. 4(2); 1979 s.21(4), Sch. 3, para. 23; 1986 s.19(2)(a); 1989 s.7, Sch. 1, para. 3(8)
(3)	1975(2) s.12, Sch. 1, para. 4(2A); 1986 s.19(2) (b)
(4)	1975(2) s.12, Sch. 1, para. 4(3); 1979 s.5, Sch. 1, para. 6; 1986 s.86, Sch. 10, para. 95(a)
(5)	1975(2) s.12, Sch. 1, para. 4(4); 1979 s.5, Sch. 1, para. 22
para. 5(1), (2)	1975(2) s.12, Sch. 1, para. 4A(1); 1979 s.5, Sch. 1, para. 7; 1986 s.19(3)
(3)	1975(2) s.12, Sch. 1, para. 4A(1A); 1986 s.19 (4)
para. 6(1), (2)	1975(2) s.12, Sch. 1, para. 4A(2); 1979 s.5, Sch. 1, para. 7; 1986 s.19(5)
(3)	1975(2) s.12, Sch. 1, para. 4A(2A)(a); 1986 s.19(6)
(4)	1975(2) s.12, Sch. 1, para. 4A(2A)(b); 1986 s.19(6)
para. 7(1)	1975(2) s.12, Sch. 1, para. 4A(3); 1979 s.5, Sch. 1, para. 7; 1986 s.86, Sch. 10, para. 95(b)
(2)	1975(2) s.60A; 1979 s.18
para. 8(1), (2)	1975(2) s.12, Sch. 1, para. 5(1), (2); 1989 Sch. 1, para. 3(9)
(3)	1975(2) s.12, Sch. 1, para. 5(3); 1989 s.7, Sch. 1, para. 3(10)
(4)	1975(2) s.12, Sch. 1, para. 5(4)
para. 9	Drafting
Sch. 6	
para. 1	1975(1) s.57(3), Sch. 8, para. 1; 1984 s.11, Sch. 4, para. 10(a)
paras. 2, 3	1975(1) s.57(3), Sch. 8, paras. 2, 3
para. 4	1975(1) s.57(3), Sch. 8, para. 4A; 1984 s.11, Sch. 4, para. 10(b)
para. 5	1975(1) s.57(3), Sch. 8, para. 5A; 1984 s.11, Sch. 4, para. 10(c)
para. 6(1), (2)	1975(1) s.57(3), Sch. 8, para. 4(1); 1982(2) s.48(5), Sch. 4, para. 17
(3)–(5)	1975(1) s.57(3), Sch. 8, para. 4(2)–(4); 1989 s.21, Sch. 3, para. 13(1)
para. 7	1975(1) s.57(3), Sch. 8, para. 5; 1989 s.21, Sch. 3, para. 13(2)
para. 8	1975(1) s.57(3), Sch. 8, para. 6
Sch. 7	
Part I	
para. 1	1986 s.39, Sch. 3, para. 4

Provision	Derivation
para. 2	1975(1) s.58
para. 3(1)	1975(1) s.59(1); 1985 s.9(4)(a); 1986 s.39, Sch. 3, para. 4
(2)	1975(1) s.59(1A)(a); 1985 s.9(4)(b); 1986 s.18 (1)
(3)	1975(1) s.59(1B)(a); 1985 s.9(4)(b); 1986 s.18 (1)
(4)	1975(1) s.59(1C)(a); 1985 s.9(4)(b); 1986 s.18 (1)
(5), (6)	1975(1) s.59(2), (3)
(7), (8)	1975(1) s.59(4); 1980(2) s.3(3)
(9)	1980(2) s.3(4)
(10)	1975(1) s.59(5)
(11)	Drafting
para. 4(1)	1975(1) s.64(1); 1975(3) s.21(1), Sch. 4, para. 21(a); 1986 s.39, Sch. 3, para. 4
(2)	1975(1) s.64(2)
(3)	1975(1) s.64(1A); 1984 s.13, Sch. 5, para. 4
(4)	1975(1) s.64(1B); 1984 s.13, Sch. 5, para. 4; Social Security (Industrial Injuries) (Dependency) (Permitted Earnings Limits) Order 1991 (S.I. 1991/546) art. 2
(5), (6)	1975(1) s.64(1C), (1D); 1984 s.13, Sch. 5, para. 4
para. 5(1)	1975(1) s.65(1); 1975(3) s.21(1), Sch. 4, para. 22(a); 1986 s.39, Sch. 3, para. 4
(2)	1975(1) s.65(2); 1975(3) s.21(1), Sch. 4, para. 22(b); 1977 s.22(3)
para. 6(1)	1975(1) s.66(1); 1975(3) s.21(1), Sch. 4, para. 23; 1980(1) s.5, Sch. 1, paras. 4 and 6; 1986 s.39, Sch. 3, para. 4
(2)	1975(1) s.66(2)
(3)–(6)	1975(1) s.66(3)–(6); 1985 s.13(5)
(7)	1975(1) s.66(7)
para. 7	1975(1) s.66A; 1984 s.14(b); 1989 s.9(3)
para. 8	1975(1) s.84A; 1989 s.31, Sch. 8, para. 7(2)
Part II	
para. 9(1), (2)	1975(1) s.57(1), (5); 1986 s.39, Sch. 3, para. 3(3)
(3)	1975(1) s.57(4); 1982(2) s.39(2); 1989 s.26, Sch. 7, para. 12
Part III	
para. 10(1)	1986 s.39, Sch. 3, para. 7
(2), (3)	1975(1) s.62
Part IV	
para. 11(1)	1975(1) s.59A(1), (10B); 1986 s.39, Sch. 3, para. 5(1); 1989 s.26, Sch. 7, para. 13; 1990 s.3(1), (4)
(2), (3)	1975(1) s.59A(1A), (1B); 1990 s.3(2)
(4)–(7)	1975(1) s.59A(2)–(5); 1986 s.39, Sch. 3, para. 5(1)
(8)	1975(1) s.59A(6); 1986 s.39, Sch. 3, para. 5(1); 1990 s.3(3)
(9)	1975(1) s.59A(7); 1986 s.39, Sch. 3, para. 5(1)
(10)	1975(1) s.59A(8); 1986 s.39, Sch. 3, para. 5(1); 1988(1) s.16, Sch. 4, para. 12(a)
(11)	1988(1) s.2(3)
(12)	1975(1) s.59A(9); 1986 s.39, Sch. 3, para. 5(1)
(13)	1975(1) s.59A(10); 1986 s.39, Sch. 3, para. 5(1)

Provision	Derivation
(14)	1975(1) s.59A(10A); 1988(1) s.16, Sch. 4, para. 12(b)
para. 12(1), (2)	1988(1) s.2(4), (5)
(3), (4)	1988(1) s.2(5A), (5B); 1989 s.17(5)
(5)	1988(1) s.2(6)
(6)	1988(1) s.2(7); 1989 s.17(6)
Part V	
para. 13(1)	1975(1) s.59B(1); 1988(1) s.2(1); 1989 s.7, Sch. 1, para. 8(2)
(2), (3)	1975(1) s.59B(2), (3); 1988(1) s.2(1)
(4)	1975(1) s.59B(5); 1988(1) s.2(1); 1989 s.7, Sch. 1, para. 8(5); Benefits Order art. 3(4) Sch. 1
(5)	1975(1) s.59B(5A); 1989 s.17(3)
(6)	1975(1) s.59B(6); 1988(1) s.2(1)
(7)	Drafting
(8), (9)	1975(1) s.59B(7), (8); 1989 s.7, Sch. 1, para. 8(6)
(10)	1975(1) s.59B(9); 1990 s.3(6)
(11)	1975(1) s.59A(10A); 1988(1) s.16, Sch. 4, para. 12(b)
Part VI	
para. 14(1)	1988(1) s.2, Sch. 1, paras. 2, 3
(2)	1975(1) s.168(1), Sch. 20 "deceased"
para. 15(1)–(3)	1975(1) s.67(1), (2); 1977 s.22(4); 1988(1) s.2, Sch. 1, para. 2
(4)	1975(1) s.67(3)
para. 16	1975(1) s.68; 1988(1) s.2, Sch. 1, para. 2
para. 17	1975(1) s.69; 1988(1) s.2, Sch. 1, para. 3
para. 18	1975(1) s.70; 1984 s.13, Sch. 5, para. 5; 1988 (1) s.2, Sch. 1, para. 2
para. 19	1975(1) s.70, Sch. 9, para. 1; 1988(1) s.2, Sch. 1, para. 2
para. 20	1975(1) s.75; 1988(1) s.2, Sch. 1, paras. 2, 6(a)
para. 21	1977 s.9; 1988(1) s.2, Sch. 1, para. 6(b)
Sch. 8	
Part I	
para. 1	1975 (Old Cases) s.1
para. 2(1)	1975 (Old Cases) s.2(1); 1990 s.16(8)(a)
(2)–(5)	1975 (Old Cases) s.2(2)–(5)
(6), (7)	1975 (Old Cases) s.2(6); The Social Security Act 1986 (Commencement No. 5) Order 1987 (S.I. 1987/354) art. 3; Benefits Order art. 6
(8)	1975 (Old Cases) s.2(7)
para. 3	1975 (Old Cases) s.3
para. 4(1)	1975 (Old Cases) s.5(1); 1990 s.16(8)(a)
(2)–(4)	1975 (Old Cases) s.5(2)–(4)
para. 5(1)	1975 (Old Cases) s.6(1)
(2)	1975 (Old Cases) s.6(2); 1980(1) s.4(3)
(3), (4)	1975 (Old Cases) s.6(3), (4)
(5)	1977 s.10, Sch. 1, para. 6
para. 6(1)	1975 (Old Cases) s.7(1)
(2), (3)	1975 (Old Cases) s.7(2); The Social Security Act 1986 (Commencement No. 5) Order 1987 (S.I. 1987/354) art. 3; Benefits Order art. 6
(4)	1975 (Old Cases) s.7(3); 1982(2) s.48(5), Sch. 4, para. 18(2); 1984 s.13, Sch. 5, para. 8(a); 1986, s.86(1), Sch. 10, para. 68(2)(a)

Provision	Derivation
(5)	1975 (Old Cases) s.7(4); 1984 s.13, Sch. 5, para. 8(b); 1986 s.86, Sch. 10, para. 68(2) (b)
(6)	1975 (Old Cases) s.7(5)
Part II	
para. 7(1)	1975(1) s.159(1)
(2)	1975(1) s.159(3)
Part III	
para. 8(1) "corresponding disablement pension rate"	1975 (Old Cases) s.14(1) "corresponding disablement pension rate"
"the 1967 Act"	Drafting
"injury pension"	1975(1) s.159(2) "injury pension"
"the original Industrial Injuries Act"	Drafting
"prescribed"	1975 (Old Cases) s.14(1) "prescribed"
"workmen's compensation"	1975 (Old Cases) s.14(1) "workmen's compensation"
"the Workmen's Compensation Acts"	1975 (Old Cases) s.14(1) "the Workmen's Compensation Acts"
(2)	1975 (Old Cases) s.14(1) "pneumoconiosis"
(3), (4)	1975 (Old Cases) s.14(2), (3)
(5)	1975 (Old Cases) s.14(4); 1977 s.11(5)
(6)	1986 s.39, Sch. 3, para. 16
Sch. 9	
paras. 1–4	1975(3) s.4(1), Sch. 1, paras. 1–4
para. 5	1975(3) s.4(1), Sch. 1, para. 5; 1984 s.11, Sch. 4, para. 13
Sch. 10	1975(3) s.4(2), Sch. 2
Sch. 11	
paras. 1–4	1982(2) s.3(3), Sch. 1, paras. 1–4
para. 5	1982(2) s.3(3), Sch. 1, para. 5; 1984 s.11, Sch. 4, para. 15(b)
paras. 6–8	1982(2) s.3(3), Sch. 1, paras. 6–8
Sch. 12	
para. 1	1982(2) s.10, Sch. 2, para. 1; 1985 s.18(6)(a)
paras. 2–4	1982(2) s.10, Sch. 2, paras. 2–4
para. 5	1982(2) s.10, Sch. 2, para. 1A; 1985 s.18(6)(b)
para. 6	1982(2) s.10, Sch. 2, para. 6
Sch. 13	
para. 1	1986 s.49, Sch. 4, para. 11; 1988(1) s.16, Sch. 4, para. 19(1)
para. 2	1986 s.49, Sch. 4, para. 11A; 1988(1) s.16, Sch. 4, para. 19(2)
para. 3	1986 s.49, Sch. 4, para. 12

TABLE OF DESTINATIONS

EDUCATION (SCOTLAND) ACT 1962
c.47

1962	c.47
s.145(16)	s.28(6)

LOCAL GOVERNMENT (SCOTLAND) ACT 1973
c.65

1973	c.65
s.129	s.28(6)
Sched. 11,	
para. 12	28(6)

INDUSTRIAL INJURIES AND DISEASES (OLD CASES) ACT 1975
c.5

1975	c.5	1975	c.5	1975	c.5
s.1	Sched. 8 Pt. I, para. 1	s.5(1)	Sched. 8 Pt. I, para. 4(1)	s.7(2)	Sched. 8 Pt. I, para. 6(2), (3)
2(1)	Sched. 8 Pt. I, para. 2(1)	(2)	Sched. 8 Pt. I, para. 4(2)–(4)	(3)	Sched. 8 Pt. I, para. 6(4)
(2)	Sched. 8 Pt. I, para. 2(2)–(5)	(3)	Sched. 8 Pt. I, para. 4(2)–(4)	(4)	Sched. 8 Pt. I, para. 6(5)
(3)	Sched. 8 Pt. I, para. 2(2)–(5)	(4)	Sched. 8 Pt. I, para. 4(2)–(4)	(5)	Sched. 8 Pt. I, para. 6(6)
(4)	Sched. 8 Pt. I, para. 2(2)–(5)	6(1)	Sched. 8 Pt. I, para. 5(1)	8(1)	175(2), 176(3)
(5)	Sched. 8 Pt. I, para. 2(2)–(5)	(2)	Sched. 8 Pt. I, para. 5(2)	14(1)	Sched. 8 Pt. I, para. 8(1), (2)
(6)	Sched. 8 Pt. I, para. 2(6), (7)	(3)	Sched. 8 Pt. I, para. 5(3), (4)	(2)	Sched. 8 Pt. I, para. 8(3), (4)
(7)	Sched. 8 Pt. I, para. 2(8)	(4)	Sched. 8 Pt. I, para. 5(3), (4)	(3)	Sched. 8 Pt. I, para. 8(3), (4)
3	Sched. 8 Pt. I, para. 3	7(1)	Sched. 8 Pt. I, para. 6(1)	(4)	Sched. 8 Pt. I, para. 8(5)
4(8)	175(2), 176(3)				

SOCIAL SECURITY ACT 1975
c.14

1975	c.14	1975	c.14	1975	c.14
s.1(1)	s.1(1)	s.2	2	s.4(6E)	9(3), (4)
(3)	1(2), (3)	3(1)	3(1)	(7)	6(5)
(4)	1(4), Sched. 1, para. 1(1), (2), (3), (4), (6), (7), (8), para. 2, para. 3(1), (2), para. 4, para. 5, para. 6(1), (2), (3), (4), (7), (8), para. 7 (1)–(10), (11), (12), (13), para. 8(1)(a)–(q), (2), (3), paras. 9–11	(1A)	4(1)	4A	10
		(1B)	4(2), (3)	7(1)	11(1)
		(1C)	4(2), (3)	(4)	11(3)
		(1D)	4(4)	(5)	11(4)
		(2)	2(2), (3)	(6)	11(5)
		(3)	2(2), (3)	7A(1)	12(1), (2)
		(4)	4(5)	(2)	12(1), (2)
		4(1)	5(1)	(3)	12(3)
		(2)	6(1), (4)	(4)–(8)	12(4)–(8)
		(3)	6(3)	8(1)	13(1)
		(4)	7	(2)	13(2)
		(5)	7	(a)	13(3)
		(6)	8(1)–(3)	(2A)	13(4)
		(6A)	8(1)–(3)	(2B)	13(5)
		(6B)	8(1)–(3)	(2C)	13(6)
(4A)	1(5)	(6C)	9(1), (4)	(2D)	13(7)
(6)	1(6)	(6D)	9(2)		

1975	c.14
s.9(1)	15(1), (2), (5)
(2)	15(3)
(3)	16(1), (2), Sched. 1
(4)	16(3), Sched. 2, para. 2, para. 3(1), (2), (3), (4), (5), para. 6(2), paras. 7–9
(5)	16(4)
(6)	16(5)
(7)	17(1), (2)
(8)	17(1), (2)
(9)	17(3)–(6)
10(1)	18(1)
(2)	18(2)
11	19(1)–(3)
12(1)	20(1)
(2)	20(2)
13(1)	21(1), (2)
(2)	22(1), (2)
(b)	84(2)
(3)	22(4)
(4)	22(5)
(5)	22(3), 23(1), (3)
(5A)	23(4)
(5AA)	22(6)
(5B)	24(1)
(5C)	24(2)
(5ZA)	23(2)
(6)	21(3), (5), Sched. 3, para. 1(1), (2), (3), (4), (5), (6), para. 2(1), (2), (3), (4), (5), (6), para. 3(1), (2), (3), para. 4(1), (2), (3), para. 5(1), (2), (3), (4), (5), (6), (7)
(7)	21(6)
(8)	21(4), Sched. 3, para. 7(1), (2), (3), (4), paras. 8–9
14	Sched. 4 Pt. I, paras. 1–2
(1)	25(1), 31(1)
(2)	25(2), 31(2)
(2A)	31(3)
(3)	25(3), 31(4)
(4)	25(4), 31(5)
(6)	25(5), (6), 31(6), (7)
(8)	25(7), 31(8)
15(1)	33(1)
(2)	33(2)
(3)	33(3)
(4)	33(4), (5)
(5)	33(6)
(5A)	33(7), (8)
(5B)	33(7), (8)
(6)	33(9)
15A(1)	33(10), (11)
(2)	33(10), (11)

1975	c.14
s.16	Sched. 4 Pt. I, para. 3
(1)	34(1), (2)
(2)	34(3)
(2B)(a)	34(4)
(2C)(a)	34(5)
(2D)(a)	34(6)
(3)	34(7)
17(1)	57(1)
(2)	57(3)
(2A)	57(4)
(2B)	57(5)
(2C)	57(6), (7)
(2D)	57(6), (7)
(3)	57(8)
(4)	57(9), (10)
(5)	57(9), (10)
18(1)	26(1)
(2)–(2B)	21(2)–(4)
(3)	26(5)
(4)	26(6)
19(1)	27(1), (2)
(1A)	21(1), 27(2)
(2)	27(3)
20A	29
(1)	28(1)
(1A)	28(2)
(2)	31(2), 32(1), 59(1), (2)
(3)	28(3), 31(2), 32(1), 59(1), (2)
(3A)	28(4)
(4)	28(5)
(5)	28(6)
(d)	32(3), 59(3)
22	Sched. 4 Pt. I, para. 4
(1)	35(1), (2), (3)
(2)	35(1), (2), (3)
(3)	35(1), (2), (3)
(4)	57(2)
(4A)	35(4)
(5)	35(5)
(6)	35(6)
(7)	35(7)
24	Sched. 4 Pt. II
(1)	36(1), (2)
(2)	36(1), (2)
(3)	36(3)
25(1)	37(1)
(2)	37(2)
(3)	37(3), (4)
(4)	37(3), (4)
26(1)	38(1)
(2)	39(4), (5)
(3)	38(2), (3)
(4)	38(2), (3)
27(2)	Sched. 3, para. 5(8)
(6)	43(1)
28(1)	44(1)
(1A)	44(2)
(7)	47(1)
(7A)(a)	47(2)
(7B)(a)	47(3)
(7C)(a)	47(4)

1975	c.14
s.28(8)	47(5)
29(1)	49(1)
(2)	49(2), (3)
(3)	49(2), (3)
(4)	49(4)
(5)	49(5)
(6)	49(6)
(7)	50(1), Sched. 4 Pt. I, para. 5
(8)	50(2)
(9)	49(7), (8)
(9A)	49(7), (8)
30(3)	54(1), (2)
(4)	54(3)
(5)	54(4)
31	56(1), (2), Sched. 4 Pt. I, para. 6
(6)	Sched. 3, para. 6
33(1)	60(1)
(2)	60(1)
(3)	60(4), (5), (6)
(4)	60(7)
34	63
35	Sched. 4 Pt. III, para. 1
(1)	64
(2)	65(1)
(2A)	65(2)
(2B)	66
(2C)	66
(3)	65(3)
(4)	65(4)
(a)	65(6)
(4A)	65(5)
(5A)	67(1)
(6)	67(2)
36	65(1), (2), (3), (4), Sched. 4 Pt. III, para. 1
(4A)	68(5)
(5)	68(6), (7)
(6)	68(6), (7)
(6A)	68(8), (9)
(6B)	68(8), (9)
(6C)	68(10)
(7)	68(11)
(8)	68(13)
36A	69, Sched. 4 Pt. III, para. 3
37	Sched. 4 Pt. III, para. 4
(1)	70(1)
(2)	70(2)
(3)	70(3), (4), (5)
(4)	70(3), (4), (5)
(5)	70(3), (4), (5)
(6)	6(10), 70(6)
(7)	70(7), (8), (9)
(8)	70(7), (8), (9)
(9)	70(7), (8), (9)
37ZA	71

1975	c.14
s.37ZB	72
37ZC	73
37ZD	75
37ZE	76
38	Sched. 4 Pt. III, para. 5
(1)	77, (7)
(2)	77(1), (2)
(3)	77(2), (3)
(4)	77(8)
(5)	77(9)
(6)	77(10)
39	Sched. 4 Pt. III, paras. 6–7
(1)(a)	78(1), (2)
(b)	78(2)
(c)	78(3), (4)
(2)	78(5)
(2A)	78(6)
(3)	78(7), (8)
(3A)	78(7), (8)
(4)	78(9)
40	79, Sched. 4 Pt. III, para. 8
41–49	Sched. 4 Pt. IV, col. (1)–(3)
41(1)	80(1)
(2)	80(2)
(2A)	80(3)
(2B)	80(4)
(2D)	80(7)
(4)	80(5), (6)
(5)	80(5), (6)
43(1)	56(1), (3), (4), 77(4), (5), 81(1), (2)
(2)	77(6), 81(3)
44(1)	82(1)
(2)	82(2)
(3)(a)	82(3)
(c)	82(4)
(4)	82(5)
45(1)	83(1)
(2)	83(2)
(2A)	83(3)
45A(1)	84(1)
(2)	84(2)
(3)	84(3)
46(1)	85(1)
(2)	85(2)
(3)	85(3)
(4)	85(4)
47(1)	86(1)
(1A)	86(2)
47A(a)	87(1)
(b)	87(2)
47B	89
48(1)	88
49	90
49A	91
50(1)	94(1)
(1A)	94(2)
(3)	94(3)
(4)	94(4)
(5)	94(5)
(6)	94(6)
50A(1)	102(1), (2)
(2)	102(1), (2)
(3)	102(3)
51	95(1)–(3)
52	98–101
54	98–101

1975	c.14
s.55	98–101
57(1)	103(1), Sched. 7 Pt. II, para. 9(1), (2)
(1A)	103(2), (3), (4)
(1B)	103(2)–(4)
(1C)	103(2)–(4)
(3)	103(5), Sched. 6, paras. 1–5, para. 6(1)–(5), para. 7, para. 8
(4)	103(6), Sched. 7 Pt. II, para. 9(3)
(5)	Sched. 4 Pt. V, para. 9, Sched. 7 Pt. II, para. 9(1), (2)
(6)	103(7), (8), Sched. 4 Pt. V, para. 1
58	Sched. 4 Pt. V, para. 5, Sched. 7 Pt. I, para. 2
59	Sched. 4 Pt. V, para. 6
(1)	Sched. 7 Pt. I, para. 3(1)
(1A)(a)	Sched. 7, para. 3(2)
(1B)	Sched. 7 Pt. IV, para. 11(2), (3)
(1C)(a)	Sched. 7 Pt. I, para. 3(4)
(2)	Sched. 7 Pt. I, para. 3(5), (6)
(3)	Sched. 7 Pt. I, para. 3(5), (6)
(4)	Sched. 7 Pt. I, para. 3(7), (8)
(5)	Sched. 7 Pt. I, para. 3(10)
(10B)	Sched. 7 Pt. IV, para. 11(1)
59A(1)	Sched. 7 Pt. IV, para. 11(1)
(1A)	Sched. 7 Pt. IV, para. 11(2), (3)
(2)	Sched. 7 Pt. IV, para. 11(4)–(7)
(3)	Sched. 7 Pt. IV, para. 11(4)–(7)
(4)	Sched. 7 Pt. IV, para. 11(4)–(7)
(5)	Sched. 7 Pt. IV, para. 11(4)–(7)
(6)	Sched. 7 Pt. IV, para. 11(8)

1975	c.14
s.59A(7)	Sched. 7 Pt. IV, para. 11(9)
(8)	Sched. 7 Pt. IV, para. 11(10)
(9)	Sched. 7 Pt. IV, para. 11(12)
(10)	Sched. 7 Pt. IV, para. 11(13)
(10A)	Sched. 7 Pt. IV, para. 11(14), Pt. V, para. 13(11)
59B(1)	Sched. 7 Pt. V, para. 13(1)
(2)	Sched. 7 Pt. V, para. 13(2), (3), (4)
(3)	Sched. 7 Pt. V, para. 13(2), (3)
(5A)	Sched. 7 Pt. V, para. 13(5)
(6)	Sched. 7 Pt. V, para. 13(6)
(7)	Sched. 7 Pt. V, para. 13(8), (9)
(8)	Sched. 7 Pt. V, para. 13(8), (9)
(9)	Sched. 7 Pt. V, para. 13(10)
61	Sched. 4 Pt. V, para. 2
(1)	104(1), (2)
(2)	104(1), (2)
(3)	104(3), (4)
(4)	104(3), (4)
62	Sched. 7 Pt. III, para. 10(2), (3)
63	105, Sched. 4 Pt. V, para. 3
64	Sched. 4 Pt. V, para. 7
(1)	Sched. 7 Pt. I, para. 4(1)
(1A)	Sched. 7 Pt. I, para. 4(3)
(1B)	Sched. 7 Pt. I, para. 4(4)
(1C)	Sched. 7 Pt. I, para. 4(5)
(1D)	Sched. 7 Pt. I, para. 4(5), (6)
(2)	Sched. 7 Pt. I, para. 4(2)
65	122(1)
(1)	Sched. 7 Pt. I, para. 5(1)
(2)	Sched. 7 Pt. I, para. 5(2)
66(1)	Sched. 7 Pt. I, para. 6(1)

1975	c.14
s.66(2)........	Sched. 4 Pt. V, para. 8, Sched. 7 Pt. I, para. 6(2)
(3)........	Sched. 7 Pt. I, para. 6(3)–(6)
(4)........	Sched. 7 Pt. I, para. 6(3)–(6)
(5)........	Sched. 7 Pt. I, para. 6(3)–(6)
(6)........	Sched. 7 Pt. I, para. 6(3)–(6)
(7)........	Sched. 7 Pt. I, para. 6(3)–(6)
66A	Sched. 7 Pt. I, para. 7
67(1)........	Sched. 7 Pt. VI, para. 15(1)–(3)
(2)........	Sched. 7 Pt. VI, para. 15(1)–(3)
(3)........	Sched. 7 Pt. VI, para. 15(4)
68	Sched. 4 Pt. V, para. 10, Sched. 7 Pt. VI, para. 16
69	Sched. 4 Pt. V, para. 11, Sched. 7 Pt. VI, para. 17
70	Sched. 4 Pt. V, para. 12, Sched. 7 Pt. VI, para. 18, para. 19
75	Sched. 7 Pt. VI, para. 20
76(1)–(4)	108(1)–(4)
(4A)	108(5)
(5)........	108(6)
77(1)........	109(1)
(2)........	109(2)
(3)........	109(3)
(4)........	109(4), (5), (6)
(5)........	103(7)
78	110
82(5)........	113(1), (2)
(6)........	113(1), (2)
83	113(3)
84(1)........	114(1), (2)
(4)........	114(3)
(5)........	114(4)
84A	92, Sched. 7 Pt. I, para. 8
91	Sched. 4 Pt. V, para. 3, para. 4
(1)........	107(1)
(2)........	107(2)
127(1).......	115(1)
(2)........	115(2), (3)
128(1)–(3) ...	116
129	117

1975	c.14
s.130	118
131	119
132(1).......	120(1)
(2)........	120(2)
(3)........	120(3)
156	97
157	96
159(1).......	Sched. 8 Pt. I, para. 7(1)
(2)........	Sched. 8 Pt. I, para. 8(1)
(3)........	Sched. 8 Pt. I, para. 7(2)
162	121, 175(3)
166(1).......	175(2)
(2)........	175(3)
(3)........	175(4)
(3A).....	175(5)
(5)........	175(7)
(6)........	175(8)
(7)........	175(9)
167(1).......	176(1)
(3)........	176(3)
168(1).......	20(2), 122(1), (4)–(6), 173, 175(1), Sched. 7 Pt. VI, para. 14(2)
(4)........	175(10)
169(2).......	Sched. 1
Sched. 1,	
para. 1(1) ...	Sched. 1, para. 1(1)
(1A) .	Sched. 1, para. 1(2)
(1B) .	Sched. 1, para. 1(3), (4)
(1C) .	Sched. 1, para. 1(3), (4)
(1D) .	Sched. 1, para. 1(6)
(2)...	Sched. 1, para. 1(7), (8)
(3)...	Sched. 1, para. 1(7), (8)
(4)...	Sched. 3, paras. 1(6), 2(6)
2	Sched. 1, para. 2
3(1)...	Sched. 1, para. 3(1)
(2)...	Sched. 1, para. 3(2)
(3)...	Sched. 1, para. 3(3)
4	Sched. 1, para. 4
4A....	Sched. 1, para. 5
5(1)...	Sched. 1, para. 6(1)
(1A) .	Sched. 1, para. 6(2)
(1B) .	Sched. 1, para. 6(3), (4)
(1C) .	Sched. 1, para. 6 (3), (4)
(2)...	Sched. 1, para. 6(7)

1975	c.14
Sched. 1—cont.	
para. 5(3) ...	Sched. 1, para. 6(8)
5A(1)–(10)	Sched. 1, para. 7(1)–(10)
(11)..	Sched. 1, para. 7(11)
(12)..	Sched. 1, para. 7(12), (13)
(13)..	Sched. 1, para. 7(12), (13)
6(1)(a)	Sched. 1, para. 8(1)(a)
(aa)	Sched. 1, para. 8(1)(b)
(b)–(e)	Sched. 1, para. 8(1)(c)–(f)
(f)	Sched. 1, para. 8(1)(g)
(g)	Sched. 1, para. 8(1)(l)
(gg)	Sched. 1, para. 8(1)(h)
(ggg)	Sched. 1, para. 8(1)(i)
(gh)	Sched. 1, para. 8(1)(j)–(k)
(gj)	Sched. 1, para. 8(1)(j)–(k)
(h)	Sched. 1, para. 8(1)(m)
(j)–(m)	Sched. 1, para. 8(1)(n)–(q)
(2)...	Sched. 1, para. 8(2), (3)
(3)...	Sched. 1, para. 8(2), (3)
7	Sched. 1, paras. (9)–(10)
8	Sched. 1, paras. 9–10
9	Sched. 1, para. 11
Sched. 2,	
para. 3(3) ...	Sched. 2, para. 3(3), (4)
(4)...	Sched. 2, para. 3(5)
4	Sched. 2, para. 9
7(1)...	Sched. 2, para. 6(1)
(2)...	Sched. 2, para. 6(2)
8	Sched. 2, paras. 7, 8
9	Sched. 2, paras. 7, 8
Sched. 3,	
para. 1(1) ...	Sched. 3, paras. 1(1), 2(1)

1975   **c.14**

Sched. 3—*cont.*
para. 1(2) ...   Sched. 3,
     paras. 1(2),
     2(2)
   (b)(i)   Sched. 3,
     para. 1(4)
    (ii)   Sched. 3,
     para. 2(4)
   (3) ...   Sched. 3,
     paras. 1(3),
     2(3)
   (b)(i)   Sched. 3,
     para. 1(3)
    (ii)   Sched. 3,
     para. 2(3)
  3(1) ...   Sched. 3,
     para. 3(1)
   (2) ...   Sched. 3,
     para. 3(2), (3)
   (3) ...   Sched. 3,
     para. 3(2), (3)
  4(1) ...   Sched. 3,
     para. 4(1), (2)
   (2) ...   Sched. 3,
     para. 4(3)
  5(1) ...   Sched. 3,
     para. 5(1)
   (2) ...   Sched. 3,
     para. 5(2)
   (3) ...   Sched. 3,
     para. 5(3), (4)
   (4) ...   Sched. 3,
     para. 5(5), (6)
   (5) ...   Sched. 3,
     para. 5(5), (6)
   (6) ...   Sched. 3,
     para. 5(7)
  6 .....   Sched. 3,
     para. 6
  8(1) ...   Sched. 3,
     para. 7(1)
   (2) ...   Sched. 3,
     para. 7(2)
   (3) ...   Sched. 3,
     para. 7(3), (4)
  10 ....   Sched. 3,
     para. 10
  13 ....   Sched. 3,
     para. 9

1975   **c.14**

Sched. 4 Pt. I,
para. 1(a) ...   Sched. 4 Pt.
     I, para. 1
   (b) ...   Sched. 4 Pt.
     I, para. 2
  3 .....   Sched. 4 Pt.
     I, para. 3
  4 .....   Sched. 4 Pt.
     I, para. 4
  9 .....   Sched. 4 Pt.
     I, para. 5
  10 ....   Sched. 4 Pt.
     I, para. 6
  Pt. IA..   Sched. 4 Pt.
     II
Pt. III,
para. 1 .....   Sched. 4 Pt.
     III, para. 1
  2 .....   Sched. 4 Pt.
     III, para. 2
  2A ....   Sched. 4 Pt.
     III, para. 3
  3 .....   Sched. 4 Pt.
     III, para. 4
  4 .....   Sched. 4 Pt.
     III, para. 5
  5 .....   Sched. 4 Pt.
     III, para. 6
  5A ....   Sched. 4 Pt.
     III, para. 7
  6 .....   Sched. 4 Pt.
     III, para. 8
Pt. IV,
col. (1) .....   Sched. 4 Pt.
     IV, col. (1)
  (2) .....   Sched. 4 Pt.
     IV, col. (2)
Pt. V,
para. 2 .....   Sched. 4 Pt.
     V, para. 9
  3 .....   Sched. 4 Pt.
     V, para. 1
  4 .....   Sched. 4 Pt.
     V, para. 5
  5 .....   Sched. 4 Pt.
     V, para. 6
  8 .....   Sched. 4 Pt.
     V, para. 3,
     para. 4

1975   **c.14**

Sched. 4—*cont.*
Pt. V—*cont.*
para. 10 ....   Sched. 4 Pt.
     V, para. 7
  12 ....   Sched. 4 Pt.
     V, para. 8
  13 ....   Sched. 4 Pt.
     V, para. 10
  14 ....   Sched. 4 Pt.
     V, para. 11
  15 ....   Sched. 4 Pt.
     V, para. 12
  16 ....   Sched. 4 Pt.
     V, para. 4
Sched. 8,
para. 1 .....   Sched. 6,
     para. 1
  2 .....   Sched. 6,
     paras. 2, 3
  3 .....   Sched. 6,
     paras. 2, 3
  4(1) ...   Sched. 6,
     para. 6(1), (2)
   (2) ...   Sched. 6,
     para. 6(3), (4),
     (5)
   (3) ...   Sched. 6,
     para. 6(3), (4),
     (5)
   (4) ...   Sched. 6,
     para. 6(3), (4),
     (5)
  4A ....   Sched. 6,
     para. 4
  5 .....   Sched. 6,
     para. 7
  5A ....   Sched. 6,
     para. 5
  6 .....   Sched. 6,
     para. 8
Sched. 9,
para. 1 .....   Sched. 7 Pt.
     VI, para. 19
Sched. 20 .....   20(2),
     122(1), (4)–(6),
     173, 175(1),
     Sched. 7 Pt.
     VI, para. 14(2)

CRIMINAL PROCEDURE (SCOTLAND) ACT 1975
C.21

1975   **c.21**

s.289F ....   Sched. 1,
     para. 3(2)
  289G ....   Sched. 1,
     para. 3(2)

SOCIAL SECURITIES PENSIONS ACT 1975
c.60

1975	c.60
s.1(1)........s.5(1)	
(2).........	5(2)
(3).........	5(3)
3(2).........	19(5)
(3).........	19(4), (5)
(4).........	19(6)
4(1).........	6(2)
(2).........	11(2)
5(1).........	14(1)
(2).........	14(2), (3)
6(1).........	44(3), (4)
(2).........	45(1)
(2A).........	45(2), (3)
(2B).........	45(4), (5)
(3).........	45(6), (7)
(4).........	44(5)
(5).........	44(6)
(6).........	44(7)
7	50(3), (4)
8(1).........	51(1)
(2).........	51(2)
(3).........	51(4)
9(1).........	52(1)
(2).........	52(2), (3)
(3).........	52(2), (3)
10(1).........	53(1)
(2).........	53(2)
12	55, Sched. 5, paras. 1, 2(1), (2), (3), (5), (6), (7), (8), 3, 4(1)–(5), 5(1)–(3), 6(1)–(4), 7(1), 8(1)–(4)
13(1).........	39(1)
(2).........	39(2)
(3).........	39(1)
14	33(3)
15(1).........	40(1)
(1A).........	40(2)
(2).........	40(3)
(3).........	40(4)
(4).........	40(5)
(5).........	40(7)
(6).........	40(8)
16(1).........	41(1)
(2).........	41(2), (3)
(3).........	41(2), (3)
(4).........	41(4), (5)
(5).........	41(7)

1975	c.60
s.16(6).........	41(8)
A	42
18(1).........	25(4), 31(5)
19(2).........	Sched. 3, para. 5(2)
(5).........	60(7)
20(1).........	48(1)
(2).........	48(3)
24(1)(b)	62(1)
(c)	62(1)
(2).........	62(2)
25(1).........	42(3), (4)
(2).........	43(5)
60A	45(6), (7), Sched. 5, paras. 2(4), 7(2)
62(1).........	176(1)
65	122(1)
(1).........	5(1), 20(1), 22(1), (2), (4), (5), (6), 31(6), (7), 33(3)–(5), 37(1), 38(1), 44(1), 50(1), 54(3), 60(4)–(6), Sched. 1, para. 8(1)(g), Sched. 4 Pt. I, para. 5, Pt. V, para. 10
Sched. 1, para. 1	Sched. 5, para. 1
2(2) ...	Sched. 5, para. 2(2)
(3) ...	Sched. 5, para. 2(3)
(4) ...	Sched. 5, para. 2(5)
(4A) .	Sched. 5, para. 2(6)
2(5) ...	Sched. 5, para. 2(7)
(6) ...	Sched. 5, para. 2(8)
3	Sched. 5, para. 3
4(1) ...	Sched. 5, para. 4(1)
(2) ...	Sched. 5, para. 4(2)

1975	c.60
Sched. 1—cont.	
para. 4(2A) .	Sched. 5, para. 4(3)
(3)...	Sched. 5, para. 4(4)
(4)...	Sched. 5, para. 4(5)
4A(1) .	Sched. 5, para. 5(1), (2)
(1A)	Sched. 5, para. 5(3)
(2)	Sched. 5, para. 6(1), (2)
(2A)(a)	Sched. 5, para. 6(3)
(b)	Sched. 5, para. 6(4)
(3) .	Sched. 5, para. 7(1)
5(1)...	Sched. 5, para. 8(1), (2)
(2)...	Sched. 5, para. 8(1), (2)
(3)...	Sched. 5, para. 8(3)
(4)...	Sched. 5, para. 8(4)
Sched. 4,	
para. 36(a) ..	5(1)
37	20(1)
38(a) ..	22(1), (2)
(b)..	22(4)
39(b)..	25(5), (6), 31(6), (7)
40(b)..	33(3)
(c)..	33(4), (5)
41	37(1)
42	38(1)
43	44(1)
44	50(1)
45	54(3)
46	60(4), (5), (6)
61	Sched. 1, para. 8(1)(g)
62	Sched. 4 Pt. I, para. 5
63	Sched. 4 Pt. V, para. 10
64	122(1)

CHILD BENEFIT ACT 1975
c.61

1975	c.61
s.1(1)........s.141	
2(1).........	142(1)
(1A).........	142(2), (3)
(1B).........	142(2), (3)
(2).........	142(4), (5)
(3).........	142(4), (5)
3(1).........	143(1), (2)

1975	c.61
s.3(3).........	143(3)
(4).........	143(4), (5)
(5).........	143(4), (5)
4(1).........	144(1), (2), Sched. 9, paras. 1–5

1975	c.61
s.4(2).........	144(3), Sched. 9, para. 5
5(1)–(4)	145(1)–(4)
9(2).........	147(5)
13	146

1975	c.61
s.21(1).......	37(1), (2),
	56(1), (2), (3),
	(4), 77(4), (5),
	(6), (9), 80(1),
	(5), (6),
	81(1)–(3),
	83(2), 85(2),
	86(1), 122(1),
	(4), (5), Sched.
	7 Pt. I, paras.
	4(1), 5(1), (2),
	6(1)
22(1).......	82(1), (2),
	(4)
(a).....	145(5)
(b).....	175(1)
(2)........	175(2)
(3)........	176(1)
(5)........	176(3)
(6)........	175(3)
(7)........	175(4)
(7A)......	175(5)
(8)........	145(6)

1975	c.61
s.22(9).......	145(7)
24(1)........	147(1)
(2)........	147(2)
(3)(b).....	147(3)
(4)........	147(4)
(5)........	147(6)
Sched. 1,	
para. 1	Sched. 9,
	paras. 1–4
2	Sched. 9,
	paras. 1–4
3	Sched. 9,
	paras. 1–4
4	Sched. 9,
	paras. 1–4
5	Sched. 9,
	para. 5
Sched. 2	Sched. 9,
	para. 5
Sched. 4,	
para. 9(a)...	37(1)
(b)...	37(2)
10	56(1), (2)

1975	c.61
Sched. 4—cont.	
para. 12(a)..	77(1)
(c)..	77(9)
13	80(1), (5),
	(6)
15(a)..	77(4), (5),
	81(1), (2)
(b)..	56(5), 77(6),
	81(3)
16(a)..	82(1), (2)
(b)..	82(4)
17	83(2)
18	85(2)
19	86(1)
21(a)..	Sched. 7,
	para. 4(1)
22(a)..	Sched. 7,
	para. 5(1)
(b)..	Sched. 7 Pt.
	I, para. 5(2)
23	Sched. 7 Pt.
	I, para. 6(1)
38	122(4), (5)

EDUCATION (SCHOOL LEAVING DATES) ACT 1976
C.5

1976	c.5
s.2(4)..........s.6(1), 11(1),	
13(1)	

SOCIAL SECURITY (MISCELLANEOUS PROVISIONS) ACT 1977
C.5

1977	c.5
s.1(3)........	Sched. 1,
	para. 1(1)
(4)........	Sched. 1,
	para. 4
(5)........14(2), (3)	
2	22(7)
3(1)(b).....	Sched. 5,
	para. 2(3)
(c)......	Sched. 5,
	para. 2(5)
(d).....	Sched. 5,
	para. 2(8)
(e).....	Sched. 5,
	para. 3
4(1)........	43(2)
(4)........	40(7), 41(7)

1977	c.5
s.8(1)........	61(1)
(2)........	61(2)
9	Sched. 7 Pt.
	VI, para. 21
10	Sched. 8 Pt.
	I, para. 5(5)
11(5).......	Sched. 8 Pt.
	I, para. 8(5)
13(1).......	74(1)
(3).......	74(2)
17(3).......	95(4), (5)
(6).......	40(6)
18(1).......	112(1), (2)
(2).......	112(3)
22(1).......	122(3)

1977	c.5
s.22(2)........	56(1), (2)
(3).......	56(5), 77(6),
	81(3), Sched. 7
	Pt. I, para.
	5(2)
(4)........	Sched. 7 Pt.
	VI, para.
	15(1)–(3)
24(1)........	40(9), 175(1)
(3)........	175(2)–(5),
	(7)
(5)........	176(3)
Sched. 1,	
para. 6	Sched. 8 Pt.
	I, para. 5(5)

NATIONAL HEALTH SERVICE ACT 1977
C.49

1977	c.49
s.129 ....s.67(2)	
Sched. 15,	
para. 63	67(2)

EMPLOYMENT PROTECTION (CONSOLIDATION) ACT 1978
C.44

1978	c.44
s.159 ....s.112(3)	
Sched. 16,	
para. 29(d)..	112(3)

SOCIAL SECURITY ACT 1979
c.18

1979	c.18
s.2(2)........s.65(1)	
(3)........ 65(2)	
(5)........ 65(6)	
(6)........ 67(1)	
5 .... 33(4), (5),	
	34(3), 41(1),
	43(2), 48(1),
	(2), 51(1),
	52(4), 53(3),
	78(3), (4),
	Sched. 3, para.
	5(7), Sched. 4
	Pt. V, para. 6,
	Sched. 5,
	paras. 4(4),
	(5), 5(1), (2),
	6(1), (2), 7(1)
14(1)........ 6(5)	
18 .... 45(6), (7),	
	Sched. 5,
	paras. 2(4),
	7(2)

1979	c.18
s.21(4)....... 23(1), 25(5),	
	(6), 31(6), (7),
	33(4), (5),
	44(5), Sched.
	3, para. 7(3),
	(4), Sched. 5,
	para. 4(1), (2)
Sched. 1,	
para. 1 ..... 33(4), (5)	
2 ..... 78(3), (4)	
3 ..... Sched. 3,	
	para. 5(7)
4 ..... 51(1)	
5 ..... 48(1)	
6 ..... Sched. 5,	
	para. 4(4)
7 ..... Sched. 5,	
	paras. 5(1),
	(2), 6(1), (2),
	7(1)
8 ..... 43(2)	

1979	c.18
Sched. 1—cont.	
para. 10(a) .. 34(3)	
13 .... Sched. 4 Pt.	
	V, para. 6
14 .... 51(1)	
15 .... 52(4)	
16 .... 53(3)	
18 .... 41(1)	
20 .... 48(2)	
22 .... Sched. 5,	
	para. 4(5)
Sched. 3,	
para. 5 .....s.23(1)	
6 ..... 25(5), (6),	
	31(6), (7)
7 ..... 33(4), (5)	
10 .... Sched. 3,	
	para. 7(3), (4)
14 .... 44(5)	
23 .... Sched. 5,	
	para. 4(1), (2)

SOCIAL SECURITY ACT 1980
c.30

1980	c.30
s.2 ....s.65(5), 82(4),	
	85(2), 86(1),
	87(1), 122(6),
	Sched. 1, para.
	1(2)
3(11)....... Sched. 5,	
	para. 2(5)
4(3)........ Sched. 8 Pt.	
	I, para. 5(2)

1980	c.30
s.5 .... Sched. 7 Pt.	
	I, para. 6(1)
18 173	
21 ....82(1), (2)	
Sched. 1,	
para. 4 ..... Sched. 7 Pt.	
	I, para. 6(1)
(a)... 82(4)	
(b)... 85(2)	

1980	c.30
Sched. 1—cont.	
para. 5(1)... 87(1)	
(2)... 82(2), 86(1)	
6 ..... Sched. 7 Pt.	
	I, para. 6(1)
7 ..... 122(6)	
8 ..... 65(5)	
16 .... Sched. 1,	
	para. 1(2)
(a).. 82(1)	

SOCIAL SECURITY ACT (NO. 2) ACT 1980
c.39

1980	c.39
s.3(1)........s.57(1)	
(3)........ 47(1), Sched.	
	7 Pt. I, para.
	3(7), (8)
(4)........ 47(6), 57(9),	
	(10), 175(1),
	Sched. 7 Pt. I,
	para. 3(9)
5 .... 57(9), (10)	

1980	c.39
s.5(1)........ 30(1)	
(1A)....... 30(2)	
(2)........ 30(3)	
(3)........ 30(4),	
	122(1), 175(1)
(4)........ 176(1)	
(6)........ 173	
7(3)........ 175(2), (3),	
	(4)

1980	c.39
s.7(4)........ 176(3)	
39(2)........ 103(6)	
(4)....... 102(1), (2),	
	(3)
48(5)....... 94(4), (6),	
	107(1)
Sched. 4,	
para. 12(2) .. 94(4)	
(3) .. 94(6)	
15 .... 107(1)	

OIL AND GAS (ENTERPRISE) ACT 1982
c.23

1982	c.23
s.37 ....s.120(2), 162	
Sched. 3,	
para. 21 .... 120(2)	
44 164	

SOCIAL SECURITY AND HOUSING BENEFITS ACT 1982
C.24

1982	c.24
s.1(1)........	s.151(1), (2)
(2)........	151(1), (2)
(3)........	151(4), (5)
(4)........	151(4), (5)
(5)........	151(6)
2(1)........	152(1), (2)
(2)........	152(1), (2)
(3)........	152(3)
(3A)......	152(4)
(4)........	152(5), (6)
(5)........	152(5), (6)
3(1)–(4).....	153(1)–(4)
(3)........	Sched. 11, paras. 1–8
(4A)......	153(5)
(5)........	153(6), (7)
(6)........	153(6), (7)
(6A)......	153(8), (9)
(6B)......	153(8), (9)
(7)........	153(10), (11)
(9)........	153(12)
4(1)........	154(1)
(2)........	154(2)
(3)........	154(3), (4)
(4)........	154(3), (4)
5(1)–(3)....	155(1)–(3)
(4)........	155(4)
(5)........	155(5)
6..........	156
7(1)........	157(1)
(1A)......	157(2)
(1B)......	176(1)
(2)........	157(3)
9(1)........	158(1)
(1B)......	158(2)
(1C)......	159
(1D)......	158(3)
(1F).......	176(1)

1982	c.24
s.9(2)........	158(4)
(3)(b).....	158(5)
(c).....	158(5)
(4)........	Sched. 1, para. 6(5)
(5)........	Sched. 1, para. 6(6)
(6)........	158(6)
10.........	Sched. 12, paras. 1–6
22.........	162
23.........	4(1)
23A(1).....	151(3), 164(6)–(7)
26(1).......	163(1)
(2).......	163(2)
(5A).....	163(6)
(6).......	163(7)
(7).......	172
27(1).......	161(1), (2)
(2).......	161(1), (2)
(3).......	161(3)
37(1).......	4(1), (2), (3)
(2)........	Sched. 1, para. 11
39(2).......	Sched. 7 Pt. II, para. 9(3)
(3)........	31(3)
44(1)(b)....	172
(c)....	172
(d)....	172
(2)(a)....	172
(b)....	172
45(1).......	175(3), (4), 175(7)
(2)........	175(2), 176(3)
47..........	175(1)

1982	c.24
s.48(5).......	4(5), 30(2), (3), 31(5), 33(9), Sched. 6, para. 6(1), (2), Sched. 8 Pt. I, para. 6(4)
Sched. 1, para. 1.....	Sched. 11, paras. 1–4
2.....	Sched. 11, paras. 1–4
3.....	Sched. 11, paras. 1–4
4.....	Sched. 11, paras. 1–4
5.....	Sched. 11, para. 5
Sched. 2, para. 1.....	Sched. 12, para. 1
1A....	Sched. 12, para. 5
2.....	Sched. 12, paras. 2–4
3.....	Sched. 12, paras. 2–4
4.....	Sched. 12, paras. 2–4
6.....	Sched. 12, para. 6
Sched. 4, para. 8.....	4(5)
9.....	31(5)
10....	33(9)
17....	Sched. 6, para. 6(1), (2)
18(2)..	Sched. 8 Pt. I, para. 6(4)
34(2)..	30(2)
(3)..	30(3)

CRIMINAL JUSTICE ACT 1982
C.48

1982	c.48
s.38..........	Sched. 1, para. 3(2)
46..........	Sched. 1, para. 3(2)
54..........	Sched. 1, para. 3(2)

THE STATUTORY SICK PAY (GENERAL) REGULATIONS 1982
S.I. 1982 No. 894

1982	894
reg. 2A.......	s.152(3)

SOCIAL SECURITY (CONTRIBUTIONS, RE-RATING) ORDER 1982
S.I. 1982 No. 1790

1982	1790
art.5(a).......	ss.15(3), 18(1)

HEALTH AND SOCIAL SECURITY ACT 1984
c.48

1984	c.48
s.11	ss.63, 90, 122(1), Sched. 4 Pt. III, para. 2, Pt. IV, col. (1), Sched. 6, paras. 1, 4, 5, Sched. 9, para. 5, Sched. 11, para. 5
(1)	68(1)–(4), (6), (7), (11)
12	84(1)
13	20(1), 80(2)–(4), (7), Sched. 7 Pt. I, para. 4(3)–(6), Pt. VI, para. 18, Sched. 8 Pt. I, para. 6(4), (5)
14(a)	89
(b)	Sched. 7 Pt. I, para. 7

1984	c.48
s.17(2)	12(1)–(8)
18(1)(a)	13(1)
(b)	13(4)
(3)	13(4), (5), (6), (7)
21	6(2), 122(1), 151(3), 154(2), 164(6)–(7)
Sched. 4, para. 3	63, 90, Sched. 4 Pt. III, para. 2, Pt. IV, col. (1)
10(a)	Sched. 6, para. 6(1)
(b)	Sched. 6, para. 4
(c)	Sched. 6, para. 5
11(a)	122(1)
(b)	122(1)
13	Sched. 9, para. 5

1984	c.48
Sched. 4—cont.	
para. 15(b)	Sched. 11, para. 5
Sched. 5,	
para. 2(a)	20(1)
3(a)	80(2)
(c)	80(3), (4), (7)
4	Sched. 7 Pt. I, para. 4(3)–(6)
5	Sched. 7 Pt. VI, para. 18
8(a)	Sched. 8 Pt. I, para. 6(4)
(b)	Sched. 8 Pt. I, para. 6(5)
Sched. 7,	
para. 2	122(1)
3(a)	6(2)
7	154(2)
8	151(3), 164(6)–(7)

SOCIAL SECURITY ACT 1985
c.53

1985	c.53
s.7(1)	s.5(1)
(2)	9(1), (2), (3), (4)
8(1)	6(5)
9(1)(a)	34(1)–(2)
(b)	34(4)–(6)
(c)	34(7)
(2)(a)	47(1)
(b)	47(1)
(c)	47(2)–(4)
(3)	50(2)
(4)	Sched. 7 Pt. I, para. 3(1)
(a)	Sched. 7 Pt. I, para. 3(1)
(b)	Sched. 7 Pt. I, para. 3(2), (4)
(5)	Sched. 5, para. 2(6)
10	28(4)

1985	c.53
s.12(1)(b)	78(6)
(2)	Sched. 4 Pt. III, para. 7
13(1)	83(3)
(2)(a)	84(1)
(b)	84(3)
(3)	85(4)
(4)(b)	86(2)
(5)	Sched. 7 Pt. I, para. 6(3)–(6)
(6)	114(3)
(8)	114(4)
18(1)	155(4)
(3)	33(10), (11)
(4)	152(4)
(5)	153(5)
(6)(a)	Sched. 12, para. 1
(b)	Sched. 12, para. 5
19	Sched. 1, para. 6(6)

1985	c.53
s.21	68(5)
29(1)	1(3), 23(4), 113(3), 122(1), 153(8), (9), 163(1), (2), Sched. 1, para. 1(2)–(4), (6)
Sched. 4,	
para. 3	68(5)
4	153(8), (9)
6	163(1)
7	163(3)–(5)
Sched. 5,	
para. 5	1(3)
6(b)	23(4)
8	113(3)
13(a)	Sched. 1, para. 1(2)
(b)	Sched. 1, para. 1(3), (4), (6)
14	122(1)

THE SOCIAL SECURITY (CONTRIBUTIONS AND CREDITS) (TRANSITIONAL AND
CONSEQUENTIAL PROVISIONS) REGULATIONS 1985
S.I. 1985 No. 1398

1985	1398
reg.4(2)	s.12(3)
(3)	13(6)

SOCIAL SECURITIES ACT 1986
c.50

1986	c.50
s.18(1)........	s.22(1), (2), 34(4)–(6), 44(3), (4), 45(1), 47(2)–(4), 52(2), (3), 53(2), 60(7), 61(1), (2), 78(3), 78(4), Sched. 7 Pt. I, para. 3(2), Pt. I, para. 3(4)
(2)........	45(1)
(3)........	44(4), (5), 45(2), (3)
(4)........	45(6), (7)
(5)........	46(2)
(6)........	46(1)
19(1)(a)	50(5)
(b)	51(3)
(c)	39(3)
(d)	41(6)
(2)(a)	Sched. 5, para. 4(1), Sched. 5, para. 4(2)
(b)	Sched. 5, para. 4(3)
(3)........	Sched. 5, para. 5(1), (2)
(4)........	Sched. 5, para. 5(3)
(5)........	Sched. 5, para. 6(1), (2)
(6)........	Sched. 5, para. 6(3), (4)
20(1)........	123(1)
(2)........	123(2)
(3)........	124(1)
(4)........	124(3)
(4A)–(4D).	125(1)–(4)
(4N)	124(2), 125(5)
(5)........	128(1)
(5A)......	128(1)
(6)........	128(3)
(6A)......	129(1)
(6B)	129(2), (3)
(6C)	129(2), (3)
(6D)	129(1)
(6E)	129(4)
(6F)	129(6)
(7)........	130(1), (2)
(8)........	130(1), (2)
(8A)......	131(1)
(8AA)	131(2)
(8B)–(8H) .	131(3)–(9)
(9)........	134(2)
(9A)......	134(3)
(10)......	128(4)
(11)......	137(1)
(12)......	137(2)
21(1)........	124(4)
(1A)	124(5), (6)
(1B)	121(5), (6)
(2)........	128(2)
(3)........	128(2)
(3A)	129(5)
(3B)	129(5)

1986	c.50
s.21(4)........	130(3)
(5)........	130(3)
(5A)......	131(10), (11)
(5B)	131(10), (11)
(6)........	130(4), (5)
(a)	128(5)
(aa)	129(8)
(c)	131(12)
(7)........	134(4)
22(1)........	135(1)–(2)
(2)........	135(1)–(2)
(2A)......	135(3)–(4)
(2B)......	135(3)–(4)
(3)........	135(5)
(4)........	135(6)
(5)........	136(1)
(6)........	134(1)
(7)........	136(2)–(3)
(8)........	136(2)–(3)
(8A)......	136(4)
22A	132
22B(1)	133(1)
(2)–(4)..	133(2)–(4)
23(1)–(4)	126(1)–(4)
(5)........	126(5)
(5A)......	126(6)
(6)........	126(7)
(7)........	126(8)
23A	127
27B(4)	129(7)
31(4)........	123(3)
31G(4)	123(4)–(6)
(5)......	123(4)–(6)
(6)......	123(4)–(6)
32(2)........	138(1)
(2A)......	138(2)
(11)......	140(5)
33(1A)......	138(3)
(2)–(4)	139(1)–(3)
(4A)	139(4)
(9)......	140(1)
(10)......	140(2)
(10A)	140(4)
(10ZA) ...	140(3)
(11)......	139(5)
36(1)........	36(1), (2)
(3)(a)	38(1)
(b)	39(4), (5)
39	60(2), (3), 94(1), 103(1)–(4), (7), (8), 104(3), (4), 109(4)–(6), 114(4), Sched. 7 Pt. I, paras. 1, 3(1), 4(1), 5(1), 6(1), Pt. II, para. 9(1), (2), Pt. III, para. 10(1), Pt. IV, para. 11(1), (4)–(10), (12), (13), Sched. 8 Pt. I, para. 8(6)
40	56(6)
43(1)........	26(6)

1986	c.50
s.43(3)(a)	28(2)
(b)	176(1)
44(1)........	27(1), (2)
(2)........	91
45(b)	77(11)
46(1)–(5)	164(1)–(5)
(6)........	164(6)–(7)
(7)........	164(8)
(8)........	164(9)
(9)........	164(10)
47(1)–(6)	165(1)–(6)
(7)........	165(7)
48(1)........	166(1)
(2)........	166(2)
(3)–(8)	166(3)–(8)
49	4(1), 57(2), 167(1)–(4), Sched. 1, para. 6(5), (6), Sched. 3, para. 3(1), Sched. 13, paras. 1–3
(2)........	35(1)–(3), (5)–(7)
50	35(6)
(1)........	171(1)
(2)........	171(2)
(2A)......	171(3)
(3)–(5)	171(4)–(6)
62(1)........	175(5)
(2)........	175(5)
(3)........	176(1)
66	148, 149, 150(1)–(4)
67(1)........	157(2), 176(1)
68	151(6)
70(1)(a)	142(1)
(b)	142(2), (3)
74(5)........	6(6), 8(4), 9(5), Sched. 1, para. 1(6)
(6)........	5(2)
75	14(1), 19(6), 21(5), 22(1), (2), (3), (4), (5), 23(1), 24(1), 44(6), Sched. 3, para. 1(2)–(5), para. 2(2)–(5), para. 4(1), (2), para. 5(2), (3), (4), para. 7(3), (4)
79(3)........	128(6), 129(9)
(4)........	169
80	170
83(1)........	175(2)–(5)
(2)........	175(6)
(3)(e)	176(1)
(4)........	176(3)
(6)........	175(7)
84(1)........	137(1), 138(4), 150(2), 171(1), 175(1)
(4)........	172

1986   **c.50**

s.86 . . . . 20(1),
21(1)–(4),
22(1), (2),
25(5), (6),
31(6), (7),
33(4), (5),
40(1), (3), (5),
112(3), 153
(12), 176(1),
Sched. 1, para.
8(1)(m),
Sched. 3,
paras. 4(1),
(2), 7(2), (3),
(4), 9, Sched.
5, paras. 2(7),
4(4), 7(1),
Sched. 8 Pt. I,
para. 6(5)
(1). . . . . Sched. 8 Pt.
I, para. 6(4)
Sched. 3,
para. 2 . . . . . 94(1)
3(1) . . . 103(1)
(2) . . . 103(2), (3),
(4)
(3) . . . Sched. 7 Pt.
II, para. 9(1),
(2)
(4) . . . 103(7), (8)
4 . . . . . 114(4),
Sched. 7 Pt. I,
paras. 1, 3(1),
4(1), 5(1), 6(1)
5(1) . . . Sched. 7 Pt.
IV, para.
11(1), (4)–(9),
(12), (13)
6 . . . . . 104(3), (4)
7 . . . . . Sched. 7 Pt.
III, para. 10(1)
10 . . . . 60(2), (3)
13 . . . . 109(4), (5),
(6), (7)

1986   **c.50**

Sched. 3—*cont.*
para. 16 . . . . 114(4),
Sched. 8 Pt. I,
para. 8(6)
Sched. 4,
para. 1 . . . . . 167(1)
2 . . . . . 167(3)
3 . . . . . Sched. 1,
para. 6(5)
4 . . . . . Sched. 1,
para. 6(6)
5 . . . . . 167(4)
10 . . . . 4(1)
11 . . . . Sched. 13,
para. 1
11A . . . Sched. 13,
para. 2
12 . . . . Sched. 13,
para. 3
13 . . . . 35(1)–(3),
(5)–(7), 57(2)
14 . . . . Sched. 3,
para. 3(1)
Sched. 6,
para. 1(1) . . . 150(1)
(2) . . . 150(2), (3),
(4)
2 148
3 149
Sched. 8,
para. 2(1) . . . 22(1), (2)
(2) . . . 22(4)
(3) . . . 22(5)
(4)(a) 23(1)
(c) 22(3)
(5) . . . 24(1)
(6) . . . 21(5)
3(1) . . . Sched. 3,
paras. 1(2),
(4), 2(2), (4)
(2) . . . Sched. 3,
paras. 1(3),
2(3)
(3) . . . Sched. 3,
paras. 1(5),
2(3), (5)

1986   **c.50**

Sched. 8—*cont.*
para. 3(4) . . . Sched. 3,
para. 4(1), (2)
(5) . . . Sched. 3,
para. 5(2)
(6) . . . Sched. 3,
para. 5(3), (4)
(7) . . . Sched. 3,
para. 7(3), (4)
5 . . . . . 19(6)
6 . . . . . 14(1)
7(1)(a) 44(6)
Sched. 10,
para. 10 . . . . Sched. 1,
para. 8(1)(m)
63 . . . . 20(1)
64 . . . . 21(1), (2)
65 . . . . 176(1)
66(a) . . Sched. 3,
para. 4(1), (2)
(b) . . Sched. 3,
para. 7(2)–(4)
(c) . . Sched. 3,
para. 9
68(2)(a) Sched. 8 Pt.
I, para. 6(4)
(b) Sched. 8 Pt.
I, para. 6(5)
70(a) . . 40(1)
(b) . . 40(3)
(c) . . 40(5)
72 . . . . 22(1), (2)
(b) . . 21(4)
74 . . . . 112(3)
77 . . . . 153(12)
83 . . . . 25(5), (6),
31(6), (7),
33(4), (5)
95(a) . . Sched. 5,
para. 2(7),
para. 4(4)
(b) . . Sched. 5,
para. 7(1)

THE STATUTORY SICK PAY (GENERAL) AMENDMENT REGULATIONS 1986
S.I. 1986 No. 477

1986   **477**
reg.2 . . . . s.152(3)

SOCIAL FUND (MATERNITY AND FUNERAL EXPENSES) ACT 1987
c.7

1987   **c.7**
s.1 . . . . s.138(1)

THE SOCIAL SECURITY ACT 1986 (COMMENCEMENT No.5) ORDER 1987
S.I. 1987 No. 354

1987   **354**
art.3 . . . . Sched. 8, Pt.
I, paras. 2(6),
(7), 6(2), (3)

TABLE OF DESTINATIONS

INCOME AND CORPORATION TAXES ACT 1988
c.1

1988	**c.1**
s.844	.ss.15(4), 126(5), 150(2), Sched. 2, paras. 3(1), (2), (5), 6(1), 9
Sched. 29, para. 14	14(4)
32	126(5), 150(2), Sched. 2, paras. 3(1), (2), (5), 6(1), 9

SOCIAL SECURITY ACT 1988
c.7

1988	**c.7**
s.1(1).	.s.64
2	60(2), (3), (8), Sched. 7 Pt. VI, paras. 14(1), 15(1)–(3), 16–21
(1).	Sched. 7 Pt. V, para. 13(1)–(4), (6)
(3).	Sched. 7 Pt. IV, para. 11(11)
(4).	Sched. 7 Pt. IV, para. 12(1), (2)
(5).	Sched. 7 Pt. IV, para. 12(1), (2)
(5A)	Sched. 7 Pt. IV, para. 12(3), (4)
(5B)	Sched. 7 Pt. IV, para. 12(3), (4)
(7).	Sched. 7 Pt. IV, para. 12(6)
3(a).	128(1)
4(1).	124(1)
(2).	124(2), 125(1)–(5)
(3).	142(1)
(4).	144(1), (2)
6(2)(a)	Sched. 3, paras. 1(2), 2(2)

1988	**c.7**
s.6(2)(b)	Sched. 3, paras. 1(3), 2(3)
7(a).	30(1)
9	23(1), (2)
11	138(2), (3), 139(4), 140(1), (4), (5)
16	35(4), 57(2), (4), 82(3), 83(2), 84(2), 94(2), 121(5), (6), 124(4), 126(6), 127, 164(9), (10), 166(2), Sched. 7, Pt. IV, para. 11(10), (14), Pt. V, para. 13(11), Sched. 13, paras. 1, 2
Sched. 1, para. 2	Sched. 7 Pt. VI, paras. 14(1), 15(1)–(3), 16, 18–20
3	Sched. 7 Pt. VI, paras. 14(1), 17
5(a) . . .	60(8)
(b) . . .	60(2), (3)
6(a) . . .	Sched. 7 Pt. VI, para. 20
(b) . . .	Sched. 7 Pt. VI, para. 21

1988	**c.7**
Sched. 2, para. 1(1)(a).	23(1)
(b).	23(2)
Sched. 3, para. 2	138(2)
7	140(5)
10	138(3)
11	139(4)
12	140(1)
13	140(4)
Sched. 4, para. 4	57(4)
5(a) . . .	57(2)
(b) . . .	35(4)
7(a) . . .	83(2)
8(a) . . .	84(2)
11	94(2)
12(a) . .	Sched. 7 Pt. IV, para. 11(10)
(b) . .	Sched. 7 Pt. IV, paras. 11(14), 13(11)
16(b) . .	82(3)
(1) . .	164(9)
(2) . .	164(10)
17	166(2)
19(1) . .	Sched. 13, para. 1
(2) . .	Sched. 13, para. 2
23(1) . .	124(4)
(2) . .	121(5), (6)
24(1) . .	126(6)
25	127

EMPLOYMENT ACT 1988
c.19

1988	**c.19**
s.27(2).	.s.28(1)
(3).	28(6)

TABLE OF DESTINATIONS

FINANCE ACT 1988
c.39

1988	c.39
s.35	Sched. 2, para. 3(4)
145	Sched. 2, para. 9
Sched. 3, para. 31	Sched. 2, para. 3(4)
Sched. 14	Sched. 2, para. 9

LOCAL GOVERNMENT FINANCE ACT 1988
c.41

1988	c.41	1988	c.41	1988	c.41
s.22(9)........	s.135(5)	Sched. 10,		Sched. 10—cont.	
135	123(1), (4)–(6), 131(1), (3)–(12), 132, 133(1), (2)–(4), 134(3), 135(5), 136(4), 137(1), 175(6)	para. 2(2)...	123(1)	para. 4(2)...	135(5)
		(3)...	131(1), (3)–(9)	(3)...	136(4)
		(4)...	134(3)	5	132, 133(1)–(4)
		(5)...	137(1)	6	123(4), (5), (6)
		3(2)...	131(10), (11)	11(2)..	175(6)
		(3)...	131(12)		

HOUSING (SCOTLAND) ACT 1988
c.43

1988	c.43
s.70(3)........	s.130(4), (5)

HOUSING ACT 1988
c.50

1988	c.50
s.121(4).......	s.130(4), (5)

UNEMPLOYMENT BENEFIT (DISQUALIFICATION PERIOD) ORDER 1988
S.I. 1988 NO. 487

1988	487
art.2	s.28(1)

TRANSFER OF FUNCTIONS (HEALTH AND SOCIAL SECURITY) ORDER 1988
S.I. 1988 NO. 1843

1988	1843
Sched. 3, para. 4(c) ...	s.123(2)

SOCIAL SECURITY ACT 1989
c.24

1989	c.24	1989	c.24	1989	c.24
s.1(1)........	s.8(1)–(3)	s.7	25(2), 31(2), 33(1), (2), 40(7), 41(7), 51(4), 54(4), 102(3), Sched. 5, paras. 1, 2(1)–(3), (7), (8), 3, 4(1), (2), 8(3), Sched. 7 Pt. V, para. 13(1), (4), (8), (9)	s.7(3)(a)	49(2), (3)
(9)........	122(1)			(4)........	55
2	Sched. 1, para. 8(1)(h)			9(1)........	30(1), (3), 176(1)
4(2)........	23(3)			(2)........	122(1)
(3)........	22(6)			(3)........	89, Sched. 7, para. 9(3)
(4)........	24(2)			(4)........	122(1)
5(1)........	137(1)			10(2).......	57(1)
6(1)........	38(4), 39(6)			(3).......	57(3)
				(4).......	57(5)
				11	26(2)–(4)

1989	c.24
s.12(1)........	28(1)
(3)........	28(5)
(4)........	29
(5)........	122(2)
13(1)........	124(1)
(2)........	137(2)
17(3)........	Sched. 7, Pt. V, para. 13(5)
(5)........	Sched. 7 Pt. IV, para. 12(3), (4)
(6)........	Sched. 7 Pt. IV, para. 12(6)
21	Sched. 6, paras. 6(3)–(5), 7
26	6(3), 9(1), 12(3), 13(6), 15(1), (2), (5), 20(1), 22(3), 36(3), 40(2), 44(6), 70(6), 103(6), 161(3), 165(7), Sched. 3, para. 7(1), Sched. 7 Pt. II, para. 9(3), Pt. IV, para. 11(1)
29(1)........	175(2), (3), (4), (5)
(3)........	176(3)
(6)........	175(7)
30(1)........	175(1)
31	92, Sched. 7 Pt. I, para. 8
(1)........	4(4), 37(3), (4), 38(2), (3), 44(1), (2), 49(7), (8), 57(6), (7), 58(1), (2), (4), (5), 65(1), (4)–(6), 68(8), (9), (11), (12), 78(7), (8), 86(1), 127, 128(3), 131(2), 133(1), 175(4)

1989	c.24
Sched. 1,	
para. 2(2) ...	54(4)
3(1) ...	Sched. 5, para. 1
(2) ...	Sched. 5, para. 2(1)
(3) ...	Sched. 5, para. 2(2)
(4) ...	Sched. 5, para. 2(3)
(5) ...	Sched. 5, para. 2(7)
(6) ...	Sched. 5, para. 2(8)
(7) ...	Sched. 5, para. 3
(8) ...	Sched. 5, para. 4(1), (2)
(9) ...	Sched. 5, para. 8(1), (2)
(10) ..	Sched. 5, para. 8(3)
4(1) ...	25(2), 31(2)
5(1) ...	33(1)
(2) ...	33(2)
8(1) ...	102(3)
(2) ...	Sched. 7 Pt. V, para. 13(1)
(5) ...	Sched. 7 Pt. 5, para. 13(4)
(6) ...	Sched. 7 Pt. V, para. (8), (9)
9(2) ...	51(4)
10(1) ..	40(7)
(2) ..	41(7)
Sched. 3,	
para. 13(1) ..	Sched. 6, para. 6(3), (4), (5)
(2) ..	Sched. 6, para. 7
Sched. 7,	
para. 2(1) ...	6(3)
(2) ...	9(1)
3(b) ...	12(3)
(c) ...	12(3)

1989	c.24
Sched. 7—*cont.*	
para. 4	13(6)
5(a) ...	15(1), (2)
(b) ...	15(1), (2)
(c) ...	15(5)
6	20(1)
7	22(3)
8	36(3)
10	70(6)
12	103(6), Sched. 7 Pt. II para. 9(3)
13	Sched. 7 Pt. IV, para. 11(1)
16	Sched. 3, para. 7(1)
19	44(6)
20(1) ..	40(2)
23	161(3)
25	165(7)
Sched. 8,	
para. 2(1) ...	58(1)
(2) ...	58(2)
(3) ...	58(3)
(4) ...	68(12)
(5) ...	68(11)
(6) ...	58(2), (4), 68(13)
(7) ...	58(5), 68(13)
3	57(6), (7)
4(1) ...	37(3), (4)
(2) ...	38(2), (3)
(3) ...	44(1)
(4) ...	44(2)
(5) ...	49(7), (8)
(6) ...	77(7), (8)
5(2) ...	65(1)
(3) ...	65(4), (6)
(4) ...	65(5)
6	68(8), (9)
7(2) ...	92, Sched. 7 Pt. I, para. 8
8	4(4)
9(2) ...	131(2)
10(1) ..	175(4)
15(1) ..	128(3)
16	127

LOCAL GOVERNMENT AND HOUSING ACT 1989
C.42

1989	c.42
s.194	s.58(4)
Sched. 11,	
para. 113 ...	58(4)

CAPITAL ALLOWANCES ACT 1990
C.1

1990	c.1
s.164	Sched. 2, para. 2
Sched. 1,	
para. 2	Sched. 2, para. 2

NATIONAL HEALTH SERVICE AND COMMUNITY CARE ACT 1990
c.19

1990	c.19
s.66(1)........s.143(3)	
Sched. 9,	
para. 15	143(3)

SOCIAL SECURITY ACT 1990
c.27

1990	c.27	1990	c.27	1990	c.27
s.1(1)........s.66		s.17(1)........	16(4)	Sched. 6,	
(2)........	65(6)	(2)........	16(5)	para. 3(1)...	60(4)–(6)
2(1)........	69	(5)........	Sched. 1,	(2)...	87(1), (2)
(2)........	Sched. 4 Pt.		para. 6(2)–(4)	(3)...	61(1)
	III, para. 3	(6)........	Sched. 1,	(4)...	61(2)
(3)........	63		para. 6(8)	4(1)...	108(5)
3(1)........	Sched. 7 Pt.	(7)........	Sched. 1,	(2)...	109(2)
	IV, para. 11(1)		para. 7(1)–(13)	8(1)...	176(3)
(2)........	Sched. 7 Pt.	(8)........	Sched. 2,	(2)...	176(1)
	IV, para.		para. 6(1)	(3)...	176(1), (3)
	11(2), (3)	(9)........	Sched. 2,	(4)...	176(3)
(3)........	Sched. 7 Pt.		para. 6(2)	(5)...	176(1)
	IV, para. 11(8)	21(1)........	58(2), (4),	(6)...	176(3)
(4)........	Sched. 7 Pt.		60(4)–(6),	(7)...	175(2),
	IV, para. 11(1)		61(1), (2),		176(3)
(6)........	Sched. 7 Pt.		68(11), 87(1),	(9)...	176(3)
	V, para. 13(10)		(2), 108(5),	(12)..	176(3)
(7)........	109(2)		109(2), 122(1),	9	Sched. 1,
4(1)........	33(3)		126(7), (8),		para. 8(1)(j)–
(2)........	40(5)		157(2), 163(6),		(k)
(3)........	40(4), (5)		171(3), 175(2),	10(1)..	Sched. 3,
5(2)........	122(1)		176(1), (3),		para. 3(1)
9	135(3)–(4)		Sched. 1, para.	11	122(1)
10(3)........	140(3)		8(1)(j)–(k),	12	175(2)
(4)........	140(4)		Sched. 3,	15(1)..	157(2)
16(1)........	1(1)		paras. 3(1),	(2)..	176(1)
(2)........	1(1), (5)		10(2)	16	163(6)
(8)(a)	Sched. 8 Pt.	Sched. 5	Sched. 1,	17(2)..	126(7)
	I, paras. 2(1),		para. 7(1)–(13)	(3)..	126(8)
	4(1)			22	171(3)
				30(2)..	58(2)
				(4)..	58(4)
				(5)..	68(11)

HUMAN FERTILISATION AND EMBRYOLOGY ACT 1990
c.37

1990	c.37
s.49 ....s.37(1)	
Sched. 4,	
para. 2	37(1)

STATUTORY SICK PAY ACT 1991
c.3

1991	c.3
s.1(1)........s.158(1)	
(3)........	158(5)
(4)........	1(5)
2(1)........	158(2), (3),
	159, 176(1)
(2)........	158(4)
(5)........	158(7)
3(1)(b)	173

TABLE OF DESTINATIONS

DISABILITY LIVING ALLOWANCE AND DISABILITY WORKING ALLOWANCE ACT 1991
C.21

1991	c.21	1991	c.21	1991	c.21
s.1(1)........s.63		s.6(6)(a)	137(1)	s.9(5)........	93
(2)........	71–73, 75, 76	(7)........	137(2)	Sched. 2,	
2(1)........	64	(8)........	129(5)	para. 3(1)...	66
4	65(3)–(5),	(9)........	129(8)	(2)...	65(3)
	66, 67(2),	7	129(9)	(3)...	65(4), (5)
	70(2), 74(1),	(1)........	129(7)	(4)...	67(2)
	150(2)	8(1)........	128(1)	4	70(2)
6(2)........	123(1)	(2)........	128(4)	7	74(1)
(3)........	123(2)	9(1)........	33(7), (8)	16	150(2)
(4)........	129(1)–(4),	(2)........	68(10)	Sched. 3,	
	(6)	(3)........	42	para. 7	129(9)

SOCIAL SECURITIES CONTRIBUTIONS ACT 1991
C.42

1991	c.42	1991	c.42	1991	c.42
s.1(2).........s.1(2)		s.2(3)(a)	Sched. 1,	s.2(5)(a)	Sched. 1,
(3)........	1(6)		para. 6(1)		para. 8(1)(b)
(5)........	10	(b)	Sched. 1,	(b)	Sched. 1,
2(1)(a)	1(4)		para. 6(2)		para. 8(1)(l)
(2)........	Sched. 1,	(4)........	Sched. 1,	(c)	Sched. 1,
	para. 5		para. 7(11)		para. 8(1)(i)

SOCIAL SECURITIES (INDUSTRIAL INJURIES) (DEPENDENCY) (PERMITTED EARNINGS LIMITS) ORDER 1991
S.I. 1991 No. 546

1991	546
art.2	Sched. 7, Pt. I, para. 4(4)

THE SOCIAL SECURITIES (CONTRIBUTIONS) (RE-RATING) NO.2 ORDER 1991
S.I. 1991 No. 2909

1991	2909
art.2(2) ....s.9(3)	
3(a)	11(1)
(b)	11(1)
4	13(1)
5	15(3), 18(1)

THE SOCIAL SECURITY BENEFITS (UP-RATING) (NO.2) ORDER 1991
S.I. 1991 No. 2910

1991	2910	1991	2910	1991	2910
art.2(3)	Sched. 4 Pt. III, para. 2	art.3(3)	Sched. 4 Pt. I, paras. 1–6,	art.11	80(4)
3(2)	Sched. 4 Pt. I, paras. 1–6, Pt. III, paras. 1–7, Pt. IV, col. (1), col. (2), col. (3), Pt. V, paras. 1–12		Pt. III, para. 1, paras. 3–7, Pt. IV, col. (1), Pt. V, paras. 1–12	16	126(7)
		(4)	Sched. 7 Pt. V, para. 13(4)	Sched. 1	Sched. 4 Pt. I, paras. 1–6, Pt. III, paras. 1–7, Pt. IV, col. (1), col. (2), col. (3), Pt. V, paras. 1–12
		4(2)	44(3), (4)		
		6	Sched. 8 Pt. I, para. 2(6), (7)		

THE STATUTORY SICK PAY (RATE OF PAYMENT) (NO.2) ORDER 1991
S.I. 1991 No. 2911

1991	2911
reg.2 ....s.157(1)	

INDEX

References are to section and schedule numbers

CHILD BENEFIT,
  entitlement to, 141
  exemptions from entitlement to, Sched. 9
  meaning of child, 142
  persons entitled to, Sched. 10
  rate of, 145
CHILD'S SPECIAL ALLOWANCE,
  existing beneficiaries, 56
CHILDREN,
  child benefit, 142
  increases for dependants, 80
  non-resident children, 81
  pension increase, 85
  restriction of increase of benefits, 81
  special allowances, 56
CONTRIBUTIONS,
  by former spouse, 48
  calculation of, 8
  Class 1, 5, Sched. 1
  Class 1A, 10
  Class 2, 11
  Class 3, 13
  Class 4, 15, Sched. 2
  classes of, 1
  contributory system, 1
  deferment of contributions, 17
  failure to satisfy conditions, 60
  incidental matters relating to, 17
  late payment of, 12
  liabilities for, 6, 11
  limits for, 5
  power to regulate liability for, 19
  recovery under Income Tax Acts, 15
  recovery under regulations, 18
  restrictions of right to pay Class 3, 14
  secondary contributors, 7
CONTRIBUTORY BENEFITS,
  conditions for, 21
  descriptions, 20
  rates of, Sched. 4
  short-term, 21
  unemployment, 25, Sched. 3
CROWN,
  armed forces, 116
  crown employments, 115, 161, 169

DISABLEMENT PENSIONS,
  entitlement to, 103
  extent of disablement, Sched. 6
  respiratory diseases, 110
  workmen's compensation, 111

EARNER,
  categories of, 3

EARNER—*cont.*
  definitions of, 2,3
  self-employed, 2
EARNINGS,
  definition of, 3
  earnings factors, 22
  earnings limits, 4
  payments treated as, 4
  records of, 24
  sums regarded as, 112

INCOME RELATED BENEFITS,
  community charge benefits, 131
  couple, 132
  disability working allowance, 129
  family credit, 128
  generally, 123
  housing benefit, 130
  income support, 124
  return to work, 127
  severe hardship, 125
  trade disputes, 126
INCOME TAX ACTS,
  application of, 16
  recovery of class 4 contributions, 15,
    Sched. 2
INDUSTRIAL INJURIES,
  accidents while meeting emergencies, 100
  illegal employments, 97
  old cases, Sched. 8
  right to benefit for, 94, Sched. 7
  sickness benefit, 102
INTERPRETATION, 122, 135, 137, 147, 150, 163,
  171, 172
INVALIDITY BENEFITS,
  conditions for, 33
  entitlement to, 42
  invalidity allowance, 34
  special provisions affecting, 58

MOBILITY,
  components of, 74, 75
  invalid carriages, 75

NATIONAL INSURANCE,
  contributions to, 1
NON-CONTRIBUTORY BENEFITS,
  attendance allowance, 64
  definitions of, 63
  disability living allowance, 71
  exclusion of, 67

Non-Contributory Benefits—*cont.*
   guardians' allowance, 77
   invalid care allowance, 70
   severe disablement allowance, 68, 69
   terminally ill persons, 66

Parliament,
   parliamentary control, 176
Pensions,
   abatement of unemployment benefit, 30
   age addition, 79
   category A, 44
   category B, 49
   categories C and D, 78
   Christmas bonus, 148
   deferred entitlement, 55, Sched. 5
   disablement pensions, 103
   entitlement to more than one, 43
   graduated retirement benefit, 62
   widow's pensions, 36, 37, 38, 39, 40

Short Title and Commencement, 177
Sickness Benefit,
   conditions for, 31, Sched. 3
   disqualification, 31
   industrial injuries for, 102
   successive accidents, 107
Social Fund,
   awards by officers, 139
   payments out of, 138
   principles of determination, 140
Statutory Maternity Pay,
   entitlement to, 164, Sched. 3
   maternity pay period, 165
   rates of payment, 166
   recovery by employers, 167
   relationship with other payments, 168, Sched. 13

Statutory Sick Pay,
   employer's liability, 151
   limitations on entitlement, 155
   notification of incapacity, 156
   period of incapacity, 152
   period of entitlement, 153
   qualifying days, 154
   rates of payment, 157
   recovery by employers, 158
   relationship with other benefits, Sched. 12
   situations where no entitlement arises, Sched. 11

Unemployment Benefits,
   abatement of, 30
   disqualifications, 28
   duration of, 26
   entitlements to, 25
   exemptions from disqualification for, 29
   trade disputes, 27

Widows. *See* Women
Women,
   couples, 132
   married and widows, 118
   married, contributions by, 19
   maternity allowance, 35
   maternity benefit, 33
   polygamous marriages, 133
   special provisions for married, 53, 121
   statutory maternity pay, 164
   widowed mothers' allowances, 37
   widows' allowances, 36
   widows' pensions, 38, 39, 40

SOCIAL SECURITY ADMINISTRATION ACT 1992*

(1992 c. 5)

ARRANGEMENT OF SECTIONS

PART I

CLAIMS FOR AND PAYMENTS AND GENERAL ADMINISTRATION OF BENEFIT

Necessity of Claim

SECT.
1. Entitlement to benefit dependent on claim.
2. Retrospective effect of provisions making entitlement to benefit dependent on claim.

Widowhood benefits

3. Late claims for widowhood benefit where death is difficult to establish.
4. Treatment of payments of benefit to certain widows.

Claims and payments regulations

5. Regulations about claims for and payments of benefit.

Community charge benefits etc.

6. Regulations about community charge benefits administration.
7. Relationship between community charge benefits and other benefits.

Industrial injuries benefit

8. Notification of accidents, etc.
9. Medical examination and treatment of claimants.
10. Obligations of claimants.

Disability working allowance

11. Initial claims and repeat claims.

The social fund

12. Necessity of application for certain payments.

Child benefit

13. Necessity of application for child benefit.

Statutory sick pay

14. Duties of employees etc. in relation to statutory sick pay.

Statutory maternity pay

15. Duties of women etc. in relation to statutory maternity pay.

Emergency payments

16. Emergency payments by local authorities and other bodies.

PART II

ADJUDICATION

Adjudication by the Secretary of State

17. Questions for the Secretary of State.
18. Appeal on question of law.
19. Review of decisions.

---

* Annotations by John Mesher, B.A., B.C.L., LL.M., Barrister, Reader in Law and Simmons & Simmons Research Fellow in Pensions Law, University of Sheffield.

Adjudication by adjudication officers

20. Claims and questions to be submitted to adjudication officer.
21. Decision of adjudication officer.

Appeals from adjudication officers—general

22. Appeal to social security appeal tribunal.
23. Appeal from social security appeal tribunal to Commissioner.
24. Appeal from Commissioners on point of law.

Reviews—general

25. Review of decisions.
26. Procedure for reviews.
27. Reviews under s.25—supplementary.
28. Appeals following reviews or refusals to review.
29. Review after claimant appeals.

Attendance allowance, disability living allowance and disability working allowance

30. Reviews of decisions of adjudication officers.
31. Further reviews.
32. Reviews of decisions as to attendance allowance, disability living allowance or disability working allowance—supplementary.
33. Appeals following reviews.
34. Appeal from social security appeal tribunals or disability appeal tribunals to Commissioners and appeals from Commissioners.
35. Reviews of decisions on appeal.

Questions first arising on appeal

36. Questions first arising on appeal.

Reference of special questions

37. Reference of special questions.

Adjudication officers and the Chief Adjudication Officer

38. Adjudication officers.
39. The Chief Adjudication Officer.

Social security appeal tribunals

40. Panels for appointment to social security appeal tribunals.
41. Constitution of social security appeal tribunals.

Disability appeal tribunals

42. Panels for appointment to disability appeal tribunals.
43. Constitution of disability appeal tribunals.

Adjudication in relation to industrial injuries and disablement benefit

44. Declaration that accident is an industrial accident.
45. Disablement questions.
46. Medical appeals and references.
47. Review of medical decisions.
48. Appeal etc. on question of law to Commissioner.

Adjudicating medical practitioners and medical appeal tribunals

49. Adjudicating medical practitioners.
50. Constitution of medical appeal tribunals.

The President and full-time chairmen of tribunals

51. The President of social security appeal tribunals, medical appeal tribunals and disability appeal tribunals and regional chairmen and other full-time chairmen.

Social Security Commissioners

52. Appointment of Commissioners.

References by authorities

53. Power of adjudicating authorities to refer matters to experts.
54. Claims relating to attendance allowance, disability living allowance and disability working allowance.
55. Medical examination etc. in relation to appeals to disability appeal tribunals.

Determination of questions of special difficulty

56. Assessors.
57. Tribunal of three Commissioners.

Regulations

58. Regulations as to determination of questions and matters arising out of, or pending, reviews and appeals.
59. Procedure.
60. Finality of decisions.
61. Regulations about supplementary matters relating to determinations.

Industrial diseases

62. Adjudication as to industrial diseases.

Housing benefit and community charge benefits

63. Adjudication.

Social fund officers and inspectors and the social fund Commissioner

64. Social fund officers.
65. The social fund Commissioner and inspectors.
66. Reviews.

Christmas bonus

67. Determination of questions.

Restrictions on entitlement to benefit following erroneous decision

68. Restrictions on entitlement to benefit in certain cases of error.
69. Determination of questions on review following erroneous decisions.

Correction of errors

70. Regulations as to correction of errors and setting aside of decisions.

PART III

OVERPAYMENTS AND ADJUSTMENTS OF BENEFIT

Misrepresentation etc.

71. Overpayments—general.
72. Special provision as to recovery of income support.

Adjustments of benefits

73. Overlapping benefits—general.
74. Income support and other payments.

Housing benefit

75. Overpayments of housing benefit.

Community charge benefits

76. Excess benefits.
77. Shortfall in benefits.

Social fund awards

78. Recovery of social fund awards.

Northern Ireland payments

79. Recovery of Northern Ireland payments.

Adjustment of child benefit

80. Child benefit—overlap with benefits under legislation of other member States.

PART IV

RECOVERY FROM COMPENSATION PAYMENTS

81. Interpretation of Part IV.

Recovery from damages etc. of sums equivalent to benefit

82. Recovery of sums equivalent to benefit from compensation payments in respect of accidents, injuries and diseases.

Payments, deductions and certificates

83. Time for making payment to Secretary of State.
84. The certificate of total benefit.
85. Exemption from deduction in cases involving small payments.
86. Multiple compensation payments.
87. Collaboration between compensators.
88. Structured settlements.
89. Insolvency.
90. Protection of legal aid charges.
91. Overpaid benefits.
92. Death.
93. Payments into court.

Administration and adjudication

94. Provision of information.
95. Applications for certificates of total benefit.
96. Liability of compensator unenforceable if certificate not issued within time limit.
97. Review of certificates of total benefit.
98. Appeals.
99. Recovery in consequence of an appeal.
100. Recovery of relevant payment in cases of default.

Miscellaneous

101. Persons in Northern Ireland.
102. Foreign compensators: duties of intended recipient.
103. Interest on damages: reductions in respect of relevant payments.
104. The Crown.

PART V

INCOME SUPPORT AND THE DUTY TO MAINTAIN

105. Failure to maintain—general.
106. Recovery of expenditure on benefit from person liable for maintenance.
107. Recovery of expenditure on income support: additional amounts and transfer of orders.
108. Reduction of expenditure on income support: certain maintenance orders to be enforceable by the Secretary of State.
109. Diversion of arrested earnings to Secretary of State—Scotland.

PART VI

ENFORCEMENT

Inspection and offences

110. Appointment and powers of inspectors.
111. Delay, obstruction etc. of inspector.
112. False representations for obtaining benefit etc.
113. Breach of regulations.
114. Offences relating to contributions.
115. Offences by bodies corporate.

Legal proceedings

116. Legal proceedings.
117. Questions arising in proceedings.

Unpaid contributions etc.

118. Evidence of non-payment.
119. Recovery of unpaid contributions on prosecution.
120. Proof of previous offences.
121. Unpaid contributions—supplementary.

PART VII

PROVISION OF INFORMATION

Inland Revenue

122. Disclosure of information by Inland Revenue.

Persons employed or formerly employed in social security administration or adjudication

123. Unauthorised disclosure of information relating to particular persons.

The Registration Service

124. Provisions relating to age, death and marriage.
125. Regulations as to notification of deaths.

Personal representatives—income support and supplementary benefit

126. Personal representatives to give information about the estate of a deceased person who was in receipt of income support or supplementary benefit.

Housing benefit

127. Information for purposes of housing benefit.

Community charge benefits

128. Information for purposes of community charge benefits.

Statutory sick pay and other benefits

129. Disclosure by Secretary of State for purpose of determination of period of entitlement to statutory sick pay.
130. Duties of employers—statutory sick pay and claims for other benefits.

Statutory maternity pay and other benefits

131. Disclosure by Secretary of State for purpose of determination of period of entitlement to statutory maternity pay.
132. Duties of employers—statutory maternity pay and claims for other benefits.

Maintenance proceedings

133. Furnishing of addresses for maintenance proceedings, etc.

PART VIII

ARRANGEMENTS FOR HOUSING BENEFIT AND COMMUNITY CHARGE BENEFITS AND RELATED SUBSIDIES

Housing benefit

134. Arrangements for housing benefit.
135. Housing benefit finance.
136. Rent allowance subsidy and determinations of rent officers.
137. Claims etc.

Community charge benefits

138. Nature of benefits.
139. Arrangements for community charge benefits.
140. Community charge benefit finance.

PART IX

ALTERATION OF CONTRIBUTIONS ETC.

141. Annual review of contributions.
142. Orders under s.141—supplementary.
143. Power to alter contributions with a view to adjusting level of National Insurance Fund.
144. Orders under s.143—supplementary.
145. Power to alter primary and secondary contributions.
146. Power to alter number of secondary earnings brackets.
147. Orders under ss.145 and 146—supplementary.
148. Revaluation of earnings factors.
149. Statutory sick pay—power to alter limit for small employers' relief.

PART X

REVIEW AND ALTERATION OF BENEFITS

150. Annual up-rating of benefits.
151. Up-rating—supplementary.
152. Rectification of mistakes in orders under section 150.
153. Annual review of child benefit.
154. Social security benefits in respect of children.

PART XI

COMPUTATION OF BENEFITS

155. Effect of alteration of rates of benefit under Parts II to V of Contributions and Benefits Act.
156. Computation of Category A retirement pension with increase under s.52(3) of Contributions and Benefits Act.
157. Effect of alteration of rates of child benefit.
158. Treatment of excess benefit as paid on account of child benefit.
159. Effect of alteration in the component rates of income support.
160. Implementation of increases in income support due to attainment of particular ages.

PART XII

FINANCE

161. National Insurance Fund.
162. Destination of contributions.
163. General financial arrangements.
164. Destination of repayments etc.
165. Adjustments between National Insurance Fund and Consolidated Fund.
166. Financial review and report.
167. The social fund.
168. Allocations from social fund.
169. Adjustments between social fund and other sources of finance.

PART XIII

ADVISORY BODIES AND CONSULTATION

The Social Security Advisory Committee and the Industrial Injuries Advisory Council

170. The Social Security Advisory Committee.
171. The Industrial Injuries Advisory Council.
172. Functions of Committee and Council in relation to regulations.
173. Cases in which consultation is not required.
174. Committee's report on regulations and Secretary of State's duties.

The Disability Living Allowance Advisory Board

175. Disability Living Allowance Advisory Board.

Housing benefit and community charge benefits

176. Consultation with representative organisations.

PART XIV

SOCIAL SECURITY SYSTEMS OUTSIDE GREAT BRITAIN

Co-ordination

177. Co-ordination with Northern Ireland.

Reciprocity

178. Reciprocal arrangements with Northern Ireland—income-related benefits and child benefit.
179. Reciprocal agreements with countries outside the United Kingdom.

PART XV

MISCELLANEOUS

Travelling expenses

180. Payment of travelling expenses by Secretary of State.

Offences

181. Impersonation of officers.
182. Illegal possession of documents.

Industrial injuries and diseases

183. Research on industrial injuries, etc.
184. Control of pneumoconiosis.

Workmen's compensation etc.

185. Administration of workmen's compensation etc.

Supplementary benefit etc.

186. Application of provisions of Act to supplementary benefit etc.

Miscellaneous

187. Certain benefit to be inalienable.
188. Exemption from stamp duty.

PART XVI

GENERAL

Subordinate legislation

189. Regulations and orders—general.
190. Parliamentary control of orders and regulations.

Supplementary

191. Interpretation—general.
192. Short title, commencement and extent.

SCHEDULES:
Schedule 1—Claims for benefit made or treated as made before 1st October 1990.
Schedule 2—Commissioners, tribunals etc.—supplementary provisions.
Schedule 3—Regulations as to procedure.
Schedule 4—Persons employed in social security administration or adjudication.
Part I—The specified persons.
Part II—Construction of references to government departments etc.
Schedule 5—Social Security Advisory Committee.
Schedule 6—Industrial Injuries Advisory Council.
Schedule 7—Regulations not requiring prior submission.
Part I—Social Security Advisory Committee.
Part II—Industrial Injuries Advisory Council.
Schedule 8—Constitution etc. of Joint Authority for Great Britain and Northern Ireland.
Schedule 9—Old Cases payments administration.
Schedule 10—Supplementary benefit etc.

An Act to consolidate certain enactments relating to the administration of social security and related matters with amendments to give effect to recommendations of the Law Commission and the Scottish Law Commission.   [13th February 1992]

PARLIAMENTARY DEBATES
Hansard, H.L. Vol. 534, col. 1480.
The Bill was discussed in Joint Committee on November 27 and December 4, 1991.

GENERAL NOTE
The Act brings together the existing social security legislation on claims, payments, adjudication and other aspects of administration. Its partner is the Social Security Contributions and Benefits Act 1992.
The Act comes into force on July 1, 1992, but there are a few amendments and omissions which take effect from the same date, by virtue of Sched. 4 to the Social Security (Consequential Provisions) Act 1992. This is to take account of provisions in the legislation which is consolidated which have not yet been brought into force.

ABBREVIATIONS

Adjudication Regulations	:	Social Security (Adjudication) Regulations 1986 (S.I. 1986 No. 2218)
AO	:	Adjudication Officer
Bonner *et al.*	:	Bonner, Hooker and White, *Non-Means Tested Benefits: the Legislation* (Sweet & Maxwell)
Claims and Payments Regulations	:	Social Security (Claims and Payments) Regulations 1987 (S.I. 1987 No. 1968)
Contributions and Benefits Act	:	Social Security Contributions and Benefits Act 1992
DAT	:	Disability Appeal Tribunal
Findlay and Ward	:	Findlay and Ward, *CPAG's Housing Benefit and Community Charge Benefit Legislation* (Child Poverty Action Group)
MAT	:	Medical Appeal Tribunal
Mesher	:	Mesher, *CPAG's Income-Related Benefits: the Legislation* (Sweet & Maxwell)
Rowland	:	Rowland, *Medical and Disability Appeal Tribunals: the Legislation* (Sweet & Maxwell)
SSAC	:	Social Security Adjudication Committee
SSAT	:	Social Security Appeal Tribunal
UBO	:	Unemployment Benefit Office

PART I

CLAIMS FOR AND PAYMENTS AND GENERAL ADMINISTRATION OF BENEFIT

Necessity of Claim

Entitlement to benefit dependent on claim

1.—(1) Except in such cases as may be prescribed, and subject to the following provisions of this section and to section 3 below, no person shall be entitled to any benefit unless, in addition to any other conditions relating to that benefit being satisfied—

(a) he makes a claim for it in the manner, and within the time, prescribed in relation to that benefit by regulations under this Part of this Act; or

(b) he is treated by virtue of such regulations as making a claim for it.

(2) Where under subsection (1) above a person is required to make a claim or to be treated as making a claim for a benefit in order to be entitled to it—

(a) if the benefit is a widow's payment, she shall not be entitled to it in respect of a death occurring more than 12 months before the date on which the claim is made or treated as made; and

(b) if the benefit is any other benefit except disablement benefit or reduced earnings allowance, the person shall not be entitled to it in respect of any period more than 12 months before that date,

except as provided by section 3 below.

(3) Where a person purports to make a claim on behalf of another—

(a) for an attendance allowance by virtue of section 66(1) of the Contributions and Benefits Act; or

(b) for a disability living allowance by virtue of section 72(5) or 73(12) of that Act,

that other shall be regarded for the purposes of this section as making the claim, notwithstanding that it is made without his knowledge or authority.

(4) In this section and section 2 below "benefit" means—

(a) benefit as defined in section 122 of the Contributions and Benefits Act; and

(b) any income-related benefit.

(5) This section (which corresponds to section 165A of the 1975 Act, as it had effect immediately before this Act came into force) applies to claims made on or after 1st October 1990 or treated by virtue of regulations under that section or this section as having been made on or after that date.

(6) Schedule 1 to this Act shall have effect in relation to other claims.

<small>DEFINITIONS</small>
"the 1975 Act": s.191.
"claim": *ibid.*
"the Contributions and Benefits Act": *ibid.*
"disablement benefit": *ibid.*
"income-related benefit": *ibid.*
"prescribe": *ibid.*

<small>GENERAL NOTE</small>

Subs. (1)
The general rule is that there cannot be entitlement to benefit unless a claim is made for it. Section 1 applies to income-related benefits, *i.e.* including income support, family credit and disability working allowance, but excluding payments from the social fund (subs. (4)). "Benefit", as defined in s.122 of the Social Security Contributions and Benefits Act 1992, does not include income-related benefits. Section 1 applies to claims made on or after October 1, 1990. Schedule 1 deals with earlier claims.

The introduction of the predecessor of s.1 was precipitated by the decision of the House of Lords in *Insurance Officer* v. *McCaffrey* [1984] 1 W.L.R. 1353 that (subject to an express provision to the contrary) a person was entitled to benefit if he met the conditions of entitlement even though he had not made a claim for that benefit. Claiming went to payability, not entitlement. This was contrary to the long-standing assumption of the DSS and was corrected with effect from September 2, 1985.

Section 3, which is excluded from the operation of s.1, deals with late claims for widow's benefits where the death of the spouse is difficult to establish.

Subs. (2)
This provision imposes an overall limit of 12 months to the entitlement to benefit before the date of claim. Not all benefits are caught by subs. (1) and there is a further exclusion in para. (b). Regulation 19 of and Sched. 4 to the Social Security (Claims and Payments) Regulations 1987 impose the ordinary time limits for claiming and allow many of those limits to be extended where the claimant proves good cause for the delay. In the case of income support, family

credit, disability working allowance and social fund maternity and funeral payments, where there is such an extension the claim is then treated as made on the first day of the period for which the claim is allowed to relate (reg. 6(3)). Although the drafting is not at all clear, the reference in subs. (2) to the 12-month limit from the date on which the claim is made or is treated as made seems to make the limit start from the date fixed by reg. 6(3). However, reg. 19(4) prevents an extension for good cause in the benefits covered by reg. 6(3) leading to entitlement earlier than 12 months before the actual date of claim. But the restriction seems to stem from that regulation and not from s.1(2), or the earlier forms set out in Sched. 1.

Retrospective effect of provisions making entitlement to benefit dependent on claim

2.—(1) This section applies where a claim for benefit is made or treated as made at any time on or after 2nd September 1985 (the date on which section 165A of the 1975 Act (general provision as to necessity of claim for entitlement to benefit), as originally enacted, came into force) in respect of a period the whole or any part of which falls on or after that date.

(2) Where this section applies, any question arising as to—

(a) whether the claimant is or was at any time (whether before, on or after 2nd September 1985) entitled to the benefit in question, or to any other benefit on which his entitlement to that benefit depends; or

(b) in a case where the claimant's entitlement to the benefit depends on the entitlement of another person to a benefit, whether that other person is or was so entitled,

shall be determined as if the relevant claim enactment and any regulations made under or referred to in that enactment had also been in force, with any necessary modifications, at all times relevant for the purpose of determining the entitlement of the claimant, and, where applicable, of the other person, to the benefit or benefits in question (including the entitlement of any person to any benefit on which that entitlement depends, and so on).

(3) In this section "the relevant claim enactment" means section 1 above as it has effect in relation to the claim referred to in subsection (1) above.

(4) In any case where—

(a) a claim for benefit was made or treated as made (whether before, on or after 2nd September 1985, and whether by the same claimant as the claim referred to in subsection (1) above or not), and benefit was awarded on that claim, in respect of a period falling wholly or partly before that date; but

(b) that award would not have been made had the current requirements applied in relation to claims for benefit, whenever made, in respect of periods before that date; and

(c) entitlement to the benefit claimed as mentioned in subsection (1) above depends on whether the claimant or some other person was previously entitled or treated as entitled to that or some other benefit,

then, in determining whether the conditions of entitlement to the benefit so claimed are satisfied, the person to whom benefit was awarded as mentioned in paragraphs (a) and (b) above shall be taken to have been entitled to the benefit so awarded, notwithstanding anything in subsection (2) above.

(5) In subsection (4) above "the current requirements" means—

(a) the relevant claim enactment, and any regulations made or treated as made under that enactment, or referred to in it, as in force at the time of the claim referred to in subsection (1) above, with any necessary modifications; and

(b) subsection (1) (with the omission of the words following "at any time") and subsections (2) and (3) above.

DEFINITIONS
"the 1975 Act": s.191.
"benefit": s.1(4).
"claim": s.191.
"claimant": *ibid.*

GENERAL NOTE

There are a number of benefits where entitlement can depend on whether a person was entitled to a benefit at some earlier date (*e.g.* on reaching pensionable age). While the predecessor of s.1 clearly governed such questions from September 2, 1985 onwards, it was arguable that in relation to earlier dates the *McCaffrey* principle (see note to s.1(1) above) had to be applied. In CS 49/1989 a Social Security Commissioner decided that this argument was correct. The predecessor of s.2 was inserted by the Social Security Act 1990 to reverse the effect of that decision and to do so retrospectively back to September 2, 1985.

The form of s.2 is complex and the retrospective effects are difficult to work out. It only applies to claims made or treated as made on or after September 2, 1985 (subs. (1)). Thus very late appeals or very long good causes for late claim might not be affected. Then on any such claim if a question of entitlement at any other date arises (including dates before September 2, 1985) that question is to be decided according to the principle of s.1 as it was in force at the relevant time (subs. (2)). The only exception to this is that if for any period benefit has been awarded following a claim, that beneficiary is to be treated as entitled to that benefit even though under the current requirements he would not be (subs. (4)).

Widowhood benefits

Late claims for widowhood benefit where death is difficult to establish

3.—(1) This section applies where a woman's husband has died or may be presumed to have died and the circumstances are such that—

(a) more than 12 months have elapsed since the date of death (whether he died, or is presumed to have died, before or after the coming into force of this section);

(b) either—

(i) the husband's body has not been discovered or identified or, if it has been discovered and identified, the woman does not know that fact; or

(ii) less than 12 months have elapsed since she first knew of the discovery and identification of the body; and

(c) no claim for any of the widowhood benefits, that is to say—

(i) widow's benefit,

(ii) an invalidity pension under section 15 of the Pensions Act, or

(iii) a Category A retirement pension by virtue of subsection (5) of that section,

was made or treated as made in respect of the death by the woman before 13th July 1990 (the coming into force of section 6 of the Social Security Act 1990, which inserted in the 1975 Act section 165C, the provision of that Act corresponding to this section).

(2) Where this section applies, notwithstanding that any time prescribed for making a claim for a widowhood benefit in respect of the death has elapsed, then—

(a) in any case falling within paragraph (b)(i) of subsection (1) above where it has been determined—

(i) under subsection (1)(b) of section 20 below on a claim made by the woman; or

(ii) under subsection (4) of that section on the submission of a question by her,

that the husband has died or is presumed to have died; or

(b) in any case falling within paragraph (b)(ii) of subsection (1) above where the identification was made not more than 12 months before

the woman first knew of the discovery and identification of the body, such a claim may be made or treated as made at any time before the expiration of the period of 12 months beginning with the date on which that determination was made or, as the case may be, the date on which she first knew of the discovery and identification.

(3) If, in a case where a claim for a widowhood benefit is made or treated as made by virtue of this section, the claimant would, apart from subsection (2) of section 1 above, be entitled to—

  (a) a widow's payment in respect of the husband's death more than 12 months before the date on which the claim is made or treated as made; or

  (b) any other widowhood benefit in respect of his death for a period more than 12 months before that date,

then, notwithstanding anything in that section, she shall be entitled to that payment or, as the case may be, to that other benefit (together with any increase under section 80(5) of the Contributions and Benefits Act).

GENERAL NOTE

The predecessor of this section was part of the Social Security Act 1990. It applies to benefits to which widows are entitled on their late husband's contributions, where the claim is made after July 12, 1990. If there is a delay in discovering or identifying the husband's body or the widow has to rely on the presumption of death, s.3 can operate to allow entitlement to be backdated beyond the normal 12 months under s.1.

If the husband's body has not to the knowledge (actual, not reasonably to be expected) of the widow been discovered and identified and his death or presumption of death has been determined in an AO's decision (subss. (1)(b)(i) and (2)(a)) a claim may be made within 12 months of that determination. Then there can be entitlement back to the date or presumed date of death, even though that goes back more than 12 months before the date of claim (subs. (3)). Where the widow does know of the discovery and identification of her husband's body she may claim within 12 months of acquiring that knowledge (subss. (1)(b)(ii) and (2)), with the same element of backdating (subs. (3)). However, if more than 12 months elapsed between the actual identification and the widow's coming to know of it, she cannot rely on s.3 (subs. (2)(b)) if she has not already done so under subs. (1)(b)(i).

Treatment of payments of benefit to certain widows

4. In any case where—

  (a) a claim for a widow's pension or a widowed mother's allowance is made, or treated as made, before 13th July 1990 (the date of the passing of the Social Security Act 1990); and

  (b) the Secretary of State has made a payment to or for the claimant on the ground that if the claim had been received immediately after the passing of that Act she would have been entitled to that pension or allowance, or entitled to it at a higher rate, for the period in respect of which the payment is made,

the payment so made shall be treated as a payment of that pension or allowance; and, if and to the extent that an award of the pension or allowance, or an award at a higher rate, is made for the period in respect of which the payment was made, the payment shall be treated as made in accordance with that award.

Claims and payments regulations

Regulations about claims for and payments of benefit

5.—(1) Regulations may provide—

  (a) for requiring a claim for a benefit to which this section applies to be made by such person, in such manner and within such time as may be prescribed;

  (b) for treating such a claim made in such circumstances as may be prescribed as having been made at such date earlier or later than that at which it is made as may be prescribed;

  (c) for permitting such a claim to be made, or treated as if made, for a period wholly or partly after the date on which it is made;

  (d) for permitting an award on such a claim to be made for such a period subject to the condition that the claimant satisfies the requirements for entitlement when benefit becomes payable under the award;

(e) for a review of any such award if those requirements are found not to have been satisfied;

(f) for the disallowance on any ground of a person's claim for a benefit to which this section applies to be treated as a disallowance of any further claim by that person for that benefit until the grounds of the original disallowance have ceased to exist;

(g) for enabling one person to act for another in relation to a claim for a benefit to which this section applies and for enabling such a claim to be made and proceeded with in the name of a person who has died;

(h) for requiring any information or evidence needed for the determination of such a claim or of any question arising in connection with such a claim to be furnished by such person as may be prescribed in accordance with the regulations;

(i) for the person to whom, time when and manner in which a benefit to which this section applies is to be paid and for the information and evidence to be furnished in connection with the payment of such a benefit;

(j) for notice to be given of any change of circumstances affecting the continuance of entitlement to such a benefit or payment of such a benefit;

(k) for the day on which entitlement to such a benefit is to begin or end;

(l) for calculating the amounts of such a benefit according to a prescribed scale or otherwise adjusting them so as to avoid fractional amounts or facilitate computation;

(m) for extinguishing the right to payment of such a benefit if payment is not obtained within such period, not being less than 12 months, as may be prescribed from the date on which the right is treated under the regulations as having arisen;

(n) for suspending payment, in whole or in part, where it appears to the Secretary of State that a question arises whether—
(i) the conditions for entitlement are or were fulfilled;
(ii) an award ought to be revised;
(iii) an appeal ought to be brought against an award;

(o) for withholding payments of a benefit to which this section applies in prescribed circumstances and for subsequently making withheld payments in prescribed circumstances;

(p) for the circumstances and manner in which payments of such a benefit may be made to another person on behalf of the beneficiary for any purpose, which may be to discharge, in whole or in part, an obligation of the beneficiary or any other person;

(q) for the payment or distribution of such a benefit to or among persons claiming to be entitled on the death of any person and for dispensing with strict proof of their title;

(r) for the making of a payment on account of such a benefit—
(i) where no claim has been made and it is impracticable for one to be made immediately;
(ii) where a claim has been made and it is impracticable for the claim or an appeal, reference, review or application relating to it to be immediately determined;
(iii) where an award has been made but it is impracticable to pay the whole immediately.

(2) This section applies to the following benefits—

(a) benefits as defined in section 122 of the Contributions and Benefits Act;

(b) income support;

(c) family credit;

(d) disability working allowance;
(e) housing benefit;
(f) any social fund payments such as are mentioned in section 138(1)(a) or (2) of the Contributions and Benefits Act;
(g) child benefit; and
(h) Christmas bonus.

(3) The reference in subsection (1)(h) above to information or evidence needed for the determination of a claim includes a reference to information or evidence required by a rent officer under section 121 of the Housing Act 1988.

(4) Subsection (1)(n) above shall have effect in relation to housing benefit as if the reference to the Secretary of State were a reference to the authority paying the benefit.

(5) Subsection (1)(g), (i), (l), (p) and (q) above shall have effect as if statutory sick pay and statutory maternity pay were benefits to which this section applies.

DEFINITIONS
"the Contributions and Benefits Act": s.191.
"prescribed": *ibid.*

GENERAL NOTE
See the Social Security (Claims and Payments) Regulations 1987 (S.I. 1987 No. 1968). The provisions relevant to particular benefits will be found in the current editions of Bonner *et al.*, Mesher and Rowland.

Community charge benefits etc.

Regulations about community charge benefits administration

6.—(1) Regulations may provide as follows as regards any community charge benefit—
(a) for requiring a claim for a benefit to be made by such person, in such manner and within such time as may be prescribed;
(b) for treating a claim made in such circumstances as may be prescribed as having been made at such date earlier or later than that at which it is made as may be prescribed;
(c) for permitting a claim to be made, or treated as if made, for a period wholly or partly after the date on which it is made;
(d) for permitting an award on a claim to be made for such a period subject to the condition that the claimant satisfies the requirements for entitlement when benefit becomes payable, or any right to a reduction or a consequential reduction becomes available, under the award;
(e) for a review of any award if those requirements are found not to have been satisfied;
(f) for the disallowance on any ground of a person's claim for a benefit to be treated as a disallowance of any further claim by that person for that benefit until the grounds of the original disallowance have ceased to exist;
(g) for enabling one person to act for another in relation to a claim for a benefit and for enabling such a claim to be made and proceeded with in the name of a person who has died;
(h) for requiring any information or evidence needed for the determination of a claim or of any question arising in connection with a claim to be furnished by such person as may be prescribed in accordance with the regulations;
(i) for the time when and manner in which any benefit (or part) which takes the form of a payment is to be paid, and for the information and evidence to be furnished in connection with the payment;

(j) for the time when the right to make a reduction or consequential reduction may be exercised;

(k) for notice to be given of any change of circumstances affecting the continuance of entitlement to a benefit;

(l) for the day on which entitlement to a benefit is to begin or end;

(m) for calculating the amount of a benefit according to a prescribed scale or otherwise adjusting it so as to avoid fractional amounts or facilitate computation;

(n) for suspending (in whole or in part) any payment or right to make a reduction or consequential reduction, where it appears to the authority which allowed a benefit that a question arises whether the conditions for entitlement to the benefit are or were fulfilled or whether the award ought to be revised or whether an appeal ought to be brought against the award;

(o) for withholding in prescribed circumstances any payment or right to make a reduction or consequential reduction, and for subsequently making in prescribed circumstances any withheld payment or restoring in prescribed circumstances any right to make a reduction or consequential reduction;

(p) in the case of any benefit (or part) which takes the form of a payment, for payment or distribution to or among persons claiming to be entitled on the death of any person, and for dispensing with strict proof of their title;

(q) in the case of any benefit (or part) which takes the form of a payment, for the circumstances and manner in which payment may be made to one person on behalf of another for any purpose, which may be to discharge, in whole or in part, an obligation of the person entitled to the benefit or any other person;

(r) for making a payment on account of a benefit, or conferring a right to make a reduction or consequential reduction on account, where no claim has been made and it is impracticable for one to be made immediately;

(s) for making a payment on account of a benefit, or conferring a right to make a reduction or consequential reduction on account, where a claim has been made but it is impracticable for the claim or an appeal, reference, review or application relating to it to be determined immediately;

(t) for making a payment on account of a benefit, or conferring a right to make a reduction or consequential reduction on account, where an award has been made but it is impracticable to institute the benefit immediately;

(u) generally as to administration.

(2) Regulations under this section may include provision in relation to community charge benefits that prescribed provisions shall apply instead of prescribed provisions of the Abolition of Domestic Rates Etc. (Scotland) Act 1987 or the Local Government Finance Act 1988, or that prescribed provisions of either of those Acts shall not apply or shall apply subject to prescribed amendments or adaptations.

(3) References in subsection (2) above to either of the Acts there mentioned include references to regulations made under the Act concerned.

DEFINITIONS
"prescribe": s.191.

GENERAL NOTE
See Parts VIII to X of the Community Charge Benefits (General) Regulations 1989 (S.I. 1989 No. 1321), in the current edition of Findlay and Ward.

Relationship between community charge benefits and other benefits

7.—(1) Regulations may provide for a claim for one relevant benefit to be treated, either in the alternative or in addition, as a claim for any other relevant benefit that may be prescribed.

(2) Regulations may provide for treating a payment made or right conferred by virtue of regulations—

(a) under section 5(1)(r) above; or

(b) under section 6(1)(r) to (t) above,

as made or conferred on account of any relevant benefit that is subsequently awarded or paid.

(3) For the purposes of subsections (1) and (2) above relevant benefits are—

(a) any benefit to which section 5 above applies; and

(b) any community charge benefit.

DEFINITIONS

"claim": s.191.

"prescribed": *ibid.*

GENERAL NOTE

Subs. (1)

See the Social Security (Claims and Payments) Regulations 1987 (S.I. 1987 No. 1968), Sched. 1. The provisions relevant to particular benefits will be found in the current editions of Bonner *et al.*, Findlay and Ward, Mesher and Rowland.

Subs. (2)

See the Social Security (Payments on account, Overpayments and Recovery) Regulations 1988 (S.I. 1988 No. 688), regs. 5–8, in the current editions of Bonner *et al.* and Mesher.

Industrial injuries benefit

Notification of accidents, etc.

8. Regulations may provide—

(a) for requiring the prescribed notice of an accident in respect of which industrial injuries benefit may be payable to be given within the prescribed time by the employed earner to the earner's employer or other prescribed person;

(b) for requiring employers—

(i) to make reports, to such person and in such form and within such time as may be prescribed, of accidents in respect of which industrial injuries benefit may be payable;

(ii) to furnish to the prescribed person any information required for the determination of claims, or of questions arising in connection with claims or awards;

(iii) to take such other steps as may be prescribed to facilitate the giving notice of accidents, the making of claims and the determination of claims and of questions so arising.

DEFINITIONS

"industrial injuries benefits": s.191.

"prescribe": *ibid.*

GENERAL NOTE

See regs. 24 and 25 of the Social Security (Claims and Payments) Regulations 1979 (S.I. 1979 No. 628), in the current edition of Bonner *et al.*

Medical examination and treatment of claimants

9.—(1) Regulations may provide for requiring claimants for disablement benefit—

(a) to submit themselves from time to time to medical examination for the purpose of determining the effect of the relevant accident, or the treatment appropriate to the relevant injury or loss of faculty;

(b) to submit themselves from time to time to appropriate medical treatment for the injury or loss of faculty.

(2) Regulations under subsection (1) above requiring persons to submit themselves to medical examination or treatment may—

(a) require those persons to attend at such places and at such times as may be required; and

(b) with the consent of the Treasury provide for the payment by the Secretary of State to those persons of travelling and other allowances (including compensation for loss of remunerative time).

DEFINITIONS
"disablement benefit": s.191.
"prescribe": *ibid.*

GENERAL NOTE
See reg. 26 of the Social Security (Claims and Payments) Regulations 1979 (S.I. 1979 No. 628), in the current edition of Bonner *et al.*

Obligations of claimants

10.—(1) Subject to subsection (3) below, regulations may provide for disqualifying a claimant for the receipt of industrial injuries benefit—

(a) for failure without good cause to comply with any requirement of regulations to which this subsection applies (including in the case of a claim for industrial death benefit, a failure on the part of some other person to give the prescribed notice of the relevant accident);

(b) for wilful obstruction of, or other misconduct in connection with, any examination or treatment to which he is required under regulations to which this subsection applies to submit himself, or in proceedings under this Act for the determination of his right to benefit or to its receipt,

or for suspending proceedings on the claim or payment of benefit as the case may be, in the case of any such failure, obstruction or misconduct.

(2) The regulations to which subsection (1) above applies are—

(a) any regulations made by virtue of section 5(1)(h), (i) or (l) above, so far as relating to industrial injuries benefit; and

(b) regulations made by virtue of section 8 or 9 above.

(3) Regulations under subsection (1) above providing for disqualification for the receipt of benefit for any of the following matters, that is to say—

(a) for failure to comply with the requirements of regulations under section 9(1) or (2) above;

(b) for obstruction of, or misconduct in connection with, medical examination or treatment,

shall not be made so as to disentitle a claimant to benefit for a period exceeding 6 weeks on any disqualification.

DEFINITION
"industrial injuries benefits": s.191.

GENERAL NOTE
See reg. 40 of the Social Security (General Benefit) Regulations 1982 (S.I. 1982 No. 1408), in the current edition of Bonner *et al.*

Disability working allowance

Initial claims and repeat claims

11.—(1) In this section—

"initial claim" means a claim for a disability working allowance made by a person—

    (a) to whom it has not previously been payable; or

    (b) to whom it has not been payable during the period of 2 years immediately preceding the date on which the claim is made or is treated as made; and

"repeat claim" means any other claim for a disability working allowance.

(2) On an initial claim a declaration by the claimant that he has a physical or mental disability which puts him at a disadvantage in getting a job is conclusive, except in such circumstances as may be prescribed, that for the purposes of section 129(1)(b) of the Contributions and Benefits Act he has such a disability (in accordance with regulations under section 129(3) of that Act).

(3) If—

    (a) a repeat claim is made or treated as made not later than the end of the period of 8 weeks commencing with the last day of the claimant's previous award; and

    (b) on the claim which resulted in that award he qualified under section 129(2) of the Contributions and Benefits Act by virtue—

        (i) of paragraph (a) of that subsection; or

        (ii) of there being payable to him a benefit under an enactment having effect in Northern Ireland and corresponding to a benefit mentioned in that paragraph,

he shall be treated on the repeat claim as if he still so qualified.

DEFINITIONS

"the Contributions and Benefits Act": s.191.

GENERAL NOTE

Section 11 supplies some special rules under which some parts of the qualifications for disability working allowance are deemed to be satisfied.

Subs. (1)

An initial claim is one made by a person who has never been entitled to disability working allowance or whose last week of entitlement was more than two years before the date of claim. Any other claim is a repeat claim.

Subs. (2)

On an initial claim a claimant's declaration, on the elaborate self-assessment claim form, that he has a disability that puts him at a disadvantage in getting a job, is conclusive. This general rule does not apply if the claim itself contains indications to the contrary or the AO has before him evidence pointing to the contrary (Disability Working Allowance (General) Regulations 1991 (S.I. 1991 No. 2887), reg. 4).

Subs. (3)

This provision applies to claimants who have been awarded disability working allowance on the basis that they were entitled to invalidity pension, severe disability allowance or income support, housing benefit or community charge benefit with the disability premium or pensioner premium for disability or any Northern Ireland equivalent (see Contributions and Benefits Act, s.129(2)(a) and (4) and Disability Working Allowance (General) Regulations 1991 (S.I. 1991 No. 2887), reg. 7). When such an award expires and the repeat claim is made within eight weeks, the claimant is deemed to satisfy the requirement. Thus if a claimant initially qualifies on this ground and continues to satisfy the other conditions of entitlement, awards may continue indefinitely.

The social fund

Necessity of application for certain payments

12.—(1) A social fund payment such as is mentioned in section 138(1)(b) of the Contributions and Benefits Act may be awarded to a person only if an application for such a payment has been made by him or on his behalf in such form and manner as may be prescribed.

(2) The Secretary of State may by regulations—

(a) make provision with respect to the time at which an application for such a social fund payment is to be treated as made;

(b) prescribe conditions that must be satisfied before any determination in connection with such an application may be made or any award of such a payment may be paid;

(c) prescribe circumstances in which such an award becomes extinguished.

DEFINITIONS
"the Contributions and Benefits Act": s.191.
"prescribe": *ibid.*

GENERAL NOTE

Subs. (1)
This provision applies to the "ordinary" social fund, not to funeral or maternity payments or cold weather payments. See the Social Fund (Applications) Regulations 1988 (S.I. 1988 No. 524), in the current edition of Mesher.

Subs. (2)
See the Social Fund (Miscellaneous Provisions) Regulations 1990 (S.I. 1990 No. 1788), in the current edition of Mesher.

Child benefit

Necessity of application for child benefit

13.—(1) Subject to the provisions of this Act, no person shall be entitled to child benefit unless he claims it in the manner, and within the time, prescribed in relation to child benefit by regulations under section 5 above.

(2) Except where regulations otherwise provide, no person shall be entitled to child benefit for any week on a claim made by him after that week if child benefit in respect of the same child has already been paid for that week to another person, whether or not that other person was entitled to it.

DEFINITIONS
"prescribe": s.191.

GENERAL NOTE

Subs. (1)
See the Social Security (Claims and Payments) Regulations 1987 (S.I. 1987 No. 1968), especially reg. 19(6), in the current edition of Bonner *et al.*

Subs. (2)
Payment of child benefit in respect of a child to one person, even if that person is not entitled to payment, generally bars payment to anyone else. See reg. 14A of the Child Benefit (General) Regulations 1976 (S.I. 1976 No. 965), in the current edition of Bonner *et al.*, for an exception.

Statutory sick pay

Duties of employees etc. in relation to statutory sick pay

14.—(1) Any employee who claims to be entitled to statutory sick pay from his employer shall, if so required by his employer, provide such information as may reasonably be required for the purpose of determining the duration of the period of entitlement in question or whether a period of entitlement exists as between them.

(2) The Secretary of State may by regulations direct—

(a) that medical information required under subsection (1) above shall, in such cases as may be prescribed, be provided in a prescribed form;

(b) that an employee shall not be required under subsection (1) above to provide medical information in respect of such days as may be prescribed in a period of incapacity for work.

(3) Where an employee asks an employer of his to provide him with a written statement, in respect of a period before the request is made, of one or more of the following—

(a) the days within that period which the employer regards as days in respect of which he is liable to pay statutory sick pay to that employee;

(b) the reasons why the employer does not so regard the other days in that period;

(c) the employer's opinion as to the amount of statutory sick pay to which the employee is entitled in respect of each of those days,

the employer shall, to the extent to which the request was reasonable, comply with it within a reasonable time.

DEFINITIONS
"prescribe": s.191.

GENERAL NOTE

Subss. (1) and (2)
There is a general obligation on the employee to provide information to the employer to enable a claim for statutory sick pay to be determined. See reg. 7 of the Statutory Sick Pay (General) Regulations 1982 (S.I. 1982 No. 894), in the current edition of Bonner *et al.*, for the time and manner of notification of incapacity for work, and the Statutory Sick Pay (Medical Evidence) Regulations 1985 (S.I. 1985 No. 1604).

Subs. (3)
See regs. 15 and 15A of the Statutory Sick Pay (General Regulations) 1982.

Statutory maternity pay

Duties of women etc. in relation to statutory maternity pay

15.—(1) A woman shall provide the person who is liable to pay her statutory maternity pay—

(a) with evidence as to her pregnancy and the expected date of confinement in such form and at such time as may be prescribed; and

(b) where she commences work after her confinement but within the maternity pay period, with such additional information as may be prescribed.

(2) Where a woman asks an employer or former employer of hers to provide her with a written statement, in respect of a period before the request is made, of one or more of the following—

(a) the weeks within that period which he regards as weeks in respect of which he is liable to pay statutory maternity pay to the woman;

(b) the reasons why he does not so regard the other weeks in that period; and

(c) his opinion as to the amount of statutory maternity pay to which the woman is entitled in respect of each of the weeks in respect of which he regards himself as liable to make a payment,

the employer or former employer shall, to the extent to which the request was reasonable, comply with it within a reasonable time.

DEFINITIONS
"prescribe": s.191.

GENERAL NOTE

Subs. (1)
See regs. 22 and 24 of the Statutory Maternity Pay (General) Regulations 1986 (S.I. 1986 No. 1960), in the current edition of Bonner *et al.*

Subs. (2)
The duty on the employer under subs. (3) to supply the woman with information about the reasons for decisions on entitlement or non-entitlement to statutory maternity pay supplements the duties in reg. 25A of the Statutory Maternity Pay (General Regulations) 1986, which apply when the woman wishes to claim another benefit.

Emergency payments

Emergency payments by local authorities and other bodies

16.—(1) The Secretary of State may make arrangements—
(a) with a local authority to which this section applies; or
(b) with any other body,
for the making on his behalf by members of the staff of any such authority or body of payments on account of benefits to which section 5 above applies in circumstances corresponding to those in which the Secretary of State himself has the power to make such payments under subsection (1)(r) of that section; and a local authority to which this section applies shall have power to enter into any such arrangements.

(2) A payment under any such arrangements shall be treated for the purposes of any Act of Parliament or instrument made under an Act of Parliament as if it had been made by the Secretary of State.

(3) The Secretary of State shall repay a local authority or other body such amount as he determines to be the reasonable administrative expenses incurred by the authority or body in making payments in accordance with arrangements under this section.

(4) The local authorities to which this section applies are—
(a) a local authority as defined by section 270(1) of the Local Government Act 1972, other than a parish or community council;
(b) the Common Council of the City of London; and
(c) a local authority as defined in section 235(1) of the Local Government (Scotland) Act 1973.

PART II

ADJUDICATION

Adjudication by the Secretary of State

Questions for the Secretary of State

17.—(1) Subject to this Part of this Act, any of the following questions shall be determined by the Secretary of State—
(a) a question whether a person is an earner and, if he is, as to the category of earners in which he is to be included;
(b) subject to subsection (2) below, a question whether the contribution conditions for any benefit are satisfied, or otherwise relating to a person's contributions or his earnings factor;
(c) a question whether a Class 1A contribution is payable or otherwise relating to a Class 1A contribution;
(d) a question whether a person is or was employed in employed earner's employment for the purposes of Part V of the Contributions and Benefits Act;
(e) a question as to whether a person was, within the meaning of regulations, precluded from regular employment by responsibilities at home;

   (f) any question as to which surpluses are to be taken into account under section 45(1) of the Contributions and Benefits Act;

   (g) any question arising under any provision of Part XI of the Contributions and Benefits Act or this Act, or under any provision of regulations under that Part, as to—

      (i) whether a person is, or was, an employee or employer of another;

      (ii) whether an employer is entitled to make any deduction from his contributions payments in accordance with regulations under section 158 of the Contributions and Benefits Act;

      (iii) whether a payment falls to be made to an employer in accordance with the regulations;

      (iv) the amount that falls to be so deducted or paid;

      (v) the amount of an employer's contributions payments for any period for the purposes of regulations under section 158(3) of the Contributions and Benefits Act; or

      (vi) whether two or more employers or two or more contracts of service are, by virtue of regulations made under section 163(5) of that Act, to be treated as one; and

   (h) any question arising under any provision of Part XII of that Act or this Act, or under any provision of regulations under that Part, as to—

      (i) whether a person is, or was, an employee or employer of another;

      (ii) whether an employer is entitled to make any deduction from his contributions payments in accordance with regulations under section 167 of the Contributions and Benefits Act;

      (iii) whether a payment falls to be made to an employer in accordance with the regulations;

      (iv) the amount that falls to be so deducted or paid; or

      (v) whether two or more employers or two or more contracts of service are, by virtue of regulations made under section 171(2) of that Act, to be treated as one,

and any question arising under regulations made by virtue of paragraph (c), (d) or (f) of section 164(9) of that Act.

   (2) Subsection (1)(b) above includes any question arising—

   (a) under section 17(1) of the Contributions and Benefits Act as to whether by regulations under that subsection a person is excepted from liability for Class 4 contributions, or his liability is deferred; or

   (b) under regulations made by virtue of section 17(3) or (4) or 18 of that Act;

but not any other question relating to Class 4 contributions, nor any question within section 20(1)(c) below.

   (3) Regulations may make provision restricting the persons who may apply to the Secretary of State for the determination of any such question as is mentioned in subsection (1) above.

   (4) The Secretary of State may, if he thinks fit, before determining any such question as is mentioned in subsection (1) above, appoint a person to hold an inquiry into the question, or any matters arising in connection with it, and to report on the question, or on those matters, to the Secretary of State.

DEFINITIONS

   "the Contributions and Benefits Act": s.191.

GENERAL NOTE

   Section 17 defines questions which are to be decided by the Secretary of State and not by the adjudicating authorities (*i.e.* AO, tribunal and Social Security Commissioner). The questions are mainly to do with the type of contributions which a person is required to pay and whether the contribution conditions for benefits are satisfied. There may well be surrounding issues, such as the identification of the relevant year in which the contribution test must be satisfied (see *R(G) 1/82*), which are for the adjudicating authorities to determine. But, in relation to subs. (1)(b), the core question of whether a claimant has made sufficient contributions for entitlement remains with the Secretary of State (*Scrivner* v. *Chief Adjudication Officer, The Times*, November 7, 1989). In that case, the question was whether contributions paid in Belgium could count for entitlement to British unemployment benefit. The Court of Appeal disapproved of the suggestion that *R(G) 1/82* meant that all issues of law were for the adjudicating authorities, with only the provision of the figures being left to the Secretary of State.

Many decisions under s.17 are taken by locally based Benefits Agency staff authorised to act on behalf of the Secretary of State, but there is also a central unit which deals mainly with difficult questions of the categorisation of earners. The inquiry procedure provided by subs. (4) is also used mainly for such questions.

For a detailed description of the history and use of the Secretary of State's powers, and a powerful critique of the present arrangements, see Partington, *The Secretary of State's Powers in Social Security Adjudication* (1991).

Appeal on question of law

18.—(1) A question of law arising in connection with the determination by the Secretary of State of any such question as is mentioned in section 17(1) above may, if the Secretary of State thinks fit, be referred for decision to the High Court or, in Scotland, to the Court of Session.

(2) If the Secretary of State determines in accordance with subsection (1) above to refer any question of law to the court, he shall give notice in writing of his intention to do so—

(a) in a case where the question arises on an application made to the Secretary of State, to the applicant; and

(b) in any case to such persons as appear to him to be concerned with the question.

(3) Any person aggrieved by the decision of the Secretary of State on any question of law within subsection (1) above which is not referred in accordance with that subsection may appeal from that decision to the court.

(4) The Secretary of State shall be entitled to appear and be heard on any such reference or appeal.

(5) Rules of court shall include provision for regulating references and appeals under this section and for limiting the time within which such appeals may be brought.

(6) Notwithstanding anything in any Act, the decision of the court on a reference or appeal under this section shall be final.

(7) On any such reference or appeal the court may order the Secretary of State to pay the costs (in Scotland, the expenses) of any other person, whether or not the decision is in that other person's favour and whether or not the Secretary of State appears on the reference or appeal.

GENERAL NOTE

Where the Secretary of State has made a formal determination under s.17, there is a right of appeal to the Court of Appeal or the Court of Session. The Secretary of State may also refer questions of law to the court. Insufficient cases proceed to the courts for the judges nominated to hear such appeals to develop any expertise in the complexities of social security contributions.

Review of decisions

19.—(1) Subject to subsection (2) below, the Secretary of State may review any decision given by him on any such question as is mentioned in section 17(1) above if—

(a) new facts have been brought to his notice; or

(b) he is satisfied that the decision—

(i) was given in ignorance of some material fact;

(ii) was based on a mistake as to some material fact; or

(iii) was erroneous in point of law.

(2) A decision shall not be reviewed while an appeal under section 18 above is pending against the decision of the Secretary of State on a question of law arising in connection with it, or before the time for so appealing has expired.

(3) On a review any question of law may be referred under subsection (1) of section 18 above or, where it is not so referred, may be the subject of an appeal under subsection (3) of that section, and the other provisions of that section shall apply accordingly.

GENERAL NOTE

The Secretary of State has wide powers to review a decision given under s.17. The fact that it is a ground of review that the decision was erroneous in point of law was seized on by the Court of Appeal in *Chief Adjudication Officer and Secretary of State for Social Security* v. *Foster* [1991] 3 W.L.R. 473 as a reason for not allowing the Social Security Commissioners (or tribunals or AOs) to determine whether regulations had been validly made. It was said that if the Commissioners could do this in determining whether a tribunal's decision was erroneous in point of law, it would mean that the Secretary of State under s.19(1)(b)(iii) could determine whether he had acted lawfully in making regulations, which would be absurd. It is far from clear that such a consequence would follow. See the notes to s.23 below.

Adjudication by adjudication officers

Claims and questions to be submitted to adjudication officer

20.—(1) Subject to section 54 below, there shall be submitted forthwith to an adjudication officer for determination in accordance with this Part of this Act—

(a) any claim for a benefit to which this section applies;

(b) subject to subsection (2) below, any question arising in connection with a claim for, or award of, such a benefit; and

(c) any question whether, if he had otherwise had a right to it, a person would be disqualified—

(i) by reason of section 28(1) of the Contributions and Benefits Act, for receiving unemployment benefit;

(ii) by reason of any regulations under section 32(1) of that Act, for receiving sickness benefit; or

(iii) by reason of any regulations under section 59(1) of that Act, for receiving invalidity benefit.

(2) Subsection (1) above does not apply to any question which falls to be determined otherwise than by an adjudication officer.

(3) Any question as to, or in connection with, entitlement to statutory sick pay or statutory maternity pay may be submitted to an adjudication officer—

(a) by the Secretary of State; or

(b) subject to and in accordance with regulations, by the employee concerned,

for determination in accordance with this Part of this Act.

(4) If—

(a) a person submits a question relating to the age, marriage or death of any person; and

(b) it appears to the adjudication officer that the question may arise if the person who has submitted it to him submits a claim to a benefit to which this section applies,

the adjudication officer may determine the question.

(5) Different aspects of the same claim or question may be submitted to different adjudication officers; and for that purpose this section and the other provisions of this Part of this Act with respect to the determination of claims and questions shall apply with any necessary modifications.

(6) This section applies to the following benefits—

(a) benefits as defined in section 122 of the Contributions and Benefits Act;
(b) income support;
(c) family credit;
(d) disability working allowance;
(e) any social fund payment such as is mentioned in section 138(1)(a) or (2) of the Contributions and Benefits Act;
(f) child benefit;
(g) statutory sick pay; and
(h) statutory maternity pay.

DEFINITIONS
"the Contributions and Benefits Act": s.191.

GENERAL NOTE

Subs. (1)
See subss. (3), (4) and (6) for the benefits to which this section applies. Subs. (2) merely confirms that questions to be determined by the Secretary of State under s.17 do not go to the AO.
In *R.* v. *Secretary of State for Social Services,* ex p. *Child Poverty Action Group* [1990] 2 Q.B. 540, the Court of Appeal decided that the duty to submit a claim "forthwith" did not arise until the DSS (now the Benefits Agency) was in possession of the basic information necessary to determine the claim. However, once that information was there, any need for verification did not justify delay in submitting the claim to the AO. It would then be for the AO to make enquiries, if he considered that verification was necessary.
In *R(SB) 29/84* the Tribunal of Commissioners (by a majority) held that the question whether payment had actually been made following an award (*i.e.* what should happen following an allegedly lost Giro) was not a "question relating to supplementary benefit" (Supplementary Benefits Act 1976, s.2(1)), and therefore was not a matter for an AO or SSAT. Any remedy was to be pursued through the courts. *R(IS) 7/91* holds, after an exhaustive review of the legislation, that the result is the same under the predecessor of subs. (1)(b). The question whether the Secretary of State has implemented an award of benefit is not a question in connection with an award of benefit.

Subs. (6)
Under para. (e), s.20 applies to funeral and maternity payments and cold-weather payments from the social fund.

Decision of adjudication officer

21.—(1) An adjudication officer to whom a claim or question is submitted under section 20 above (other than a claim which under section 30(12) or (13) or 35(7) below falls to be treated as an application for a review) shall take it into consideration and, so far as practicable, dispose of it, in accordance with this section, and with procedure regulations under section 59 below, within 14 days of its submission to him.
(2) Subject to subsection (3) and section 37 below, the adjudication officer may decide a claim or question himself or refer it to a social security appeal tribunal.
(3) The adjudication officer must decide a claim for or question relating to an attendance allowance, a disability living allowance or a disability working allowance himself.
(4) Where an adjudication officer refers a question as to, or in connection with, entitlement to statutory sick pay or statutory maternity pay to a social security appeal tribunal, the employee and employer concerned shall each be given notice in writing of the reference.
(5) In any other case notice in writing of the reference shall be given to the claimant.
(6) Where—
(a) a case has been referred to a social security appeal tribunal ("the tribunal"); and

(b) the claimant makes a further claim which raises the same or similar questions; and

(c) that further claim is referred to the tribunal by the adjudication officer,

then the tribunal may proceed to determine the further claim whether or not notice has been given under subsection (4) or (5) above.

GENERAL NOTE

Subs. (1)

The general rule is that the AO should make a decision within 14 days, once the claim or question is submitted to him under s.20. In *R.* v. *Secretary of State for Social Services*, ex p. *Child Poverty Action Group* [1990] 2 Q.B. 540, the Court of Appeal upheld Schiemann J.'s decision that there was no breach of the predecessor of subs. (1) if a heavy workload prevented an AO from disposing of the claim or question within the 14 days. It was clear that the Act intended that claims should be dealt with expeditiously, but this was merely one factor which the Secretary of State had to consider in exercising his discretion as to the number of AOs to appoint. He was under no duty to appoint enough AOs to deal with all claims within 14 days.

It also appears that the need to obtain verification of information may make it not practicable to reach a decision within 14 days. Although the obligation of a claimant under reg. 7 of the Social Security (Claims and Payments) Regulations 1987 (S.I. 1987 No. 1968) to provide such evidence, information, etc., as required by the Secretary of State (mentioned in *R(SB) 29/83* as relevant to practicability) is now presumably relevant to s.21, the rest of the decision probably holds. After a reasonable length of time, even if further information is not forthcoming, the AO must make a decision on the evidence available to him. Then, if the decision is adverse, the claimant has something to appeal against and the adequacy of the information before the AO can be dealt with by the SSAT. Note that there is no longer a power for the Secretary of State to deem a claim to have been withdrawn if the information required under reg. 7 is not produced.

It has been held that an AO does not "discharge responsibilities of a judicial nature" (Glidewell L.J. in *Jones* v. *Department of Employment* [1988] 1 All E. R. 725, 733), but clearly the AO's administrative decisions must be reached in a judicial manner. The investigatory functions most recently emphasised in the CPAG case do not extend to a duty to investigate the claimant's entire financial situation on a review (*Duggan* v. *Chief Adjudication Officer, The Times*, December 19, 1988; *R(SB) 13/89*).

The Court of Appeal in *Chief Adjudication Officer and Secretary of State for Social Security* v. *Foster* [1991] 3 W.L.R. 473 has decided that the AO (as well as social security appeal tribunals and Social Security Commissioners) must reach decisions on the basis that all regulations are validly made. Only the High Court or the Court of Appeal has the jurisdiction to declare regulations *ultra vires*. While this is true, the proposition that an adjudicating authority must apply a provision which is not validly part of English law is very dubious and is to be challenged in the appeal to the House of Lords which will be heard in October 1992. The Court of Appeal in *Foster* does not refer to earlier cases in which the Court of Appeal has raised no objection to the Social Security Commissioners dealing with the validity of regulations (*Bhatia* v. *Birmingham*, appendix to *R(S) 8/83*, and *Kilburn* v. *Chief Adjudication Officer*, appendix to *R(SB) 9/87*).

An AO cannot be bound by any assurance given by an employee of the DSS or the Benefits Agency about a claimant's entitlement, but must come to a proper decision on the law applicable to the case. Even if a claimant had relied on a statement from or on behalf of an AO, this requirement to carry out the statutory duty prevents an estoppel arising (*R(SB) 14/88*, *R(SB) 14/89*, and Woolf L.J. refusing leave to appeal in *R(SB) 4/91*).

The claims excluded from the operation of subs. (1) by the words in brackets are certain claims for disability living allowance or disability working allowance. Under ss.30(12) and 35(7), if an award of either of those benefits has been made for a period a further claim made within that period is treated as an application to review the existing award. Under s.30(13), where an AO's decision is not to award one of those benefits or attendance allowance, any further claim made during the period prescribed for applying for a review of that decision on any ground (*i.e.* eight weeks: Social Security (Adjudication) Regulations 1986 (S.I. 1986 No. 2218), reg. 26A) is treated as an application for review.

Subs. (2)

The AO no longer has express power to decide questions in any particular way. The power to make references to the SSAT is used mainly where there is a conflict of evidence which the AO feels unable to resolve. The most common situation is where the accounts of a claimant of unemployment benefit and his ex-employer of the reasons why employment was ended conflict. The question of whether a disqualification for misconduct or leaving voluntarily without just cause should be imposed may then be referred to the SSAT. Another use is where a further claim is made following on from a period which is to be dealt with by the SSAT in determining an appeal (see subs. (6)).

The effect of subs. (3) is that such references cannot be made in disability working allowance cases. Section 37 is concerned with the reference of special questions.

Subs. (3)

In these cases the AO must determine the claim or question himself, and so cannot refer a matter to a SSAT or DAT. This is no doubt because the process of appeal for these benefits must start with a review by another AO before there can be an appeal to the SSAT or DAT.

Subss. (4) and (5)

Subsections (4) and (5) do not prescribe any particular period in advance of the hearing for the written notice of a reference to be given. The Tribunal of Commissioners in *R(S) 5/86* decided that whatever is a reasonable time in the circumstances is the test. The same decision holds that the requirement that the reference is to be in writing cannot be waived by the claimant. Note the exception introduced by subs. (6), which has been in operation since April 1990.

Subs. (6)

Once a case has been properly referred to a SSAT under subs. (2) a further claim raising similar questions may be referred to the SSAT for decision without notice in writing being given to the claimant. It is obviously desirable that notice that the SSAT is to be asked to deal with the further claim should be given to the claimant if possible.

Appeals from adjudication officers—general

Appeal to social security appeal tribunal

22.—(1) Subject to subsection (3) below, where the adjudication officer has decided a claim or question other than a claim or question relating to an attendance allowance, a disability living allowance or a disability working allowance—

    (a) if it relates to statutory sick pay or statutory maternity pay, the employee and employer concerned shall each have a right to appeal to a social security appeal tribunal; and

    (b) in any other case the claimant shall have a right to do so.

(2) A person with a right of appeal under this section shall be given such notice of a decision falling within subsection (1) above and of that right as may be prescribed.

(3) No appeal lies under this section where—

    (a) in connection with the decision of the adjudication officer there has arisen any question which under or by virtue of this Act falls to be determined otherwise than by an adjudication officer; and

    (b) the question has been determined; and

    (c) the adjudication officer certifies that the decision on that question is the sole ground of his decision.

(4) Regulations may make provision as to the manner in which, and the time within which, appeals are to be brought.

(5) Where an adjudication officer has determined that any amount, other than an amount—

    (a) of an attendance allowance;

    (b) of a disability living allowance;

    (c) of a disability working allowance;

    (d) of statutory sick pay; or

    (e) of statutory maternity pay,

is recoverable under or by virtue of section 71 or 74 below, any person from whom he has determined that it is recoverable shall have the same right of appeal to a social security appeal tribunal as a claimant.

(6) In any case where—

(a) an adjudication officer has decided any claim or question under Part V of the Contributions and Benefits Act; and

(b) the right to benefit under that Part of that Act of any person other than the claimant is or may be, under Part VI of Schedule 7 to that Act, affected by that decision,

that other person shall have the like right of appeal to a social security appeal tribunal as the claimant.

(7) Subsection (2) above shall apply to a person with a right of appeal under subsection (5) or (6) above as it applies to a claimant.

GENERAL NOTE

Subs. (1)

There is a general right of appeal to a SSAT for a claimant against any decision of an AO on any claim or question. Note that under subs. (5) a person from whom an overpayment of most benefits has been determined to be recoverable has the same right of appeal as a claimant. Subsection (1) does not cover attendance allowance, disability living allowance and disability working allowance, where the appeal on most questions is to a DAT. See ss.30–33.

Subs. (2)

See the Social Security (Adjudication) Regulations 1986 (S.I. 1986 No. 2218), particularly regs. 20 and 63, in the current editions of Bonner *et al.* and Mesher.

Subs. (3)

There can be no valid appeal to the SSAT where the AO certifies that the sole ground of his decision was the determination of a question which is for another authority (*e.g.* the Secretary of State) to determine.

Subs. (4)

See reg. 3 of and Sched. 2 to the Adjudication Regulations (above), in the current editions of Bonner *et al.* and Mesher.

Subs. (5)

A person from whom it is determined that an overpayment of most benefits is recoverable has a right to appeal against the AO's decision to that effect. This applies to overpayments under s.71 (misrepresentation or failure to disclose) and s.74 (duplication of income support and other payments). A person falling within subs. (5) must be given notice of the decision and the right of appeal (subss. (2) and (7)).

The benefits listed in paras. (a)–(e) are excluded from the operation of subs. (5). See s.32(9) for rights of appeal against decisions on the recoverability of attendance allowance, disability living allowance and disability working allowance.

Subs. (6)

Part V of the Contributions and Benefits Act concerns industrial injuries benefits. Part VI of Sched. 7 concerns industrial death benefit, which can only be awarded in respect of deaths before April 11, 1988. Subsection (6) preserves a right of appeal for the surviving spouse in relation to decisions about the deceased's entitlement to industrial injuries benefit. Outside that situation, an appeal abates on the death of the claimant, but is revived by appointment of a personal representative of the estate or of an appointee under the Social Security (Claims and Payments) Regulations 1987 (S.I. 1987 No. 1968) (*R(SB) 8/88* and *R(SB) 5/90*).

Appeal from social security appeal tribunal to Commissioner

23.—(1) Subject to the provisions of this section, an appeal lies to a Commissioner from any decision of a social security appeal tribunal under section 22 above on the ground that the decision of the tribunal was erroneous in point of law.

(2) In the case of statutory sick pay or statutory maternity pay an appeal lies under this section at the instance of any of the following—

(a) an adjudication officer;

(b) the employee concerned;

(c) the employer concerned;

(d) a trade union, where—

(i) the employee is a member of the union at the time of the appeal and was so immediately before the question at issue arose; or

(ii) the question at issue is a question as to or in connection with entitlement of a deceased person who was at the time of his death a member of the union;

(e) an association of employers of which the employer is a member at the time of the appeal and was so immediately before the question at issue arose.

(3) In any other case an appeal lies under this section at the instance of any of the following—

(a) an adjudication officer;

(b) the claimant;

(c) in any of the cases mentioned in subsection (5) below, a trade union; and

(d) a person from whom it is determined that any amount is recoverable under section 71(1) or 74 below.

(4) In a case relating to industrial injuries benefit an appeal lies under this section at the instance of a person whose right to benefit is, or may be, under Part VI of Schedule 7 to the Contributions and Benefits Act, affected by the decision appealed against, as well as at the instance of any person or body such as is mentioned in subsection (3) above.

(5) The following are the cases in which an appeal lies at the instance of a trade union—

(a) where the claimant is a member of the union at the time of the appeal and was so immediately before the question at issue arose;

(b) where that question in any way relates to a deceased person who was a member of the union at the time of his death;

(c) where the case relates to industrial injuries benefit and the claimant or, in relation to industrial death benefit, the deceased, was a member of the union at the time of the relevant accident.

(6) Subsections (2), (3) and (5) above, as they apply to a trade union, apply also to any other association which exists to promote the interests and welfare of its members.

(7) Where the Commissioner holds that the decision was erroneous in point of law, he shall set it aside and—

(a) he shall have power—

(i) to give the decision which he considers the tribunal should have given, if he can do so without making fresh or further findings of fact; or

(ii) if he considers it expedient, to make such findings and to give such decision as he considers appropriate in the light of them; and

(b) in any other case he shall refer the case to a tribunal with directions for its determination.

(8) Subject to any direction of the Commissioner, the tribunal on a reference under subsection (7)(b) above shall consist of persons who were not members of the tribunal which gave the erroneous decision.

(9) No appeal lies under this section without the leave—

(a) of the person who was the chairman of the tribunal when the decision was given or, in a prescribed case, the leave of some other chairman; or

(b) subject to and in accordance with regulations, of a Commissioner.

(10) Regulations may make provision as to the manner in which, and the time within which, appeals are to be brought and applications made for leave to appeal.

DEFINITIONS
  "Commissioner": s.191.
  "prescribed": *ibid.*

GENERAL NOTE

Subs. (1)
  There may only be an appeal from a decision under s.22 to the Commissioner on the ground that the SSAT made an error of law. See s.34 for attendance allowance, disability living allowance and disability working allowance cases. Note also the requirement under subs. (10) for leave to appeal to be given by the SSAT chairman (or a substitute) or a Commissioner.
  There are a number of other parts of the Commissioners' jurisdiction where appeal is on a point of law only and the well-established tests have been taken over here. In *R(SB) 6/81* the most accurate and concise summary is said to be that set out in *R(A) 1/72*. The Social Security Commissioner there held that a decision would be wrong in law if (i) it contained a false proposition of law on its face; (ii) it was supported by no evidence; or (iii) the facts found were such that no person acting judicially and properly instructed as to the relevant law could have come to the determination in question.
  CSB 29/81 refers to *R(I) 14/75*, which sets out the three heads quoted above and adds (iv) breach of the requirements of natural justice; and (v) failure to state adequate reasons.
  The formula of five headings is adopted in *R(SB) 11/83* (although by reference to decisions of the courts rather than the Commissioners) and is now clearly accepted.
  The result of the Court of Appeal's decision in the *Foster* case (see notes to s.21(1)) is that it is not an error of law under head (i) for a SSAT to apply a regulation which has not been validly made, but which has not been declared to be *ultra vires* in judicial review proceedings.
  In determining whether there is an error of law under head (iii) it is necessary to look at all the evidence presented to the tribunal, not only that recorded in the findings of fact or the chairman's notes of evidence. It is only if a decision cannot be supported looking at the totality of the evidence presented that an error of law is committed (*CSB 15/82, R(SB) 16/82, R(S) 1/88*). If an item of evidence was not before the SSAT, it cannot in itself be an error of law not to have considered it. The Commissioners have held that they are not restricted to looking at the formal SSAT documents but may consider any reliable account of what evidence was presented (*CSB 34/81, R(SB) 10/82, R(SB) 18/83*). However, the approach to such accounts is somewhat cautious. The Commissioner in *R(SB) 10/82* suggested an over-elaborate procedure for producing an account agreed between the parties to be referred to the SSAT chairman. That approach is rejected in *R(M)1/89*. The Tribunal of Commissioners there holds that it is a matter for the Commissioner's discretion what evidence about the proceedings to admit.

Subss. (2)–(6)
  These provisions define the parties who may make an appeal from a SSAT in various kinds of cases and deal with trade unions and other organisations.

Subs. (7)
  This important provision on the powers of the Commissioner seems oddly placed in the middle of s.23. Paragraph (a)(i) confirms the power of the Commissioner to give the decision the SSAT should have given where no further findings of fact are necessary. Paragraph (a)(ii) gives the power (new in 1987) for the Commissioner, when he considers it expedient, to make fresh or further findings of fact and then to give a decision in the light of those findings. The power has been used by Commissioners in a large number of appeals, including *R(SB) 11/88* and *CSB 176/1987*. In the first decision, the Commissioner held that the power existed from April 6, 1987 and that it did not matter that the SSAT decision was before that date. In the second, the Commissioner called for quite a lot of new evidence, although there was no real dispute over the facts. A Commissioner is more likely to send factual disputes back to a SSAT, although practice varies. The power is most often used where the SSAT has failed to make express findings on matters which are not in dispute or on which the result of the existing evidence is clear. There may be some difficulty if a Commissioner is making a decision partly on his own assessment of evidence and partly on the SSAT's assessment of evidence which the Commissioner has not directly heard or seen.
  If para. (a) does not apply, then under para. (b) the case must be referred to a SSAT with directions. These have normally included a direction that no members of the original SSAT should be on the new one, as is now expressly required by subs. (8) unless the Commissioner directs otherwise.

Subs. (9)

A party who wishes to appeal from a SSAT decision must get leave from either the chairman of the SSAT (or a substitute under reg. 26(4) of the Social Security (Adjudication) Regulations 1986 (S.I. 1986 No. 2218)) or a Commissioner. Regulation 26 deals with the procedure for applying for leave to the chairman, and the time limit is three months (Adjudication Regulations, Sched. 2, para. 7). If the chairman refuses leave, a party has 42 days to apply to a Commissioner for leave (Social Security Commissioners Procedure Regulations 1987 (S.I. 1987 No. 214), reg. 3). A Commissioner may deal with late applications if, for special reasons, he thinks fit (reg. 3(2) and (5)).

A mere assertion of a mistake of law is not enough for leave to be granted. There must be some material in the case indicating that there is a sensible argument in support (*R(SB) 1/81*). There is, in the nature of things, not much further guidance given to chairmen about whether to give leave or not. The most helpful statement is in para. 30 of *R(S) 4/82*. The Tribunal of Commissioners stresses that the chairman's discretion is unfettered provided that it is exercised in a judicial manner, but says that chairmen should bear in mind that the object of requiring leave to be given is to restrict appeals to those which are neither hopeless nor frivolous and raise a serious issue. If the conduct of the tribunal's proceedings is seriously in question, leave should be given, but if the allegations are general, with no supporting detail, leave should be refused. The party always has another chance by applying to the Commissioner for leave.

It is suggested that if the grounds put forward by the claimant or the AO do not contain any allegations of error of law (either expressly or by obvious implication) then the SSAT chairman should refuse leave to appeal. In particular, if the complaint is that the SSAT should have made a different decision on the facts, or that there is some new or different evidence which was not put to the SSAT (*R(S) 1/88*), that is not good enough. It is suggested that normally the chairman should not give leave simply because, on looking beyond the application, he considers that there might be some error of law in the SSAT's decision, such as inadequate findings of fact or reasons. That is something which is better dealt with by a Commissioner if the claimant or the AO makes a further application for leave to appeal.

If the Commissioner refuses leave to appeal that is not a decision within the meaning of s.24 below and so cannot be appealed to the Court of Appeal (*Bland* v. *Chief Supplementary Benefit Officer* [1983] 1 W.L.R. 262, *R(SB) 12/83*). There is no right of appeal from a refusal of leave by a chairman. The only right of appeal is from a decision of a SSAT.

Subs. (10)

See the Social Security (Adjudication) Regulations 1986 (S.I. 1986 No. 2218), regs. 3 and 26 and Sched. 2 (see the current editions of Bonner *et al.* and Mesher), and the Social Security Commissioners Procedure Regulations 1987 (S.I. 1987 No. 214).

Appeal from Commissioners on point of law

24.—(1) Subject to subsections (2) and (3) below, an appeal on a question of law shall lie to the appropriate court from any decision of a Commissioner [¹or given in consequence of a reference under section 112(4) of the 1975 Act (which enabled a medical appeal tribunal to refer a question of law to a Commissioner)].

(2) No appeal under this section shall lie from a decision except—

(a) with the leave of the Commissioner who gave the decision or, in a prescribed case, with the leave of a Commissioner selected in accordance with regulations; or

(b) if he refuses leave, with the leave of the appropriate court.

(3) An application for leave under this section in respect of a Commissioner's decision may only be made by—

(a) a person who, before the proceedings before the Commissioner were begun, was entitled to appeal to the Commissioner from the decision to which the Commissioner's decision relates;

(b) any other person who was a party to the proceedings in which the first decision mentioned in paragraph (a) above was given;

(c) the Secretary of State, in a case where he is not entitled to apply for leave by virtue of paragraph (a) or (b) above;

(d) any other person who is authorised by regulations to apply for leave; and regulations may make provision with respect to the manner in which and the time within which applications must be made to a Commissioner for leave under this section and with respect to the procedure for dealing with such applications.

(4) On an application to a Commissioner for leave under this section it shall be the duty of the Commissioner to specify as the appropriate court—

    (a) the Court of Appeal if it appears to him that the relevant place is in England or Wales;

    (b) the Court of Session if it appears to him that the relevant place is in Scotland; and

    (c) the Court of Appeal in Northern Ireland if it appears to him that the relevant place is in Northern Ireland,

except that if it appears to him, having regard to the circumstances of the case and in particular to the convenience of the persons who may be parties to the proposed appeal, that he should specify a different court mentioned in paragraphs (a) to (c) above as the appropriate court, it shall be his duty to specify that court as the appropriate court.

    (5) In this section—

        "the appropriate court", except in subsection (4) above, means the court specified in pursuance of that subsection;

        "the relevant place", in relation to an application for leave to appeal from a decision of a Commissioner, means the premises where the authority whose decision was the subject of the Commissioner's decision usually exercises its functions.

    (6) The powers to make regulations conferred by this section shall be exercisable by the Lord Chancellor.

AMENDMENT

1. Social Security (Consequential Provisions) Act 1992, Sched. 4, paras. 1 and 12 (until the repeal of s.14(7) of the Social Security Act 1980 in Sched. 9 to the Social Security Act 1989 comes into force).

DEFINITIONS

    "the 1975 Act": s.191.
    "the Commissioner": *ibid.*
    "prescribed": *ibid.*

GENERAL NOTE

    This section provides for an appeal on a point of law to the Court of Appeal, Court of Session or Court of Appeal in Northern Ireland, as appropriate, from a decision of a Commissioner, with the leave of a Commissioner or the court. See the Social Security Commissioners Procedure Regulations 1987 (S.I. 1987 No. 214).

    For the procedure applicable in Scotland, see Books of Sederunt, Rules of Court, rr. 290 and 293B (inserted by S.I. 1980 No. 1745 (s.151)).

    A decision of a Commissioner to grant or refuse leave to appeal to the Commissioner is not a "decision" from which an appeal may lie under this section (*Bland* v. *Chief Supplementary Benefit Officer* [1983] 1 W.L.R. 262).

Reviews—general

Review of decisions

    25.—(1) Subject to the following provisions of this section, any decision under this Act of an adjudication officer, a social security appeal tribunal or a Commissioner (other than a decision relating to an attendance allowance, a disability living allowance or a disability working allowance) may be reviewed at any time by an adjudication officer or, on a reference by an adjudication officer, by a social security appeal tribunal, if—

    (a) the officer or tribunal is satisfied that the decision was given in ignorance of, or was based on a mistake as to, some material fact; or

    (b) there has been any relevant change of circumstances since the decision was given; or

    (c) it is anticipated that a relevant change of circumstances will so occur; or

    (d) the decision was based on a decision of a question which under or by virtue of this Act falls to be determined otherwise than by an adjudication officer, and the decision of that question is revised; or

(e) the decision falls to be reviewed under section 57(4) or (5) of the Contributions and Benefits Act.

(2) Any decision of an adjudication officer (other than a decision relating to an attendance allowance, a disability living allowance or a disability working allowance) may be reviewed, upon the ground that it was erroneous in point of law, by an adjudication officer or, on a reference from an adjudication officer, by a social security appeal tribunal.

(3) Regulations may provide that a decision may not be reviewed on the ground mentioned in subsection (1)(a) above unless the officer or tribunal is satisfied as mentioned in that paragraph by fresh evidence.

(4) In their application to family credit, subsection (1)(b) and (c) above shall have effect subject to section 128(3) of the Contributions and Benefits Act (change of circumstances not to affect award or rate during specified period).

(5) Where a decision is reviewed on the ground mentioned in subsection (1)(c) above, the decision given on the review—

(a) shall take effect on the day prescribed for that purpose by reference to the date on which the relevant change of circumstances is expected to occur; and

(b) shall be reviewed again if the relevant change of circumstances either does not occur or occurs otherwise than on that date.

DEFINITIONS

"Commissioner": s.191.
"the Contributions and Benefits Act": *ibid.*
"prescribed": *ibid.*

GENERAL NOTE

Section 25 does not apply to attendance allowance, disability living allowance or disability working allowance. See ss.30 to 35 for reviews and appeals in those benefits.

Subs. (1)

Any decision to which s.25 applies may be reviewed by an AO on one of the five grounds set out in paras. (a)–(e). Where, as is normally the case for many benefits, an award is for an indefinite period (Social Security (Claims and Payments) Regulations 1987 (S.I. 1987 No. 1968), reg. 17(1)), any alteration to that award must be by way of review and revision. The principle flows from the fundamental rule in s.60 of this Act that a decision on a claim, for whatever period covered by the decision, is final, subject to the processes of appeal or review (see *CSSB 544/1989* and the Common Appendix to the group of decisions including *CSSB 281/1989*).

There are a number of potential exceptions to this general principle. The first is under reg. 17(4) of the Claims and Payments Regulations, which is being used as the basis for submissions that awards made for days after the date of claim may be terminated whenever the claimant ceases to satisfy the conditions of entitlement. See the current edition of Mesher for the argument that reg. 17(4) may be *ultra vires* in so far as it has this effect. The second potential exception is that ss.155, 157, 159 and 160 below provide for most alterations in rates of benefit and some prescribed figures to take effect automatically without the need for a decision by an AO. Where some kind of transitional addition to income support is in payment, review by an AO under reg. 69(3A) of the Social Security (Adjudication) Regulations 1986 (S.I. 1986 No. 2218) is necessary. Some powers of review in income support cases are given directly by reg. 69(4) and reg. 69(2) sets out circumstances in which review under s.25(1) is not to take place. However, outside these circumstances s.25(1) provides the general rule.

The significance of this is that it is clearly established (see, *e.g. CSB 376/1983*, applying *R(I) 1/71* and *CI 11/77*) that the onus lies on the person wanting the review to establish both facts justifying the review and the correctness of the subsequent revised decision. Thus if, as in *CSB 376/1983*, the AO withdraws benefit on a change of circumstances when there is insufficient information to work out benefit, he has to justify the decision on the balance of probabilities. He cannot simply rely on the claimant's not having proved his right to benefit. The same approach is taken in *CIS 1/1988* and *CIS 125/1989*. If it is the claimant requesting the review (*e.g.* by raising the question whether a previous decision denying benefit should be revised (*R(SB) 9/84*), then the onus is on him. Although s.26(1) mentions an application in writing to the AO, a request for review may be oral or even implied (*CSB 336/1987*).

A number of recent Commissioner's decisions have illuminated the general area of review through a detailed examination of review in supplementary benefit cases (see the individual decisions noted in the 1991 Supplement to Mesher). The most general point is that in principle it is for the party seeking a review to identify the decision which he wishes to have reviewed. Only once that is done can any potential grounds for review be properly identified. However, if, as was often the case, the claimant was not properly notified of the exact terms of an AO's decision (see Adjudication Regulations, reg. 63), due allowances must be made (*CSSB 470/1989*). If what is being put forward is a change of circumstances after the date of the decision, it will not be so important to establish the grounds of the original decision.

Secondly, doubt is cast on the proposition in *R(A) 2/90* that once one ground of review of a determination is established the whole determination is open to reconsideration (*CSSB 238/1989*). Even if this were right about an attendance allowance decision, the Commissioner held that it does not apply to supplementary benefit decisions. Supplementary benefit awards (and, it would seem by analogy, income support awards) are made up of a continuing award co-existing with a series of review adjustments to particular elements of the award (*CSSB 238/189* and the Common Appendix to the group of decisions including *CSSB 281/1989*). Thus where there are grounds for review of one element this does not in itself allow review of any other elements, and if one element is revised on review, that does not affect the existence of the underlying continuing award or the other elements of it. Previous decisions appearing to suggest that a decision on review completely supersedes the decision reviewed are shown to be limited to decisions which are different in nature and are indivisible, such as decisions that an overpayment is recoverable (*CSB 64/1986* and *R(SB) 15/87*) or attendance allowance cases where the review is in effect the first stage of an appeal (*R(A) 5/89*). See also *R(SB) 1/82* and *R(P) 1/82*.

Perhaps the most controversial and difficult part of these decisions is the proposition that a request for review must be directed at the last operative decision dealing with the element of which review is sought (Common Appendix to group of decisions including *CSSB 281/1989*, as explained and expanded in *CSSB 238/1989* and *CSSB 544/1989*). If there has been a series of review decisions on that element, the chain must be traced backwards, at each decision asking whether grounds for review of the immediately preceding decision exist. However, the basis for this proposition has not yet been clearly established, and its application could cause considerable problems for claimants and for the DSS. For instance, if an old award is discovered to have been based on a misrepresentation of a material fact, must the AO trace a chain of review back to the relevant decision in order to carry out the review and revision which is a necessary basis of a decision on recoverability of the overpayment under s.71?

Paras. (a)–(c)

The Social Security Commissioners have drawn a distinction between material facts and conclusions of fact (*e.g.* that a person is incapable of work, or is cohabiting). In *R(I) 3/75* (applied in *R(S) 4/86*) it is held that review is not allowed if the AO is simply satisfied that a mistaken inference was drawn from the evidence. He must go further and prove "that the inference might not have been drawn, or that a different inference might have been drawn, if the determining authority had not been ignorant of some specific fact of which it could have been aware, or had not been mistaken as to some specific fact which it took into consideration". This principle was also applied in *R(A) 2/81*. The Court of Appeal in *Saker* v. *Secretary of State for Social Services*, *The Times*, January 16, 1988 (*R(I) 2/88*) expressly decided that for a fact to be material it is not necessary that knowledge of it would have altered the decision. It is enough that the fact is one which would have called for serious consideration by the authority which made the decision and might well have affected its decision.

In *CA 90/1987*, the Commissioner applied this approach to the question of when a change of circumstances is relevant. This throws doubt on decisions such as *R(I) 56/54* and *R(A) 4/81*, where it is said that the change of circumstances must make the original decision cease to be correct. This test may be too stringent, given the authority of *Saker*, but a reported decision would clarify this important area. It is accepted that merely obtaining a different medical opinion is not a change of circumstances, although it may be evidence of an underlying change (*R(S) 6/78, R(S) 4/86*). A change in the law may amount to a change of circumstances (*R(A) 4/81*).

It is not clear quite how subs. (2) allowing review where a decision was erroneous in law affects the principles noted above. If a wrong inference is drawn from correct primary facts because the wrong legal test is applied, that is clearly an error of law. If no person properly directing himself as to the law could have drawn that inference from those primary facts, then that will be an error of law (*cf. R(A) 1/72, R(I) 14/75*). But if the AO simply changes his mind about an "inference of fact" there has been no error of law.

Para. (d)

This paragraph applies where the benefit decision was based on a decision made by someone other than the AO, typically the Secretary of State. If that other decision is revised, the benefit decision is to be reviewed and revised in line with it.

Para. (e)

These provisions of the Contributions and Benefits Act deal with availability and actively seeking work in unemployment benefit.

Regulations 65–71 of the Adjudication Regulations prevent any revision on review in most cases from making benefit payable or increasing the amount of benefit payable before certain dates. The precise rule varies according to the benefit concerned. The test is usually of so many weeks before the date of the request for review. However, these provisions are now subject to reg. 64A, which has replaced the controversial reg. 72, allowing the limit to be lifted in deserving cases.

Subs. (2)

Note that only AO decisions may be reviewed on the ground of error of law, not decisions of SSATs or the Commissioners. Otherwise the provisions on appeals would be undermined. See the notes to s.23 for "error of law." Review on this ground is subject to the restrictions of regs. 65–69 and 70 of the Adjudication Regulations, with the exemptions in reg. 64A.

Subs. (3)

No regulations have yet been made prescribing circumstances in which fresh evidence is required to trigger review.

Subs. (4)

Awards of family credit, which are normally made for a fixed period of 26 weeks, may not generally be reviewed on the ground of an actual or anticipated change of circumstances. See s.128(3) of the Contributions and Benefits Act.

Subs. (5)

There are special rules where there is a review in advance of an anticipated change of circumstances under subs. (1)(c). The decision on review takes effect on the date identified by para. 7 of Sched. 7 to the Claims and Payments Regulations. There must be a further review if the change does not happen at all, or happens on a different date.

Procedure for reviews

26.—(1) A question may be raised with a view to a review under section 25 above by means of an application in writing to an adjudication officer, stating the grounds of the application.

(2) On receipt of any such application, the adjudication officer shall proceed to deal with or refer any question arising on it in accordance with sections 21 to 23 above.

(3) Regulations may provide for enabling, or requiring, in prescribed circumstances, a review under section 25 above notwithstanding that no application for a review has been made under subsection (1) above.

GENERAL NOTE

Subs. (1)

Although this provides a useful procedure, it is not compulsory (*CSB 336/1987*). On general principle, a review should occur at any time if the AO is satisfied that the conditions are met, wherever the evidence comes from. But doubt was cast on this conclusion by the introduction of the predecessor of subs. (3) in 1987, after the time relevant to *CSB 336/1987*. In the Common Appendix to the group of decisions including *CSSB 281/1989*, the Commissioner suggests that the duty is on the Secretary of State to submit in writing to the AO any requests for review received, in whatever form, from claimants.

Subs. (3)

This power is only doubtfully necessary (see notes to subs. (1)). No regulations have yet been made.

Reviews under s.25—supplementary

27.—(1) Regulations—

(a) may prescribe what are, or are not, relevant changes of circumstances for the purposes of section 25 above; and

(b) may make provision restricting the payment of any benefit, or any increase of benefit, to which a person would, but for this subsection, be entitled by reason of a review in respect of any period before or after the review (whether that period falls wholly or partly before or after the making of the regulations).

(2) Regulations under subsection (1)(b) above shall not restrict the payment to or for a woman of so much of—

(a) any widow's benefit, any invalidity pension under section 40 of the Contributions and Benefits Act or any Category A or Category B retirement pension; or

(b) any increase of such a benefit or pension,

as falls to be paid by reason of a review which takes place by virtue of section 25(1)(a) or (1)(b) above in consequence of a claim for a widowhood benefit, within the meaning of section 3 above, which is made or treated as made by virtue of that section.

DEFINITIONS

"prescribe": s.191.

GENERAL NOTE

Subs. (1)

On para. (a), see reg. 51 of the Family Credit (General) Regulations 1987 (S.I. 1987 No. 1973) and reg. 56 of the Disability Working Allowance (General) Regulations 1991 (S.I. 1991 No. 2887) in the current edition of Mesher. On para. (b) see regs. 65–71 of the Social Security (Adjudication) Regulations 1986 (S.I. 1986 No. 2218), in the current editions of Bonner *et al.* and Mesher.

Subs. (2)

There is a special rule removing the limits on backdating of increases on review of other benefits where a claim for widowhood benefits is made under s.3.

Appeals following reviews or refusals to review

28. A decision given on a review under section 25 above, and a refusal to review a decision under that section, shall be subject to appeal in like manner as an original decision, and sections 21 to 23 above shall, with the necessary modifications, apply in relation to a decision given on such a review as they apply to the original decision of a question.

GENERAL NOTE

The ordinary rights to appeal arise from a revised decision given on review or a refusal to review. This can be a useful way of getting round the time limits on appealing against an AO's decision. A request to review the decision will, if it does not produce all that the claimant wants, generate a fresh right of appeal.

Review after claimant appeals

29. Where a claimant has appealed against a decision of an adjudication officer and the decision is reviewed by an adjudication officer under section 25 above—

(a) if the adjudication officer considers that the decision which he has made on the review is the same as the decision that would have been made on the appeal had every ground of the claimant's appeal succeeded, the appeal shall lapse; but

(b) in any other case, the review shall be of no effect and the appeal shall proceed accordingly.

GENERAL NOTE

The predecessor of this provision made an important change in the relationship between review and appeals. Previously, it was established, at least in relation to some types of decision, that if a decision was reviewed it ceased to exist, being replaced by the decision made on review (*R(SB) 1/82, R(SB) 15/87*). The effect was that any appeal already lodged against the original decision would "lapse," because there was nothing left for the appeal to bite on (see *R(A) 5/89*, which contains an authoritative review of all the earlier decisions). It is now clear from *CSSB 238/1989* that this only applies to decisions which are in their nature indivisible, like decisions that an overpayment is recoverable (*R(SB) 15/87*) or attendance allowance decisions reviewed in what is effectively the first stage of the appeal process (*R(A) 5/89*). In other cases, a review of one element of a decision leaves the rest of it intact (*R(P) 1/82*). Commissioners had in any event been able to get round the inconvenient effects of this principle in some circumstances, by treating the appeal as against the revised decision although no notice of appeal had been given (*R(SB) 15/87*). The suggestion in *R(SB) 1/82* that if an appeal had been lodged a decision should not be reviewed unless the revised decision gave the claimant everything that could have been obtained in the appeal, was only patchily applied.

Now, for reviews after April 5, 1990, if there is an appeal pending from an AO decision, a review is only of effect if the AO considers that the revised decision is the same as would have been made if every ground of the claimant's appeal had succeeded. In this case, but no other, the appeal lapses. This effect turns on the AO's opinion, but, as a matter of general principle, if the claimant disputes that the revised decision is the same as if every ground of the appeal had succeeded, the issue ought to go to the SSAT in the original appeal, although the amendment to reg. 24(1) of the Social Security (Adjudication) Regulations 1986 (S.I. 1986 No. 2218) (see the current editions of Bonner *et al.* and Mesher) suggests otherwise. Note that the grounds set out in the claimant's appeal are the crucial elements, not further arguments which might be raised against the AO's decision (see reg. 3(5) of the Adjudication Regulations).

Note also that s.29 only applies to reviews of AO decisions, not to reviews of SSAT or Commissioners' decisions.

Attendance allowance, disability living allowance and disability working allowance

Reviews of decisions of adjudication officers

30.—(1) On an application under this section made within the prescribed period, a decision of an adjudication officer under section 21 above which relates to an attendance allowance, a disability living allowance or a disability working allowance may be reviewed on any ground subject, in the case of disability working allowance, to section 129(6) of the Contributions and Benefits Act.

(2) On an application under this section made after the end of the prescribed period, a decision of an adjudication officer under section 21 above which relates to an attendance allowance or a disability living allowance may be reviewed if—

(a) the adjudication officer is satisfied that the decision was given in ignorance of, or was based on a mistake as to, some material fact; or

(b) there has been any relevant change of circumstances since the decision was given; or

(c) it is anticipated that a relevant change of circumstances will so occur; or

(d) the decision was erroneous in point of law; or

(e) the decision was to make an award for a period wholly or partly after the date on which the claim was made or treated as made but subject to a condition being fulfilled and that condition has not been fulfilled,

but regulations may provide that a decision may not be reviewed on the ground mentioned in paragraph (a) above unless the officer is satisfied as mentioned in that paragraph by fresh evidence.

(3) Regulations may prescribe what are, or are not, relevant changes of circumstances for the purposes of subsection (2)(b) and (c) above.

(4) On an application under this section made after the end of the prescribed period, a decision of an adjudication officer under section 21

above that a person is or was at any time terminally ill for the purposes of section 66(1), 72(5) or 73(12) of the Contributions and Benefits Act may be reviewed if there has been a change of medical opinion with respect to his condition or his reasonable expectation of life.

(5) On an application under this section made after the end of the prescribed period, a decision of an adjudication officer under section 21 above which relates to a disability working allowance may be reviewed if—

   (a) the adjudication officer is satisfied that the decision was given in ignorance of, or was based on a mistake as to, some material fact; or

   (b) subject to section 129(6) of the Contributions and Benefits Act, there has been any prescribed change of circumstances since the decision was given; or

   (c) the decision was erroneous in point of law; or

   (d) the decision was to make an award for a period wholly or partly after the date on which the claim was made or treated as made but subject to a condition being fulfilled and that condition has not been fulfilled,

but regulations may provide that a decision may not be reviewed on the ground mentioned in paragraph (a) above unless the officer is satisfied as mentioned in that paragraph by fresh evidence.

(6) The claimant shall be given such notification as may be prescribed of a decision which may be reviewed under this section and of his right to a review under subsection (1) above.

(7) A question may be raised with a view to a review under this section by means of an application made in writing to an adjudication officer stating the grounds of the application and supplying such information and evidence as may be prescribed.

(8) Regulations—

   (a) may provide for enabling or requiring, in prescribed circumstances, a review under this section notwithstanding that no application under subsection (7) above has been made; and

   (b) if they do so provide, shall specify under which provision of this section a review carried out by virtue of any such regulations falls.

(9) Reviews under this section shall be carried out by adjudication officers.

(10) Different aspects of any question which arises on such a review may be dealt with by different adjudication officers; and for this purpose this section and the other provisions of this Part of this Act which relate to reviews under this section shall apply with any necessary modifications.

(11) If a review is under subsection (1) above, the officer who took the decision under review shall not deal with any question which arises on the review.

(12) Except in prescribed circumstances, where a claim for a disability living allowance in respect of a person already awarded such an allowance by an adjudication officer is made or treated as made during the period for which he has been awarded the allowance, it shall be treated as an application for a review under this section.

(13) Where—

   (a) a claim for an attendance allowance, a disability living allowance or a disability working allowance in respect of a person has been refused; and

   (b) a further claim for the same allowance is made in respect of him within the period prescribed under subsection (1) above,

the further claim shall be treated as an application for a review under that subsection.

DEFINITIONS
    "the Contributions and Benefits Act": s.191.
    "prescribe": *ibid.*

GENERAL NOTE
    Section 30 deals with two types of review in attendance allowance, disability living allowance and disability working allowance cases. The first, under subs. (1), is review as the first stage of appeal against the initial AO's decision. The second, under subs. (2) or (5), is the "ordinary" review, on similar grounds to those provided in s.25(1).

Subs. (1)
    There is no provision in the legislation for an appeal from the initial decision of an AO under s.21 on an attendance allowance, disability living allowance or disability working allowance claim. Therefore, a claimant dissatisfied with the initial decision must apply for a review under this provision. The application must be made within the prescribed period, *i.e.* three months from the date on which notice of the AO's decision was given (Social Security (Adjudication) Regulations 1986 (S.I. 1986 No. 2218), reg. 26A, in the current editions of Mesher and Rowland). It seems that because review can only be considered "on an application under this section", the claimant must make an application and it must, under subs. (7), be made in writing to an AO. Although the words of subs. (7) are merely permissive, the words of subs. (1) seem to produce a different result from those of s.26(1). This is unfortunate, because review on specified grounds under subs. (2) or (5) is not available until after the end of the prescribed period unless there has already been a review under subs. (1). If, for instance, an AO notices just after an initial decision has been issued to the claimant that there has been an error of law, it appears that the decision cannot be reviewed unless the AO invites the claimant to apply for a review. Possibly an application could be made to the AO by a person acting on behalf of the Secretary of State.
    Once an application has been made, review may be on any ground. This obviously covers mistake or ignorance of material facts as at the date of the decision or an error of law. But it can also cover a difference of opinion as to what conclusion to draw from the material facts and changes of circumstances after the date of the decision. However, there are a number of limitations. First, if the AO had made an award of disability working allowance, there can be no review on the basis of a change of circumstances (Contributions and Benefits Act, s.129(6)). Second, if the AO's initial decision was not to make an award, any revised decision on review under subs. (1) cannot take effect before the date of the application for review (Adjudication Regulations, regs. 65(4C) and 70B(1)). This rule seems completely wrong if review is the first stage of the appeal process and it reveals that the decision has been mistaken from the outset, but is clearly set out in the regulations.
    If, after a decision refusing an award, a claimant makes a new claim during the prescribed period, it is to be treated as an application for review under subs. (1) (subs. (13)). The review is to be carried out by a different AO from the AO who made the initial decision (subs. (9) and (11)). The claimant has a right of appeal to a tribunal under s.33(1).

Subs. (2)
    Subsection (2) applies to attendance allowance and disability living allowance. See the notes to subs. (1) for the argument that the opening words of this subsection mean that an application in writing to the AO is necessary before review can be considered. The argument that an application can be made on behalf of the Secretary of State is much stronger here, otherwise there would be no way of reviewing an award wrongly made to a claimant.
    Normally an application under subs. (2) has to be made after the end of the prescribed period of three months from the date on which notice of the AO's initial decision was given (Adjudication Regulations, reg. 26A(1)). But if there has been a decision on review under subs. (1), whether favourable or unfavourable to the claimant, then an application under subs. (2) can be made at any time to review that decision (s.31(1)).
    See the notes to s.25(1)(a)–(c) and (2) for review under paras. (a)–(d). No regulations have been made requiring fresh evidence to be produced for para. (a), but see reg. 65(4A) of the Adjudication Regulations.
    Paragraph (e) is roughly equivalent to reg.17(4) of the Social Security (Claims and Payments) Regulations 1987, which appears to apply a condition to awards of benefit including attendance allowance and disability living allowance.
    If a person is dissatisfied with a refusal to review or a decision on review, then there must be an application for a further review under the conditions of subs. (1) before there can be an appeal to a tribunal (s.31(2)).

Subs. (3)

No regulations prescribing what counts or does not count as relevant changes of circumstances have yet been made.

Subs. (4)

Attendance allowance and the care component of disability living allowance can be awarded on the ground of terminal illness. Such awards are made for life. Subsection (4) allows review of such awards where there is a change of medical opinion about the claimant's condition or how long he is expected to live. Normally a change of medical opinion, as opposed to a change in the underlying facts, is not a change of circumstances (*R(S) 4/86*).

Subs. (5)

This provision applies to disability working allowance. See the notes to subs. (2) for the need for an application in writing.

See the notes to s.25(1)(a) and (b) and (2) for review under paras. (a), (b) and (c). Section 129(6) of the Contributions and Benefits Act prevents review of an award of disability working allowance, or of the level of benefit, on the ground of change of circumstances. No regulations have been made requiring fresh evidence to be produced for para. (a), but see reg. 70B(2) of the Adjudication Regulations.

Paragraph (d) is roughly equivalent to reg. 17(4) of the Claims and Payments Regulations, which appears to apply a condition to awards of benefit including disability working allowance. If a person is dissatisfied with a refusal to review or a decision on review, then there must be an application for a further review under the conditions of subs. (1) before there can be an appeal to a tribunal (s.31(2)).

Subs. (6)

Separate provision needs to be made for requiring notice of initial attendance allowance, disability living allowance and disability working allowance decisions and the right to apply for review under subs. (1) because of the exclusion in s.22(1).

Subs. (7)

This subsection only says that review "may" be started by an application in writing to an AO, but the wording of subss. (1), (2) and (5) seems to require there to be such an application. In the ordinary case the application will be made by the claimant, but if circumstances showing that a ground for review has arisen come to the DSS's attention a person acting on behalf of the Secretary of State should make an application to the AO. Otherwise, there is no way of reviewing a decision based on a misrepresentation or failure to disclose material facts by the claimant. The principle should hold where the review would be in favour of the claimant. No regulations have been made specifying any particular information or evidence to be supplied with the application.

Subs. (8)

No regulations have been made under subs. (8).

Subss. (9)–(11)

Applications for review must be decided initially by an AO. There is no power for the AO to refer a question to a tribunal (cf. s.21(3)).

Where the review is under subs. (1) the AO who carries out the review must be a different person from the AO who made the initial decision.

Subs. (12)

If a person has an award of disability living allowance and makes another claim for the allowance during the period of the award, the claim is to be treated as an application for review. A common situation will be where a person has an award of one component of the allowance and makes a claim for the other component. See s.32(2)–(4) for the issues which arise on such a review.

Subs. (13)

If an AO's decision is to refuse the claim and another claim is made within the prescribed period (three months from the date of notice of the AO's decision: Adjudication Regulations, reg. 26A(1)), the claim is to be treated as an application for review under subs. (1). The first claim is then to be treated as having been made on the date of the second claim (Claims and Payments Regulations, reg. 6(11)). In any case any award made on the review could only take effect from that date (Adjudication Regulations, regs. 65(4A) and 70B(1)).

Further reviews

31.—(1) Subsections (2), (4) and (5) of section 30 above shall apply to a decision on a review under subsection (1) of that section as they apply to a decision of an adjudication officer under section 21 above but as if the words "made after the end of the prescribed period" were omitted from each subsection.

(2) Subsections (1), (2), (4) and (5) of section 30 above shall apply—

(a) to a decision on a review under subsection (2), (4) or (5) of that section; and

(b) to a refusal to review a decision under subsection (2), (4) or (5) of that section,

as they apply to a decision of an adjudication officer under section 21 above.

(3) The claimant shall be given such notification as may be prescribed—

(a) of a decision on a review under section 30 above;

(b) if the review was under section 30(1), of his right of appeal under section 33 below; and

(c) if it was under section 30(2), (4) or (5), of his right to a further review under section 30(1).

Subs. (1)
A decision on a review under s.30(1) may be reviewed as if it were an initial decision by an AO, but with no need to wait the prescribed three months.

Subs. (2)
If a person wishes to challenge a refusal to review under s.30(2), (4) or (5), there must first be an application for further review under s.30(1) before there can be an appeal to a tribunal.

Subs. (3)
Notice must be given to the claimant of all decisions on review under s.30 (which must include a refusal to review under s.30(5)) and of the appropriate rights of appeal or further review (Adjudication Regulations, reg. 20(1)). Separate provision is necessary because of the exclusion in s.22(1).

Reviews of decisions as to attendance allowance, disability living allowance or disability working allowance—supplementary

32.—(1) An award of an attendance allowance, a disability living allowance or a disability working allowance on a review under section 30 above replaces any award which was the subject of the review.

(2) Where a person who has been awarded a disability living allowance consisting of one component applies or is treated as applying for a review under section 30 above and alleges that he is also entitled to the other component, the adjudication officer need not consider the question of his entitlement to the component which he has already been awarded or the rate of that component.

(3) Where a person who has been awarded a disability living allowance consisting of both components applies or is treated as applying for a review under section 30 above and alleges that he is entitled to one component at a rate higher than that at which it has been awarded, the adjudication officer need not consider the question of his entitlement to the other component or the rate of that component.

(4) Where a person has been awarded a component for life, on a review under section 30 above the adjudication officer shall not consider the question of his entitlement to that component or the rate of that component or the period for which it has been awarded unless—

(a) the person awarded the component expressly applies for the consideration of that question; or

(b) information is available to the adjudication officer which gives him reasonable grounds for believing that entitlement to the component, or entitlement to it at the rate awarded or for that period, ought not to continue.

(5) No decision which relates to an attendance allowance or a disability living allowance shall be reviewed under section 30 above on the ground that the person is or was at any time terminally ill, within the meaning of section 66(2) of the Contributions and Benefits Act, unless an application for review is made expressly on that ground either—

(a) by the person himself; or

(b) by any other person purporting to act on his behalf, whether or not that other person is acting with his knowledge or authority;

and a decision may be so reviewed on such an application, notwithstanding that no claim under section 66(1) or 72(5) or 73(12) of that Act has been made.

(6) Where a decision is reviewed under section 30 above on the ground that it is anticipated that a change of circumstances will occur, the decision given on review—

(a) shall take effect on the day prescribed for that purpose by reference to the date on which the change of circumstances is expected to occur; and

(b) shall be reviewed again if the change of circumstances either does not occur or occurs otherwise than on that date.

(7) Where a claimant has appealed against a decision of an adjudication officer under section 33 below and the decision is reviewed again under section 30(2), (4) or (5) above by an adjudication officer, then—

(a) if the adjudication officer considers that the decision which he has made on the review is the same as the decision that would have been made on the appeal had every ground of the appeal succeeded, then the appeal shall lapse; but

(b) in any other case, the review shall be of no effect and the appeal shall proceed accordingly.

(8) Regulations may make provision restricting the payment of any benefit, or any increase of benefit, to which a person would, but for this subsection, be entitled by reason of a review in respect of any period before or after the review (whether that period falls wholly or partly before or after the making of the regulations).

(9) Where an adjudication officer has determined that any amount paid by way of an attendance allowance, a disability living allowance or a disability working allowance is recoverable under or by virtue of section 71 below, any person from whom he has determined that it is recoverable shall have the same right of review under section 30 above as a claimant.

(10) This Act and the Contributions and Benefits Act shall have effect in relation to a review by virtue of subsection (9) above as if any reference to the claimant were a reference to the person from whom the adjudication officer has determined that the amount in question is recoverable.

DEFINITIONS
  "the Contributions and Benefits Act": s.191.
  "prescribed": *ibid.*

GENERAL NOTE

Subs. (1)
  See reg. 65(4C) of the Social Security (Adjudication) Regulations 1986 (S.I. 1986 No. 2218) for the date from which a replacement award of attendance allowance or disability living allowance on review can take effect. See reg. 70B(1) for disability working allowance.

Subs. (2)
Where a person who has an award of one component of disability living allowance applies for the other component (either by way of application for review or a purported fresh claim (see s.30(12)) the AO need not consider entitlement to the component which has already been awarded. However, the AO may consider that entitlement, subject to the restrictions in the case of life awards applied by subs. (4) below.

Subs. (3)
Subsection (3) applies a similar rule to that of subs. (2) to a case where a person has been awarded both components and applies for one of those components to be increased.

Subs. (4)
Where a person has been awarded a component of disability allowance for life, that award cannot be reviewed under s.30 unless either he specifically applies for review of that component (thus modifying subss. (2) and (3) above) or the AO has reasonable grounds for believing that entitlement to the particular level of component ought not to continue. This second condition is obviously necessary in order to allow review of awards in the case of unexpected improvement or mistaken initial decisions, where review will be initiated by the AO, but it can also apply where the review is initiated by the claimant.

Subs. (5)
Claims for attendance allowance or disability living allowance on the ground of terminal illness must be made expressly by reference to that ground (Contributions and Benefits Act, ss.66(2) and 72(5)). This provision applies similar rules where there is an application to increase an existing award on that ground.

Subs. (6)
See s.30(2)(c).

Subs. (7)
See notes to s.29.

Subs. (8)
See regs. 65(4A) and 70B(2) of the Adjudication Regulations.

Subss. (9) and (10)
Where an AO has decided that an overpayment of attendance allowance, disability living allowance or disability working allowance has been made and is recoverable under s.71, the review and appeal process is the same as for an initial claim.

Appeals following reviews

33.—(1) Where an adjudication officer has given a decision on a review under section 30(1) above, the claimant or such other person as may be prescribed may appeal—
(a) in prescribed cases, to a disability appeal tribunal; and
(b) in any other case, to a social security appeal tribunal.
(2) Regulations may make provision as to the manner in which, and the time within which, appeals are to be brought.
(3) An award on an appeal under this section replaces any award which was the subject of the appeal.
(4) Where a person who has been awarded a disability living allowance consisting of one component alleges on an appeal that he is also entitled to the other component, the tribunal need not consider the question of his entitlement to the component which he has already been awarded or the rate of that component.
(5) Where a person who has been awarded a disability living allowance consisting of both components alleges on an appeal that he is entitled to one component at a rate higher than that at which it has been awarded, the tribunal need not consider the question of his entitlement to the other component or the rate of that component.

(6) The tribunal shall not consider—

(a) a person's entitlement to a component which has been awarded for life; or

(b) the rate of a component so awarded; or

(c) the period for which a component has been so awarded,

unless—

(i) the appeal expressly raises that question; or

(ii) information is available to the tribunal which gives it reasonable grounds for believing that entitlement to the component, or entitlement to it at the rate awarded or for that period, ought not to continue.

DEFINITIONS

"prescribed": s.191.

GENERAL NOTE

Subs. (1)

Where there has been a review under s.30(1) following an initial decision on attendance allowance, disability living allowance or disability working allowance by an AO, the claimant may appeal to a tribunal. The effect of paras. (a) and (b) seems to be that if appeal to a disability appeal tribunal (DAT) is possible, that is where the appeal must go. It is only where appeal to the DAT is not possible that the appeal goes to the SSAT. Regulation 26C(1) of the Social Security (Adjudication) Regulations 1986 (S.I. 1986 No. 2218) prescribes that the claimant may appeal to the DAT where either a disability question or both a disability question and any other question relating to attendance allowance, disability living allowance or disability working allowance arises. Regulation 26C(2) defines what are disability questions. Broadly they are the medical issues arising on entitlement. Thus a SSAT may never consider a disability question, since if such a question first arises in the course of an appeal properly made to a SSAT, the SSAT cannot deal with it (s.36(2)). But a DAT has to consider all the conditions of entitlement to an allowance if a disability question arises along with other matters.

Subs. (2)

See Sched. 2 to the Adjudication Regulations.

Subs. (3)

This provision confirms that an award of attendance allowance, disability living allowance or disability working allowance by a tribunal on appeal replaces any award made by the AO.

Subss. (4)–(6)

See the notes to s.32(2)–(4).

Appeal from social security appeal tribunals or disability appeal tribunals to Commissioners and appeals from Commissioners

34.—(1) Subject to the provisions of this section, an appeal lies to a Commissioner from any decision of a social security appeal tribunal or disability appeal tribunal under section 33 above on the ground that the decision of the tribunal was erroneous in point of law.

(2) An appeal lies under this section at the instance of any of the following—

(a) an adjudication officer;

(b) the claimant;

(c) a trade union—

(i) where the claimant is a member of the union at the time of the appeal and was so immediately before the question at issue arose;

(ii) where that question in any way relates to a deceased person who was a member of the union at the time of his death; and

(d) a person from whom it is determined that any amount is recoverable under section 71(1) below.

(3) Subsection (2) above, as it applies to a trade union, applies also to any other association which exists to promote the interests and welfare of its members.

(4) Subsections (7) to (10) of section 23 above have effect for the purposes of this section as they have effect for the purposes of that section.

(5) Section 24 above applies to a decision of a Commissioner under this section as it applies to a decision of a Commissioner under section 23 above.

DEFINITIONS
"Commissioner": s.191.

GENERAL NOTE

Subs. (1)
See notes to s.23(1).

Subss. (2) and (3)
See notes to s.23(3), (5) and (6).

Subs. (4)
See notes to s.23(7)–(10).

Subs. (5)
See notes to s.24. Subsection (5) is probably redundant as s.24 was finally drafted.

Reviews of decisions on appeal

35.—(1) Any decision under this Act of a social security appeal tribunal, a disability appeal tribunal or a Commissioner which relates to an attendance allowance or a disability living allowance may be reviewed at any time by an adjudication officer if—

(a) he is satisfied that the decision was given in ignorance of, or was based on a mistake as to, some material fact; or

(b) there has been any relevant change of circumstances since the decision was given; or

(c) it is anticipated that a relevant change of circumstances will so occur; or

(d) the decision was that a person is or was at any time terminally ill for the purposes of section 66(1), 72(5) or 73(12) of the Contributions and Benefits Act and there has been a change of medical opinion with respect to his condition or his reasonable expectation of life; or

(e) the decision was to make an award for a period wholly or partly after the date on which the claim was made or treated as made but subject to a condition being fulfilled and that condition has not been fulfilled,

but regulations may provide that a decision may not be reviewed on the ground mentioned in paragraph (a) above unless the officer is satisfied as mentioned in that paragraph by fresh evidence.

(2) Regulations may prescribe what are, or are not, relevant changes of circumstances for the purposes of subsection (1)(b) and (c) above.

(3) Any decision under this Act of a social security appeal tribunal, a disability appeal tribunal or a Commissioner which relates to a disability working allowance may be reviewed at any time by an adjudication officer if—

(a) he is satisfied that the decision was given in ignorance of, or was based on a mistake as to, some material fact; or

(b) subject to section 129(7) of the Contributions and Benefits Act, there has been any prescribed change of circumstances since the decision was given; or

(c) the decision was to make an award for a period wholly or partly after the date on which the claim was made or treated as made but subject to a condition being fulfilled and that condition has not been fulfilled,

but regulations may provide that a decision may not be reviewed on the ground mentioned in paragraph (a) above unless the officer is satisfied as mentioned in that paragraph by fresh evidence.

(4) A question may be raised with a view to a review under this section by means of an application made in writing to an adjudication officer, stating the grounds of the application and supplying such information and evidence as may be prescribed.

(5) Regulations may provide for enabling or requiring, in prescribed circumstances, a review under this section notwithstanding that no application for a review has been made under subsection (4) above.

(6) Reviews under this section shall be carried out by adjudication officers.

(7) Except in prescribed circumstances, where a claim for a disability living allowance in respect of a person already awarded such an allowance on an appeal is made or treated as made during the period for which he has been awarded the allowance, it shall be treated as an application for a review under this section.

(8) Subsections (1), (2), (4) and (5) of section 30 above shall apply—

(a) to a decision on a review under this section; and

(b) to a refusal to review a decision such as is mentioned in subsection (1) above,

as they apply to a decision of an adjudication officer under section 21 above.

(9) The person whose claim was the subject of the appeal the decision on which has been reviewed under this section shall be given such notification as may be prescribed—

(a) of the decision on the review; and

(b) of his right to a further review under section 30(1) above.

(10) Regulations may make provision restricting the payment of any benefit, or any increase of benefit, to what a person would, but for this subsection, be entitled by reason of a review in respect of any period before or after the review (whether that period falls wholly or partly before or after the making of the regulations).

(11) Where a decision is reviewed on the ground mentioned in subsection (1)(c) above, the decision given on the review—

(a) shall take effect on the day prescribed for that purpose by reference to the date on which the relevant change of circumstances is expected to occur; and

(b) shall be reviewed again if the relevant change of circumstances either does not occur or occurs otherwise than on that date.

(12) Section 30(10) above and section 32(1) to (5) above shall apply in relation to a review under this section as they apply to a review under section 30 above.

DEFINITIONS

"Commissioner": s.191.

"the Contributions and Benefits Act": *ibid.*

"prescribed": *ibid.*

GENERAL NOTE

Subs. (1)

Subsection (1) applies to attendance allowance and disability living allowance (see the notes to s.30(2)). A decision of a SSAT, a DAT or a Commissioner cannot be reviewed as being erroneous in point of law, otherwise the appeal process would be subverted.

Note that review under subs. (1) does not have to be "on an application made under this section". Therefore it seems that an application under subs. (4) is just one way of raising the question of review and that an AO can carry out a review without an application having been made.

Subs. (2)

No regulations have yet been made under this provision.

Subs. (3)

Subsection (3) applies to disability working allowance. See the notes to subs. (1) above, with the substitution of s.30(5). To make sense, the reference in para. (b) should be to s.129(6) of the Contributions and Benefits Act, not s.129(7). See reg. 56 of the Disability Working Allowance (General) Regulations 1991 (S.I. 1991 No. 2887).

Subss. (4) and (5)

See notes to s.26(1) and (3). No regulations have been made under this subsection prescribing any information to be provided.

Subs. (7)

See s.30(12).

Subs. (8)

If the claimant is dissatisfied with the decision on a review under this section he must apply for a further review under s.30(1) before he can appeal to a tribunal.

Subs. (9)

See reg. 20(1)(a) of the Adjudication Regulations.

Subs. (10)

See notes to s.30(8).

Questions first arising on appeal

Questions first arising on appeal

36.—(1) Where a question which but for this section would fall to be determined by an adjudication officer first arises in the course of an appeal to a social security appeal tribunal, a disability appeal tribunal or a Commissioner, the tribunal, subject to subsection (2) below, or the Commissioner may, if they or he think fit, proceed to determine the question notwithstanding that it has not been considered by an adjudication officer.

(2) A social security appeal tribunal may not determine a question by virtue of subsection (1) above if an appeal in relation to such a question would have lain to a disability appeal tribunal.

DEFINITIONS

"Commissioner": s.191.

GENERAL NOTE

Subs. (1)

A provision in similar terms to this has existed for some time for benefits which fell directly under the Social Security Act 1975. There was an extension to social fund, supplementary benefit and family income supplement in April 1987.

Now s.36 applies generally. What is its effect? It might at first sight appear to allow a SSAT, DAT or Commissioner to go outside the purview of the appeal and decide any question about entitlement raised by the claimant. The Commissioner in *R(I) 4/75* says that the "useful" provision should be liberally construed. However, s.36 applies only to questions which arise in the course of an appeal. This does not mean in the course of the hearing of the appeal (*CS 101/1986*). The question must be connected with whatever question is properly before the tribunal or the Commissioner in the appeal. Similarly, it is confirmed in *CS 104/1987* that s.36 can only be invoked where the question first arises in the course of an appeal. Thus if an AO has decided a question, from which decision no appeal has been made, the tribunal cannot deal with that question under s.36 as it does not first arise in the course of the appeal. The suggestion in *CS 101/1986* that the section could be used where a question might have been referred to the SSAT, but was not, must then be restricted to cases where the AO has not made a decision on that question. In addition, there are two controls. First, the tribunal or the Commissioner has a discretion to decide the new question. It may consider the argument that when the only appeal from the tribunal is on the ground of error of law, the claimant may be deprived of a stage in the appeal process if the tribunal, rather than the AO, makes an initial decision. Second, the principles of natural justice would require that a tribunal or Commissioner should not make a decision on a new point if all parties have not had a fair opportunity of dealing with it (*R(F) 1/72*).

Subs. (2)

If a SSAT is hearing an appeal on attendance allowance, disability living allowance or disability working allowance and a disability question arises for the first time, then the SSAT cannot deal with that question. If there is such a disability question (with or without some other point in dispute) when an appeal is made, the whole appeal goes to the DAT (s.33(1) and Social Security (Adjudication) Regulations 1986 (S.I. 1986 No. 2218), reg. 26C). It appears, however, that if an appeal has properly gone to the SSAT before the disability question first arises, then the SSAT should continue to deal with the questions raised in the original appeal. By definition, the disability question must have been decided by the AO under s.30(1) in the claimant's favour, otherwise the appeal would already be before the DAT. If something comes to light in the SSAT appeal which casts doubt on that, but the SSAT determines all the other questions in the claimant's favour, there is a difficult question on the SSAT's proper course of action. Should it make an award of benefit, and leave the AO to review that award under s.35(3), or simply determine the questions before it and leave the AO to review the disability question? On balance, the first alternative seems more in line with the scheme of the legislation.

Reference of special questions

Reference of special questions

37.—(1) Subject to subsection (2) below—

(a) if on consideration of any claim or question an adjudication officer is of opinion that there arises any question which under or by virtue of this Act falls to be determined otherwise than by an adjudication officer, he shall refer the question for such determination; and

(b) if on consideration of any claim or question a social security appeal tribunal or Commissioner is of opinion that any such question arises, the tribunal or Commissioner shall direct it to be referred by an adjudication officer for such determination.

(2) The person or tribunal making or directing the reference shall then deal with any other question as if the referred question had not arisen.

(3) The adjudication officer, tribunal or Commissioner may—

(a) postpone the reference of, or dealing with, any question until other questions have been determined;

(b) in cases where the determination of any question disposes of a claim or any part of it, make an award or decide that an award cannot be made, as to the claim or that part of it, without referring or dealing with, or before the determination of, any other question.

DEFINITIONS

"Commissioner": s.191.

GENERAL NOTE

If an AO, a SSAT or a Commissioner considers that a question arises which has to be decided by someone else (*e.g.* the Secretary of State under s.17) then that question must be referred to the other person.

Adjudication officers and the Chief Adjudication Officer

Adjudication officers

38.—(1) Adjudication officers shall be appointed by the Secretary of State, subject to the consent of the Treasury as to number, and may include—

(a) officers of the Department of Employment appointed with the concurrence of the Secretary of State in charge of that Department; or

(b) officers of the Northern Ireland Department appointed with the concurrence of that Department.

(2) An adjudication officer may be appointed to perform all the functions of adjudication officers under any enactment or such functions of such officers as may be specified in his instrument of appointment.

DEFINITIONS
  "the Northern Ireland Department": s.191.

GENERAL NOTE

Subs. (1)
  The Secretary of State is not obliged to appoint enough AOs to dispose of all claims submitted to them within 14 days under s.21(1) (*R.* v. *Secretary of State for Social Services*, ex p. *Child Poverty Action Group* [1990] 2 Q.B. 540).

Subs. (2)
  The current instrument of appointment was signed by the Secretary of State on March 28, 1991 and is reproduced as Appendix 1 to Part 01 of the Adjudication Officers' Guide. It directs that all persons appointed shall carry out all the functions of AOs, unless specifically designated to exercise only specified functions. In practice, most AOs will deal with only a limited number of benefits, but will formally have the power to carry out any AO function.
  See reg. 64 of the Adjudication Regulations for the consequences of the limited practical range of expertise of individual AOs.

The Chief Adjudication Officer

39.—(1) The Secretary of State shall appoint a Chief Adjudication Officer.

(2) It shall be the duty of the Chief Adjudication Officer to advise adjudication officers on the performance of their functions under this or any other Act.

(3) The Chief Adjudication Officer shall keep under review the operation of the system of adjudication by adjudication officers and matters connected with the operation of that system.

(4) The Chief Adjudication Officer shall report annually in writing to the Secretary of State on the standards of adjudication and the Secretary of State shall publish his report.

GENERAL NOTE
  The Chief Adjudication Officer combines the functions of the former Chief Insurance Officer and the Chief Supplementary Benefit Officer. However, his advisory duties were given statutory expression for the first time in 1984. The duty to report publicly on standards of adjudication was also new. The CAO's first report was published in 1986. This and the subsequent annual reports contain much interesting and critical material. The more recent reports contain fascinating material on the relationship of the adjudication system with the Benefits Agency.

Social security appeal tribunals

Panels for appointment to social security appeal tribunals

40.—(1) The President shall constitute for the whole of Great Britain, to act for such areas as he thinks fit and be composed of such persons as he thinks fit to appoint, panels of persons to act as members of social security appeal tribunals.

(2) The panel for an area shall be composed of persons appearing to the President to have knowledge or experience of conditions in the area and to be representative of persons living or working in the area.

(3) Before appointing members of a panel, the President shall take into consideration any recommendations from such organisations or persons as he considers appropriate.

(4) The members of the panels shall hold office for such period as the President may direct, but the President may at any time terminate the appointment of any member of a panel.

DEFINITIONS
  "President": s.191.

GENERAL NOTE
The President of social security appeal tribunals, etc., is to appoint members to a national panel and assign them to particular areas.

There is now one panel of members. The temporary survival after April 1984 of the two panels left over from the old supplementary benefit appeal tribunals and national insurance local tribunals, conceded in order to get the Health and Social Services and Social Security Adjudication Act 1983 through Parliament before the 1983 General Election, came to an end on September 26, 1984. This was in fulfilment of the Government's original intention.

The test for appointment under subs. (2) is a dual one. The member must have knowledge or experience of conditions in the area to which the appointment applies and be representative of persons living or working in the area. The first part seems to be a watered-down version of the old supplementary benefit appeal tribunal test for "Secretary of State's" members, omitting the requirement of knowledge or experience of the problems of people living on low incomes. This requirement was presumably thought inappropriate to the wider jurisdiction of the SSAT, but it is a pity that it should be lost altogether. It is far from clear what the "representative" test requires. The intention apparently is that the range of organisations consulted about membership under subs. (3) should be widened out from Trade Councils, Chambers of Commerce, etc. to include groups representing ethnic minorities, the disabled, one-parent families, etc. This is laudable in an attempt to secure a balanced panel, although of course it does not secure any specific balance on an individual tribunal. However, the member does not have to be nominated by an organisation. The test is not of a representative in that sense. The test is whether a person is representative of the local population. Individuals who do not belong to groups or organisations are also eligible, and may have much to offer.

Constitution of social security appeal tribunals

41.—(1) A social security appeal tribunal shall consist of a chairman and two other persons.

(2) The members other than the chairman shall be drawn from the appropriate panel constituted under section 40 above.

(3) The President shall nominate the chairman.

(4) The President may nominate as chairman—

(a) himself;

(b) one of the full-time chairmen appointed under section 51(1) below; or

(c) a person drawn from the panel appointed by the Lord Chancellor or, as the case may be, the Lord President of the Court of Session under section 7 of the Tribunals and Inquiries Act 1971.

(5) No person shall be appointed chairman of a tribunal under subsection (4)(c) above unless he has a 5 year general qualification or he is an advocate or solicitor in Scotland of at least 5 years' standing.

(6) If practicable, at least one of the members of the appeal tribunal hearing a case shall be of the same sex as the claimant.

(7) Schedule 2 to this Act shall have effect for supplementing this section.

DEFINITIONS
"5-year general qualification": s.191.
"President": *ibid.*

GENERAL NOTE

Subs. (1)
For the appointment of chairmen, see subss. (3)–(5). For the appointment of the other members, see subs. (2). For an overriding condition on the composition of each particular tribunal hearing an appeal, see subs. (6).

Subs. (2)
There is now one panel for each area from which members of a particular tribunal are chosen. The old division between the Trades Council members and the Secretary of State's members on supplementary benefit appeal tribunals and between employers' and employees' representatives on national insurance local tribunals has gone. There is no longer any guarantee of having a member from any particular background on any individual tribunal. Members need no longer be summoned in turn to sit on tribunals. See s.40 for appointment to the panel of members.

Subs. (4)

The panel referred to in para. (c) is of the ordinary part-time chairmen of SSATs, appointed by the Lord Chancellor (or the Lord President in Scotland). The President assigns chairmen to act in particular areas.

See s.51 for Regional and other full-time chairmen.

Subs. (5)

Since 1984, part-time chairmen have had to have professional legal qualifications. This was a controversial provision, which required the discarding of some highly experienced and knowledgeable supplementary benefit appeal tribunal chairmen. However, it was probably inevitable in view of the excessive legalisation of the supplementary benefit system. What remains controversial is the requirement of professional legal qualifications (which, to put it kindly, do not guarantee any knowledge of, or interest in, social security law), rather than some other evidence of legal skills (*e.g.* a law degree).

From January 1, 1991, the nature of the required professional legal qualification in England and Wales has changed, following the reforms embodied in the Courts and Legal Services Act 1990. A person has a general qualification under s.71 of that Act if he has a right of audience, granted by an authorised body, in relation to any class of proceedings in the Supreme Court or all proceedings in county courts or magistrates' courts. To meet tests of having had a qualification for a particular length of time a person must currently hold the qualification and have held it for the required number of years, not necessarily consecutive (s.71(5)). There are transitional provisions under which solicitors and barristers admitted or called before 1991 are deemed to have been granted the appropriate right of audience.

Subs. (6)

This provision causes difficulty while only about 25 per cent. of members are women. The President's policy on appointments is to attempt to redress this imbalance. The Commissioner in *R(SB) 2/88* holds that practicability imposes quite a strict requirement. The provision is mandatory, and if the SSAT does not have a member of the same sex as the claimant it must be shown that it was not practicable to do otherwise. This cannot be presumed. The chairman should ask the clerk about the circumstances, and endorse the record of decision (AT3) accordingly. If non-practicability cannot be proved, the SSAT's decision will be in error of law even though the claimant consents to the hearing's continuing. If it is not practicable to have a member of the same sex as the claimant it might be appropriate to offer the claimant an adjournment.

Disability appeal tribunals

Panels for appointment to disability appeal tribunals

42.—(1) The President shall constitute for the whole of Great Britain, to act for such areas as he thinks fit and be composed of such persons as he thinks fit to appoint, panels of persons to act as members of disability appeal tribunals.

(2) There shall be two panels for each area.

(3) One panel shall be composed of medical practitioners.

(4) The other shall be composed of persons who are experienced in dealing with the needs of disabled persons—

(a) in a professional or voluntary capacity; or

(b) because they are themselves disabled,

but may not include medical practitioners.

(5) In considering the appointment of members of the panels the President shall have regard to the desirability of appointing disabled persons.

(6) Before appointing members of a panel, the President shall take into consideration any recommendations from such organisations or persons as he considers appropriate.

(7) The members of the panels shall hold office for such periods as the President may direct, but the President may at any time terminate the appointment of any member of a panel.

DEFINITIONS
  "President": s.191.

GENERAL NOTE

See s.40 for the general pattern. The distinctive feature of disability appeal tribunals is that the members other than the chairman must come one each from the two panels set up under s.42. One panel is of medical practitioners. In practice, these are general practitioners, rather than those of consultant status who sit on medical appeal tribunals. The second panel is of people experienced in dealing with the needs of disabled persons, either because of personal disability or professional or voluntary experience. Because of the issues dealt with by DATs and the move away from medical testing, such people are considered to be particularly qualified to assess the needs of disabled people. There is no guarantee that the member of the DAT deciding a particular claimant's appeal will have any experience of the claimant's particular needs.

Constitution of disability appeal tribunals

43.—(1) A disability appeal tribunal shall consist of a chairman and two other persons.

(2) Of the members of a tribunal other than the chairman, one shall be drawn from the panel mentioned in subsection (3) of section 42 above.

(3) The other shall be drawn from the panel mentioned in subsection (4) of that section.

(4) The President shall nominate the chairman.

(5) The President may nominate as chairman—

(a) himself;

(b) one of the full-time chairmen appointed under section 51(1) below; or

(c) a person drawn from the panel appointed by the Lord Chancellor or, as the case may be, the Lord President of the Court of Session under section 7 of the Tribunals and Inquiries Act 1971.

(6) No person shall be appointed chairman of a tribunal under subsection (5)(c) above unless he has a 5 year general qualification or he is an advocate or solicitor in Scotland of at least 5 years' standing.

(7) In summoning members of a panel to serve on a tribunal, the clerk to the tribunal shall have regard to the desirability of at least one of the members of the tribunal being a disabled person.

(8) If practicable, at least one of the members of the tribunal shall be of the same sex as the claimant.

(9) Schedule 2 to this Act shall have effect for supplementing this section.

DEFINITIONS

"President": s.191.

GENERAL NOTE

See s.41. One member must be drawn from each of the two panels set up under s.42. Subsection (7) requires the clerk to consider the desirability of one of the disability appeal tribunal members being disabled. The chairman and the medical practitioner member can count for this purpose, and there is no definition of disability. The requirement cannot be more extensive or carers would rarely be able to sit as members.

Adjudication in relation to industrial injuries and disablement benefit

Declaration that accident is an industrial accident

44.—(1) Where, in connection with any claim for industrial injuries benefit, it is determined that the relevant accident was or was not an industrial accident, an express declaration of that fact shall be made and recorded and (subject to subsection (3) below) a claimant shall be entitled to have the question whether the relevant accident was an industrial accident determined notwithstanding that his claim is disallowed on other grounds.

(2) Subject to subsection (3) below and to section 60 below, any person suffering personal injury by accident shall be entitled, if he claims the accident was an industrial accident, to have that question determined and a declaration made and recorded accordingly, notwithstanding that no claim

for benefit has been made in connection with which the question arises; and this Part of this Act applies for that purpose as if the question had arisen in connection with a claim for benefit.

(3) The adjudication officer, social security appeal tribunal or Commissioner (as the case may be) may refuse to determine the question whether an accident was an industrial accident if satisfied that it is unlikely to be necessary to determine the question for the purposes of any claim for benefit; but any such refusal of an adjudication officer or social security appeal tribunal shall be subject to appeal to a social security appeal tribunal or Commissioner, as the case may be.

(4) Subject to the provisions of this Part of this Act as to appeal and review, any declaration under this section that an accident was or was not an industrial accident shall be conclusive for the purposes of any claim for industrial injuries benefit in respect of that accident.

(5) Where subsection (4) above applies—
(a) in relation to a death occurring before 11th April 1988; or
(b) for the purposes of section 60(2) of the Contributions and Benefits Act,
it shall have effect as if at the end there were added the words "whether or not the claimant is the person at whose instance the declaration was made".

(6) For the purposes of this section (but subject to section 60(3) below), an accident whereby a person suffers personal injury shall be deemed, in relation to him, to be an industrial accident if—
(a) it arises out of and in the course of his employment;
(b) that employment is employed earner's employment for the purposes of Part V of the Contributions and Benefits Act;
(c) payment of benefit is not under section 94(5) of that Act precluded because the accident happened while he was outside Great Britain.

(7) A decision under this section shall be final except that sections 25 to 29 above apply to a decision under this section that an accident was or was not an industrial accident as they apply to a decision under sections 21 to 23 above if, but only if, the adjudication officer or social security appeal tribunal, as the case may be, is satisfied that the decision under this section was given in consequence of any wilful non-disclosure or misrepresentation of a material fact.

DEFINITIONS
"Commissioner": s.191.
"the Contributions and Benefits Act": *ibid.*
"industrial injuries benefit": *ibid.*

GENERAL NOTE
A declaration that a person has suffered an industrial accident may be obtained even though no current award of benefit is made, or even claimed, provided that it might be relevant to some future claim.

Disablement questions

45.—(1) In relation to industrial injuries benefit and severe disablement allowance, the "disablement questions" are the questions—
(a) in relation to industrial injuries benefit, whether the relevant accident has resulted in a loss of faculty;
(b) in relation to both benefits, at what degree the extent of disablement resulting from a loss of faculty is to be assessed, and what period is to be taken into account by the assessment;
but questions relating to the aggregation of percentages of disablement resulting from different accidents are not disablement questions (and accordingly fall to be determined by an adjudication officer).

(2) Subject to and in accordance with regulations, the disablement questions shall be referred to and determined—

(a) by an adjudicating medical practitioner; or
(b) by two or more adjudicating medical practitioners; or
(c) by a medical appeal tribunal; or
(d) in such cases relating to severe disablement allowance as may be prescribed, by an adjudication officer.

(3) Where—
(a) the case of a claimant for disablement benefit has been referred by the adjudication officer to one or more adjudicating medical practitioners for determination of the disablement questions; and
(b) on that or any subsequent reference, the extent of the disablement is provisionally assessed,

the case shall again be referred under this section, to one or more adjudicating medical practitioners as regulations may provide for the purposes of such subsequent references, not later than the end of the period taken into account by the provisional assessment.

(4) Where, in the case of a claimant for disablement benefit, the extent of any disablement of his resulting from an aggregable accident (that is to say, an accident other than the one which is the basis of the claim in question) has been assessed in accordance with paragraph 6(3) of Schedule 6 to the Contributions and Benefits Act at less than 14 per cent., then—
(a) the adjudication officer may refer the disablement questions relating to the aggregable accident to one or more adjudicating medical practitioners for fresh determination; and
(b) on any such reference—
(i) those questions shall be determined as at the first day of the common period; and
(ii) the period to be taken into account shall be the period beginning with that day.

(5) In subsection (4) above "the first day of the common period" means whichever is the later of—
(a) the first day of the period taken into account by the assessment of the extent of the claimant's disablement resulting from the accident which is the basis of the claim in question;
(b) the first day of the period taken into account by the assessment of the extent of his disablement resulting from the aggregable accident.

(6) In the following provisions of this Act "adjudicating medical practitioner" means, in relation to any case, one such practitioner, unless regulations applicable to cases of that description provide for references to more than one.

DEFINITIONS
"industrial injuries benefit": s.191.

GENERAL NOTE
See the detailed discussion in the current edition of Rowland. "Disablement questions" are subject to a special route for adjudication. The initial determination is normally by one or two adjudicating medical practitioners, with an appeal to a medical appeal tribunal. See Section D of Pt. III of the Social Security (Adjudication) Regulations 1986 (S.I. 1986 No. 2218). "Disablement questions" are whether there is a loss of faculty in an industrial injuries benefits case, and at what percentage the resulting disablement should be assessed, and the percentage of disablement in severe disablement allowance cases.

Medical appeals and references

46.—(1) This section has effect where the case of a claimant for disablement benefit or severe disablement allowance has been referred by the adjudication officer to an adjudicating medical practitioner for determination of the disablement questions.

(2) Subject to subsection (3) below, if the claimant is dissatisfied with the decision of the adjudicating medical practitioner, he may appeal in the

prescribed manner and within the prescribed time, and the case shall be referred to a medical appeal tribunal.

(3) If—

(a) the Secretary of State notifies the adjudication officer within the prescribed time that he is of the opinion that any decision of the adjudicating medical practitioner ought to be considered by a medical appeal tribunal; or

(b) the adjudication officer is of the opinion that any such decision ought to be so considered,

the adjudication officer shall refer the case to a medical appeal tribunal for their consideration, and the tribunal may confirm, reverse or vary the decision in whole or in part as on an appeal.

GENERAL NOTE

Section 46 provides for a right of appeal by a claimant from a decision of adjudicating medical practitioners to a medical appeal tribunal. The adjudication officer may refer such a decision to a MAT under the conditions in subs. (3).

Review of medical decisions

47.—(1) Any decision under this Act of an adjudicating medical practitioner or a medical appeal tribunal may be reviewed at any time by an adjudicating medical practitioner if satisfied that the decision was given in ignorance of a material fact or was based on a mistake as to a material fact.

(2) Any decision under this Act of an adjudicating medical practitioner may be reviewed at any time by such a practitioner if he is satisfied that the decision was erroneous in point of law.

(3) Regulations may provide that a decision may not be reviewed under subsection (1) above unless the adjudicating medical practitioner is satisfied as mentioned in that subsection by fresh evidence.

(4) Any assessment of the extent of the disablement resulting from the relevant loss of faculty may also be reviewed by an adjudicating medical practitioner if he is satisfied that since the making of the assessment there has been unforeseen aggravation of the results of the relevant injury.

(5) Where in connection with a claim for disablement benefit made after 25th August 1953 it is decided that the relevant accident had not resulted in a loss of faculty, the decision—

(a) may be reviewed under subsection (4) above as if it were an assessment of the extent of disablement resulting from a relevant loss of faculty; but

(b) subject to any further decision on appeal or review, shall be treated as deciding the question whether the relevant accident had so resulted both for the time about which the decision was given and for any subsequent time.

(6) For the purposes of subsection (5) above, a final assessment of the extent of the disablement resulting from a loss of faculty made for a period limited by reference to a definite date shall be treated as deciding that at that date the relevant accident has not resulted in a loss of faculty.

(7) An assessment made, confirmed or varied by a medical appeal tribunal shall not be reviewed under subsection (4) above without the leave of a medical appeal tribunal, and (notwithstanding the provisions of Part V of the Contributions and Benefits Act) on a review under that subsection the period to be taken into account by any revised assessment shall only include a period before the date of the application for the review if and in so far as regulations so provide.

(8) Subject to the foregoing provisions of this section, an adjudicating medical practitioner may deal with a case on a review in any manner in which he could deal with it on an original reference to him, and in particular may in

any case relating to disablement benefit make a provisional assessment notwithstanding that the assessment under review was final.

(9) Section 46 above applies to an application for a review under this section and to a decision of an adjudicating medical practitioner in connection with such an application as it applies to an original claim for disablement benefit or severe disablement allowance, as the case may be, and to a decision of an adjudicating medical practitioner in connection with such a claim.

(10) In subsection (6) above the reference to a final assessment does not include an assessment made for the purpose of section 12(1)(a) or (b) of the National Insurance (Industrial Injuries) Act 1946 as originally enacted and having the effect that benefit is not payable.

DEFINITIONS
"the Contributions and Benefits Act": s.191.

GENERAL NOTE
See the detailed discussion in the current edition of Rowland.

Subs. (1)
Decisions of an adjudicating medical practitioner or a MAT may be reviewed on the ground of ignorance of or mistake as to a material fact (see notes to s.25(1)). No regulations have yet been made under subs. (3).

Subs. (2)
Decisions of adjudicating medical practitioners, but not MATs, can be reviewed for error of law.

Subs. (4)
This is an important provision in the scheme of industrial injuries benefits. An assessment of disablement (including by virtue of subss. (5) and (6) a decision that there is no loss of faculty) is to be reviewed if there has been unforeseen aggravation of the results of the industrial injury or disease since the assessment was made. Thus an assessment can be varied upwards if the outcome turns out to be worse than was originally thought or the disablement continues for longer than was originally thought.

Any revised assessment can only take effect from a date three months before the date of the application for review (subs. (7) and Social Security (Adjudication) Regulations 1986 (S.I. 1986 No. 2218), reg. 68)).

Subs. (7)
An assessment made by a MAT cannot be reviewed under subs. (4) unless leave has been given by a MAT.

As to the date from which a revised assessment can take effect, see the note to subs. (4).

Appeal etc. on question of law to Commissioner

48.—(1) Subject to this section, an appeal lies to a Commissioner from any decision of a medical appeal tribunal (if given after 27th September 1959) on the ground that the decision is erroneous in point of law, at the instance of—

(a) an adjudication officer;
(b) the claimant;
(c) a trade union of which the claimant was a member at the time of the relevant accident or, in a case relating to severe disablement allowance, at the prescribed time; or
(d) the Secretary of State.

(2) Subsection (1) above, as it applies to a trade union, applies also to any other association which exists to promote the interests and welfare of its members.

(3) No appeal lies under subsection (1) above without the leave—

(a) of the person who was the chairman of the medical appeal tribunal when the decision was given or, in a prescribed case, the leave of some other chairman of a medical appeal tribunal; or

(b) subject to and in accordance with regulations, of a Commissioner,

and regulations may make provision as to the manner in which, and the time within which, appeals are to be brought and applications made for leave to appeal.

(4) On any such appeal, the question of law arising for the decision of the Commissioner and the facts on which it arises shall be submitted for his consideration in the prescribed manner.

(5) Where the Commissioner holds that the decision was erroneous in point of law, he shall set it aside and refer the case to a medical appeal tribunal with directions for its determination.

(6) Subject to any direction of the Commissioner, the tribunal on a reference under subsection (5) above shall consist of persons who were not members of the tribunal which gave the erroneous decision.

DEFINITIONS
　"claimant": s.191.
　"Commissioner": ibid.

GENERAL NOTE
　See the detailed discussion in the current edition of Rowland. An appeal lies from a decision of a medical appeal tribunal to the Social Security Commissioner on the ground that the decision was erroneous in point of law. Leave must be given by the MAT chairman or by the Commissioner. If the Commissioner decides that the decision was erroneous in point of law the case must be referred to a new MAT (subss. (5) and (6)).

Adjudicating medical practitioners and medical appeal tribunals

Adjudicating medical practitioners

49.—(1) Adjudicating medical practitioners shall be appointed by the Secretary of State.

(2) Subject to subsection (1) above, their appointment shall be determined by regulations.

Constitution of medical appeal tribunals

50.—(1) A medical appeal tribunal shall consist of a chairman and two other persons.

(2) The members other than the chairman shall be medical practitioners appointed by the President after consultation with such academic medical bodies as appear to him to be appropriate.

(3) The President shall nominate the chairman.

(4) The President may nominate as chairman—

(a) himself;

(b) one of the full-time chairmen appointed under section 51(1) below; or

(c) a person drawn from the panel appointed by the Lord Chancellor or, as the case may be, the Lord President of the Court of Session under section 7 of the Tribunals and Inquiries Act 1971.

(5) No person shall be appointed chairman of a tribunal under subsection (4)(c) above unless he has a 5 year general qualification, or he is an advocate or solicitor in Scotland of at least 5 years' standing.

(6) Subject to subsections (1) to (5) above, the constitution of medical appeal tribunals shall be determined by regulations.

(7) Schedule 2 to this Act shall have effect for supplementing this section.

DEFINITIONS
　"5-year general qualification": s.191.
　"President": ibid.

GENERAL NOTE

See the notes to s.41. The medical practitioners appointed as members are of consultant status. There is no longer any extra qualification for MAT chairmen over those for SSAT and DAT chairmen.

The President and full-time chairmen of tribunals

The President of social security appeal tribunals, medical appeal tribunals and disability appeal tribunals and regional chairmen and other full-time chairmen

51.—(1) The Lord Chancellor may, after consultation with the Lord Advocate, appoint—

(a) a President of social security appeal tribunals, medical appeal tribunals and disability appeal tribunals; and

(b) regional and other full-time chairmen of such tribunals.

(2) A person is qualified to be appointed President if he has a 10 year general qualification or he is an advocate or solicitor in Scotland of at least 10 years' standing.

(3) A person is qualified to be appointed a full-time chairman if he has a 5 year general qualification or he is an advocate or solicitor in Scotland of at least 5 years' standing.

(4) Schedule 2 to this Act shall have effect for supplementing this section.

DEFINITIONS

"5 year general qualification": s.191.

"10 year general qualification": *ibid.*

GENERAL NOTE

One of the major innovations in the reform of tribunals in 1984 was the appointment of a President who took over the appointment of social security appeal tribunal and medical appeal tribunal members and clerks as well as the training of chairmen and members. In effect, the administration of SSATs and MATs has been removed from the DSS into the hands of an entirely independent agency. The reality of this independence has largely been secured, but still depends on the resources allowed to the President by the Treasury. The President has now added disability appeal tribunals to his remit.

The first incumbent, Judge H.J. Byrt, took up his post towards the end of 1983 and completed his initial term of office in 1988. He was replaced by Judge Derek Holden in February 1990.

Section 51 also provides for the appointment of regional chairmen and full-time chairmen. Regional chairmen have been appointed for each of the seven (now reduced to six) DSS regions in Britain. This innovation can be seen as a reflection of the success of the four senior chairmen who had previously been responsible for supplementary benefit appeal tribunals and did a great deal to improve the standards of independence and expertise in those tribunals. The regional chairmen have smaller geographical areas to cope with, but must deal also with former national insurance local tribunals, MATs and now DATs and probably in 1993 child support appeal tribunals. The regional chairmen carry out many of the statutory functions of the President, *e.g.* training, arranging meetings and appointing members, within the overall framework set by the President.

Power is also given to appoint other full-time chairmen. Initially seven were appointed, but following the recent extensions in the tribunals' jurisdiction, some additional appointments have been made. In the past, they seem to have acted mainly as "troubleshooters", a resource to be called in to help clear backlogs of appeals in particular places or maybe to take particularly difficult cases. They have also had a large rôle in training, and with the number of tribunals expanding beyond what an individual Regional Chairman can handle, are likely increasingly to take on an administrative rôle.

Some dislike the development of full-time chairmen as much as the requirement of professional legal qualifications for part-time chairmen, as eroding the connections of chairmen with the local community. With the further expansion of the range of tribunals under the President's supervision, it may be that more full-time chairmen will be appointed. It is certainly becoming increasingly unrealistic to expect part-time chairmen to keep on top of the entire range of the SSAT's jurisdiction, as well as possibly DATs and MATs, and maintain the expertise to exercise a true independence of judgment.

Social Security Commissioners

Appointment of Commissioners

52.—(1) Her Majesty may from time to time appoint, from among persons who have a 10 year qualification or advocates or solicitors in Scotland of at least 10 years' standing—

(a) a Chief Social Security Commissioner; and

(b) such number of other Social Security Commissioners as Her Majesty thinks fit.

(2) If the Lord Chancellor considers that, in order to facilitate the disposal of the business of Social Security Commissioners, he should make an appointment in pursuance of this subsection, he may appoint—

(a) a person who has a 10 year general qualification; or

(b) an advocate or solicitor in Scotland of at least 10 years' standing; or

(c) a member of the bar of Northern Ireland or solicitor of the Supreme Court of Northern Ireland of at least 10 years' standing,

to be a Social Security Commissioner (but to be known as a deputy Commissioner) for such period or on such occasions as the Lord Chancellor thinks fit.

(3) When the Lord Chancellor proposes to exercise the power conferred on him by subsection (2) above, it shall be his duty to consult the Lord Advocate with respect to the proposal.

(4) Schedule 2 to this Act shall have effect for supplementing this section.

DEFINITIONS
"10-year general qualification": s.191.

References by authorities

Power of adjudicating authorities to refer matters to experts

53.—(1) An authority to which this section applies may refer any question of special difficulty arising for decision by the authority to one or more experts for examination and report.

(2) The authorities to which this section applies are—

(a) an adjudication officer;

(b) an adjudicating medical practitioner, or two or more such practitioners acting together;

(c) a specially qualified adjudicating medical practitioner appointed by virtue of section 62 below, or two or more such practitioners acting together;

(d) a social security appeal tribunal;

(e) a disability appeal tribunal;

(f) a medical appeal tribunal;

(g) a Commissioner;

(h) the Secretary of State.

(3) Regulations may prescribe cases in which a Commissioner shall not exercise the power conferred by subsection (1) above.

(4) In this section "expert" means a person appearing to the authority to have knowledge or experience which would be relevant in determining the question of special difficulty.

DEFINITIONS
"Commissioner": s.191.
"prescribed": *ibid.*

GENERAL NOTE
This general power may be useful to SSATs in exceptional circumstances, perhaps being more relevant to AOs or MATs and DATs. The question must be of special difficulty and needs

to be carefully specified. The power should not be used to get the tribunal off the hook of coming to a decision on conflicting evidence.

Claims relating to attendance allowance, disability living allowance and disability working allowance

54.—(1) Before a claim for an attendance allowance, a disability living allowance or a disability working allowance or any question relating to such an allowance is submitted to an adjudication officer under section 20 above the Secretary of State may refer the person in respect of whom the claim is made or the question is raised to a medical practitioner for such examination and report as appears to him to be necessary—

(a) for the purpose of providing the adjudication officer with information for use in determining the claim or question; or

(b) for the purpose of general monitoring of claims for attendance allowances, disability living allowances and disability working allowances.

(2) An adjudication officer may refer—

(a) a person in respect of whom such a claim is made or such a question is raised;

(b) a person who has applied or is treated as having applied for a review under section 30 or 35 above,

to a medical practitioner for such examination and report as appears to the adjudication officer to be needed to enable him to reach a decision on the claim or question or the matter under review.

(3) The Secretary of State may direct adjudication officers to refer for advice to a medical practitioner who is an officer of the Secretary of State any case falling within a specified class of cases relating to attendance allowance or disability living allowance, and an adjudication officer may refer for advice any case relating to attendance allowance or disability living allowance to such a medical practitioner without such a direction.

(4) An adjudication officer may refer for advice any case relating to disability working allowance to such a medical practitioner.

(5) A medical practitioner who is an officer of the Secretary of State and to whom a case or question relating to an attendance allowance or a disability living allowance is referred under section 53 above or subsection (3) above may refer the case or question to the Disability Living Allowance Advisory Board for advice.

(6) Such a medical practitioner may obtain information about such a case or question from another medical practitioner.

(7) A medical practitioner who is an officer of the Secretary of State and to whom a question relating to disability working allowance is referred under section 53 above may obtain information about it from another medical practitioner.

(8) Where—

(a) the Secretary of State has exercised the power conferred on him by subsection (1) above or an adjudication officer has exercised the power conferred on him by subsection (2) above; and

(b) the medical practitioner requests the person referred to him to attend for or submit himself to medical examination; but

(c) he fails without good cause to do so,

the adjudication officer shall decide the claim or question or matter under review against him.

GENERAL NOTE

The powers contained in this section will in disability working allowance cases mainly be used in relation to the disability question under s.129(1)(b) of the Contributions and Benefits Act. They are more likely to be used in attendance allowance and disability living allowance cases. Although the philosophy of the scheme in force from April 1992 is of self-assessment, there will be cases where what is put on the claim form is inconsistent or improbable or where a claimant is appealing against an adverse decision and medical examination is necessary. A random sample of all claims will be referred for medical examination, mainly for monitoring purposes.

Medical examination etc. in relation to appeals to disability appeal tribunals

55.—(1) Where an appeal has been brought under section 33(1)(a) above, a person who may be nominated as chairman of a disability appeal tribunal may, if prescribed conditions are satisfied, refer the claimant to a medical practitioner for such examination and report as appears to him to be necessary for the purpose of providing a disability appeal tribunal with information for use in determining the appeal.

(2) At a hearing before a disability appeal tribunal, except in prescribed circumstances, the tribunal—

(a) may not carry out a physical examination of the claimant; and
(b) may not require the claimant to undergo any physical test for the purpose of determining whether he satisfies the condition mentioned in section 73(1)(a) of the Contributions and Benefits Act.

GENERAL NOTE

Subs. (1)
A chairman of a DAT may refer a claimant for medical examination and report. In contrast, the power in s.53 can only be exercised by the DAT as a whole and there must be a question of special difficulty. The prescribed conditions, in reg. 26F of the Social Security (Adjudication) Regulations 1986 (S.I. 1986 No. 2218), are that the chairman is satisfied that the appeal cannot be properly determined unless the claimant is examined by a medical practitioner who provides the DAT with information for use in determining the appeal. The need for such a power arises because subs. (2) prevents a DAT from itself physically examining a claimant. The intention is that the power in subs. (1) should be used only in unusual cases, in line with the philosophy of self-assessment. However, there is no express reference to this philosophy in the legislation and it remains to be seen how far DATs feel able to discharge their judicial functions without the benefit of reports of medical examinations.

Subs. (2)
A DAT may not carry out a physical examination of the claimant or require him to undergo a physical test to determine whether he is unable or virtually unable to walk by reason of physical disablement. No regulations have as yet prescribed any exceptions.
These limitations appear to be in reaction to the unpopularity of medical examinations and of the "walking tests" carried out by medical boards and medical appeal tribunals for mobility allowance purposes. Now, medical examinations by DATs are prohibited. If such an examination is necessary the powers in s.53 or subs. (1) must be used. Walking tests, for the mobility component of disability living allowance, are not prohibited, but may not be required. A claimant may therefore volunteer to undergo a walking test, but difficulties can be foreseen if DATs attempt to offer the claimant a choice of doing so. It will be almost impossible to avoid an impression that some pressure is being put on the claimant to agree. The result is to leave DATs in acute difficulties in mobility component appeals, for self-assessment of walking ability is inherently unreliable.

Determination of questions of special difficulty

Assessors

56.—(1) Where it appears to an authority to which this section applies that a matter before the authority involves a question of fact of special difficulty, then, unless regulations otherwise provide, the authority may direct that in dealing with that matter they shall have the assistance of one or more assessors.

(2) The authorities to which this section applies are—
(a) two or more adjudicating medical practitioners acting together;
(b) two or more specially qualified adjudicating medical practitioners, appointed by virtue of section 62 below, acting together;

(c) a social security appeal tribunal;
(d) a disability appeal tribunal;
(e) a medical appeal tribunal;
(f) a Commissioner;
(g) the Secretary of State.

GENERAL NOTE

Presumably the principles laid down in *R(I) 14/51* in relation to earlier legislation will continue to apply. The assessor's rôle is to assist the authority to understand the factual issues and to evaluate the evidence. He does not himself give evidence and so cannot be questioned by the parties to the proceedings. His advice should be summarised and the parties given the opportunity to comment on it.

Tribunal of three Commissioners

57.—(1) If it appears to the Chief Social Security Commissioner (or, in the case of his inability to act, to such other of the Commissioners as he may have nominated to act for the purpose) that an appeal falling to be heard by one of the Commissioners involves a question of law of special difficulty, he may direct that the appeal be dealt with, not by that Commissioner alone, but by a Tribunal consisting of any 3 of the Commissioners.

(2) If the decision of the Tribunal is not unanimous, the decision of the majority shall be the decision of the Tribunal.

GENERAL NOTE

Under the legislation in force before April 1984 there was no express power for the Chief Commissioner to convene a Tribunal of Commissioners in supplementary benefit or family income supplement cases. The power was found by implication (*R(FIS) 1/82*). It is often invoked where individual Commissioners have reached conflicting decisions. Individual Commissioners are bound to follow a decision of a Tribunal of Commissioners, unless there are compelling reasons to the contrary (*R(I) 12/75* and *CM 44/1991*). A Tribunal of Commissioners may depart from a previous Tribunal decision if satisfied that it was wrong (*R(U) 4/88*).

With the expansion in the number of Commissioners it can no longer be guaranteed that the approach adopted by the three Commissioners on a Tribunal will be accepted by the Commissioners as a whole. In recent years, a number of Tribunal decisions have been left unreported. This may be because of lack of support by the Commissioners as a whole, but it is impossible from the outside to tell. A tribunal or an AO must follow a Tribunal's decision, whether reported or unreported, in preference to a decision of an individual Commissioner. Possibly, if the individual Commissioner finds compelling reasons for departing from an unreported Tribunal decision, a tribunal would be entitled to follow the individual Commissioner's decision.

Regulations

Regulations as to determination of questions and matters arising out of, or pending, reviews and appeals

58.—(1) Subject to the provisions of this Act, provision may be made by regulations for the determination—
(a) by the Secretary of State; or
(b) by a person or tribunal appointed or constituted in accordance with the regulations,
of any question arising under or in connection with the Contributions and Benefits Act or the former legislation, including a claim for benefit.

(2) In this section "the former legislation" means the National Insurance Acts 1965 to 1974 and the National Insurance (Industrial Injuries) Acts 1965 to 1974 and the 1975 Act and Part II of the 1986 Act.

(3) Regulations under subsection (1) above may modify, add to or exclude any provisions of this Part of this Act, so far as relating to any questions to which the regulations relate.

(4) It is hereby declared for the avoidance of doubt that the power to make regulations under subsection (1) above includes power to make regulations for the determination of any question arising as to the total or partial recoupment of unemployment benefit in pursuance of regulations under section 132 of the Employment Protection (Consolidation) Act 1978 (including any decision as to the amount of benefit).

(5) Regulations under subsection (1) above may provide for the review by the Secretary of State of decisions on questions determined by him.

(6) The Lord Chancellor may by regulations provide—

(a) for officers authorised—
  (i) by the Lord Chancellor; or
  (ii) in Scotland, by the Secretary of State,
  to determine any question which is determinable by a Commissioner and which does not involve the determination of any appeal, application for leave to appeal or reference;

(b) for the procedure to be followed by any such officer in determining any such question;

(c) for the manner in which determinations of such questions by such officers may be called in question.

(7) A determination which would have the effect of preventing an appeal, application for leave to appeal or reference being determined by a Commissioner is not a determination of the appeal, application or reference for the purposes of subsection (6) above.

(8) Regulations under subsection (1) above may provide—

(a) for the reference to the High Court or, in Scotland, the Court of Session for decision of any question of law arising in connection with the determination of a question by the Secretary of State; and

(b) for appeals to the High Court or Court of Session from the decision of the Secretary of State on any such question of law;

and subsections (5) to (7) of section 18 above shall apply to a reference or appeal under this subsection as they apply to a reference or appeal under subsections (1) to (3) of that section.

DEFINITIONS
  "the 1975 Act": s.191.
  "the 1986 Act": *ibid.*
  "the Contributions and Benefits Act": *ibid.*

Procedure

59.—(1) Regulations (in this section referred to as "procedure regulations") may make any such provision as is specified in Schedule 3 to this Act.

(2) Procedure regulations may deal differently with claims and questions relating to—

(a) benefit under Parts II to IV of the Contributions and Benefits Act;

(b) industrial injuries benefit;

(c) each of the other benefits to which section 20 above applies.

(3) At any inquiry held by virtue of procedure regulations the witnesses shall, if the person holding the inquiry thinks fit, be examined on oath; and the person holding the inquiry shall have power to administer oaths for that purpose.

(4) In proceedings for the determination of a question mentioned in section 17(1)(c) above (including proceedings on an inquiry)—

(a) in England and Wales, there shall be available to a witness (other than the person who is liable, or alleged to be liable, to pay the Class 1A contribution in question) any privilege against self-incrimination or incrimination of a spouse which is available to a witness in legal proceedings; and

(b) in Scotland, section 3 of the Evidence (Scotland) Act 1853 (competence and compellability of witnesses) shall apply as it applies to civil proceedings.

(5) Procedure regulations prescribing the procedure to be followed in cases before a Commissioner shall provide that any hearing shall be in public except in so far as the Commissioner for special reasons otherwise directs.

(6) It is hereby declared—

(a) that the power to prescribe procedure includes power to make provision as to the representation of one person, at any hearing of a case, by another person whether having professional qualifications or not; and

(b) that the power to provide for the manner in which questions arising for determination by the Secretary of State are to be raised includes power to make provision with respect to the formulation of any such questions, whether arising on a reference under section 117 below or otherwise.

(7) Except so far as it may be applied in relation to England and Wales by procedure regulations, the Arbitration Act 1950 shall not apply to any proceedings under this Part of this Act.

DEFINITIONS
"the Contributions and Benefits Act": s.191.
"industrial injuries benefit": *ibid.*

GENERAL NOTE
See Sched. 3 and the Social Security (Adjudication) Regulations 1986 (S.I. 1986 No. 2218), in the current editions of Bonner *et al.*, Mesher and Rowland.

Finality of decisions

60.—(1) Subject to the provisions of this Part of this Act, the decision of any claim or question in accordance with the foregoing provisions of this Part of this Act shall be final; and subject to the provisions of any regulations under section 58 above, the decision of any claim or question in accordance with those regulations shall be final.

(2) Subsection (1) above shall not make any finding of fact or other determination embodied in or necessary to a decision, or on which it is based, conclusive for the purpose of any further decision.

(3) A decision (given under subsection (2) of section 44 above or otherwise) that an accident was an industrial accident is to be taken as determining only that paragraphs (a), (b) and (c) of subsection (5) of that section are satisfied in relation to the accident, and neither any such decision nor the reference to an adjudicating medical practitioner or a medical appeal tribunal under section 45 above of the disablement questions in connection with any claim to or award of disablement benefit is to be taken as importing a decision as to the origin of any injury or disability suffered by the claimant, whether or not there is an event identifiable as an accident apart from any injury that may have been received; but—

(a) a decision that on a particular occasion when there was no such event a person had an industrial accident by reason of an injury shall be treated as a decision that, if the injury was suffered by accident on that occasion, the accident was an industrial accident; and

(b) a decision that an accident was an industrial accident may be given, and a declaration to that effect be made and recorded in accordance with section 44 above, without its having been found that personal injury resulted from the accident (saving always the discretion under subsection (3) of that section to refuse to determine the question if it is unlikely to be necessary for the purposes of a claim for benefit).

(4) Notwithstanding anything in subsection (2) or (3) above (but subject to the provisions of this Part of this Act as to appeal and review), where for purposes of disablement pension or disablement gratuity in respect of an accident it has been found by an adjudicating medical practitioner or a medical appeal tribunal, on the determination or last determination of the disablement questions, that an injury resulted in whole or in part from the accident, then for purposes of industrial death benefit in respect of that accident the finding shall be conclusive that the injury did so result.

(5) Subsections (2) to (4) above shall apply as regards the effect to be given in any proceedings to any decision, or to a reference under section 45 above, whether the decision was given or reference made or the proceedings were commenced before or after the passing of the National Insurance Act 1972 (section 5 of which originally contained the provisions contained in this section), except that it shall not affect the determination of any appeal under section 48 above from a decision of a medical appeal tribunal given before the passing of that Act, nor affect any proceedings consequent on such an appeal from a decision so given; and accordingly—

(a) any decision given before the passing of that Act that a claimant was not entitled to industrial death benefit may be reviewed in accordance with this Part of this Act to give effect to subsection (4) above; and

(b) the references in subsections (2) and (3) above to provisions of this Act, and the reference in this subsection to section 45 above shall (so far as necessary) include the corresponding provisions of previous Acts.

GENERAL NOTE

Jones v. *Department of Employment* [1988] 1 All E.R. 725 decided that an AO cannot be sued for negligently making a decision, partly because of the effect of s.60.

Although decisions are final, under subs. (2) findings of fact or other determinations are not conclusive for further decisions. It used to be the case that decisions of the insurance officer on certain questions were conclusive for supplementary benefit purposes. This issue is now covered by reg. 64 of the Social Security (Adjudication) Regulations 1986 (S.I. 1986 No. 2218). The issue is only really a live one before a tribunal, and here it is clear from reg. 64 that, although an AO must first make a decision on a relevant question, the SSAT can deal with both income support and the national insurance or child benefit question together.

Subsection (2) also confirms that on a fresh claim, issues of fact and law are for decision afresh. For instance, if an income support claim is rejected on the ground that a claimant has notional capital under the deprivation rule, a claim a month or a week later cannot be rejected simply by reference to the earlier decision.

Regulations about supplementary matters relating to determinations

61.—(1) Regulations may make provision as respects matters arising—

(a) pending the determination under this Act (whether in the first instance or on an appeal or reference, and whether originally or on review)—

(i) of any claim for benefit to which this section applies; or

(ii) in any question affecting any person's right to such benefit or its receipt; or

(iii) of any person's liability for contributions under Part I of the Contributions and Benefits Act; or

(b) out of the revision on appeal or review of any decision under this Act on any such claim or question.

(2) Without prejudice to the generality of subsection (1) above, regulations under that subsection may include provision as to the date from which any decision on a review is to have effect or to be deemed to have had effect.

(3) Regulations under subsection (1) above as it applies to child benefit may include provision as to the date from which child benefit is to be payable to a person in respect of a child in a case where, before the benefit was

awarded to that person, child benefit in respect of the child was awarded to another person.

(4) This section applies—
(a) to benefit as defined in section 122 of the Contributions and Benefits Act;
(b) to child benefit;
(c) to statutory sick pay;
(d) to statutory maternity pay;
(e) to income support;
(f) to family credit;
(g) to disability working allowance; and
(h) to any social fund payments such as are mentioned in section 138(1) (a) or (2) of the Contributions and Benefits Act.

DEFINITIONS
"the Contributions and Benefits Act": s.191.

GENERAL NOTE
See the Social Security (Adjudication) Regulations 1986 (S.I. 1986 No. 2218) and the Social Security (Claims and Payments) Regulations 1987 (S.I. 1987 No. 1968), in the current editions of Bonner *et al.*, Mesher and Rowland.

Industrial diseases

Adjudication as to industrial diseases

62.—(1) Regulations shall provide for applying, in relation—
(a) to claims for benefit under sections 108 to 110 of the Contributions and Benefits Act; and
(b) to questions arising in connection with such claims or with awards of such benefit,
the provisions of this Part of this Act subject to any prescribed additions or modifications.

(2) Regulations for those purposes may in particular provide—
(a) for the appointment of specially qualified adjudicating medical practitioners and the appointment of medical officers for the purposes of the regulations (which shall be taken to include, in the case of specially qualified adjudicating medical practitioners, the purposes for which adjudicating medical practitioners are appointed and medical appeal tribunals are established); and
(b) for the payment by the prescribed persons of fees of the prescribed amount in connection with any medical examination by specially qualified adjudicating medical practitioners or any such officer and their return in any prescribed cases, and (so far as not required to be returned) their payment into the National Insurance Fund and recovery as sums due to that Fund.

DEFINITIONS
"the Contributions and Benefits Act": s.191.

GENERAL NOTE
See Section A of Pt. IV of the Social Security (Adjudication) Regulations 1986 (S.I. 1986 No. 2281), in the current edition of Rowland.

Housing benefit and community charge benefits

Adjudication

63.—(1) Regulations shall provide that, where a person has claimed—
(a) housing benefit; or
(b) a community charge benefit as regards a personal or collective community charge of a charging authority; or

(c) a community charge benefit as regards a personal or collective community charge payable to a levying authority,

the authority shall notify the person of its determination of the claim.

(2) Any such notification shall be given in such form as may be prescribed.

(3) Regulations shall make provision for reviews of determinations relating to housing benefit or community charge benefits.

GENERAL NOTE

See reg. 77 of the Housing Benefits (General) Regulations 1987 (S.I. 1987 No. 1971) and reg. 65 of the Community Charge Benefits (General) Regulations 1989 (S.I. 1989 No. 1321), in the current edition of Findlay and Ward.

Social fund officers and inspectors and the social fund Commissioner

Social fund officers

64.—(1) The Secretary of State shall appoint officers, to be known as "social fund officers", for the purpose of performing functions in relation to payments out of the social fund such as are mentioned in section 138(1)(b) of the Contributions and Benefits Act.

(2) A social fund officer may be appointed to perform all the functions of social fund officers or such functions of such officers as may be specified in his instrument of appointment.

(3) The Secretary of State may nominate for an area a social fund officer who shall issue general guidance to the other social fund officers in the area about such matters relating to the social fund as the Secretary of State may specify.

DEFINITIONS

"the Contributions and Benefits Act": s.191.

GENERAL NOTE

Subs. (3)

See s.140(5) of the Contributions and Benefits Act and s.66(9) below for the status of guidance issued by area social fund officers.

The social fund Commissioner and inspectors

65.—(1) There shall continue to be an officer, to be known as "the social fund Commissioner" (in this section referred to as "the Commissioner").

(2) The Commissioner shall be appointed by the Secretary of State.

(3) The Commissioner—

(a) shall appoint such social fund inspectors; and

(b) may appoint such officers and staff for himself and for social fund inspectors,

as he thinks fit, but with the consent of the Secretary of State and the Treasury as to numbers.

(4) Appointments under subsection (3) above shall be made from persons made available to the Commissioner by the Secretary of State.

(5) It shall be the duty of the Commissioner—

(a) to monitor the quality of decisions of social fund inspectors and give them such advice and assistance as he thinks fit to improve the standard of their decisions;

(b) to arrange such training of social fund inspectors as he considers appropriate; and

(c) to carry out such other functions in connection with the work of social fund inspectors as the Secretary of State may direct.

(6) The Commissioner shall report annually in writing to the Secretary of State on the standards of reviews by social fund inspectors and the Secretary of State shall publish his report.

GENERAL NOTE
The rôle of the social fund Commissioner is to appoint social fund inspectors, who deal with applications for review from social fund officers under s.66(3), and to oversee their operation. The Annual Reports of the Social Fund Commissioner contain much interesting material. Inspectors have been recruited from outside and inside the DSS and have established an independence of operation.

Reviews

66.—(1) A social fund officer—
(a) shall review a determination made under the Contributions and Benefits Act by himself or some other social fund officer, if an application for a review is made within such time and in such form and manner as may be prescribed by or on behalf of the person who applied for the payment to which the determination relates; and
(b) may review such a determination in such other circumstances as he thinks fit;
and may exercise on a review any power exercisable by an officer under Part VIII of the Contributions and Benefits Act.

(2) The power to review a determination conferred on a social fund officer by subsection (1) above includes power to review a determination made by a social fund officer on a previous review.

(3) On an application made by or on behalf of the person to whom a determination relates within such time and in such form and manner as may be prescribed a determination of a social fund officer which has been reviewed shall be further reviewed by a social fund inspector.

(4) On a review a social fund inspector shall have the following powers—
(a) power to confirm the determination made by the social fund officer;
(b) power to make any determination which a social fund officer could have made;
(c) power to refer the matter to a social fund officer for determination.

(5) A social fund inspector may review a determination under subsection (3) above made by himself or some other social fund inspector.

(6) In determining a question on a review a social fund officer or social fund inspector shall have regard, subject to subsection (7) below, to all the circumstances of the case and, in particular, to the matters specified in section 140(1)(a) to (e) of the Contributions and Benefits Act.

(7) An officer or inspector shall determine any question on a review in accordance with any general directions issued by the Secretary of State under section 140(2) of the Contributions and Benefits Act and any general directions issued by him with regard to reviews and in determining any such question shall take account of any general guidance issued by him under that subsection or with regard to reviews.

(8) Directions under this section may specify—
(a) the circumstances in which a determination is to be reviewed; and
(b) the manner in which a review is to be conducted.

(9) In reviewing a question under this section a social fund officer shall take account (subject to any directions or guidance issued by the Secretary of State under this section) of any guidance issued by the social fund officer nominated for his area under section 64(3) above.

(10) A social fund inspector reviewing a determination shall be under the same duties in relation to such guidance as the social fund officer or inspector who made the determination.

DEFINITIONS
"the Contributions and Benefits Act": s.191.

GENERAL NOTE

Subss. (1) and (3)
See the Social Fund (Application for Review) Regulations 1988 (S.I. 1988 No. 34). Sub-

section (1) establishes the review of an initial SFO decision by another SFO as the first stage of challenge by a claimant. Subsection (3) establishes the further stage of review by a social fund inspector.

Subs. (4)

A social fund inspector (see s.65) may confirm the SFO's decision, give any decision which the SFO could have made or refer the matter back to a SFO. However, a social fund inspector is as bound by the factors listed in s.140(1)(a)–(e) of the Contributions and Benefits Act and by directions and guidance from the Secretary of State or the area SFO as the SFO (subss. (6), (7), (9) and (10)). There is an additional duty to follow the directions specified in subs. (8).

Subss. (7) and (8)

See directions 31–42 of the Secretary of State's directions to SFOs and the directions to SFIs, together with the notes to those directions, in the current edition of Mesher.

Christmas bonus

Determination of questions

67.—(1) A determination by the competent authority that a person is entitled or not entitled to payment of a qualifying benefit in respect of a period which includes a day in the relevant week shall be conclusive for the purposes of section 148 of the Contributions and Benefits Act; and in this subsection "competent authority" means, in relation to a payment of any description of a qualifying benefit, an authority that ordinarily determines whether a person is entitled to such a payment.

(2) Any question arising under that section other than one determined or falling to be determined under subsection (1) above shall be determined by the Secretary of State whose decision shall except as provided by subsection (3) below be final.

(3) The Secretary of State may reverse a decision under subsection (2) above on new facts being brought to his notice or if he is satisfied that the decision was given in ignorance of, or was based on a mistake as to, some material fact.

(4) Expressions used in this section to which a meaning is assigned by section 150 of the Contributions and Benefits Act have that meaning in this section.

Restrictions on entitlement to benefit following erroneous decision

Restrictions on entitlement to benefit in certain cases of error

68.—(1) This section applies where—

(a) on the determination, whenever made, of a Commissioner or the court (the "relevant determination"), a decision made by an adjudicating authority is or was found to have been erroneous in point of law; and

(b) after both—

(i) 13th July 1990 (the date of the coming into force of section 165D of the 1975 Act, the provision of that Act corresponding to this section); and

(ii) the date of the relevant determination,

a claim which falls, or which would apart from this section fall, to be decided in accordance with the relevant determination is made or treated under section 7(1) above as made by any person for any benefit.

(2) Where this section applies, any question which arises on, or on the review of a decision which is referable to, the claim mentioned in subsection (1)(b) above and which relates to the entitlement of the claimant or any other party to any benefit—

(a) in respect of a period before the relevant date; or

(b) in the case of a widow's payment, in respect of a death occurring before that date,

shall be determined as if the decision referred to in subsection (1)(a) above had been found by the Commissioner or court in question not to have been erroneous in point of law.

(3) In determining whether a person is entitled to benefit in a case where—

(a) his entitlement depends on his having been entitled to the same or some other benefit before attaining a particular age; and

(b) he attained that age—

(i) before both the date of the relevant determination and the date of the claim referred in subsection (1)(b) above, but

(ii) not before the earliest day in respect of which benefit could, apart from this section, have been awarded on that claim,

subsection (2) above shall be disregarded for the purpose only of determining the question whether he was entitled as mentioned in paragraph (a) above.

(4) In this section—

"adjudicating authority" means—

(a) an adjudication officer or, where the original decision was given on a reference under section 21(2) or 25(1) above, a social security appeal tribunal, a disability appeal tribunal or a medical appeal tribunal;

(b) any of the following former bodies or officers, that is to say, the National Assistance Board, the Supplementary Benefits Commission, the Attendance Allowance Board, a benefit officer, an insurance officer or a supplement officer; or

(c) any of the officers who, or tribunals or other bodies which, in Northern Ireland correspond to those mentioned in paragraph (a) or (b) above;

"benefit" means—

(a) benefit as defined in section 122 of the Contributions and Benefits Act; and

(b) any income-related benefit;

"the court" means the High Court, the Court of Appeal, the Court of Session, the High Court or Court of Appeal in Northern Ireland, the House of Lords or the Court of Justice of the European Community;

"the relevant date" means whichever is the latest of—

(a) the date of the relevant determination;

(b) the date which falls 12 months before the date on which the claim referred to in subsection (1)(b) above is made or treated under section 7(1) above as made; and

(c) the earliest date in respect of which the claimant would, apart from this section, be entitled on that claim to the benefit in question.

(5) For the purposes of this section—

(a) any reference in this section to entitlement to benefit includes a reference to entitlement—

(i) to any increase in the rate of a benefit; or

(ii) to a benefit, or increase of benefit, at a particular rate; and

(b) any reference to a decision which is "referable to" a claim is a reference to—

(i) a decision on the claim,

(ii) a decision on a review of the decision on the claim, or

(iii) a decision on a subsequent review of the decision on the review,

and so on.

(6) The date of the relevant determination shall, in prescribed cases, be determined for the purposes of this section in accordance with any regulations made for that purpose.

DEFINITIONS
"the 1975 Act": s.191.
"Commissioner": *ibid.*
"the Contributions and Benefits Act": *ibid.*
"income-related benefit": *ibid.*

GENERAL NOTE

See the notes to s.69 below for the general background and effect of ss.68 and 69, and for discussion of the definitions in s.68(4).

Section 68 can only apply when a claim is actually made after the date of some Commissioner's or court decision which finds the DSS view of the law to be wrong. Then, in so far as the claim can be treated as for a period before the date of claim and the claimant would otherwise be entitled to benefit, entitlement for any period before the "relevant date" is to be determined as if the decision had gone the other way (subs. (2)). The "relevant date" is either the date of the decision or 12 months before the actual date of claim, if later (subs. (4), paras. (a) and (b) of the definition).

Paragraph (c) of the definition merely seems to confirm what would be the case anyway.

There is a small exception in subs. (3), where payment of the particular benefit at the date in question is not in issue, but merely the establishment of an entitlement to the benefit at a particular age.

Determination of questions on review following erroneous decisions

69.—(1) Subsection (2) below applies in any case where—

(a) on the determination, whenever made, of a Commissioner or the court (the "relevant determination"), a decision made by an adjudicating authority is or was found to have been erroneous in point of law; and

(b) in consequence of that determination, any other decision—

  (i) which was made before the date of that determination; and

  (ii) which is referable to a claim made or treated as made by any person for any benefit,

falls (or would, apart from subsection (2) below, fall) to be revised on a review carried out under section 25(2) above on or after 13th July 1990 (the date of the passing of the Social Security Act 1990, which added to the 1975 Act sections 104(7) to (10), corresponding to this section) or on a review under section 30 above on the ground that the decision under review was erroneous in point of law.

(2) Where this subsection applies, any question arising on the review referred to in subsection (1)(b) above, or on any subsequent review of a decision which is referable to the same claim, as to any person's entitlement to, or right to payment of, any benefit—

(a) in respect of any period before the date of the relevant determination; or

(b) in the case of widow's payment, in respect of a death occurring before that date,

shall be determined as if the decision referred to in subsection (1)(a) above had been found by the Commissioner or court in question not to have been erroneous in point of law.

(3) In determining whether a person is entitled to benefit in a case where his entitlement depends on his having been entitled to the same or some other benefit before attaining a particular age, subsection (2) above shall be disregarded for the purpose only of determining the question whether he was so entitled before attaining that age.

(4) For the purposes of this section—

(a) "adjudicating authority" and "the court" have the same meaning as they have in section 68 above;

(b) any reference to—
>>> (i) a person's entitlement to benefit; or
>>> (ii) a decision which is referable to a claim,
>> shall be construed in accordance with subsection (5) of that section; and
> (c) the date of the relevant determination shall, in prescribed cases, be determined in accordance with any regulations made under subsection (6) of that section.

DEFINITIONS
"the 1975 Act": s.191.
"Commissioner": *ibid.*

GENERAL NOTE

J decision
The predecessor of s.69 formed a package with the predecessor of s.68 on claims when they were introduced in 1990. The aim is that where an established interpretation of the law is overturned by a decision of a Social Security Commissioner or a higher court, effect can only be given to the new interpretation for other claimants on review or a fresh claim with effect from the date of that decision (the decision is referred to below as the J decision and the date as the J Day).

Background
The general rule on claims for benefit is that there can be no entitlement for a period more than 12 months before the actual date of claim, however good the cause for delay in claiming (s.1(2) above; Social Security Act 1975, s.165A(2)). This limit does not apply to disablement benefit or reduced earnings allowance. Thus if a possible entitlement is revealed by the J decision and the person has not previously claimed, that limit applies.
    If the person has already had a decision on a claim and applies for a review of that decision based on the new interpretation, again there is a general limit of 12 months before the date of the request for review (Social Security (Adjudication) Regulations 1986 (S.I. 1986 No. 2281), regs. 65 and 69–71). However, there was until August 31, 1991 an exemption from this limit under reg. 72(1) of the Adjudication Regulations where, among other things, the decision to be reviewed was erroneous by reason of a mistake made by an adjudication officer (AO). Acting on a mistaken view of the law could obviously come within reg. 72(1) (*R(SB) 10/91* and *CIS 11/1991*), so that a revision on review triggered by the J decision could go back to the date of the original decision. Alarm about this effect led to the insertion of reg. 72(2) from September 1, 1987, which provided that reg. 72 should not apply where review was on the ground that the original decision was erroneous in law by reason of the J decision. The result was that in such cases the normal 12-month limit applied. The argument that the original decision was not erroneous by reason of the J decision, but was simply revealed to have been erroneous all along, was rejected in *R(SB) 11/89*.
    In an investigation by the Parliamentary Commissioner for Administration (the Ombudsman) into the decision of the Secretary of State about how extensively to trawl back for past entitlements following a Commissioner's decision on the offsetting of payments of occupational pension against dependency additions to invalidity benefit, the Ombudsman raised the effect of reg. 72(2) of the Adjudication Regulations (*C191/88*, Fourth Report of the PCA for 1989–90). He was concerned that the longer the delay in identifying a claimant's case as requiring review the more benefit was lost, because of the absolute time limit recently reintroduced. He was not convinced that this effect was brought to Ministers' attention. In the course of responding to that point the DSS said that it would introduce a common start date for entitlement on review in such cases, but gave no indication of what sort of date would be chosen. The new provisions introduced by the Social Security Act 1990 were said to be in fulfilment of this undertaking. See *Hansard*, H.L. Vol. 519, cols. 684–6 (Lord Henley).
    Regulation 72 of the Adjudication Regulations has been replaced with effect from August 31, 1991 by reg. 64A, which also allows the 12-month limit on review to be lifted, but uses a more restricted approach to errors of law. See the notes to that regulation in the current edition of Mesher.

The new provisions
    The new provisions came into force on July 13, 1990. Because, as discussed below, there has been a significant change in the legislation in this Act, in force from July 1, 1992, it is necessary

carefully to separate the legal position before July 1, 1992 from the position after that date. The current provisions on review (s.69) and claims (s.68) apply where "on a determination, whenever made, of a Commissioner or the court . . . , a decision made by an adjudicating authority is or was found to have been erroneous in point of law" (subs. (1)(a)). Note that appeals from initial decisions (including reviews and refusals to review) which are not affected by the new rules are not within the scope of either section at all.

An "adjudicating authority" was originally defined to cover an AO or any of his legislative predecessors, a social security appeal tribunal, a medical appeal tribunal, the Attendance Allowance Board, the Supplementary Benefits Commission or the National Assistance Board. The disability appeal tribunal was added in April 1991. However, the form of words in the 1992 Act (s.68(4)) has introduced a significant change. Tribunals are only included where the original decision was given on a reference by the AO to a SSAT under s.21(2) or 25(1). There was no condition of this kind in the pre-July 1992 legislation. The change is not covered by a Law Commission recommendation (see the Report on the consolidation of certain enactments relating to Social Security: Law Com. No. 203). Therefore, it must have been considered to come within the corrections and minor improvements which can properly be authorised by s.2 of the Consolidation of Enactments (Procedure) Act 1949. The Joint Committee on Consolidation Bills (H.L. Paper 23-I, H.C. Paper 141-I, Session 1991–2) gave their opinion that this was so (although they also considered that this Act and the Contributions and Benefits Act represented "pure consolidation" of the existing law), so that presumably the new form has to be accepted. See below for some of the resulting problems.

"The court" includes everything above the Commissioner (s.68(4)). If any decision made before J Day falls to be revised on review carried out on or after July 13, 1990 "in consequence of that determination" (s.69(1)(b)), entitlement before J Day is to be determined as if the adjudicating authority's decision had been found not to be erroneous in point of law (s.69(2)). In addition, reg. 64B of the Adjudication Regulations requires the revised decision on review to take effect only from J Day. Alternatively, if a new claim is made after J Day, entitlement before that date is to be decided on the same assumption (s.68(2)). These provisions do not seem to achieve the intended aim, and give rise to a number of problems.

The problems

The aim of the provisions is clear—a common start date for revising other claimants' entitlements when an appeal overturns the previously accepted DSS interpretation of the law. The main political argument against their introduction was that the start date was placed unacceptably and unfairly late at J Day. While reg. 72(2) of the Adjudication Regulations still existed there was only a common start date when the review took place within 12 months of J Day. For reviews which take place after reg. 64A has taken over, the 12-month limit will only be lifted if the J decision shows that the previous interpretation involved errors of law of particular kinds (see reg. 64A(3)). But the form of the new provisions both before and after July 1, 1992 raises more fundamental problems.

The argument on the pre-July 1992 form of the provisions is as follows. For the new rules to apply, a Commissioner or higher court must have found an adjudicating authority's decision to be erroneous in point of law. Thus, if a SSAT adopts the AO's view of the law and the Commissioner holds the SSAT to have made an error of law, the new rules apply. But if a SSAT differs from the AO and the Commissioner holds that the SSAT has not made an error of law, the condition in the predecessor of ss.68(1)(a) and 69(1)(a) is not met. The Commissioner's jurisdiction is only to determine whether the SSAT has made an error of law. Although the reasons for his determination may include an indication that the AO's decision was erroneous in point of law, this is not something which is "found" "on the determination". The words "erroneous in point of law" are precisely those used in describing the Commissioner's powers on an appeal from a SSAT (see s.23(7)). A similar point can be made if the AO's view is accepted by the SSAT and the Commissioner, but the Court of Appeal finds the Commissioner to have been in error of law. The Commissioner is not within the definition of "adjudicating authority". The Court of Appeal will not have "found" an adjudicating authority's decision to be erroneous in point of law and the new rules do not apply.

On this view, there might seem to be no point in the inclusion of the AO in the definition of "adjudicating authority", for there is no way in which a Commissioner or court within the normal appeal structure can "find" an AO's decision to be erroneous in point of law. However, an AO's decision may be taken directly to a court in an application for judicial review. Under the Court of Appeal's decision in *Chief Adjudication Officer and Secretary of State for Social Security* v. *Foster* [1991] 3 W.L.R. 473, this is the only way in which an argument that a regulation is *ultra vires* can be raised. It is therefore arguable that if the Divisional Court or some other court decides that a regulation relied on by an AO is *ultra vires*, this involves finding that the AO's decision was erroneous in point of law.

If this general argument is correct, the pre-July 1992 rules applied capriciously, depending on the precise history of the appeal before the J decision. This view was not shared by the DSS and there has not yet been any authoritative ruling on it. The contrary view is that "found" does not have any technical meaning, so that if a Commissioner or a court takes a different view of the law from that taken by an AO, this amounts to finding the decision made by the AO to be erroneous in point of law. However, there remains considerable scope for argument that the new rules do not apply in the circumstances identified above. It may be that the change in the legislation from July 1, 1992 was an attempt to "clarify" the law, but what is clear is that it cannot affect the proper interpretation of the legislation as it stood before July 1, 1992.

The form of the definition of "adjudicating authority" in force with effect from July 1, 1992 (s.68(4), applied in s.69(4)(a)) adds even further difficulties. It appears to exclude SSATs, DATs and MATs except where the original decision was given on a reference under s.21(2) or s.25(2). Under these provisions, an AO need not make a decision on a claim or an application for review, but may refer the claim or application to a SSAT for decision. The SSAT then makes the original decision on the claim or review. Thus a SSAT deciding an appeal is not an adjudicating authority. In the case of DATs or MATs the original decision cannot have been given on a reference under either of those provisions, which only apply to SSATs. Since the condition seems to govern SSATs, DATs and MATs, this has the effect of excluding DATs and MATs from the definition entirely. If tribunals are excluded from the definition except in the case where the SSAT makes an original decision on a reference, the argument put forward above about the pre-July 1992 law would mean that no Commissioner or court decision which put forward a different interpretation of the law from that adopted by an AO in an original decision could "find" a decision of an adjudicating authority erroneous in point of law, whether it upheld the view of an SSAT or not. This would give ss.68 and 69 such a very narrow application that it must bolster the contrary argument mentioned above, on the basis that otherwise there would be little point in legislating ss.68 and 69. But the contrary argument still has to overcome formidable obstacles in the form of the actual words of ss.68(1)(a) and 69(1)(a). It is highly unsatisfactory that the law should remain in such confusion. If the argument made above about the pre-July 1992 law is right, and the Administration Act has succeeded in changing the law, either to widen the application of ss.68 and 69 or to narrow it, that goes well beyond the correction or minor improvement which is allowable in a consolidation Act. If the argument about the pre-July 1992 law is wrong, so that the change made by this Act is merely clarificatory, it is clarification in an exceptionally underhand and oblique way.

There are also difficulties on other issues. If the new rules apply, the decision of the relevant adjudicating authority is to be assumed not to have been erroneous in point of law. What if the AO decides according to the accepted DSS interpretation, the SSAT reaches the same result but for peculiar and different reasons and the Commissioner decides that a third approach is correct? It appeared before July 1, 1992 to be the SSAT decision which had to be assumed not to be erroneous in law, thus incorporating its reasons rather than the DSS interpretation. Similarly, if the SSAT decision was erroneous in several respects, only one of which was the matter which would trigger the review, it appeared that all the errors must be assumed not to be errors. However, if the contrary argument mentioned above is correct, it was the AO's decision which had to be assumed not to be erroneous in point of law. This has to be the case from July 1, 1992 onwards in whatever circumstances ss.68 and 69 apply. Regulation 64B of the Adjudication Regulations has rendered these points academic in the case of review.

There is a link to the problem of identifying which of a series of decisions ought to count as the J decision. The question is when it is a consequence of one decision that decisions on other claimant's claims should be revised on review as erroneous in point of law. AOs commonly do not carry out such reviews if a single Commissioner's decision goes against the DSS view, especially if an appeal is being taken to the Court of Appeal. If the Court of Appeal then confirms the Commissioner's decision, the J Day ought to be the date of the Commissioner's decision. But if there are a series of equally authoritative decisions, which one establishes the J Day? It ought to be the earliest one. If the decision which therefore is to be reviewed and revised as erroneous in point of law was made after this J Day, the review based on the effect of the J decision is free of the new rules. The condition in subs. (1)(b)(i) is not met.

Finally, the new provisions are almost certainly ineffective in relation to rulings on the effect of European Community law by the European Court of Justice (see the definition of "court" in s.68(4)) and by British courts. For the British legislature to remove a person's entitlement based on such a ruling would be a breach of the obligation in E.C. law to provide an adequate remedy (see *Von Colson* [1984] E.C.R. 1891).

Correction of errors

Regulations as to correction of errors and setting aside of decisions

70.—(1) Regulations may make provision with respect to—
(a) the correction of accidental errors in any decision or record of a

decision given with respect to a claim or question arising under or in connection with any relevant enactment by a body or person authorised to decide the claim or question; and
(b) the setting aside of any such decision in a case where it appears just to set the decision aside on the ground that—
(i) a document relating to the proceedings in which the decision was given was not sent to, or was not received at an appropriate time by, a party to the proceedings or a party's representative or was not received at an appropriate time by the body or person who gave the decision; or
(ii) a party to the proceedings or a party's representative was not present at a hearing related to the proceedings.

(2) Nothing in section (1) above shall be construed as derogating from any power to correct errors or set aside decisions which is exercisable apart from regulations made by virtue of that subsection.

(3) In this section "relevant enactment" means any enactment contained in—
(a) the National Insurance Acts 1965 to 1974;
(b) the National Insurance (Industrial Injuries) Act 1965 to 1974;
(c) the Industrial Injuries and Diseases (Old Cases) Act 1967 to 1974;
(d) the Social Security Act 1973;
(e) the Social Security Acts 1975 to 1991;
(f) the Old Cases Act;
(g) the Child Benefit Act 1975;
(h) the Family Income Supplements Act 1970;
(i) the Supplementary Benefits Act 1976; or
(j) the Contributions and Benefits Act.

DEFINITIONS
"the Contributions and Benefits Act": s.191.
"the Old Cases Act": *ibid.*

GENERAL NOTE
See regs. 10 to 12 of the Social Security (Adjudication) Regulations 1986 (S.I. 1986 No. 2218), in the current editions of Bonner *et al.*, Mesher and Rowland. The form of subs. (1)(b), which reproduces the earlier legislation, only authorises the making of reg. 11(a) and (b). Regulation 11(c) is made under the predecessor of para. 2 of Sched. 3 (*R(U) 3/89*).

PART III

OVERPAYMENTS AND ADJUSTMENTS OF BENEFIT

Misrepresentation etc.

Overpayments—general

71.—(1) Where it is determined that, whether fraudulently or otherwise, any person has misrepresented, or failed to disclose, any material fact and in consequence of the misrepresentation or failure—
(a) a payment has been made in respect of a benefit to which this section applies; or
(b) any sum recoverable by or on behalf of the Secretary of State in connection with any such payment has not been recovered,
the Secretary of State shall be entitled to recover the amount of any payment which he would not have made or any sum which he would have received but for the misrepresentation or failure to disclose.

(2) Where any such determination as is referred to in subsection (1) above is made on an appeal or review, there shall also be determined in the course of the appeal or review the question whether any, and if so what, amount is recoverable under that subsection by the Secretary of State.

(3) An amount recoverable under subsection (1) above is in all cases recoverable from the person who misrepresented the fact or failed to disclose it.

(4) In relation to cases where payments of benefit to which this section applies have been credited to a bank account or other account under arrangements made with the agreement of the beneficiary or a person acting for him, circumstances may be prescribed in which the Secretary of State is to be entitled to recover any amount paid in excess of entitlement; but any such regulations shall not apply in relation to any payment unless before he agreed to the arrangements such notice of the effect of the regulations as may be prescribed was given in such manner as may be prescribed to the beneficiary or to a person acting for him.

(5) Except where regulations otherwise provide, an amount shall not be recoverable under subsection (1) above or regulations under subsection (4) above unless—

    (a) the determination in pursuance of which it was paid has been reversed or varied on an appeal or revised on a review; and

    (b) it has been determined on the appeal or review that the amount is so recoverable.

(6) Regulations may provide—

    (a) that amounts recoverable under subsection (1) above or regulations under subsection (4) above shall be calculated or estimated in such manner and on such basis as may be prescribed;

    (b) for treating any amount paid to any person under an award which it is subsequently determined was not payable—

        (i) as properly paid; or

        (ii) as paid on account of a payment which it is determined should be or should have been made,

and for reducing or withholding any arrears payable by virtue of the subsequent determination;

    (c) for treating any amount paid to one person in respect of another as properly paid for any period for which it is not payable in cases where in consequence of a subsequent determination—

        (i) the other person is himself entitled to a payment for that period; or

        (ii) a third person is entitled in priority to the payee to a payment for that period in respect of the other person,

and for reducing or withholding any arrears payable for that period by virtue of the subsequent determination.

(7) Circumstances may be prescribed in which a payment on account by virtue of section 5(1)(r) above may be recovered to the extent that it exceeds entitlement.

(8) Where any amount paid is recoverable under—

    (a) subsection (1) above;

    (b) regulations under subsection (4) or (7) above; or

    (c) section 74 below,

it may, without prejudice to any other method of recovery, be recovered by deduction from prescribed benefits.

(9) Where any amount paid in respect of a married or unmarried couple is recoverable as mentioned in subsection (8) above, it may, without prejudice to any other method of recovery, be recovered, in such circumstances as may be prescribed, by deduction from prescribed benefits payable to either of them.

(10) Any amount recoverable under the provisions mentioned in subsection (8) above—

    (a) if the person from whom it is recoverable resides in England and Wales and the county court so orders, shall be recoverable by execution issued from the county court or otherwise as if it were payable under an order of that court; and

   (b) if he resides in Scotland, shall be enforced in like manner as an extract registered decree arbitral bearing a warrant for execution issued by the sheriff court of any sheriffdom in Scotland.

   (11) This section applies to the following benefits—

   (a) benefits as defined in section 122 of the Contributions and Benefits Act;

   (b) subject to section 72 below, income support;

   (c) family credit;

   (d) disability working allowance;

   (e) any social fund payments such as are mentioned in section 138(1)(a) or (2) of the Contributions and Benefits Act; and

   (f) child benefit.

DEFINITIONS

"the Contributions and Benefits Act": s.191.
"married couple": Contributions and Benefits Act, s.137.
"prescribed": s.191.
"unmarried couple": Contributions and Benefits Act, s.137.

GENERAL NOTE

The predecessor of s.71 was intended to produce a common rule on overpayments across all social security benefits. Since the new rule was based on the old supplementary benefit rule (Supplementary Benefits Act 1976, s.20), many of the existing principles developed in Commissioners' decisions will continue to be relevant. The currently authoritative view, following the decision of the Court of Appeal in *Secretary of State for Social Security* v. *Tunnicliffe* [1991] 2 All E.R. 712, is that s.53 of the Social Security Act 1986 (now replaced by this section) applies to determinations of overpayments as part of reviews carried out on or after April 6, 1987, when the section came into force, whenever the overpayment occurred.

Section 71 applies to the benefits specified in subs. (11) and, by virtue of para. 4(1) of Sched. 10, to benefits under the National Assistance Act 1948, the Supplementary Benefit Act 1966, the Supplementary Benefits Act 1976 and the Family Income Supplements Act 1970, among others. It does not matter how far back the overpayments occurred, provided that they were made under one of these pieces of legislation. The time limits of the Limitation Act 1980 do not start to run until there has been a determination under s.71 or one of its predecessors giving the Secretary of State the right of recovery (*R(SB) 5/91* and *R(A) 2/86*).

Subs. (1)

This expresses the general rule on recovery of overpayments. There is no provision for the recovery of administrative costs, and if payments are made which go beyond what has been awarded by an AO, recovery is a matter for the civil law (see *CSB 830/1985* on the old s.20).

Before considering the main elements of the rule, note the important condition imposed by subss. (2) and (5) that an overpayment determination can only be made in the course of a review of the decision awarding benefit (or an appeal from that decision). A SSAT must be satisfied that a valid review and revision has taken place before considering the rest of s.71. This is often overlooked, which causes great difficulties. See the notes to subs. (5) for further details.

For the right of recovery to exist, a person must have misrepresented or failed to disclose a material fact. Then it must be shown that a payment of benefit, or non-recovery, was a consequence of the misrepresentation or failure to disclose. Finally, the amount recoverable must be determined. *R(SB) 2/92* decides that the words "whether fraudulently or otherwise" do not impose any further condition of there having been some kind of dishonesty. This decision was upheld by the Court of Appeal in *Page* v. *Chief Adjudication Officer* (*The Times*, July 4, 1991 and appendix to *R(SB) 2/92*). The Court of Appeal holds that the plain meaning of the words is "whether fraudulently or not".

It was clearly established under the old s.20 that the burden of proof of all issues lay on the AO (*R(SB) 34/83*). The same will apply to s.71. It was also established that if an initial decision is based on a failure to disclose (or misrepresentation), it is open to a SSAT to base its decision on misrepresentation (or failure to disclose), provided that the claimant has had a fair opportunity of dealing with that new point (*R(SB) 40/84*).

Material fact

Section 71 only applies where there has been a misrepresentation of or a failure to disclose a material fact. There is often a concentration on the circumstances of a failure to disclose or a misrepresentation and the significance of whether something is a material fact or not is forgotten. There are three main limitations imposed. First, matters of law are not covered. It is established for purposes of review that a mistake of law is not a mistake of material fact (*R(G) 18/52*). Entitlement to benefit is a conclusion of law based on findings of fact. Therefore, a representation by a claimant that he is entitled to benefit is not a representation of fact unless it involves, either expressly or by implication, some representation of fact, *e.g.* that circumstances have not changed. Signing the declaration on a benefit order that the claimant is entitled to benefit cannot in itself found a recovery under s.71. Even if a claimant knows that he is not entitled to benefit and has been asked to return the order book, there is no misrepresentation of material fact when the claimant signs a standard declaration that he is entitled to the payment. Often there will be no misrepresentation of material fact in the second part of that declaration, that the claimant has correctly reported any facts which could affect the amount of the payment, for that will be why the order book is to be returned.

These points seem to have been overlooked in *CIS 359/1990*, where the Commissioner criticises as unfair the requirement on the claimant to declare his entitlement, on penalty of being guilty of misrepresentation if he gets it wrong. The unfairness is lessened if such a misrepresentation of law does not found recovery under s.71. It may found recovery under some other legal principles, but not through the mechanism of s.71. Unfortunately, in an unstarred decision, *CSB 249/1989*, the Commissioner has upheld recoverability under the old s.53 based on a misrepresentation of entitlement. There, however, the point argued was that the misrepresentation was not made to the Secretary of State. The fundamental issue was not raised, and it is open to SSATs to draw a distinction between matters of material fact and law.

Second, in the context of the powers to review contained in s.25(1), the Commissioners have drawn a distinction between material facts and conclusions of fact, or inferences from primary fact (*R(I) 3/75, R(A) 2/81* and *R(S) 4/86*, discussed in the note to s.25). The same principle should apply here, so that only misrepresentations or failures to disclose primary facts can found recovery under s.71. So a representation that the claimant was incapable of work would not be enough in itself, unless it contained by necessary implication a representation that the claimant's underlying condition had not changed.

The third requirement is that the fact in issue is a material fact. In the context of review, the Court of Appeal in *Saker* v. *Secretary of State for Social Services, The Times,* January 16, 1988 (*R(I) 2/88*) has decided that for a fact to be material it is not necessary that knowledge of it would have altered the decision. It is enough that the fact is one which would have called for serious consideration by the authority which made the decision and which might well have affected the decision. No doubt the same interpretation should be given to "material fact" here, as was effectively done in *CSB 1006/1985*, but since it is only benefit which would not have been paid but for the misrepresentation or failure to disclose which can be recovered under s.71, it is necessary that knowledge of the material fact would have altered the decision awarding benefit. In *R(SB) 2/91* a student was alleged to have failed to disclose that his course was full-time. The Commissioner held that since a student's own opinion of whether the course was full-time was irrelevant (the objective classification of the course being the issue) disclosure was not reasonably to be expected. Although the Commissioner does not expressly say that the student's opinion was not a material fact, the points he makes about the relevant information having to be gathered from the institution at which the claimant was studying lead inevitably to that conclusion.

There is, however, an extra complication in s.71 cases. When considering review, only facts material to the question of entitlement are relevant. Under s.71 it may be that facts relevant to the payment of benefit are also relevant. So if a claimant wrongly declares that he has correctly reported any fact which could affect the amount of his payment, this does not seem to be a misrepresentation of a material fact in the review sense, but if the test under s.71 is whether the fact is material to payment of benefit, then there will have been a misrepresentation of a material fact. It has not yet been explicitly determined which approach is correct, although several of the decisions mentioned below under *Misrepresentation* proceed on the assumption that the second approach is correct.

Misrepresentation

The meaning of misrepresentation is fairly clear. It requires an actual statement to have been made which is untrue (*CSB 1006/1985*). The statement of material fact may be oral or written, or in some circumstances may arise from conduct, *e.g.* cashing a Giro-cheque. But in this last case there must be some positive conduct from which a statement can be implied, rather than a failure to act. An example where this principle worked in the claimant's favour is *R(SB) 18/85*. The claimant had signed a statement of his resources which omitted his Army pension, but he had produced his pension book to the officer who had filled in the form. The Commissioner holds that the circumstances surrounding the completion of a form must be looked at in deciding what has been represented. If the claimant had qualified the written form by saying that the Army pension should be taken into account, the writing could only be taken into account subject to that qualification. The same result would follow if he had indicated by his actions (*e.g.* producing the pension book) that the pension should be taken into account.

Even where there is a straightforward written statement, its precise terms must be considered. In *CSB 1006/1985* the declaration on the B1 form (since changed) signed by the claimant was "as far as I know the information on this form is true and complete". Although a capital resource was omitted from the form, there was no misrepresentation because the claimant honestly believed that the resource was not available to him. In *CSB 790/1988* the claimant had signed this declaration on a benefit order: "I declare that I have read and understand all the instructions in this order book, that I have correctly reported any fact which could affect the amount of my payment and that I am entitled to the above sum". The Commissioner, somewhat surprisingly, concluded that this was only a representation of what the claimant believed she had to disclose on the basis of the instructions given to her. In view of the plain words of the declaration, the decision to the contrary in *CIS 359/1990* must be right. The Commissioner holds that it is an unqualified representation that the factual position is as the claimant has reported it. By contrast, in *R(SB) 9/85* the claimant regularly signed declarations that his circumstances had not changed although (unknown to him) his wife's earnings had gone up. The Commissioner says that the claimant should have added something like "not to my knowledge" to his declaration. It is not known what would happen if a claimant tried writing something like this on an order in an order book or crossing out some of the declaration.

R(SB) 9/85 illustrates that a wholly innocent misrepresentation may trigger recovery. The section applies whether the person acts "fraudulently or otherwise" (see *Page* v. *Chief Adjudication Officer*, above). In *R(SB) 9/85* the rule that the absence of knowledge of the facts which make the statement untrue is irrelevant is justified on the ground that misrepresentation is based on positive and deliberate action. Similarly, the reasonableness of any belief that a fact was not material is irrelevant (*R(SB) 18/85*). In *R(SB) 3/90* it is suggested that a future case might have to determine whether mental incapacity could prevent there being a misrepresentation at all. On the facts, where the claimant was at the crucial time recovering from a nervous breakdown and treatment including ECT and drugs, there was a misrepresentation, but it was wholly innocent. Possibly, a person would have not to realise the nature of what he was doing to be said not to have made a misrepresentation at all.

Failure to disclose

A failure to disclose is a much more troublesome concept, and there is a good deal of confusing case-law. An essential background is that reg. 32 of the Social Security (Claims and Payments) Regulations 1987 (S.I. 1987 No. 1968) (in the current editions of Bonner *et al.* and Mesher) imposes a duty on claimants entitled to benefit to notify the Secretary of State in writing of any change of circumstance specified in the notice of determination or order book or any other change which the person might reasonably be expected to know might affect the right to benefit. However, there is not a straightforward link with s.71. For example, recovery may be pursued against any person who fails to disclose or misrepresents a material fact (see, *e.g. R(SB) 21/82* (spouse) and *R(SB) 28/83* (receiver of a mentally infirm person's estate)). Such persons may not be covered by reg. 32. Secondly, the right of recovery only arises under the conditions of s.71. If an order book required a claimant to notify the Secretary of State of a fact which was not material, a failure to do so would not trigger s.71. See above for what amounts to a material fact. Although reg. 32 requires notification in writing, it has long been settled that an oral disclosure is as effective as one in writing for the purposes of s.71 (*CSB 688/1982* and *R(SB) 40/84*).

What does disclosure mean? In *R(SB)15/87* a Tribunal of Commissioners holds, adopting an opinion in an Australian case, that it is a statement of a fact so as to reveal that which so far as the discloser knows was previously unknown to the person to whom the statement is made. This is in line with the ordinary everyday meaning of "disclose". Once disclosure has been made to a particular person there can be no question of there being an obligation to repeat that disclosure to the same person. The question of to whom disclosure is to be made is considered below.

The Act uses the words "fails to disclose", not "does not disclose". Therefore it is necessary to consider what amounts to such a failure. In *CSB 53/1981* (a decision of a Tribunal of Commissioners, but not reported) the statement of Diplock J. in *R.* v. *Medical Appeal Tribunal (North Midland Region),* ex p. *Hubble* [1958] 2 Q.B. 228, 242 was applied to the old section 20 of the Supplementary Benefits Act 1976. " 'Non-disclosure' in the context of the subsection, where it is coupled with misrepresentation, means a failure to disclose a fact known to the person who does not disclose it . . . It is innocent if the person failing to disclose the fact does not appreciate its materiality, fraudulent if he does". In *CSB 53/1981*, the claimant had either overlooked or failed to appreciate the relevance of £1,000 of Premium Bonds, so was innocent, but had still failed to disclose. This approach gives the impression that if a fact is material and is known to the person, no other factors are relevant. It is certainly the case that knowledge of the fact is an essential requirement. Where the person is the owner of an asset and has once known of its existence, he will normally be fixed with that knowledge even if he later forgets about it (*R(SB) 21/82*, para. 20(4)). However, in some cases a person may not be mentally capable of knowing that he continues to possess the asset. This was so in *R(SB) 28/83*, where the Commissioner says that it must be shown that the person either knew or with reasonable diligence ought to have known that he possessed the assets. In *R(SB) 40/84* there was a possibility that, in view of her advanced age, the claimant had never known that her superannuation had been increased. Similar arguments can be applied, for instance, to the addition of interest to building society accounts. Knowledge of this process can normally be assumed if a person knows of the account, but, depending on the medical evidence, may not exist in some circumstances. If the person from whom recovery is sought is not the owner of the asset, it seems that there is less room for assumptions and that knowledge of its existence must be proved (*R(SB) 21/82*, para. 20(4)). Some doubt is expressed in para. 22(2) whether constructive knowledge (*i.e.* what a person ought to know) is enough, but it probably is, since no dishonesty or fraud has to be shown (*Page* v. *Chief Adjudication Officer, R(SB) 2/92*).

Once it is proved that the person has sufficient knowledge of a material fact, there must still be something which amounts to a "failure". In para. 4(2) of *R(SB) 21/82* the Commissioner says that this "necessarily imports the concept of some breach of obligation, moral or legal—*i.e.* the non-disclosure must have occurred in circumstances in which, at lowest, disclosure by the person in question was reasonably to be expected". This statement has been accepted in many decisions, including *R(SB) 28/83*, *R(SB) 54/83* and *R(SB) 15/87*, but does not provide a simple solution to problems when it is also clear that an innocent failure to disclose can trigger the right to recover. In *CSB 1006/1985* it is suggested that the statement does not apply at all where non-disclosure by the claimant himself of an asset of his own is being considered. This is probably going too far, but it is necessary to attempt to spell out some limitations. First, the test is an objective one (*cf. 26/1990*). It must depend on what a reasonable person in the position of the person from whom recovery is sought, with that person's knowledge, would have done. Thus, in general the fact that, as in *CSB 1006/1985*, the claimant did not consider that an asset was relevant, would be irrelevant. A reasonable person would not take that view. But if, say, a DSS official had expressly assured the claimant that an undoubtedly material fact did not need to be disclosed, this surely would create a situation in which disclosure was not reasonably to be expected. This would be in line with the result of *R(SB) 3/81* where a course of conduct which had evolved over several years between the DSS and the claimant concerning the handing over of P60s was held to have affected the claimant's obligation.

A slight extension is shown in *CSB 727/1987*, where it is held that the terms of a DSS form and the answers given by the claimant are relevant to whether a later disclosure is reasonably to be expected. The claim for supplementary benefit was made soon after the birth of the claimant's child. On the claim form she said that she was owed family allowance and had applied for child benefit and one-parent benefit. Supplementary benefit was awarded without any deduction for child benefit or one-parent benefit. The claimant's child benefit and one-parent benefit order book was sent to her on December 17, 1984. She did not notify the local supplementary benefit office until February 24, 1986 and in the meantime supplementary benefit was paid without taking account of the income from child benefit and one-parent benefit. Most SSATs would have regarded this as an open-and-shut case of failure to disclose, but the Commissioner held that in these circumstances disclosure was not reasonably to be expected. The claimant had given detailed answers about her claims and made it clear that she regarded child benefit and one-parent benefit as due to her. She might then expect not to have to report their actual receipt. Although her supplementary benefit did not go down, she might well have thought that such benefits did not affect the amount of supplementary benefit. The questions on the claim form could easily have led her to think that her answers were all the information the DSS required unless they expressly asked for more. Nor did the instructions in the supplementary benefit order book alter the situation, since they concerned reporting income or benefit not already reported to the Issuing Office. The claimant could justifiably think that she had already reported the benefits. The decision must depend on its particular facts, and some of the Commissioner's assumptions might not have held up under close examination of the claimant's actual knowledge, but it does indicate the necessity to consider what is reasonably to be expected in a broad context.

The general principle has been applied in a number of unreported decisions. In *CSB 677/1986* a supplementary benefit claimant was also in receipt of sickness benefit, both being administered in the same local office. He received a notification from the local office that he had progressed from sickness benefit to invalidity benefit (paid at a higher rate). The claimant did not inform the supplementary benefit section, but the Commissioner held that he could not reasonably be expected to inform the office which had informed him, especially if the notes in his order book turned out to refer simply to the "issuing office". In *CSB 1246/1986* it was held that there was no obligation to disclose the annual up-rating of unemployment benefit, since this was public knowledge. *CSB 790/1988* takes the same line as *CSB 677/1986* on whether, when an order book instructs a claimant to report changes to "the issuing office", a claimant would reasonably expect to have to report to one part of an integrated local office receipt of benefit from another part. Precise proof of what instructions were included in the order book actually issued to the claimant was crucial in *CP 20/1990*. An increase of benefit for the claimant's wife was improperly awarded, then excluded from payment by an administrative procedure, but allegedly actually paid to the claimant. The Commissioner says that in an ordinary case where proper awards are made, a photocopy of the Departmental record of the award and the issue of order books, together with a specimen of the order books current at the time, will suffice to show the instructions given in the book about disclosure. But here it could not be assumed that the appropriate order book with the appropriate instructions had been issued.

More recently, in *R(SB) 2/91* the Commissioner held that a claimant could not reasonably be expected to disclose a matter which was irrelevant to the question on which entitlement depended. However, it is expecting too much for a claimant to assess whether a matter is relevant or not, and this case would have been better dealt with on the basis that what was not disclosed was not a material fact (see above).

CSB 510/1987 decided that advice from the claimant's solicitor and barrister that she did not need to tell the Department about an increase in her children's maintenance payments could make disclosure not reasonably expected. If one is concerned with disclosure by the claimant of someone else's asset (*e.g.* in *R(SB) 54/83*, the fact that the claimant's wife was working), the *R(SB) 21/82* test may be useful in marginal cases. Its most direct application will be, as in *R(SB) 21/82* itself, in deciding whether some person other than the claimant is under an obligation to disclose. *R(SB) 28/83* is a further example. Since the receiver of the mentally infirm claimant knew of his assets and knew or ought to have known that he was receiving supplementary benefit, he came under an obligation to disclose.

The next issue is to whom must disclosure be made. The leading decision is now *R(SB) 15/87*. Since the concern under the old s.20 of the Supplementary Benefits Act 1976 was with breaches of the obligation to disclose which had the consequence that the Secretary of State incurred expenditure, it was held that the obligation was to disclose to a member or members of staff of an office of the Department handling the transaction giving rise to the expenditure. Although the wording of s.71 is somewhat different, it is thought that the obligation would be similar, relating to the office handling the claim giving rise to the payment of benefit alleged to have been overpaid. The Tribunal rejects the argument that disclosure to any member of the staff of the Department or to anyone in the "integrated office" in which the claimant was claiming would do. It is accepted that the claimant cannot be expected to identify the precise person dealing with his claim, but the Tribunal is then rather vague about how the obligation is to be fulfilled. They say it is best fulfilled by disclosure to the local office either on a claim form or making sufficient reference to the claim for the information to be referred to the proper person. If this is done, then there can be no further duty to disclose that matter. In the case of a claimant who is required to be available for work and thus has to deliver his claim form to the unemployment benefit office (UBO), disclosure on a claim form delivered there fulfils the duty. The Tribunal also accepts the decision in *R(SB) 54/83* that if an officer in another office accepts information in circumstances which make it reasonable for the claimant to think that the information will be passed on to the proper local office the duty is fulfilled. It holds that it is only in this kind of situation that there is a continuing duty of disclosure, as suggested in para. 18 of *R(SB) 54/83*. If the claimant should subsequently have realised that the information had not reached the proper person then a further obligation to disclose to the proper person would arise. The Tribunal expressly leaves open the question whether the claimant must actually know that the information has not got through.

Although the decision in *R(SB) 15/87* clears up a number of points, it does still leave some uncertainties. The major one is in what circumstances disclosure to the UBO might fulfil an income support claimant's obligation. It was suggested in *R(SB) 54/83* that in the case of a supplementary benefit claimant who was required to declare his availability for work at, and is paid through, the UBO, the UBO is the agent of the supplementary benefit office, so that notice to the UBO would be imputed to the supplementary benefit office (and now the office dealing with income support). The Commissioner did not have to decide the point, but the issue was exhaustively discussed by a Tribunal of Commissioners in *R(SB) 36/84* and *CSB 397/1983*. There is an identical appendix in both decisions, setting out in detail the arrangements between the DHSS and the Department of Employment (DE), who administer UBOs. The preliminary conclusion is that having regard to the past 40 years' arrangements, in particular those under which payment to claimants required to register or be available for work is made on the instructions of the UBO, there is an agency relationship. The decisions were not directly to do with recovery of overpayments, but the result in this context would be as suggested in *R(SB) 54/83*, regardless of the fact that the two Departments are otherwise independent. Some earlier decisions like *CSB 14/82* must now be rejected as being based on mistaken assumptions about the independence of Departments (although it is clear that the principle can only apply in the special case of claimants paid through the UBO). However, the point has been treated as one of fact for each SSAT, rather than a matter on which a definite legal answer has been given (*R(SB) 10/85*).

The Tribunal of Commissioners in *R(SB) 15/87* certainly does not expressly reject the agency argument. Some doubt is raised because the Tribunal mention several ways of fulfilling the duty of disclosure, including delivering a claim form to the UBO, without mentioning the general agency argument. There is an obscure passage (para. 30) on causation (see below) which refers to para. 6549 of the S Manual. This does not seem to be relevant, but para. 6548 said that claimants who were required to be available were required to declare their earnings at the UBO. This reinforces the agency argument, but the context in the Tribunal's decision is of a situation where the claimant is said to have failed to disclose. Until there is clarification, the approach of *R(SB) 36/84* should be followed until expressly disapproved. In *R(SB) 2/91* it was accepted by the representative of the Chief Adjudication Officer that the DE were the agents of the DHSS for the purposes of the payment of supplementary benefit, so that information given to the UBO constituted information given to the supplementary benefit section of the DHSS. This view was approved by the Commissioner. The weight of the decisions is clearly that the DE now acts as the agent of the DSS in cases in which income support is paid through the UBO, so that in those cases disclosure to the UBO is disclosure to the office dealing with the claim.

In *CSB 699/1986* the Commissioner considers the circumstances in which, once disclosure has been made, there is no further obligation to disclose "the same matter". He suggests that the "same matter" is not restricted to one-off events, but could extend to a continuing state of affairs, such as the receipt of another benefit. But a transition from sickness to invalidity benefit would be a different matter. Similarly, disclosure on the claim form on a previous claim for the same benefit does not lift the duty to disclose on a fresh claim (*R(SB) 3/90*).

R(SB) 15/87 also deals with the question of by whom disclosure can be made in order to fulfil the claimant's obligation. One daughter, for whom the claimant had received benefit as a dependant, had made a claim in her own right for supplementary benefit at the same office. In respect of another child who started a YTS course, the child benefit book had been surrendered to the contributory benefits section of the same office by the claimant's wife. The Tribunal holds that neither of these actions was sufficient disclosure. Disclosure can be made by a third party on behalf of the claimant, but if this is done in the course of a separate transaction, the information must be given to the relevant benefit office and the claimant must know that it has been done and reasonably believe that it is unnecessary for him to take any action himself.

CSB 347/1983 (approved in *R(SB) 10/85*) holds that while an AO might discharge his initial burden of proof by showing that there is no official record of a change of circumstances, thus leaving it for the claimant to prove on a balance of probabilities that he had made a disclosure, this only applies if a proper foundation is laid by evidence (not mere assertion) as to the instructions for recording information and how these are in practice carried out. The distinction between evidence and assertion is strongly supported in *CSB 1195/1984*. The claimant said that she had told two visiting officers that she was receiving unemployment benefit, but there was no official record of such a statement. The Commissioner stresses that what the claimant says about her own acts is evidence, while what a presenting officer says is not evidence unless backed up by personal knowledge of the facts. He says that the new SSAT should call the two visiting officers to give evidence. If they failed to appear without adequate excuse, the weight of the assertions alleged to have been made by them would be reduced to little or nothing. In *CSB 615/1985* it is stressed that there is no rule that only documentary evidence is admissible or that oral evidence requires corroboration.

Causation

It must be shown by the AO that any overpayment resulted from the misrepresentation or failure to disclose. In *R(SB) 3/81* the SBAT simply failed to look at the issue. In *R(SB) 21/82* the Commissioner holds that the right to recovery arises "only on a clearly stipulated causal basis". In that case the claimant's wife had made declarations in 1969 and 1971, but made no more until after the claimant's death in 1979. It was not clear how far any overpayment of benefit was in consequence of those earlier declarations when there were many intervening declarations by the claimant. It is clear that if a claimant has disclosed a material fact to the relevant office in relation to the relevant claim there can be no recovery of subsequent benefit based on a failure to disclose that fact. This was decided in *CSB 688/1982* and *CSB 347/1983*, and confirmed in *R(SB) 15/87*. On principle, it would seem that proper disclosure would rob a subsequent misrepresentation of any causative effect. This appeared to be the result in *CSB 688/1982*, where the claimant orally disclosed to an officer that he had a mine-worker's pension. The officer omitted this from the statement which the claimant then signed as a true and complete statement of his circumstances. The Commissioner holds that the disclosure was fatal to the right of recovery. Although this had been put only on the ground of failure to disclose, the Commissioner felt able to make the decision that the overpayment was not recoverable. Since there had obviously been a misrepresentation, it looked as though the Commissioner must have considered that it could have no legal effect. However, in the very similar case of *R(SB) 18/85*, the same Commissioner concentrates on the misrepresentation (see above) and makes no mention of the causation issue. It may be that since the appeal had to be sent back to the SBAT for proper findings of fact, the decision should be regarded as neutral on the causation issue. The better view is that disclosure does rob a subsequent misrepresentation of causative effect, but the point is not authoritatively decided. In *R(SB) 3/90* the basic principle was applied that if a misrepresentation induces a person to act it is irrelevant that the person had a means of verifying the information. But during the currency of one claim the principle of *R(SB) 15/87* would undermine that approach where the means of verification stems from the claimant's disclosure.

The most controversial issue here is the effect of the breakdown of procedures within the DSS for notifying the income support office that a person has been awarded some other benefit (see, *e.g.* Income Support Manual, paras. 3.1207–1212 for the child benefit procedure). The argument is that even though a claimant may have failed to disclose receipt of the other benefit, the operative cause of the overpayment is the failure of the administrative procedure to get notice of entitlement to the other benefit from the other section concerned to the income support office. This argument has been rejected in a number of Commissioner's decisions, most recently in *CSB 64/1986* and *R(SB) 3/90*. The question asked there is would the Secretary of State have avoided the relevant expenditure if the claimant had not failed to disclose the relevant material fact? If the answer is "yes", then the failure is the cause of the expenditure. The DSS procedure is in that sense a back-up one. The validity of this approach is confirmed by the Court of Appeal in *Duggan* v. *Chief Adjudication Officer, The Times*, December 18, 1988 (*R(SB) 13/89*). The claimant had failed to disclose his wife's unemployment benefit, but argued that on a review the AO should have investigated the full financial situation. It is held that if one cause of the overpayment was the failure to disclose, the overpayment is recoverable. The new wording in s.71, describing the amount recoverable as any payment which the Secretary of State would not have made but for the misrepresentation or failure to disclose, reinforces this conclusion.

However, it is vital to note that the above principles only apply when the other section of the DSS fails to inform the income support section. It is different if the information is received, but the income support section fails to act on it. The Tribunal of Commissioners in *R(SB) 15/87* recognise that if the DSS procedure works it may break the causal link between the claimant's failure and the overpayment. This is now explicitly dealt with in *CIS 159/1990*, where the Child Benefit Centre informed the local office dealing with the income support claim of the issue of an order book with an increased amount of child benefit, plus some arrears. The claimant did not report the arrival of the order book. The Commissioner held that the overpayment was not in consequence of the failure to disclose, because the local office already knew of the material fact.

Note that if income support is paid while a claimant is waiting for a decision on entitlement for another benefit and arrears of the other benefit are paid for this period, any excess income support cannot be recovered under this section, since it does not result from a failure to disclose. But s.74 and the Social Security (Payments on account, Overpayments and Recovery) Regulations 1988 (S.I. 1988 No. 664) (the "Payments Regulations" in the current editions of Bonner *et al.* and Mesher) will operate to allow the excess to be deducted from the arrears of the other benefit or recovered from the recipient.

Amount of overpayment

The calculation of the amount to be recovered has given considerable problems in the past. Subsection (6)(a) below allows regulations to be made on this issue. Regulations 13 and 14 of the Payments Regulations are relevant.

The starting point is the amount of benefit which would not have been paid but for the overpayment or failure to disclose. This is in line with the approach set out in *R(SB) 20/84* and *R(SB) 10/85* of looking at what the revised decision would be when the full facts were known. Normally there is no difficulty in determining the amount of benefit which was actually paid, but there may be exceptional cases, like *CP 20/1990*, where evidence of the amounts of payment, rather than a second-hand description, is required.

A controversial question under the pre-April 1987 law was how far it was possible to take account of underpayments of benefit against the overpayment. Regulation 13(b) of the Payments Regulations provides that from the gross amount of the overpayment is to be deducted any additional amount of benefit which should have been awarded on the basis of the claim as originally presented or with the addition of the facts misrepresented or not disclosed. This allows a somewhat more extensive set-off than under the old law (for which, see *R(SB) 20/84*, *R(SB) 10/85* and *R(SB) 11/86*). *CSIS 49/1990* confirms that the reg. 13(b) deduction is not limited to the period after the beginning of the overpayment, but can go back to the date of claim. But the examination of the additional amount which would have been payable must be based on the claim as originally presented, or with the addition of the material facts misrepresented or not disclosed. Thus, if, for instance, evidence suggesting that a premium should have been allowed is produced for the first time once an overpayment has been determined by an AO, the amount of that premium is not to be offset against the gross amount of the overpayment (confirming the result of *CSB 615/1985*). In that case, any arrears must be obtained through the ordinary process of review under s.25, and subject to the 12-month limit imposed by regs. 45 and 67–71 of the Adjudication Regulations. If the award of benefit has been reviewed, *e.g.* to include a premium, but the arrears have not yet been paid when the overpayment is determined, there can be an offset under regs. 5(2) (Case 1) and 14(a). Any other offset under reg. 5 is to be deducted, but no other deduction for underpayments is to be made.

Another problem now dealt with by regulations arises when the misrepresentation or failure to disclose is of capital resources. If it emerged that a claimant who had been in receipt of income support or family credit for a few years throughout had capital of £1 over the limit, it would be most unfair to require repayment of the whole amount of benefit. If the capital had been properly taken into account, so that benefit was not initially awarded, the capital would have immediately been reduced below the limit in order to provide for living expenses. The Commissioners applied the "diminishing capital" principle (*CSB 53/1981*, *CSBO* v. *Leary*, appendix to *R(SB) 6/85* and *R(SB) 15/85*). The position is now governed by reg. 14 of the Payments Regulations. This provides for the reduction of the figure of capital resources at quarterly intervals from the beginning of the overpayment period by the amount overpaid in income support or family credit in the previous quarter. No other reduction of the actual amount of capital resources is allowed (reg. 15(2)). Under the Commissioners' approach the notional reduction had to be made week by week. It will be considerably easier to make the calculation at 13-week intervals, but the tendency will be for higher amounts of overpayments to be produced.

It is for the AO to prove the existence and amount of capital taken into account in calculating an overpayment (*R(SB) 21/82*). Here, sums had suddenly appeared in building society accounts and there was no evidence as to where they had come from. The Commissioner commends the adoption of a lower figure of overpayment rather than a higher one based on the assumption that the capital assets had been possessed before any evidence existed about them. The Commissioner in *R(SB) 34/83* agrees strongly on the burden of proof, but points out that if the person concerned was alive and failed to give any proper explanation of the origin of such sums, adverse inferences could be drawn against him, enabling the AO to discharge his burden of proof. He goes on to hold that the estate of a deceased person should be in the same position. Therefore, a heavy responsibility devolved on the executor to make every reasonable enquiry as to the origin of the money. If, however, after such efforts there was no evidence as to where the money came from, the burden of proof would not have been discharged.

It is essential that on an appeal a SSAT should clearly state the amount which is recoverable, and state how that amount is calculated (*R(SB) 9/85*). If the SSAT cannot make the calculation at the time of their initial decision they can refer the matter back to the AO for recalculation on the basis determined by the SSAT, but only if the decision expressly allows the matter to be referred back to the SSAT if agreement cannot be reached on the recalculation (*R(SB) 11/86*, *R(SB) 15/87*). One reason why SSATs must be careful to specify the amount recoverable is that often differing amounts are calculated by the AO after his initial decision. If this is done there is, at least before April 1990, no bar to this operating as a review and revision of the initial decision. The initial decision, being on a single indivisible question, will thus be replaced and any appeal lodged against it will lapse. However, appeals in these circumstances are commonly continued as though they have not lapsed. In *CSB 64/1986*, where the claimant's representative insisted that the appeal was against the initial decision, the Commissioner held that the SSAT's decision was given without authority, as the appeal had lapsed. In *R(SB) 15/87*, the appeal was treated as against the revised decision, although no notice of appeal against that decision had been given. The Tribunal of Commissioners held that in this case the failure to comply with the procedural requirements did not make the SSAT's proceedings a nullity. There had been substantial compliance with the requirements, there was no public interest in strict compliance and the claimant would be prejudiced if the procedural failure was not ignored, since the time for appealing against the revised decision had expired. The predecessor of s.29 of this Act provided from April 1990 that once an appeal has been lodged, a review is to be of no effect unless it gives the claimant everything that the claimant could possibly obtain in the appeal.

Subs. (2)
See notes to subs. (5).

Subs. (3)
This provision confirms that amounts are recoverable from the person who made the misrepresentation or failed to make disclosure. Presumably the principle that after the person's death the overpayment is recoverable from his estate (*Secretary of State for Social Services* v. *Solly* [1974] 3 All E.R. 922, *R(SB) 21/82*, *R(SB) 28/83*) is not affected. Note that the time limit of the Limitation Act 1980 does not begin to run until there is a determination of an overpayment by an AO which gives the Secretary of State the right of recovery (*R(SB) 5/91*, *R(A) 2/86*).

Subs. (4)
This provision applies where benefit is directly credited to an account. See reg. 21 of the Claims and Payments Regulations and reg. 11 of the Payments Regulations.

Subs. (5)
The general rule here is taken over from that for contributory benefits, that recovery of an overpayment should follow a revision on review of the decision awarding benefit or its variation on appeal. The result is that if the conditions for review are not met, then even though the initial decision was incorrect, no overpayment can be recovered. However, regulations may provide otherwise and have done so. Regulation 12 of the Payments Regulations provides that subs. (5) shall not apply where the fact and circumstances of the misrepresentation or non-disclosure do not provide a basis for reviewing and revising the initial decision. This formulation is rather obscure, but it seems to mean that if the conditions for review and revision do not exist there can still be a determination that an overpayment is recoverable. If those conditions do exist, then the determination of the recoverable overpayment must be made as part of the review decision or not at all (see also subs. (2)). This has now been decided in *R(SB) 7/91*.

A number of decisions have held that (outside the exception in reg. 12 of the Payments Regulations) it is an essential pre-condition of an overpayment determination that there should be proof of a valid revision of entitlement on review. See *CSSB 105/1989*, followed in *CIS 179/1990* and *CIS 360/1990*, and *R(SB) 7/91*. The principle is accepted in *CSSB 316/1989*, where the Commissioner also deals with the requirement of subs. (5) that the overpayment determination must be made "on the appeal or review". He says "[the] earliest possible correction of a continuing award which has been found to be incorrect is obviously desirable and I accept that an effective decision for the purposes of section 53(1), (1A) and (4) can be made notwithstanding that grounds of review and revisal of the award for the past and the future, which must of course be appropriate, are established at a date prior to the making of the decision establishing the detail of the overpayment".

There remains some uncertainty about what a SSAT should do if faced with an overpayment decision when there has not been a valid revision of entitlement on review. In *CSSB 105/1989*, *CSSB 316/1989* and *CSSB 540/1989*, the Commissioner suggests that the SSAT should simply determine that no valid AO's decision on the overpayment has been made. In *R(SB) 7/91*, the Commissioner held that if the AO made no review decision, the SSAT should determine that the AO's overpayment decision was of no force or effect. However, this seems to leave the possibility of an AO's reviewing the defective AO's decision for error of law under s.25(2) of this Act (suggested in *CSSB 105/1989*) or of the AO's starting the overpayment procedure all over again by a valid revision of entitlement on review. A SSAT's decision in this form does not decide that an overpayment can never be recovered. It secures that the proper process must be applied. But the final result may be the same and the claimant has to appeal yet again to challenge it. It may therefore be asked why the SSAT should not follow the general principle put forward in *CSSB 540/1989* that on appeal a SSAT can correct a defective review decision. In *CSB 1272/1989* the Commissioner, in an effort to avoid the expense and delay of starting the whole process again, suggests that where in overpayments cases the AO has omitted to carry out a review, the SSAT should make good the omission, using its power under s.36 of the Administration Act (1975 Act, s.102) to determine questions first arising in the course of the appeal. This approach seems rather dubious, since the review question seems to be part and parcel of the overpayment question already before the AO and the SSAT, and not one which first arises in the course of the appeal. In addition, none of the decisions mentioned earlier are cited in *CSB 1272/1989*. The current position thus remains unresolved until some authoritative decision emerges from the Commissioners. At the moment the weight of authority would seem to be in favour of a SSAT determining that no valid overpayment decision has been made. There is in any case a difficulty in "correcting" an AO's decision where no review decision at all has been made. There may, however, be exceptional circumstances, for instance where a SSAT is clear that an overpayment would not be recoverable under s.71, where a SSAT should deal with the review issue (*cf. CSB 274/1990*).

If there is no doubt that the AO has carried out a review and revision it is not an error of law for a SSAT to fail to mention the issue, although it is desirable for it to be dealt with (*CSIS 62/1991*).

Subs. (6)
The Payments Regulations have been made under these powers.

Subs. (7)
See Pt. II of the Payments Regulations.

Subs. (8)
The benefits from which deductions may be made are prescribed by reg. 15 of the Payments Regulations. They include most social security benefits. Limits to the weekly amounts which may be deducted from income support and family credit are set by reg. 16. Regulation 20(2) of the Social Security (Claims and Payments) Regulations 1987 (S.I. 1987 No. 1968) provides that subs. (8) also applies to amounts recoverable under any enactment repealed by the 1986 Act or regulation revoked by the 1987 Regulations. The Divisional Court in *R. v. Secretary of State for Social Services*, ex p. *Britnell (Alan)*, *The Times*, January 27, 1989 decided that reg. 20(2) did not offend the rule of construction against retrospection. Its effect was merely to provide an additional method of recovery where there was no dispute that a liability to repay existed. In the Court of Appeal (*The Times*, February 16, 1990) and the House of Lords ([1991] 1 W.L.R. 198), the point on retrospection was not argued and reg. 20(2) was found to have been validly made under s.89(1) of the 1986 Act.

Subs. (9)
See reg. 17 of the Payments Regulations.

Special provision as to recovery of income support

72.—(1) Where—
(a) a direction under section 125(1) of the Contributions and Benefits Act is revoked; and
(b) it is determined by an adjudication officer that, whether fraudulently or otherwise, any person has misrepresented, or failed to disclose, any material fact and in consequence of the misrepresentation or failure a payment of income support has been made during the relevant period to the person to whom the direction related,
an adjudication officer may determine that the Secretary of State shall be entitled to recover the amount of the payment.

(2) In subsection (1) above "the relevant period" means—
(a) if the revocation is under subsection (3) of section 125 of the Contributions and Benefits Act, the period beginning with the date of the change of circumstances and ending with the date of the revocation; and
(b) if the revocation is under subsection (4) of that section, the period during which the direction was in force.

(3) Where a direction under section 125(1) of the Contributions and Benefits Act is revoked, the Secretary of State may certify whether there has been misrepresentation of a material fact or failure to disclose a material fact.

(4) If he certifies that there has been such misrepresentation or failure to disclose, he may also certify—

(a) who made the misrepresentation or failed to make the disclosure; and

(b) whether or not a payment of income support has been made in consequence of the misrepresentation or failure.

(5) If he certifies that a payment has been made, he may certify the period during which income support would not have been paid but for the misrepresentation or failure to disclose.

(6) A certificate under this section shall be conclusive for the purposes of this section as to any matter certified.

(7) Section 71(3) and (6) to (11) above apply to income support recoverable under subsection (1) above as they apply to income support recoverable under section 71(1) above.

(8) The other provisions of section 71 above do not apply to income support recoverable under subsection (1) above.

DEFINITIONS
"the Contributions and Benefits Act": s.191.

GENERAL NOTE
Section 125(1) of the Contributions and Benefits Act enables the Secretary of State to direct that a person under the age of 18 is to qualify for income support in order to avoid severe hardship. The direction may be revoked under s.125(3) on the ground of change of circumstances or under s.125(4) on the ground that a mistake or ignorance of material fact led to the determination that severe hardship would result if income support were not to be paid. A special provision is needed for recovery in cases of misrepresentation or failure to disclose because the revocation of the direction is not a review which can found action under s.71. Although the determination is made by the AO under subs. (1), the Secretary of State's certificate is conclusive on almost every issue (subss. (3)–(6)). The provisions of s.71 about the mechanics of recovery apply.

Adjustments of benefits

Overlapping benefits—general

73.—(1) Regulations may provide for adjusting benefit as defined in section 122 of the Contributions and Benefits Act which is payable to or in respect of any person, or the conditions for its receipt, where—

(a) there is payable in his case any such pension or allowance as is described in subsection (2) below; or

(b) the person is, or is treated under the regulations as, undergoing medical or other treatment as an in-patient in a hospi· ıl or similar institution.

(2) Subsection (1)(a) above applies to any pension, allowance or benefit payable out of public funds (including any other benefit as so defined, whether it is of the same or a different description) which is payable to or in respect of—

(a) the person referred to in subsection (1);

(b) that person's wife or husband;

(c) any child or adult dependant of that person; or

(d) the wife or husband of any adult dependant of that person.

(3) Where but for regulations made by virtue of subsection (1)(a) above two persons would both be entitled to an increase of benefit in respect of a third person, regulations may make provision as to their priority.

(4) Regulations may provide for adjusting benefit as defined in section 122 of the Contributions and Benefits Act payable to or in respect of any person where there is payable in his case any such benefit as is described in subsection (5) below.

(5) Subsection (4) above applies to any benefit payable under the legislation of any member State other than the United Kingdom which is payable to or in respect of—

(a) the person referred to in that subsection;

(b) that person's wife or husband;

(c) any child or adult dependant of that person; or

(d) the wife or husband of any adult dependant of that person.

DEFINITIONS

"the Contributions and Benefits Act": s.191.

GENERAL NOTE

See the Social Security (Overlapping Benefits) Regulations 1979 (S.I. 1979 No. 597), in the current edition of Bonner *et al.*

Income support and other payments

74.—(1) Where—

(a) a payment by way of prescribed income is made after the date which is the prescribed date in relation to the payment; and

(b) it is determined that an amount which has been paid by way of income support would not have been paid if the payment had been made on the prescribed date,

the Secretary of State shall be entitled to recover that amount from the person to whom it was paid.

(2) Where—

(a) a prescribed payment which apart from this subsection falls to be made from public funds in the United Kingdom or under the law of any other member State is not made on or before the date which is the prescribed date in relation to the payment; and

(b) it is determined that an amount ("the relevant amount") has been paid by way of income support that would not have been paid if the payment mentioned in paragraph (a) above had been made on the prescribed date,

then—

(i) in the case of a payment from public funds in the United Kingdom, the authority responsible for making it may abate it by the relevant amount; and

(ii) in the case of any other payment, the Secretary of State shall be entitled to receive the relevant amount out of the payment.

(3) Where—

(a) a person (in this subsection referred to as A) is entitled to any prescribed benefit for any period in respect of another person (in this subsection referred to as B); and

(b) either—

(i) B has received income support for that period; or

(ii) B was, during that period, a member of the same family as some person other than A who received income support for that period; and

(c) the amount of the income support has been determined on the basis that A has not made payments for the maintenance of B at a rate equal to or exceeding the amount of the prescribed benefit,

the amount of the prescribed benefit may, at the discretion of the authority administering it, be abated by the amount by which the amounts paid by way of income support exceed what it is determined that they would have been had A, at the time the amount of the income support was determined, been making payments for the maintenance of B at a rate equal to the amount of the prescribed benefit.

(4) Where an amount could have been recovered by abatement by virtue of subsection (2) or (3) above but has not been so recovered, the Secretary of State may recover it otherwise than by way of abatement—

   (a) in the case of an amount which could have been recovered by virtue of subsection (2) above, from the person to whom it was paid; and

   (b) in the case of an amount which could have been recovered by virtue of subsection (3) above, from the person to whom the prescribed benefit in question was paid.

(5) Where a payment is made in a currency other than sterling, its value in sterling shall be determined for the purposes of this section in accordance with regulations.

DEFINITIONS
"prescribed": s.191.

GENERAL NOTE
Most of this section was originally, in substance, s.12 of the Supplementary Benefits Act 1976. There are changes in form from the old s.12, but the overall aim is the same, to prevent a claimant from getting a double payment when other sources of income are not paid on time. The predecessor of s.74, s.27 of the Social Security Act 1986, came into force on April 6, 1987 for supplementary benefit purposes and otherwise on April 11, 1988. It would seem to be the provision in force at the date on which the overpayment determination is made which governs, as under s.71.

Section 71 is an important provision, which is often overlooked.

Subs. (1)
Prescribed income is defined in reg. 7(1) of the Social Security (Payments on account, Overpayments and Recovery) Regulations 1988 (S.I. 1988 No. 664) ("the Payments Regulations") as any income which is to be taken into account under Pt. V of the Income Support (General) Regulations 1987 (S.I. 1987 No. 1967). The prescribed date under reg. 7(2) is, in general, the first day of the period to which that income relates. If as a result of that income being paid after the prescribed date, more income support is paid than would have been paid if the income had been paid on the prescribed date, the excess may be recovered. Note that the right to recover is absolute and does not depend on lack of care on the claimant's part, or on the effect of this section having been pointed out. An example would be where a claimant has not been paid part-time earnings when they were due and as a result has been paid income support on the basis of having no earnings. Once the arrears of wages are received, the excess benefit would be recoverable. Late payment of most social security benefits is covered in subss. (2) and (4), but can also come within subs. (1). For instance, if a claim is made for child benefit and while a decision is awaited, income support is paid without any deduction for the amount of the expected child benefit, then if arrears of child benefit are eventually paid in full (*i.e.* the abatement procedure of subs. (2) does not work) the "excess" income support for the period covered by the arrears is recoverable under subs. (1) or (4).

Subs. (2)
Prescribed payments are listed in reg. 8(1) of the Payments Regulations and include most social security benefits, training allowances and social security benefits from other EC countries. As under subs. (1), a claimant is not to keep excess income support resulting from late payment of one of the prescribed payments. However, the primary mechanism here where the payment is due from public funds in the U.K. is for the arrears due to be abated (*i.e.* reduced) by the amount of the excess income support (subs. (2)(a) and (i)). Note that the abatement may be applied to benefits due to another member of the claimant's family (*e.g.* retirement pension due to the wife of the income support claimant in *CSB 383/1988*). If this mechanism breaks down and the arrears are paid in full, then under subs. (1) or (4) the Secretary of State can recover the excess from the income support recipient.

In the case of other payments (which will normally be benefits due from other EC countries), recovery is the primary mechanism (subs. (2)(ii)). If the payment is routed through the DSS, as was the case for the arrears of a German invalidity pension in *R(IS) 3/91*, a deduction can be made before the arrears are paid over to the claimant. Although reg. 8(1)(g) of the Payments Regulations makes a reference to EC Regulation 1408/71, the s.74 procedure is not limited to benefits obtained by virtue of the Regulation.

Once again, the operation of the provision is automatic. Any undertaking by the claimant to repay seems superfluous. However, the Secretary of State might choose not to enforce his right to recovery.

Under s.71(8)(c), amounts may be recovered by deduction from most benefits.

Subs. (3)

Prescribed benefits are listed in reg. 9 of the Payments Regulations. They are benefits, like child benefit, which can be claimed if a person (A) is contributing to the support of another person (B) at at least the rate of the benefit. If income support has been paid for B on the basis that this contribution was not paid, the prescribed benefit may be abated by the amount of the excess income support. If the abatement mechanism breaks down, the Secretary of State may recover the excess under subs. (4). Under s.71(8)(c), amounts may be recovered by deduction from most benefits.

Subs. (4)

See notes to subss. (2) and (3).

Subs. (5)

R(SB) 28/85 had revealed problems in valuing a payment of arrears in a foreign currency which might cover quite a long period during which exchange rates varied. This provision authorises regulations to be made to deal with the conversion. See reg. 10 of the Payments Regulations, which appears to require the actual net amount received to be taken into account, reversing the effect of *R(SB) 28/85*.

Housing benefit

Overpayments of housing benefit

75.—(1) Except where regulations otherwise provide, any amount of housing benefit paid in excess of entitlement may be recovered in such manner as may be prescribed either by the Secretary of State or by the authority which paid the benefit.

(2) Regulations may require such an authority to recover such an amount in such circumstances as may be prescribed.

(3) An amount recoverable under this section is in all cases recoverable from the person to whom it was paid; but, in such circumstances as may be prescribed, it may also be recovered from such other person as may be prescribed.

(4) Any amount recoverable under this section may, without prejudice to any other method of recovery, be recovered by deduction from prescribed benefits.

GENERAL NOTE

See Pt. XIII of the Housing Benefit (General) Regulations 1987, in the current edition of Findlay and Ward.

Community charge benefits

Excess benefits

76.—(1) Regulations may make provision as to any case where a charging authority or a levying authority has allowed a community charge benefit to a person and the amount allowed exceeds the amount to which he is entitled in respect of the benefit.

(2) As regards any case where the benefit is in respect of a personal community charge the regulations may provide that—

    (a) a sum equal to the excess shall be due from the person concerned to the authority (whatever the form the benefit takes);

    (b) any liability under any provision included under paragraph (a) above shall be met by such method mentioned in subsection (3) below as is prescribed as regards the case concerned, or by such combination of two or all three of the methods as is prescribed as regards the case concerned.

(3) The methods are—

    (a) payment by the person concerned;

    (b) addition to any amount in respect of the charge concerned;

(c) deduction from prescribed benefits.

(4) As regards any case where the benefit is in respect of a contribution period the regulations may provide that—

(a) a sum equal to the excess shall be due from the person concerned to the authority (whatever the form the benefit takes);

(b) any liability under any provision included under paragraph (a) above shall be met by such method mentioned in subsection (5) below as is prescribed as regards the case concerned, or by such combination of the methods as is prescribed as regards the case concerned;

(c) there is to be no adjustment as between the person concerned and the charge payer, or as between the charge payer and the authority concerned.

(5) The methods are—

(a) payment by the person concerned;

(b) deduction from prescribed benefits.

(6) In a case where the regulations provide that a sum or part of a sum is to be paid, and the sum or part is not paid on or before such day as may be prescribed, the regulations may provide that the sum or part shall be recoverable in a court of competent jurisdiction.

(7) For the purposes of the subsection (4) above the charge payer is—

(a) in relation to England and Wales, the person who is liable to pay an amount in respect of the collective community charge concerned under section 15 of the Local Government Finance Act 1988;

(b) in relation to Scotland, the person who is liable to pay the collective community charge under section 11(5) of the Abolition of Domestic Rates Etc. (Scotland) Act 1987.

(8) The regulations may provide that they are not to apply as regards any case falling within a prescribed category.

DEFINITIONS
"charging authority": s.191.
"levying authority": *ibid.*
"prescribed": *ibid.*

GENERAL NOTE
See Pt. XI of the Community Charge Benefits (General) Regulations 1989 (S.I. 1989 No. 1321), in the current edition of Findlay and Ward.

Shortfall in benefits

77.—(1) Regulations may make provision as to any case where a charging authority or a levying authority has allowed a community charge benefit to a person and the amount allowed is less than the amount to which he is entitled in respect of the benefit.

(2) In particular, as regards any prescribed case where the benefit is in respect of a contribution period the regulations may provide that—

(a) a sum equal to the difference shall be due from the authority to the person concerned;

(b) any liability under any provision included under paragraph (a) above shall be met by payment and not by such reductions as are mentioned in section 138(4) below (whatever the form the benefit actually allowed takes);

(c) there is to be no adjustment as between the person concerned and the charge payer, or as between the charge payer and the authority concerned.

(3) For the purposes of subsection (2) above the charge payer is—

(a) in relation to England and Wales, the person who is liable to pay an amount in respect of the collective community charge concerned under section 15 of the Local Government Finance Act 1988;

(b) in relation to Scotland, the person who is liable to pay the collective community charge under section 11(5) of the Abolition of Domestic Rates Etc. (Scotland) Act 1987.

DEFINITIONS
"charging authority": s.191.
"levying authority": *ibid.*
"prescribed": *ibid.*

GENERAL NOTE
See reg. 79 of the Community Charge Benefits (General) Regulations 1989 (S.I. 1989 No. 1321), in the current edition of Findlay and Ward.

Social fund awards

Recovery of social fund awards

78.—(1) A social fund award which is repayable shall be recoverable by the Secretary of State.

(2) Without prejudice to any other method of recovery, the Secretary of State may recover an award by deduction from prescribed benefits.

(3) The Secretary of State may recover an award—

(a) from the person to or for the benefit of whom it was made;

(b) where that person is a member of a married or unmarried couple, from the other member of the couple;

(c) from a person who is liable to maintain the person by or on behalf of whom the application for the award was made or any person in relation to whose needs the award was made.

(4) Payments to meet funeral expenses may in all cases be recovered, as if they were funeral expenses, out of the estate of the deceased, and (subject to section 71 above) by no other means.

(5) In this section—

"married couple" means a man and woman who are married to each other and are members of the same household;

"unmarried couple" means a man and woman who are not married to each other but are living together as husband and wife otherwise than in circumstances prescribed under section 132 of the Contributions and Benefits Act.

(6) For the purposes of this section—

(a) a man shall be liable to maintain his wife and any children of whom he is the father;

(b) a woman shall be liable to maintain her husband and any children of whom she is the mother;

(c) a person shall be liable to maintain another person throughout any period in respect of which the first-mentioned person has, on or after 23rd May 1980 (the date of the passing of the Social Security Act 1980) and either alone or jointly with a further person, given an undertaking in writing in pursuance of immigration rules within the meaning of the Immigration Act 1971 to be responsible for the maintenance and accommodation of the other person; and

(d) "child" includes a person who has attained the age of 16 but not the age of 19 and in respect of whom either parent, or some person acting in the place of either parent, is receiving income support.

(7) Any reference in subsection (6) above to children of whom the man or the woman is the father or the mother shall be construed in accordance with section 1 of the Family Law Reform Act 1987.

(8) Subsection (7) above does not apply in Scotland, and in the application of subsection (6) above to Scotland any reference to children of whom the man or the woman is the father or the mother shall be construed as a reference to any such children whether or not their parents have ever been married to one another.

(9) A document bearing a certificate which—
(a) is signed by a person authorised in that behalf by the Secretary of State; and
(b) states that the document apart from the certificate is, or is a copy of, such an undertaking as is mentioned in subsection (6)(c) above,

shall be conclusive of the undertaking in question for the purposes of this section; and a certificate purporting to be so signed shall be deemed to be so signed until the contrary is proved.

DEFINITIONS
"prescribed": s.191.

GENERAL NOTE

Subss. (1)–(3)
These provisions give the framework for recovery of social fund loans. See the Social Fund (Recovery by Deductions from Benefits) Regulations 1988 (S.I. 1988 No. 35), in the current edition of Mesher.

Subs. (4)
Subsection (4) contains an important provision for the recovery of any social fund payment for funeral expenses out of the estate of the deceased. Regulation 8 of the Social Fund Maternity and Funeral Expenses (General) Regulations 1987 lists sums to be deducted in calculating the amount of a funeral payment. These include assets of the deceased which are available before probate or letters of administration have been granted. The old reg. 8(3)(a) of the Supplementary Benefit (Single Payments) Regulations 1987 required the deduction of the value of the deceased's estate, but since it might take some time for the estate to become available, the provision in subs. (4) is preferable.

The funeral payment is to be recovered as if it were funeral expenses. Funeral expenses are a first charge on the estate, in priority to anything else (see *R(SB) 18/84*, paras. 8 and 10, for the law in England and Scotland). *CIS 616/1990* decides that the right to recover is given to the Secretary of State. The AO (and the SSAT) has no rôle in subs. (4).

The only other method of recovery is under s.71, which applies generally where there has been misrepresentation or a failure to disclose and does depend on a review of entitlement by an AO, followed by a determination of an overpayment.

Subss. (6)–(9)
See the notes to s.105.

Northern Ireland payments

Recovery of Northern Ireland payments

79. Without prejudice to any other method of recovery—
(a) amounts recoverable under any enactment or instrument having effect in Northern Ireland and corresponding to an enactment or instrument mentioned in section 71(8) above shall be recoverable by deduction from benefits prescribed under that subsection;
(b) amounts recoverable under any enactment having effect in Northern Ireland and corresponding to section 75 above shall be recoverable by deduction from benefits prescribed under subsection (4) of that section; and
(c) awards recoverable under Part III of the Northern Ireland Administration Act shall be recoverable by deduction from benefits prescribed under subsection (2) of section 78 above and subsection (3) of that section shall have effect in relation to such awards as it has effect in relation to awards out of the social fund under this Act.

DEFINITIONS
"the Northern Ireland Administration Act": s.191.
"prescribed": *ibid.*

Adjustment of child benefit

Child benefit—overlap with benefits under legislation of other member States

80. Regulations may provide for adjusting child benefit payable in respect of any child in respect of whom any benefit is payable under the legislation of any member State other than the United Kingdom.

PART IV

RECOVERY FROM COMPENSATION PAYMENTS

Interpretation of Part IV

81.—(1) In this Part of this Act—
"benefit" means any benefit under the Contributions and Benefits Act except child benefit and, subject to regulations under subsection (2) below, the "relevant benefits" are such of those benefits as may be prescribed for the purposes of this Part of this Act;
"certificate of deduction" means a certificate given by the compensator specifying the amount which he has deducted and paid to the Secretary of State in pursuance of section 82(1) below;
"certificate of total benefit" means a certificate given by the Secretary of State in accordance with this Part of this Act;
"compensation payment" means any payment falling to be made (whether voluntarily, or in pursuance of a court order or an agreement, or otherwise)—
> (a) to or in respect of the victim in consequence of the accident, injury or disease in question, and
> (b) either—
>> (i) by or on behalf of a person who is, or is alleged to be, liable to any extent in respect of that accident, injury or disease; or
>> (ii) in pursuance of a compensation scheme for motor accidents,
but does not include benefit of an exempt payment or so much of any payment as is referable to costs incurred by any person;
"compensation scheme for motor accidents" means any scheme or arrangement under which funds are available for the payment of compensation in respect of motor accidents caused, or alleged to have been caused, by uninsured or unidentified persons;
"compensator", "victim" and "intended recipient" shall be construed in accordance with section 82(1) below;
"payment" means payment in money or money's worth, and cognate expressions shall be construed accordingly;
"relevant deduction" means the deduction required to be made from the compensation payment in question by virtue of this Part of this Act;
"relevant payment" means the payment required to be made to the Secretary of State by virtue of this Part of this Act;
"relevant period" means—
> (a) in the case of a disease, the period of 5 years beginning with the date on which the victim first claims a relevant benefit in consequence of the disease; or
> (b) in any other case, the period of 5 years immediately following the day on which the accident or injury in question occurred;
but where before the end of that period the compensator makes a compensation payment in final discharge of any claim made by or

in respect of the victim and arising out of the accident, injury or disease, the relevant period shall end on the date on which that payment is made; and

"total benefit" means the gross amount referred to in section 82(1)(a) below.

(2) If statutory sick pay is prescribed as a relevant benefit, the amount of that benefit for the purposes of this Part of this Act shall be a reduced amount determined in accordance with regulations by reference to the percentage from time to time specified in section 158(1)(a) of the Contributions and Benefits Act (percentage of statutory sick pay recoverable by employers by deduction from contributions).

(3) For the purposes of this Part of this Act the following are the "exempt payments"—

(a) any small payment, as defined in section 85 below;

(b) any payment made to or for the victim under section 35 of the Powers of Criminal Courts Act 1973 or section 58 of the Criminal Justice (Scotland) Act 1980;

(c) any payment to the extent that it is made—

(i) in consequence of an action under the Fatal Accidents Act 1976; or

(ii) in circumstances where, had an action been brought, it would have been brought under that Act;

(d) any payment to the extent that it is made in respect of a liability arising by virtue of section 1 of the Damages (Scotland) Act 1976;

(e) without prejudice to section 6(4) of the Vaccine Damage Payments Act 1979 (which provides for the deduction of any such payment in the assessment of any award of damages), any payment made under that Act to or in respect of the victim;

(f) any award of compensation made to or in respect of the victim by the Criminal Injuries Compensation Board under section 111 of the Criminal Justice Act 1988;

(g) any payment made in the exercise of a discretion out of property held subject to a trust in a case where no more that 50 per cent. by value of the capital contributed to the trust was directly or indirectly provided by persons who are, or are alleged to be, liable in respect of—

(i) the accident, injury or disease suffered by the victim in question; or

(ii) the same or any connected accident, injury or disease suffered by another;

(h) any payment made out of property held for the purposes of any prescribed trust (whether the payment also falls within paragraph (g) above or not);

(i) any payment made to the victim by an insurance company within the meaning of the Insurance Companies Act 1982 under the terms of any contract of insurance entered into between the victim and the company before—

(i) the date on which the victim first claims a relevant benefit in consequence of the disease in question; or

(ii) the occurrence of the accident or injury in question;

(j) any redundancy payment falling to be taken into account in the assessment of damages in respect of an accident, injury or disease.

(4) Regulations may provide that any prescribed payment shall be an exempt payment for the purposes of this Part of this Act.

(5) Except as provided by any other enactment, in the assessment of damages in respect of an accident, injury or disease the amount of any relevant benefits paid or likely to be paid shall be disregarded.

(6) If, after making the relevant deduction from the compensation payment, there would be no balance remaining for payment to the intended

recipient, any reference in this Part to the making of the compensation payment shall be construed in accordance with regulations.

(7) This Part of this Act shall apply in relation to any compensation payment made on or after 3rd September 1990 (the date of the coming into force of section 22 of the Social Security Act 1989 which, with Schedule 4 to that Act, made provision corresponding to that made by this Part) to the extent that it is made in respect of—

(a) an accident or injury occurring on or after 1st January 1989; or

(b) a disease, if the victim's first claim for a relevant benefit in consequence of the disease is made on or after that date.

DEFINITIONS
"the Contributions and Benefits Act": s.191.
"prescribed": *ibid.*

GENERAL NOTE
See the annotations in Current Law Statutes 1989 BV2 to s.22 of and Sched. 4 to the Social Security Act 1989 for the general structure of the system of recovery from compensation payments and to Sched. 1 to the Social Security Act 1990 BV2 for some significant amendments.

Recovery from damages etc. of sums equivalent to benefit

Recovery of sums equivalent to benefit from compensation payments in respect of accidents, injuries and diseases

82.—(1) A person ("the compensator") making a compensation payment, whether on behalf of himself or another, in consequence of an accident, injury or disease suffered by any other person ("the victim") shall not do so until the Secretary of State has furnished him with a certificate of total benefit and shall then—

(a) deduct from the payment an amount, determined in accordance with the certificate of total benefit, equal to the gross amount of any relevant benefits paid or likely to be paid to or for the victim during the relevant period in respect of that accident, injury or disease;

(b) pay to the Secretary of State an amount equal to that which is required to be so deducted; and

(c) furnish the person to whom the compensation payment is or, apart from this section, would have been made ("the intended recipient") with a certificate of deduction.

(2) Any right of the intended recipient to receive the compensation payment in question shall be regarded as satisfied to the extent of the amount certified in the certificate of deduction.

DEFINITIONS
"certificate of deduction": s.81
"certificate of total benefit": *ibid.*
"compensation payment": *ibid.*

GENERAL NOTE
See the note to s.81.

Payments, deductions and certificates

Time for making payment to Secretary of State

83. The compensator's liability to make the relevant payment arises immediately before the making of the compensation payment, and he shall make the relevant payment before the end of the period of 14 days following the day on which the liability arises.

DEFINITIONS
"compensation payment": s.81.
"compensator": *ibid.*
"relevant payment": *ibid.*

GENERAL NOTE
See the note to s.81.

The certificate of total benefit

84.—(1) It shall be for the compensator to apply to the Secretary of State for the certificate of total benefit and he may, subject to subsection (5) below, from time to time apply for fresh certificates.

(2) The certificate of total benefit shall specify—

(a) the amount which has been, or is likely to be, paid on or before a specified date by way of any relevant benefit which is capable of forming part of the total benefit;

(b) where applicable—

(i) the rate of any relevant benefit which is, has been, or is likely to be paid after the date so specified and which would be capable of forming part of the total benefit; and

(ii) the intervals at which any such benefit is paid and the period for which it is likely to be paid;

(c) the amounts (if any) which, by virtue of this Part of this Act, are to be treated as increasing the total benefit; and

(d) the aggregate amount of any relevant payments made on or before a specified date (reduced by so much of that amount as has been paid by the Secretary of State to the intended recipient before that date in consequence of this Part of this Act).

(3) On issuing a certificate of total benefit, the Secretary of State shall be taken to have certified the total benefit as at every date for which it is possible to calculate an amount that would, on the basis of the information so provided, be the total benefit as at that date, on the assumption that payments of benefit are made on the days on which they first become payable.

(4) The Secretary of State may estimate, in such manner as he thinks fit, any of the amounts, rates or periods specified in the certificate of total benefit.

(5) A certificate of total benefit shall remain in force until such date as may be specified in the certificate for that purpose and no application for a fresh certificate shall be made before that date.

(6) Where a certificate ceases to be in force, the Secretary of State may issue a fresh certificate, whether or not an application has been made to him for such a certificate.

(7) The compensator shall not make the compensation payment at any time when there is no certificate of total benefit in force in respect of the victim, unless his liability to make the relevant deduction and the relevant payment has ceased to be enforceable by virtue of section 96 below.

DEFINITIONS
"certificate of total benefit": s.81.
"compensator": *ibid.*
"intended recipient": *ibid.*
"relevant benefit": *ibid.*
"relevant deduction": *ibid.*
"relevant payment": *ibid.*
"total benefit": *ibid.*
"victim": *ibid.*

GENERAL NOTE
See the note to s.81.

Exemption from deduction in cases involving small payments

85.—(1) Regulations may make provision exempting persons from liability to make the relevant deduction or the relevant payment in prescribed cases where the amount of the compensation payment in question, or the aggregate amount of two or more connected compensation payments, does not exceed the prescribed sum.

(2) Regulations may make provision for cases where an amount has been deducted and paid to the Secretary of State which, by virtue of regulations under subsection (1) above, ought not to have been so deducted and paid, and any such regulations may, in particular, provide for him to pay that amount to the intended recipient or the compensator or to pay a prescribed part of it to each of them.

(3) The reference in section 81(3)(a) above to a "small payment" is a reference to a payment from which by virtue of this section no relevant deduction falls to be made.

(4) For the purposes of this section—

(a) two or more compensation payments are "connected" if each is made to or in respect of the same victim and in respect of the same accident, injury or disease; and

(b) any reference to a compensation payment is a reference to a payment which would be such a payment apart from section 81(3)(a) above.

DEFINITIONS
"compensation payment": s.81.
"intended recipient": *ibid.*
"prescribed": s.191.
"relevant deduction": s.81.
"relevant payment": *ibid.*

GENERAL NOTE
See the note to s.81.

Multiple compensation payments

86.—(1) This section applies where—

(a) a compensation payment (an "earlier payment") has been made to or in respect of the victim; and

(b) subsequently another such payment (a "later payment") falls to be made to or in respect of the same victim in respect of the same accident, injury or disease (whether by the same or another compensator).

(2) In determining the amount of the relevant deduction and payment required to be made in connection with the later payment, the amount referred to in section 82(1)(a) above shall be reduced by the amount of any relevant payment made in connection with the earlier payment, or, if more than one, the aggregate of those relevant payments.

(3) In relation to the later payment, the compensator shall take the amount of the reduction required by subsection (2) above to be such as may be specified under section 84(2)(d) above in the certificate of total benefit issued to him in connection with that later payment.

(4) In any case where—

(a) the relevant payment made in connection with an earlier payment is not reflected in the certificate of total benefit in force in relation to a later payment, and

(b) in consequence, the aggregate of the relevant payments made in relation to the later payment and every earlier payment exceeds what it would have been had that relevant payment been so reflected,

the Secretary of State shall pay the intended recipient an amount equal to the excess.

(5) In determining any rights and liabilities in respect of contribution or indemnity, relevant payments shall be treated as damages paid to or for the intended recipient in respect of the accident, injury or disease in question.

DEFINITIONS
  "certificate of total benefit": s.81.
  "compensation payment": *ibid.*
  "compensator": *ibid.*
  "intended recipient": *ibid.*
  "relevant deduction": *ibid.*
  "relevant payment": *ibid.*
  "victim": *ibid.*

GENERAL NOTE
  See the note to s.81.

Collaboration between compensators

87.—(1) This section applies where compensation payments in respect of the same accident, injury or disease fall (or apart from this Part would fall) to be made to or in respect of the same victim by two or more compensators.

(2) Where this section applies, any two or more of those compensators may give the Secretary of State notice that they are collaborators in respect of compensation payments in respect of that victim and that accident, injury or disease.

(3) Where such a notice is given and any of the collaborators makes a relevant payment in connection with such a compensation payment, each of the other collaborators shall be treated as if the aggregate amount of relevant payments specified in his certificate of total benefit, as in force at the time of that relevant payment, or in a fresh certificate which does not purport to reflect the payment, were increased by the amount of that payment.

DEFINITIONS
  "certificate of total benefit": s.81.
  "compensation payment": *ibid.*
  "compensator": *ibid.*
  "relevant payment": *ibid.*
  "victim": *ibid.*

GENERAL NOTE
  See the note to s.81.

Structured settlements

88.—(1) This section applies where—
  (a) in final settlement of a person's claim, an agreement is entered into—
      (i) for the making of periodical payments (whether of an income or capital nature) to or in respect of the victim; or
      (ii) for the making of such payments and one or more lump sum payments; and
  (b) apart from this section, those payments would fall to be regarded for the purposes of this Part of this Act as compensation payments.

(2) Where this section applies, this Part of this Act (other than this section) shall have effect on the following assumptions, that is to say—
  (a) the relevant period in the case of the compensator in question shall be taken to end (if it has not previously done so) on the day of settlement;
  (b) the compensator in question shall be taken—
      (i) to have been liable to make on that day a single compensation payment of the amount referred to in section 82(1)(a) above

(reduced or increased in accordance with such of the provisions of
this Part as would have applied in the case of a payment on that
day); and

    (ii) to have made from that single payment a relevant deduction
of an amount equal to it; and

(c) the payments under the agreement referred to in subsection (1) above
shall be taken to be exempt payments.

(3) The intended recipient shall not by virtue of anything in this section
become entitled to be paid any sum, whether by the compensator or the
Secretary of State, and if on a review or appeal under section 97 or 99 below
it appears that the amount paid by a compensator in pursuance of this
section was either greater or less than it ought to have been, then—

(a) any excess shall be repaid to the compensator instead of to the
intended recipient; but

(b) any deficiency shall be paid to the Secretary of State by the intended
recipient.

(4) Where any further compensation payment falls to be made to or in
respect of the victim otherwise than under the agreement in question,
subsection (2)(a) above shall be disregarded for the purpose of determining
the end of the relevant period in relation to that further payment.

(5) In any case where—

(a) the person making the periodical payments ("the secondary party")
does so in pursuance of arrangements entered into with another (as in
a case where an insurance company purchases an annuity for the
victim from another such company), and

(b) apart from those arrangements, that other ("the primary party")
would have been regarded as the compensator,

then for the purposes of this Part, the primary party shall be regarded as the
compensator and the secondary party shall not be so regarded.

(6) In determining for the purposes of this section whether any periodical
payments would fall to be regarded as compensation payments, section
81(3)(a) above shall be disregarded.

(7) In this section "the day of settlement" means—

(a) if the agreement referred to in subsection (1) above is approved by a
court, the day on which that approval is given; and

(b) in any other case, the day on which the agreement is entered into.

DEFINITIONS
"compensation payment": s.81.
"compensator": *ibid.*
"intended recipient": *ibid.*
"relevant deduction": *ibid.*
"relevant period": *ibid.*
"victim": *ibid.*

GENERAL NOTE
See the note to s.81.

Insolvency

89.—(1) Where the intended recipient is subject to a bankruptcy order,
nothing in the Insolvency Act 1986 shall affect the operation of this Part of
this Act.

(2) Where the estate of the intended recipient is sequestrated, the relevant
deduction from the compensation payment shall not form part of the whole
estate of the debtor, within the meaning of section 31(8) of the Bankruptcy
(Scotland) Act 1985.

DEFINITIONS
"compensation payment": s.81.
"intended recipient": *ibid.*
"relevant deduction": *ibid.*

GENERAL NOTE
See the note to s.81.

Protection of legal aid charges

90.—(1) In any case where—
(a) the compensation payment is subject to any charge under the Legal
    Aid Act 1974 or the Legal Aid Act 1988, and
(b) after the making of the relevant deduction, the balance of the com-
    pensation payment is insufficient to satisfy that charge,
the Secretary of State shall make such a payment as will secure that the
deficiency is made good to the extent of the relevant payment.

(2) Where the Secretary of State makes a payment under this section, then
for the purposes of section 84 above, the amount of the payment shall be
treated as increasing the total benefit.

(3) In the application of this section to Scotland, references in subsection
(1) above to a charge under the Acts specified shall be construed as references to any provisions of the Legal Aid (Scotland) Act 1986 for the
repayment to the Scottish Legal Aid Fund of sums paid by it on behalf of the
intended recipient in respect of the proceedings in which the compensation
payment is made.

DEFINITIONS
"compensation payment": s.81.
"relevant deduction": *ibid.*
"relevant payment": *ibid.*
"total benefit": *ibid.*

GENERAL NOTE
See the note to s.81.

Overpaid benefits

91. In any case where—
(a) during the relevant period, there has, in respect of the accident,
    injury or disease, been paid to or for the victim any relevant benefit to
    which he was not entitled ("the overpaid benefit"), and
(b) the amount of the relevant payment is such that, after taking account
    of the rest of the total benefit, there remains an amount which
    represents the whole or any part of the overpaid benefit,
then, notwithstanding anything in section 71 above or any regulations under
that section or section 53 of the 1986 Act, the receipt by the Secretary of
State of the relevant payment shall be treated as the recovery of the whole
or, as the case may be, that part of the overpaid benefit.

DEFINITIONS
"the 1986 Act": s.191.
"relevant payment": s.81.
"relevant period": *ibid.*
"total benefit": *ibid.*

GENERAL NOTE
See the note to s.81.

Death

92. In the case of any compensation payment the whole or part of which is
made—
(a) in consequence of an action under the Fatal Accidents Act 1976, or

(b) in circumstances where, had an action been brought, it would have been brought under that Act, or

(c) in respect of a liability arising by virtue of section 1 of the Damages (Scotland) Act 1976,

regulations may make provision for estimating or calculating the portion of the payment which is to be regarded as so made for the purposes of section 81(3)(c) or (d) above.

GENERAL NOTE
See the note to s.81.

Payments into court

93.—(1) Nothing in this Part of this Act requires a court to make any relevant deduction or payment in connection with money in court.

(2) Where a party to an action makes a payment into court which, had it been paid directly to the other party, would have constituted a compensation payment, the making of that payment shall be regarded for the purposes of this Part of this Act as the making of a compensation payment, but the compensator—

(a) may either—

(i) withhold from the payment into court an amount equal to the relevant deduction; or

(ii) make such a payment into court before the certificate of total benefit has been issued to him; and

(b) shall not become liable to make the relevant payment, or to furnish a certificate of deduction, until he has been notified that the whole or any part of the payment into court has been paid out of court to or for the other party.

(3) Where a person making a payment into court withholds an amount in accordance with subsection (2)(a)(i) above—

(a) he shall, at the time when he makes that payment, furnish the court with a certificate of the amount so withheld; and

(b) the amount paid into court shall be regarded as increased by the amount so certified,

but no person shall be entitled by virtue of this subsection to the payment out of court of any amount which has not in fact been paid into court.

(4) Where a payment into court is made as mentioned in subsection (2)(a)(ii) above, the compensator—

(a) shall apply for the certificate of total benefit no later than the day on which the payment into court is made; and

(b) shall become liable to make the relevant payment as mentioned in subsection (2)(b) above, notwithstanding that the relevant deduction has not been made.

(5) Where any such payment into court as is mentioned in subsection (2) above is accepted by the other party to the action within the initial period, then, as respects the compensator in question, the relevant period shall be taken to have ended on the day on which the payment into court (or, if there were two or more such payments, the last of them) was made; but where the payment into court is not so accepted, then—

(a) the relevant period as respects that compensator shall end on the day on which he is notified that the payment has been paid out of court to or for that other party; and

(b) in determining the amount of the relevant payment, that compensator shall be treated as if his payment into court had been made on that day.

(6) In subsection (5) above "the initial period" means the period of 21 days following the making of the payment into court (or, if there were two or more such payments, the last of them), but rules of court may make provision varying the length of that period.

(7) Where a payment into court is paid out wholly to or for the party who made the payment (otherwise than to or for the other party to the action) the making of the payment into court shall cease to be regarded as the making of a compensation payment.

(8) Rules of court may make provision regulating or prescribing the practice and procedure to be followed in relation to such payments into court as are mentioned in subsection (2) above.

(9) This section does not extend to Scotland.

DEFINITIONS
"certificate of deduction": s.81.
"certificate of total benefit": *ibid.*
"compensation payment": *ibid.*
"compensator": *ibid.*
"relevant deduction": *ibid.*
"relevant payment": *ibid.*
"relevant period": *ibid.*

GENERAL NOTE
See the note to s.81.

Administration and adjudication

Provision of information

94.—(1) Any person who is, or is alleged to be, liable in respect of an accident, injury or disease, or any person acting on his behalf, shall furnish the Secretary of State with the prescribed information relating to any person seeking compensation, or in respect of whom compensation is sought, in respect of that accident, injury or disease.

(2) Any person who claims a relevant benefit or who has been in receipt of such a benefit or, if he has died, the personal representatives of such a person, shall furnish the Secretary of State with the prescribed information relating to any accident, injury or disease suffered by that person.

(3) A person who makes any payment (whether a compensation payment or not) on behalf of himself or another—

(a) in consequence of any accident, injury or disease suffered, or any damage to property sustained, by any other person, or

(b) which is referable to any costs, or, in Scotland, expenses, incurred by any such other person by reason of such an accident, injury, disease or damage,

shall, if the Secretary of State so requests him in writing, furnish the Secretary of State with such particulars relating to the size and composition of the payment as may be specified in the request.

(4) Any person—

(a) who is the employer of a person who suffers or has suffered an accident, injury or disease, or

(b) who has been the employer of such a person at any time during the relevant period,

shall furnish the Secretary of State with the prescribed information relating to the payment of statutory sick pay in respect of that person.

(5) In subsection (4) above "employer" has the same meaning as it has in Part XI of the Contributions and Benefits Act.

(6) Any person furnishing information under this section shall do so in the prescribed manner, at the prescribed place and within the prescribed time.

GENERAL NOTE
  See the note to s.81.

Applications for certificates of total benefit

95.—(1) If at any time before he makes the compensation payment in question the compensator requests the Secretary of State to furnish him with a certificate of total benefit relating to the victim in question—

  (a) the Secretary of State shall comply with that request before the end of the period of 4 weeks, or such other number of weeks as may be prescribed, following the day on which the request is, or is deemed in accordance with regulations to be, received, and
  (b) any certificate so furnished shall, in particular, specify for the purposes of section 84(2)(a) above a date not earlier than the date of the request.

(2) Where the Secretary of State furnishes any person with a certificate of total benefit, he shall also provide the information contained in that certificate to the person who appears to him to be the victim in relation to the compensation payment in question.

(3) The victim may apply to the Secretary of State for particulars of the manner in which any amount, rate or period specified in a certificate of total benefit has been determined.

DEFINITIONS
  "certificate of total benefit": s.81.
  "compensation payment": *ibid.*
  "compensator": *ibid.*
  "prescribed": s.191.
  "victim": s.81.

GENERAL NOTE
  See the note to s.81.

Liability of compensator unenforceable if certificate not issued within time limit

96.—(1) The liability of the compensator to make the relevant deduction and payment relating to the first compensation payment after the default date shall not be enforceable if—

  (a) he has made a request under section 95(1) above which—
    (i) accurately states the prescribed particulars relating to the victim and the accident, injury or disease in question; and
    (ii) specifies the name and address of the person to whom the certificate is to be sent;
  (b) he has in his possession a written acknowledgment, sent to him in accordance with regulations, of the receipt of the request; and
  (c) the Secretary of State does not, within the time limit referred to in section 95(1) above, send the certificate to the person specified in the request as the person to whom the certificate is to be sent, at the address so specified;

and accordingly, where those liabilities cease to be enforceable, nothing in this Part of this Act shall prevent the compensator from making that compensation payment.

(2) In any case where—

(a) the liability to make the relevant deduction and payment becomes unenforceable by virtue of this section, but

(b) the compensator nevertheless makes that deduction and payment, he shall be treated for all purposes as if the liability had remained enforceable.

(3) Where the compensator, in reliance on this section, does not make the relevant deduction and payment, then—

(a) he shall within 14 days of the default date give the Secretary of State notice of that fact together with such other particulars as may be prescribed; and

(b) in determining the amount of the relevant deduction and payment to be made in connection with any subsequent compensation payment made by the same or any other compensator, the amount which, apart from this section, would have fallen to be deducted and paid by him shall continue to form part of the total benefit and shall not be treated as if it had been paid.

(4) If, in the opinion of the Secretary of State, circumstances have arisen which adversely affect normal methods of communication—

(a) he may by order provide that no liability shall become unenforceable by virtue of this section during a specified period not exceeding three months; and

(b) he may continue any such order in force for further periods not exceeding three months at a time.

(5) In this section "the default date" means the date on which the time limit mentioned in subsection (1)(c) above expires.

DEFINITIONS
  "compensation payment": s.81.
  "compensator": ibid.
  "prescribed": s.191.
  "relevant deduction": s.81.
  "relevant payment": ibid.
  "total benefit": ibid.
  "victim": ibid.

GENERAL NOTE
  See the note to s.81.

Review of certificates of total benefit

97.—(1) The Secretary of State may review any certificate of total benefit if he is satisfied that it was issued in ignorance of, or was based on a mistake as to, some material fact or that a mistake (whether in computation or otherwise) has occurred in its preparation.

(2) On any such review the Secretary of State may either—

(a) confirm the certificate, or

(b) issue a fresh certificate containing such variations as he considers appropriate,

but he shall not so vary the certificate as to increase the total benefit.

(3) In any case where—

(a) one or more relevant payments have been made, and

(b) in consequence of a review under this section, it appears that the aggregate amount so paid exceeds the amount that ought to have been paid,

the Secretary of State shall pay the intended recipient an amount equal to the excess.

DEFINITIONS
  "certificate of total benefit": s.81.
  "intended recipient": ibid.

"relevant payment": *ibid.*
"total benefit": *ibid.*

GENERAL NOTE
See the note to s.81.

Appeals

98.—(1) An appeal shall lie in accordance with this section against any certificate of total benefit at the instance of the compensator, the victim or the intended recipient, on the ground—
   (a) that any amount, rate or period specified in the certificate is incorrect, or
   (b) that benefit paid or payable otherwise than in consequence of the accident, injury or disease in question has been brought into account.
   (2) No appeal shall be brought under this section until—
   (a) the claim giving rise to the compensation payment has been finally disposed of; and
   (b) the relevant payment, or where more than one such payment may fall to be made, the final relevant payment, has been made.
   (3) Notwithstanding subsection (2) above, where—
   (a) an award of damages ("provisional damages") has been made under or by virtue of—
       (i) section 32A(2)(a) of the Supreme Court Act 1981;
       (ii) section 12(2)(a) of the Administration of Justice Act 1982; or
       (iii) section 51(2)(a) of the County Courts Act 1984; and
   (b) the relevant payment or, where more than one such payment falls to be made, the final relevant payment in relation to the provisional damages so awarded has been made,
an appeal may be brought under this section against any certificate of total benefit by reference to which the amount of that relevant payment, or any of those relevant payments, was made.
   (4) Regulations may make provision—
   (a) as to the manner in which, and the time within which, appeals under this section are to be brought, and
   (b) for the purpose of enabling any such appeal to be treated as an application for review under section 97 above,
and regulations under paragraph (b) above may, in particular, provide that the circumstances in which such a review may be carried out shall not be restricted to those specified in section 97 above.
   (5) If any of the medical questions arises for determination on an appeal under this section, the Secretary of State shall refer that question to a medical appeal tribunal, whose determination shall be binding, for the purposes of the appeal, on any social security appeal tribunal to whom a question is referred under subsection (7) below.
   (6) A medical appeal tribunal, in determining any of the medical questions, shall take into account any decision of any court relating to the same, or any similar, issue arising in connection with the accident, injury or disease in question.
   (7) If any question concerning any amount, rate or period specified in the certificate of total benefit arises for determination on an appeal under this section, the Secretary of State shall refer that question to a social security appeal tribunal, but where any medical questions arising on the appeal have been referred to a medical appeal tribunal—
   (a) he shall not refer any question to the social security appeal tribunal until he has received the determination of the medical appeal tribunal on the questions referred to them; and
   (b) he shall notify the social security appeal tribunal of the determinations of the medical appeal tribunal.

(8) On a reference under subsection (7) above a social security appeal tribunal may either—

    (a) confirm the amounts, rates and periods specified in the certificate of total benefit; or

    (b) specify any increases, reductions or other variations which are to be made on the issue of the fresh certificate under subsection (9) below.

(9) When the Secretary of State has received the determinations of the tribunals on the questions referred to them under subsections (5) and (7) above, he shall in accordance with those determinations either—

    (a) confirm the certificate against which the appeal was brought, or

    (b) issue a fresh certificate.

(10) Regulations may make provision with respect to the procedure for the reference under this section of questions to medical appeal tribunals or social security appeal tribunals.

(11) An appeal shall lie to a Commissioner at the instance of the Secretary of State, the compensator, the victim or the intended recipient from a decision of a medical appeal tribunal or a social security appeal tribunal under this section on the ground that the decision was erroneous in point of law; and for the purposes of appeals under this subsection—

    (a) section 23(7) to (10) above shall apply in relation to an appeal from the decision of a social security appeal tribunal; and

    (b) section 48(3) above shall apply in relation to an appeal from the decision of a medical appeal tribunal.

(12) In this section "the medical questions" means—

    (a) any question whether, as the result of a particular occurrence, the victim suffered an injury, sickness or disease;

    (b) any question as to the period for which the victim suffered any injury, sickness or disease.

DEFINITIONS
    "benefit": s.81.
    "certificate of total benefit": *ibid.*
    "compensation payment": *ibid.*
    "compensator": *ibid.*
    "intended recipient": *ibid.*
    "relevant payment": *ibid.*
    "victim": *ibid.*

GENERAL NOTE
    See the note to s.81.

Recovery in consequence of an appeal

99.—(1) Where it appears, in consequence of an appeal under section 98 above, that the aggregate amount of the relevant payment or payments actually made exceeds the amount that ought to have been paid, the Secretary of State shall pay the intended recipient an amount equal to that excess.

(2) Where it appears, in consequence of such an appeal, that the aggregate amount of the relevant payment or payments actually made is less than the amount that ought to have been paid, the intended recipient shall pay the Secretary of State an amount equal to the deficiency.

(3) Without prejudice to any other method of enforcement, an amount payable under subsection (2) above may be recovered by deduction from any benefits which are prescribed benefits for the purposes of section 71 above.

DEFINITIONS
    "benefit": s.81.
    "intended recipient": *ibid.*
    "prescribed": s.191.
    "relevant payment": s.81.

GENERAL NOTE
See the note to s.81.

Recovery of relevant payment in cases of default

100.—(1) This section applies in any case where the compensator has made a compensation payment but—

(a) has not requested a certificate of total benefit in respect of the victim, or

(b) if he has done so, has not made the relevant payment within the time limit imposed by section 83 above.

(2) Where this section applies, the Secretary of State may—

(a) if no certificate of total benefit has been issued to the compensator, issue to him such a certificate and a demand for the relevant payment to be made forthwith, or

(b) if a certificate of total benefit has been issued to the compensator, issue to him a copy of that certificate and such a demand,

and the amount so certified shall, to the extent that it does not exceed the amount of the compensation payment, be recoverable by the Secretary of State from the compensator.

(3) Any amount recoverable under this section shall—

(a) if the compensator resides or carries on business in England and Wales and a county court so orders, be recoverable by execution issued from the county court or otherwise as if it were payable under an order of that court; or

(b) if the compensator resides or carries on business in Scotland, be enforced in like manner as an extract registered decree arbitral bearing a warrant for execution issued by the sheriff court of any sheriffdom in Scotland.

(4) A document bearing a certificate which—

(a) is signed by a person authorised in that behalf by the Secretary of State, and

(b) states that the document, apart from the certificate, is a record of the amount recoverable under this section,

shall be conclusive evidence that that amount is so recoverable; and a certificate purporting to be signed as aforesaid shall be deemed to be so signed unless the contrary is proved.

(5) Where this section applies in relation to two or more connected compensators, the Secretary of State may proceed against them as if they were jointly and severally liable for an amount equal to the difference between—

(a) the total benefit determined in accordance with the latest connected certificate of total benefit issued to any of them, and

(b) the aggregate amount of any connected relevant payments previously made.

(6) Nothing in subsection (5) above authorises the recovery from any person of an amount in excess of the compensation payment by virtue of which this section applies to him (or, if there are two or more such payments which are connected, the aggregate amount of those payments).

(7) In subsections (5) and (6) above, "connected" means relating to the same victim and the same accident, injury or disease.

DEFINITIONS
"certificate of total benefit": s.81.
"compensation payment": *ibid.*
"compensator": *ibid.*
"relevant payment": *ibid.*
"victim": *ibid.*

Miscellaneous

Persons in Northern Ireland

101.—(1) Where, immediately before making a compensation payment to or in respect of a victim, the compensator—

(a) is not resident and does not have a place of business in Great Britain, but

(b) is resident or has a place of business in Northern Ireland,

this Part of this Act (other than this subsection and subsection (2) below) shall apply in relation to him as if at that time he were resident or had a place of business in the relevant part of Great Britain.

(2) Where, immediately before making a Northern Ireland compensation payment to or in respect of a Northern Ireland victim, a Northern Ireland compensator—

(a) is not resident and does not have a place of business in Northern Ireland, but

(b) is resident or has a place of business in any part of Great Britain,

the Northern Ireland provisions (other than subsection (1) above and this subsection) shall apply in relation to him as if at that time he were resident or had a place of business in Northern Ireland.

(3) Where an address in Northern Ireland is the first address notified in writing to the compensator by or on behalf of the victim as his residence (or, if the victim has died, by or on behalf of the intended recipient as the victim's last residence) then—

(a) the compensator shall apply, as a Northern Ireland compensator, for a Northern Ireland certificate in accordance with the Northern Ireland provisions (and shall not make any separate application for a certificate of total benefit under this Part);

(b) any Northern Ireland certificate which is issued to the compensator in relation to the victim and the accident, injury or disease in question—

(i) shall contain a statement that it is to be treated as including a certificate of total benefit so issued by the Secretary of State and that any relevant payment required to be made to him by reference thereto is to be paid to the Northern Ireland Department as his agent; and

(ii) shall be taken to include such a certificate of total benefit; and

(c) any payment made by the compensator to the Northern Ireland Department in pursuance of such a Northern Ireland certificate shall be applied—

(i) first towards discharging his liability under the Northern Ireland provisions; and

(ii) then, as respects any remaining balance, towards discharging his liability under this Part,

in respect of the relevant victim and that accident, injury or disease.

(4) Where an address in any part of Great Britain is the first address notified in writing to a Northern Ireland compensator by or on behalf of a Northern Ireland victim as his residence (or, if the Northern Ireland victim has died, by or on behalf of the Northern Ireland intended recipient as the Northern Ireland victim's last residence) then—

(a) the Northern Ireland compensator shall apply, as a compensator, for a certificate of total benefit in accordance with this Part of this Act (and shall not make any separate application for a Northern Ireland certificate under the Northern Ireland provisions);

(b) any certificate of total benefit which is issued to the Northern Ireland compensator in relation to the Northern Ireland victim and the accident, injury or disease in question—

(i) shall contain a statement that it is to be treated as including a Northern Ireland certificate so issued by the Northern Ireland Department and that any Northern Ireland relevant payment required to be made to that Department by reference thereto is to be paid to the Secretary of State as its agent; and

(ii) shall be taken to include such a Northern Ireland certificate; and

(c) any payment made by the Northern Ireland compensator to the Secretary of State in pursuance of such a certificate shall be applied—

(i) first towards discharging his liability under this Part of this Act; and

(ii) then, as respects any remaining balance, towards discharging his liability under the Northern Ireland provisions,

in respect of the relevant victim and that accident, injury or disease.

(5) For the purposes of subsection (1) above, "the relevant part of Great Britain", in relation to a compensator, means—

(a) if the compensator has been notified in writing—

(i) by or on behalf of the victim, or

(ii) if the victim has died, by or on behalf of the intended recipient,

that the victim is or was at any time resident at an address in any part of Great Britain, that part of Great Britain (or, if more than one such notification has been given, the part in which he was so notified that the victim was most recently so resident); or

(b) in any other case, such part of Great Britain as the Secretary of State may determine in accordance with regulations.

(6) In this section—

"Northern Ireland certificate" means a certificate of total benefit, within the meaning of the Northern Ireland provisions;

"Northern Ireland compensation payment" means a compensation payment, within the meaning of the Northern Ireland provisions, and includes a payment which would be such a payment if the person making it were resident or had a place of business in Northern Ireland;

"Northern Ireland compensator" means a compensator, within the meaning of the Northern Ireland provisions, and includes a person who would be such a compensator if he were resident or had a place of business in Northern Ireland;

"the Northern Ireland intended recipient" means the intended recipient, within the meaning of the Northern Ireland provisions, in relation to a Northern Ireland compensation payment;

"the Northern Ireland provisions" means—

(a) any legislation corresponding to this Part (other than this section) and having effect in Northern Ireland; and

(b) this section;

"Northern Ireland relevant payment" means a relevant payment within the meaning of the Northern Ireland provisions;

"Northern Ireland victim" means a person who is the victim, within the meaning of the Northern Ireland provisions, in relation to a Northern Ireland compensation payment;

"the relevant victim" means the person who is the victim or the Northern Ireland victim (or both), as the case may be.

DEFINITIONS
"certificate of total benefit": s.81.
"compensation payment": *ibid.*
"compensator": *ibid.*

"intended recipient": *ibid.*
"victim": *ibid.*

GENERAL NOTE
See the note to s.81.

Foreign compensators: duties of intended recipient

102.—(1) Where, immediately before the making of the compensation payment, the compensator is not resident and does not have a place of business in any part of the United Kingdom, any deduction, payment or other thing which would, apart from this section, fall to be made or done under this Part of this Act by the compensator shall instead be made or done by the intended recipient and references to the compensator shall be construed accordingly.

(2) The Secretary of State may by regulations make such provision as he considers expedient for the purpose of modifying this Part of this Act in its application in such a case.

DEFINITIONS
"compensation payment": s.81.
"compensator": *ibid.*
"intended recipient": *ibid.*

GENERAL NOTE
See the note to s.81.

Interest on damages: reductions in respect of relevant payments

103. In assessing the amount of interest payable in respect of an award of damages, the amount of the award shall be treated as reduced by a sum equal to the amount of the relevant payment (if any) required to be made in connection with the payment of the damages and—
  (a) in England and Wales, if both special and general damages are awarded, any such reductions shall be treated as made first against the special damages and then, as respects any remaining balance, against the general damages; and
  (b) in Scotland, if damages are awarded both for patrimonial loss and for solatium, any such reductions shall be treated as made first against the damages for patrimonial loss and then, as respects any remaining balance, against the damages for solatium.

DEFINITIONS
"relevant payment": s.81.

GENERAL NOTE
See the note to s.81.

[¹The Crown

104. This Part of this Act applies in relation to the making of a compensation payment by the Crown as it applies in relation to the making of a compensation payment by any other compensator.]

AMENDMENT
  1. Omitted until s.27 of the Social Security Act 1989 is brought into force: Social Security (Consequential Provisions) Act 1992, Sched. 4, paras. 1 and 13.

PART V

INCOME SUPPORT AND THE DUTY TO MAINTAIN

Failure to maintain—general

105.—(1) If—
  (a) any person persistently refuses or neglects to maintain himself or any person whom he is liable to maintain; and

   (b) in consequence of his refusal or neglect income support is paid to or in respect of him or such a person,
he shall be guilty of an offence and liable on summary conviction to imprisonment for a term not exceeding 3 months or to a fine of an amount not exceeding level 4 on the standard scale or to both.

(2) For the purposes of subsection (1) above a person shall not be taken to refuse or neglect to maintain himself or any other person by reason only of anything done or omitted in furtherance of a trade dispute.

(3) Subsections (6) to (9) of section 78 above shall have effect for the purposes of this Part of this Act as they have effect for the purposes of that section.

GENERAL NOTE

Subs. (1)

The criminal offence created by subs. (1) of refusing or neglecting to maintain oneself is at first sight rather extraordinary, but it is only committed if as a consequence income support is paid. Prosecution is very much a last resort after the ordinary sanctions against voluntary unemployment have been used. In 1984/5 there were none (NACRO, Enforcement of the Law Relating to Social Security, para. 8.6). Prosecution of those who refuse or neglect to maintain others is more common.

Liability to maintain

Under subs. (3), liability to maintain another person for the purposes of Pt. V is tested according to s.78(6)–(9). Both men and women are liable to maintain their spouses and children. The definition of child goes beyond the usual meaning in s.137 of the Contributions and Benefits Act of a person under 16 to include those under 19 who count as a dependant in someone else's income support entitlement (s.78(6)(d)). The effect of the reference in s.78(4) to s.1 of the Family Law Reform Act 1987 is that in determining whether a person is the father or mother of a child it is irrelevant whether the person was married to the other parent at the time of the birth or not. If a married couple divorce, their liability to maintain each other ceases for the purposes of Pt. V, but the obligation to maintain their children remains. This, then, is the remnant of the old family means-test that used to extend much wider until the Poor Law was finally "abolished" by the National Assistance Act 1948. For the enforcement of this liability, see ss.106–108, and, for a criminal offence, subs. (1).

Section 78(6)(c) was new in 1980. In *R. v. West London Supplementary Benefits Appeal Tribunal*, ex p. *Clarke* [1975] 1 W.L.R. 1396, SB7, the court had held that the sponsor of an immigrant was under no obligation to maintain the immigrant for supplementary benefit purposes. This position is now reversed, and s.78(9) provides for conclusive certificates of an undertaking to maintain to be produced. The liability to maintain is enforced under s.106. The SBC policy struck down in *Clarke's* case had deemed the immigrant to be receiving the support from his sponsor even where it was not forthcoming. This is not now the case. It is only a resource when actually received.

Recovery of expenditure on benefit from person liable for maintenance

106.—(1) Subject to the following provisions of this section, if income support is claimed by or in respect of a person whom another person is liable to maintain or paid to or in respect of such a person, the Secretary of State may make a complaint against the liable person to a magistrates' court for an order under this section.

(2) On the hearing of a complaint under this section the court shall have regard to all the circumstances and, in particular, to the income of the liable person, and may order him to pay such sum, weekly or otherwise, as it may consider appropriate, except that in a case falling within section 78(6)(c) above that sum shall not include any amount which is not attributable to income support (whether paid before or after the making of the order).

(3) In determining whether to order any payments to be made in respect of income support for any period before the complaint was made, or the amount of any such payments, the court shall disregard any amount by

which the liable person's income exceeds the income which was his during that period.

(4) Any payments ordered to be made under this section shall be made—

(a) to the Secretary of State in so far as they are attributable to any income support (whether paid before or after the making of the order);

(b) to the person claiming income support or (if different) the dependant; or

(c) to such other person as appears to the court expedient in the interests of the dependant.

(5) An order under this section shall be enforceable as a magistrates' court maintenance order within the meaning of section 150(1) of the Magistrates' Courts Act 1980.

(6) In the application of this section to Scotland, subsection (5) above shall be omitted and for the references to a complaint and to a magistrates' court there shall be substituted respectively references to an application and to the sheriff.

(7) On an application under subsection (1) above a court in Scotland may make a finding as to the parentage of a child for the purpose of establishing whether a person is, for the purposes of section 105 above and this section, liable to maintain him.

DEFINITIONS
"child": ss.105(3) and 78(6)(b).

GENERAL NOTE
This section gives the DSS an independent right to enforce the liability to maintain in s.78(6), which now covers both spouses and children, by an order in the magistrates' court, provided that income support has been claimed or paid for the person sought to be maintained. Note that from April 1993 the Child Support Act 1991 will introduce an entirely new system of determining and enforcing liability to maintain children, through the Child Support Agency.

Spouses
The usual procedure was last described in detail in Chapter 13 of the Supplementary Benefits Handbook (1984 ed.) and will presumably continue to apply, since it is repeated in essence in the DSS Guide to Income Support, although there have recently been some administrative changes. The most common situation is where a breakdown of marriage leads to separation or divorce and the woman claims income support. The same procedures can apply if it is the man who claims benefit. If there has already been a divorce then there is no liability to maintain between the ex-spouses, although there still is for children, and the amount of any court order for maintenance will be relevant to the calculation of income. If there has merely been a separation, the wife is entitled to benefit as a single person, but there will be an investigation of the circumstances to ensure that the separation is genuine. If the husband is already paying maintenance under a court order or the wife has taken proceedings herself which are reasonably advanced, no approach to the husband will be made by the DSS. Otherwise, the wife will be asked for information about the whereabouts of the liable relative (although producing the information cannot be made a condition of receiving benefit) and he will be contacted as soon as possible. The husband is asked to pay as much as he can, if possible enough to remove the need for income support to be paid to the wife and any children.

In deciding what level of payment is acceptable on a voluntary basis, the DHSS used a formula which was first revealed in the Report of the Finer Committee on One-Parent Families (Cmnd. 5629, paras. 4.188–4.189) and is most recently described in para. 13.10 of the Handbook. The supplementary benefit scale rates for the man and any partner or children living with him were taken, plus full rent or mortgage payments (including capital), plus rates. To this was added a margin of £5 or a quarter of the new family's net income (the £5 appeared in the Finer Report, but is obviously out of date and is not mentioned in the Handbook). The excess over this figure was regarded as available to be used for maintenance, but the Handbook emphasised that the excess was to be used only as a basis for discussion and that payment of a lesser amount might be agreed, if there were special expenses. Thus if the man himself were receiving supplementary benefit he would not be expected to pay anything.

It is assumed that a similar approach, substituting income support applicable amounts, plus net housing costs (after deducting any housing benefit or income support for such costs), will be applied now.

If the husband is unwilling to make a payment voluntarily, although the DSS believe that he has sufficient income, then legal proceedings may be considered. The first step will be to see if the wife will take action. The official policy is that the wife will merely be advised on the advantages of taking proceedings herself (that she may get enough maintenance to lift her off benefit and that an order for maintenance will continue if she ceases to be entitled to income support, as by working full-time). The first advantage is likely to be real in only a small minority of cases and the force of the second has been reduced by the introduction of the procedure in s.107(3)–(14). The choice should be left entirely to the woman, although staff have recently been instructed to stress the advantages of reflecting the husband's responsibilities in the maintenance arrangements, especially if children are involved. A wife may of course take proceedings herself even though the DSS have accepted voluntary payments from the husband.

The courts have refused to adopt the "liable relative formula" in private proceedings by wives or ex-wives (*Shallow* v. *Shallow* [1979] Fam. 1) and will only have regard to the man's subsistence level. By this they mean the ordinary scale rates of benefit plus housing costs. A more realistic approach may have been presaged by *Allen* v. *Allen* [1986] 2 F.L.R. 265, where the Court of Appeal used the long-term scale rate (now disappeared) as a yardstick. In *Delaney* v. *Delaney* [1990] 2 F.L.R. 457, the Court of Appeal accepted the principle that where the man had insufficient resources after taking account of his reasonable commitments to a new family properly to maintain his former wife and family, a maintenance order should not financially cripple him where the wife is entitled to social security benefits. But no calculation of the man's income support level was made.

If the wife does not take proceedings, then the DSS may. The court is to have regard to all the circumstances, in particular the husband's resources, and may order him to pay whatever sum is appropriate (subs. (2)). Presumably, the same principles will govern the amount of an order as in a private application. There are some new provisions in s.107(1) in cases where the order includes amounts for children, but it is not at all clear how these interact with the general test of appropriateness under subs. (2). The wife's adultery or desertion or other conduct is only a factor to be taken into account, not a bar to any order. Nor is the existence of a separation agreement under which the wife agrees not to claim maintenance a bar (*National Assistance Board* v. *Parkes* [1955] 2 Q.B. 506). Although *Hulley* v. *Thompson* [1981] 1 W.L.R. 159 concerned only the liability to maintain children, because there had been a divorce, it showed that not even a consent order, under which the man transferred the matrimonial home to his ex-wife and she agreed to receive no maintenance for herself or the children, barred the statutory liability to maintain the children. However, it seems that the existence of the order could be taken into account in deciding what amount it is appropriate for the man to pay.

Proceedings by the DSS are relatively rare. In 1979 there were only 431 (SBC Annual Report for 1979 (Cmnd. 8033), para. 8.30).

Unmarried and divorced parents

The position of an unmarried mother is in many ways the same as that of a divorced wife. She is entitled to income support as a single person. Payments from the father of her child only affect her benefit when they are actually received. Equally, a father who has care of children may receive payments from the mother. The procedure to be adopted by the DSS was described in detail in the Supplementary Benefits Handbook (1984 ed.), paras. 13.13–13.19 and will presumably continue under income support. The woman will be approached after the birth of the child if it is clear that it is not being offered for adoption and benefit is likely to be paid for some time. If she is already receiving maintenance for her child or her own proceedings are reasonably far advanced, information will only be requested about amounts for the calculation of resources. Otherwise, information about the father will be requested, although the Handbook emphasised that it should be made clear that her benefit will continue if she does not give the information. "Provided that the mother has no objection to an approach being made" (para. 13.16) the alleged father will be contacted. If he is willing to meet the full amount of benefit for the child or pay what the DSS considers reasonable (using the "liable relative formula"—see above) payments will be accepted on a voluntary basis. If the man denies paternity or refuses to make payments, then proceedings will be discussed. No pressure should be put on the mother to take her own proceedings, but the advantages of her doing so will now be stressed. If the DSS take their own action, she will be asked for information about her relationship with the alleged father and what evidence she can produce to support the allegation of paternity. Once again it is stressed that she does not have to provide such information, although the "normal expectation" is that she will. The policy is thus that no pressure at all should be put on the woman, as was admittedly the case in the past. But everything will depend on how the policy is actually operated, when the appearance of pressure in an emotionally fraught situation may be very subtle. The White Paper *Children Come First* (Cm. 1264) made a controversial proposal to reduce a lone parent's benefit if she declines to take maintenance proceedings or to provide information to the DSS (para. 5.33), which has been incorporated in the Child Support Act 1991. The provision will come into operation in April 1993.

See the discussion above under *Spouses* for the court's approach to the level of an order to be made, and s.107(1) for some other factors.

Not many actions are brought by the DSS (519 in 1979: SBC Annual Report for 1979 (Cmnd. 8033), para. 8.20.). The DSS's right to an order is independent of that of the mother (*National Assistance Board* v. *Mitchell* [1956] 1 Q.B. 53, *National Assistance Board* v. *Tugby* [1957] 1 Q.B. 506). It does not matter even that the mother's own action has been dismissed for insufficient evidence (*Clapham* v. *National Assistance Board* [1961] 2 Q.B. 77). See also *Hulley* v. *Thompson* [1981] 1 W.L.R. 159, under *Spouses* above.

Recovery of expenditure on income support: additional amounts and transfer of orders

107.—(1) In any case where—

(a) the claim for income support referred to in section 106(1) above is or was made by the parent of one or more children in respect of both himself and those children; and

(b) the other parent is liable to maintain those children but, by virtue of not being the claimant's husband or wife, is not liable to maintain the claimant,

the sum which the court may order that other parent to pay under subsection (2) of that section may include an amount, determined in accordance with regulations, in respect of any income support paid to or for the claimant by virtue of such provisions as may be prescribed.

(2) Where the sum which a court orders a person to pay under section 106 above includes by virtue of subsection (1) above an amount (in this section referred to as a "personal allowance element") in respect of income support by virtue of paragraph 1(2) of Schedule 2 to the Income Support (General) Regulations 1987 (personal allowance for lone parent) the order shall separately identify the amount of the personal allowance element.

(3) In any case where—

(a) there is in force an order under subsection (2) of section 106 above made against a person ("the liable parent") who is the parent of one or more children, in respect of the other parent or the children; and

(b) payments under the order fall to be made to the Secretary of State by virtue of subsection (4)(a) of that section; and

(c) that other parent ("the dependent parent") ceases to claim income support,

the Secretary of State may, by giving notice in writing to the court which made the order and to the liable parent and the dependent parent, transfer to the dependent parent the right to receive the payments under the order, exclusive of any personal allowance element, and to exercise the relevant rights in relation to the order, except so far as relating to that element.

(4) Notice under subsection (3) above shall not be given (and if purportedly given, shall be of no effect) at a time when there is in force a maintenance order made against the liable parent—

(a) in favour of the dependent parent or one or more of the children; or

(b) in favour of some other person for the benefit of the dependent parent or one or more of the children;

and if such a maintenance order is made at any time after notice under that subsection has been given, the order under section 106(2) above shall cease to have effect.

(5) In any case where—

(a) notice is given to a magistrates' court under subsection (3) above,

(b) payments under the order are required to be made by any method of payment falling within section 59(6) of the Magistrates' Courts Act 1980 (standing order, etc.), and

(c) the clerk to the justices for the petty sessions area for which the court is acting decides that payment by that method is no longer possible,

the clerk shall amend the order to provide that payments under the order shall be made by the liable parent to the clerk.

(6) Except as provided by subsections (8) and (12) below, where the Secretary of State gives notice under subsection (3) above, he shall cease to be entitled—

(a) to receive any payment under the order in respect of any personal allowance element; or

(b) to exercise the relevant rights, so far as relating to any such element,

notwithstanding that the dependent parent does not become entitled to receive any payment in respect of that element or to exercise the relevant rights so far as so relating.

(7) If, in a case where the Secretary of State gives notice under subsection (3) above, a payment under the order is or has been made to him wholly or partly in respect of the whole or any part of the period beginning with the day on which the transfer takes effect and ending with the day on which the notice under subsection (3) above is given to the liable parent, the Secretary of State shall—

(a) repay to or for the liable parent so much of the payment as is referable to any personal allowance element in respect of that period or, as the case may be, the part of it in question; and

(b) pay to or for the dependent parent so much of any remaining balance of the payment as is referable to that period or part;

and a payment under paragraph (b) above shall be taken to discharge, to that extent, the liability of the liable parent to the dependent parent under the order in respect of that period or part.

(8) If, in a case where the Secretary of State has given notice under subsection (3) above, the dependent parent makes a further claim for income support, then—

(a) the Secretary of State may, by giving a further notice in writing to the court which made the order and to the liable parent and the dependent parent, transfer back from the dependent parent to himself the right to receive the payments and to exercise the relevant rights; and

(b) that transfer shall revive the Secretary of State's right to receive payment under the order in respect of any personal allowance element and to exercise the relevant rights so far as relating to any such element.

(9) Subject to subsections (10) and (11) below, in any case where—

(a) notice is given to a magistrates' court under subsection (8) above, and

(b) the method of payment under the order which subsists immediately before the day on which the transfer under subsection (8) above takes effect differs from the method of payment which subsisted immediately before the day on which the transfer under subsection (3) above (or, if there has been more than one such transfer, the last such transfer) took effect,

the clerk to the justices for the petty sessions area for which the court is acting shall amend the order by reinstating the method of payment under the order which subsisted immediately before the day on which the transfer under subsection (3) above (or, as the case may be, the last such transfer) took effect.

(10) The clerk shall not amend the order under subsection (9) above if the Secretary of State gives notice in writing to the clerk, on or before the day on which the notice under subsection (8) above is given, that the method of payment under the order which subsists immediately before the day on which the transfer under subsection (8) above takes effect is to continue.

(11) In any case where—
(a) notice is given to a magistrates' court under subsection (8) above,
(b) the method of payment under the order which subsisted immediately before the day on which the transfer under subsection (3) above (or, if there has been more than one such transfer, the last such transfer) took effect was any method of payment falling within section 59(6) of the Magistrates' Courts Act 1980 (standing order, etc.), and
(c) the clerk decides that payment by that method is no longer possible,
the clerk shall amend the order to provide that payments under the order shall be made by the liable parent to the clerk.

(12) A transfer under subsection (3) or (8) above does not transfer or otherwise affect the right of any person—
(a) to receive a payment which fell due to him at a time before the transfer took effect; or
(b) to exercise the relevant rights in relation to any such payment;
and, where notice is given under subsection (3), subsection (6) above does not deprive the Secretary of State of his right to receive such a payment in respect of any personal allowance element or to exercise the relevant rights in relation to such a payment.

(13) For the purposes of this section—
(a) a transfer under subsection (3) above takes effect on the day on which the dependent parent ceases to be in receipt of income support in consequence of the cessation referred to in paragraph (c) of that subsection, and
(b) a transfer under subsection (8) above takes effect on—
    (i) the first day in respect of which the dependent parent receives income support after the transfer under subsection (3) above took effect, or
    (ii) such later day as may be specified for the purpose in the notice under subsection (8),
irrespective of the day on which notice under the subsection in question is given.

(14) Any notice required to be given to the liable parent under subsection (3) or (8) above shall be taken to have been given if it has been sent to his last known address.

(15) In this section—
"child" means a person under the age of 16, notwithstanding section 78(6)(d) above;
"court" shall be construed in accordance with section 106 above;
"maintenance order"—
    (a) in England and Wales, means—
        (i) any order for the making of periodical payments or for the payment of a lump sum which is, or has at any time been, a maintenance order within the meaning of the Attachment of Earnings Act 1971;
        (ii) any order under Part III of the Matrimonial and Family Proceedings Act 1984 (overseas divorce) for the making of periodical payments or for the payment of a lump sum;
    (b) in Scotland, has the meaning assigned by section 106 of the Debtors (Scotland) Act 1987, but disregarding paragraph (h) (alimentary bond or agreement);
"the relevant rights", in relation to an order under section 106(2) above, means the right to bring any proceedings, take any steps or do any other thing under or in relation to the order which the Secretary of State could have brought, taken or done apart from any transfer under this section.

GENERAL NOTE

The predecessors of this section and s.108 formed one of the central strategic objectives of the Social Security Act 1990 (*Hansard*, H.C. Vol. 170, col. 1137, April 3, 1990 (Tony Newton); *Hansard*, H.L. Vol. 518, col. 234, April 20, 1990 (Lord Henley)), but were only introduced at the Report stage in the Commons. They therefore received relatively little Parliamentary discussion due to the operation of the guillotine. The Government has carried out a general review of the maintenance system, based on a survey of work in U.K. courts and DSS offices and study of overseas systems, and has produced radical proposals in *Children Come First* (Cm. 1264). These proposals have been embodied in the Child Support Act 1991, which is due to come into operation in April 1993. Action had already been taken to tighten up the assessment of an absent parent's ability to pay maintenance for his family on income support. The new provisions are regarded as desirable in the short term to improve the effectiveness of the present system, pending the more radical reform (*Hansard*, H.C. Vol. 170, col. 566).

Section 107 contains two elements. The first relates to the situation where a lone parent is receiving income support, but the absent parent of the child(ren) is not liable to maintain the parent under s.78(6) because the parents are not or are no longer married. Where the DSS seeks its own order against the absent parent, courts are empowered to take into account income support relating to the lone parent in calculating the amount to be paid for the child(ren) and the DSS may of course take this into account in negotiating voluntary agreements. The second is to allow a DSS order to be transferred to the lone parent when that person comes off income support, rather than the lone parent having to obtain a separate private maintenance order.

Subss. (1) and (2)

These provisions comprise the first element identified above. They apply when both of conditions (a) and (b) in subs. (1) are satisfied. Under para. (a), s.106 gives the DSS power to obtain an order against a person who is liable to maintain a claimant of income support or a person included in the family for claiming purposes. Section 78(6) defines liability to maintain for this purpose. There is a liability to maintain a spouse and any children. Under s.78(6)(d) "child" includes a person aged 16 to 18 (inclusive) who is still a member of the claimant's family for income support purposes (*e.g.* because still in full-time education). However, subs. (15) provides that for the purposes of s.107 "child" is restricted to a person under the age of 16. Thus, lone parent claimants whose children are all over 15 will fall outside this provision. Under para. (b) the absent parent must not be married to the lone parent, so that the obligation to maintain under s.78(6) is only in respect of the child(ren). If both these conditions are met, a court may include whatever amount the regulations determine in respect of the income support paid for the lone parent. The Income Support (Liable Relatives) Regulations 1990 specify in general the children's personal allowances, family premium, lone parent premium, disabled child premium and the carer premium in respect of care for a child.

The intention was said to be that the regulation-making power "will be used to specify that once having looked at the allowances and premiums that are paid because there are children, the court should also have regard to the income support personal allowance paid for the mother" (*Hansard*, H.C. Vol. 170, col. 567, March 28, 1990). The Liable Relatives Regulations provide that if the liable parent has the means to pay in addition to the amounts already specified, a court order may include some or all of the dependent parent's personal allowance.

It is said that in a private maintenance order for children the court can take account of the parent's care costs and that social security law is thus being brought into line with family law. However, there is nothing as specific as s.107 in family law. The existing power of the court on orders sought by the DSS is already wide and it is not clear how much real difference the new powers will make. Under s.106(2) the court may order payment of such sum as it may consider appropriate. The assumption seems to be that not only could the personal allowance for a child under 16 be considered under this provision, but also the family premium (paid to all claimants with a child or young person (16–18) in the family) and the additional lone-parent premium. If such amounts can be considered under the existing law (and they might be considered to reflect the care costs of the lone parent) there seems no reason why the court could not also consider some part of the parent's personal allowance if that was considered "appropriate". However, subs. (1) and the Liable Relatives Regulations make the position clear, which should be an advantage.

It is notable that the court retains a discretion as to what amounts to consider and that the overriding factor under s.106(2) is what is appropriate. Under para. 1 of Sched. 2 to the Income

Support (General) Regulations 1987 (S.I. 1987 No. 1967) the personal allowance for a lone parent aged under 18 or over 24 is the same as for a single person with no dependants. There is only a difference (£8.75 p.w. in April 1992) for those aged 18 to 24.

Subsection (2) provides that if the lone parent's personal allowance under Sched. 2 is covered by the order, this element must be separately identified. This has no bearing on subs. (1), but is relevant to the procedure set up by subss. (3)–(14).

Subss. (3)–(15)

These provisions contain the important procedure allowing the transfer of a DSS order to the lone parent on coming off income support. The conditions for transfer under subs. (3) are that in such a case (remembering that "child" is defined to cover only those under 16 (subs. (15)) the Secretary of State gives notice to the court which made the order and to both the parents. Then the right to enforce or apply for variation of the order (apart from any personal allowance element identified under subs. (2)) is transferred to the lone parent (known as "the dependent parent"). Thus, the personal allowance element, which is of no net benefit to the lone parent while she is on income support, is removed at the point when its value would actually be felt by the lone parent. The DSS can no longer enforce the personal allowance element of the order (subs. (6)). Under subs. (13)(a) the transfer takes effect on the day on which the dependent parent ceases to receive income support in consequence of ceasing to claim. This is a peculiar way of putting things. If the dependent parent's circumstances change (*e.g.* her capital goes over the cut-off limit or she starts full-time work) her entitlement to income support may be terminated on review by the AO under s.25. She may well then choose not to claim income support again, as it would be a useless exercise. The dependent parent could with some strain be said to cease to claim income support and so to satisfy subs. (3)(c), but the cessation of receipt of income support is not in consequence of the cessation of claiming but of the review and revision by the AO.

Subsection (3) is not to apply if a private maintenance order (see subs. (15) for definition) is in existence, and if the dependent parent obtains one after a transfer, the right to enforce the DSS order disappears (subs. (4)).

If, after a transfer, the dependent parent makes another claim for income support (presumably only while still having children under 16), the Secretary of State may by giving notice to all parties retransfer to the DSS the right to enforce the order and revive the personal allowance element on the dependent parent becoming entitled to income support (subss. (8) and (13)(b)). Presumably, the revival of the personal allowance element depends on the conditions of subss. (1) and (2) being met at the date of revival.

Reduction of expenditure on income support: certain maintenance orders to be enforceable by the Secretary of State

108.—(1) This section applies where—
(a) a person ("the claimant") who is the parent of one or more children is in receipt of income support either in respect of those children or in respect of both himself and those children; and
(b) there is in force a maintenance order made against the other parent ("the liable person")—
    (i) in favour of the claimant or one or more of the children, or
    (ii) in favour of some other person for the benefit of the claimant or one or more of the children;
and in this section "the primary recipient" means the person in whose favour that maintenance order was made.

(2) If, in a case where this section applies, the liable person fails to comply with any of the terms of the maintenance order—
(a) the Secretary of State may bring any proceedings or take any other steps to enforce the order that could have been brought or taken by or on behalf of the primary recipient; and
(b) any court before which proceedings are brought by the Secretary of State by virtue of paragraph (a) above shall have the same powers in connection with those proceedings as it would have had if they had been brought by the primary recipient.

(3) The Secretary of State's powers under this section are exercisable at his discretion and whether or not the primary recipient or any other person consents to their exercise; but any sums recovered by virtue of this section

shall be payable to or for the primary recipient, as if the proceedings or steps in question had been brought or taken by him or on his behalf.

(4) The powers conferred on the Secretary of State by subsection (2)(a) above include power—

    (a) to apply for the registration of the maintenance order under—

        (i) section 17 of the Maintenance Orders Act 1950;

        (ii) section 2 of the Maintenance Orders Act 1958; or

        (iii) the Civil Jurisdiction and Judgments Act 1982; and

    (b) to make an application under section 2 of the Maintenance Orders (Reciprocal Enforcement) Act 1972 (application for enforcement in reciprocating country).

(5) Where this section applies, the prescribed person shall in prescribed circumstances give the Secretary of State notice of any application—

    (a) to alter, vary, suspend, discharge, revoke, revive or enforce the maintenance order in question; or

    (b) to remit arrears under that maintenance order;

and the Secretary of State shall be entitled to appear and be heard on the application.

(6) Where, by virtue of this section, the Secretary of State commences any proceedings to enforce a maintenance order, he shall, in relation to those proceedings, be treated for the purposes of any enactment or instrument relating to maintenance orders as if he were a person entitled to payment under the maintenance order in question (but shall not thereby become entitled to any such payment).

(7) Where, in any proceedings under this section in England and Wales, the court makes an order for the whole or any part of the arrears due under the maintenance order in question to be paid as a lump sum, the Secretary of State shall inform the Legal Aid Board of the amount of that lump sum if he knows—

    (a) that the primary recipient either—

        (i) received legal aid under the Legal Aid Act 1974 in connection with the proceedings in which the maintenance order was made, or

        (ii) was an assisted party, within the meaning of the Legal Aid Act 1988, in those proceedings; and

    (b) that a sum remains unpaid on account of the contribution required of the primary recipient—

        (i) under section 9 of the Legal Aid Act 1974 in respect of those proceedings, or

        (ii) under section 16 of the Legal Aid Act 1988 in respect of the costs of his being represented under Part IV of that Act in those proceedings,

        as the case may be.

(8) In this section "maintenance order" has the same meaning as it has in section 107 above but does not include any such order for the payment of a lump sum.

GENERAL NOTE

Section 108 enables the DSS to enforce certain private maintenance orders in favour of lone-parent claimants of income support. Only lone parents are covered by subs. (1)(a), and not mere separated or divorced spouses, but the maintenance order may be in favour either of the parent or the child(ren) or both. The Secretary of State may at his discretion and without the consent of the lone parent take steps (including those specified in subs. (5)) to enforce the order as if he were the person entitled to payment under the order (subss. (2), (3) and (6)). Any sums recovered, however, are payable to the primary recipient under the order (subss. (3) and (6)). Under subs. (5), regulations may specify who has to inform the DSS of applications to vary, suspend, etc., the private order, or to remit arrears. Regulation 3 of the Income Support (Liable Relatives) Regulations 1990 specifies various court officials. The Secretary of State is given the right to be heard on any such application, but has no power to make such an application, *e.g.* to increase the amount of an order. This is because subs. (2) only operates when there is a failure to comply with the terms (*i.e.* the existing terms) of the order.

Subsection (7) requires the Secretary of State to inform the Legal Aid Board when a lump sum of arrears is to be paid, when the Board might be able to recover a contribution out of the lump sum.

Overall, s.108 is a powerful weapon for the DSS to enforce the payment of maintenance orders. If the lone parent has her own order, which is not being paid, income support will make up the shortfall. There is thus no great incentive for the lone parent to go through all the inconvenience of enforcement, and there may be other circumstances making her reluctant to take action. The DSS will have no such inhibitions.

The Secretary of State predicted that the amount of maintenance recovered by the DSS in respect of lone parents on income support would rise to about £260 million in 1990–91, having gone up from £155 million in 1988–89 to £180 million in 1989–90 (*Hansard*, H.C. Vol. 170, col. 571, March 28, 1990). The predicted increase was partly based on the provisions now contained in ss.107 and 108 and partly on giving greater priority and resources to such work, with changes in the administrative guidance. These changes are to point up the need to stress to lone parents on benefits the advantages of reflecting the absent parent's proper responsibilities in the maintenance arrangements from the outset and also to indicate that the "normal expectation" should be that a lone parent will co-operate in establishing where responsibility lies. It is, however, recognised that there may be circumstances in which lone parents will not wish to name the father of a child. The White Paper *Children Come First* proposes reductions in the lone parent's benefit if she declines without good cause to take maintenance proceedings. See now the Child Support Act 1991, due to come into operation in April 1993.

Diversion of arrested earnings to Secretary of State—Scotland

109.—(1) Where in Scotland a creditor who is enforcing a maintenance order or alimentary bond or agreement by a current maintenance arrestment or a conjoined arrestment order is in receipt of income support, the creditor may in writing authorise the Secretary of State to receive any sums payable under the arrestment or order until the creditor ceases to be in receipt of income support or in writing withdraws the authorisation, whichever occurs first.

(2) On intimation by the Secretary of State—

(a) to the employer operating the current maintenance arrestment; or

(b) to the sheriff clerk operating the conjoined arrestment order;

of an authorisation under subsection (1) above, the employer or sheriff clerk shall, until notified by the Secretary of State that the authorisation has ceased to have effect, pay to the Secretary of State any sums which would otherwise be payable under the arrestment or order to the creditor.

PART VI

ENFORCEMENT

Inspection and offences

Appointment and powers of inspectors

110.—(1) For the purposes of the Acts to which this section applies the Secretary of State may appoint such inspectors, and pay to them such salaries or remuneration, as he may determine with the consent of the Treasury.

(2) An inspector appointed under this section shall, for the purposes of the execution of those Acts have the following powers—

(a) to enter at all reasonable times any premises liable to inspection under this section;

(b) to make such examination and inquiry as may be necessary—

(i) for ascertaining whether the provisions of the Acts are being, or have been, complied with in any such premises; or

(ii) for investigating the circumstances in which any accident, injury or disease which has given or may give rise to a claim for industrial injuries benefit, or for any benefit which is a relevant benefit, occurred or may have occurred, or was or may have been received or contracted;

(c) to examine, either alone or in the presence of any other person, as he thinks fit, in relation to any matters under the Acts on which he may reasonably require information, every person whom he finds in any such premises or whom he has reasonable cause to believe to be or to have been a person liable to pay—

    (i) contributions under Part I of the Contributions and Benefits Act; or

    (ii) a state scheme premium; or

    (iii) a compensation payment or a relevant payment,

and to require every such person to be so examined;

(d) to exercise such other powers as may be necessary for carrying the Acts into effect.

(3) The premises liable to inspection under this section are any where an inspector has reasonable grounds for supposing that—

(a) any persons are employed; or

(b) there is being carried on any agency or other business for the introduction or supply to persons requiring them of persons available to do work or to perform services; or

(c) a personal or occupational pension scheme is being administered; or

(d) any person—

    (i) who is the compensator in relation to any such accident, injury or disease as is referred to in subsection (2)(b)(ii) above; or

    (ii) on whose behalf any such compensator has or may have made, or may make, a compensation payment,

carries on business or is to be found,

but do not include any private dwelling-house not used by, or by permission of, the occupier for the purposes of a trade or business.

(4) Every inspector shall be furnished with a certificate of his appointment, and on applying for admission to any premises for the purpose of the Acts shall, if so required, produce the certificate.

(5) Where any premises are liable to be inspected by an inspector or officer appointed or employed by, or are under the control of, some other government department, the Secretary of State may make arrangements with that department for any of the powers or duties of inspectors under this section to be carried out by an inspector or officer employed by that department.

(6) In accordance with this section, persons shall furnish to an inspector all such information, and produce for his inspection all such documents, as he may reasonably require for the purpose of ascertaining—

(a) whether—

    (i) any contribution under Part I of the Contributions and Benefits Act; or

    (ii) any state scheme premium; or

    (iii) any compensation payment or relevant payment,

is or has been payable, or has been duly paid, by or in respect of any person; or

(b) whether benefit is or was payable to or in respect of any person.

(7) The following persons are under the duty imposed by subsection (6) above—

(a) the occupier of any premises liable to inspection under this section;

(b) any person who is or has been an employer or an employee within the meaning of any provision of the Contributions and Benefits Act;

(c) any person carrying on an agency or other business for the introduction or supply to persons requiring them of persons available to do work or to perform services;

(d) any person who is or has at any time been a trustee or manager of a personal or occupational pension scheme;

(e) any person who is or has been liable—

(i) to pay contributions or state scheme premiums; or

(ii) to make any compensation payment or relevant payment;

(f) the servants or agents of any such person as is specified in any of the preceding paragraphs,

but no one shall be required under this section to answer any questions or to give evidence tending to incriminate himself or, in the case of a person who is married, his or her spouse.

(8) This section applies to the following Acts—

(a) the Social Security Act 1973;

(b) the Contributions and Benefits Act;

(c) this Act;

(d) the Pensions Act; and

(e) Part I of the 1986 Act.

(9) In this section "relevant benefit" and "relevant payment" mean a relevant benefit and relevant payment within the meaning of Part IV of this Act.

DEFINITIONS
  "the 1986 Act": s.191.
  "the Contributions and Benefits Act": *ibid.*
  "industrial injuries benefit": *ibid.*
  "occupational pension scheme": *ibid.*
  "the Pensions Act": *ibid.*
  "personal pension scheme": *ibid.*

Delay, obstruction etc. of inspector

111.—(1) If a person—

(a) intentionally delays or obstructs an inspector in the ᴄrcise of any power under this Act; or

(b) refuses or neglects to answer any question or to furnish any information or to produce any document when required to do so under this Act,

he shall be guilty of an offence and liable on summary conviction to a fine not exceeding level 3 on the standard scale.

(2) Where a person is convicted of an offence under subsection (1)(b) above and the refusal or neglect is continued by him after his conviction, he shall be guilty of a further offence and liable on summary conviction to a fine not exceeding £40 for each day on which it is continued.

False representations for obtaining benefit etc.

112.—(1) If a person for the purpose of obtaining any benefit or other payment under the legislation to which section 110 above applies whether for himself or some other person, or for any other purpose connected with that legislation—

(a) makes a statement or representation which he knows to be false; or

(b) produces or furnishes, or knowingly causes or knowingly allows to be produced or furnished, any document or information which he knows to be false in a material particular,

he shall be guilty of an offence.

(2) A person guilty of an offence under subsection (1) above shall be liable on summary conviction to a fine not exceeding level 5 on the standard scale, or to imprisonment for a term not exceeding 3 months, or to both.

Breach of regulations

113. Regulations and schemes under any of the Acts to which section 110 above applies may provide for contravention of, or failure to comply with, any provision contained in regulations made under that Act to be an offence under that Act and for the recovery, on summary conviction of any such offence, of penalties not exceeding—

  (a) for any one offence, level 3 on the standard scale; or
  (b) for an offence of continuing any such contravention or failure after conviction, £40 for each day on which it is so continued.

Offences relating to contributions

114.—(1) If a person fails to pay, at or within the time prescribed for the purpose, any contribution which he is liable under Part I of the Contributions and Benefits Act to pay, he shall be guilty of an offence and liable on summary conviction to a fine not exceeding level 3 on the standard scale.

(2) If a person fails to pay at or within the time prescribed for the purpose any sums which he is required by regulations made by virtue of paragraph 6 of Schedule 1 to the Contributions and Benefits Act to pay, he shall be liable to be proceeded against and punished under subsection (1) above without proof of his failure so to pay any particular contribution.

(3) Subsection (1) above does not apply to Class 4 contributions recoverable by the Inland Revenue.

(4) If a person—

  (a) buys, sells or offers for sale, takes or gives in exchange, or pawns or takes in pawn a contribution card or a used contribution stamp; or
  (b) affixes a used contribution stamp to a contribution card,

he shall be guilty of an offence and liable on summary conviction to a fine not exceeding level 5 on the standard scale or to imprisonment for a term not exceeding 3 months, or to both.

(5) In any proceedings under subsection (4) above with respect to used stamps a stamp shall be deemed to have been used if it has been affixed to a contribution card or cancelled or defaced in any way whatsoever and whether or not it has actually been used for the payment of a contribution.

(6) In this Act "contribution card" means any card issued under regulations for the purpose of payment of contributions by affixing stamps to it.

DEFINITIONS
  "the Contributions and Benefits Act": s.191.
  "prescribed": *ibid.*

Offences by bodies corporate

115.—(1) Where an offence under this Act which has been committed by a body corporate is proved to have been committed with the consent or connivance of, or to be attributable to any neglect on the part of, a director, manager, secretary or other similar officer of the body corporate, or any person who was purporting to act in any such capacity, he, as well as the body corporate, shall be guilty of that offence and be liable to be proceeded against accordingly.

(2) Where the affairs of a body corporate are managed by its members, subsection (1) above applies in relation to the acts and defaults of a member in connection with his functions of management as if he were a director of the body corporate.

Legal proceedings

Legal proceedings

116.—(1) Any person authorised by the Secretary of State in that behalf may conduct any proceedings under this Act before a magistrates' court although not a barrister or solicitor.

(2) Notwithstanding anything in any Act—

(a) proceedings for an offence under this Act other than an offence relating to housing benefit or community charge benefits may be begun at any time within the period of 3 months from the date on which evidence, sufficient in the opinion of the Secretary of State to justify a prosecution for the offence, comes to his knowledge or within a period of 12 months from the commission of the offence, whichever period last expires; and

(b) proceedings for an offence under this Act relating to housing benefit or community charge benefits may be begun at any time within the period of 3 months from the date on which evidence, sufficient in the opinion of the appropriate authority to justify a prosecution for the offence, comes to the authority's knowledge or within a period of 12 months from the commission of the offence, whichever period last expires.

(3) For the purposes of subsection (2) above—

(a) a certificate purporting to be signed by or on behalf of the Secretary of State as to the date on which such evidence as is mentioned in paragraph (a) of that subsection came to his knowledge shall be conclusive evidence of that date; and

(b) a certificate of the appropriate authority as to the date on which such evidence as is mentioned in paragraph (b) of that subsection came to the authority's knowledge shall be conclusive evidence of that date.

(4) In subsections (2) and (3) above "the appropriate authority" means, in relation to an offence which relates to housing benefit and concerns any dwelling—

(a) if the offence relates to rate rebate, the authority who are the appropriate rating authority by virtue of section 134 below; and

(b) if it relates to a rent rebate, the authority who are the appropriate housing authority by virtue of that subsection; and

(c) if it relates to rent allowance, the authority who are the appropriate local authority by virtue of that subsection.

(5) In subsections (2) and (3) above "the appropriate authority" means, in relation to an offence relating to community charge benefits, such authority as is prescribed in relation to the offence.

(6) Any proceedings in respect of any act or omission of an adjudication officer which, apart from this subsection, would fall to be brought against a person appointed by virtue of section 38(1)(b) above who is resident in Northern Ireland, other than proceedings for an offence, may instead be brought against the Chief Adjudication Officer; and, for the purposes of any proceedings so brought, the acts or omissions of the adjudication officer shall be treated as the acts or omissions of the Chief Adjudication Officer.

(7) In the application of this section to Scotland, the following provisions shall have effect in substitution for subsections (1) to (5) above—

(a) proceedings for an offence under this Act may, notwithstanding anything in section 331 of the Criminal Procedure (Scotland) Act 1975, be commenced at any time within the period of 3 months from the date on which evidence, sufficient in the opinion of the Lord Advocate to justify proceedings, comes to his knowledge, or within the period of 12 months from the commission of the offence, whichever period last expires;

(b) for the purposes of this subsection—

(i) a certificate purporting to be signed by or on behalf of the Lord Advocate as to the date on which such evidence as is mentioned above came to his knowledge shall be conclusive evidence of that date; and

(ii) subsection (3) of section 331 of the said Act of 1975 (date of commencement of proceedings) shall have effect as it has effect for the purposes of that section.

Questions arising in proceedings

117.—(1) Where in any proceedings—
(a) for an offence under this Act; or
(b) involving any question as to the payment of contributions (other than a Class 4 contribution recoverable by the Inland Revenue); or
(c) for the recovery of any sums due to the Secretary of State or the National Insurance Fund,
any such question arises as is mentioned in section 17(1) above, the decision of the Secretary of State shall be conclusive for the purposes of the proceedings.
(2) If—
(a) a decision of any such question is necessary for the determination of proceedings; and
(b) the decision of the Secretary of State has not been obtained or a question has been raised with a view to a review of the decision obtained,
the question shall be referred to the Secretary of State for determination or review in accordance (subject to any necessary modifications) with Part II of this Act.
(3) Subsection (1) above does not apply if—
(a) an appeal under section 18 above is pending; or
(b) the time for appealing has not expired; or
(c) a question has been raised with a view to a review of the Secretary of State's decision under section 19 above,
and the court dealing with the case shall adjourn the proceedings until such time as a final decision on the question has been obtained.

Unpaid contributions etc.

Evidence of non-payment

118.—(1) Subsection (2) below applies with respect to any period during which, under regulations made by virtue of paragraph 5(1) of Schedule 1 to the Contributions and Benefits Act (deduction with P.A.Y.E.), contributions fall to be paid in like manner as income tax.
(2) A certificate of a collector of taxes that any amount by way of contributions which a person is liable to pay to that collector for any period has not been paid—
(a) to him; or
(b) to the best of his knowledge and belief, to any other person to whom it might lawfully be paid,
shall until the contrary is proved be sufficient evidence in any proceedings before any court that the sum mentioned in the certificate is unpaid and due.
(3) A document purporting to be such a certificate shall be deemed to be such a certificate until the contrary is proved.
(4) A statutory declaration by an officer of the Secretary of State that the searches specified in the declaration for a particular contribution card or for a record of the payment of a particular contribution have been made, and that the card in question or a record of the payment of the contribution in question has not been found, is admissible in any proceedings for an offence as evidence of the facts stated in the declaration.
(5) Nothing in subsection (4) above makes a statutory declaration admissible as evidence in proceedings for an offence except in a case where, and to the extent to which, oral evidence to the like effect would have been admissible in those proceedings.
(6) Nothing in subsections (4) and (5) above makes a statutory declaration admissible as evidence in proceedings for an offence—
(a) unless a copy of it has, not less than 7 days before the hearing or trial,

been served on the person charged with the offence in any manner in which a summons or, in Scotland, a citation in a summary prosecution may be served; or

(b) if that person, not later than 3 days before the hearing or trial or within such further time as the court may in special circumstances allow, gives notice to the prosecutor requiring the attendance at the trial of the person by whom the declaration was made.

DEFINITIONS

"contribution card": s.191.

"the Contributions and Benefits Act": *ibid.*

Recovery of unpaid contributions on prosecution

119.—(1) Where—

(a) a person has been convicted of an offence under section 114(1) above of failing to pay a contribution at or within the time prescribed for the purpose; and

(b) the contribution remains unpaid at the date of the conviction,

he shall be liable to pay to the Secretary of State a sum equal to the amount which he failed to pay.

(2) Where—

(a) a person is convicted of an offence—

(i) under section 114(3)(b) above; or

(ii) under section 13 of the Stamp Duties Management Act 1891 as applied by regulations made under paragraph 7(3) of Schedule 1 to the Contributions and Benefits Act; or

(iii) of contravening or failing to comply with regulations; and

(b) the evidence on which he is convicted shows that he, for the purposes of paying any contribution which he was liable or entitled to pay, has affixed to any contribution card any used contribution stamp; and

(c) the contribution (not being a Class 3 contribution) in respect of which the stamp was affixed remains unpaid at the date of the conviction,

he shall be liable to pay to the Secretary of State a sum equal to the amount of the contribution.

DEFINITIONS

"the Contributions and Benefits Act": s.191.

Proof of previous offences

120.—(1) Subject to and in accordance with subsections (2) to (5) below, where a person is convicted of an offence mentioned in section 119(1) or (2)(a) above, evidence may be given of any previous failure by him to pay contributions within the time prescribed for the purpose; and in those subsections "the conviction" and "the offence" mean respectively the conviction referred to in this subsection and the offence of which the person is convicted.

(2) Such evidence may be given only if notice of intention to give it is served with the summons or warrant or, in Scotland, the complaint on which the person appeared before the court which convicted him.

(3) If the offence is one of failure to pay a Class 1 contribution, evidence may be given of failure on his part to pay (whether or not in respect of the same person) such contributions or any Class 1A contributions or state scheme premiums on the date of the offence, or during the 2 years preceding that date.

(4) If the offence is one of failure to pay Class 1A contribution, evidence may be given of failure on his part to pay (whether or not in respect of the

same person or the same car) such contributions, or any Class 1 contributions or state scheme premiums, on the date of the offence, or during the 2 years preceding that date.

(5) If the offence—

(a) is one of failure to pay Class 2 contributions; or

(b) is one of those mentioned in section 119(2)(a) above,

evidence may be given of his failure to pay such contributions during those 2 years.

(6) On proof of any matter of which evidence may be given under subsection (3), (4), or (5) above, the person convicted shall be liable to pay to the Secretary of State a sum equal to the total of all amounts which he is so proved to have failed to pay and which remain unpaid at the date of the conviction.

Unpaid contributions—supplementary

121.—(1) Where in England and Wales a person charged with an offence mentioned in section 119(1) or (2)(a) above is convicted of that offence in his absence under section 12(2) of the Magistrates' Courts Act 1980, then if—

(a) it is proved to the satisfaction of the court, on oath or in the manner prescribed by rules under section 144 of that Act, that notice under section 120(2) above has been duly served specifying the other contributions in respect of which the prosecutor intends to give evidence; and

(b) the clerk of the court has received a statement in writing purporting to be made by the accused or by a solicitor acting on his behalf to the effect that if the accused is convicted in his absence of the offence charged he desires to admit failing to pay the other contributions so specified or any of them,

section 120 above shall have effect as if the evidence had been given and the failure so admitted had been proved, and the court shall proceed accordingly.

(2) In England and Wales, where a person is convicted of an offence mentioned in section 119(1) or (2)(a) above and an order is made under Part I of the Powers of Criminal Courts Act 1973 placing the offender on probation or discharging him absolutely or conditionally, sections 119 and 120 above, and subsection (1) above, shall apply as if it were a conviction for all purposes.

(3) In Scotland, where a person is convicted on indictment of, or is charged before a court of summary jurisdiction with, any such offence, and an order is made under Part I of the Criminal Procedure (Scotland) Act 1975 discharging him absolutely or placing him on probation, sections 119 and 120 above shall apply as if—

(a) the conviction on indictment were a conviction for all purposes; or

(b) (as the case may be) the making of the order by the court of summary jurisdiction were a conviction.

(4) In England and Wales, any sum which a person is liable to pay under section 119 or 120 above or under subsection (1) above shall be recoverable from him as a penalty.

(5) Sums recovered by the Secretary of State under the provisions mentioned in subsection (4) above, so far as representing contributions of any class, are to be treated for all purposes of the Contributions and Benefits Act and this Act (including in particular the application of section 162 below) as contributions of that class received by the Secretary of State.

(6) Without prejudice to subsection (5) above, in so far as such sums represent primary Class 1 or Class 2 contributions, they are to be treated as contributions paid in respect of the person in respect of whom they were

originally payable; and enactments relating to earnings factors shall apply accordingly.

PART VII

PROVISION OF INFORMATION

Inland Revenue

Disclosure of information by Inland Revenue

122.—(1) No obligation as to secrecy imposed by statute or otherwise on a person employed in relation to the Inland Revenue shall prevent information obtained or held in connection with the assessment or collection of income tax from being disclosed—

(a) to the Secretary of State;

(b) to the Northern Ireland Department; or

(c) to an officer of either of them authorised to receive such information in connection with the operation of the Contributions and Benefits Act or this Act or any enactment of Northern Ireland legislation corresponding to either of them.

(2) In relation to persons who are carrying on or have carried on a trade, profession or vocation income from which is chargeable to tax under Case I or II of Schedule D, disclosure under subsection (1) above relating to that trade, profession or vocation shall be limited to information about the commencement or cessation of, and employed earners engaged in, the trade, profession or vocation, but sufficient information may also be given to identify the persons concerned.

(3) Subsection (1) above extends only to disclosure by or under the authority of the Commissioners of Inland Revenue; and information which is subject to disclosure to any person by virtue of that subsection shall not be further disclosed to any person except where the further disclosure is made—

(a) to a person to whom disclosure could by virtue of that subsection have been made by or under the authority of the Commissioners of Inland Revenue; or

(b) for the purposes of proceedings (civil or criminal) in connection with the operation of the Contributions and Benefits Act or this Act or of any enactment of Northern Ireland legislation corresponding to either of them; or

(c) for any purposes of sections 17 to 62 above and any corresponding provisions of Northern Ireland legislation.

DEFINITIONS
"the Contributions and Benefits Act": s.191.

Persons employed or formerly employed in social security administration or adjudication

Unauthorised disclosure of information relating to particular persons

123.—(1) A person who is or has been employed in social security administration or adjudication is guilty of an offence if he discloses without lawful authority any information which he acquired in the course of his employment and which relates to a particular person.

(2) A person who is or has been employed in the audit of expenditure or the investigation of complaints is guilty of an offence if he discloses without lawful authority any information—

(a) which he acquired in the course of his employment;

(b) which is, or is derived from, information acquired or held by or for the purposes of any of the government departments or other bodies or persons referred to in Part I of Schedule 4 to this Act or Part I of Schedule 3 to the Northern Ireland Administration Act; and

(c) which relates to a particular person.

(3) It is not an offence under this section—

(a) to disclose information in the form of a summary or collection of information so framed as not to enable information relating to any particular person to be ascertained from it; or

(b) to disclose information which has previously been disclosed to the public with lawful authority.

(4) It is a defence for a person charged with an offence under this section to prove that at the time of the alleged offence—

(a) he believed that he was making the disclosure in question with lawful authority and had no reasonable cause to believe otherwise; or

(b) he believed that the information in question had previously been disclosed to the public with lawful authority and had no reasonable cause to believe otherwise.

(5) A person guilty of an offence under this section shall be liable—

(a) on conviction on indictment, to imprisonment for a term not exceeding two years or a fine or both; or

(b) on summary conviction, to imprisonment for a term not exceeding six months or a fine not exceeding the statutory maximum or both.

(6) For the purposes of this section, the persons who are "employed in social security administration or adjudication" are—

(a) any person specified in Part I of Schedule 4 to this Act or in any corresponding enactment having effect in Northern Ireland;

(b) any other person who carries out the administrative work of any of the government departments or other bodies or persons referred to in that Part of that Schedule or that corresponding enactment; and

(c) any person who provides, or is employed in the provision of, services to any of those departments, persons or bodies;

and "employment", in relation to any such person, shall be construed accordingly.

(7) For the purposes of subsections (2) and (6) above, any reference in Part I of Schedule 4 to this Act or any corresponding enactment having effect in Northern Ireland to a government department shall be construed in accordance with Part II of that Schedule or any corresponding enactment having effect in Northern Ireland, and for this purpose "government department" shall be taken to include—

(a) the Commissioners of Inland Revenue; and

(b) the Scottish Courts Administration.

(8) For the purposes of this section, the persons who are "employed in the audit of expenditure or the investigation of complaints" are—

(a) the Comptroller and Auditor General;

(b) the Comptroller and Auditor General for Northern Ireland;

(c) the Parliamentary Commissioner for Administration;

(d) the Northern Ireland Parliamentary Commissioner for Administration;

(e) the Health Service Commissioner for England;

(f) the Health Service Commissioner for Wales;

(g) the Health Service Commissioner for Scotland;

(h) the Northern Ireland Commissioner for Complaints;

(i) any member of the staff of the National Audit Office or the Northern Ireland Audit Office;

(j) any other person who carries out the administrative work of either of those Offices, or who provides, or is employed in the provision of, services to either of them; and

(k) any officer of any of the Commissioners referred to in paragraphs (c) to (h) above;

and "employment", in relation to any such person, shall be construed accordingly.

(9) For the purposes of this section a disclosure is to be regarded as made with lawful authority if, and only if, it is made—

  (a) in accordance with his official duty—
        (i) by a civil servant; or
        (ii) by a person employed in the audit of expenditure or the investigation of complaints, who does not fall within subsection (8)(j) above;

  (b) by any other person either—
        (i) for the purposes of the function in the exercise of which he holds the information and without contravening any restriction duly imposed by the person responsible; or
        (ii) to, or in accordance with an authorisation duly given by, the person responsible;

  (c) in accordance with any enactment or order of a court;

  (d) for the purpose of instituting, or otherwise for the purposes of, any proceedings before a court or before any tribunal or other body or person referred to in Part I of Schedule 4 to this Act or Part I of Schedule 3 to the Northern Ireland Administration Act; or

  (e) with the consent of the appropriate person;

and in this subsection "the person responsible" means the Secretary of State, the Lord Chancellor or any person authorised by the Secretary of State or the Lord Chancellor for the purposes of this subsection and includes a reference to "the person responsible" within the meaning of any corresponding enactment having effect in Northern Ireland.

(10) For the purposes of subsection (9)(e) above, "the appropriate person" means the person to whom the information in question relates, except that if the affairs of that person are being dealt with—

  (a) under a power of attorney;

  (b) by a receiver appointed under section 99 of the Mental Health Act 1983 or a controller appointed under Article 101 of the Mental Health (Northern Ireland) Order 1986;

  (c) by a Scottish mental health custodian, that is to say—
        (i) a curator bonis, tutor or judicial factor, or
        (ii) the managers of a hospital acting on behalf of that person under section 94 of the Mental Health (Scotland) Act 1984; or

  (d) by a mental health appointee, that is to say—
        (i) a person directed or authorised as mentioned in sub-paragraph (a) of rule 41(1) of the Court of Protection Rules 1984 or sub-paragraph (a) of rule 38(1) of Order 109 of the Rules of the Supreme Court (Northern Ireland) 1980; or
        (ii) a receiver ad interim appointed under sub-paragraph (b) of the said rule 41(1) or a controller ad interim appointed under sub-paragraph (b) of the said rule 38(1),

the appropriate person is the attorney, receiver, controller, custodian or appointee, as the case may be, or, in a case falling within paragraph (a) above, the person to whom the information relates.

DEFINITIONS
"the Northern Ireland Administration Act": s.191.

The Registration Service

Provisions relating to age, death and marriage

124.—(1) Regulations made by the Registrar General under section 20 of the Registration Service Act 1953 or section 54 of the Registration of Births, Deaths and Marriages (Scotland) Act 1965 may provide for the furnishing by superintendent registrars and registrars, subject to the payment of such fee as may be prescribed by the regulations, of such information for the purposes—

(a) of the provisions of the Contributions and Benefits Act to which this section applies; and

(b) of the provisions of this Act so far as they have effect in relation to matters arising under those provisions,

including copies or extracts from the registers in their custody, as may be so prescribed.

(2) This section applies to the following provisions of the Contributions and Benefits Act—

(a) Parts I to VI except section 108;

(b) Part VII, so far as it relates to income support and family credit;

(c) Part VIII, so far as it relates to any social fund payment such as is mentioned in section 138(1)(a) or (2);

(d) Part IX;

(e) Part XI; and

(f) Part XII.

(3) Where the age, marriage or death of a person is required to be ascertained or proved for the purposes mentioned in subsection (1) above, any person—

(a) on presenting to the custodian of the register under the enactments relating to the registration of births, marriages and deaths in which particulars of the birth, marriage or death (as the case may be) of the first-mentioned person are entered, a duly completed requisition in writing in that behalf; and

(b) on payment of a fee of £1.50 in England and Wales and £4.00 in Scotland,

shall be entitled to obtain a copy, certified under the hand of the custodian, of the entry of those particulars.

(4) Requisitions for the purposes of subsection (3) above shall be in such form and contain such particulars as may from time to time be specified by the Registrar General, and suitable forms of requisition shall, on request, be supplied without charge by superintendent registrars and registrars.

(5) In this section—

(a) as it applies to England and Wales—

"Registrar General" means the Registrar General for England and Wales; and

"superintendent registrar" and "registrar" mean a superintendent registrar or, as the case may be, registrar for the purposes of the enactments relating to the registration of births, deaths and marriages; and

(b) as it applies to Scotland—

"Registrar General" means the Registrar General of Births, Deaths and Marriages for Scotland;

"registrar" means a district registrar, senior registrar or assistant registrar for the purposes of the enactments relating to the registration of births, deaths and marriages.

Regulations as to notification of deaths

125.—(1) Regulations may provide that it shall be the duty of any of the following persons—

(a) the Registrar General for England and Wales;

(b) the Registrar General of Births, Deaths and Marriages for Scotland;

(c) each registrar of births and deaths,
to furnish the Secretary of State, for the purpose of his functions under the Contributions and Benefits Act and this Act and the functions of the Northern Ireland Department under any Northern Ireland legislation corresponding to either of them, with the prescribed particulars of such deaths as may be prescribed.

(2) The regulations may make provision as to the manner in which and times at which the particulars are to be furnished.

DEFINITIONS
    "the Contributions and Benefits Act": s.191.
    "the Northern Ireland Department": *ibid.*
    "prescribed": *ibid.*

Personal representatives—income support and supplementary benefit

Personal representatives to give information about the estate of a deceased person who was in receipt of income support or supplementary benefit

126.—(1) The personal representatives of a person who was in receipt of income support or supplementary benefit at any time before his death shall provide the Secretary of State with such information as he may require relating to the assets and liabilities of that person's estate.

(2) If the personal representatives fail to supply any information within 28 days of being required to do so under subsection (1) above, then—

(a) the appropriate court may, on the application of the Secretary of State, make an order directing them to supply that information within such time as may be specified in the order, and

(b) any such order may provide that all costs (or, in Scotland, expenses) of and incidental to the application shall be borne personally by any of the personal representatives.

(3) In this section "the appropriate court" means—

(a) in England and Wales, a county court;

(b) in Scotland, the sheriff;

and any application to the sheriff under this section shall be made by summary application.

GENERAL NOTE
    Under s.71(3) an overpayment which would have been recoverable from a person is recoverable from that person's estate (*Secretary of State for Social Services* v. *Solly* [1974] 3 All E.R. 922). Section 126 provides a specific obligation for the estate to provide information about the assets in it. However, s.126 only applies to the estates of income support or supplementary benefit claimants. It does not apply to family credit, family income supplement, disability working allowance, housing benefit or community charge benefit claimants, all of whom can be overpaid because they have concealed capital. Nor does it apply to anyone other than a recipient of income support or supplementary benefit. Sometimes a person other than a recipient may become liable to recovery by making a misrepresentation or failing to disclose a material fact (*R(SB) 21/82* and *R(SB) 28/83*).

Housing benefit

Information for purposes of housing benefit

127.—(1) The Secretary of State may supply to authorities such information of a prescribed description obtained by reason of the exercise of any of his functions under the Contributions and Benefits Act or this Act as they may require in connection with any of their functions relating to housing benefit.

(2) Authorities shall supply to the Secretary of State such information of a prescribed description obtained by reason of the exercise of their functions relating to housing benefit as he may require in connection with any of his functions under the Contributions and Benefits Act or this Act.

(3) It shall also be the duty of an authority to supply the Secretary of State, in the prescribed manner and within the prescribed time—

(a) with such information as he may require concerning their performance of any of their functions relating to housing benefit; and

(b) with such information as he may require to enable him—

　(i) to prepare estimates of likely future amounts of housing benefit expenditure; and

　(ii) to decide questions relating to the development of housing benefit policy.

DEFINITIONS

"the Contributions and Benefits Act": s.191.

"prescribed": *ibid.*

Community charge benefits

Information for purposes of community charge benefits

128.—(1) The Secretary of State may supply to charging authorities and levying authorities such information of a prescribed description obtained by reason of the exercise of any of his functions under the Contributions and Benefits Act or this Act as they may require in connection with any of their functions relating to community charge benefits.

(2) Charging authorities and levying authorities shall supply to the Secretary of State such information of a prescribed description obtained by reason of the exercise of their functions relating to community charge benefits as he may require in connection with any of his functions under those Acts.

(3) It shall also be the duty of each charging authority and of each levying authority to supply the Secretary of State, in the prescribed manner and within the prescribed time—

(a) with such information as he may require concerning its performance of any of its functions relating to community charge benefits;

(b) with such information as he may require to enable him to prepare estimates of likely future amounts of community charge benefit subsidy; and

(c) with such information as he may require to enable him to decide questions relating to the development of policy as regards community charge benefits.

DEFINITIONS

"charging authority": s.191.

"the Contributions and Benefits Act": *ibid.*

"levying authority": *ibid.*

"prescribed": *ibid.*

Statutory sick pay and other benefits

Disclosure by Secretary of State for purpose of determination of period of entitlement to statutory sick pay

129. Where the Secretary of State considers that it is reasonable for information held by him to be disclosed to an employer, for the purpose of enabling that employer to determine the duration of a period of entitlement under Part XI of the Contributions and Benefits Act in respect of an employee, or whether such a period exists, he may disclose the information to that employer.

Duties of employers—statutory sick pay and claims for other benefits

130.—(1) Regulations may make provision requiring an employer, in a case falling within subsection (3) below to furnish information in connection with the making, by a person who is, or has been, an employee of that employer, of a claim for—

(a) sickness benefit;

(b) a maternity allowance;

(c) an invalidity pension under section 33, 40 or 41 of the Contributions and Benefits Act;

(d) industrial injuries benefit; or

(e) a severe disablement allowance.

(2) Regulations under this section shall prescribe—

(a) the kind of information to be furnished in accordance with the regulations;

(b) the person to whom information of the prescribed kind is to be furnished; and

(c) the manner in which, and period within which, it is to be furnished.

(3) The cases are—

(a) where, by virtue of paragraph 2 of Schedule 11 to the Contributions and Benefits Act or of regulations made under paragraph 1 of that Schedule, a period of entitlement does not arise in relation to a period of incapacity for work;

(b) where a period of entitlement has come to an end but the period of incapacity for work which was running immediately before the period of entitlement came to an end continues; and

(c) where a period of entitlement has not come to an end but, on the assumption that—

(i) the period of incapacity for work in question continues to run for a prescribed period; and

(ii) there is no material change in circumstances,

the period of entitlement will have ended on or before the end of the prescribed period.

(4) Regulations—

(a) may require employers to maintain such records in connection with statutory sick pay as may be prescribed;

(b) may provide for—

(i) any person claiming to be entitled to statutory sick pay; or

(ii) any other person who is a party to proceedings arising under Part XI of the Contributions and Benefits Act,

to furnish to the Secretary of State, within a prescribed period, any information required for the determination of any question arising in connection therewith; and

(c) may require employers who have made payments of statutory sick pay to furnish to the Secretary of State such documents and information, at such times, as may be prescribed.

GENERAL NOTE

See regs. 13 to 15 of the Statutory Sick Pay (General) Regulations 1982 (S.I. 1982 No. 894), in the current edition of Bonner *et al.*

Statutory maternity pay and other benefits

Disclosure by Secretary of State for purpose of determination of period of entitlement to statutory maternity pay

131. Where the Secretary of State considers that it is reasonable for information held by him to be disclosed to a person liable to make payments of statutory maternity pay for the purpose of enabling that person to determine—

(a) whether a maternity pay period exists in relation to a woman who is or has been an employee of his; and

(b) if it does, the date of its commencement and the weeks in it in respect of which he may be liable to pay statutory maternity pay,

he may disclose the information to that person.

Duties of employers—statutory maternity pay and claims for other benefits

132.—(1) Regulations may make provision requiring an employer in prescribed circumstances to furnish information in connection with the making of a claim by a woman who is or has been his employee for—

(a) a maternity allowance;

(b) sickness benefit;

(c) an invalidity pension under section 33, 40 or 41 of the Contributions and Benefits Act; or

(d) a severe disablement allowance.

(2) Regulations under this section shall prescribe—

(a) the kind of information to be furnished in accordance with the regulations;

(b) the person to whom information of the prescribed kind is to be furnished; and

(c) the manner in which, and period within which, it is to be furnished.

(3) Regulations—

(a) may require employers to maintain such records in connection with statutory maternity pay as may be prescribed;

(b) may provide for—

(i) any woman claiming to be entitled to statutory maternity pay; or

(ii) any other person who is a party to proceedings arising under Part XII of the Contributions and Benefits Act,

to furnish to the Secretary of State, within a prescribed period, any information required for the determination of any question arising in connection therewith; and

(c) may require persons who have made payments of statutory maternity pay to furnish to the Secretary of State such documents and information, at such time, as may be prescribed.

DEFINITIONS

"the Contributions and Benefits Act": s.191.

GENERAL NOTE

See regs. 25 to 26 of the Statutory Maternity Pay (General) Regulations 1986 (S.I. 1986 No. 1960), in the current edition of Bonner *et al.*

Maintenance proceedings

Furnishing of addresses for maintenance proceedings, etc.

133. The Secretary of State may incur expenses for the purpose of furnishing the address at which a man or woman is recorded by him as residing, where the address is required for the purpose of taking or carrying on legal proceedings to obtain or enforce an order for the making by the man or woman of payments—

   (a) for the maintenance of the man's wife or former wife, or the woman's husband or former husband; or

   (b) for the maintenance or education of any person as being the son or daughter of the man or his wife or former wife, or of the woman or her husband or former husband.

PART VIII

ARRANGEMENTS FOR HOUSING BENEFIT AND COMMUNITY CHARGE BENEFITS AND RELATED SUBSIDIES

Housing benefit

Arrangements for housing benefit

134.—(1) Housing benefit provided by virtue of a scheme under section 123 of the Contributions and Benefits Act (in this Act referred to as "the housing benefit scheme")—

   (a) is to be in the form of a rate rebate funded and administered by the appropriate rating authority, if it is in respect of payments by way of rates;

   (b) is to be in the form of a rent rebate or, in prescribed cases, of a rent allowance, funded and administered by the appropriate housing authority, if it is in respect of payments, other than payments by way of rates, to be made to a housing authority; and

   (c) is in any other case to be in the form of a rent allowance funded and administered by the appropriate local authority.

(2) The rebates and allowances referred to in subsection (1) above may take any of the following forms, that is to say—

   (a) a payment or payments by the authority to the person entitled to the benefit;

   (b) a reduction in the amount of any payments which that person is liable to make to the authority by way of rent or rates; or

   (c) such a payment or payments and such a reduction;

and in any enactment or instrument (whenever passed or made) "pay", in relation to housing benefit, includes discharge in any of those forms.

(3) Regulations may provide that in prescribed cases a payment made by a person entitled to a rent allowance shall be treated for the purposes of subsection (1)(a) above as being, to such extent as may be prescribed, a payment by way of rates.

(4) For the purposes of this section in its application to any dwelling—

   (a) the appropriate rating authority is the rating authority for the area in which it is situated;

   (b) the appropriate housing authority is the housing authority to whom the occupier of the dwelling is liable to make payments; and

   (c) the appropriate local authority is the local authority for the area in which the dwelling is situated.

(5) Authorities may agree that one shall carry out responsibilities relating to housing benefit on another's behalf.

(6) Circumstances may be prescribed in which a rate rebate may be treated as if it fell to be paid as a rent allowance.

(7) The cases that may be prescribed under subsection (1)(b) above do not include any case where the payment in respect of which the housing benefit is granted is a payment in respect of a dwelling which, within the meaning of Part VI of the Local Government and Housing Act 1989, is a house or other property of an authority within the authority's Housing Revenue Account.

(8) An authority may modify any part of the housing benefit scheme administered by the authority—

    (a) so as to provide for disregarding, in determining a person's income (whether he is the occupier of a dwelling or any other person whose income falls to be aggregated with that of the occupier of a dwelling), the whole or part of any war disablement pension or war widow's pension payable to that person;

    (b) to such extent in other respects as may be prescribed,

and any such modification may be adopted by resolution of an authority.

(9) Modifications other than such modifications as are mentioned in subsection (8)(a) above shall be so framed as to secure that, in the estimate of the authority adopting them, the total of the rebates or allowances which will be granted by the authority in any year will not exceed the permitted total of rebates or allowances for that year.

(10) An authority who have adopted modifications may by resolution revoke or vary them.

(11) If the housing benefit scheme includes power for an authority to exercise a discretion in awarding housing benefit, the authority shall not exercise that discretion so that the total of the rebates or allowances granted by them in any year exceeds the permitted total of rebates or allowances for that year.

(12) In relation to any authority the permitted total of rebates or allowances for any year shall be calculated, in the manner specified by an order made by the Secretary of State, by reference to the total housing benefit granted by that authority during the year, less such deductions as are specified in the order.

(13) In this section "modifications" includes additions, omissions and amendments, and related expressions shall be construed accordingly.

DEFINITIONS
    "the Contributions and Benefits Act": s.191.
    "dwelling": *ibid.*
    "housing authority": *ibid.*
    "local authority": *ibid.*
    "prescribed": *ibid.*
    "rates": *ibid.*
    "rating authority": *ibid.*

GENERAL NOTE
    See the notes in the current edition of Findlay and Ward.

Housing benefit finance

    135.—(1) For each year the Secretary of State shall pay—

    (a) a subsidy to be known as "rate rebate subsidy" to each rating authority;

    (b) a subsidy to be known as "rent rebate subsidy" to each housing authority; and

    (c) a subsidy to be known as "rent allowance subsidy" to each local authority.

    (2) The subsidy under subsection (1) above which is to be paid to an authority—

    (a) shall be calculated, in the manner specified by an order made by the Secretary of State, by reference—

        (i) in the case of an authority in England and Wales, to the relevant benefit; and

        (ii) in the case of an authority in Scotland, to the total housing benefit,

    and by reference also, in the case of an authority in England and

Wales or Scotland, to any rebate or allowance within the meaning of the Social Security and Housing Benefits Act 1982 granted by that authority during the year with any additions specified in the order but subject to any deductions so specified; and

(b) shall be subject to deduction of any amount which the Secretary of State considers it unreasonable to meet out of money provided by way of subsidy under subsection (1) above.

(3) In subsection (2) above "relevant benefit", in relation to an authority, means total housing benefit excluding any Housing Revenue Account rebates granted by them.

(4) Nothing in this section shall be taken to imply that any such addition or deduction as is mentioned in subsection (2)(a) or (b) above may not be determined by reference to—

(a) an authority's expenditure in respect of any housing benefit, or in respect of any rebate or allowance within the meaning of the Social Security and Housing Benefits Act 1982, granted during any previous year; or

(b) any subsidy under this section or that Act paid to an authority in respect of any previous year.

(5) For each year the Secretary of State may pay to an authority as part of the subsidy under subsection (1) above an additional sum calculated, in the manner specified by an order made by the Secretary of State, in respect of the costs of administering housing benefit.

(6) Rent rebate subsidy shall be payable—

(a) in the case of a local authority in England and Wales, subject to subsection (7) below, for the credit of a revenue account of theirs which is not a Housing Revenue Account or a Housing Repairs Account;

(b) in the case of a local authority in Scotland, for the credit of their rent rebate account;

(c) in the case of a new town corporation in England and Wales or the Development Board for Rural Wales, for the credit of their housing account; and

(d) in the case of a new town corporation in Scotland or Scottish Homes, for the credit of the account to which rent rebates granted by them, or it, are debited.

(7) Rent rebate subsidy for a year beginning before 1st April 1990 shall be payable in the case of a local authority in England and Wales—

(a) for the credit of their Housing Revenue Account to the extent that it is calculated by reference to Housing Revenue Account rebates and any costs of administering such rebates; and

(b) for the credit of their general rate fund to the extent that it is not so calculated.

(8) Every local housing authority in England and Wales shall for each year carry to the credit of their Housing Revenue Account from some other revenue account of theirs which is not a Housing Repairs Account an amount equal to the aggregate of—

(a) so much of each Housing Revenue Account rebate granted by them during the year as was granted in the exercise of a discretion conferred by the housing benefit scheme or in pursuance of such modifications of that scheme as are mentioned in paragraph (b) of section 134(8) above; and

(b) unless the authority otherwise determine, so much of each such rebate as was granted in pursuance of such modifications of that scheme as are mentioned in paragraph (a) of that subsection.

(9) Every local authority in Scotland shall make for each year a rate fund contribution to their Housing Revenue Account of an amount equal to the difference between—

(a) so much of their rent rebate subsidy for the year as is credited to that Account; and
(b) the total of—
    (i) the Housing Revenue Account rebates granted by them during the year; and
    (ii) the cost of administering such rebates.
(10) Rent allowance subsidy shall be payable—
(a) in the case of a local authority in England and Wales and subsidy payable for a year beginning before 1st April 1990, for the credit of their general rate fund; and
(b) in the case of a local authority in Scotland, for the credit of their rent allowance account.
(11) Subsidy under this section shall be payable by the Secretary of State at such time and in such manner as the Treasury may direct.
(12) The amount of any subsidy payable to an authority shall be calculated to the nearest pound, by disregarding an odd amount of 50 pence or less and by treating an odd amount exceeding 50 pence as a whole pound.
(13) In subsection (7) above "general rate fund" means—
(a) in relation to the Council of the Isles of Scilly, their general fund; and
(b) in relation to the Common Council of the City of London, their general rate.
(14) In this section "modifications" includes additions, omissions and amendments and related expressions shall be construed accordingly.

DEFINITIONS
"housing benefit scheme": s.191.
"local authority": *ibid.*
"new town corporation": *ibid.*
"rate rebate": *ibid.*
"rent allowance": *ibid.*
"rent rebate": *ibid.*

GENERAL NOTE
See the notes in the current edition of Findlay and Ward.

Rent allowance subsidy and determinations of rent officers

136.—(1) In relation to rent allowance subsidy, the Secretary of State—
(a) may provide for any calculation under paragraph (a) of section 135(2) above to be made,
(b) may specify any such additions and deductions as are referred to in that paragraph; and
(c) may exercise his discretion as to what is unreasonable for the purposes of paragraph (b) of that subsection,
by reference to determinations made by rent officers in exercise of functions conferred on them under section 121 of the Housing Act 1988 or section 70 of the Housing (Scotland) Act 1988 ("the Housing Act functions").
(2) The Secretary of State may by regulations require a local authority in any prescribed case to apply to a rent officer for a determination to be made in pursuance of the Housing Act functions and any such authority shall comply with prescribed requirements as to the time for making such an application.
(3) Where a local authority would have been required to apply to a rent officer for a determination under the Housing Act functions in a pre-commencement case, had the first regulations under section 30(2B) of the 1986 Act (which corresponded to subsection (2) above) come into force on 1st April 1989, regulations may make provision—
(a) requiring the authority in prescribed circumstances to apply within a prescribed period to the rent officer for that determination to be made; and

(b) requiring the rent officer in prescribed circumstances to make that determination on prescribed assumptions.

(4) In subsection (3) above "pre-commencement case" means any case which arose before the date on which the first regulations under section 30(2B) of the 1986 Act in fact came into force.

  "the 1986 Act": s.191.
  "local authority": *ibid.*
  "prescribed": *ibid.*

GENERAL NOTE
  See reg. 12A of the Housing Benefit (General) Regulations 1987 (S.I. 1987 No. 1971) and the Rent Officers (Additional Functions) Order 1990 (S.I. 1990 No. 428), in the current edition of Findlay and Ward.

Claims etc.

137.—(1) Subsidy under section 135 above shall not be payable to an authority until either—
  (a) they have made a claim for it in such form as the Secretary of State may determine; or
  (b) if they have not made such a claim, the amount of subsidy payable to them (apart from subsection (6) below) has been estimated under subsection (3) below.

(2) The Secretary of State may withhold from an authority so much of any subsidy under section 135 above as he thinks fit until either—
  (a) the authority has supplied him with prescribed particulars relating to their claim for subsidy and complied with prescribed conditions as to records, certificates, audit or otherwise; or
  (b) he is satisfied that there is a good reason for the authority's failure to supply those particulars or comply with those conditions.

(3) If an authority has not—
  (a) made a claim for subsidy;
  (b) supplied the prescribed particulars referred to in paragraph (a) of subsection (2) above; or
  (c) complied with the prescribed conditions referred to in that paragraph,
within the prescribed period, then the Secretary of State may estimate the amount of subsidy payable to them (apart from subsection (6) below) and employ for that purpose such criteria as he considers relevant.

(4) If the Secretary of State considers it reasonable to do so in any particular case, he may give the authority in question written notice extending any of the periods prescribed under subsection (3) above for the purposes of paragraph (a), (b) or (c) of that subsection, as the case may be.

(5) If an authority fails to make a claim for subsidy within such period as the Secretary of State considers reasonable, he may withhold from them such part of the subsidy as he thinks fit for so long as he thinks fit.

(6) Where the amount of subsidy paid to an authority for any year is found to be incorrect, the amount payable to them for any subsequent year may be adjusted for the purpose of rectifying that mistake in whole or in part.

DEFINITIONS
  "prescribed": s.191.

GENERAL NOTE
  See the note in the current edition of Findlay and Ward.

Community charge benefits

Nature of benefits

138.—(1) In relation to England and Wales, regulations shall provide that where a person is entitled to a community charge benefit in respect of a charging authority's personal community charge the benefit shall take such of the following forms as is prescribed in the case of the person—
(a) a payment or payments by the authority to the person;
(b) a reduction in the amount the person is or becomes liable to pay to the authority in respect of the charge as it has effect for the relevant or any subsequent chargeable financial year;
(c) both such payment or payments and such reduction.
(2) In relation to Scotland, regulations shall provide that where a person is entitled to a community charge benefit in respect of a personal community charge determined by a regional, islands or district council the benefit shall take such of the following forms as is prescribed in the case of the person—
(a) a payment or payments to the person by the levying authority to which the charge is payable;
(b) a reduction in the amount the person is or becomes liable to pay in respect of the charge as it has effect for the relevant or any subsequent chargeable financial year;
(c) both such payment or payments and such reduction.
(3) Regulations shall provide that where a person is entitled to a community charge benefit in respect of a contribution period the benefit shall take such of the following forms as is prescribed in the case of the person—
(a) a payment or payments by the relevant authority to the person;
(b) the reductions mentioned in subsection (4) below;
(c) both such payment or payments and such reductions.
(4) The reductions are—
(a) a reduction in the amount the person is liable to pay to the charge payer in respect of the contribution period, and
(b) a consequential reduction in the amount the charge payer is liable to pay in respect of the charge concerned as it has effect for the relevant chargeable financial year.
(5) For the purposes of subsections (1) and (2) above the relevant chargeable financial year is the chargeable financial year in which the relevant day falls; and the relevant day is the day in respect of which the person concerned is entitled to the benefit.
(6) For the purposes of subsection (3) above the relevant authority is—
(a) in relation to England and Wales, the authority to which an amount is payable in respect of the collective community charge concerned under section 15 of the Local Government Finance Act 1988 ("the 1988 Act");
(b) in relation to Scotland, the levying authority to which the collective community charge is payable.
(7) For the purposes of subsection (4) above the charge payer is—
(a) in relation to England and Wales, the person who is liable to pay an amount in respect of the collective community charge concerned under section 15 of the 1988 Act;
(b) in relation to Scotland, the person who is liable to pay the collective community charge under section 11(5) of the Abolition of Domestic Rates Etc. (Scotland) Act 1987 ("the 1987 Act").
(8) For the purposes of subsection (4) above the relevant chargeable financial year is the chargeable financial year in which the contribution period falls.
(9) Regulations under subsection (1), or (2) or (3) above may include such supplementary, incidental or consequential provisions as appear to the

Secretary of State to be necessary or expedient; and any such provisions may include provisions amending or adapting provisions of the 1987 Act or the 1988 Act.

DEFINITIONS
  "chargeable financial year": s.191.
  "charging authority": *ibid.*
  "levying authority": *ibid.*

GENERAL NOTE
  See the note in the current edition of Findlay and Ward.

Arrangements for community charge benefits

139.—(1) Any community charge benefit provided for by virtue of a scheme under section 123 of the Contributions and Benefits Act (in this Act referred to as a community charge benefit scheme) is to be administered by the appropriate authority.

(2) For the purposes of this section in its application to England and Wales, the appropriate authority in relation to a particular benefit is the charging authority as regards whose personal or collective community charge a person is entitled to the benefit.

(3) For the purposes of this section in its application to Scotland, the appropriate authority in relation to a particular benefit is the levying authority—

  (a) to which the personal community charge is payable by a person entitled to the benefit; or

  (b) in whose area is situated the premises in respect of residence in which for a contribution period a collective community charge contribution is payable.

(4) Charging authorities may agree that one shall carry out responsibilities relating to community charge benefits on another's behalf.

(5) Levying authorities may agree that one shall carry out responsibilities relating to community charge benefits on another's behalf.

(6) A charging authority or levying authority may modify any part of the community charge benefit scheme administered by the authority—

  (a) so as to provide for disregarding, in determining a person's income, the whole or part of any war disablement pension or war widow's pension payable to that person or to his partner or to a person to whom he is polygamously married;

  (b) to such extent in other respects as may be prescribed,
and any such modifications may be adopted by resolution of an authority.

(7) Modifications other than such modifications as are mentioned in subsection (6)(a) above shall be so framed as to secure that, in the estimate of the authority adopting them, the total of the benefits which will be allowed by the authority for any year will not exceed the permitted total of benefits for that year.

(8) An authority which has adopted modifications may by resolution revoke or vary them.

(9) If the community charge benefits scheme includes power for an authority to exercise a discretion in allowing community charge benefits, the authority shall not exercise that discretion so that the total of the benefits allowed by it for any year exceeds the permitted total of benefits for that year.

(10) In relation to any authority the permitted total of benefits for any year shall be such amount as is calculated in accordance with rules contained in an order made by the Secretary of State.

(11) In this section—

"modifications" includes additions, omissions and amendments, and related expressions shall be construed accordingly;

"partner", in relation to a person, means the other member of the couple concerned;

"war disablement pension" means—

(a) any retired pay, pension or allowance granted in respect of disablement under powers conferred by or under the Air Force (Constitution) Act 1917, the Personal Injuries (Emergency Provisions) Act 1939, the Pensions (Navy, Army, Air Force and Mercantile Marine) Act 1939, the Polish Resettlement Act 1947 or Part VII or section 151 of the Reserve Forces Act 1980;

(b) without prejudice to paragraph (a) of this definition, any retired pay or pension to which subsection (1) of section 315 of the Income and Corporation Taxes Act 1988 applies; and

"war widow's pension" means any widow's pension or allowance granted in respect of a death due to service or war injury and payable by virtue of any enactment mentioned in paragraph (a) of the preceding definition or a pension or allowance for a widow granted under any scheme mentioned in section 315(2)(e) of the Income and Corporation Taxes Act 1988.

DEFINITIONS
"the Contributions and Benefits Act": s.191.
"charging authority": *ibid.*
"levying authority": *ibid.*

GENERAL NOTE
See the note in the current edition of Findlay and Ward.

Community charge benefit finance

140.—(1) For each year the Secretary of State shall pay a subsidy (to be known as community charge benefit subsidy) to each charging authority and to each levying authority.

(2) The amount of community charge benefit subsidy to be paid to a charging authority or a levying authority for a year shall be calculated in such manner as may be specified by an order made by the Secretary of State.

(3) Any calculation under subsection (2) above shall be made by reference to the total amount of the community charge benefits allowed by the authority during the year with any additions specified in the order but subject to any deduction so specified.

(4) The Secretary of State may deduct, from the amount which would (apart from this subsection) be payable to a charging or levying authority by way of community charge benefit subsidy for a year, such amount as he considers it unreasonable to pay by way of such subsidy.

(5) The Secretary of State may pay to an authority, as part of the amount of community charge benefit subsidy payable to the authority for a year, an additional sum in respect of the costs of administering community charge benefits; and any such additional sum shall be calculated in a manner specified by an order made by the Secretary of State.

(6) Nothing in this section shall be taken to imply that any such addition or deduction as is mentioned in subsection (3) or (4) above may not be determined by reference to—

(a) an authority's expenditure in respect of community charge benefits allowed during any previous year; or

(b) any subsidy paid under this section to an authority in respect of any previous year.

(7) Subsidy under this section shall be payable by the Secretary of State at such time and in such manner as the Treasury may direct; and section 137

above shall apply in relation to a charging authority or a levying authority and subsidy under this section as they apply in relation to a rating authority, a housing authority or local authority and subsidy under that section.

(8) The amount of any subsidy payable to an authority shall be calculated to the nearest pound, by disregarding an odd amount of 50 pence or less and by treating an odd amount exceeding 50 pence as a whole pound.

DEFINITIONS
  "charging authority": s.191.
  "levying authority": *ibid.*

GENERAL NOTE
  See the note in the current edition of Findlay and Ward.

PART IX

ALTERATION OF CONTRIBUTIONS ETC.

Annual review of contributions

141.—(1) In each tax year the Secretary of State shall carry out a review of the general level of earnings in Great Britain taking into account changes in that level which have taken place since his last review under this section, with a view to determining whether, in respect of Class 2, 3 or 4 contributions, an order should be made under this section, to have effect in relation to the next following tax year.

(2) For the purposes of any review under this section, the Secretary of State—

  (a) shall estimate the general level of earnings in such manner as he thinks fit; and

  (b) shall take into account any other matters appearing to him to be relevant to his determination whether or not an order should be made under this section, including the current operation of the Contributions and Benefits Act.

(3) If the Secretary of State determines, as a result of a review under this section, that having regard to changes in the general level of earnings which have taken place, and to any other matters taken into account on the review, an order under this section should be made for the amendment of Part I of the Contributions and Benefits Act, he shall prepare and lay before each House of Parliament a draft of such an order framed so as to give effect to his conclusions on the review.

(4) An order under this section may amend Part I of the Contributions and Benefits Act by altering any one or more of the following figures—

  (a) the figure specified in section 11(1) as the weekly rate of Class 2 contributions;

  (b) the figure specified in section 11(4) as the amount of earnings below which regulations under that subsection may except an earner from liability for Class 2 contributions;

  (c) the figure specified in section 13(1) as the amount of a Class 3 contribution;

  (d) the figures specified in section 15(3) as the lower and upper limits of profits or gains which are to be taken into account for the purposes of Class 4 contributions.

(5) If an order under this section contains an amendment altering either of the figures specified in section 15(3) of the Contributions and Benefits Act, it shall make the same alteration of the corresponding figure specified in section 18(1) of that Act.

(6) If the Secretary of State determines as a result of a review under this section that, having regard to his conclusions in respect of the general level

of earnings and otherwise, no such amendments of Part I of the Contributions and Benefits Act are called for as can be made for the purposes of subsection (4) above, and determines accordingly not to lay a draft of an order before Parliament, he shall instead prepare and lay before each House of Parliament a report explaining his reasons for that determination.

(7) In subsection (1) above in its application to the tax year 1992–93 the reference to the last review under this section shall be construed as a reference to the last review under section 120 of the 1975 Act.

DEFINITIONS
    "the Contributions and Benefits Act": s.191.
    "tax year": *ibid.*

GENERAL NOTE
    Section 141 provides for the annual up-rating of contributions, having regard to the movement in average earnings.

Orders under s.141—supplementary

142.—(1) Where the Secretary of State lays before Parliament a draft of an order under section 141 above, he shall lay with it a copy of a report by the Government Actuary or the Deputy Government Actuary on the effect which, in that Actuary's opinion, the making of such an order may be expected to have on the National Insurance Fund; and, where he determines not to lay a draft order, he shall with the report laid before Parliament under section 141(6) above lay a copy of a report by the Government Actuary or the Deputy Government Actuary on the consequences for the Fund which may, in that Actuary's opinion, follow from that determination.

(2) Where the Secretary of State lays before Parliament a draft of an order under section 141 above, then if the draft is approved by a resolution of each House, the Secretary of State shall make an order in the form of the draft.

(3) An order under section 141 above shall be made so as to be in force from the beginning of the tax year following that in which it receives Parliamentary approval, and to have effect for that year and any subsequent tax year (subject to the effect of any subsequent order under this Part of this Act); and for this purpose the order is to be taken as receiving Parliamentary approval on the date on which the draft of it is approved by the second House to approve it.

DEFINITIONS
    "tax year": s.191.

Power to alter contributions with a view to adjusting level of National Insurance Fund

143.—(1) Without prejudice to section 141 above, the Secretary of State may at any time, if he thinks it expedient to do so with a view to adjusting the level at which the National Insurance Fund stands for the time being and having regard to the sums which may be expected to be paid from the Fund in any future period, make an order amending Part I of the Contributions and Benefits Act by altering any one or more of the following figures—
    (a) the percentage rate specified—
        (i) as the initial primary percentage in section 8(2)(a);
        (ii) as the main primary percentage in section 8(2)(b);
    (b) the percentage rate for secondary Class 1 contributions specified as the appropriate rate for Bracket 4 in section 9(3);
    (c) the figure specified in section 11(1) as the weekly rate of Class 2 contributions;
    (d) the figure specified in section 13(1) as the amount of a Class 3 contribution;

(e) the percentage rate for Class 4 contributions specified in section 15(3).

(2) If an order under subsection (1) above contains an amendment altering the percentage rate for Class 4 contributions specified in section 15(3) of the Contributions and Benefits Act, it shall make the same alteration of the percentage rate specified in section 18(1) of that Act.

(3) An order under subsection (1) above may if it contains an amendment altering the figure specified in section 11(1) of the Contributions and Benefits Act as the weekly rate of Class 2 contributions and the Secretary of State thinks it expedient in consequence of that amendment, amend section 11(4) of that Act by altering the figure there specified as the amount of earnings below which regulations under that subsection may except an earner from liability for Class 2 contributions.

(4) No order shall be made under this section so as—

(a) to increase for any tax year—
    (i) the percentage rate of the initial or main primary percentage; or
    (ii) the percentage rate for secondary Class 1 contributions,
  to a percentage rate more than 0.25 per cent. higher than the percentage rate applicable at the end of the preceding tax year for the primary percentage or secondary Class 1 contribution in question; or

(b) to increase the percentage rate for Class 4 contributions to more than 8.25 per cent.

DEFINITIONS
"the Contributions and Benefits Act": s.191.
"tax year": *ibid.*

GENERAL NOTE
Section 143 gives the Secretary of State very broad powers to alter the percentage rates of contributions.

Orders under s.143—supplementary

144.—(1) Where (in accordance with section 190 below) the Secretary of State lays before Parliament a draft of an order under section 143 above, he shall lay with it a copy of a report by the Government Actuary or the Deputy Government Actuary on the effect which, in that Actuary's opinion, the making of such an order may be expected to have on the National Insurance Fund.

(2) An order under section 143 above shall be made so as to be in force from the beginning of the tax year following that in which it received Parliamentary approval, and to have effect for that year and any subsequent tax year (subject to the effect of any subsequent order under this Part of this Act); and for this purpose the order is to be taken as receiving Parliamentary approval on the date on which the draft of it is approved by the second House to approve it.

DEFINITIONS
"tax year": s.191.

Power to alter primary and secondary contributions

145.—(1) For the purpose of adjusting amounts payable by way of primary Class 1 contributions, the Secretary of State may at any time make an order altering—

(a) the percentage rate specified as the initial primary percentage in section 8(2)(a) of the Contributions and Benefits Act;

(b) the percentage rate specified as the main primary percentage in section 8(2)(b) of that Act.

(2) For the purpose of adjusting amounts payable by way of secondary Class 1 contributions, the Secretary of State may at any time make an order amending section 9(3) of that Act by altering any one or more of the following figures—
(a) the upper weekly earnings figure specified in respect of Bracket 1;
(b) the weekly earnings figures specified in respect of Brackets 2 to 4; and
(c) the percentage rates specified as the appropriate rates for Brackets 1 to 3.
(3) No order shall be made under this section so as—
(a) to alter the percentage rate of the initial or main primary percentage to a percentage rate more than 0.25 per cent. higher than applicable at the end of the preceding tax year for the primary percentage in question; or
(b) to alter any of the percentage rates specified as the appropriate rates for Brackets 1 to 3 in section 9(3) of the Contributions and Benefits Act to a rate higher than the percentage rate which at the time the order comes into force is specified as the appropriate rate for Bracket 4.
(4) Without prejudice to section 141 or 143 above, the Secretary of State may make such order—
(a) amending section 11(1) of the Contributions and Benefits Act by altering the figure specified in that subsection as the weekly rate of Class 2 contributions;
(b) amending section 13(1) of that Act by altering the figure specified in that subsection as the amount of a Class 3 contribution,
as he thinks fit in consequence of the coming into force of an order made or proposed to be made under subsection (1) above.

DEFINITIONS
"the Contributions and Benefits Act": s.191.

Power to alter number of secondary earnings brackets

146. The Secretary of State may by order alter the number of secondary earnings brackets below the highest bracket specified in section 9(3) of the Contributions and Benefits Act.

DEFINITIONS
"the Contributions and Benefits Act": s.191.

Orders under ss.145 and 146—supplementary

147.—(1) An order under section 145 or 146 above may make such amendments of any enactment as appear to the Secretary of State to be necessary or expedient in consequence of any alteration made by it.
(2) Where (in accordance with section 190 below) the Secretary of State lays before Parliament a draft of an order under section 145 or 146 above, he shall lay with it a copy of a report by the Government Actuary or the Deputy Government Actuary on the effect which, in that Actuary's opinion, the making of such an order may be expected to have on the National Insurance Fund.
(3) An order under section 145 or 146 above shall be made so as to come into force—
(a) on a date in the tax year in which it receives Parliamentary approval; or
(b) on a date in the next tax year.
(4) Such an order shall have effect for the remainder of the tax year in which it comes into force and for any subsequent tax year (subject to the effect of any subsequent order under this Part of this Act).

(5) Such an order shall be taken as receiving Parliamentary approval on the date on which the draft of it is approved by the second House to approve it.

Revaluation of earnings factors

148.—(1) This section shall have effect for the purpose of securing that earnings factors which are relevant—
  (a) to the calculation—
      (i) of the additional pension in the rate of any long-term benefit; or
      (ii) of any guaranteed minimum pension; or
  (b) to any other calculation required under Part III of the Pensions Act (including that Part as modified by or under any other enactment),
maintain their value in relation to the general level of earnings obtaining in Great Britain.

(2) The Secretary of State shall in each tax year review the general level of earnings obtaining in Great Britain and any changes in that level which have taken place since the end of the period taken into account for the last review under this section; and for the purposes of any such review the Secretary of State shall estimate the general level of earnings in such manner as he thinks fit.

(3) If on any such review the Secretary of State concludes, having regard to earlier orders under this section, that earnings factors for any previous tax year (not being earlier than 1978–79) have not, during the period taken into account for that review, maintained their value in relation to the general level of earnings, he shall make an order under this section.

(4) An order under this section shall be an order directing that, for the purposes of any such calculation as is mentioned in subsection (1) above, the earnings factors referred to in subsection (3) above shall be increased by such percentage of their amount, apart from earlier orders under this section, as the Secretary of State thinks necessary to make up that fall in their value, during the period taken into account for the review together with other falls in their value which had been made up by such earlier orders.

(5) Subsections (3) and (4) above do not require the Secretary of State to direct any increase where it appears to him that the increase would be inconsiderable.

(6) If on any such review the Secretary of State determines that he is not required to make an order under this section, he shall instead lay before each House of Parliament a report explaining his reasons for arriving at that determination.

(7) For the purposes of this section—
  (a) any review under section 21 of the Pensions Act (which made provision corresponding to this section) shall be treated as a review under this section; and
  (b) any order under that section shall be treated as an order under this section,
(but without prejudice to sections 16 and 17 of the Interpretation Act 1978).

GENERAL NOTE

Section 148 provides for the revaluing of earnings factors (earned by earnings-related contributions) in line with average earnings. The most important rôle of earnings factors is calculating entitlements under the state earnings-related pension scheme (SERPS).

Statutory sick pay—power to alter limit for small employers' relief

149. If and so long as regulations under section 158(3) of the Contributions and Benefits Act prescribe an amount which an employer's contributions payments must not exceed if he is to be a small employer for the purposes of that section, the Secretary of State shall in each tax year consider whether that amount should be increased, having regard to any increase in the aggregate amount of all primary and secondary Class 1 contributions payable in Great Britain and such other matters as he considers appropriate.

DEFINITIONS
    "the Contributions and Benefits Act": s.191.

PART X

REVIEW AND ALTERATION OF BENEFITS

Annual up-rating of benefits

150.—(1) The Secretary of State shall in each tax year review the sums—
  (a) specified in the following provisions of the Contributions and Benefits Act—
      (i) Schedule 4;
      (ii) section 44(4); and
      (iii) paragraphs 2(6)(c) and 6(2)(b) of Schedule 8;
  (b) specified in regulations under section 72(3) or 73(10) of that Act;
  (c) which are the additional pensions in long-term benefits;
  (d) which are the increases in the rates of retirement pensions under Schedule 5 to the Contributions and Benefits Act;
  (e) which are—
      (i) payable by virtue of section 35(6) of the Pensions Act to a person who is also entitled to a Category A or Category B retirement pension (including sums payable by virtue of section 36(3)); or
      (ii) payable to such a person as part of his Category A or Category B retirement pension by virtue of an order made under this section by virtue of this paragraph or made under section 126A of the 1975 Act or section 63(1)(d) of the 1986 Act;
  (f) specified in section 80(4) of the Contributions and Benefits Act;
  (g) falling to be calculated under paragraph 13(4) of Schedule 7 to that Act;
  (h) prescribed for the purposes of section 128(5) or 129(8) of that Act or specified in regulations under section 135(1);
  (i) specified by virtue of section 145(1) of that Act;
  (j) specified in section 157(1) of that Act or in regulations under section 166(3);
in order to determine whether they have retained their value in relation to the general level of prices obtaining in Great Britain estimated in such manner as the Secretary of State thinks fit.

    (2) Where it appears to the Secretary of State that the general level of prices is greater at the end of the period under review than it was at the beginning of that period, he shall lay before Parliament the draft of an up-rating order—
  (a) which increases each of the sums to which subsection (3) below applies by a percentage not less than the percentage by which the general level of prices is greater at the end of the period than it was at the beginning; and
  (b) if he considers it appropriate, having regard to the national economic situation and any other matters which he considers relevant, which also increases by such a percentage or percentages as he thinks fit any

of the sums mentioned in subsection (1) above but to which subsection (3) below does not apply; and

(c) stating the amount of any sums which are mentioned in subsection (1) above but which the order does not increase.

(3) This subsection applies to sums—

(a) specified in Part I, paragraph 1, 2, 4, 5 or 6 of Part III, Part IV or Part V of Schedule 4 to the Contributions and Benefits Act;

(b) mentioned in subsection (1)(a)(ii) or (iii), (b), (c), (d), (e) or (g) above.

(4) Subsection (2) above shall not require the Secretary of State to provide for an increase in any case in which it appears to him that the amount of the increase would be inconsiderable.

(5) The Secretary of State may, in providing for an increase in pursuance of subsection (2) above, adjust the amount of the increase so as to round any sum up or down to such extent as he thinks appropriate.

(6) Where subsection (2) above requires the Secretary of State to lay before Parliament the draft of an order increasing any sum that could be reduced under section 154(1) below, the order may make such alteration to that sum as reflects the combined effect of that increase and of any reduction that could be made under that subsection.

(7) If the Secretary of State considers it appropriate to do so, he may include in the draft of an up-rating order, in addition to any other provisions, provisions increasing any of the sums for the time being specified in regulations under Part VII of the Contributions and Benefits Act or which are additions to income support under regulations made under section 89 of the 1986 Act.

(8) The Secretary of State shall lay with any draft order under this section a copy of a report by the Government Actuary or the Deputy Government Actuary giving that Actuary's opinion on the likely effect on the National Insurance Fund of such parts of the order as relate to sums payable out of that Fund.

(9) If a draft order laid before Parliament in pursuance of this section is approved by a resolution of each House, the Secretary of State shall make the order in the form of the draft.

(10) An order under this section—

(a) shall be framed so as to bring the alterations to which it relates into force—

(i) in the week beginning with the first Monday in the tax year; or

(ii) on such earlier date in April as may be specified in the order;

(b) may make such transitional provision as the Secretary of State considers expedient in respect of periods of entitlement—

(i) to family credit;

(ii) to disability working allowance; or

(iii) to statutory sick pay,

running at the date when the alterations come into force.

(11) So long as sections 36 and 37 of the National Insurance Act 1965 (graduated retirement benefit) continue in force by virtue of regulations made under Schedule 3 to the Social Security (Consequential Provisions) Act 1975 or under Schedule 3 to the Consequential Provisions Act, regulations may make provision for applying the provisions of this section to the amount of graduated retirement benefit payable for each unit of graduated contributions and to increases of such benefit under any provisions made by virtue of section 24(1)(b) of the Pensions Act or section 62(1)(a) of the Contributions and Benefits Act.

DEFINITIONS

"the 1986 Act": s.191.

"the Consequential Provisions Act": *ibid.*

"the Contributions and Benefits Act": *ibid.*
"the Pensions Act": *ibid.*
"tax year": *ibid.*

GENERAL NOTE
Section 150 provides for the annual up-rating of levels of benefit, having regard to movements in prices, rather than earnings. The benefits specified in subs. (3) must be up-rated in line with any increase in prices (subs. (2)(a)). Other benefits, excluding child benefit (on which see s.153), need only be increased if the Secretary of State considers it appropriate (subs. (2)(b)).

Up-rating—supplementary

151.—(1) Any increase under section 150 above of the sums mentioned in subsection (1)(c) of that section shall take the form of a direction that those sums shall be increased by a specified percentage of their amount apart from the order and shall apply only in relation to additional pensions calculated under section 45 of the Contributions and Benefits Act by reference to final relevant years which are—
  (a) earlier than the tax year preceding that in which the order comes into force; or
  (b) if the order comes into force on or after 6th May in any tax year, earlier than that year.

(2) Any increase under section 150 above of the sums mentioned in subsection (1)(d) or (e) of that section shall take the form of a direction that those sums shall be increased by a specified percentage of their amount apart from the order and shall apply only in relation to sums calculated under Schedule 5 to the Contributions and Benefits Act by reference to periods of deferment which have ended before the coming into force of the order.

(3) An increase in a sum such as is specified in section 150(1)(e)(ii) above shall form part of the Category A or Category B retirement pension of the person to whom it is paid and an increase in a sum such as is specified in section 150(1)(e)(i) above shall be added to and form part of that pension but shall not form part of the sum increased.

(4) Where any increment under section 35(6) of the Pensions Act—
  (a) is increased in any tax year by an order under section 37A of that Act; and
  (b) in that tax year also falls to be increased by an order under section 150 above,
the increase under that section shall be the amount that would have been specified in the order, but for this subsection, less the amount of the increase under section 37A.

(5) Where sums are payable to a person by virtue of section 35(6) of the Pensions Act (including such sums payable by virtue of section 36(3) of that Act) during a period ending with the date on which he became entitled to a Category A or Category B retirement pension, then, for the purpose of determining the amount of his Category A or Category B retirement pension, orders made under section 150 above during that period shall be deemed to have come into force (consecutively in the order in which they were made) on the date on which he became entitled to that pension.

(6) Any increase under section 150 above of any of the sums which are additions to income support mentioned in section 150(7) above shall take the form of a direction that any such sum shall be increased by a specified percentage of its amount apart from the order.

DEFINITIONS
  "the Contributions and Benefits Act": s.191.
  "the Pensions Act": *ibid.*
  "tax year": *ibid.*

Rectification of mistakes in orders under section 150

152.—(1) If the Secretary of State is satisfied that a mistake (whether in computation or otherwise) has occurred in the preparation of the previous order under section 150 above, he may by order vary the amount of any one or more of the sums specified in an enactment mentioned in subsection (1)(a) of that section by increasing or reducing it to the level at which it would have stood had the mistake not occurred.

(2) Where the amount of any such sum is varied under this section, then, for the purposes of the next review and order under that section, the amount of the sum shall be taken to be, and throughout the period under review to have been, its amount as so varied.

[¹Annual review of child benefit

153. The Secretary of State shall review the level of child benefit in April of each year, taking account of increases in the Retail Price Index and other relevant external factors.]

AMENDMENT
   1. Omitted until s.5 of the Social Security Act 1988 is brought into force: Social Security (Consequential Provisions) Act 1992, Sched. 4, paras. 1 and 16.

GENERAL NOTE
   Child benefit is to be excluded from the general provision about up-rating in s.150, but the Secretary of State is required to review its level each year.

Social security benefits in respect of children

154.—(1) Regulations may, with effect from any day on or after that on which there is an increase in the rate or any of the rates of child benefit, reduce any sum specified in any of the provisions mentioned in subsection (2) below to such extent as the Secretary of State thinks appropriate having regard to that increase.

(2) The provisions referred to in subsection (1) above are the following provisions of Schedule 4 to the Contributions and Benefits Act—
   (a) paragraph 6 of Part I (child's special allowance);
   (b) paragraph 5 of Part III (guardian's allowance);
   (c) column (2) of Part IV (increase for child dependants);
   (d) paragraph 7 of Part V (increase of weekly rate of disablement pension in respect of child dependants);
   (e) paragraph 12 of Part V (allowance in respect of deceased's children).

DEFINITIONS
   "the Contributions and Benefits Act": s.191.

PART XI

COMPUTATION OF BENEFITS

Effect of alteration of rates of benefit under Parts II to V of Contributions and Benefits Act

155.—(1) This section has effect where the rate of any benefit to which this section applies is altered—
   (a) by an Act subsequent to this Act;
   (b) by an order under section 150 or 152 above; or
   (c) in consequence of any such Act or order altering any maximum rate of benefit;
and in this section "the commencing date" means the date fixed for payment of benefit at an altered rate to commence.

(2) This section applies to benefit under Part II, III, IV or V of the Contributions and Benefits Act.

(3) Subject to such exceptions or conditions as may be prescribed, where—

(a) the weekly rate of a benefit to which this section applies is altered to a fixed amount higher or lower than the previous amount; and

(b) before the commencing date an award of that benefit has been made (whether before or after the passing of the relevant Act or the making of the relevant order),

except as respects any period falling before the commencement date, the benefit shall become payable at the altered rate without any claim being made for it in the case of an increase in the rate of benefit or any review of the award in the case of a decrease, and the award shall have effect accordingly.

(4) Where—

(a) the weekly rate of a benefit to which this section applies is altered; and

(b) before the commencing date (but after that date is fixed) an award is made of the benefit,

the award either may provide for the benefit to be paid as from the commencing date at the altered rate or may be expressed in terms of the rate appropriate at the date of the award.

(5) Where in consequence of the passing of an Act, or the making of an order, altering the rate of disablement pension, regulations are made varying the scale of disablement gratuities, the regulations may provide that the scale as varied shall apply only in cases where the period taken into account by the assessment of the extent of the disablement in respect of which the gratuity is awarded begins or began after such day as may be prescribed.

(6) Subject to such exceptions or· conditions as may be prescribed, where—

(a) for any purpose of any Act or regulations the weekly rate at which a person contributes to the cost of providing for a child, or to the maintenance of an adult dependant, is to be calculated for a period beginning on or after the commencing date for an increase in the weekly rate of benefit; but

(b) account is to be taken of amounts referable to the period before the commencing date,

those amounts shall be treated as increased in proportion to the increase in the weekly rate of benefit.

(7) So long as sections 36 and 37 of the National Insurance Act 1965 (graduated retirement benefit) continue in force by virtue of regulations made under Schedule 3 to the Social Security (Consequential Provisions) Act 1975 or under Schedule 3 to the Consequential Provisions Act, regulations may make provision for applying the provisions of this section to the amount of graduated retirement benefit payable for each unit of graduated contributions and to increases of such benefit under any provisions made by virtue of section 24(1)(b) of the Pensions Act or section 62(1)(a) of the Contributions and Benefits Act.

DEFINITIONS
"the Consequential Provisions Act": s.191.
"the Contributions and Benefits Act": *ibid.*
"the Pensions Act": *ibid.*

GENERAL NOTE
Section 155 provides for up-rated amounts of benefit under Pts. II–V of the Contributions and Benefits Act to take effect automatically without the need for any claim or review.

Computation of Category A retirement pension with increase under s.52(3) of Contributions and Benefits Act

156. Where a person is entitled to a Category A retirement pension with an increase under section 52(3) of the Contributions and Benefits Act in the additional pension and the circumstances are such that—

(a) the deceased spouse to whose contributions that increase is referable died during that part of the tax year which precedes the date on which the order under section 150 above comes into force ("the initial up-rating order"); and

(b) the deceased spouse's final relevant year for the purposes of section 44 of the Contributions and Benefits Act is the tax year immediately preceding that in which the death occurred,

then, in determining the amount of the additional pension which falls to be increased by the initial up-rating order, so much of that pension as is attributable to the increase under section 52(3) of the Contributions and Benefits Act shall be disregarded.

DEFINITIONS
"the Contributions and Benefits Act": s.191.
"tax year": *ibid.*

Effect of alteration of rates of child benefit

157.—(1) Subsections (3) and (4) of section 155 above shall have effect where there is an increase in the rate or any of the rates of child benefit as they have effect in relation to the rate of benefit to which that section applies.

(2) Where in connection with child benefit—

(a) any question arises in respect of a period after the date fixed for the commencement of payment of child benefit at an increased rate—

(i) as to the weekly rate at which a person is contributing to the cost of providing for a child; or

(ii) as to the expenditure that a person is incurring in respect of a child; and

(b) in determining that question account falls to be taken of contributions made or expenditure incurred for a period before that date,

the contributions made or expenditure incurred before that date shall be treated as increased in proportion to the increase in the rate of benefit.

GENERAL NOTE
The amount of payment of child benefit increases automatically on an up-rating under s.153.

Treatment of excess benefit as paid on account of child benefit

158.—(1) In any case where—

(a) any benefit as defined in section 122 of the Contributions and Benefits Act or any increase of such benefit ("the relevant benefit or increase") has been paid to a person for a period in respect of a child; and

(b) subsequently child benefit for that period in respect of the child becomes payable at a rate which is such that, had the relevant benefit or increase been awarded after the child benefit became payable, the rate of the relevant benefit or increase would have been reduced,

then, except in so far as regulations otherwise provide, the excess shall be treated as paid on account of child benefit for that period in respect of the child.

(2) In subsection (1) above "the excess" means so much of the relevant benefit or increase as is equal to the difference between—

(a) the amount of it which was paid for the period referred to in that subsection; and

(b) the amount of it which would have been paid for that period if it had been paid at the reduced rate referred to in paragraph (b) of that subsection.

DEFINITIONS
"the Contributions and Benefits Act": s.191.

Effect of alteration in the component rates of income support

159.—(1) Subject to such exceptions and conditions as may be prescribed, where—

(a) an award of income support is in force in favour of any person ("the recipient"); and

(b) there is an alteration in any of the relevant amounts, that is to say—

(i) any of the component rates of income support;

(ii) any of the other sums specified in regulations under Part VII of the Contributions and Benefits Act; or

(iii) the recipient's benefit income; and

(c) the alteration affects the computation of the amount of income support to which the recipient is entitled,

then subsection (2) or (3) below (as the case may be) shall have effect.

(2) Where, in consequence of the alteration in question, the recipient becomes entitled to an increased or reduced amount of income support ("the new amount"), then, as from the commencing date, the amount of income support payable to or for the recipient under the award shall be the new amount, without any further decision of an adjudication officer, and the award shall have effect accordingly.

(3) Where, notwithstanding the alteration in question, the recipient continues on and after the commencing date to be entitled to the same amount of income support as before, the award shall continue in force accordingly.

(4) In any case where—

(a) there is an alteration in any of the relevant amounts; and

(b) before the commencing date (but after that date is fixed) an award of income support is made in favour of a person,

the award either may provide for income support to be paid as from the commencing date, in which case the amount shall be determined by reference to the relevant amounts which will be in force on that date, or may provide for an amount determined by reference to the amounts in force at the date of the award.

(5) In this section—

"alteration" means—

(a) in relation to—

(i) the component rates of income support; or

(ii) any other sums specified in regulations under Part VII of the Contributions and Benefits Act,

their alteration by or under any enactment whether or not contained in that Part; and

(b) in relation to a person's benefit income, the alteration of any of the sums referred to in section 150 above—

(i) by any enactment; or

(ii) by an order under section 150 or 152 above,

to the extent that any such alteration affects the amount of his benefit income;

"benefit income", in relation to any person, means so much of his income as consists of—

(a) benefit under the Contributions and Benefits Act, other than income support; or

(b) a war disablement pension or war widow's pension;

"the commencing date" in relation to an alteration, means the date on which the alteration comes into force in the case of the person in question;

"component rate", in relation to income support, means the amount of—

(a) the sum referred to in section 126(5)(b)(i) and (ii) of the Contributions and Benefits Act; or

    (b) any of the sums specified in regulations under section
        135(1) of that Act; and
"relevant amounts" has the meaning given by subsection (1)(b) above.

DEFINITIONS
  "the Contributions and Benefits Act": s.191.

GENERAL NOTE
  The general rule under s.159 is that if there is an alteration in the prescribed figures for
income support personal allowances, premiums, the relevant sum (*i.e.* assumed "strike pay" in
trade dispute cases), or any social security benefits which count as income for income support
purposes (subss. (1) and (5)), then any consequent change in the amount of income support
which is payable takes effect automatically without the need for a decision by an AO (subs. (2)).
Thus no right of appeal arises against the change in the amount, although the claimant can
always request a review of the decision awarding benefit, as altered under s.159. The former
power to review an award of income support in such circumstances has been removed by the
amendment to reg. 69(3) of the Social Security (Adjudication) Regulations 1986 (S.I. 1986 No.
2218), except where some kind of transitional addition is in payment. In this latter case, there
must be a review under reg. 69(3A) to give effect to the change. See the current edition of
Mesher.

Implementation of increases in income support due to attainment of particular ages

  160.—(1) This section applies where—
  (a) an award of income support is in force in favour of a person ("the
      recipient"); and
  (b) there is a component which becomes applicable, or applicable at a
      particular rate, in his case if he or some other person attains a
      particular age.
  (2) If, in a case where this section applies, the recipient or other person
attains the particular age referred to in paragraph (b) of subsection (1) above
and, in consequence,—
  (a) the component in question becomes applicable, or applicable at a
      particular rate, in the recipient's case (whether or not some other
      component ceases, for the same reason, to be applicable, or applic-
      able at a particular rate, in his case); and
  (b) after taking account of any such cessation, the recipient becomes
      entitled to an increased amount of income support,
then, except as provided by subsection (3) below, as from the day on which
he becomes so entitled, the amount of income support payable to or for him
under the award shall be that increased amount, without any further decision of an adjudication officer, and the award shall have effect accordingly.
  (3) Subsection (2) above does not apply in any case where, in consequence
of the recipient or other person attaining the age in question, some question
arises in relation to the recipient's entitlement to any benefit under the
Contributions and Benefits Act, other than—
  (a) the question whether the component concerned, or any other compo-
      nent, becomes or ceases to be applicable, or applicable at a particular
      rate, in his case; and
  (b) the question whether, in consequence, the amount of his income
      support falls to be varied.
  (4) In this section "component", in relation to a person and his income
support, means any of the sums specified in regulations under section 135(1)
of the Contributions and Benefits Act.

DEFINITIONS
  "the Contributions and Benefits Act": s.191.

GENERAL NOTE
Section 160 extends the process begun by s.159 of taking routine adjustments in the amount of income support out of the ordinary mechanism of review by an AO under s.25.

PART XII

FINANCE

National Insurance Fund

161.—(1) The National Insurance Fund shall continue to be maintained under the control and management of the Secretary of State.

(2) Accounts of the National Insurance Fund shall be prepared in such form, and in such manner and at such times, as the Treasury may direct, and the Comptroller and Auditor-General shall examine and certify every such account and shall lay copies of it, together with his report on it, before Parliament.

(3) Any money in the National Insurance Fund may from time to time be paid over to the National Debt Commissioners and be invested by them, in accordance with such directions as may be given by the Treasury, in any such manner for the time being specified in Part II of Schedule 1 to the Trustee Investments Act 1961 as the Treasury may specify by an order of which a draft has been laid before Parliament.

(4) The National Debt Commissioners shall present to Parliament annually an account of the securities in which money in the National Insurance Fund is for the time being invested.

Destination of contributions

162.—(1) Contributions received by the Secretary of State under Part I of the Contributions and Benefits Act shall be paid by him into the National Insurance Fund after deducting from contributions of any class, the appropriate national health service allocation in the case of contributions of that class.

(2) The contributions referred to in subsection (1) above include those paid over to the Secretary of State by the Inland Revenue under section 16(4) of the Contributions and Benefits Act and paragraph 6(8) of Schedule 1 to that Act, but subsection (1) above is subject to section 16(5) of that Act as respects contributions from Northern Ireland.

(3) The additions paid under section 1(5) of the Contributions and Benefits Act shall be paid, in accordance with any directions given by the Treasury, into the National Insurance Fund.

(4) The sums paid to the Secretary of State by the Inland Revenue under section 16(4)(b) of the Contributions and Benefits Act and paragraphs 6(8)(b) and 7(7) of Schedule 1 to that Act in respect of interest and penalties recovered by them in connection with contributions of any class shall, subject to section 16(5) of that Act, be paid, in accordance with any directions given by the Treasury, into the National Insurance Fund.

(5) In subsection (1) above "the appropriate national health service allocation" means—

    (a) in the case of primary Class 1 contributions, 1.05 per cent. of the amount estimated to be that of the earnings in respect of which those contributions were paid at the main primary percentage rate;

    (b) in the case of secondary Class 1 contributions, 0.9 per cent. of the amount estimated to be that of the earnings in respect of which those contributions were paid;

    (c) in the case of Class 1A contributions, 0.9 per cent. of the amount estimated to be the aggregate of the cash equivalents of the benefits of the cars and car fuel used in calculating those contributions;

(d) in the case of Class 2 contributions, 15.5 per cent. of the amount estimated to be the total of those contributions;

(e) in the case of Class 3 contributions, 15.5 per cent. of the amount estimated to be the total of those contributions; and

(f) in the case of Class 4 contributions, 1.15 per cent. of the amount estimated to be that of the earnings in respect of which those contributions were paid.

(6) In subsection (5) above "estimated" means estimated by the Secretary of State in any manner which after consulting the Government Actuary or the Deputy Government Actuary he considers to be appropriate and which the Treasury has approved.

(7) The Secretary of State may, with the consent of the Treasury, by order amend any of paragraphs (a) to (f) of subsection (5) above in relation to any tax year, by substituting for the percentage for the time being specified in that paragraph a different percentage.

(8) No order under subsection (7) above shall substitute a figure which represents an increase or decrease in the appropriate national health service allocation of more than—

(a) 0.1 per cent. of the relevant earnings, in the case of paragraph (a) or (b);

(b) 0.1 per cent. of the relevant aggregate, in the case of paragraph (c);

(c) 4 per cent. of the relevant contributions, in the case of paragraph (d) or (e); or

(d) 0.2 per cent. of the relevant earnings, in the case of paragraph (f).

(9) From the national health service allocation in respect of contributions of any class there shall be deducted such amount as the Secretary of State may estimate to be the portion of the total expenses incurred by him or any other government department in collecting contributions of that class which is fairly attributable to that allocation, and the remainder shall, in the hands of the Secretary of State, be taken as paid towards the cost—

(a) of the national health service in England;

(b) of that service in Wales; and

(c) of that service in Scotland,

in such shares as the Treasury may determine.

(10) The Secretary of State shall pay any amounts deducted in accordance with subsection (9) above into the Consolidated Fund.

(11) Any estimate by the Secretary of State for the purposes of subsection (9) above shall be made in accordance with any directions given by the Treasury.

(12) The Secretary of State may make regulations modifying this section, in such manner as he thinks appropriate, in relation to the contributions of persons referred to in the following sections of the Contributions and Benefits Act—

(a) section 116(2) (H.M. forces);

(b) section 117(1) (mariners, airmen, etc.);

(c) section 120(1) (continental shelf workers),

and in relation to any contributions which are reduced under section 6(5) of that Act.

DEFINITIONS
"the Contributions and Benefits Act": s.191.

General financial arrangements

163.—(1) There shall be paid out of the National Insurance Fund—

(a) benefit under Part II of the Contributions and Benefits Act;

(b) guardian's allowance;

(c) Christmas bonus if the relevant qualifying benefit is payable out of that Fund;

(d) any sum falling to be paid by or on behalf of the Secretary of State under regulations relating to statutory sick pay or maternity pay; and

(e) any expenses of the Secretary of State in making payments under section 85, 97 or 99 above to the extent that he estimates that those payments relate to sums paid into the National Insurance Fund.

(2) There shall be paid out of money provided by Parliament—

(a) any administrative expenses of the Secretary of State or other government department in carrying into effect the Contributions and Benefits Act or this Act;

(b) benefit under Part III of that Act, other than guardian's allowance;

(c) benefit under Part V of that Act;

(d) any sums payable by way of the following—
  (i) income support;
  (ii) family credit;
  (iii) disability working allowance;
  (iv) rate rebate subsidy;
  (v) rent rebate subsidy;
  (vi) rent allowance subsidy;
  (vii) community charge benefit subsidy;

(e) payments by the Secretary of State into the social fund under section 167(3) below;

(f) child benefit;

(g) Christmas bonus if the relevant qualifying benefit is payable out of such money;

(h) any sums falling to be paid by the Secretary of State under or by virtue of this Act by way of travelling expenses;

(i) any expenses of the Secretary of State in making payments under section 85, 97 or 99 above to the extent that he estimates that those payments relate to sums paid into the Consolidated Fund;

except in so far as they may be required by any enactment to be paid or borne in some other way.

(3) The administrative expenses referred to in subsection (2)(a) above include those in connection with any inquiry undertaken on behalf of the Secretary of State with a view to obtaining statistics relating to the operation of Parts I to VI and XI of the Contributions and Benefits Act.

(4) Any sums required by a secondary contributor for the purpose of paying any secondary Class 1 contributions which are payable by him in respect of an earner in consequence of the earner's employment in an office of which the emoluments are payable out of the Consolidated Fund shall be paid out of that Fund.

(5) Any expenditure in respect of the payment of interest or repayment supplements under or by virtue of paragraph 6 of Schedule 1 to the Contributions and Benefits Act or paragraph 6 of Schedule 2 to that Act shall be defrayed out of the National Insurance Fund in accordance with any directions given by the Treasury.

DEFINITIONS
  "Christmas bonus": s.191.
  "the Contributions and Benefits Act": *ibid.*

Destination of repayments etc.

164.—(1) Subject to the following provisions of this section, so far as it relates to payments out of money provided by Parliament, any sum recovered by the Secretary of State under or by virtue of this Act shall be paid into the Consolidated Fund.

(2) So far as any such sum relates to a payment out of the National Insurance Fund, it shall be paid into that Fund.

(3) So far as any such sum relates to a payment out of the social fund, it shall be paid into that fund.

(4) Sums repaid by virtue of paragraph 1(4)(e) of Schedule 9 to this Act as it has effect for the purposes of schemes under paragraph 2 or 4 of Schedule 8 to the Contributions and Benefits Act shall be paid into the Consolidated Fund.

(5) There shall be paid into the National Insurance Fund—

  (a) fees so payable under regulations made by virtue of section 62(2)(b) above; and

  (b) sums recovered by the Secretary of State by virtue of a scheme under paragraph 2 or 4 of Schedule 8 to the Contributions and Benefits Act making provision by virtue of paragraph 4 of Schedule 9 to this Act.

(6) Any sums paid to the Secretary of State in pursuance of section 82 above shall be paid—

  (a) into the Consolidated Fund, to the extent that the Secretary of State estimates that those sums relate to payments out of money provided by Parliament; and

  (b) into the National Insurance Fund, to the extent that he estimates that they relate to payments out of that Fund.

[¹(7) Any sums repaid to the Secretary of State in pursuance of section 119(1) of the 1975 Act (which related to the effect of adjudication and was repealed subject to a saving in relation to certain reviews and appeals) shall—

  (a) be paid by him into the Consolidated Fund in so far as they represent benefit which under section 163 above is payable out of money provided by Parliament and not out of the National Insurance Fund; and

  (b) otherwise, be paid by him into that Fund.]

AMENDMENT
  1 Inserted until the repeal of s.135(b) of the Social Security Act 1975 in Sched. 11 of the Social Security Act 1986 is brought into force: Social Security (Consequential Provisions) Act 1992, Sched. 4, paras. 1 and 19.

DEFINITIONS
  "the 1975 Act": s.191.
  "the Contributions and Benefits Act": *ibid.*

Adjustments between National Insurance Fund and Consolidated Fund

165.—(1) There shall be made out of the National Insurance Fund into the Consolidated Fund, or out of money provided by Parliament into the National Insurance Fund, such payments by way of adjustment as the Secretary of State determines (in accordance with any directions of the Treasury) to be appropriate in consequence of the operation of any enact-ment or regulations relating to—

  (a) family credit;

  (b) disability working allowance;

  (c) statutory sick pay;

  (d) statutory maternity pay; or

  (e) the repayment or offsetting of benefit as defined in section 122 of the Contributions and Benefits Act or other payments.

(2) Where any such payments as are specified in subsection (3) below fall to be made by way of adjustment, then, subject to subsection (4) below,—

  (a) the amounts of the payments to be made shall be taken to be such, and

  (b) payments on account of them shall be made at such times and in such manner,

as may be determined by the Secretary of State in accordance with any directions given by the Treasury.

(3) The payments mentioned in subsection (2) above are the following, that is to say—

    (a) any payments falling to be made by way of adjustment by virtue of subsection (1)(a) to (d) above;

    (b) any payments falling to be made by way of adjustment in consequence of the operation of any enactment or regulations relating to child benefit—

        (i) out of the National Insurance Fund into the Consolidated Fund, or

        (ii) into the National Insurance Fund out of money provided by Parliament; and

    (c) any payments falling to be made by way of adjustment in circumstances other than those mentioned in subsection (1) or paragraph (b) above—

        (i) out of the National Insurance Fund either to the Secretary of State or another government department or into the Consolidated Fund; or

        (ii) into the National Insurance Fund out of money provided by Parliament.

(4) In relation to payments falling within paragraph (a) or (c) of subsection (3) above, subsection (2) above only applies in such cases or classes of case as may be specified by the Secretary of State by order.

(5) There shall be paid out of the National Insurance Fund into the Consolidated Fund, at such times and in such manner as the Treasury may direct, such sums as the Secretary of State may estimate (in accordance with any directions given by the Treasury) to be the amount of the administrative expenses incurred as mentioned in section 163(2)(a) above, excluding—

    (a) expenses attributable to the carrying into effect of provisions of the Contributions and Benefits Act or this Act relating to the benefits which by virtue of section 163(2) above are payable out of money provided by Parliament; and

    (b) any other category of expenses which the Treasury may direct, or any enactment may require, to be excluded from the Secretary of State's estimate under this subsection;

but none of the administrative expenses of the Christmas bonus shall be excluded from that estimate by virtue of paragraph (a) or (b) above.

DEFINITIONS

   "Christmas bonus": s.191.

   "the Contributions and Benefits Act": *ibid.*

Financial review and report

    166.—(1) As from the end of the period of 5 years beginning with 6th April 1990, or such shorter period as the Secretary of State may direct, the Government Actuary or the Deputy Government Actuary shall review the operation during that period of the 1975 Act and of Parts I to VI of the Contributions and Benefits Act (except Part I of Schedule 8) and this Act so far as it relates to those Parts.

    (2) As from the end of each review period, the Government Actuary or Deputy Government Actuary shall review the operation during that period of Parts I to VI of the Contributions and Benefits Act (except Part I of Schedule 8) and this Act, so far as it relates to those Parts.

    (3) For the purposes of subsection (2) above, a review period is—

    (a) the period of five tax years, or

    (b) such shorter period as the Secretary of State may direct in respect of any review,

from the end of the last period to be subject to a review under this section.

    (4) It shall be the object of a review under this section to determine the extent to which the level at which the National Insurance Fund stands from year to year may be expected in the longer term to bear a proper relation to

demands in respect of payments of benefit; and for this purpose the Actuary shall take into account—

(a) current rates of contributions;

(b) the yield to be expected from contributions in the longer term; and

(c) such other matters as he considers to be relevant as affecting the present and future level of the Fund.

(5) After completing his review, the Government Actuary or Deputy Government Actuary shall report to the Secretary of State his opinion on the question referred to in subsection (4) above; and the Secretary of State shall lay a copy of the report before Parliament.

DEFINITIONS
"the Contributions and Benefits Act": s.191.
"tax year": *ibid.*

The social fund

167.—(1) The fund known as the social fund shall continue in being by that name.

(2) The social fund shall continue to be maintained under the control and management of the Secretary of State and payments out of it shall be made by him.

(3) The Secretary of State shall make payments into the social fund of such amounts, at such times and in such manner as he may with the approval of the Treasury determine.

(4) Accounts of the social fund shall be prepared in such form, and in such manner and at such times, as the Treasury may direct, and the Comptroller and Auditor General shall examine and certify every such account and shall lay copies of it, together with his report, before Parliament.

(5) The Secretary of State shall prepare an annual report on the social fund.

(6) A copy of every such report shall be laid before each House of Parliament.

Allocations from social fund

168.—(1) The Secretary of State shall allocate amounts for payments from the social fund such as are mentioned in section 138(1)(b) of the Contributions and Benefits Act in a financial year.

(2) The Secretary of State may specify the amounts either as sums of money or by reference to money falling into the social fund on the repayment or partial repayment of loans, or partly in the former and partly in the latter manner.

(3) Allocations—

(a) may be for payments by a particular social fund officer or group of social fund officers;

(b) may be of different amounts for different purposes;

(c) may be made at such time or times as the Secretary of State considers appropriate; and

(d) may be in addition to any other allocation to the same officer or group of officers or for the same purpose.

(4) The Secretary of State may at any time re-allocate amounts previously allocated, and subsections (2) and (3) above shall have effect in relation to a re-allocation as they have effect in relation to an allocation.

(5) The Secretary of State may give general directions to social fund officers or groups of social fund officers, or to any class of social fund officers, with respect to the control and management by social fund officers or groups of social fund officers of the amounts allocated to them under this section.

DEFINITIONS
"the Contributions and Benefits Act": s.191.

GENERAL NOTE

See the social fund directions in the current edition of Mesher. The existence of a fixed budget for each office of the Benefits Agency for the purposes of loans and grants respectively is the most distinctive feature of the social fund. The amount allocated each year is entirely within the discretion of the Secretary of State.

Adjustments between social fund and other sources of finance

169.—(1) There shall be made—

(a) out of the social fund into the Consolidated Fund or the National Insurance Fund;

(b) into the social fund out of money provided by Parliament or the National Insurance Fund,

such payments by way of adjustment as the Secretary of State determines (in accordance with any directions of the Treasury) to be appropriate in consequence of any enactment or regulations relating to the repayment or offsetting of a benefit or other payment under the Contributions and Benefits Act.

(2) Where in any other circumstances payments fall to be made by way of adjustment—

(a) out of the social fund into the Consolidated Fund or the National Insurance Fund; or

(b) into the social fund out of money provided by Parliament or the National Insurance Fund,

then, in such cases or classes of case as may be specified by the Secretary of State by order, the amounts of the payments to be made shall be taken to be such, and payments on account of it shall be made at such times and in such manner, as may be determined by the Secretary of State in accordance with any direction given by the Treasury.

DEFINITIONS

"the Contributions and Benefits Act": s.191.

PART XIII

ADVISORY BODIES AND CONSULTATION

The Social Security Advisory Committee and the Industrial Injuries Advisory Council

The Social Security Advisory Committee

170.—(1) The Social Security Advisory Committee (in this Act referred to as "the Committee") constituted under section 9 of the Social Security Act 1980 shall continue in being by that name—

(a) to give (whether in pursuance of a reference under this Act or otherwise) advice and assistance to the Secretary of State in connection with the discharge of his functions under the relevant enactments;

(b) to give (whether in pursuance of a reference under this Act or otherwise) advice and assistance to the Northern Ireland Department in connection with the discharge of its functions under the relevant Northern Ireland enactments; and

(c) to perform such other duties as may be assigned to the Committee under any enactment.

(2) Schedule 5 to this Act shall have effect with respect to the constitution of the Committee and the other matters there mentioned.

(3) The Secretary of State may from time to time refer to the Committee for consideration and advice such questions relating to the operation of any of the relevant enactments as he thinks fit (including questions as to the advisability of amending any of them).

(4) The Secretary of State shall furnish the Committee with such information as the Committee may reasonably require for the proper discharge of its functions.

(5) In this Act—

"the relevant enactments" means—

(a) the provisions of the Contributions and Benefits Act and this Act, except as they apply to industrial injuries benefit and Old Cases payments; and

(b) the provisions of Part II of Schedule 3 to the Consequential Provisions Act, except as they apply to industrial injuries benefit; and

"the relevant Northern Ireland enactments" means—

(a) the provisions of the Northern Ireland Contributions and Benefits Act and the Northern Ireland Administration Act, except as they apply to Northern Ireland industrial injuries benefit and payments under Part I of Schedule 8 to the Northern Ireland Contributions and Benefits Act; and

(b) the provisions of Part II of Schedule 3 to the Social Security (Consequential Provisions) (Northern Ireland) Act 1992, except as they apply to Northern Ireland industrial injuries benefit; and

(c) Article 52A(10), Part VA, Articles 69J and 70ZA of the Social Security Pensions (Northern Ireland) Order 1975;

and in this definition—

(i) "Northern Ireland Contributions and Benefits Act" means the Social Security Contributions and Benefits (Northern Ireland) Act 1992;

(ii) "Northern Ireland industrial injuries benefit" means benefit under Part V of the Northern Ireland Contributions and Benefits Act other than under Schedule 8 to that Act.

DEFINITIONS

"the Consequential Provisions Act": s.191.
"the Contributions and Benefits Act": *ibid.*
"industrial injuries benefit": *ibid.*
"the Northern Ireland Administration Act": *ibid.*
"Old Cases payments": *ibid.*

GENERAL NOTE

The Secretary of State is obliged under ss.172–174 to consult the Social Security Advisory Committee on proposals to make certain regulations and to publish the SSAC's recommendations when they are laid before Parliament. The SSAC in appropriate cases carries out a public consultation exercise (although often inadequately publicised). Its recommendations are sometimes trenchant and have resulted in wholesale changes in proposed regulations.

The SSAC also keeps under review the general area of social security policy within its remit and publishes annual reports and occasional papers. These contain much valuable material. The SSAC's independence of view is firmly established, but the weight of its influence is hard to assess.

The Industrial Injuries Advisory Council

171.—(1) The Industrial Injuries Advisory Council (in this Act referred to as "the Council") constituted under section 62 of the National Insurance (Industrial Injuries) Act 1965 shall continue in being by that name.

(2) Schedule 6 to this Act shall have effect with respect to the constitution of the Council and the other matters there mentioned.

(3) The Secretary of State may from time to time refer to the Council for consideration and advice such questions as he thinks fit relating to industrial injuries benefit or its administration.

(4) The Council may also give advice to the Secretary of State on any other matter relating to such benefit or its administration.

GENERAL NOTE
The Industrial Injuries Advisory Council carries out similar functions to the SSAC (see s.170) in its more limited area.

Functions of Committee and Council in relation to regulations

172.—(1) Subject—
(a) to subsection (3) below; and
(b) to section 173 below,
where the Secretary of State proposes to make regulations under any of the relevant enactments, he shall refer the proposals, in the form of draft regulations or otherwise, to the Committee.
(2) Subject—
(a) to subsection (4) below; and
(b) to section 173 below,
where the Secretary of State proposes to make regulations relating only to industrial injuries benefit or its administration, he shall refer the proposals, in the form of draft regulations or otherwise, to the Council for consideration and advice.
(3) Subsection (1) above does not apply to the regulations specified in Part I of Schedule 7 to this Act.
(4) Subsection (2) above does not apply to the regulations specified in Part II of that Schedule.
(5) In relation to regulations required or authorised to be made by the Secretary of State in conjunction with the Treasury, the reference in subsection (1) above to the Secretary of State shall be construed as a reference to the Secretary of State and the Treasury.

DEFINITIONS
"industrial injuries benefit": s.191.

GENERAL NOTE
See notes to ss.170 and 171.

Cases in which consultation is not required

173.—(1) Nothing in any enactment shall require any proposals in respect of regulations to be referred to the Committee or the Council if—
(a) it appears to the Secretary of State that by reason of the urgency of the matter it is inexpedient so to refer them; or
(b) the relevant advisory body have agreed that they shall not be referred.
(2) Where by virtue only of subsection (1)(a) above the Secretary of State makes regulations without proposals in respect of them having been referred, then, unless the relevant advisory body agrees that this subsection shall not apply, he shall refer the regulations to that body as soon as practicable after making them.
(3) Where the Secretary of State has referred proposals to the Committee or the Council, he may make the proposed regulations before the Committee have made their report or, as the case may be the Council have given their advice, only if after the reference it appears to him that by reason of the urgency of the matter it is expedient to do so.
(4) Where by virtue of this section regulations are made before a report of the Committee has been made, the Committee shall consider them and make a report to the Secretary of State containing such recommendations with regard to the regulations as the Committee thinks appropriate; and a copy of any report made to the Secretary of State on the regulations shall be laid by him before each House of Parliament together, if the report contains recommendations, with a statement—

(a) of the extent (if any) to which the Secretary of State proposes to give effect to the recommendations; and

(b) in so far as he does not propose to give effect to them, of his reasons why not.

(5) Except to the extent that this subsection is excluded by an enactment passed after 25th July 1986, nothing in any enactment shall require the reference to the Committee or the Council of any regulations contained in either—

(a) a statutory instrument made before the end of the period of 6 months beginning with the coming into force of the enactment under which those regulations are made; or

(b) a statutory instrument—

(i) which states that it contains only regulations made by virtue of, or consequential upon, a specified enactment; and

(ii) which is made before the end of the period of 6 months beginning with the coming into force of that specified enactment.

(6) In relation to regulations required or authorised to be made by the Secretary of State in conjunction with the Treasury, any reference in this section to the Secretary of State shall be construed as a reference to the Secretary of State and the Treasury.

(7) In this section "regulations" means regulations under any enactment, whenever passed.

Committee's report on regulations and Secretary of State's duties

174.—(1) The Committee shall consider any proposals referred to it by the Secretary of State under section 172 above and shall make to the Secretary of State a report containing such recommendations with regard to the subject-matter of the proposals as the Committee thinks appropriate.

(2) If after receiving a report of the Committee the Secretary of State lays before Parliament any regulations or draft regulations which comprise the whole or any part of the subject-matter of the proposals referred to the Committee, he shall lay with the regulations or draft regulations a copy of the Committee's report and a statement showing—

(a) the extent (if any) to which he has, in framing the regulations, given effect to the Committee's recommendations; and

(b) in so far as effect has not been given to them, his reasons why not.

(3) In the case of any regulations laid before Parliament at a time when Parliament is not sitting, the requirements of subsection (2) above shall be satisfied as respects either House of Parliament if a copy of the report and statement there referred to are laid before that House not later than the second day on which the House sits after the laying of the regulations.

(4) In relation to regulations required or authorised to be made by the Secretary of State in conjunction with the Treasury any reference in this section to the Secretary of State shall be construed as a reference to the Secretary of State and the Treasury.

The Disability Living Allowance Advisory Board

Disability Living Allowance Advisory Board

175.—(1) The Disability Living Allowance Advisory Board (in this section referred to as "the Board") constituted under section 3(1) of the Disability Living Allowance and Disability Working Allowance Act 1991 shall continue in being by that name.

(2) Regulations shall confer on the Board such functions relating to disability living allowance or attendance allowance as the Secretary of State thinks fit and shall make provision for—

(a) the Board's constitution;

(b) the qualifications of its members;

(c) the method of their appointment;

(d) the term of office and other terms of appointment of its members;

(e) their removal.

(3) Regulations may also make provision—

(a) enabling the Board to appoint persons as advisers to it on matters on which in its opinion they are specifically qualified;

(b) for the appointment of officers and servants of the Board;

(c) enabling the Board to act notwithstanding any vacancy among its members;

(d) enabling the Board to make rules for regulating its procedure (including its quorum).

(4) The expenses of the Board to such an amount as may be approved by the Treasury shall be paid by the Secretary of State out of money provided by Parliament.

(5) There may be paid as part of the expenses of the Board—

(a) to all or any of the members of the Board, such salaries or other remuneration and travelling and other allowances;

(b) to advisers to the Board, such fees; and

(c) to such other persons as may be specified in regulations such travelling and other allowances (including compensation for loss of remunerative time),

as the Secretary of State may with the consent of the Treasury determine.

(6) The Secretary of State may furnish the Board with such information as he considers that it may need to enable it to discharge its functions.

Housing benefit and community charge benefits

Consultation with representative organisations

176.—(1) Subject to subsection (2) below, before making—

(a) regulations relating to house benefit or community charge benefits (other than regulations of which the effect is to increase any amount specified in regulations previously made);

(b) an order under section 134(12), 135, 139 or 140 above,

the Secretary of State shall consult with organisations appearing to him to be representative of the authorities concerned.

(2) Nothing in subsection (1) above shall require the Secretary of State to undertake consultations if—

(a) it appears to him that by reason of the urgency of the matter it is inexpedient to do so; or

(b) the organisations have agreed that consultations should not be undertaken.

(3) Where the Secretary of State has undertaken such consultations, he may make any regulations or order to which the consultations relate without completing the consultations if it appears to him that by reason of the urgency of the matter it is expedient to do so.

PART XIV

SOCIAL SECURITY SYSTEMS OUTSIDE GREAT BRITAIN

Co-ordination

Co-ordination with Northern Ireland

177.—(1) The Secretary of State may with the consent of the Treasury make arrangements with the Northern Ireland Department ("the joint arrangements") for co-ordinating the operation of the legislation to which this section applies with a view to securing that, to the extent allowed for in the arrangements, it provides a single system of social security for the United Kingdom.

(2) The Joint Authority consisting of the Secretary of State and the Head of the Northern Ireland Department shall continue in being by that name for the purposes of the enactments mentioned in subsection (5) below; and Schedule 8 to this Act has effect with respect to the Joint Authority.

(3) The responsibility of the Joint Authority shall include that of giving effect to the joint arrangements, with power—

(a) to make any necessary financial adjustments between the National Insurance Fund and the Northern Ireland National Insurance Fund; and

(b) to discharge such other functions as may be provided under the joint arrangements.

(4) The Secretary of State may make regulations for giving effect to the joint arrangements; and any such regulations may for the purposes of the arrangements provide—

(a) for adapting legislation (including subordinate legislation) for the time being in force in Great Britain so as to secure its reciprocal operation with Northern Ireland;

(b) without prejudice to paragraph (a) above, for securing that acts, omissions and events having any effect for the purposes of the enactments in force in Northern Ireland have a corresponding effect in relation to Great Britain (but not so as to confer any double benefit); and

(c) for determining, in cases where rights accrue both in relation to Great Britain and in relation to Northern Ireland, which of those rights shall be available to the person concerned.

(5) This section applies—

(a) to the Contributions and Benefits Act and this Act; and

(b) to the Northern Ireland Contributions and Benefits Act and the Northern Ireland Administration Act,

except in relation to the following benefits—

(i) income support;

(ii) family credit;

(iii) disability working allowance;

(iv) housing benefit;

(v) child benefit;

(vi) Christmas bonus;

(vii) statutory sick pay; and

(viii) statutory maternity pay.

DEFINITIONS

"Christmas bonus": s.191.
"the Contributions and Benefits Act": *ibid.*
"the Northern Ireland Administration Act": *ibid.*
"the Northern Ireland Contributions and Benefits Act": s.170(5).

Reciprocity

Reciprocal arrangements with Northern Ireland—income-related benefits and child benefit

178.—(1) The Secretary of State may with the consent of the Treasury make reciprocal arrangements with the authority administering any scheme in force in Northern Ireland and appearing to him to correspond substantially with a scheme contained in the Contributions and Benefits Act and this Act concerning any of the benefits to which this section applies for co-ordinating the operation of those schemes, and such arrangements may include provision for making any necessary financial adjustments.

(2) This section applies to the following benefits—

(a) income support;

(b) family credit;

(c) disability working allowance;

(d) housing benefit; or

(e) child benefit.

(3) Regulations may make provision for giving effect to any such arrangements; and such regulations may in particular provide—

(a) for modifying any provision of this Act or the Contributions and Benefits Act concerning any of the benefits to which this section applies or any regulations made under such a provision;

(b) without prejudice to paragraph (a) above, for securing that acts, omissions and events having any effect for the purposes of the scheme in force in Northern Ireland shall have a corresponding effect for the purposes of this Act and the Contributions and Benefits Act (but not so as to confer any double benefit);

(c) for determining, in cases where rights accrue both under that scheme and under this Act and the Contributions and Benefits Act, which of those rights shall be available to the person concerned.

DEFINITIONS
"the Contributions and Benefits Act": s.191.

Reciprocal agreements with countries outside the United Kingdom

179.—(1) For the purpose of giving effect—

(a) to any agreement with the government of a country outside the United Kingdom providing for reciprocity in matters relating to payments for purposes similar or comparable to the purposes of legislation to which this section applies, or

(b) to any such agreement as it would be if it were altered in accordance with proposals to alter it which, in consequence of any change in the law of Great Britain, the government of the United Kingdom has made to the other government in question,

Her Majesty may by Order in Council make provision for modifying or adapting such legislation in its application to cases affected by the agreement or proposed alterations.

(2) An Order made by virtue of subsection (1) above may, instead of or in addition to making specific modifications or adaptations, provide generally that legislation to which this section applies shall be modified to such extent as may be required to give effect to the provisions contained in the agreement or, as the case may be, alterations in question.

(3) The modifications which may be made by virtue of subsection (1) above include provisions—

(a) for securing that acts, omissions and events having any effect for the purposes of the law of the country in respect of which the agreement is made have a corresponding effect for the purposes of this Act and the Contributions and Benefits Act (but not so as to confer a right to double benefit);

(b) for determining, in cases where rights accrue both under such legislation and under the law of that country, which of those rights is to be available to the person concerned;

(c) for making any necessary financial adjustments.

(4) This section applies—

(a) to the Contributions and Benefits Act; and

(b) to this Act,

except in relation to the following benefits—

(i) community charge benefits;
(ii) payments out of the social fund;
(iii) Christmas bonus;
(iv) statutory sick pay; and
(v) statutory maternity pay.

(5) The power conferred by subsection (1) above shall also be exercisable in relation to regulations made under the Contributions and Benefits Act or this Act and concerning—

(a) income support;
(b) family credit;
(c) disability working allowance;
(d) housing benefit; or
(e) child benefit.

DEFINITIONS
"Christmas bonus": s.191.
"the Contributions and Benefits Act": *ibid.*

PART XV

MISCELLANEOUS

Travelling expenses

Payment of travelling expenses by Secretary of State

180. The Secretary of State may pay such travelling expenses as, with the consent of the Treasury, he may determine—

(a) to persons required by him to attend any interview in connection with the operation of the Contributions and Benefits Act or this Act;
(b) to persons attending local offices in connection with the operation—
  (i) of the Contributions and Benefits Act or this Act; or
  (ii) of any prescribed enactment.

DEFINITIONS
"the Contributions and Benefits Act": s.191.
"prescribed": *ibid.*

Offences

Impersonation of officers

181. If any person, with intent to deceive, falsely represents himself to be a person authorised by the Secretary of State for Social Security to act in any capacity (whether under this Act or otherwise) he shall be guilty of an offence and liable on summary conviction to a fine not exceeding level 4 on the standard scale.

Illegal possession of documents

182.—(1) If any person—

(a) as a pledge or a security for a debt; or
(b) with a view to obtaining payment from the person entitled to it of a debt due either to himself or to any other person,

receives, detains or has in his possession any document issued by or on behalf of the Secretary of State for Social Security in connection with any benefit, pension or allowance (whether payable under the Contributions and Benefits Act or otherwise) he shall be guilty of an offence.

(2) If any such person has such a document in his possession without lawful authority or excuse (the proof whereof shall lie on him) he shall be guilty of an offence.

(3) A person guilty of an offence under this section shall be liable on summary conviction to imprisonment for a term not exceeding 3 months or to a fine not exceeding level 4 on the standard scale or to both.

DEFINITIONS
"the Contributions and Benefits Act": s.191.

Industrial injuries and diseases

Research on industrial injuries, etc.

183.—(1) The Secretary of State may promote research into the causes and incidence of accidents arising out of and in the course of employment, or injuries and diseases which—
  (a) are due to the nature of employment; or
  (b) it is contemplated might be prescribed for the purposes of section 108 to 110 of the Contributions and Benefits Act,
either by himself employing persons to conduct such research or by contributing to the expenses of, or otherwise assisting, other persons engaged in such research.

(2) The Secretary of State may pay to persons so employed by him such salaries or remuneration, and such travelling and other allowances, as he may determine with the consent of the Treasury.

DEFINITIONS
"the Contributions and Benefits Act": s.191.

Control of pneumoconiosis

184. As respects pneumoconiosis, regulations may provide—
  (a) for requiring persons to be medically examined before, or within a prescribed period after, becoming employed in any occupation in relation to which pneumoconiosis is prescribed, and to be medically examined periodically while so employed, and to furnish information required for the purposes of any such examination;
  (b) for suspending from employment in any such occupation, and in such other occupations as may be prescribed, persons found on such an examination—
      (i) to be suffering from pneumoconiosis or tuberculosis, or
      (ii) to be unsuitable for such employment, having regard to the risk of pneumoconiosis and such other matters affecting their susceptibility to pneumoconiosis as may be prescribed;
  (c) for the disqualification for the receipt of benefit as defined in section 122 of the Contributions and Benefits Act in respect of pneumoconiosis of any person who fails without good cause to submit himself to any such examination or to furnish information required by the regulations or who engages in any employment from which he has been suspended as mentioned in paragraph (b) above;
  (d) for requiring employers—
      (i) to provide facilities for such examinations,
      (ii) not to employ in any occupation a person who has been suspended as mentioned in paragraph (b) above from employment in that occupation or who has failed without good cause to submit himself to such an examination,
      (iii) to give to such officer as may be prescribed the prescribed notice of the commencement of any prescribed industry or process;
  (e) for the recovery on summary conviction of monetary penalties in respect of any contravention of or failure to comply with any such requirement as is mentioned in paragraph (d) above, so, however,

that such penalties shall not exceed £5.00 for every day on which the contravention or failure occurs or continues;

(f) for such matters as appear to the Secretary of State to be incidental to or consequential on provisions included in the regulations by virtue of paragraphs (a) to (d) above or section 110(1) of the Contributions and Benefits Act.

DEFINITIONS
"the Contributions and Benefits Act": s.191.

GENERAL NOTE
See Section B of Pt. V of the Social Security (Industrial Injuries) (Prescribed Diseases) Regulations 1985 (S.I. 1985 No. 967).

Workmen's compensation etc.

Administration of workmen's compensation etc.

185.—(1) Schedule 9 to this Act shall have effect in relation to schemes under paragraphs 2 and 4 of Schedule 8 to the Contributions and Benefits Act.

(2) Regulations may provide for applying in relation to payments under Part II of that Schedule the provisions of this Act relating to the making of claims and the determination of claims and questions in so far as those provisions apply in relation to—

(a) an unemployability supplement;

(b) an increase of a disablement pension in respect of a child or adult dependant; or

(c) an increase of a disablement pension in respect of the need for constant attendance or exceptionally severe disablement,

(as the case may be) subject to any additions or modifications.

DEFINITIONS
"the Contributions and Benefits Act": s.191.

Supplementary benefit etc.

Application of provisions of Act to supplementary benefit etc.

186. Schedule 10 to this Act shall have effect for the purpose of making provision in relation to the benefits there mentioned.

Miscellaneous

Certain benefit to be inalienable

187.—(1) Subject to the provisions of this Act, every assignment of or charge on—

(a) benefit as defined in section 122 of the Contributions and Benefits Act;

(b) any income-related benefit; or

(c) child benefit,

and every agreement to assign or charge such benefit shall be void; and, on the bankruptcy of a beneficiary, such benefit shall not pass to any trustee or other person acting on behalf of his creditors.

(2) In the application of subsection (1) above to Scotland—

(a) the reference to assignment of benefit shall be read as a reference to assignation, "assign" being construed accordingly;

(b) the reference to a beneficiary's bankruptcy shall be read as a reference to the sequestration of his estate or the appointment on his estate of a judicial factor under section 41 of the Solicitors (Scotland) Act 1980.

(3) In calculating for the purposes of section 5 of the Debtors Act 1869 or section 4 of the Civil Imprisonment (Scotland) Act 1882 the means of any beneficiary, no account shall be taken of any increase of disablement benefit in respect of a child or of industrial death benefit.

DEFINITIONS
   "the Contributions and Benefits Act": s.191.
   "income-related benefit": *ibid.*

Exemption from stamp duty

188.—(1) Stamp duty shall not be chargeable on any document to which this subsection applies.
   (2) Subsection (1) above applies to any document authorised by virtue—
   (a) of Parts I to VI of the Contributions and Benefits Act; or
   (b) of any provision of this Act so far as it operates in relation to matters to which those Parts relate,
or otherwise required in order to give effect to those Parts or to any such provision so far as it so operates or in connection with any description of business thereunder.
   (3) Stamp duty shall not be chargeable—
   (a) upon such documents used in connection with business under paragraphs 2 and 3 of Schedule 8 to the Contributions and Benefits Act and paragraph 1 of Schedule 9 to this Act as may be specified in a scheme made under paragraph 2 of Schedule 8 to the Contributions and Benefits Act; or
   (b) upon such documents used in connection with business under paragraphs 4 to 6 of that Schedule and paragraph 2 of Schedule 9 to this Act as may be specified in a scheme made under paragraph 4 of Schedule 8 to the Contributions and Benefits Act.

DEFINITIONS
   "the Contributions and Benefits Act": s.191.

PART XVI

GENERAL

Subordinate legislation

Regulations and orders—general

189.—(1) Subject to subsection (2) below and to any other express provision of this Act, regulations and orders under this Act shall be made by the Secretary of State.
   (2) Regulations with respect to proceedings before the Commissioners (whether for the determination of any matter or for leave to appeal to or from the Commissioners) shall be made by the Lord Chancellor.
   (3) Powers under this Act to make regulations or orders are exercisable by statutory instrument.
   (4) Except in the case of regulations under section 24 or 175 above and in so far as this Act otherwise provides, any power conferred by this Act to make an Order in Council, regulations or an order may be exercised—
   (a) either in relation to all cases to which the power extends, or in relation to those cases subject to specified exceptions, or in relation to any specified cases or classes of case;
   (b) so as to make, as respects the cases in relation to which it is exercised—
      (i) the full provision to which the power extends or any less provision (whether by way of exception or otherwise);

(ii) the same provision for all cases in relation to which the power is exercised, or different provision for different cases or different classes of case or different provision as respects the same case or class of case for different purposes of this Act;

(iii) any such provision either unconditionally or subject to any specified condition;

and where such a power is expressed to be exercisable for alternative purposes it may be exercised in relation to the same case for any or all of those purposes; and powers to make an Order in Council, regulations or an order for the purposes of any one provision of this Act are without prejudice to powers to make regulations or an order for the purposes of any other provision.

(5) Without prejudice to any specific provision in this Act, a power conferred by this Act to make an Order in Council, regulations or an order (other than the power conferred by section 24 above) includes power to make thereby such incidental, supplementary, consequential or transitional provision as appears to Her Majesty, or the authority making the regulations or order, as the case may be, to be expedient for the purposes of the Order in Council, regulations or order.

(6) Without prejudice to any specific provisions in this Act, a power conferred by any provision of this Act, except sections 14, 24, 130 and 175, to make an Order in Council, regulations or an order includes power to provide for a person to exercise a discretion in dealing with any matter.

(7) Any power conferred by this Act to make orders or regulations relating to housing benefit or community charge benefits shall include power to make different provision for different areas.

(8) An order under section 135, 140, 150, 152, 165(4) or 169 above and regulations prescribing relevant benefits for the purposes of Part IV of this Act or under section 85 above shall not be made without the consent of the Treasury.

(9) Any power of the Secretary of State under any provision of this Act, except under sections 80, 154, 175 and 178, to make any regulations or order, where the power is not expressed to be exercisable with the consent of the Treasury, shall if the Treasury so direct be exercisable only in conjunction with them.

(10) Where the Lord Chancellor proposes to make regulations under this Act, other than under section 24 above, it shall be his duty to consult the Lord Advocate with respect to the proposal.

(11) A power under any of sections 177 to 179 above to make provision by regulations or Order in Council for modifications or adaptations of the Contributions and Benefits Act or this Act shall be exercisable in relation to any enactment passed after this Act which is directed to be construed as one with them, except in so far as any such enactment relates to a benefit in relation to which the power is not exercisable; but this subsection applies only so far as a contrary intention is not expressed in the enactment so passed, and is without prejudice to the generality of any such direction.

(12) Any reference in this section or section 190 below to an Order in Council, or an order or regulations, under this Act includes a reference to an Order in Council, an order or regulations made under any provision of an enactment passed after this Act and directed to be construed as one with this Act; but this subsection applies only so far as a contrary intention is not expressed in the enactment so passed, and without prejudice to the generality of any such direction.

Parliamentary control of orders and regulations

190.—(1) Subject to the provisions of this section, a statutory instrument containing (whether alone or with other provisions)—

(a) an order under section 141, 143, 145, 146, 150, 152 or 162(7) above; or
(b) regulations under section 102(2) or 154 above,
shall not be made unless a draft of the instrument has been laid before Parliament and been approved by a resolution of each House of Parliament.

(2) Subsection (1) above does not apply to a statutory instrument by reason only that it contains regulations under section 154 above which are to be made for the purpose of consolidating regulations to be revoked in the instrument.

(3) A statutory instrument—
(a) which contains (whether alone or with other provisions) orders or regulations made under this Act by the Secretary of State; and
(b) which is not subject to any requirement that a draft of the instrument be laid before and approved by a resolution of each House of Parliament,
shall be subject to annulment in pursuance of a resolution of either House of Parliament.

(4) A statutory instrument—
(a) which contains (whether alone or with other provisions) regulations made under this Act by the Lord Chancellor; and
(b) which is not subject to any requirement that a draft of the instrument be laid before and approved by a resolution of each House of Parliament,
shall be subject to annulment in pursuance of a resolution of either House of Parliament.

GENERAL NOTE

Section 190 defines which regulations under the Act are subject to the affirmative resolution procedure before Parliament and which to the negative resolution procedure.

Supplementary

Interpretation—general

191. In this Act, unless the context otherwise requires—
"the 1975 Act" means the Social Security Act 1975;
"the 1986 Act" means the Social Security Act 1986;
"benefit" means benefit under the Contributions and Benefits Act;
"chargeable financial year" and "charging authority" have the same meanings as in the Local Government Finance Act 1988;
"Christmas bonus" means a payment under Part X of the Contributions and Benefits Act;
"claim" is to be construed in accordance with "claimant";
"claimant" (in relation to contributions under Part I and to benefit under Parts II to IV of the Contributions and Benefits Act) means—
(a) a person whose right to be excepted from liability to pay, or to have his liability deferred for, or to be credited with, a contribution, is in question;
(b) a person who has claimed benefit;
and includes, in relation to an award or decision a beneficiary under the award or affected by the decision;
"claimant" (in relation to industrial injuries benefit) means a person who has claimed such a benefit and includes—
(a) an applicant for a declaration under section 44 above that an accident was or was not an industrial accident; and
(b) in relation to an award or decision, a beneficiary under the award or affected by the decision;

"Commissioner" means the Chief Social Security Commissioner or any other Social Security Commissioner and includes a tribunal of 3 Commissioners constituted under section 57 above;

"compensation payment" and "compensator" have the meanings assigned to them respectively by sections 81 and 82 above;

"the Consequential Provisions Act" means the Social Security (Consequential Provisions) Act 1992;

"contribution card" has the meaning assigned to it by section 114(6) above;

"the Contributions and Benefits Act" means the Social Security Contributions and Benefits Act 1992;

"disablement benefit" is to be construed in accordance with section 94(2)(a) of the Contributions and Benefits Act;

"the disablement questions" is to be construed in accordance with section 45 above;

"dwelling" means any residential accommodation, whether or not consisting of the whole or part of a building and whether or not comprising separate and self-contained premises;

"5 year general qualification" is to be construed in accordance with section 71 of the Courts and Legal Services Act 1990;

"housing authority" means a local authority, a new town corporation, Scottish Homes or the Development Board for Rural Wales;

"housing benefit scheme" is to be construed in accordance with section 134(1) above;

"income-related benefit" means—

    (a) income support;
    (b) family credit;
    (c) disability working allowance;
    (d) housing benefit; and
    (e) community charge benefits;

"industrial injuries benefit" means benefit under Part V of the Contributions and Benefits Act, other than under Schedule 8;

"invalidity benefit" has the meaning assigned to it by section 20(1)(c) of that Act;

"levying authority" has the same meaning as in the Abolition of Domestic Rates Etc. (Scotland) Act 1987;

"local authority" means—

    (a) in relation to England and Wales, the council of a district or London borough, the Common Council of the City of London or the Council of the Isles of Scilly; and
    (b) in relation to Scotland, an islands or district council;

"medical examination" includes bacteriological and radiographical tests and similar investigations, and "medically examined" has a corresponding meaning;

"medical practitioner" means—

    (a) a registered medical practitioner; or
    (b) a person outside the United Kingdom who is not a registered medical practitioner, but has qualifications corresponding (in the Secretary of State's opinion) to those of a registered medical practitioner;

"medical treatment" means medical, surgical or rehabilitative treatment (including any course of diet or other regimen), and references to a person receiving or submitting himself to medical treatment are to be construed accordingly;

"new town corporation" means—

    (a) in relation to England and Wales, a development corporation established under the New Towns Act 1981 or the Commission for the New Towns; and

(b) in relation to Scotland, a development corporation established under the New Towns (Scotland) Act 1968;

"the Northern Ireland Department" means the Department of Health and Social Services for Northern Ireland;

"the Northern Ireland Administration Act" means the Social Security (Northern Ireland) Administration Act 1992;

"occupational pension scheme" has the same meaning as in section 66(1) of the Pensions Act;

"the Old Cases Act" means the Industrial Injuries and Diseases (Old Cases) Act 1975;

"Old Cases payments" means payments under Part I of Schedule 8 to the Contributions and Benefits Act;

"the Pensions Act" means the Social Security Pensions Act 1975;

"personal pension scheme" has the meaning assigned to it by section 84(1) of the 1986 Act;

"prescribe" means prescribe by regulations;

"President" means the President of social security appeal tribunals, disability appeal tribunals and medical appeal tribunals;

"rate rebate", "rent rebate" and "rent allowance" shall be construed in accordance with section 134 above;

"rates", in relation to England and Wales, has the same meaning as in the General Rate Act 1967 and, in relation to Scotland, the meaning given to "rate" by section 26(2)(a) of the Abolition of Domestic Rates Etc. (Scotland) Act 1987;

"rating authority", in relation to England and Wales, has the same meaning as in the General Rate Act 1967 and, in relation to Scotland, the meaning given by section 109 of the Local Government (Scotland) Act 1973;

"tax year" means the 12 months beginning with 6th April in any year;

"10 year general qualification" is to be construed in accordance with section 71 of the Courts and Legal Services Act 1990; and

"widow's benefit" has the meaning assigned to it by section 20(1)(e) of the Contributions and Benefits Act.

Short title, commencement and extent

192.—(1) This Act may be cited as the Social Security Administration Act 1992.

(2) This Act is to be read, where appropriate, with the Contributions and Benefits Act and the Consequential Provisions Act.

(3) The enactments consolidated by this Act are repealed, in consequence of the consolidation, by the Consequential Provisions Act.

(4) Except as provided in Schedule 4 to the Consequential Provisions Act, this Act shall come into force on 1st July 1992.

(5) The following provisions extend to Northern Ireland—

section 24;

section 101;

section 170 (with Schedule 5);

section 177 (with Schedule 8); and

this section.

(6) Except as provided by this section, this Act does not extend to Northern Ireland.

DEFINITIONS

"the Consequential Provisions Act": s.191.

"the Contributions and Benefits Act": *ibid.*

SCHEDULES

SCHEDULE 1

CLAIMS FOR BENEFIT MADE OR TREATED AS MADE BEFORE 1ST OCTOBER 1990

Claims made or treated as made on or after 2nd September 1985 and before 1st October 1986

1. Section 1 above shall have effect in relation to a claim made or treated as made on or after 2nd September 1985 and before 1st October 1986 as if the following subsections were substituted for subsections (1) to (3)—

"(1) Except in such cases as may be prescribed, no person shall be entitled to any benefit unless, in addition to any other conditions relating to that benefit being satisfied—

(a) he makes a claim for it—
(i) in the prescribed manner; and
(ii) subject to subsection (2) below, within the prescribed time; or
(b) by virtue of a provision of Chapter VI of Part II of the 1975 Act or of regulations made under such a provision he would have been treated as making a claim for it.

(2) Regulations shall provide for extending, subject to any prescribed conditions, the time within which a claim may be made in cases where it is not made within the prescribed time but good cause is shown for the delay.

(3) Notwithstanding any regulations made under this section, no person shall be entitled to any benefit (except disablement benefit or industrial death benefit) in respect of any period more than 12 months before the date on which the claim is made.".

Claims made or treated as made on or after 1st October 1986 and before 6th April 1987

2. Section 1 above shall have effect in relation to a claim made or treated as made on or after 1st October 1986 and before 6th April 1987 as if the subsections set out in paragraph 1 above were substituted for subsections (1) to (3) but with the insertion in subsection (3) of the words ", reduced earnings allowance" after the words "disablement benefit".

Claims made or treated as made on or after 6th April 1987 and before 21st July 1989

3. Section 1 above shall have effect in relation to a claim made or treated as made on or after 6th April 1987 and before 21st July 1989, as if—

(a) the following subsection were substituted for subsection (1)—
"(1) Except in such cases as may be prescribed, no person shall be entitled to any benefit unless, in addition to any other conditions relating to that benefit being satisfied—
(a) he makes a claim for it in the prescribed manner and within the prescribed time; or
(b) by virtue of regulations made under section 51 of the 1986 Act he would have been treated as making a claim for it."; and
(b) there were omitted—
(i) from subsection (2), the words "except as provided by section 3 below"; and
(ii) subsection (3).

Claims made or treated as made on or after 21st July 1989 and before 13th July 1990

4. Section 1 above shall have effect in relation to a claim made or treated as made on or after 21st July 1989 and before 13th July 1990 as if there were omitted—
(a) from subsection (1), the words "and subject to the following provisions of this section and to section 3 below";
(b) from subsection (2), the words "except as provided by section 3 below"; and
(c) subsection (3).

Claims made or treated as made on or after 13th July 1990 and before 1st October 1990

5. Section 1 above shall have effect in relation to a claim made or treated as made on or after 13th July 1990 and before 1st October 1990 as if there were omitted—
(a) from subsection (1), the words "the following provisions of this section and to"; and
(b) subsection (3).

DEFINITIONS
"disablement benefit": s.191.
"prescribe": *ibid.*

GENERAL NOTE
See notes to s.1.

COMMISSIONERS, TRIBUNALS ETC—SUPPLEMENTARY PROVISIONS

Tenure of offices

1.—(1) Subject to the following provisions of this paragraph, the President and the regional and other full-time chairmen of social security appeal tribunals, medical appeal tribunals and disability appeal tribunals shall hold and vacate office in accordance with the terms of their appointment.

(2) Commissioners, the President and the full-time chairmen shall vacate their offices at the end of the completed year of service in which they attain the age of 72.

(3) Where the Lord Chancellor considers it desirable in the public interest to retain a Commissioner, the President or a full-time chairman in office after the time at which he would be required by sub-paragraph (2) above to vacate it, the Lord Chancellor may from time to time authorise his continuance in office until any date not later than that on which he attains the age of 75.

(4) A Commissioner, the President and a full-time chairman may be removed from office by the Lord Chancellor on the ground of incapacity or misbehaviour.

(5) Where the Lord Chancellor proposes to exercise a power conferred on him by sub-paragraph (3) or (4) above, it shall be his duty to consult the Lord Advocate with respect to the proposal.

(6) Nothing in sub-paragraph (2) or (3) above or in section 13 or 32 of the Judicial Pensions Act 1981 (which relate to pensions for Commissioners) shall apply to a person by virtue of his appointment in pursuance of section 52(2) above.

(7) Nothing in sub-paragraph (2) or (4) above applies to a Commissioner appointed before 23rd May 1980.

Remuneration etc. for President and Chairmen

2. The Secretary of State may pay, or make such payments towards the provision of, such remuneration, pensions, allowances or gratuities to or in respect of the President and full-time chairmen as, with the consent of the Treasury, he may determine.

Officers and staff

3. The President may appoint such officers and staff as he thinks fit—
   (a) for himself;
   (b) for the regional and other full-time chairmen;
   (c) for social security appeal tribunals;
   (d) for disability appeal tribunals; and
   (e) for medical appeal tribunals,
with the consent of the Secretary of State and the Treasury as to numbers and as to remuneration and other terms and conditions of service.

Clerks to social security appeal tribunals and disability appeal tribunals

4.—(1) The President shall assign clerks to service the social security appeal tribunal for each area and the disability appeal tribunal for each area.

(2) The duty of summoning members of a panel to service on such a tribunal shall be performed by the clerk to the tribunal.

Miscellaneous administrative duties of President

5. It shall be the duty of the President—
   (a) to arrange—
          (i) such meetings of chairmen and members of social security appeal tribunals, chairmen and members of disability appeal tribunals and chairmen and members of medical appeal tribunals;
          (ii) such training for such chairmen and members,
       as he considers appropriate; and
   (b) to secure that such works of reference relating to social security law as he considers appropriate are available for the use of chairmen and members of social security appeal tribunals, disability appeal tribunals and medical appeal tribunals.

Remuneration etc.

6. The Lord Chancellor shall pay to a Commissioner such salary or other remuneration, and

such expenses incurred in connection with the work of a Commissioner or any tribunal presided over by a Commissioner, as may be determined by the Treasury.

7.—(1) The Secretary of State may pay—

(a) to any person specified in sub-paragraph (2) below, such remuneration and such travelling and other allowances;

(b) to any person specified in sub-paragraph (3) below, such travelling and other allowances; and

(c) subject to sub-paragraph (4) below, such other expenses in connection with the work of any person, tribunal or inquiry appointed or constituted under any provision of this Act,

as the Secretary of State with the consent of the Treasury may determine.

(2) The persons mentioned in sub-paragraph (1)(a) above are—

(a) any person (other than a Commissioner) appointed under this Act to determine questions or as a member of, or assessor to, a social security appeal tribunal, a disability appeal tribunal or a medical appeal tribunal; and

(b) a medical officer appointed under regulations under section 62 above.

(3) The persons mentioned in sub-paragraph (1)(b) above are—

(a) any person required to attend at any proceedings or inquiry under this Act; and

(b) any person required under this Act (whether for the purposes of this Act or otherwise) to attend for or to submit themselves to medical or other examination or treatment.

(4) Expenses are not payable under sub-paragraph (1)(c) above in connection with the work—

(a) of a tribunal presided over by a Commissioner; or

(b) of a social fund officer, a social fund inspector or the social fund Commissioner.

(5) In this paragraph references to travelling and other allowances include references to compensation for loss of remunerative time but such compensation shall not be paid to any person in respect of any time during which he is in receipt of remuneration under this paragraph.

Certificates of decisions

8. A document bearing a certificate which—

(a) is signed by a person authorised in that behalf by the Secretary of State; and

(b) states that the document, apart from the certificate, is a record of a decision—

(i) of a Commissioner;

(ii) of a social security appeal tribunal;

(iii) of a disability appeal tribunal; or

(iv) of an adjudication officer,

shall be conclusive evidence of the decision; and a certificate purporting to be so signed shall be deemed to be so signed unless the contrary is proved.

DEFINITIONS

"Commissioner": s.191.

"President": *ibid.*

GENERAL NOTE

Para. 4

Of the President's detailed powers and duties, the duty to assign the clerk to SSATs and DATs (but, oddly, not to MATs) under para. 4 is particularly important. The fact that supplementary benefit appeal tribunal clerks were in the past DHSS employees had long been a source of criticism, although their rôle had become less prominent as SBATs themselves became stronger. The President's own regional offices have now been established for some years. Clerks work from these offices as part of the President's own staff and the independence of this system is now clearly established.

Para. 5

The President's powers to arrange training and to provide materials are unlimited, but he is constrained by the budget allowed to him for these purposes.

Section 59   SCHEDULE 3

REGULATIONS AS TO PROCEDURE

Interpretation

1. In this Schedule "competent tribunal" means—
(a) a Commissioner;
(b) a social security appeal tribunal;
(c) a disability appeal tribunal;
(d) a medical appeal tribunal;
(e) an adjudicating medical practitioner.

Provision which may be made

2. Provision prescribing the procedure to be followed in connection with the consideration and determination of claims and questions by the Secretary of State, an adjudication officer and a competent tribunal, or in connection with the withdrawal of a claim.

3. Provision as to the striking out of proceedings for want of prosecution.

4. Provision as to the form which is to be used for any document, the evidence which is to be required and the circumstances in which any official record or certificate is to be sufficient or conclusive evidence.

5. Provision as to the time to be allowed—
(a) for producing any evidence; or
(b) for making an appeal.

6. Provision as to the manner in which, and the time within which, a question may be raised with a view to its decision by the Secretary of State under Part II of this Act or with a view to the review of a decision under that Part.

7. Provision for summoning persons to attend and give evidence or produce documents and for authorising the administration of oaths to witnesses.

8. Provision for authorising a competent tribunal consisting of two or more members to proceed with any case, with the consent of the claimant, in the absence of any member.

9. Provision for giving the chairman or acting chairman of a competent tribunal consisting of two or more members a second or casting vote where the number of members present is an even number.

10. Provision for empowering the chairman of a social security appeal tribunal, a disability appeal tribunal or a medical appeal tribunal to give directions for the disposal of any purported appeal which he is satisfied that the tribunal does not have jurisdiction to entertain.

11. Provision for the non-disclosure to a person of the particulars of any medical advice or medical evidence given or submitted for the purposes of a determination.

12. Provision for requiring or authorising the Secretary of State to hold, or to appoint a person to hold, an inquiry in connection with the consideration of any question by the Secretary of State.

GENERAL NOTE
See the Social Security (Adjudication) Regulations 1986, in the current editions of Bonner *et al.*, Mesher and Rowland.

Section 123   SCHEDULE 4

PERSONS EMPLOYED IN SOCIAL SECURITY ADMINISTRATION OR ADJUDICATION

PART I

THE SPECIFIED PERSONS

Government departments

A civil servant in—
(a) the Department of Social Security;
(b) the Department of Employment;
(c) the Lord Chancellor's Department.

Other public departments and offices

A member or officer of the Commissioners of Inland Revenue.
A civil servant in the Scottish Courts Administration.

Adjudication officers

The Chief Adjudication Officer.
An adjudication officer.

Adjudicating bodies

The clerk to, or other officer or member of the staff of, any of the following bodies—
(a) a social security appeal tribunal;
(b) a disability appeal tribunal;
(c) a medical appeal tribunal;
(d) a vaccine damage tribunal;
(e) a Pensions Appeal Tribunal constituted under the Pensions Appeal Tribunals Act 1943.

The Disability Living Allowance Advisory Board

A member of the Disability Living Allowance Advisory Board.
An officer or servant of that Board.

The Occupational Pensions Board

The chairman or deputy chairman of the Occupational Pensions Board.
A member of that Board.
A member of the staff of that Board.

The Social Fund

The Social Fund Commissioner.
A social fund officer.
A social fund inspector.
A member of any staff employed in connection with the social fund.

Former Officers

An officer or other member of the staff of—
(a) the former Supplementary Benefits Commission;
(b) the former National Assistance Board;
(c) the former Attendance Allowance Board.
A benefit officer.
An insurance officer.
A supplement officer.

PART II

CONSTRUCTION OF REFERENCES TO GOVERNMENT DEPARTMENTS ETC.

1. The reference in Part I of this Schedule to the Department of Social Security includes a reference to—
(a) the former Department of Health and Social Security,
(b) the former Ministry of Pensions and National Insurance,
(c) the former Ministry of Social Security, and
(d) any other former government department,
but, in the case of paragraphs (a) and (d) above, only to the extent that the functions carried out in the former department related to social security or to occupational or personal pension schemes or to war pensions.
2. The reference in Part I of this Schedule to the Department of Employment is a reference to that Department only to the extent that the functions carried out in it relate to unemployment benefit or income support or related to the former supplementary benefit.
3. Any reference in Part I of this Schedule to the Lord Chancellor's Department or the Scottish Courts Administration is a reference to that Department or Administration only to the extent that the functions carried out by persons in its employ are, or are connected with—
(a) functions of the Chief, or any other, Social Security Commissioner; or
(b) functions of the Council on Tribunals or the Scottish committee of that Council which relate to social security or to occupational or personal pension schemes or to war pensions.
4. The reference in Part I of this Schedule to the Commissioners of Inland Revenue is a reference to those Commissioners only to the extent that the functions carried out by them or any officer of theirs relate to—

(a) any of the following aspects of social security—
    (i) National Insurance contributions;
    (ii) statutory sick pay;
    (iii) statutory maternity pay; or
(b) the tax treatment of occupational or personal pension schemes.

5. In this Part of this Schedule "war pension" has the meaning given by section 25(4) of the Social Security Act 1989.

Section 170   SCHEDULE 5

SOCIAL SECURITY ADVISORY COMMITTEE

1. The Committee shall consist of a chairman appointed by the Secretary of State and not less than 10 nor more than 13 other members so appointed.

2.—(1) Each member of the Committee shall be appointed to hold office for such period of not more than 5 years, nor less than 3 years, as the Secretary of State shall determine.

(2) The Secretary of State may, at any time before the expiration of the term of office of any member, extend or further extend that member's term of office; but no one extension shall be for a period of more than 5 years from the date when the term of office would otherwise expire.

(3) Any member—
(a) shall be eligible for reappointment from time to time on or after the expiration of his term of office;
(b) may by notice in writing to the Secretary of State resign office at any time, while remaining eligible for reappointment.

3.—(1) Of the members of the Committee (other than the chairman) there shall be appointed—
(a) one after consultation with organisations representative of employers;
(b) one after consultation with organisations representative of workers; and
(c) one after consultation with the Head of the Northern Ireland Department;
and the Committee shall include at least one person with experience of work among, and of the needs of, the chronically sick and disabled.

(2) In selecting a person with such experience regard shall be had to the desirability of having a chronically sick or disabled person.

4. The Secretary of State may remove a member of the Committee on the ground of incapacity or misbehaviour.

5. The Secretary of State shall appoint a secretary to the Committee and may appoint such other officers and such servants to the Committee, and there shall be paid to them by the Secretary of State such salaries and allowances, as the Secretary of State may with the consent of the Treasury determine.

6. The expenses of the Committee to such an amount as may be approved by the Treasury shall be paid by the Secretary of State.

7. There may be paid as part of the expenses of the Committee—
(a) to all or any of the members of the Committee, such salaries or other remuneration and travelling and other allowances; and
(b) to persons attending its meetings at the request of the Committee, such travelling and other allowances (including compensation for loss of remunerative time),
as the Secretary of State may with the consent of the Treasury determine.

8.—(1) The Secretary of State may pay or make provision for paying, to or in respect of any member of the Committee, such sums by way of pensions, superannuation allowances and gratuities as the Secretary of State may determine with the consent of the Treasury.

(2) Where a person ceases to be a member of the Committee otherwise than on the expiry of his term of office and it appears to the Secretary of State that there are special circumstances which make it right for the person to receive compensation the Secretary of State may make to him a payment of such amount as the Secretary of State may determine with the consent of the Treasury.

9. The Committee may act notwithstanding any vacancy among the members.

10. The Committee may make rules for regulating its procedure (including the quorum of the Committee).

Section 171   SCHEDULE 6

INDUSTRIAL INJURIES ADVISORY COUNCIL

1.—(1) The Council shall consist of a chairman appointed by the Secretary of State and such number of other members so appointed as the Secretary of State may determine.

(2) The members other than the chairman shall include an equal number of persons appointed by the Secretary of State, after consultation with such organisations as he thinks fit, to represent employers and employed earners respectively.

2.—(1) The Secretary of State may pay—

(a) to the chairman and other members of the Council, such salaries or other remuneration;

(b) to persons who are not members of the Council but who at the Council's invitation are joined with its members as advisers at a Council meeting or a meeting of any committee of the Council held to consider questions on which they are specially qualified, such fees; and

(c) to the chairman and other members of the Council and to persons attending meetings at the Council's request or attending meetings of any committee of the Council at the Council's or committee's request, such expenses and travelling and other allowances,

as the Secretary of State may with the consent of the Treasury determine.

(2) Any payment under paragraph (a) of sub-paragraph (1) above may be made either in lieu of or in addition to any payment to the recipient under paragraph (c) of that sub-paragraph.

(3) Any payment under sub-paragraph (1)(b) above may be either in lieu of or in addition to any expenses or travelling or other allowances payable to the recipient apart from that sub-paragraph.

Section 172   SCHEDULE 7

REGULATIONS NOT REQUIRING PRIOR SUBMISSION

PART I

SOCIAL SECURITY ADVISORY COMMITTEE

Disability living allowance

1. Regulations under section 72(3) or 73(10) of the Contributions and Benefits Act.

Industrial injuries

2. Regulations relating only to industrial injuries benefit.

Up-rating etc.

3. Regulations contained in a statutory instrument which states that it contains only provisions in consequence of an order under one or more of the following provisions—

(a) section 141, 143 or 145 above;

(b) section 150 above.

Earnings limits

4. Regulations under section 5 of the Contributions and Benefits Act or regulations contained in a statutory instrument which states that it contains only regulations to make provision consequential on regulations under that section.

Married women and widows—reduced rate contributions

5. Regulations under section 19(4)(a) of the Contributions and Benefits Act.

Child benefit

6. Regulations prescribing the rate or any of the rates of child benefit in Great Britain.

7. Regulations varying social security benefits following an increase of the rate or any of the rates of child benefit in Great Britain.

Statutory maternity pay and statutory sick pay

8. Regulations under section 158 of 167 of the Contributions and Benefits Act.

Procedural rules for tribunals

9. Regulations in so far as they consist only of procedural rules for a tribunal in respect of which consultation with the Council on Tribunals is required by section 10(1) of the Tribunals and Inquiries Act 1971.

Consolidation

10. Regulations made for the purpose only of consolidating other regulations revoked by them.

Part II

Industrial Injuries Advisory Council

11. Regulations under section 121(1)(b) of the Contributions and Benefits Act.

12. Regulations contained in a statutory instrument which states that it contains only provisions in consequence of an order under section 141, 143 or 150 above.

13. Regulations contained in a statutory instrument made within a period of 6 months from the date of any Act passed after this Act and directed to be construed as one with this Act, where the statutory instrument states that it contains only regulations to make provision consequential on the passing of the Act, and the Act does not exclude this paragraph in respect of the regulations.

14. Regulations in so far as they consist only of procedural rules for a tribunal in respect of which consultation with the Council on Tribunals is required by section 10(1) of the Tribunals and Inquiries Act 1971.

15. Regulations contained in a statutory instrument which states that it contains only regulations making with respect to industrial injuries benefit or its administration the same or substantially the same provision as has been, or is to be, made with respect to other benefit as defined in section 122(1) of the Contributions and Benefits Act or its administration.

16. Regulations contained in a statutory instrument which states that the only provision with respect to industrial injuries benefit or its administration that is made by the regulations is the same or substantially the same as provision made by the instrument with respect to other benefit as defined in section 122(1) of the Contributions and Benefits Act or its administration.

17. Regulations made for the purpose only of consolidating other regulations revoked by them.

Definitions

"the Contributions and Benefits Act": s.191.

Section 177   SCHEDULE 8

Constitution etc. of Joint Authority for Great Britain and Northern Ireland

1. The Joint Authority shall be a body corporate by the name of the National Insurance Joint Authority, and shall have an official seal which shall be officially and judicially noticed, and the seal of the Authority may be authenticated by either member of, or the secretary to, the Authority, or by any person authorised by the Authority to act on behalf of the secretary.

2. Either member of the Joint Authority shall be entitled, subject to and in accordance with any rules laid down by the Authority, to appoint a deputy to act for him at meetings of the Authority at which he is unable to be present.

3. The Documentary Evidence Act 1868 shall apply to the Joint Authority as if the Authority were included in the first column of the Schedule to that Act, and as if either member or the secretary, or any person authorised to act on behalf of the secretary, of the Authority were mentioned in the second column of that Schedule, and as if the regulations referred to in that Act included any document issued by the Authority.

Section 185   SCHEDULE 9

Old Cases payments administration

Provisions ancillary to paragraph 2 of Schedule 8 to the Contributions and Benefits Act

1.—(1) The provisions of this paragraph shall have effect with respect to schemes under paragraph 2 of Schedule 8 to the Contributions and Benefits Act and any such scheme is hereafter in this paragraph referred to as "scheme".

(2) A scheme may make such incidental, supplementary, consequential or transitional provision as appears to the Secretary of State to be necessary or expedient for the purposes of that paragraph.

(3) A scheme shall in particular make provision with respect to the making of claims for allowances, with respect to the determination of questions arising on or in connection with any such claim or the payment of allowances, and with respect to any other matters necessary for the proper administration of any scheme; and, subject to any provisions of a scheme for reviewing decisions, the decision in accordance with a scheme of any question arising under a scheme shall be final for the purposes of paragraph 2 of Schedule 8 to the Contributions and Benefits Act.

(4) Without prejudice to the generality of sub-paragraph (2) above, a scheme may make provision—

(a) for the Secretary of State to be charged with the general administration of any scheme and (subject to any provisions of a scheme) with the determination of questions arising under any scheme, and for enabling the decision of the Secretary of State on any such question to be proved in legal proceedings by means of a certificate or otherwise;

(b) for enabling any class or description of such questions to be determined as if they had arisen under Parts II to VI of the Contributions and Benefits Act;

(c) for applying, with or without modifications, section 187(1) and (2) above, or for making provision corresponding to them;

(d) for requiring persons claiming or receiving allowances to furnish information and evidence and to undergo medical or other examination, for summoning persons to attend and give evidence or produce documents at any hearing for the purpose of determining questions arising under a scheme, and for authorising the administration of oaths to witnesses at any such hearing;

(e) for requiring the repayment to the Secretary of State in whole or in part of payments under paragraph 2 of Schedule 8 to the Contributions and Benefits Act subsequently found not to have been due, for the deduction of any sums so required to be repaid from payments under that paragraph or by way of industrial injuries benefits, and for the deduction from payments under that paragraph of any sums which may by virtue of any provision of this Act be recovered by deduction from any payment by way of such benefit.

(5) The Secretary of State may make such payments in connection with the administration of any scheme (including payments on account of travelling expenses or loss of remunerative time or both to persons required to undergo medical or other examination or to attend any hearing for the purpose of determining questions arising under any such scheme), as he may with the consent of the Treasury determine.

(6) Notwithstanding anything in this Act or the Contributions and Benefits Act, a scheme shall not require a person to submit himself to medical treatment.

(7) A scheme varying an earlier scheme may do so in such a way as to make allowances payable, or payable at an increased rate, under the earlier scheme in respect of periods before the making of the later scheme.

Provisions ancillary to paragraph 4 of Schedule 8

2.—(1) Subject to sub-paragraph (2) below, sub-paragraphs (2) to (6) of paragraph 1 above shall have effect for the purposes of paragraph 4 of Schedule 8 to the Contributions and Benefits Act as if in those sub-paragraphs—

(a) any reference to a scheme were a reference to a scheme under paragraph 4;

(b) any reference to paragraph 2 of Schedule 8 to the Contributions and Benefits Act were a reference to paragraph 4;

(c) any reference to allowances (other than the reference in sub-paragraph (4)) included a reference to any other payment under paragraph 4.

(2) Nothing in this Schedule or in Schedule 8 to that Act shall authorise the recovery of sums by deduction from payments under paragraph 4 of that Schedule in respect of the death of any person, or the abatement of such payments.

(3) Without prejudice to the powers conferred by paragraph 1 above as applied by this paragraph, a scheme under paragraph 4 may in particular make provision for the determination by a medical board of questions of such classes as may be prescribed by the scheme.

(4) Without prejudice to the provision made by sub-paragraphs (1) and (3) above with respect to the determination of questions, such a scheme may, where it appears to the Secretary of State expedient so as to avoid the introduction or working of the scheme being impeded, provide that, in any circumstances prescribed by the scheme, a person shown to be disabled by a disease shall be presumed for the purposes of the scheme to have been disabled by that disease for such period previously, and the disablement to have been during that period or any part of it of such a nature and degree, as may be so prescribed.

Adjustment of benefit in certain cases

3.—(1) A scheme under paragraph 2 or 4 of Schedule 8 to the Contributions and Benefits Act may include provisions for adjusting the rate of, or extinguishing any right to, an allowance under the paragraph in question or under the other of those paragraphs in a case where the same person is, or would otherwise be, entitled separately in respect of two or more injuries or diseases to an allowance under the paragraph in question or, as the case may be, to both such an allowance and an allowance under the other of those paragraphs.

(2) Where immediately before 22nd June 1967 (the commencement of the Industrial Injuries and Diseases (Old Cases) Act 1967) a person was receiving payments by virtue of section 3(2) of the Workmen's Compensation and Benefit (Amendment) Act 1965 of a greater amount or

aggregate amount than, but for the provisions of this sub-paragraph, he would have been entitled to receive on or after 6th April 1975 (the commencement of the Old Cases Act) by way of allowances under section 2 or 5 of that Act, he shall continue to be entitled to that greater amount or aggregate amount for any period commencing on or after that date for which he would have so continued if neither Act had been passed.

Overpayments

4. A scheme under paragraph 2 or 4 of Schedule 8 to the Contributions and Benefits Act may make provision in relation to allowances under that Schedule corresponding to the provision made by section 71 above in relation to the benefits to which it applies.

DEFINITIONS
"the Contributions and Benefits Act": s.191.
"the Old Cases Act": *ibid.*

Section 186   SCHEDULE 10

SUPPLEMENTARY BENEFIT ETC.

Interpretation

1. In this Schedule—
   "the former National Insurance Acts" means the National Insurance Act 1946 and the National Insurance Act 1965; and
   "the former Industrial Injuries Acts" means the National Insurance (Industrial Injuries) Act 1946 and the National Insurance (Industrial Injuries) Act 1965.

Claims and payments

2.—(1) Section 5 above shall have effect in relation to the benefits specified in sub-paragraph (2) below as it has effect in relation to the benefits to which it applies by virtue of subsection (2).
   (2) The benefits mentioned in sub-paragraph (1) above are benefits under—
   (a) the former National Insurance Acts;
   (b) the former Industrial Injuries Acts;
   (c) the National Assistance Act 1948;
   (d) the Supplementary Benefit Act 1966;
   (e) the Supplementary Benefits Act 1976;
   (f) the Family Income Supplements Act 1970.

Adjudication

3.—(1) Sections 20 to 29, 36 to 43, 51 to 61 and section 124 above shall have effect for the purposes of the benefits specified in paragraph 2(2) above as they have effect for the purposes of benefit within the meaning of section 122 of the Contributions and Benefits Act other than attendance allowance, disability living allowance and disability working allowance.
   (2) Procedure regulations made under section 59 above by virtue of sub-paragraph (1) may make different provision in relation to each of the benefits specified in paragraph 2(2) above.

Overpayments etc.

4.—(1) Section 71 above shall have effect in relation to the benefits mentioned in paragraph 2(2) above as it has effect in relation to the benefits to which it applies by virtue of subsection (11).
   (2) Section 74 above shall have effect in relation to supplementary benefit as it has effect in relation to income support.
   (3) The reference to housing benefit in section 75 above includes a reference to housing benefits under Part II of the Social Security and Housing Benefits Act 1982.

Inspection

5. Section 110 above shall have effect as if it also applied to—
   (a) the Supplementary Benefits Act 1976;
   (b) the Family Income Supplements Act 1970.

Legal proceedings

6. Section 116 above shall have effect as if any reference to this Act in that section included—

(a) the National Assistance Act 1948;
(b) the Supplementary Benefit Act 1966;
(c) the Supplementary Benefits Act 1976;
(d) the Family Income Supplements Act 1970.

DEFINITIONS
"the Contributions and Benefits Act": s.191.

TABLE OF DERIVATIONS

Note:

1. Abbreviations used in this Table are the same as those used in the Table of Derivations for the Social Security Contributions and Benefits Act. They are set out at the beginning of that Table.
2. The Table does not acknowledge the general change made by paragraph 1 of Schedule 8 to the Health and Social Services and Social Security Adjudications Act 1983. That paragraph transferred adjudication functions to adjudication officers and social security appeal tribunals.
3. The Table does not contain any entries in respect of section 66(2) of the Social Security Pensions Act 1975 (c.60) which provides that, with certain exceptions, that Act and the Social Security Act 1975 (c.14) shall have effect as if the provisions of the Social Security Pensions Act 1975 were contained in the Social Security Act 1975. The effect is that the general provisions of the Social Security Act 1975 apply to the provisions of the Social Security Pensions Act 1975.
4. The Table does not show the effect of transfer of functions orders.

Provision	Derivation
1(1)	1975(1) s.165A(1); 1986 s.86(1), Sch. 10, para. 87; 1989 s.31(1), Sch. 8, para. 9(1); 1990 s.6(1)(a)
(2)	1975(1) s.165A(2); 1986 s.86(1), Sch. 10, para. 87; 1990 s.6(1)(b)
(3)	1975(1) s.165A(3); 1990 s.1(6); 1991(2) s.4, Sch. 1, para. 19
(4)	1975(1) s.165A(1); 1986 s.86, Sch. 10, para. 48(b); 1990 s.5(4)
(5), (6)	Drafting
2(1)	1975(1) s.165B(1); 1990 s.5(1)
(2), (3)	1975(1) s.165B(2); 1990 s.5(1)
(4), (5)	1975(1) s.165B(3), (4); 1990 s.5(1)
3	1975(1) s.165C; 1990 s.6(2)
4	1990 s.21(1), Sch. 6, para. 27(2)
5(1)(a)–(h)	1986 s.51(1)(a)–(h)
(i)–(r)	1986 s.51(1)(k)–(t)
(2)	1986 s.51(2); 1988(1) s.11, Sch. 3, para. 16; 1991(2) s.7, Sch. 3, para. 1
(3)	Housing Act 1988 (c. 50) s.121(6)
(4), (5)	1986 s.51(3), (4)
6(1)(a)–(k)	1986 s.51A(1)(a)–(k); 1988(2) s.135, Sch. 10, para. 8
(l)	1986 s.51A(1)(kk); 1989 s.31(1), Sch. 8, para. 9(6)(a)
(m)–(p)	1986 s.51A(1)(l)–(o); 1988(2) s.135, Sch. 10, para. 8
(q)	1986 s.51A(1)(oo); 1989 s.31(1), Sch. 8, para. 9(6)(b)
(r)–(u)	1986 s.51A(1)(p)–(s); 1988(2) s.135, Sch. 10, para. 8
(2), (3)	1986 s.51A(2), (3); 1988(2) s.135, Sch. 10, para. 8
7	1986 s.51B; 1988(2) s.135, Sch. 10, para. 8
8	1975(1) s.88
9	1975(1) s.89
10(1)	1975(1) s.90(2); 1988(1) s.2, Sch. 1, para. 6
(2)	1975(1) s.90(3); 1986 s.86, Sch. 10, para. 85

Provision	Derivation
(3)	1975(1) s.90(4)
11	1986 s.27B(1)–(3); 1991(2) s.7(1)
12(1)	1986 s.33(1); 1988(1) s.11, Sch. 3, para. 9
(2)	1986 s.33(13); 1990 s.10(5)
13(1)	1975(3) s.6(1); 1989 s.26, Sch. 7, para. 22
(2)	1975(3) s.6(3)
14(1)	1982(2) s.17(2)
(2)	1982(2) s.17(2A); 1985 s.20
(3)	1982(2) s.17(3)
15(1)	1986 s.49, Sch. 4, para. 6
(2)	1986 s.49, Sch. 4, para. 7
16	1988(1) s.8
17(1)(a), (b)	1975(1) s.93(1)(a), (b)
(c)	1975(1) s.93(1)(bb); 1991(3) s.3(1)
(d)	1975(1) s.93(1)(d)
(e)	1975(1) s.93(1)(e); 1977 s.22(5)
(f)	1975(2) s.60(1)(a)
(g)(i)–(iv)	1986 s.52(2), Sch. 5, Part II, para. (b)(i)–(iv)
(v)	1986 s.52(2), Sch. 5, Part II, para. (b)(vi); 1991(1) s.2(3)
(vi)	1986 s.52(2), Sch. 5, Part II, para. b(v)
(h)	1986 s.52(2), Sch. 5, Part II, para. (c)
(2)	1975(1) s.93(2)
(3)	1975(1) s.93(2A); 1989 s.21, Sch. 3, para. 1(1); R8
(4)	1975(1) s.93(3); R8
18(1)	1975(1) s.94(1); R8
(2)–(5)	1975(1) s.94(2)–(5)
(6), (7)	1975(1) s.94(7), (8)
19(1)	1975(1) s.96(1); 1986 s.52(1), Sch. 5, para. 3; R8
(2), (3)	1975(1) s.96(2); 1980(1) ss.2, 21, Sch. 1, para. 9
20(1)	1975(1) s.98(1); 1991(2) s.4, Sch. 1, para. 2
(2)	1975(1) s.98(2); 1986 s.52(1), Sch. 5, para. 4
(3)	1975(1) s.98(1); 1986 s.52(3), (7)(a); 1991(2) s.4, Sch. 2, para. 15(a)
(4)	1975(1) s.98(2A); 1986 s.52(1), Sch. 5, para. 4
(5)	1975(1) s.98(3)
(6)	1975(1) s.98(1); 1986 s.52(3)(a), (3A), (6); 1988(1), s.11, Sch. 3, para. 16; 1991(2) ss.4, 7, Sch. 2, para. 15(a), Sch. 3, para. 3(1)
21(1)	1975(1) s.99(1); 1991(2) s.4, Sch. 1, para. 3(1)
(2)	1975(1) s.99(2); 1986 s.52(1), Sch. 5, para. 5; 1991(2) s.4, Sch. 1, para. 3(2)
(3)	1975(1) s.99(2A); 1986 s.52(3A); 1991(2) ss.4, 7, Sch. 1, para. 3(3), Sch. 3, para. 3(1)
(4), (5)	1975(1) s.99(3); 1986 s.52(7)(b)
(6)	1975(1) s.99(4); 1989 s.21, Sch. 3, para. 2
22(1)	1975(1) s.100(1); 1986 s.52(3A), (7)(c)(i); 1991(2) ss.4, 7, Sch. 1, para. 4(a), Sch. 3, para. 3(1)
(2)	1975(1) s.100(2); 1986 s.52(1), (7)(c)(ii), Sch. 5, para. 6(b); 1991(2) s.4, Sch. 1, para. 4(b)
(3)	1975(1) s.100(3); 1986 s.52(1), Sch. 5, para. 6(c)
(4)	1975(1) s.100(4); 1986 s.52(1), Sch. 5, para. 6(d)
(5)	1975(1) s.100(7); 1986 s.52(1), (7)(c)(iii), Sch. 5, para. 6(e); 1991(2) s.4, Sch. 1, para. 4(c)

Provision	Derivation
(6), (7)	1975(1) s.100(8), (9); 1990 s.21(1), Sch. 6, para. 6(1)
23(1)	1975(1) s.101(1); 1986 s.52(1), Sch. 5, para. 7(1)
(2)	1975(1) s.101(2); 1986 s.52(7)(d)
(3)	1975(1) s.101(2)(a), (b), (c), (d); 1986 s.52 (1), Sch. 5, para. 7(2)
(4)	1975(1) s.101(2)(bb); 1990 s.21(1), Sch. 6, para. 6(2)
(5)	1975(1) s.101(3); 1990 s.21(1), Sch. 6, para. 6(3)
(6)	1975(1) s.101(4)
(7), (8)	1975(1) s.101(5); 1986 s.52(1), Sch. 5, para. 7(3); 1989 s.21, Sch. 3, para. 6
(9), (10)	1975(1) s.101(5A), (5B); 1986 s.52(1), Sch. 5, para. 7(3)
24(1)–(5)	1980(1) s.14(1)–(5)
(6)	1980(1) s.14(8)(a); The Transfer of Functions (Social Security Commissioners) Order 1984 (S.I. 1984/1818) art. 3
25(1)	1975(1) s.104(1); 1986 s.52(1), (3)(a), (3A), (6), Sch. 5, para. 10(a); 1988(1) ss.11, 16, Sch. 3, para. 16, Sch. 4, para. 14; 1989 ss.10(5), 21, Sch. 3, para. 11(1); 1991(2) ss.4, 7, Sch. 1, para. 8(a), Sch. 3, para. 3(1)
(2)	1975(1) s.104(1A); 1983 s.25, Sch. 8, para. 3; 1986 s.52(3A); 1991(2) ss.4, 7, Sch. 1, para. 8(b), Sch. 3, para. 3(1)
(3)	1975(1) s.104(1); 1986 s.52(1), Sch. 5, para. 10(a)
(4)	1986 s.52(8); R9
(5)	1975(1) s.104(1ZA); 1989 s.25, Sch. 3, para. 11(2)
26(1), (2)	1975(1) s.104(2), (3)
(3)	1975(1) s.104(3A); 1986 s.52(1), Sch. 5, para. 10(c)
27(1)	1975(1) s.104(5); 1986 s.52(1), Sch. 5, para. 10(d); 1989 s.21, Sch. 3, para. 11(4)
(2)	1975(1) s.104(6); 1990 s.6(3)
28	1975(1) s.104(4)
29	1975(1) s.104(3B); 1989 s.21, Sch. 3, para. 7
30(1)	1975(1) s.100A(1); 1986 s.52(3A), (10); 1991 (2) ss.4, 7, Sch. 1, para. 5, Sch. 3, para. 3(1), (3)
(2)	1975(1) s.100A(2); 1991(2) s.4, Sch. 1, para. 5
(3)	1975(1) s.100A(3); 1991(2) s.4, Sch. 1, para. 5
(4)	1975(1) s.100A(4); 1991(2) s.4, Sch. 1, para. 5
(5)	1975(1) s.100A(2); 1986 s.52(3A), (9)(a), (b), (10); 1991(2) ss.4, 7, Sch. 1, para. 5, Sch. 3, para. 3(1), (3)
(6)–(11)	1975(1) s.100A(5)–(10); 1986 s.52(3A); 1991 (2) ss.4, 7, Sch. 1, para. 5, Sch. 3, para. 3(1)
(12)	1975(1) s.100A(11); 1991(2) s.4, Sch. 1, para. 5
(13)	1975(1) s.100A(12); 1986 s.52(3A); 1991(2) ss.4, 7, Sch. 1, para. 5, Sch. 3, para. 3(1)
31	1975(1) s.100B; 1986 s.52(3A); 1991(2) ss.4, 7, Sch. 1, para. 5, Sch. 3, para. 3(1)
32(1)	1975(1) s.100C(1); 1986 s.52(3A); 1991(2) ss.4, 7, Sch. 1, para. 5, Sch. 3, para. 3(1)

Provision	Derivation
(2)–(5)	1975(1) s.100C(2)–(5); 1991(2) s.4, Sch. 1, para. 5
(6), (7)	1975(1) s.100C(6), (7); 1986 s.52(3A); 1991 (2) ss.4, 7, Sch. 1, para. 5, Sch. 3, para. 3(1)
(8)	1975(1) ss.100C(8)(a), 104(5)(b); 1986 s.52 (3A); 1991(2) ss.4, 7, Sch. 1, para. 5, Sch. 3, para. 3(1)
(9), (10)	1975(1) s.100C(9), (10); 1986 s.52(3A); 1991 (2) ss.4, 7, Sch. 1, para. 5, Sch. 3, para. 3(1)
33	1975(1) s.100D(1)–(6); 1986 s.52(3A); 1991 (2) ss.4, 7, Sch. 1, para. 5, Sch. 3, para. 3(1)
34(1)	1975(1) s.101(1); 1986 s.52(3A); 1991(2) ss.4, 7, Sch. 1, para. 6(a), Sch. 3, para. 3(1)
(2)	1975(1) s.101(2), (3); 1986 s.52(3A); 1991(2) s.7, Sch. 3, para. 3(1)
(3)	1975(1) s.101(4); 1986 s.52(3A); 1991(2) s.7, Sch. 3, para. 3(1)
(4)	1975(1) s.101(5)–(5B); 1991(2) s.7, Sch. 3, para. 3(1)
(5)	1980(1) s.14(1)–(5), (8)(a)
35(1), (2)	1975(1) s.104A(1), (2); 1991(2) s.4, Sch. 1, para. 9
(3)	1975(1) s.104A(1); 1986 s.52(3A), (9)(a), (b), (10); 1991(2) ss.4, 7, Sch. 1, para. 9, Sch. 3, para. 3(1), (3)
(4)	1975(1) s.104A(3); 1986 s.52(3A); 1991(2) ss.4, 7, Sch. 1, para. 9, Sch. 3, para. 3(1)
(5)	1975(1) ss.104(3A), 104A(9); 1986 s.52(3A), (9)(c); 1991(2) ss.4, 7, Sch. 1, para. 9, Sch. 3, para. 3(1), (3)(c)
(6)–(9)	1975(1) s.104A(4)–(7); 1986 s.52(3A); 1991 (2) ss.4, 7, Sch. 1, para. 9, Sch. 3, para. 3(1)
(10)	1975(1) ss.104(5)(b), 104A(9)(c); 1986 s.52 (3A), (9)(c); 1991(2) ss.4, 7, Sch. 1, para. 9, Sch. 3, para. 3(1), (3)(c)
(11)	1975(1) ss.104(1ZA), 104A(9)(a); 1991(2) s.4, Sch. 1, para. 9
(12)	1975(1) s.104A(8); 1986 s.52(3A); 1991(2) ss.4, 7, Sch. 1, para. 9, Sch. 3, para. 3(1)
36(1)	1975(1) s.102(1), (2); 1986 s.52(1), Sch. 5, para. 8; 1991(2) s.4, Sch. 1, para. 7(1)
(2)	1975(1) s.102(3); 1991(2) s.4, Sch. 1, para. 7(2)
37(1)	1975(1) s.103(1); 1986 s.52(1), Sch. 5, para. 9
(2)	1975(1) s.103(2); 1986 s.52(1), Sch. 5, para. 9; 1989 s.21, Sch. 3, para. 15
(3)	1975(1) s.103(3); 1986 s.52(1), Sch. 5, para. 9
38(1)	1975(1) s.97(1); 1983 s.25, Sch. 8, para. 2; 1990 s.21(1), Sch. 6, para. 5(1)
(2)	1975(1) s.97(1A); 1983 s.25, Sch. 8, para. 2
39	1975(1) s.97(1B)–(1E); 1983 s.25, Sch. 8, para. 2
40(1)	1975(1) s.97(4), Sch. 10, para. 1(1); 1983 s.25, Sch. 8, para. 7
(2), (3)	1975(1) s.97(4), Sch. 10, para. 1(2), (2A); 1984 s.16(b)
(4)	1975(1) s.97(4), Sch. 10, para. 1(6); 1983 s.25, Sch. 8, para. 7
41(1)	1975(1) s.97(2); 1983 s.25, Sch. 8, para. 2
(2)	1975(1) s.97(2A); 1984 s.16(a)

Provision	Derivation
(3), (4)	1975(1) s.97(2C), (2D); 1983 s.25, Sch. 8, para. 2
(5)	1975(1) s.97(2E); 1983 s.25, Sch. 8, para. 2; Courts and Legal Services Act 1990 (c. 41) s.71(2), Sch. 10, para. 37(1)
(6)	1975(1) s.97(4), Sch. 10, para. 1(8); 1983 s.25, Sch. 8, para. 7
(7)	Drafting
42(1)–(5)	1975(1) s.100D(7), Sch. 10A, paras. 3–7; 1991 (2) s.4, Sch. 1, paras. 5, 16
(6)	1975(1) ss.97(4), 100D(7), Sch. 10, para. 1(2A); Sch. 10A, para. 8; 1991(2) s.4, Sch. 1, paras. 5, 16
(7)	1975(1) ss.97(4), 100D(7), Sch. 10, para. 1(6); Sch. 10A, para. 8; 1991(2) s.4, Sch. 1, paras. 5, 16
43(1)	1975(1) s.100D(7), Sch. 10A, para. 1; 1991(2) s.4, Sch. 1, paras. 5, 16
(2), (3)	1975(1) s.100D(7), Sch. 10A, paras. 9, 10; 1991(2) s.4, Sch. 1, paras. 5, 16
(4)–(6)	1975(1) ss.97(2C)–(2E), 100D(7), Sch. 10A, para. 2; 1991(2) s.4, Sch. 1, paras. 5, 16
(7), (8)	1975(1) s.100D(7), Sch. 10A, paras. 12, 13; 1991(2) s.4, Sch. 1, paras. 5, 16
(9)	Drafting
44(1)–(3)	1975(1) s.107(1)–(3)
(4), (5)	1975(1) s.107(4); 1988 s.2, Sch. 1, para. 6
(6)	1975(1) s.107(5)
(7)	1975(1) s.107(6); 1986 s.52(1), Sch. 5, para. 12(a)
45(1)	1975(1) s.108(1); 1984 s.11(2), Sch. 4, para. 5; 1986 s.39, Sch. 3, para. 14(a); 1989 s.21, Sch. 3, para. 12(1)
(2)	1975(1) s.108(2); 1983 s.25, Sch. 8, para. 21(1); 1984 s.11(2), Sch. 4, para. 6
(3)	1975(1) s.108(4); 1983, s.25, Sch. 8, para. 21(3)
(4), (5)	1975(1) s.108(4A), (4B); 1989 s.21, Sch. 3, para. 12(2)
(6)	1975(1) s.108(5); 1983 s.25, Sch. 8, para. 21(3)
46(1)	1975(1) s.109(1); 1983 s.25, Sch. 8, para. 22(a); 1984, s.11(2), Sch. 4, para. 7
(2)	1975(1) s.109(2); 1983 s.25, Sch. 8, para. 22(b)(i)
(3)	1975(1) s.109(3); 1983 s.25, Sch. 8, para. 22(c); 1986 s.52(1), Sch. 5, para. 13
47(1)	1975(1) s.110(1); 1979 s.21(4), Sch. 3, para. 8; 1983 s.25, Sch. 8, para. 23(a)
(2), (3)	1975(1) s.110(1A), (1B); 1986 s.52(1), Sch. 5, para. 14(b)
(4)	1975(1) s.110(2); 1983 s.25, Sch. 8, para. 23(b)
(5)–(7)	1975(1) s.110(3)–(5)
(8)	1975(1) s.110(6); 1983 s.25, Sch. 8, para. 23(c); 1984 s.11(2), Sch. 4, para. 8(a)
(9)	1975(1) s.110(7); 1983 s.25, Sch. 8, para. 23(d); 1984 s.11(2), Sch. 4, para. 8(b)
(10)	Social Security (Consequential Provisions) Act 1975 (c. 18) ss.2, 4, Sch. 3, para. 20

Provision	Derivation
48(1)	1975(1) s.112(1); 1984 s.11(2), Sch. 4, para. 9; 1986 s.52(1), Sch. 5, para. 15(a)
(2)	1975(1) s.112(2)
(3)	1975(1) s.112(3); 1986 s.52(1), Sch. 5, para. 15(b)
(4)	1975(1) s.112(5)
(5), (6)	1975(1) s.112(6), (7); 1989 s.21, Sch. 3, para. 9(2)
49(1)	1975(1) s.108(3), Sch. 12, para. 1; 1983 s.25, Sch. 8, paras. 21(2), 27(a)
(2)	1975(1) s.108(3), Sch. 12, para. 3; 1983 s.25, Sch. 8, paras. 21(2), 27(b)
50(1)	1975(1) s.108(3), Sch. 12, para. 2(1); 1983 s.25, Sch. 8, paras. 9, 21(2)
(2)	1975(1) s.108(3), Sch. 12, para. 2(2); 1983 s.25, Sch. 8, paras. 9, 21(2); 1986 s.52(1), Sch. 5, para. 18
(3), (4)	1975(1) s.108(3), Sch. 12, para. 2(3), (4); 1983 s.25, Sch. 8, paras. 9, 21(2)
(5)	1975(1) s.108(3), Sch. 12, para. 2(5); 1983 s.25, Sch. 8, paras. 9, 21(2); 1989 ss.21, 26, Sch. 3, para. 18, Sch. 7, para. 17; Courts and Legal Services Act 1990 (c. 41) s.71(2), Sch. 10, para. 37(4)
(6)	1975(1) s.108(3), Sch. 12, para. 3; 1983 s.25, Sch. 8, paras. 21(2), 27(b)
(7)	Drafting
51(1)	1975(1) s.97(4), Sch. 10, para. 1A(1); 1991(2) s.4, Sch. 1, para. 15
(2)	1975(1) s.97(4), Sch. 10, para. 1A(2); 1983 s.25, Sch. 8, para. 8; Courts and Legal Services Act 1990 (c. 41) s.71(2), Sch. 10, para. 37(2)
(3)	1975(1) s.97(4), Sch. 10, para. 1A(3); 1983 s.25, Sch. 8, para. 8; Courts and Legal Services Act 1990 (c. 41) s.71(2), Sch. 10, para. 37(3)
(4)	Drafting
52(1)	1975(1) s.97(3); 1980(1) s.12; Courts and Legal Services Act 1990 (c. 41) s.71(2), Sch. 10, para. 36
(2)	1980(1) s.13(5); Courts and Legal Services Act 1990 (c. 41) s.71(2), Sch. 10, para. 46
(3)	1980(1) s.13(6)
(4)	Drafting
53(1)	1975(1) s.115A(1); 1989 s.21, Sch. 3, para. 3(1)
(2)	1975(1) s.115A(2); 1989 s.21, Sch. 3, para. 3(1); 1991(2) s.4, Sch. 1, para. 11
(3), (4)	1975(1) s.115A(3), (4); 1989 s.21, Sch. 3, para. 3(1)
54(1), (2)	1975(1) s.115C(1), (2); 1986 s.52(3A); 1991 (2) ss.4, 7, Sch. 1, para. 13, Sch. 3, para. 3(1)
(3)	1975(1) s.115C(3); 1991(2) s.4, Sch. 1, para. 13
(4)	1975(1) s.115C(3); 1986 s.52(3A), (9)(d); 1991(2) s.7, Sch. 3, para. 3(1), (3)
(5)	1975(1) s.115C(4); 1986 s.52(3A), (9)(b); 1991(2) ss.4, 7, Sch. 1, para. 13, Sch. 3, para. 3(1), (2)

Provision	Derivation
(6)	1975(1) s.115C(5); 1991(2) s.4, Sch. 1, para. 13
(7)	1975(1) s.115C(5); 1986 s.52(3A), (9)(e); 1991(2) s.7, Sch. 3, para. 3(1), (3)
(8)	1975(1) s.115C(6); 1986 s.52(3A); 1991(2) ss.4, 7, Sch. 1, para. 13, Sch. 3, para. 3(1)
55	1975(1) s.115D; 1986 s.52(3A)(c); 1991(2) ss.4, 7, Sch. 1, para. 13, Sch. 3, para. 3(1)
56(1)	1975(1) s.115B(1); 1989 s.21, Sch. 3, para. 3(1)
(2)	1975(1) s.115B(2); 1989 s.21, Sch. 3, para. 3(1); 1991(2) s.4, Sch. 1, para. 12
57(1)	1975(1) s.116(1); 1980(1) s.12
(2)	1975(1) s.116(2)
58(1), (2)	1975(1) s.114(1); 1986 s.52(3)(b), (3A), (6); 1988(1) s.11, Sch. 3, para. 16; 1991(2) s.7, Sch. 3, para. 3(1)
(3)	1975(1) s.114(2)
(4)	1975(1) s.114(2A); Employment Protection (Consolidation) Act 1978 (c. 44) s.159, Sch. 16, para. 19(1)
(5)–(7)	1975(1) s.114(2B)–(2D); 1986 s.52(1), Sch. 5, para. 16(a)
(8)	1975(1) s.114(5)
59(1)	1975(1) s.115(1), (2); 1986 s.52(3)(c), (3A) (6); 1988(1) s.11, Sch. 3, para. 16; 1991(2) s.7, Sch. 3, para. 3(1)
(2)	1975(1) s.115(3); 1986 s.52(4); 1991 s.7, Sch. 3, para. 3(2)
(3)	1975(1) s.115(4)
(4)	1975(1) s.115(4A); 1991(3) s.3(2)
(5)	1975(1) s.115(5)
(6)	1975(1) s.115(6); 1989 s.21, Sch. 3, para. 1(2)
(7)	1975(1) s.115(7)
60(1)	1975(1) s.117(1); 1983 s.25, Sch. 8, para. 6; 1986 s.52(3)(d), (3A), (6); 1988(1) s.11, Sch. 3, para. 16; 1991(2) s.7, Sch. 3, para. 3(1)
(2)	1975(1) s.117(2)
(3)	1975(1) s.117(3); 1983 s.25, Sch. 8, para. 26
(4)	1975(1) s.117(4); 1988(1) s.2, Sch. 1, para. 6
(5)	1975(1) s.117(5); 1988(1) s.2, Sch. 1, para. 6
61(1)	1975(1) s.119(3)
(2)	1975(1) s.119(4)(a)
(3)	1977 s.17(5)
(4)	1975(1) s.119(3); 1986 s.52(3)(e), (3A), (6); 1988(1) s.11, Sch. 3, para. 16; 1991(2) s.7, Sch. 3, para. 3(1)
62(1)	1975(1) s.113(1)
(2)	1975(1) s.113(2)(a), (b); 1983 s.25, Sch. 8, para. 24(a)
63(1)	1986 ss.29(1), 31C(1); 1988(2) s.135, Sch. 10, para. 6
(2)	1986 ss.29(2), 31C(2); 1988(2) s.135, Sch. 10, para. 6
(3)	1986 ss.29(3), 31C(3); 1988(2) s.135, Sch. 10, para. 6
64(1), (2)	1986 s.32(8), (9)
(3)	1986 s.32(10); 1988(1) s.11, Sch. 3, para. 7; 1990 s.10(2)
65	1986 s.35
66(1)–(8)	1986 s.34

Provision	Derivation
(9), (10)	1986 s.32(11), (12); 1988(1) s.11, Sch. 3, para. 7
67	1986 s.66, Sch. 6, para. 4
68(1)–(3)	1975(1) s.165D(1)–(3); 1990 s.21(1), Sch. 6, para. 7(2)
(4)	1975(1) s.165D(4); 1986 s.86, Sch. 10, para. 48(c); 1990 s.21(1), Sch. 6, para. 7(2), (3); 1991(2) s.4, Sch. 2, para. 5
(5), (6)	1975(1) s.165D(5), (6); 1990 s.21(1), Sch. 6, para. 7(2)
69(1)	1975(1) ss.100C(8)(b), 104(7); 1986 s.52(3)(a), (3A); 1990 s.21(1), Sch. 6, para. 7(1); 1991(2) ss.4, 7, Sch. 1, para. 5, Sch. 2, para. 15(a), Sch. 3, para. 3(1)
(2)–(4)	1975(1) s.104(8)–(10); 1990 s.21(2), Sch. 6, para. 7(1)
70(1)	National Insurance Act 1974 (c. 14) s.6(1)
(2)	National Insurance Act 1974 s.6(3)
(3)	National Insurance Act 1974 s.6(1); Social Security (Consequential Provisions) Act 1975 (c. 18) s.1(3), Sch. 2, para. 70; 1975(2) s.65, Sch. 4, para. 35; 1975(3) s.21(1), Sch. 4, para. 8; Supplementary Benefits Act 1976 (c. 71) s.35(2), Sch. 7, para. 36; 1990 s.21(1), Sch. 6, para. 31(a); 1991(1) s.3(1)(a); 1991(2) s.15(1); 1991(3) s.6(1)
71(1)	1986 s.53(1)
(2)	1986 s.53(1A); 1989 s.21, Sch. 3, para. 14(1)
(3), (4)	1986 s.53(2), (3)
(5)	1986 s.53(4); 1989 s.21, Sch. 3, para. 14(2)
(6)–(8)	1986 s.53(5)–(7)
(9), (10)	1986 s.53(8), (9)
(11)	1986 s.53(10); 1988(1) ss.11, 16, Sch. 3, para. 16, Sch. 4, para. 30(1); 1991(2) s.7, Sch. 3, para. 4
72(1)	1986 s.20(4E); 1988(1) s.4(2)
(2)	1986 s.20(4H); 1988(1) s.4(2)
(3)–(6)	1986 s.20(4J)–(4M); 1988(1) s.4(2)
(7), (8)	1986 s.20(4F), (4G); 1986 s.53(10A); 1988(1) ss.4(2), 16, Sch. 4, para. 30(2)
73(1)	1975(1) s.85(1)
(2)	1975(1) s.85(2); 1975(3) s.21(1), Sch. 4, para. 28
(3)	1975(1) s.85(3)
(4), (5)	1975(1) s.85(4), (5); 1979 s.15(1)
74	1986 s.27
75	1986 s.29(4)–(7)
76(1), (2)	1986 s.31D(1), (2); 1988(2) s.135, Sch. 10, para. 6
(3)	1986 s.31D(3); 1988(2) s.135, Sch. 10, para. 6; 1989 s.31(1), Sch. 8, para. 9(4)
(4)	1986 s.31D(4); 1988(2) s.135, Sch. 10, para. 6
(5)	1986 s.31D(5); 1988(2) s.135, Sch. 10, para. 6; 1989 s.31(1), Sch. 8, para. 9(4)
(6)–(8)	1986 s.31D(6)–(8); 1988(2) s.135, Sch. 10, para. 6
77	1986 s.31E; 1988(2) s.135, Sch. 10, para. 6
78(1)–(3)	1986 s.33(5)–(7)
(4)	1986 s.32(4)
(5)	1986 s.33(12)
(6)	1986 ss.26(3), 33(8); 1989 s.5(2)

Provision	Derivation
(7)	1986 ss.26(4), 33(8); Family Law Reform Act 1987 (c. 42) s.33(1), Sch. 2, para. 93; 1989 s.5(3)
(8)	1986 ss.26(5), 33(8); 1989 s.5(4)
(9)	1986 ss.26(6), 33(8)
79(a)	1986 s.53(7A); 1988 s.16, Sch. 4, para. 28
(b)	1986 s.29(8); 1988 s.16, Sch. 4, para. 26
(c)	1986 s.33(8A); 1988 s.16, Sch. 4, para. 27
80	1975(3) s.4A; 1979 s.15(3)
81(1) "benefit"	1989 s.22(3) "benefit"; 1991(1) s.1(5)
"certificate of deduction"	1989 s.22(3) "certificate of deduction"
"certificate of total benefit"	1989 s.22(3) "certificate of total benefit"
"compensation payment"	1989 s.22(3) "compensation payment"; 1990 s.7, Sch. 1, para. 1(1)
"compensation scheme for motor accidents"	1989 s.22(3) "compensation scheme for motor accidents"; 1990 s.7, Sch. 1, para. 1(2)
"compensator"; "victim"; "intended recipient"	Drafting
"payment"	1989 s.22(3) "payment"
"relevant deduction"	1989 s.22(7), Sch. 4, para. 1(1) "relevant deduction"
"relevant payment"	1989 s.22(7), Sch. 4, para. 1(1) "relevant payment"
"relevant period"	1989 s.22(3) "relevant period"
"total benefit"	1989 s.22(7), Sch. 4, para. 1(1) "total benefit"
(2)	1989 s.22(3A); 1991(1) s.1(5)
(3)–(5)	1989 s.22(4)–(6)
(6)	1989 s.22(7), Sch. 4, para. 1(2)
(7)	1989 s.22(8)
82	1989 s.22(1), (2)
83	1989 s.22(7), Sch. 4, para. 2
84	1989 s.22(7), Sch. 4, para. 3
85	1989 s.22(7), Sch. 4, para. 4
86	1989 s.22(7), Sch. 4, para. 5
87	1989 s.22(7), Sch. 4, para. 6
88	1989 s.22(7), Sch. 4, para. 7
89	1989 s.22(7), Sch. 4, para. 8
90	1989 s.22(7), Sch. 4, para. 9
91	1989 s.22(7), Sch. 4, para. 10
92	1989 s.22(7), Sch. 4, para. 11
93(1)	1989 s.22(7), Sch. 4, para. 12(1)
(2)	1989 s.22(7), Sch. 4, para. 12(2); 1990 s.7, Sch. 1, para. 2(1)
(3), (4)	1989 s.22(7), Sch. 4, para. 12(3), (4)
(5)	1989 s.22(7), Sch. 4, para. 12(5); 1990 s.7, Sch. 1, para. 2(2)
(6)	1989 s.22(7), Sch. 4, para. 12(6); 1990 s.7, Sch. 1, para. 2(3)
(7)	1989 s.22(7), Sch. 4, para. 12(6A); 1990 s.7 Sch. 1, para. 2(4)
(8), (9)	1989 s.22(7), Sch. 4, para. 12(7), (8)
94(1), (2)	1989 s.22(7), Sch. 4, para. 13(1), (2)
(3)	1989 s.22(7), Sch. 4, para. 13(2A); 1990 s.7, Sch. 1, para. 1(4)
(4)–(6)	1989 s.22(7), Sch. 4, para. 13(3)–(5)
95	1989 s.22(7), Sch. 4, para. 14
96	1989 s.22(7), Sch. 4, para. 15
97	1989 s.22(7), Sch. 4, para. 16
98(1), (2)	1989 s.22(7), Sch. 4, para. 17(1), (2)

Provision	Derivation
(3)	1989 s.22(7), Sch. 4, para. 17(3); 1990 s.7, Sch. 1, para. 3
(4)–(10)	1989 s.22(7), Sch. 4, para. 17(4)–(10)
(11)	1989 s.22(7), Sch. 4, para. 17(11); 1990 s.7, Sch. 1, para. 4
(12)	1989 s.22(7), Sch. 4, para. 17(12)
99	1989 s.22(7), Sch. 4, para. 18
100	1989 s.22(7), Sch. 4, para. 19
101	1989 s.22(7), Sch. 4, para. 20A; 1990 s.7, Sch. 1, para. 5(1)
102(1)	1989 s.22(7), Sch. 4, para. 21(1); 1990 s.7, Sch. 1, para. 5(2)
(2)	1989 s.22(7), Sch. 4, para. 21(2)
103	1989 s.22(7), Sch. 4, para. 24; 1990 s.7, Sch. 1, para. 6
104	1989 s.27
105(1), (2)	1986 s.26(1), (2)
(3)	1986 s.26(3)–(6); 1990 s.8(3)
106(1)	1986 s.24(1)
(2)–(4)	1986 s.24(4)–(6)
(5)	1986 s.24(7); Family Law Reform Act 1987 (c. 42) s.33(1), Sch. 2, para. 91
(6), (7)	1986 s.24(8), (9)
107(1)–(4)	1986 s.24A(1)–(4); 1990 s.8(1)
(5)	1986 s.24A(4A); Maintenance Enforcement Act 1991 (c. 17) s. 9(1)
(6)–(8)	1986 s.24A(5)–(7); 1990 s.8(1)
(9)–(11)	1986 s.24A(7A)–(7C); Maintenance Enforcement Act 1991 s.9(2)
(12)–(15)	1986 s.24A(8)–(11); 1990 s.8(1)
108	1986 s.24B; 1990 s.8(1)
109	1986 s.25A; Debtors (Scotland) Act 1987 (c. 18) s.68
110(1)	1986 s.58(1)
(2)	1986 s.58(2); 1989 s.22, Sch. 4, para. 20(2), (3)
(3)	1986 s.58(3); 1989 s.22, Sch. 4, para. 20(4)
(4), (5)	1986 s.58(4), (5)
(6)	1986 s.58(6); 1989 s.22, Sch. 4, para. 20(5)
(7)	1986 s.58(7); 1989 s.22, Sch. 4, para. 20(6)
(8)	1986 s.84(1) "the benefit Acts"
(9) "relevant benefit"	1986 s.58(2)(b)(ii), (10); 1989 s.22, Sch. 4, para. 20(2), (7)
"relevant payment"	1986 s.58(c)(iii), (6)(a)(iii), (7)(e), (10); 1989 s.22, Sch. 4, para. 20(3), (5)–(7)
111	1986 s.58(8), (9); R10
112	1986 s.55
113	1986 s.54
114(1)	1975(1) s.146(1); Criminal Procedure (Scotland) Act 1975 (c. 21) s.289G; Criminal Justice Act 1982 (c. 48) ss.46, 54
(2)	1975(1) s.1(4), Sch. 1, para. 5(2)
(3)	1975(1) s.146(2)
(4)	1975(1) s.146(3); Criminal Procedure (Scotland) Act 1975 (c. 21) s.289G; Criminal Justice Act 1982 (c. 48) ss.46, 54
(5), (6)	1975(1) s.146(4)
115	1986 s.57
116(1)	1986 s.56(1)
(2)	1986 s.56(2); 1988(2) s.135, Sch. 10, para. 9(2)

Provision	Derivation
(3)	1986 s.56(3)
(4)	1986 s.56(4); 1988(2) s.135, Sch. 10, para. 9(3)
(5)	1986 s.56(4A), 1988(2) s.135, Sch. 10, para. 9(4)
(6)	1986 s.56(4B); 1990 s.21(1), Sch. 6, para. 5(2)
(7)	1986 s.56(5); 1988(2) s.135, Sch. 10, para. 9(5)
117(1)	1975(1) s.148(1); 1986 s.52(5); R8
(2), (3)	1975(1) s.148(2), (3)
118	1975(1) s.149
119	1975(1) s.150
120(1), (2)	1975(1) s.151(1), (2)
(3)	1975(1) s.151(3); 1991(3) s.2(6)(a)
(4)	1975(1) s.151(3A); 1991(3) s.2(6)(b)
(5)	1975(1) s.151(4)
(6)	1975(1) s.151(5); 1991(3) s.2(6)(c)
121(1)	1975(1) s.152(1); Magistrates' Courts Act 1980 (c. 43) s.154, Sch. 7, para. 135
(2)	1975(1) s.152(2); 1975(2) s.65, Sch. 4, para. 67
(3)	1975(1) s.152(3)
(4)–(6)	1975(1) s.152(5)–(7)
122(1)	1986 s.59(1); 1989 s.20(a)
(2)	1986 s.59(2); 1989 s.20(b)
(3)	1986 s.59(3)
123(1)–(6)	1989 s.19(1)–(6)
(7)	1989 s.19(7); 1990 s.21(1), Sch. 6, para. 28(1)
(8)	1989 s.19(8)
(9)	1989 s.19(9); 1990 s.2i(1), Sch. 6, para. 28(2)
(10)	1989 s.19(10); 1990 s.21(1), Sch. 6, para. 28(3)
124(1), (2)	1975(1) s.160(1); 1975 (Old Cases) s.11; 1986 s.52(3)(f), (3A) (6); 1988(1) s.11, Sch. 3, para. 16; 1991(2) s.7, Sch. 3, para. 3(1)
(3)	1975(1) s.160(2); Registration of Births, Deaths and Marriages (Fees) (No. 2) Order 1990 (S.I. 1990/2515) art. 2, Sch.; Registration of Births, Deaths and Marriages (Fees) (Scotland) Order 1990 (S.I. 1990/2637) art. 2, Sch.
(4), (5)	1975(1) s.160(3), (4)
125	1986 s.60
126	1986 s.27A; 1989 s.31(1), Sch. 8, para. 17
127	1986 s.31(1)–(3)
128	1986 s.31G(1)–(3); 1988(2), s.135, Sch. 10, para. 6
129	1982(2) s.17(1)
130(1)	1982(2) s.18(1); 1984 s.11, Sch. 4, para. 15(a)
(2), (3)	1982(2) s.18(2), (3)
(4)(a), (b)	1982(2) (s.17(4)
(c)	1982(2) s.9(3)(a)
131	1986 s.49, Sch. 4, para. 9
132(1), (2)	1986, s.49, Sch. 4, para. 8A; 1989 s.31(1), Sch. 8, para. 18
(3)	1986 s.49, Sch. 4, para. 8
133	1975(1) s.161(1)
134(1)	1986 s.28(1); 1990 s.21(1), Sch. 6, para. 18
(2)	1986 s.28(1A); 1989 s.14(1)
(3)–(6)	1986 s.28(2)–(5)
(7)	1986 s.28(5A); 1990 s.21(1), Sch. 6, para. 18

Provision	Derivation
(8)–(12)	1986 s.28(6)–(10)
(13)	1986 s.84(1) "modifications"
135(1)	1986 s.30(1)
(2), (3)	1986 s.30(2); Local Government and Housing Act 1989 (c. 42) s.81(1); The Housing Benefit (Transitional) Amendment Regulations 1988 reg. 3 (S.I. 1988/458)
(4)	1986 s.30(2ZA); 1990 s.21(1), Sch. 6, para. 19(1)
(5)	1986 s.30(3)
(6), (7)	1986 s.30(5); Housing (Scotland) Act 1988 (c. 43) ss.1, 3, Sch. 2, para. 1; Local Government and Housing Act 1989 s.81(2)
(8), (9)	1986 s.30(6); Local Government and Housing Act 1989 s.81(3)
(10)	1986 s.30(7); R11
(11)	1986 s.30(8); 1989 s.15(2)
(12)	1986 s.30(9)
(13)	1986 s.84(3)
(14)	1986 s.84(1) "modifications"
136(1)	1986 s.30(2A); 1989 s.15(1); 1990 s.21(1), Sch. 6, para. 19(2)
(2)–(4)	1986 s.30(2B), (2C); 1989 s.15(1)
137	1986 s.30(8A)–(8F); 1989 s.15(2)
138(1), (2)	1986 s.31A(1), (2); 1988(2) s.135, Sch. 10, para. 6; 1990 s.21(1), Sch. 6, para. 20
(3)–(9)	1986 s.31A(3)–(9); 1988(2) s.135, Sch. 10, para. 6
139(1)–(5)	1986 s.31B(1)–(5); 1988(2) s.135, Sch. 10, para. 6
(6)	1986 s.31B(6); 1988(2) s.135, Sch. 10, para. 6; the Community Charge Benefits (General) Regulations 1989 reg. 11(1) (S.I. 1989/1321)
(7)–(10)	1986 s.31B(7)–(10); 1988(2) s.135, Sch. 10, para. 6
(11)	1986 s.84(1) "modifications", "war disablement pension", "war widow's pension"; the Income and Corporation Taxes Act 1988 (c. 1) s.844, Sch. 29, para. 32, Table; the Community Charge Benefits (General) Regulations 1989 reg. 11(2)
140(1), (2)	1986 s.31F(1), (2); 1988(2) s.135, Sch. 10, para. 6
(3)	1986 s.31F(3); 1990 s.21(1), Sch. 6, para. 21(1)
(4), (5)	1986 s.31F(4), (5); 1988(2) s.135, Sch. 10, para. 6
(6)	1986 s.31F(5A); 1990 s.21(1), Sch. 6, para. 21(2)
(7)	1986 s.31F(6); 1990 s.21(1), Sch. 6, para. 21(3)
(8)	1986 s.31F(7); 1988(2) s.135, Sch. 10, para. 6
141(1)	1975(1) s.120(2); 1975(2) s.65(1), Sch. 4, para. 50(b)
(2)–(6)	1975(1) s.120(3)–(7)
(7)	Transitional
142(1)	1975(1) ss.121(1), 165
(2)	1975(1) s.121(2)
(3)	1975(1) s.121(3); 1990 s.21(1), Sch. 6, para. 1(2)(a)

Provision	Derivation
143(1)	1975(1) s.122(1); 1985 s.29(1), Sch. 5, para. 9(a); 1989 s.1(3)
(2)	1975(1) s.122(2)
(3)	1975(1) s.122(3)(a)
(4)	1975(1) s.122(6); 1980(1) s.2, Sch. 1, para. 13; 1989 s.1(5)
144(1)	1975(1) ss.123(2), 165
(2)	1975(1) s.123(3); 1990 s.21(1), Sch. 6, para. 1(2)(b)
145(1)	1975(1) s.123A(1); 1989 s.1(6)
(2)	1975(1) s.123A(2); 1985 s.7(5)
(3)	1975(1) s.123A(3); 1985 s.7(5); 1989 s.1(7)
(4)	1975(1) s.123A(4); 1985 s.7(5)
146	1975(1) s.4(6F); 1985 s.7(2)
147(1)	1975(1) ss.4(6G), 123A(5); 1985 s.7(2), (5)
(2)	1975(1) ss.4(6HH), 123A(6A), 165; 1986 s.74 (1), (2)
(3)	1975(1) ss.4(6J), 123A(7); 1985 s.7(2), (5)
(4), (5)	1975(1) ss.4(6K), 123A(8); 1985 s.7(2), (5); 1990 s.21(1), Sch. 6, para. 1(1), (2)(c)
148(1)	1975(2) s.21(1); 1985 s.4, Sch. 3, para. 1; 1986 s.18(1)
(2)	1975(2) s.21(2); 1979 s.10(2)
(3), (4)	1975(2) s.21(3); 1979 s.10(3); 1980(1) s.3(3)
(5)	1975(2) s.21(4)
(6)	1975(2) s.21(5); 1980(1) s.3(3)
(7)	Transitional
149	1982(2) s.9(1E); 1991(1) s.2(1)
150(1)(a)(i)	1986 s.63(1)(a)(i)
(ii)	1986 s.63(1)(a)(iv)
(iii)	1986 s.63(1)(a)(iii)
(b)	1986 s.63(1)(aa); 1991(2) s.4, Sch. 2, para. 16(a)
(c)–(f)	1986 s.63(1)(b)–(e)
(g)	1986 s.63(1)(ee); 1988(1) s.2(2)(a)
(h)	1986 s.63(1)(i); 1991(2) s.7, Sch. 3, para. 5(a)
(i)	1986 s.63(1)(f)
(j)	1986 s.63(1)(g), (h)
(2)	1986 s.63(2)
(3)	1986 s.63(3); 1988(1) s.2(2)(b); 1991(2) s.4, Sch. 2, para. 16(b)
(4)–(6)	1986 s.63(4)–(6)
(7)	1986 s.63(10); Social Security Act 1986 (Consequential) Amendment Regulation 1988 (S.I. 1998/961) reg. 2(a)
(8)	1986 s.63(11); 1990 s.21(1), Sch. 6, para. 23
(9)	1986 s.63(12)
(10)	1986 s.63(13); 1989 s.31(1), Sch. 8, para. 15(2); 1991(2) s.7, Sch. 3, para. 5(b)
(11)	1975(2) s.24(1)(a); 1986 s.86, Sch. 10, para. 92
151(1)	1975(2) s.23(2); 1986 ss.18(1), 86, Sch. 10, para. 91
(2)	1975(2) s.23(3); 1986 s.86, Sch. 10, para. 91
(3)–(5)	1986 s.63(7)–(9)
(6)	1986 s.63(10A); Social Security Act 1986 (Consequential) Amendment Regulation 1988 (S.I. 1988/961) reg. 2(b)
152	1986 s.63A; 1989 s.17(1)
153	1988(1) s.5
154	1975(3) s.17(1), (2)

Provision	Derivation
155(1)	1986 s.64(1); 1989 s.17(2)(a)
(2)	1986 s.64(6)
(3)–(6)	1986 s.64(2)–(5)
(7)	1975(2) s.24(1)(a); 1986 s.86, Sch. 10, para. 92
156	1975(2) s.23(2A); 1989 s.31(1), Sch. 8, para. 11
157(1)	1975(3) s.5(6), Sch. 3, paras. 1, 2; 1986 s.86, Sch. 10, para. 97
(2)	1975(3) s.5(6), Sch. 3, para. 3
158	1977 s.17(4)
159	1986 s.64A; 1989 s.18
160	1986 s.64B; 1990 s.21(1), Sch. 6, para. 24
161(1), (2)	1975(1) s.133(1), (2)
(3)	1975(1) s.133(3); Finance Act 1980 (c. 48) s.120, Sch. 19, para. 5(4)
(4)	1975(1) s.133(4)
162(1)	1975(1) s.134(1)(a)
(2)	1975(1) s.134(2); 1989 s.26, Sch. 7, para. 15
(3)	1975(1) s.134(2A); 1990 s.16(3)
(4)	1975(1) s.134(2B); 1990 s.17(3)
(5)(a)	1975(1) s.134(4)(a); 1985 s.29(1), Sch. 5, para. 11; 1989 s.1(8); The Social Security (Contributions and Allocation of Contributions) (Re-rating) Order 1989 (S.I. 1989/26) art. 6
(b)	1975(1) s.134(4)(b); 1985 s.29(1), Sch. 5, para. 11; The Social Security (Contributions and Allocation of Contributions) (Re-rating) Order 1989 (S.I. 1989/26) art. 6
(c)	1975(1) s.134(4)(bb); 1991(3) s.4(a)
(d)–(f)	1975(1) s.134(4)(c)–(e); 1985 s.29(1), Sch. 5, para. 11; The Social Security (Treasury Supplement to and Allocation of Contributions) (Re-rating) Order 1987 (S.I. 1987/48) art. 3
(6)	1975(1) ss.134(4), 165; 1985 s.29(1), Sch. 5, para. 11
(7)	1975(1) s.134(4A); 1981(1) s.3(3)
(8)(a)	1975(1) s.134(4B)(a); 1981(1) s.3(3)
(b)	1975(1) s.134(4B)(aa); 1991(3) s.4(b)
(c), (d)	1975(1) s.134(4B)(b), (c); 1981(1) s.3(3)
(9)–(11)	1975(1) s.134(5)
(12)	1975(1) s.134(6); 1979 s.14(2)
163(1)(a), (b)	1975(1) s.135(1), (2); 1975(2) s.65(1), Sch. 4, para. 52; 1984 s.11, Sch. 4, para. 3; 1990 s.16(4); 1991(2) s.4, Sch. 1, para. 17
(c)	1986 s.85(3)(d)
(d)	1982(2) ss.1(6), 9(7); 1985 s.19; 1986 ss.68, 85(3)(c)
(e)	1989 s.28(4)(b)
(2)(a)	1975(1) s.135(3)(a); 1975(2) s.64(1)(a); 1975(3) s.23(1)(a); 1977 s.23(1)(a); 1980(1) s.19(1); 1982(2) s.46(1)(a); 1986 s.85(1)(e), (f); 1988(1) s.15(1)(a); 1989 s.28(1)(a); 1990 s.18(1)(a); 1991(1) s.4(3)
(b)	1975(1) s.135(2)(a)–(f), (3)(b); 1984 s.11, Sch. 4, para. 3; 1991(2) s.4, Sch. 1, para. 18
(c)	1975(1) ss.135(2)(h), (3)(b), 159(4); 1975 (Old Cases) ss.2(1), 5(1); 1990 s.16(4), (7), (8)(a)

Provision	Derivation
(d)	1986 s.85(1)(a); 1988(2) s.135, Sch. 10, para. 12; 1991(2) s.7, Sch. 3, para. 8(a)
(e)	1986 s.85(1)(b)
(f)	1975(3) s.1(2)
(g)	1986 s.85(1)(c)
(h)	1986 s.85(1)(d)
(i)	1989 s.28(4)(a)
(3)	1975(1) s.135(4); 1982(2) s.46(2)
(4)	1977 s.1(2)
(5)	1975(1) s.135(7); 1990 s.17(4)
164(1)–(3)	1986 s.85(5)–(7)
(4)	1975 (Old Cases) s.4(4)(e); 1990 s.16(8)(b)
(5)	1975(1) s.113(2)(b); 1983 s.25, Sch. 8, para. 24; 1986 s.85(8)
(6)	1989 s.28(3)
165(1)	1975(1) s.133(5); 1986 s.85(9); 1991(2) s.7, Sch. 3, para. 8(b)
(2)–(4)	1975(1) s.133(6); 1975(3) s.23(4); 1986 s.85 (10)
(5)	1975(1) s.135(5); 1975(2) s.64(2); 1975(3) s.23(4); 1977 s.23(2); 1980(1) s.19(3); 1980 (2) s.7(1); 1986 s.85(4); 1988(1) s.15(2); 1989 s.28(2); 1990 ss.16(5), 18(2)
166(1)–(3)	1975(1) ss.137(2), 165
(4), (5)	1975(1) ss.137(3), (4), 165
167(1)	1986 s.32(1)
(2)–(4)	1986 s.32(5)–(7)
(5), (6)	1986 s.32(7A), (7B); 1988(1) s.11, Sch. 3, para. 4
168(1)–(4)	1986 s.32(8A)–(8D); 1988(1) s.11, Sch. 3, para. 6
(5)	1986 s.32(8E); 1990 s.10(1)
169	1986 s.85(11), (12)
170(1)–(4)	1980(1) s.9(1)–(4)
(5)	1980(1) s.9(7); 1982(2) s.48(5), Sch. 4, para. 30; 1991(1) s.3(1)(b); R12
171(1), (2)	1975(1) s.141(1)
(3)	1975(1) s.141(3)
(4)	1975(1) s.141(4); 1982 s.48(5), Sch. 4, para. 16
172(1)	1980(1) s.10(1); 1986 s.86, Sch. 10, para. 98(a)
(2)	1975(1) s.141(2); 1981(2) s.8, Sch. 2, para. 2; 1986 s.86, Sch. 10, para. 86
(3)	1980(1) s.10(2)
(4)	1975(1) s.141(2)
(5)	1980(1) s.10(9)
173(1), (2)	1986 s.61(1), (2)
(3)	1986 s.61(3); 1989 s.26, Sch. 7, para. 27
(4)	1986 s.61(4)
(5)	1986 s.61(5); 1989 s.31(1), Sch. 8, para. 12(3)
(6)	1980(1) s.10(9)
(7)	1986 s.61(10) "regulations"; 1989 s.31(1), Sch. 8, para. 12(4)
174(1)–(3)	1980(1) s.10(3)–(5)
(4)	1980(1) s.10(9)
175	1991(2) s.3(1)–(6)
176(1)	1986 s.61(7); 1988(2) s.135, Sch.10, para. 10
(2), (3)	1986 s.61(8), (9)
177(1)–(3)	1975(1) s.142(1)–(3)

Provision	Derivation
(4)	1975(1) s.142(4); 1975(2) s.65(2), Sch. 4, para. 66; 1986 s.65(1)
(5)	1975(1) s.142(1)
178(1), (2)	1975(3) s.14(1); 1986 s.65(4); 1991(2) s.7, Sch. 3, para. 6
(3)	1975(3) s.14(2)
179(1)	1975(1) s.143(1); 1975(3) s.15(1); 1977 s.20 (1), (2); 1986 s.65(2)(a)
(2)	1975(1) s.143(1A); 1975(3) s.15(1A); 1981(2) s.6(1), (2)
(3)	1975(1) s.143(2); 1975(3) s.15(2)
(4)	1975(1) s.143(1); 1975(3) s.15(1); 1986 s.65 (4); 1991(2) s.7, Sch. 3, para. 6
(5)	1975(3) s.15(1); 1986 s.65(4); 1991(2) s.7, Sch. 3, para. 6
180	1986 s.78
181	Supplementary Benefits Act 1976 (c. 71) s.22; 1980(1) s.6(1), (3), Sch. 2, Part I, para. 21, Part II; Criminal Procedure (Scotland) Act 1975 (c. 21) s.298G; Criminal Justice Act 1982 (c. 48) ss.46, 54; The Transfer of Functions (Health and Social Security) Order 1988 (S.I. 1988/1843) Sch. 3, para. 2(c)
182	Supplementary Benefits Act 1976 s.23; 1980 (1) s.6(3), Sch. 2, Part II; Criminal Procedure (Scotland) Act 1975 s.298G; Criminal Justice Act 1982 ss.46, 54; The Transfer of Functions (Health and Social Security) Order 1988 Sch. 3, para. 2(c)
183	1975(1) s.154
184	1975(1) s.155
185(1)	Drafting
(2)	1975(1) s.159(3)(c)
186	Drafting
187(1)	1975(1) s.87(1); 1975(3) s.12(1); 1986 s.86, Sch. 10, para. 48(a)
(2)	1975(1) s.87(2); 1975(3) s.12(2); Solicitors (Scotland) Act 1980 (c. 46) s.66, Sch. 6, para. 2
(3)	1975(1) s.87(3)
188(1), (2)	1975(1) s.163
(3)	1975 (Old Cases) s.12
189(1), (2)	1975(1) s.168(1), Sch. 20, "regulations"; 1975 (3) s.22(1); 1977 s.24(1) "regulations"; 1982(2) s.47 "regulations"; 1986 ss.52, 84(1) "regulations", Sch. 5, para. 20, 1989 s.30(1) "regulations"; 1991(2) s.3(8)
(3)	1975(1) s.166(1); 1975(3) s.22(2); 1977 s.24 (3); 1980(1) s.14(8); 1982(2) s.45(2); 1986 s.83(1); 1989 s.29(1); 1990 s.21(1), Sch. 6, para. 8(7); 1991(2) s.3(8)
(4)	1975(1) s.166(2); 1975(3) s.22(6); 1977 s.24 (3); 1982(2) s.45(1); 1986 s.83(1); 1989 s.29 (1)
(5)	1975(1) ss.113(2)(c), 166(3); 1975(3) s.22(7); 1977 s.24(3); 1982(2) s.45(1); 1986 s.83(1); 1989 ss.29(1), 31(1), Sch. 8, para. 10(1); 1991(2) s.3(7); R6
(6)	1975(1) s.166(3A); 1975(3) s.22(7A); 1977 s.24(3); 1986 ss.62(1), (2), 83(1); 1989 s.29 (1)

Provision	Derivation
(7)	1986 s.83(2); 1988(2) s.135, Sch. 10, para. 11(2)
(8)	1975(1) s.133(6); 1986 s.83(5); 1988(2) s.135, Sch. 10, para. 11(4); 1989 ss.17(2)(c), s.9(5)
(9)	1975(1) s.166(5); 1977 s.24(3); 1982(2) s.45 (1); 1986 s.83(6); 1989 s.29(6); 1991 s.12(3)
(10)	1975(1) s.166(5A); 1986 s.52(1), Sch. 5, para. 17
(11)	1975(1) s.166(7); 1975(3) ss.14(3), 15(3); 1986 s.65(4); 1991(2) s.7, Sch. 3, para. 6
(12)	1975(1) s.168(4)
190(1)	1975(1) s.167(1)(b); 1975(3) s.22(3); 1981(1) s.4(5)(b), 1986 ss.62(3), 83(3)(d); 1989 ss.17(2)(b), 29(2)(h)
(2)	1975(3) s.22(4); 1990 s.21(1), Sch. 6, para. 8(3)
(3)	1975(1) s.167(3); 1975(3) s.22(5); 1977 s.24 (5); 1982(2) s.45(2); 1986 s.83(4); 1989 s.29 (3); 1990 s.21(1), Sch. 6, para. 8(1), (3), (4), (7), (9), (12); 1991(2) s.12(2)
(4)	1975(1) s.167(4); 1980(1) s.14(8); 1990 s.21 (1), Sch. 6, para. 8(1); R13
191	
"the 1975 Act"; "the 1986 Act"; "benefit"	Drafting
"chargeable financial year"; "charging authority"	1986 s.20(11), "chargeable financial year"; "charging authority"; 1988(2) s.135, Sch. 10, para. 2(5)
"Christmas bonus"	Drafting
"claim"	1975(1) s.168(1), Sch. 20, "claim"
"claimant"	1975(1) s.168(1), Sch. 20, "claimant"
"Commissioner"; "compensation payment"; "compensator"; "the Consequential Provisions Act"; "contribution card"; "the Contributions and Benefits Act"; "disablement benefit"; "the disablement questions"	Drafting
"dwelling"	1986 s.84(1) "dwelling"
"5 year general qualification"	Drafting
"housing authority"	1986 s.84(1) "housing authority"; Housing (Scotland) Act 1988 (c. 43) ss.1, 3, Sch. 2, para. 1
"housing benefit scheme"	1986 s.84(1) "housing benefit scheme"
"income-related benefit"	Drafting
"industrial injuries benefit"	1975(1) s.168(1), Sch. 20, "industrial injuries benefit"
"invalidity benefit"	Drafting
"levying authority"	1986 s.20(11) "levying authority"; 1988(2) s.135, Sch. 10, para. 2(5)
"local authority"	1986 s.84(1) "local authority"
"medical examination"	1975(1) s.168(1), Sch. 20, "medical examination"
"medical practitioner"	1975(1) s.168(1), Sch. 20, "medical practitioner"
"medical treatment"	1975(1) s.168(1), Sch. 20, "medical treatment"
"new town corporation"	1986 s.84(1) "new town corporation"
"the Northern Ireland Department"	1975(1) s.168(1) Sch. 20, "the Northern Ireland Department"
"the Northern Ireland Administration Act"; "occupational pension scheme"; "the Old Cases Act"; "Old Cases payments"; "the Pensions Act"; "personal pension scheme"	Drafting

Provision	Derivation
"prescribe"	1975 s.168(1), Sch. 20, "prescribe"
"President"	1975(1) s.168(1), Sch. 20, "President"; 1991 (2) s.4, Sch. 1, para. 20
"rate rebate"; "rent rebate"; "rent allowance"	Drafting
"rates"	1986 s.84(1) "rates"; Abolition of Domestic Rates Etc. (Scotland) Act 1987 (c. 47) s.26 (2)(a)
"rating authority"	1986 s.84(1) "rating authority"
"tax year"	1975(1) s.168(1), Sch. 20, "tax year"
"10 year general qualification"	Drafting
"widow's benefit"	Drafting
192	Short title, commencement and extent
Sch. 1	
para. 1	1975(1) s.165A; 1985 ss.17, 32(3)
para. 2	1975(1) s.165A; 1985 s.17; 1986 s.86, Sch. 10, para. 88; Social Security Act 1986 (Commencement No. 1) Order 1986 (S.I. 1986/ 1609)
para. 3	1975(1) s.165A; 1986 s.86, Sch. 10, para. 87; Social Security Act 1986 (No. 4) Commencement Order 1986 (S.I. 1986/1959)
para. 4	1975(1) s.165A; 1986 s.86, Sch. 10, para. 87; 1989 ss.31(1), 33(2), (3), Sch. 8, para. 9(1)
para. 5	1975(1) s.165A; 1986 s.86, Sch. 10, para. 87; 1989 s.31(1), Sch. 8, para. 9(1); 1990 ss.6(1), 23(2), (3)
Sch. 2	
para. 1(1)	1975(1) s.97(4), Sch. 10, para. 1A(4); 1983 s.25, Sch. 8, para. 8
(2)–(4)	1975(1) s.97(4), Sch. 10, para. 1A(5)–(7); 1980(1) s.13(1)–(3); 1983 s.25, Sch. 8, para. 8
(5)	1975(1) s.97(4), Sch. 10, para. 1A(9); 1980(1) s.13(6); 1983 s.25, Sch. 8, para. 8
(6)	1980(1) s.13(5)(a); Judicial Pensions Act 1981 (c. 20) s.36, Sch. 3, para. 10
(7)	1980(1) s.13(1)
para. 2	1975(1) s.97(4), Sch. 10, para. 1A(10); 1983 s.25, Sch. 8, para. 8
para. 3	1975(1) ss.97(4), 100D(7), 108(3), Sch. 10, para. 1A(11), Sch. 10A, para. 11, Sch. 12, paras. 5A, 7; 1983 s.25, Sch. 8, paras. 8, 10; 1991(2) s.4, Sch. 1, paras. 5, 16
para. 4(1), (2)	1975(1) ss.97(4), 100D(7), Sch. 10, paras. 1B, 1C, Sch. 10A, para. 11; 1983 s.25, Sch. 8, para. 8; 1991(2) s.4, Sch. 1, paras. 5, 16
para. 5	1975(1) ss.97(4), 100D(7), 108(3), Sch. 10, para. 1D, Sch. 10A, para. 11, Sch. 12, para. 9; 1983 s.25, Sch. 8, paras. 8, 11; 1991(2) ss.4, Sch. 1, paras. 5, 16
para. 6	1975(1) s.97(4), Sch. 10, para. 4; 1980(1) s.12; The Transfer of Functions (Social Security Commissioners) Order 1984 (S.I. 1984/ 1818) art. 3
para. 7	1975(1) ss.97(4), 100D(7), 108(3), 113(3), Sch. 10, para. 3, Sch. 10A, para. 11, Sch. 12, paras. 4, 5, 6, 7; 1983 s.25, Sch. 8, para. 27(b); 1991(2) s.4, Sch. 1, paras. 5, 16
para. 8	1980(1) s.17; 1991(2) s.4, Sch. 2, para. 10
Sch. 3	

Provision	Derivation
para. 1	1975(1) s.115(2) "competent tribunal"; 1983 s.25, Sch. 8, paras. 5, 25; 1991(2) s.4, Sch. 1, para. 10
para. 2	1975(1) s.115, Sch. 13, para. 1; 1989 s.21, Sch. 3, para. 4
para. 3	1975(1) s.115, Sch. 13, para. 1A; 1986 s.52(1), Sch. 5, para. 19(a)
paras. 4–9	1975(1) s.115, Sch. 13, paras. 2–7
para. 10	1975(1) s.115, Sch. 13, para. 7A; 1989 s.21, Sch. 3, para. 10; 1991(2) s.4, Sch. 1, para. 17
para. 11	1975(1) s.115, Sch. 13, para. 10; 1986 s.52(1), Sch. 5, para. 19(b)
para. 12	1975(1) s.115, Sch. 13, para. 11
Sch. 4	
Part I	1989 s.19, Sch. 2, Part I; 1990 s. 21(1), Sch. 6, para. 28(4), (5); 1991(2) s.4, Sch. 2, para. 19
Part II	1989 s.19, Sch. 2, Part II; 1990 s.21(1), Sch. 6, para. 28(6)
Sch. 5	
para. 1	1980(1) s.9(2), Sch. 3, para. 1; 1982(2) s.48 (5), Sch. 4, para. 32(2)
para. 2	1980(1) s.9(2), Sch. 3, para. 2; 1982(2) s.48 (5), Sch. 4, para. 32(3)
paras. 3–10	1980(1) s.9(2), Sch. 3, paras. 3–10
Sch. 6	1975(1) s.141, Sch. 16, Part 1
Sch. 7	
Part I	
para. 1	1980(1) s.10(2), Sch. 3, para. 12(4); 1991(2) s.4, Sch. 2, para. 11
para. 2	1980(1) s.10(2), Sch. 3, para. 12(1)
para. 3	1980(1) s.10(2), Sch. 3, para. 12(2); 1986 s.86, Sch. 10, para. 99
para. 4	1980(1) s.10(2), Sch. 3, para. 13(1)
para. 5	1980(1) s.10(2), Sch. 3, para. 13(1A); 1986 s.86, Sch. 10, para. 106
paras. 6, 7	1980(1) s.10(2), Sch. 3, para. 14
para. 8	1980(1) s.10(2), Sch. 3, paras. 15A, 15AA; 1982(2) s.48(5), Sch. 4, para. 33(3); 1986 s.86, Sch. 10, para. 107; 1989 s.31(1), Sch. 8, para. 12(6)
paras. 9, 10	1980(1) s.10(2), Sch. 3, paras. 19, 20
Part II	R14
para. 11	1975(1) s.141, Sch. 16, para. 5
para. 12	1975(1) s.141, Sch. 16, para. 8; 1986 s.86, Sch. 10, para. 90
paras. 13–15	1975(1) s.141, Sch. 16, paras. 9–11
para. 16	1980(1) s.11(2)(a)
para. 17	1975(1), s.141, Sch. 16, para. 12
Sch. 8	1975(1) s.142(2); Sch. 17
Sch. 9	
para. 1(1)	1975 (Old Cases) s.4(1)
(2)	1975 (Old Cases) s.4(2); 1989 s.31(1), Sch. 8, para. 10(1)
(3)	1975 (Old Cases) s.4(3)
(4)	1975 (Old Cases) s.4(4); 1977 s.11(1)(a); 1990 s.16(8)(b)
(5)–(7)	1975 (Old Cases) s.4(5)–(7)
paras. 2, 3	1975 (Old Cases) ss.8, 9
para. 4	1986 s.53(11)

Provision	Derivation
Sch. 10	
para. 1	Drafting
para. 2	1986 s.73, Sch. 7, para. 3
para. 3(1)	1986 s.73, Sch. 7, para. 4(1); 1991(2) s.4, Sch. 2, para. 15(b)
(2)	1986 s.73, Sch. 7, para. 4(2)
para. 4(1)	1986 s.73, Sch. 7, para. 5(1)
(2)	1986 s.73, Sch. 7, para. 2
(3)	1986 s.73, Sch. 7, para. 5(2)
para. 5	1986 s.73, Sch. 7, para. 7
para. 6	1986 s.73, Sch. 7, para. 6

TABLE OF DESTINATIONS

NATIONAL INSURANCE ACT 1974
c.14

1974	c.14
s.6(1)........	s.70(1), (3)
(3)........	70(2)

SOCIAL SECURITY ACT 1975
c.14

1975	c.14	1975	c.14	1975	c.14
s.1(4)........	s.114(2)	s.98(1)......	20(1), (3), (6)	s.101(3)......	23(5), 34(2)
4(6F).......	146	(2).......	20(2)	(4)......	23(6), 34(3)
(6G).......	147(1)	(2A).....	20(4)	(5)......	23(7), (8),
(6HH).....	147(2)	(3).......	20(5)		34(4)
(6J).......	147(3)	99(1).......	21(1)	(5A).....	23(9),
(6K).......	147(4), (5)	(2).......	21(2)		(10), 34(4)
23(2).......	151(1)	(2A).....	21(3)	(5B).....	23(9), (10),
85(1).......	73(1)	(3).......	21(4), (5)		34(4)
(2).......	73(2)	(4).......	21(6)	102(1)......	36(1)
(3).......	73(3)	100(1)......	22(1)	(2)......	36(1)
(4).......	73(4), (5)	(2).......	22(2)	(3)......	36(2)
(5).......	73(4), (5)	(3).......	22(3)	103(1)......	37(1)
87(1)......	187(1)	(4).......	22(4)	(2)......	37(2)
(2).......	187(2)	(7).......	22(5)	(3)......	37(3)
(3).......	187(3)	(8).......	22(6), (7)	104(1)......	25(1), (3)
88..........	8	(9).......	22(6), (7)	(1A)......	25(2)
89..........	9	100A(1)......	30(1)	(1ZA)...	25(5), 35(11)
90(2).......	10(1)	(2)....	30(2), (5)	(2)......	26(1), (2)
(3).......	10(2)	(3)....	30(3)	(3)......	26(1), (2)
(4).......	10(3)	(4)....	30(4)	(3A).....	26(3), 35(5)
93(1)(a)(b)..	17(1)(a)(b)	(5)....	30(6)–(11)	(3B).....	29
(bb)....	17(1)(c)	(6)....	30(6)–(11)	(4)......	28
(d)....	17(1)(d)	(7)....	30(6)–(11)	(5)......	27(1)
(e)....	17(1)(e)	(8)....	30(6)–(11)	(b)....	32(8), 35(10)
(2).......	17(2)	(9)....	30(6)–(11)	(6)......	27(2)
(2A).....	17(3)	(10)....	30(6)–(11)	(7)......	69(1)
(3).......	17(4)	(11)....	30(12)	(8)......	69(2)–(4)
94(1).......	18(1)	(12)....	30(13)	(9)......	69(2)–(4)
(2).......	18(2)–(5)	100B........	31	(10).....	69(2)–(4)
(3).......	18(2)–(5)	100C(1).....	32(1)	104A(1)....	35(1)–(3)
(4).......	18(2)–(5)	(2)....	32(2)–(5)	(2)....	35(1), (2)
(5).......	18(2)–(5)	(3)....	32(2)–(5)	(3)....	35(4)
(7).......	18(6), (7)	(4)....	32(2)–(5)	(4)....	35(6)–(9)
(8).......	18(6), (7)	(5)....	32(2)–(5)	(5)....	35(6)–(9)
96(1).......	19(1)	(6)....	32(6), (7)	(6)....	35(6)–(9)
(2).......	19(2), (3)	(7)....	32(6), (7)	(7)....	35(6)–(9)
97(1).......	38(1)	(8)(a)...	32(8)	(8)....	35(12)
(1A).....	38(2)	(b)..	69(1)	(9)....	35(5)
(1B)......	39	(9)....	32(9), (10)	(a)..	35(11)
(1C)......	39	(10)....	32(9), (10)	(c)..	35(10)
(1D)......	39	100D(1)....	33	107(1).......	44(1)–(3)
(1E)......	39	(2)....	33	(2).......	44(1)–(3)
(2).......	41(1)	(3)....	33	(3).......	44(1)–(3)
(2A).....	41(2)	(4)....	33	(4).......	44(4), (5)
(2C)......	41(3), (4),	(5)....	33	(5).......	44(6)
	43(4)–(6)	(6)....	33	(6).......	44(7)
(2D).....	41(3), (4),	(7)....	42(1)–(7),	108(1).......	45(1)
	43(4)–(6)		43(1)–(8),	(2)......	45(2)
(2E)......	41(5), 43(4)–		Sched. 2,	(3)......	49(1), (2),
	(6)		paras. 3,		50(1)–(6)
(3).......	52(1)		4(1), (2), 5, 7		Sched. 2,
(4).......	40(1)–(4),	101(1).......	23(1), 34(1)		paras. 3, 5, 7
	41(6), 42(6),	(2).......	23(2), 34(2)	(4)......	45(3)
	(7), 51(1)–(3)	(a)....	23(3)	(4A).....	45(4), (5)
	Sched. 2,	(b)....	23(3)	(4B).....	45(4), (5)
	paras. 1(1),	(bb)...	23(4)	(5)......	45(6)
	(5), 2, 3, 4(1),	(c)....	23(3)	109(1).......	46(1)
	(2), 5, 6, 7	(d)....	23(3)	(2)......	46(2)

1975	c.14
s.109(3)	46(3)
110(1)	47(1)
(1A)	47(2), (3)
(1B)	47(2), (3)
(2)	47(4)
(3)	47(5)–(7)
(4)	47(5)–(7)
(5)	47(5)–(7)
(6)	47(8)
(7)	47(9)
112(1)	48(1)
(2)	48(2)
(3)	48(3)
(5)	48(5)
(6)	48(5), (6)
(7)	48(5), (6)
113(1)	62(1)
(2)(a)	62(2)
(b)	62(2), 164(5)
(c)	189(5)
(3)	Sched. 2, para. 7
114(1)	58(1), (2)
(2)	58(3)
(2A)	58(3)
(2B)	58(5)–(7)
(2C)	58(5)–(7)
(2D)	58(5)–(7)
(5)	58(8)
115	Sched. 3, paras. 2–12
(1)	59(1)
(2)	59(1), Sched. 3, para. 1
(3)	59(2)
(4)	59(3)
(4A)	59(4)
(5)	59(5)
(6)	59(6)
(7)	59(7)
115A(1)	53(1)
(2)	53(2)
(3)	53(3), (4)
(4)	53(3), (4)
115B(1)	56(1)
(2)	56(2)
115C(1)	54(1), (2)
(2)	54(1), (2)
(3)	54(3), (4)
(4)	54(5)
(5)	54(6), (7)
(6)	54(8)
115D	55
116(1)	57(1)
(2)	57(1)
117(1)	60(1)
(2)	60(2)
(3)	60(3)
(4)	60(4)
(5)	60(5)
119(3)	61(1), (4)
(4)(a)	61(2)
120(2)	141(1)
(3)	141(2)–(6)
(4)	141(2)–(6)
(5)	141(2)–(6)
(6)	141(2)–(6)
(7)	141(2)–(6)
121(1)	142(1)
(2)	142(2)
s.121(3)	142(3)
s.122(1)	143(1)
(2)	143(2)
(3)(a)	143(3)
(6)	143(4)
123(2)	144(1)
(3)	144(2)
123A(1)	145(1)
(2)	145(2)
(3)	145(3)
(4)	145(4)
(5)	147(1)
(6A)	147(2)
(7)	147(3)
(8)	147(4), (5)
133(1)	161(1), (2)
(2)	161(1), (2)
(3)	161(3)
(4)	161(4)
(5)	165(1)
(6)	165(2)–(4), 189(8)
134(1)(a)	162(1)
(2)	162(2)
(2A)	162(3)
(2B)	162(4)
(4)	162(6)
(a)	162(5)(a)
(b)	162(5)(b)
(bb)	162(5)(c)
(c)	162(5)(d)–(f)
(d)	162(5)(d)–(f)
(e)	162(5)(d)–(f)
(4A)	162(7)
(4B)(a)	162(8)(a)
(aa)	162(8)(b)
(b)	162(8)(c), (d)
(c)	162(8)(c), (d)
(5)	162(9)–(11)
(6)	162(12)
135(1)	163(1)(a), (b)
(2)	163(1)(a), (b)
(a)	163(2)(b)
(b)	163(2)(b)
(c)	163(2)(b)
(d)	163(2)(b)
(e)	163(2)(b)
(f)	163(2)(b)
(h)	163(2)(c)
(3)(a)	163(2)(a)
(b)	163(2)(b), (c)
(4)	163(3)
(5)	165(5)
(7)	163(5)
137(2)	166(1)–(3)
(3)	166(4), (5)
(4)	166(4), (5)
141	Sched. 6, Sched. 7, Part II, paras. 11, 12, 17
(1)	171(1), (2)
(2)	172(2), (4)
(3)	171(3)
(4)	171(4)
142(1)	177(1)–(5)
(2)	177(1)–(3), Sched. 8
s.142(3)	177(1)–(3)
(4)	177(4)
143(1)	179(1), (4)
(1A)	179(2)
(2)	179(3)
146(1)	114(1)
(2)	114(3)
(3)	114(4)
(4)	114(5), (6)
148(1)	117(1)
(2)	117(2), (3)
(3)	117(2), (3)
149	118
150	119
151(1)	120(1), (2)
(2)	120(1), (2)
(3)	120(3)
(3A)	120(4)
(4)	120(5)
(5)	120(6)
152(1)	121(1)
(2)	121(2)
(3)	121(3)
(5)	121(4)–(6)
(6)	121(4)–(6)
(7)	121(4)–(6)
154	183
155	184
159(3)(c)	185(2)
(4)	163(2)(c)
160(1)	124(1), (2)
(2)	124(3)
(3)	124(4), (5)
(4)	124(4), (5)
161(1)	133
163	188(1), (2)
165	142(1), 144(1), 147(2), 162(6), 166(1)–(5)
165A	Sched. 1, paras. 1–5
(1)	1(1), (4)
(2)	1(2)
(3)	1(3)
165B(1)	2(1)
(2)	2(2), (3)
(3)	2(4), (5)
(4)	2(4), (5)
165C	3
165D(1)	68(1)–(3)
(2)	68(1)–(3)
(3)	68(1)–(3)
(4)	68(4)
(5)	68(5), (6)
(6)	68(5), (6)
166(1)	189(3)
(2)	189(4)
(3)	189(5)
(3A)	189(6)
(5)	189(9)
(5A)	189(10)
(7)	189(11)
167(1)(b)	190(1)
(3)	190(3)
(4)	190(4)
168(1)	189(1), (2), 191
(4)	189(12)
Sched. 1, para. 5(2)	114(2)

1975 **c.14**
Sched. 3,
  para. 3(1) ... 32(6), (7)
Sched. 10,
  para. 1(1) ... 40(1)
       (2) ... 40(2), (3)
       (2A) . 40(2), (3),
              42(6)
       (6) ... 40(4), 42(7)
       (8) ... 41(6)
       1A(1) . 51(1)
       (2) . 51(2)
       (3) . 51(3)
       (5) .Sched. 2,
              para. 1(2)–
              (4)
       (6) .Sched. 2,
              para. 1(2)–
              (4)
       (7) .Sched. 2,
              para. 1(2)–
              (4)
       (9) .Sched. 2,
              para. 1(5)
       (10) Sched. 2,
              para. 2
       (11) Sched. 2,
              para. 3
       1B ....Sched. 2,
              para. 4(1),
              (2)
       1C ....Sched. 2,
              para. 4(1),
              (2)
       1D ....Sched. 2,
              para. 5
       3 .....Sched. 2,
              para. 7
       4 .....Sched. 2,
              para. 6

1975 **c.14**
Sched. 10A,
  para. 1 ..... 43(1)
       2 ..... 43(4)–(6)
       3 ..... 42(1)–(5)
       4 ..... 42(1)–(5)
       5 ..... 42(1)–(5)
       6 ..... 42(1)–(5)
       7 ..... 42(1)–(5)
       8 ..... 42(6), (7)
       9 ..... 43(2), (3)
       10 .... 43(2), (3)
       11 ....Sched. 2,
              paras. 3,
              4(1), (2), 5, 7
       12 .... 43(7), (8)
       13 .... 43(7), (8)
Sched. 12,
  para. 1 ..... 49(1)
       2(1) ... 50(1)
       (2) ... 50(2)
       (3) ... 50(3), (4)
       (4) ... 50(3), (4)
       (5) ... 50(5)
       3 ..... 49(2), 50(6)
       4 .....Sched. 2,
              para. 7
       5 .....Sched. 2,
              para. 7
       5A ....Sched. 2,
              para. 3
       6 .....Sched. 2,
              para. 7
       7 .....Sched. 2,
              paras. 3, 7
       9 .....Sched. 2,
              para. 5
Sched. 13,
  para 1 ......Sched. 3,
              para. 2

1975 **c.14**
Sched. 13—cont.
  para. 1A ....Sched. 3,
              para. 3
       2 .....Sched. 3,
              paras. 4–9
       3 .....Sched. 3,
              paras. 4–9
       4 .....Sched. 3,
              paras. 4–9
       5 .....Sched. 3,
              paras. 4–9
       6 .....Sched. 3,
              paras. 4–9
       7 .....Sched. 3,
              paras. 4–9
       7A ....Sched. 3,
              para. 10
       10 ....Sched. 3,
              para. 11
       11 ....Sched. 3,
              para. 12
Sched. 16,
  para. 5 .....Sched. 7,
              Part II,
              para. 11
       8 .....Sched. 7,
              Part II,
              para. 12
       9 .....Sched. 7,
              Part II,
              paras. 13–15
       10 ....Sched. 7,
              Part II,
              paras. 13–15
       12 ....Sched. 7,
              Part II,
              para. 17
  Part 1 ......Sched. 6
Sched. 17 .....Sched. 8
Sched. 20 .....189(1), (2), 191

SOCIAL SECURITY PENSIONS ACT 1975
c.60

1975 **c.60**
s.21(1)........ s.148(1)
   (2)........ 148(2)
   (3)........ 148(2), (3)
   (4)........ 148(5)
   (5)........ 148(6)
23(2A) 156
   (3)........ 151(2)
24(1)(a) ..... 150(11), 155
              (7)

1975 **c.60**
s.60(1)(a) ..... 17(1)(f)
64(1)(a) ..... 163(2)(a)
   (2)........ 165(5)
65 .... 70(3), 121(2)
   (1)........ 141(1), 163
              (1)(a), (b)
   (2)........ 177(4)

1975 **c.60**
Sched. 4,
  para. 35 .... 70(3)
       50(b).. 141(1)
       52 .... 163(1)(a),
              (b)
       66 .... 177(4)
       67 .... 121(2)

CHILD BENEFIT ACT 1975
c.61

1975 **c.61**
s.1(2)........ s.163(2)(f)
4A 80
5(6)........ 157(1), (2)
6(1)........ 13(1)
   (3)........ 13(2)
12(1)........ 187(1)
   (2)........ 187(2)
14(1)........ 178(1), (2)
   (2)........ 178(3)
   (3)........ 189(11)
15(1)........ 179(1), (4),
              (5)

1975 **c.61**
s.15(1A) ...... 179(2)
   (2)........ 179(3)
   (3)........ 189(11)
17(1)........ 154
   (2)........ 154
21(1)........ 70(3), 73(2)
22(1)........ 189(1), (2)
   (2)........ 189(3)
   (3)........ 190(1)
   (4)........ 190(2)
   (5)........ 190(3)
   (6)........ 189(4)

1975 **c.61**
s.22(7)........ 189(5)
   (7A) ...... 189(6)
23(1)(a) ..... 163(2)(a)
   (4)........ 165(2)–(5)
Sched. 3,
  para. 1 ..... 157(1)
       2 .... 157(1)
       3 .... 157(2)
Sched. 4,
  para. 8 ..... 70(3)
       28 .... 73(2)

INDUSTRIAL INJURIES AND DISEASES (OLD CASES) ACT 1975
c.16

1975	c.16
s.2(1).........	s.163(2)(c)
4(1).........	Sched. 9,
	para. 1(1)
(2).........	Sched. 9,
	para. 1(2)
(3).........	Sched. 9,
	para. 1(3)
(4).........	Sched. 9,
	para. 1(4)
(e)......	164(4)

1975	c.16
s.4(5).........	Sched. 9,
	para. 1(5)–
	(7)
(6).........	Sched. 9,
	para. 1(5)–
	(7)
(7).........	Sched. 9,
	para. 1(5)–
	(7)

1975	c.16
s.5(1).........	163(2)(c)
8	Sched. 9,
	paras. 2, 3
9	Sched. 9,
	paras. 2, 3
11	124(1), (2)
12	188(3)

SOCIAL SECURITY (CONSEQUENTIAL PROVISIONS) ACT 1975
c.18

1975	c.18
s.1(3).........	s.70(3)
2	47(10)
4	47(10)
Sched. 2,	
para. 70	70(3)
Sched. 3,	
para. 20	47(10)

CRIMINAL PROCEDURE (SCOTLAND) ACT 1975
c.21

1975	c.21
s.289G	s.114(1), (4),
	181, 182

SUPPLEMENTARY BENEFITS ACT 1976
c.71

1976	c.71
s.22	s.181
23	182
35(2).........	70(3)
Sched. 7,	
para. 36	70(3)

SOCIAL SECURITY (MISCELLANEOUS PROVISIONS) ACT 1977
c.5

1977	c.5
s.1(2).........	s.163(4)
11(1)(a)	Sched. 9,
	para 1(4)
17(4).........	158
(5).........	61(3)

1977	c.5
s.20(1)........	179(1)
(2).........	179(1)
22(5).........	17(1)(e)
23(1)(a)	163(2)(a)

1977	c.5
s.23(2).........	165(5)
24(1).........	189(1), (2)
(3).........	189(3)–(6),
	(9)
(5).........	190(3)

EMPLOYMENT PROTECTION (CONSOLIDATION) ACT 1978
c.44

1978	c.44
s.159	s.58(4)
Sched. 16,	
para. 19(1) ..	58(4)

SOCIAL SECURITY ACT 1979
c.18

1979	c.18
s.10(2)........	s.148(2)
(3)........	148(3), (4)
14(2)........	162(12)
15(1)........	73(4), (5)
(3)........	80
21(4)........	47(1)
Sched. 3,	
para. 8	47(1)

SOCIAL SECURITY ACT 1980
c.30

1980	c.30	1980	c.30	1980	c.30
s.2	s.19(2), (3),	s.13(6)........	52(3),	Sched. 3—*cont.*	
	143(4)		Sched. 2,	para. 7 .....Sched. 5,	
3(3)........	148(3), (4),		para. 1(5)		paras. 3–10
	(6)	14(1)........	24(1)–(5),	8 .....Sched. 5,	
6(1)........	181		34(5)		paras. 3–10
(3)........	181, 182	(2)........	24(1)–(5),	9 .....Sched. 5,	
9(1)........	170(1)–(4)		34(5)		paras. 3–10
(2)........	170(1)–(4),	(3)........	24(1)–(5),	10 ....Sched. 5,	
	Sched. 5,		34(5)		paras. 3–10
	paras. 1–10	(4)........	24(1)–(5),	12(1) ..Sched. 7,	
(3)........	170(1)–(4)		34(5)		Part 1,
(4)........	170(1)–(4)	(5)........	24(1)–(5),		para. 2
(7)........	170(5)		34(5)	(2) ..Sched. 7,	
10(1)........	172(1)	(8)........	189(3), 190		Part 1,
(2)........	172(3),	(4)			para. 3
	Sched. 7,	(a)	24(6), 34(5)	(4) ..Sched. 7,	
	Part I,	17 ....Sched. 2,			Part 1,
	paras. 1–10		para. 8		para. 1
10(3)........	174(1)–(3)	19(1)........	163(2)(a)	13(1) ..Sched. 7,	
(4)........	174(1)–(3)	(3)........	165(5)		Part 1,
(5)........	174(1)–(3)	21	19(2), (3)		para. 4
(9)........	172(5), 173	Sched. 1,		(1A) Sched. 7,	
	(6), 174(4)	para. 9 .....19(2), (3)			Part 1,
11(2)(a) .....Sched. 7,		13	143(4)		para. 5
	Part II,	Sched. 2,		14 ....Sched. 7,	
	para. 16	Part I,			Part 1,
12	52(1), 57(1),	para. 21	181		paras. 6, 7
	Sched. 2,	Part II	181, 182	15A ...Sched. 7,	
	para. 6	Sched. 3,			Part 1,
13(1).......Sched. 2,		para. 1 .....Sched. 5,			para. 8
	para. 1(2)–		para. 1	15AA .Sched. 7,	
	(4), (7)	2 .....Sched. 5,			Part 1,
(2).......Sched. 2,			para. 2		para. 8
	para. 1(2)–	3 .....Sched. 5,		19 ....Sched. 7,	
	(4)		paras. 3–10		Part 1,
(3).......Sched. 2,		4 .....Sched. 5,			paras. 9, 10
	para. 1(2)–		paras. 3–10	20 ....Sched. 7,	
	(4)	5 .....Sched. 5,			Part 1,
(5)........	52(2)		paras. 3–10		paras. 9, 10
(a) .....Sched. 2,		6 .....Sched. 5,			
	para. 1(6)		paras. 3–10		

SOCIAL SECURITY (No. 2) ACT 1980
c.39

1980	c.39
s.7(1).........	s.165(5)

TABLE OF DESTINATIONS

FINANCE ACT 1980
c.48

1980	c.48
s.120	s.161(3)
Sched. 19,	
para. 5(4) ...	161(3)

MAGISTRATES' COURTS ACT 1980
c.43

1980	c.43
s.154	121(1)
Sched. 7,	
para. 135 ...	121(1)

SOLICITORS (SCOTLAND) ACT 1980
c.46

1980	c.46
s.66	s.187(2)
Sched. 6,	
para. 2	187(2)

SOCIAL SECURITY (CONTRIBUTIONS) ACT 1981
c.1

1981	c.1
s.3(3).........	s.162(7), (8)
	(a), (c), (d)
4(5)(b)	190(1)

SOCIAL SECURITY ACT 1981
c.33

1981	c.33
s.6(1).........	s.179(2)
(2).........	179(2)
8	172(2)
Sched. 2,	
para. 2	172(2)

JUDICIAL PENSIONS ACT 1981
c.20

1981	c.20
s.36 ....Sched. 2,	
	para. 1(6)
Sched. 3,	
para. 10 ....Sched. 2,	
	para. 1(6)

SOCIAL SECURITY (CONTRIBUTIONS) ACT 1982
c.2

1982	c.2
s.48(5)........	s.171(4)
Sched. 4,	
para. 16	171(4)

5–214

SOCIAL SECURITY AND HOUSING BENEFITS ACT 1982
c.24

1982	c.24
s.1(6).........	s.163(1)(d)
9(1E)	149
(3)(a)	130(4)(c)
(7)........	163(1)(d)
17(1).......	129
(2).......	14(1)
(2A)	14(2)
(3).......	14(3)
(4).......	130(4)(a), (b)

1982	c.24
s.18(1).......	130(1)
(2).......	130(2), (3)
(3).......	130(2), (3)
45(1).......	189(4), (5)(a)
(2).......	189(3), 190 (3)
46(1)(a)	163(2)(a)
(2)........	163(3)
47	189(1), (2)
48(5).......	170(5), Sched. 5, paras. 1, 2, Sched. 7, Part 1, para. 8

1982	c.24
Sched. 4,	
para. 30	170(5)
32(2) ..	Sched. 5, paras. 1, 2
33(3) ..	Sched. 7, Part 1, para. 8

CRIMINAL JUSTICE ACT 1982
c.48

1982	c.48
s.46	s.114(1), (4), 181, 182
54	114(1), (4), 181, 182

HEALTH AND SOCIAL SERVICES AND SOCIAL SECURITY ADJUDICATIONS ACT 1983
c.41

1983	c.41
s.25	s.25(2), 38(1), (2), 39, 40(1), (4), 41(1), (3)– (6), 45(2), (3), (6), 46(1)–(3), 47(1), (4), (8), (9), 49(1), (2), 50(1), (2)–(6), 51(2), (3), 60(1), (3), 62(2), 164(5)
	Sched. 2, paras, 1(2)– (5), 2, 3, 4(1), (2), 5, 7, Sched. 3, para. 1
Sched. 8,	
para. 2	38(1), (2), 39, 41(1), (3)– (5)

1983	c.41
Sched. 8—cont.	
para. 3	25(2)
5	Sched. 3, para. 1
6	60(1)
7	40(1), (4), 41(6)
8	51(2), (3) Sched. 2, paras. 1(2)– (5), 2, 3, 4(1), (2), (5)
9	50(1)–(5)
10	Sched. 2, para. 3
11	Sched. 2, para. 5
21(1) ..	45(2)
(2) ..	49(1), (2), 50(1)–(6)
(3) ..	45(3), (6)

1983	c.41
Sched. 8—cont.	
para. 22(a) ..	46(1)
(b)(i)	46(2)
(c) ..	46(3)
23(a) ..	47(1)
(b) ..	47(4)
(c) ..	47(8)
(d) ..	47(9)
24	164(5)
(a) ..	62(2)
25	Sched. 3, para. 1
26	60(3)
27(a) ..	49(1)
(b) ..	49(2), 50(6), Sched. 2, para. 7

HEALTH AND SOCIAL SECURITY ACT 1984
c.48

1984	c.48
s.11	s.130(1), 163 (1)(a), (b), (2) (b)
(2).......	45(1), (2), 46(1), 47(8), (9), 48(1)

1984	c.48
s.16(a).......	41(2)
(b)	40(2), (3)
Sched. 4,	
para. 3	163(1)(a), (b), (2)(b)
5	45(1)

1984	c.48
Sched. 4—cont.	
para. 6	45(2)
7	46(1)
8(a)...	47(8)
(b)...	47(9)
9	48(1)
15(a) ..	130(1)

TRANSFER OF FUNCTIONS (SOCIAL SECURITY COMMISSIONERS) ORDER 1984
S.I. 1984 No. 1818

1984	S.I. 1818
art. 3	s.24(6),
	Sched. 2,
	para. 6

SOCIAL SECURITY ACT 1985
c.53

1985	c.53	1985	c.53	1985	c.53
s.4	s.148(1)	s.19	163(1)(d)	Sched. 3,	
7(2)	146, 147(1),	20	14(2)	para. 1	148(1)
	(3)–(5)	29(1)	143(1), 162	Sched. 5,	
(5)	145(2), (3),		(5)(a), (b), (d)–	para. 9(a) . . .	143(1)
	(4), 147(1), (3)–		(f), (6)	11	162(5)(a),
	(5)	32(3)	Sched. 1,		(b), (d)–(f), (6)
17	Sched. 1,		para. 1		
	paras. 1, 2				

SOCIAL SECURITY ACT 1986
c.50

1986	c.50	1986	c.50	1986	c.50
s.18(1)	148(1), 151	s.27B(3)	11	s.31A(6)	138(3)–(9)
	(1)	28(1)	134(1)	(7)	138(3)–(9)
20(4E)	72(1)	(1A)	134(2)	(8)	138(3)–(9)
(4F)	72(7), (8)	(2)	134(3)–(6)	(9)	138(3)–(9)
(4G)	72(7), (8)	(3)	134(3)–(6)	31B(1)	139(1)–(5)
(4H)	72(2)	(4)	134(3)–(6)	(2)	139(1)–(5)
(4J)	72(3)–(6)	(5)	134(3)–(6)	(3)	139(1)–(5)
(4K)	72(3)–(6)	(5A)	134(7)	(4)	139(1)–(5)
(4L)	72(3)–(6)	(6)	134(8)–(12)	(5)	139(1)–(5)
(4M)	72(3)–(6)	(7)	134(8)–(12)	(6)	139(6)
(11)	191	(8)	134(8)–(12)	(7)	139(7)–(10)
24(1)	106(1)	(9)	134(8)–(12)	(8)	139(7)–(10)
(4)	106(2)–(4)	(10)	134(8)–(12)	(9)	139(7)–(10)
(5)	106(2)–(4)	29(1)	63(1)	(10)	139(7)–(10)
(6)	106(2)–(4)	(2)	63(2)	31C(1)	63(1)
(7)	106(5)	(4)	75	(2)	63(2)
(8)	106(6), (7)	(5)	75	31D(1)	76(1), (2)
(9)	106(6), (7)	(6)	75	(2)	76(1), (2)
24A(1)	107(1)–(4)	(7)	75	(3)	76(3)
(2)	107(1)–(4)	(8)	79(b)	(4)	76(4)
(3)	107(1)–(4)	30(1)	135(1)	(5)	76(5)
(4)	107(1)–(4)	(2)	135(2), (3)	(6)	76(6)–(8)
(4A)	107(5)	(2A)	136(1)	(7)	76(6)–(8)
(5)	107(6)–(8)	(2B)	136(2)–(4)	(8)	76(6)–(8)
(6)	107(6)–(8)	(2C)	136(2)–(4)	31E	77
(7)	107(6)–(8)	(2ZA)	135(4)	31F(1)	140(1), (2)
(7A)	107(9)–(11)	(3)	135(5)	(2)	140(1), (2)
(7B)	107(9)–(11)	(5)	135(6), (7)	(3)	140(3)
(7C)	107(9)–(11)	(6)	135(8), (9)	(4)	140(4), (5)
(8)	107(12)–(15)	(7)	135(10)	(5)	140(4), (5)
(9)	107(12)–(15)	(8)	135(11)	(5A)	140(6)
(10)	107(12)–(15)	(8A)	137	(6)	140(7)
(11)	107(12)–(15)	(8B)	137	(7)	140(8)
24B	108	(8C)	137	31G(1)	128
25A	109	(8D)	137	(2)	128
26(1)	105(1), (2)	(8E)	137	(3)	128
(2)	105(1), (2)	(8F)	137	32(1)	167(1)
(3)	78(6); 105(3)	(9)	135(12)	(4)	78(4)
(4)	78(7); 105(3)	31(1)	127	(5)	167(2)–(4)
(5)	78(8); 105(3)	(2)	127	(6)	167(2)–(4)
(6)	78(9)	(3)	127	(7)	167(2)–(4)
(7)	105(3)	31A(1)	138(1), (2)	(7A)	167(5), (6)
27	74	(2)	138(1), (2)	(7B)	167(5), (6)
27A	126	(3)	138(3)–(9)	(8)	64(1), (2)
27B(1)	11	(4)	138(3)–(9)	(8A)	168(1)–(4)
(2)	11	(5)	138(3)–(9)	(8B)	168(1)–(4)

1986	c.50
s.32(8C)	168(1)–(4)
(8D)	168(1)–(4)
(8E)	168(5)
(9)......	64(1), (2)
(10)......	64(3)
(11)......	66(9), (10)
(12)......	66(9), (10)
33(1)......	12(1)
(5).......	78(1)–(3)
(6).......	78(1)–(3)
(7).......	78(1)–(3)
(8).......	78(6)–(9)
(8A).....	79(C)
(12)......	78(5)
(13)......	12(2)
34	66(1)–(8)
35	65
39	45(1)
49	15(1), (2); 131; 132(1), (2), (3)
51(1)(a)–(h) .	5(1)(a)–(h)
(k)–(t)..	5(1)(i)–(r)
(2).......	5(2)
(3).......	5(4), (5)
(4).......	5(4), (5)
51A(1)(a)–	
(k) ..	6(1)(a)–(k)
(kk) ..	6(1)(l)
(l)–(o)	6(1)(m)–(p)
(oo) ..	6(1)(q)
(p)–(s)	6(1)(r)–(u)
(2), (3) ..	6(2), (3)
51B........	7
52	189(1), (2)
(1).......	19(1), 20(2), (4), 21(2), 22(2)–(5), 23(1), (3), (7), (8), 23(9), (10), 25(1), (3), 26(3), 27(1), 36(1), 37(1), (2), (3), 4(7), 46(3), 47(2), (3), 48(1), (3), 50(2), 58(5)– (7), 189(10), Sched. 3 paras. 3, 11
(2).......	17(1)(g), (i)– (vi), (h)
(3).......	20(3)
(a)	20(6), 25(1), 69(1)
(b)	58(1), (2)
(c)	59(1)
(d)	60(1)
(e)	61(4)
(f)	124(1), (2)

1986	c.50
s.52(3A)	20(6), 21(3), 22(1), 25(1), (2), 30(1), (5)–(11), (13), 31, 32(1), (6)–(10), 33, 34(1)–(3), 35(3)–(10), (12), 54(1), (2), (4), (5), (7), (8), 58(1), (2), 59(1), 60(1), 61(4), 69(1), 124(1), (2)
52(3A).....	30(6)–(11)
(c) ...	55
(4).......	59(2)
(5).......	117(1)
(6).......	20(6), 25(1), 58(1), (2), 59(1), 60(1), 61(4), 124(1), (2)
(7)(a)	20(3)
(b)	21(4), (5)
(c)(i) ..	22(1)
(ii) ..	22(2)
(iii) ..	22(5)
(d)	23(2)
(8).......	25(4)
(9)(a)	30(5); 35(3)
(b)	30(5); 35(3); 54(5)
(c)	35(5), (10)
(d)	54(4)
(e)	54(7)
(10)......	30(1), (5); 35(3)
53(1).......	71(1)
(1A).......	71(2)
(2).......	71(3), (4)
(3).......	71(3), (4)
(4).......	71(5)
(5).......	71(6)–(8)
(6).......	71(6)–(8)
(7).......	71(6)–(8)
(7A).......	79(a)
(8).......	71(9), (10)
(9).......	71(9), (10)
(10)......	71(11)
(10A)....	72(7), (8)
(11)......	Sched. 9, para. 4
54	113
55	112
56(1).......	116(1)
(2).......	116(2)
(3).......	116(3)
(4).......	116(4)
(4A)	116(5)
(4B)	116(6)
(5).......	116(7)
57	115
58(c)(iii)	110(9)
(1).......	110(1)
(2).......	110(2)
(b)(ii) ..	110(9)
(3).......	110(3)
(4).......	110(4), (5)

1986	c.50
s.58(5).......	110(4), (5)
(6).......	110(6)
(a)(iii)..	110(9)
(7).......	110(7)
(e).......	110(9)
(8).......	111
(9).......	111
(10)......	110(9)
59(1).......	122(1)
(2).......	122(2)
(3).......	122(3)
60	125
61(1).......	173(1), (2)
(2).......	173(1), (2)
(3).......	173(3)
(4).......	173(4)
(5).......	173(5)
(7).......	176(1)
(8).......	176(2), (3)
(9).......	176(2), (3)
(10)......	173(7)
62(1).......	189(6)
(2).......	189(6)
(3).......	190(1)
63(1)(a)(i) ...	150(1)(a)(i)
(iii)..	150(1)(a)(iii)
(iv)..	150(1)(a)(ii)
(aa)	150(1)(b)
(b)	150(1)(c)–(f)
(c)	150(1)(c)–(f)
(d)	150(1)(c)–(f)
(e)	150(1)(c)–(f)
(ee)	150(1)(g)
(f)	150(1)(i)
(g)	150(1)(j)
(h)	150(1)(j)
(i)	150(1)(h)
(2)........	150(2)
(3)........	150(3)
(4)........	150(4)–(6)
(5)........	150(4)–(6)
(6)........	150(4)–(6)
(7)........	151(3)–(5)
(8)........	151(3)–(5)
(9)........	151(3)–(5)
(10)......	150(7)
(10A).....	151(6)
(11).......	150(8)
(12).......	150(9)
(13).......	150(10)
63A	152
64(1)........	155(1)
(2)........	155(3)–(6)
(3)........	155(3)–(6)
(4)........	155(3)–(6)
(5)........	155(3)–(6)
(6)........	155(2)
64A	159
64B	160
65(1)........	177(4)
(2)(a)	179(1)
(4)........	178(1), (2), 179(4), (5), 189(11)
66	67
68	163(1)(d)
73	Sched. 10 paras. 2, 3(1), (2), 4(1)–(3), 5, 6

1986	c.50
74(1)........	147(2)
(2)........	147(2)
78	180
83(1)........	189(3)–(6)
(2)........	189(7)
(3)(d)	190(1)
(4)........	190(3)
(5)........	189(8)
(6)........	189(9)
84(1)........	110(8), 134(13), (14), 139(11), 189(1), (2), 191
(3)........	135(13)
85(1)(a)	163(2)(d)
(b)	163(2)(e)
(c)	163(2)(g)
(d)	163(2)(h)
(e)	163(2)(a)
(f)	163(2)(a)
(3)(c)	163(1)(d)
(d)	163(1)(c)
(4)........	165(5)
(5)........	164(1)–(3)
(6)........	164(1)–(3)
(7)........	164(1)–(3)
(8)........	164(5)
(9)........	165(1)
(10)........	165(2)–(4)
(11)........	169
(12)........	169
86	1(4), 10(2), 68(4), 150(11), 151(1), (2), 155 (7), 157(1), 172 (1), (2), 187(1) Sched. 1 paras. 2–5 Sched. 7 Part 1 paras. 3, 5, 8 Part II para. 12
86(1)........	1(1), (2)

1986	c.50
Sched. 3	
para. 14(a) ..	45(1)
Sched. 4	
para. 6	15(1)
7	15(2)
8	132(3)
8A....	132(1), (2)
9	131
Sched. 5	
para. 3	19(1)
4	20(2), (4)
5	21(2)
6(b)...	22(2)
(c)...	22(3)
(d)...	22(4)
(e)...	22(5)
7(1)...	23(1)
(2)...	23(3)
(3)...	23(7)–(10)
8	36(1)
9	37(1)–(3)
10(a)..	25(1), (3)
(c)..	26(3)
(d)..	27(1)
12(a)..	44(7)
13	46(3)
14(b)..	47(2), (3)
15(b)..	48(3)
(1)..	48(1)
16(a)..	58(5)–(7)
17	189(10)
18	50(2)
19(a) ..Sched. 3 para. 3	
(b)..Sched. 3 para. 11	
20	189(1), (2)
Part II	
para. (b)	
(i)–(iv)	17(1)(g)(i)–(iv)
(v) .	17(1)(g)(vi)
(vi).	17(1)(g)(v)
(c)	17(1)(h)

1986	c.50
Sched. 6	
para. 4	67
Sched. 7	
para. 2 .....Sched. 10 para. 4(2)	
3 .....Sched. 10, para. 2	
4(1)...Sched. 10, para. 3(1)	
(2)...Sched. 10, para. 3(2)	
5(1)...Sched. 10, para. 4(1)	
(2)...Sched. 10, para. 4(3)	
6 .....Sched. 10, para. 6	
7 .....Sched. 10, para. 5	
Sched. 10	
para. 48(a) ..	187(1)
(b)..	1(4)
(c)..	68(4)
85	10(2)
86	172(2)
87	1(1), (2), Sched. 1 paras. 3, 4, 5
88 ....Sched. 1 para. 2	
90 ....Sched. 7 Part II para. 12	
91	151(1), (2)
92	150(11), 155 (7)
97	157(1)
98(a)..	172(1)
99 ....Sched. 7 Part I para. 3	
106 ...Sched. 7 Part I para. 5	
107 ...Sched. 7 Part I para. 8	

SOCIAL SECURITY ACT 1986 (COMMENCEMENT NO. 1) ORDER 1986
S.I. 1986 No. 1609

1986	S.I.1609
s.0 ....Sched. 1 paras. 2, 3	

FAMILY LAW REFORM ACT 1987
c.42

1986	c.42
s.33(1)........	s.78(7), 106(5)
Sched. 2,	
para. 91	106(5)
93	78(7)

SOCIAL SECURITY (TREASURY SUPPLEMENT TO AND ALLOCATION OF CONTRIBUTIONS) (RE-RATING) ORDER 1987
S.I. 1987 No. 48

1987	S.I. 48
art. 3........	s.162(5)(d)–(f)

TABLE OF DESTINATIONS

DEBTORS (SCOTLAND) ACT 1987
c.18

1987	S.I. 48
s.68	s.109

ABOLITION OF DOMESTIC RATES ETC. (SCOTLAND) ACT 1987
c.47

1987	c.47
s.26(2)(a)	s.191

SOCIAL SECURITY ACT 1988
c.7

1988	c.7
s.2	s.10(1), 44(4), (5), 60(4), (5)
(a).	150(1)(g)
(b)	150(3)
4(2).	72(1)–(8)
5	153
8	16
11	5(2), 12(1), 20(6), 25(1), 58(1), (2), 59(1), 60(1);61 (4), 64(3), 66(9), (10), 71(11), 124(1), (2), 167(5), (6), 168(1)–(4)

1988	c.7
s.15(1)(a)	163(2)(a)
(2).	165(5)
16	25(1), 71(11), 72(7), (8), 79(a), (b), (c)
Sched. 1	
para. 6	10(1), 44(4), (5), 60(4), (5)
Sched. 3	
para. 4	167(5), (6)
6	168(1)–(4)
7	64(3), 66(9), (10)
9	12(1)

1988	c.7
Sched. 3—cont.	
para. 16	5(2), 20(6), 25(1), 58(1), (2), 59(1), 60(1), 61(4), 71(11), 124(1), (2)
Sched. 4	
para. 14	25(1)
26	79(b)
27	79(c)
28	79(a)
30(1) . .	71(11)
(2) . .	72(7), (8)

LOCAL GOVERNMENT FINANCE ACT 1988
c.41

1988	c.41
s.135	s.6(1)(a)–(u), (2), (3), 7, 63(1), (2), 76(1)–(8), 77, 116(2), (4), (5), (7), 128, 138(1)–(9), 139(1)–(10), 140(1), (2), (4), (5), (8), 163(2)(d), 176(1), 189(7), (8), 191

1988	c.41
Sched. 10	
para. 2(5) . . .	191
6	63(1), (3), 76(1)–(8), 77, 128, 138(1)–(9), 139(1)–(10), 140(1), (2), (4), (5), (8)
8	6(1)(a)–(u), (2), (3), 7

1988	c.41
Sched. 10—cont.	
para. 9(2) . . .	116(2)
(3) . . .	116(4)
(4) . . .	116(5)
(5) . . .	116(7)
10	176(1)
11(2) . .	189(7)
11(4) . .	189(8)
12	163(2)(d)

HOUSING ACT 1988
c.50

1988	c.50
s.121(6).	s.5(3)

INCOME AND CORPORATION TAXES ACT 1988
c.1

1988	C.1
s.844	s.139(11)
Sched. 29	
para. 32	139(11)

HOUSING BENEFIT (TRANSITIONAL) AMENDMENT REGULATIONS 1988
S.I. 1988 No. 458

1988	S.I. 458
reg. 3	s.135(2), (3)

TABLE OF DESTINATIONS

SOCIAL SECURITY ACT 1988 (CONSEQUENTIAL) AMENDMENT REGULATIONS 1988
S.I. 1988 No. 961

1988	S.I. 961
reg. 2(a)	s.150(7)
(b)	151(6)

TRANSFER OF FUNCTIONS (HEALTH AND SOCIAL SECURITY) ORDER 1988
S.I. 1988 No. 1843

1988	S.I. 1843
Sched. 3	
para. 2(c) ...	181, 182

HOUSING (SCOTLAND) ACT 1988
c.43

1988	c.43
s.1	s.135(6), (7), 191
3	135(6), (7), 191
Sched. 2	
para. 1	135(6), (7), 191

SOCIAL SECURITY ACT 1989
c.24

1989	c.24	1989	c.24	1989	c.24
s.1(3).........	s.143(1)	s.21	17(3), 21(6),	s.29(2)(h)	190(1)
(5).........	143(4)		23(7), (8),	(3)........	190(3)
(6).........	145(1)		25(1), 27(1),	(6)........	189(9)
(7).........	145(3)		29, 37(2),	30(1)........	189(1), (2)
(8).........	162(5)(a)		45(1), (4), (5),	31(1)........	1(1), 6(1)(l),
5(2).........	78(6)		48(5), (6),		(q), 76(3), (5),
(3).........	78(7)		50(5), 53(1)–		126, 132(1),
(4).........	78(8)		(4), 56(1), (2),		(2), 150(10),
9(5).........	189(8)		59(6), 71(2),		156, 173(5),
10(5).......	25(1)		(5)		(7), 189(5)
14(1).......	134(2)	Sched. 3		Sched. 1	
15(1).......	136(1)–(4)	paras. 2, 10		paras, 4, 5	
(2).......	135(11), 137	22	110(2), (3),	Sched. 7	
17(1).......	152		(6), (7), (9)	Part 1	
(2)(a)	155(1)	(1).......	82	para. 8	
(b)	190(1)	(2)........	82	Sched. 9	
(c)	189(8)	(3).......	81(1)	para. 1(2)	
18	159	(3A)......	81(2)	(2)........	Sched. 1
19 ....Sched. 4		(4).......	81(3)–(5)		para. 4
Part I		(5).......	81(3)–(5)	(3)........	Sched. 1
Part II		(6).......	81(3)–(5)		para. 4
(1).......	123(1)–(6)	(7).......	81(1), (6),	Sched. 2	
(2).......	123(1)–(6)		83, 84, 85, 86,	Part I.......	Sched. 4
(3).......	123(1)–(6)		87, 88, 89, 90,		Part I
(4).......	123(1)–(6)		91, 92, 93(1)–	Part II	Sched. 4
(5).......	123(1)–(6)		(8)(a), 94(1)–		Part II
(6).......	123(1)–(6)		(6), 95, 96, 97,	Sched. 3	
(7).......	123(7)		98(1)–(12), 99,	para. 1(1) ...	17(3)
(8).......	123(8)		100, 101,	(2) ...	59(6)
(9).......	123(9)		102(1), (2), 103	2	21(6)
(10)......	123(10)	(8).......	81(7)	3(1) ...	53(1)–(4),
20(a).......	122(1)	25	25(5)		56(1), (2)
(b)	122(2)	26	13(1), 50(5),	4 .....Sched. 3
			162(2), 173(3)		para. 2
		27	104	6	23(7), (8)
		28(1)(a)	163(2)(a)	7	29
		(2).......	165(5)	9(2) ...	48(5), (6)
		(3).......	164(6)	10 ....Sched. 3
		(4)(a)	163(2)(i)		para. 10
		(b)	163(1)(e)	11(1) ..	25(1)
		29(1).......	189(3)–(6)	(2) ..	25(5)

1989	c.24
Sched. 3—*cont.*	
para. 11(4) ..	27(1)
12(1) ..	45(1)
(2) ..	45(4), (5)
14(1) ..	71(2)
(2) ..	71(5)
15	37(2)
18	50(5)
Sched. 4	
para. 1(1) ...	81(1)
(2) ...	81(6)
2	83
3	84
4	85
5	86
6	87
7	88
8	89
9	90
10	91
11	92
12(1) ..	93(1)
(2) ..	93(2)
(3) ..	93(3), (4)
(4) ..	93(3), (4)
(5) ..	93(5)
(6) ..	93(6)
(6A)	93(7)
(7) ..	93(8), (9)
(8) ..	93(8), (9)
13(1) ..	94(1), (2)

1989	c.24
Sched. 4—*cont.*	
para. 13(2) ..	94(1), (2)
(2A)	94(3)
(3) ..	94(4)–(6)
(4) ..	94(4)–(6)
(5) ..	94(4)–(6)
14	95
15	96
16	97
17(1) ..	98(1), (2)
(2) ..	98(1), (2)
(3) ..	98(3)
20(2) ..	110(2), (9)
(3) ..	110(2), (9)
(4) ..	110(3)
(5) ..	110(6), (9)
(6) ..	110(7), (9)
(7) ..	110(9)
Sched. 7	
para. 15	162(2)
17	50(5)
(4) ..	98(4)–(10)
(5) ..	98(4)–(10)
(6) ..	98(4)–(10)
(7) ..	98(4)–(10)
(8) ..	98(4)–(10)
(9) ..	98(4)–(10)
(10) .	98(4)–(10)
(11) .	98(11)
(12) .	98(12)

1989	c.24
Sched. 7—*cont.*	
para. 18	99
19	100
20A ...	101
21(1) ..	102(1)
(2) ..	102(2)
22	13(1)
24	103
Sched. 7	
para. 27	173(3)
Sched. 8	
para. 9(1) ...	1(1), Sched. 1 paras. 4, 5
(4) ...	76(3), (5)
(6)(a)	6(1)(l)
(b)	6(1)(q)
10(1) ..	189(5), Sched. 9 para. 1(2)
11	156
12(3) ..	173(5)
(4) ..	173(7)
(6) ..	Sched. 7 Part I para. 8
15(2) ..	150(10)
17	126
18	132(1), (2)

LOCAL GOVERNMENT AND HOUSING ACT 1989
c.42

1989	c.42
s.81(1)........	s.135(2), (3)
(2)........	135(6), (7)
(3)........	135(8), (9)

COMMUNITY CHARGE BENEFITS (GENERAL) REGULATIONS 1989
S.I. 1989 No. 1321

1989	S.I. 1321
reg. 11(1)	s.139(6)
(2)	139(11)

SOCIAL SECURITY (CONTRIBUTIONS AND ALLOCATION OF CONTRIBUTIONS) (RE-RATING) ORDER 1989
S.I. 1989 No. 26

1989	S.I. 26
art. 6........	s.162(5)(a), (b)

SOCIAL SECURITY ACT 1990
c.27

1990	c.27
s.1(6)........	s.1(3)
5(1)........	2(1)–(5)
(4)........	1(4)
6(1)........	Sched. 1, para. 5
(a)	1(1)
(b)	1(2)
(2)........	3
(3)........	27(2)

1990	c.27
s.7	81(1), 93(2), (5)–(7), 94(3), 98(3), (11), 101, 102(1), 103
8(1)........	107(1)–(8), (12)–(15), 108
10(1)........	168(5)
(2)........	64(3)
(5)........	12(2)
16(3)........	162(3)
(4)........	163(1)(a), (b), (2)(c)

1990	c.27
s.16(5)........	165(5)
(7)........	163(2)(c)
(8)(a)	163(2)(c)
(b)	164(4), Sched. 9, para. 1(4)
17(3)........	162(4)
(4)........	163(5)
18(1)(a)	163(2)(a)
(2)........	165(5)

1990	c.27
21(1)........	22(6), (7), 23(4), (5), 38(1), 68(1)– (6), 69(1), 70(3), 116(6), 123(7), (9), (10), 134(1), (7), 135(4), 136(1), 138(1), (2), 140(3), (6), (7), 142(3), 144(2), 147(4), (5), 150(8), 160, 189(3), 190(2), (3), (4), Sched. 4, Part I Part II
(2).........	4, 69(2)–(4)
23(2)........	Sched. 1, para. 5
(3)........	Sched. 1, para. 5

1990	c.27
Sched. 1,	
para. 1(1)...	81(1)
(2)...	81(1)
(4)...	94(3)
2(1)...	93(2)
(2)...	93(5)
(3)...	93(6)
(4)...	93(7)
3	98(3)
4	98(11)
5(1)...	101
(2)...	102(1)
6	103
Sched. 6,	
para. 1(1)...	147(4), (5)
(2)(a)	142(3)
(b)	144(2)
(c)	147(4), (5)
5(1)...	38(1)
(2)...	116(6)
6(1)...	22(6), (7)
(2)...	23(4)
(3)...	23(5)
7(1)...	69(1)–(4)
(2)...	68(1)–(6)
(3)...	68(4)
8(1)...	190(3), (4)

1990	c.27
Sched. 6—*cont.*	
para. 8(3)...	190(2), (3)
(4)...	190(3)
(7)...	189(3), 190(3)
(9)...	190(3)
(12)...	190(3)
18	134(1), (7)
19(1)..	135(4)
(2)..	136(1)
20	138(1), (2)
21(1)..	140(3)
(2)..	140(6)
(3)..	140(7)
23	150(8)
24	160
27(2)..	4
28(1)..	123(7)
(2)..	123(9)
(3)..	123(10)
(4)..Sched. 4, Part I
(5)..Sched. 4, Part I
(6)..Sched. 4, Part II
31(a)..70(3)

COURTS AND LEGAL SERVICES ACT 1990
c.41

1990	c.41
s.71(2)........	s.41(5), 50(5), 51(2), (3), 52(1), (2)
Sched. 10,	
para. 36	52(1)
37(1)..	41(5)
(2)..	51(2)
(3)..	51(3)
(4)..	50(5)
46	52(2)

REGISTRATION OF BIRTHS, DEATHS AND MARRIAGES (FEES) (No. 2) ORDER 1990
S.I. 1990 No. 2515

1990	S.I. 2515
art. 2.........	s.124(3)
Sched........	124(3)

REGISTRATION OF BIRTHS, DEATHS AND MARRIAGES (FEES) (SCOTLAND) ORDER 1990
S.I. 1990 No. 2637

1990	S.I. 2637
art. 2.........	s.124(3)
Sched........	124(3)

STATUTORY SICK PAY ACT 1991
c.3

1991	c.3
s.1(5)........	s.81(1)
2(1)........	149
(3)........	17(1)(g)(v)
3(1)(a)	70(3)
(b)	170(5)
4(3)........	163(2)(a)

DISABILITY LIVING ALLOWANCE AND DISABILITY WORKING ALLOWANCE ACT 1991
c.21

1991   c.21
s.3(1)........ s.175
(2)......... 175
(3)......... 175
(4)......... 175
(5)......... 175
(6)......... 175
(7)......... 189(5)
(8)........ 189(1)–(3)
4 .... 1(3), 20(1),
(3), (6),
21(1)–(3),
22(1), (2), (5),
25(1), (2),
30(1)–(13), 31,
32(1)–(10), 33,
34(1), 35(1)–
(12), 36(1),
(2), 42(1)–(7),
43(1)–(8),
51(1), 53(2),
54(1)–(3), (5),
(6), (8), 55,
56(2), 68(4),
69(1), 150(1)
(b), (3),
163(1)(a), (b),
(2)(b), 191
Sched. 2,
paras. 3,
4(1), (2), 5, 7,
8,
Sched. 3,
paras. 1, 10,
Sched. 4,
Part I,
Sched. 7,
Part I,
para. 1
Sched. 10,
para. 3(1)
7 .... 5(2), 20(6),
21(3), 22(1),
25(1), (2),
30(1), (5)–(11),
31, 32(1),
(6)–(10), 33,
34(1)–(4),
35(3)–(10),
(12), 54(1),

1991   c.21
s.7—cont...... (2), (4), (5),
(7), (8), 55,
58(1), (2),
59(1), 60(1),
61(4), 69(1),
71(11), 124(1),
(2), 150(1)(h),
(10), 163(2)(d),
165(1), 178(1),
(2), (4), (5),
189(11)
(1)......... 11
12(2)........ 190(3)
15(1)........ 70(3)
Sched. 1,
para. 2 ..... 20(1)
3(1) ... 21(1)
(2) ... 21(2)
(3) ... 21(3)
4(a) ... 22(1)
(b) ... 22(2)
(c) ... 22(5)
5 ..... 30(1)–(13),
31, 32(1)–(10),
33, 42(1)–(7),
43(1)–(8),
69(1)
Sched. 2,
paras. 3,
4(1), (2), 5, 7
6(a) ... 34(1)
7(1) ... 36(1)
(2) ... 36(2)
8(a) ... 25(1)
(b) ... 25(2)
9 ..... 35(1)–(12)
10 ....Sched. 3,
para. 1
11 .... 53(2)
12 .... 56(2)
13 .... 54(1)–(3),
(5), (6), (8), 55
15 .... 51(1)
16 .... 42(1)–(7),
43(1)–(8)
Sched. 2,
paras. 3,
4(1), (2), 5, 7

1991   c.21
Sched. 1—cont.
para. 17 .... 163(1)(a),
(b),
Sched. 3,
para. 10
18 .... 163(2)(b)
19 .... 1(3)
20 191
Sched. 2,
para. 5 ..... 68(4)
10 ....Sched. 2,
para. 8
11 ....Sched. 7,
Part I
para. 1
15(a) .. 20(3), (6),
69(1)
(b) . .Sched. 10,
para. 3(1)
16(a) .. 150(1)(b)
(b) .. 150(3)
19 ....Sched. 4,
Part I
Sched. 3,
para. 1 ..... 5(2)
3(1) ... 20(6), 21(3),
22(1), 25(1),
(2), 30(1),
(5)–(11), (13),
31, 32(1),
(8)–(10), 33,
34(1)–(4),
35(3)–(10),
54(1), (2), (4),
(5), (7), (8),
55, 58(1), (2),
59(1), 60(1),
61(4), 69(1),
124(1), (2)
(2) ... 54(5)
(3) ... 30(1),   (5),
35(3), 54(4), (7)
(c) 35(5), (10)
4 ..... 71(11)
5(a) ... 150(1)(h)
(b) ... 150(10)
6 ..... 178(1),   (2),
179(4), (5), 189
(11)
8(a) ... 163(2)(d)
(b) ... 165(1)

SOCIAL SECURITY (CONTRIBUTIONS) ACT 1991
c.42

1991   c.42
s.2(6)(a) ...... s.120(3)
(b) ...... 120(4)
(c) ..... 120(6)
3(1)......... 17(1)(c)
(2)......... 59(4)
4(a)......... 162(5)(c)
(b) .... 162(8)(b)
6(1)......... 70(3)

TABLE OF DESTINATIONS

MAINTENANCE ENFORCEMENT ACT 1991
c.17

1991	c.17
s.9(1).........	s.107(5)
(2).........	107(9)–(11)

INDEX

References are to section number

ADJUDICATION,
  authority, 53
    appointment of assessors, 56
  commissioner. *See* COMMISSIONER
  disability appeals tribunal,
  officer, 20, 94
    appointment of, 39
    decisions of, 21
      appeal against, 22
  reference of special questions, 37
  Secretary of State, by. *See* SECRETARY OF
    STATE
ADVISORY BODIES,
  consultation of, 173, 176
  Disability Living Allowance Advisory
    Board, 175
  functions of, 172
  Industrial Advisory Council, 171, Sched. 6
  reports of, 174
  Social Security Advisory Committee, 170,
    Sched. 5
APPEALS, 48
  questions first arising on, 36

BENEFIT. *See also* CLAIMS 186, Sched. 10
  adjustments to, 71, 73
  annual up-rating, 150
  certificate of. *See* COMPENSATION PAYMENTS
  compensation payments. *See* COMPENSA-
    TION PAYMENTS
  Contributions and Benefits Act,
    alterations under, 155, 156, 157, 158, 159
  death and, 92
  entitlement,
    error in, 68, 70
  inalienable, 187
  information for. *See* INFORMATION
  overpayment of, 91
  recovery of, 72
  rectification of, 152
  underpayment of, 77

CLAIMS, 137, Sched. 1
  attendance allowance, 54
  bonus and, 67
  child benefit, 13, 80, 154
    annual review of, 153
  community charge benefit, 63, 138, 139
    information. *See* INFORMATION
    overpayment of, 76
  disability living allowances, 54
  duty of employers, 130, 132
  housing benefit, 63
    overpayment, 75

CLAIMS—*cont.*
  housing benefit—*cont.*
    subsidies, 134, 135
  income support, 72, 74
    attainment of age due to, 160
    duty to maintain and, 105
    maintenance and, 107
      recovery of, 106, 107, 108
      Scotland, 109
  late, 3
  regulations for, 5
  rent allowance, 136
  statutory sick pay, 130, 131, 149
COMMENCEMENT, 192
COMMISSIONER, Sched. 2
  appeal from, 24, 34
  appeal to, 23
  appointment of, 52
COMMUNITY CHARGE,
  benefits for, 6, 7
COMPENSATION PAYMENTS, 81
  benefit and, 82
    deductions from, 83, 85
    certificate of total benefit, 84, 95, 96
      appeals against, 98
      review of, 97
  compensators, 87
    foreign, 102
  Crown and, 104
  insolvency and, 89
  interest and, 103
  legal aid charges and, 90
  multiple, 86
  payment into court and, 93
  recovery of benefits and, 100
  structured settlements, 88
CONTRIBUTIONS, 114
  alteration of, 121, 143, 145, 146
  annual review of, 141
  destination of, 162
  evidence of non-payment, 118, 120
  National Insurance Fund, 161, 163
    Consolidated Fund and, 165
    repayments from, 164
  orders under s.141, 142, 144, 147
  orders under s.145, 147
  orders under s.146 147
  recovery of, 119
CONTRIBUTIONS AND BENEFITS ACT,
  payments under, Sched. 9

DISABILITY ALLOWANCE,
  initial claims, 11
  repeat claims, 11

DISABILITY APPEALS TRIBUNAL, 34
   chairman of, 51
   constitution of, 43
   panels for, 42
   request for medical examination, 55

EMERGENCY PAYMENTS, 16
ENFORCEMENT,
   inspectors, 110
     obstruction of, 111
     powers of, 110
   legal proceedings and, 116, 117
ENTITLEMENT, 1
   false representations as to, 112
   retrospective, 2

FOREIGN COUNTRIES,
   reciprocal arrangements with, 179

INDUSTRIAL INJURIES,
   claimants,
     medical examination of, 9
     obligations of, 10
   declaration of industrial accidents, 44
   disablement, 45
   diseases, 62
   medical references, 46
     review of, 47
   notification of accidents, 8
   research into, 183
INFORMATION,
   community charge, 128
   housing benefit, 127
   disclosure of,
     Inland revenue, by 122
     unauthorised, 123
   statutory sick pay, 129
   personal representative supply by, 126
INTERPRETATION, 191

MEDICAL APPEAL TRIBUNALS, 50
   chairman of, 51
   constitution of, 50

NORTHERN IRELAND, 79, 101, Sched. 8
   co-ordination with, 177
   reciprocal arrangements with, 178

PAYMENTS,
   regulations for, 5
PNEUMOCONIOSIS,
   control of, 184

REGISTRATION SERVICE, 124
   death,
     notification to, 125
REGULATIONS, 189, Sched. 3, Sched. 7
   arising from appeals or reviews, 58
     finality of, 60
   breach of, 113
   parliamentary control of, 190
   procedure, 59
   supplementary, 61
REVIEWS, 31, 32
   appeals against, 28, 33
   certificate of benefit. *See* COMPENSATION
     PAYMENTS
   Contributions and Benefits Act and, 166
   decisions of, 25
     adjudication officers of, 30
   decisions on appeal of, 35
   following claimant appeals, 29
   industrial injuries. *See* INDUSTRIAL INJURIES
   procedure for, 26
   questions for determination, 69
   social fund, of, 66
   under s.25, 27

SECRETARY OF STATE,
   adjudication by, 17, 18
     review of, 19
   documents issued by,
     illegal possession of, 182
   officers of,
     impersonation of, 181
SHORT TITLE, 192
SOCIAL SECURITY PERSONNEL, Sched. 4
SOCIAL FUND, 12, 167
   adjustments to, 169
   allocations from, 168
   awards,
     recovery of, 78
   commissioners, 65
   inspectors, 65
   officers, 64
SOCIAL SECURITY APPEAL TRIBUNAL,
   appeal from, 23, 34
   appeal to, 22
   chairman of, 51
   constitution of, 41
   panel for, 40
STAMP DUTY,
   exemption from, 188
STATUTORY MATERNITY PAY, 15
STATUTORY SICK PAY, 14

TRAVELLING EXPENSES, 180

WIDOWS,
   provisions for, 4
WORKMEN'S COMPENSATION, 185

SOCIAL SECURITY (CONSEQUENTIAL PROVISIONS) ACT 1992

(1992 c. 6)

ARRANGEMENT OF SECTIONS

SECT.
1. Meaning of "the consolidating Acts".
2. Continuity of the law.
3. Repeals.
4. Consequential amendments.
5. Transitional provisions and savings.
6. Transitory modifications.
7. Short title, commencement and extent.

SCHEDULES:
Schedule 1—Lands.
Schedule 2—Consequential amendments.
Schedule 3—Transitional provisions and savings (including some transitional provisions retained from previous Acts).
Part I—General and miscellaneous.
Part II—Specific transitional provisions and savings (including some derived from previous Acts).
Schedule 4—Transitory modifications.
Part I—Provisions not yet in force.
Part II—Other transitory modifications.

An Act to make provision for repeals, consequential amendments, transitional and transitory matters and savings in connection with the consolidation of enactments in the Social Security Contributions and Benefits Act 1992 and the Social Security Administration Act 1992 (including provisions to give effect to recommendations of the Law Commission and the Scottish Law Commission). [13th February 1992]

PARLIAMENTARY DEBATES
Hansard, H.L. Vol. 532, col. 1268; Vol. 534, col. 1488; Vol. 535, col. 348.

INTRODUCTION
This Act together with the Social Security Contributions and Benefits Act and the Social Security Administration Act provides for the consolidation of legislation relating to social security for the U.K., except Northern Ireland, for which separate legislation has been enacted. This Act will facilitate the efficient and effective consolidation by providing for the necessary repeals, consequential amendments and transitory and transitional measures.

Meaning of "the consolidating Acts"

1. In this Act—
"the consolidating Acts" means the Social Security Contributions and Benefits Act 1992 ("the Contributions and Benefits Act"), the Social Security Administration Act 1992 ("the Administration Act") and, so far as it reproduces the effect of the repealed enactments, this Act; and
"the repealed enactments" means the enactments repealed by this Act.

Continuity of the law

2.—(1) The substitution of the consolidating Acts for the repealed enactments does not affect the continuity of the law.

(2) Anything done or having effect as if done under or for the purposes of a provision of the repealed enactments has effect, if it could have been done under or for the purposes of the corresponding provision of the consolidating Acts, as if done under or for the purposes of that provision.

(3) Any reference, whether express or implied, in the consolidating Acts or any other enactment, instrument or document to a provision of the consolidating Acts shall, so far as the context permits, be construed as including, in relation to the times, circumstances and purposes in relation to which the corresponding provision of the repealed enactments has effect, a reference to that corresponding provision.

(4) Any reference, whether express or implied, in any enactment, instrument or document to a provision of the repealed enactments shall be construed, so far as is required for continuing its effect, as including a reference to the corresponding provision of the consolidating Acts.

Repeals

3.—(1) The enactments mentioned in Schedule 1 to this Act are repealed to the extent specified in the third column of that Schedule.

(2) Those repeals include, in addition to repeals consequential on the consolidation of provisions in the consolidating Acts, repeals in accordance with Recommendations of the Law Commission and the Scottish Law Commission, of section 30(6)(b) of the Social Security Act 1975, paragraphs 2 to 8 of Schedule 9 to that Act, paragraph 2(1) of Schedule 10 to that Act and section 10 of the Social Security Act 1988.

(3) The repeals have effect subject to any relevant savings in Schedule 3 to this Act.

Consequential amendments

4. The enactments mentioned in Schedule 2 to this Act shall have effect with the amendments there specified (being amendments consequential on the consolidating Acts).

Transitional provisions and savings

5.—(1) The transitional provisions and savings in Schedule 3 to this Act shall have effect.

(2) Nothing in that Schedule affects the general operation of section 16 of the Interpretation Act 1978 (general savings implied on repeal) or of the previous provisions of this Act.

Transitory modifications

6. The transitory modifications in Schedule 4 to this Act shall have effect.

Short title, commencement and extent

7.—(1) This Act may be cited as the Social Security (Consequential Provisions) Act 1992.

(2) This Act shall come into force on 1st July 1992.

(3) Section 2 above and this section extend to Northern Ireland.

(4) Subject to subsection (5) below, where any enactment repealed or amended by this Act extends to any part of the United Kingdom, the repeal or amendment extends to that part.

(5) The repeals—

(a) of provisions of sections 10, 13 and 14 of the Social Security Act 1980 and Part II of Schedule 3 to that Act;

(b) of enactments amending those provisions;

(c) of paragraph 2 of Schedule 1 to the Capital Allowances Act 1990; and

(d) of section 17(8) and (9) of the Social Security Act 1990,

do not extend to Northern Ireland.

(6) Section 6 above and Schedule 4 to this Act extend to Northern Ireland in so far as they give effect to transitory modifications of provisions of the consolidating Acts which so extend.

(7) Except as provided by this section, this Act does not extend to Northern Ireland.

(8) Section 4 above extends to the Isle of Man so far as it relates to paragraphs 53 and 54 of Schedule 2 to this Act.

SCHEDULES

Section 3

SCHEDULE 1

REPEALS

Chapter	Short title	Extent of repeal
1974 c. 14.	National Insurance Act 1974.	Section 6(1) and (3).
1975 c. 14.	Social Security Act 1975.	The whole Act.
1975 c. 16.	Industrial Injuries and Diseases (Old Cases) Act 1975.	The whole Act.
1975 c. 18.	Social Security (Consequential Provisions) Act 1975.	In Schedule 2, paragraphs 6, 8 and 9, 11, 69 and 70. In Schedule 3, paragraphs 1 to 20.
1975 c. 60.	Social Security Pensions Act 1975.	Part I. Sections 6 to 10. Sections 12 to 16A. Sections 18 to 21. Sections 23 to 25. Section 51A(13). Section 60(1)(a). In section 60A, the words "6(3)" and ", and paragraphs 2(3) and 4A of Schedule 1 to,". Section 62(1) and (3). In section 64(2), the words from "and as respects" to the end. Section 65(4). In section 66(2), in paragraph (a), the words "Part I and" and in paragraph (b) the words "except section 22)". Schedule 1. In Schedule 4, paragraphs 35 to 46, 49, 50, 53 to 64 and 66 and 67.
1975 c. 61.	Child Benefit Act 1975.	The whole Act.
1976 c. 5.	Education (School-leaving Dates) Act 1976.	Section 2(4).
1976 c. 71.	Supplementary Benefits Act 1976.	Sections 22 and 23. In Schedule 7, paragraph 36.
1977 c. 5.	Social Security (Miscellaneous Provisions) Act 1977.	Sections 1 and 2. Section 3(1). Sections 4 to 6. Sections 8 to 11. Section 13. Sections 17 and 18. Section 20(1) and (2). Section 22(1) to (5). In section 23(2), the words from "and as respects" to the end. In section 24, in subsection (1), the definition of "the Old Cases Act", and subsections (2) and (4). Schedule 1.
1977 c. 49.	National Health Service Act 1977.	In Schedule 15, paragraphs 63, 64 and 67.

Chapter	Short title	Extent of repeal
1978 c. 29.	National Health Service (Scotland) Act 1978.	In Schedule 16, paragraph 40.
1978 c. 44.	Employment Protection (Consolidation) Act 1978.	In Schedule 16, paragraphs 19 and 29.
1979 c. 18.	Social Security Act 1979.	Section 2. Sections 4 and 5. Section 9(1). Section 10. Sections 14 and 15. Section 19. Section 20(3). Schedule 1. Schedule 2. In Schedule 3, paragraphs 4 to 8, 10 and 11, in paragraph 13, the words "6(3) and" and paragraphs 14, 15, 23, 29, 31 and 32.
1980 c. 30.	Social Security Act 1980.	Section 2. In section 3, subsections (1) to (3) and (11). Section 4(3), (5) and (6). Section 5(1). Section 6(2) and (4). In section 9, subsections (1) and (2), in subsection (3), the words from the beginning to "and", in the second place where it occurs, in subsection (4), the words "The Secretary of State and" and subsections (5) and (7). In section 10, subsections (1) to (5) and in subsection (9) the words "the Secretary of State in conjunction with the Treasury or by", "or section 61 of the Social Security Act 1986" and "the Secretary of State or". Section 11. Section 13(1) to (3), (5) and (6). Section 14. Sections 17 and 18. Section 19(3). Schedule 1. In Schedule 2, paragraph 21. Schedule 3. In Schedule 4, paragraphs 10 and 14.
1980 c. 39.	Social Security (No. 2) Act 1980.	The whole Act.
1980 c. 43.	Magistrates' Courts Act 1980.	In section 65(1), the paragraph (m) inserted by paragraph 54 of Schedule 10 to the Social Security Act 1986. In Schedule 7, paragraph 135.
1980 c. 48.	Finance Act 1980.	In Schedule 19, in paragraph 5(4), the words "section 133(3) of the Social Security Act 1975".
1981 c. 1.	Social Security (Contributions) Act 1981.	The whole Act.
1981 c. 20.	Judicial Pensions Act 1981.	In Schedule 3, paragraph 10.
1981 c. 33.	Social Security Act 1981.	Sections 5 and 6. Section 8(2). In Schedule 1, paragraphs 3(a), 6 and 7. In Schedule 2, paragraph 2.
1982 c. 2.	Social Security (Contributions) Act 1982.	The whole Act.
1982 c. 23.	Oil and Gas (Enterprise) Act 1982.	In Schedule 3, paragraphs 21 and 44.

Chapter	Short title	Extent of repeal
1982 c. 24.	Social Security and Housing Benefits Act 1982.	Sections 1 to 7. Section 9. Sections 17 and 18. Sections 22, 23 and 23A. Sections 26 and 27. Section 37. Section 39(1) to (4). Section 44. Section 46(2). Section 48(2). Schedule 1. In Schedule 2, paragraphs 1 to 4. In Schedule 4, paragraphs 7 to 10, 12 and 13, 15 to 18, 30 to 34 and 39.
1982 c. 34.	Forfeiture Act 1982.	In section 4(5), the entry relating to the Child Benefit Act 1975.
1983 c. 41.	Health and Social Services and Social Security Adjudications Act 1983.	Schedule 8, except paragraphs 1(3)(a) and 29.
1984 c. 48.	Health and Social Security Act 1984.	Sections 11 to 14. Sections 16 to 18. Schedule 4. Schedule 5. In Schedule 7, paragraphs 1 to 3 and 6 to 8.
1985 c. 53.	Social Security Act 1985.	Section 7. Section 8(1). Sections 9 to 13. Section 18. Section 20. Section 27. Section 30. In Schedule 3, paragraph 1. In Schedule 4, paragraphs 3 to 7. In Schedule 5, paragraphs 5, 8 and 9, 11 and 13 to 15.
1986 c. 50.	Social Security Act 1986.	Sections 18 to 29. Section 30(1) to (9) and (11). Sections 31 to 36. Section 37(1). Section 38. Sections 40 to 51. Section 52(3) to (10). Section 53. Section 54(2). Section 55. In section 56, in subsection (2)(a), the words "other than an offence relating to housing benefit or community charge benefits", subsection (2)(b) and the word "and" immediately preceding it, subsection (3)(b) and the word "and" immediately preceding it, subsections (4) to (4B). Section 58. In section 61, in subsection (1), the words "the Committee, the Council or", in subsection (3), the words "the Committee, the Council or" and "or, in the case of the Council, given their advice,", in subsection (4), the words "Committee or", in

Chapter	Short title	Extent of repeal
		each place where they occur, in subsection (5), the words "the Committee, the Council or", subsections (7) to (9) and in subsection (10), the definitions of "the Committee" and "the Council".
		Sections 62 to 69.
		Section 70(1).
		Sections 73 and 74.
		Section 79(3) and (4).
		In section 80(1), the words "and V".
		Section 81.
		In section 83, subsection (2), subsection (3) (b) to (e), and in subsection (5), the words from "30" to "section", in the second place where it occurs.
		In section 84, in subsection (1), the definition of "applicable amount", paragraphs (c) and (d) of the definition of "the benefit Acts", the definitions of "dwelling", "housing authority", "housing benefit scheme", "Housing Revenue Account dwelling", "income-related benefit", "local authority", long-term benefit", "new town corporation", "primary Class I contributions", "secondary Class I contributions", "qualifying benefit", "rate rebate", "rent rebate", "rent allowance", "rates", "rating authority", "trade dispute", "war disablement pension" and "war widow's pension", and subsection (3).
		In section 85, subsection (1)(a) to (c) and (f), subsection (3)(c) and (d), subsection (4), in subsection (5), the words "and (7)", subsection (7), in subsection (8), the words from "and sums" to the end and subsections (9) to (12).
		Schedule 3, except paragraph 17.
		Schedule 4.
		In Schedule 5, paragraphs 2 to 20 and in Part II, paragraphs (b) and (c).
		Schedules 6 and 7.
		In Schedule 8, paragraphs 1 to 3 and 5 to 7.
		In Schedule 10, paragraphs 10, 34, 40, 48, 54, 62 to 67, 68(2), 69, 70, 72, 74, 77, 83 to 88, 90 to 92, 95, 97 to 100, 103(a) and (b), 104 to 107 and 108(a).
1987 c. 7.	Social Fund (Maternity and Funeral Expenses) Act 1987.	The whole Act.
1987 c. 18.	Debtors (Scotland) Act 1987.	Section 68.
1987 c. 42.	Family Law Reform Act 1987.	Section 2(1)(g). In Schedule 2, paragraphs 59 and 91 to 93.
1988 c. 1.	Income and Corporation Taxes Act 1988.	In Schedule 29, in paragraph 14, the words "the Social Security Act 1975 and", and in paragraph 32, the entries relating to the Social Security Act 1975 and the Social Security Act 1986.

Chapter	Short title	Extent of repeal
1988 c. 7.	Social Security Act 1988.	Sections 1 to 8. Sections 10 and 11. Section 17. In section 18, in subsection (2), the words from "section 1" to "that Act". Schedule 1. In Schedule 2, paragraph 1(1). Schedule 3. In Schedule 4, paragraphs 3 to 20 and 23 to 30.
1988 c. 19.	Employment Act 1988.	Section 27.
1988 c. 34.	Legal Aid Act 1988.	Section 34(14).
1988 c. 39.	Finance Act 1988.	In Schedule 3, in paragraph 31, the words "the Social Security Act 1975 and".
1988 c. 41.	Local Government Finance Act 1988.	In Schedule 4, in paragraph 28(2), the words "Part III of the Social Security Act 1975,". Schedule 10, except paragraphs 1, 9(1) and (5).
1988 c. 50.	Housing Act 1988.	Section 121(4) to (6).
1989 c. 24.	Social Security Act 1989.	Sections 1 to 3. Section 4(1) to (4). Section 5(1) to (4). Section 6(1). Section 7(1) to (5). Sections 9 to 19. Section 21. Section 22(1) to (6) and (8). Section 27. In section 28, in subsection (2), the words "1 to 4" and "9 to 12 and 22" and subsections (3) and (4). In section 29, subsections (2) and (5). In section 30(1), the definitions of "the 1982 Act" and "the Old Cases Act". Section 32. In Schedule 1, paragraphs 1 to 10. Schedules 2 and 3. In Schedule 4, paragraphs 1 to 21 and 24. Schedule 7, except paragraphs 1, 14, 21 and 27. In Schedule 8, paragraphs 1 to 7, 9, 10(1), 11, 12(2), (5) and (6) and 14 to 18 and 19(a) and (b).
1989 c. 42.	Local Government and Housing Act 1989.	Section 81. In Schedule 11, paragraph 113.
1990 c. 1.	Capital Allowances Act 1990.	In Schedule 1, paragraph 2.
1990 c. 19.	National Health Service and Community Care Act 1990.	In Schedule 9, paragraph 15.
1990 c. 27.	Social Security Act 1990.	Sections 1 to 5. Section 6(1) to (3). Sections 8 to 10. Section 16. Section 17(1) to (9). In section 20, the definitions of "the 1982 Act", "the 1986 Act", "the 1989 Act" and "the Old Cases Act". Section 22(1).

Chapter	Short title	Extent of repeal
		In Schedule 1, paragraphs 1 to 4, 5(1) and (2) and 6. Schedule 5. In Schedule 6, paragraphs 1, 3, 4(1) and (2), 5 to 7, 8(1), (3), (5), (7), (8) and (11), 9 to 12, 14 to 26, 27(2), 28, 30 and 31(a) and (b).
1990 c. 37.	Human Fertilisation and Embryology Act 1990.	In Schedule 4, paragraph 2.
1990 c. 41.	Courts and Legal Services Act 1990.	In Schedule 10, paragraphs 36, 37 and 46. In Schedule 11, in the entry beginning "Social Security Commissioner", the words "appointed under section 97 of the Social Security Act 1975". In Schedule 18, paragraph 24.
1991 c. 3.	Statutory Sick Pay Act 1991.	Sections 1 and 2. Section 3(1)(a) and (b) and (3) to (5). Section 4(5).
1991 c. 17.	Maintenance Enforcement Act 1991.	Section 9.
1991 c. 21.	Disability Living Allowance and Disability Working Allowance Act 1991.	Section 1. Section 2(1). Section 3. Section 4(1). Sections 5 and 6. Section 7(1). Sections 8 and 9. Sections 11 to 14. Schedule 1. In Schedule 2, paragraphs 2(2), 3 to 5, 8, 10 and 11, 15 to 17 and 19. In Schedule 3, Part I.
1991 c. 42.	Social Security (Contributions) Act 1991.	The whole Act.
1991 c. 48.	Child Support Act 1991.	In Schedule 3, in paragraph 1(1), the words "under Schedule 10 to the Social Security Act 1975" and in paragraph 3(2)(c) the words "under paragraph 1A of Schedule 10 to the Social Security Act 1975".

Section 4

SCHEDULE 2

CONSEQUENTIAL AMENDMENTS

National Assistance Act 1948

1. In section 64(1) of the National Assistance Act 1948, for the definition of "trade dispute", there shall be substituted—
   " "trade dispute" has the same meaning as in section 27 of the Social Security Contributions and Benefits Act 1992".

Law Reform (Personal Injuries) Act 1948

2. In section 2 of the Law Reform (Personal injuries) Act 1948 (measure of damages)—
   (a) in subsection (1)(a), for the words "section 22 of the Social Security Act 1989" there shall be substituted the words "section 81 of the Social Security Administration Act 1992"; and
   (b) in subsection (1A), for the words "paragraph 4(1) of Schedule 4 to the Social Security Act 1989" there shall be substituted the words "section 85(1) of the Social Security Administration Act 1992".

Maintenance Orders Act 1950

3.—(1) In the following provisions of the Maintenance Orders Act 1950 (jurisdiction of and enforcement by courts)—
  (a) section 4(1)(d);
  (b) section 9(1)(d);
  (c) section 12(1)(d);
  (d) section 16(2)(a)(viii);
  (e) section 16(2)(b)(ix); and
  (f) section 16(2)(c)(viii),
for the words "section 24 of the Social Security Act 1986", in each place where they occur, there shall be substituted the words "section 106 of the Social Security Administration Act 1992".
  (2) In sections 4(2) and 9(2) of that Act for "24", in each place where it occurs, there shall be substituted "106".

Agriculture Act 1967

4. In subsection (3)(e) of section 67 of the Agriculture Act 1967 (sick pay for agricultural workers) for the words "payable under Part II of the Social Security Act 1975" there shall be substituted the words "payable under Parts II to V of the Social Security Contributions and Benefits Act 1992".

Public Expenditure and Receipts Act 1968

5. In paragraph 1(b) of Schedule 3 to the Public Expenditure and Receipts Act 1968 for the words "The Social Security Act 1975 (c. 14), section 160(2)" there shall be substituted the words "The Social Security Administration Act 1992 (c. 5) section 124(3)".

Administration of Justice Act 1970

Attachment of Earnings Act 1971

6. In paragraph 3A of Schedule 4 to the Administration of Justice Act 1970 and paragraph 3A of Schedule 2 to the Attachment of Earnings Act 1971 for the words "Social Security Act 1975" there shall be substituted the words "Social Security Contributions and Benefits Act 1992".
  7. In paragraph 6 of Schedule 8 to the Administration of Justice Act 1970 and paragraph 7 of Schedule 1 to the Attachment of Earnings Act 1971 (maintenance orders) the word "or" where first occurring shall be omitted and after "1986" there shall be inserted the words "or section 106 of the Social Security Administration Act 1992".

Tribunals and Inquiries Act 1971

8. In section 7(3) of the Tribunals and Inquiries Act 1971 (chairmen etc.) for "(c) or (d)" there shall be substituted "(b), (c) or (e)".
  9. The following paragraph shall be substituted for paragraph 30A of Schedule 1 to that Act (tribunals under general supervision of Council on Tribunals)—

"Social Security...	30A	(a) Social security appeal tribunals constituted under section 41 of the Social Security Administration Act 1992; (b) disability appeal tribunals constituted under section 43 of that Act; (c) medical appeal tribunals constituted under section 50 of that Act; (d) a Commissioner appointed under section 52 of that Act and any tribunal presided over by a Commissioner so appointed; (e) a tribunal constituted under regulations made under section 58 of that Act.".

Employment and Training Act 1973

10. In subsection (3) of section 11 of the Employment and Training Act 1973 (financial provisions) for the words "Part II of the Social Security Act 1975" there shall be substituted the words "Part II to V of the Social Security Contributions and Benefits Act 1992".

11. In section 12(2) of that Act (duty of local education authorities to furnish Secretary of State with information in connection with determination of questions relating to contributions or benefit) for the words from "under" to the end of paragraph (b) there shall be substituted the words "under the Social Security Contributions and Benefits Act 1992".

Social Security (Northern Ireland) Act 1975

12. The following subsection shall be inserted after subsection (4) of section 155 of the Social Security (Northern Ireland) Act 1975 (orders and regulations (general provisions))—
  "(4A) If the Treasury so direct, regulations under section 123(2) or (3) above shall be made only in conjunction with them.".
13. The following section shall be inserted after that section—

"Regulations under section 123(2) or (3) (Parliamentary control).
  155A. Section 176 of the Social Security Contributions and Benefits Act 1992 as it applies to regulations made by the Secretary of State under section 116(2) or (3) of that Act applies also to regulations made by him under section 123(2) or (3) above.".
14. In section 158 of that Act—
(a) at the beginning of subsection (2) there shall be inserted the words "Subject to subsection (2A) below,"; and
(b) the following subsection shall be inserted after that subsection—
  "(2A) Section 123(2) above extends to Great Britain as well as Northern Ireland.".

Social Security (Consequential Provisions) Act 1975

15. In section 2(3)(a) of the Social Security (Consequential Provisions) Act 1975 (transitional provisions and savings) for the words "sections 166 and 167(3) of the Social Security Act 1975" there shall be substituted the words "sections 189 and 190(3) of the Social Security Administration Act 1992".

House of Commons Disqualification Act 1975

16. In Part I (judicial offices disqualifying for membership) of Schedule 1 to the House of Commons Disqualification Act 1975, in the first entry beginning "Chief or other Social Security Commissioner", for the words "excluding a person appointed in pursuance of section 13(5) of the Social Security Act 1980)" there shall be substituted the words "(not including a deputy Commissioner)".
17. In Part III (other disqualifying offices)—
(a) in the entry beginning "Adjudicating medical practitioner" for the words "Part III of the Social Security Act 1975" there shall be substituted the words "Part II of the Social Security Administration Act 1992"; and
(b) in the entry beginning "Member of a Medical Appeal Tribunal appointed" for the words "paragraph 2(2) of Schedule 12 to the Social Security Act 1975" there shall be substituted the words "section 50 of the Social Security Administration Act 1992".

Northern Ireland Assembly Disqualification Act 1975

18. In Part I (judicial offices disqualifying for membership) of Schedule I to the Northern Ireland Assembly Disqualification Act 1975 for the entry beginning "Chief or other Social Security Commissioner (not including a deputy Commissioner)" there shall be substituted the following entry—
  "Chief or other Social Security Commissioner (not including a deputy Commissioner)".

Social Security Pensions Act 1975

19. The Social Security Pensions Act 1975 shall be amended as follows.
20.—(1) In subsection (1)(a) of section 26 (contracting-out of full contributions and benefits) for the words "the principal Act" there shall be substituted the words "the Contributions and Benefits Act".
  (2) The following subsection shall be inserted after that subsection—
  "(1A) This Part of this Act shall also have effect, where an occupational pension scheme so provides or falls to be treated as so providing, for the purpose of making provision in relation—
      (a) to invalidity allowance under section 34 of the Contributions and Benefits Act;
      (b) to increases of Category A retirement pensions for invalidity under section 47 of that Act; and
      (c) to increases of unemployability supplement under paragraph 3 of Schedule 7 to that Act.".

21. In subsection (5) of section 27 (contracted-out rates of Class I contributions) for the words "section 3 above" there shall be substituted the words "section 19(4) of the Contributions and Benefits Act".

22. In subsection (1) of section 28 (review and alteration of contracted-out rates of Class I contributions)—
- (a) in paragraph (a), after the words "Government Actuary" there shall be inserted the words "or the Deputy Government Actuary", and
- (b) in paragraph (b), for the words "Government Actuary's report," there shall be substituted the words "report of the Government Actuary or Deputy Government Actuary,".

23.—(1) In subsection (1)(a) of section 29 (contracted-out rates of benefit) for the words "section 16 above" there shall be substituted the words "section 41 of the Contributions and Benefits Act".

(2) In subsections (2) and (2A) of that section for "16(2B), 28(7A) and 59(1A) of the principal Act" there shall be substituted "29A, 29B and 29C below".

(3) In subsection (3) after the word "section", in the first place where it occurs, there shall be inserted the words "and in sections 29A, 29B and 29C below".

24. The following sections shall be inserted after that section—

"Contracting-out and invalidity allowance

29A.—(1) Where for any period—
- (a) a person is entitled to one or more guaranteed minimum pensions; and
- (b) he is also entitled to an invalidity pension under section 33 of the Contributions and Benefits Act; and
- (c) the weekly rate of his invalidity pension includes an additional pension such as is mentioned in section 44(3)(b) of that Act,

for that period section 34 of that Act shall have effect as if the following subsection were substituted for subsection (5)—

"(5) In this section "the relevant amount" means an amount equal to the aggregate of—
- (a) an amount equal to the additional pension; and
- (b) an amount equal to the weekly rate or aggregate weekly rates of the guaranteed minimum pension or pensions,

reduced by the amount of any reduction in the weekly rate of the invalidity pension made by virtue of section 29 of the Pensions Act.".

(2) Where for any period—
- (a) a person is entitled to one or more guaranteed minimum pensions; and
- (b) he is also entitled to an invalidity pension under section 33 of the Contributions and Benefits Act; and
- (c) the weekly rate of his invalidity pension does not include an additional pension such as is mentioned in section 44(3)(b) of that Act,

for that period the relevant amount shall be deducted from the appropriate weekly rate of invalidity allowance and he shall be entitled to invalidity allowance only if there is a balance after the deduction and, if there is such a balance, at a weekly rate equal to it.

(3) In subsection (2) above "the relevant amount" means an amount equal to the weekly rate or aggregate weekly rates of the guaranteed minimum pension or pensions reduced by the amount of any reduction in the weekly rate of the invalidity pension made by virtue of section 29 above.

(4) Where subsection (2) above applies, section 34(7) of the Contributions and Benefits Act shall have effect as if for the words "subsection (4) above" there were substituted the words "section 29A(2) of the Pensions Act".

Contracting-out and increases of Category A retirement pension for invalidity

29B.—(1) Where for any period—
- (a) a person is entitled to one or more guaranteed minimum pensions; and
- (b) he is also entitled to a Category A retirement pension under section 44 of the Contributions and Benefits Act; and
- (c) the weekly rate of his pension includes an additional pension such as is mentioned in section 44(3)(b) of that Act,

for that period section 47 of that Act shall have effect as if the following subsection were substituted for subsection (3)—

"(3) In subsection (2) above "the relevant amount" means an amount equal to the aggregate of—

(a) an amount equal to the additional pension; and

(b) an amount equal to the weekly rate or aggregate weekly rates of the guaranteed minimum pension or pensions,

reduced by the amount of any reduction in the weekly rate of the Category A retirement pension made by virtue of section 29 of the Pensions Act.".

(2) Where for any period—

(a) a person is entitled to one or more guaranteed minimum pensions; and

(b) he is also entitled to a Category A retirement pension under section 44 of the Contributions and Benefits Act; and

(c) the weekly rate of his Category A retirement pension does not include an additional pension such as is mentioned in section 44(3)(b) of that Act,

for that period the relevant amount shall be deducted from the amount that would otherwise be the increase under section 47(1) of that Act and the pensioner shall be entitled to an increase under that subsection only if there is a balance remaining after that deduction and, if there is such a balance, of an amount equal to it.

(3) In subsection (2) above "the relevant amount" means an amount equal to the weekly rate or aggregate weekly rates of the guaranteed minimum pension or pensions reduced by the amount of any reduction in the weekly rate of the Category A retirement pension made by virtue of section 29 above.

Contracting-out and increases of unemployability supplement

29C.—(1) Where for any period—

(a) a person is entitled to one or more guaranteed minimum pensions; and

(b) he is also entitled—

(i) to an invalidity pension under section 33 of the Contributions and Benefits Act;

(ii) to a Category A retirement pension under section 44; or

(iii) to a Category B retirement pension under section 49; and

(c) the weekly rate of the pension includes an additional pension such as is mentioned in section 44(3)(b) of that Act,

for that period paragraph 3 of Schedule 7 to that Act shall have effect as if the following sub-paragraph were substituted for sub-paragraph (3)—

"(3) In this paragraph "the relevant amount" means an amount equal to the aggregate of—

(a) an amount equal to the additional pension; and

(b) an amount equal to the weekly rate or aggregate weekly rates of the guaranteed minimum pension or pensions,

reduced by the amount of any reduction in the weekly rate of the pension made by virtue of section 29 of the Pensions Act.".

(2) Where for any period—

(a) a person is entitled to one or more guaranteed minimum pensions; and

(b) he is also entitled to any of the pensions under the Contributions and Benefits Act mentioned in subsection (1)(b) above; and

(c) the weekly rate of the pension does not include an additional pension such as is mentioned in section 44(3)(b) of that Act,

for that period the relevant amount shall be deducted from the amount that would otherwise be the increase under that paragraph and the beneficiary shall be entitled to an increase only if there is a balance after that deduction and, if there is such a balance, only to an amount equal to it.

(3) In subsection (2) above "the relevant amount" means an amount equal to the weekly rate or aggregate weekly rates of the guaranteed minimum pension or pension.".

25. In subsection (1B) of section 30 (contracted-out employment) for the words "section 4(2) and (6) of the principal Act" there shall be substituted the words "sections 6(1) and 8(3) of the Contributions and Benefits Act".

26. In subsection (1A) of section 33 (requisite benefit for earner) for the words "section 3 of this Act" there shall be substituted the words "section 19(4) of the Contributions and Benefits Act".

27.—(1) In subsection (2ZA) of section 35 (earner's guaranteed minimum) for the words "section 3 of this Act" there shall be substituted the words "section 19(4) of the Contributions and Benefits Act".

(2) In subsections (5) and (7) of that section for the words "section 21 above" there shall be substituted the words "section 148 of the Administration Act".

28. In subsection (6) of section 36 (requisite benefit for widow) for the words "section 27(6) of the principal Act" there shall be substituted the words "section 43(1) of the Contributions and Benefits Act".

29. In subsection (7) of section 37A (annual increases of guaranteed minimum pensions) for the words from "sections" to "above" there shall be substituted the words "sections 29(1), 29A(1) and (2), 29B(1) and (2) and 29C(1) and (2) above".

30. In subsection (4A) of section 41C (supplementary provisions) and in subsection (3)(a) of section 45 (premium where guaranteed minimum pension excluded from full revaluation) for the words "section 21 above" there shall be substituted the words "section 148 of the Administration Act".

31. In subsection (6)(a) of section 44 (premium on termination of contracted-out scheme) for the words "section 21 above" there shall be substituted the words "section 148 of the Administration Act".

32. In subsection (10) of section 51A (refusal and cancellation of contracting-out certificates) for the words "section 4(3) of the principal Act" there shall be substituted the words "section 6(3) of the Contributions and Benefits Act".

33. In subsection (1) of section 52D (guaranteed minimum pensions under contracted-out schemes-supplementary) for the words "sections 16(2B), 28(7A) and 59(1A) of the principal Act and section 29(1) above" there shall be substituted the words "sections 29(1), 29A, 29B and 29C above".

34. In subsection (1) of section 59 (official pensions) for the words from "section 23" to "1986" there shall be substituted the words "section 151 of the Administration Act a direction is given that the sums mentioned in section 150(1)(c) of that Act".

35. In section 60 (determination of questions)—
(a) in subsection (1), for the words "section 93(1) of the principal Act" there shall be substituted the words "section 17(1) of the Administration Act"; and
(b) in subsection (3), for the words "section 93(1) nor section 98(1) of the principal Act" there shall be substituted the words "section 17(1) nor section 20(1) of the Administration Act".

36. The following sections shall be inserted after section 60ZA—

"Offences relating to state scheme premiums
60ZB. If a person fails to pay, at or within the time prescribed for the purpose, any state scheme premium which is payable by him, he shall be guilty of an offence and liable on summary conviction to a fine not exceeding level 3 on the standard scale.

Questions arising in proceedings
60ZC.—(1) Where in any proceedings—
(a) for an offence under this Act; or
(b) involving any question as to payment of a state scheme premium,
any such question arises as is mentioned in section 60(1) above, the decision of the Secretary of State shall be conclusive for the purposes of the proceedings.
(2) If—
(a) a decision of any such question is necessary for the determination of proceedings; and
(b) the decision of the Secretary of State has not been obtained or a question has been raised with a view to a review of the decision obtained,
the question shall be referred to the Secretary of State for determination or review in accordance (subject to any necessary modification) with sections 17 to 19 of the Administration Act.
(3) Subsection (1) above does not apply if—
(a) an appeal under section 18 of that Act is pending; or
(b) the time for appealing has not expired; or
(c) a question has been raised with a view to a review of the Secretary of State's decision under section 19,
and the court dealing with the case shall adjourn the proceedings until such time as a final decision on the question has been obtained.

Recovery of unpaid state scheme premiums on prosecution
60ZD. Where—
(a) a person has been convicted of an offence under section 60ZB above of failing to pay a state scheme premium at or within the time prescribed for the purpose; and
(b) the premium remains unpaid at the date of the conviction,
he shall be liable to pay to the Secretary of State a sum equal to the amount which he failed to pay.

Proof of previous offences

60ZE.—(1) Subject to subsection (2) below, where a person is convicted of an offence mentioned in section 60ZD above, evidence may be given of any previous failure by him to pay state scheme premiums within the time prescribed for the purpose; and in that section "the conviction" and "the offence" mean respectively the conviction referred to in this subsection and the offence of which the person is convicted.

(2) Such evidence may be given only if notice of intention to give it is served with the summons or warrant or, in Scotland, the complaint on which the person appeared before the court which convicted him.

Unpaid premiums—supplementary

60ZF.—(1) Where in England and Wales a person charged with an offence to which section 60ZD above applies is convicted of that offence in his absence under section 12(2) of the Magistrates' Courts Act 1980, then if—

(a) it is proved to the satisfaction of the court, on oath or in the manner prescribed by rules under section 144 of that Act, that notice under section 60ZE(2) above has been duly served specifying the other state scheme premiums in respect of which the prosecutor intends to give evidence; and

(b) the clerk of the court has received a statement in writing purporting to be made by the accused or by a solicitor acting on his behalf to the effect that if the accused is convicted in his absence of the offence charged he desires to admit failing to pay the other premiums so specified or any of them,

section 60ZE above shall have effect as if the evidence had been given and the failure so admitted had been proved, and the court shall proceed accordingly.

(2) In England and Wales, where—

(a) a person is convicted of an offence to which section 60ZD above applies; and

(b) an order is made under Part I of the Powers of Criminal Courts Act 1973 placing the offender on probation or discharging him absolutely or conditionally,

sections 60ZD and 60ZE above and subsection (1) above shall apply as if it were a conviction for all purposes.

(3) In Scotland, where—

(a) a person is convicted on indictment of, or is charged before a court of summary jurisdiction with, any such offence; and

(b) an order is made under Part I of the Criminal Procedure (Scotland) Act 1975 discharging him absolutely or placing him on probation,

sections 60ZD and 60ZE above shall apply as if—

(i) the conviction on indictment were a conviction for all purposes; or

(ii) (as the case may be) the making of the order by the court of summary jurisdiction were a conviction.

(4) In England and Wales, any sum which a person is liable to pay under sections 60ZD and 60ZE above and subsection (1) above shall be recoverable from him as a penalty.

(5) State scheme premiums recovered by the Secretary of State under those provisions are to be treated for all purposes as premiums paid to the Secretary of State in the respect of the person in respect of whom they were originally payable.".

37. The following sections shall be inserted after section 61—

"Consultation with Social Security Advisory Committee about certain regulations

61A.—(1) Subject to section 173 of the Administration Act, where the Secretary of State proposes to make regulations under section 51A(10) above, he shall refer the proposals, in the form of draft regulations or otherwise, to the Social Security Advisory Committee ("the Committee").

(2) The Committee shall consider any proposals referred to it by the Secretary of State under subsection (1) above and shall make to the Secretary of State a report containing such recommendations with regard to the subject-matter of the proposals as the Committee thinks appropriate.

(3) If after receiving a report of the Committee the Secretary of State lays before Parliament any regulations which comprise the whole or any part of the subject-matter of the proposals referred to the Committee, he shall lay with the regulations a copy of the Committee's report and a statement showing—

(a) the extent (if any) to which he has, in framing the regulations, given effect to the Committee's recommendations; and

(b) in so far as effect has not been given to them, his reasons why not.

(4) In the case of any regulations laid before Parliament at a time when Parliament is not sitting, the requirements of subsection (3) above shall be satisfied as respects either House of Parliament if a copy of the report and statement there referred to are laid before that House not later than the second day on which the House sits after the laying of the regulations.

Orders and regulations (general provisions)

61B.—(1) Powers under this Act to make regulations or orders, except any power of the Occupational Pensions Board to make orders, are exercisable by statutory instrument.

(2) Except in so far as this Act otherwise provides, any power conferred thereby to make regulations or an order may be exercised—

(a) either in relation to all cases to which the power extends, or in relation to those cases subject to specified exceptions, or in relation to any specified cases or classes of case;

(b) so as to make, as respects the cases in relation to which it is exercised—

(i) the full provision to which the power extends or any less provision (whether by way of exception or otherwise),

(ii) the same provision for all cases in relation to which the power is exercised, or different provision for different cases or different classes of case or different provision as respects the same case or class of case for different purposes of this Act,

(iii) any such provision either unconditionally or subject to any specified condition;

and where such a power is expressed to be exercisable for alternative purposes it may be exercised in relation to the same case for any or all of those purposes; and powers to make regulations or an order for the purposes of any one provision of this Act are without prejudice to powers to make regulations or an order for the purposes of any other provision.

(3) Without prejudice to any specific provision in this Act, a power conferred by this Act to make regulations or an order includes power to make thereby such incidental, supplementary, consequential or transitional provision as appears to the authority making the regulations or order to be expedient for the purposes of the regulations or order.

(4) Without prejudice to any specific provisions in this Act, a power conferred by this Act to make regulations or an order includes power to provide for a person to exercise a discretion in dealing with any matter.

(5) A power conferred on the Secretary of State to make any regulations or order, where the power is not expressed to be exercisable with the consent of the Treasury, shall if the Treasury so direct be exercisable only in conjunction with them.".

38. The following subsection shall be substituted for section 62(2)—

"(2) A statutory instrument—

(a) which contains (whether alone or with other provisions) any order or regulations made under this Act by the Secretary of State, other than an order which, under any provision of this Act, is required to be laid before Parliament after being made; and

(b) which is not subject to any requirement that a draft of the instrument shall be laid before and approved by a resolution of each House of Parliament,

shall be subject to annulment in pursuance of a resolution of either House of Parliament.".

39. In section 64(2)—

(a) for the words "Subsection (5) of section 135 of the principal Act" there shall be substituted the words "Section 165(5) of the Administration Act"; and

(b) for the words "subsection (3)(a) of that section" there shall be substituted the words "section 163(2)(a) of that Act".

40.—(1) In section 66(1)—

(a) the following definition shall be inserted before the definition of "average salary benefits"—

" "the Administration Act" means the Social Security Administration Act 1992;"; and

(b) the following definition shall be inserted after that definition—

" "the Contributions and Benefits Act" means the Social Security Contributions and Benefits Act 1992;".

(2) In section 66(2), for the words "section 29" there shall be substituted the words "sections 29 and 29C".

41. In paragraph 8 of Schedule 1A (revaluation of pensions) for the words "section 23(2) above" there shall be substituted the words "section 151(1) of the Administration Act".

42. In paragraph 6(3)(c) of Schedule 2 (contracting-out regulations) for the words "the principal Act" there shall be substituted the words "the Contributions and Benefits Act".

Employment Protection Act 1975

43. In section 124(6) of the Employment Protection Act 1975 (financial provisions)—
(a) for the words "section 135(3)(a) of the Social Security Act 1975" there shall be substituted the words "section 163(2)(a) of the Social Security Administration Act 1992"; and
(b) for the words "subsection (5) of that section" there shall be substituted the words "section 165(5) of that Act".

Social Security (Miscellaneous Provisions) Act 1977

44.—(1) In subsection (1)(a) of section 21 of the Social Security (Miscellaneous Provisions) Act 1977 (calculation of guaranteed minimum pensions preserved under approved arrangements) after the words "Pensions Act" there shall be inserted the words "or section 148 of the Social Security Administration Act 1992".
(2) The following subsection shall be substituted for subsection (3) of that section—
"(3) In this section—
"earner" and "earnings" are to be construed in accordance with sections 3, 4 and 112 of the Social Security Contributions and Benefits Act 1992;
"earnings factors" is to be construed in accordance with sections 22 and 23 of that Act;
"tax year" means the 12 months beginning with 6th April in any year,
and expressions used in Part III of the Pensions Act have the same meanings as in that Part.".
45. In section 23(2) of that Act (financial provisions)—
(a) for the words "Subsection (5) of section 135 of the principal Act" there shall be substituted the words "Section 165(5) of the Social Security Administration Act 1992"; and
(b) for the words "subsection (3)(a) of that section" there shall be substituted the words "section 163(2)(a) of that Act".
46. In section 24(3) of that Act (supplemental)—
(a) for the words "Subsections (1) to (5) of section 166 of the principal Act" there shall be substituted the words "Subsections (3) to (6) and (9) of section 189 of the Social Security Administration Act 1992";
(b) for the words "subsections (2) to (4) of the said section 166" there shall be substituted the words "subsections (4) to (6) of that section"; and
(c) for the words from "and for the purposes" to end there shall be substituted the words "and a power under any of sections 116 to 120 of the Social Security Contributions and Benefits Act 1992 or 177 to 179 of the Social Security Administration Act 1992 to make provision by regulations or Order in Council for modifications or adaptations of those Acts shall be exercisable in relation to any enactment contained in this Act.".

Rent Act 1977

47. The following section shall be inserted after section 72 of the Rent Act 1977—

"Amounts attributable to services
72A. In order to assist authorities to give effect to the housing benefit scheme under Part VII of the Social Security Contributions and Benefits Act 1992, where a rent is registered, there shall be noted on the register the amount (if any) of the registered rent which, in the opinion of the rent officer or rent assessment committee, is fairly attributable to the provision of services, except any amount which is negligible in the opinion of the officer or, as the case may be, the committee.".

Rating (Disabled Persons) Act 1978

48. In section 4(9) of the Rating (Disabled Persons) Act 1978 (rebates for lands and heritages with special facilities for disabled persons), for "1986)" there shall be substituted "1986 or section 134 of the Social Security Administration Act 1992)".

Employment Protection (Consolidation) Act 1978

49. In subsection (4) of section 123 of the Employment Protection (Consolidation) Act 1978 (payment of unpaid contributions to pension schemes) for "1986," there shall be substituted "1986 or Part XII of the Social Security Contributions and Benefits Act 1992,".
50.—(1) In subsection (4) of section 132 of that Act (recoupment of benefit) for the words "the Social Security Act 1986" there shall be substituted the words "Part III or V of the Social Security Administration Act 1992".

(2) In subsection (6) of that section, in the definition of "unemployment benefit", for the words "the Social Security Act 1975" there shall be substituted the words "the Social Security Contributions and Benefits Act 1992".

51.—(1) In sub-paragraph (1)(b) of paragraph 14 of Schedule 13 to that Act (redundancy payments where employment wholly or partly abroad)—
   (a) the following sub-paragraph shall be inserted before sub-paragraph (i)—
      "(ia) where the week is a week of employment beginning after 1st July 1992, an employed earner for the purposes of the Social Security Contributions and Benefits Act 1992 in respect of whom a secondary Class 1 contribution was payable under that Act; or"; and
   (b) in sub-paragraph (i) after "1976" there shall be inserted the words "and not falling within sub-paragraph (ia) above".

(2) In sub-paragraph (4)(b) of that paragraph after "1975" there shall be inserted the words "or the Social Security Contributions and Benefits Act 1992".

Capital Gains Tax Act 1979

52. In sub-paragraph (2) of paragraph 5 of Schedule 1 to the Capital Gains Tax Act 1979 (application of provisions about reliefs in relation to property held on trust for disabled persons)—
   (a) for the words "35 of the Social Security Act 1975 or" there shall be substituted the words "64 of the Social Security Contributions and Benefits Act 1992 or section 35 of"; and
   (b) for the words "37ZA of the Social Security Act 1975" there shall be substituted the words "71 of the Social Security Contributions and Benefits Act 1992".

Vaccine Damage Payments Act 1979

53. In section 1(4) of the Vaccine Damage Payments Act 1979 (assessment of disablement) for the words "section 57 of the Social Security Act 1975 or" there shall be substituted the words "section 103 of the Social Security Contributions and Benefits Act 1992 or section 57 of".

54. In subsection (2) of section 12 of that Act (financial provisions) for the words "Schedule 20 to the Social Security Act 1975" there shall be substituted the words "section 191 of the Social Security Administration Act 1992".

Pneumoconiosis etc. (Workers' Compensation) Act 1979

55.—(1) In subsection (3) of section 2 of the Pneumoconiosis etc. (Workers' Compensation) Act 1979 (conditions of entitlement), in the definition of "death benefit"—
   (a) for the words "section 76 of the Social Security Act 1975" there shall be substituted the words "section 108 of the Social Security Contributions and Benefits Act 1992"; and
   (b) for the words "section 5 of the Industrial Injuries and Diseases (Old Cases) Act 1975" there shall be substituted the words "paragraph 4 of Schedule 8 to the Social Security Contributions and Benefits Act 1992".

(2) In the definition of "disablement benefit", after "1975"—
   (a) in the first place where it occurs, there shall be inserted the words "or section 108 of the Social Security Contributions and Benefits Act 1992"; and
   (b) in the second place where it occurs, there shall be inserted the words "or paragraph 4 of Schedule 8 to the Social Security Contributions and Benefits Act 1992".

56. In section 4(3) of that Act (appeal on question of law)—
   (a) for the words "94 of the Social Security Act 1975" there shall be substituted the words "18 of the Social Security Administration Act 1992"; and
   (b) for "93(1)" there shall be substituted "17(1)".

57. In section 10(2) of that Act (construction)—
   (a) for the words "the Social Security Act 1975" there shall be substituted the words "the Social Security Contributions and Benefits Act 1992 or the Social Security Administration Act 1992"; and
   (b) for the words "that Act" there shall be substituted the words "either of those Acts".

Justices of the Peace Act 1979

58. In section 58(2)(b) of the Justices of the Peace Act 1979 for the words "Social Security Act 1975" there shall be substituted the words "Social Security Contributions and Benefits Act 1992".

Social Security Act 1980

59. In section 21(3) of the Social Security Act 1980 (supplemental) for the words "Subsections

(2) and (3) of section 166 of the principal Act" there shall be substituted the words "Section 175(3) and (4) of the Social Security Contributions and Benefits Act 1992".

Magistrates' Courts Act 1980

60. The following paragraph shall be inserted after the paragraph which paragraph 82 of Schedule 2 to the Family Law Reform Act 1987 inserted in subsection (1) of section 65 of the Magistrates' Courts Act 1980 (domestic proceedings)—
"(n) section 106 of the Social Security Administration Act 1992;".

Local Government, Planning and Land Act 1980

61. In subsection (1) of section 154 of the Local Government, Planning and Land Act 1980 (rent rebates) for the words "Part II of the Social Security Act 1986" there shall be substituted the words "Part VII of the Social Security Contributions and Benefits Act 1991 and the Social Security Administration Act 1992".

Civil Jurisdiction and Judgments Act 1982

62. In paragraph 5(c) of Schedule 5 to the Civil Jurisdiction and Judgments Act 1982 (proceedings excluded from Schedule 4) for the words "or any enactment applying in Northern Ireland and corresponding to it," there shall be substituted the words "section 106 of the Social Security Administration Act 1992 to any enactment applying in Northern Ireland and corresponding to either of them,".

Forfeiture Act 1982

63.—(1) In subsection (2) of section 4 of the Forfeiture Act 1982 (Commissioner to decide whether rule applies to social security benefits) for the words "section 115 of the Social Security Act 1975" there shall be substituted the words "section 59 of the Social Security Administration Act 1992".
(2) In subsection (4) of that section for the words "Section 166(2) to (3A) of the Social Security Act 1975" there shall be substituted the words "Section 175(3) to (5) of the Social Security Contributions and Benefits Act 1992".
(3) In subsection (5) of that section—
(a) in the definition of "Commissioner", for the words "Social Security Act 1975" there shall be substituted the words "Social Security Administration Act 1992"; and
(b) in the definition of "relevant enactment" the following entry shall be added after the entry relating to the Social Security Acts 1975 to 1991—
"the Social Security Contributions and Benefits Act 1992,".

Transport Act 1982

64. In section 70(2)(a) of the Transport Act 1982 (payments in respect of applications for exemption from wearing seat belts)—
(a) in sub-paragraph (i) for the words "35 of the Social Security Act 1975" there shall be substituted the words "64 of the Social Security Contributions and Benefits Act 1992";
(b) in sub-paragraph (iA) for "37ZA" there shall be substituted "71"; and
(c) in sub-paragraph (iii) for "57" there shall be substituted "103" and for "61(1)", "104(1)".

Value Added Tax Act 1983

65. In the seventh note to Group 14 (drugs, medicines, aids for the handicapped) of Schedule 5 (zero-rating) to the Value Added Tax Act 1983 for the words "37ZA of the Social Security Act 1975" there shall be substituted the words "71 of the Social Security Contributions and Benefits Act 1992".

Inheritance Tax Act 1984

66.—(1) In paragraph (b) of sections 74(4) and 89(4) of the Inheritance Tax Act 1984 (disabled persons for purposes of provisions about trusts for disabled persons) for the words "35 of the Social Security Act 1975 or" there shall be substituted the words "64 of the Social Security Contributions and Benefits Act 1992 or section 35 of".
(2) In paragraph (c) of those subsections for the words "37ZA of the Social Security Act 1975" there shall be substituted the words "71 of the Social Security Contributions and Benefits Act 1992".

Social Security Act 1985

67.—(1) At the end of subsection (1) of section 5 of the Social Security Act 1985 (managers of occupational pension schemes) there shall be added the words "or

(c) of Part VI of the Social Security Administration Act 1992.".

(2) In subsection (2) of that section for the words "Section 166 of the Social Security Act 1975" there shall be substituted the words "Section 61B of the Social Security Pensions Act 1975".

68. In section 32(8) of that Act (commencement) for the words "Subsections (2) and (3) of section 166 of the Social Security Act 1975" there shall be substituted the words "Section 175(3) and (4) of the Social Security Contributions and Benefits Act 1992".

Bankruptcy (Scotland) Act 1985

69. In section 31 of the Bankruptcy (Scotland) Act 1985 (vesting of debtor's estate at date of sequestration) in subsection (8) for the words "and to paragraph 8(2) of Schedule 4 to the Social Security Act 1989" there shall be substituted the words "and to section 89(2) of the Social Security Administration Act 1992".

Housing Act 1985

70. In subsection (2)(b) of section 425 of the Housing Act 1985 (the local contribution differential) for the words "section 30 of the Social Security Act 1986" there shall be substituted the words "section 135 of the Social Security Administration Act 1992".

71. In Item 4 in Part I of Schedule 14 to that Act (items to be credited to the Housing Revenue Account) for the words "Part II of the Social Security Act 1986" there shall be substituted the words "section 135 of the Social Security Administration Act 1992".

72. In paragraph 3 of Part IV of that Schedule (rate fund contributions to the Housing Revenue Account) for the words "section 30(6) of the Social Security Act 1986" there shall be substituted the words "section 135(7) of the Social Security Administration Act 1992".

Insolvency Act 1986

73. In paragraph 6 of Schedule 6 to the Insolvency Act 1986 (preferential debts) for the words "Social Security Act 1975" there shall be substituted the words "Social Security Contributions and Benefits Act 1992".

Wages Act 1986

74. In subsection (1) of section 7 of the Wages Act 1986 (meaning of "wages")—

(a) in paragraph (e), after "1982" there shall be added the words "or Part XI of the Social Security Contributions and Benefits Act 1992"; and

(b) at the end of paragraph (f) there shall be added the words "or Part XII of the Social Security Contributions and Benefits Act 1992,".

Social Security Act 1986

75. The Social Security Act 1986 shall be amended as follows.

76. In section 3(4) (amount of minimum contributions) for the words "section 4(2) and (6) of the Social Security Act 1975" there shall be substituted the words "sections 6(1) and 8(3) of the Social Security Contributions and Benefits Act 1992".

77. In section 4(1) (effect of payment of minimum contributions on rate of certain benefits) for the words from "sections 16(2B)" to "section 29" there shall be substituted the words "sections 34(4) and 47(2) of the Social Security Contributions and Benefits Act 1992, paragraph 3(2) of Schedule 7 to that Act and sections 29 to 29C".

78. In section 7(5) (schemes becoming contracted-out between 1986 and 1993) for the words "section 4(2) and (6) of the Social Security Act 1975" there shall be substituted the words "sections 6(1) and 8(3) of the Social Security Contributions and Benefits Act 1992".

79. In subsection (5) of section 9 (guaranteed minimum pensions) for the words "section 16(5) of that Act" there shall be substituted the words "section 41(7) of the Social Security Contributions and Benefits Act 1992".

80. In subsection (4)(a) of section 16 (actuarial tables) after the words "Government Actuary" there shall be inserted the words "or the Deputy Government Actuary".

81. In subsection (1) of section 17A (reciprocity as to pensions with other countries) for the words "Section 143 of the Social Security Act 1975" there shall be substituted the words "Section 179 of the Social Security Administration Act 1992".

82. In section 52(2) (questions for determination by Secretary of State) for the words "section 93(1) of the Social Security Act 1975" there shall be substituted the words "section 17(1) of the Social Security Administration Act 1992".

83. In subsection (3)(c) of section 59 (disclosure of information) for the words "Part III of the Social Security Act 1975 including that Part as extended by section 52(3) above" there shall be substituted the words "sections 17 to 62 of the Social Security Administration Act 1992".

84. In section 83(1) (general provisions about orders and regulations) for the words "Section 166(1) to (3A) of the Social Security Act 1975" there shall be substituted the words "Section 61B(1) to (4) of the Social Security Pensions Act 1975".

Abolition of Domestic Rates Etc. (Scotland) Act 1987

85. The Abolition of Domestic Rates Etc. (Scotland) Act 1987 shall be amended as follows.

86. In subsection (7) of section 9 (reduced liability for personal community charge) for the words "the Social Security Act 1986" there shall be substituted the words "Part VII of the Social Security Contributions and Benefits Act 1992".

87. At the end of section 20B(2)(a) (regulations regarding use of social security information) there shall be added the words "the Social Security Contributions and Benefits Act 1992 or the Social Security Administration Act 1992".

88. In paragraph 4(2) of Schedule 1A (exemptions of the severely mentally impaired from personal community charge)—
   (a) for paragraphs (a), (b), (d) and (e) there shall be substituted the following paragraphs—
      "(a) he is entitled to an invalidity pension under section 33, 40 or 41 of the Social Security Contributions and Benefits Act 1992;
       (b) he is entitled to a severe disablement allowance under section 68 of that Act;
       (e) he is entitled to unemployability supplement under Part I of Schedule 7 to that Act;"; and
   (b) for paragraphs (g) and (h), there shall be substituted the following paragraphs—
      "(g) he is entitled to an attendance allowance under section 64 of the Social Security Contributions and Benefits Act 1992;
       (h) he is entitled to an increase of the weekly rate of his disablement pension under section 104 of that Act;".

89. In paragraph 5 of Schedule 1A (exemption of children from personal community charge) for the words "Schedule 1 to the Child Benefit Act 1975" there shall be substituted the words "Schedule 9 to the Social Security Contributions and Benefits Act 1992".

90. In paragraph 4 of Schedule 2 (payment of community charges)—
   (a) in sub-paragraph (7) for the words "or community charge benefit in pursuance of Part II of the Social Security Act 1986" there shall be substituted the words "in pursuance of the Social Security Act 1986 or community charge benefit in pursuance of Part VII of the Social Security Contributions and Benefits Act 1992"; and
   (b) in sub-paragraph (12) for the words "section 20(11) of the Social Security Act 1986" there shall be substituted the words "section 137(1) of the Social Security Contributions and Benefits Act 1992".

91. In paragraph 5 of that Schedule in each of sub-paragraphs (1) and (7)(c) for the words "or community charge benefit in pursuance of Part II of the Social Security Act 1986" there shall be substituted the words "in pursuance of the Social Security Act 1986 or community charge benefit in pursuance of Part VII of the Social Security Contributions and Benefits Act 1992".

92. In paragraph 7A(1) of that Schedule for the words "the Social Security Act 1986" there shall be substituted the words "Part VII of the Social Security Contributions and Benefits Act 1992".

Income and Corporation Taxes Act 1988

93.—(1) Section 617 of the Income and Corporation Taxes Act 1988 (treatment of social security benefits and contributions for tax purposes) shall be amended as follows.

(2) In subsection (1) for the words from "Chapters", where it first occurs, to "Pensions Act 1975" there shall be substituted the words "Parts II to IV of the Social Security Contributions and Benefits Act 1992".

(3) In subsection (2)—
   (a) in paragraph (a), for the words "the Social Security Act 1986" there shall be substituted the words "Part VII of the Social Security Contributions and Benefits Act 1992"; and
   (b) in paragraph (aa), for the words "section 70 of the Social Security Act 1975" there shall be substituted the words "paragraph 18 of Schedule 7 to the Social Security Contributions and Benefits Act 1992".

(4) In subsection (3)(a) for the words "Act 1975" there shall be substituted the words "Contributions and Benefits Act 1992".

(5) In subsection (4) for the words "the Social Security Act 1975" there shall be substituted the words "Part I of the Social Security Contributions and Benefits Act 1992".

(6) In subsection (5) for the words "(2) of section 9 of the Social Security Act 1975 or" there shall be substituted the words "(3) of section 15 of the Social Security Contributions and Benefits Act 1992 or subsection (2) of section 9".

Social Security Act 1988

94. In section 13(4)(e) of the Social Security Act 1988 (schemes for distribution of welfare foods) for the words "the Social Security Act 1975" there shall be substituted the words "the Social Security Administration Act 1992".

95. In section 15(2) of that Act (financial provision) for the words "sections 2, 6, 7, 9 and 10" there shall be substituted the words "section 9".

96. In section 15A(1) of that Act (regulations and orders) for the words "Section 166(1) to (3A) of the Social Security Act 1975" there shall be substituted the words "Section 175(2) to (5) of the Social Security Contributions and Benefits Act 1992".

Legal Aid Act 1988

97. In section 34(6) of the Legal Aid Act 1988 (calculation of income or capital) for the words "social security benefits" there shall be substituted the words "benefits under Part VII of the Social Security Contributions and Benefits Act 1992 (income-related benefits)".

Local Government Finance Act 1988

98. The following paragraph shall be substituted for sub-paragraph (2) of paragraph 4 (exemption of the severely mentally impaired from personal community charge) of Schedule 1 to the Local Government Finance Act 1988—

"(2) The conditions are that—
(a) he is entitled for the day to an invalidity pension under section 33 of the Social Security Contributions and Benefits Act 1992;
(b) he is entitled for the day to a severe disablement allowance under section 68 of that Act;
(c) he is on the day of pensionable age within the meaning given by section 122 of that Act.".

99. At the end of paragraph 14(2)(a) of Schedule 2 to that Act (community charges: administration) there shall be added the words "the Social Security Contributions and Benefits Act 1992 or the Social Security Administration Act 1992,".

100. In paragraph 6(1) of Schedule 4 to that Act (community charges: enforcement) for the words "the Social Security Act 1986" there shall be substituted the words "Part VII of the Social Security Contributions and Benefits Act 1992".

101. In paragraph 28(2) of that Schedule after "1979," there shall be inserted the words "sections 17 to 62 of the Social Security Administration Act 1992".

Housing (Scotland) Act 1988

102. The following section shall be inserted after section 48 of the Housing (Scotland) Act 1988—

"Amounts attributable to services
48A. In order to assist authorities to give effect to the housing benefit scheme under Part VIII of the Social Security Contributions and Benefits Act 1992, where a rent is determined under section 25 or 34 above, the rent assessment committee shall note in their determination the amount (if any) of the rent which, in the opinion of the committee, is fairly attributable to the provision of services, except where that amount is in their opinion negligible; and the amounts so noted may be included in the information specified in an order under section 49 below.".

Housing Act 1988

103. The following section shall be inserted after section 41 of the Housing Act 1988—

"Amounts attributable to services
41A. In order to assist authorities to give effect to the housing benefit scheme under Part VII of the Social Security Contributions and Benefits Act 1992, where a rent is determined under section 14 or 22 above, the rent assessment committee shall note in their determination the amount (if any) of the rent which, in the opinion of the committee, is fairly attributable to the provision of services, except where that amount is in their opinion negligible; and the amount so noted may be included in the information specified in an order under section 42 below.".

104. The following subsection shall be substituted for subsection (7) of section 121 of that Act (rent officers: additional functions relating to housing benefits etc.)—

"(7) In this section—

"housing benefit" means housing benefit under Part VII of the Social Security Contributions and Benefits Act 1992; and

"rent allowance subsidy" has the meaning assigned to it by section 135 of the Social Security Administration Act 1992.".

Social Security Act 1989

105.—(1) In subsection (7) of section 6 of the Social Security Act 1989 (benefits for women widowed before 11th April 1988) for the words "section 104 of the principal Act" there shall be substituted the words "section 25 of the Social Security Administration Act 1992".

(2) In subsection (9) of that section—

(a) for the words "Subsection (4) of section 104 of the principal Act" there shall be substituted the words "Section 28 of the Social Security Administration Act 1992"; and

(b) for the words "that section" there shall be substituted the words "section 25 of that Act".

106. In section 29(1) of that Act (general provisions about regulations and orders) for the words "subsections (1) to (3A) of section 166 of the principal Act" there shall be substituted the words "Section 175(2) to (5) of the Social Security Contributions and Benefits Act 1992".

Finance Act 1989

107. In section 178 of the Finance Act 1989 (rates of interest) in subsection (2)(gg) for the words "paragraph 5 of Schedule 1 to the Social Security Act 1975" there shall be substituted the words "paragraph 6 of Schedule 1 to the Social Security Contributions and Benefits Act 1992".

Children Act 1989

108. In the following provisions of the Children Act 1989—

(a) section 17(9) (no repayment of assistance);

(b) section 29(3) (no recoupment of costs); and

(c) paragraph 21(4) of Part III of Schedule 2 (no liability to contribute to maintenance),

for the words "Social Security Act 1986" there shall be substituted the words "Part VII of the Social Security Contributions and Benefits Act 1992".

Capital Allowances Act 1990

109. In the following provisions of the Capital Allowances Act 1990—

(a) section 22(6)(a) (first-year allowances: transitional relief for regional projects); and

(b) section 36(4)(a) (definition of "motor car"),

for the words "Social Security Act 1975" there shall be substituted the words "Social Security Contributions and Benefits Act 1992".

Social Security Act 1990

110. In section 18(2) of the Social Security Act 1990 (general financial provisions) for the words from "sections 4" to "26" there shall be substituted the words "paragraphs 2".

111. In section 19(1) of that Act (general provisions about regulations and orders) for the words "subsections (1) to (3A) of section 166 of the principal Act" there shall be substituted the words "section 175(2) to (5) of the Social Security Contributions and Benefits Act 1992".

112.—(1) In sub-paragraph (3) of paragraph 27 of Schedule 6 to that Act (benefits for women widowed before 11th April 1988) for the words "section 104 of the principal Act" there shall be substituted the words "section 25 of the Social Security Administration Act 1992".

(2) In sub-paragraph (5) of that paragraph for the words "Subsection (4) of section 104 of the principal Act" there shall be substituted "Section 28 of the Social Security Administration Act 1992".

Child Support Act 1991

113. In subsection (2) of section 43 of the Child Support Act 1991 (contribution to maintenance by deduction from benefit) for the words "section 51 of the Social Security Act 1986 by virtue of subsection (1)(r)," there shall be substituted the words "section 5 of the Social Security Administration Act 1992 by virtue of subsection (1)(t),".

114. In section 45 of that Act (interpretation)—

(a) in the definition of "benefit Acts" for the words "Social Security Acts 1975 to 1991" there shall be substituted the words "Social Security Contributions and Benefits Act 1992 and the Social Security Administration Act 1992"; and

(b) in the definition of "disability living allowance" for the words "Social Security Act 1975" there shall be substituted the words "benefit Acts".

Section 5   SCHEDULE 3

TRANSITIONAL PROVISIONS AND SAVINGS (INCLUDING SOME TRANSITIONAL PROVISIONS RETAINED FROM PREVIOUS ACTS)

PART I

GENERAL AND MISCELLANEOUS

Questions relating to contributions and benefits

1.—(1) A question other than a question arising under any of sections 1 to 3 of the Administration Act—
(a) whether a person is entitled to benefit in respect of a time before 1st July 1992;
(b) whether a person is liable to pay contributions in respect of such a time,
and any other question not arising under any of those sections with respect to benefit or contributions in respect of such a time is to be determined, subject to section 68 of the Administration Act, in accordance with provisions in force or deemed to be in force at that time.

(2) Subject to sub-paragraph (1) above, the consolidating Acts apply to matters arising before their commencement as to matters arising after it.

General saving for old savings

2. The repeal by this Act of an enactment previously repealed subject to savings (whether or not in the repealing enactment) does not affect the continued operation of those savings.

Documents referring to repealed enactments

3. Any document made, served or issued after this Act comes into force which contains a reference to any of the repealed enactments shall be construed, except so far as a contrary intention appears, as referring or, as the context may require, including a reference to the corresponding provision of the consolidating Acts.

Provisions relating to the coming into force of other provisions

4. The repeal by this Act of a provision providing for or relating to the coming into force of a provision reproduced in the consolidating Acts does not affect the operation of the first provision, in so far as it remains capable of having effect, in relation to the enactment reproducing the second provision.

Containing powers to make transitional etc. regulations

5. Where immediately before 1st July 1992 the Secretary of State has power under any provision of the Social Security Acts 1975 to 1991 not reproduced in the consolidating Acts by regulations to make provision or savings in preparation for or in connection with the coming into force of a provision repealed by this Act but reproduced in the consolidating Acts, the power shall be construed as having effect in relation to the provision reproducing the repealed provision.

Powers to make preparatory regulations

6. The repeal by this Act of a power by regulations to make provision or savings in preparation for or in connection with the coming into force of a provision reproduced in the consolidating Acts does not affect the power, in so far as it remains capable of having effect, in relation to the enactment reproducing the second provision.

Provisions contained in enactments by virtue of orders or regulations

7.—(1) Without prejudice to any express provision in the consolidating Acts, where this Act repeals any provision contained in any enactment by virtue of any order or regulations and the provision is reproduced in the consolidating Acts, the Secretary of State shall have the like power to make orders or regulations repealing or amending the provision of the consolidating Acts which reproduces the effect of the repealed provision as he had in relation to that provision.

(2) Sub-paragraph (1) above applies to a repealed provision which was amended by Schedule 7 to the Social Security Act 1989 as it applies to a provision not so amended.

Amending orders made after passing of Act

8. An order which is made under any of the repealed enactments after the passing of this Act and which amends any of the repealed enactments shall have the effect also of making a corresponding amendment of the consolidating Acts.

PART II

SPECIFIC TRANSITIONAL PROVISIONS AND SAVINGS (INCLUDING SOME DERIVED FROM PREVIOUS ACTS)

Interpretation

9. In this Part of this Schedule—
   "the 1965 Act" means the National Insurance Act 1965;
   "the 1973 Act" means the Social Security Act 1973;
   "the 1975 Act" means the Social Security Act 1975;
   "the former Consequential Provisions Act" means the Social Security (Consequential Provisions) Act 1975; and
   "the 1986 Act" means the Social Security Act 1986;

Social Security Pensions Act 1975

10. The repeal by this Act of any provision contained in the 1975 Act or any enactment amending such a provision does not affect the operation of that provision by virtue of section 66(2) of the Social Security Pensions Act 1975.

Additional pensions

11. The repeal by this Act of section 18(1) of the 1986 Act (which substituted in any enactment or instrument made under an enactment a reference to a basic pension for any reference to the basic component of a long-term benefit and a reference to an additional pension for any reference to an additional component of such a benefit) does not affect the construction of any enactment or instrument amended by that subsection.

Supersession of National Insurance Acts—provisions derived from Schedule 3 to former Consequential Provisions Act

12. Regulations may provide that, in relation to—
   (a) persons who ceased by virtue of paragraph 2 of Schedule 3 to the former Consequential Provisions Act to be insured under the 1965 Act,
   (b) persons to or in respect of whom benefit under that Act was, or but for a disqualification or forfeiture would have been, payable immediately before 6th April 1975, and
   (c) persons who had a prospective right to, or expectation of, any benefit under that Act immediately before that day,
the Contributions and Benefits Act and the Administration Act (so far as they represent provisions of the 1973 Act) shall have effect subject to such modifications as may be prescribed with a view to securing continuity of the law.

13. Without prejudice to the generality of the powers conferred by paragraph 12 above, regulations under that paragraph may in particular provide for the taking into account, for such purposes and in such manner and subject to such conditions as may be prescribed, of contributions paid or credited or deemed to be, or treated as, paid or credited under the 1965 Act or the National Insurance Act 1946 or any enactment repealed by that Act.

14. Regulations may provide that the Contributions and Benefits Act and the Administration Act (so far as they represent the 1973 Act) and this Part of this Schedule (except this paragraph) shall have effect subject to prescribed modifications in relation to persons who attained the age of 16 before 6th April 1975 and who, immediately before that day, were not insured under the 1965 Act.

15. Notwithstanding any repeal effected by the 1973 Act, provision may be made by regulations for continuing in force, with or without prescribed modifications, such provisions of the 1965 Act or any other enactments specified in the third column of Schedule 28 to the 1973 Act (repeals) as the Secretary of State considers appropriate for the purpose of preserving rights to benefit under that Act or those enactments in those cases (if any) in which in his opinion adequate alternative rights to benefit under the Contributions and Benefits Act are

not conferred in pursuance of paragraph 12 above, or for temporarily retaining the effect of those provisions for transitional purposes.

16. In the foregoing provisions of this Part of this Schedule, any reference to benefit under the 1965 Act includes a reference to such other benefit, pension or allowance as is mentioned in paragraph 17(2)(b) of Schedule 11 to that Act (pre-1948 beneficiaries).

17.—(1) Any instrument (except regulations, an Order in Council or another order) and any appointment which is in force immediately before 1st July 1992 and was made or has effect as if made under an enactment repealed by the 1973 Act shall, in so far as a corresponding instrument or appointment is capable of being made under any provision of the Contributions and Benefits Act or the Administration Act representing a provision in the 1973 Act, be deemed to be so made except to the extent that regulations otherwise provide.

(2) A reference in any document to an enactment repealed and re-enacted by the 1973 Act with or without modifications shall, in so far as the context permits, be construed as a reference to the Contributions and Benefits Act or, as the case may be, the Administration Act or to the corresponding enactment therein.

Housing benefit—provision derived from section 30(11) of 1986 Act

18.—(1) The Secretary of State may by order make provision for the modification or termination of rights to subsidy under Part II of the Social Security and Housing Benefits Act 1982 in respect of benefit paid in excess of entitlement.

(2) Any expenses of the Secretary of State under this paragraph shall be paid out of money provided by Parliament.

(3) The power conferred by this paragraph includes power to make different provision for different areas.

Industrial injuries—provision derived from paragraph 12 of Schedule 3 to 1986 Act

19.—(1) The Secretary of State may by regulations provide for the payment of prescribed amounts in prescribed circumstances to persons who immediately before the repeal of sections 71 to 73 of the 1975 Act were entitled to any benefit by virtue of any of those sections, but in determining the amount which is to be payable in any case or class of cases the Secretary of State may take into account—
(a) the extent to which the weekly rate of industrial death benefit has been modified in that case or class of cases by virtue of section 74;
(b) the age of the beneficiary and of any person or persons formerly maintained by the deceased; and
(c) the length of time that entitlement to the benefit would have been likely to continue if those sections had not been repealed.

(2) In this paragraph "prescribed" means specified in or determined in accordance with regulations.

(3) Any expenses of the Secretary of State under this paragraph shall be paid out of money provided by Parliament.

Attendance allowance—provision derived from section 1 of Social Security Act 1988

20. For the purposes—
(a) of any determination following a claim made before 15th March 1988 (the date of the passing of the Social Security Act 1988);
(b) of any review following an application made before that date; and
(c) of any review following a decision to conduct a review made before that date,
section 64 of the Contributions and Benefits Act shall have effect as if the following subsection were substituted for subsection (3)—
"(3) A person satisfies the night attendance condition if he is so severely disabled physically or mentally that, at night, he requires from another person either—
(a) prolonged or repeated attention during the night in connection with his bodily functions; or
(b) continued supervision throughout the night in order to avoid substantial danger to himself or others."

Supplementary benefit and former housing-related benefits—provision derived from section 16 of Social Security Act 1989

21.—(1) Any expenses of the Secretary of State in making payments to persons falling within sub-paragraph (2) or (3) below may be paid out of money provided by Parliament.

(2) A person falls within this sub-paragraph if—
(a) he was entitled to supplementary benefit immediately before 11th April 1988, but

(b) he did not become entitled to income support in respect of the week beginning with that day.

(3) A person falls within this sub-paragraph if he was entitled to any one or more of the former housing-related benefits in respect of a qualifying week but either—

(a) he did not become entitled to housing benefit under Part II of the 1986 Act in respect of the commencement week, or

(b) the amount of any such housing benefit to which he became entitled in repect of that week was less than the amount of the former housing-related benefits to which he had been entitled in respect of the qualifying week.

(4) In this paragraph—

"commencement day" means the day on which the new provisions came into force in the case of the person in question (1st or 4th April 1988, according to the circumstances);

"commencement week", in relation to any person, means the week beginning with the commencement day in his case;

"the former housing-related benefits" means—

(a) rent rebates, rate rebates and rent allowances, within the meaning of Part II of the Social Security and Housing Benefits Act 1982; and

(b) housing benefit supplement;

"the new provisions" means the following provisions of Part II of the 1986 Act, so far as relating to housing benefit, that is to say, sections 20 to 22, 28 and 29;

"qualifying week", in relation to any person, means any week beginning on or after 21st March 1988 and ending before the commencement day in his case;

"week" means a period of 7 days.

(5) For the purposes of this paragraph—

(a) a person shall be regarded as having been entitled to housing benefit supplement in respect of a week if an amount was applicable in respect of him under regulation 19 of the Supplementary Benefit (Requirements) Regulations 1983 in respect of that week; and

(b) the amount of housing benefit supplement to which he was entitled in respect of that week shall be taken to be an amount equal to the amount so applicable.

Substitution of disability living allowance for attendance allowance and mobility allowance and dissolution of Attendance Allowance Board—provision derived from section 5 of Disability Living Allowance and Disability Working Allowance Act 1991

22.—(1) The Secretary of State may make such regulations as appear to him necessary or expedient in relation to the substitution of disability living allowance for attendance allowance and mobility allowance and the dissolution of the Attendance Allowance Board.

(2) Without prejudice to the generality of this paragraph, regulations under this paragraph—

(a) may provide for the termination or cancellation of awards of attendance allowance and awards of mobility allowance;

(b) may direct that a person whose award of either allowance has been terminated or cancelled by virtue of the regulations or who is a child or such a person shall by virtue of the regulations be treated as having been awarded one or more disability living allowances;

(c) may direct that a disability living allowance so treated as having been awarded shall consist of such component as the regulations may specify or, if the regulations so specify, of both components, and as having been awarded either component at such weekly rate and for such period as the regulations may specify;

(d) may provide for the termination in specified circumstances of an award of disability living allowance;

(e) may direct that in specified circumstances a person whose award of disability living allowance has been terminated by virtue of the regulations shall by virtue of the regulations be treated as having been granted a further award of a disability living allowance consisting of such component as the regulations may specify or, if the regulations so specify, of both components, and as having been awarded on the further award either component at such weekly rate and for such period as the regulations may specify;

(f) may provide for the review of awards made by virtue of paragraph (b) or (e) above and for the treatment of claims for disability living allowance in respect of beneficiaries with such awards;

(g) may direct that for specified purposes certificates issued by the Attendance Allowance Board shall be treated as evidence of such matters as may be specified in the regulations;

(h) may direct that for specified purposes the replacement of attendance allowance and mobility allowance by disability living allowance shall be disregarded;

(i) may direct that a claim for attendance allowance or mobility allowance shall be treated in specified circumstances and for specified purposes as a claim for disability living allowance or that a claim for disability living allowance shall be treated in specified circumstances and for specified purposes as a claim for attendance allowance or mobility allowance or both;

(j) may direct that in specified circumstances and for specified purposes a claim for a disability living allowance shall be treated as having been made when no such claim was in fact made;

(k) may direct that in specified circumstances a claim for attendance allowance, mobility allowance or disability living allowance shall be treated as not having been made;

(l) may direct that in specified circumstances where a person claims attendance allowance or mobility allowance or both, and also claims disability living allowance, his claims may be treated as a single claim for such allowances for such periods as the regulations may specify;

(m) may direct that cases relating to mobility allowance shall be subject to adjudication in accordance with the provisions of Part II of the Administration Act relating to disability living allowance; and

(n) may direct that, at a time before the Attendance Allowance Board is dissolved, in specified circumstances cases relating to attendance allowance shall be subject to adjudication under the system of adjudication for such cases introduced by the Disability Living Allowance and Disability Working Allowance Act 1991.

(3) Regulations under this paragraph may provide that any provision to which this sub-paragraph applies—

(a) shall have effect subject to modifications, additions or amendments; or

(b) shall not have effect.

(4) Sub-paragraph (3) above applies—

(a) to any provision of the 1975 Act which relates to mobility allowance, so far as it so relates;

(b) to any provision of Part VI of the 1986 Act which is relevant to mobility allowance;

(c) to any provision of the Contributions and Benefits Act which relates to disability living allowance or attendance allowance, so far as it so relates; and

(d) to any provision of the Administration Act which is relevant to disability living allowance or attendance allowance.

Regulations and orders—supplementary

23.—(1) Regulations under this Part of this Schedule shall be made by the Secretary of State.

(2) Powers under this Part of this Schedule to make regulations or orders are exercisable by statutory instrument.

(3) Any power conferred by this Part of this Schedule to make regulations or orders may be exercised—

(a) either in relation to all cases to which the power extends, or in relation to those cases subject to specified exceptions, or in relation to any specified cases or classes of case;

(b) so as to make, as respects the cases in relation to which it is exercised—

(i) the full provision to which the power extends or any less provision (whether by way of exception or otherwise);

(ii) the same provision for all cases in relation to which the power is exercised, or different provision for different cases or different classes of case or different provision as respects the same case or class of case for different purposes of this Part of this Schedule;

(iii) any such provision either unconditionally or subject to any specified condition.

(4) The powers to make regulations or orders conferred by any provision of this Part of this Schedule other than paragraph 22 above include powers to make thereby such incidental, supplementary, consequential or transitional provision as appears to the Secretary of State to be expedient for the purposes of the regulations.

(5) A power conferred by this Part of this Schedule to make regulations or an order includes power to provide for a person to exercise a discretion in dealing with any matter.

(6) If the Treasury so direct, regulations or orders under this Part of this Schedule shall be made only in conjunction with them.

(7) A statutory instrument—

(a) which contains (whether alone or with other provisions) orders or regulations made under this Part of this Schedule, and

(b) which is not subject to any requirement that a draft of the instrument be laid before and approved by a resolution of each House of Parliament,

shall be subject to annulment in pursuance of a resolution of either House of Parliament.

SCHEDULE 4

TRANSITORY MODIFICATIONS

PART I

PROVISIONS NOT YET IN FORCE

Introductory

1.—(1) If—
(a) no date has been appointed as the date on which a provision mentioned in column 1 of the
    following Table is to come into force before 1st July 1992; or
(b) a date has been appointed which is later than 1st July 1992,
then the paragraph of this Schedule mentioned in column 2 of the Table opposite that provision
shall have effect until the appointed day.

TABLE

Provision	*Paragraph of this Schedule*
Paragraph 7(1)(b) of Schedule 8 to the Social Security Act 1986 (c. 50).	Paragraph 3.
The repeal in Schedule 11 to the Social Security Act 1986 of section 135(6) of the Social Security Act 1975 (c. 14).	Paragraph 19.
The repeal in Schedule 11 to the Social Security Act 1986 of paragraph 18 of Schedule 3 to the Social Security (Consequential Provisions) Act 1975 (c. 18).	Paragraph 20.
The repeal in Schedule 11 to the Social Security Act 1986 of the words "Subject to subsection (5A) below," in section 6(5) of the Social Security Pensions Act 1975 (c. 60).	Paragraph 2.
Section 5 of the Social Security Act 1988 (c. 7).	Paragraph 16.
Section 27 of the Social Security Act 1989 (c. 24).	Paragraph 13.
Paragraph 8(8) of Schedule 1 to the Social Security Act 1989.	Paragraphs 10 and 11.
The repeal in Schedule 9 to the Social Security Act 1989 of section 14(7) of the Social Security Act 1980 (c. 30).	Paragraph 12.
Paragraph 15 of Schedule 9 to the National Health Service and Community Care Act 1990 (c. 19).	Paragraph 5.
Section 9 of the Social Security Act 1990 (c. 27).	Paragraph 4.
Section 17(3) of the Social Security Act 1990.	Paragraph 17.
Section 17(4) of the Social Security Act 1990.	Paragraph 18.
Section 17(5) of the Social Security Act 1990.	Paragraph 6.
Section 17(6) of the Social Security Act 1990.	Paragraph 7.
Section 17(8) of the Social Security Act 1990.	Paragraph 8.
Section 17(9) of the Social Security Act 1990.	Paragraph 9.
Section 9(1) of the Maintenance Enforcement Act 1991 (c. 17).	Paragraph 14.
Section 9(2) of the Maintenance Enforcement Act 1991.	Paragraph 15.

(2) If—
(a) a date has been appointed as the date on which a provision mentioned in column 1 of the
    Table in sub-paragraph (1) is to come into force for some purposes of that provision but
    not for others; and
(b) that date is on or before 1st July 1992,
then the paragraph of this Schedule mentioned in column 2 of the Table opposite that provision
shall have effect for those other purposes of that provision (in so far as it is capable of doing so)
until the relevant appointed day.
(3) In this paragraph "the appointed day" means—
(a) in the case mentioned in paragraph (a) of sub-paragraph (1) above, such day as may be
    appointed by the Secretary of State by order made by statutory instrument; and
(b) in the case mentioned in paragraph (b) of that sub-paragraph, the day appointed as the
    day on which the provision mentioned in column 1 of the Table is to come into force.

(4) An order under sub-paragraph (3) above may appoint different days for different provisions or different purposes of the same provision.

(5) An order under sub-paragraph (3) above relating to paragraph 5 of this Schedule may—

(a) appoint different days for different purposes and for different areas or descriptions of area; and

(b) contain such transitional provisions and savings (whether or not involving the modification of any statutory provision) as appear to the Secretary of State necessary or expedient in connection with the order.

The Contributions and Benefits Act

2. At the beginning of subsection (6) of section 44 of the Contributions and Benefits Act there shall be inserted the words "Subject to subsection (7A) below".

3. The following subsection shall be inserted after subsection (7) of that section—

"(7A) The Secretary of State may prescribe circumstances in which pensioners' earnings factors for any relevant year may be calculated in such manner as may be prescribed.".

4. In section 135 of that Act subsections (3) and (4) shall be omitted.

5. In section 143(3)(c) of that Act the following sub-paragraphs shall be substituted for sub-paragraphs (i) to (iii)—

"(i) paragraph 2 of Schedule 8 to the National Health Service Act 1977;

(ii) the Children Act 1989; or

(iii) section 37 of the National Health Service (Scotland) Act 1978.".

6. In paragraph 6 of Schedule 1 to that Act sub-paragraphs (2) to (4) shall be omitted.

7. The following sub-paragraph shall be substituted for paragraph 6(8) of that Schedule—

"(8) The Inland Revenue shall, at such times, and in such manner as the Treasury may direct, account to the Secretary of State for, and pay to him, the sums estimated by the Inland Revenue, in such manner as may be so directed, to have been received by them as contributions in accordance with regulations made by virtue of this paragraph.".

8. The following sub-paragraph shall be substituted for paragraph 6(1) of Schedule 2 to that Act—

"(1) Section 88(1), (4) and (5)(a) and (b) of the Taxes Management Act 1970 (interest on tax recovered to make good loss due to taxpayer's fault) shall apply in relation to any amount due in respect of Class 4 contributions as it applies in relation to income tax; but section 86 of that Act (interest on amounts overdue) shall not apply.".

9. Paragraph 6(2) of that Schedule shall be omitted.

10. The following sub-paragraph shall be inserted after paragraph 11(12) of Schedule 7 to that Act—

"(12A) The reference in sub-paragraph (11) above to a person who has retired from regular employment includes a reference—

(a) to a person who under subsection (3) of section 27 of the 1975 Act was treated for the purposes of that Act as having retired from regular employment; and

(b) to a person who under subsection (5) of that section was deemed for those purposes to have retired from it.".

11. At the end of paragraph 12 of Schedule 7 to that Act there shall be inserted—

"(7) The reference in sub-paragraph (1) above to a person who has retired from regular employment includes a reference—

(a) to a person who under subsection (3) of section 27 of the 1975 Act was treated for the purposes of that Act as having retired from regular employment; and

(b) to a person who under subsection (5) of that section was deemed for those purposes to have retired from it.".

The Administration Act

12. In section 24 of the Administration Act—

(a) at the end of subsection (1) there shall be inserted the words "or given in consequence of a reference under section 112(4) of the 1975 Act (which enabled a medical appeal tribunal to refer a question of law to a Commissioner)"; and

(b) the following subsection shall be inserted after subsection (5)—

"(5A) In relation to a decision of a Commissioner which was given in consequence of a reference under section 112(4) of the 1975 Act subsections (3) and (5) of this section shall have effect with such modifications as may be prescribed by regulations.".

13. Section 104 of that Act shall be omitted.

14. Subsection (5) of section 107 of that Act shall be omitted.

15. Subsections (9) to (11) of that section shall be omitted.

16. Section 153 of that Act shall be omitted.

17. In section 162 of that Act subsection (4) shall be omitted.

18. In section 163 of that Act subsection (5) shall be omitted.

19. The following subsection shall be inserted at the end of section 164 of that Act—

"(7) Any sums repaid to the Secretary of State in pursuance of section 119(1) of the 1975 Act (which related to the effect of adjudication and was repealed subject to a saving in relation to certain reviews and appeals) shall—

(a) be paid by him into the Consolidated Fund in so far as they represent benefit which under section 163 above is payable out of money provided by Parliament and not out of the National Insurance fund; and

(b) otherwise, be paid by him into that Fund.".

This Act

20. In Schedule 3 to this Act—

(a) in the heading before paragraph 18 for the words "provision derived from" there shall be substituted the words "provisions derived from paragraph 18 of Schedule 3 to former Consequential Provisions Act and"; and

(b) the following paragraph shall be inserted after that heading—

"17A. In determining a woman's right—

(a) to a pension or allowance in respect of a deceased person under section 67, 68, 71, 72 or 73 of the 1975 Act; or

(b) to a pension in respect of a deceased person under paragraph 15 or 16 of Schedule 7 to the Contributions and Benefits Act,

for any period after 25th February 1962, or her right on her re-marriage after that date to a gratuity under section 67 of the 1975 Act, her cohabitation with a man at any time after the deceased's death but before that date shall be disregarded; but a right to benefit arising by virtue of this paragraph shall not, under Schedule 9 to that Act or Schedule 7 to the Contributions and Benefits Act, affect the right of any other persons to benefit awarded before that date.".

Part II

Other transitory modifications

Transition from mobility allowance to disability living allowance

21. In the application of subsection (2) of section 129 of the Contributions and Benefits Act to claims made or treated as made before the first day in respect of which disability living allowance is payable paragraph (b) of that subsection shall have effect as if the following sub-paragraph were substituted for sub-paragraph (ii)—

"(ii) a mobility allowance under section 37A of the 1975 Act;".

Amendment of Schedule 1 to the Attachment of Earnings Act 1971 (c. 32)

22. Until such time as there comes into force an amendment of Schedule 1 to the Attachment of Earnings Act 1971 (maintenance orders to which the Act applies) which has the effect of including among the orders specified in that Schedule any order for periodical or other payments made or having effect as if made under Schedule 1 to the Children Act 1989, the definition of "maintenance order" in section 107(15) of the Administration Act shall have effect as if, in paragraph (a), after sub-paragraph (ii) there were inserted—

"(iii) any order under paragraph 1(2)(a), (b) or (c) of Schedule 1 to the Children Act 1989 (financial provision for children against their parents);".

INDEX

References are to sections.

COMMENCEMENT, 7(2)
CONSEQUENTIAL AMENDMENTS, 4, Sched. 2
CONSOLIDATING ACTS,
   meaning of, 1
CONTINUITY OF THE LAW, 2

EXTENT, 7(3)–(8)

REPEALED ENACTMENTS, 3, Sched. 1
   meaning, 1

SAVINGS, 5(2)
SHORT TITLE, 7(1)

TRANSITIONAL PROVISIONS, 5(1), Sched. 3
TRANSITORY MODIFICATIONS, 6, Sched. 4

SOCIAL SECURITY CONTRIBUTIONS AND BENEFITS (NORTHERN IRELAND) ACT 1992*

(1992 c. 7)

ARRANGEMENT OF SECTIONS

PART I

CONTRIBUTIONS

Preliminary

SECT.
1. Outline of contributory system.
2. Categories of earners.
3. "Earnings" and "earner".
4. Payments treated as remuneration and earnings.

Class 1 contributions

5. Earnings limits for Class 1 contributions.
6. Liability for Class 1 contributions.
7. "Secondary contributor".
8. Calculation of primary Class 1 contributions.
9. Calculation of secondary Class 1 contributions.

Class 1A contributions

10. Class 1A contributions.

Class 2 contributions

11. Liability for Class 2 contributions.
12. Late paid Class 2 contributions.

Class 3 contributions

13. Class 3 contributions.
14. Restriction on right to pay Class 3 contributions.

Class 4 contributions

15. Class 4 contributions recoverable under the Income Tax Acts.
16. Destination of Class 4 contributions.
17. Exceptions, deferment and incidental matters relating to Class 4 contributions.
18. Class 4 contributions recoverable under regulations.

General

19. General power to regulate liability for contributions.

PART II

CONTRIBUTORY BENEFITS

Preliminary

20. Descriptions of contributory benefits.
21. Contribution conditions.
22. Earnings factors.
23. Provisions supplemental to ss.21 and 22.
24. Records of earnings and calculation of earnings factors in absence of records.

Unemployment benefit

25. Unemployment benefit.

---

* Annotations by Ray Geary, LL.B., LL.M., Laura Lundy, LL.B., both Lecturers in Law, Queen's University of Belfast, and N. J. Wikeley, M.A. (Cantab.), Barrister, Lecturer in Law, University of Birmingham.

26. Duration of unemployment benefit.
27. Interruption of employment in connection with trade dispute.
28. Unemployment benefit—other disqualifications, etc.
29. Exemptions from disqualification for unemployment benefit.
30. Abatement of unemployment benefit on account of payments of occupational or personal pension.

Sickness benefit

31. Sickness benefit.
32. Sickness benefit—disqualifications, etc.

Invalidity benefits

33. Invalidity pension.
34. Invalidity allowance.

Maternity

35. State maternity allowance.

Benefits for widows and widowers

36. Widow's payment.
37. Widowed mother's allowance.
38. Widow's pension.
39. Rate of widowed mother's allowance and widow's pension.
40. Invalidity pension for widows.
41. Invalidity pension for widowers.
42. Entitlement to invalidity pension on termination of employment after period of entitlement to disability working allowance.

Retirement pensions (Categories A and B)

43. Persons entitled to more than one retirement pension.
44. Category A retirement pension.
45. The additional pension in a Category A retirement pension.
46. Modifications of s.45 for calculating the additional pension in certain benefits.
47. Increase of Category A retirement pension for invalidity.
48. Use of former spouse's contributions.
49. Category B retirement pension for women.
50. Rate of Category B retirement pension for women.
51. Category B retirement pension for widowers.
52. Special provision for surviving spouses.
53. Special provision for married women.
54. Category A and Category B retirement pensions: supplemental provisions.
55. Increase of retirement pension where entitlement is deferred.

Child's special allowance

56. Child's special allowance—existing beneficiaries.

Provisions relating to unemployment benefit, sickness benefit and invalidity benefit

57. Determination of days for which benefit is payable.
58. Incapacity for work: work as councillor to be disregarded.

Invalidity benefit—disqualifications, etc.

59. Invalidity benefit—disqualifications, etc.

Partial satisfaction of contribution conditions

60. Partial satisfaction of contribution conditions.
61. Exclusion of increase of benefit for failure to satisfy contribution condition.

Graduated retirement benefit

62. Graduated retirement benefit.

PART III

NON-CONTRIBUTORY BENEFITS

63. Descriptions of non-contributory benefits.

Attendance allowance

64. Entitlement.
65. Period and rate of allowance.
66. Attendance allowance for the terminally ill.
67. Exclusions by regulation.

Severe disablement allowance

68. Entitlement and rate.
69. Severe disablement allowance: age related addition.

Invalid care allowance

70. Invalid care allowance.

Disability living allowance

71. Disability living allowance.
72. The care component.
73. The mobility component.
74. Mobility component for certain persons eligible for invalid carriages.
75. Persons 65 or over.
76. Disability living allowance—supplementary.

Guardian's allowance

77. Guardian's allowance.

Benefits for the aged

78. Category C and Category D retirement pensions and other benefits for the aged.
79. Age addition.

PART IV

INCREASES FOR DEPENDANTS

Child dependants

80. Beneficiary's dependent children.
81. Restrictions on increase—child not living with beneficiary, etc.

Adult dependants

82. Short-term benefit: increase for adult dependants.
83. Pension increase (wife).
84. Pension increase (husband).
85. Pension increase (person with care of children).
86. Increase of woman's invalidity pension (husband).
87. Rate of increase where associated retirement pension is attributable to reduced contributions.
88. Pension increases to be in respect of only one adult dependant.

Miscellaneous

89. Earnings to include occupational and personal pensions for purposes of provisions relating to increases of benefits in respect of child or adult dependants.
90. Beneficiaries under sections 68 and 70.
91. Effect of trade disputes on entitlement to increases.
92. Dependency increases: continuation of awards in cases of fluctuating earnings.
93. Dependency increases on termination of employment after period of entitlement to disability working allowance.

PART V

BENEFIT FOR INDUSTRIAL INJURIES

General provisions

94. Right to industrial injuries benefit.
95. Relevant employments.
96. Persons treated as employers for certain purposes.
97. Accidents in course of illegal employments.
98. Earner acting in breach of regulations, etc.
99. Earner travelling in employer's transport.
100. Accidents happening while meeting emergency.
101. Accident caused by another's misconduct, etc.

Sickness benefit

102. Sickness benefit in respect of industrial injury.

Disablement pension

103. Disablement pension.
104. Increase where constant attendance needed.
105. Increase for exceptionally severe disablement.

Other benefits and increases

106. Benefits and increases subject to qualifications as to time.

Successive accidents

107. Adjustments for successive accidents.

Prescribed industrial diseases, etc.

108. Benefit in respect of prescribed industrial diseases, etc.
109. General provisions relating to benefit under s.108.
110. Respiratory diseases.

Old cases

111. Workmen's compensation, etc.

PART VI

MISCELLANEOUS PROVISIONS RELATING TO PARTS I TO V

Earnings

112. Certain sums to be earnings.

Disqualification and suspension

113. General provisions as to disqualification and suspension.

Persons maintaining dependants, etc.

114. Persons maintaining dependants, etc.

Special cases

115. Crown employment—Parts I to VI.
116. Her Majesty's forces.
117. Mariners, airmen, etc.
118. Married women and widows.
119. Persons outside Northern Ireland.
120. Treatment of certain marriages.

Interpretation

121. Interpretation of Parts I to VI and supplementary provisions.

Part VII

Income-Related Benefits

General

122. Income-related benefits.

Income support

123. Income support.
124. Severe hardship cases.
125. Trade disputes.
126. Effect of return to work.

Family credit

127. Family credit.

Disability working allowance

128. Disability working allowance.

Housing benefit

129. Housing benefit.

General

130. Exclusions from benefit.
131. The applicable amount.
132. Income and capital.
133. Interpretation of Part VII and supplementary provisions.

Part VIII

The Social Fund

134. Payments out of the social fund.
135. Awards by social fund officers.
136. Principles of determination.

Part IX

Child Benefit

137. Child benefit.
138. Meaning of "child".
139. Meaning of "person responsible for child".
140. Exclusions and priority.
141. Rate of child benefit.
142. Persons outside Northern Ireland.
143. Interpretation of Part IX and supplementary provisions.

Part X

Christmas bonus for pensioners

144. Entitlement of pensioners to Christmas bonus.
145. Provisions supplementary to s.144.
146. Interpretation of Part X.

Part XI

Statutory Sick Pay

147. Employer's liability.

The qualifying conditions

148. Period of incapacity for work.
149. Period of entitlement.
150. Qualifying days.

Limitations on entitlement, etc.

151. Limitations on entitlement.
152. Notification of incapacity for work.

Rate of payment, etc.

153. Rate of payment.
154. Recovery by employers of amounts paid by way of statutory sick pay.
155. Power to substitute provisions for s.154(2).

Miscellaneous

156. Relationship with benefits and other payments, etc.
157. Crown employment—Part XI.
158. Special classes of persons.
159. Interpretation of Part XI and supplementary provisions.

PART XII

STATUTORY MATERNITY PAY

160. Statutory maternity pay—entitlement and liability to pay.
161. The maternity pay period.
162. Rates of payment.
163. Recovery of amounts paid by way of statutory maternity pay.
164. Relationship with benefits and other payments, etc.
165. Crown employment—Part XII.
166. Special classes of persons.
167. Interpretation of Part XII, etc.

PART XIII

GENERAL

Interpretation

168. Application of Act in relation to territorial waters.
169. Age.
170. Interpretation.

Subordinate legislation

171. Regulations and orders—general.
172. Assembly, etc. control of regulations and orders.

Supplementary

173. Short title, commencement and extent.

SCHEDULES:
Schedule 1—Supplementary provisions relating to contributions of Classes 1, 1A, 2 and 3.
Schedule 2—Schedule 2 to the Social Security Contributions and Benefits Act 1992: levy of Class 4 contributions with income tax.
Schedule 3—Contribution conditions for entitlement to benefit.
   Part I—The conditions.
   Part II—Satisfaction of conditions in early years of contribution.
Schedule 4—Rates of benefits, etc.
   Part I—Contributory periodical benefits.
   Part II—Widow's payment.

Part III—Non-contributory periodical benefits.
Part IV—Increases for dependants.
Part V—Rate of industrial injuries benefit.
Schedule 5—Increase of pension where entitlement is deferred.
Schedule 6—Assessment of extent of disablement.
Schedule 7—Industrial injuries benefits.
    Part I—Unemployability supplement.
    Part II—Disablement gratuity.
    Part III—Increase of disablement pension during hospital treatment.
    Part IV—Reduced earnings allowance.
    Part V—Retirement allowance.
    Part VI—Industrial death benefit.
Schedule 8—Industrial injuries and diseases (old cases).
    Part I—Workmen's compensation and industrial diseases benefit in respect of
        employment before 5th July 1948.
    Part II—Regulations providing for benefit for pre-1948 cases.
    Part III—Interpretation.
Schedule 9—Exclusions from entitlement to child benefit.
Schedule 10—Priority between persons entitled to child benefit.
Schedule 11—Circumstances in which periods of entitlement to statutory sick pay do
      not arise.
Schedule 12—Relationship of statutory sick pay with benefits and other payments, etc.
Schedule 13—Relationship of statutory maternity pay with benefits and other pay-
      ments, etc.

An Act to consolidate for Northern Ireland certain enactments relating to social security contributions and benefits, with corrections and minor improvements under the Consolidation of Enactments (Procedure) Act 1949.   **[13th February 1992]**

PARLIAMENTARY DEBATES
Hansard, H.L. Vol. 534, col. 1489; Vol. 535, cols. 240, 348.

INTRODUCTION AND GENERAL NOTE

The consolidation of social security law has been long overdue. The Social Security Contributions and Benefits (Northern Ireland) Act 1992 is one of three statutes which seeks to achieve this objective so far as Northern Ireland is concerned. This Act deals with the contributions on which certain benefits depend, and the primary legislation governing individual benefits. The Social Security Administration (Northern Ireland) Act 1992 covers such matters as claims for, and payments of, benefit, adjudication, appeals, enforcement and uprating. The Social Security (Consequential Provisions) (Northern Ireland) Act 1992 contains repeals, consequential and transitional provisions arising out of the other two Acts. The Social Security (Northern Ireland) Act 1975 is repealed in its entirety, as are the Child Benefit (Northern Ireland) Order 1975 (S.I. 1975 No. 1504 (N.I. 16)) and the Social Security (Contributions) (Northern Ireland) Orders of 1981 (S.I. 1981 No. 230 (N.I. 16)), 1982 (S.I. 1982 No. 158 (N.I. 4)) and 1991 (S.I. 1991 No. 2294 (N.I. 22)). There are substantial repeals of the Social Security (Northern Ireland) Orders 1979 (S.I. 1979 No. 396 (N.I. 5)), 1980 (S.I. 1980 No. 870 (N.I. 8)), 1985 (S.I. 1985 No. 1209 (N.I. 16)), 1986 (S.I. 1986 No. 1888 (N.I. 18)), 1988 (S.I. 1988 No. 594 (N.I. 2)), 1989 (S.I. 1989 No. 1342 (N.I. 13)) and 1990 (S.I. 1990 No. 1511 (N.I. 15)). Three further Acts deal with Great Britain (see General Note to s.173).

The Law Commission and the Scottish Law Commission's report on the consolidating legislation was published in November 1991 (Cm. 1726).

There is a presumption that Parliament, in enacting consolidating legislation, does not intend to alter the existing law. Furthermore, in interpreting a consolidating Act, reference should only be made to legislative antecedents if the words are unclear (*Farrell* v. *Alexander* [1977] A.C. 59; see also *Morton* v. *Chief Adjudication Officer* [1988] I.R.L.R. 444 on the construction of consolidating regulations). Decisions of the Social Security Commissioners and the courts on the earlier provisions will still be precedents. Some of the most important authorities are mentioned in these annotations, but, for a full analysis of this complex area of law, reference should be made to the latest annual edition of Bonner, Mesher, Findlay and Ward or Rowland as appropriate (see below). This is especially important given the frequent changes to regulations.

[*N.B.* Unless otherwise stated (*i.e.* stated to be decisions of the Northern Ireland Commissioners), references to commissioners' decisions are to decisions of the Great Britain Commissioners. These are frequently cited in the Northern Ireland Tribunals and are considered to be highly persuasive but not binding].

COMMENCEMENT
The Act came into force on July 1, 1992, subject to the modifications contained in the Social Security (Consequential Provisions) (Northern Ireland) Act 1992, Sched. 4 (s.173(4)).

ABBREVIATIONS

AO	:	adjudication officer
BNIL	:	Bulletin of Northern Ireland Law
Bonner	:	*Non-Means Tested Benefits: The Legislation*, by D. Bonner, I. Hooker and R. White
DLADWAO 1991	:	Disability Living Allowance and Disability Working Allowance (Northern Ireland) Order 1991 (S.I. 1991 No. 1712 (N.I. 17))
DHSS	:	Department of Health and Social Security
Findlay and Ward	:	*CPAG's Housing Benefit and Community Charge Legislation*, by L. Findlay and M. Ward
ICTA	:	Income and Corporation Taxes Act 1988
Lewis	:	*Compensation for Industrial Injury* (1987)
Mesher	:	*CPAG's Income Support, The Social Fund and Family Credit: The Legislation*, by J. Mesher
Ogus and Barendt	:	*The Law of Social Security* (3rd ed., 1988)
Rowland	:	*Medical and Disability Appeal Tribunals: The Legislation*, by M. Rowland
Secretary of State	:	Secretary of State for Social Security
SERPS	:	State earnings-related pension scheme
SS(N.I.)A 1975	:	Social Security (Northern Ireland) Act 1975
SS(N.I.)O 1982	:	Social Security (Northern Ireland) Order 1982 (S.I. 1982 No. 1084 (N.I. 16))
SS(N.I.)O 1986	:	Social Security (Northern Ireland) Order 1986 (S.I. 1986 No. 1888 (N.I. 18))
SS(N.I.)O 1988	:	Social Security (Northern Ireland) Order 1988 (S.I. 1988 No. 594 (N.I. 2))
SS(N.I.)O 1989	:	Social Security (Northern Ireland) Order 1989 (S.I. 1989 No. 1342 (N.I. 13))
SS(N.I.)O 1990	:	Social Security (Northern Ireland) Order 1990 (S.I. 1990 No. 1511 (N.I. 15))
SSA(N.I.)A 1992	:	Social Security Administration (Northern Ireland) Act 1992
SS(CP)(N.I.)A 1992	:	Social Security (Consequential Provisions) (Northern Ireland) Act 1992
SSP(N.I.)O 1975	:	Social Security Pensions (Northern Ireland) Order 1975 (S.I. 1975 No. 1503 (N.I. 15))
SSP(N.I.)O 1991	:	Statutory Sick Pay (Northern Ireland) Order 1991 (S.I. 1991 No. 765 (N.I. 9))
SSAT	:	social security appeal tribunal
The Way Ahead	:	*The Way Ahead: Benefits for Disabled People* (Cm. 917, 1990)
Williams	:	*National Insurance Contributions, Statutory Sick Pay and Statutory Maternity Pay* (1987, looseleaf)

PART I

CONTRIBUTIONS

Preliminary

Outline of contributory system

1.—(1) The funds required—
  (a) for paying such benefits under this Act as are payable out of the National Insurance Fund and not out of other public money; and
  (b) for the making of payments under section 142 of the Administration Act towards the cost of the health service,

shall be provided by means of contributions payable to the Department by earners, employers and others, together with the additions under subsection (5) below.

(2) Contributions under this Part of this Act shall be of the following five classes—

    (a) Class 1, earnings-related, payable under section 6 below, being—

        (i) primary Class 1 contributions from employed earners; and

        (ii) secondary Class 1 contributions from employers and other persons paying earnings;

    (b) Class 1A, payable under section 10 below in respect of cars made available for private use and car fuel by persons liable to pay secondary Class 1 contributions and certain other persons;

    (c) Class 2, flat-rate, payable weekly under section 11 below by self-employed earners;

    (d) Class 3, payable under section 13 below by earners and others voluntarily with a view to providing entitlement to benefit, or making up entitlement; and

    (e) Class 4, payable under section 15 below in respect of the profits or gains of a trade, profession or vocation, or under section 18 below in respect of equivalent earnings.

(3) The amounts and rates of contributions in this Part of this Act and the other figures in it which affect the liability of contributors shall—

    (a) be subject to regulations under sections 19(4) and 116 to 119 below; and

    (b) to the extent provided provided for by section 129 of the Administration Act be subject to alteration by orders made under that section,

and the provisions of this Part of this Act are subject to the provisions of Part IV of the Pensions Order (contracting-out—reduced rates of contributions).

(4) Schedule 1 to this Act—

    (a) shall have effect with respect to the computation, collection and recovery of contributions of Classes 1, 1A, 2 and 3, and otherwise with respect to contributions of those classes; and

    (b) shall also, to the extent provided by regulations made under section 18 below, have effect with respect to the computation, collection and recovery of Class 4 contributions, and otherwise with respect to such contributions, where under that section provision is made for contributions of that class to be recovered by the Department and not by the Inland Revenue under section 16(1) to (3) of the Great Britain Contributions and Benefits Act.

(5) For each financial year there shall, by way of addition to contributions, be paid out of money hereafter appropriated for that purpose, in such manner and at such times as the Department of Finance and Personnel may determine, amounts the total of which for any such year is equal to the aggregate of all statutory sick pay and statutory maternity pay recovered by employers and others in that year, as estimated by the Department.

(6) No person shall—

    (a) be liable to pay Class 1, Class 1A or Class 2 contributions unless he fulfils prescribed conditions as to residence or presence in Northern Ireland;

    (b) be entitled to pay Class 3 contributions unless he fulfils such conditions; or

    (c) be entitled to pay Class 1, Class 1A or Class 2 contributions other than those which he is liable to pay, except so far as he is permitted by regulations to pay them.

DEFINITIONS
"the Administration Act": s.170.
"benefit": s.121(1).

"earner": ss.3(1) and 121(1).
"employed earner": ss.2(1) and 121(1).
"Northern Ireland": s.168.
"Inland Revenue": s.121(1).
"the Pensions Act": s.170.
"prescribe": s.121(1).
"self-employed earner": ss.2(1) and 121(1).

GENERAL NOTE

The basic structure of the National Insurance scheme was established in its present form as from April 6, 1975. Since then it has been subject to frequent amendment (see Report by the Government Actuary, National Insurance Fund Long Term Financial Estimates (H.C. 582, Session 1989–90)). The National Insurance Fund is used principally to pay contributory benefits, but allocations are also made to the National Health Service (subs. (1)(b)). The cost of providing industrial injuries benefits, statutory sick pay and statutory maternity pay was transferred from the National Insurance Fund to general taxation by SS(N.I.)O 1990, art. 18. In the case of the latter two benefits this actually operates by way of a transfer of the appropriate sums from the Consolidated Fund to the National Insurance Fund (subs. (5)). The Redundancy Fund was merged with the National Insurance Fund by the Redundancy Fund (Abolition) (Northern Ireland) Order 1991 (S.I. 1991 No. 196 (N.I. 2)), art. 3.

The finances of the National Insurance Fund (excluding investment income) are derived from two sources: insured persons (either employees or self-employed persons) and employers (subs. (1)). The Exchequer contribution was abolished by SS(N.I.)O 1989, art. 5. On the administration of the Fund, see SSA(N.I.)A 1992, Pt. XI.

There are now five classes of contributions (subs. (2)):

Class 1: earnings-related contributions by employed earners (primary Class 1 contributions) and their employers (secondary Class 1 contributions): ss.5–9.

Class 1A: graduated contributions by employers in respect of cars and fuel provided to directors and certain employees where private use is allowed: s.10.

Class 2: flat-rate contributions from self-employed earners: ss.11 and 12.

Class 3: voluntary flat-rate contributions by earners and others: ss.13 and 14.

Class 4: contributions from self-employed earners payable on profits or gains: ss.15–18.

The National Insurance Fund is financed on a pay-as-you-go basis with the contribution rates set from year to year so as to generate the income required to meet current expenditure on benefits and administration costs (subs. (3)).

Regulations made under subs. (3) also enable special provision to be made for married women and widows, members of H.M. forces, mariners and airmen, etc., persons outside Northern Ireland and those employed at sea.

Further detailed provision is made in Sched. 1 and in the Social Security (Contributions) (Northern Ireland) Regulations 1979 (S.I. 1979 No. 186).

Categories of earners

2.—(1) In this Part of this Act and Parts II to V—

(a) "employed earner" means a person who is gainfully employed in Northern Ireland either under a contract of service, or in an office (including elective office) with emoluments chargeable to income tax under Schedule E; and

(b) "self-employed earner" means a person who is gainfully employed in Northern Ireland otherwise than in employed earner's employment (whether or not he is also employed in such employment).

(2) Regulations may provide—

(a) for employment of any prescribed description to be disregarded in relation to liability for contributions otherwise arising from employment of that description;

(b) for a person in employment of any prescribed description to be treated, for the purposes of this Act, as falling within one or other of the categories of earner defined in subsection (1) above, notwithstanding that he would not fall within that category apart from the regulations.

(3) Where a person is to be treated by reference to any employment of his as an employed earner, then he is to be so treated for all purposes of this Act;

and references throughout this Act to employed earner's employment shall be construed accordingly.

(4) Subsections (1) to (3) above are subject to the provision made by section 95 below as to the employments which are to be treated, for the purposes of industrial injuries benefit, as employed earner's employments.

(5) For the purposes of this Act, a person shall be treated as a self-employed earner as respects any week during any part of which he is such an earner (without prejudice to his being also treated as an employed earner as respects that week by reference to any other employment of his).

DEFINITIONS
"contract of service": s.121(1).
"Department": s.170.
"earner": ss.3(1) and 121(1).
"employed earner": subs. (1).
"employment": s.121(1).
"industrial injuries benefit": s.121(1).
"Northern Ireland": s.168.
"self-employed earner": s.121(1).
"week": s.121(1).

GENERAL NOTE
This section seeks to define the concepts of an "employed earner" and a "self-employed earner". This is primarily important for ascertaining an individual's liability to pay contributions in any given class.

Subs. (1)
The distinction between an employed earner and a self-employed earner is fundamental to the National Insurance scheme. Employed earners are liable to pay Class 1 contributions and may qualify for all contributory benefits. Self-employed earners are liable to pay Class 2 contributions (and those for Class 4 where profits or gains exceed the relevant threshold) and are eligible for all contributory benefits except unemployment benefit (s.21(2)). The decision on classification of an individual's working status is one for the Department, not the usual independent statutory adjudicating authorities. A question of law arising from such a decision may be referred for final determination to the Court of Appeal: SSA(N.I.)A 1992, ss.15 and 16.

Employed earner. There are two types of employed earners: those gainfully employed under a contract of service, and those gainfully employed in an office with emoluments chargeable to income tax under Sched. E. Each of these three terms merits separate treatment.

Gainfully employed. Earlier legislation used the concept of being "gainfully occupied". The significance of the change in terminology in 1975 is not entirely clear, but it appears that the meaning of the phrase remains substantially unchanged. In the context of the definition of employed earner the term is probably otiose. It may, however, have some significance in the definition of self-employed earner, as a self-employed earner who has recently become "gainfully employed" may voluntarily contribute even if not currently liable to contribute. See further *Vandyk* v. *Minister of Pensions and National Insurance* [1955] 1 Q.B. 29.

Contract of service. The distinction between a contract of service and a contract for services is much litigated in various spheres of law. The definition of contract of service proffered by s.121(1) is only of very limited assistance, and so guidance must be sought from the case law. The preferred view of the courts today, in determining whether a contractual relationship is properly characterised as a contract of service or for services, is that account must be taken of a whole range of factors, no one of which is conclusive. Furthermore, the significance of any one factor may vary as it may have different weight attached to it in different cases. This is sometimes known as the "multiple factors" test: *Ready Mixed Concrete South East* v. *Minister of Pensions and National Insurance* [1968] 2 Q.B. 497. This approach was approved in the Northern Ireland decision, *Maguire* v. *P.L. Lagan Contractors* [1976] N.I. 49, O'Donnell L.J.

Relevant considerations will usually include: closeness of supervision of work, powers of appointment and dismissal, form of remuneration, duration of contract, responsibility for equipment, place of work, mutuality of obligations and discretion as to hours of work. Sometimes the courts resort to the "economic reality" test, which appears to be shorthand for the multiple factors test, *i.e.* "is the worker in business on his or her own account?" (see *Lee Ting Sang* v. *Chung Chi-Keung* [1990] A.C. 374).

Extensive case law exists for Great Britain in this area. For further comment see the Social Security Contributions and Benefits Act 1992 (c. 4), s.2 in Current Law Statutes Annotated.

Office. This alternative basis for categorisation as an employed earner was introduced in 1973 in order to simplify the collection of contributions by correlating Class 1 contributors with Sched. E taxpayers. On the meaning of office-holder, see *Edwards (Inspector of Taxes)* v. *Clinch* [1982] A.C. 845.

Self-employed earner. This negatively-framed formulation defines self-employed earners as all those persons who are gainfully employed (see above) in Northern Ireland otherwise than under a contract of service or in an office (including elective office) with emoluments chargeable to income tax under Sched. E (s.2(1)). Persons will be regarded as self-employed for Class 2 purposes if they are self-employed for any part of a week, even just one day (subs. (5)).

Further provision in connection with self-employed earners is made by the Social Security (Categorisation of Earners) Regulations (Northern Ireland) 1978 (S.I. 1978 No. 401). For a detailed analysis of this concept, see Williams.

Subs. (2)

This enables the Department to shift particular groups of earners from one class of contributors to another by provisions in regulations. This power has been extensively used: see Social Security (Categorisation of Earners) Regulations (Northern Ireland) 1978 (S.I. 1978 No. 401). Some employments are treated as Class 1 occupations (*e.g.* office cleaners, certain part-time lecturers, teachers and instructors, etc.) where they might otherwise be characterised as falling within Class 2.

Other forms of employment are disregarded, *i.e.* excluded from Classes 1 or 2 (*e.g.* self-employment, where it is not the person's ordinary occupation).

Subs. (4)

The concept of "employed earner's employment" is modified in certain respects for the purposes of industrial injuries benefits by virtue of s.95: see further Social Security (Employed Earners' Employments for Industrial Injuries Purposes) Regulations (Northern Ireland) 1975 (S.I. 1975 No. 90).

"Earnings" and "earner"

3.—(1) In this Part of this Act and Parts II to V—
  (a) "earnings" includes any remuneration or profit derived from an employment; and
  (b) "earner" shall be construed accordingly.
(2) For the purposes of this Part of this Act and of Parts II to V other than those of Schedule 8—
  (a) the amount of a person's earnings for any period; or
  (b) the amount of his earnings to be treated as comprised in any payment made to him or for his benefit,
shall be calculated or estimated in such manner and on such basis as may be prescribed.

(3) Regulations made for the purposes of subsection (2) above may prescribe that payments of a particular class or description made or falling to be made to or by a person shall, to such extent as may be prescribed, be disregarded or, as the case may be, be deducted from the amount of that person's earnings.

DEFINITIONS
  "earner": subs. (1).
  "earnings": subs. (1).
  "employment": s.121(1).
  "prescribe": s.121(1).

GENERAL NOTE

The concept of "earnings" is important in two ways in the social security scheme. First, it is relevant for calculating the appropriate level of National Insurance contributions. Secondly, it is necessary in order to determine entitlement to certain benefits (*e.g.* for increases of benefit for dependants). In either case the starting point under this section is that earnings are computed on the basis of the individual's gross remuneration from his or her employment(s) (subs. (1)). "Employment" itself is defined as "any trade, business, profession, office or vocation" (s.121(1)).

The underlying distinction is between income which is derived from an employment in this broad sense, and payments which the individual receives in some other capacity. Thus earnings include any payments received in connection with an employment. These include directors' fees, even if the duties involved are very limited (*R(G) 14/56*), and allowances paid to councillors (*R(P) 2/76*). See also Northern Ireland decision *R2/79(UB)*. Genuinely *ex gratia* payments do not constitute earnings (*R(P) 4/67*), but further income from the same source may be regarded as earnings, especially where it has been the subject of income tax relief (*R(P) 1/69*). Income received by an individual as a shareholder does not count as earnings (*R(P) 22/64*). The same principle would apply to other investment income.

The calculation of earnings is based on the sums which the individual is entitled to receive in respect of a given period, not those actually received (*R(P) 5/53*). On the calculation of earnings from self-employment, see *R(U) 3/88*.

Further provision on the calculation of earnings is made by s.4. The concept of earnings is also modified by the Social Security Benefit (Computation of Earnings) Regulations (Northern Ireland) 1978 (S.I. 1978 No. 371), made under subs. (2). These provide for certain permissible deductions from earnings (*e.g.* expenses incurred in connection with employment and National Insurance contributions, but not income tax). The regulations also allow for certain disregards (*e.g.* the value of meals provided at the place of work) and deal with situations in which earnings cannot be immediately ascertained.

Payments treated as remuneration and earnings

4.—(1) For the purposes of section 3 above there shall be treated as remuneration derived from employed earner's employment—

   (a) any sum paid to or for the benefit of a person in satisfaction (whether in whole or in part) of any entitlement of that person to—
      (i) statutory sick pay; or
      (ii) statutory maternity pay; and
   (b) any sickness payment made—
      (i) to or for the benefit of the employed earner; and
      (ii) in accordance with arrangements under which the person who is the secondary contributor in relation to the employment concerned has made, or remains liable to make, payments towards the provision of that sickness payment.

(2) Where the funds for making sickness payments under arrangements of the kind mentioned in paragraph (b) of subsection (1) above are attributable in part to contributions to those funds made by the employed earner, regulations may make provision for disregarding, for the purposes of that subsection, the prescribed part of any sum paid as a result of the arrangements.

(3) For the purposes of subsections (1) and (2) above "sickness payment" means any payment made in respect of absence from work due to incapacity for work, within the meaning of section 57 below.

(4) For the purposes of section 3 above there shall be treated as remuneration derived from an employed earner's employment any sum paid to or for the benefit of an employed earner which is chargeable to tax by virtue of section 313 of the Income and Corporation Taxes Act 1988 (taxation of consideration for certain restrictive undertakings) otherwise than by virtue of subsection (4) of that section.

(5) For the purposes of section 3 above regulations may make provision for treating as remuneration derived from an employed earner's employment any payment made by a body corporate to or for the benefit of any of its directors where that payment would, when made, not be earnings for the purposes of this Act.

Definitions
   "employed earner": ss.2(1) and 121(1).
   "employment": s.121(1).
   "prescribe": s.121(1).
   "sickness payment": subs. (3).

GENERAL NOTE

Further to the general definition in s.3, earnings include statutory maternity pay and both statutory and contractual sick pay (subs. (1)). Earnings also include payments on termination of certain employments which represent consideration for entering into restrictive undertakings chargeable to income tax under ICTA 1988, s.313 (subs. (4)). This allows Class 1 contributions to be levied on such payments.

Class 1 contributions

Earnings limits for Class 1 contributions

5.—(1) For the purposes of this Act there shall for every tax year be—

(a) a lower earnings limit for Class 1 contributions, being the level of weekly earnings at which employed earners become liable for such contributions in respect of the earnings from their employments; and

(b) an upper earnings limit for Class 1 contributions, being the maximum amount of weekly earnings in respect of which primary Class 1 contributions are payable;

and those limits shall be the amounts specified for that year by regulations made in accordance with subsections (2) and (3) below.

(2) The amount specified as the lower earnings limit for any tax year shall be an amount equal to or not more than 99p less than—

(a) the sum which at the beginning of that year is specified in section 44(4) below as the weekly rate of the basic pension in a Category A retirement pension; or

(b) that sum as increased by any Act, Measure or order passed, enacted or made before the beginning of that year and taking effect before 6th May in that year.

(3) The amount specified as the upper earnings limit for any tax year shall be an amount which either—

(a) is equal to 7 times the sum by reference to which the lower earnings limit for that year is specified in accordance with subsection (2) above; or

(b) exceeds or falls short of 7 times that sum by an amount not exceeding half that sum.

DEFINITIONS

"earnings": ss.3(1) and 121(1).
"employed earner": ss.2(1) and 121(1).
"employment": s.121(1).
"lower earnings limit": subs. (1)(a).
"tax year": s.121(1).
"upper earnings limit": subs. (1)(b).

GENERAL NOTE

Class 1 contributions (and those for other classes) are paid on the basis of the tax year (*e.g.* April 6, 1992–April 5, 1993: s.121(1)). For the purpose of Class 1 contributions, weekly lower and upper earnings limits are laid down for each tax year (subs. (1)). The lower earnings limit represents a threshold for contributions to the National Insurance scheme. It was originally set under the Social Security Act 1973 at a figure approximately equal to one-quarter of national average male industrial earnings (Williams, Social Security Taxation (1982), p. 90). The upper earnings limit represents a ceiling in that currently employees do not pay contributions on income in excess of that prescribed maximum. The lower earnings limit for any tax year must be set at a level equivalent to (or not more than 99p less than) the standard Category A retirement pension (subs. (2)). The upper earnings limit for any tax year must be set at a level which is between 6½ and 7½ times the lower earnings limit (subs. (3)). For further details on liability for Class 1 contributions, see ss.6–9.

Liability for Class 1 contributions

6.—(1) Where in any tax week earnings are paid to or for the benefit of an earner in respect of any one employment of his which is employed earner's employment and—

(a) he is over the age of 16; and

(b) the amount paid is equal to or exceeds the current lower earnings limit for Class 1 contributions (or the prescribed equivalent in the case of earners paid otherwise than weekly),

a primary and a secondary Class 1 contribution shall be payable in accordance with this section and sections 8 and 9 below.

(2) Except as may be prescribed, no primary Class 1 contribution shall be payable in respect of earnings paid to or for the benefit of an employed earner after he attains pensionable age, but without prejudice to any liability to pay secondary Class 1 contributions in respect of any such earnings.

(3) The primary and secondary Class 1 contributions referred to in subsection (1) above are payable as follows—

(a) the primary contribution shall be the liability of the earner; and

(b) the secondary contribution shall be the liability of the secondary contributor;

but nothing in this subsection shall prejudice the provisions of paragraph 3 of Schedule 1 to this Act relating to the manner in which the earner's liability falls to be discharged.

(4) Except as provided by this Act, the primary and secondary Class 1 contributions in respect of earnings paid to or for the benefit of an earner in respect of any one employment of his shall be payable without regard to any other such payment of earnings in respect of any other employment of his.

(5) Regulations may provide for reducing primary or secondary Class 1 contributions which are payable in respect of persons to whom section 11 of the Contracts of Employment and Redundancy Payments Act (Northern Ireland) 1965 (redundancy payments) does not apply by virtue of section 26(1) or (5) of that Act.

(6) The power conferred by subsection (1) above to prescribe an equivalent of the lower earnings limit includes power to prescribe an amount which exceeds, by not more than £1.00, the amount which is the arithmetical equivalent of that limit.

DEFINITIONS

"current": s.121(1).
"earner": ss.3(1) and 121(1).
"earnings": ss.3(1) and 121(1).
"employed earner": ss.2(1) and 121(1).
"employment": s.121(1).
"lower earnings limit": ss.5(1)(a) and 121(1).
"pensionable age": s.121(1).
"prescribe": s.121(1).
"secondary contributor": s.7(1).
"tax week": s.121(1).

GENERAL NOTE

Liability to pay Class 1 contributions only arises where an employed earner is aged 16 or over (but under pensionable age: subs. (2)) and has earnings in excess of the current lower earnings limit (subs. (1)). Where these conditions are met, the employed earner is liable to pay primary Class 1 contributions (subs. (3) and s.8) and the employer (technically the "secondary contributor": see s.7) is responsible for secondary Class 1 contributions (subs. (3) and s.9). Where earners are paid otherwise than weekly, regulations detail equivalent figures for the lower and upper earnings limits (and see subs. (6)).

In practice the employer is responsible for the collection and payment over of contributions (Sched. 1, para. 3). Although an employed earner who has attained pensionable age is not liable for primary Class 1 contributions, the employer must pay secondary Class 1 contributions (subs. (2)).

Where a person has two or more employed earner's employments (or offices), for which there are separate secondary contributors, a liability arises to pay Class 1 contributions in respect of each employment, irrespective of the existence of the other employment(s) (subs. (4)). There are, however, rules which mitigate the overpayment of contributions in cases of multiple employments: see Social Security (Contributions) Regulations (Northern Ireland) 1979 (S.I. 1979 No. 186), regs. 10–13 and 48–49.

Reduced contributions may be payable where there is a special redundancy scheme in operation (subs. (5)).

"Secondary contributor"

7.—(1) For the purposes of this Act, the "secondary contributor" in relation to any payment of earnings to or for the benefit of an employed earner, is—
- (a) in the case of an earner employed under a contract of service, his employer;
- (b) in the case of an earner employed in an office with emoluments, either—
  - (i) such person as may be prescribed in relation to that office; or
  - (ii) if no person is prescribed, the government department, public authority or body of persons responsible for paying the emoluments of the office;

but this subsection is subject to subsection (2) below.

(2) In relation to employed earners who—
- (a) are paid earnings in a tax week by more than one person in respect of different employments; or
- (b) work under the general control or management of a person other than their immediate employer,

and in relation to any other case for which it appears to the Department that such provision is needed, regulations may provide that the prescribed person is to be treated as the secondary contributor in respect of earnings paid to or for the benefit of an earner.

DEFINITIONS
"contract of service": s.121(1).
"Department": s.170.
"earner": ss.3(1) and 121(1).
"earnings": ss.3(1) and 121(1).
"employed earner": ss.2(1) and 121(1).
"employment": s.121(1).
"prescribe": s.121(1).
"secondary contributor": s.7(1).
"tax week": s.121(1).

GENERAL NOTE
This section defines the secondary contributor for the purposes of liability to pay secondary Class 1 contributions. In the usual case, where the earner is an employee, the secondary contributor is the employer (subs. (1)(a)). Where the earner is employed in an office with emoluments, the bodies detailed in subs. (1)(b) will be liable as secondary contributors.

Where the employee has multiple employments, or works under the control or management of a person other than his or her immediate employer (*e.g.* for an agency), the Department has the power to transfer liability to another prescribed person (subs. (2)). The Department may also exercise this power more generally wherever it appears "that such provision is needed". See further Social Security (Categorisation of Earners) Regulations (Northern Ireland) 1978 (S.I. 1978 No. 371), Sched. 3.

Calculation of primary Class 1 contributions

8.—(1) Where a primary Class 1 contribution is payable, the amount of that contribution shall be the aggregate of—
- (a) the initial primary percentage of so much of the earner's earnings paid in the tax week, in respect of the employment in question, as does not exceed the current lower earnings limit; and

(b) the main primary percentage of so much of those earnings as exceeds
    that limit but does not exceed the current upper earnings limit;
but this subsection is subject to regulations under section 6(5) above and
sections 116 to 119 below and to Article 29 of the Pensions Order (contracted-out rates).

(2) For the purposes of this Act the primary percentages shall be as
follows—

(a) the initial primary percentage shall be 2 per cent.; and
(b) the main primary percentage shall be 9 per cent.;
but the rates of those primary percentages are subject to alteration under
section 129 of the Administration Act.

(3) In the case of earners paid otherwise than weekly, any reference in
subsection (1) above to the current upper, or (as the case may be) lower,
earnings limit shall be taken as a reference to the prescribed equivalent of
that limit.

(4) The power conferred by subsection (3) above to prescribe an equivalent of a limit includes power to prescribe an amount which exceeds, by not
more than £1.00, the amount which is the arithmetical equivalent of that
limit.

DEFINITIONS
    "the Administration Act": s.170.
    "Department": s.170.
    "earner": ss.3(1) and 121(1).
    "earnings": ss.3(1) and 121(1).
    "employment": s.121(1).
    "Great Britain Administration Act": s.170.
    "lower earnings limit": s.5(1)(a).
    "the Pensions Act": s.170.
    "prescribe": s.121(1).
    "upper earnings limit": s.5(1)(b).
    "tax week": s.121(1).

GENERAL NOTE
    The basis of calculating primary Class 1 contributions has undergone a number of changes in
recent years. Under the original scheme, employed earners with earnings above the lower
earnings limit paid contributions at a set rate on all their earnings up to the upper earnings limit.
In 1985 the contribution rates were graduated (five, seven and nine per cent. respectively) for
those with earnings between three different brackets. This was thought to create a disincentive
effect, and so in 1989 a new structure was introduced, now embodied in subss. (1) and (2). As
before, the lower earnings limit represents the threshold for entry to the National Insurance
scheme. Primary Class 1 contributions are then payable on the basis of two per cent. of earnings
up to that level (the "initial primary percentage") and nine per cent on the remainder up to the
upper earnings limit. These rates may be altered in Great Britain by the Secretary of State in
accordance with ss.143 and 145 of the Great Britain Administration Act. If the rates in Great
Britain are altered then the Department may make a corresponding order for Northern Ireland
(SSA(N.I.)A 1992, s.129).
    As before, special rates apply to those who have opted out of SERPS (SSP(N.I.)O 1975, art.
29). This group pays the same initial primary percentage but pays two per cent. less than that
due from contracted-in employees on earnings between the lower and upper earnings limits.

Calculation of secondary Class 1 contributions

9.—(1) Where a secondary Class 1 contribution is payable, the amount of
that contribution shall be the appropriate secondary percentage of the
earnings paid in the week in respect of the employment in question.

(2) For the purposes of subsection (1) above, the "appropriate secondary
percentage", in relation to the earner's earnings, is the percentage specified
in subsection (3) below as appropriate to the secondary earnings bracket (or
the prescribed equivalent in the case of earners paid otherwise than weekly)
into which those earnings fall.

(3) The secondary earnings brackets and the percentages appropriate to
them shall be as set out below—

	Weekly earnings	Appropriate percentage
Bracket 1	Current lower earnings limit to £89.99	4.6 per cent.
Bracket 2	£90.00 to £134.99	6.6 per cent.
Bracket 3	£135.00 to £189.99	8.6 per cent.
Bracket 4	£190.00 or more	10.4 per cent.

(4) Subsections (1) and (3) above are subject as mentioned below, that is to say—

(a) subsection (1) is subject to Article 29 of the Pensions Order and to regulations under section 6(5) above and sections 116 to 119 below;

(b) subsection (3) is subject to any order under section 129 of the Administration Act.

(5) The power conferred by subsection (2) above to prescribe an equivalent of a bracket includes power to prescribe an amount which exceeds, by not more than £1.00, the amount which is the arithmetical equivalent of that bracket.

DEFINITIONS
"the Administration Act": s.170.
"appropriate secondary percentage": subs. (2).
"current": s.121(1).
"Department": s.170.
"earner": ss.3(1) and 121(1).
"earnings": ss.3(1) and 121(1).
"employment": s.121(1).
"Great Britain Administration Act": s.170.
"lower earnings limit": s.5(1)(a).
"the Pensions Act": s.170.
"prescribe": s.121(1).
"week": s.121(1).

GENERAL NOTE
This section sets out the basis for calculating secondary Class 1 contributions, *i.e.* those contributions paid by employers and other secondary contributors (s.7). The progressive bands of contribution rates introduced in 1985 have been retained for secondary Class 1 contributions, unlike for those paid by employed earners (see General Note to s.8). Accordingly there is no liability for secondary Class 1 contributions where earnings are below the lower earnings limit. For earnings above that level, contributions are computed on the basis of a percentage of all earnings, according to the relevant band (subs. (3)). The number of these brackets may be altered in Great Britain by order by the Secretary of State under s.146 of the Great Britain Administration Act. If such an order is made then the Department may make a corresponding order for Northern Ireland (SSA(N.I.)A 1992, s.129). Secondary Class 1 contributions are payable on earnings above the upper earnings limit, unlike the present position for employed earners' contributions. A reduction of 3.8 per cent. on earnings between the lower and earnings limits applies for contracted-out employees (SSP(N.I.)A 1975, s.29(2)).

Class 1A contributions

Class 1A contributions

10.—(1) Where—

(a) for any tax year an amount in respect of a car is by virtue of section 157 of the Income and Corporation Taxes Act 1988 chargeable on an earner to income tax under Schedule E; and

(b) the employment by reason of which the car is made available is employed earner's employment,

a Class 1A contribution shall be payable for that tax year, in accordance with this section, in respect of the earner and car in question.

(2) The Class 1A contribution referred to in subsection (1) above is payable by—

(a) the person who is liable to pay the secondary Class 1 contribution relating to the last (or only) relevant payment of earnings in the tax year in relation to which there is a liability to pay such a contribution; or

(b) if no such contribution is payable in relation to a relevant payment of earnings in the tax year, the person who would be liable but for section 6(1)(b) above to pay a secondary Class 1 contribution relating to the last (or only) relevant payment of earnings in the tax year.

(3) A payment of earnings is a "relevant payment of earnings" for the purposes of subsection (2) above if it is made to or for the benefit of the earner in respect of the employment by reason of which the car is made available.

(4) The amount of the Class 1A contribution referred to in subsection (1) above shall be—

(a) the Class 1A percentage of the cash equivalent of the benefit of the car to the earner in the tax year; or

(b) where for the tax year an amount in respect of fuel for the car is by virtue of section 158 of the Income and Corporation Taxes Act 1988 also chargeable on the earner to income tax under Schedule E, the aggregate of—

(i) the Class 1A percentage of the cash equivalent of the benefit of the fuel to the earner in the tax year; and

(ii) the amount mentioned in paragraph (a) above,

the cash equivalents of the benefit of a car or fuel being ascertained, subject to the provisions of this section, in accordance with section 157 or, as the case may be, 158 of the Income and Corporation Taxes Act 1988 and Schedule 6 to that Act.

(5) In subsection (4) above "the Class 1A percentage" means a percentage rate equal to the percentage rate for secondary Class 1 contributions specified in section 9(3) above as appropriate for the highest secondary earnings bracket for the tax year in question.

(6) In calculating for the purposes of subsection (4) above the cash equivalent of the benefit of a car or fuel—

(a) the car shall not be treated as being unavailable on a day by virtue of paragraph 2(2)(b) of Schedule 6 to the Income and Corporation Taxes Act 1988 for the purposes of section 158(5) of that Act or paragraph 2(2), 3(2) or 5(2) of that Schedule, unless the person liable to pay the contribution has information to show that the condition specified in paragraph 2(2)(b) is satisfied as regards that day;

(b) the use of the car for the earner's business travel shall be taken—

(i) for the purposes of section 158(5) of that Act and sub-paragraph (1) of paragraph 3 of that Schedule to have amounted to less than 18,000 miles (or such lower figure as is applicable by virtue of sub-paragraph (2) of that paragraph); and

(ii) for the purposes of sub-paragraph (1) of paragraph 5 of that Schedule to have amounted to not more than 2,500 miles (or such lower figure as is applicable by virtue of sub-paragraph (2) of that paragraph),

unless in either case the person liable to pay the contribution has information to show the contrary; and

(c) for the purposes of paragraph 5(3) of that Schedule, the car shall be treated as not having been the car used to the greatest extent for the employee's business travel, unless the person liable to pay the contribution has information to show the contrary.

(7) Regulations may make such amendments of this section as appear to the Department to be necessary or expedient in consequence of any alteration to section 157 or 158 of the Income and Corporation Taxes Act 1988 or Schedule 6 to that Act.

(8) A person shall be liable to pay different Class 1A contributions in respect of different earners, different cars and different tax years.

(9) Regulations may provide—

(a) for persons to be excepted in prescribed circumstances from liability to pay Class 1A contributions;

(b) for reducing Class 1A contributions in prescribed circumstances.

DEFINITIONS

"Class 1A percentage": subs. (5).
"earner": ss.3(1) and 121(1).
"earnings": ss.3(1) and 121(1).
"employed earner": ss.2(1) and 121(1).
"employment": s.121(1).
"prescribe": s.121(1).
"relevant payment of earnings": subs. (3).
"secondary earnings bracket": s.9(3).
"tax year": s.121(1).

GENERAL NOTE

Class 1A contributions were introduced by the Social Security (Contributions) (Northern Ireland) Order 1991 (S.I. 1991 No. 2294 (N.I. 22)) and became payable from April 6, 1991. Class 1A contributions must be paid by the employer in respect of any car provided for a director or employee (or for members of their families or households) by reason of their employment if the car is also available for private use. Contributions must also be paid on fuel provided for private use in that car. Contributions are calculated on the basis of 10.4 per cent. (subs. (5)) of the appropriate scale charge (*i.e.* the car/fuel cash equivalent).

The directors or employees concerned must be in employed earner's employment and must be liable under s.157 of ICTA 1988 on the scale charge value of the car (and, where appropriate, under s.158 for private fuel). The employer's liability applies to cars and fuel made available to directors irrespective of their earnings (subject to certain exceptions) but only to employees with emoluments of £8,500 or more a year (including taxable benefits and expenses).

So far as payments (*e.g.* by petrol vouchers or petrol charge cards) by employers to employees to cover their private motoring costs are concerned, it has been held that both primary and secondary Class 1 contributions are payable: *R.* v. *Secretary of State for Social Security*, ex p. *Overdrive Credit Card* [1991] 1 W.L.R. 635.

Class 2 contributions

Liability for Class 2 contributions

11.—(1) Every self-employed earner who is over the age of 16 shall be liable to pay Class 2 contributions at the rate of £5.35 a week, subject to the provisions of this section and sections 12 and 19(4)(b) below.

(2) No Class 2 contributions shall be payable by an earner in respect of any period after he attains pensionable age.

(3) Regulations may make provision so that an earner is liable for a weekly rate of Class 2 contributions higher than that specified in subsection (1) above where—

(a) in respect of any employment of his, he is treated by regulations under section 2(2)(b) above as being a self-employed earner; and

(b) in any period or periods he has earnings from that employment and—

(i) those earnings are such that (disregarding their amount) he would be liable for Class 1 contributions in respect of them if he were not so treated in respect of the employment, and

(ii) no Class 4 contribution is payable in respect of the earnings by virtue of regulations under section 18(1) below.

(4) Regulations may provide for an earner otherwise liable for Class 2 contributions in respect of employment as a self-employed earner to be excepted from the liability in respect of any period in which his earnings from such employment are, or are treated by regulations as being, less than £3,030 a tax year.

(5) Regulations made for the purposes of subsection (4) above shall not except a person from liability to pay contributions otherwise than on his own application, but may provide for so excepting a person with effect from any date not earlier than 13 weeks before the date on which his application was made.

DEFINITIONS
"Department": s.170.
"earner": ss.3(1) and 121(1).
"earnings": ss.3(1) and 121(1).
"employment": s.121(1).
"Great Britain Administration Act": s.170.
"pensionable age": s.121(1).
"self-employed earner": ss.2(1) and 121(1).
"tax year": s.121(1).

GENERAL NOTE
Class 2 contributions are paid by the self-employed. Class 2 contributions give rise to entitlement to all contributory benefits except unemployment benefit (s.21(2)). Contributors must be over 16 years and under pensionable age (subss. (1) and (2)). Modifications are laid down in the Social Security (Contributions) Regulations (Northern Ireland) 1979 (S.I. 1979 No. 186), Pt. III. Class 2 contributions are assessed on a weekly flat-rate basis (subs. (1)), with special rates for share fishermen and volunteer development workers overseas (who, unlike usual Class 2 contributors, qualify for unemployment benefit).

Self-employed people may be excepted from liability to pay Class 2 contributions on the grounds of low earnings, the threshold being £3,030 for 1992–93 (subs. (4)). Certificates of exception can only be backdated up to 13 weeks before the date of application (subs. (5)), although the regulations now provide for repayment of contributions (Social Security (Contributions) Regulations (Northern Ireland) 1979 (S.I. 1979 No. 186), reg. 26A). Payment is also excused on the grounds of inability to earn (reg. 23). Contributions may still be made voluntarily. Where self-employed earnings exceed a higher threshold (at present £6,120), an additional liability to pay Class 4 contributions arises (ss.15–18).

The weekly contribution rate (subs. (1)) and low earnings threshold (subs. (4)) are both liable to annual review under the Great Britain Administration Act, s.141. If the Secretary of State makes an order altering the weekly contribution rate and lower earnings threshold in Great Britain as a result of such a review then the Department may make a corresponding order for Northern Ireland (SSA(N.I.)A 1992, s.129).

Late paid Class 2 contributions

12.—(1) This section applies to any Class 2 contribution paid in respect of a week falling within a tax year ("the contribution year") earlier than the tax year in which it is paid ("the payment year").

(2) Subject to subsections (3) to (5) below, the amount of a contribution to which this section applies shall be the amount which the earner would have had to pay if he had paid the contribution in the contribution year.

(3) Subject to subsections (4) to (6) below, in any case where—

(a) the earner pays an ordinary contribution to which this section applies after the end of the tax year immediately following the contribution year; and

(b) the weekly rate of ordinary contributions for the week in respect of which the contribution was payable in the contribution year differs from the weekly rate applicable at the time of payment in the payment year, the amount of the contribution shall be computed by reference to the highest weekly rate of ordinary contributions in the period beginning with the week in respect of which the contribution is paid and ending with the day on which it is paid.

(4) The Department may by regulations direct that subsection (3) above shall have effect in relation to a higher-rate contribution to which this section applies subject to such modifications as may be prescribed.

(5) Subject to subsection (6) below, for the purposes of proceedings in any court relating to an earner's failure to pay Class 2 contributions, the amount of each contribution which he is to be treated as having failed to pay is the amount which he would have paid in accordance with subsections (1) to (3) above or regulations under subsection (6) below if he had paid that contribution on the date on which the proceedings commenced.

(6) The Department may by regulations provide that the amount of any contribution which, apart from the regulations, would fall to be computed in accordance with subsection (3) or (5) above shall instead be computed by reference to a tax year not earlier than the contribution year but earlier—

(a) in a case falling within subsection (3) above, than the payment year; and

(b) in a case falling within subsection (5) above, than the tax year in which the proceedings commenced.

(7) For the purposes of this section—

(a) proceedings in the High Court or a county court commence when an action commences; and

(b) proceedings under section 108 of the Administration Act (offences relating to contributions) commence when a complaint is made.

(8) In this section—

"ordinary contribution" means a contribution under section 11(1) above; and

"higher-rate contribution" means a contribution under regulations made under section 11(3) above.

DEFINITIONS
"the Administration Act": s.170.
"contribution year": subs. (1).
"earner": ss.3(1) and 121(1).
"higher-rate contribution": s.121(1).
"ordinary contribution": s.121(1).
"payment year": subs. (1).
"prescribe": s.121(1).
"tax year": s.121(1).
"week": s.121(1).

GENERAL NOTE
This section concerns the late payment of Class 2 contributions. Class 2 contributions should technically be paid in the week in which they fall due. They may still count for benefit purposes if paid later, providing they are paid within six years of the end of the tax year in which they were due.

Class 3 contributions

Class 3 contributions

13.—(1) Regulations shall provide for earners and others, if over the age of 16, to be entitled if they so wish, but subject to any prescribed conditions, to pay Class 3 contributions; and, subject to the following provisions of this section, the amount of a Class 3 contribution shall be £5.25.

(2) Payment of Class 3 contributions shall be allowed only with a view to enabling the contributor to satisfy contribution conditions of entitlement to

benefit by acquiring the requisite earnings factor for the purposes described in section 22 below.

(3) Regulations may provide for Class 3 contributions, although paid in one tax year, to be appropriated in prescribed circumstances to the earnings factor of another tax year.

(4) The amount of a Class 3 contribution in respect of a tax year earlier than the tax year in which it is paid shall be the same as if it had been paid in the earlier year and in respect of that year, unless it falls to be calculated in accordance with subsection (6) below or regulations under subsection (7) below.

(5) In this section—

"the payment year" means the tax year in which a contribution is paid; and

"the contribution year" means the earlier year mentioned in subsection (4) above.

(6) Subject to subsection (7) below, in any case where—

(a) a Class 3 contribution is paid after the end of the next tax year but one following the contribution year; and

(b) the amount of a Class 3 contribution applicable had the contribution been paid in the contribution year differs from the amount of a Class 3 contribution applicable at the time of payment in the payment year,

the amount of the contribution shall be computed by reference to the highest of those two amounts and of any other amount of a Class 3 contribution in the intervening period.

(7) The Department may by regulations provide that the amount of a contribution which apart from the regulations would fall to be computed in accordance with subsection (6) above shall instead be computed by reference to the amount of a Class 3 contribution for a tax year earlier than the payment year but not earlier than the contribution year.

DEFINITIONS
"benefit": s.121(1).
"contribution year": subs. (5).
"Department": s.170.
"earner": s.121(1).
"earnings factor": s.22(1).
"Great Britain Administration Act": s.170.
"payment year": subs. (5).
"prescribe": s.121(1).
"tax year": s.121(1).

GENERAL NOTE
Class 3 contributions are entirely voluntary. They may be paid by people contributing in Class 1 or 2, but with deficiencies in their contribution records, or by persons who are outside the labour market. Payment of Class 3 contributions only gives rise to entitlement to widows' benefits and Category A and B retirement pensions (s.21(2)). Class 3 contributions are not payable if the individual's earnings factor in the given year is otherwise sufficient to meet the second contribution condition for these benefits (s.14). The contribution required is a weekly flat-rate sum, just less than the Class 2 contribution, and is reviewed annually in Great Britain in accordance with s.141 of the Great Britain Administration Act. If the Secretary of State alters the rate in Great Britain as a result of such a review then the Department may make a corresponding order for Northern Ireland (SSA(N.I.)A 1992, s.129).

Further provision is made by the Social Security (Contributions) Regulations (Northern Ireland) 1979 (S.I. 1979 No. 186), Pt. III.

Restriction on right to pay Class 3 contributions

14.—(1) No person shall be entitled to pay a Class 3 contribution in respect of any tax year if his earnings factor, or the aggregate of his earnings factors, for that year derived—

(a) in the case of 1987–88 or any subsequent year, from earnings upon which Class 1 contributions have been paid or treated as paid or from Class 2 contributions actually paid; or

(b) in the case of any earlier year, from contributions actually paid,

is equal to or exceeds the qualifying earnings factor for that year; and regulations may provide for precluding the payment of Class 3 contributions in other cases.

(2) Regulations may provide for the repayment of Class 3 contributions that have been paid in cases where their payment was precluded by, or by regulations made under, subsection (1) above.

(3) Contributions repayable by virtue of regulations under subsection (2) above shall, for the purpose of determining the contributor's entitlement to any benefit, be treated as not having been paid (but nothing in this subsection shall be taken to imply that any other repayable contributions are to be treated for the purposes of benefit as having been paid).

DEFINITIONS
"benefit": s.121(1).
"Department": s.170.
"earnings": ss.3(1) and 121(1).
"earnings factor": s.22(1).
"qualifying earnings factor": s.121(1).
"tax year": s.121(1).

GENERAL NOTE
See General Note to s.13.

Class 4 contributions

Class 4 contributions recoverable under the Income Tax Acts

15.—(1) Class 4 contributions shall be payable for any tax year in respect of all annual profits or gains which—

(a) are immediately derived from the carrying on or exercise of one or more trades, professions or vocations, and

(b) are profits or gains chargeable to income tax under Case I or Case II of Schedule D for the year of assessment corresponding to that tax year.

(2) Class 4 contributions in respect of profits or gains shall be payable—

(a) in the same manner as any income tax which is, or would be, chargeable in respect of those profits or gains (whether or not income tax in fact falls to be paid), and

(b) by the person on whom the income tax is (or would be) charged,

in accordance with assessments made from time to time under the Income Tax Acts as applied and modified by section 16(1) to (3) of the Great Britain Contributions and Benefits Act.

(3) A Class 4 contribution for any tax year shall be an amount equal to 6.3 per cent. of so much of the profits or gains referred to in subsection (1) above (as computed in accordance with Schedule 2 to the Great Britain Contributions and Benefits Act, the text of which is set out as Schedule 2 to this Act) as exceeds £6,120 and does not exceed £21,060.

(4) The reference in subsection (1) above to profits or gains chargeable to income tax under Case I or Case II of Schedule D shall be taken to include a reference to profits or gains consisting of a payment of enterprise allowance chargeable to income tax under Case VI of Schedule D by virtue of section 127(2) of the Income and Corporation Taxes Act 1988.

(5) For the purposes of this section the year of assessment which corresponds to a tax year is the year of assessment (within the meaning of the Tax Acts) which consists of the same period as that tax year.

DEFINITIONS
"Great Britain Administration Act": s.170.
"Income Tax Acts": Interpretation Act 1978, s.5 and Sched. 1.
"tax year": s.121(1).

GENERAL NOTE
Class 4 contributions are earnings-related payments by the self-employed. Liability for Class 4 contributions is largely coincident with liability under Sched. D of the Income Tax Acts (but see s.17) and is levied at the rate of 6.3 per cent. of profits and gains between an upper and lower limit (subs. (3)). These limits are reviewed annually in Great Britain in accordance with s.141 of the Great Britain Administration Act. If the Secretary of State alters the limits in Great Britain as a result of such a review then the Department may make a corresponding order for Northern Ireland (SSA(N.I.)A 1992, s.129). Where an individual is liable to pay both Class 1 and 4 contributions, the total is limited to the maximum liability under one class only. For this and further provisions, see the Social Security (Contributions) Regulations (Northern Ireland) 1979 (S.I. 1979 No. 186), Pt. VII.

Destination of Class 4 contributions

16. Any money paid over by the Secretary of State under section 16(5) of the Great Britain Contributions and Benefits Act (Class 4 contributions collected from Northern Ireland) shall be treated as Class 4 contributions collected by the Department for the purposes of this Act.

DEFINITIONS
"Department": s.170.
"Great Britain Contributions and Benefits Act": s.170.
"Income Tax Acts": Interpretation Act 1978, s.5 and Sched. 1.
"Inland Revenue": s.121(1).

GENERAL NOTE
Section 16 of the Great Britain Contributions and Benefits Act applies the provisions of the Income Tax Acts as to the assessment, collection, repayment and recovery of taxes, etc., to Class 4 contributions. These powers are subject to provision made under regulations (subs. (2); see ss.17 and 18) and in Sched. 2 (subs. (3)).

Exceptions, deferment and incidental matters relating to Class 4 contributions

17.—(1) The Department may by regulations made with the concurrence of the Inland Revenue provide—
  (a) for excepting persons from liability to pay Class 4 contributions in accordance with section 15(1) to (3) above and section 16(1) to (3) of the Great Britain Contributions and Benefits Act; or
  (b) for deferring any person's liability,
and may certify from time to time to the Inland Revenue the persons who are excepted from liability, or whose liability is to be deferred, and who accordingly are not required (except in accordance with the regulations) to be assessed for contributions.

(2) Exception from liability, or deferment, under subsection (1) above may, in particular, be by reference—
  (a) to a person otherwise liable for contributions being under a prescribed age at the beginning of a tax year;
  (b) to a person having attained pensionable age;
  (c) to a person being in receipt of earnings in respect of which primary Class 1 contributions are, or may be, payable; or
  (d) to a person not satisfying prescribed conditions as to residence or presence in the United Kingdom.

(3) Regulations may provide for any incidental matters arising out of the payment of any Class 4 contributions recovered by the Inland Revenue, including in particular the return, in whole or in part, of such contributions in cases where—

(a) payment has been made in error; or

(b) repayment ought for any other reason to be made.

(4) Regulations may provide for any matters arising out of the deferment of liability for Class 4 contributions under subsection (1) above, including in particular provision for the amount of a person's profits or gains (as computed in accordance with the Great Britain Contributions and Benefits Act) to be certified by the Inland Revenue to the Department and the person liable.

(5) No such certificate as is referred to in subsection (4) above shall relate to a person's profits or gains so far as they exceed the higher of the two money sums for the time being specified in section 15(3) above.

(6) Any regulations under subsection (3) or (4) above must be made with the concurrence of the Inland Revenue.

DEFINITIONS
"Department": s.170.
"earnings": s.121(1).
"Great Britain Contributions and Benefits Act": s.170.
"Inland Revenue": s.121(1).
"pensionable age": s.121(1).
"prescribe": s.121(1).
"primary Class 1 contributions": s.6(3).
"tax year": s.121(1).
"United Kingdom": s.168

GENERAL NOTE
This section enables the Department to make regulations excluding certain groups from liability for Class 4 contributions. This allows for some differences between assessment for Class 4 contributions and under Sched. D for income-tax purposes. For example, liability for Class 4 contributions is confined to persons aged 16 or over but under pensionable age (subs. (2)): see further the Social Security (Contributions) Regulations (Northern Ireland) 1979 (S.I. 1979 No. 186), Pt. VII.

Class 4 contributions recoverable under regulations

18.—(1) Provision may be made by regulations so that where—

(a) an earner, in respect of any one or more employments of his, is treated by regulations under section 2(2)(b) above as being self-employed; and

(b) in any tax year he has earnings from any such employment (one or more) which fall within paragraph (b)(i) of subsection (3) of section 11 above but is not liable for a higher weekly rate of Class 2 contributions by virtue of regulations under that subsection; and

(c) the total of those earnings exceeds £6,120,

he is to be liable, in respect of those earnings, to pay a Class 4 contribution of an amount equal to 6.3 per cent. of so much of the total as exceeds £6,120 and does not exceed £21,060.

(2) It shall be for the Department and not the Inland Revenue, to recover Class 4 contributions payable by virtue of regulations under this section and generally to be responsible for the relevant administration; and, in relation to contributions so payable, regulations may—

(a) apply any of the provisions of Schedule 1 to this Act (except a provision conferring power to make regulations); and

(b) make any such provision as may be made by regulations under that Schedule, except paragraph 6.

DEFINITIONS
"Department": s.170.
"earner": s.121(1).
"earnings": s.121(1).

"employment": s.121(1).
"Inland Revenue": s.121(1).
"tax year": s.121(1).

GENERAL NOTE
  Where persons have earnings chargeable to income tax under Sched. E, but are also paying Class 2 contributions, they are subject to the same liability to pay Class 4 contributions as other self-employed earners. Liability is deferred until the end of the relevant tax year and collection is the responsibility of the Department, not the Inland Revenue.

General

General power to regulate liability for contributions

  19.—(1) Regulations may provide either generally or in relation to—
  (a) any prescribed category of earners; or
  (b) earners in any prescribed category of employments,
that their liability in a particular tax year in respect of contributions of prescribed classes is not to exceed such maximum amount or amounts as may be prescribed.
  (2) Regulations made for the purposes of subsection (1) above may provide—
  (a) for an earner whose liability is subject to a maximum prescribed under that subsection to be liable in the first instance for the full amount of any contributions due from him apart from the regulations, or to be relieved from liability for such contributions in prescribed circumstances and to the prescribed extent; and
  (b) for contributions paid in excess of any such maximum to be repaid at such times, and in accordance with such conditions, as may be prescribed.
  (3) Regulations may provide, in relation to earners otherwise liable for contributions of any class, for excepting them from the liability for such periods, and in such circumstances, as may be prescribed.
  (4) As respects any woman who was married or a widow on 6th April 1977 (the date of the coming into force of the repeal of the old provisions that primary Class 1 contributions might be paid at a reduced rate and Class 2 contributions need not be paid by a married woman or a widow) regulations shall provide—
  (a) for enabling her to elect that her liability in respect of primary Class 1 contributions shall be a liability to contribute at such reduced rate as may be prescribed; and
  (b) either for enabling her to elect that her liability in respect of Class 2 contributions shall be a liability to contribute at such reduced rate as may be prescribed or for enabling her to elect that she shall be under no liability to pay such contributions; and
  (c) for enabling her to revoke any such election.
  (5) Regulations under subsection (4) above may—
  (a) provide for the making or revocation of any election under the regulations to be subject to prescribed exceptions and conditions;
  (b) preclude a person who has made such an election from paying Class 3 contributions while the election has effect;
  (c) provide for treating an election made or revoked for the purpose of any provision of the regulations as made or revoked also for the purpose of any other provision of the regulations;
  (d) provide for treating an election made in accordance with regulations under section 125(2) of the 1975 Act as made for the purpose of regulations under subsection (4) above.
  (6) Regulations may provide for earnings factors to be derived, for such purposes as may be prescribed, as follows, that is to say—

(a) in the case of earnings factors for 1987–88 or any subsequent tax year—
    (i) from earnings upon which primary Class 1 contributions are paid at a reduced rate by virtue of regulations under subsection (4) above; or
    (ii) from Class 2 contributions paid at a reduced rate by virtue of such regulations; and
(b) in the case of earnings factors for any earlier tax year, from contributions which are paid at a reduced rate by virtue of regulations under subsection (4) above;

and if provision is made for a person to have earnings factors so derived for the purpose of establishing entitlement to any benefit, the regulations may, in relation to that person, vary or add to the requirements for entitlement to that benefit.

DEFINITIONS
"the 1975 Act": s.170.
"benefit": s.121(1).
"earner": s.121(1).
"earnings factor": s.22(1).
"employment": s.121(1).
"prescribe": s.121(1).
"tax year": s.121(1).

GENERAL NOTE
This is a general regulation-making provision. See further the Social Security (Contributions) Regulations (Northern Ireland) 1979 (S.I. 1979 No. 186).

PART II

CONTRIBUTORY BENEFITS

Preliminary

Descriptions of contributory benefits

20.—(1) Contributory benefits under this Part of this Act are of the following descriptions, namely—
(a) unemployment benefit (with increase for adult and, where the beneficiary is over pensionable age, child dependants);
(b) sickness benefit (with increase for adult and, where the beneficiary is over pensionable age, child dependants);
(c) invalidity benefit, comprising—
    (i) invalidity pension under section 33, 40 or 41 below (with increase for adult and child dependants);
    (ii) invalidity allowance;
(d) maternity allowance (with increase for adult dependants);
(e) widow's benefit, comprising—
    (i) widow's payment;
    (ii) widowed mother's allowance (with increase for child dependants);
    (iii) widow's pension;
(f) retirement pensions of the following categories—
    (i) Category A, payable to a person by virtue of his own contributions (with increase for adult and child dependants); and
    (ii) Category B, payable to a woman by virtue of her husband's contributions or payable to a man by virtue of his late wife's contributions (with increase for child dependants);
(g) for existing beneficiaries only, child's special allowance.

(2) In this Act—
"long-term benefit" means—
(a) an invalidity pension under section 33, 40 or 41 below;
(b) a widowed mother's allowance;
(c) a widow's pension; and
(d) a Category A or Category B retirement pension; and
"short-term benefit" means—
(a) unemployment benefit;
(b) sickness benefit; and
(c) maternity allowance.
(3) The provisions of this Part of this Act are subject to the provisions of Part IV of the Pensions Order (contracting-out—reduced rates of benefit).

DEFINITIONS
"the Pensions Act": s.170.
"beneficiary": s.121(1).
"benefit": s.121(1).
"child": s.121(1).
"long-term benefit": subs. (2).
"pensionable age": s.121(1).
"the Pensions Act": s.170.
"short-term benefit": subs. (2).

GENERAL NOTE
Subsection (1) simply sets out the contributory benefits payable under Pt. II of the Act, while subs. (2) is a definition provision. Subsection (3) had no immediate statutory forerunner but is a drafting measure to draw attention to the inter-relationship with Pt. IV of the SSP(N.I.)O 1975.

Contribution conditions

21.—(1) Entitlement to any benefit specified in section 20(1) above, other than invalidity benefit, depends on contribution conditions being satisfied (either by the claimant or by some other person, according to the particular benefit).

(2) The class or classes of contribution which, for the purposes of subsection (1) above, are relevant to each of those benefits are as follows—

Short-term benefit

Unemployment benefit	Class 1
Sickness benefit	Class 1 or 2
Maternity allowance	Class 1 or 2

Other benefits

Widow's payment	Class 1, 2 or 3
Widowed mother's allowance	Class 1, 2 or 3
Widow's pension	Class 1, 2 or 3
Category A retirement pension	Class 1, 2 or 3
Category B retirement pension	Class 1, 2 or 3
Child's special allowance	Class 1, 2 or 3

(3) The relevant contribution conditions in relation to the benefits specified in subsection (2) above are those specified in Part I of Schedule 3 to this Act.

(4) Part II of Schedule 3 to this Act shall have effect as to the satisfaction of contribution conditions for benefit, other than maternity allowance, in certain cases where a claim for short-term benefit or a widow's payment is, or has on a previous occasion been, made in the first or second year after that in which the contributor concerned first became liable for primary Class 1 or Class 2 contributions.

(5) In subsection (4) above and Schedule 3 to this Act—
(a) "the contributor concerned", for the purposes of any contribution condition, means the person by whom the condition is to be satisfied;
(b) "a relevant class", in relation to any benefit, means a class of contributions specified in relation to that benefit in subsection (2) above;
(c) "the earnings factor"—
(i) where the year in question is 1987–88 or any subsequent tax year, means, in relation to a person, the aggregate of his earnings factors derived from all his earnings upon which primary Class 1 contributions have been paid or treated as paid and from his Class 2 and Class 3 contributions; and
(ii) where the year in question is any earlier tax year, means, in relation to a person's contributions of any class or classes, the aggregate of his earnings factors derived from all those contributions;
(d) except in the expression "benefit year", "year" means a tax year.
(6) In this Part of this Act "benefit year" means a period—
(a) beginning with the first Sunday in January in any calendar year, and
(b) ending with the Saturday immediately preceding the first Sunday in January in the following calendar year;
but for any prescribed purposes of this Part of this Act "benefit year" may by regulations be made to mean such other period (whether or not a period of 12 months) as may be specified in the regulations.

DEFINITIONS
"a relevant class": subs. (5).
"benefit year": subs. (6).
"benefit": s.121(1).
"contributor concerned": subs. (5).
"earnings factor": subs. (5).
"prescribe": s.121(1).
"short-term benefit": s.20(2).
"year": subs. (5).

GENERAL NOTE
This section details those benefits to which entitlement may arise by virtue of contributions of the various classes. Under subs. (2) only persons who have paid Class 1 contributions can qualify for unemployment benefit. Exceptions to this principle are made by regulations for share fishermen and volunteer development workers (Social Security (Contributions) Regulations (Northern Ireland) 1979 (S.I. 1979 No. 186), regs. 96 and 115A–F). Class 2 contributions confer title to any contributory benefit except unemployment benefit. Voluntary Class 3 contributions only enable a person to qualify for widow's benefits and Category A or B retirement pensions (child's special allowance is preserved only for existing beneficiaries: s.56). The specific contribution conditions required for each benefit are listed in Pt. I of Sched. 3. Class 4 contributions give rise to no benefit entitlement.

Earnings factors

22.—(1) A person shall, for the purposes specified in subsection (2) below, be treated as having annual earnings factors derived—
(a) in the case of 1987–88 or any subsequent tax year, from those of his earnings upon which primary Class 1 contributions have been paid or treated as paid and from Class 2 and Class 3 contributions; and
(b) in the case of any earlier tax year, from his contributions of any of Classes 1, 2 and 3;
but subject to the following provisions of this section and those of section 23 below.
(2) The purposes referred to in subsection (1) above are those of—
(a) establishing, by reference to the satisfaction of contribution condi-

tions, entitlement to any benefit specified in section 20(1) above, other than maternity allowance; and
(b) calculating the additional pension in the rate of a long-term benefit.
(3) Separate earnings factors may be derived for 1987–88 and subsequent tax years—
(a) from earnings upon which primary Class 1 contributions have been paid or treated as paid;
(b) from earnings which have been credited;
(c) from contributions of different classes paid or credited in the same tax year;
(d) by any combination of the methods mentioned in paragraphs (a) to (c) above,
and may be derived for any earlier tax year from contributions of different classes paid or credited in the same tax year, and from contributions which have actually been paid, as opposed to those not paid but credited.
(4) Subject to regulations under section 19(4) to (6) above, no earnings factor shall be derived—
(a) for 1987–88 or any subsequent tax year, from earnings upon which primary Class 1 contributions are paid at the reduced rate, or
(b) for any earlier tax year, from primary Class 1 contributions paid at the reduced rate or from secondary Class 1 contributions.
(5) Regulations may provide for crediting—
(a) for 1987–88 or any subsequent tax year, earnings or Class 2 or Class 3 contributions, or
(b) for any earlier tax year, contributions of any class,
for the purpose of bringing a person's earnings factor for that tax year to a figure which will enable him to satisfy contribution conditions of entitlement to any prescribed description of benefit (whether his own entitlement or another person's).
(6) Regulations may impose limits with respect to the earnings factors which a person may have or be treated as having in respect of any one tax year.
(7) The power to amend regulations made before 30th March 1977 (the making of the Social Security (Miscellaneous Provisions) (Northern Ireland) Order 1977) under subsection (5) above may be so exercised as to restrict the circumstances in which and the purposes for which a person is entitled to credits in respect of weeks before the coming into force of the amending regulations; but not so as to affect any benefit for a period before the coming into force of the amending regulations if it was claimed before 18th March 1977.

DEFINITIONS
"benefit": s.121(1).
"earnings": s.121(1).
"earnings factor": s.21(5).
"long-term benefit": s.20(2).
"prescribe": s.121(1).
"tax year": s.121(1).
"week": s.121(1).

GENERAL NOTE
This section (together with s.23) lays down the basic framework for computing earnings factors. Earnings factors are used to calculate whether the contribution conditions set out in Sched. 3 have been met for contributory benefits (except maternity allowance). They are also significant in calculating the additional pension under SERPS (subs. (2)). In the case of Class 1 contributions, the earnings factor is the amount of earnings upon which contributions have been paid (s.23(3)(a)). For Class 2 or Class 3 contributions, the earnings factor is the lower earnings limit for Class 1 multiplied by the number of contributions made in the relevant tax

year (s.23(3)). For further details, see Social Security (Earnings Factor) Regulations (Northern Ireland) 1975 (S.I. 1975 No. 82).

Provisions supplemental to ss.21 and 22

23.—(1) Earnings factors derived as mentioned in section 22(1)(a) above, including earnings factors as increased by any order under section 130 of the Administration Act—

(a) shall be expressed, subject to subsection (2) below, as whole numbers of pounds; and

(b) shall be made ascertainable from tables or rules to be drawn up by the Department and embodied in regulations.

(2) Subsection (1) above does not require earnings factors in respect of the tax year 1978–79 or any subsequent tax year which have been revalued for the purpose of calculating guaranteed minimum pensions under the Pensions Order to be expressed as whole numbers of pounds.

(3) The tables and rules referred to in subsection (1) above shall be drawn up so that, in general—

(a) in respect of the tax year 1987–88 and any subsequent tax year, the amount of earnings upon which primary Class 1 contributions have been paid or treated as paid gives rise, subject to subsection (4) below, to an earnings factor for that year equal or approximating to the amount of those earnings; and

(b) any number of Class 2 or Class 3 contributions in respect of a tax year gives rise to an earnings factor for that tax year equal or approximating to that year's lower earnings limit for Class 1 contributions multiplied by the number of contributions.

(4) The Department may by regulations make such modifications of subsection (3)(a) above as appear to the Department to be appropriate in consequence of section 8(2) above.

DEFINITIONS
"the Administration Act": s.170.
"earnings": s.121(1).
"earnings factor": s.22(1).
"lower earnings limit": s.5(1)(a).
"the Pensions Order": s.170.
"tax year": s.121(1).

GENERAL NOTE
See General Note to s.22. The legislative history of subs. (4) is dealt with by the Law Commissions (Cm. 1726, 1991), para. 1.

Records of earnings and calculation of earnings factors in absence of records

24.—(1) Regulations may provide for requiring persons to maintain, in such form and manner as may be prescribed, records of such earnings paid by them as are relevant for the purpose of calculating earnings factors, and to retain such records for so long as may be prescribed.

(2) Where the Department is satisfied that records of earnings relevant for the purpose of calculating a person's earnings factors for the tax year 1987–88 or any subsequent tax year have not been maintained or retained or are otherwise unobtainable, then, for the purpose of determining those earnings factors, the Department may—

(a) compute, in such manner as it thinks fit, an amount which shall be regarded as the amount of that person's earnings on which primary Class 1 contributions have been paid or treated as paid; or

(b) take the amount of those earnings to be such sum as it may specify in the particular case.

DEFINITIONS
  "Department": s.170.
  "earnings": s.121(1).
  "earnings factor": s.22(1).
  "prescribe": s.121(1).
  "tax year": s.121(1).

GENERAL NOTE
  Subsection (1) enables the Department to make regulations requiring employers to keep records of earnings for the purpose of calculating earnings factors. Subsection (2) empowers the Department to calculate earnings factors in the absence of proper records, so as to protect the potential benefit entitlement of employees.

Unemployment benefit

Unemployment benefit

25.—(1) Subject to the provisions of this section, a person who satisfies any of the three conditions of subsection (2) below shall be entitled to unemployment benefit in respect of any day of unemployment which forms part of a period of interruption of employment.
  (2) The conditions of this subsection are that—
  (a) the person is under pensionable age on the day in question and satisfies the contribution conditions specified for unemployment benefit in Schedule 3, Part I, paragraph 1;
  (b) on that day the person—
          (i) is over pensionable age, but not more than 5 years over that age; and
          (ii) would be entitled to a Category A retirement pension if his entitlement had not been deferred or if he had not made an election under section 54(1) below; or
  (c) on that day the person—
          (i) is over pensionable age, but not more than 5 years over that age; and
          (ii) would be entitled to a Category B retirement pension by virtue of the contributions of his deceased spouse, but for any such deferment or election.
  (3) A person shall not be entitled to unemployment benefit for the first three days of any period of interruption of employment.
  (4) In the case of a person entitled under paragraph (a) of subsection (2) above unemployment benefit shall be payable at the weekly rate specified in Schedule 4, Part I, paragraph 1.
  (5) In the case of any person over pensionable age who is entitled under paragraph (b) or (c) of subsection (2) above, unemployment benefit shall be payable at the weekly rate at which the retirement pension referred to in the applicable paragraph of that subsection would have been payable; but in determining that rate for the purposes of this subsection any increase specified in subsection (6) below shall be disregarded.
  (6) The increases to be disregarded for the purposes of subsection (5) above are the following—
  (a) any increase (for invalidity) under section 47(1) below;
  (b) any increase (for married women) under section 53(2) below or (for deferred entitlement) under Schedule 5 to this Act;
  (c) any increase (for dependants) under section 80, 83 or 85 below;
  (d) any increase (for Category A or Category B pensioners) under section 132 of the Administration Act which corresponds to an increase under section 150 of the Great Britain Administration Act.

(7) The amount payable by way of benefit under this section for any day of unemployment or of incapacity for work shall be one sixth of the appropriate weekly rate.

DEFINITIONS
"the Administration Act": s.170.
"deferred": s.121(1).
"entitled": s.121(1).
"pensionable age": s.121(1).
"period of interruption of employment": s.57(1)(d).

GENERAL NOTE
This section deals with the basic conditions of entitlement to unemployment benefit. Benefit is payable in respect of "any day of unemployment which forms part of a period of interruption of employment" (subs. (1)). The preliminary requirements are that the claimant has met the contribution conditions in Sched. 3, and is either under pensionable age or is no more than five years over pensionable age and has deferred entitlement to a contributory retirement pension.

The first question then to be determined is whether the claimant is indeed unemployed. Under the Social Security (Unemployment, Sickness, and Invalidity Benefit) Regulations (Northern Ireland) 1984 (S.I. 1984 No. 245), benefit is not payable where the claimant is "engaged in any employment" (reg. 7(1)(g)). On the broad meaning of employment, see s.121(1). The underlying principle is that a person is unemployed if he or she is not engaged in an activity from which it is intended to derive remuneration or profit. The concept of being in employment is thus wider than simply working under a contract of service: see Ogus and Barendt, pp. 67–71.

The second issue to be decided is whether the day for which benefit is claimed is indeed a "day of unemployment". There is no single definition of this term to be found in the Act or the regulations. Rather, it is a technical construct, the meaning of which must be derived from various provisions in the Act (see s.57), the regulations (see especially reg. 7) and the case law.

Thirdly, the day of unemployment must be part of a "period of interruption of employment"; in determining this, account must be taken of the linking rules (s.57(1)(d)). Finally, reference must also be made to the requirement that the claimant is capable of work, available for employment and actively seeking such employment (s.57(1)(a)) and that there is no disqualification by virtue of involvement in a trade dispute (s.27) or for "voluntary" unemployment (s.28).

Unemployment benefit is not payable for the first three "waiting days" of a period of interruption of employment (subs. (3)). It is paid at a flat rate, which may be supplemented by an increase for a dependent spouse. The daily rate is one-sixth of the weekly rate (subs. (7)) as Sundays (or appropriate substituted days) do not count for these purposes (s.57(1)(e)).

Special rules apply to men aged 65–70, and women aged 60–65, who have not retired, but who would have been entitled to a Category A or Category B retirement pension if they had retired. They are paid at the current rate of the appropriate pension (subs. (5), disregarding the increases mentioned in subs. (6)). These special rules are potentially discriminatory as contrary to Art. 4 of the E.C. Directive on Equal Treatment 79/7: see *Secretary of State for Social Security* v. *Thomas* [1991] 2 W.L.R. 886 and also Webb (1992) 55 M.L.R. 393.

Duration of unemployment benefit

26.—(1) A person who, in respect of any period of interruption of employment, has been entitled to unemployment benefit for 312 days shall not thereafter be entitled to that benefit for any day of unemployment (whether in the same or a subsequent period of interruption of employment) unless before that day he has requalified for benefit.

(2) A person who has exhausted his right to unemployment benefit requalifies for it on the next occasion when, having again been in employment as an employed earner, he makes a claim for that benefit in circumstances such that the requalification conditions are satisfied with respect to each of at least 13 weeks in the period of 26 weeks immediately preceding—

(a) the day on which the claim is made, or
(b) if he would not requalify by reference to that day, his first day of unemployment since he was last in employment as an employed earner.

(3) For the purposes of subsection (2) above the requalification conditions are satisfied with respect to any week if—

(a) the person in question has been in employment as an employed earner in that week;

(b) he has worked in such employment for at least 16 hours in that week; and

(c) the week begins after the last day for which he was entitled to unemployment benefit.

(4) Subsection (2) above shall have effect in prescribed cases with the substitution for the reference to 26 weeks of a reference to such longer period as may be prescribed.

(5) Where a person requalifies for unemployment benefit, subsection (1) above shall again apply to him but, in a case where the period of interruption of employment in which he exhausted his right to that benefit continues after his requalification, as if the part before and the part after his requalification were distinct periods of interruption of employment.

(6) Regulations may provide for a person who would be entitled to unemployment benefit but for the operation of any provision of this Act or of regulations disentitling him to it or disqualifying him for it to be treated as if entitled to it for the purposes of this section.

DEFINITIONS
  "claim": s.121(1).
  "employed earner": s.121(1).
  "employment": s.121(1).
  "entitled": s.121(1).
  "period of interruption of employment": s.57(1)(d).
  "prescribe": s.121(1).
  "week": s.121(1).

GENERAL NOTE
  Under subs. (1) the right to unemployment benefit is exhausted after the claimant has been entitled for 312 days in any one period of interruption of employment (in effect one year, subject to the linking rule and allowing for the disregard of Sundays or alternate days: s.57(1)(e)). A person can requalify for unemployment benefit after the 312 days if he or she has been in employment as an employed earner for at least 13 weeks within the 26 weeks immediately before reclaiming, and in each of those weeks has been employed for at least 16 hours (subss. (2) and (3)). See *R(U) 3/82* and *R(U) 5/88*. Exceptions are prescribed for the purposes of the 13 weeks in 26 weeks rule: Social Security (Unemployment, Sickness, and Invalidity Benefit) Regulations (Northern Ireland) 1984 (S.I. 1984 No. 245), reg. 6A.
  Once a person has requalified for benefit, entitlement runs for a further maximum duration of 312 days in any period of interruption of employment (subs. (5)). Subsection (6) enables rules to be made preventing claimants from extending their entitlement to benefit by manipulating the rules relating to periods of interruption of employment. See further Ogus and Barendt, p. 125 and regs. 16 and 28.

Interruption of employment in connection with trade dispute

27.—(1) Subject to the following provisions of this section—

(a) an employed earner who has lost employment as an employed earner by reason of a stoppage of work due to a trade dispute at his place of employment is disqualified for receiving unemployment benefit for any day during the stoppage unless he proves that he is not directly interested in the dispute; and

(b) an employed earner who has withdrawn his labour in furtherance of a trade dispute, but does not fall within paragraph (a) above, is disqualified for receiving unemployment benefit for any day on which his labour remains withdrawn.

(2) A person disqualified under subsection (1)(a) above for receiving unemployment benefit shall cease to be so disqualified if he proves that during the stoppage—

(a) he has become bona fide employed elsewhere;

(b) his employment has been terminated by reason of redundancy within the meaning of section 11(2) of the Contracts of Employment and Redundancy Payments Act (Northern Ireland) 1965; or

(c) he has bona fide resumed employment with his employer but has subsequently left for a reason other than the trade dispute.

(3) In this Act—

(a) "place of employment" in relation to any person, means the factory, workshop, farm or other premises or place at which he was employed, so however that, where separate branches of work which are commonly carried on as separate businesses in separate premises or at separate places are in any case carried on in separate departments on the same premises or at the same place, each of those departments shall for the purpose of this paragraph be deemed to be a separate factory or workshop or farm or separate premises or a separate place, as the case may be;

(b) "trade dispute" means any dispute between employers and employees, or between employees and employees, which is connected with the employment or non-employment or the terms of employment or the conditions of employment of any persons, whether employees in the employment of the employer with whom the dispute arises, or not.

DEFINITIONS

"employed earner": s.121(1).
"employment": s.121(1).
"place of employment": subs. (3)(a).
"trade dispute": subs. (3)(b).

GENERAL NOTE

Claimants are disqualified from unemployment benefit if they have lost their employment by reason of a stoppage of work due to a trade dispute at their place of employment (subs. (1)(a)). There are exceptions to this rule (see proviso to subs. (1)(a) and subs. (2)). Alternatively, even if a claimant is not debarred by virtue of subs. (1)(a), disqualification will ensue under subs. (1)(b) where the person's labour has been withdrawn in furtherance of a trade dispute.

Subs. (1)(a)

In order for a claimant to be disqualified under this head, the adjudication officer must show on the balance of probabilities that (1) there is a trade dispute (subs. (3)(b)); (2) at the claimant's place of employment (subs. (3)(a)); (3) resulting in a stoppage of work; and (4) as a result of that stoppage the claimant lost employment (*R(U) 17/52*).

Stoppage of work. A stoppage of work means "a situation in which operations are being stopped or hindered otherwise than to a negligible extent" (*R(U) 1/87*). It must be "in the nature of a strike or lock-out, that is to say it must be a move in a contest between an employer and his employees, the object of which is that employment shall be resumed on certain conditions" (*R(U) 17/52*).

In principle the disqualification lasts as long as the stoppage (not the trade dispute) is in existence. The disqualification will end earlier if the stoppage is no longer part of the trade dispute (*R(U) 1/65*) or has ended for some other reason (*R(U) 15/80*).

Claimants may also be able to invoke the proviso, *i.e.* that they are not directly interested in the trade dispute. In practice this will be very difficult as in essence claimants have to demonstrate that they have nothing to gain, either financially or in terms of their conditions of employment, from the outcome of the dispute: *Presho* v. *Department of Health and Social Security (Insurance Officer)* [1984] A.C. 310 and *Cartlidge* v. *Chief Adjudication Officer* [1986] Q.B. 360. The direct interest may terminate if the employer effects a genuine severance of all relations with the employees in question (*R(U) 1/87*); dismissal as a tactical gambit in a dispute would not be sufficient. This approach was adopted by the Northern Ireland Commissioners in

R 5/86 (UB). But see the Northern Ireland decision reported at BNIL *89/9/94*, where it was decided that direct interest continued after dismissal.

A claimant may, moreover, be able to escape the impact of the disqualification by relying upon one of the grounds detailed in subs. (2).

Lost employment by reason of. . . The claimant need not be an active participant in strike action; under subs. (1)(a) it is sufficient that he or she has "lost employment. . . by reason of a stoppage of work", *i.e.* the disqualification covers people who are laid off or unable to go to work because of picketing. (See, for example, Northern Ireland decision *R2/80 (UB)*). Furthermore, once a claimant has lost some days due to this cause, the disqualification applies for the duration of the stoppage: *Cartlidge* v. *Chief Adjudication Officer* [1986] Q.B. 360; see also above; but note subs. (2).

Subs. (1)(b)
This head of disqualification was introduced in 1986. It is essentially a catch-all provision to disbar strikers who might escape disqualification through a lacuna in subs. (1)(a). The only requirement is that the individual has withdrawn his or her labour in furtherance of a trade dispute. There is no need for a stoppage of work or for the trade dispute to be at the claimant's place of employment. The disqualification applies for so long as the person's labour is withdrawn.

Subs. (2)
These special grounds enable claimants to escape any disqualification imposed under subs. (1)(a) (but not under subs. (1)(b)).

Bona fide employed elsewhere. The onus is on the claimant to show that the employment elsewhere which has subsequently ceased was genuine and taken up for an honest motive (*R(U) 39/56, R(U) 6/74*).

His employment has been terminated. This deals with the perceived injustice in *Cartlidge* v. *Chief Adjudication Officer* [1986] Q.B. 360, in which a miner under notice of redundancy, who had sought to work out his notice, was disqualified under the trade dispute rule because the stoppage of work continued after his employment had ended.

Bona fide resumed employment. This provision, similarly inspired by *Cartlidge*, is designed as an escape clause for claimants who have withdrawn their labour, then returned to work, and later still left for some other reason (*e.g.* a resignation on grounds of ill-health).

Subs. (3)
Place of employment. Under subs. (1)(a) the trade dispute must be at the claimant's place of employment. The essence of this convoluted definition is that it may be open to the claimant to show that the trade dispute is taking place in a separate department which fulfils the criteria set out. See further *R(U) 4/58, R(U) 4/62, R(U) 1/70* and *CU66/1986* (discussed in Bonner).

Trade dispute. This broad definition, which is relevant to disqualification under both subs. (1)(a) and (1)(b), covers official and unofficial strikes, lock-outs and demarcation disputes. It is therefore wider than the current definition used for the purposes of conferring immunity in tort for strike action. The dispute must have reached "a certain stage of contention" before it may be regarded as a trade dispute (*R(U) 21/59*).

Unemployment benefit—other disqualifications, etc.

28.—(1) Subject to section 29 below a person shall be disqualified for receiving unemployment benefit for such period not exceeding 26 weeks as may be determined in accordance with Part II of the Administration Act if—

    (a) he has lost his employment as an employed earner through his misconduct, or has voluntarily left such employment without just cause;

    (b) after a situation in any employment has been properly notified to him as vacant or about to become vacant, he has without good cause refused or failed to apply for that situation or refused to accept that situation when offered to him;

    (c) he has without good cause neglected to avail himself of a reasonable opportunity of employment;

    (d) he has without good cause refused or failed to carry out any official recommendations given to him with a view to assisting him to find employment, being recommendations which were reasonable having regard to his circumstances and to the means of obtaining that employment usually adopted in the district in which he resides;

(e) he has lost his place on an approved training scheme through his misconduct, or has voluntarily left such a place without good cause;

(f) after a place on an approved training scheme has been properly notified to him as vacant or about to become vacant, he has without good cause refused or failed to apply for that place or refused to accept that place when offered to him; or

(g) he has without good cause neglected to avail himself of a reasonable opportunity of a place on an approved training scheme.

(2) The Department may by order substitute a shorter period for the period for the time being mentioned in subsection (1) above.

(3) Regulations may also provide for imposing, in the case of any prescribed category of persons—

(a) additional conditions with respect to the receipt of unemployment benefit; and

(b) restrictions on the rate and duration of unemployment benefit,

if, having regard to special circumstances, it appears to the Department necessary to do so for the purpose of preventing inequalities, or injustice to the general body of employed earners, or of earners generally, as the case may be.

(4) For the purposes of this section a person who has been dismissed by his employer by reason of redundancy within the meaning of section 11(2) of the Contracts of Employment and Redundancy Payments Act (Northern Ireland) 1965 after volunteering or agreeing so to be dismissed shall not be deemed to have left his employment voluntarily.

(5) For the purposes of subsection (1) above regulations may—

(a) prescribe matters which are or are not to be taken into account in determining whether a person does or does not have good cause for any act or omission; or

(b) prescribe circumstances in which a person is or is not to be regarded as having or not having good cause for any act or omission;

but, subject to any such regulations, in determining for the purposes of that subsection whether a person does or does not have good cause for any act or omission, there shall be disregarded any matter relating to the level of remuneration in the employment in question.

(6) For the purposes of this section—

(a) "properly notified", in subsection (1)(b) and (f) above, means notified by the Department of Economic Development or some other recognised agency, or by or on behalf of an employer;

(b) "official recommendations", in subsection (1)(d) above, means recommendations in writing made by an officer of the Department of Economic Development;

(c) "approved training scheme", in subsection (1)(e), (f) and (g) above, means a scheme under which persons—

(i) are trained for employment; or

(ii) acquire work-experience for the purpose of becoming or keeping fit for entry to or return to regular employment,

and which is approved by the Department of Economic Development for the purposes of this section;

(d) "week" means any period of 7 days.

DEFINITIONS
"the Administration Act": s.170.
"approved training scheme": subs. (6)(c).
"earner": s.121(1).
"employed earner": s.121(1).

"employment": s.121(1).
"official recommendations": subs. (6)(b).
"prescribe": s.121(1).
"properly notified": subs. (6)(a).
"week": subs. (6)(e).

GENERAL NOTE
This important section provides for claimants to be disqualified from unemployment benefit in cases of "voluntary" unemployment. In practice by far the most common ground for disqualification is under subs. (1)(a), which is concerned with the manner in which the claimant lost his or her previous job. Far fewer disqualifications are imposed on the grounds concerned with the claimant's subsequent behaviour and job-search activity while unemployed, or with conduct in connection with training schemes (subs. (1)(b)–(g)).

The length of the period of disqualification may be as little as one day or as much as 26 weeks (subs. (1)). On the way in which this discretion should be exercised, see *R(U) 8/74* and *R(U) 4/87*. The underlying purpose of the rule is said to be to protect the National Insurance Fund against unwarranted claims (*CU 190/50*).

All these heads of disqualification are subject to s.29, which provides for certain exemptions in connection with refusals of offers of employment. In practice this means that the proviso "Subject to s.29 below" has no application to subss. (1)(e)–(g), which concern training schemes.

Subs. (1)(a)
This provision contains two quite distinct grounds for disqualification: loss of job through misconduct and voluntarily leaving without just cause.

Misconduct. This has been defined as "conduct which is causally but not necessarily directly connected with the employment, and having regard to the relationship of employer and employee and the rights and duties of both, can fairly be described as blameworthy, reprehensible and wrong" (*R(U) 2/77*). In *R(U) 7/57* the test was formulated as follows: was the claimant's conduct such as would cause a reasonable employer to dispense with the employee's services on the ground that, having regard to the conduct in question, he or she was not a fit person to hold that position?

Misconduct need not be deliberate, but only more serious forms of negligence will amount to such behaviour (*R(U) 8/57*). The misconduct need not occur at work, but where it occurs outside working hours there must still be some nexus with the job (*e.g.* a lorry driver losing his licence whilst driving his own car: *R(U) 7/57*, but see *R(U) 1/71*). See specifically the Northern Ireland decisions *R3/79 (UB)* and BNIL 91/6/99.

The onus of establishing misconduct lies on the adjudication officer (*R(U) 2/60*). On the relevance of other legal proceedings, see *R(U) 10/54* and Northern Ireland decision *R1/84(UB)* (criminal court) and *R(U) 2/74* (industrial tribunal).

Voluntarily left. Three conditions must be satisfied before disqualification can be imposed on this ground. First, the claimant must have left the employment in question. Secondly, the leaving must have been voluntary. Thirdly, it must have been without just cause (see below). The onus is on the adjudication officer to establish both that the claimant left the employment and that this was voluntary (*R(U) 20/64*). Although most cases under this head involve resignation, the concept also covers losing a job through absenteeism and, exceptionally, cases of dismissal prompted by the claimant's actions (*R(U) 16/52*). Taking early retirement can amount to voluntarily leaving employment (*Crewe* v. *Social Security Commissioner* [1982] 1 W.L.R. 1209, but see *R(U) 3/81* and subs. (4)). *R(U) 3/81* was distinguished in the Northern Ireland Commissioner's Decision *R1/82 (UB)*.

Without just cause. Whereas "good cause" as it applies to subss. (1)(b)–(g) is now regulated by statute, the concept of "just cause" is defined by reference to case law. According to *Crewe* v. *Social Security Commissioner* [1982] 1 W.L.R. 1209, the issue is not what is in the claimant's interests or even in the broader public interest. Rather, just cause means that the interests of the claimant and those of other contributors to the National Insurance Fund need to be balanced. Just cause has been found to exist where claimants have left jobs because of grievances at work or where personal or domestic circumstances have made it impossible for them to continue. See further *R(U) 4/87*, and Bonner for a fuller discussion of case law.

Subs. (1)(b)
This applies the sanction to claimants who refuse to apply for, or fail to apply for, or refuse to accept a vacancy when offered to them. Until 1989 there was a requirement that the employment in question be "suitable". Although this has now disappeared, there is still a "good cause" proviso. Good cause, however, is determined solely in accordance with statute (subs. (5) and

Social Security (Unemployment, Sickness, and Invalidity Benefit) Regulations (Northern Ireland) 1984 (S.I. 1984 No. 245), reg. 12E). See further Bonner. On "properly notified", see subs. (6)(a).

Subs. (1)(c)
There is a degree of overlap between this head of disqualification and that in subs. (1)(b). Until 1989 there was a requirement that the opportunity of employment be "suitable". Although this has now disappeared, there is the "good cause" proviso. For relevant pre-amendment case law, see *R(U) 28/55* and *R(U) 5/71*.

Subs. (1)(d)
The concept of "good cause" here has the same meaning as in the parallel provisions in this section. On "official recommendations", see subs. (6)(b).

Subs. (1)(e)–(g)
These provisions, introduced in 1989, are intended to apply the same grounds of disqualification in respect of a claimant losing a place on an approved training scheme, and associated forms of behaviour, as relate to the employment grounds in subs. (1)(a)–(c). The only difference is that subs. (1)(a) applies the sanction in cases of leaving employment "without just cause", whereas subs. (1)(e) only applies where the claimant has left an approved training scheme (on which see subs. (6)(c)) "without good cause". In principle "just cause" may be more difficult to establish than "good cause" (*Crewe* v. *Social Security Commissioner* [1982] 1 W.L.R. 1209), but whereas the principles governing just cause are purely a matter of case law, good cause is now determined solely in accordance with statute (subs. (5) and Social Security (Unemployment, Sickness, and Invalidity Benefit) Regulations (Northern Ireland) 1984 (S.I. 1984 No. 245), reg. 12E). On the inapplicability of the proviso relating to s.29, see the General Note above.

Subs. (4)
This provision, implemented in 1985, is unfortunately drafted. Its purpose is to ensure that individuals who volunteer for (or agree to) redundancy should not face disqualification for voluntarily leaving without just cause. Technically the operative words should read "after volunteering or agreeing so to be dismissed shall be deemed not to have left his employment voluntarily." In order to rely on this escape clause, the claimant must be dismissed *and* the reason for dismissal must be redundancy within the meaning of the employment protection legislation. Difficulties may arise in showing that the claimant has actually been dismissed, rather than that he has agreed a consensual termination of the contract of employment (*Birch* v. *University of Liverpool* [1985] I.C.R. 470). See further the Rosyth Dockyard cases, *CSU/33/88*, *CSU/34/88* and *CSU/21/90*.

Subs. (5)
See Social Security (Unemployment, Sickness, and Invalidity Benefit) Regulations (Northern Ireland) 1984 (S.I. 1984 No. 245), reg. 12E.

Exemptions from disqualification for unemployment benefit

29.—(1) Nothing in section 28 above or in regulations under that section shall be taken to disqualify a person for receiving unemployment benefit by reason only of his refusal—
  (a) to seek or accept employment in a situation which is vacant in consequence of a stoppage of work due to a trade dispute; or
  (b) to seek or accept during the permitted period any employment other than employment in his usual occupation at a level of remuneration not lower than he is accustomed to receive.
(2) Regulations shall make provision for the purpose of enabling any person of a prescribed description to accept any employed earner's employment without being disqualified under—
  (a) subsection (1)(a) of section 28 above, so far as it relates to a person who voluntarily leaves such employment without just cause, or
  (b) subsection (1)(c) of that section,

should he leave that employment voluntarily and without just cause at any time after the end of the 6th week, but not later than the end of the 12th week, of a trial period.

(3) In this section—

"permitted period", in relation to any person, means such period, whether expired or not, as may be determined in accordance with regulations by an adjudication officer on the submission of the question whether that person is disqualified under section 28 above for receiving unemployment benefit; and any such regulations may prescribe—

(a) the day on which any such period shall be regarded as having commenced in any case;

(b) the shortest and longest periods which may be so determined in any case; and

(c) criteria to which the adjudication officer is to have regard in determining the permitted period in any case;

"trial period" means a period of 12 weeks beginning with the commencement of the employment in question; but regulations may—

(a) make provision for the purpose of determining the day on which a person's employment is to be regarded as commencing; and

(b) provide that, for the purpose of determining the time at which the 6th or 12th week of a trial period ends, prescribed periods may be disregarded in prescribed circumstances.

DEFINITIONS

"employed earner": s.121(1).
"employment": s.121(1).
"permitted period": subs. (3).
"prescribe": s.121(1).
"trade dispute": s.27(3)(b).
"trial period": subs. (3).
"week": s.121(1).

GENERAL NOTE

This section has two purposes. First, subs. (1) provides a degree of relief from the disqualification provisions in s.28. Claimants are not subject to the sanction if they refuse to seek or accept employment which has become available as a result of a stoppage of work due to a trade dispute. Equally, disqualification may not be imposed during the permitted period when claimants decline work, other than their normal employment, which is paid at a lower rate than they are accustomed to receive.

Permitted period. See subs. (3) and Social Security (Unemployment, Sickness, and Invalidity Benefit) Regulations (Northern Ireland) 1984 (S.I. 1984 No. 245), reg. 12F.

Secondly, subs. (2) suspends the operation of the disqualification rule for certain claimants. Those who meet the conditions laid down in Social Security (Unemployment, Sickness, and Invalidity Benefit) Regulations (Northern Ireland) 1984 (S.I. 1984 No. 245), reg. 12G are not liable to disqualification even though they voluntarily leave a job without just cause, provided that they leave between the end of the sixth week and the end of a twelfth week of a trial period (subs. (3)). The intention is to act as an incentive to unemployed claimants to take up opportunities where they may be unsure as to whether the job is right for them.

Abatement of unemployment benefit on account of payments of occupational or personal pension

30.—(1) If payments by way of occupational or personal pension which in the aggregate exceed the maximum sum are made for any week to a person who has attained the age of 55, the rate of any unemployment benefit to which apart from this section he is entitled for that week shall be reduced by 10 pence for each 10 pence of the excess; and in this subsection "the maximum sum" means such sum not less than £35 as is prescribed.

(2) Where a reduction in the rate of unemployment benefit payable to a person falls to be made under this section the reduction shall be made, so far as is necessary—

(a) initially against so much of the benefit as falls to be paid by virtue of section 25(4) or (5) above or of regulations under section 60 below;

(b) then against any increase in the benefit payable under section 82 below; and

(c) finally against any increase in the benefit payable under section 80 below.

(3) Regulations may provide—

(a) for such sums as are specified in or determined under the regulations to be disregarded for the purposes of this section;

(b) for securing that no reduction in pursuance of subsection (1) above is made in the unemployment benefit for any day before the day which in pursuance of the regulations is treated as that on which relevant payments by way of occupational or personal pension begin;

(c) for this section to apply, in cases where—

(i) a lump sum is paid to a person in connection with a former employment of his or arrangements are made for a lump sum to be so paid;

(ii) benefits of any description are made available to a person in connection with a former employment of his or arrangements are made for them to be made so available; or

(iii) payments by way of occupational or personal pension to a person are assigned, reduced or postponed or are made otherwise than weekly,

as if there were made to the person such weekly payments by way of occupational or personal pension as are specified in or determined under the regulations;

(d) for the method of determining whether payments by way of occupational or personal pension are made to a person for any week and the amount of any such payments which are so made;

(e) for section 26(1) above and section 57(1) below to have effect, in relation to a person whose rate of unemployment benefit is reduced by virtue of this section, with such modifications as are prescribed.

(4) In this section—

"employer" means—

(a) in relation to an employment under a contract of service, the employer under the contract;

(b) in relation to an employment in an office with emoluments, the person responsible for paying the emoluments;

"employment" means an employment under a contract of service or in an office with emoluments;

"modifications" includes additions, omissions and amendments;

and the reference in subsection (1) above to unemployment benefit includes any increase of the benefit on account of dependants.

DEFINITIONS

"employer": subs. (4).
"employment": subs. (4).
"entitled": s.121(1).
"maximum sum": subs. (1).
"modifications": subs. (4).
"payments by way of occupational or personal pension": s.121(1).
"prescribe": s.121(1).
"week": s.121(1).

GENERAL NOTE

This section introduces a significant element of means-testing into unemployment benefit for those approaching retirement age. Where the claimant is 55 or over, and has an occupational or personal pension which exceeds £35.00 per week, unemployment benefit is reduced by 10p for every 10p that the pension exceeds the threshold. The £35.00 limit has remained unchanged since this rule was first enacted in 1980. A Tribunal of Commissioners has held that, notwithstanding that more men are likely to be affected by it than women, this provision is not in breach of the E.C. Directive on Equal Treatment 79/7 (*R(U) 10/88*).

Payments by way of occupational or personal pension. The definition in s.121(1) is very wide: see *R(U) 4/85* and *R(U) 1/89*. Broadly, the statutory definition covers all periodical payments made in connection with the ending of an employment from money provided wholly or partly by the employer, or from money provided under legislation, or from specified types of pension scheme. However, sums paid in respect of redundancy and not part of an occupational pension scheme are disregarded (Social Security (Unemployment, Sickness, and Invalidity Benefit) Regulations (Northern Ireland) 1984 (S.I. 1984 No. 245), reg. 25), as are lump sums paid instead of periodical payments (*R(U) 5/85*; but see also reg. 27). Where no benefit is received for a given day because of the operation of this section, the day still counts as a day of unemployment for the purposes of the rule limiting entitlement to 312 days (reg. 28).

Sickness benefit

Sickness benefit

31.—(1) Subject to the provisions of this section, a person who satisfies any of the three conditions of subsection (2) below shall be entitled to sickness benefit in respect of any day of incapacity for work which forms part of a period of interruption of employment.

(2) The conditions of this subsection are that—

(a) the person is under pensionable age on the day in question and satisfies the contribution conditions specified for sickness benefit in Schedule 3, Part I, paragraph 2;

(b) on that day the person—

(i) is over pensionable age, but not more than 5 years over that age; and

(ii) would be entitled to a Category A retirement pension if his entitlement had not been deferred or if he had not made an election under section 54(1) below; or

(c) on that day the person—

(i) is over pensionable age, but not more than 5 years over that age; and

(ii) would be entitled to a Category B retirement pension by virtue of the contributions of his deceased spouse, but for any such deferment or election.

(3) Subsection (1) above is subject to the provision made by section 102 below in relation to entitlement to sickness benefit in cases of industrial injury.

(4) A person shall not be entitled to sickness benefit for the first 3 days of any period of interruption of employment.

(5) In the case of a person entitled under paragraph (a) of subsection (2) above (including a person entitled by virtue of that paragraph and section 102 below) sickness benefit shall be payable at the weekly rate specified in Schedule 4, Part I, paragraph 2.

(6) In the case of any person over pensionable age who is entitled under paragraph (b) or (c) of subsection (2) above, sickness benefit shall be payable at the weekly rate at which the retirement pension referred to in the applicable paragraph of that subsection would have been payable; but in determining that rate for the purposes of this subsection any increase specified in subsection (7) below shall be disregarded.

(7) The increases to be disregarded for the purposes of subsection (6) above are the following—

(a) any increase (for married women) under section 53(2) below or (for deferred entitlement) under Schedule 5 to this Act;

(b) any increase (for dependants) under section 80, 83 or 85 below; and
(c) any increase (for Category A or Category B pensioners) under section 132 of the Administration Act which corresponds to an increase under section 150 of the Great Britain Administration Act.

(8) The amount payable by way of benefit under this section for any day of incapacity for work shall be one-sixth of the appropriate weekly rate.

DEFINITIONS
"the Administration Act": s.170.
"day of incapacity for work": ss.57(1)(a) and 121(1).
"deferred": s.121(1).
"entitled": s.121(1).
"pensionable age": s.121(1).
"period of interruption of employment": s.57(1)(d).

GENERAL NOTE
Sickness benefit is now a residual benefit for claimants who do not qualify for statutory sick pay (under Pt. XI) for some reason. The structure of this section is very similar to s.25 governing unemployment benefit (previously both benefits were dealt with together in SS(N.I.)A 1975, s.14). Benefit is payable for any day of incapacity for work (see s.57(1)(a)(ii) and 121(1)) which forms part of a period of interruption of employment (see General Note to s.25). The conditions set out in subs. (2) are the same as for unemployment benefit. Where the contribution conditions are not satisfied, sickness benefit is still payable where the claimant has become incapable of work due to an industrial accident or disease (subs. (3) and s.102).

As with unemployment benefit, there are three waiting days (subs. (4)) and the daily rate is one-sixth of the weekly rate (subs. (8)). The special rules as regards the rate of benefit for those who are over pensionable age but within five years of that age also apply (subs. (6)), although the invalidity increase in respect of Category A retirement pensions is not disregarded (subs. (7); compare s.25(6)(a)). See the General Note to s.25 on possible E.C. implications of these rules in so far as they are discriminatory. See also s.32 on the disqualification provisions.

Sickness benefit—disqualifications, etc.

32.—(1) Regulations may provide for disqualifying a person for receiving sickness benefit for such period not exceeding 6 weeks as may be determined in accordance with Part II of the Administration Act if—
(a) he has become incapable of work through his own misconduct; or
(b) he fails without good cause to attend for, or to submit himself to, such medical or other examination or treatment as may be required in accordance with the regulations, or to observe any prescribed rules of behaviour.

(2) Regulations may also provide for imposing, in the case of any prescribed category of persons—
(a) additional conditions with respect to the receipt of sickness benefit; and
(b) restrictions on the rate and duration of sickness benefit,
if, having regard to special circumstances, it appears to the Department necessary to do so for the purpose of preventing inequalities, or injustice to the general body of employed earners, or of earners generally, as the case may be.

(3) For the purposes of this section "week" means any period of 7 days.

DEFINITIONS
"the Administration Act": s.170.
"earner": s.121(1).
"employed earner": s.121(1).
"medical examination": s.121(1).
"medical treatment": s.121(1).
"prescribe": s.121(1).
"week": subs. (3).

GENERAL NOTE

This section allows regulations to be made disqualifying claimants from receiving sickness benefit for up to six weeks (not 26 weeks, as with unemployment benefit). The purpose of these rules has been described as three-fold: to protect the National Insurance Fund against fraudulent claims, to exclude those who are incapacitated through their own deliberate misconduct, and to reinforce the machinery for the control and administration of the scheme (Ogus and Barendt, p. 156). See further Social Security (Unemployment, Sickness and Invalidity Benefit) Regulations (Northern Ireland) 1984 (S.I. 1984 No. 245), reg. 17. Section 59 is a parallel enabling provision for invalidity benefit. There are no equivalent provisions governing statutory sick pay.

Invalidity benefits

Invalidity pension

33.—(1) Where in respect of any period of interruption of employment a person has been entitled to sickness benefit for 168 days (including, in the case of a woman, any day for which she was entitled to a maternity allowance) then—

(a)　he shall cease to be entitled to that benefit for any subsequent day of incapacity for work falling within that period; and

(b)　he shall be entitled to an invalidity pension under this section for any day of incapacity for work in that period for which, by virtue only of paragraph (a) above, he is not entitled to sickness benefit if on that day either—

(i) he is under pensionable age, or

(ii) being over that age but not more than 5 years over it he satisfies either of the conditions of subsection (2) below;

and any day in the first 3 days of a period of interruption of employment which was a day of incapacity for work shall be treated for the purposes of this subsection as a day on which he was so entitled.

(2) The conditions of this subsection are that on that day—

(a)　the person would be entitled to a Category A retirement pension if his entitlement had not been deferred or if he had not made an election under section 54(1) below; or

(b)　the person would be entitled to a Category B retirement pension by virtue of the contributions of his deceased spouse, but for any such deferment or election.

(3) Except as provided by subsection (4) below, the weekly rate of an invalidity pension under this section shall for any period of interruption of employment be determined in accordance with the provisions of sections 44 and 45 below as they apply in the case of a Category A retirement pension, but—

(a)　with the modification provided by section 46(1) below, and

(b)　with the substitution for section 44(7) below of the following—

"(7) In the application of this section for the purpose of determining the weekly rate of a person's invalidity pension for any period of interruption of employment—

(a)　"relevant year" means any tax year, being neither earlier than the tax year 1978–79 nor later than the tax year 1990-91, in the period which—

(i) begins with the tax year in which the invalidity pensioner attained the age of 16; and

(ii) ends with the tax year immediately preceding the tax year which includes or included the first day of entitlement to the pension in respect of that period of interruption of employment; and

(b)　"final relevant year" means the last tax year which is a relevant year in relation to the invalidity pensioner.".

(4) In the case of a person over pensionable age who is entitled to an invalidity pension under paragraph (a) or (b) of subsection (2) above, the pension shall be payable at the weekly rate at which the retirement pension referred to in the applicable paragraph of that subsection would have been payable, apart from any increase to be disregarded by virtue of subsection (5) below.

(5) The increases to be disregarded for the purposes of subsection (4) above are the following—

(a) if he is also entitled to an invalidity allowance, any increase under section 47(1) or 50(2) below;

(b) any increase (for married women) under section 53(2) below or (for deferred entitlement) under Schedule 5 to this Act;

(c) any increase (for dependants) under section 80, 83 or 85 below; and

(d) any increase (for Category A or Category B pensioners) under section 132 of the Administration Act which corresponds to an increase under section 150 of the Great Britain Administration Act.

(6) The amount payable by way of an invalidity pension under this section shall for any day of incapacity for work be one sixth of the appropriate weekly rate.

(7) Where—

(a) a person who is engaged and normally engaged in remunerative work ceases to be so engaged; and

(b) he is entitled to a disability working allowance for the week in which there falls the last day on which he is so engaged; and

(c) he qualified for a disability working allowance for that week by virtue of an invalidity pension under this section having been payable to him; and

(d) the first relevant day after he ceases to be engaged as mentioned in paragraph (a) above is for him a day of incapacity for work and falls not later than the end of the period of 2 years beginning with the last day for which he was entitled to such a pension,

any day since that day which fell within a week for which he was entitled to a disability working allowance shall be treated for the purposes of any claim for such a pension for a period commencing after he ceases to be engaged as mentioned in paragraph (a) above as having been a day of incapacity for work.

(8) Any day other than a Sunday or a day prescribed under section 57(1)(e) below is a relevant day for the purposes of subsection (7) above.

(9) Regulations may make provision in relation to entitlement to invalidity pension under this section—

(a) corresponding to that made by or under section 102 below in relation to sickness benefit for persons who have attained pensionable age;

(b) restricting entitlement to invalidity pension under this section in cases where in respect of one or more of the 168 days mentioned in subsection (1) above the person claiming invalidity pension (whether or not he has attained pensionable age) would not have been entitled to sickness benefit but for the provision so made.

(10) The Department may by regulations provide that, for the purpose of entitlement to invalidity pension under this section, such days as may be prescribed, in respect of which a person is or has been entitled to statutory sick pay, shall be days in respect of which he is deemed to be or to have been entitled to sickness benefit.

(11) A person under pensionable age who is deemed in accordance with regulations under subsection (10) above to have been entitled to sickness benefit for the whole or any part of a period of 168 days such as is mentioned in subsection (1) above shall not be entitled to invalidity pension under this section unless he would have satisfied the contribution conditions for sickness benefit had he claimed that benefit on the first of those days.

DEFINITIONS
"the Administration Act": s.170.
"day of incapacity of work": ss.57(1)(a) and 121(1).
"deferred": s.121(1).
"entitled": s.121(1).
"final relevant year": subs. (3).
"pensionable age": s.121(1).
"period of interruption of employment": s.57(1)(d).
"prescribe": s.121(1).
"relevant year": subs. (3).
"tax year": s.121(1).

GENERAL NOTE

Invalidity benefit is a contributory benefit for people incapable of work whose incapacity extends beyond the maximum period of entitlement to statutory sick pay or sickness benefit (*i.e.* 168 days, or 28 weeks). It consists of an invalidity pension, governed by this section, and, where appropriate, an invalidity allowance (s.34). Invalidity pension is payable to claimants under pensionable age and to those not more than five years above that age (subs. (1)). (The question as to whether this contravenes E.C. Directive 79/7 has been referred to the European Court of Justice: *R.* v. *Secretary of State for Social Security*, ex p. *Smithson* [1992] 1 C.M.L.R. 1601.) The day of claim must be a day of incapacity for work which falls within the same period of interruption of employment as that in which the maximum entitlement to sickness benefit (or maternity allowance) ended. Where a claimant has been in receipt of statutory sick pay, this requirement is deemed to be met (subs. (10)). There are special rules for widows so far as the qualifying period is concerned (s.40).

For claimants under pensionable age invalidity pension is essentially paid at the same rate as a Category A retirement pension (subs. (3)). Claimants who are over pensionable age have to meet the extra condition specified in subs. (2) and are paid at the appropriate rate equivalent to a category A or B retirement pension, excluding the specified increases (subss. (4) and (5)). As with unemployment benefit and sickness benefit, the daily rate is one-sixth of the weekly rate (subs. (6)). For the disqualification rules, see s.59.

As a general rule, claimants who leave invalidity benefit are exempt from the 28-week qualifying rule if they reclaim within eight weeks of the end of their earlier claim (s.57). The period under this linking rule is extended to two years for those in receipt of disability working allowance (subs. (7)).

Invalidity allowance

34.—(1) If a person is more than 5 years below pensionable age on the qualifying date in any period of interruption of employment then, subject to the following provisions of this section, in respect of every day of that period in respect of which he is entitled to an invalidity pension, he shall also be entitled to an invalidity allowance at the appropriate weekly rate specified in Schedule 4, Part I, paragraph 3.

(2) In this section "the qualifying date" means the first day in the period of interruption of employment in question (whether that day falls before the coming into force of this section or later) which is a day of incapacity for work or such earlier day as may be prescribed.

(3) An invalidity allowance shall be payable—

(a) at the higher rate specified in Schedule 4, Part I, paragraph 3, if—

　　(i) the qualifying date fell before 5th July 1948; or

　　(ii) on the qualifying date the beneficiary was under the age of 35; or

　　(iii) on the qualifying date the beneficiary was under the age of 40 and had not attained pensionable age before 6th April 1979;

(b) at the middle rate so specified if paragraph (a) above does not apply and either—

　　(i) on the qualifying date the beneficiary was under the age of 45; or

　　(ii) on the qualifying date the beneficiary was under the age of 50 and had not attained pensionable age before 6th April 1979;

(c) at the lower rate so specified if paragraphs (a) and (b) above do not apply, and on the qualifying date the beneficiary was a man under the age of 60 or a woman under the age of 55.

(4) Where for any period the weekly rate of the invalidity pension to which the beneficiary is entitled includes an additional pension such as is mentioned in section 44(3)(b) below, for that period the relevant amount shall be deducted from the appropriate weekly rate of invalidity allowance and he shall be entitled to invalidity allowance only if there is a balance after the deduction and, if there is such a balance, at a weekly rate equal to it.

(5) In this section "the relevant amount" means an amount equal to the additional pension reduced by the amount of any reduction in the weekly rate of the invalidity pension made by virtue of Article 31 of the Pensions Order.

(6) In this section references to an additional pension are references to that pension after any increase under section 52(3) below but without any increase under paragraphs 1 and 2 of Schedule 5 to this Act.

(7) The amount payable by way of invalidity allowance shall for any day of incapacity for work be one sixth of the appropriate weekly rate or, where subsection (4) above applies, of the weekly rate payable under that subsection.

DEFINITIONS
"beneficiary": s.121(1).
"day of incapacity for work": ss.57(1)(a) and 121(1).
"entitled": s.121(1).
"pensionable age": s.121(1).
"the Pensions Act": s.170.
"period of interruption of employment": s.57(1)(d).
"qualifying date": subs. (2).
"relevant amount": subs. (5).

GENERAL NOTE
Invalidity allowance is paid as a supplement to invalidity benefit for men who are aged under 60 and women under 55 on the first day of incapacity for work in a period of interruption of employment. The rate of benefit depends on the individual's age on the qualifying date: the highest rate is presently payable to those under 40, the middle rate to those aged between 40 and 49, and the lower rate for men aged 50–59 and women aged 50–54 (subs. (3)).

The discrimination against women aged 55–59 would appear to be unlawful under Art. 4 of E.C. Directive 79/7: see *Thomas* v. *Chief Adjudication Officer and Secretary of State for Social Security*; *Cooze* v. *Same*; *Beard* v. *Same*; *Murphy* v. *Same*; *Morley* v. *Same* [1991] 2 W.L.R. 886 and General Note to s.25.

Amounts received by way of earnings-related components or guaranteed minimum pension are deducted from the allowance (subss. (4)–(6)).

Maternity

State maternity allowance

35.—(1) A woman shall be entitled to a maternity allowance at the weekly rate specified in Schedule 4, Part I, paragraph 4, if—

(a) she has become pregnant and has reached, or been confined before reaching, the commencement of the 11th week before the expected week of confinement; and

(b) she has been engaged in employment as an employed or self-employed earner for at least 26 weeks in the 52 weeks immediately preceding the 14th week before the expected week of confinement; and

(c) she satisfies the contribution condition for a maternity allowance specified in Schedule 3, Part I, paragraph 3; and

(d) she is not entitled to statutory maternity pay for the same week in respect of the same pregnancy.

(2) Subject to the following provisions of this section, a maternity allowance shall be payable for the period ("the maternity allowance period") which, if she were entitled to statutory maternity pay, would be the maternity pay period under section 161 below.

(3) Regulations may provide—

(a) for disqualifying a woman for receiving a maternity allowance if—

(i) during the maternity allowance period she does any work in employment as an employed or self-employed earner, or fails without good cause to observe any prescribed rules of behaviour; or

(ii) at any time before she is confined she fails without good cause to attend for, or submit herself to, any medical examination required in accordance with the regulations;

(b) that this section and Schedule 3, Part I, paragraph 3 shall have effect subject to prescribed modifications in relation to cases in which a woman has been confined and—

(i) has not made a claim for a maternity allowance in expectation of that confinement (other than a claim which has been disallowed); or

(ii) has made a claim for a maternity allowance in expectation of that confinement (other than a claim which has been disallowed), but she was confined more than 11 weeks before the expected week of confinement.

(4) A woman who has become entitled to a maternity allowance shall cease to be entitled to it if she dies before the beginning of the maternity allowance period; and if she dies after the beginning, but before the end, of that period, the allowance shall not be payable for any week subsequent to that in which she dies.

(5) Where for any purposes of this Part of this Act or of regulations it is necessary to calculate the daily rate of a maternity allowance—

(a) Sunday or such other day in each week as may be prescribed shall be disregarded; and

(b) the amount payable by way of that allowance for any other day shall be taken as one sixth of the weekly rate of the allowance.

(6) In this section "confinement" means—

(a) labour resulting in the issue of a living child, or

(b) labour after 28 weeks of pregnancy resulting in the issue of a child whether alive or dead,

and "confined" shall be construed accordingly; and where a woman's labour begun on one day results in the issue of a child on another day she shall be taken to be confined on the day of the issue of the child or, if labour results in the issue of twins or a greater number of children, she shall be taken to be confined on the day of the issue of the last of them.

(7) The fact that the mother of a child is being paid maternity allowance shall not be taken into consideration by any court in deciding whether to order payment of expenses incidental to the birth of the child.

DEFINITIONS

"claim": s.121(1).
"confined": subs. (6).
"confinement": subs. (6).
"employed earner": s.121(1).
"employment": s.121(1).
"entitled": s.121(1).
"maternity allowance period": subs. (2).
"prescribe": s.121(1).
"self-employed earner": s.121(1).
"week": s.121(1).

GENERAL NOTE

The state maternity allowance is a residual contributory benefit and replaced the old maternity allowance. Most women workers will be entitled to statutory maternity pay (under Pt. XII) in the event of pregnancy. Entitlement to statutory maternity pay and state maternity allowance are mutually exclusive (subs. (1)(d)). State maternity allowance is payable to women who do not qualify for statutory maternity pay, *e.g.* because they are self-employed or fail to meet the continuous employment test for that benefit.

There are four main conditions for entitlement to state maternity allowance. The claimant must:

(1) satisfy the contribution condition (subs. (1)(c); see Sched. 3, Pt. I, para. 3);

(2) have been employed for at least 26 weeks in the 52 weeks ending before the 14th week before the expected week of confinement (subs. (1)(b));

(3) either be expecting a child within the next 11 weeks or have recently given birth (subs. (1)(a); and see *R(G) 4/56* and *R(G) 12/59*); and

(4) not be working (and see regulations below).

Like statutory maternity pay, state maternity allowance is payable for 18 weeks, commencing not earlier than the 11th week before the expected week of confinement (subs. (2)).

The Social Security (Maternity Allowance) Regulations (Northern Ireland) 1987 (S.I. 1987 No. 170), made under subs. (3), provide for certain disqualifications for benefit and for modifications of the maternity allowance period.

Benefits for widows and widowers

Widow's payment

36.—(1) A woman who has been widowed shall be entitled to a widow's payment of the amount specified in Schedule 4, Part II if—

(a) she was under pensionable age at the time when her late husband died, or he was then not entitled to a Category A retirement pension under section 44 below; and

(b) her late husband satisfied the contribution condition for a widow's payment specified in Schedule 3, Part I, paragraph 4.

(2) The payment shall not be payable to a widow if she and a man to whom she is not married are living together as husband and wife at the time of her husband's death.

(3) A widow's payment is payable only in cases where the husband dies on or after 11th April 1988 (the coming into operation of Article 37 of the 1986 Order, which introduced the widow's payment by making provision corresponding to this section).

DEFINITIONS

"the 1986 Act": s.170.
"entitled": s.121(1).
"late husband": s.121(1).
"pensionable age": s.121(1).

GENERAL NOTE

The widow's payment is a lump-sum payment which replaced the widow's allowance (a weekly benefit paid for the first six months of widowhood) from April 1988. Under subs. (1) this benefit is only payable if the widow was under pensionable age when her husband died (or if he was not entitled to a Category A retirement pension) and if her husband satisfied the contribution conditions (or died as a result of an industrial accident or disease: s.60(2)). No benefit is payable where the widow is cohabiting with another man at the time of her husband's death (subs. (2); and see General Note to s.38).

Widowed mother's allowance

37.—(1) A woman who has been widowed shall be entitled to a widowed mother's allowance at the rate determined in accordance with section 39 below if her late husband satisfied the contribution conditions for a widowed mother's allowance specified in Schedule 3, Part I, paragraph 5 and either—

(a) the woman is entitled to child benefit in respect of a child falling within subsection (2) below;

(b) the woman is pregnant by her late husband; or

(c) if the woman and her late husband were residing together immediately before the time of his death, the woman is pregnant as the result of being artificially inseminated before that time with the semen of some person other than her husband, or as the result of the placing in her before that time of an embryo, of an egg in the process of fertilisation, or of sperm and eggs.

(2) A child falls within this subsection if one of the conditions specified in section 81(2) below is for the time being satisfied with respect to the child and the child is either—

(a) a son or daughter of the woman and her late husband;

(b) a child in respect of whom her late husband was immediately before his death entitled to child benefit; or

(c) if the woman and her late husband were residing together immediately before his death, a child in respect of whom she was then entitled to child benefit.

(3) The widow shall not be entitled to the allowance for any period after she remarries, but, subject to that, she shall continue to be entitled to it for any period throughout which she satisfies the requirements of subsection (1)(a), (b) or (c) above.

(4) A widowed mother's allowance shall not be payable—

(a) for any period falling before the day on which the widow's entitlement is to be regarded as commencing for that purpose by virtue of section 5(1)(l) of the Administration Act; or

(b) for any period during which she and a man to whom she is not married are living together as husband and wife.

DEFINITIONS

"the Administration Act": s.170.
"child": s.121(1).
"entitled": s.121(1).
"late husband": s.121(1).

GENERAL NOTE

Widowed mother's allowance is a weekly benefit for which two conditions have to be satisfied. First, the widow's late husband must have met the contribution conditions (or have died as a result of an industrial accident or disease: s.60(2)). Secondly, the widow must be receiving child benefit for a child falling within subs. (2), or be pregnant with her husband's child, or pregnant by A.I.D. (so long as she was residing with her husband immediately before his death). Widowed mother's allowance ends on remarriage and is suspended during any period of cohabitation (subss. (3) and (4); see General Note to s.38). Once it ceases (*e.g.* because child benefit is no longer payable for any child), a widow's pension may be payable under s.38.

Widow's pension

38.—(1) A woman who has been widowed shall be entitled to a widow's pension at the rate determined in accordance with section 39 below if her late husband satisfied the contribution conditions for a widow's pension specified in Schedule 3, Part I, paragraph 5 and either—

(a) she was, at the husband's death, over the age of 45 but under the age of 65; or

(b) she ceased to be entitled to a widowed mother's allowance at a time when she was over the age of 45 but under the age of 65.

(2) The widow shall not be entitled to the pension for any period after she remarries, but, subject to that, she shall continue to be entitled to it until she attains the age of 65.

(3) A widow's pension shall not be payable—
(a) for any period falling before the day on which the widow's entitlement is to be regarded as commencing for that purpose by virtue of section 5(1)(l) of the Administration Act;
(b) for any period for which she is entitled to a widowed mother's allowance; or
(c) for any period during which she and a man to whom she is not married are living together as husband and wife.

(4) In the case of a widow whose late husband died before 11th April 1988 and who either—
(a) was over the age of 40 but under the age of 55 at the time of her husband's death; or
(b) is over the age of 40 but under the age of 55 at the time when she ceases to be entitled to a widowed mother's allowance,
subsection (1) above shall have effect as if for "45" there were substituted "40".

DEFINITIONS
"the Administration Act": s.170.
"entitled": s.121(1).
"late husband": s.121(1).

GENERAL NOTE
The widow's pension is a weekly benefit payable to widows aged under 65 who are not entitled to widowed mother's allowance (s.37) and whose late husband satisfied the contributions requirement (or whose death was due to an industrial accident or disease: s.60(2)). Finally, if the husband died on or after April 11, 1988, the widow must have been over 45 but under 65 at the time of his death or when she was no longer eligible for widowed mother's allowance (subs. (1)). Alternatively, where the husband died before April 11, 1988 the widow need only have been over 40 but under 65 on either of these dates (subs. (4)). The basic rate of benefit is the same as the Category A retirement pension, but is reduced if the claimant was under 55 at the relevant date, or 50 where the bereavement was before April 11, 1988 (s.39(4)–(6)).

It is fundamental to widowhood that (a) there was a valid marriage in existence at the time of the husband's death, and (b) that the husband is in fact dead. So far as (a) is concerned, this is usually evidenced by production of a copy of the marriage certificate. Difficulties may arise in connection with Scottish marriages, which may be proved by "cohabitation with habit and repute" (*R(G) 2/82, R(G) 5/83* and *R(G) 4/84*), or with foreign marriages (*R(G) 2/71*): see Bonner. Marriage may be brought to an end by decree absolute of divorce or nullity, although a void marriage has no legal effect at any time.

As regards (b), this is again usually evidenced by production of a copy of the relevant certificate. See SSA(N.I.)A 1992, s.3, in cases where death is difficult to establish, and Bonner for discussion of the position where the husband is presumed dead. Where the widow is herself responsible for her late husband's death, the provisions of the Forfeiture (Northern Ireland) Order 1982 apply. (But see unreported Northern Ireland decision BNIL *89/2/101.*)

Entitlement to widow's pension terminates on remarriage or attaining the age of 65 (subs. (2)). Benefit is suspended so long as the widow is living with another man as husband and wife. For analysis of this expression, see annotations to s.137. The principles governing the same term in the context of income support (formerly supplementary benefit) apply equally to widow's benefits (*R(SB) 17/81* and *R(G) 3/81*).

Rate of widowed mother's allowance and widow's pension

39.—(1) The weekly rate of—
(a) a widowed mother's allowance,
(b) a widow's pension,
shall be determined in accordance with the provisions of sections 44 and 45 below as they apply in the case of a Category A retirement pension, but subject, in particular, to the following provisions of this section and section 46(2) below.

(2) In the application of sections 44 and 45 below by virtue of subsection (1) above—

    (a) where the woman's husband was over pensionable age when he died, references in those sections to the pensioner shall be taken as references to the husband, and

    (b) where the husband was under pensionable age when he died, references in those sections to the pensioner and the tax year in which he attained pensionable age shall be taken as references to the husband and the tax year in which he died.

(3) In the case of a woman whose husband dies after 5th April 2000, the additional pension falling to be calculated under sections 44 and 45 below by virtue of subsection (1) above shall (before making any reduction required by subsection (4) below) be one half of the amount which it would be apart from this subsection.

(4) Where a widow's pension is payable to a woman who was under the age of 55 at the time when the applicable qualifying condition was fulfilled, the weekly rate of the pension shall be reduced by 7 per cent. of what it would be apart from this subsection multiplied by the number of years by which her age at that time was less than 55 (any fraction of a year being counted as a year).

(5) For the purposes of subsection (4) above, the time when the applicable qualifying condition was fulfilled is the time when the woman's late husband died or, as the case may be, the time when she ceased to be entitled to a widowed mother's allowance.

(6) In the case of a widow whose late husband died before 11th April 1988 and who either—

    (a) was over the age of 40 but under the age of 55 at the time of her husband's death; or

    (b) is over the age of 40 but under the age of 55 at the time when she ceases to be entitled to a widowed mother's allowance,

subsection (4) above shall have effect as if for "55" there were substituted "50".

DEFINITIONS

    "entitled": s.121(1).
    "late husband": s.121(1).
    "pensionable age": s.121(1).
    "tax year": s.121(1)

GENERAL NOTE

    This section deals with the rate at which the weekly benefits under ss.37 and 38 are payable. Essentially both benefits are paid at the same rate as the Category A retirement pension. The widow's pension is reduced in the case of younger widows (subss. (4)–(6); see General Note to s.38). Claimants widowed after April 5, 2000 will be entitled to only half the increase under SERPS that is payable in relation to deaths before that date (subs. (3)).

Invalidity pension for widows

40.—(1) Subject to subsection (2) below, this section applies to a woman who—

    (a) on her late husband's death is not entitled to a widowed mother's allowance or subsequently ceases to be entitled to such an allowance; and

    (b) is incapable of work at the time when he dies or when she subsequently ceases to be so entitled; and

    (c) either—

        (i) would have been entitled to a widow's pension if she had been over the age of 45 when her husband died or when she ceased to be entitled to a widowed mother's allowance; or

(ii) is entitled to such a pension with a reduction under section 39(4) above.

(2) This section does not apply to a woman unless—

(a) her husband died after 5th April 1979; or

(b) she ceased to be entitled to a widowed mother's allowance after that date (whenever her husband died).

(3) Subject to subsection (7) below, a woman to whom this section applies shall be entitled to an invalidity pension under this section for any day of incapacity for work which—

(a) falls in a period of interruption of employment that began before the time when her late husband died or she subsequently ceased to be entitled to a widowed mother's allowance; and

(b) is after that time and after the first 168 days of incapacity for work in that period.

(4) An invalidity pension under this section shall be payable at the higher of—

(a) the weekly rate which would apply if the pension were payable under section 33 above; or

(b) the weekly rate specified in subsection (5) below.

(5) The weekly rate referred to in subsection (4)(b) above is—

(a) if the woman is not entitled to a widow's pension, a weekly rate equal to that of the widow's pension to which she would have been entitled if she had been over the age of 55 when her husband died; and

(b) if she is entitled to a widow's pension with a reduction under section 39(4) above, a weekly rate equal to the difference between the weekly rate of that pension and what it would have been without the reduction,

but, in calculating the weekly rate of a widow's pension for the purposes of paragraph (a) above, or the weekly rate of a widow's pension without reduction, for the purposes of paragraph (b) above, any additional pension by virtue of section 44(3) below as it applies for the purposes of section 39 above shall be determined without reference to any surpluses in her late husband's earnings factors for tax years after 1990–91.

(6) For the purpose of calculating the rate of an invalidity pension for a woman to whom this section applies by virtue of subsection (1)(c)(ii) above, subsections (4) and (5) above shall have effect with such modifications as are prescribed.

(7) A woman shall not be entitled to an invalidity pension under this section if she is over pensionable age and is entitled to a Category A or Category B retirement pension; but if she has attained pensionable age, and the period of interruption of employment mentioned in subsection (3)(a) above did not terminate earlier than the day before she attained that age—

(a) she shall, if not otherwise entitled to a Category A retirement pension, be entitled to such a pension; and

(b) the weekly rate of the Category A retirement pension to which she is entitled (whether by virtue of paragraph (a) above or otherwise) shall be determined in the prescribed manner.

(8) No invalidity pension shall be payable under section 33 above for any day of incapacity for which an invalidity pension is payable under this section.

(9) In subsection (6) above "modifications" includes additions, omissions and amendments.

DEFINITIONS

"day of incapacity for work": ss.57(1)(a) and 121(1).

"entitled": s.121(1).

"late husband": s.121(1).

"modifications": subs. (9).
"pensionable age": s.121(1).
"period of interruption of employment": s.57(1)(d).
"prescribe": s.121(1).
"tax year": s.121(1).

GENERAL NOTE

A widow who falls within subss. (1) and (2) may claim invalidity benefit after 168 days of incapacity even though she does not satisfy the normal requirement of receipt of statutory sick pay or sickness benefit during this period (subs. (3)). The additional component is calculated on the basis of her own contributions or those of her late husband, whichever is the more favourable to her (subs. (4)). The same principle applies to widowers (s.41(3)).

Invalidity pension for widowers

41.—(1) This section applies to a man whose wife has died on or after 6th April 1979 and who either—
   (a) was incapable of work at the time when she died; or
   (b) becomes incapable of work within the prescribed period after that time.
(2) Subject to subsection (7) below, a man to whom this section applies shall be entitled to an invalidity pension under this section for any day of incapacity for work which—
   (a) falls in a period of interruption of employment that began before the time when his wife died or within the prescribed period after that time; and
   (b) is after that time and after the first 168 days of incapacity for work in that period.
(3) An invalidity pension under this section shall be payable at the higher of—
   (a) the weekly rate which would apply if the pension were payable under section 33 above; or
   (b) the weekly rate specified in subsection (4) below.
(4) The weekly rate mentioned in subsection (3)(b) above is a rate determined in accordance with the provisions of sections 44 and 45 below as they apply in the case of a Category A retirement pension, but subject in particular, to subsections (5) and (6) and section 46(2) below.
(5) In the application of sections 44 and 45 below by virtue of subsection (4) above—
   (a) where the man's wife was over pensionable age when she died, references in those sections to the pensioner shall be taken as references to the wife; and
   (b) where the man's wife was under pensionable age when she died, references in those sections to the pensioner and the tax year in which he attained pensionable age shall be taken as references to the wife and the tax year in which she died; and
   (c) any additional pension shall be determined without reference to any surpluses in her earnings factors for tax years after 1990–91.
(6) In the case of a widower whose wife dies after 5th April 2000, the additional pension falling to be calculated under sections 44 and 45 below by virtue of subsection (4) above shall be one half of the amount which it would be apart from this subsection.
(7) A man shall not be entitled to an invalidity pension under this section if he is over pensionable age and is entitled to a Category A or Category B retirement pension; but if he has attained pensionable age, and the period of interruption of employment mentioned in subsection (2)(a) above did not terminate earlier than the day before he attained that age—
   (a) he shall, if not otherwise entitled to a Category A retirement pension

and also not entitled to a Category B retirement pension by virtue of section 51 below, be entitled to a Category A retirement pension; and
(b) the weekly rate of the Category A retirement pension to which he is entitled (whether by virtue of paragraph (a) above or otherwise) shall be determined in the prescribed manner.

(8) No invalidity pension shall be payable under section 33 above for any day of incapacity for which an invalidity pension is payable under this section.

DEFINITIONS
"day of incapacity for work": ss.57(1)(a) and 121(1).
"earnings factor": s.22(1).
"entitled": s.121(1).
"pensionable age": s.121(1).
"period of interruption of employment": s.57(1)(d).
"prescribe": s.121(1).
"tax year": s.121(1).

GENERAL NOTE
The contributory benefits scheme has no special benefits for widowers. This section provides one concession in that a man who falls within subs. (1) is entitled to an invalidity pension, based on either his own contributions or those of his late wife, whichever produces the higher rate.

Entitlement to invalidity pension on termination of employment after period of entitlement to disability working allowance

42.—(1) Where—
(a) a person who is engaged and normally engaged in remunerative work ceases to be so engaged; and
(b) he is entitled to a disability working allowance for the week in which there falls the last day on which he is so engaged; and
(c) he qualified for a disability working allowance for that week by virtue of an invalidity pension under section 40 or 41 above having been payable to him; and
(d) the first relevant day after he ceases to be engaged as mentioned in paragraph (a) above is a day on which he is incapable of work and falls not later than the end of the period of 2 years beginning with the last day for which he was entitled to such a pension,
any day since that day which fell within a week for which he was entitled to a disability working allowance shall be treated for the purposes of any claim for such a pension for a period commencing after he ceases to be engaged as mentioned in paragraph (a) above as having been a day on which he was incapable of work.

(2) Any day other than a Sunday or a day prescribed under section 57(1)(e) below is a relevant day for the purposes of this section.

DEFINITIONS
"entitled": s.121(1).
"prescribe": s.121(1).

GENERAL NOTE
This is an analogous provision to the linking rule under s.33(7) but in relation to claims for invalidity pension by people over pensionable age.

Retirement pensions (Categories A and B)

Persons entitled to more than one retirement pension

43.—(1) A person shall not be entitled for the same period to more than one retirement pension under this Part of this Act except as provided by subsection (2) below.

(2) A person who, apart from subsection (1) above, would be entitled for the same period to both—

(a) a Category A or a Category B retirement pension under this Part; and

(b) a Category C or a Category D retirement pension under Part III of this Act,

shall be entitled to both of those pensions for that period, subject to any adjustment of them in pursuance of regulations under section 71 of the Administration Act.

(3) A person who, apart from subsection (1) above, would be entitled—

(a) to both a Category A and a Category B retirement pension under this Part for the same period, or

(b) to both a Category C and a Category D retirement pension under Part III of this Act for the same period,

may from time to time give notice in writing to the Department specifying which of the pensions referred to in paragraph (a) or, as the case may be, paragraph (b) above he wishes to receive.

(4) If a person gives such a notice, the pension so specified shall be the one to which he is entitled in respect of any week commencing after the date of the notice.

(5) If no such notice is given, the person shall be entitled to whichever of the pensions is from time to time the most favourable to him (whether it is the pension which he claimed or not).

DEFINITIONS

"the Administration Act": s.170.

"entitled": s.121(1).

"week": s.121(1).

GENERAL NOTE

There are four types of retirement pension:

Category A: paid on the basis of the claimant's own contribution record (s.44).

Category B: paid to married women on the basis of their husband's contribution record and also to certain widows and widowers on the basis of their deceased spouse's contributions (ss.49–51).

Category C: paid to those who were already over pensionable age on July 5, 1948 or whose husband was then over that age (s.78).

Category D: paid to those aged over 80 years of age who do not qualify for another retirement pension (s.78).

The general rule, not surprisingly, is that a claimant is not entitled to more than one retirement pension at a time (subs. (1)). A special rule operates in the cases mentioned in subss. (2) and (3).

Category A retirement pension

44.—(1) A person shall be entitled to a Category A retirement pension if—

(a) he is over pensionable age; and

(b) he satisfies the contribution conditions for a Category A retirement pension specified in Schedule 3, Part I, paragraph 5;

and, subject to the provisions of this Act, he shall become so entitled on the day on which he attains pensionable age and his entitlement shall continue throughout his life.

(2) A Category A retirement pension shall not be payable in respect of any period falling before the day on which the pensioner's entitlement is to be regarded as commencing for that purpose by virtue of section 5(1)(l) of the Administration Act.

(3) A Category A retirement pension shall consist of—

(a) a basic pension payable at a weekly rate; and

(b) an additional pension payable where there are one or more surpluses in the pensioner's earnings factors for the relevant years.

(4) The weekly rate of the basic pension shall be £54.15 except that, so far as the sum is relevant for the purpose of calculating the rate of sickness benefit under section 31(6) above, it shall be £51.95.

(5) For the purposes of this section and section 45 below—
 (a) there is a surplus in the pensioner's earnings factor for a relevant year if that factor exceeds the qualifying earnings factor for the final relevant year; and
 (b) the amount of the surplus is the amount of that excess;
and for the purposes of paragraph (a) above the pensioner's earnings factor for any relevant year shall be taken to be that factor as increased by the last order under section 130 of the Administration Act to come into force before the end of the final relevant year.

(6) Any reference in this section or section 45 below to the pensioner's earnings factor for any relevant year is a reference—
 (a) where the relevant year is 1987–88 or any subsequent tax year, to the aggregate of—
  (i) his earnings factors derived from earnings upon which primary Class 1 contributions were paid or treated as paid in respect of that year, and
  (ii) his earnings factors derived from Class 2 and Class 3 contributions actually paid in respect of it; and
 (b) where the relevant year is an earlier tax year, to the aggregate of his earnings factors derived from contributions actually paid by him in respect of that year.

(7) In this section—
 (a) "relevant year" means 1978–79 or any subsequent tax year in the period between—
  (i) (inclusive) the tax year in which the pensioner attained the age of 16, and
  (ii) (exclusive) the tax year in which he attained pensionable age;
 (b) "final relevant year" means the last tax year which is a relevant year in relation to the pensioner.

(8) For the purposes of this section any order under Article 23 of the Pensions Order (which made provision corresponding to section 130 of the Administration Act) shall be treated as an order under section 130 (but without prejudice to sections 16 and 17 of the Interpretation Act 1978).

DEFINITIONS
 "additional pension": s.45(1).
 "the Administration Act": s.170.
 "earnings": s.121(1).
 "earnings factor": s.22(1).
 "entitled": s.121(1).
 "final relevant year": subs. (7)(b).
 "pensionable age": s.121(1).
 "the Pensions Order": s.170.
 "qualifying earnings factor": s.121(1).
 "relevant year": subs. (7)(a).
 "tax year": s.121(1).

GENERAL NOTE
 The Category A retirement pension is the standard old-age pension. The two eligibility conditions are that the claimant has reached pensionable age and has satisfied the necessary contribution requirements (subs. (1)). The retirement condition and the earnings rule were abolished by SS(N.I.)O 1989, so a pension may be drawn when the above two conditions are met, irrespective of whether the claimant intends to remain in regular employment. Reduced rate pensions are payable where the claimant has an incomplete contributions record (Social Security (Widow's Benefit and Retirement Pensions) Regulations (Northern Ireland) 1979 (S.I. 1979 No. 243), reg. 6).

The weekly Category A retirement pension consists of a flat-rate basic component and an earnings-related additional component (subs. (3)). Subsections (4)–(6) and s.45 deal with the calculation of this benefit. A Category A pension may be increased by the age addition of 25p per week for claimants over 80 (s.79), a higher pension by deferring entitlement (s.55), a graduated retirement benefit based on earnings between 1961 and 1975 (s.62) and, in certain cases, invalidity allowance (s.47). The Christmas bonus (s.144) is also payable.

Subs. (1)
The difference in pensionable ages for men and women (s.121(1)) is permitted by Art. 7 of E.C. Directive 79/7: *R(P)3/90.*

Subs. (6)
Note the transitory modification in SS(CP)(N.I.)A 1992, Sched. 4, paras. 2 and 3.

The additional pension in a Category A retirement pension

45.—(1) The weekly rate of the additional pension in a Category A retirement pension in any case where the pensioner attained pensionable age in a tax year before 6th April 1999 shall be the weekly equivalent of 1 1/4 per cent. of the amount of the surpluses mentioned in section 44(3)(b) above.

(2) The weekly rate of the additional pension in a Category A retirement pension in any case where the pensioner attained pensionable age in a tax year after 5th April 1999 shall be—
- (a) in relation to any surpluses in the pensioner's earnings factors for the tax years in the period beginning with 1978–79 and ending with 1987–88, the weekly equivalent of 25/N per cent. of the amount of those surpluses; and
- (b) in relation to any surpluses in the pensioner's earnings factors in a tax year after 1987–88, the weekly equivalent of the relevant percentage of the amount of those surpluses.

(3) In subsection (2)(b) above, "relevant percentage" means—
- (a) 20/N per cent., where the pensioner attained pensionable age in 2009–10 or any subsequent tax year;
- (b) $(20+X)/N$ per cent., where the pensioner attained pensionable age in a tax year falling within the period commencing with 1999–2000 and ending with 2008–9.

(4) In this section—
- (a) $X = 0.5$ for each tax year by which the tax year in which the pensioner attained pensionable age precedes 2009–10; and
- (b) $N =$ the number of tax years in the pensioner's working life which fall after 5th April 1978;

but paragraph (b) above is subject, in particular, to subsection (5) and, where applicable, section 46 below.

(5) Regulations may direct that in prescribed cases or classes of cases any tax year shall be disregarded for the purpose of calculating N under subsection (4)(b) above, if it is a tax year after 5th April 1978 in which the pensioner—
- (a) was credited with contributions or earnings under this Act by virtue of regulations under section 22(5) above, or
- (b) was precluded from regular employment by responsibilities at home, or
- (c) in prescribed circumstances, would have been treated as falling within paragraph (a) or (b) above,

but not so as to reduce the number of years below 20.

(6) For the purposes of subsections (1) and (2) above, the weekly equivalent of the amount of any surpluses shall be calculated by dividing that amount by 52 and rounding the result to the nearest whole penny, taking any 1/2p as nearest to the next whole penny.

(7) Where the amount falling to be rounded under subsection (6) above is a sum less than 1/2p, the amount calculated under that subsection shall be taken to be zero, notwithstanding any other provision of this Act or the Administration Act.

(8) The sums which are the weekly rate of the additional pension in a Category A retirement pension are subject to alteration by orders made by the Department under section 132 of the Administration Act.

DEFINITIONS
"the Administration Act": s.170.
"earnings factor": s.22(1).
"pensionable age": s.121(1).
"prescribe": s.121(1).
"relevant percentage": subs. (3).
"tax year": s.121(1).

GENERAL NOTE
This details the method of calculation for the additional pension under s.44(3)(b), but subject to the modifications under s.46.

Modifications of s.45 for calculating the additional pension in certain benefits

46.—(1) For the purpose of determining the additional pension falling to be calculated under section 45 above by virtue of section 33(3) above, the following definition shall be substituted for the definition of "N" in section 45(4)(b) above—

"N = the number of tax years which begin after 5th April 1978 and end before the first day of entitlement to the additional pension in the period of interruption of employment in which that day falls, except that if—
(i) in a case where the person entitled to the pension is a man, that number would be greater than 49; or
(ii) in a case where the person so entitled is a woman, that number would be greater than 44,
N = 49 or 44, as the case may be".

(2) For the purpose of determining the additional pension falling to be calculated under section 45 above by virtue of section 39(1) or 41(4) above or section 50(3) below in a case where the deceased spouse died under pensionable age, the following definition shall be substituted for the definition of "N" in section 45(4)(b) above—

"N = the number of tax years which begin after 5th April 1978 and end before the date when the entitlement to the additional pension commences, except that if—
(i) in a case where the deceased spouse was a man, that number would be greater than 49, or
(ii) in a case where the deceased spouse was a woman, that number would be greater than 44,
N = 49 or 44, as the case may be".

DEFINITIONS
"additional pension": s.45(1).
"pensionable age": s.121(1).
"period of interruption of employment": s.57(1)(d).
"tax year": s.121(1).

GENERAL NOTE
See General Note to s.45.

Increase of Category A retirement pension for invalidity

47.—(1) Subject to section 61 below, the weekly rate of a Category A retirement pension shall be increased if the pensioner was entitled to an invalidity allowance in respect of—

(a) any day falling within the period of 8 weeks ending immediately before the day on which he attains pensionable age; or

(b) the last day before the beginning of that period;

and the increase shall, subject to subsection (2) below, be of an amount equal to the appropriate weekly rate of the invalidity allowance on that day.

(2) Where for any period the weekly rate of a Category A retirement pension includes an additional pension, for that period the relevant amount shall be deducted from the amount that would otherwise be the increase under subsection (1) above and the pensioner shall be entitled to an increase under that subsection only if there is a balance remaining after that deduction and, if there is such a balance, of an amount equal to it.

(3) In subsection (2) above the "relevant amount" means an amount equal to the additional pension, reduced by the amount of any reduction in the weekly rate of the Category A retirement pension made by virtue of Article 31 of the Pensions Order.

(4) In this section any reference to an additional pension is a reference to that pension after any increase under section 52(3) below but without any increase under paragraphs 1 and 2 of Schedule 5 to this Act.

(5) In ascertaining for the purposes of subsection (1) above the rate of a pensioner's invalidity allowance, regard shall be had to the rates in force from time to time.

(6) Regulations may provide that subsection (1) above shall have effect as if for the reference to 8 weeks there were substituted a reference to a larger number of weeks specified in the regulations.

DEFINITIONS
  "entitled": s.121(1).
  "pensionable age": s.121(1).
  "the Pensions Order": s.170.
  "relevant amount": subs. (3).
  "week": s.121(1).

GENERAL NOTE
  A claimant in receipt of invalidity allowance (s.34) in the period immediately before attaining pensionable age may keep that benefit as a supplement to a Category A retirement pension. If the claimant is also entitled to an increased pension by virtue of SERPS (or its equivalent if contracted-out), such an increase is set against the invalidity allowance and only the balance becomes payable. This section is subject to s.61, which excludes increases of benefit where there has been a failure to satisfy a contribution condition.

Use of former spouse's contributions

48.—(1) Where a person—

(a) has been married, and

(b) in respect of the tax year in which the marriage terminated or any previous tax year, does not with his own contributions satisfy the contribution conditions for a Category A retirement pension,

then, for the purpose of enabling him to satisfy those conditions (but only in respect of any claim for a Category A retirement pension), the contributions of his former spouse may to the prescribed extent be treated as if they were his own contributions.

(2) Subsection (1) above shall not apply in relation to any person who attained pensionable age before 6th April 1979 if the termination of his marriage also occurred before that date.

(3) Where a person has been married more than once this section applies only to the last marriage and the references to his marriage and his former spouse shall be construed accordingly.

DEFINITIONS
"pensionable age": s.121(1).
"prescribe": s.121(1).
"tax year": s.121(1).

GENERAL NOTE
A widow or widower who has not attained pensionable age before his or her spouse died, and who has not remarried before that age, can rely on that deceased spouse's contributions record. See further Social Security (Widow's Benefit and Retirement Pensions) Regulations (Northern Ireland) 1979 (S.I. 1979 No. 243), reg. 8 and Sched. 1.

Category B retirement pension for women

49.—(1) A woman who is or has been married, and has attained pensionable age, shall be entitled to a Category B retirement pension by virtue of the contributions of her husband; and the cases in which a woman is so entitled are those specified in subsections (2) to (5) below.

(2) The first case of entitlement is where the woman is married to that husband at the time when she attains pensionable age and—
  (a) he also has attained pensionable age and has become entitled to a Category A retirement pension; and
  (b) he satisfies the relevant contribution conditions.

(3) The second case of entitlement is where the woman marries after attaining pensionable age and—
  (a) her husband has also attained pensionable age and has become entitled to a Category A retirement pension; and
  (b) he satisfies the relevant contribution conditions.

(4) The third case of entitlement is where the woman's husband is dead and his death was after she attained pensionable age, and—
  (a) she was married to him when he died; and
  (b) before his death he satisfied the relevant contribution conditions.

(5) The fourth case of entitlement is where the woman's husband is dead and his death was before she attained pensionable age, and—
  (a) she was a widow immediately before attaining pensionable age and is entitled (or is treated by regulations as entitled) to a widow's pension; and
  (b) she became entitled to the pension in consequence of the husband's death.

(6) The relevant contribution conditions for the purposes of the first, second and third cases of entitlement are those specified in Schedule 3, Part I, paragraph 5

(7) Subject to the provisions of this Act, a woman's entitlement to a Category B retirement pension shall commence on the day on which the conditions of entitlement become satisfied in her case and shall continue throughout her life.

(8) A woman's Category B retirement pension shall not be payable for any period falling before the day on which the pensioner's entitlement is to be regarded as commencing for that purpose by virtue of section 5(1)(l) of the Administration Act.

DEFINITIONS
"the Administration Act": s.170.
"entitled": s.121(1).
"pensionable age": s.121(1).

GENERAL NOTE
A married woman or widow can claim a Category B retirement pension on the basis of her husband's contributions record, providing she has attained pensionable age, in any of the circumstances set out in subss. (2)–(5). A Category B pension may be supplemented by the age

addition of 25p per week for claimants over 80 (s.79), a higher pension by deferring entitlement (s.55) and the Christmas bonus (s.144).

Rate of Category B retirement pension for women

50.—(1) A woman's Category B retirement pension—
(a) in the first and second cases of entitlement under section 49 above, shall—
    (i) during any period in which the husband is alive, be payable at the weekly rate specified in Schedule 4, Part I, paragraph 5, and
    (ii) during any period after he is dead, be payable at a weekly rate ascertained in accordance with subsection (3) below;
(b) in the third case of entitlement under that section, shall be payable at a weekly rate ascertained in accordance with subsection (3) below; and
(c) in the fourth case of entitlement under that section, shall be payable at the same weekly rate as her widow's pension.
(2) In any case where—
(a) a woman would, apart from section 43(1) above, be entitled both to a Category A and to a Category B retirement pension, and
(b) subsection (1) of section 47 above would apply for the increase of the Category A retirement pension,
that subsection shall be taken as applying also for the increase of the Category B retirement pension, subject to reduction or extinguishment of the increase by the application of section 47(2) above or Article 31B(2) of the Pensions Order.
(3) The weekly rate referred to in paragraphs (a)(ii) and (b) of subsection (1) above for a woman's Category B retirement pension shall determined in accordance with the provisions of sections 44 and 45 above as they apply in the case of a Category A retirement pension, but subject, in particular—
(a) to section 46(2) above; and
(b) to subsections (4) and (5) below.
(4) In the application of sections 44 and 45 above by virtue of subsection (3) above—
(a) references in those sections to the pensioner shall be taken as references to the husband, and
(b) where, in the third case of entitlement under section 49 above, the husband was under pensionable age when he died, references in those sections to the pensioner and the tax year in which he attained pensionable age shall be taken as references to the husband and the tax year in which he died.
(5) In the case of a widow whose husband dies after 5th April 2000, the additional pension falling to be calculated under sections 44 and 45 above by virtue of subsection (3) above shall be one half of the amount which it would be apart from this subsection.

DEFINITIONS
    "additional pension": s.45(1).
    "entitled": s.121(1).
    "pensionable age": s.121(1).
    "the Pensions Order": s.170.
    "tax year": s.121(1).

GENERAL NOTE
    This section deals with the method of calculating the rate of a Category B retirement pension. The additional pension will be reduced to half that of her husband if he dies after April 5, 2000 (subs. (5)).

Category B retirement pension for widowers

51.—(1) A man shall be entitled to a Category B retirement pension if—
(a) he has had a wife and she has died on or after 6th April 1979, and he was married to her when she died; and
(b) they were both over pensionable age when she died; and
(c) before her death she satisfied the contribution conditions for a Category A retirement pension in Schedule 3, Part I, paragraph 5.

(2) The weekly rate of a man's Category B retirement pension under this section shall, subject to subsection (3) below, be determined in accordance with the provisions of sections 44 and 45 above as they apply in the case of a Category A retirement pension, taking references in those sections to the pensioner as references to the wife.

(3) In the case of a widower whose wife dies after 5th April 2000, the additional pension falling to be calculated under sections 44 and 45 above by virtue of subsection (2) above shall be one half of the amount which it would be apart from this subsection.

(4) Subject to the provisions of this Act, a man shall become entitled to a Category B retirement pension on the day on which the conditions of entitlement become satisfied in his case and his entitlement shall continue throughout his life.

DEFINITIONS
"additional pension": s.45(1).
"entitled": s.121(1).
"pensionable age": s.121(1).

GENERAL NOTE
The SSP(N.I.)O 1975 extended entitlement to a Category B retirement pension to a widower whose wife died on or after April 6, 1979, providing they were both over pensionable age when she died and that before her death she satisfied the contribution conditions for a Category A retirement pension. As under s.50, widowers will only receive half their partner's additional pension if she dies after April 5, 2000 (subs. (3)). Unlike widows, a widower cannot qualify for a Category B pension if his wife dies before he reached pensionable age.

Special provision for surviving spouses

52.—(1) This section has effect where, apart from section 43(1) above, a person would be entitled both—
(a) to a Category A retirement pension; and
(b) to a Category B retirement pension—
(i) under section 49 above by virtue of the contributions of a husband who has died; or
(ii) under section 51 above.

(2) If by reason of a deficiency of contributions the basic pension in the Category A retirement pension falls short of the full amount, that basic pension shall be increased by the lesser of—
(a) the amount of the shortfall, or
(b) the amount of the basic pension in the rate of the Category B retirement pension,
"full amount" meaning for this purpose the sum specified in section 44(4) above as the weekly rate of the basic pension in a Category A retirement pension.

(3) If the additional pension in the category A retirement pension falls short of the prescribed maximum, that additional pension shall be increased by the lesser of—
(a) the amount of the shortfall, or
(b) the amount of the additional pension in the Category B retirement pension.

(4) This section does not apply in any case where the death of the wife or husband, as the case may be, occurred before 6th April 1979 and the surviving spouse had attained pensionable age before that date.

DEFINITIONS
"additional pension": s.45(1).
"entitled": s.121(1).
"full amount": subs. (2).
"pensionable age": s.121(1).

GENERAL NOTE
This section applies where a person's spouse died on or after April 6, 1979, and he himself had not attained pensionable age before that date. If his own contribution record does not entitle him to a full Category A retirement pension, a "composite" pension is payable using all or part of the Category B pension entitlement to raise the Category A pension to the full basic pension rate (subs. (2)). The same principle applies to the additional earnings-related element (subs. (3)).

Special provision for married women

53.—(1) This section has effect where, apart from section 43(1) above, a married woman would be entitled both—
 (a) to a Category A retirement pension; and
 (b) to a Category B retirement pension by virtue of the contributions of her husband.
 (2) If by reason of a deficiency of contributions the basic pension in the Category A retirement pension falls short of the weekly rate specified in Schedule 4, Part I, paragraph 5, that basic pension shall be increased by the lesser of—
 (a) the amount of the shortfall, or
 (b) the amount of the weekly rate of the Category B retirement pension.
 (3) This section does not apply in any case where both the husband and wife attained pensionable age before 6th April 1979.

DEFINITIONS
"entitled": s.121(1).
"pensionable age": s.121(1).

GENERAL NOTE
This section enables a married woman to add a husband's pension rights to her own in order to obtain a composite Category A retirement pension. This option is not open to divorced women.

Category A and Category B retirement pensions: supplemental provisions

54.—(1) Regulations may provide that in the case of a person of any prescribed description who—
 (a) has become entitled to a Category A or Category B retirement pension but is, in the case of a woman, under the age of 65 or, in the case of a man, under the age of 70; and
 (b) elects in such manner and in accordance with such conditions as may be prescribed that the regulations shall apply in his case,
this Part of this Act shall have effect as if that person had not become entitled to such a retirement pension.
 (2) Regulations under subsection (1) above may make such modifications of the provisions of this Part of this Act, or of those of Part II of the Administration Act as those provisions apply in a case where a person makes an election under the regulations, as may appear to the Department necessary or expedient.
 (3) Where a husband and wife have both become entitled to retirement pensions and—

(a) the husband's pension is Category A; and
(b) the wife's pension is—
    (i) Category B by virtue of that husband's contributions, or
    (ii) Category A with an increase under section 53(2) above by virtue of that husband's contributions,
the husband shall not be entitled to make an election in accordance with regulations made under subsection (1) above without the consent of the wife, unless that consent is unreasonably withheld.

(4) In any case where—
(a) a person claims a Category A or Category B retirement pension; and
(b) the date specified in the claim as the date on which entitlement to the pension is to commence falls after the date when the claim was made, such a pension may be awarded as from the date so specified but, if so awarded, shall be conditional on the person's not ceasing to be entitled to the pension in consequence of any election under subsection (1) above.

DEFINITIONS
"the Administration Act": s.170.
"entitled": s.121(1).
"prescribe": s.121(1).

GENERAL NOTE
This section enables a retirement pensioner under 65 (for a woman) or 70 (for a man) to "de-retire" by notifying the authorities in the prescribed manner (subs. (1)). Such a decision may be cancelled at any time, although it is not possible to "de-retire" a second time thereafter (Social Security (Widow's Benefit and Retirement Pensions) Regulations (Northern Ireland) 1979 (S.I. 1979 No. 243), reg. 2). This facility is also subject to the wife's consent (unless unreasonably withheld) where she is entitled to a Category B retirement pension based on his contributions or a "composite" Category A pension based in part on such contributions (subs. (3)).

The question as to whether the different ages for "de-retiring" are discriminatory has been referred to the European Court of Justice: *R.* v. *Secretary of State for Social Security*, ex p. *Smithson* [1991] 1 C.M.L.R. 1601.

Increase of retirement pension where entitlement is deferred

55.—(1) Where a person's entitlement to a Category A or Category B retirement pension is deferred, Schedule 5 to this Act shall have effect for increasing the rate of his pension.

(2) For the purposes of this Act, a person's entitlement to a Category A or Category B retirement pension is "deferred" if and so long as he does not become entitled to that pension by reason only—
(a) that he has not satisfied the conditions of section 1 of the Administration Act (entitlement to benefit dependent on claim); or
(b) that, in the case of a woman's Category B retirement pension by virtue of her husband's contributions, her husband has not satisfied those conditions with respect to his Category A retirement pension; and, in relation to any such pension, "period of deferment" shall be construed accordingly.

DEFINITIONS
"the Administration Act": s.170.
"deferred": subs. (2).
"period of deferment": subs. (2).

GENERAL NOTE
This section introduces Sched. 5, which provides for the deferment of retirement. During the first five years after attaining pensionable age, claimants are able to defer entitlement to a Category A or B retirement pension. This gives rise to a higher rate of benefit once the pension is actually taken up. See Ogus and Barendt, pp. 222–4.

Child's special allowance

Child's special allowance—existing beneficiaries

56.—(1) Subject to the provisions of this Act (and in particular to those of section 81 below), a woman whose marriage has been terminated by divorce shall be entitled to a child's special allowance at the weekly rate specified in Schedule 4, Part I, paragraph 6, if—

(a) the husband of that marriage is dead and satisfied the contribution condition for a child's special allowance specified in Schedule 3, Part I, paragraph 6; and

(b) she is entitled to child benefit in respect of a child and either—

(i) she was so entitled immediately before that husband's death; or

(ii) in such circumstances as may be prescribed, he was then so entitled; and

(c) either—

(i) that husband had before his death been contributing at not less than the prescribed weekly rate to the cost of providing for that child; or

(ii) at the date of that husband's death she was entitled, under an order of a court, trust or agreement which she has taken reasonable steps to enforce, to receive (whether from that husband or from another person) payments in respect of that child at not less than that rate provided or procured by that husband.

(2) A child's special allowance shall not be payable to a woman—

(a) for any period after her remarriage; or

(b) for any period during which she and a man to whom she is not married are living together as husband and wife.

(3) Where, apart from this subsection, a person is entitled to receive, in respect of a particular child, payment of an amount by way of a child's special allowance, that amount shall not be payable unless one of the conditions specified in subsection (4) below is satisfied.

(4) Those conditions are—

(a) that the beneficiary would be treated for the purposes of Part IX of this Act as having the child living with him; or

(b) that the requisite contributions are being made to the cost of providing for the child.

(5) The condition specified in subsection (4)(b) above is to be treated as satisfied if, but only if—

(a) such contributions are being made at a weekly rate not less than the amount referred to in subsection (3) above—

(i) by the beneficiary; or

(ii) where the beneficiary is one of two spouses residing together, by them together; and

(b) except in prescribed cases, the contributions are over and above those required for the purpose of satisfying section 139(1)(b) below.

(6) A child's special allowance shall not be payable for any period after 5th April 1987 except to a woman who immediately before 6th April 1987—

(a) satisfied the conditions set out in paragraphs (a) to (c) of subsection (1) above; and

(b) was not barred from payment of the allowance for either of the reasons mentioned in subsection (2) above,

and who has so continued since 6th April 1987.

DEFINITIONS

"beneficiary": s.121(1).

"child": s.121(1).

"entitled": s.121(1).
"prescribe": s.121(1).

GENERAL NOTE
   The child's special allowance was designed to provide a degree of assistance to a woman who failed to qualify for a widowed mother's allowance (see now s.37) because she was divorced from her former husband before he died. The child's special allowance was abolished as from April 6, 1987 by SS(N.I.)O 1986, art. 41, except for existing beneficiaries. Such entitlement ceases where the claimant is no longer entitled to child benefit for the child, or remarries or lives with a man as husband and wife (subs. (6)). For a full analysis, see Ogus and Barendt (2nd ed., pp. 236–9).

Provisions relating to unemployment benefit, sickness benefit and invalidity benefit

Determination of days for which benefit is payable

   57.—(1) For the purposes of any provisions of this Act relating to unemployment benefit, sickness benefit or invalidity benefit—
   (a) subject to the provisions of this Act, a day shall not be treated in relation to any person—
      (i) as a day of unemployment unless on that day he is capable of work and he is, or is deemed in accordance with regulations to be, available to be employed in employed earner's employment and that day falls in a week in which he is, or is deemed in accordance with regulations to be, actively seeking such employment; or
      (ii) as a day of incapacity for work unless on that day he is, or is deemed in accordance with regulations to be, incapable of work by reason of some specific disease or bodily or mental disablement,
      ("work", in this paragraph, meaning work which the person can reasonably be expected to do);
   (b) where a person is an employed earner and his employment as such has not been terminated, then in any week a day on which in the normal course that person would not work in that employment or in any other employed earner's employment shall not be treated as a day of unemployment unless each other day in that week (other than the day referred to in paragraph (e) below) on which in the normal course he would so work is a day of interruption of employment;
   (c) "day of interruption of employment" means a day which is a day of unemployment or of incapacity for work;
   (d) the following periods; namely—
      (i) any 2 days of unemployment, whether consecutive or not, within a period of 6 consecutive days,
      (ii) any 4 or more consecutive days of incapacity for work,
      shall be treated as a period of interruption of employment, and any 2 such periods not separated by a period of more than 8 weeks ("week" for this purpose meaning any period of 7 days) shall be treated as one period of interruption of employment;
   (e) Sunday or such other day in each week as may be prescribed shall not be treated as a day of unemployment or of incapacity for work and shall be disregarded in computing any period of consecutive days.
   (2) Any day which falls within the maternity allowance period as defined in section 35(2) above shall be treated for the purposes of any provision of this Act relating to unemployment benefit, sickness benefit or invalidity benefit as a day of incapacity for work unless the woman is disqualified for receiving a maternity allowance in respect of that day by virtue of regulations under section 35(3)(a) above.
   (3) Regulations may—

(a) make provision (subject to subsections (1) and (2) above) as to the days which are or are not to be treated for the purposes of unemployment benefit, sickness benefit and invalidity benefit as days of employment or of incapacity for work;

(b) make provision with respect to—

(i) steps which a person is required to take in any week if he is to be regarded as actively seeking employed earner's employment in that week;

(ii) the meaning of "week" in subsection (1)(a)(i) above or in any other provision relating to a person's actively seeking employed earner's employment;

(c) prescribe respective circumstances in which, for the purposes of subsection (1)(b) above—

(i) employment which has not been terminated may be treated as if it had been terminated; or

(ii) a day which falls in a period when an employed earner's employment is suspended but does not fall to be so treated and which, apart from the regulations, would not fall to be treated as a day of interruption of employment may be treated as such a day.

(4) Where it has been determined that a person is to be deemed in accordance with regulations to be available for employment in employed earner's employment in respect of any day, the question of his actual availability for such employment in respect of that day may be subsequently determined on a review of the determination as to his deemed availability.

(5) Where it has been determined that a person is to be deemed in accordance with regulations to be actively seeking employed earner's employment in any week, the question of his actually doing so in that week may be subsequently determined on a review of the determination as to his deemed doing so.

(6) If regulations under paragraph (a) of subsection (3) above provide that for the purposes of unemployment benefit days falling in a post-employment period are not to be treated in relation to a person as days of unemployment, then, for the purpose of determining that period, the regulations may, in particular, make provision—

(a) for calculating or estimating the amount or value of any payment made, or goods or services provided, to or for that person by his employer;

(b) for calculating or estimating that person's level of earnings in the employment in question during any period or for treating him as having such a level of earnings as may be prescribed; and

(c) for calculating or estimating the amount or value of any other sum which falls to be taken into account under the regulations.

(7) In subsection (6) above "post-employment period" means a period following the termination of a person's employment and falling to be determined in accordance with the regulations by reference to the amount or value of payments made, or goods or services provided, to or for the person by his employer at the time of, or within a prescribed period before or after, the termination of the employment.

(8) Subsections (1) and (3) above shall, on and after such day as the Department may by order appoint, have effect—

(a) with the substitution for paragraph (b) of subsection (1) of the following paragraph—

"(b) where a person is an employed earner and his employment as such has not been terminated but has been suspended by the employer, a day shall not be treated in relation to that person as a day of unemployment unless it is the 7th or a later day in a continuous period of days on which that suspension has lasted, there being disregarded for the purposes of determining the first 6 days of the period (but for no other purpose)—

(i) Sunday or such other day in each week as may have been prescribed under paragraph (e) of this subsection,

(ii) any day of recognised or customary holiday in connection with the suspended employment,

(iii) such other day or days as may be prescribed;"; and

(b) with the substitution for paragraph (c) of subsection (3) of the following paragraph—

"(c) prescribe respective circumstances in which for the purposes of subsection (1)(b) above an employed earner's employment may be treated—

(i) as having been or, as the case may be, as not having been terminated, or

(ii) as having been or, as the case may be, as not having been suspended.".

(9) Regulations may provide—

(a) that paragraph (d) of subsection (1) above shall have effect as if for the reference to 8 weeks there were substituted a reference to a larger number of weeks specified in the regulations; and

(b) that sub-paragraph (ii) of that paragraph shall have effect in such cases as may be specified in the regulations, as if—

(i) the period of 4 days mentioned there were such lesser period as may be specified, and

(ii) the word "consecutive" were omitted.

(10) Regulations under subsection (9)(b) above may be made to have effect from such date, not earlier than 14th September 1980, as may be specified in the regulations.

DEFINITIONS
"day of incapacity for work": subs. (1)(a)(ii).
"day of interruption of employment": subs. (1)(c).
"earnings": s.121(1).
"employed earner": s.121(1).
"employment": s.121(1).
"period of interruption of employment": subs. (1)(d).
"post-employment period": subs. (7).
"prescribe": s.121(1).
"week": subs. (1)(d) and s.121(1).
"work": subs. (1)(a).

GENERAL NOTE
It would have been more helpful if this section could have been placed immediately after ss.25–34. It lays down some basic principles as to the days for which unemployment benefit, sickness benefit and invalidity benefit are payable. The key provisions are contained in subs. (1). The rest of the section consists of consequential or enabling provisions.

So far as unemployment benefit is concerned, to qualify as a day of unemployment (*e.g.* for the purpose of s.25(1)) the claimant must on that day be capable of work, be available to be employed in employed earner's employment and be actively seeking such employment (subs. (1)(a)(i)). Days of incapacity for work for the purpose of sickness and invalidity benefits are dealt with by subs. (1)(a)(ii).

Subs. (1)(a)(i)
Day of unemployment. There is no comprehensive statutory definition of this concept. See General Note to s.25.
Capable of work. This requirement makes it clear that those unable to work through ill-health are not entitled to unemployment benefit.
Available to be employed. The law requires that the claimant be available for employed earner's employment. This does not mean that a job has to be shown to be available to the claimant (*R(U) 44/53*). Availability for part-time work may suffice (*CU/109/48(KL)*), but not

for self-employed work only (*R(U) 14/51*). "Work" means work that the person can reasonably be expected to do.

Availability may be either actual or deemed. Actual availability is determined in accordance with Commissioners' case law and the Social Security (Unemployment, Sickness, and Invalidity Benefit) Regulations (Northern Ireland) 1984 (S.I. 1984 No. 245), reg. 7B. In *R(U) 5/80* it was said that availability "means being available in an active, positive sense, that is by making oneself available. Availability implies some active step by the person concerned to draw attention to his availability: it is not a passive state in which a person may be said to be available provided he is sought out and his location is ascertained." See also Northern Ireland decision *R3/78 (UB)*.

The case law demonstrates that two further conditions have to be met in order for the claimant to be available for employment. First, there must be a reasonable prospect of the claimant finding employment on his stated terms of the type for which he holds himself out as available (leaving aside any wider issues as to the impact of an economic recession). See *R(U) 12/52*, *R(U) 44/53* and reg. 7B. Secondly, the claimant must be willing and able to accept employment (*R(U) 1/53*, *R(U) 1/85* and *R(U) 2/90*). See Bonner for detailed analysis of both conditions. On deemed availability, see regs. 9–14.

Actively seeking such employment. Since October 1988, as well as being available for employment, claimants must be actively seeking such employment. As with availability, claimants may be actively seeking work or be deemed to be so doing. The detailed provisions are set out in regs. 12B–D (see Bonner).

Subs. (1)(a)(ii)

Day of incapacity for work. The concept of a day of incapacity for work is fundamental to entitlement to sickness benefit, statutory sick pay, invalidity benefit, severe disablement allowance and invalidity pensions for widows or widowers. A claimant is incapable of work if he or she is suffering from a disease or bodily or mental disablement such that he or she is incapable of doing any work which it would be reasonable to expect such a person to do; but see Northern Ireland decision *R2/84 (SB)*. Some claimants who are able to work may be deemed to be incapable of work (*e.g.* Social Security (Unemployment, Sickness, and Invalidity Benefit) Regulations (Northern Ireland) 1984 (S.I. 1984 No. 245), reg. 3). See further Ogus and Barendt, pp. 149–56 and Bonner.

See also subs. (2), deeming days within the maternity allowance period (s.35(2)) as days of incapacity for work for the purposes of unemployment benefit, sickness benefit or invalidity benefit (unless the claimant is disqualified).

Subs. (1)(b)

This is the basis for the so-called normal idle day rule, under which a claimant is not entitled to unemployment benefit for a day on which he or she would not have worked in any event. The rule is inapplicable where the claimant's employment has been terminated, where there is no recognised or customary working week or where the claimant does not regularly work for the same number of days each week. In practice it is not used as widely as the "full extent normal" rule (reg. 7(1)(e)), but it may be applicable in situations where workers have been temporarily put on short-time. See further the Social Security (Unemployment, Sickness, and Invalidity Benefit) Regulations (Northern Ireland) 1984 (S.I. 1984 No. 245), reg. 19.

Subs. (1)(d)

A day of unemployment for the purposes of entitlement to unemployment benefit must form part of a period of interruption of employment (s.25(1)). The same principle applies to days of incapacity for work so far as incapacity benefits are concerned (*e.g.* s.31(1)). This paragraph embodies the "continuity" and "linking" rules: see Bonner.

Subs. (1)(e)

See Social Security (Unemployment, Sickness, and Invalidity Benefit) Regulations (Northern Ireland) 1984 (S.I. 1984 No. 245), reg. 4 and *R(S) 3/88*.

Subs. (2)

See annotations to subs. (1)(a)(ii).

Subs. (3)

See Social Security (Unemployment, Sickness, and Invalidity Benefit) Regulations (Northern Ireland) 1984 (S.I. 1984 No. 245).

Subs. (4)

Where a query has arisen over a claimant's availability for work, he or she is deemed to be so available until such time as a decision on the matter is taken (Social Security (Unemployment, Sickness, and Invalidity Benefit) Regulations (Northern Ireland) 1984 (S.I. 1984 No. 245), reg. 12A). This section enables the claimant's actual availability to be determined subsequently on review.

Subs. (5)

This is an analogous provision to subs. (4) but in relation to the "actively seeking work" requirement.

Subs. (6)

This is an enabling power which elaborates on that contained in subs. (3)(a). It provides the authority for the regulations disentitling claimants from receiving unemployment benefit for a period after they have received a payment in connection with the termination of their previous employment. See the Social Security (Unemployment, Sickness, and Invalidity Benefit) Regulations (Northern Ireland) 1984 (S.I. 1984 No. 245), reg. 7(1)(d) and (6).

Subs. (8)

No order was ever made bringing into force the predecessor to this provision, but the Social Security (Unemployment, Sickness, and Invalidity Benefit) Regulations (Northern Ireland) 1984 (S.I. 1984 No. 245), regs. 6, 7(1)(h) and 19 borrow the concepts used in subs. (8)(a).

Incapacity for work: work as councillor to be disregarded

58.—(1) In determining for the purposes of any of the provisions of this Part of this Act which relate to sickness benefit or invalidity benefit whether any day is to be treated as a day of incapacity for work in relation to a person, there shall be disregarded any work which that person has undertaken, or is capable of undertaking, as a councillor.

(2) Where the net amount of councillor's allowance to which a person is entitled in respect of any week exceeds the permitted earnings limit, an amount equal to the excess shall be deducted from the amount of any sickness benefit or invalidity benefit to which he is entitled in respect of that week, and only the balance remaining (if any) shall be payable.

(3) In determining whether a person satisfies the conditions of entitlement for any such benefit, he shall be treated as having been incapable of work on any day which falls in the pre-commencement period and which—

(a) would have been treated as a day on which he was so incapable, were there disregarded any work which he undertook (or was capable of undertaking) as a councillor; but

(b) would not have been so treated apart from this subsection.

(4) In this section—

"councillor" means a member of a district council;

"councillor's allowance" means such payments for or in connection with the work which a person undertakes as a councillor as the Department may prescribe for the purposes of this section; and where any such payments are made otherwise than weekly, an amount calculated or estimated in accordance with regulations shall be regarded as the weekly amount of the payments;

"net amount", in relation to any councillor's allowance to which a person is entitled, means the aggregate amount of the councillor's allowance or allowances to which he is entitled for the week in question, reduced by the amount of any expenses incurred by him in that week in connection with his membership of the council or councils in question;

"permitted earnings limit" means the amount specified in regulation 3(3) of the Social Security (Unemployment, Sickness and Invalidity Benefit) Regulations (Northern Ireland) 1984;

"pre-commencement period" means the period beginning with 11th May 1987 and ending immediately before 9th October 1989 (the coming into operation of paragraph 2 of Schedule 8 to the Social Security (Northern Ireland) Order 1989 which made provision corresponding to the provision made by this section).

(5) Any reference in this section to the work which a person undertakes, or is capable of undertaking, as a councillor shall be taken to include a reference to any work which he undertakes, or is capable of undertaking, as a member of any body established under any statutory provision of which he is a member by virtue of his being a councillor.

DEFINITIONS
    "councillor": subs. (4).
    "councillor's allowance": subs. (4).
    "day of incapacity for work": s.121(1).
    "net amount": subs. (4).
    "permitted earnings limit": subs. (4).
    "pre-commencement period": subs. (4).
    "week": s.121(1).

GENERAL NOTE
    Entitlement to sickness benefit (ss.31–32) and invalidity benefit (ss.33–34) are dependent upon proof of incapacity for work. The therapeutic earnings rule (Social Security (Unemployment, Sickness and Invalidity Benefit) Regulations (Northern Ireland) 1984 (S.I. 1984 No. 245), reg. 3(3))—here described as the "permitted earnings limit" (subs. (4))—provides a limited exception to this requirement. For this purpose attendance allowances paid to local government councillors are counted as earnings (*R(S) 3/86* and *R(S) 6/86*).
    This section, which originally appeared as SS(N.I.)O 1989, Sched. 8, para. 2, provides that work undertaken by councillors is to be disregarded in assessing incapacity for work (subs. (1)). Furthermore, the earnings rule is modified so that benefit is withdrawn on a tapered basis. Accordingly, incapacity benefits are reduced only in so far as the attendance allowance exceeds the permitted earnings limit (subs. (2)). This relaxation is backdated to the period starting with May 11, 1987 (subs. (3)).

Invalidity benefit—disqualifications, etc.

Invalidity benefit—disqualifications, etc.

   59.—(1) Regulations may provide for disqualifying a person for receiving invalidity benefit for such period not exceeding 6 weeks as may be determined in accordance with Part II of the Administration Act if—
   (a) he has become incapable of work through his own misconduct; or
   (b) he fails without good cause to attend for, or to submit himself to, such medical or other examination or treatment as may be required in accordance with the regulations, or to observe any prescribed rules of behaviour.
   (2) Regulations may also provide for imposing, in the case of any prescribed category of persons—
   (a) additional conditions with respect to the receipt of invalidity benefit; and
   (b) restrictions on the rate and duration of invalidity benefit,
if, having regard to special circumstances, it appears to the Department necessary to do so for the purpose of preventing inequalities, or injustice to the general body of employed earners, or of earners generally, as the case may be.
   (3) For the purpose of this section "week" means any period of 7 days.

DEFINITIONS
    "the Administration Act": s.170.
    "earner": s.121(1).

"employed earner": s.121(1).
"medical examination": s.121(1).
"medical treatment": s.121(1).
"prescribe": s.121(1).
"week": subs. (3).

GENERAL NOTE
   See General Note to s.32, the parallel provision in relation to sickness benefit. It is not obvious why this section could not have been located immediately after those relating to the substantive conditions for invalidity benefit (ss.33 and 34).

Partial satisfaction of contribution conditions

Partial satisfaction of contribution conditions

   60.—(1) Subject to the provisions of this section, regulations may provide for persons to be entitled to any of the following benefits, namely—
   (a) a widowed mother's allowance,
   (b) a widow's pension,
   (c) a Category A retirement pension,
   (d) a Category B retirement pension,
in cases where the first contribution condition specified in relation to that benefit in paragraph 5 of Schedule 3 to this Act is satisfied and the second contribution condition so specified is not.
   (2) Subject to subsection (8) below, in any case where—
   (a) an employed earner who is married dies as a result of—
      (i) a personal injury of a kind mentioned in section 94(1) below, or
      (ii) a disease or injury such as is mentioned in section 108(1) below, and
   (b) the contribution conditions are not wholly satisfied in respect of him, those conditions shall be taken to be satisfied for the purposes of his widow's entitlement to any of the benefits specified in subsection (3) below.
   (3) The benefits referred to in subsection (2) above are the following—
   (a) a widow's payment;
   (b) a widowed mother's allowance;
   (c) a widow's pension;
   (d) a Category B retirement pension payable to a woman which is payable to her at the same rate as her widow's pension or which falls within section 49(4) above.
   (4) Subject to subsections (6) and (7) below, regulations under subsection (1) above shall provide for benefit payable by virtue of any such regulations to be payable at a rate, or to be of an amount, less than that which would be applicable under this Part of this Act had both of the relevant contribution conditions been fully satisfied.
   (5) Subject to subsections (6) and (7) below, the rate or amount prescribed by regulations under subsection (1) above may vary with the extent to which the relevant contribution conditions are satisfied (and may be nil).
   (6) The amount prescribed by regulations under subsection (1) above for any increase of benefit in respect of a child shall, subject to subsection (7) below, be the same as if both of the relevant contribution conditions had been fully satisfied.
   (7) Regulations may provide that where—
   (a) a person is entitled by virtue of subsection (1) above to a Category A or Category B retirement pension consisting only of the additional pension with no basic pension, and
   (b) that retirement pension, and any graduated retirement benefit to which he may be entitled, together amount to less than the prescribed rate,

that person's entitlement as respects that retirement pension shall be satisfied either altogether or for a prescribed period by the making of a single payment of the prescribed amount.

(8) Subsection (2) above only has effect where the employed earner's death occurred on or after 11th April 1988.

DEFINITIONS
"child": s.121(1).
"employed earner": s.121(1).
"entitled": s.121(1).
"prescribe": s.170.

GENERAL NOTE
This section provides for a reduced rate of benefit of certain long-term benefits where the second contribution condition has only been partially satisfied. Regulations made under the predecessor to subs. (1) specify that the basic component is calculated according to the proportion of reckonable years (*i.e.* years in which the qualifying earnings factor has been attained) to the number of years prescribed for the particular benefit concerned (see the Social Security (Widow's Benefit and Retirement Pensions) Regulations (Northern Ireland) 1979 (S.I. 1979 No. 243), reg. 6). The second contribution condition must have been met in at least 25 per cent. of the years in question. Increases for adult dependants are subject to the same reduction but increases for child dependants are unaffected (subs. (6)).

Widows whose husbands died as a result of an industrial accident or disease on or after April 11, 1988 are deemed to have met the contribution conditions for widows' benefits and the Category B retirement pension (subss. (2) and (3)). This is the only form in which the industrial preference continues for women widowed on or after that date.

Exclusion of increase of benefit for failure to satisfy contribution condition

61.—(1) A Category A or Category B retirement pension which is payable by virtue of section 60(1) above and a widowed mother's allowance which is so payable shall not be increased under section 47(1) above or under Part IV below on account of a child or an adult if the pension or allowance contains no basic pension in consequence of a failure to satisfy a contribution condition.

(2) Where a person is entitled—
(a) to unemployment benefit at a rate determined under section 25(5) above;
(b) to sickness benefit at a rate determined under section 31(6) above; or
(c) to an invalidity pension at a rate determined under section 33(4) above,

and the retirement pension by reference to which the rate of the benefit or invalidity pension is determined—
(i) would have been payable only by virtue of section 60 above; and
(ii) would, in consequence of a failure to satisfy a contribution condition, have contained no basic pension,

the benefit or invalidity pension shall not be increased under section 47(1) above or under Part IV below on account of a child or an adult.

DEFINITIONS
"child": s. 121(1).

GENERAL NOTE
See General Note to s.47.

Graduated retirement benefit

Graduated retirement benefit

62.—(1) So long as sections 35 and 36 of the National Insurance Act (Northern Ireland) 1966 (graduated retirement benefit) continue in force by virtue of regulations made under Schedule 3 to the Social Security (Consequential Provisions) Act 1975 or under Schedule 3 to the Consequential Provisions Act, regulations may make provision—

(a) for replacing section 35(4) of the National Insurance Act (Northern Ireland) 1966 (increase of graduated retirement benefit in cases of deferred retirement) with provisions corresponding to those of paragraphs 1 to 3 of Schedule 5 to this Act;

(b) for extending section 36 of that Act (increase of woman's retirement pension by reference to her late husband's graduated retirement benefit) to men and their late wives.

(2) This section is without prejudice to any power to modify those sections conferred by Schedule 3 to the Consequential Provisions Act.

DEFINITIONS
"the Consequential Provisions Act": s.170.
"late husband": s.121(1).

GENERAL NOTE
Graduated retirement benefit is payable to all those who paid graduated Class 1 National Insurance contributions between April 1961 and April 1975 in addition to the standard flat-rate contributions. See the Social Security (Graduated Retirement Benefit) (No. 2) Regulations (Northern Ireland) 1978 (S.I. 1978 No. 78).

PART III

NON-CONTRIBUTORY BENEFITS

Descriptions of non-contributory benefits

63. Non-contributory benefits under this Part of this Act are of the following descriptions, namely—

(a) attendance allowance;

(b) severe disablement allowance (with age related addition and increase for adult and child dependants);

(c) invalid care allowance (with increase for adult and child dependants);

(d) disability living allowance;

(e) guardian's allowance;

(f) retirement pensions of the following categories—

(i) Category C, payable to certain persons who were over pensionable age on 5th July 1948 and their wives and widows (with increase for adult and child dependants), and

(ii) Category D, payable to persons over the age of 80;

(g) age addition payable, in the case of persons over the age of 80, by way of increase of a retirement pension of any category or of a pension or allowance to which section 79(2) below applies.

DEFINITIONS
"child": s.121(1).
"pensionable age": s.121(1).

GENERAL NOTE
This lists the various non-contributory benefits. Mobility allowance, which appeared in the predecessor to this section (SS(N.I.)A 1975, s.34, as amended), was abolished by the DLAD-WAO 1991 as it was superseded by the mobility component of disability living allowance (s.73 below).

Attendance allowance

Entitlement

64.—(1) A person shall be entitled to an attendance allowance if he is aged

65 or over, he is not entitled to the care component of a disability living allowance and he satisfies either—
  (a) the condition specified in subsection (2) below ("the day attendance condition"), or
  (b) the condition specified in subsection (3) below ("the night attendance condition"),
and prescribed conditions as to residence and presence in Northern Ireland.

(2) A person satisfies the day attendance condition if he is so severely disabled physically or mentally that, by day, he requires from another person either—
  (a) frequent attention throughout the day in connection with his bodily functions, or
  (b) continual supervision throughout the day in order to avoid substantial danger to himself or others.

(3) A person satisfies the night attendance condition if he is so severely disabled physically or mentally that, at night,—
  (a) he requires from another person prolonged or repeated attention in connection with his bodily functions, or
  (b) in order to avoid substantial danger to himself or others he requires another person to be awake for a prolonged period or at frequent intervals for the purpose of watching over him.

DEFINITIONS
  "entitled": s.121(1).
  "Northern Ireland": s.168.
  "prescribe": s.121(1).

GENERAL NOTE
  As a result of amendments made by the DLADWAO 1991, attendance allowance is now a benefit for elderly people whose care needs arise too late in life for them to be entitled to disability living allowance (for DLA, see ss.72 and 75). The attendance allowance provisions are less generous than those for DLA in that there is no third lower tier of attendance allowance and claimants have to wait six months (rather than three) before payment begins (s.65). (But see s.66 for those who are terminally ill). This form of attendance allowance is known as AA65+. For the special review and appeals procedure, see SSA(N.I.)A 1992, ss.28–33.

Subs. (1)
  The qualifying conditions for the receipt of attendance allowance were modified in two respects by the DLADWAO 1991. The first change was of a technical nature to clarify that a claimant must satisfy prescribed criteria as to both residence and presence in Northern Ireland. See Social Security (Attendance Allowance) Regulations (Northern Ireland) 1992 (S.I. 1992 No. 20), reg. 2. The decision of the European Court of Justice in *Case 356/89, Newton* v. *Chief Adjudication Officer* [1992] 1 C.M.L.R. 149 implied by analogy that such conditions could not disentitle a British worker in receipt of attendance allowance who goes to live in another member state (but see the Reservation discussed in the annotations to s.71(6)).
  Secondly, and more importantly, attendance allowance is now restricted to those claimants who are aged 65 or over and are not entitled to the care component of DLA (s.72). People with disabilities who qualify for DLA before they reach 65 will continue to receive the new benefit after that age, providing they continue to satisfy the qualifying conditions. People who fulfil the care criteria only after attaining the age of 65 are only eligible for attendance allowance (*i.e.* AA65+).

Subs. (2)
  So severely disabled physically or mentally. This relates to a condition of body or mind that is capable of medical definition. It is not meant to cover anti-social behaviour which is not related to serious mental illness: *R(A) 2/92.*

Subs. (2)(a)

Frequent attention. This means, according to Lord Denning M.R.'s rather unhelpful explanation, "several times—not once or twice" (*R.* v. *National Insurance Commissioner*, ex p. *Secretary of State for Social Services* [1981] 1 W.L.R. 1017 at p. 1022, C.A.—the *Packer* case).

Throughout the day. Commissioners' decisions have stressed the importance of looking at the overall pattern of care needs (*R(A) 2/74*). The attention must therefore be required "at intervals spread over the day" (*CA/281/1989*).

In connection with his bodily functions. Lord Denning M.R., in a much-cited passage in the *Packer* case, defined "bodily functions" as including:

> "breathing, hearing, seeing, eating, drinking, walking, sitting, sleeping, getting in and out of bed, dressing, undressing, eliminating waste products—and the like—all of which an ordinary person—who is not suffering from any disability—does for himself. But they do not include cooking, shopping or any of the other things which a wife or daughter does as part of her domestic duties: or generally which one of the household normally does for the rest of the family" (p. 1022).

Subsequently the House of Lords has held that the phrase "bodily functions" is a restricted and precise one, narrower than "bodily needs" (*Woodling* v. *Secretary of State for Social Services* [1984] 1 W.L.R. 348 at p. 352, *per* Lord Bridge).

Somewhat more problematic has been the requirement that the attention be "in connection with" the claimant's bodily functions. Lord Denning M.R. gave the following guidance in the *Packer* case:

> "I would hold that ordinary domestic duties such as shopping, cooking meals, making tea or coffee, laying the table or the tray, carrying it into the room, making the bed or filling the hot-water bottle, do not qualify as 'attention . . . in connection with [the] bodily functions' of the disabled person. But that duties that are out of the ordinary—doing for the disabled person what a normal person would do for himself—such as cutting up food, lifting the cup to the mouth, helping to dress or undress or at the toilet—all do qualify as 'attention . . . in connection with [the] bodily functions of the disabled person'" (p. 1022).

Lord Bridge, approving dicta of Dunn L.J. in the *Packer* case, held in rather more abstract terms that the phrase "connotes a high degree of personal intimacy between the person giving and the person receiving the attention" (*Woodling, supra*, at p. 352).

The test is ultimately therefore one of proximity and remoteness, and it is difficult to resolve such issues at the borderline. It would appear to be an error of law to hold that an activity which is an "ordinary" household duty (*e.g.* cooking or washing clothes or bedding) is necessarily not in connection with the claimant's bodily functions. In *R(A) 1/87* (where the carer had to prepare and control a very specialised diet for a child suffering from phenylketonuria (PKU)) it was held that the preparation of food could be part of the attention required in connection with the disabled person's bodily functions. See also *R(A) 1/91*.

Subs. (2)(b)

Continual supervision throughout the day in order to avoid substantial danger to himself or others. A Tribunal of Commissioners has held that this alternative requirement for the day condition involves four elements (*R(A) 1/83*). First, the claimant's medical condition must be such that there is a substantial danger to her/himself or to someone else. This is ultimately a question of fact and should not be construed too narrowly (*R(A) 1/73, R(A) 2/91*). Secondly, that danger must not be too remote a possibility. Thus the remoteness of the risk should be weighed against the seriousness of the consequences should the risk actually arise (*R(A) 2/89, R(A) 3/89* and *R(A) 6/89*). Thirdly, supervision by another person must be required in order to avoid the danger. It must be needed in order to effect a real reduction in the risk of harm, not in order to eliminate all substantial danger: *R(A) 3/92* and unreported Northern Ireland decision BNIL 89/9/72. Supervision is, however, a more passive concept than attention, and covers being in a position to intervene if necessary in an emergency (*R(A) 6/72* and *Moran* v. *Secretary of State for Social Services*, reported as appendix to *R(A) 1/88*). The decision of the Great Britain Commissioner in *R(A) 1/88* on the question of continual supervision and epilepsy was set out in the judgment of the Northern Ireland Court of Appeal case of *Young* v. *Department of Health and Social Services* with approval BNIL 91/1/90. Fourthly, the supervision must be "continual". The "characteristic nature of supervision is overseeing or watching over considered with reference to its frequency or regularity of occurrence" (*R(A) 2/75*). In *Moran* the English Court of Appeal held that the relative frequency or infrequency of attacks is immaterial to the question of whether supervision is continual, so long as the risk of substantial danger is not so remote a possibility that it ought reasonably to be disregarded. A need for periodic supervision is therefore insufficient: *Devlin* v. *Secretary of State for Social Services* (1991) S.L.T. 815.

Prolonged or repeated attention. Official guidance issued by the former Attendance Allowance Board (AAB) stated that:

"The Board accept as prolonged that attention which reasonably, in the light of medical expertise, can be claimed to last for 20 minutes or more. Repeated attention is attention which is needed on more than one occasion during the same night, not necessarily for the same purpose each time" (DHSS/AAB, *Handbook for Delegated Medical Practitioners* (1988), HMSO, p. 27).

This suggests that a smaller amount of care will be needed to satisfy the night-time criteria for the middle rate than will be required during the day for the lower rate.

In connection with his bodily functions. See note to subs. (2)(a) above.

He requires another person to be awake for a prolonged period or at frequent intervals for the purpose of watching over him. Originally the wording of this condition was identical to the parallel day condition. The English Court of Appeal in *Moran* (see above) held that such continual supervision could be provided at night where the carer was asleep nearby, ready to be summoned if need be. The formulation of the alternative night condition was amended by SS(N.I.)O 1988, art. 3, such that the claimant now needs the carer "to be awake for a prolonged period or at frequent intervals for the purpose of watching over him". It was explained at the time that the amendment was designed to "restore the law to what it was believed to be by emphasising that for the night-time condition to be satisfied active supervision was envisaged—a wakeful and watchful presence." (*Per* Mr J. Moore, *Hansard*, H.C. Vol. 121, col. 661, November 2, 1987).

Period and rate of allowance

65.—(1) Subject to the following provisions of this Act, the period for which a person is entitled to an attendance allowance shall be—

(a) a period throughout which he has satisfied or is likely to satisfy the day or the night attendance condition or both; and

(b) a period preceded immediately, or within such period as may be prescribed, by one of not less than 6 months throughout which he satisfied, or is likely to satisfy, one or both of those conditions.

(2) For the purposes of subsection (1) above a person who suffers from renal failure and is undergoing such form of treatment as may be prescribed shall, in such circumstances as may be prescribed, be deemed to satisfy or to be likely to satisfy the day or the night attendance condition or both.

(3) The weekly rate of the attendance allowance payable to a person for any period shall be the higher rate specified in Schedule 4, Part III, paragraph 1, if both as regards that period and as regards the period of 6 months mentioned in subsection (1)(b) above he has satisfied or is likely to satisfy both the day and the night attendance conditions, and shall be the lower rate in any other case.

(4) A person shall not be entitled to an attendance allowance for any period preceding the date on which he makes, or is treated as making, a claim for it.

(5) Notwithstanding anything in subsection (4) above, provision may be made by regulations for a person to be entitled to an attendance allowance for a period preceding the date on which he makes or is treated as making a claim for it if such an allowance has previously been paid to or in respect of him.

(6) Except in so far as regulations otherwise provide and subject to section 66(1) below—

(a) a claim for an attendance allowance may be made during the period of 6 months immediately preceding the period for which the person to whom the claim relates is entitled to the allowance; and

(b) an award may be made in pursuance of a claim so made, subject to the condition that, throughout that period of 6 months, that person satisfied—

(i) both the day and the night attendance conditions, or

(ii) if the award is at the lower rate, one of those conditions.

DEFINITIONS
  "claim": s.121(1).
  "entitled": s.121(1).
  "prescribe": s.121(1).

GENERAL NOTE
  A claimant for attendance allowance must have satisfied either or both of the conditions specified in s.64 for a period of six months before the claim (subs. (1)). It is possible to make a claim in anticipation of satisfying that requirement (subs. (6)). Awards are made for a fixed number of years (in which case a renewal claim may be made on expiry) or for life. There is no upper age limit to attendance allowance. The higher rate of attendance allowance is payable if both the day and night attendance conditions are met; otherwise the lower rate applies (subs. (3)).
  Special provision is made in the Social Security (Attendance Allowance) Regulations (Northern Ireland) 1992 (S.I. 1992 No. 20) for claimants on dialysis (subs. (2) and reg. 5).

Attendance allowance for the terminally ill

66.—(1) If a terminally ill person makes a claim expressly on the ground that he is such a person, then—
  (a) he shall be taken—
      (i) to satisfy, or to be likely to satisfy, both the day attendance condition and the night attendance condition for the remainder of his life, beginning with the date of the claim or, if later, the first date on which he is terminally ill; and
      (ii) to have satisfied those conditions for the period of 6 months immediately preceding that date (so however that no allowance shall be payable by virtue of this sub-paragraph for any period preceding that date); and
  (b) the period for which he is entitled to attendance allowance shall be the remainder of the person's life, beginning with that date.
(2) For the purposes of subsection (1) above—
  (a) a person is "terminally ill" at any time if at that time he suffers from a progressive disease and his death in consequence of that disease can reasonably be expected within 6 months; and
  (b) where a person purports to make a claim for an attendance allowance by virtue of that subsection on behalf of another, that other shall be regarded as making the claim, notwithstanding that it is made without his knowledge or authority.

DEFINITIONS
  "claim": s.121(1).
  "terminally ill": subs. (2).

GENERAL NOTE
  Claimants who are terminally ill are treated as special cases and are granted automatic entitlement to the higher rate of attendance allowance for the remainder of their life. Subsection (1) deems the terminally ill to be satisfying both the day and night attendance conditions for the relevant period (including the six-month qualifying period). The definition of "terminally ill" (subs. (2)(b)) is somewhat problematic. In practice the great majority of claims on this basis are successful. Even if death does not follow within six months or so, as a matter of practice claims are only reconsidered by the Benefits Agency Medical Service in Great Britain once a period of 15 months has elapsed.

Exclusions by regulation

67.—(1) Regulations may provide that, in such circumstances, and for such purposes as may be prescribed, a person who is, or is treated under the regulations as, undergoing treatment for renal failure in a hospital or other similar institution otherwise than as an in-patient shall be deemed not to satisfy or to be unlikely to satisfy the day attendance condition or the night attendance condition, or both of them.

(2) Regulations may provide that an attendance allowance shall not be payable in respect of a person for any period when he is a person for whom accommodation is provided—

    (a) in pursuance of Article 5, 7, 15 or 36 of the Health and Personal Social Services (Northern Ireland) Order 1972;

    (b) in circumstances in which the cost is, or may be, borne wholly or partly out of public or local funds, in pursuance of those enactments or of any other enactment relating to persons under disability.

DEFINITIONS
    "prescribe": s.121(1).

GENERAL NOTE
    Special provision is made under subs. (1) for claimants receiving renal dialysis (Social Security (Attendance Allowance) Regulations (Northern Ireland) 1992 (S.I. 1992 No. 20), reg. 5). Various categories of claimant who receive state subsidy for their accommodation are excluded from entitlement to attendance allowance by virtue of subs. (2) (regs. 6–8).

Severe disablement allowance

Entitlement and rate

68.—(1) Subject to the provisions of this section, a person shall be entitled to a severe disablement allowance for any day ("the relevant day") if he satisfies—

    (a) the conditions specified in subsection (2) below; or

    (b) the conditions specified in subsection (3) below.

    (2) The conditions mentioned in subsection (1)(a) above are that—

    (a) on the relevant day he is incapable of work; and

    (b) he has been incapable of work for a period of not less than 196 consecutive days—

        (i) beginning not later than the day on which he attained the age of 20; and

        (ii) ending immediately before the relevant day.

    (3) The conditions mentioned in subsection (1)(b) above are that—

    (a) on the relevant day he is both incapable of work and disabled; and

    (b) he has been both incapable of work and disabled for a period of not less than 196 consecutive days ending immediately before the relevant day.

    (4) A person shall not be entitled to a severe disablement allowance if—

    (a) he is under the age of 16;

    (b) he is receiving full-time education;

    (c) he does not satisfy the prescribed conditions—

        (i) as to residence in Northern Ireland; or

        (ii) as to presence there; or

    (d) he has attained pensionable age and—

        (i) was not entitled to a severe disablement allowance immediately before he attained that age; and

        (ii) is not treated by regulations as having been so entitled immediately before he attained that age.

    (5) A person shall not be entitled to a severe disablement allowance for any day which as between him and his employer falls within a period of entitlement for the purposes of statutory sick pay.

    (6) A person is disabled for the purposes of this section if he suffers from loss of physical or mental faculty such that the extent of the resulting disablement assessed in accordance with Schedule 6 to this Act amounts to not less than 80 per cent.

    (7) A severe disablement allowance shall be paid at the weekly rate specified in Schedule 4, Part III, paragraph 2.

(8) The amount of severe disablement allowance payable for any relevant day shall be one sixth of the weekly rate referred to in subsection (7) above.

(9) In any case where—

(a) a severe disablement allowance is payable to a woman in respect of one or more relevant days in a week; and

(b) an amount of statutory maternity pay becomes payable to her on any day in that week,

the amount of the severe disablement allowance (including any increase for a child or adult dependant under section 90(a) below) so payable shall be reduced by the amount of the statutory maternity pay, and only the balance (if any) shall be payable.

(10) Where—

(a) a person who is engaged and normally engaged in remunerative work ceases to be so engaged; and

(b) he is entitled to a disability working allowance for the week in which there falls the last day on which he is so engaged; and

(c) he qualified for a disability working allowance for that week by virtue of a severe disablement allowance having been payable to him; and

(d) the first day after he ceases to be engaged as mentioned in paragraph (a) above is a day on which he is incapable of work and falls not later than the end of the period of two years beginning with the last day for which he was entitled to a severe disablement allowance,

any day since that day which fell within a week for which he was entitled to a disability working allowance shall be treated for the purposes of any claim for a severe disablement allowance for a period commencing after he ceases to be engaged as mentioned in paragraph (a) above as having been a day on which he was both incapable of work and disabled.

(11) Regulations—

(a) may direct that persons who—

(i) have attained retiring age; and

(ii) were entitled to a severe disablement allowance immediately before they attained that age,

shall continue to be so entitled notwithstanding that they do not satisfy the conditions specified in subsection (2) or (3) above;

(b) may direct—

(i) that persons who have previously been entitled to a severe disablement allowance shall be entitled to such an allowance notwithstanding that they do not satisfy the conditions specified in subsection (2)(b) or (3)(b) above;

(ii) that subsections (2)(b) and (3)(b) above shall have effect in relation to such persons subject to such modifications as may be specified in the regulations;

(c) may prescribe the circumstances in which a person is or is not to be treated—

(i) as incapable of work; or

(ii) as receiving full-time education;

(d) may provide that, where the net amount of councillor's allowance (within the meaning of section 58 above) to which a person is entitled in respect of any week exceeds a prescribed sum, then, except in prescribed cases, an amount equal to the excess shall be deducted from the amount of any severe disablement allowance to which he is entitled in respect of that week, and only the balance remaining (if any) shall be payable; and

(e) may provide for disqualifying a person from receiving a severe disablement allowance for such period not exceeding 6 weeks as may be determined in accordance with the Administration Act if—

(i) he has become incapable of work through his own misconduct; or

(ii) he fails without good cause to attend for, or to submit himself to, such medical or other examination or treatment as may be required in accordance with the regulations, or to observe any prescribed rules of behaviour.

(12) In determining whether a person satisfies the conditions specified in subsections (2)(b) and (3)(b) above he shall be treated as having been incapable of work on any day which falls in the pre-commencement period and which—

(a) would have been treated as a day on which he was so incapable, were there disregarded any work which he undertook (or was capable of undertaking) as a councillor, but

(b) would not have been so treated apart from this subsection.

(13) In this section—

"councillor" and "pre-commencement period" have the meanings assigned to them by section 58(4) above;

"retiring age" means 70 in the case of a man and 65 in the case of a woman,

and section 58(5) above has effect for the purposes of subsection (12) above as it has effect for the purposes of section 58 above.

DEFINITIONS
"the Administration Act": s.170.
"child": s.121(1).
"councillor": subs. (13).
"councillor's allowance": s.58(4).
"entitled": s.121(1).
"medical examination": s.121(1).
"medical treatment": s.121(1).
"Northern Ireland": s.168.
"pensionable age": s.121(1).
"pre-commencement period": subs. (13).
"prescribe": s.121(1).
"relevant day": subs. (1).
"retiring age": subs. (13).
"week": s.121(1).

GENERAL NOTE
Severe disablement allowance (SDA) is a non-contributory benefit paid to people who have been incapable of work and have satisfied an extra condition of severe disability for a continuous period of 196 days (28 weeks). SDA replaced the non-contributory invalidity pension in 1984. It is paid at a lower rate than the contributory invalidity benefit but may be supplemented by age-related additions (s.69).

All SDA claimants must be incapable of work and have been so for 196 days immediately before the date of claim. Claimants must then satisfy any one of three separate further conditions:

(i) *Incapacity when young.* The claimant must show that the 196 days of incapacity began on or before his or her twentieth birthday (subs. (2)). There is a special concession which allows young people to work for no more than 182 days without losing entitlement to benefit under this route (Social Security (Severe Disablement Allowance) Regulations (Northern Ireland) 1984 (S.I. 1984 No. 317), reg. 7(3)). Those who take advantage of this facility need not satisfy the disablement test under subs. (3).

(ii) *The severely disabled.* Any claimant under pensionable age may qualify for SDA by showing that he or she is 80 per cent. disabled or more (subss. (3) and (6)). The assessment criteria used under the industrial injuries scheme apply in this context. Individuals with certain types of disability are deemed to meet the 80 per cent. threshold without the need for a medical examination (reg. 10).

(iii) *Prior entitlement to SDA.* Transitional rules apply to those formerly entitled to the non-contributory invalidity pension (reg. 20). The E.C.J. has held that these provisions contravene Art. 4(1) of E.C. Directive 7917: *Johnson* v. *Chief Adjudication Officer (Case C-31/90)* [1992] 2 All E.R. 705.

Finally, claimants must not fall within the exclusions specified in subss. (4) or (5). The rules of entitlement as to residence and presence are elaborated upon in regulations. The exclusion of persons of pensionable age has been found to be contrary to E.C. Directive 79/7: *Thomas* v. *Chief Adjudication Officer and Secretary of State for Social Security*; *Cooze* v. *Same*; *Beard* v. *Same*; *Murphy* v. *Same*; *Morley* v. *Same* [1991] 2 W.L.R. 886.

Severe disablement allowance: age related addition

69.—(1) If a person was under the age of 60 on the day on which he qualified for severe disablement allowance, the weekly rate of his severe disablement allowance shall be increased by an age related addition at whichever of the weekly rates specified in the second column of paragraph 3 of Part III of Schedule 4 to this Act is applicable in his case, that is to say—

    (a) the higher rate, if he was under the age of 40 on the day on which he qualified for severe disablement allowance;

    (b) the middle rate, if he was between the ages of 40 and 50 on that day; or

    (c) the lower rate, if he was between the ages of 50 and 60 on that day.

(2) Subject to subsection (4) below, for the purposes of this section the day on which a person qualified for severe disablement allowance is his first day of incapacity for work in the period of not less than 196 consecutive days mentioned in section 68(2)(b) or (3)(b) above, as the case may be, which preceded the first day in his current period of entitlement.

(3) For the purposes of this section, a person's "current period of entitlement" is a current period—

    (a) which consists of one or more consecutive days on which he is or has been entitled to a severe disablement allowance; and

    (b) which begins immediately after the last period of one or more consecutive days for which he was not entitled to such an allowance.

(4) Regulations—

    (a) may prescribe cases where a person is to be treated for the purposes of this section as having qualified for severe disablement allowance on a prescribed day earlier than the day ascertained in accordance with subsection (2) above;

    (b) may provide for days which are not days of incapacity for work in relation to a person to be treated as days of incapacity for work for the purpose of determining under this section the day on which he qualified for severe disablement allowance; and

    (c) may make provision for disregarding prescribed days in computing any period of consecutive days for the purposes of subsection (3) above.

DEFINITIONS
   "current period of entitlement": subs. (3).
   "day of incapacity for work": s.121(1).
   "prescribe": s.121(1).

GENERAL NOTE
   The basic rate of severe disablement allowance is less than that for invalidity benefit. SS(N.I.)O 1990, art. 4(1) introduced age-related additions for SDA (set at the same levels as the invalidity allowance rates) to help narrow this gap. The higher rate is payable to claimants who are below the age of 40 on the first day of the 196-day qualifying period. A middle rate is payable to those who are aged 40–49 on qualifying, and a lower rate for those aged 50–59. This reform followed the proposals set out in The Way Ahead which were designed to assist those disabled early in life.

Invalid care allowance

Invalid care allowance

70.—(1) A person shall be entitled to an invalid care allowance for any day on which he is engaged in caring for a severely disabled person if—

    (a) he is regularly and substantially engaged in caring for that person;

(b) he is not gainfully employed; and
(c) the severely disabled person is either such relative of his as may be prescribed or a person of any such other description as may be prescribed.

(2) In this section, "severely disabled person" means a person in respect of whom there is payable either an attendance allowance or a disability living allowance by virtue of entitlement to the care component at the highest or middle rate or such other payment out of public funds on account of his need for attendance as may be prescribed.

(3) A person shall not be entitled to an allowance under this section if he is under the age of 16 or receiving full-time education.

(4) A person shall not be entitled to allowance under this section unless he satisfies prescribed conditions as to residence or presence in Northern Ireland.

(5) Subject to subsection (6) below, a person who has attained pensionable age shall not be entitled to an allowance under this section unless he was so entitled (or is treated by regulations as having been so entitled) immediately before attaining that age.

(6) Regulations may make provision whereby a person who has attained retiring age, and was entitled to an allowance under this section immediately before attaining that age, continues to be so entitled notwithstanding that he is not caring for a severely disabled person or no longer satisfies the requirements of subsection (1)(a) or (b) above.

(7) No person shall be entitled for the same day to more than one allowance under this section; and where, apart from this subsection, two or more persons would be entitled for the same day to such an allowance in respect of the same severely disabled person, one of them only shall be entitled and that shall be such one of them—
(a) as they may jointly elect in the prescribed manner, or
(b) as may, in default of such an election, be determined by the Department in its discretion.

(8) Regulations may prescribe the circumstances in which a person is or is not to be treated for the purposes of this section as engaged, or regularly and substantially engaged, in caring for a severely disabled person, as gainfully employed or as receiving full-time education.

(9) An invalid care allowance shall be payable at the weekly rate specified in Schedule 4, Part III, paragraph 4.

(10) In this section "retiring age" means 70 in the case of a man and 65 in the case of a woman.

DEFINITIONS
"Department": s.170.
"entitled": s.121(1).
"pensionable age": s.121(1).
"prescribe": s.121(1).
"relative": s.121(1).
"retiring age": subs. (10).
"severely disabled person": subs. (2).

GENERAL NOTE
Invalid care allowance (ICA) is a non-contributory benefit payable to those who provide regular and substantial care for a person who receives attendance allowance, the care component of disability living allowance at the higher or middle rate or (as prescribed by the Social Security (Invalid Care Allowance) Regulations (Northern Ireland) 1976 (S.I. 1976 No. 99), reg. 3) constant attendance allowance in respect of industrial or war disablement (subs. (2)). Claimants under the age of 16 (subs. (3)) and over pensionable age are not eligible for ICA (subs. (5), but see *Thomas* v. *Chief Adjudication Officer and Secretary of State for Social Security*; *Cooze* v. *Same*; *Beard* v. *Same*; *Murphy* v. *Same*; *Morley* v. *Same* [1991] 2 W.L.R. 886), but those in receipt of ICA before reaching pensionable age may retain their entitlement.

Subs. (1)

Regularly and substantially engaged. Although subs. (1) refers to ICA as a daily benefit, reg. 4 establishes a threshold of at least 35 hours of care a week (subject to a concession where there is a temporary break in caring).

Not gainfully employed. Claimants are regarded as not being in gainful employment if they earn no more than a weekly limit set by reg. 8 (£40 for 1992/93). ICA is not therefore restricted to those who give up paid work completely to look after an invalid.

The disabled person is either such relative. No distinction is made in the regulations between invalids who are related or not to the carer (reg. 6).

Subs. (3)

Receiving full-time education. This concept is left to the discretion of the Department to define (reg. 5). The former restriction on married women and those cohabiting was repealed following the decision of the E.C.J. in *Drake* v. *Chief Adjudication Officer (No. 150/85)* [1987] Q.B. 166.

Subs. (4)

Residence or presence. See reg. 9, which as a general rule requires the claimant to be present and ordinarily resident in Northern Ireland.

Subs. (7)

ICA is only payable in respect of the care provided for one invalid. There is no provision for entitlement where the carer looks after two individuals, neither of whom is entitled to one of the prescribed benefits, but whose care needs together amount to more than 35 hours a week.

Disability living allowance

Disability living allowance

71.—(1) Disability living allowance shall consist of a care component and a mobility component.

(2) A person's entitlement to a disability living allowance may be an entitlement to either component or to both of them.

(3) A person may be awarded either component for a fixed period or for life, but if his award of a disability living allowance consists of both components, he may not be awarded the components for different fixed periods.

(4) The weekly rate of a person's disability living allowance for a week for which he has been only awarded one component is the appropriate weekly rate for that component as determined in accordance with this Act or regulations under it.

(5) The weekly rate of a person's disability living allowance for a week for which he has been awarded both components is the aggregate of the appropriate weekly rates for the two components as so determined.

(6) A person shall not be entitled to a disability living allowance unless he satisfies prescribed conditions as to residence and presence in Northern Ireland.

DEFINITIONS
   "Department": s.170.
   "entitled": s.121(1).
   "Northern Ireland": s.168.
   "week": s.121(1).

GENERAL NOTE

Disability living allowance (DLA) was created by merging attendance allowance and mobility allowance and by extending their coverage to include people with less severe disabilities. These changes came into effect in April 1992 under the DLADWAO 1991. DLA is a composite benefit with three possible rates for the care component (as against two for attendance allowance) and two rates for the mobility component (as against one for the former mobility allowance). Attendance allowance is preserved only for claimants who are aged 65 or over when they qualify for the first time under the care criteria (see ss.64–67), while mobility allowance has been abolished.

The highest and middle rates of the care component are equivalent to the two rates of attendance allowance. The higher of the two rates for the mobility component is equivalent to the old mobility allowance (MobA). The new lower rate of the care component was designed for "people who need help with self-care during the day but less frequently than those who currently qualify for AA" (*The Way Ahead*, para. 4.12). The lower rate of the mobility component is for "people who are not independently mobile and who do not otherwise fulfil the current criteria for MobA" (para. 4.13). DLA is therefore something of a misnomer in that it fails to provide assistance with the many other extra living costs faced by disabled people.

Sections 71–76 set out the basic framework for DLA. Matters of detail are dealt with in the Social Security (Disability Living Allowance) Regulations (Northern Ireland) 1992 (S.I. 1992 No. 32). DLA has been designed so far as possible to enable self-assessment in claiming benefit. For the special review and appeals procedure, see SSA(N.I.)A 1992, ss.28–33. Advice in relation to DLA is offered to the Department by the Disability Living Allowance Advisory Board for Northern Ireland (SSA(N.I.)A 1992, s.152).

Subs. (2)
Consequently there are 11 different rates of payment for DLA, ranging from the lowest rate of just one component to the top rate of both components.

Subs. (3)
A DLA component may be awarded for a fixed period or for life. If a claimant is entitled to both components of the new benefit, they may not be awarded for different fixed periods. This means that a claimant with care and mobility needs will find one award shortened to align it with the other, unless one of the awards is for life. The rationale for this is partly in the claimants' interests by minimising the need for repeated assessment and adjudication but also partly for reasons of administrative convenience.

Subs. (6)
The residence and presence criteria for DLA are dealt with in regulations. The claimant must be ordinarily resident in Northern Ireland, present in Northern Ireland for an aggregate of not less than 26 weeks in the 12 months preceding the date of claim and present in Northern Ireland throughout the claim. The residence and presence conditions apply to terminally ill claimants for the care component, who are otherwise excused from the retrospective and prospective qualifying periods under s.72(2) below (see s.72(5)).

These rules are necessarily subject to the relevant E.C. legislation, and in particular Reg. 1408/71. In *Newton* v. *Chief Adjudication Officer* [1992] 1 C.M.L.R. 149 the European Court of Justice held that mobility allowance could not be withdrawn from a British national who had been awarded benefit but then moved to live in France. As from May 1, 1992, however, various income-related and non-contributory benefits (including mobility allowance and disability living allowance) have become non-exportable: See Reg. 1408/71, art. 10a and Annex IIa, inserted by Reg. 1247/92.

The care component

72.—(1) Subject to the provisions of this Act, a person shall be entitled to the care component of a disability living allowance for any period throughout which—

    (a) he is so severely disabled physically or mentally that—

        (i) he requires in connection with his bodily functions attention from another person for a significant portion of the day (whether during a single period or a number of periods); or

        (ii) he cannot prepare a cooked main meal for himself if he has the ingredients;

    (b) he is so severely disabled physically or mentally that, by day, he requires from another person—

        (i) frequent attention throughout the day in connection with his bodily functions; or

        (ii) continual supervision throughout the day in order to avoid substantial danger to himself or others; or

    (c) he is so severely disabled physically or mentally that, at night,—

        (i) he requires from another person prolonged or repeated attention in connection with his bodily functions; or

   (ii) in order to avoid substantial danger to himself or others he
  requires another person to be awake for a prolonged period or at
  frequent intervals for the purpose of watching over him.
 (2) Subject to the following provisions of this section, a person shall not be
entitled to the care component of a disability living allowance unless—
  (a) throughout—
    (i) the period of 3 months immediately preceding the date on
   which the award of that component would begin; or
    (ii) such other period of 3 months as may be prescribed,
  he has satisfied or is likely to satisfy one or other of the conditions
  mentioned in subsection (1)(a) to (c) above; and
  (b) he is likely to continue to satisfy one or other of those conditions
  throughout—
    (i) the period of 6 months beginning with that date; or
    (ii) (if his death is expected within the period of 6 months
   beginning with that date) the period so beginning and ending with
   his death.
 (3) Three weekly rates of the care component shall be prescribed.
 (4) The weekly rate of the care component payable to a person for each
week in the period for which he is awarded that component shall be—
  (a) the highest rate, if he falls within subsection (2) above by virtue of
  having satisfied or being likely to satisfy both the conditions mentioned in subsection (1)(b) and (c) above throughout both the period
  mentioned in paragraph (a) of subsection (2) above and that mentioned in paragraph (b) of that subsection;
  (b) the middle rate, if he falls within that subsection by virtue of having
  satisfied or being likely to satisfy one or other of those conditions
  throughout both those periods; and
  (c) the lowest rate in any other case.
 (5) For the purposes of this section, a person who is terminally ill, as
defined in section 66(2) above, and makes a claim expressly on the ground
that he is such a person, shall be taken—
  (a) to have satisfied the conditions mentioned in subsection (1)(b) and (c)
  above for the period of 3 months immediately preceding the date of
  the claim, or, if later, the first date on which he is terminally ill (so
  however that the care component shall not be payable by virtue of this
  paragraph for any period preceding that date); and
  (b) to satisfy or to be likely to satisfy those conditions for the remainder of
  his life beginning with that date.
 (6) For the purposes of this section in its application to a person for any
period in which he is under the age of 16—
  (a) sub-paragraph (ii) of subsection (1)(a) above shall be omitted; and
  (b) neither the condition mentioned in sub-paragraph (i) of that paragraph nor any of the conditions mentioned in subsection (1)(b) and
  (c) above shall be taken to be satisfied unless—
    (i) he has requirements of a description mentioned in subsection
   (1)(a), (b) or (c) above substantially in excess of the normal
   requirements of persons of his age; or
    (ii) he has substantial requirements of any such description which
   younger persons in normal physical and mental health may also
   have but which persons of his age and in normal physical and
   mental health would not have.
 (7) Subject to subsections (5) and (6) above, circumstances may be
prescribed in which a person is to be taken to satisfy or not to satisfy such of
the conditions mentioned in subsection (1)(a) to (c) above as may be
prescribed.
 (8) Regulations may provide that a person shall not be paid any amount in
respect of a disability living allowance which is attributable to entitlement to

the care component for a period when he is a person for whom accommodation is provided—
   (a) in pursuance of Article 5, 7, 15 or 36 of the Health and Personal Social Services (Northern Ireland) Order 1972; or
   (b) in circumstances in which the cost is, or may be, borne wholly or partly out of public or local funds, in pursuance of those enactments or of any other enactment relating to persons under disability or to young persons or to education or training.

DEFINITIONS
   "claim": s.121(1).
   "entitled": s.121(1).
   "prescribe": s.121(1).

GENERAL NOTE
   This section deals with entitlement to and payment of the care component of disability living allowance. Three separate criteria for the award of the care component of DLA are specified. A claimant who only meets either of the conditions set out in subs. (1)(a) will receive the lowest rate of care component (subs. (4)(c)). A claimant who meets the criteria in either subs. (1)(b) or (c) will qualify for the middle rate of this component (subs. (4)(b)), whilst a claimant who satisfies both of the conditions in subs. (1)(b) and (c) will be awarded the highest rate (subs. (4)(a)).

Subs. (1)(a)
   This condition is the basis for the lowest rate of the care component. It is therefore designed for people whose care needs would not be regarded as severe enough for them to qualify under the rules for attendance allowance. It comprises two quite distinct and alternative tests:
   (i) *He requires in connection with his bodily functions* . . . The first limb of the day condition for DLA (subs. (1)(b)(i)) is only satisfied if the claimant requires "frequent attention throughout the day in connection with his bodily functions". The wording of this subsection is intended to enable people who need a lower level of care to qualify for DLA, so long as it is required "for a significant portion of the day (whether during a single period or a number of periods)". The Government envisaged "'significant portion' being interpreted as an hour or thereabouts. For example, this route will help people who need help getting in and out of bed or a bath, or people who require assistance in administering courses of injections or medicines" (*per* Lord Henley, *Hansard*, H.L. Vol. 526, col. 884, February 26, 1991). For discussion of the meaning of "in connection with his bodily functions", see annotations to s.64(2)(a) above.
   (ii) *He cannot prepare a cooked main meal for himself* . . . This condition is purely hypothetical and is to be determined in accordance with the principle of self-assessment.

Subs. (1)(b)
   The wording of these alternative heads of entitlement is identical in all material respects to the day condition for attendance allowance (s.64(2) above) and so the case law on that provision will remain relevant.

Subs. (1)(c)
   The wording of these alternative heads of entitlement is identical in all material respects to the night condition for attendance allowance (s.64(3) above) and so the case law on that provision will remain relevant.

Subs. (2)
   In addition to meeting the care criteria specified in subs. (1), claimants for the care component must also satisfy the qualifying period conditions laid down in this subsection (except those who are terminally ill: see subs. (5)). These conditions, which apply equally to the mobility component (see s.73(9)), are a compromise between the previous requirements for attendance allowance and mobility allowance.

Subs. (3)
   The three weekly rates of the care component are specified in regulations. The top and middle rates are equivalent to the two rates of attendance allowance, whilst the third and lower rate was introduced in April 1992.

Subs. (4)
   This subsection details the level of care component to be awarded in any given case: see General Note.

Subs. (5)

This makes special provision for claimants who are terminally ill. A person is terminally ill if "he suffers from a progressive disease and his death in consequence of that disease can reasonably be expected within six months" (s.66(2)). People who meet this criterion are deemed to satisfy the qualifying period. People who are terminally ill must still satisfy the residence and presence conditions prescribed under s.71(6) above.

Subs. (6)

As with the original form of attendance allowance, special rules apply where the disabled person is a child. Children aged under 16 will only qualify for the lower rate of care component if they satisfy the test in subs. (1)(a)(i) above—the abstract cooking test in subs. (1)(a)(ii) being inappropriate. Furthermore, with regard to both the test in subs. (1)(a)(i) and those under subs. (1)(b) and (c), the additional condition detailed in subs. (6)(b) must be met. This formulation emphasises that disabled children should not be denied benefit merely because they have substantial care or attention needs which may be shared by younger but physically and mentally healthy children.

Subs. (7)

This is an enabling provision permitting regulations to specify circumstances in which a person is deemed to satisfy or not to satisfy the care criteria in subs. (1) above. Special rules are made under this power for claimants on renal dialysis.

Subs. (8)

This enabling provision allows the payment of benefit to be restricted where people are being cared for in residential accommodation which is paid for out of public funds. Under the regulations the care component ceases to be payable once the claimant has been in such accommodation (or has been in hospital) for 28 days. Different rules apply to the mobility component; see further s.73(14).

The mobility component

73.—(1) Subject to the provisions of this Act, a person shall be entitled to the mobility component of a disability living allowance for any period in which he is over the age of 5 and throughout which—

(a) he is suffering from physical disablement such that he is either unable to walk or virtually unable to do so;

(b) he falls within subsection (2) below;

(c) he falls within subsection (3) below; or

(d) he is able to walk but is so severely disabled physically or mentally that, disregarding any ability he may have to use routes which are familiar to him on his own, he cannot take advantage of the faculty out of doors without guidance or supervision from another person most of the time.

(2) A person falls within this subsection if—

(a) he is both blind and deaf; and

(b) he satisfies such other conditions as may be prescribed.

(3) A person falls within this subsection if—

(a) he is severely mentally impaired; and

(b) he displays severe behavioural problems; and

(c) he satisfies both the conditions mentioned in section 72(1)(b) and (c) above.

(4) For the purposes of this section in its application to a person for any period in which he is under the age of 16, the condition mentioned in subsection (1)(d) above shall not be taken to be satisfied unless—

(a) he requires substantially more guidance or supervision from another person than persons of his age in normal physical and mental health would require; or

(b) persons of his age in normal physical and mental health would not require such guidance or supervision.

(5) Subject to subsection (4) above, circumstances may be prescribed in which a person is to be taken to satisfy or not to satisfy a condition mentioned in subsection (1)(a) or (d) or subsection (2)(a) above.

(6) Regulations shall specify the cases which fall within subsection (3)(a) and (b) above.

(7) A person who is to be taken for the purposes of section 72 above to satisfy or not to satisfy a condition mentioned in subsection (1)(b) or (c) of that section is to be taken to satisfy or not to satisfy it for the purposes of subsection (3)(c) above.

(8) A person shall not be entitled to the mobility component for a period unless during most of that period his condition will be such as permits him from time to time to benefit from enhanced facilities for locomotion.

(9) A person shall not be entitled to the mobility component of a disability living allowance unless—

    (a) throughout—

        (i) the period of 3 months immediately preceding the date on which the award of that component would begin; or

        (ii) such other period of 3 months as may be prescribed,

    he has satisfied or is likely to satisfy one or other of the conditions mentioned in subsection (1) above; and

    (b) he is likely to continue to satisfy one or other of those conditions throughout—

        (i) the period of 6 months beginning with that date; or

        (ii) (if his death is expected within the period of 6 months beginning with that date) the period so beginning and ending with his death.

(10) Two weekly rates of the mobility component shall be prescribed.

(11) The weekly rate of the mobility component payable to a person for each week in the period for which he is awarded that component shall be—

    (a) the higher rate, if he falls within subsection (9) above by virtue of having satisfied or being likely to satisfy one or other of the conditions mentioned in subsection (1)(a), (b) and (c) above throughout both the period mentioned in paragraph (a) of subsection (9) above and that mentioned in paragraph (b) of that subsection; and

    (b) the lower rate in any other case.

(12) For the purposes of this section in its application to a person who is terminally ill, as defined in section 66(2) above, and who makes a claim expressly on the ground that he is such a person—

    (a) subsection (9)(a) above shall be omitted; and

    (b) subsection (11)(a) above shall have effect as if for the words from "both" to "subsection", in the fourth place where it occurs, there were substituted the words "the period mentioned in subsection (9)(b) above".

(13) Regulations may prescribe cases in which a person who has the use—

    (a) of an invalid carriage or other vehicle provided under Article 30(1) of the Health and Personal Social Services (Northern Ireland) Order 1972 or provided by the Secretary of State under section 5(2)(a) of the National Health Service Act 1977 and Schedule 2 to that Act or under section 46 of the National Health Service (Scotland) Act 1978; or

    (b) of any prescribed description of appliance supplied under that Order being such an appliance as is primarily designed to afford a means of personal and independent locomotion out of doors,

is not to be paid any amount attributable to entitlement to the mobility component or is to be paid disability living allowance at a reduced rate in so far as it is attributable to that component.

(14) A payment to or in respect of any person which is attributable to his entitlement to the mobility component, and the right to receive such a

payment, shall (except in prescribed circumstances and for prescribed purposes) be disregarded in applying any enactment or instrument under which regard is to be had to a person's means.

DEFINITIONS
"entitled": s.121(1).
"prescribe": s.121(1).
"week": s.121(1).

GENERAL NOTE

This section specifies the criteria for the award of the mobility component. Two conditions must be satisfied under subs. (1): the age condition and the mobility condition. So far as age is concerned, the mobility component is not payable to children aged under five (in contrast, there is no lower age limit for the care component, subject to the initial qualifying period). Claims made by children aged five or over must also satisfy the additional condition laid down in subs. (4). At the other end of the age spectrum, initial claims for the mobility component are generally not possible by people over 65 (see s.75).

The claimant must then meet one of the four mobility conditions set out in subs. (1)(a)–(d), as elaborated upon by subss. (2) and (3). Criteria (a) and (b) replicate tests which were used for the former mobility allowance and, together with condition (c), give rise to entitlement to the higher rate of the mobility component. The fourth condition only qualifies the claimant for the lower rate.

Subs. (1)

(a) He is suffering from physical disablement such that he is either unable to walk or virtually unable to do so. The formula adopted is elaborated upon in the Social Security (Disability Living Allowance) Regulations (Northern Ireland) 1992 (S.I. 1992 No. 32), reg. 12. The crucial point is that the inability to walk must result from a physical rather than a psychological cause (*Lees* v. *Secretary of State for Social Services* [1985] A.C. 930, and *Harrison* v. *Secretary of State for Social Services*, reported as appendix to *R(M) 1/88*). *Lees* demonstrates that an individual will be not "unable to walk"—and so will be ineligible for mobility allowance—if he can put one foot in front of another without the assistance of a third party, even though guidance may be required. This type of case may now fall within any of subs. (1)(b)–(d) below.

The meaning of "virtually unable to walk" is a question of law (*R(M) 1/78*). The base point is a total inability to walk, but this is extended to take in people who can technically walk but only to an insignificant extent. An inability to walk to the shops or to the bus stop and so to lead a normal life is not sufficient to ground entitlement: *R(M) 3/78*, *R(M) 1/91*.

(b) He falls within subsection (2) below. Special provision for the deaf-blind to claim mobility allowance was made as from April 1990. Under the regulations this is defined as 100 per cent. sight loss and at least 80 per cent. hearing loss.

(c) He falls within subsection (3) below. The decision of the House of Lords in *Lees* made it very difficult for claimants with behavioural problems to claim mobility allowance. A Tribunal of three Commissioners ruled that the essential question in such cases was "whether the claimant could not walk, as distinct from would not walk" (*R(M) 3/86*, para. 8). In that case it was held that claims were possible where the disabled person's condition was such that he or she behaved erratically, sometimes running off and sometimes stopping completely. The formula set out in subs. (3) first appeared in the DLADWAO 1991 and was designed to extend the higher rate of the mobility component to a group of some 8,000 to 9,000 people who suffer from severe mental handicap and severe behavioural problems.

(d) He is able to walk but is so severely disabled physically or mentally . . . This head of entitlement was introduced by the DLADWAO 1991 and is entirely hypothetical. It was designed so that "a person who can go by himself to the local corner shop because he is familiar with the journey but needs help to go anywhere else should receive benefit" (*per* Lord Henley, *Hansard*, H.L. Vol. 526, col. 1578, March 7, 1991). Where the claimant is a person aged under 16, the additional condition set out in subs. (4) must be satisfied.

Subs. (3)

(a) He is severely mentally impaired. The regulations define this as where a person suffers "from a state of arrested development or incomplete physical development of the brain, which includes severe impairment of intelligence and social functioning" (Social Security (Disability Living Allowance) Regulations (Northern Ireland) 1992 (S.I. 1992 No. 32), reg. 12(5)).

(b) He displays severe behavioural problems. The regulations define this as where a person exhibits disruptive behaviour which is (i) extreme, (ii) regularly requires another person to

intervene and physically restrain him in order to prevent him causing physical injury to himself or another, or damage to property, and (iii) is so unpredictable that he requires another person to be present and watching over him whenever he is awake (reg. 12(6)).

Entitlement only arises if the claimant also satisfies both the day and night conditions for the care component. See further Rowland.

Subs. (4)

This is analogous to the additional condition for children aged under 16 in relation to the care component (s.72(6) above). It does not apply to the first three mobility conditions set out in subs. (1)(a)–(c).

Subs. (5)

This enables regulations to prescribe the circumstances in which a person is to be taken to satisfy or not to satisfy the various mobility conditions specified. These include provision for people who have had both legs amputated to be awarded the mobility component automatically.

Subs. (7)

This means, for example, that a person who is terminally ill and is thereby deemed to meet the care criteria in s.72 above is regarded as also satisfying those conditions for the purpose of qualifying for the mobility component under subs. (3)(c).

Subs. (8)

This excludes from entitlement people whom it is unsafe to move at all and persons so severely mentally handicapped that a high degree of supervision and restraint is needed to prevent them from injuring themselves or a third party (*R(M) 2/83*).

Subs. (9)

See annotations to s.72(2) above, which applies the same tests to the care component.

Subs. (10)

Regulations set out the two rates for the mobility component. The higher rate is equivalent to the old mobility allowance whilst the lower rate will be available to those who meet the conditions specified in subs. (1)(d) above.

Subs. (11)

This subsection specifies the level of mobility component to be awarded. Claimants who meet any of the criteria in subs. (1)(a)–(c) above throughout the qualifying period mentioned in subs. (9) are entitled to the higher rate. People who only qualify under subs. (1)(d) receive the lower rate. Recipients of the lower rate are not exempt from vehicle excise duty, unlike claimants on the higher rate (Vehicles (Excise) (Northern Ireland) Act 1972, s.7(2), as amended).

Subs. (12)

As with the care component, claimants who are terminally ill are exempted from the prior qualifying period. They must still satisfy the residence and presence conditions prescribed under s.71(6) above.

Subs. (13)

This enables regulations to be made to avoid duplicate provision by ensuring that the mobility component is not payable, or is payable at a reduced rate, to people who have the use of such an invalid vehicle.

Subs. (14)

The mobility component of DLA, unlike the care component (see s.72(8)), is generally to be disregarded in any means-testing.

Mobility component for certain persons eligible for invalid carriage

74.—(1) Regulations may provide for the issue, variation and cancellation of certificates in respect of prescribed categories of persons to whom this section applies; and a person in respect of whom such a certificate is issued shall, during any period while the certificate is in force, be deemed for the purposes of section 73 above to satisfy the condition mentioned in sub-section (1)(a) of that section and to fall within paragraph (a) or (b) of subsection (9) by virtue of having satisfied or being likely to satisfy that condition throughout both the periods mentioned in those paragraphs.

(2) This section applies to any person whom the Department considers—

(a) was on 1st January 1976 in possession of an invalid carriage or other vehicle provided in pursuance of Article 30 of the Health and Personal Social Services (Northern Ireland) Order 1972 (which relates to vehicles for persons suffering from physical defect or disability) or receiving payments in pursuance of paragraph (3) of that Article;

(b) had at that date, or at a later date specified by the Department made an application which the Department approved for such a carriage or vehicle or for such payments;

(c) was, both at some time during a prescribed period before that date and at some time during a prescribed period after that date, in possession of such a carriage or vehicle or receiving such payments; or

(d) would have been, by virtue of any of the preceding paragraphs, a person to whom this section applies but for some error or delay for which in the opinion of the Department the person was not responsible and which was brought to the attention of the Department within the period of one year beginning with 30th March 1977 (the date of the making of the Social Security (Miscellaneous Provisions) (Northern Ireland) Order 1977, Article 10 of which made provision corresponding to the provision made by this section).

DEFINITIONS
"prescribe": s.121(1).

GENERAL NOTE
Regulations made under this section enable people who have a small car or tricycle under the pre-1976 Invalid Vehicle Scheme to transfer automatically to the mobility component of DLA as and when they give up use of such a vehicle.

Persons 65 or over

75.—(1) Except to the extent to which regulations provide otherwise, no person shall be entitled to either component of a disability living allowance for any period after he attains the age of 65 otherwise than by virtue of an award made before he attains that age.

(2) Regulations may provide in relation to persons who are entitled to a component of a disability living allowance by virtue of subsection (1) above that any provision of this Act which relates to disability living allowance, other than section 74 above, so far as it so relates, and any provision of the Administration Act which is relevant to disability living allowance—

(a) shall have effect subject to modifications, additions or amendments; or

(b) shall not have effect.

DEFINITIONS
"the Administration Act": s.170.
"entitled": s.121(1).

GENERAL NOTE
This section restricts the entitlement to DLA of people aged 65 or over to those who have already been receiving the benefit before that age. In doing so it follows the pattern of mobility allowance. There is, however, no upper limit to receipt of DLA.

Subs. (1)
The basic rule is that claimants whose disabilities start on or after their 65th birthday are not

eligible for DLA. Thus a person who, after attaining 65, for the first time satisfies the test for the middle or higher rate of the care component is only eligible for attendance allowance (see s.64 above). A person who, after reaching 65, qualifies for the first time for what would be the lower rate of the care component or either rate of the mobility component is not eligible for benefit at all. People who qualify for DLA before the age of 65 are still entitled, providing they make a claim before they reach 66 (as with mobility allowance: see *R(M) 3/89*). More generally, claimants already in receipt of DLA before the age of 65 will continue to be eligible after that age, assuming the other criteria are still satisfied.

Subs. (2)
Regulations made under this provision ensure that people receiving DLA are not treated differently from other claimants if their circumstances change after they reach the age of 65.

Disability living allowance—supplementary

76.—(1) Subject to subsection (2) below, a person shall not be entitled to a disability living allowance for any period preceding the date on which a claim for it is made or treated as made by him or on his behalf.

(2) Notwithstanding anything in subsection (1) above, provision may be made by regulations for a person to be entitled to a component of a disability living allowance for a period preceding the date on which a claim for such an allowance is made or treated as made by him or on his behalf if he has previously been entitled to that component.

(3) For the purposes of sections 72(5) and 73(12) above, where—
  (a) a person purports to make a claim for a disability living allowance on behalf of another; and
  (b) the claim is made expressly on the ground that the person on whose behalf it purports to be made is terminally ill,
that person shall be regarded as making the claim notwithstanding that it is made without his knowledge or authority.

Definitions
  "claim": s.121(1).
  "entitled": s.121(1).

General Note

Subs. (1)
Entitlement to DLA cannot be backdated, subject to the narrow exception in subs. (2). There is therefore no provision for "good cause" to enable backdating of claims, unlike with claims for industrial injuries benefits, invalidity benefit, severe disablement allowance and other benefits.
  Or treated as made. This is a useful relaxation of an otherwise harsh rule. Under the regulations, the date of claim for a claim form which is received within six weeks of a request for a form is the date of receipt of such a request.

Subs. (2)
This allows regulations to be made ensuring that there are no gaps in entitlement where repeat claims are delayed.

Subs. (3)
This follows the special provision for claims on behalf of the terminally ill for attendance allowance (s.66(2)(b) above).

Guardian's allowance

Guardian's allowance

77.—(1) A person shall be entitled to a guardian's allowance in respect of a child if—
  (a) he is entitled to child benefit in respect of that child, and

(b) the circumstances are any of those specified in subsection (2) below;
but this subsection is subject, in particular, to section 81 below.

(2) The circumstances referred to in subsection (1)(b) above are—

(a) that both of the child's parents are dead;

(b) that one of the child's parents is dead and the person claiming a guardian's allowance shows that he was at the date of the death unaware of, and has failed after all reasonable efforts to discover, the whereabouts of the other parent; or

(c) that one of the child's parents is dead and the other is in prison.

(3) There shall be no entitlement to a guardian's allowance in respect of a child unless at least one of the child's parents satisfies, or immediately before his death satisfied, such conditions as may be prescribed as to nationality, residence, place of birth or other matters.

(4) Where, apart from this subsection, a person is entitled to receive, in respect of a particular child, payment of an amount by way of a guardian's allowance, that amount shall not be payable unless one of the conditions specified in subsection (5) below is satisfied.

(5) Those conditions are—

(a) that the beneficiary would be treated for the purposes of Part IX of this Act as having the child living with him; or

(b) that the requisite contributions are being made to the cost of providing for the child.

(6) The condition specified in subsection (5)(b) above is to be treated as satisfied if, but only if—

(a) such contributions are being made at a weekly rate not less than the amount referred to in subsection (4) above—

(i) by the beneficiary; or

(ii) where the beneficiary is one of two spouses residing together, by them together; and

(b) except in prescribed cases, the contributions are over and above those required for the purposes of satisfying section 139(1)(b) below.

(7) A guardian's allowance in respect of a child shall be payable at the weekly rate specified in Schedule 4, Part III, paragraph 5.

(8) Regulations—

(a) may modify subsection (2) or (3) above in relation to cases in which a child has been adopted or is illegitimate, or the marriage of a child's parents has been terminated by divorce;

(b) shall prescribe the circumstances in which a person is to be treated for the purposes of this section as being in prison (by reference to his undergoing a sentence of imprisonment for life or of a prescribed minimum duration, or to his being in legal custody in prescribed circumstances); and

(c) may, for cases where entitlement to a guardian's allowance is established by reference to a person being in prison, provide—

(i) for requiring him to pay to the National Insurance Fund sums paid by a way of guardian's allowance;

(ii) for suspending payment of an allowance where a conviction, sentence or order of a court is subject to appeal, and for the matters arising from the decision of an appeal;

(iii) for reducing the rate of an allowance in cases where the person in prison contributes to the cost of providing for the child.

(9) Where a husband and wife are residing together and, apart from this subsection, they would each be entitled to a guardian's allowance in respect of the same child, only the wife shall be entitled, but payment may be made either to her or to him unless she elects in the prescribed manner that payment is not to be made to him.

(10) Subject to subsection (11) below, no person shall be entitled to a guardian's allowance in respect of a child of which he or she is the parent.

(11) Where a person—
(a) has adopted a child; and
(b) was entitled to guardian's allowance in respect of the child imme-
    diately before the adoption,
subsection (10) above shall not terminate his entitlement.

DEFINITIONS
    "beneficiary": s.121(1).
    "child": s.121(1).
    "entitled": s.121(1).
    "prescribe": s.121(1).

GENERAL NOTE
    Guardian's allowance (GA) is a benefit paid to those who are looking after children who are
orphans (although in certain cases only one parent need be dead). The claimant does not have
to be the child's guardian in any formal sense (*e.g.* as appointed under the Guardianship of
Infants Act 1886, s.2).

Subs. (1)
    The claimant must be entitled to child benefit for the child for whom the allowance is claimed.
This emphasises the need for something approximating a parent–child relationship. Note also
the further requirements relating to the claimant laid down in subss. (5) and (6).

Subs. (2)
    The first basis of entitlement is the conventional meaning of orphanhood. It is not possible to
be awarded GA merely because both parents are missing, however diligent the claimant's
enquiries have been. The second and third situations cover cases where one parent is dead and
the other parent is missing or in prison. The presumption of death after seven years' absence
may be relied upon for GA claims (*R(G) 11/52*).
    The onus under subs. (2)(b) is on the claimant to show that "all reasonable efforts" have been
made to discover the whereabouts of the missing parent, *i.e.* "efforts that would be reasonably
expected to be made by a person who wanted to find [that] person" (*R(G) 2/83*). Commissioners in Northern Ireland appear to have taken a markedly more generous approach to the
interpretation of this provision than those in Great Britain (see Bonner, and Northern Ireland
decisions *R31/74 (P)* and *R31/75 (P)*).
    Regulations define being "in prison" as serving a sentence of imprisonment of five years or
more (including life sentences) or being detained at Her Majesty's pleasure (Social Security
(Guardian's Allowance) Regulations (Northern Ireland) 1975 (S.I. 1975 No. 98), reg. 5). This
has been held not to cover cases of detention under the Mental Health Act 1983 (Mental Health
(Northern Ireland) Order 1986) (*R(G) 4/65, R(G) 2/80*). These heads of entitlement are
modified for certain special cases by regulations made under subs. (8) below.

Subs. (3)
    One of the child's parents must either have been born in the U.K. or at the date of death of
the parent whose death gave rise to the claim have been present in Northern Ireland for at least
52 weeks in any period of two years after attaining the age of 16 (reg. 6).

Subss. (5) and (6)
    No GA is payable unless the claimant has the child living with him or her for the purposes of
child benefit or contributes to the child's maintenance at a weekly rate which is at least
equivalent to the amount of addition over and above any contribution being made to qualify for
child benefit.

Subs. (8)
    Where a child has been adopted, the adopters count as the parents (reg. 2). It is therefore
possible, if the adoptive parents die, for the natural parents to become entitled to GA (*Secretary
of State for Social Services* v. *Smith* [1983] 1 W.L.R. 1110). Adoptive parents may continue to
receive GA if they were entitled to it immediately before the adoption (subs. (11)).
    Where a child's parents were not married to each other at the time of his or her birth, GA is
payable after the death of the mother only, unless paternity had been found by a court or
otherwise admitted or established (reg. 3).
    Where the child's parents were divorced, and one parent has died and the other did not have
custody of the child (nor was maintaining the child or liable to do so under a court order), then a
claimant other than the surviving parent is eligible for GA (reg. 4).

Subs. (10)

Step-parents do not count as parents. Thus a step-parent is not debarred from receiving GA under subs. (10), nor does the existence of a step-parent disentitle a person looking after the child.

Benefits for the aged

Category C and Category D retirement pensions and other benefits for the aged

78.—(1) A person who was over pensionable age on 5th July 1948 and who satisfies such conditions as may be prescribed shall be entitled to a Category C retirement pension at the appropriate weekly rate.

(2) If a woman whose husband is entitled to a Category C retirement pension—

(a) is over pensionable age; and

(b) satisfies such other conditions as may be prescribed,

she shall be entitled to a Category C retirement pension at the appropriate weekly rate.

(3) A person who is over the age of 80 and satisfies such conditions as may be prescribed shall be entitled to a Category D retirement pension at the appropriate weekly rate if—

(a) he is not entitled to a Category A, Category B or Category C retirement pension; or

(b) he is entitled to such a pension, but it is payable at a weekly rate which, disregarding those elements specified in subsection (4) below, is less than the appropriate weekly rate.

(4) The elements referred to in subsection (3)(b) above are—

(a) any additional pension;

(b) any increase so far as attributable to—

(i) any additional pension, or

(ii) any increase in a guaranteed minimum pension;

(c) any graduated retirement benefit; and

(d) any increase (for dependants) under section 80, 83 or 85 below.

(5) The appropriate weekly rate of a Category C retirement pension—

(a) shall be the lower rate specified in Schedule 4, Part III, paragraph 6, where—

(i) the pensioner is a married woman, and

(ii) she has not, at any time since she become entitled to her pension, ceased to be a married woman; and

(b) shall be the higher rate so specified in any other case.

(6) The appropriate weekly rate of a Category D retirement pension shall be that specified in Schedule 4, Part III, paragraph 7.

(7) Entitlement to a Category C or Category D retirement pension shall continue throughout the pensioner's life.

(8) A Category C or Category D retirement pension shall not be payable for any period falling before the day on which the pensioner's entitlement is to be regarded as commencing for that purpose by virtue of section 5(1)(l) of the Administration Act.

(9) Regulations may provide for the payment—

(a) to a widow whose husband was over pensionable age on 5th July 1948; or

(b) to a woman whose marriage to a husband who was over pensionable age on that date was terminated otherwise than by his death,

of a Category C retirement pension or of benefit corresponding to a widow's pension or a widowed mother's allowance; and any such retirement pension or any such benefit shall be at the prescribed rate.

DEFINITIONS
    "additional pension": s.45(1).
    "the Administration Act": s.170.
    "entitled": s.121(1).
    "graduated retirement benefit": s.62.
    "pensionable age": s.121(1).
    "prescribe": s.121(1).

GENERAL NOTE
    The Category C non-contributory retirement pension was introduced in 1970. Initially it applied to persons who were excluded from the National Insurance scheme because they were over pensionable age on July 5, 1948. This is obviously a rapidly diminishing group. The Category C retirement pension also applies to certain dependants of such people. In 1971 the Category D non-contributory pension was brought in. This is available to persons who are aged 80 or more, satisfy the residence tests and either fail to qualify for a contributory retirement pension or qualify for one at a lower rate than the Category C pension. There were only some 32,000 non-contributory retirement pensions in payment in Great Britain in September 1990 (Social Security Statistics 1991, p. 108) and 3,027 in Northern Ireland in March 1990 (N.I. Abstract of Statistics 1991).

Age addition

79.—(1) A person who is over the age of 80 and entitled to a retirement pension of any category shall be entitled to an increase of the pension, to be known as "age addition".

(2) Where a person is in receipt of a pension or allowance payable by virtue of any prescribed enactment or instrument (whether passed or made before or after this Act) and—

(a) he is over the age of 80; and

(b) he fulfils such other conditions as may be prescribed,

he shall be entitled to an increase of that pension or allowance, also known as age addition.

(3) Age addition shall be payable for the life of the person entitled, at the weekly rate specified in Schedule 4, Part III, paragraph 8.

DEFINITIONS
    "entitled": s.121(1).
    "prescribe": s.121(1).

GENERAL NOTE
    All retirement pensions are increased by an extra 25p a week if the recipient is aged 80 or over. The age addition also applies to certain other benefits prescribed under subs. (2). This addition is paid automatically and so does not need a separate claim. The value of the age addition has not been uprated since its introduction in 1971.

PART IV

INCREASES FOR DEPENDANTS

Child dependants

Beneficiary's dependent children

80.—(1) Subject to section 61 above and to the following provisions of this Part of this Act, the weekly rate of any benefit to which this subsection applies shall, for any period for which the beneficiary is entitled to child benefit in respect of a child or children, be increased in respect of that child, or each respectively of those children, by the amount specified in relation to the benefit in question in Schedule 4, Part IV, column (2).

(2) Subsection (1) above applies to—

(a) unemployment benefit where the beneficiary is over pensionable age;

(b) sickness benefit where the beneficiary is over pensionable age;
(c) invalidity pension; and
(d) Category A, Category B or Category C retirement pension.
(3) In any case where—
(a) a beneficiary is one of two persons who are—
(i) spouses residing together; or
(ii) an unmarried couple; and
(b) the other person had earnings in any week,
the beneficiary's right to payment of increases for the following week under subsection (1) above shall be determined in accordance with subsection (4) below.
(4) No such increase shall be payable—
(a) in respect of the first child where the earnings were £115 or more; and
(b) in respect of a further child for each complete £15 by which the earnings exceeded £115.
(5) Subject to section 81 below, the weekly rate of a widowed mother's allowance payable by virtue of subsection (1)(a) of section 37 above shall be increased for any period in respect of the child or, if more than one, each respectively of the children falling within subsection (2)(a), (b) or (c) of that section in respect of whom she is for the time being entitled to child benefit by the amount specified in relation to that allowance in Schedule 4, Part IV, column (2).
(6) Subject to section 81 below, the weekly rate of child's special allowance shall, for any period for which the beneficiary is entitled to child benefit in respect of two or more children with respect to whom the conditions specified in section 56(1)(b) and (c) above are satisfied, be increased in respect of each respectively of those children other than the elder or eldest by the amount specified in relation to that allowance in Schedule 4, Part IV, column (2).
(7) In this section—
"unmarried couple" means a man and a woman who are not married to each other but are living together as husband and wife; and
"week" means such period of 7 days as may be prescribed for the purposes of this section.

Definitions
"beneficiary": s.121(1).
"benefit": s.121(1).
"child": s.121(1).
"child benefit": s.137.
"earnings": s.121(1).
"entitled": s.121(1).
"pensionable age": s.121(1).
"unmarried couple": subs. (7).
"week": subs. (7).

General Note
Where any of the benefits listed in subs. (2) are payable, they may be supplemented by increases for child dependants. Three criteria need to be met in such cases.
First, the claimant must be entitled to child benefit in respect of the child(ren) in question (see Pt. IX). These rules are modified in certain respects by the Social Security Benefit (Dependency) Regulations (Northern Ireland) 1977 (S.I. 1977 No. 74), regs. 4A and 4B.
Secondly, the child(ren) must be living with the claimant or the claimant must be contributing to the cost of their upkeep at a weekly rate of not less than the amount of the increase, over and above any amount received by way of child benefit (s.81).
Thirdly, the increase is not payable where either the claimant or partner earns more than the amount specified in subs. (4). "Earnings" include occupational or personal pensions (s.89(1)).
Subsections (5) and (6) contain special rules in relation to widowed mother's allowance and child's special allowance.

Restrictions on increase—child not living with beneficiary, etc.

81.—(1) Where, apart from this subsection, a person is entitled to receive, in respect of a particular child, payment of an amount by way of an increase under section 80 above of any benefit, that amount shall not be payable unless one of the conditions specified in subsection (2) below is satisfied.

(2) Those conditions are—

(a) that the beneficiary would be treated for the purposes of Part IX of this Act as having the child living with him; or

(b) that the requisite contributions are being made to the cost of providing for the child.

(3) The condition specified in subsection (2)(b) above is to be treated as satisfied if, but only if—

(a) such contributions are being made at a weekly rate not less than the amount referred to in subsection (1) above—

(i) by the beneficiary; or

(ii) where the beneficiary is one of two spouses residing together, by them together; and

(b) except in prescribed cases, the contributions are over and above those required for the purpose of satisfying section 139(1)(b) below.

DEFINITIONS
"beneficiary": s.121(1).
"benefit": s.121(1).
"child": s.121(1).
"entitled": s.121(1).
"prescribe": s.121(1).

GENERAL NOTE
See General Note to s.80 and *R(U) 14/62.*

Adult dependants

Short-term benefit: increase for adult dependants

82.—(1) Subject to section 61 above and section 87 below, the weekly rate of unemployment benefit or sickness benefit shall be increased by the amount specified in relation to the benefit in question in Schedule 4, Part IV, column (3), for any period during which—

(a) the beneficiary is—

(i) residing with his wife, or

(ii) contributing to the maintenance of his wife at a weekly rate not less than that amount; and

(b) his wife does not have weekly earnings which exceed that amount.

(2) Subject, in particular, to subsection (5) and section 87 below, the weekly rate—

(a) of unemployment benefit or sickness benefit in the case of a beneficiary not entitled to an increase under subsection (1) above, and

(b) of a maternity allowance in any case,

shall be increased by the amount specified in relation to the benefit in question in Schedule 4, Part IV, column (3) ("the amount of the relevant increase") for any period to which this subsection applies by virtue of subsection (3) or (4) below.

(3) Subsection (2) above applies by virtue of this subsection to any period during which—

(a) the beneficiary's husband does not have weekly earnings which exceed that amount of the relevant increase, and

(b) either she and her husband are residing together or she is contributing to his maintenance at a weekly rate not less than that amount.

(4) Subsection (2) above applies by virtue of this subsection to any period during which a person—

(a) who is neither the spouse of the beneficiary nor a child, and

(b) in respect of whom such further conditions as may be prescribed are fulfilled,

has the care of a child or children in respect of whom the beneficiary is entitled to child benefit.

(5) A beneficiary shall not under subsection (2) above be entitled for the same period to an increase of benefit in respect of more than one person.

DEFINITIONS

"amount of the relevant increase": subs. (2).
"beneficiary": s.121(1).
"child": s.121(1).
"earnings": s.121(1).
"prescribe": s.121(1).

GENERAL NOTE

This section enables increases to be paid for adult dependants to supplement unemployment benefit, sickness benefit or maternity allowance. A claimant is entitled to such an increase for a spouse where two conditions are satisfied. First, the husband and wife must be residing together or (where separated) the claimant must be paying weekly maintenance at a level at least equal to the increase (subss. (1)(a) and (3)(a)). Secondly, the spouse's weekly earnings must not exceed the amount of the increase (subs. (1)(b) and (3)(a)). "Earnings" include occupational or personal pensions (s.89(1)). Increases are alternatively payable where some other adult is looking after a child or children (subs. (4)).

Subs. (1)

Wife. The marriage must be one which is recognised in the U.K. and subsisting at the time of the event giving rise to the claim for benefit. Cohabitees are excluded (*R(S) 6/89*). For detailed analysis, see Bonner.

Residing with. See Social Security Benefit (Persons Residing Together) Regulations (Northern Ireland) 1977 (S.I. 1977 No. 166), *R(P) 1/90* and Ogus and Barendt, pp. 343–5.

Pension increase (wife)

83.—(1) This section applies to—

(a) a Category A or Category C retirement pension;

(b) an invalidity pension under section 33 or 41 above.

(2) Subject to subsection (3) below, the weekly rate of a pension to which this section applies, when payable to a man, shall be increased by the amount specified in relation to the pension in Schedule 4, Part IV, column (3)—

(a) for any period during which the pensioner is residing with his wife; or

(b) for any period during which the pensioner is contributing to the maintenance of his wife at a weekly rate not less than that amount, and his wife does not have weekly earnings which exceed that amount.

(3) Regulations may provide that for any period during which the pensioner is residing with his wife and his wife has earnings—

(a) the increase of benefit under this section shall be subject to a reduction in respect of the wife's earnings; or

(b) there shall be no increase of benefit under this section.

DEFINITIONS

"earnings": s.121(1).

GENERAL NOTE

This section provides for a married man to receive an increase for his wife in the case of the benefits mentioned in subs. (1). The conditions are that they are either residing together and she is earning no more than the amount of the increase (Social Security Benefit (Dependency) Regulations (Northern Ireland) 1977 (S.I. 1977 No. 74), reg. 8) or that they are residing apart but he is contributing to her maintenance at a weekly rate not less than the amount of the increase. "Earnings" include occupational or personal pensions (s.89(1)). On the meaning of "wife" and "residing with", see General Note to s.82. Only one such addition is payable (s.88).

Pension increase (husband)

84.—(1) Where a Category A retirement pension is payable to a woman for any period—
(a) which began immediately upon the termination of a period for which the pensioner was entitled to an increase in unemployment benefit, sickness benefit or invalidity pension by virtue of section 82(3) above or 86(1) below, and
(b) during which the requirements of either paragraph (a) or (b) of subsection (2) below are satisfied (without interruption),
then, the weekly rate of the pensioner's Category A retirement pension shall be increased by the amount specified in relation to that pension in Schedule 4, Part IV, column (3) ("the specified amount").
(2) The requirements referred to in subsection (1)(b) above are—
(a) that the pensioner is residing with her husband;
(b) that the pensioner is contributing to the maintenance of her husband at a weekly rate not less than the specified amount, and her husband does not have weekly earnings which exceed that amount.
(3) Regulations may provide that for any period during which the pensioner is residing with her husband and her husband has earnings—
(a) the increase of benefit under this section shall be subject to a reduction in respect of the husband's earnings; or
(b) there shall be no increase of benefit under this section.

DEFINITIONS
"earnings": s.121(1).
"entitled": s.121(1).
"specified amount": subs. (1).

GENERAL NOTE
This provision enables a wife to receive an addition for her husband as an increase to her Category A retirement pension on similar terms to those under s.83 for a man. Only one such addition is payable (s.88).
An extra requirement is laid down by subs. (1): the woman must become entitled to that pension immediately after being entitled to an increase for the husband to one of those benefits specified in subs. (1)(a). Although apparently discriminatory, the validity of this rule was upheld in *R(P) 3/88*. This decision may itself now be open to challenge in the light of the English Court of Appeal's decision in *Thomas* v. *Chief Adjudication Officer and Secretary of State for Social Security*; *Cooze* v. *Same*; *Beard* v. *Same*; *Murphy* v. *Same*; *Morley* v. *Same* [1991] 2 W.L.R. 886.

Pension increase (person with care of children)

85.—(1) This section applies to—
(a) a Category A retirement pension;
(b) a Category C retirement pension payable by virtue of section 78(1) above;
(c) an invalidity pension under section 33, 40 or 41 above.
(2) Subject to the following provisions, the weekly rate of a pension to which this section applies shall be increased by the amount specified in relation to that pension in Schedule 4, Part IV, column (3) for any period during which a person who is neither the spouse of the pensioner nor a child has the care of a child or children in respect of whom the pensioner is entitled to child benefit.

(3) Subsection (2) above does not apply if the pensioner is a man whose wife is entitled to a Category B retirement pension, or to a Category C retirement pension by virtue of section 78(2) above or in such other cases as may be prescribed.

(4) Regulations may, in a case within subsection (2) above in which the person there referred to is residing with the pensioner and fulfils such further conditions as may be prescribed, authorise an increase of benefit under this section, but subject, taking account of the earnings of the person residing with the pensioner, other than such of that person's earnings as may be prescribed, to provisions comparable to those that may be made by virtue of section 83(3) above.

DEFINITIONS
"benefit": s.121(1).
"child": s.121(1).
"entitled": s.121(1).
"earnings": s.121(1).
"prescribe": s.121(1).

GENERAL NOTE
This section provides for an increase in the benefits listed in subs. (1) for a person caring for the claimant's child(ren). The claimant must be entitled to child benefit (subs. (2)), or treated as so entitled (Social Security Benefit (Dependency) Regulations (Northern Ireland) 1977 (S.I. 1977 No. 74), regs. 4A and 4B). For further conditions see Social Security (Dependency) Regulations (Northern Ireland) 1977 (S.I. 1977 No. 74), regs. 8 and 10. "Earnings" include occupational or personal pensions (s.89(1)). Only one such addition is payable (s.88).

Increase of woman's invalidity pension (husband)

86.—(1) Subject to section 87 below, the weekly rate of an invalidity pension payable to a woman shall be increased by the amount specified in relation to an invalidity pension in Schedule 4, Part IV, column (3) for any period during which either—
  (a) the pensioner and her husband are residing together and he does not have earnings at a weekly rate in excess of the amount specified in Schedule 4, Part I, paragraph 1; or
  (b) they are not residing together, he does not have earnings at a weekly rate in excess of the amount specified in relation to an invalidity pension in Schedule 4, Part IV, column (3) and she is contributing to his maintenance at a weekly rate not less than the amount so specified.

(2) Regulations may provide that—
  (a) the increase of benefit under this section shall be subject to a reduction in respect of the husband's earnings; or
  (b) there shall be no increase of benefit under this section.

DEFINITIONS
"earnings": s.121(1).

GENERAL NOTE
A married woman may be entitled to an increase in invalidity pension for her husband on the same terms as under s.83(2). "Earnings" include occupational or personal pensions (s.89(1)). Only one such addition is payable (s.88).

Rate of increase where associated retirement pension is attributable to reduced contributions

87.—(1) Where a person—
  (a) is entitled—
      (i) to unemployment benefit by virtue of section 25(2)(b) or (c) above, or

(ii) to sickness benefit by virtue of section 31(2)(b) or (c) above, or
(iii) to an invalidity pension by virtue of section 33(2) above; and
(b) would have been entitled only by virtue of section 60(1) above to the retirement pension by reference to which the rate of that benefit or invalidity pension is determined,
the amount of any increase of the benefit or invalidity pension attributable to sections 82 to 86 above shall not be determined in accordance with those sections but shall be determined in accordance with regulations.

(2) The regulations shall not provide for any such increase in a case where the retirement pension by reference to which the rate of the said benefit or invalidity pension is determined—
(a) would have been payable only by virtue of section 60 above; and
(b) would, in consequence of a failure to satisfy a contribution condition, have contained no basic pension.

DEFINITIONS
"entitled": s.121(1).

GENERAL NOTE
Where a person is entitled to one of the benefits listed in subs. (1), the amount of any increase in that benefit in respect of an adult dependant is to be determined according to regulations. See Social Security Benefits (Dependency) Regulations (Northern Ireland) 1977 (S.I. 1977 No. 74), reg. 13.

Pension increases to be in respect of only one adult dependant

88. A pensioner shall not under sections 83 to 86 above be entitled for the same period to an increase of benefit in respect of more than one person.

DEFINITIONS
"benefit": s.121(1).
"entitled": s.121(1).

Miscellaneous

Earnings to include occupational and personal pensions for purposes of provisions relating to increases of benefits in respect of child or adult dependants

89.—(1) Except as may be prescribed, in section 80 and sections 82 to 86 above any reference to earnings includes a reference to payments by way of occupational or personal pension.

(2) For the purposes of the provisions mentioned in subsection (1) above, the Department may by regulations provide, in relation to cases where payments by way of occupational or personal pension are made otherwise than weekly, that any necessary apportionment of the payments shall be made in such manner and on such basis as may be prescribed.

DEFINITIONS
"earnings": s.121(1).
"payments by way of occupational or personal pension": s.121(1).
"prescribe": s.121(1).

GENERAL NOTE
See *R(U) 1/89* on civil service pensions.

Beneficiaries under sections 68 and 70

90. The weekly rates—
(a) of a severe disablement allowance, and

(b) of an invalid care allowance,

shall, in such circumstances as may be prescribed, be increased for child or adult dependants by the appropriate amount specified in relation to the allowance in question in Schedule 4, Part IV.

DEFINITIONS
  "child": s.121(1).
  "prescribe": s.121(1).

GENERAL NOTE
  This section enables increases to be paid for child and adult dependants to supplement severe disablement allowance and invalid care allowance. See Social Security (Dependency) Regulations (Northern Ireland) 1977 (S.I. 1977 No. 74), reg. 12.

Effect of trade disputes on entitlement to increases

91.—(1) A beneficiary shall not be entitled—

(a) to an increase in any benefit under sections 82 to 88 above; or

(b) to an increase in benefit for an adult dependant by virtue of regulations under section 90 above,

if the person in respect of whom he would entitled to the increase falls within subsection (2) below.

(2) A person falls within this subsection if—

(a) he is disqualified under section 27 above for receiving unemployment benefit; or

(b) he would be so disqualified if he were otherwise entitled to that benefit.

DEFINITIONS
  "beneficiary": s.121(1).
  "entitled": s.121(1).

GENERAL NOTE
  This provision, first introduced in 1986, disentitles claimants from receiving dependants' increases where they have been disqualified from unemployment benefit under s.27 or would have been so disqualified had they claimed that benefit.

Dependency increases: continuation of awards in cases of fluctuating earnings

92.—(1) Where a beneficiary—

(a) has been awarded an increase of benefit under this Part of this Act, but

(b) ceases to be entitled to the increase by reason only that the weekly earnings of some other person ("the relevant earner") exceed the amount of the increase or, as the case may be, some specified amount,

then, if and so long as the beneficiary would have continued to be entitled to the increase, disregarding any such excess of earnings, the award shall continue in force but the increase shall not be payable for any week if the earnings relevant to that week exceed the amount of the increase or, as the case may be, the specified amount.

(2) In this section the earnings which are relevant to any week are those earnings of the relevant earner which, apart from this section, would be taken into account in determining whether the beneficiary is entitled to the increase in question for that week.

DEFINITIONS
  "beneficiary": s.121(1).
  "earnings": s.121(1).
  "entitled": s.121(1).

"relevant earner": subs. (1).
"week": s.121(1).

GENERAL NOTE
The purpose of this infelicitously drafted section is to ensure that once a dependency increase is awarded, it will not end merely because the relevant person's income has exceeded the specified amount. It is a technical provision which ensures that a repeat claim does not become necessary every time earnings fall below the earnings limit.

Dependency increases on termination of employment after period of entitlement to disability working allowance

93. Where—
(a) a person becomes entitled to an invalidity pension or a severe disablement allowance by virtue of section 33(7), 42 or 68(10) above; and
(b) when he was last entitled to that pension or allowance, it was increased in respect of a dependant by virtue of—
    (i) regulation 8(6) of the Social Security Benefit (Dependency) Regulations (Northern Ireland) 1977;
    (ii) regulation 3 of the Social Security Benefit (Dependency) (Amendment) Regulations (Northern Ireland) 1984;
    (iii) regulation 2 of the Social Security (Savings for Existing Beneficiaries) Regulations (Northern Ireland) 1984; or
    (iv) regulation 4 of the Social Security Benefit (Dependency and Computation of Earnings) (Amendment) Regulations (Northern Ireland) 1989,
for the purpose of determining whether his pension or allowance should be increased by virtue of that regulation for any period beginning with the day on which he again becomes entitled to his pension or allowance, the increase in respect of that dependant shall be treated as having been payable to him on each day between the last day on which his pension or allowance was previously payable and the day on which he again becomes entitled to it.

DEFINITIONS
"entitled": s.121(1).

GENERAL NOTE
This section is concerned with disability working allowance recipients who have to leave work and go back on to invalidity benefit or severe disablement allowance under the two-year linking rule. In such cases their benefit will be calculated in the same way as before, including any increases for dependants.

PART V

BENEFIT FOR INDUSTRIAL INJURIES

General provisions

Right to industrial injuries benefit

94.—(1) Industrial injuries benefit shall be payable where an employed earner suffers personal injury caused after 4th July 1948 by accident arising out of and in the course of his employment, being employed earner's employment.
(2) Industrial injuries benefit consists of the following benefits—
(a) disablement benefit payable in accordance with sections 103 to 105 below, paragraphs 2 and 3 of Schedule 7 to this Act and Parts II and III of that Schedule;
(b) reduced earnings allowance payable in accordance with Part IV of that Schedule;

(c) retirement allowance payable in accordance with Part V of that Schedule; and

(d) industrial death benefit, payable in accordance with Part VI of that Schedule.

(3) For the purposes of industrial injuries benefit an accident arising in the course of an employed earner's employment shall be taken, in the absence of evidence to the contrary, also to have arisen out of that employment.

(4) Regulations may make provision as to the day which, in the case of night workers and other special cases, is to be treated for the purposes of industrial injuries benefit as the day of the accident.

(5) Subject to sections 117 and 119 below, industrial injuries benefit shall not be payable in respect of an accident happening while the earner is outside Northern Ireland.

(6) In the following provisions of this Part of this Act "work" in the contexts "incapable of work" and "incapacity for work" means work which the person in question can be reasonably expected to do.

(7) Subsection (5) above shall cease to have effect on such day as the Head of the Department may by order appoint.

DEFINITIONS
"earner": s.121(1).
"employed earner": s.121(1).
"employed earner's employment": s.95(1).
"industrial injuries benefit": subs. (2) and s.121(1).
"Northern Ireland": s.168.
"work": subs. (6).

GENERAL NOTE
The industrial injuries scheme today is radically different from that established in 1948. All the important changes have taken place since 1980. Since the abolition of industrial injury benefit (1982), industrial death benefit (1988) and reduced earnings allowance and retirement allowance (1990), the principal benefit under the scheme has been disablement benefit (s.103). The list of benefits contained in subs. (2) is therefore potentially misleading, as those mentioned in subs. (2)(b)–(d) are only payable where the accident or the onset of the disease occurred before October 1, 1990 (reduced earnings allowance and retirement allowance) or the relevant death occurred before April 11, 1988 (industrial death benefit): see s.106. The principal adjudication provisions are contained in SSA(N.I.)A 1992, ss.42–48.

Subs. (1)
The definition of entitlement to industrial injuries benefit contained in subs. (1) has been the subject of a wealth of case law. There are four basic elements:
(a) the claimant must be "an employed earner . . . in employed earner's employment"; (b) the claimant must suffer "personal injury"; (c) the personal injury must be "caused after 4 July 1948 by accident"; and (d) the accident must arise "out of and in the course of his employment".
An employed earner . . . in employed earner's employment. The self-employed are hence excluded. See further s.95.
Suffers personal injury. This means some "hurt to body or mind" (*Jones* v. *Secretary of State for Social Services* [1972] A.C. 944 at 1020, *per* Lord Simon). A temporary strain is unlikely to be sufficient; there must be some discernible physiological worsening of the claimant's condition (*R(19/60)*, *R(I) 1/76*). See further Lewis, pp. 43–45.
Caused after 4th July 1948 by accident. This apparently straightforward formulation has given rise to much litigation. There are two difficult areas of interpretation, relating to the meaning of "accident" and "caused by".
Accident. The standard definition of accident is "an unlooked-for mishap or an untoward event which is neither expected nor designed" (*Fenton* v. *J. Thorley & Co.* [1903] A.C. 443 at 448, *per* Lord Macnaghten). The incident may still be an accident if deliberately caused by a third party (*Trim Joint District School Board* v. *Kelly* [1914] A.C. 667).
The distinction between accident and process is especially problematic: "There must come a time when the indefinite number of so-called accidents and the length of time over which they occur take away the element of accident and substitute that of process": *Roberts* v. *Dorothea Slate Quarries* [1948] 2 All E.R. 201, *per* Lord Porter). The significance of this is that an injury

caused by an accident gives rise to entitlement to benefit, whereas one caused by a process does not, unless the resultant condition is scheduled as a prescribed disease (s.108). At times this has led to some very fine if not arbitrary distinctions. For example, in *R(I) 43/61* digital neuritis caused by less than three days' use of scissors was held to be due to an accident, while in *R(I) 19/56* osteoarthritis of the fingers caused by three days of stitching was found to be the cumulative result of a process. For a recent controversial illustration, see *R(I) 6/91* (asthma brought on by passive smoking held on special facts to be a series of accidents).

Difficulties may also arise where the injury sustained is alleged to be the accident for the purposes of entitlement to benefit: see *R(I) 11/80* and *R(I) 6/82*. See further Bonner and Lewis, pp. 38–43.

Caused by. The onus is on the claimant to establish that the accident caused the injury (*R(I) 14/51*). The claimant must also show that but for the accident the injury would not have occurred, and that the accident is an effective cause of the injury. See Lewis, pp. 45–49.

Arising out of and in the course of his employment. This expression dates back to the Workmen's Compensation Act 1897. The underlying intention is to restrict the industrial injuries scheme to injuries which may be regarded as work-related and to exclude those which are the result of the ordinary risks of life (*e.g. R(I) 62/53*). As a general rule a claimant will establish a prima-facie case if he can show that the accident occurred at his normal place of work and during his normal hours of work. Inevitably the application of this principle to individual cases has caused considerable difficulty. See the Northern Ireland decisions *R2/79 (II)*, *R1/81 (II)*, *R1/83 (II)* and BNIL *91/2/87*.

Authoritative guidance on the meaning of this phrase has been given in *Nancollas* v. *Insurance Officer* [1985] 2 All E.R. 833, and (albeit in a different context) *Smith* v. *Stages* [1989] A.C. 928. For recent Commissioners' decisions, see *R(I) 1/88* and *R(I) 1/91* and, for a full analysis of this difficult area, Ogus and Barendt, pp. 261-78, Lewis, pp. 50–89 and Bonner.

Note that the concept of work-related accidents is extended by the deeming provisions in ss.98–101 (especially s.99, concerning earners sustaining accidents while travelling in their employer's transport).

Subs. (3)
This presumption is of limited value as the claimant must still prove that the accident occurred in the course of the employment and there must be no evidence to the contrary.

Subs. (5)
As a general principle industrial injuries benefit is not payable in respect of accidents occurring outside Northern Ireland. The statute contains special provisions for mariners and airmen (ss.117 and 119). Accidents occurring abroad may also give rise to benefit under the Social Security Benefit (Persons Abroad) Regulations (Northern Ireland) 1975 (S.I. 1975 No. 103). Where the accident occurs in another member state of the European Community the claimant may be able to rely on E.C. Regulations 1408/71 and 574/72. In respect of other states there may be special provision in the relevant reciprocal convention on social security.

Relevant employments

95.—(1) In section 94 above, this section and sections 98 to 109 below "employed earner's employment" shall be taken to include any employment by virtue of which a person is, or is treated by regulations as being for the purposes of industrial injuries benefit, an employed earner.

(2) Regulations may provide that any prescribed employment shall not be treated for the purposes of industrial injuries benefit as employed earner's employment notwithstanding that it would be so treated apart from the regulations.

(3) For the purposes of the provisions of this Act mentioned in subsection (1) above an employment shall be an employed earner's employment in relation to an accident if (and only if) it is, or is treated by regulations as being, such an employment when the accident occurs.

(4) Any reference in the industrial injuries and diseases provisions to an "employed earner" or "employed earner's employment" is to be construed, in relation to any time before 6th April 1975, as a reference respectively to an "insured person" or "insurable employment" within the meaning of the provisions relating to industrial injuries and diseases which were in force at that time.

(5) In subsection (4) above "the industrial injuries and diseases provisions" means—
- (a) this section and sections 96 to 110 below;
- (b) any other provisions of this Act so far as they relate to those sections; and
- (c) any provisions of the Administration Act so far as they so relate.

<small>DEFINITIONS</small>
"the Administration Act": s.170.
"Department": s.170.
"employed earner": subs. (4) and s.121(1).
"employed earner's employment": subss. (1) and (4).
"employment": s.121(1).
"industrial injuries and diseases provisions": subs. (5).
"industrial injuries benefit": s.121(1).
"prescribe": s.121(1).

<small>GENERAL NOTE</small>
This section enables the Department by regulation to extend or exclude certain categories of earners for the purposes of the scheme (see also s.2(4)). See Social Security (Employed Earners' Employments for Industrial Injuries Purposes) Regulations (Northern Ireland) 1975 (S.I. 1975 No. 90). Decisions as to whether a claimant is or was employed in employed earner's employment are for the Department, not the independent statutory authorities (SSA(N.I.)A 1992, s.15(1)(d)). There is therefore no right of appeal to a SSAT.

Persons treated as employers for certain purposes

96. In relation to —
- (a) a person who is an employed earner for the purposes of this Part of this Act otherwise than by virtue of a contract of service or apprenticeship; or
- (b) any other employed earner—
  - (i) who is employed for the purpose of any game or recreation and is engaged or paid through a club; or
  - (ii) in whose case it appears to the Department there is special difficulty in the application of all or any of the provisions of this Part of this Act relating to employers,

regulations may provide for a prescribed person to be treated in respect of industrial injuries benefit and its administration as the earner's employer.

<small>DEFINITIONS</small>
"contract of service": s.121(1).
"employed earner": s.121(1).
"industrial injuries benefit": s.121(1).
"prescribe": s.121(1).

<small>GENERAL NOTE</small>
See Social Security (Employed Earners' Employments for Industrial Injuries Purposes) Regulations (Northern Ireland) 1975 (S.I. 1975 No. 90).

Accidents in course of illegal employments

97.—(1) Subsection (2) below has effect in any case where—
- (a) a claim is made for industrial injuries benefit in respect of an accident, or of a prescribed disease or injury; or
- (b) an application is made under section 42 of the Administration Act for a declaration that an accident was an industrial accident, or for a corresponding declaration as to a prescribed disease or injury.

(2) The Department may direct that the relevant employment shall, in relation to that accident, disease or injury, be treated as having been employed earner's employment notwithstanding that by reason of a contra-

vention of, or non-compliance with, some provision contained in or having effect under an enactment passed for the protection of employed persons or any class of employed persons, either—
  (a) the contract purporting to govern the employment was void; or
  (b) the employed person was not lawfully employed in the relevant employment at the time when, or in the place where, the accident happened or the disease or injury was contracted or received.
  (3) In subsection (2) above "relevant employment" means—
  (a) in relation to an accident, the employment out of and in the course of which the accident arises; and
  (b) in relation to a prescribed disease or injury, the employment to the nature of which the disease or injury is due.

DEFINITIONS
  "the Administration Act": s.170.
  "Department": s.170.
  "employed earner": s.121(1).
  "employment": s.121(1).
  "industrial injuries benefit": s.121(1).
  "relevant employment": subs. (3).

GENERAL NOTE
  This section enables the Department to direct that a particular employment is covered by the industrial injuries scheme, notwithstanding that the employment is illegal or the contract of service void. This could provide some protection for children who are illegally employed (Lewis, p. 33).

Earner acting in breach of regulations, etc.

  98. An accident shall be taken to arise out of and in the course of an employed earner's employment, notwithstanding that he is at the time of the accident acting in contravention of any statutory or other regulations applicable to his employment, or of any orders given by or on behalf of his employer, or that he is acting without instructions from his employer, if—
  (a) the accident would have been taken so to have arisen had the act not been done in contravention of any such regulations or order, or without such instructions, as the case may be; and
  (b) the act is done for the purposes of and in connection with the employer's trade or business.

DEFINITIONS
  "employed earner's employment": s.95(1).
  "employment": s.121(1).
  "trade or business": s.121(1).

GENERAL NOTE
  As a general principle an employee who is injured while acting in contravention of regulations or orders has not suffered an accident which arises out of and in the course of the employment. This principle is modified by this section, which deems certain accidents to be attributable to the employment if two conditions are satisfied. It is always necessary in such cases to consider as a preliminary issue whether the claim can succeed under the general principles relating to s.94(1) (*CI 210/50*).
  The section requires first that the accident would have met the statutory test under s.94(1) had the employee not been acting against or without authority. Secondly, the act done without such authority must have been performed for the purposes of and in connection with the employer's trade or business.
  In cases where the injured employee was doing something which was the duty of another employee, whose duties were not interchangeable with those of the victim, it may be impossible to rely on this deeming provision (*R(I) 12/61, R(I) 1/66*). See further Lewis, pp. 70–73.

Earner travelling in employer's transport

99.—(1) An accident happening while an employed earner is, with the express or implied permission of his employer, travelling as a passenger by any vehicle to or from his place of work shall, notwithstanding that he is under no obligation to his employer to travel by that vehicle, be taken to arise out of and in the course of his employment if—

   (a) the accident would have been taken so to have arisen had he been under such an obligation; and

   (b) at the time of the accident, the vehicle—

      (i) is being operated by or on behalf of his employer or some other person by whom it is provided in pursuance of arrangements made with his employer; and

      (ii) is not being operated in the ordinary course of a public transport service.

(2) In this section references to a vehicle include a ship, vessel, hovercraft or aircraft.

DEFINITIONS
   "employed earner": s.121(1).
   "vehicle": subs. (2).

GENERAL NOTE
Accidents which occur while travelling have given rise to a considerable body of case law in the industrial injuries scheme. The starting point is that travel to or from the claimant's usual place of work is normally outside the scope of the employment. This section provides an exception to this principle so far as a narrow class of commuting accidents are concerned. Journeys to and from work are deemed to arise out of and in the course of the claimant's employment provided that:

   (a) the claimant is travelling as a passenger to or from his or her place of work;

   (b) the vehicle is operated by or on behalf of the employer or provided by some third party under an arrangement with the employer;

   (c) the claimant has the employer's permission to travel by the vehicle;

   (d) the vehicle is not being operated in the ordinary course of a public transport service; and

   (e) the accident would have qualified under s.94 had the claimant been under an obligation to travel in the vehicle.

See further Lewis (pp. 80–82).

Accidents happening while meeting emergency

100. An accident happening to an employed earner in or about any premises at which he is for the time being employed for the purposes of his employer's trade or business shall be taken to arise out of and in the course of his employment if it happens while he is taking steps, on an actual or supposed emergency at those premises, to rescue, succour or protect persons who are, or are thought to be or possibly to be, injured or imperilled, or to avert or minimise serious damage to property.

DEFINITIONS
   "employed earner": s.121(1).
   "employment": s.121(1).
   "trade or business": s.121(1).

GENERAL NOTE
As a general principle, irrespective of this section, most employees injured whilst acting in an emergency will qualify for industrial injuries benefits. Case law establishes that an employee may claim where he or she acts in response to an emergency in a manner which is reasonable, in the employer's interests and reasonably incidental to the employment. These conditions have historically been construed in a broad fashion: see *R(I) 46/60* and the discussion in Lewis, pp. 67–69.

In the relatively unusual case where the claimant is unable to rely upon the general principles outlined above, recourse may be had to this section. It is wider than the general principles in that the employee need not be acting in the employer's interests (*e.g. R(I) 6/63*, where a milkman was injured while trying to rescue children trapped in a bungalow on fire). It is narrower, however, in that the emergency must be "in or about" premises connected with the employment.

Accident caused by another's misconduct, etc.

101. An accident happening after 19th December 1961 shall be treated for the purposes of industrial injuries benefit, where it would not apart from this section be so treated, as arising out of an employed earner's employment if—
  (a) the accident arises in the course of the employment; and
  (b) the accident either is caused—
      (i) by another person's misconduct, skylarking or negligence, or
      (ii) by steps taken in consequence of any such misconduct skylarking or negligence, or
      (iii) by the behaviour or presence of an animal (including a bird, fish or insect),
      or is caused by or consists in the employed earner being struck by any object or by lightning; and
  (c) the employed earner did not directly or indirectly induce or contribute to the happening of the accident by his conduct outside the employment or by any act not incidental to the employment.

DEFINITIONS
  "industrial injuries benefit": s.121(1).
  "employed earner": s.121(1).
  "employed earner's employment": s.95(1).

GENERAL NOTE
  This provision was first introduced in 1961 to reverse the effect of *R.* v. *National Insurance (Industrial Injuries) Commissioner*, ex p. *Richardson* [1958] 1 W.L.R. 851. In that case the Divisional Court had held that a bus conductor, who was the subject of what appeared to be an indiscriminate attack by a gang of youths, could not claim under the industrial injuries scheme as his position was no different from that of any other member of the public. The section effectively deems various accidents at work to be arising out of insured employment. There is no obvious common thread between the situations detailed in subs. (b).
  There has been little reported case law on this provision. See, however, *R(I) 3/67* and Northern Ireland decision *R1/81 (I.I.)* and the discussion in Lewis, pp. 86–88.

Sickness benefit

Sickness benefit in respect of industrial injury

102.—(1) In any case where—
  (a) an employed earner is incapable of work as a result of a personal injury of a kind mentioned in section 94(1) above; and
  (b) the contribution conditions are not satisfied in respect of him,
those conditions shall be taken to be satisfied for the purposes of paragraph (a) or, as the case may be, paragraph (b) of section 31(2) above.
  (2) In the case of a person who—
  (a) is entitled, by virtue of this section, to sickness benefit under subsection (2)(b) of section 31 above, and
  (b) is not also entitled to sickness benefit under subsection (2)(c) of that section,
the weekly rate at which sickness benefit is payable shall be determined in accordance with regulations.
  (3) In subsection (1) above "contribution conditions" means—
  (a) in the case of a person who is made under pensionable age, the contribution conditions specified for sickness benefit in Schedule 3, Part I, paragraph 2; and

(b) in the case of a person who has attained pensionable age but who is not for the time being entitled to a Category A or Category B retirement pension, the contribution conditions for a Category A retirement pension specified in Schedule 3, Part I, paragraph 5.

DEFINITIONS
"contribution conditions": subs. (3).
"employed earner": s.121(1).
"pensionable age": s.121(1).
"work": s.94(6).

GENERAL NOTE
This section was introduced as a result of the abolition of short-term industrial injury benefit in 1982. It deems industrial injury claimants to have satisfied the contribution conditions for sickness benefit. This protects the few industrial accident victims who would otherwise have failed to qualify for this incapacity benefit.

Disablement pension

Disablement pension

103.—(1) Subject to the provisions of this section, an employed earner shall be entitled to disablement pension if he suffers as the result of the relevant accident from loss of physical or mental faculty such that the assessed extent of the resulting disablement amounts to not less than 14 per cent or, on a claim made before 19th November 1986, 20 per cent.

(2) In the determination of the extent of an employed earner's disablement for the purposes of this section there may be added to the percentage of the disablement resulting from the relevant accident the assessed percentage of any present disablement of his—

(a) which resulted from any other accident after 4th July 1948 arising out of and in the course of his employment, being employed earner's employment, and

(b) in respect of which a disablement gratuity was not paid to him after a final assessment of his disablement,

(as well as any percentage which may be so added in accordance with regulations under subsection (2) of section 109 below made by virtue of subsection (4)(b) of that section).

(3) Subject to subsection (4) below, where the assessment of disablement is a percentage between 20 and 100 which is not a multiple of 10, it shall be treated—

(a) if it is a multiple of 5, as being the next higher percentage which is a multiple of 10, and

(b) if it is not a multiple of 5, as being the nearest percentage which is a multiple of 10,

and where the assessment of disablement on a claim made on or after 19th November 1986 is less than 20 per cent., but not less than 14 per cent., it shall be treated as 20 per cent.

(4) Where subsection (2) above applies, subsection (3) above shall have effect in relation to the aggregate percentage and not in relation to any percentage forming part of the aggregate.

(5) In this Part of this Act "assessed", in relation to the extent of any disablement, means assessed in accordance with Schedule 6 to this Act; and for the purposes of that Schedule there shall be taken to be no relevant loss of faculty when the extent of the resulting disablement, if so assessed, would not amount to 1 per cent.

(6) A person shall not be entitled to a disablement pension until after the expiry of the period of 90 days (disregarding Sundays) beginning with the day of the relevant accident.

(7) Subject to subsection (8) below, where disablement pension is payable for a period, it shall be paid at the appropriate weekly rate specified in Schedule 4, Part V, paragraph 1.

(8) Where the period referred to in subsection (7) above is limited by reference to a definite date, the pension shall cease on the death of the beneficiary before that date.

DEFINITIONS
"assessed": subs. (6).
"beneficiary": s.121(1).
"employed earner": s.121(1).
"employed earner's employment": s.95(1).
"employment": s.121(1).
"loss of physical faculty": s.121(1).

GENERAL NOTE
Disablement pension, or disablement benefit as it is more commonly known, is now the most important feature of the industrial injuries scheme. There are three conditions of entitlement:
  (1) the claimant must suffer from a loss of physical or mental faculty, as a result of one or more industrial accidents or prescribed diseases or injuries;
  (2) the resultant disablement must be assessed as being at least 14 per cent. (except for pneumoconiosis, byssinosis and diffuse mesothelioma: see General Note to s.110);
  (3) 90 days (excluding Sundays, *i.e.* 15 weeks) must have passed since the date of the accident or the onset of the prescribed disease or injury.
The claimant must of course also be an employed earner (so excluding the self-employed), but there is no need to establish any contribution conditions.
Condition (2) was introduced as from November 19, 1986 (subs. (1)). Before that date disablement benefit was paid in respect of any injury or disease where the level of disablement was assessed at one per cent. Under the old rules any assessment of less than 20 per cent. led to the payment of a lump-sum disablement gratuity rather than a pension. Since 1986 assessments of between 14 and 19 per cent. have been paid at the 20 per cent. rate (subs. (3)). There is also an administrative practice of making assessments in steps of 10 per cent, so the special respiratory conditions mentioned above will attract a 10 per cent. award as a minimum (awards for mesothelioma, a fatal cancer, are customarily much higher). Guidance as to the assessment of disablement is contained in Sched. 6 (subs. (5)); see also the tariff in Sched. 2 to the Social Security (General Benefit) (Northern Ireland) Regulations 1984 (S.I. 1984 No. 92).
Historically disablement benefit was capable of being supplemented by one or more of various special increases. Constant attendance allowance and exceptionally severe disablement allowance (ss.104 and 105) are still available, but unemployability supplement and hospital treatment allowance (s.106 and Sched. 7) were abolished as from April 6, 1987, except for existing claimants. Special hardship allowance, to compensate for lower earnings, was a supplement to disablement benefit until it was replaced in 1986 by reduced earnings allowance, a benefit in its own right. This latter benefit has itself since been abolished, with savings for those already entitled (s.106 and Sched. 7).

Increase where constant attendance needed

104.—(1) Where a disablement pension is payable in respect of an assessment of 100 per cent., then, if as the result of the relevant loss of faculty the beneficiary requires constant attendance, the weekly rate of the pension shall be increased by an amount, not exceeding the appropriate amount specified in Schedule 4, Part V, paragraph 2 determined in accordance with regulations by reference to the extent and nature of the attendance required by the beneficiary.

(2) An increase of pension under this section shall be payable for such period as may be determined at the time it is granted, but may be renewed from time to time.

(3) The Department may by regulations direct that any provision of sections 64 to 67 above shall have effect, with or without modifications, in relation to increases of pension under this section.

(4) In subsection (3) above, "modifications" includes additions and omissions.

General Note

Constant attendance allowance is payable where a claimant is entitled to an ordinary industrial disablement pension based on a degree of disablement assessed at 100 per cent. and, because of the relevant loss of faculty, requires constant attendance. The criteria governing the different rates of constant attendance allowance are set out in the Social Security (General Benefit) Regulations (Northern Ireland) 1984 (S.I. 1984 No. 92), reg. 17. See further Lewis, pp. 159–161 and 250–1. Decisions on entitlement to constant attendance allowance are for the Department and not the independent statutory adjudicating authorities (Social Security (Adjudication) Regulations (Northern Ireland) 1987 (S.I. 1987 No. 828), reg. 19(1)(a)), so there is no right of appeal to a SSAT.

Increase for exceptionally severe disablement

105.—(1) Where a disablement pension is payable to a person—

(a) who is or, but for having received medical or other treatment as an in-patient in a hospital or similar institution, would be entitled to an increase of the weekly rate of the pension under section 104 above, and the weekly rate of the increase exceeds the amount specified in Schedule 4, Part V, paragraph 2(a); and

(b) his need for constant attendance of an extent and nature qualifying him for such an increase at a weekly rate in excess of that amount is likely to be permanent,

the weekly rate of the pension shall, in addition to any increase under section 104 above, be further increased by the amount specified in Schedule 4, Part V, paragraph 3.

(2) An increase under this section shall be payable for such period as may be determined at the time it is granted, but may be renewed from time to time.

General Note

Exceptionally severe disablement allowance is a further addition to disablement benefit payable to claimants who are entitled to the higher rate of constant attendance allowance (or would be if they were not in hospital) and whose need for such attendance is likely to be permanent. As with constant attendance allowance (s.104), decisions on entitlement are taken on behalf of the Department so there is no right of appeal.

Other benefits and increases

Benefits and increases subject to qualifications as to time

106. Schedule 7 to this Act shall have effect in relation—

(a) to unemployability supplement;
(b) to disablement gratuity;
(c) to increase of disablement pension during hospital treatment;
(d) to reduced earnings allowance;
(e) to retirement allowance; and
(f) to industrial death benefit,

for all of which the qualifications include special qualifications as to time.

General Note

This section introduces Sched. 7, which contains various savings provisions for benefits under

the industrial injuries scheme which have been abolished in recent years for new claimants. The key dates for the benefits in question are as follows:
(a) unemployability supplement: April 6, 1987,
(b) disablement gratuity: November 19, 1986,
(c) increases to disablement pension during hospital treatment: April 6, 1987,
(d) reduced earnings allowance: October 1, 1990,
(e) retirement allowance: April 10, 1989,
(f) industrial death benefit: April 11, 1988.

On the consolidation of legislation relating to industrial death benefit, see the report of the Law Commissions (Cm. 1726, 1991), para. 16.

Successive accidents

Adjustments for successive accidents

107.—(1) Where a person suffers two or more successive accidents arising out of and in the course of his employed earner's employment—
   (a) he shall not for the same period be entitled (apart from any increase of benefit mentioned in subsection (2) below) to receive industrial injuries benefit by way of two or more disablement pensions at an aggregate weekly rate exceeding the appropriate amount specified in Schedule 4, Part V, paragraph 4; and
   (b) regulations may provide for adjusting—
      (i) disablement benefit, or the conditions for the receipt of that benefit, in any case where he has received or may be entitled to a disablement gratuity;
      (ii) any increase of benefit mentioned in subsection (2) below, or the conditions for its receipt.

(2) The increases of benefit referred to in subsection (1) above are those under the following provisions of this Act—
    section 104,
    section 105,
    paragraph 2, 4 or 6 of Schedule 7.

DEFINITIONS
"employed earner": s.121(1).
"employed earner's employment": s.95(1).

GENERAL NOTE
As a general principle a claimant who has the misfortune to suffer from disablement caused by two successive accidents (or diseases) is entitled to an assessment based on the aggregate of the respective degrees of disablement. The aggregate amount cannot exceed the weekly amount payable in respect of 100 per cent. disablement (subs. (1)(a)). See also Security (General Benefit) Regulations (Northern Ireland) 1984 (S.I. 1984 No. 92), regs. 36 and 37.

Prescribed industrial diseases, etc.

Benefit in respect of prescribed industrial diseases, etc.

108.—(1) Industrial injuries benefits shall, in respect of a person who has been in employed earner's employment, be payable in accordance with this section and sections 109 and 110 below in respect of—
   (a) any prescribed disease, or
   (b) any prescribed personal injury (other than an injury caused by accident arising out of and in the course of his employment),
which is a disease or injury due to the nature of that employment and which developed after 4th July 1948.

(2) A disease or injury may be prescribed in relation to any employed earners if the Department is satisfied that—

(a) it ought to be treated, having regard to its causes and incidence and any other relevant considerations, as a risk of their occupations and not as a risk common to all persons; and

(b) it is such that, in the absence of special circumstances, the attribution of particular cases to the nature of the employment can be established or presumed with reasonable certainty.

(3) Regulations prescribing any disease or injury for those purposes may provide that a person who developed the disease or injury on or at any time after a date specified in the regulations (being a date before the regulations came into force but not before 5th July 1948) shall be treated, subject to any prescribed modifications of this section or section 109 or 110 below, as if the regulation had been in force when he developed the disease or injury.

(4) Provision may be made by regulations for determining—

(a) the time at which a person is to be treated as having developed any prescribed disease or injury; and

(b) the circumstances in which such a disease or injury is, where the person in question has previously suffered from it, to be treated as having recrudesced or as having been contracted or received afresh.

(5) Notwithstanding any other provision of this Act, the power conferred by subsection (4)(a) above includes power to provide that the time at which a person shall be treated as having developed a prescribed disease or injury shall be the date on which he first makes a claim which results in the payment of benefit by virtue of this section or section 110 below in respect of that disease or injury.

(6) Nothing in this section or in section 109 or 110 below affects the right of any person to benefit in respect of a disease which is a personal injury or accident within the meaning of this Part of this Act, except that a person shall not be entitled to benefit in respect of a disease as being an injury by accident arising out of and in the course of any employment if at the time of the accident the disease is in relation to him a prescribed disease by virtue of the occupation in which he is engaged in that employment.

DEFINITIONS

"benefit": s.121(1).
"employed earner": s.121(1).
"employed earner's employment": s.95(1).
"employment": s.121(1).
"industrial injuries benefit": s.121(1).
"prescribe": s.121(1).

GENERAL NOTE

The concept of a prescribed disease dates back to the Workmen's Compensation Act 1906. The system of prescribed diseases enables benefit to be paid to individuals who suffer from defined occupational hazards. As such, it provides a degree of flexibility which avoids the difficult problems of "accident" or "process" (see annotations to s.94). The list of currently prescribed diseases and injuries is contained in Sched. 1 to the Social Security (Industrial Injuries) (Prescribed Diseases) Regulations (Northern Ireland) 1983 (S.I. 1983 No. 19).

The issue as to whether a particular condition should be prescribed for the purposes of the industrial injuries scheme is normally referred to the Industrial Injuries Advisory Council (IIAC), constituted under the Great Britain Social Security Administration Act 1992 (s.171 and Sched. 6). IIAC has a specialist Research Working Group to examine such matters and to keep diseases as yet unprescribed under review. The traditionally cautious approach of IIAC in deciding whether the prescription test (subs. (2)) has been satisfied in the case of any given condition has been the subject of criticism (Lewis, pp. 92–97).

Special adjudication arrangements apply in cases of industrial disease: see SSA(N.I.)A 1992, s.60.

General provisions relating to benefit under s.108

109.—(1) Subject to the power to make different provision by regulations, and to the following provisions of this section and section 110 below—

(a) the benefit payable under section 108 above in respect of a prescribed disease or injury, and

(b) the conditions for receipt of benefit,

shall be the same as in the case of personal injury by accident arising out of and in the course of employment.

(2) In relation to prescribed diseases and injuries, regulations may provide—

(a) for modifying any provisions contained in this Act or the Administration Act which relate to disablement benefit or reduced earnings allowance or their administration; and

(b) for adapting references in this Act and that Act to accidents,

and for the purposes of this subsection the provisions of the Administration Act which relate to the administration of disablement benefit or reduced earnings allowance shall be taken to include section 1 and any provision which relates to the administration of both the benefit in question and other benefits.

(3) Without prejudice to the generality of subsection (2) above, regulations under that subsection may in particular include provision—

(a) for presuming any prescribed disease or injury—

    (i) to be due, unless the contrary is proved, to the nature of a person's employment where he was employed in any prescribed occupation at the time when, or within a prescribed period or for a prescribed length of time (whether continuous or not) before, he developed the disease or injury,

    (ii) not to be due to the nature of a person's employment unless he was employed in some prescribed occupation at the time when, or within a prescribed period or for a prescribed length of time, (whether continuous or not) before, he developed the disease or injury;

(b) for such matters as appear to the Department to be incidental to or consequential on provisions included in the regulations by virtue of subsection (2) and paragraph (a) above.

(4) Regulations under subsection (2) above may also provide—

(a) that, in the determination of the extent of an employed earner's disablement resulting from a prescribed disease or injury, the appropriate percentage may be added to the percentage of that disablement; and

(b) that, in the determination of the extent of an employed earner's disablement for the purposes of section 103 above, the appropriate percentage may be added to the percentage of disablement resulting from the relevant accident.

(5) In subsection (4)(a) above "the appropriate percentage" means the assessed percentage of any present disablement of the earner which resulted—

(a) from any accident after 4th July 1948 arising out of and in the course of his employment, being employed earner's employment, or

(b) from any other prescribed disease or injury due to the nature of that employment and developed after 4th July 1948,

and in respect of which a disablement gratuity was not paid to him after a final assessment of his disablement.

(6) In subsection (4)(b) above "the appropriate percentage" means the assessed percentage of any present disablement of the earner—

(a) which resulted from any prescribed disease or injury due to the nature of his employment and developed after 4th July 1948, and

(b) in respect of which a disablement gratuity was not paid to him after a final assessment of his disablement.

(7) Where regulations under subsection (2) above—

(a) make provision such as is mentioned in subsection (4) above, and
(b) also make provision corresponding to that in section 103(3) above,
they may also make provision to the effect that those corresponding provisions shall have effect in relation to the aggregate percentage and not in relation to any percentage forming part of the aggregate.

DEFINITIONS
  "the Administration Act": s.170.
  "appropriate percentage": subss. (5) and (6).
  "benefit": s.121(1).
  "employed earner": s.121(1).
  "employment": s.121(1).
  "prescribe": s.121(1).

GENERAL NOTE
  See further the Social Security (Industrial Injuries) (Prescribed Diseases) Regulations (Northern Ireland) 1983 (S.I. 1983 No. 19).

Respiratory diseases

  110.—(1) As respects pneumoconiosis, regulations may further provide that, where a person is found to be suffering from pneumoconiosis accompanied by tuberculosis, the effects of the tuberculosis shall be treated for the purposes of this section and sections 108 and 109 above as if they were effects of the pneumoconiosis.

  (2) Subsection (1) above shall have effect as if after "tuberculosis" (in both places) there were inserted "emphysema or chronic bronchitis", but only in relation to a person the extent of whose disablement resulting from pneumoconiosis, or from pneumoconiosis accompanied by tuberculosis, would (if his physical condition were otherwise normal) be assessed at not less than 50 per cent.

  (3) A person found to be suffering from pneumoconiosis shall be treated for the purposes of this Act as suffering from a loss of faculty such that the assessed extent of the resulting disablement amounts to not less than 1 per cent.

DEFINITIONS
  "pneumoconiosis": s.121(1).

GENERAL NOTE
  This section makes special provision for certain respiratory diseases. Regulations made under subs. (1) enable the effects of tuberculosis to be taken into account where it accompanies pneumoconiosis (see Social Security (Industrial Injuries) (Prescribed Diseases) Regulations (Northern Ireland) 1983 (S.I. 1983 No. 19), reg. 34). The same principle applies to emphysema or chronic bronchitis, provided that the assessment attributable to pneumoconiosis (with or without tuberculosis) is at least 50 per cent. (subs. (2) and reg. 35).
  Some claimants with pneumoconiosis may also benefit from the rule in subs. (3) that where the condition is diagnosed there must be an assessment of at least one per cent. (This could occur where pneumoconiosis is diagnosed in the absence of any present respiratory disablement). The non-statutory administrative practice of making assessments in steps of 10 per cent. means that a pneumoconiosis sufferer is guaranteed an assessment of at least 10 per cent. Awards in respect of pneumoconiosis (which includes asbestosis: s.121(1)) are not subject to the 14 per cent. threshold (reg. 33).
  The qualification for byssinosis in subs. (4) has been disapplied by regulations (reg. 33(2)).

Old cases

Workmen's compensation, etc.

  111. Schedule 8 to this Act shall have effect—
  (a) to continue workmen's compensation;

(b) to enable regulations—
    (i) to supplement workmen's compensation; and
    (ii) to provide for the payment of allowances or other benefits for industrial diseases in respect of employment before 5th July 1948; and
(c) to enable regulations to confer rights to payments in respect of such employment.

DEFINITIONS
"employment": s.121(1).

GENERAL NOTE
This section, introducing Sched. 8, is a saving provision. Sched. 8 itself re-enacts the relevant sections of the Industrial Injuries and Diseases (Northern Ireland Old Cases) Act 1975 (which itself consolidated earlier legislation). The Schedule provides for benefits to be paid out of the National Insurance Fund in respect of accidents which happened as a result of (or diseases caused by) employment before July 5, 1948. The Workmen's Compensation (Supplementation) Regulations (Northern Ireland) 1983 (S.I. 1983 No. 101) deals with such cases. On administrative arrangements, see SSA(N.I.)A 1992, s.161 and Sched. 6.

PART VI

MISCELLANEOUS PROVISIONS RELATING TO PART I TO V

Earnings

Certain sums to be earnings

112.—(1) Regulations may provide—
(a) that any employment protection entitlement shall be deemed for the purposes of Parts I to V of this Act to be earnings payable by and to such persons as are prescribed and to be so payable in respect of such periods as are prescribed; and
(b) that those periods shall, so far as they are not periods of employment, be deemed for those purposes to be periods of employment.
(2) In subsection (1) above "employment protection entitlement" means—
(a) any sum, or a prescribed part of any sum, mentioned in subsection (3) below; and
(b) prescribed amounts which the regulations provide are to be treated as related to any of those sums.
(3) The sums referred to in subsection (2) above are the following—
(a) a sum payable in respect of arrears of pay in pursuance of an order for reinstatement or re-engagement under the Industrial Relations (Northern Ireland) Order 1976;
(b) a sum payable by way of pay in pursuance of an order under that Order for the continuation of a contract of employment;
(c) a sum payable by way of remuneration in pursuance of a protective award under that Order.

DEFINITIONS
"earnings": s.121(1).
"employment": s.121(1).
"employment protection entitlement": subs. (2).
"prescribe": s.121(1).

GENERAL NOTE
See Social Security (Contributions) (Amendment) Regulations (Northern Ireland) 1977 (S.I. 1977 No. 93).

Disqualification and suspension

General provisions as to disqualification and suspension

113.—(1) Except where regulations otherwise provide, a person shall be disqualified for receiving any benefit under Parts II to V of this Act, and an increase of such benefit shall not be payable in respect of any person as the beneficiary's wife or husband, for any period during which the person—

(a) is absent from Northern Ireland; or

(b) is undergoing imprisonment or detention in legal custody.

(2) Regulations may provide for suspending payment of such benefit to a person during any period in which he is undergoing medical or other treatment as an in-patient in a hospital or similar institution.

(3) Regulations may provide for a person who would be entitled to any such benefit but for the operation of any provision of this Act or the Administration Act to be treated as if entitled to it for the purposes of any rights or obligations (whether his own or another's) which depend on his entitlement, other than the right to payment of the benefit.

DEFINITIONS
"the Administration Act": s.170.
"beneficiary": s.121(1).
"benefit": s.121(1).
"entitled": s.121(1).
"Northern Ireland": s.168.
"medical treatment": s.121(1).

GENERAL NOTE
This section provides the authority for the disqualification or suspension of claimants from receiving benefit under Pts. II to V in the specified instances.

Subs. (1)
Is absent from Northern Ireland. The test for absence is simply whether the person is "not physically present" (*R(U) 16/62*). Presence at any time in the past is not necessary. This basic principle as to disqualification is subject to the Social Security Benefit (Persons Abroad) Regulations (Northern Ireland) 1975 (S.I. 1975 No. 103). The position is also complicated by the existence of a considerable body of European Community law and of a large number of reciprocal conventions (see further Bonner).

Is undergoing imprisonment or detention in legal custody. The imprisonment must be imposed by a court exercising criminal jurisdiction (*R(S) 8/79*), so imprisonment for non-payment of maintenance does not of itself disqualify a claimant from receiving benefit. Further provision, including certain exceptions, is made in the Social Security (General Benefit) Regulations (Northern Ireland) 1984 (S.I. 1984 No. 92), regs. 2 and 3.

Persons maintaining dependants, etc

Persons maintaining dependants, etc.

114.—(1) Regulations may provide for determining the circumstances in which a person is or is not to be taken, for the purposes of Parts II to V of this Act—

(a) to be wholly or mainly, or to a substantial extent, maintaining, or to be contributing at any weekly rate to the maintenance of, another person; or

(b) to be, or have been, contributing at any weekly rate to the cost of providing for a child.

(2) Regulations under this section may provide, for the purposes of the provisions relating to an increase of benefit under Parts II to V of this Act in respect of a wife or other adult dependant, that where—

(a) a person is partly maintained by each of two or more beneficiaries, each of whom would be entitled to such an increase in respect of that person if he were wholly or mainly maintaining that person, and

(b) the contributions made by those two or more beneficiaries towards the maintenance of that person amount in the aggregate to sums which would, if they had been contributed by one of those beneficiaries, have been sufficient to satisfy the requirements of regulations under this section,

that person shall be taken to be wholly or mainly maintained by such of those beneficiaries as may be prescribed.

(3) Regulations may provide for any sum or sums paid by a person by way of contribution towards either or both of the following, that is to say—

(a) the maintenance of his or her spouse, and

(b) the cost of providing for one or more children,

to be treated for the purposes of any of the provisions of this Act specified in subsection (4) below as such contributions, of such respective amounts equal in the aggregate to the said sum or sums, in respect of such persons, as may be determined in accordance with the regulations so as to secure as large a payment as possible by way of benefit in respect of the dependants.

(4) The provisions in question are sections 56, 81 to 84, 86 and paragraphs 5 and 6 of Schedule 7 to this Act.

DEFINITIONS
"beneficiary": s.121(1).
"benefit": s.121(1).
"child": s.121(1).
"prescribe": s.121(1).

GENERAL NOTE
See Social Security Benefit (Dependency) Regulations (Northern Ireland) 1977 (S.I. 1977 No. 74).

Special cases

Crown employment—Parts I to VI

115.—(1) Subject to the provisions of this section, Parts I to V and this Part of this Act apply to persons employed by or under the Crown in like manner as if they were employed by a private person.

(2) Subsection (1) above does not apply to persons serving as members of Her Majesty's forces in their capacity as such.

(3) Employment as a member of Her Majesty's forces and any other prescribed employment under the Crown are not, and are not to be treated as, employed earner's employment for any of the purposes of Part V of this Act.

(4) The references to Parts I to V of this Act in this section and sections 116, 117, 119 and 120 below do not include references to section 111 above.

DEFINITIONS
"employed earner": s.121(1).
"employed earner's employment": s.95(1).
"employment": s.121(1).
"prescribe": s.121(1).

GENERAL NOTE
Crown employees are in principle in the same position as ordinary employees so far as the National Insurance scheme is concerned, but there are special rules governing members of HM forces (see s.116).

Her Majesty's forces

116.—(1) Subject to section 115(2) and (3) above and to this section, a

person who is serving as a member of Her Majesty's forces shall, while he is so serving, be treated as an employed earner, in respect of his membership of those forces, for the purposes—
(a) of Parts I to V and this Part of this Act; and
(b) of any provision of the Administration Act in its application to him as an employed earner.

(2) The Secretary of State may make regulations modifying Parts I to V and this Part of this Act, and any provision of Part II of the Administration Act which replaces provisions of Part III of the 1975 Act, in such manner as he thinks proper, in their application to persons who are or have been members of Her Majesty's forces; and regulations under this section may in particular provide—
(a) in the case of persons who are employed earners in respect of their membership of those forces, for reducing the rate of the contributions payable in respect of their employment and for determining—
(i) the amounts payable on accounts of those contributions by the Secretary of State and the time and manner of payment, and
(ii) the deductions (if any) to be made on account of those contributions from the pay of those persons;
(b) for preventing a person who is discharged from Her Majesty's forces at his own request from being thereby disqualified for receiving unemployment benefit on the ground that he has voluntarily left his employment without just cause.

(3) For the purposes of Parts I to V and this Part of this Act, Her Majesty's forces shall be taken to consist of such establishments and organisations as may be prescribed by regulations made by the Secretary of State being establishments and organisations in which persons serve under the control of the Defence Council.

DEFINITIONS
"the Administration Act": s.170.
"employed earner": s.121(1).
"Her Majesty's forces": subs. (3).

GENERAL NOTE
See, *e.g.* Social Security (Benefit) (Members of the Forces) Regulations 1975 (S.I. 1975 No. 493) and Social Security (Contributions) Regulations 1979 (S.I. 1979 No. 591), Pt. VIII, Case E.

Mariners, airmen, etc.

117.—(1) The Department may make regulations modifying provisions of Parts I to V and this Part of this Act, and any provision of Part II of the Administration Act which replaces provisions of Part III of the 1975 Act, in such manner as the Department thinks proper, in their application to persons who are or have been, or are to be, employed on board any ship, vessel, hovercraft or aircraft.

(2) Regulations under subsection (1) above may in particular provide—
(a) for any such provision to apply to such persons, notwithstanding that it would not otherwise apply;
(b) for excepting such persons from the application of any such provision where they neither are domiciled nor have a place of residence in Northern Ireland;
(c) for requiring the payment of secondary Class I contributions in respect of such persons, whether or not they are (within the meaning of Part I of this Act) employed earners;
(d) for the taking of evidence, for the purposes of any claim to benefit, in a country or territory other than Northern Ireland, by a British consular official or such other person as may be prescribed;

(e) for enabling persons who are or have been so employed to authorise the payment of the whole or any part of any benefit to which they are or may become entitled to such of their dependants as may be prescribed.

DEFINITIONS
"the 1975 Act": s.170.
"the Administration Act": s.170.
"employed earner": s.121(1).
"entitled": s.121(1).
"Northern Ireland": s.168.
"prescribe": s.121(1).

GENERAL NOTE
See, *e.g.* Social Security (Airmen's Benefits) Regulations (Northern Ireland) 1975 (S.I. 1975 No. 101), Social Security (Mariners' Benefits) Regulations (Northern Ireland) 1975 (S.I. 1975 No. 108) and Social Security (Contributions) Regulations (Northern Ireland) 1979 (S.I. 1979 No. 186), Pt. VIII, Cases A and B.

Married women and widows

118. The Department may make regulations modifying any of the following provisions of this Act, namely—
(a) Part I;
(b) Part II (except section 60); and
(c) Parts III and IV,
in such manner as the Department thinks proper, in their application to women who are or have been married.

GENERAL NOTE
Historically, married women have been subject to differential treatment under the social security system. Until April 1977 married women and widows could elect to pay National Insurance contributions at a reduced rate (with lesser entitlements). Such an election may be revoked, but, once lost, the right to pay reduced contributions cannot be reclaimed. The details are set out in the Social Security (Contributions) Regulations (Northern Ireland) 1979 (S.I. 1979 No. 186), Pt. VIII, Case C (on which see Williams). The impact of European Community law has narrowed the range of situations in which differential treatment is still permissible.

Persons outside Northern Ireland

119. The Department may make regulations modifying Parts I to V of this Act, and any provision of Part II of the Administration Act which replaces provisions of Part III of the 1975 Act, in such manner as the Department thinks proper, in their application to persons who are or have been outside Northern Ireland at any prescribed time or in any prescribed circumstances.

DEFINITIONS
"the 1975 Act": s.170.
"the Administration Act": s.170.
"Northern Ireland": s.168.
"prescribe": s.121(1).

GENERAL NOTE
See, *e.g.* Social Security Benefit (Persons Abroad) Regulations (Northern Ireland) 1975 (S.I. 1975 No. 103) and Social Security (Contributions) Regulations (Northern Ireland) 1979 (S.I. 1979 No. 186), Pt. VIII, Case D.

Treatment of certain marriages

120.—(1) Regulations may provide—
(a) for a voidable marriage which has been annulled, whether before or after the date when the regulations come into force, to be treated for

the purposes of the provisions to which this subsection applies as if it had been a valid marriage which was terminated by divorce at the date of annulment;

(b) as to the circumstances in which, for the purposes of the enactment to which this section applies—

(i) a marriage celebrated under a law which permits polygamy; or

(ii) any marriage during the subsistence of which a party to it is at any time married to more than one person,

is to be treated as having, or not having, the consequences of a marriage celebrated under a law which does not permit polygamy.

(2) Subsection (1) above applies—

(a) to any enactment contained in Parts I to V or this Part of this Act; and

(b) to regulations under any such enactment.

GENERAL NOTE
See Ogus and Barendt, pp. 351–3.

Interpretation

Interpretation of Parts I to VI and supplementary provisions

121.—(1) In Parts I to V above and this Part of this Act, unless the context otherwise requires—

"beneficiary", in relation to any benefit, means the person entitled to that benefit;

"benefit" means—

(a) benefit under Parts II to V of this Act other than Old Cases payments;

(b) as respects any period before 1st July 1992 but not before 6th April 1975, benefit under Part II of the 1975 Act; or

(c) as respects any period before 6th April 1975, benefit under—

(i) the National Insurance Act (Northern Ireland) 1946 or 1966; or

(ii) the National Insurance (Industrial Injuries) Act (Northern Ireland) 1946 or 1966;

"child" means a person under the age of 19 who would be treated as a child for the purposes of Part IX of this Act or such other person under that age as may be prescribed;

"claim" is to be construed in accordance with "claimant";

"claimant", in relation to benefit other than industrial injuries benefit, means a person who has claimed benefit;

"claimant", in relation to industrial injuries benefit, means a person who has claimed industrial injuries benefit;

"contract of service" means any contract of service or apprenticeship whether written or oral and whether express or implied;

"current", in relation to the lower and upper earnings limits under section 5(1) above, means for the time being in force;

"day of incapacity for work" and "day of interruption of employment" have the meanings assigned to them by section 57 above;

"deferred" and "period of deferment" have the meanings assigned to them by section 55 above;

"earner" and "earnings" are to be construed in accordance with sections 3, 4 and 112 above;

"employed earner" has the meaning assigned to it by section 2 above;

"employment" includes any trade, business, profession, office or vocation and "employed" has a corresponding meaning;

"entitled", in relation to any benefit, is to be construed in accordance
with—
> (a) the provisions specifically relating to that benefit;
> (b) in the case of a benefit specified in section 20(1) above,
> section 21 above; and
> (c) sections 1 to 3 and 66 of the Administration Act;

"government department" means, or as the case may require, includes,
a Northern Ireland department;

"industrial injuries benefit" means benefit under Part V of this Act,
other than under Schedule 8 to this Act;

"initial primary percentage" is to be construed in accordance with
section 8(1) and (2) above and as referring to the percentage rate
from time to time specified in section 8(2)(a) above as the initial
primary percentage;

"the Inland Revenue" means the Commissioners of Inland Revenue;

"late husband", in relation to a woman who has been more than once
married, means her last husband;

"long-term benefit" has the meaning assigned to it by section 20(2)
above;

"loss of physical faculty" includes disfigurement whether or not accompanied by any loss of physical faculty;

"lower earnings limit" and "upper earnings limit" are to be construed in
accordance with section 5(1) above and references to the lower or
upper earnings limit of a tax year are to whatever is (or was) for
that year the limit in force under that subsection;

"medical examination" includes bacteriological and radiographical
tests and similar investigations and "medically examined" has a
corresponding meaning;

"medical treatment" means medical, surgical or rehabilitative treatment (including any course or diet or other regimen), and references to a person receiving or submitting himself to medical
treatment are to be construed accordingly;

"Old Cases payments" means payments under Part I of Schedule 8 to
this Act;

"payments by way of occupational or personal pension" means, in
relation to a person, periodical payments which, in connection
with the coming to an end of an employment of his, fall to be made
to him—
> (a) out of money provided wholly or partly by the employer or
> under arrangements made by the employer;
> (b) out of money provided under an enactment or instrument
> having the force of law in any part of the United Kingdom or
> elsewhere;
> (c) under a personal pension scheme as defined in Article 2(2)
> of the 1986 Order;
> (d) under a contract or trust scheme approved under Chapter
> III of Part XIV of the Income and Corporation Taxes Act 1988;
> or
> (e) under a personal pension scheme approved under Chapter
> IV of that Part of that Act,

and such other payments as are prescribed;

"pensionable age" means—
> (a) the age of 65, in the case of man; and
> (b) the age of 60, in the case of a woman;

"pneumoconiosis" means fibrosis of the lungs due to silica dust, asbestos dust, or other dust, and includes the condition of the lungs
known as dust-reticulation;

"prescribe" means prescribe by regulations;

"primary percentage" is to be construed in accordance with section 8(1) and (2) above;

"qualifying earnings factor" means an earnings factor equal to the lower earnings limit for the year in question multiplied by 52;

"relative" includes a person who is a relative by marriage and a person who would be a relative if some person born illegitimate had been born legitimate;

"relevant accident" means the accident in respect of which industrial injuries benefit is claimed or payable;

"relevant injury" means the injury in respect of which industrial injuries benefit is claimed or payable;

"relevant loss of faculty" means—

    (a) in relation to severe disablement allowance, the loss of faculty which results in the disablement; or

    (b) in relation to industrial injuries benefit, the loss of faculty resulting from the relevant injury;

"self-employed earner" has the meaning assigned to it by section 2 above;

"short-term benefit" has the meaning assigned to it by section 20(2) above;

"tax week" means one of the successive periods in a tax year beginning with the first day of that year and every seventh day thereafter, the last day of a tax year (or, in the case of a tax year ending in a leap year, the last two days) to be treated accordingly as a separate tax week;

"tax year" means the twelve months beginning with 6th April in any year, the expression "1978–79" meaning the tax year beginning with 6th April 1978, and any correspondingly framed reference to a pair of successive years being construed as a reference to the tax year beginning with 6th April in the earlier of them;

"trade or business" includes, in relation to a public or local authority, the exercise and performance of the powers and duties of that authority;

"trade union" means an association of employed earners;

"week", except in relation to disability working allowance, means a period of 7 days beginning with Sunday.

(2) Regulations may make provision modifying the meaning of "employment" for the purposes of any provision of Parts I to V and this Part of this Act.

(3) Provision may be made by regulations as to the circumstances in which a person is to be treated as residing or not residing with another person for any of the purposes of Parts I to V and this Part of this Act and as to the circumstances in which persons are to be treated for any of those purposes as residing or not residing together.

(4) A person who is residing with his spouse shall be treated for the purposes of Parts I to V of this Act and this Part as entitled to any child benefit to which his spouse is entitled.

(5) Regulations may, for the purposes of any provision of those Parts under which the right to any benefit or increase of benefit depends on a person being or having been entitled to child benefit, make provision whereby a person is to be treated as if he were or had been so entitled or as if he were not or had not been so entitled.

(6) For the purposes of Parts I to V of this Act and this Part a person is "permanently incapable of self-support" if (but only if) he is incapable of supporting himself by reason of physical or mental infirmity and is likely to remain so incapable for the remainder of his life.

"the 1975 Act": s.170.
"the 1986 Order": s.170.
"the Administration Act": s.170.
"permanently incapable of self-support": subs. (6).

GENERAL NOTE

Subs. (6)
Permanently incapable of self-support. This term appears to be relevant solely in the context of industrial death benefit, which itself is only payable in respect of deaths before April 11, 1988 (see s.106). See, for example, Sched. 7, Pt. VI, paras. 16(2)(c) and 17(1)(b).

PART VII

INCOME-RELATED BENEFITS

General

Income-related benefits

122.—(1) Prescribed schemes shall provide for the following benefits (in this Act referred to as "income-related benefits")—
(a) income support;
(b) family credit;
(c) disability working allowance;
(d) housing benefit.
(2) The Department shall make copies of schemes prescribed under subsection (1)(a), (b) or (c) above available for public inspection at social security offices of the Department at all reasonable hours without payment.
(3) The Department of the Environment and the Executive—
(a) shall take such steps as appear to them appropriate for the purpose of securing that persons who may be entitled to housing benefit become aware that they may be entitled to it; and
(b) shall makes copies of the housing benefit scheme available for public inspection at their offices at all reasonable hours without payment.

DEFINITIONS
"the Administration Act": s.170.
"Department": s.170.
"the Executive": s.133(1).
"income-related benefits": subs. (1).
"prescribes": s.137(1).

GENERAL NOTE
    This section sets out the income-related or means-tested benefits (subs. (1)). It also imposes a duty on the Department to make available for inspection copies of the rules relating to the income support, family credit and disability working allowance schemes at DHSS local offices. Such a facility must be available at all reasonable hours and free of charge (subs. (2)). An analogous duty is imposed on the Department of Environment and the Housing Executive in respect of the housing benefit scheme (subs. (3)(b) and (6)). The DOE and Housing Executive are also under an obligation to take such steps as appear to them appropriate for the purpose of securing that persons who may be entitled to housing benefit become aware that they are so entitled (subs. (3)(a)). No parallel duty is imposed on the Department to publicise the principal schemes listed in subs. (1)(a)–(c).

Income support

Income support

123.—(1) A person in Northern Ireland is entitled to income support if—

(a) he is of or over the age of 18 or, in prescribed circumstances and for a prescribed period, of or over the age of 16 or he is a person to whom section 124(1) below applies;

(b) he has no income or his income does not exceed the applicable amount;

(c) he is not engaged in remunerative work and, if he is a member of a married or unmarried couple, the other member is not so engaged; and

(d) except in such circumstances as may be prescribed—
    (i) he is available for, and actively seeking, employment;
    (ii) he is not receiving relevant education.

(2) In subsection (1)(a) above "period" includes—

(a) a period of a determinate length;

(b) a period defined by reference to the happening of a future event; and

(c) a period of a determinate length but subject to earlier determination upon the happening to a future event.

(3) Circumstances may be prescribed in which a person must not only satisfy the condition specified in subsection (1)(d)(i) above but also be registered in the prescribed manner for employment.

(4) Subject to subsection (5) below, where a person is entitled to income support, then—

(a) if he has no income, the amount shall be the applicable amount; and

(b) if he has income, the amount shall be the difference between his income and the applicable amount.

(5) Where a person is entitled to income support for a period to which this subsection applies, the amount payable for that period shall be calculated in such manner as may be prescribed.

(6) Subsection (5) above applies—

(a) to a period of less than a week which is the whole period for which income support is payable; and

(b) to any other period of less than a week for which it is payable.

DEFINITIONS
    "Department": s.170.
    "married couple": s.133(1).
    "Northern Ireland": s.168.
    "period": subs. (2).
    "prescribed": s.133(1).
    "unmarried couple": s.133(1).

GENERAL NOTE
This section establishes the framework for entitlement to income support. The basic conditions are laid down in subs. (1) and amplified by the Income Support (General) Regulations (Northern Ireland) 1987 (S.I. 1987 No. 459). See further Mesher on the equivalent Great Britain Regulations, *i.e.* the Income Support (General) Regulations 1987 (S.I. 1987 No. 1968).

As a general rule, income support is payable only to persons who have reached the age of 18. Some 16- and 17-year-olds may qualify for benefit by either of two routes. Some may be eligible by virtue of falling into one of the categories prescribed under subs. (1)(a), while others may be awarded benefit on the basis that otherwise they will suffer severe hardship (s.124). Decisions in the first category are made by adjudication officers (with a right of appeal to a SSAT) while decisions under s.124 are made by the Department (with no right of appeal).

Subsection (1)(b) sets out the income means-test (see further subs. (4)). There is also a capital limit (currently £8,000) laid down in regulations under s.130(1). In addition, claimants (or their partners) must not be engaged in remunerative work (defined as 16 hours a week or more from April 7, 1992: Income Support (General) Amendment No. 3 Regulations (Northern Ireland) 1991 (S.I. 1991 No. 338)). Unless excepted by regulations, they must also be available for and actively seeking employment and not receiving relevant education. See further Mesher.

The rate of income support is calculated in accordance with the appropriate applicable amount. Where the claimant has no income, the applicable amount is paid. Where the claimant has some income, this is set against the applicable amount and the balance represents the benefit payable (subs. (5)). Subsections (5) and (6) enable regulations to deal with entitlement to income support for part weeks.

The inter-relationship between income support and maintenance is dealt with by SSA(N.I.)A 1992, Pt. V (ss.100–103).

Severe hardship cases

124.—(1) If it appears to the Department—
(a) that a person of or over the age of 16 but under the age of 18 is not entitled to income support; and
(b) that severe hardship will result to that person unless income support is paid to him,
the Department may direct that this subsection shall apply to him.

(2) Any such direction may specify a period for which subsection (1) above is to apply to the person to whom the direction relates.

(3) The person to whom such a direction relates shall be treated in accordance with it, but if at any time it appears to the Department that there has been a change of circumstances as a result of which failure to receive income support need no longer result in severe hardship to him, the Department may revoke the direction.

(4) The Department may also revoke the direction if—
(a) it is satisfied that the direction was given in ignorance of some material fact or was based on a mistake as to some material fact; and
(b) it considers that but for its ignorance or mistake it would not have determined that failure to receive income support would result in severe hardship.

(5) In this section "period" includes—
(a) a period of a determinate length;
(b) a period defined by reference to the happening of a future event; and
(c) a period of a determinate length but subject to earlier determination upon the happening of a future event.

DEFINITIONS
"Department": s.170.
"period": subs. (5).

GENERAL NOTE
As a general rule, entitlement to income support does not arise until a person attains the age of 18 (s.123(1)(a)). This section, however, enables some 16- and 17-year-olds to qualify for benefit. This is only possible where both (i) the individual in question does not fall into one of the special categories of 16- and 17-year-olds prescribed in regulations under s.124(1)(a) and (ii) severe hardship will result unless income support is paid. Decisions on awards of benefit under this section are made in the name of the Department, rather than by an adjudication officer. There is therefore no right of appeal to a SSAT. Even if both subs. (1)(a) and (b) are satisfied, the Department retains a discretion as to whether to make an award. Awards may be for a fixed period or until the happening of some future event and may be revoked if there is a change in circumstances (subss. (2)–(5)).

Trade disputes

125.—(1) This section applies to a person, other than a child or a person of a prescribed description—
(a) who is disqualified under section 27 above for receiving unemployment benefit; or
(b) who would be so disqualified if otherwise entitled to that benefit,
except during any period shown by the person to be a period of incapacity for work by reason of disease or bodily or mental disablement or to be within the maternity period.

(2) In subsection (1) above "the maternity period" means the period commencing at the beginning of the 6th week before the expected week of

confinement and ending at the end of the 7th week after the week in which confinement takes place.

(3) For the purpose of calculating income support—

(a) so long as this section applies to a person who is not a member of a family, the applicable amount shall be disregarded;

(b) so long as it applies to a person who is a member of a family but is not a member of a married or unmarried couple, the portion of the applicable amount which is included in respect of him shall be disregarded;

(c) so long as it applies to one of the members of a married or unmarried couple—

(i) if the applicable amount consists only of an amount in respect of them, it shall be reduced to one-half; and

(ii) if it includes other amounts, the portion of it which is included in respect of them shall be reduced to one-half and any further portion of it which is included in respect of the member of the couple to whom this section applies shall be disregarded;

(d) so long as it applies to both the members of a married or unmarried couple—

(i) if neither of them is responsible for a child or person of a prescribed description who is a member of the same household, the applicable amount shall be disregarded; and

(ii) in any other case, the portion of the applicable amount which is included in respect of them and any further portion of it which is included in respect of either of them shall be disregarded.

(4) Where a reduction under subsection (3)(c) above would not produce a sum which is a multiple of 5p, the reduction shall be to the nearest lower sum which is such a multiple.

(5) Where this section applies to a person for any period, then, except so far as regulations provide otherwise—

(a) in calculating the entitlement to income support of that person or a member of his family the following shall be treated as his income and shall not be disregarded—

(i) any payment which he or a member of his family receives or is entitled to obtain by reason of the person to whom this section applies being without employment for that period; and

(ii) without prejudice to the generality of sub-paragraph (i) above, any amount which becomes or would on an application duly made become available to him in that period by way of repayment of income tax deducted from his emoluments in pursuance of section 203 of the Income and Corporation Taxes Act 1988 (PAYE); and

(b) any payment by way of income support for that period or any part of it which apart from this paragraph would be made to him, or to a person whose applicable amount is aggregated with his—

(i) shall not be made if the weekly rate of payment is equal to or less than the relevant sum; or

(ii) if it is more than the relevant sum, shall be at a weekly rate equal to the difference.

(6) In respect of any period less than a week, subsection (5) above shall have effect subject to such modifications as may be prescribed.

(7) Subject to subsection (8) below, "the relevant sum" for the purposes of subsection (5) above shall be £22.50.

(8) If an order under section 132 of the Administration Act (annual uprating) has the effect of increasing payments of income support, from the time when the order comes into operation there shall be substituted, in subsection (5)(b) above, for the references to the sum for the time being mentioned in it references to a sum arrived at by—

(a) increasing that sum by the percentage by which the personal allowance under paragraph 1(1) of Part I of Schedule 2 to the Income Support (General) Regulations (Northern Ireland) 1987 for a single person aged not less than 25 has been increased by the order; and

(b) if the sum as so increased is not a multiple of 50p, disregarding the remainder if it is 25p and, if it is not, rounding it up or down to the nearest 50p,

and the order shall state the substituted sum.

DEFINITIONS
"the Administration Act": s.170.
"child": s.133(1).
"family": s.133(1).
"married couple": s.133(1).
"maternity period": subs. (2).
"prescribed": s.133(1).
"relevant sum": subs. (7).
"unmarried couple": s.133(1).

GENERAL NOTE
This section lays down the rules relating to income support where the claimant is disqualified for unemployment benefit under s.27 (or would be so disqualified if otherwise entitled) by reason of involvement in a trade dispute. The section only comes into play once the s.27 question has been determined. The income support trade dispute rule does not apply if the claimant is incapable of work or within the maternity period (proviso to subs. (1)).

The two principal modifications to income support entitlement where this section applies relate to the calculation of the relevant applicable amount (subs. (3)) and to the assessment of the claimant's income (subs. (5)). In particular, the applicable amounts to which claimants are entitled are much reduced. Furthermore, claimants caught by the operation of this rule are assumed to receive the "relevant sum" by way of strike pay, irrespective of whether the person is on strike (as opposed to locked-out or laid off), is a member of a union or whether his union offers strike pay. For 1992/93 the "relevant sum" is £22.50 per week. See further Mesher.

Effect of return to work

126. If a person returns to work with the same employer after a period during which section 125 above applies to him, and whether or not his return is before the end of any stoppage of work in relation to which he is or would be disqualified for receiving unemployment benefit—

(a) that section shall cease to apply to him at the commencement of the day on which he returns to work; and

(b) until the end of the period of 15 days beginning with that day, section 123(1) above shall have effect in relation to him as if the following paragraph were substituted for paragraph (c)—
   "(c) in the case of a member of a married or unmarried couple, the other member is not engaged in remunerative work; and"; and

(c) any sum paid by way of income support for that period of 15 days to him or, where he is a member of a married or unmarried couple, to the other member of that couple, shall be recoverable in accordance with the regulations from the person to whom it was paid or from any prescribed person or, where the person to whom it was paid is a member of a married or unmarried couple, from the other member of the couple.

DEFINITIONS
"married couple": s.133(1).
"prescribed": s.133(1).
"unmarried couple": s.133(1).

GENERAL NOTE
This section enables income support to be paid for the first 15 days following a return to work

after a trade dispute. In such cases benefit would otherwise be precluded by virtue of s.123(1)(c).

Family credit

Family credit

127.—(1) Subject to regulations under section 5(1)(a) of the Administration Act, a person in Northern Ireland is entitled to family credit if, when the claim for it is made or is treated as made—

    (a) his income—

        (i) does not exceed the amount which is the applicable amount at such date as may be prescribed; or

        (ii) exceeds it, but only by such an amount that there is an amount remaining if the deduction for which subsection (2)(b) below provides is made;

    (b) he or, if he is a member of a married or unmarried couple, he or the other member of the couple, is engaged and normally engaged in remunerative work;

    (c) except in such circumstances as may be prescribed, neither he nor any member of his family is entitled to a disability working allowance; and

    (d) he or, if he is a member of a married or unmarried couple, he or the other member, is responsible for a member of the same household who is a child or a person of a prescribed description.

(2) Where a person is entitled to family credit, then—

    (a) if his income does not exceed the amount which is the applicable amount at the date prescribed under subsection (1)(a)(i) above, the amount of the family credit shall be the amount which is the appropriate maximum family credit in his case; and

    (b) if his income exceeds the amount which is the applicable amount at that date, the amount of the family credit shall be what remains after the deduction from the appropriate maximum family credit of a prescribed percentage of the excess of his income over the applicable amount.

(3) Family credit shall be payable for a period of 26 weeks or such other period as may be prescribed and, subject to regulations, an award of family credit and the rate at which it is payable shall not be affected by any change of circumstances during that period or by any order under section 132 of the Administration Act.

(4) Regulations may provide that an award of family credit shall terminate—

    (a) if a person who was a member of the family at the date of the claim becomes a member of another family and some member of that family is entitled to family credit; or

    (b) if income support or a disability working allowance becomes payable in respect of a person who was a member of the family at the date of the claim for family credit.

(5) Regulations shall prescribe the manner in which the appropriate maximum family credit is to be determined in any case.

(6) The provisions of this Act relating to family credit apply in relation to persons employed by or under the Crown as they apply in relation to persons employed otherwise than by or under the Crown.

DEFINITIONS

    "the Administration Act": s.170.

    "child": s.133(1).

    "family": s.133(1).

    "married couple": s.133(1).

    "Northern Ireland": s.168.

"prescribed": s.133(1).
"unmarried couple": s.133(1).

GENERAL NOTE
   This section establishes the framework for entitlement to family credit. The basic conditions are laid down in subs. (1) and amplified by the Family Credit (General) Regulations (Northern Ireland) 1987 (S.I. 1987 No. 463).
   Family credit is payable to single claimants or couples who are responsible for a child or children (subs. (1)(d)). Claimants (or their partners) must also be engaged and normally engaged in remunerative work (the threshold for which is 16 hours per week from April 7, 1992: Family Credit (General) Amendment Regulations (Northern Ireland) 1991 (S.I. 1991 No. 326)).
   As with the other income-related benefits, determination of the rate of benefit in any given case depends on the relationship between the claimant's income and his or her applicable amount. Maximum family credit is payable where the claimant's income (as aggregated with the rest of his or her family) does not exceed the relevant applicable amount (subss. (1)(a)(i) and (2)(a)). Where income exceeds the applicable amount, the maximum family credit payable is reduced by a percentage of the excess (currently 70 per cent.) (subs. (1)(a)(ii) and (2)(b)). There is also a capital limit (at present £8,000) laid down in regulations under s.130(1).
   Once an award of family credit is made, it will run for 26 weeks, regardless of any uprating orders issued during that time or (as a general rule) any changes in circumstances (subs. (3)). Subsection (4) enables regulations to be made preventing duplication of awards of family credit or where a member of the family starts to receive income support or disability working allowance.

Disability working allowance

Disability working allowance

   128.—(1) A person in Northern Ireland who has attained the age of 16 and qualifies under subsection (2) below is entitled to a disability working allowance if, when the claim for it is made or is treated as made—
   (a) he is engaged and normally engaged in remunerative work;
   (b) he has a physical or mental disability which puts him at a disadvantage in getting a job;
   (c) his income—
      (i) does not exceed the amount which is the applicable amount at such date as may be prescribed; or
      (ii) exceeds it, but only by such an amount that there is an amount remaining if the deduction for which subsection (5)(b) below provides is made; and
   (d) except in such circumstances as may be prescribed, neither he nor, if he has a family, any member of it, is entitled to family credit.
   (2) Subject to subsection (4) below, a person qualifies under this sub-section if—
   (a) for one or more of the 56 days immediately preceding the date when the claim for a disability working allowance is made or is treated as made there was payable to him one or more of the following—
      (i) an invalidity pension under section 33, 40 or 41 above;
      (ii) a severe disablement allowance;
      (iii) income support or housing benefit,
   or a corresponding benefit under any statutory provision having effect in Great Britain;
   (b) when the claim for a disability working allowance is made or is treated as made, there is payable to him one or more of the following—
      (i) an attendance allowance;
      (ii) a disability living allowance;
      (iii) an increase of disablement pension under section 104 above;
      (iv) an analogous pension increase under a war pension scheme or the industrial injuries regulations;

or a corresponding benefit under any statutory provision having effect in Great Britain; or

(c) when the claim for a disability working allowance is made or is treated as made, he has an invalid carriage or other vehicle provided under Article 30(1) of the Health and Personal Social Services (Northern Ireland) Order 1972 or provided by the Secretary of State under section 5(2)(a) of the National Health Service Act 1977 and Schedule 2 to that Act or under section 46 of the National Health Service (Scotland) Act 1978.

(3) For the purposes of subsection (1) above a person has a disability which puts him at a disadvantage in getting a job only if he satisfies prescribed conditions, or prescribed circumstances exist in relation to him.

(4) If the only benefit mentioned in paragraph (a) of subsection (2) above which is payable to a person as there mentioned is—

(a) a benefit mentioned in sub-paragraph (iii) of that paragraph; or

(b) a corresponding benefit under any statutory provision having effect in Great Britain,

he only qualifies under that subsection in prescribed circumstances.

(5) Where a person is entitled to a disability working allowance, then—

(a) if his income does not exceed the amount which is the applicable amount at the date prescribed under subsection (1)(c)(i) above, the amount of the disability working allowance shall be the amount which is the appropriate maximum disability working allowance in his case; and

(b) if his income exceeds that amount, the amount of the disability working allowance shall be what remains after the deduction from the appropriate maximum disability working allowance of a prescribed percentage of the excess of his income over that amount.

(6) A disability working allowance shall be payable for a period of 26 weeks or such other period as may be prescribed and, subject to regulations, an award of a disability working allowance and the rate at which it is payable shall not be affected by any change of circumstances during that period or by any order under section 132 of the Administration Act.

(7) Regulations may provide that an award of a disability working allowance to a person shall terminate if—

(a) a disability working allowance becomes payable in respect of some other person who was a member of his family at the date of his claim for a disability working allowance; or

(b) income support or family credit becomes payable in respect of a person who was a member of the family at that date.

(8) Regulations shall prescribe the manner in which the appropriate maximum disability working allowance is to be determined in any case.

(9) The provisions of this Act relating to disability working allowance apply in relation to persons employed by or under the Crown as they apply in relation to persons employed otherwise than by or under the Crown.

DEFINITIONS

"the Administration Act": s.170.
"Department": s.170.
"family": s.133(1).
"industrial injuries scheme": s.133(1).
"Northern Ireland": s.168.
"prescribed": s.133(1).
"war pension scheme": s.133(1).

GENERAL NOTE

Disability working allowance was introduced by the DLADWAO 1991 and first became payable in April 1992. It was devised to tackle a longstanding weakness of the social security scheme, namely the absence of any partial incapacity benefit. The main income replacement benefit for people who are incapable of work is invalidity benefit, a contributory benefit paid under s.34 above. Invalidity benefit is payable only to people who are incapable of all work, although claimants may engage in therapeutic work and earn up to £39 per week (at 1991–92 rates) without losing benefit (Social Security (Unemployment, Sickness and Invalidity Benefit) Regulations (Northern Ireland) 1984 (S.I. 1984 No. 245), reg. 3). The Way Ahead announced a new benefit, disability employment credit, designed along the same lines as family credit as a work-incentive benefit, except that it would be available to single disabled people and couples without children. This would be for disabled people who were only partially incapable for work and would involve a tapered withdrawal of benefit as income increased. The DLADWAO 1991 retitled this benefit disability working allowance (DWA).

DWA was designed to be cost-neutral in the long term. As is inevitable with a means-tested benefit, not all eligible claimants will be better off on DWA (although most will be). A relatively small group of people will be worse off if they take a low-paid job supplemented by DWA. This consists of some claimants with mortgages and others with children whose total income takes them just above income support levels with consequential loss of free school meals. Invalidity benefit claimants will be worse off if they have a large extra pension or other income or capital, or a partner in work, or if they are taking advantage of the therapeutic earnings rule.

The basic conditions for entitlement to DWA are set out in subs. (1) as amplified by the Disability Working Allowance (General) Regulations (Northern Ireland) 1992 (S.I. 1992 No. 78). They are closely modelled on those for family credit. Where a person has a choice between claiming either of these benefits, DWA will generally be the better option as it includes an amount equivalent to a single person's income support disability premium. However, recipients of DWA are not automatically exempt from prescription charges and charges for dental and optical services. Nor does DWA act as a passport for reimbursement of fares to hospital. These exemptions do apply to family-credit claimants. DWA claimants may still qualify under the low-income scheme operated by the DHSS (Travelling Expenses and Remission of Charges) Regulations (Northern Ireland) 1988 (S.I. 1988 No. 150)).

A further and important condition of eligibility is that the claimant satisfies the qualifying benefits criterion in subs. (2). This means that many people partially capable of work are not eligible for DWA because they do not qualify for one of these passporting benefits.

For rules governing initial and repeat claims, see SSA(N.I.)A 1992, s.9, and for the special review and appeals procedure, see ss.28–33. See generally Rowland.

Subs. (1)

This subsection specifies the conditions of entitlement to DWA and is closely modelled on the analogous provision for family credit (s.127). The preliminary conditions are that the claimant is in Northern Ireland, is aged 16 years or more and meets the qualifying criteria set out in subs. (2) below. The four main conditions are then:

(a) *He is engaged and normally engaged in remunerative work.* This is defined by regulations as 16 hours a week, which also represents the starting point for most employment protection rights. Disabled people working fewer than 16 hours a week will still be able to claim income support with the higher rate of disregard and some claimants may be eligible to take advantage of the therapeutic earnings rule in relation to invalidity benefit or severe disablement allowance.

The fact that this condition is expressed in the present tense means that disabled people are not able to make a claim in advance of starting work, which may act as a disincentive. Assurances have been given that such claims are to be given the highest priority, the aim being to clear the vast majority within five days (*per* Mr N. Scott, Standing Committee E, col. 190, January 17, 1991).

(b) *He has a physical or mental disability which puts him at a disadvantage in getting a job.* This concept is defined in regulations made under subs. (3) below. This condition is in addition to the qualifying benefits condition under subs. (2) which acts to passport the claimant to DWA.

(c) *His income — ....* The claimant's income must not exceed the prescribed applicable amount, or exceed it only by such an amount that there is an amount remaining after the application of the income taper prescribed under s.128(5)(b). Where income does not exceed the applicable amount, the maximum level of DWA will be awarded, depending on the composition of the family. Where income exceeds the applicable amount, benefit will be reduced by a proportion of the claimant's income above the applicable amount. There is also a capital limit (currently £16,000) laid down in regulations under s.130(1).

(d) *Except in such circumstances as may be prescribed.* Neither the claimant nor a member of his family must be entitled to family credit.

Subs. (2)

This subsection defines the qualifying benefit criterion for entitlement to DWA. The claimant must satisfy one of the conditions set out in subs. (2)(a)–(c). The advantage of this extra condition is that it makes the traditional medical examination for incapacity benefits unnecessary, and hence has permitted the streamlining of the adjudication arrangements. As with DLA, there is an emphasis on self-assessment in claiming. The chief disadvantage is that many disabled people are not eligible for DWA because they do not qualify for one of the benefits listed in this subsection.

Subs. (2)(a)

This means that, in at least one of the eight weeks immediately before the date of claim, invalidity benefit, severe disablement allowance, income support, or housing benefit must have been payable to the claimant. The choice of eight weeks rather than any longer period is directly related to the linking rule for incapacity benefits. Extra conditions so far as those in receipt of the last two benefits are specified in regulations made under subs. (4) below. These provide that the claimant must qualify for the disability premium for one of these benefits.

Subs. (2)(b)

This provides a second route to qualifying: at the point of claim attendance allowance, DLA, constant attendance allowance or an analogous pension increase under a war pension or industrial injuries scheme must be payable to the claimant. In subs. (2)(b)(ii) the words "a mobility allowance under section 37A of the 1975 Act" should be substituted in respect of claims made (or treated as made) before the first day for which disability living allowance became payable (April 6, 1992): see SS(CP)(N.I.)A 1992, Sched. 3, para. 21.

Subs. (2)(c)

The third and final possible qualifying condition is that the claimant has an invalid carriage or other vehicle (instead of the mobility component to DLA).

Subs. (3)

This enabling provision allows the Department to prescribe in regulations the circumstances in which a person meets the condition set out in subs. (1)(b) above. The Disability Working Allowance (General) Regulations (Northern Ireland) 1992 (S.I. 1992 No. 78) list a range of relevant physical and mental disabilities.

Subs. (4)

See annotations to subs. (2)(a) above.

Subs. (5)

This specifies the method for calculating DWA and follows the parallel provision for family credit (s.127(2)).

Subs. (6)

This provides that DWA is to be awarded for a fixed period of 26 weeks. Subject to exceptions to be prescribed, the award is not affected by changes in the claimant's circumstances or any uprating order under SSA(N.I.)A 1992, s.132. The same rules govern the family credit scheme.

Housing benefit

Housing benefit

129.—(1) A person is entitled to housing benefit if—

(a) he is liable to make payments in respect of a dwelling in Northern Ireland which he occupies as his home;

(b) there is an appropriate maximum housing benefit in his case; and

(c) either—

(i) he has no income or his income does not exceed the applicable amount; or

(ii) his income exceeds that amount, but only by so much that there is an amount remaining if the deduction for which subsection (3)(b) below provides is made.

(2) In subsection (1) above "payments in respect of a dwelling" means such payments as may be prescribed, but the power to prescribe payments does not include power to prescribe mortgage payments.

(3) Where a person is entitled to housing benefit, then—

(a) if he has no income or his income does not exceed the applicable amount, the amount of the housing benefit shall be the amount which is the appropriate maximum housing benefit in his case; and

(b) if his income exceeds the applicable amount, the amount of the housing benefit shall be what remains after the deduction from the appropriate maximum housing benefit of prescribed percentages of the excess of his income over the applicable amount.

(4) Regulations shall prescribe the manner in which the appropriate maximum housing benefit is to be determined in any case.

DEFINITIONS
"dwelling": s.133(1).
"the Executive": s.133.
"Northern Ireland": s.168.
"payments in respect of a dwelling": subs. (2).
"prescribed": s.133(1).

GENERAL NOTE
This section establishes the framework for entitlement to housing benefit, which is administered by the Executive and not the DHSS. The basic conditions are laid down in subs. (1) and amplified by the Housing Benefit (General) Regulations (Northern Ireland) 1987 (S.I. 1987 No. 461) (see Findlay and Ward for the Great Britain equivalents, *i.e.* the Housing Benefit (General) Regulations 1987 (S.I. 1987 No. 1971)). As with the other income-related benefits, determination of the rate of benefit in any given case depends on the relationship between the claimant's income and his or her applicable amount. Individuals who have no income, or income not in excess of the applicable amount, receive the maximum housing benefit appropriate to their situation (subss. (1)(c)(i) and (3)(a)). Claimants with more income than their applicable amount receive a proportion of their maximum entitlement after the application of a taper (subss. (1)(c)(ii) and (3)(b)). There is also a capital limit (currently £16,000) laid down in regulations under s.130(1).

Housing benefit is payable in respect of prescribed categories of payments in respect of dwellings, but not for mortgage payments (subs. (2)). Assistance with mortgage payments is only available under the income support scheme (Income Support (General) Regulations (Northern Ireland) 1987 (S.I. 1987 No. 459), Sched. 3).

Financial and administrative arrangements for housing benefit are provided for by SSA(N.I.)A 1992, Pt. VIII (ss.126–128).

General

Exclusions from benefit

130.—(1) No person shall be entitled to an income-related benefit if his capital or a prescribed part of it exceeds the prescribed amount.

(2) Except in prescribed circumstances the entitlement of one member of a family to any one income-related benefit excludes entitlement to that benefit for any other member for the same period.

(3) Where the amount of any income-related benefit would be less than a prescribed amount, it shall not be payable except in prescribed circumstances.

DEFINITIONS
"family": s.133(1).
"income-related benefit": s.122(1).
"prescribed": s.133(1).

GENERAL NOTE
The actual maximum capital limits (subs. (1)) for the income-related benefits are laid down in

regulations. For 1992/93 they are £8,000 (income support and family credit) and £16,000 (disability working allowance and housing benefit). Generally, where one member of a family receives a benefit listed in s.122(1), other members of the family are precluded from receiving the same benefit for the same period (subs. (2)). Subsection (3) allows for regulations to specify that *de minimis* entitlements to benefit are not to be payable (*e.g.* less than 50p per week in the case of family credit: Social Security (Claims and Payments) Regulations (Northern Ireland) 1987 (S.I. 1987 No. 465), reg. 27(2)).

The applicable amount

131.—(1) The applicable amount, in relation to any income-related benefit, shall be such amount or the aggregate of such amounts as may be prescribed in relation to that benefit.

(2) The power to prescribe applicable amounts conferred by subsection (1) above includes power to prescribe nil as an applicable amount.

(3) In prescribing, for the purposes of income support, amounts under subsection (1) above in respect of accommodation in any area for qualifying persons in cases where prescribed conditions are fulfilled, the Department shall take into account—

(a) the amounts which the Department has agreed to pay, and

(b) information provided by the Board or other prescribed persons with respect to the amounts which the Board or such persons have agreed to pay,

for the provision of accommodation in relevant premises in that area.

(4) In subsection (3) above—

"accommodation" includes any board or care;

"the Board" means the Health and Social Services Board for that area;

"qualifying persons" means persons who are ordinarily resident in relevant premises and the Department may by regulations prescribe the circumstances in which persons are to be treated as being ordinarily resident in relevant premises for the purposes of this subsection;

"relevant premises" means subject to such exemptions as may be prescribed—

(a) nursing homes in respect of which a person is registered under section 1 of the Nursing Homes and Nursing Agencies Act (Northern Ireland) 1971;

(b) homes for persons in need in respect of which a person is registered under Article 35 of, and Schedule 5 to, the Health and Personal Social Services (Northern Ireland) Order 1972.

(5) In relation to income support and housing benefit, the applicable amount for a severely disabled person shall include an amount in respect of his being a severely disabled person.

(6) Regulations may specify circumstances in which persons are to be treated as being or as not being severely disabled.

DEFINITIONS

"accommodation": subs. (4).
"Board": subs. (4).
"Department": s.170.
"income-related benefit": s.122(1).
"prescribed": s.133(1).
"qualifying person": subs. (4).
"relevant premises": subs. (4).

GENERAL NOTE

Subss. (1) and (2)
The applicable amount is a crucial factor in determining the rate of entitlement to an income-related benefit (see, *e.g.* s.123(4)). The applicable amounts are laid down in regulations

and uprated each year. See, *e.g.* Income Support (General) Regulations (Northern Ireland) 1987 (S.I. 1987 No. 459), Pt. IV and Sched. 2.

Subss. (3) and (4)
   These provisions, first enacted by SS(N.I.)O 1990, art. 11, are concerned with the Government's changes in community care. When those reforms are implemented (in April 1993) new residents in residential care and nursing homes will receive financial support from the Board, who will negotiate prices and contracts with care suppliers. Existing residents will still be supported by income support, so the weekly limits set out in Sched. 4 of the Income Support (General) Regulations (Northern Ireland) 1987 (S.I. 1987 No. 459) will remain important. Subsection (3) requires the Department to take into account information supplied by the Board about price levels. There is no statutory obligation to maintain the income support limits in line with market prices.
   Note the transitory modification in SS(CP)(N.I.)A 1992, Sched. 4, para. 4.

Subss. (5) and (6)
   These provisions, originally inserted in the SSO 1986 by the House of Lords against the wishes of the Government, were the subject of the controversial decision in *Chief Adjudication Officer and Secretary of State for Social Security* v. *Foster* [1992] 1 Q.B. 31. The majority of the Court of Appeal (Lord Donaldson M.R. dissenting) held that the conditions laid down for the receipt of the severe disability premium for income support were *intra vires* of these provisions inasmuch as they entitled the Secretary of State to specify requirements extraneous to the individual's disability (*e.g.* the presence of a non-dependant in the claimant's household). See also Income Support (General) Regulations (Northern Ireland) 1987 (S.I. 1987 No. 459), Sched. 2, para. 13. The English Court of Appeal also held unanimously that a Social Security Commissioner (and therefore a SSAT or an AO) had no power to determine the *vires* of such regulations. An appeal in this case is expected to be heard by the House of Lords in the latter part of 1992.

Income and capital

132.—(1) Where a person claiming an income-related benefit is a member of a family, the income and capital of any member of that family shall, except in prescribed circumstances, be treated as the income and capital of that person.
   (2) Regulations may provide that capital not exceeding the amount prescribed under section 130(1) above but exceeding a prescribed lower amount shall be treated, to a prescribed extent, as if it were income of a prescribed amount.
   (3) Income and capital shall be calculated or estimated in such manner as may be prescribed.
   (4) Circumstances may be prescribed in which—
   (a) a person is treated as possessing capital or income which he does not possess;
   (b) capital or income which a person does possess is to be disregarded;
   (c) income is to be treated as capital;
   (d) capital is to be treated as income.

DEFINITIONS
   "Department": see s.170.
   "family": s.133(1).
   "income-related benefit": s.122(1).
   "prescribed": s.133(1).

GENERAL NOTE
   The general rule for income-related benefits is that income and capital resources belonging to family members are aggregated (subs. (1)). The principal exceptions prescribed under the regulations relate to children and young persons. Subsection (2) enables regulations to provide that capital between the lower limit (£3,000 for 1992/93) and the appropriate maximum limit (£8,000 or £16,000: see General Note to s.130) shall be assumed to generate a certain tariff income. Subsections (3)–(5) give the Department sweeping powers to prescribe how resources

are to be calculated, including the remarkable powers to deem income to be capital and vice versa (sub-paras. (c) and (d)).

Interpretation of Part VII and supplementary provisions

133.—(1) In this Part of this Act—
"child" means a person under the age of 16;
"the Executive" means the Northern Ireland Housing Executive;
"family" means—
> (a) a married or unmarried couple;
> (b) a married or unmarried couple and a member of the same household for whom one of them is or both are responsible and who is a child or a person of a prescribed description;
> (c) except in prescribed circumstances, a person who is not a member of a married or unmarried couple and a member of the same household for whom that person is responsible and who is a child or a person of a prescribed description;

"industrial injuries regulations" means the regulations made under Schedule 8 to this Act or section 150 of the 1975 Act or under the Old Cases Act;
"married couple" means a man and woman who are married to each other and are members of the same household;
"prescribed" means specified in or determined in accordance with regulations;
"unmarried couple" means a man and woman who are not married to each other but are living together as husband and wife otherwise than in prescribed circumstances;
"war pension scheme" means a scheme under which war pensions (as defined in section 25(4) of the Social Security Act 1989) are provided.

(2) Regulations may make provision for the purposes of this Part of this Act—
> (a) as to circumstances in which a person is to be treated as being or not being in Northern Ireland;
> (b) continuing a person's entitlement to benefit during periods of temporary absence from Northern Ireland;
> (c) as to what is or is not to be treated as remunerative work or as employment;
> (d) as to circumstances in which a person is or is not to be treated as—
> > (i) engaged or normally engaged in remunerative work;
> > (ii) available for employment; or
> > (iii) actively seeking employment;
> (e) as to what is or is not to be treated as relevant education;
> (f) as to circumstances in which a person is or is not to be treated as receiving relevant education;
> (g) specifying the descriptions of pension increases under war pension schemes or the industrial injuries regulations that are analogous to the benefits mentioned in section 128(2)(b)(i) to (iii) above;
> (h) as to circumstances in which a person is or is not to be treated as occupying a dwelling as his home;
> (i) for treating any person who is liable to make payments in respect of a dwelling as if he were not so liable;
> (j) for treating any person who is not liable to make payments in respect of a dwelling as if he were so liable;
> (k) for treating as included in a dwelling any land used for the purposes of the dwelling;
> (l) as to circumstances in which persons are to be treated as being or not being members of the same household;

(m) as to circumstances in which one person is to be treated as responsible or not responsible for another.

DEFINITIONS
"the 1975 Act": s.170.
"Great Britain Contributions and Benefit Act": s.170.
"Northern Ireland": s.168.
"the Old Cases Act": s.170.

GENERAL NOTE
This section includes a number of important definitions for the purposes of the income-related benefits.
Child. Although the age of majority is 18, a child is defined as a person under the age of 16. See also the definition of young person in the Income Support (General) Regulations (Northern Ireland) 1987 (S.I. 1987 No. 459), reg. 14.
Family. This means, in other words, married and unmarried couples, with or without a child or children, and single claimants with a child or children. As to the test of membership of a household and children, see, *e.g. England* v. *Secretary of State for Social Services* (1982) 3 F.L.R. 222. There are deeming rules in the various sets of regulations.
Married couple. The key point of this definition is the concept of household. It is quite possible to have more than one household in any one house: see *R(SB) 4/83*, and the unreported Northern Ireland decision [1989] 7 BNLI 153 and matrimonial cases such as *Fuller* v. *Fuller* [1973] 1 W.L.R. 730.
Unmarried couple. The concept of living together as husband and wife (sometimes known as the cohabitation rule) gives rise to some of the most difficult issues which SSATs have to determine. The rule is important in two main types of case. First, in relation to the income-related benefits, resources are aggregated within a family unit, and the applicable amount for a couple is less than twice that for a single claimant. Secondly, widow's benefits (ss.36–38) are not payable so long as a widow is living together with a man as husband and wife. The same principles should apply as between income support and widow's benefits (*R(SB) 17/81* and *R(G) 3/81*) and between the income-related benefits themselves (*R.* v. *Penwith District Council Housing Benefits Review Board*, ex p. *Menear* (1992) 24 H.L.R. 114).
According to *R(G) 3/71*, three main factors have to be considered in determining whether a man and woman are living together as husband and wife: "(1) their relationship in relation to sex; (2) their relationship in relation to money; (3) their general relationship. Although all three are as a rule relevant, no single one of them is necessarily conclusive". These factors were amplified in the Supplementary Benefit Handbook for Northern Ireland (1985, DHSS), and an earlier version of the corresponding Great Britain official guidelines was approved in *Crake* v. *Supplementary Benefits Commission*; *Butterworth* v. *Same* [1982] 1 All E.R. 498. These six pointers have remained the basis of decision-making by AOs and SSATs in this area. The factors are: (1) members of the same household; (2) stability; (3) financial support; (4) sexual relationship; (5) children; and (6) public acknowledgment.
It is not necessary that all six aspects should be found to exist in any given situation. For example, a couple may be regarded as living together as husband and wife even though they have no children and keep their own names, bank accounts, etc. However, the parties must in any event be living in the same household. This concept is in itself by no means unproblematic (see *R(SB) 30/83*, *R(SB) 8/85* and *R(SB) 19/85*).
The other factors to be considered are equally not without difficulty. For example, in deciding whether there is a stable relationship, time is not the only matter to be considered. The true nature of the relationship must also be explored, as the parties may have a stable relationship as landlady and lodger, or as two members of the opposite sex living together for mutual support, rather than specifically as husband and wife. See *Crake (supra)*, *Robson* v. *Secretary of State for Social Services* (1982) 3 F.L.R. 232), *Kaur* v. *Secretary of State for Social Services* (1982) 3 F.L.R. 237, *R(SB) 17/81* and *R(SB) 35/85*.

PART VIII

THE SOCIAL FUND

Payments out of the social fund

134.—(1) Payments may be made out of the social fund, in accordance with this Part of this Act—

(a) of prescribed amounts, whether in respect of prescribed items or otherwise, to meet, in prescribed circumstances, maternity expenses and funeral expenses; and

(b) to meet other needs in accordance with directions given or guidance issued by the Department.

(2) Payments may also be made out of that fund, in accordance with this Part of this Act, of a prescribed amount or a number of prescribed amounts to prescribed descriptions of persons, in prescribed circumstances to meet expenses for heating which appear to the Department to have been or to be likely to be incurred in cold weather.

(3) The power to make a payment out of the social fund such as is mentioned in subsection (1)(b) above may be exercised by making a payment to a third party with a view to the third party providing, or arranging for the provision of, goods or services for the applicant.

(4) In this section "prescribed" means specified in or determined in accordance with regulations.

DEFINITIONS
    "the Department": s.170.
    "prescribed": subs. (4).

GENERAL NOTE
    The introduction of the social fund in April 1988 was one of the most controversial aspects of the reform of the social security scheme instigated by the Fowler Review. The previous system of regulation-based single payments and urgent needs payments was abandoned when income support superseded supplementary benefit. In its place the social fund was established to provide loans and grants to those unable to finance certain purchases or costs out of the ordinary weekly rate of benefit. On the financial arrangements for the social fund, see SSA(N.I.)A 1992, ss.146–8.
    The social fund falls into two distinct parts. First, there is a regulation-based system of payments for maternity, funeral and cold-weather payments (subss. (1)(a) and (2)). These payments are akin to single payments under the pre-1988 scheme in that entitlement is a matter of right once the conditions in the regulations have been satisfied. Decisions under this part of the social fund are made by AOs and can be challenged on appeal before a SSAT. There is a further right of appeal (with leave and on a point of law only) in the ordinary way to a Social Security Commissioner.
    The bulk of social fund payments fall into the second category: the discretionary part of the social fund. These take the form of budgeting loans, crisis loans and community care grants (subs. (1)(b) and the Social Fund Manual). On the necessity for applications for such payments to be in the prescribed form, see SSA(N.I.)A 1992, s.10. Social fund officers, and not adjudication officers, decide whether to grant applications for discretionary payments from the social fund. In reaching their decisions, social fund officers must have regard to all the circumstances of the case and in particular the factors listed in s.136(1). Furthermore, social fund officers must follow the Department's directions and must take account of any guidance issued by the Department (s.136(2)). In particular, the discretionary part of the social fund is subject to budgetary control (s.136(3)). Social fund officers' decisions cannot be appealed to a SSAT; instead there is the opportunity for an internal review to be carried out. If the applicant remains dissatisfied, a further review may be conducted by a social fund inspector: see SSA(N.I.)A 1992, s.64. The only recourse to the courts is by way of judicial review.

Subs. (1)(a)
    The regulation-based part of the social fund is not subject to any budgetary limit. Decisions are made by AOs with the normal right of appeal to a SSAT. Details of entitlement are provided in the Social Fund Maternity and Funeral Expenses (General) Regulations (Northern Ireland) 1987 (S.I. 1987 No. 150). See Mesher on the Great Britain equivalents, *i.e.* Social Fund (Maternity and Funeral Expenses) (General) Regulations 1987 (S.I. 1987 No. 481). Note also that non-discretionary payments may also be made for cold-weather costs (subs. (2)).

Subs. (1)(b)
    This subsection empowers the Department (Secretary of State in Great Britain) to issue directions and guidance in connection with the discretionary part of the social fund. The ambit of the equivalent Great Britain provision was considered in *R.* v. *Secretary of State for Social Security,* ex p. *Stitt*; *R.* v. *Social Security Fund Inspector,* ex p. *Sherwin*; *R.* v. *Same*; ex p.

Roberts [1991] C.O.D. 68 and in *R.* v. *Secretary of State for Social Services,* ex p. *Stitt*; *R.* v. *Same*, ex p. *Healey*; *R.* v. *Social Fund Inspector,* ex p. *Ellison, The Times,* December 19, 1991. In *ex p. Stitt* [1991] C.O.D. 68 both the Divisional Court and the Court of Appeal held that a direction excluding community care grants from the social fund for domestic assistance were validly made. The Divisional Court and Purchas L.J. in the Court of Appeal concluded that such directions could be made in exercise of the Secretary of State's control and management functions (see now the Great Britain SSAA 1992, s.167(2), and s.146(2) of the Northern Ireland SSAA 1992). Butler-Sloss L.J. and Sir Patrick Connor held that the power arose under what is now s.138(1)(b) and s.140(2) of the Great Britain SSAA 1992 (s.134(1)(b) and s.136(2) of the Northern Ireland SSAA 1992). All the members of the Court of Appeal expressed their surprise at the breadth of the powers granted to the Secretary of State.

Following this decision, the Court of Appeal in *ex p. Healey* held that it was not irrational for the Secretary of State to exclude from payment from the social fund needs which, on social grounds, are as worthy as those which are eligible for payment. This principle applies even where such needs cannot be met elsewhere in the public sector, since social considerations are immaterial to the lawfulness of the decision to exclude a given need.

Subs. (2)
As with payments made from the social fund under subs. (1)(a) above, cold-weather payments are not subject to budgetary control. Decisions are made by AOs with the normal right of appeal to a SSAT. Details of entitlement are provided in the Social Fund Cold Weather Payments (General) Regulations (Northern Ireland) 1988 (S.I. 1988 No. 368). See Mesher on the equivalent Great Britain Regulations, *i.e.* Social Fund Cold Weather Payments (General) Regulations 1988 (S.I. 1988 No. 1724).

Subs. (3)
This power is only appropriate in special cases, as indicated in the Social Fund Manual.

Awards by social fund officers

135.—(1) The questions whether a payment such as is mentioned in section 134(1)(b) above is to be awarded and how much it is to be shall be determined by a social fund officer.

(2) A social fund officer may determine that an award shall be payable in specified instalments at specified times.

(3) A social fund officer may determine that an award is to be repayable.

(4) An award that is to be repayable shall be repayable upon such terms and conditions as before the award is paid the Department notifies to the person by or on behalf of whom the application for it was made.

(5) Payment of an award shall be made to the applicant unless the social fund officer determines otherwise.

DEFINITIONS
"social fund officer": SSA(N.I.)A 1992, s.62(1).
"the Department": s.170.

GENERAL NOTE
The Department's (Secretary of State's in Great Britain) directions and guidance as to how social fund officers should exercise their functions under this section are contained in the Social Fund Manual. See also Mesher.

Principles of determination

136.—(1) In determining whether to make an award to the applicant or the amount or value to be awarded a social fund officer shall have regard, subject to subsection (2) below, to all the circumstances of the case and, in particular—

(a) the nature, extent and urgency of the need;
(b) the existence of resources from which the need may be met;
(c) the possibility that some other person or body may wholly or partly meet it;

(d) where the payment is repayable, the likelihood of repayment and the time within which repayment is likely;

(e) any relevant allocation under section 147(1) to (4) of the Administration Act.

(2) A social fund officer shall determine any question in accordance with any general directions issued by the Department and in determining any question shall take account of any general guidance issued by the Department.

(3) Without prejudice to the generality of subsection (2) above, the Department may issue directions under that subsection for the purpose of securing that a social fund officer or group of social fund officers shall not in any specified period make awards of any specified description which in the aggregate exceed the amount, or a specified portion of the amount, allocated to that officer or group of officers under section 147(1) to (4) of the Administration Act for payments under awards of that description in that period.

(4) Without prejudice to the generality of subsection (2) above, the power to issue general directions conferred on the Department by that subsection includes power to direct—

(a) that in circumstances specified in the direction a social fund officer shall not determine an application and, without prejudice to the generality of this paragraph, that a social fund officer shall not determine an application which is made before the end of a specified period after the making of an application by the same person for a payment such as is mentioned in section 134(1)(b) above to meet the same need and without there having been any relevant change of circumstances since the previous application;

(b) that for a category of need specified in the direction a social fund officer shall not award less than an amount specified in the direction;

(c) that for a category of need specified in the direction a social fund officer shall not award more than an amount so specified;

(d) that payments to meet a category of need specified in the direction shall in all cases or in no case be made by instalments;

(e) that payments to meet a category of need specified in the direction shall in all cases or in no case be repayable; and

(f) that a payment such as is mentioned in section 134(1)(b) above shall only be awarded to a person if either—

(i) he is in receipt of a benefit which is specified in the direction and the circumstances are such as are so specified; or

(ii) in a case where the conditions specified in subparagraph (i) above are not satisfied, the circumstances are such as are specified in the direction,

and the power to issue general guidance conferred on the Department by that subsection includes power to give social fund officers guidance as to any matter to which directions under that subsection may relate.

(5) In determining a question a social fund officer shall take account (subject to any directions or guidance issued by the Department under this section) of any guidance issued by the social fund officer nominated for his area under section 62(3) of the Administration Act.

DEFINITIONS
"the Administration Act": s.170.
"social fund officer": SSA(N.I.)A 1992, s.62(1).

GENERAL NOTE
Social fund officers, in deciding whether to grant an application, must consider all the circumstances of the case and especially the five factors listed in subs. (1). Their apparent discretion under subs. (1) is severely constrained by subs. (2), which requires officers to follow

directions and to take into account guidance issued by the Department (see Social Fund Manual). The crucial distinction is that directions are mandatory (assuming they are *intra vires*) whereas guidance is not. The state of the budget is merely one factor amongst several under subs. (1), but directions issued under subs. (3) give it a higher status. Subsection (3) was inserted in the Social Security Act 1986 by the Social Security Act 1990 and thus subsequently into the Northern Ireland equivalent, SS(N.I.)O 1986, by SS(N.I.)O 1990 in order to overturn the effect of the Divisional Court's ruling in *R.* v. *Social Fund Inspector and Secretary of State for Social Security,* ex p. *Roberts* (*The Times,* February 23, 1990) (affirmed in *R.* v. *Secretary of State for Social Services,* ex p. *Stitt; R.* v. *Social Fund Inspector,* ex p. *Sherwin; R.* v. *Same,* ex p. *Roberts* [1991] C.O.D. 68 on other grounds) that the original guidance in the Social Fund Manual on budgets was unlawful.

PART IX

CHILD BENEFIT

Child benefit

137. A person who is responsible for one or more children in any week shall be entitled, subject to the provisions of this Part of this Act, to a benefit (to be known as "child benefit") for that week in respect of the child or each of the children for whom he is responsible.

DEFINITIONS
"child": s.138(1).
"responsible for": s.139(1).
"week": s.143(1).

GENERAL NOTE
Child benefit was introduced by the Child Benefit (Northern Ireland) Order 1975 (S.I. 1975 No. 1504 (N.I. 16)). The new benefit, which in part replaced family allowances, came into operation between 1977 and 1980 as children's tax allowances were phased out. During the 1980s the real value of child benefit declined to the extent that there were serious doubts as to the Government's commitment to this universal benefit (Brown, Child Benefit: Investing in the Future (1988)). These concerns were mollified by the decision to uprate child benefit in 1991.

Entitlement to child benefit turns on two principal issues. These are (1) whether the child is one in respect of whom benefit is payable (s.138), and (2) whether the claimant is a person who is "responsible for" the child or children (s.139). On the necessity for an application for benefit, see SSA(N.I.)A 1992, s.11.

Meaning of "child"

138.—(1) For the purposes of this Part of this Act a person shall be treated as a child for any week in which—
  (a) he is under the age of 16;
  (b) he is under the age of 18 and not receiving full-time education and prescribed conditions are satisfied in relation to him; or
  (c) he is under the age of 19 and receiving full-time education either by attendance at a recognised educational establishment or, if the education is recognised by the Department, elsewhere.
  (2) The Department may recognise education provided otherwise than at a recognised educational establishment for a person who, in the opinion of the Department, could reasonably be expected to attend such an establishment only if the Department is satisfied that education was being so provided for that person immediately before he attained the age of 16.
  (3) Regulations may prescribe the circumstances in which education is or is not to be treated for the purposes of this Part of this Act as full-time.
  (4) In determining for the purposes of paragraph (c) of subsection (1) above whether a person is receiving full-time education as mentioned in that paragraph, no account shall be taken of such interruptions as may be prescribed.

(5) Regulations may provide that a person who in any week ceases to fall within subsection (1) above shall be treated as continuing to do so for a prescribed period; but no person shall by virtue of any such regulations be treated as continuing to fall within that subsection for any week after that in which he attains the age of 19.

DEFINITIONS
"child": subs. (1).
"prescribed": s.143(1).
"recognised educational establishment": s.143(1).
"week": s.143(1).

GENERAL NOTE
The starting point for the statutory meaning of "child" in the context of child benefit is subs. (1). This provides for a normal age limit of 16, but in certain cases the upper age limit is raised to 18 or 19. This general rule is then modified by the Child Benefit (General) Regulations (Northern Ireland) 1976 (S.I. 1976 No. 226).

For example, children who have just left school and are under 19 are deemed to be in full-time education for a specified period, subject to certain exceptions (reg. 7). Child-benefit entitlement therefore continues for this period, and may be extended if the young person is under 18 and satisfies further conditions, *e.g.* as to registration as to availability for work or youth training, etc. (reg. 7D). The continuation of child benefit during this "extension period" reflects the withdrawal of income-support entitlement from most 16- and 17-year-olds in their own right. Child benefit may also be payable to children under 19 who are in "full-time education". This concept is defined in great detail in regs. 5 and 6. For a full analysis on the equivalent Great Britain Regulations, *i.e.* Child Benefit (General) Regulations 1976 (S.I. 1976 No. 965), see Bonner.

Meaning of "person responsible for child"

139.—(1) For the purposes of this Part of this Act a person shall be treated as responsible for a child in any week if—
  (a) he has the child living with him in that week; or
  (b) he is contributing to the cost of providing for the child at a weekly rate which is not less than the weekly rate of child benefit payable in respect of the child for that week.

(2) Where a person has had a child living with him at some time before a particular week he shall be treated for the purposes of this section as having the child living with him in that week notwithstanding their absence from one another unless, in the 16 weeks preceding that week, they were absent from one another for more than 56 days not counting any day which is to be disregarded under subsection (3) below.

(3) Subject to subsection (4) below, a day of absence shall be disregarded for the purposes of subsection (2) above if it is due solely to the child's—
  (a) receiving full-time education by attendance at a recognised educational establishment;
  (b) undergoing medical or other treatment as an in-patient in a hospital or similar institution; or
  (c) being, in such circumstances as may be prescribed, in residential accommodation pursuant to arrangements made under Article 7 of the Health and Personal Social Services (Northern Ireland) Order 1972.

(4) The number of days that may be disregarded by virtue of subsection (3)(b) or (c) above in the case of any child shall not exceed such number as may be prescribed unless the person claiming to be responsible for the child regularly incurs expenditure in respect of the child.

(5) Regulations may prescribe the circumstances in which a person is or is not to be treated—
  (a) as contributing to the cost of providing for a child as required by subsection (1)(b) above; or

(b) as regularly incurring expenditure in respect of a child as required by subsection (4) above;

and such regulations may in particular make provision whereby a contribution made or expenditure incurred by two or more persons is to be treated as made or incurred by one of them or whereby a contribution made or expenditure incurred by one of two spouses residing together is to be treated as made or incurred by the other.

DEFINITIONS
"child": s.138(1).
"prescribed": s.143(1).
"recognised educational establishment": s.143(1).
"week": s.143(1).

GENERAL NOTE
Entitlement to child benefit is not based on the blood tie between parent and child. Instead, child benefit is payable to a person who is "responsible for" the child. This is defined by subs. (1) as either a person with whom the child is living or a person who is contributing to the child's maintenance by an amount which is at least as much as the appropriate rate of weekly child benefit. Where more than one person is responsible for the child, priorities are determined by s.140(3) and Sched. 10.

Subs. (1)
He has the child living with him. This concept was discussed in *R(F) 2/79* by Commissioner Hallett, who held that "living with" is not synonymous with "residing together". In determining whether the child lives with the claimant all the relevant evidence must be considered, including such factors as who has *de facto* care and control of the children and where they regard home as being (see also *R(F) 2/81*). Note that certain temporary absences may be disregarded for these purposes by virtue of subss. (2)–(4) and reg. 4.
He is contributing to the cost of providing for the child. The alternative (and in practice much rarer) route to qualifying for child benefit is where the claimant contributes to the child's upkeep at the level of at least the current rate of child benefit. For guidance see *R(F) 8/61* and *R(F) 9/61*.

Exclusions and priority

140.—(1) Regulations may provide that child benefit shall not be payable by virtue—
(a) of paragraph (b) of section 138(1) above and regulations made under that paragraph; or
(b) of paragraph (c) of that subsection,
in such cases as may be prescribed.
(2) Schedule 9 to this Act shall have effect for excluding entitlement to child benefit in other cases.
(3) Where, apart from this subsection, two or more persons would be entitled to child benefit in respect of the same child for the same week, one of them only shall be entitled; and the question which of them is entitled shall be determined in accordance with Schedule 10 to this Act.

DEFINITIONS
"child": s.138(1).
"prescribed": s.143(1).
"week": s.143(1).

GENERAL NOTE
Schedule 9, introduced by subs. (2), excludes entitlement to child benefit in certain circumstances. These situations are essentially where (1) the child has been in prison, detained in custody or in the care of a Health and Social Services Board; (2) the child is aged 16 or more but under 19 and is in full-time employment because of some office or employment held (*e.g.* apprentices); (3) the child is married; or (4) the U.K. income of the claimant (or spouse) is exempt from tax under various provisions. These rules are subject to the provisions of the Child

Benefit (General) Regulations (Northern Ireland) 1976 (S.I. 1976 No. 226): see also Bonner on the equivalent Great Britain Regulations, *i.e.* Child Benefit (General) Regulations 1976 (S.I. 1976 No. 965).

Schedule 10, introduced by subs. (3), deals with the position where more than one person is regarded as being responsible for the child under s.139. Priority is accorded in the first instance to the person with whom the child is living. The order of priority is then wife (where residing with husband), parent, mother (where residing with father but not married to him) and, as between others, the individual agreed amongst the claimants. Failing such agreement, the Department may nominate the recipient.

Rate of child benefit

141.—(1) Child benefit shall be payable by the Department at such weekly rate as may be prescribed.

(2) Different rates may be prescribed in relation to different cases, whether by reference to the age of the child in respect of whom the benefit is payable or otherwise.

(3) The power to prescribe different rates under subsection (2) above shall be exercised so as to bring different rates into force on such day as the Department may by order specify.

(4) No rate prescribed in place of a rate previously in force shall be lower than the rate that it replaces.

(5) Regulations under this section shall be made by the Department in conjunction with the Department of Finance and Personnel.

DEFINITIONS
    "child": s.138(1).
    "parent": s.143(3).
    "prescribed": s.143(1).

GENERAL NOTE
Since April 1991 child benefit has been paid at an enhanced rate for the first or only child in the family. In October 1991 the basic rate of child benefit was increased for the first time since April 1987.

Persons outside Northern Ireland

142.—(1) Regulations may modify the provisions of this Part of this Act in their application to persons who are or have been outside Northern Ireland at any prescribed time or in any prescribed circumstances.

(2) Subject to any regulations under subsection (1) above, no child benefit shall be payable in respect of a child for any week unless—

    (a) he is in Northern Ireland in that week; and

    (b) either he or at least one of his parents has been in Northern Ireland for more than 182 days in the 52 weeks preceding that week.

(3) Subject to any regulations under subsection (1) above, no person shall be entitled to child benefit for any week unless—

    (a) he is in Northern Ireland in that week; and

    (b) he has been in Northern Ireland for more than 182 days in the 52 weeks preceding that week.

DEFINITIONS
    "child": s.138(1).
    "Northern Ireland": s.168.
    "prescribed": s.143(1).
    "week": s.143(1).

GENERAL NOTE
This section lays down two general rules relating to entitlement to child benefit. First, the child in question must be in Northern Ireland for the relevant week and either the child or the parent must have been in Northern Ireland for more than 182 days in the previous 52 weeks

(subs. (2); see *R(F) 1/88*). Secondly, the person claiming child benefit must be in Northern Ireland for that week and for 182 days out of the previous 52 weeks. These rules are subject to the qualifications contained in the Child Benefit (Residence and Persons Abroad) Regulations (Northern Ireland) 1976 (S.I. 1976 No. 227).

Interpretation of Part IX and supplementary provisions

143.—(1) In this Part of this Act—
"prescribed" means prescribed by regulations;
"recognised educational establishment" means an establishment recognised by the Department as being, or as comparable to, a university, college or school;
"voluntary organisation" means any association carrying on or proposing to carry on any activities otherwise than for the purpose of gain by the association or by individual members of the association;
"week" means a period of 7 days beginning with a Monday.
(2) Subject to any provision made by regulations, references in this Part of this Act to any condition being satisfied or any facts existing in a week shall be construed as references to the condition being satisfied or the facts existing at the beginning of that week.
(3) References in this part of this Act to a parent, father or mother of a child shall be construed—
(a) as including references to the natural parent, father or mother of an illegitimate child;
(b) as including references to a step-parent, step-father or step-mother.
(4) Regulations may prescribe the circumstances in which persons are or are not to be treated for the purposes of this Part of this Act as residing together.
(5) Regulations may make provision as to the circumstances in which—
(a) a marriage celebrated under a law which permits polygamy; or
(b) a marriage during the subsistence of which a party to it is at any time married to more than one person,
is to be treated for the purposes of this Part of this Act as having, or not having, the consequences of a marriage celebrated under a law which does not permit polygamy.
(6) Nothing in this Part of this Act shall be construed as conferring a right to child benefit on any body corporate; but regulations may confer such a right on voluntary organisations and for that purpose may make such modifications as the Department thinks fit—
(a) of any provision of this Part of this Act; or
(b) of any provision of the Administration Act relating to child benefit.

DEFINITIONS
"the Administration Act": s.170.

GENERAL NOTE
The meaning of "week" (subs. (1)) was considered by the Commissioners in *R(F) 1/82*. The principal Regulations made under this section are the Child Benefit (General) Regulations (Northern Ireland) 1976 (S.I. 1976 No. 226). See Bonner for commentary on the equivalent Great Britain Regulations, *i.e.* Child Benefit (General) Regulations 1976 (S.I. 1976 No. 965).

PART X

CHRISTMAS BONUS FOR PENSIONERS

Entitlement of pensioners to Christmas bonus

144.—(1) Any person who in any year—
(a) is present or ordinarily resident in the United Kingdom or any other member State at any time during the relevant week; and

  (b) is entitled to a payment of a qualifying benefit in respect of a period which includes a day in that week or is to be treated as entitled to a payment of a qualifying benefit in respect of such a period,

shall, subject to the following provisions of this Part of this Act and to section 1 of the Administration Act, be entitled to payment under this subsection in respect of that year.

(2) Subject to the following provisions of this Part of this Act, any person who is a member of a couple and is entitled to a payment under subsection (1) above in respect of a year shall also be entitled to payment under this subsection in respect of that year if—

  (a) both members have attained pensionable age not later than the end of the relevant week; and

  (b) the other member satisfies the condition mentioned in subsection (1)(a) above; and

  (c) either—

      (i) he is entitled or treated as entitled, in respect of the other member, to an increase in the payment of the qualifying benefit; or

      (ii) the only qualifying benefit to which he is entitled is income support.

(3) A payment under subsection (1) or (2) above—

  (a) is to be made by the Department; and

  (b) is to be of £10 or such larger sum as the Department may by order specify.

(4) Where the only qualifying benefit to which a person is entitled is income support, he shall not be entitled to a payment under subsection (1) above unless he has attained pensionable age not later than the end of the relevant week.

(5) Only one sum shall be payable in respect of any person.

DEFINITIONS

  "the Administration Act": s.170.

  "couple": s.146(3).

  "pensionable age": s.146(1).

  "qualifying benefit": s.146(1).

  "the relevant week": s.146(4).

  "United Kingdom": ss.145(1) and 168.

GENERAL NOTE

  The Christmas bonus was introduced in 1972. As Ogus and Barendt note, "in social policy terms, it serves little obvious purpose except that of courting political popularity" (p. 372). The amount payable (£10: subs. (3)) has not changed since 1972. The qualifying benefits are set out in s.146(1). On the determination of questions, see SSA(N.I.)A 1992, s.65.

Provisions supplementary to s.144

  145.—(1) For the purposes of section 144 above the Channel Islands, the Isle of Man and Gibraltar shall be treated as though they were part of the United Kingdom.

(2) A person shall be treated for the purposes of section 144(1)(b) above as entitled to a payment of a qualifying benefit if he would be so entitled—

  (a) in the case of a qualifying benefit other than income support, but for the fact that he or, if he is a member of a couple, the other member is entitled to receive some other payment out of public funds;

  (b) in the case of income support, but for the fact that his income or, if he is a member of a couple, the income of the other member was exceptionally of an amount which resulted in his having ceased to be entitled to income support.

(3) A person shall be treated for the purposes of section 144(2)(c)(i) above as entitled in respect of the other member of the couple to an increase in a payment of a qualifying benefit if he would be so entitled—

  (a) but for the fact that he or the other member is entitled to receive some other payment out of public funds;

  (b) but for the operation of any provision of section 83(2) or (3) above or paragraph 6(4) of Schedule 7 to this Act or any regulations made under paragraph 6(3) of that Schedule whereby entitlement to benefit is affected by the amount of a person's earnings in a given period.

(4) For the purposes of section 144 above a person shall be taken not to be entitled to a payment of a war disablement pension unless not later than the end of the relevant week he has attained the age of 70 in the case of a man or 65 in the case of a woman.

(5) A sum payable under section 144 above shall not be treated as benefit for the purposes of any enactment or instrument under which entitlement to the relevant qualifying benefit arises or is to be treated as arising.

(6) A payment and the right to receive a payment—

  (a) under section 144 above or any enactment corresponding to it in Great Britain; or

  (b) under regulations relating to widows which are made by the Secretary of State under any enactment relating to police and which contain a statement that the regulations provide for payments corresponding to payments under that section,

shall be disregarded for all purposes of income tax and for the purposes of any enactment or instrument under which regard is had to a person's means.

DEFINITIONS
  "United Kingdom": subs. (1) and s.168.

Interpretation of Part X

146.—(1) In this Part of this Act "qualifying benefit" means—

  (a) a retirement pension;

  (b) an invalidity pension;

  (c) a widowed mother's allowance or widow's pension;

  (d) a severe disablement allowance;

  (e) an invalid care allowance;

  (f) industrial death benefit;

  (g) an attendance allowance;

  (h) an unemployability supplement or allowance;

  (i) a war disablement pension;

  (j) a war widow's pension;

  (k) income support.

(2) In this Part of this Act—

  "attendance allowance" means—

      (a) an attendance allowance;

      (b) a disability living allowance;

      (c) an increase of disablement pension under section 104 or 105 above;

      (d) a payment under regulations made in exercise of the powers in section 150(3)(b) of the 1975 Act or paragraph 4(2) of Schedule 8 to this Act;

      (e) an increase of allowance under Article 8 of the Pneumoconiosis, Byssinosis and Miscellaneous Diseases Benefit Scheme 1983 (constant attendance allowance for certain persons to whom that Scheme applies) or under the corresponding provision of any Scheme which may replace that Scheme;

(f) an allowance in respect of constant attendance on account of disablement for which a person is in receipt of war disablement pension, including an allowance in respect of exceptionally severe disablement;

"pensionable age" means—

(a) in the case of a man, the age of 65;

(b) in the case of a woman, the age of 60;

"retirement pension" includes graduated retirement benefit, if paid periodically;

"unemployability supplement or allowance" means—

(a) an unemployability supplement payable under Part I of Schedule 7 to this Act; or

(b) any corresponding allowance payable—

(i) by virtue of paragraph 6(4)(a) of Schedule 8 to the Great Britain Contributions and Benefits Act;

(ii) by way of supplement to retired pay or pension exempt from income tax under section 315(1) of the Income and Corporation Taxes Act 1988;

(iii) under the Personal Injuries (Emergency Provisions) Act 1939; or

(iv) by way of supplement to retired pay or pension under the Polish Resettlement Act 1947;

"war disablement pension" means—

(a) any retired pay, pension or allowance granted in respect of disablement under powers conferred by or under the Air Force (Constitution) Act 1917, the Personal Injuries (Emergency Provisions) Act 1939, the Pensions (Navy, Army, Air Force and Mercantile Marine) Act 1939, the Polish Resettlement Act 1947, or Part VII or section 151 of the Reserve Forces Act 1980;

(b) without prejudice to paragraph (a) of this definition, any retired pay or pension to which subsection (1) of section 315 of the Income and Corporation Taxes Act 1988 applies;

"war widow's pension" means any widow's pension or allowance granted in respect of a death due to service or war injury and payable by virtue of any enactment mentioned in paragraph (a) of the preceding definition or a pension or allowance for a widow granted under any scheme mentioned in subsection (2)(e) of the said section 315;

and each of the following expressions, namely "attendance allowance", "unemployability supplement or allowance", "war disablement pension" and "war widow's pension", includes any payment which the Department accepts as being analogous to it.

(3) References in this Part of this Act to a "couple" are references to a married or unmarried couple; and for this purpose "married couple" and "unmarried couple" are to be construed in accordance with Part VII of this Act and any regulations made under it.

(4) In this Part of this Act "the relevant week", in relation to any year, means the week beginning with the first Monday in December or such other week as may be specified in an order made by the Department.

DEFINITIONS
"the 1975 Act": s.170.
"attendance allowance": subs. (2).
"couple": subs. (3).
"married couple": subs. (3).
"pensionable age": subs. (2).
"relevant week": subs. (4).
"retirement pension": subs. (2).

"unemployability supplement or allowance": subs. (2).
"unmarried couple": subs. (3).
"war disablement pension": subs. (2).
"war widow's pension": subs. (2).

Part XI

Statutory Sick Pay

Employer's liability

147.—(1) Where an employee has a day of incapacity for work in relation to his contract of service with an employer, that employer shall, if the conditions set out in sections 148 to 150 below are satisfied, be liable to make him, in accordance with the following provisions of this Part of this Act, a payment (to be known as "statutory sick pay") in respect of that day.

(2) Any agreement shall be void to the extent that it purports—

(a) to exclude, limit or otherwise modify any provision of this Part of this Act, or

(b) to require an employee to contribute (whether directly or indirectly) towards any costs incurred by his employer under this Part of this Act.

(3) For the avoidance of doubt, any agreement between an employer and an employee authorising any deductions from statutory sick pay which the employer is liable to pay to the employee in respect of any period shall not be void by virtue of subsection (2)(a) above if the employer—

(a) is authorised by that or another agreement to make the same deductions from any contractual remuneration which he is liable to pay in respect of the same period, or

(b) would be so authorised if he were liable to pay contractual remuneration in respect of that period.

(4) For the purposes of this Part of this Act a day shall not be treated as a day of incapacity for work in relation to any contract of service unless on that day the employee concerned is, or is deemed in accordance with regulations to be, incapable by reason by some specific disease or bodily or mental disablement of doing work which he can reasonably be expected to do under that contract.

(5) In any case where an employee has more than one contract of service with the same employer the provisions of this Part of this Act shall, except in such cases as may be prescribed and subject to the following provisions of this Part of this Act, have effect as if the employer were a different employer in relation to each contract of service.

(6) Circumstances may be prescribed in which, notwithstanding the provisions of subsections (1) to (5) above, the liability to make payments of statutory sick pay is to be a liability of the Department.

Definitions
"contract of service": s.159(1).
"employee": s.159(1).
"employer": s.159(1).
"prescribed": s.159(1).

General Note
Statutory sick pay was brought in by the SS(N.I.)O 1982 and supersedes sickness benefit so far as most employees are concerned. It is administered by employers, although disputes may be referred to the normal social security adjudication machinery. As originally implemented, employers received 100 per cent. reimbursement for payments under the scheme. This was reduced under the SSP(N.I.)O 1991 to an 80 per cent. refund for all bar small employers (see s.154).

As a preliminary issue, the claimant must be an employee (subs. (1) and Statutory Sick Pay (General) Regulations (Northern Ireland) 1982 (S.I. 1982 No. 263), reg. 16). Furthermore, in order for a claimant to qualify for statutory sick pay, the day in question must:

(1) form part of a period of incapacity for work (s.148);

(2) fall within a period of entitlement (s.149); and

(3) be a qualifying day (s.150).

Limitations on entitlement appear in s.151, while s.152 deals with notification of incapacity for work. Section 153 concerns rates of payment and ss.154 and 155 provide for refunds to employers of payments. The duties of employees and employers in respect of statutory sick pay are prescribed under SSA(N.I.)A 1992, ss.12 and 122 respectively.

The qualifying conditions

Period of incapacity for work

148.—(1) The first condition is that the day in question forms part of a period of incapacity for work.

(2) In this Part of this Act "period of incapacity for work" means any period of four or more consecutive days, each of which is a day of incapacity for work in relation to the contract of service in question.

(3) Any two periods of incapacity for work which are separated by a period of not more than 8 weeks shall be treated as a single period of incapacity for work.

(4) The Department may by regulations direct that a larger number of weeks specified in the regulations shall be substituted for the number of weeks for the time being specified in subsection (3) above.

(5) No day of the week shall be disregarded in calculating any period of consecutive days for the purposes of this section.

(6) A day may be a day of incapacity for work in relation to a contract of service, and so form part of a period of incapacity for work, notwithstanding that—

(a) it falls before the making of the contract or after the contract expires or is brought to an end; or

(b) it is not a day on which the employee concerned would be required by that contract to be available for work.

DEFINITIONS

"contract of service": s.159(1).

"day of incapacity for work": s.147(4).

"employee": s.159(1).

"period of incapacity for work": subs. (2).

"week": s.159(1).

GENERAL NOTE

The first condition for entitlement to statutory sick pay is that the day in question falls within a period of incapacity for work. This means a period of four or more consecutive days of incapacity, whether or not they are normally working days (subss. (2) and (5)). A linking rule operates by virtue of subs. (3), so that any two periods separated by not more than eight weeks can be aggregated as one period of incapacity for work, so avoiding a duplication of the three "waiting days" (s.151(1)).

Period of entitlement

149.—(1) The second condition is that the day in question falls within a period which is, as between the employee and his employer, a period of entitlement.

(2) For the purposes of this Part of this Act a period of entitlement, as between an employee and his employer, is a period beginning with the commencement of a period of incapacity for work and ending with whichever of the following first occurs—

(a) the termination of that period of incapacity for work;

(b) the day on which the employee reaches, as against the employer concerned, his maximum entitlement to statutory sick pay (determined in accordance with section 151 below);

(c) the day on which the employee's contract of service with the employer concerned expires or is brought to an end;

(d) in the case of an employee who is, or has been, pregnant, the day immediately preceding the beginning of the disqualifying period.

(3) Schedule 11 to this Act has effect for the purpose of specifying circumstances in which a period of entitlement does not arise in relation to a particular period of incapacity for work.

(4) A period of entitlement as between an employee and an employer of his may also be, or form part of, a period of entitlement as between him and another employer of his.

(5) The Department may by regulations—

(a) specify circumstances in which, for the purpose of determining whether an employee's maximum entitlement to statutory sick pay has been reached in a period of entitlement as between him and an employer of his, days falling within a previous period of entitlement as between the employee and any person who is or has in the past been an employer of his are to be counted; and

(b) direct that in prescribed circumstances an employer shall provide a person who is about to leave his employment, or who has been employed by him in the past, with a statement in the prescribed form containing such information as may be prescribed in relation to any entitlement of the employee to statutory sick pay.

(6) Regulations may provide, in relation to prescribed cases, for a period of entitlement to end otherwise than in accordance with subsection (2) above.

(7) In a case where the employee's contract of service first takes effect on a day which falls within a period of incapacity for work, the period of entitlement begins with that day.

(8) In a case where the employee's contract of service first takes effect between two periods of incapacity for work which by virtue of section 148(3) above are treated as one, the period of entitlement begins with the first day of the second of those periods.

(9) In any case where, otherwise than by virtue of section 6(1)(b) above, an employee's earnings under a contract of service in respect of the day on which the contract takes effect do not attract a liability to pay secondary Class 1 contributions, subsections (7) and (8) above shall have effect as if for any reference to the contract first taking effect there were substituted a reference to the first day in respect of which the employee's earnings attract such a liability.

(10) Regulations shall make provision as to an employer's liability under this Part of this Act to pay statutory sick pay to an employee in any case where the employer's contract of service with that employee has been brought to an end by the employer solely, or mainly, for the purpose of avoiding liability for statutory sick pay.

(11) Subsection (2)(d) above does not apply in relation to an employee who has been pregnant if her pregnancy terminated, before the beginning of the disqualifying period, otherwise than by confinement.

(12) In this section—

"confinement" is to be construed in accordance with section 167(1) below;

"disqualifying period" means—

(a) in relation to a woman entitled to statutory maternity pay, the maternity pay period; and

(b) in relation to a woman entitled to maternity allowance, the maternity allowance period;
"maternity allowance period" has the meaning assigned to it by section 35(2) above, and
"maternity pay period" has the meaning assigned to it by section 161(1) below.

DEFINITIONS
"confinement": subs. (12).
"contract of service": s.159(1).
"disqualifying period": subs. (12).
"employee": s.159(1).
"employer": s.159(1).
"maternity allowance period": subs. (12).
"maternity pay period": subs. (12).
"period of entitlement": subs. (2).
"period of incapacity for work": s.148(2).
"prescribed": s.159(1).

GENERAL NOTE
The claimant's period of entitlement generally begins with the period of incapacity for work (but see special rules in subss. (7)–(9)) and ends on the occurrence of any of the events listed in subs. (2) or under regulations, *e.g.* Statutory Sick Pay (General) Regulations (Northern Ireland) 1982 (S.I. 1982 No. 263), reg. 3. The maximum period of entitlement is 28 weeks.

Subsection (3) introduces Sched. 11, which in turn sets out various circumstances in which employees are precluded from claiming statutory sick pay (*e.g.* where they are earning less than the National Insurance lower earnings limit currently in force); see further Bonner.

Qualifying days

150.—(1) The third condition is that the day in question is a qualifying day.

(2) The days which are for the purposes of this Part of this Act to be qualifying days as between an employee and an employer of his (that is to say, those days of the week on which he is required by his contract of service with that employer to be available for work or which are chosen to reflect the terms of that contract) shall be such day or days as may, subject to regulations, be agreed between the employee and his employer or, failing such agreement, determined in accordance with regulations.

(3) In any case where qualifying days are determined by agreement between an employee and his employer there shall, in each week (beginning with Sunday), be at least one qualifying day.

(4) A day which is a qualifying day as between an employee and an employer of his may also be a qualifying day as between him and another employer of his.

DEFINITIONS
"contract of service": s.159(1).
"employee": s.159(1).
"employer": s.159(1).
"week": s.159(1).

GENERAL NOTE
In essence, a qualifying day is a day on which the employee is required to be available for work. Employers and employees are granted a degree of flexibility by subs. (2) to agree which days count as qualifying days (but note subs. (3)). Further provision is made by the Statutory Sick Pay (General) Regulations (Northern Ireland) 1982 (S.I. 1982 No. 263), reg. 5.

Subs. (2)
Required by his contract of service. This means, not days where an employee is merely "asked" to work overtime: *R(SSP) 1/82.*

Limitations on entitlement, etc.

Limitations on entitlement

151.—(1) Statutory sick pay shall not be payable for the first three qualifying days in any period of entitlement.

(2) An employee shall not be entitled, as against any one employer, to an aggregate amount of statutory sick pay in respect of any one period of entitlement which exceeds his maximum entitlement.

(3) The maximum entitlement as against any one employer is reached on the day on which the amount to which the employee has become entitled by way of statutory sick pay during the period of entitlement in question first reaches or passes the entitlement limit.

(4) The entitlement limit is an amount equal to 28 times the appropriate weekly rate set out in section 153 below.

(5) Regulations may make provision for calculating the entitlement limit in any case where an employee's entitlement to statutory sick pay is calculated by reference to different weekly rates in the same period of entitlement.

DEFINITIONS
"employee": s.159(1).
"employer": s.159(1).
"period of entitlement": s.149(2).
"qualifying day": s.150.

GENERAL NOTE
As with unemployment benefit and sickness benefit, no statutory sick pay is payable for the first three qualifying days or "waiting days" (subs. (1)). An employee's maximum entitlement is determined in accordance with subss. (2)–(4) and amounts to 28 weeks.

Notification of incapacity for work

152.—(1) Regulations shall prescribe the manner in which, and the time within which, notice of any day of incapacity for work is to be given by or on behalf of an employee to his employer.

(2) An employer who would, apart from this section, be liable to pay an amount of statutory sick pay to an employee in respect of a qualifying day (the "day in question") shall be entitled to withhold payment of that amount if—

(a) the day in question is one in respect of which he has not been duly notified in accordance with regulations under subsection (1) above; or

(b) he has not been so notified in respect of any of the first three qualifying days in a period of entitlement (a "waiting day") and the day in question is the first qualifying day in that period of entitlement in respect of which the employer is not entitled to withhold payment—
   (i) by virtue of paragraph (a) above; or
   (ii) in respect of an earlier waiting day by virtue of this paragraph.

(3) Where an employer withholds any amount of statutory sick pay under this section—

(a) the period of entitlement in question shall not be affected; and

(b) for the purposes of calculating his maximum entitlement in accordance with section 151 above the employee shall not be taken to have become entitled to the amount so withheld.

DEFINITIONS
"employee": s.159(1).
"employer": s.159(1).

"period of entitlement": s.149(2).
"qualifying day": s.150.
"waiting day": subs. (2)(b).

GENERAL NOTE
This section is amplified by the Statutory Sick Pay (General) Regulations (Northern Ireland) 1982 (S.I. 1982 No. 263), reg. 7. Where the employer has not been duly notified of the day of incapacity for work, statutory sick pay may be withheld (subs. (2)), but such days do not affect the period of entitlement, and nor do they count towards the employee's maximum entitlement (subs. (3)).

Rate of payment, etc.

Rate of payment

153.—(1) Statutory sick pay shall be payable by an employer at the weekly rate of—

(a) £52.50, in a case where the employee's normal weekly earnings under his contract of service with that employer are not less than £190.00; or
(b) £45.30, in any other case.
(2) The Department may by order—
(a) substitute alternative provisions for the paragraphs of subsection (1) above; and
(b) make such consequential amendments as appear to the Department to be required of any provision contained in this Part of this Act.
(3) The amount of statutory sick pay payable by any one employer in respect of any day shall be the weekly rate applicable on that day divided by the number of days which are, in the week (beginning with Sunday) in which that day falls, qualifying days as between that employer and the employee concerned.

DEFINITIONS
"contract of service": s.159(1).
"earnings": Statutory Sick Pay (General) Regulations (Northern Ireland) 1982 (S.I. 1982 No. 263), reg. 17.
"employee": s.159(1).
"employer": s.159(1).
"normal weekly earnings": s.159(2) and Statutory Sick Pay (General) Regulations (Northern Ireland) 1982 (S.I. 1982 No. 263), reg. 19.
"qualifying day": s.150.
"week": s.159(1)

GENERAL NOTE
There are two rates of statutory sick pay, the higher rate being payable where the employee's normal weekly earnings exceed a prescribed amount. Unlike sickness benefit, statutory sick pay has never had to be uprated in line with inflation. In 1990 employees became eligible for the higher rate if they earned £125 per week or more; this threshold was raised to £185 in 1991, and to £190 for 1992. The higher rate itself has not been uprated since April 1990.
    The concepts of "earnings" and "normal weekly earnings" are defined in the Statutory Sick Pay (General) Regulations (Northern Ireland) 1982 (S.I. 1982 No. 263).

Recovery by employers of amounts paid by way of statutory sick pay

154.—(1) Regulations shall make provisions—
(a) entitling, except in prescribed circumstances, any employer who has made one or more payments of statutory sick pay in a prescribed period to recover an amount equal to the sum of—
        (i) the aggregate of such of those payments as qualify for small employers' relief; and
        (ii) an amount equal to 80 per cent. of the aggregate of such of those payments as do not so qualify,
    by making one or more deductions from his contributions payments; and

(b) for the payment, in prescribed circumstances, by or on behalf of the Department of sums to employers who are unable so to recover the whole, or any part, of the amounts which they are entitled to recover by virtue of paragraph (a) above.

(2) For the purposes of this section, a payment of statutory sick pay which an employer is liable to make to an employee for any day which forms part of a period of incapacity for work qualifies for small employers' relief if—

(a) on that day the employer is a small employer who has been liable to pay statutory sick pay in respect of that employee for earlier days forming part of that period of incapacity for work; and

(b) the aggregate amount of those payments exceeds the entitlement threshold, that is to say, an amount equal to W x R, where—

W is a prescribed number of weeks; and

R is the appropriate weekly rate set out in section 153 above;

and regulations may make provision for calculating the entitlement threshold in any case where the employee's entitlement to statutory sick pay is calculated by reference to different weekly rates in the same period of incapacity for work.

(3) For the purposes of this section, "small employer" shall have the meaning assigned to it by regulations, and, without prejudice to the generality of the foregoing, any such regulations—

(a) may define that expression by reference to the amount of an employer's contributions payments for any prescribed period; and

(b) if they do so, may in that connection make provision for the amount of those payments for that prescribed period—

(i) to be determined without regard to any deductions that may be made from them under this section or under any other statutory provision; and

(ii) in prescribed circumstances, to be adjusted, estimated or otherwise attributed to him by reference to their amount in any other prescribed period.

(4) In this section "contributions payments", in relation to an employer, means any payments which the employer is required, by or under any statutory provision, to make in discharge of any liability in respect of primary or secondary Class 1 contributions.

(5) Regulations under this section may, in particular,—

(a) provide for any deduction made in accordance with the regulations to be disregarded for prescribed purposes; and

(b) provide for the rounding up or down of any fraction of a penny which would otherwise result from calculating the amount which an employer is entitled to recover from any period by virtue of subsection (1)(a) above.

(6) Where, in accordance with any provision of regulations made under this section, an amount has been deducted from an employer's contributions payments, the amount so deducted shall (except in such cases as may be prescribed) be treated for the purposes of any provision made by or under any statutory provision in relation to primary or secondary Class 1 contributions as having been—

(a) paid (on such date as may be determined in accordance with the regulations); and

(b) received by the Department,

towards discharging the liability mentioned in subsection (4) above.

(7) Any day of incapacity for work falling before 6th April 1991 shall be left out of account for the purposes of subsection (2) above.

DEFINITIONS
"contributions payments": subs. (4).

"employee": s.159(1).
"employer": s.159(1).
"period of incapacity for work": s.148(2).
"prescribed": s.159(1).
"small employer": subs. (3).
"week": s.159(1).

GENERAL NOTE

Statutory sick pay is indirectly financed by social security contributions, in that employers' payments are offset against their contributions liability under arrangements made under this section. Originally this offset represented 100 per cent. of the cost of statutory sick pay payments, but reimbursement was reduced to 80 per cent. by the SSP(N.I.)O 1991. Small employers continue to receive 100 per cent. reimbursement (subs. (1)(a)(i) and (2); but see also s.155). A small employer is defined (for 1992/93) as one who pays (or is liable to pay) £16,000 or less in gross national insurance contributions in the relevant tax year (Statutory Sick Pay (Small Employers' Relief) Amendment Regulations (Northern Ireland) 1992 (S.I. 1992 No. 139)). The SSP(N.I.)O 1991 also abolished the compensatory sum previously paid to employers to cover administrative costs and contributions paid during periods of statutory sick pay.

Power to substitute provisions for s.154(2)

155.—(1) If the Department by order so provides for any tax year, the following subsections shall have effect for that tax year in substitution for section 154(2) above—

"(2A) For the purposes of this section, a payment of statutory sick pay which an employer is liable to make to an employee for any day in a tax year qualifies for small employers' relief if—

  (a) on that day the employer is a small employer who has been liable to make payments of statutory sick pay for earlier days in that tax year in respect of any employees of his; and

  (b) the aggregate of any such payments for those earlier days exceeds a prescribed sum.

(2B) In any case where—

  (a) an employer is liable to make two or more payments of statutory sick pay for the same day in a tax year; and

  (b) by virtue of the condition in subsection (2A)(b) above, none of those payments would qualify for small employers' relief; but

  (c) that condition would have been fulfilled in relation to a proportion of the aggregate amount of those payments, had he been liable—

    (i) to pay as statutory sick pay for an earlier day in that tax year, instead of for the day in question, the smallest part of that aggregate that would enable that condition to be fulfilled; and

    (ii) to pay the remainder as statutory sick pay for the day in question,

he shall be treated for the purposes of subsection (2A) above as if he had been liable to make payments of statutory sick pay as mentioned in paragraph (c) above instead of as mentioned in paragraph (a) above.

(2C) If, in a case not falling within subsection (2B) above—

  (a) an employer is liable to make a single payment of statutory sick pay for a day in a tax year; and

  (b) by virtue of the condition in subsection (2A)(b) above, that payment would not qualify for small employers' relief; but

  (c) that condition would have been fulfilled in relation to a proportion of that payment, had he been liable—

    (i) to pay as statutory sick pay for an earlier day in that tax year, instead of for the day in question, the smallest part of that payment that would enable that condition to be fulfilled; and

(ii) to pay the remainder as statutory sick pay for the day in question,

he shall be treated for the purposes of subsection (2A) above as if he had been liable to make payments of statutory sick pay as mentioned in paragraph (c) above instead of the payment mentioned in paragraph (a) above.".

(2) Without prejudice to section 171(4) below, the Department may by regulations make such transitional or consequential provision or savings as the Department considers necessary or expedient in connection with the coming into force of an order under subsection (1) above or the expiry or revocation of any such order and the consequent revival of section 154(2) above.

"employee": s.159(1).
"employer": s.159(1).
"prescribed": s.159(1).
"small employer": s.154(3).

GENERAL NOTE
This provides for an alternative basis for small employers' relief under s.154(2).

Miscellaneous

Relationship with benefits and other payments, etc.

156. Schedule 12 to this Act has effect with respect to the relationship between statutory sick pay and certain benefits and payments.

GENERAL NOTE
This section introduces Sched. 12, which provides that no day of incapacity (whether or not it is also a qualifying day) within a period of entitlement to statutory sick pay can count as part of a period of interruption of employment. Consequently there can be no entitlement to sickness benefit in such a case.

Crown employment—Part XI

157.—(1) Subject to subsection (2) below, the provisions of this Part of this Act apply in relation to persons employed by or under the Crown as they apply in relation to persons employed otherwise than by or under the Crown.

(2) The provisions of this Part of this Act do not apply in relation to persons serving as members of Her Majesty's forces, in their capacity as such.

(3) For the purposes of this section Her Majesty's forces shall be taken to consist of such establishments and organisations as may be prescribed by regulations made by the Secretary of State, being establishments and organisations in which persons serve under the control of the Defence Council.

GENERAL NOTE
Employees of the Crown are eligible for statutory sick pay unless they are members of HM forces (an exception which does not apply to statutory maternity pay: see s.165).

Special classes of persons

158.—(1) The Department may make regulations modifying this Part of this Act in such manner as the Department thinks proper in their application to any person who is, has been or is to be—

(a) employed on board any ship, vessel, hovercraft or aircraft; or
(b) outside Northern Ireland at any prescribed time or in any prescribed circumstances.
(2) Regulations under subsection (1) above may in particular provide—
(a) for any provision of this Part to apply to any such person, notwithstanding that it would not otherwise apply;
(b) for any such provision not to apply to any such person, notwithstanding that it would otherwise apply;
(c) for excepting any such person from the application of any such provision where he neither is domiciled nor has a place of residence in Northern Ireland;
(d) for the taking of evidence, for the purposes of the determination of any question arising under any such provision, in a country or territory other than Northern Ireland, by a British consular official or such other person as may be determined in accordance with the regulations.

DEFINITIONS
"Northern Ireland": s.168.
"prescribed": s.159(1).

GENERAL NOTE

Subs. 2(d)
On the drafting of this provision, see the Law Commissions' report (Cm. 1726, 1991), para. 4.

Interpretation of Part XI and supplementary provisions

159.—(1) In this Part of this Act—
"contract of service" (except in paragraph (a) of the definition below of "employee") includes any arrangement providing for the terms of appointment of an employee;
"employee" means a person who is—
(a) gainfully employed in Northern Ireland either under a contract of service or in an office (including elective office) with emoluments chargeable to income tax under Schedule E; and
(b) over the age of 16;
but subject to regulations, which may provide for cases where any such person is not to be treated as an employee for the purposes of this Part of this Act and for cases where any person who would not otherwise be an employee for those purposes is to be treated as an employee for those purposes;
"employer", in relation to an employee and a contract of service of his, means a person who under section 6 above is, or but for subsection (1)(b) of that section would be, liable to pay secondary Class 1 contributions in relation to any earnings of the employee under the contract;
"period of entitlement" has the meaning given by section 149 above;
"period of incapacity for work" has the meaning given by section 148 above;
"period of interruption of employment" has the same meaning as it has in the provisions of this Act relating to unemployment benefit, sickness benefit and invalidity benefit by virtue of section 57(1)(d) above;
"prescribed" means prescribed by regulations;
"qualifying day" has the meaning given by section 150 above;
"week" means any period of 7 days.
(2) For the purposes of this Part of this Act an employee's normal weekly earnings shall, subject to subsection (4) below, be taken to be the average

weekly earnings which in the relevant period have been paid to him or paid for his benefit under his contract of service with the employer in question.

(3) For the purposes of subsection (2) above, the expressions "earnings" and "relevant period" shall have the meaning given to them by regulations.

(4) In such cases as may be prescribed an employee's normal weekly earnings shall be calculated in accordance with regulations.

(5) Without prejudice to any other power to make regulations under this Part of this Act, regulations may specify cases in which, for the purposes of this Part of this Act or such of its provisions as may be prescribed—

(a) two or more employers are to be treated as one;

(b) two or more contracts of service in respect of which the same person is an employee are to be treated as one.

(6) Where, in consequence of the establishment of one or more Health and Social Services trusts under the Health and Personal Social Services (Northern Ireland) Order 1991, a person's contract of employment is treated by a scheme under that Order as divided so as to constitute two or more contracts, regulations may make provision enabling him to elect for all of those contracts to be treated as one contract for the purposes of this Part of this Act or of such provisions of this Part of this Act as may be prescribed; and any such regulations may prescribe—

(a) the conditions that must be satisfied if a person is to be entitled to make such an election;

(b) the manner in which, and the time within which, such an election is to be made;

(c) the persons to whom, and the manner in which, notice of such an election is to be given;

(d) the information which a person who makes such an election is to provide, and the persons to whom, and the time within which, he is to provide it;

(e) the time for which such an election is to have effect;

(f) which one of the person's employers under the two or more contracts is to be regarded for the purposes of statutory sick pay as his employer under the one contract;

and the powers conferred by this subsection are without prejudice to any other power to make regulations under this Part of this Act.

(7) Regulations may provide for periods of work which begin on one day and finish on the following day to be treated, for the purposes of this Part of this Act, as falling solely within one or other of those days.

Definitions
"Northern Ireland": s.168.

General Note
See further the Statutory Sick Pay (General) Regulations (Northern Ireland) 1982 (S.I. 1982 No. 263).

Part XII

Statutory Maternity Pay

Statutory maternity pay—entitlement and liability to pay

160.—(1) Where a woman who is or has been an employee satisfies the conditions set out in this section, she shall be entitled, in accordance with the following provisions of this Part of this Act, to payments to be known as "statutory maternity pay".

(2) The conditions mentioned in subsection (1) above are—

(a) that she has been in employed earner's employment with an employer for a continuous period of at least 26 weeks ending with the week immediately preceding the 14th week before the expected week of confinement but has ceased to work for him, wholly or partly because of pregnancy or confinement;

(b) that her normal weekly earnings for the period of 8 weeks ending with the week immediately preceding the 14th week before the expected week of confinement are not less than the lower earnings limit in force under section 5(1)(a) above immediately before the commencement of the 14th week before the expected week of confinement; and

(c) that she has become pregnant and has reached, or been confined before reaching, the commencement of the 11th week before the expected week of confinement.

(3) The liability to make payments of statutory maternity pay to a woman is a liability of any person of whom she has been an employee as mentioned in subsection (2)(a) above.

(4) Except in such cases as may be prescribed, a woman shall be entitled to payments of statutory maternity pay only if—

(a) she gives the person who will be liable to pay it notice that she is going to be absent from work with him, wholly or partly because of pregnancy or confinement; and

(b) the notice is given at least 21 days before her absence from work is due to begin or, if that is not reasonably practicable, as soon as is reasonably practicable.

(5) The notice shall be in writing if the person who is liable to pay the woman statutory maternity pay so requests.

(6) Any agreement shall be void to the extent that it purports—

(a) to exclude, limit or otherwise modify any provision of this Part of this Act; or

(b) to require an employee or former employee to contribute (whether directly or indirectly) towards any costs incurred by her employer or former employer under this Part of this Act.

(7) For the avoidance of doubt, any agreement between an employer and an employee authorising any deductions from statutory maternity pay which the employer is liable to pay to the employee in respect of any period shall not be void by virtue of subsection (6)(a) above if the employer—

(a) is authorised by that or another agreement to make the same deductions from any contractual remuneration which he is liable to pay in respect of the same period, or

(b) would be so authorised if he were liable to pay contractual remuneration in respect of that period.

(8) Regulations shall make provision as to a former employer's liability to pay statutory maternity pay to a woman in any case where the former employer's contract of service with her has been brought to an end by the former employer solely, or mainly, for the purpose of avoiding liability for statutory maternity pay.

(9) The Department may by regulations—

(a) specify circumstances in which, notwithstanding subsections (1) to (8) above, there is to be no liability to pay statutory maternity pay in respect of a week;

(b) specify circumstances in which, notwithstanding subsections (1) to (8) above, the liability to make payments of statutory maternity pay is to be a liability of the Department;

(c) specify in what circumstances employment is to be treated as continuous for the purposes of this Part of this Act;

(d) provide that a woman is to be treated as being employed for a continuous period of at least 26 weeks where—

    (i) she has been employed by the same employer for at least 26 weeks under two or more separate contracts of service; and

(ii) those contracts were not continuous;
(e) provide that any of the provisions specified in subsection (10) below shall have effect subject to prescribed modifications—
    (i) where a woman has been dismissed from her employment;
    (ii) where a woman is confined before the beginning of the 14th week before the expected week of confinement; and
    (iii) in such other cases as may be prescribed;
(f) provide for amounts earned by a woman under separate contracts of service with the same employer to be aggregated for the purposes of this Part of this Act; and
(g) provide that—
    (i) the amount of a woman's earnings for any period, or
    (ii) the amount of her earnings to be treated as comprised in any payment made to her or for her benefit,
shall be calculated or estimated in such manner and on such basis as may be prescribed and that for that purpose payments of a particular class or description made or falling to be made to or by a woman shall, to such extent as may be prescribed, be disregarded or, as the case may be, be deducted from the amount of her earnings.

(10) The provisions mentioned in subsection (9)(e) above are—
(a) subsection (2)(a) and (b) above; and
(b) section 162(2), (4) and (5) below.

DEFINITIONS
"confined": s.167(1).
"confinement": s.167(1).
"Department": s.170.
"dismissed": s.167(1).
"employee": s.167(1).
"employer": s.167(1).
"prescribed": s.167(1).
"week": s.167(1).

GENERAL NOTE

Statutory maternity pay came into being in April 1987. It superseded the maternity pay provisions under the employment protection legislation and effectively replaced maternity allowance for most women employees. Maternity allowance remains in existence for employees who are not entitled to statutory maternity pay (s.35). Statutory maternity pay is analogous to statutory sick pay in that it is administered by employers (subs. (3)) and disputes can be referred to the normal social security adjudication machinery.

An employee is entitled to statutory maternity pay if she satisfies four main conditions:

(1) she has been continuously employed in employed earner's employment for 26 weeks up to and including the 15th week (the qualifying week) before the expected week of confinement (subs. (2)(a)). Regulations (see below) provide for certain disregards in calculating this period;

(2) her average weekly earnings in the eight weeks before the qualifying week exceeded the current lower earnings limit for National Insurance contributions (subs. (2)(b)). Regulations (see below) define earnings and normal weekly earnings. Note, however, that there are no contributions conditions as such;

(3) she is pregnant and has reached (or has been confined by) the 11th week before the expected week of confinement (subs. (2)(c)). Regulations (see below) provide for modifications where a woman has been dismissed by an employer solely or mainly for the purpose of avoiding liability to pay statutory maternity pay;

(4) she gives notice of her absence for pregnancy or confinement at least 21 days before such absence (or, if that is not reasonably practicable, as soon as is reasonably practicable) (subss. (4) and (5)). On the interpretation of this requirement, see by analogy *Nu-Swift International* v. *Mallison* [1979] I.C.R. 157.

This basic scheme is modified by regulations made by the Department under subss. (8) and (9): see the Statutory Maternity Pay (General) Regulations (Northern Ireland) 1987 (S.I. 1987 No. 30). The duties of employees and employers in respect of statutory maternity pay are prescribed under SSA(N.I.)A 1992, ss.13 and 124 respectively.

The maternity pay period

161.—(1) Statutory maternity pay shall be payable, subject to the provisions of this Part of this Act, in respect of each week during a prescribed period ("the maternity pay period") of a duration not exceeding 18 weeks.

(2) Subject to subsections (3) and (7) below, the first week of the maternity pay period shall be the 11th week before the expected week of confinement.

(3) Cases may be prescribed in which the first week of the period is to be a prescribed week later than the 11th week before the expected week of confinement, but not later than the 6th week before the expected week of confinement.

(4) Statutory maternity pay shall not be payable to a woman by a person in respect of any week during any part of which she works under a contract of service with him.

(5) It is immaterial for the purposes of subsection (4) above whether the work referred to in that subsection is work under a contract of service which existed immediately before the maternity pay period or a contract of service which did not so exist.

(6) Except in such cases as may be prescribed, statutory maternity pay shall not be payable to a woman in respect of any week after she has been confined and during any part of which she works for any employer who is not liable to pay her statutory maternity pay.

(7) Regulations may provide that this section shall have effect subject to prescribed modifications in relation—

(a) to cases in which a woman has been confined before the 11th week before the expected week of confinement; and

(b) to cases in which—

(i) a woman is confined during the period beginning with the 11th week, and ending with the 7th week, before the expected week of confinement; and

(ii) the maternity pay period has not then commenced for her.

DEFINITIONS
"confinement": s.167(1).
"employer": s.167(1).
"maternity pay period": subs. (1).
"modifications": s.167(1).
"prescribed": s.167(1).
"week": s.167(1).

GENERAL NOTE.
Statutory maternity pay is payable for a maximum of 18 weeks (subs. (1)). This "maternity pay period" must begin no earlier than 11 weeks before the expected week of confinement (subs. (2)). The start of this period of 18 weeks' entitlement may be postponed to begin no later than six weeks before the expected week of confinement (subs. (3)). This allows women a degree of flexibility. These rules are modified by the Statutory Maternity Pay (General) Regulations (Northern Ireland) 1987 (S.I. 1987 No. 30), Pt. II, for special cases.

No statutory maternity pay is payable for any week in which the woman works for an employer liable to pay her this benefit (subss. (4) and (5)). Nor is a woman entitled to the benefit where she works for another employer after her confinement (subs. (6), but see reg. 8). Further exclusions of entitlement are provided for in the regulations.

Rates of payment

162.—(1) There shall be two rates of statutory maternity pay, in this Act referred to as "the higher rate" and "the lower rate".

(2) The higher rate is a weekly rate equivalent to nine-tenths of a woman's normal weekly earnings for the period of 8 weeks immediately preceding the

14th week before the expected week of confinement or the weekly rate prescribed under subsection (3) below, whichever is the higher.

(3) The lower rate is such weekly rate as may be prescribed.

(4) Subject to the following provisions of this section, statutory maternity pay shall be payable at the higher rate to a woman who for a continuous period of at least 2 years ending with the week immediately preceding the 14th week before the expected week of confinement has been an employee in employed earner's employment of any person liable to pay it to her, and shall be so paid by any such person in respect of the first 6 weeks in respect of which it is payable.

(5) Statutory maternity pay shall not be payable at the higher rate to a woman whose relations with the person liable to pay it are or were governed by a contract of service which normally involves or involved employment for less than 16 hours weekly unless during a continuous period of at least 5 years ending with the week immediately preceding the 14th week before the expected week of confinement her contract of service normally involved employment for 8 hours or more weekly.

(6) The Department may by regulations make provision as to when a contract of service is to be treated for the purposes of subsection (5) above as normally involving or having involved employment—

(a) for less than 16 hours weekly; or

(b) for 8 hours or more weekly,

or as not normally involving or having involved such employment.

(7) Statutory maternity pay shall be payable to a woman at the lower rate if she is entitled to statutory maternity pay but is not entitled to payment at the higher rate.

(8) If a woman is entitled to statutory maternity pay at the higher rate, she shall be entitled to it at the lower rate in respect of the portion of the maternity pay period after the end of the 6 week period mentioned in subsection (4) above.

DEFINITIONS

   "confinement": s.167(1).
   "employee": s.167(1).
   "higher rate": subs. (2).
   "lower rate": subs. (3).
   "prescribed": s.167(1).
   "week": s.167(1).

GENERAL NOTE

   There are two rates of statutory maternity pay. The higher rate is 90 per cent. of the average weekly earnings in the eight weeks preceding the qualifying week (subs. (2)). This rate is only payable to women who have been employed by the relevant employer for at least 16 hours a week for a continuous period of two years immediately before the qualifying week (or for at least eight hours a week for the previous five years): subss. (4)–(5). The lower rate is a flat-rate sum payable both to those who do not qualify for the higher rate (subs. (7)) and for the remaining 12 weeks of entitlement for those who qualify for six weeks on the higher rate (subs. (8)).

Recovery of amounts paid by way of statutory maternity pay

163.—(1) Regulations shall make provision—

(a) entitling, except in prescribed circumstances, any person who has made a payment of statutory maternity pay to recover the amount so paid by making one or more deductions from his contributions payments;

(b) for the payment, in prescribed circumstances, by the Department or by the Commissioners of Inland Revenue on behalf of the Department, of sums to persons who are unable so to recover the whole, or any part, of any payments of statutory maternity pay which they have made;

(c) giving any person who has made a payment of statutory maternity pay a right, except in prescribed circumstances, to an amount, determined in such manner as may be prescribed;

(d) providing for the recovery, in prescribed circumstances, of the whole or any part of any such amount from contributions payments;

(e) for the payment, in prescribed circumstances, by the Department or by the Commissioners of Inland Revenue on behalf of the Department, of the whole or any part of any such amount.

(2) In this section "contributions payments", in relation to an employer, means any payments which the employer is required, by or under any enactment, to make in discharge of any liability in respect of primary or secondary Class 1 contributions.

(3) Regulations under subsection (1) above may, in particular, provide for any deduction made in accordance with the regulations to be disregarded for prescribed purposes.

(4) Where, in accordance with any provision of regulations made under this section, an amount has been deducted from an employer's contributions payments, the amount so deducted shall (except in such cases as may be prescribed) be treated for the purposes of any provision made by or under any statutory provision in relation to primary or secondary Class 1 contributions as having been—

(a) paid (on such date as may be determined in accordance with the regulations); and

(b) received by the Department,

towards discharging the employer's liability in respect of such contributions.

DEFINITIONS
"contributions payments": subs. (2).
"employer": s.167(1).
"prescribed": s.167(1).

GENERAL NOTE

Subs. (2)
The inclusion of a specific definition of "contributions payments", equivalent to that for statutory maternity pay (s.154(4)), follows the recommendation of the Law Commissions (Cm. 1726, 1991), para. 5.

Relationship with benefits and other payments, etc.

164. Schedule 13 to this Act has effect with respect to the relationship between statutory maternity pay and certain benefits and payments.

GENERAL NOTE
This section introduces Sched. 13, which provides that as a general principle entitlement to statutory maternity pay precludes any entitlement to maternity allowance, statutory sick pay, sickness benefit or unemployment benefit in respect of the same period.

Crown employment—Part XII

165. The provisions of this Part of this Act apply in relation to women employed by or under the Crown as they apply in relation to women employed otherwise than by or under the Crown.

GENERAL NOTE
The exclusion of women members of HM Forces from receiving statutory maternity pay was ended by SS(N.I.)O 1990, Sched. 6, para. 14. In this respect statutory maternity pay differs from statutory sick pay (s.157).

Special classes of persons

166.—(1) The Department may make regulations modifying this Part of this Act in such manner as the Department thinks proper in their application to any person who is, has been or is to be—

(a) employed on board any ship, vessel, hovercraft or aircraft;

(b) outside Northern Ireland at any prescribed time or in any prescribed circumstances; or

(c) in prescribed employment in connection with continental shelf operations.

(2) Regulations under subsection (1) above may in particular provide—

(a) for any provision of this Part to apply to any such person, notwithstanding that it would not otherwise apply;

(b) for any such provision not to apply to any such person, notwithstanding that it would otherwise apply;

(c) for excepting any such person from the application of any such provision where he neither is domiciled nor has a place of residence in any part of Northern Ireland;

(d) for the taking of evidence, for the purposes of the determination of any question arising under any such provision, in a country or territory other than Northern Ireland, by a British consular official or such other person as may be determined in accordance with the regulations.

(3) In this section "continental shelf operations" means any activities which, if paragraphs (a) and (d) of subsection (6) of section 23 of the Oil and Gas (Enterprise) Act 1982 (application of civil law to certain offshore activities) were omitted, would nevertheless fall within subsection (2) of that section.

DEFINITIONS
"Northern Ireland": s.168.

GENERAL NOTE
See further the Statutory Maternity Pay (Persons Abroad and Mariners) Regulations (Northern Ireland) 1987 (S.I. 1987 No. 171).

Subs. (2)(d)
See General Note to s.158(2) above.

Interpretation of Part XII, etc.

167.—(1) In this Part of this Act—
"confinement" means—
　　　(a) labour resulting in the issue of a living child, or
　　　(b) labour after 28 weeks of pregnancy resulting in the issue of a child whether alive or dead,
　　and "confined" shall be construed accordingly; and where a woman's labour begun on one day results in the issue of a child on another day she shall be taken to be confined on the day of the issue of the child or, if labour results in the issue of twins or a greater number of children, she shall be taken to be confined on the day of the issue of the last of them;
"dismissed" is to be construed in accordance with Article 21(2) to (5) of the Industrial Relations (Northern Ireland) Order 1976;
"employee" means a woman who is—
　　　(a) gainfully employed in Northern Ireland either under a contract of service or in an office (including elective office) with emoluments chargeable to income tax under Schedule E; and
　　　(b) over the age of 16;

but subject to regulations which may provide for cases where any such woman is not to be treated as an employee for the purposes of this Part of this Act and for cases where a woman who would not otherwise be an employee for those purposes is to be treated as an employee for those purposes;

"employer", in relation to a woman who is an employee, means a person who under section 6 above is, or but for subsection (1)(b) of that section would be, liable to pay secondary Class 1 contributions in relation to any of her earnings;

"maternity pay period" has the meaning assigned to it by section 161(1) above;

"modifications" includes additions, omissions and amendments, and related expressions shall be construed accordingly;

"prescribed" means specified in or determined in accordance with regulations;

"week" means a period of 7 days beginning with Sunday or such other period as may be prescribed in relation to any particular case or class of cases.

(2) Without prejudice to any other power to make regulations under this Part of this Act, regulations may specify cases in which, for the purposes of this Part of this Act or of such provisions of this Part of this Act as may be prescribed—

(a) two or more employers are to be treated as one;

(b) two or more contracts of service in respect of which the same woman is an employee are to be treated as one.

(3) Where, in consequence of the establishment of one or more Health and Social Services trusts under the Health and Personal Social Services (Northern Ireland) Order 1991, a woman's contract of employment is treated by a scheme under that Order as divided so as to constitute two or more contracts, regulations may make provision enabling her to elect for all of those contracts to be treated as one contract for the purposes of this Part of this Act or of such provisions of this Part of this Act as may be prescribed; and any such regulations may prescribe—

(a) the conditions that must be satisfied if a woman is to be entitled to make such an election;

(b) the manner in which, and the time within which, such an election is to be made;

(c) the persons to whom, and the manner in which, notice of such an election is to be given;

(d) the information which a woman who makes such an election is to provide, and the persons to whom, and the time within which, she is to provide it;

(e) the time for which such an election is to have effect;

(f) which one of the woman's employers under the two or more contracts is to be regarded for the purposes of statutory maternity pay as her employer under the one contract;

and the powers conferred by this subsection are without prejudice to any other power to make regulations under this Part of this Act.

(4) For the purposes of this Part of this Act a woman's normal weekly earnings shall, subject to subsection (6) below, be taken to be the average weekly earnings which in the relevant period have been paid to her or paid for her benefit under the contract of service with the employer in question.

(5) For the purposes of subsection (4) above "earnings" and "relevant period" shall have the meanings given to them by regulations.

(6) In such cases as may be prescribed a woman's normal weekly earnings shall be calculated in accordance with regulations.

DEFINITIONS
"Northern Ireland": s.168.

GENERAL NOTE
See further the Statutory Maternity Pay (General) Regulations (Northern Ireland) 1987 (S.I. 1987 No. 30).

PART XIII

GENERAL

Interpretation

Application of Act in relation to territorial waters

168. In this Act—
(a) any reference to Northern Ireland includes a reference to the territorial waters of the United Kingdom adjacent to Northern Ireland;
(b) any reference to the United Kingdom includes a reference to the territorial waters of the United Kingdom.

Age

169. For the purposes of this Act a person—
(a) is over or under a particular age if he has or, as the case may be, has not attained that age; and
(b) is between two particular ages if he has attained the first but not the second.

Interpretation

170. In this Act—
"the 1975 Act" means the Social Security (Northern Ireland) Act 1975;
"the 1986 Order" means the Social Security (Northern Ireland) Order 1986;
"the Administration Act" means the Social Security Administration (Northern Ireland) Act 1992;
"the Consequential Provisions Act" means the Social Security (Consequential Provisions) (Northern Ireland) Act 1992;
"the Department" means the Department of Health and Social Services for Northern Ireland;
"the Department of Economic Development" means the Department of Economic Development in Northern Ireland;
"the Department of the Environment" means the Department of the Environment for Northern Ireland;
"the Department of Finance and Personnel" means the Department of Finance and Personnel in Northern Ireland;
"the Great Britain Administration Act" means the Social Security Administration Act 1992;
"the Great Britain Contributions and Benefits Act" means the Social Security Contributions and Benefits Act 1992;
"the National Insurance Fund" means the Northern Ireland National Insurance Fund;
"the Old Cases Act" means the Industrial Injuries and Diseases (Northern Ireland Old Cases) Act 1975;
"the Pensions Order" means the Social Security Pensions (Northern Ireland) Order 1975;
"statutory provision" has the meaning assigned by section 1(f) of the Interpretation Act (Northern Ireland) 1954.

Subordinate legislation

Regulations and orders—general

171.—(1) Subject to any specific provision of this Act, regulations and orders under this Act shall be made by the Department.

(2) Any power conferred by this Act to make regulations (except regulations made by the Secretary of State under section 116 or 157) or orders is exercisable by statutory rule for the purposes of the Statutory Rules (Northern Ireland) Order 1979.

(3) Except in the case of an order under section 141(3) above and in so far as this Act otherwise provides, any power conferred by this Act to make regulations or an order may be exercised—

    (a) either in relation to all cases to which the power extends, or in relation to those cases subject to specified exceptions, or in relation to any specified cases or classes of case;

    (b) so as to make, as respects the cases in relation to which it is exercised—

        (i) the full provision to which the power extends or any less provision (whether by way of exception or otherwise),

        (ii) the same provision for all cases in relation to which the power is exercised, or different provision for different cases or different classes of case or different provisions as respects the same case or class of case for different purposes of this Act,

        (iii) any such provision either unconditionally or subject to any specified condition;

and where such a power is expressed to be exercisable for alternative purposes it may be exercised in relation to the same case for any or all of those purposes; and powers to make regulations or an order for the purposes of any one provision of this Act are without prejudice to powers to make regulations or an order for the purposes of any other provision.

(4) Without prejudice to any specific provision of this Act, any power conferred by this Act to make regulations or an order (other than the power conferred by section 141(3)) includes power to make thereby such incidental, supplementary, consequential or transitional provision as appears to the authority making the regulations or order to be expedient for the purposes of the regulations or order.

(5) Without prejudice to any specific provision of this Act, a power conferred by any provision of this Act except—

    (a) sections 30, 47(6), 57(9)(a) and 141(3) and paragraph 3(9) of Schedule 7; and

    (b) section 121(1) in relation to the definition of "payments by way of occupational or personal pension"; and

    (c) Part XI,

to make regulations or an order includes power to provide for a person to exercise a discretion in dealing with any matter.

(6) Any power conferred by this Act to make regulations relating to housing benefit shall include power to make different provision for different areas.

(7) Any power of the Department under any provision of this Act, except the provisions mentioned in subsection (5)(a) and (b) above and Part IX, to make any regulations or order, where the power is not expressed to be exercisable with the consent of the Department of Finance and Personnel shall if that Department so directs be exercisable only in conjunction with it.

(8) Any power under any of sections 116 to 119 above to modify provisions of this Act or the Administration Act extends also to modifying so much of any other provision of this Act or that Act as re-enacts provisions of the 1975

Act which replaced provisions of the National Insurance (Industrial Injuries) Measures (Northern Ireland) 1966 to 1974.

(9) A power to make regulations under any of sections 116 to 119 above shall be exercisable in relation to any enactment passed or made after this Act which is directed to be construed as one with this Act, but this subsection applies only so far as a contrary intention is not expressed in the enactment, and is without prejudice to the generality of any such direction.

(10) Any power of the Secretary of State under section 116 or 157 above to make regulations is exercisable by statutory instrument; and subsections (3) to (5) above apply to those regulations as they apply to regulations made by the Department.

(11) Any power of the Secretary of State under section 116 or 157 above to make regulations shall if the Treasury so direct be exercisable only in conjunction with them.

(12) Any reference in this section or section 172 below to an order or regulations under this Act includes a reference to an order or regulations made under any provision of an enactment passed or made after this Act which is directed to be construed as one with this Act; but this subsection applies only so far as a contrary intention is not expressed in the enactment, and is without prejudice to the generality of any such direction.

DEFINITIONS
"the 1975 Act": s.170.
"the Administration Act": s.170.

Assembly, etc. control of regulations and orders

172.—(1) The regulations and orders to which this subsection applies shall be laid before the Assembly after being made and shall take effect on such date as may be specified in the regulations or order, but shall (without prejudice to validity of anything done thereunder or to the making of new regulations or a new order) cease to have effect upon the expiration of a period of six months from that date unless at some time before the expiration of that period the regulations have, or the order has, been approved by a resolution of the Assembly.

(2) Subsection (1) above applies to—

(a) regulations made by the Department under section 11(3), 18(1), 19(4) to (6), 28(3), 32(2), 59(2), 104(3), 117, 118, 141 or 154(2) or (3) above;

(b) regulations prescribing payments for the purposes of the definition of "payments by way of occupational or personal pension" in section 121(1) above;

(c) an order made by the Department under section 28(2), 57(8), 144(3) (b), 153(2) or 155(1) above.

(3) Subsection (1) above does not apply to—

(a) regulations under section 117 which states that they are made for the purpose of making provision consequential on the making of an order under section 129 of the Administration Act;

(b) regulations under any provision mentioned in subsection (2)(a) above (other than section 154(2) or (3)) which are to be made for the purpose of consolidating regulations thereby revoked;

(c) regulations which, in so far as they are made under any provision mentioned in subsection (2)(a) above (other than section 141 or 154(2) or (3)), only replace provisions of previous regulations with new provisions to the same effect.

(4) Subject to subsection (7) below, all regulations and orders made by the Department under this Act, other than regulations or orders to which subsection (1) above applies, shall be subject to negative resolution.

(5) Section 41(3) of the Interpretation Act (Northern Ireland) 1954 (laying statutory instruments or statutory documents before the Assembly) shall apply in relation to any instrument or document which by virtue of any provision of this Act is required to be laid before the Assembly as if it were a statutory instrument or statutory document within the meaning of that Act.

(6) This subsection applies to any regulations or order made under this Act which—

(a) but for subsection (7) below, would be subject to negative resolution, and

(b) are or is contained in a statutory rule which includes any regulations or order subject to the confirmatory procedure.

(7) Any regulations or order to which subsection (6) above applies shall not be subject to negative resolution, but shall be subject to the confirmatory procedure.

(8) During the interim period (as defined by section 1(4) of the Northern Ireland Act 1974), subsections (1) and (4) above have effect subject to paragraph 3 of Schedule 1 to that Act.

(9) Subject to subsection (10) below, regulations made under this Act by the Secretary of State shall be subject to annulment in pursuance of a resolution of either House of Parliament.

(10) This subsection applies to any regulations made under this Act which—

(a) but for subsection (11) below, would be subject to annulment in pursuance of a resolution of either House of Parliament, and

(b) are, or is, contained in an instrument which is subject to any requirement that a draft of the instrument be laid before and approved by a resolution of each House of Parliament.

(11) Any regulations to which subsection (9) above applies shall not be subject as mentioned in paragraph (a) of that subsection, but shall be subject to the procedure described in paragraph (b) of that subsection.

(12) In this section—

"the Assembly" means the Northern Ireland Assembly;

"the confirmatory procedure" means the procedure described in subsection (1) above;

"subject to negative resolution" has the meaning assigned by section 41(6) of the Interpretation Act (Northern Ireland) 1954 (but as if the regulations or orders in question were statutory instruments within the meaning of that Act).

DEFINITIONS
"the Administration Act": s.170.

GENERAL NOTE
The Northern Ireland Assembly has been dissolved since 1986. Regulations and orders which are subject to the Assembly's negative procedure (*i.e.* those specified in subs. (2)) are subject to the negative procedure at Westminster. Regulations and orders subject to negative resolution by the Assembly (*i.e.* everything other than those specified in subs. (2)) are simply laid before Westminster.

Supplementary

Short title, commencement and extent

173.—(1) This Act may be cited as the Social Security Contributions and Benefits (Northern Ireland) Act 1992.

(2) This Act is to be read, where appropriate, with the Administration Act and the Consequential Provisions Act.

(3) The enactments consolidated by this Act are repealed, in consequence of the consolidation, by the Consequential Provisions Act.

(4) Except as provided in Schedule 4 to the Consequential Provisions Act, this Act shall come into force on 1st July 1992.

(5) Except as provided by this section, this Act extends to Northern Ireland only.

(6) Section 116(2) and this section also extend to Great Britain.

DEFINITIONS
  "the Administration Act": s.170.
  "the Consequential Provisions Act": s.170.

GENERAL NOTE

Subss. (5) and (6)
  General provision for Great Britain is made by the Social Security Contributions and Benefits Act 1992, the Social Security Administration Act 1992 and the Social Security (Consequential Provisions) Act 1992.

SCHEDULES

Section 1(4)

SCHEDULE 1

SUPPLEMENTARY PROVISIONS RELATING TO CONTRIBUTIONS OF CLASSES 1, 1A, 2 AND 3

Class 1 contributions where earner employed in more than one employment

1.—(1) For the purposes of determining whether Class 1 contributions are payable in respect of earnings paid to an earner in a given week and, if so, the amount of the contributions—
  (a) all earnings paid to him or for his benefit in that week in respect of one or more employed earner's employments under the same employer shall, except as may be provided by regulations, be aggregated and treated as a single payment of earnings in respect of one such employment; and
  (b) earnings paid to him or for his benefit in that week by different persons in respect of different employed earner's employments shall in prescribed circumstances be aggregated and treated as a single payment of earnings in respect of one such employment;
and regulations may provide that the provisions of this sub-paragraph shall have effect in cases prescribed by the regulations as if for any reference to a week there were substituted a reference to a period prescribed by the regulations.

(2) Where earnings in respect of employments which include any contracted-out employment and any employment which is not a contracted-out employment are aggregated under sub-paragraph (1) above and the aggregated earnings are not less than the current lower earnings limit, then, except as may be provided by regulations—
  (a) the amount of the primary Class 1 contribution in respect of the aggregated earnings shall be determined in accordance with sub-paragraph (3) below; and
  (b) the amount of the secondary Class 1 contribution in respect of the aggregated earnings shall be determined in accordance with sub-paragraph (6) below.

(3) The amount of the primary Class 1 contribution shall be the aggregate of the amounts obtained—
  (a) by applying the rates of primary Class 1 contributions that would apply if the aggregated earnings were all attributable to contracted-out employments—
    (i) to the part of the aggregated earnings attributable to any such employments, or
    (ii) if that part exceeds the current upper earnings limit, to so much of that part as does not exceed that limit; and
  (b) if that part is less than that limit, by applying the rate of primary Class 1 contributions that would apply if the aggregated earnings were all attributable to employments which are not contracted-out to so much of the remainder of the aggregated earnings as, when added to that part, does not exceed that limit.

(4) In relation to earners paid otherwise than weekly, any reference in sub-paragraph (2) or (3) above to the lower or upper earnings limit shall be construed as a reference to the prescribed equivalent of that limit.

(5) The power under sub-paragraph (4) above to prescribe an equivalent of a limit includes power to prescribe an amount which exceeds, by not more than £1.00, the amount which is the arithmetical equivalent of that limit.

(6) The amount of the secondary Class 1 contribution shall be the aggregate of the amounts obtained—

(a) by applying the rates of secondary Class 1 contributions that would apply if the aggregated earnings were all attributable to contracted-out employments to the part of the aggregated earnings attributable to any such employments; and

(b) by applying the rate of secondary Class 1 contributions that would apply if the aggregated earnings were all attributable to employments which are not contracted-out to the remainder of the aggregated earnings.

(7) Where any single payment of earnings is made in respect of two or more employed earner's employments under different employers, liability for Class 1 contributions shall be determined by apportioning the payment to such one or more of the employers as may be prescribed, and treating a part apportioned to any employer as a separate payment of earnings by him.

(8) Where earnings are aggregated under sub-paragraph (1)(b) above, liability (if any) for the secondary contribution shall be apportioned, in such manner as may be prescribed, between the secondary contributors concerned.

Earnings not paid at normal intervals

2. Regulations may, for the purposes of Class 1 contributions, make provision as to the intervals at which payments of earnings are to be treated as made.

Method of paying Class 1 contributions

3.—(1) Where earnings are paid to an employed earner and in respect of that payment liability arises for primary and secondary Class 1 contributions, the secondary contributor shall (except in prescribed circumstances), as well as being liable for his own secondary contribution, be liable in the first instance to pay also the earner's primary contribution, on behalf of and to the exclusion of the earner; and for the purposes of this Act and the Administration Act contributions paid by the secondary contributor on behalf of the earner shall be taken to be contributions paid by the earner.

(2) Notwithstanding any contract to the contrary, no secondary contributor shall be entitled—

(a) to make, from earnings paid by him, any deduction in respect of his own or any other person's secondary Class 1 contributions, or

(b) otherwise to recover such contributions from any earner to whom he pays earnings.

(3) A secondary contributor shall be entitled, subject to and in accordance with regulations, to recover from an earner the amount of any primary Class 1 contribution paid or to be paid by him on behalf of the earner; and notwithstanding anything in any enactment, regulations under this sub-paragraph shall provide for recovery to be made by deduction from the earner's earnings, and for it not to be made in any other way.

General provisions as to Class 1 contributions

(4) Regulations may, in relation to Class 1 contributions, make provision—

(a) for calculating the amounts payable according to a scale prepared from time to time by the Department or otherwise adjusting them so as to avoid fractional amounts or otherwise facilitate computations;

(b) for requiring that the liability in respect of a payment made in a tax week, in so far as the liability depends on any conditions as to a person's age or retirement, shall be determined as at the beginning of the week or as at the end of it;

(c) for securing that liability is not avoided or reduced by a person following in the payment of earnings any practice which is abnormal for the employment in respect of which the earnings are paid; and

(d) without prejudice to sub-paragraph (c) above, for enabling the Department, where it is satisfied as to the existence of any practice in respect of the payment of earnings whereby the incidence of Class 1 contributions is avoided or reduced by means of irregular or unequal payments, to give directions for securing that such contributions are payable as if that practice were not followed.

Class 1A contributions where car made available by reasons of more than one employment

5. Regulations may modify section 10 above in relation to cases where a car is made available by reason of two or more employed earner's employment under different employers.

Power to combine collection of contributions with tax

6.—(1) Regulations made with the concurrence of the Inland Revenue may—

(a) provide for Class 1, Class 1A or Class 2 contributions to be paid, accounted for and recovered in like manner as income tax deducted from the emoluments of an office or employment by virtue of regulations under section 203 of the Income and Corporation Taxes Act 1988 (PAYE);

(b) apply or extend with or without modification in relation to such contributions any of the provisions of the Income Tax Acts or of regulations under that section;

(c) make provision for the appropriation of the payments made by any person between his liabilities in respect of income tax and contributions.

(2) Without prejudice to the generality of sub-paragraph (1) above, the provision that may be made by virtue of paragraph (a) of that sub-paragraph includes in relation to Class 1 or Class 1A contributions—

(a) provision for requiring the payment of interest on sums due in respect of Class 1 or Class 1A contributions which are not paid by the due date, for determining the date (being, in the case of Class 1 contributions, not less than 14 days after the end of the tax year in respect of which the sums are due) from which such interest is to be calculated and for enabling the repayment or remission of such interest;

(b) provision for requiring the payment of interest on sums due in respect of Class 1 or Class 1A contributions which fall to be repaid and for determining the date (being not less than one year after the end of the tax year in respect of which the sums are due) from which such interest is to be calculated;

(c) provision for, or in connection with, the imposition and recovery of penalties in relation to any returns required to be made which relate to Class 1 or Class 1A contributions, but subject to sub-paragraph (7) and paragraph 7 below;

and any reference to contributions or income tax in paragraph (b) or (c) of sub-paragraph (1) above shall be construed as including a reference to any interest or penalty in respect of contributions or income tax, as the case may be.

(3) The rate of interest applicable for any purpose of this paragraph shall be—

(a) the rate from time to time prescribed for that purpose under section 178 of the Finance Act 1989 for the purpose of any enactment (whether or not extending to Northern Ireland) if prescribed by regulations made by virtue of this paragraph; or

(b) such other rate as may be prescribed by such regulations.

(4) Regulations under this paragraph may require the payment of interest on sums due in respect of contributions, notwithstanding that a question arising in relation to the contributions has not been determined under section 15 of the Administration Act by the Department, except that where—

(a) any such question arises which affects a person's liability for, or the amount of, any such interest, and

(b) either—

(i) that person requires the question to be determined under section 15, or

(ii) a question of law arising in accordance with the determination of the question is, or is to be, referred to the Court of Appeal under section 16 of the Administration Act,

the regulations shall not require the payment of any such interest until the question has been determined under section 15 of the Administration Act by the Department or the reference has been finally disposed of under section 16 of that Act, as the case may be; but, subject to that, this paragraph is without prejudice to sections 15 to 17 of the Administration Act.

(5) The power to make regulations under this paragraph includes power to make such provision as the Department considers expedient in consequence of any provision made by or under section 154 or 163 above.

(6) Provision made in regulations under this paragraph, by virtue of sub-paragraph (5) above, may in particular require the inclusion—

(a) in returns, certificates and other documents; or

(b) in any other form of record;

which the regulations require to be kept or produced or to which those regulations otherwise apply, of such particulars relating to statutory sick pay, statutory maternity pay or deductions or payments made by virtue of section 163(1) above as may be prescribed by those regulations.

(7) Section 98 of the Taxes Management Act 1970 shall apply in relation to regulations made by virtue of this paragraph as it applies in relation to regulations made under section 203 of the Income and Corporation Taxes Act 1988 (PAYE).

(8) The Inland Revenue shall, at such times and in such manner as the Department of Finance and Personnel may direct, account to the Department for, and pay to it—

(a) the sums estimated by the Inland Revenue, in such manner as may be so directed, to have been received by them as contributions in accordance with regulations made by virtue of this paragraph; and

(b) so much of any interest recovered by the Inland Revenue by virtue of this paragraph as remains after the deduction by them of any administrative costs attributable to its recovery.

7.—(1) This paragraph applies where regulations under paragraph 6 above make provision requiring any return which is to be made in accordance with a specified provision of regulations under that paragraph (the "contributions return") to be made—

(a) at the same time as any specified return required to be made in accordance with a provision of regulations made by the Inland Revenue under section 203(2) (PAYE) or 566(1) (sub-contractors) of the Income and Corporation Taxes Act 1988 to which section 98A of the Taxes Management Act 1970 applies (the "tax return"); or

(b) if the circumstances are such that the return mentioned in paragraph (a) above does not fall to be made, at a time defined by reference to the time for making that return, had it fallen to be made;

and, in a case falling within paragraph (b) above, any reference in the following provisions of this paragraph to the tax return shall be construed as a reference to the return there mentioned.

(2) Where this paragraph applies, regulations under paragraph 6 above may provide that section 98A of the Taxes Management Act 1970 (penalties for late, fraudulent or negligent returns) shall apply in relation to any specified provision of regulations in accordance with which the contributions return is required to be made; and where they so provide then, subject to the following provisions of this paragraph—

(a) that section shall apply in relation to the contributions return as it applies in relation to the tax return; and

(b) sections 100 to 100D and 102 to 104 of that Act shall apply in relation to a penalty under section 98A of that Act to which a person is liable by virtue of this sub-paragraph as they apply in relation to any other penalty under that section.

(3) Where a person is liable to a penalty under paragraph (a) of subsection (2) of section 98A of that Act (first 12 months' default) in consequence of a failure in respect of a tax return, he shall not also be liable to a penalty under that paragraph in respect of any failure in respect of the associated contributions return.

(4) In any case where—

(a) a person is liable to a penalty under subsection (2)(b) or (4) of that section (tax-related penalties) in respect of both a tax return and its associated contributions return, and

(b) an officer of the Inland Revenue authorised for the purposes of section 100 of that Act has determined that a penalty is to be imposed under that provision in respect of both returns,

the penalty so imposed shall be a single penalty of an amount not exceeding the limit determined under sub-paragraph (5) below.

(5) The limit mentioned in sub-paragraph (4) above is an amount equal to the sum of—

(a) the maximum penalty that would have been applicable under subsection (2)(b) or (4) of section 98A of that Act (as the case may be) for a penalty in relation to the tax return only; and

(b) the maximum penalty that would have been so applicable in relation to the associated contributions return only.

(6) So much of any single penalty imposed by virtue of sub-paragraph (4) above as is recovered by the Inland Revenue shall, after the deduction of any administrative costs of the Inland Revenue attributable to its recovery, be apportioned between the Inland Revenue and the Department in the ratio T:C, where—

T is the maximum penalty that could have been imposed under the provision in question in relation to the tax return only; and

C is the maximum penalty that could have been so imposed in relation to the associated contributions return only.

(7) The Inland Revenue shall, at such times and in such manner as the Department of Finance and Personnel may direct, account to the Department for, and pay to it—

(a) the amounts apportioned to the Department under sub-paragraph (6) above in respect of such penalties as are there mentioned; and

(b) so much of any penalty otherwise imposed by virtue of this paragraph and recovered by the Inland Revenue as remains after the deduction by them of any administrative costs attributable to its recovery.

(8) Sub-paragraphs (6) and (7) above shall have effect notwithstanding any provision which treats a penalty under section 98A of that Act as if it were tax charged in an assessment and due and payable.

(9) In the application of section 98A of that Act by virtue of this paragraph, any reference to a year of assessment shall be construed, in relation to a contributions return, as a reference to the tax year corresponding to that year of assessment.

(10) In the application of section 100D of that Act (court proceedings for penalties in cases of fraud) by virtue of this paragraph—

(a) subsection (2) shall have effect with the omission of the words "England, Wales or" and paragraphs (a) and (b); and

(b) subsection (3) shall have effect with the omission of the words from "instituted in England and Wales" to "and any such proceedings" and the substitution for "that Part of that Act" of "Part II of the Crown Proceedings Act 1947".

(11) In the application of section 103 of that Act (time limit for recovery) by virtue of this paragraph—

(a) any reference in subsection (1) to tax shall be taken to include a reference to Class 1 and Class 1A contributions;

(b) any penalty by virtue of sub-paragraph (4) above shall be regarded as a penalty in respect of the tax return in question; and

(c) where, by virtue of subsection (2) (death), subsection (1)(b) does not apply in relation to a penalty under section 98A(2)(b) or (4) of that Act in respect of a tax return, it shall also not apply in relation to a penalty so imposed in respect of the associated contributions return.

(12) A penalty under section 98A of that Act as it applies by virtue of this paragraph may be imposed notwithstanding that a question arising in relation to contributions has not been determined under section 15 of the Administration Act by the Department except that where—

(a) any such question arises which affects a person's liability for, or the amount of, the penalty, and

(b) either—

(i) that person requires the question to be determined under section 15, or

(ii) a question of law arising in connection with the determination of the question is, or is to be, referred to the Court of Appeal under section 16 of the Administration Act,

the penalty shall not be imposed until the question has been determined under section 15 of the Administration Act by the Department or the reference has been finally disposed of under section 16 of that Act, as the case may be; but, subject to that, this paragraph is without prejudice to sections 15 to 17 of the Administration Act.

(13) For the purposes of this paragraph—

(a) "contributions return" and "tax return" shall be construed in accordance with sub-paragraph (1) above; and

(b) a contributions return and a tax return are "associated" if the contributions return is required to be made—

(i) at the same time as the tax return, or

(ii) where sub-paragraph (1)(b) above applies, at a time defined by reference to the time for making the tax return.

General regulation-making powers

8.—(1) Regulations may provide—

(a) for requiring persons to maintain, in such form and matter as may be prescribed, records—

(i) of the earnings paid by them to and in respect of earners, and

(ii) of the contributions paid or payable in respect of earnings so paid,

for the purpose of enabling the incidence of liability for contributions of any class to be determined, and to retain the records for so long as may be prescribed;

(b) for requiring persons to maintain, in such form and manner as may be prescribed, records of such matter as may be prescribed for the purpose of enabling the incidence of liability for Class 1A contributions to be determined, and to retain the records for so long as may be prescribed;

(c) for treating primary Class 1 contributions, when payable on the primary contributor's behalf by the secondary contributor, but not paid, as actually paid where the failure to pay is shown not to have been with the consent or connivance of, or attributable to any negligence on the part of, the primary contributor and, in the case of contributions so treated, for treating them also as paid at a prescribed time or in respect of a prescribed period;

(d) for treating, for the purpose of any entitlement to benefit, contributions paid at or after any prescribed time as paid at some other time (whether earlier or later) or, in the case of contributions paid after the due date for payment, or at such later date as may be prescribed, as not having been paid;

(e) for enabling contributions to be treated as paid in respect of a tax year earlier or later than that in respect of which they were actually paid;

(f) for treating (for the purposes of Class 2 contributions) a week which falls partly in one, and partly in another, tax year as falling wholly within one or the other of those tax years;

(g) for treating contributions of the wrong class, or at the wrong rate, or of the wrong amount, as paid on account of contributions properly payable (notwithstanding section 14 above, in the case of Class 3 contributions) or as paid (wholly or in part) in discharge of a liability for a state scheme premium;

(h) for the repayment, in prescribed cases, of the whole or a prescribed part of any contributions paid by reference to earnings which have become repayable;

(i) for the repayment, in prescribed cases, of a prescribed part of any Class 1A contribution as to which the Department is satisfied in the light of information of a kind mentioned in section 10(6)(a), (b) or (c) above that has become available to it, that too much has been paid;

(j) for the repayment, on the making of an application in the prescribed manner and within the prescribed time, of Class 2 contributions paid by a person in respect of a period which consists of, or falls within, a tax year for which his earnings from employment as a self-employed earner were, or were such as to be treated by regulations under subsection (4) of section 11 above as being, at a lower rate than the one specified in that subsection for that year;

(k) for excepting a person from liability for contributions repaid by virtue of paragraph (j) above, to the extent that he would not have been so excepted by virtue of section 11(4) above;

(l) without prejudice to paragraph (g) above, for enabling—
  (i) the whole or part of any payment of secondary Class 1 contributions to be treated as a payment of Class 1A contributions;
  (ii) the whole or part of any payment of Class 1A contributions to be treated as a payment of secondary Class 1 contributions or Class 2 contributions;
  (iii) the whole or part of any payment of Class 2 contributions to be treated as a payment of secondary Class 1 contributions or Class 1A contributions;

(m) for the return of the whole or any prescribed part of any contributions paid either in error or in such circumstances that, under any provision of Part I of this Act or of regulations, they fall to be repaid;

(n) for treating a person as being an employed earner, notwithstanding that his employment is outside Northern Ireland;

(o) for treating a person's employment as continuing during periods of holiday, unemployment or incapacity for work and in such other circumstances as may be prescribed;

(p) for requiring persons to apply to the Department for the allocation of a national insurance number;

(q) for any other matters incidental to the payment, collection or return of contributions.

(2) Regulations made by the Department under sub-paragraph (1) above providing for the payment of Class 2 or Class 3 contributions (at the option of the persons liable to pay) either—

(a) by means of adhesive stamps; or

(b) by some alternative method, the use of which involves greater expense in administration to the government departments concerned than would be incurred if the contributions were paid by means of such stamps,

may include provision for the payment to the Department by any person who adopts any alternative method, and for the recovery by the Department, of the prescribed fees in respect of any difference in the expense in administration.

(3) Where under regulations made by virtue of sub-paragraph (1) above contributions are payable by means of adhesive stamps, the Department—

(a) may, with the consent of the Department of Finance and Personnel, arrange for the preparation and sale of those stamps, and

(b) may by regulations provide for applying, with the necessary modifications as respects those stamps, all or any of the provisions of the Stamp Duties Management Act 1891, section 9 of the Stamp Act 1891 and section 63 of the Post Office Act 1953.

9. Regulations may provide that—

(a) for the purpose of determining whether a contribution is payable in respect of any person, or

(b) for determining the amount or rate of any contribution,

he is to be treated as having attained at the beginning of a week, or as not having attained until the end of a week, any age which he attains during the course of that week.

Sickness payments counting as remuneration

10.—(1) Regulations may make provision as to the manner in which, and the person through whom, any sickness payment which, by virtue of section 4(1) above, is to be treated as remuneration derived from employed earner's employment is to be made.

(2) In any case where regulations made under sub-paragraph (1) above have the effect of requiring a registered friendly society (within the meaning of the Friendly Societies Act (Northern Ireland) 1970) to make amendments to its rules, the amendments may, notwithstanding any provision of those rules, be made in accordance with the procedure prescribed by regulations made by the Registrar of Friendly Societies for Northern Ireland for the purposes of this paragraph.

(3) Regulations made under sub-paragraph (2) above shall be subject to negative resolution within the meaning of section 41(6) of the Interpretation Act (Northern Ireland) 1954 as if they were statutory instruments within the meaning of that Act.

GENERAL NOTE

This Schedule consolidates SS(N.I.)A 1975, Sched. 1 (as amended) and concerns the rules and regulation-making powers governing the computation, collection and recovery of National Insurance contributions under Classes 1, 1A, 2 and 3. It also applies to Class 4 contributions in so far as they are collected by the Department rather than the Inland Revenue (s.1(4)(b)).

Para. 6

Note the transitory modifications in SS(CP)(N.I.)A 1992, Sched. 4, paras. 5 and 6.

Section 15(3)　　　　　　　　　SCHEDULE 2

SCHEDULE 2 TO THE SOCIAL SECURITY CONTRIBUTIONS AND BENEFITS ACT 1992: LEVY OF CLASS 4 CONTRIBUTIONS WITH INCOME TAX

Interpretation

1. In this Schedule—
(a) "the Act of 1988" means the Income and Corporation Taxes Act 1988;
(b) "the Act of 1990" means the Capital Allowances Act 1990;
(c) "year" means year of assessment within the meaning of the Act of 1988.

Method of computing profits or gains

2. Subject to the following paragraphs, Class 4 contributions shall be payable in respect of the full amount of all profits or gains of any relevant trade, profession or vocation chargeable to income tax under Case I or II Schedule D, subject to—
(a) deductions for—
(i) allowances which under section 140(2) of the Act of 1990 fall to be made as a deduction in charging the profits or gains to income tax, and
(ii) any allowance the amount of which falls to be given by way of discharge or repayment of income tax under section 141 of that Act,
where in either case the allowance arises from activities of any relevant trade, profession or vocation; and
(b) additions for any such charges as under section 140(7) of that Act fall to be made for purposes of income tax on the profits or gains.

Reliefs

3.—(1) For the purposes of computing the amount of profits or gains in respect of which Class 4 contributions are payable, relief shall be available under, and in the manner provided by, the following provisions of the Act of 1988—
(a) sections 380 and 381 (set-off of trade losses against general income), but only where loss arises from activities the profits or gains of which would be brought into computation for the purposes of Class 4 contributions;
(b) section 383 (extension of right of set-off to capital allowances);
(c) section 385 (carry-forward of loss against subsequent profits); and
(d) sections 388 and 389 (carry-back of terminal losses).
(2) The following relief provisions of the Act of 1988 shall not apply, that is to say—
(a) Chapter I of Part VII (personal reliefs);
(b) section 353 (relief for payment of interest);

   (c) section 387 (carry-forward as losses of amounts to be taxed under section 350);

   (d) section 390 (treatment of interest as a loss for purposes of carry-forward or carry-back);

   (e) section 617(5) (relief for Class 4 contributions); and

   (f) sections 619 and 620 (premiums or other consideration under annuity contracts and trust schemes).

(3) Where in the year 1989-90 or any previous year of assessment for which a person claims and is allowed relief by virtue of sub-paragraph (1) above—

   (a) there falls to be made in computing his total income for income tax purposes, or that of his spouse, a deduction in respect of any loss, and

   (b) the deduction or part of it falls to be so made from income other than profits or gains of a trade, profession or vocation,

the amount of the deduction made from the other income shall be treated as reducing the person's profits or gains (that is to say the profits or gains of any relevant trade, profession or vocation as computed for the purpose of the charge to Class 4 contributions) for subsequent years (being deducted as far as may be from those of the immediately following year, whether or not he claims or is entitled to claim relief under this paragraph for that year, and, so far as it cannot be so deducted, then from those of the next year, and so on).

(4) Where in the year 1990–1991 or any subsequent year of assessment for which a person claims and is allowed relief by virtue of sub-paragraph (1) above there falls to be made in computing his total income for income tax purposes a deduction in respect of any loss in any relevant trade, profession or vocation—

   (a) the amount of the deduction shall, as far as may be, be treated for the purpose of the charge to Class 4 contributions as reducing the person's profits or gains for that year of any relevant trade, profession or vocation, and

   (b) any excess shall be treated for that purpose as reducing such profits or gains for subsequent years (being deducted as far as may be from those of the immediately following year, whether or not the person claims or is entitled to claim relief under this paragraph for that year, and, so far as it cannot be so deducted, then from those of the next year, and so on).

(5) Relief shall be allowed, in respect of—

   (a) payments under section 348 or 349(1) of the Act of 1988 (annuities and other annual payments, etc.); or

   (b) payments under section 353 of that Act (relief for payment of interest), being payments for which relief from income tax is or can be given,

so far as incurred wholly or exclusively for the purposes of any relevant trade, profession or vocation, by way of deduction from or set-off against profits or gains chargeable to Class 4 contributions for the year in which the payments are made; and, in the case of any insufficiency of the profits or gains of that year, the payments shall be carried forward and deducted from or set off against the profits or gains of any subsequent year (being deducted or set off as far as may be from or against the profits or gains of the immediately following year, whether or not relief can be claimed under this paragraph for that year, and so far as it cannot be so deducted, from or against those of the next year, and so on).

Partnerships

4.—(1) Where a trade or profession is carried on by two or more persons jointly, the liability of any one of them in respect of Class 4 contributions shall arise in respect of his share of the profits or gains of that trade or profession (so far as immediately derived by him from carrying it on); and for this purpose his share shall be aggregated with his share of the profits or gains of any other trade, profession or vocation (so far as immediately derived by him from carrying it on or exercising it).

(2) Where sub-paragraph (1) above applies, the Class 4 contributions for which a person is liable in respect of the profits or gains of the trade or profession carried on jointly (aggregated, where appropriate, as mentioned in that sub-paragraph) may either be charged on him separately or (to the extent only that the liability arises in respect of the profits or gains of that partnership) be the subject of a joint assessment to contributions made in the partnership name; and sections 111 to 115 of the Act of 1988 shall apply accordingly, but substituting this paragraph for section 111.

Trustees, etc.

5. In any circumstances in which apart from this paragraph a person would—

   (a) under section 72 of the Taxes Management Act 1970 be assessable and chargeable to

Class 4 contributions as trustee, guardian, tutor, curator, or committee of an incapacitated person in respect of the profits or gains of a trade, profession or vocation, or

(b) by virtue of section 59 of the Act of 1988 be assessed and charged to such contributions in respect of profits or gains received or receivable by him in the capacity of trustee,

such contributions shall not be payable either by him or by any other person.

Other provisions

6.—(1) Sections 86 and 88(1), (4) and (5)(a) and (b) of the Taxes Management Act 1970 (interest on amounts overdue, and on tax recovered to make good loss due to taxpayer's fault) shall apply in relation to any amount due in respect of Class 4 contributions as they apply in relation to income tax; and section 824 of the Act of 1988 (repayment supplements) shall, with the necessary modifications, apply in relation to Class 4 contributions as it applies in relation to income tax.

(2) The Inland Revenue shall have the same powers under section 1 of the Taxes Management Act 1970 (general functions of care and management) in relation to the remission of interest payable under section 86 or 88 of that Act by virtue of this paragraph as they have in relation to the remission of interest payable under either of those sections on tax.

7. Where an assessment has become final and conclusive for the purposes of income tax for any year, that assessment shall also be final and conclusive for the purposes of computing liability for Class 4 contributions; and no allowance or adjustment of liability, on the ground of diminution of income or loss, shall be taken into account in computing profits or gains chargeable to Class 4 contributions unless that allowance or adjustment has previously been made on an application under the special provisions of the Income Tax Acts relating to it, or falls to be allowed under paragraph 3(5) of this Schedule.

8. The provisions of Part V of the Taxes Management Act 1970 (appeals, etc.) shall apply with the necessary modifications in relation to Class 4 contributions as they apply in relation to income tax; but nothing in the Income Tax Acts shall apply with respect to the determination of any question arising—

(a) under subsection (1) of section 17 above or subsection (1) of section 17 of the Northern Ireland Contributions and Benefits Act as to whether by regulations under that subsection a person is expected from liability for Class 4 contributions, or his liability is deferred; or

(b) under regulations made by virtue of section 17(3) or (4) or 18 above or section 17(3) or (4) or 18 of the Northern Ireland Contributions and Benefits Act.

Husband and wife—1989–90 and previous years of assessment

9.—(1) For the year 1989–90 and previous years of assessment Chapter II of Part VII of the Act of 1988 shall apply for the purposes of Class 4 contributions as it applies for those of income tax and an application by a husband or wife for separate assessment under section 283 of that Act, and an election by them under section 287 of that Act (separate taxation of wife's earnings) shall operate as respects liability for such contributions as it does for income tax, the wife being liable for Class 4 contributions in respect of her own profits or gains.

(2) Such an application or election as is referred to in sub-paragraph (1) above shall not be made separately for the purposes of Class 4 contributions apart from those of income tax.

(3) Where section 279 of the Act of 1988 applies and there is no separate assessment under section 283 of that Act and no election under section 287 of that Act, the wife's profits and gains are to be computed, for the purposes of Class 4 contributions as if section 279 did not apply, but the contributions shall be assessed on, and recoverable from, the husband.

(4) In this paragraph "year of assessment" has the meaning assigned to it by section 832 of the Act of 1988.

GENERAL NOTE

This Schedule consolidates SS(N.I.)A 1975, Sched. 2 (as amended) and concerns the rules governing the levying of Class 4 National Insurance contributions.

Para. 6

Note the transitory modifications in SS(CP)(N.I.)A 1992, Sched. 4, paras. 7 and 8.

CONTRIBUTION CONDITIONS FOR ENTITLEMENT TO BENEFIT

PART I

THE CONDITIONS

Unemployment benefit

1.—(1) The contribution conditions for unemployment benefit are the following.

(2) The first condition is that—

(a) the claimant must have actually paid contributions of a relevant class in respect of one of the last two complete years before the beginning of the relevant benefit year, and those contributions must have been paid before the relevant time; and

(b) the earnings factor derived as mentioned in sub-paragraph (4) below must be not less than that year's lower earnings limit multiplied by 25.

(3) The second condition is that—

(a) the claimant must in respect of the last two complete years before the beginning of the relevant benefit year have either paid or been credited with contributions of a relevant class or been credited (in the case of 1987–88 or any subsequent year) with earnings; and

(b) the earnings factor derived as mentioned in sub-paragraph (5) below must be not less in each of those years than the year's lower earnings limit multiplied by 50.

(4) The earnings factor referred to in paragraph (b) of sub-paragraph (2) above is that which is derived—

(a) if the year in question is 1987–88 or any subsequent year from earnings upon which primary Class 1 contributions have been paid or treated as paid; or

(b) if the year in question is an earlier year, from the contributions paid as mentioned in paragraph (a) of that sub-paragraph.

(5) The earnings factor referred to in paragraph (b) of sub-paragraph (3) above is that which is derived—

(a) if the year in question is 1987–88 or any subsequent year from earnings upon which primary Class 1 contributions have been paid or treated as paid or from earnings credited; or

(b) if the year in question is an earlier year, from the contributions referred to in paragraph (a) of that sub-paragraph.

(6) For the purposes of these conditions—

(a) "the relevant time" is the day in respect of which benefit is claimed;

(b) "the relevant benefit year" is the benefit year in which there falls the beginning of the period of interruption of employment which includes the relevant time.

Sickness benefit

2.—(1) The contribution conditions for sickness benefit are the following.

(2) The first condition is that—

(a) the claimant must have actually paid contributions of a relevant class in respect of any one year, and those contributions must have been paid before the relevant time; and

(b) the earnings factor derived as mentioned in sub-paragraph (4) below must be not less than that year's lower earnings limit multiplied by 25.

(3) The second condition is that—

(a) the claimant must in respect of the last two complete years before the beginning of the relevant benefit year have either paid or been credited with contributions of a relevant class or been credited (in the case of 1987–88 or any subsequent year) with earnings; and

(b) the earnings factor derived as mentioned in sub-paragraph (5) below must be not less in each of those years than the year's lower earnings limit multiplied by 50.

(4) The earnings factor referred to in paragraph (b) of sub-paragraph (2) above is that which is derived—

(a) if the year in question is 1987–88 or any subsequent year—

(i) from earnings upon which primary Class 1 contributions have been paid or treated as paid; or

(ii) from Class 2 contributions; or

(b) if the year in question is an earlier year, from the contributions paid as mentioned in paragraph (a) of that sub-paragraph.

(5) The earnings factor referred to in paragraph (b) of sub-paragraph (3) above is that which is derived—

  (a) if the year in question is 1987–88 or any subsequent year—
        (i) from earnings upon which primary Class 1 contributions have been paid or treated as paid or from earnings credited; or
        (ii) from Class 2 contributions; or
  (b) if the year in question is an earlier year, from the contributions referred to in paragraph (a) of that sub-paragraph.
  (6) For the purposes of these conditions—
  (a) "the relevant time" is the day in respect of which benefit is claimed;
  (b) "the relevant benefit year" is the benefit year in which there falls the beginning of the period of interruption of employment which includes the relevant time.

Maternity allowance

  3.—(1) Subject to sub-paragraph (2) below, the contribution condition for a maternity allowance is—
  (a) that the claimant must, in respect of at least 26 weeks in the 52 weeks immediately preceding the 14th week before the expected week of confinement, have actually paid contributions of a relevant class; and
  (b) in the case of Class 1 contributions, that they were not secondary contributions and were paid otherwise than at the reduced rate.
  (2) In the case of a claimant who is or has been paid otherwise than weekly, any week—
  (a) in respect of which she did not pay contributions of a relevant class; but
  (b) for which her earnings were such that, had she been paid weekly, she would have been required to pay primary Class 1 contributions in respect of that week; and
  (c) for which no such election as is mentioned in section 19(4)(a) above was in force in her case,
shall be treated for the purposes of sub-paragraph (1) above as a week in respect of which she actually paid such contributions otherwise than at a reduced rate.
  (3) For the purposes of sub-paragraph (2) above, the amount of the claimant's earnings for any week shall be determined in accordance with regulations.

Widow's payment

  4.—(1) The contribution condition for a widow's payment is that—
  (a) the contributor concerned must in respect of any one relevant year have actually paid contributions of a relevant class; and
  (b) the earnings factor derived as mentioned in sub-paragraph (2) below must be not less than that year's lower earnings limit multiplied by 25.
  (2) The earnings factor referred to in paragraph (b) of sub-paragraph (1) above is that which is derived—
  (a) if the year in question is 1987–88 or any subsequent year, from earnings upon which primary Class 1 contributions have been paid or treated as paid and from Class 2 and Class 3 contributions, or
  (b) if the year in question is an earlier year, from the contributions referred to in paragraph (a) of that sub-paragraph.
  (3) For the purposes of this condition a relevant year is any year ending before the date on which the contributor concerned attained pensionable age or died under that age.

Widowed mother's allowance and widow's pension; retirement pensions (Categories A and B)

  5.—(1) The contribution conditions for a widowed mother's allowance, a widow's pension or a Category A or Category B retirement pension are the following.
  (2) The first condition is that—
  (a) the contributor concerned must in respect of any one relevant year have actually paid contributions of a relevant class; and
  (b) the earnings factor derived—
        (i) if that year is 1987–88 or any subsequent year, from earnings upon which such of those contributions as are primary Class 1 contributions were paid or treated as paid and any Class 2 or Class 3 contributions, or
        (ii) if that year is an earlier year, from the contributions referred to in paragraph (a) above,
    must be not less than the qualifying earnings factor for that year.
  (3) The second condition is that—
  (a) the contributor concerned must, in respect of each of not less than the requisite number

of years of his working life, have paid or been credited with contributions of a relevant
class; and
(b) in the case of each of those years, the earnings factor derived as mentioned in sub-
paragraph (4) below must be not less than the qualifying earnings factor for that year.
(4) For the purposes of paragraph (b) of sub-paragraph (3) above, the earnings factor—
(a) in the case of 1987–88 or any subsequent year, is that which is derived from—
(i) any earnings upon which such of the contributions mentioned in paragraph (a) of
that sub-paragraph as are primary Class 1 contributions were paid or treated as paid or
earnings credited; and
(ii) any Class 2 or Class 3 contributions for the year; or
(b) in the case of any earlier year, is that which is derived from the contributions mentioned
in paragraph (a) of that sub-paragraph.
(5) For the purposes of the first condition, a relevant year is any year ending before that in
which the contributor concerned attained pensionable age or died under that age; and the
following table shows the requisite number of years for the purpose of the second condition, by
reference to a working life of a given duration—

Duration of working life	Requisite number of years
10 years or less	The number of years of the working life, minus 1.
20 years or less (but more than 10)	The number of years of the working life, minus 2.
30 years or less (but more than 20)	The number of years of the working life, minus 3.
40 years or less (but more than 30)	The number of years of the working life, minus 4.
More than 40 years	The number of years of the working life, minus 5.

(6) The first condition shall be taken to be satisfied if the contributor concerned was entitled
to an invalidity pension at any time during—
(a) the year in which he attained pensionable age or died under that age, or
(b) the year immediately preceding that year.
(7) The second condition shall be taken to be satisfied notwithstanding that paragraphs (a)
and (b) of sub-paragraph (3) above are not complied with as respects each of the requisite
number of years if—
(a) those paragraphs are complied with as respects at least half that number of years (or at
least 20 of them, if that is less than half); and
(b) in each of the other years the contributor concerned was, within the meaning of regulations, precluded from regular employment by responsibilities at home.
(8) For the purposes of this paragraph a person's working life is the period between—
(a) (inclusive) the tax year in which he attained the age of 16; and
(b) (exclusive) the tax year in which he attained pensionable age or died under that age.

Child's special allowance

6.—(1) The contribution condition for a child's special allowance is that—
(a) the contributor concerned must in respect of any one relevant year have actually paid
contributions of a relevant class; and
(b) the earnings factor derived from those contributions must be not less than that year's
lower earnings limit multiplied by 50.
(2) For the purposes of this condition, a relevant year is any year ending before the date on
which the contributor concerned attained pensionable age or died under that age.

PART II

SATISFACTION OF CONDITIONS IN EARLY YEARS OF CONTRIBUTION

7.—(1) Sub-paragraph (3) below shall apply where a claim is made for a widow's payment
and the last complete year before the beginning of the benefit year in which the relevant time
falls was either—
(a) the year in which the contributor concerned first became liable for primary Class 1 or
Class 2 contributions; or

(b) the year preceding that in which he first became so liable.

(2) The relevant time for the purposes of this paragraph is the date on which the contributor concerned attained pensionable age or died under that age.

(3) For the purposes of satisfaction by the contributor concerned of paragraph (b) of the contribution condition for a widow's payment, all earnings factors falling within sub-paragraph (4) below may be aggregated and that aggregate sum shall be treated as his earnings factor for the last complete year before the beginning of the benefit year in which the relevant time falls.

(4) The earnings factors referred to in sub-paragraph (3) above are—

  (a) the contributor's earnings factors for 1987–88 and each subsequent year derived from the aggregate of his earnings upon which primary Class 1 contributions were paid or treated as paid and from Class 2 contributions actually paid by him before the relevant time; and

  (b) his earnings factors for each earlier year, derived from his contributions of a relevant class actually paid by him before the relevant time.

8. Where a person claims sickness benefit, he shall be taken to satisfy the first contribution condition for the benefit if on a previous claim for any short-term benefit he has satisfied the first contribution condition for that benefit by virtue of paragraph 8 of Schedule 3 to the 1975 Act, with contributions of a class relevant to sickness benefit.

9. Where a woman claims a widow's payment, the contributor concerned for the purposes of the claim shall be taken to satisfy the contribution condition for the payment if on a claim made in the past for any short-term benefit he has satisfied the first contribution condition for the benefit, by virtue of paragraph 8 of Schedule 3 to the 1975 Act, with contributions of a class relevant to widow's payment.

GENERAL NOTE

This Schedule consolidates SS(N.I.)A 1975, Sched. 3 (as amended) and sets out the contribution conditions for the benefits listed in s.20, the main conditions for which are detailed elsewhere in Pt. II.

Parts II to V   SCHEDULE 4

RATES OF BENEFITS, ETC.

Note: This Schedule is subject to alteration by orders made by the Department under section 132 of the Administration Act.

PART I

CONTRIBUTORY PERIODICAL BENEFITS

Description of benefit	*Weekly rate*
1. Unemployment benefit.	£43.10.
2. Sickness benefit.	£41.20.
3. Invalidity allowance.	(a) higher rate ... ... £11.55 (b) middle rate ... ... £7.20 (c) lower rate ... ... £3.60 (the appropriate rate being determined in accordance with section 34(3)).
4. Maternity allowance.	£42.25.
5. Category B retirement pension where section 50(1)(a)(i) applies.	£32.55.
6. Child's special allowance.	£10.85.

PART II

WIDOW'S PAYMENT

WIDOW'S PAYMENT.	£1,000.00

PART III

NON-CONTRIBUTORY PERIODICAL BENEFITS

Description of benefit	*Weekly rate*
1. Attendance allowance.	(a) higher rate £43.35
	(b) lower rate £28.95
	(the appropriate rate being determined in accordance with section 65(3)).
2. Severe disablement allowance.	£32.55.
3. Age related addition.	(a) higher rate £11.55
	(b) middle rate £7.20
	(c) lower rate £3.60
	(the appropriate rate being determined in accordance with section 69(1)).
4. Invalid care allowance.	£32.55.
5. Guardian's allowance.	£10.85.
6. Category C retirement pension.	(a) lower rate £19.45
	(b) higher rate £32.55
	(the appropriate rate being determined in accordance with section 78(5)).
7. Category D retirement pension.	The higher rate for Category C retirement pensions under paragraph 6 above.
8. Age addition (to a pension of any category, and otherwise under section 79).	£0.25.

PART IV

INCREASES FOR DEPENDANTS

Benefit to which increase applies	*Increase for qualifying child*	*Increase for adult dependant*
(1)	*(2)* £	*(3)* £
1. Unemployment or sickness benefit—		
(a) unemployment benefit, where the beneficiary is under pensionable age	—	26.60
(b) unemployment benefit, where the beneficiary is over pensionable age	10.85	32.55
(c) sickness benefit, where the beneficiary is under pensionable age	—	25.50
(d) sickness benefit, where the beneficiary is over pensionable age	10.85	31.20
2. Invalidity pension.	10.85	32.55
3. Maternity allowance.	—	25.50
4. Widowed mother's allowance.	10.85	—
5. Category A or B retirement pension.	10.85	32.55

Benefit to which increase applies	Increase for qualifying child	Increase for adult dependant
(1)	*(2)* £	*(3)* £
6. Category C retirement pension.	10.85	19.45
7. Child's special allowance.	10.85	—
8. Severe disablement allowance.	10.85	19.45
9. Invalid care allowance.	10.85	19.45

PART V

RATE OF INDUSTRIAL INJURIES BENEFIT

Description of benefit, etc.	*Rate*
1. Disablement pension (weekly rates).	For the several degrees of disablement set out in column (1) of the following Table, the respective amounts in that Table, using— (a) column (2) for any period during which the beneficiary is over the age of 18 or is entitled to an increase of benefit in respect of a child or adult dependant; (b) column (3) for any period during which the beneficiary is not over the age of 18 and not so entitled;

TABLE

Degree of disablement	Amount	
(1) Per cent.	*(2)* £	*(3)* £
100	88.40	54.15
90	79.56	48.74
80	70.72	43.32
70	61.88	37.91
60	53.04	32.49
50	44.20	27.08
40	35.36	21.66
30	26.52	16.25
20	17.68	10.83

2. Maximum increase of weekly rate of disablement pension where constant attendance needed.	(a) except in cases of exceptionally severe disablement ... ... £35.40 (b) in any case of exceptionally severe disablement £70.80
3. Increase of weekly rate of disablement pension (exceptionally severe disablement).	£35.40
4. Maximum of aggregate of weekly benefit payable for successive accidents.	(a) for any period during which the beneficiary is over the age of 18 or is entitled to an increase in benefit in respect of a child or adult dependant ... ... £88.40 (b) for any period during which the beneficiary is not over the age of 18 and not so entitled £54.15
5. Unemployability supplement under paragraph 2 of Schedule 7.	£54.15

6. Increase under paragaph 3 of Schedule 7 of weekly rate of unemployability supplement.

   (a) if on the qualifying date the beneficiary was under the age of 35 or if that date fell before 5th July 1948 ... ... £11.55

   (b) if head (a) above does not apply and on the qualifying date the beneficiary was under the age of 40 and he had not attained pensionable age before 6th April 1979 ... ... £11.55

   (c) if heads (a) and (b) above do not apply and on the qualifying date the beneficiary was under the age of 45 ... ... £7.20

   (d) if heads (a), (b) and (c) above do not apply and on the qualifying date the beneficiary was under the age of 50 and had not attained pensionable age before 6th April 1979 ... ...£7.20

   (e) in any other case £3.60

7. Increase under paragraph 4 of Schedule 7 of weekly rate of disablement pension.

   £10.85

8. Increase under paragraph 6 of Schedule 7 of weekly rate of disablement pension.

   £32.55

9. Maximum disablement gratuity under paragraph 9 of Schedule 7.

   £5,870.00

10. Widow's pension (weekly rates).

   (a) initial rate £57.65
   (b) higher permanent rate £54.15
   (c) lower permanent rate 30
   per cent. of the first sum specified in section 44(4) (Category A basic retirement pension) (the appropriate rate being determined in accordance with paragraph 16 of Schedule 7).

11. Widower's pension (weekly rate).

   £54.15

12. Weekly rate of allowance in respect of children under paragraph 18 of Schedule 7.

   In respect of each qualifying child £10.85

GENERAL NOTE

This Schedule sets out the various rates of benefit. Uprating takes place in April of each year. See further SSA(N.I.)A 1992, ss.132–134.

Section 55   SCHEDULE 5

INCREASE OF PENSION WHERE ENTITLEMENT IS DEFERRED

Increase of pension where pensioner's entitlement is deferred

1. Where a person's entitlement to a Category A or Category B retirement pension is deferred, the rate of his Category A or Category B retirement pension shall be increased by an amount equal to the aggregate of the increments to which he is entitled under paragraph 2 below, but only if that amount is enough to increase the rate of the pension by at least 1 per cent.

2.—(1) Subject to paragraph 3 below, a person is entitled to an increment under this paragraph for each complete incremental period in his period of enhancement.

(2) In this Schedule—

"incremental period" means any period of six days which are treated by regulations as days of increment for the purposes of this Schedule in relation to the person and the pension in question; and

"the period of enhancement", in relation to that person and that pension, means the period which—

(a) begins on the same day as the period of deferment in question; and

(b) ends on the same day as that period or, if earlier, on the day before the 5th anniversary of the beginning of that period.

(3) Subject to paragraph 3 below, the amount of the increment for any such incremental period shall be 1/7th per cent. of the weekly rate of the Category A or Category B retirement pension to which that person would have been entitled for the period if his entitlement had not been deferred.

(4) Where an amount is required to be calculated in accordance with the provisions of sub-paragraph (3) above—

(a) the amount so calculated shall be rounded to the nearest penny, taking any 1/2p as nearest to the next whole penny above; and

(b) where the amount so calculated would, apart from this sub-paragraph, be a sum less than 1/2p, that amount shall be taken to be zero, notwithstanding any other provision of this Act, the Pensions Order or the Administration Act.

(5) For the purposes of sub-paragraph (3) above the weekly rate of pension for any period shall be taken—

(a) to include any increase under section 47(1) above and any increase under paragraph 4, 5 or 6 below, but

(b) not to include any increase under section 80, 83 or 85 above or any graduated retirement benefit.

(6) The reference in sub-paragraph (5) above to any increase under subsection (1) of section 47 above shall be taken as a reference to any increase that would take place under that subsection if subsection (2) of that section and Article 31B(2) of the Pensions Order were disregarded.

(7) Where one or more orders have come into force under section 132 of the Administration Act during the period of enhancement the rate for any incremental period shall be determined as if the order or orders had come into force before the beginning of the period of enhancement.

(8) Where a pensioner's rights premium is paid in respect of a person who is, or if his entitlement had not been deferred would be, entitled to a Category A or Category B retirement pension, then, in calculating any increment under this paragraph which falls to be paid to him in respect of such a pension after the date on which the premium is paid there shall be disregarded any guaranteed minimum pension to which the pensioner was entitled in connection with the employment to which the premium relates.

3.—(1) Regulations may provide that sub-paragraphs (1) to (3) of paragraph 2 above shall have effect with such additions, omissions and amendments as are prescribed in relation to a person during whose period of enhancement there has been a change, other than a change made by such an order as is mentioned in sub-paragraph (7) of that paragraph, in the rate of the Category A or Category B retirement pension to which he would have been entitled if his entitlement to the pension had commenced on attaining pensionable age.

(2) Any regulations under this paragraph may make such consequential additions, omissions and amendments in paragraph 8(3) below as the Department considers are appropriate in consequence of any changes made by virtue of this paragraph in paragraph 2 above.

Increase of pension where pensioner's deceased spouse has deferred entitlement

4.—(1) Subject to sub-paragraph (3) below, where a woman is entitled to a Category A or Category B retirement pension and—

(a) she has had a husband and he had died, and she was married to him when he died; and

(b) the husband either—

(i) was entitled to a Category A or Category B retirement pension with an increase under this Schedule; or

(ii) would have been so entitled if his period of deferment had ended on the day before his death,

the rate of her pension shall be increased by an amount equal to the increase to which he was or would have been entitled under this Schedule apart from paragraph 6.

(2) Subject to sub-paragraph (3) below, where a man is entitled to a Category A or Category B retirement pension and—

(a) he has had a wife and she has died, and he was married to her when she died;

(b) he was over pensionable age when she died; and

(c) the wife either—

(i) was entitled to a Category A or Category B retirement pension with an increase under this Schedule; or

(ii) would have been so entitled if her period of deferment had ended on the day before her death, the rate of his pension shall be increased by an amount equal to the increase to which she was or woud have been entitled under this Schedule apart from paragraph 5.

(3) If a married person dies after April 5, 2000, the rate of the retirement pension for that person's widow or widower shall be increased by an amount equivalent to the sum of—

    (a) the increase in the basic pension to which the deceased spouse was entitled; and

    (b) one-half of the increase in the additional pension.

(4) In any case where—

    (a) there is a period between the death of the former spouse and the date on which the surviving spouse becomes entitled to a Category A or Category B retirement pension, and

    (b) one or more orders have come into force under section 132 of the Administration Act during that period,

the amount of the increase to which the surviving spouse is entitled under this paragraph shall be determined as if the order or orders had come into force before the beginning of that period.

(5) This paragraph does not apply in any case where the deceased spouse died before April 6, 1979 and the widow or widower attained pensionable age before that date.

5.—(1) Where a woman is entitled to a Category A or Category B retirement pension and—

    (a) she has a husband and he has died, and she was married to him when he died; and

    (b) the husband either—

        (i) was entitled to a guaranteed minimum pension with an increase under Article 37(6) of the Pensions Order, or

        (ii) would have been so entitled if he had retired on the date of his death,

the rate of her pension shall be increased by an amount equal to the sum of the amounts set out in sub-paragraph (2) or, as the case may be, (3) below.

(2) Where the husband dies before April 6, 2000, the amounts referred to in sub-paragraph (1) above are the following—

    (a) an amount equal to the increase mentioned in paragraph (b) of that sub-paragraph;

    (b) the appropriate amount; and

    (c) an amount equal to any increase to which she had been entitled under paragraph 6 below.

(3) Where the husband dies after April 5, 2000, the amounts referred to in sub-paragraph (1) above are the following—

    (a) one-half of the appropriate amount after it has been reduced by the amount of any increases under Article 39A of the Pensions Order; and

    (b) one-half of any increase to which the husband had been entitled under paragraph 6 below.

6.—(1) Where a man is entitled to a Category A or Category B retirement pension and—

    (a) he has had a wife and she has died, and he was married to her when she died;

    (b) he was over pensionable age when she died; and

    (c) the wife either—

        (i) was entitled to a guaranteed minimum pension with an increase under Article 37(6) of the Pensions Order; or

        (ii) would have been so entitled if she had retired on the date of her death.

the rate of his pension shall be increased by an amount equal to the sum of the amounts set out in sub-paragraph (2) or, as the case may be, (3) or (4) below.

(2) Where the wife dies before April 6, 1989, the amounts referred to in sub-paragraph (1) above are the following—

    (a) an amount equal to the increase mentioned in paragraph (c) of that sub-paragraph;

    (b) the appropriate amount; and

    (c) an amount equal to any increase to which she had been entitled under paragraph 5 above.

(3) Where the wife dies after April 5, 1989 but before April 6, 2000, the amounts referred to in sub-paragraph (1) above are the following—

    (a) the increase mentioned in paragraph (c) of that sub-paragraph, so far as attributable to employment before April 6, 1988;

    (b) one-half of that increase, so far as attributable to employment after April 5, 1988;

    (c) the appropriate amount reduced by the amount of any increases under Article 39A of the Pensions Order; and

    (d) any increase to which she had been entitled under paragraph 5 above.

(4) Where the wife dies after April 5, 2000, the amounts referred to in sub-paragraph (1) above are the following—

    (a) one-half of the increase mentioned in paragraph (c) of that sub-paragraph, so far as attributable to employment before April 6, 1988;

    (b) one-half of the appropriate amount after it has been reduced by the amount of any increases under Article 39A of the Pensions Order; and

    (c) one-half of any increase to which she had been entitled under paragraph 5 above.

7.—(1) For the purposes of paragraphs 5 and 6 above, the "appropriate amount" means the greater of—

(a) the amount by which the deceased person's Category A or Category B retirement pension had been increased under section 132 of the Administration Act corresponding to an order under section 150(1)(e) of the Great Britain Administration Act; or

(b) the amount by which his Category A or Category B retirement pension would have been so increased had he died immediately before his surviving spouse became entitled to a Category A or Category B retirement pension.

(2) Where an amount is required to be calculated in accordance with the provisions of paragraph 5 or 6 or sub-paragraph (1) above—

(a) the amount so calculated shall be rounded to the nearest penny, taking any 1/2p as nearest to the next whole penny above; and

(b) where the amount so calculated would, apart from this sub-paragraph, be a sum less than 1/2p, that amount shall be taken to be zero, notwithstanding any other provision of this Act, the Pensions Order or the Administration Act.

Married women

8.—(1) For the purposes of paragraphs 1 to 3 above in their application to a Category B retirement pension to which a married woman is entitled by virtue of her husband's contributions, a married woman who would have become entitled to such a pension on an earlier day if her husband's entitlement to his Category A retirement pension had not been deferred shall be treated as having (in addition to any other period of enhancement) a period of enhancement which begins on that earlier day and ends on the same day as her husband's period of enhancement.

(2) The reference in sub-paragraph (1) above to the day on which the woman's husband's period of enhancement ends shall, where the marriage is terminated before that day, be construed as a reference to the day on which the marriage is terminated.

(3) In the case of—

(a) a Category B retirement pension to which a married woman is entitled by virtue of her husband's contributions; or

(b) a married woman's Category A retirement pension with an increase under section 53(2) above attributable to her husband's contributions,

the reference in paragraph 2(3) above to the pension to which a person would have been entitled if his entitlement had not been deferred shall be construed as a reference to the pension to which she would have been entitled if neither her nor her husband's entitlement to a retirement pension had been deferred.

(4) Paragraph 4(2)(c) above shall not apply to a Category B retirement pension to which the wife was or would have been entitled by virtue of the man's contributions; and where the Category A retirement pension to which the wife was or would have been entitled includes an increase under section 53(2) above attributable to his contributions, the increase to which he is entitled under that paragraph shall be calculated as if there had been no increase under that section.

Uprating

9. The sums which are the increases in the rates of retirement pensions under this Schedule are subject to alteration by orders made by the Department under section 132 of the Administration Act.

GENERAL NOTE
See General Note to s.55.

Sections 68(6) and 103(5)   SCHEDULE 6

ASSESSMENT OF EXTENT OF DISABLEMENT

General provisions as to method of assessment

1. For the purposes of section 68 or 103 above and Part II of Schedule 7 to this Act, the extent of disablement shall be assessed, by reference to the disabilities incurred by the claimant as a result of the relevant loss of faculty, in accordance with the following general principles—

(a) except as provided in paragraphs (b) to (d) below, the disabilities to be taken into account shall be all disabilities so incurred (whether or not involving loss of earning power or additional expense) to which the claimant may be expected, having regard to his physical and mental condition at the date of the assessment, to be subject during the period taken into account by the assessment as compared with a person of the same age and sex whose physical and mental condition is normal;

(b) except in the case of an assessment for the purposes of section 68 above, regulations may make provision as to the extent (if any) to which any disabilities are to be taken into account where they are disabilities which, though resulting from the relevant loss of faculty, also result, or without the relevant accident might have been expected to result, from a cause other than the relevant accident;

(c) the assessment shall be made without reference to the particular circumstances of the claimant other than age, sex, and physical and mental condition;

(d) the disabilities resulting from such loss of faculty as may be prescribed shall be taken as amounting to 100 per cent. disablement and other disabilities shall be assessed accordingly.

2. Provision may be made by regulations for further defining the principles on which the extent of disablement is to be assessed and such regulations may in particular direct that a prescribed loss of faculty shall be treated as resulting in a prescribed degree of disablement; and, in connection with any such direction, nothing in paragraph 1(c) above prevents the making of different provision, in the case of loss of faculty in or affecting hand or arm, for right-handed and for left-handed persons.

3. Regulations under paragraph 1(d) or 2 above may include provision—

(a) for adjusting or reviewing an assessment made before the date of the coming into force of those regulations;

(b) for any resulting alteration of that assessment to have effect as from that date;

so however that no assessment shall be reduced by virtue of this paragraph.

Severe disablement allowance

4.—(1) In the case of an assessment of any person's disablement for the purposes of section 68 above, the period to be taken into account for any such assessment shall be the period during which that person has suffered and may be expected to continue to suffer from the relevant loss of faculty beginning not later than—

(a) the first claim day if his entitlement to benefit falls to be determined in accordance with section 68(3)(b) above as modified by regulations under section 68(11)(b);

(b) where his disablement has previously been assessed for the purposes of section 68 above at a percentage which is not less than 80 per cent.—

(i) if the period taken into account for that assessment was or included the period of 196 days ending immediately before the first claim day, the first claim day, or

(ii) if the period so taken into account included any day falling within that period of 196 days, the day immediately following that day or, if there is more than one such day, the last such day;

(c) in any other case, 196 days before the first claim day;

and, in any case, ending not later than the day on which that person attains the age of 65, if a woman, or 70, if a man.

(2) In this paragraph "the first claim day" means the first day in respect of which the person concerned has made the claim in question for a severe disablement allowance.

5.—(1) An assessment of any person's disablement for the purposes of section 68 above shall state the degree of disablement in the form of a percentage and shall specify the period taken into account by the assessment.

(2) For the purposes of any such assessment—

(a) a percentage which is not a whole number shall be rounded to the nearest whole number or if it falls equally near two whole numbers shall be rounded up to the higher; and

(b) a percentage between 5 and 100 which is not a multiple of 10 shall be treated, if it is a multiple of 5, as being the next higher percentage which is a multiple of 10 and, in any other case, as being the nearest percentage which is a multiple of 10.

(3) If on the assessment the person's disablement is found to be less than 5 per cent. that degree of disablement shall for the purposes of section 68 above be disregarded and, accordingly, the assessment shall state that he is not disabled.

Disablement benefit

6.—(1) Subject to sub-paragraphs (2) and (3) below, the period to be taken into account by an assessment for the purposes of section 103 above and Part II of Schedule 7 to this Act of the extent of a claimant's disablement shall be the period (beginning not earlier than the end of the period of 90 days referred to in section 103(6) above and in paragraph 9(3) of that Schedule and limited by reference either to the claimant's life or to a definite date) during which the claimant has suffered and may be expected to continue to suffer from the relevant loss of faculty.

(2) If on any assessment the condition of the claimant is not such, having regard to the possibility of changes in that condition (whether predictable or not), as to allow of a final assessment being made up to the end of the period provided by sub-paragraph (1) above, then, subject to sub-paragraph (3) below—

(a) a provisional assessment shall be made, taking into account such shorter period only as seems reasonable having regard to his condition and that possibility; and

(b) on the next assessment the period to be taken into account shall begin with the end of the period taken into account by the provisional assessment.

(3) Where the assessed extent of a claimant's disablement amounts to less than 14 per cent. then, subject to sub-pararaphs (4) and (5) below, that assessment shall be a final assessment and the period to be taken into account by it shall not end before the earliest date on which it seems likely that the extent of the disablement will be less than 1 per cent.

(4) Sub-paragraph (3) above does not apply in any case where it seems likely that—

(a) the assessed extent of the disablement will be aggregated with the assessment extent of any present disablement, and

(b) that aggregate will amount to 14 per cent. or more.

(5) Where the extent of the claimant's disablement is assessed at different percentages for different parts of the period taken into account by the assessment, then—

(a) sub-paragraph (3) above does not apply in relation to the assessment unless the percentage assessed for the latest part of that period is less than 14 per cent., and

(b) in any such case that sub-paragraph shall apply only in relation to that part of that period (and subject to sub-paragraph (4) above).

7. An assessment for the purposes of section 103 above and Part II of Schedule 7 to this Act shall—

(a) state the degree of disablement in the form of a percentage;

(b) specify the period taken into account by the assessment; and

(c) where that period is limited by reference to a definite date, specify whether the assessment is provisional or final;

but the percentage and the period shall not be specified more particularly than is necessary for the purpose of determining in accordance with section 103 above and Parts II and IV of Schedule 7 to this Act the claimant's rights as to disablement pension and gratuity and reduced earnings allowance (whether or not a claim has been made).

Special provision as to entitlement to constant attendance allowance, etc.

8.—(1) For the purpose of determining whether a person is entitled—

(a) to an increase of a disablement pension under section 104 above; or

(b) to a corresponding increase of any other benefit by virtue of paragraph 4(2)(b) of Schedule 8 to this Act,

regulations may provide for the extent of the person's disablement resulting from the relevant injury or disease to be determined in such manner as may be provided for by the regulations by reference to all disabilities to which that person is subject which result either from the relevant injury or disease or from any other injury or disease in respect of which there fall to be made to the person payments of any of the descriptions listed in sub-paragraph (2) below.

(2) Those payments are payments—

(a) by way of disablement pension;

(b) by way of benefit under paragraph 4(1) of Schedule 8 to this Act; or

(c) in such circumstances as may be prescribed by way of such other benefit as may be prescribed (being benefit in connection with any hostilities or with service as a member of Her Majesty's forces or of such other organisation as may be specified in the regulations).

GENERAL NOTE

This Schedule consolidates SS(N.I.)A 1975, Sched. 8 (as amended) and specifies the rules governing the assessment of disablement for the purposes of severe disablement allowance, disablement benefit and constant attendance allowance. See Lewis, Chap. 5.

Section 106   SCHEDULE 7

INDUSTRIAL INJURIES BENEFITS

PART I

UNEMPLOYABILITY SUPPLEMENT

Availability

1. This Part of this Schedule applies only in relation to persons who were beneficiaries in

receipt of unemployability supplement under section 58 of the 1975 Act immediately before 6th April 1987.

Rate and duration

2.—(1) The weekly rate of a disablement pension shall, if as the result of the relevant loss of faculty the beneficiary is incapable of work and likely to remain so permanently, be increased by the amount specified in Schedule 4, Part V, paragraph 5.

(2) An increase of pension under this paragraph is referred to in this Act as an "unemployability supplement."

(3) For the purposes of this paragraph a person may be treated as being incapable of work and likely to remain so permanently, notwithstanding that the loss of faculty is not such as to prevent him being capable of work, if it is likely to prevent his earnings in a year exceeding a prescribed amount not less than £104.

(4) An unemployability supplement shall be payable for such period as may be determined at the time it is granted, but may be renewed from time to time.

Increase of unemployability supplement

3.—(1) Subject to the following provisions of this paragraph, if on the qualifying date the beneficiary was—

(a) a man under the age of 60, or
(b) a woman under the age of 55,

the weekly rate of unemployability supplement shall be increased by the appropriate amount specified in Schedule 4, Part V, paragraph 6.

(2) Where for any period the beneficiary is entitled to a Category A or Category B retirement pension or an invalidity pension and the weekly rate of the pension includes an additional pension such as is mentioned in section 44(3)(b) above, for that period the relevant amount shall be deducted from the amount that would otherwise be the increase under this paragraph and the beneficiary shall be entitled to an increase only if there is a balance after that deduction and, if there is such a balance, only of an amount equal to it.

(3) In this paragraph "the relevant amount" means an amount equal to the additional pension reduced by the amount of any reduction in the weekly rate of the retirement or invalidity pension made by virtue of Article 31 of the Pensions Order.

(4) In this paragraph references to an additional pension are references to that pension after any increase under section 52(3) above but without any increase under paragraphs 1 and 2 of Schedule 5 to this Act.

(5) In this paragraph "the qualifying date" means, subject to sub-paragraphs (6) and (7) below, the beginning of the first week for which the beneficiary qualified for unemployability supplement.

(6) If the incapacity for work in respect of which unemployability supplement is payable forms part of a period of interruption of employment which has continued from a date earlier than the date fixed under sub-paragraph (5) above, the qualifying date means the first day in that period which is a day of incapacity for work, or such earlier day as may be prescribed.

(7) Subject to sub-paragraph (6) above, if there have been two or more periods for which the beneficiary was entitled to unemployability supplement, the qualifying date shall be, in relation to unemployability supplement for a day in any one of those periods, the beginning of the first week of that period.

(8) For the purposes of sub-paragraph (7) above—

(a) a break of more than 8 weeks in entitlement to unemployability supplement means that the periods before and after the break are two different periods; and
(b) a break of 8 weeks or less is to be disregarded.

(9) Regulations may provide that sub-paragraph (8) above shall have effect as if for the references to 8 weeks there were substituted references to a larger number of weeks specified in the regulations.

(10) In this paragraph "period of interruption of employment" has the same meaning as it has for the purposes of unemployment benefit.

(11) The provisions of this paragraph are subject to Article 31C of the Pensions Order (contracting-out and increases of unemployability supplement).

Increase for beneficiary's dependent children

4.—(1) Subject to the provisions of this paragraph and paragraph 5 below, the weekly rate of a disablement pension where the beneficiary is entitled to an unemployability supplement shall be increased for any period during which the beneficiary is entitled to child benefit in respect of a child or children.

(2) The amount of the increase shall be as specified in Schedule 4, Part V, paragraph 7.

(3) In any case where—

(a) a beneficiary is one of two persons who are—
    (i) spouses residing together, or
    (ii) an unmarried couple, and
(b) the other person had earnings in any week,

the beneficiary's right to payment of increases for the following week under this paragraph shall be determined in accordance with sub-paragraph (4) below.

(4) No such increase shall be payable—

(a) in respect of the first child where the earnings were £110 or more; and
(b) in respect of a further child for each complete £14 by which the earnings exceeded £110.

(5) The Department may by order substitute larger amounts for the amounts for the time being specified in sub-paragraph (4) above.

(6) In this paragraph "week" means such period of 7 days as may be prescribed by regulations made for the purposes of this paragraph.

Additional provisions as to increase under paragraph 4

5.—(1) An increase under paragraph 4 above of any amount in respect of a particular child shall for any period be payable only if during that period one or other of the following conditions is satisfied with respect to the child—

(a) the beneficiary would be treated for the purposes of Part IX of this Act as having the child living with him; or
(b) the requisite contributions are being made to the cost of providing for the child.

(2) The condition specified in paragraph (b) of sub-paragraph (1) above is to be treated as satisfied if, and only if—

(a) such contributions are being made at a weekly rate not less than the amount referred to in that sub-paragraph—
    (i) by the beneficiary, or
    (ii) where the beneficiary is one of two spouses residing together, by them together; and
(b) except in prescribed cases, the contributions are over and above those required for the purposes of satisfying section 139(1)(b) above.

Increase for adult dependants

6.—(1) The weekly rate of a disablement pension where the beneficiary is entitled to an unemployability supplement shall be increased under this paragraph for any period during which—

(a) the beneficiary is—
    (i) residing with his spouse, or
    (ii) contributing to the maintenance of his spouse at the requisite rate; or
(b) a person—
    (i) who is neither the spouse of the beneficiary nor a child, and
    (ii) in relation to whom such further conditions as may be prescribed are fulfilled,
    has the care of a child or children in respect of whom the beneficiary is entitled to child benefit.

(2) The amount of the increase under this paragraph shall be that specified in Schedule 4, Part V, paragraph 8 and the requisite rate for the purposes of sub-paragraph (1)(a) above is a weekly rate not less than that amount.

(3) Regulations may provide that, for any period during which—

(a) the beneficiary is contributing to the maintenance of his or her spouse at the requisite rate, and
(b) the weekly earnings of the spouse exceed such amount as may be prescribed,

there shall be no increase of benefit under this paragraph.

(4) Regulations may provide that, for any period during which the beneficiary is residing with his or her spouse and the spouse has earnings—

(a) the increase of benefit under this paragraph shall be subject to a reduction in respect of the spouse's earnings; or
(b) there shall be no increase of benefit under this paragraph.

(5) Regulations may, in a case within sub-paragraph (1)(b) above in which the person there referred to is residing with the beneficiary and fulfils such further conditions as may be prescribed, authorise an increase of benefit under this paragraph, but subject, taking account of

the earnings of the person residing with the beneficiary, other than such of that person's earnings from employment by the beneficiary as may be prescribed, to provisions comparable to those that may be made by virtue of sub-paragraph (4) above.

(6) Regulations under this paragraph may, in connection with any reduction or extinguishment of an increase in benefit in respect of earnings, prescribe the method of calculating or estimating the earnings.

(7) A beneficiary shall not be entitled to an increase of benefit under this paragraph in respect of more than one person for the same period.

Earnings to include occupational and personal pensions for purposes of disablement pension

7.—(1) Except as may be prescribed, any reference to earnings in paragraph 4 or 6 above includes a reference to payments by way of occupational or personal pension.

(2) For the purposes of those paragraphs, the Department may by regulations provide, in relation to cases where payments by way of occupational or personal pension are made otherwise than weekly, that any necessary apportionment of the payments shall be made in such manner and on such basis as may be prescribed.

Dependency increases: continuation of awards in cases of fluctuating earnings

8.—(1) Where a beneficiary—
(a) has been awarded an increase of benefit under paragraph 4 or 6 above, but
(b) ceases to be entitled to the increase by reason only that the weekly earnings of some other person ("the relevant earner") exceed the amount of the increase or, as the case may be, some specified amount,
then, if and so long as the beneficiary would have continued to be entitled to the increase, disregarding any such excess of earnings, the award shall continue in force but the increase shall not be payable for any week if the earnings relevant to that week exceed the amount of the increase or, as the case may be, the specified amount.

(2) In this paragraph the earnings which are relevant to any week are those earnings of the relevant earner which, apart from this paragraph, would be taken into account in determining whether the beneficiary is entitled to the increase in question for that week.

Part II

Disablement Gratuity

9.—(1) An employed earner shall be entitled to a disablement gratuity, if—
(a) he made a claim for disablement benefit before 19th November 1986;
(b) he suffered as the result of the relevant accident from loss of physical or mental faculty such that the extent of the resulting disablement assessed in accordance with Schedule 6 to this Act amounts to not less than 1 per cent.; and
(c) the extent of the disablement is assessed for the period taken into account as amounting to less than 20 per cent.

(2) A disablement gratuity shall be—
(a) of an amount fixed, in accordance with the length of the period and the degree of the disablement, by a prescribed scale, but not in any case exceeding the amount specified in Schedule 4, Part V, paragraph 9; and
(b) payable, if and in such cases as regulations so provide, by instalments.

(3) A person shall not be entitled to disablement gratuity until after the expiry of the period of 90 days (disregarding Sundays) beginning with the day of the relevant accident.

Part III

Increase of Disablement Pension During Hospital Treatment

10.—(1) This Part of this Schedule has effect in relation to a period during which a person is receiving medical treatment as an in-patient in a hospital or similar institution and which—
(a) commenced before 6th April 1987; or
(b) commenced after that date but within a period of 28 days from the end of the period during which he last received an increase of benefit under section 62 of the 1975 Act or this paragraph in respect of such treatment for the relevant injury or loss of faculty.

(2) Where a person is awarded disablement benefit, but the extent of his disablement is assessed for the period taken into account by the assessment at less than 100 per cent., it shall be treated as assessed at 100 per cent. for any part of that period, whether before or after the

making of the assessment or the award of benefit, during which he receives, as an in-patient in a hospital or similar institution, medical treatment for the relevant injury or loss of faculty.

(3) Where the extent of the disablement is assessed for that period at less than 20 per cent., sub-paragraph (2) above shall not affect the assessment; but in the case of a disablement pension payable by virtue of this paragraph to a person awarded a disablement gratuity wholly or partly in respect of the same period, the weekly rate of the pension (after allowing for any increase under Part V of this Act) shall be reduced by the amount prescribed as being the weekly value of his gratuity.

Part IV

Reduced Earnings Allowance

11.—(1) Subject to the provisions of this paragraph, an employed earner shall be entitled to reduced earnings allowance if—
(a) he is entitled to a disablement pension or would be so entitled if that pension were payable where disablement is assessed at not less than 1 per cent.; and
(b) as a result of the relevant loss of faculty, he is either—
(i) incapable, and likely to remain permanently incapable, of following his regular occupation; and
(ii) incapable of following employment of an equivalent standard which is suitable in his case,

or is, and has at all times since the end of the period of 90 days referred to in section 103(6) above been, incapable of following that occupation or any such employment;
but a person shall not be entitled to reduced earnings allowance to the extent that the relevant loss of faculty results from an accident happening on or after 1st October 1990 (the day on which Article 5 of the Social Security (Northern Ireland) Order 1990 came into operation).

(2) A person—
(a) who immediately before that date is entitled to reduced earnings allowance in consequence of the relevant accident; but
(b) who subsequently ceases to be entitled to that allowance for one or more days,
shall not again be entitled to reduced earnings allowance in consequence of that accident; but this sub-paragraph does not prevent the making at any time of a claim for, or an award of, reduced earnings allowance in consequence of that accident for a period which commences not later than the day after that on which the claimant was last entitled to that allowance in consequence of that accident.

(3) For the purposes of sub-paragraph (2) above—
(a) a person who, apart from section 103(6) above, would have been entitled to reduced earnings allowance immediately before 1st October 1990 shall be treated as entitled to that allowance on any day (including a Sunday) on which he would have been entitled to it apart from that provision;
(b) regulations may prescribe other circumstances in which a person is to be treated as entitled, or as having been entitled, to reduced earnings allowance on any prescribed day.

(4) The Department may by regulations provide that in prescribed circumstances employed earner's employment in which a claimant was engaged when the relevant accident took place but which was not his regular occupation is to be treated as if it had been his regular occupation.

(5) In sub-paragraph (1) above—
(a) references to a person's regular occupation are to be taken as not including any subsidiary occupation, except to the extent that they fall to be treated as including such an occupation by virtue of regulations under sub-paragraph (4) above; and
(b) employment of an equivalent standard is to be taken as not including employment other than employed earner's employment;
and in assessing the standard of remuneration in any employment, including a person's regular occupation, regard is to be had to his reasonable prospect of advancement.

(6) For the purposes of this Part of this Schedule a person's regular occupation is to be treated as extending to and including employment in the capacities to which the persons in that occupation (or a class or description of them to which he belonged at the time of the relevant accident) are in the normal course advanced, and to which, if he had continued to follow that occupation without having suffered the relevant loss of faculty, he would have had at least the normal prospects of advancement; and so long as he is, as a result of the relevant loss of faculty, deprived in whole or in part of those prospects, he is to be treated as incapable of following that occupation.

(7) Regulations may for the purposes of this Part of this Schedule provide that a person is not to be treated as capable of following an occupation or employment merely because of his working thereat during a period of trial or for purposes of rehabilitation or training or in other prescribed circumstances.

(8) Reduced earnings allowance shall be awarded—

(a) for such period as may be determined at the time of the award; and

(b) if at the end of that period the beneficiary submits a fresh claim for the allowance, for such further period, commencing as mentioned in sub-paragraph (2) above, as may be determined.

(9) The award may not be for a period longer than the period to be taken into account under paragraph 4 or 6 of Schedule 6 to this Act.

(10) Reduced earnings allowance shall be payable at a rate determined by reference to the beneficiary's probable standard of remuneration during the period for which it is granted in any employed earner's employments which are suitable in his case and which he is likely to be capable of following as compared with that in the relevant occupation, but in no case at a rate higher than 40 per cent. of the maximum rate of a disablement pension or at a rate such that the aggregate of disablement pension (not including increases in disablement pension under any provision of this Act) and reduced earnings allowance awarded to the beneficiary exceeds 140 per cent. of the maximum rate of a disablement pension.

(11) Sub-paragraph (10) above shall have effect in the case of a person who retired from regular employment before 6th April 1987 with the substitution for "140 per cent." of "100 per cent.".

(12) In sub-paragraph (10) above "the relevant occupation" means—

(a) in relation to a person who is entitled to reduced earnings allowance by virtue of regulations under sub-paragraph (4) above, the occupation in which he was engaged when the relevant accident took place; and

(b) in relation to any other person who is entitled to reduced earnings allowance, his regular occupation within the meaning of sub-paragraph (1) above.

(13) On any award except the first the probable standard of his remuneration shall be determined in such manner as may be prescribed; and, without prejudice to the generality of this sub-paragraph, regulations may provide in prescribed circumstances for the probable standard of remuneration to be determined by reference—

(a) to the standard determined at the time of the last previous award of reduced earnings allowance; and

(b) to scales or indices of earnings in a particular industry or description of industries or any other data relating to such earnings.

(14) In this paragraph "maximum rate of a disablement pension" means the rate specified in the first entry in column (2) of Schedule 4, Part V, paragraph 1 and does not include increases in disablement pension under any provision of this Act.

Supplementary

12.—(1) A person who on 10th April 1988 or 9th April 1989 satisfies the conditions—

(a) that he has attained pensionable age;

(b) that he has retired from regular employment; and

(c) that he is entitled to reduced earnings allowance,

shall be entitled to that allowance for life.

(2) In the case of any beneficiary who is entitled to reduced earnings allowance by virtue of sub-paragraph (1) above, the allowance shall be payable, subject to any enactment contained in Part V or VI of this Act or in the Administration Act and to any regulations made under any such enactment, at the weekly rate at which it was payable to the beneficiary on the relevant date or would have been payable to him on that date but for any such enactment or regulations.

(3) For the purpose of determining under sub-paragraph (2) above the weekly rate of reduced earnings allowance payable in the case of a qualifying beneficiary, it shall be assumed that the weekly rate at which the allowance was payable to him on the relevant date was—

(a) £25.84, where that date is 10th April 1988, or

(b) £26.96, where that date is 9th April 1989.

(4) In sub-paragraph (3) above "qualifying beneficiary" means a person entitled to reduced earnings allowance by virtue of sub-paragraph (1) above who—

(a) did not attain pensionable age before 6th April 1987, or

(b) did not retire from regular employment before that date,

and who, on the relevant date, was entitled to the allowance at a rate which was restricted under paragraph 11(10) above by reference to 40 per cent. of the maximum rate of disablement pension.

(5) For a beneficiary who is entitled to reduced earnings allowance by virtue of satisfying the conditions in sub-paragraph (1) above on 10th April 1988 the relevant date is that date.

(6) For a beneficiary who is entitled to it by virtue only of satisfying those conditions on 9th April 1989 the relevant date is that date.

PART V

RETIREMENT ALLOWANCE

13.—(1) Subject to the provisions of this Part of this Schedule, a person who—
(a) has attained pensionable age; and
(b) gives up regular employment on or after 10th April 1989; and
(c) was entitled to reduced earnings allowance (by virtue either of one award or a number of awards) on the day immediately before he gave up such employment,
shall cease to be entitled to reduced earnings allowance as from the day on which he gives up regular employment.

(2) If the day before a person ceases under sub-paragraph (1) above to be entitled to reduced earnings allowance he is entitled to the allowance (by virtue either of one award or of a number of awards) at a weekly rate or aggregate weekly rate of not less than £2.00, he shall be entitled to a benefit, to be known as "retirement allowance".

(3) Retirement allowance shall be payable to him (subject to any enactment contained in Part V or VI of this Act or in the Administration Act and to any regulations made under any such enactment) for life.

(4) Subject to sub-paragraph (6) below, the weekly rate of a beneficiary's retirement allowance shall be—
(a) 25 per cent. of the weekly rate at which he was entitled to reduced earnings allowance; or
(b) 10 per cent. of the maximum rate of a disablement pension,
whichever is the less.

(5) For the purpose of determining under sub-paragraph (4) above the weekly rate of retirement allowance in the case of a beneficiary who—
(a) retires or is deemed to have retired on 10th April 1989, and
(b) on 9th April 1989 was entitled to reduced earnings allowance at a rate which was restricted under paragraph 11(10) above by reference to 40 per cent. of the maximum rate of disablement pension,
it shall be assumed that the weekly rate of reduced earnings allowance to which he was entitled on 9th April 1989 was £26.96.

(6) If the weekly rate of the beneficiary's retirement allowance—
(a) would not be a whole number of pence; and
(b) would exceed the whole number of pence next below it by 1/2p or more,
the beneficiary shall be entitled to retirement allowance at a rate equal to the next higher whole number of pence.

(7) The sums falling to be calculated under sub-paragraph (4) above are subject to alteration by orders made by the Department under section 132 of the Administration Act.

(8) Regulations may—
(a) make provision with respect to the meaning of "regular employment" for the purposes of this paragraph; and
(b) prescribe circumstances in which, and periods for which, a person is or is not to be regarded for those purposes as having given up such employment.

(9) Regulations under sub-paragraph (8) above may, in particular—
(a) provide for a person to be regarded—
  (i) as having given up regular employment, notwithstanding that he is or intends to be an earner; or
  (ii) as not having given up regular employment, notwithstanding that he has or may have one or more days of interruption of employment; and
(b) prescribe circumstances in which a person is or is not to be regarded as having given up regular employment by reference to—
  (i) the level or frequency of his earnings during a prescribed period; or
  (ii) the number of hours for which he works during a prescribed period calculated in a prescribed manner.

(10) "Day of interruption of employment" has the same meaning for the purposes of this paragraph as it has for the purposes of provisions of this Act relating to unemployment benefit, sickness benefit or invalidity benefit.

(11) In this paragraph "maximum rate of a disablement pension" means the rate specified in the first entry in column (2) of Schedule 4, Part V, paragraph 1 and does not include increases in disablement pension under any provision of this Act.

PART VI

INDUSTRIAL DEATH BENEFIT

Introductory

14.—(1) This Part of this Schedule only has effect in relation to deaths before 11th April 1988.
(2) In this Part of this Schedule "the deceased" means the person in respect of whose death industrial death benefit is claimed or payable.

Widow's benefit (entitlement)

15.—(1) The widow of the deceased shall be entitled to death benefit if at his death either—
(a) she was residing with him; or
(b) she was receiving or entitled to receive, or would but for the relevant accident have been receiving or entitled to receive, from him periodical payments for her maintenance of not less than the prescribed amount.
(2) In the case of a widow, death benefit shall be a pension commencing from the death of the deceased and payable, at the weekly rate for the time being applicable under paragraph 16 below for life or until she remarries.
(3) A pension under this paragraph shall not be payable for any period during which the beneficiary is living as husband and wife with a man not her husband.
(4) In this paragraph—
(a) references to a widow receiving or being entitled to receive payments from the deceased are only to her receiving or being entitled to receive (whether from him or from another) payments provided or procured by the deceased; and
(b) "entitled" means, in relation to any such payments, entitled under any order of a court, trust or agreement which the widow has taken reasonable steps to enforce.

Widow's benefit (rate)

16.—(1) The weekly rate of a pension payable under paragraph 15 above shall, for the period of 26 weeks next following the deceased's death, be the initial rate specified in Schedule 4, Part V, paragraph 10.
(2) The weekly rate of the pension shall, after the end of that period, be the higher permanent rate specified in that paragraph—
(a) for any period for which the widow is entitled, or is treated by regulations as entitled, to an allowance for children under paragraph 18 below;
(b) where the widow was over the age of 50 at the deceased's death or was over the age of 40 at the end of the period for which she was entitled to such an allowance;
(c) where the widow at the deceased's death was permanently incapable of self-support; or
(d) while the widow is pregnant by the deceased.
(3) After the end of the period of 26 weeks referred to in sub-paragraph (1) above, the weekly rate of the pension shall, in any case not within sub-paragraph (2) above, be the lower permanent rate specified in Schedule 4, Part V, paragraph 10.

Widower's benefit (entitlement and rate)

17.—(1) The widower of the deceased shall be entitled to death benefit if at her death he—
(a) was being wholly or mainly maintained by her or would but for the relevant accident have been so maintained; and
(b) was permanently incapable of self-support.
(2) In the case of a widower, death benefit shall be a pension at the weekly rate specified in Schedule 4, Part V, paragraph 11 commencing from the death of the deceased and payable for life.

Children of deceased's family

18.—(1) Subject to paragraph 19 below, where at his death the deceased was entitled to child benefit in respect of a child or children, then, for any period for which—
(a) the widow of the deceased is entitled—
(i) to death benefit (other than a gratuity) under paragraphs 15 and 16 above; and

(ii) to child benefit in respect of that child or one or more of those children; or
(b) such other person as may be prescribed is entitled to child benefit in respect of that child or one or more of those children,

the widow or, as the case may be, the person so prescribed shall be entitled in respect of that child, or in respect of each respectively of those children, to death benefit by way of an allowance at the weekly rate specified in Schedule 4, Part V, paragraph 12.

(2) Paragraph 5 above applies in relation to an allowance under this paragraph as it applies in relation to an increase of benefit under paragraph 4 above.

Limits of entitlement to industrial death benefit in respect of children

19. Where two or more persons satisfy the conditions, in respect of the same death, for receipt of an allowance or allowances under paragraph 18 above for any period—
(a) not more than one of those persons shall be entitled for that period to such an allowance in respect of the same child;
(b) where the deceased leaves a widow or widower, then for any period for which she or he is entitled to death benefit as the deceased's widow or widower and satisfies the conditions for receipt of such an allowance in respect of a child, she or he shall be entitled to the allowance in respect of that child;
(c) subject to sub-paragraph (b) above, regulations may make provision as to the priority in any prescribed circumstances of two or more persons satisfying the said conditions.

Death of person with constant attendance allowance

20.—(1) If a person dies at a time when—
(a) he is entitled to an increase under section 104 above of a disablement pension and the amount of the increase is not less than the amount which at that time is specified in Schedule 4, Part V, paragraph 2(a); or
(b) he would have been so entitled but for having received medical or other treatment as an in-patient in a hospital or similar institution,

he is to be regarded for the purposes of entitlement to industrial death benefit as having died as a result of the injury in respect of which the disablement pension was payable.

(2) The reference in sub-paragraph (1) above to an increase under section 104 above includes only a payment by way of increase of a disablement pension, and in particular does not include any payment for constant attendance under paragraph 4(2)(b) of Schedule 8 to this Act.

(3) Sub-paragraph (1) above does not affect death benefit where the death occurred before 26th July 1971.

Pulmonary disease

21.—(1) If a person dies as a result of any pulmonary disease and—
(a) he was entitled, for a period which includes the date of his death, to disablement pension or gratuity in respect of pneumoconiosis or byssinosis or pneumoconiosis accompanied by tuberculosis; and
(b) the extent of the disablement in respect of which the benefit was payable was assessed for such a period at not less than 50 per cent.,

then, subject to sub-paragraph (2) below, his death shall be treated, for the purposes of this Part of this Schedule, as having been caused by the disease in respect of which the benefit was payable.

(2) Unless regulations provide otherwise, the requirements of paragraph (b) of sub-paragraph (1) above shall be treated as unsatisfied in a case where, had the physical condition of the deceased at the time of the assessment been normal, apart from the diseases mentioned in paragraph (a) of that sub-paragraph, the extent of the disablement in question would have been assessed at less than 50 per cent.

(3) This paragraph does not affect death benefit where the death occurred before 30th March 1977.

GENERAL NOTE
    This Schedule deals with various benefits under the industrial injuries scheme which have been phased out in recent years. See General Note to ss.94 and 106.

Paras. 11 and 12
    Note the transitory modifications in SS(CP)(N.I.)A 1992, Sched. 4, paras. 9 and 10.

SCHEDULE 8

INDUSTRIAL INJURIES AND DISEASES (OLD CASES)

PART I

WORKMEN'S COMPENSATION AND INDUSTRIAL DISEASES BENEFIT IN RESPECT OF EMPLOYMENT BEFORE 5th JULY 1948

Continuation of workmen's compensation

1. The Workmen's Compensation Acts and any other enactment repealed by section 88 of the National Insurance (Industrial Injuries) Act (Northern Ireland) 1946 shall continue to apply to any cases to which, if the Supplementation Act had not been passed, they would have applied by virtue of that section, being certain cases where a right to compensation arises or has arisen in respect of employment before 5th July 1948.

Regulations to provide for supplementing workmen's compensation

2.—(1) The Department may, with the consent of the Department of Finance and Personnel, make regulations (in this Schedule referred to as "the regulations") conferring a right to allowances on persons who are, or have at any time after 23rd July 1951 been, entitled to weekly payments by way of workmen's compensation, other than a person whose entitlement to such payments—
   (a) arose in consequence of an accident happening after 31st December 1923; and
   (b) ceased before 24th July 1956.
   (2) Subject to the provisions of this Schedule, the right to such an allowance or to a payment on account of such an allowance shall be subject to such conditions, and the rate of the allowance shall be such, as may be provided by the regulations.
   (3) The allowances for the payment of which the regulations may make provision shall be—
   (a) where the relevant accident happened before 1st January 1924, an allowance (in this paragraph referred to as a "basic allowance") in respect of any period such as is mentioned in sub-paragraph (8) below;
   (b) an allowance in respect of any period such as is mentioned in sub-paragraph (8)(a) below (in this paragraph referred to as a "major incapacity allowance");
   (c) subject to sub-paragraphs (4) and (5) below, an allowance in respect of any period such as is mentioned in sub-paragraph (8)(b) below (in this paragraph referred to as a "lesser incapacity allowance");
and a major incapacity allowance or lesser incapacity allowance in respect of any period shall be payable whether or not a basic allowance is also payable in respect of that period.
   (4) A lesser incapacity allowance—
   (a) shall not be payable to any person in respect of any period unless there is or may be expected to be (or, but for the cesser at a time after 28th February 1966 of that person's entitlement to workmen's compensation, would or might be expected to have been) payable to that person in respect of that period either a weekly payment by way of basic allowance or a weekly payment by way of workmen's compensation which is not a notional payment;
   (b) except to a person who immediately before 1st March 1966 was receiving an allowance under a scheme made under the Workmen's Compensation (Supplementation) Act (Northern Ireland) 1951, shall not be payable if the relevant accident happened after 31st December 1923 and the claimant's entitlement to workmen's compensation in consequence of it ceased before 1st March 1966.
   (5) For the purposes of a lesser incapacity allowance, a weekly payment by way of workmen's compensation shall be treated as a notional payment if awarded or paid for the purpose of safeguarding a potential entitlement to compensation and not related to any existing loss of earnings; and the regulations may provide that—
   (a) in such circumstances or cases as may be specified in the regulations; and
   (b) in particular, in cases where weekly payments by way of such compensation are being paid to a person to whom such payments were not made, or were made at a lower rate, during the period of 12 months immediately preceding such date not earlier than 30th November 1965 as may be specified in the regulations,
a weekly payment by way of such compensation shall be deemed to be a notional payment unless the contrary is proved.
   (6) The weekly rate—

(a) of a basic allowance shall not exceed £2 less the amount of the recipient's workmen's compensation and, in respect of a period such as is mentioned in sub-paragraph (8)(b) below which is a period of partial incapacity only, shall also not exceed the difference between 2/3rds of the amount representing his weekly loss of earnings determined in accordance with the regulations and the amount of his workmen's compensation;

(b) of a major incapacity allowance shall be the corresponding disablement pension rate;

(c) of a lesser incapacity allowance shall not exceed £32.55.

(7) Sub-paragraph (6)(b) above shall have effect in relation to any person who has retired, or is treated as having retired, from regular employment, for the purposes of Parts I to VI of this Act, for so long as he continues to be treated as retired for those purposes, as if at the end of the paragraph there were added the words "less the amount of the recipient's workmen's compensation and less the amount of his basic allowance, if any".

(8) The periods referred to in sub-paragraph (3) above are—

(a) any period during which the person claiming or receiving an allowance under this paragraph—
  (i) being or having been entitled to his workmen's compensation in respect of any injury or disease, is as a result of that injury or disease totally incapable of work and likely to remain so incapable for a considerable period; or
  (ii) being or having been entitled to his workmen's compensation in respect of two or more injuries or diseases, is as the joint result of those injuries or diseases totally incapable of work and likely to remain so incapable for a considerable period;

(b) any period which, not being a period such as is mentioned in paragraph (a) above, is a period of total or partial incapacity for work resulting from the relevant injury or disease.

Provisions supplementary to paragraph 2

3.—(1) For the purposes of paragraph 2 above—

(a) the expressions "relevant accident" and "relevant injury or disease" mean the accident in consequence of which or, as the case may be, the injury or disease in respect of which, an entitlement to weekly payments by way of workmen's compensation arose;

(b) any reference to the happening of an accident shall, in relation to a case of disease, be construed in the same way as for the purposes of the Workmen's Compensation Acts;

(c) a payment—
  (i) under the Workmen's Compensation (War Addition) Acts 1917 and 1919; or
  (ii) under the Workmen's Compensation (Supplementary Allowances) Act (Northern Ireland) 1940 as amended by the Workmen's Compensation (Temporary Increases) Act (Northern Ireland) 1943,
shall be treated as a weekly payment by way of workmen's compensation.

(2) For the purposes of paragraph 2(1) above, a person shall be deemed to be or have been entitled to weekly payments by way of workmen's compensation at any time if he would be or, as the case may be, have been so entitled at that time if—

(a) the amount of any payment, allowance or benefit received by him otherwise than by way of workmen's compensation; or

(b) where the relevant accident happened before 1st January 1924, either that amount, or the amount he is earning or able to earn in some suitable employment or business, or both those amounts,
were sufficiently reduced.

(3) Subject to sub-paragraph (7) below, for the purpose of the reference in paragraph 2(8)(b) above to a period of total incapacity for work resulting from the relevant injury or disease, a person who is or has been unable to obtain employment shall be treated as subject to such an incapacity if he is treated as being so for the purposes of his workmen's compensation in respect of the relevant injury or disease and in such other circumstances as may be provided by the regulations.

(4) Any reference in paragraph 2 above or this paragraph to the amount of a person's workmen's compensation shall (subject to sub-paragraphs (5) to (7) below) be taken as referring to the amount, if any, of the weekly payments to which for the time being he is, or would but for the determination of his right be, entitled in respect of the relevant injury or disease so, however, that—

(a) where in fixing the amount of those weekly payments under the provisions relating to them regard was had to any payment, allowance or benefit which he might receive during the period of his incapacity from the person liable for the compensation, and the amount is shown to have been reduced in consequence, the amount of those weekly payments shall for the purposes of this sub-paragraph be taken to be the reduced amount so fixed with the addition of the amount of the reduction; and

(b) where the amount of those weekly payments has not been fixed under the said provisions, it shall be fixed for the purposes of this sub-paragraph without regard to any such payment, allowance or benefit.

(5) The regulations may include provision that, in such special circumstances or cases and for such purposes as may be specified in the regulations, any reference in paragraph 2 above or this paragraph to the amount of a person's workmen's compensation shall be taken as referring to such amount as it may be determined in manner provided by the regulations ought reasonably and properly to have been the amount of the weekly payments referred to in sub-paragraph (4) above.

(6) Where a person is, or has at any time after 23rd July 1951 been, entitled to payments under the enactments referred to in sub-paragraph (1)(c)(i) or (ii) above but ceased before 24th July 1951 to be entitled to any other weekly payments by way of workmen's compensation in respect of the relevant injury or disease, the amount of his workmen's compensation shall for the purposes of paragraph 2 above be calculated as if he had not ceased to be entitled to such other payments.

(7) The regulations may provide for modifying the operation of sub-paragraphs (3) to (5) above in relation to a person whose workmen's compensation is or was compensation under a contracting-out scheme in such manner as appears to the Department to be proper having regard to the provisions of the contracting-out scheme.

PART II

REGULATIONS PROVIDING FOR BENEFIT FOR PRE-1948 CASES

4.—(1) This paragraph applies to any person who is or has been at any time after 4th July 1948—
   (a) entitled in respect of any injury or disease to weekly payments by way of compensation under the Workmen's Compensation Acts; or
   (b) entitled to payments on account of an injury pension under or by virtue of any enactment in respect of an injury received or disease contracted by him before 5th July 1948 or in respect of his retirement in consequence of such an injury or disease.

(2) Regulations may provide—
   (a) for conferring on persons to whom this paragraph applies who as a result of the injury or disease in question are, or could for the purpose of the provisions of this Act relating to unemployability supplement and any provisions of the Administration Act, so far as they so relate, be treated as being, incapable of work and likely to remain permanently so incapable—
       (i) the like right to payments under Schedule 7 to this Act by way of unemployability supplement; and
       (ii) the like right to payments under Schedule 7 to this Act in respect of a child or adult dependant,
   as if the injury or disease were one in respect of which a disablement pension were for the time being payable;
   (b) for conferring on persons to whom this paragraph applies who as a result of the injury or disease in question require constant attendance—
       (i) the like right to payments under this Act in respect of the need for constant attendance; and
       (ii) the like right to an increase for exceptionally severe disablement,
   as if the injury or disease were one in respect of which a disablement pension were for the time being payable in respect of an assessment of 100 per cent.;
   (c) for applying in relation to payments under this paragraph the provisions of this Act relating to industrial injuries benefit, in so far as those provisions apply in relation to—
       (i) an unemployability supplement;
       (ii) an increase of a disablement pension in respect of a child or adult dependant; or
       (iii) an increase of a disablement pension in respect of the need for constant attendance or exceptionally severe disablement,
   (as the case may be) subject to any additions or modifications.

PART III

INTERPRETATION

5.—(1) In this Schedule, except where the context otherwise requires—
   "corresponding disablement pension rate" means the weekly rate for the time being of a disablement pension in respect of an assessment of 100 per cent.;

"injury pension" includes any pension or similar benefit payable in respect of a person's employment or former employment, being a pension or benefit which would not be payable or would be payable at a less rate but for an injury or disease referable to that employment;

"the regulations" has the meaning given by paragraph 2(1) above;

"the Supplementation Act" means the Workmen's Compensation (Supplementation) Act (Northern Ireland) 1966;

"workmen's compensation" means compensation under any of the Workmen's Compensation Acts or under any contracting-out scheme duly certified under any of those Acts;

"the Workmen's Compensation Acts" means the Workmen's Compensation Acts (Northern Ireland) 1927 to 1943, or the enactments repealed by the Workmen's Compensation Act (Northern Ireland) 1927 or the enactments repealed by the Workmen's Compensation Act 1906.

(2) For the purposes of this Schedule—

(a) a period shall be treated as considerable if it lasts or can be expected to last for not less than 13 weeks;

(b) a person may be treated as being, as the result of an injury or disease or as the joint result of two or more injuries or diseases, totally incapable of work and likely to remain so incapable for a considerable period notwithstanding that the disability resulting from the injury or disease or, as the case may be, from the injuries or diseases taken together is not such as to prevent him from being capable of work, if it is likely to prevent his earnings (including any remuneration or profit derived from a gainful occupation) exceeding in a year such amount as is for the time being prescribed for purposes of unemployability supplement.

(3) For the purposes of paragraph 4 above, paragraph 4 of Schedule 3 to the 1986 Order and paragraph 1 of Schedule 7 to this Act shall be deemed not to have been enacted.

GENERAL NOTE

This Schedule consolidates the Industrial Injuries and Diseases (Northern Ireland Old Cases) Act 1975 (as amended) and concerns claims in respect of industrial accidents or diseases which occurred before July 5, 1948. See General Note to s.111.

Section 140(2) SCHEDULE 9

EXCLUSIONS FROM ENTITLEMENT TO CHILD BENEFIT

Children in detention, care, etc.

1.—(1) Except where regulations otherwise provide, no person shall be entitled to child benefit in respect of a child for any week if in that week the child—

(a) is undergoing imprisonment or detention in a young offenders centre;

(b) is authorised under—

(i) any provision of the Children and Young Persons Act (Northern Ireland) 1968; or

(ii) paragraph 7 of Schedule 13 to the Education and Libraries (Northern Ireland) Order 1986;

to be detained in a training school, and is not absent from the school on licence;

(c) is liable to be detained by virtue of section 73 of that Act of 1968 and is not discharged on licence;

(d) is the subject of an order under that Act of 1968 committing him to custody in any place to which he may be committed on remand;

(e) is subject to a provision of a supervision order made under that Act of 1968 requiring him to reside in an institution;

(f) is—

(i) in the care of the Department; or

(ii) the subject of a parental rights order under section 104 of that Act of 1968,

in such circumstances as may be prescribed.

(2) In sub-paragraph (1) above the reference to a child in the care of the Department includes a reference to a child in the care of a Health and Social Services Board.

Employed trainees, etc.

2.—(1) No person shall be entitled to child benefit by virtue of section 138(1)(c) above in respect of a child if the education in question is received by that child by virtue of his employment or of any office held by him.

(2) Regulations may specify the circumstances in which a child is or is not to be treated as receiving education as mentioned in sub-paragraph (1) above.

Married children

3. Except where regulations otherwise provide, no person shall be entitled to child benefit in respect of a child who is married.

Persons exempt from tax

4. Except where regulations otherwise provide, no person shall be entitled to child benefit in respect of a child if either that person or such other person as may be prescribed is exempt from tax under such provisions as may be prescribed.

Children entitled to severe disablement allowance

5. Except where regulations otherwise provide, no person shall be entitled to child benefit in respect of a child for any week in which the child is entitled to a severe disablement allowance.

GENERAL NOTE
This Schedule consolidates Sched. 1 to the Child Benefit (Northern Ireland) Order 1975 (S.I. 1975 No. 1504 (N.I. 16)) (as amended) and specifies various exclusions from entitlement to child benefit. See General Note to s.140.

Section 140(3) SCHEDULE 10

PRIORITY BETWEEN PERSONS ENTITLED TO CHILD BENEFIT

Person with prior award

1.—(1) Subject to sub-paragraph (2) below, as between a person claiming child benefit in respect of a child for any week and a person to whom child benefit in respect of that child for that week has already been awarded when the claim is made, the latter shall be entitled.

(2) Sub-paragraph (1) above shall not confer any priority where the week to which the claim relates is later than the third week following that in which the claim is made.

Person having child living with him

2. Subject to paragraph 1 above, as between a person entitled for any week by virtue of paragraph (a) of subsection (1) of section 139 above and a person entitled by virtue of paragraph (b) of that subsection the former shall be entitled.

Husband and wife

3. Subject to paragraphs 1 and 2 above, as between a husband and wife residing together the wife shall be entitled.

Parents

4.—(1) Subject to paragraphs 1 to 3 above, as between a person who is and one who is not a parent of the child the parent shall be entitled.

(2) Subject as aforesaid, as between two persons residing together who are parents of the child but not husband and wife, the mother shall be entitled.

Other cases

5. As between persons not falling within paragraphs 1 to 4 above, such one of them shall be entitled as they may jointly elect or, in default of election, as the Department may in its discretion determine.

Supplementary

6.—(1) Any election under this Schedule shall be made in the prescribed manner.

(2) Regulations may provide for exceptions from and modifications of the provisions of paragraphs 1 to 5 above in relation to such cases as may be prescribed.

GENERAL NOTE
    This Schedule consolidates Sched. 2 to the Child Benefit (Northern Ireland) Order 1975 (S.I. 1975 No. 1504 (N.I. 16)) and details the rules governing priority among claimants for child benefit. See General Note to s.140.

Section 149(3)   SCHEDULE 11

CIRCUMSTANCES IN WHICH PERIODS OF ENTITLEMENT TO STATUTORY SICK PAY DO NOT ARISE

1. A period of entitlement does not arise in relation to a particular period of incapacity for work in any of the circumstances set out in paragraph 2 below or in such other circumstances as may be prescribed.
2. The circumstances are that—
(a) at the relevant date the employee is over pensionable age;
(b) the employee's contract of service was entered into for a specified period of not more than three months;
(c) at the relevant date the employee's normal weekly earnings are less than the lower earnings limit then in force under section 5(1)(a) above;
(d) the employee had—
(i) in the period of 57 days ending immediately before the relevant date, at least one day which formed part of a period of interruption of employment; and
(ii) at any time during that period of interruption of employment, an invalidity pension day (whether or not the day referred to in paragraph (i) above);
(e) in the period of 57 days ending immediately before the relevant date the employee had at least one day on which—
(i) he was entitled to sickness benefit (or on which he would have been so entitled if he had satisfied the contribution conditions for sickness benefit mentioned in section 31(2)(a) above), or
(ii) she was entitled to a maternity allowance;
(f) the employee has done no work for his employer under his contract of service;
(g) on the relevant date there is, within the meaning of section 27 above, a stoppage of work due to a trade dispute at the employee's place of employment;
(h) the employee is, or has been, pregnant and the relevant date falls within the disqualifying period (within the meaning of section 149(12) above).
3. In this Schedule "relevant date" means the date on which a period of entitlement would begin in accordance with section 149 above if this Schedule did not prevent it arising.
4.—(1) Paragraph 2(b) above does not apply in any case where—
(a) at the relevant date the contract of service has become a contract for a period exceeding three months; or
(b) the contract of service (the "current contract") was preceded by a contract of service entered into by the employee with the same employer (the "previous contract") and—
(i) the interval between the date on which the previous contract ceased to have effect and that on which the current contract came into effect was not more than 8 weeks; and
(ii) the aggregate of the period for which the previous contract had effect and the period specified in the current contract (or, where that period has been extended, the specified period as so extended) exceeds 13 weeks.
(2) For the purposes of sub-paragraph (1)(b)(ii) above, in any case where the employee entered into more than one contract of service with the same employer before the current contract, any of those contracts which came into effect not more than 8 weeks after the date on which an earlier one of them ceased to have effect shall be treated as one with the earlier contract.
5.—(1) In paragraph 2(d) above "invalidity pension day" means a day—
(a) for which the employee in question was entitled to an invalidity pension, a non-contributory invalidity pension (under section 36 of the 1975 Act) or a severe disablement allowance; or
(b) for which he was not so entitled but which was the last day of the invalidity pension qualifying period.
(2) In sub-paragraph (1)(b) above the "invalidity pension qualifying period" means the period mentioned in section 33(1) or, as the case may be, 40(3) or 41(2) above as falling within the period of interruption of employment referred to in whichever of those provisions is applicable.

6. For the purposes of paragraph 2(f) above, if an employee enters into a contract of service which is to take effect not more than 8 weeks after the date on which a previous contract of service entered into by him with the same employer ceased to have effect, the two contracts shall be treated as one.

7. Paragraph 2(g) above does not apply in the case of an employee who proves that at no time on or before the relevant date did have a direct interest in the trade dispute in question.

8. Paragraph 2(h) above does not apply in relation to an employee who has been pregnant if her pregnancy terminated, before the beginning of the disqualifying period, otherwise than by confinement (as defined for the purposes of statutory maternity pay in section 167(1) above).

GENERAL NOTE
This Schedule consolidates SS(N.I.)O 1982, Sched. 1, and specifies the situations in which periods of entitlement to statutory sick pay do not arise. See General Note to s.149.

Section 156   SCHEDULE 12

RELATIONSHIP OF STATUTORY SICK PAY WITH BENEFITS AND OTHER PAYMENTS, ETC.

The general principle

1. Any day which—
(a) is a day of incapacity for work in relation to any contract of service; and
(b) falls within a period of entitlement (whether or not it is also a qualifying day),
shall not be treated for the purposes of this Act as a day of incapacity for work for the purposes of determining whether a period is a period of interruption of employment.

Contractual remuneration

2.—(1) Subject to sub-paragraphs (2) and (3) below, any entitlement to statutory sick pay shall not affect any right of an employee in relation to remuneration under any contract of service ("contractual remuneration").
(2) Subject to sub-paragraph (3) below—
(a) any contractual remuneration paid to an employee by an employer of his in respect of a day of incapacity for work shall go towards discharging any liability of that employer to pay statutory sick pay to that employee in respect of that day; and
(b) any statutory sick pay paid by an employer to an employee of his in respect of a day of incapacity for work shall go towards discharging any liability of that employer to pay contractual remuneration to that employee in respect of that day.
(3) Regulations may make provision as to payments which are, and those which are not, to be treated as contractual remuneration for the purposes of sub-paragraph (1) or (2) above.

Sickness benefit

3.—(1) This paragraph applies in any case where—
(a) a period of entitlement as between an employee and an employer of his comes to an end; and
(b) the first day immediately following the day on which the period of entitlement came to an end—
(i) is a day of incapacity for work in relation to that employee; and
(ii) is not prevented by paragraph 1 above from being treated as a day of incapacity for work for the purposes of determining whether a period is a period of interruption of employment.
(2) In a case to which this paragraph applies, the day of incapacity for work mentioned in sub-paragraph (1)(b) above shall, except in prescribed cases, be or as the case may be form part of a period of interruption of employment notwithstanding section 57(1)(d)(ii) above.
(3) Where each of the first two consecutive days, or the first three consecutive days, following the day on which the period of entitlement came to an end is a day falling within sub-paragraphs (i) and (ii) of sub-paragraph (1)(b) above, sub-paragraph (2) above shall have effect in relation to the second day or, as the case may be, the second and third days, as it has effect in relation to the first day.
(4) Any day which is, by virtue of section 57(1)(e) above to be disregarded in computing any period of consecutive days for the purposes of Part II of this Act shall be disregarded in determining, for the purposes of this paragraph, whether a day is the first day following the end of a period of entitlement or, as the case may be, the second or third consecutive such day.

4.—(1) This paragraph applies in any case where—

(a) a period of entitlement as between an employee and an employer of his comes to an end; and

(b) that employee has a day of incapacity for work which—
(i) is, or forms part of, a period of interruption of employment; and
(ii) falls within the period of 57 days immediately following the day on which the period of entitlement came to an end.

(2) In a case to which this paragraph applies, section 31(4) above shall not apply in relation to a day of incapacity for work of a kind mentioned in sub-paragraph (1)(b) above or to any later day in the period of interruption of employment concerned.

Invalidity pension for widows and widowers

5. Paragraph 1 above does not apply for the purpose of determining whether the conditions specified in section 40(3) or 41(2) above are satisfied.

Unemployability supplement

6. Paragraph 1 above does not apply in relation to paragraph 3 of Schedule 7 to this Act and accordingly the references in paragraph 3 of that Schedule to a period of interruption of employment shall be construed as if the provisions re-enacted in this Part of this Act had not been enacted.

GENERAL NOTE
This Schedule consolidates SS(N.I.)O 1982, Sched. 2, and deals with the inter-relationship between statutory sick pay and other benefits. See General Note to s.156.

Section 164   SCHEDULE 13

RELATIONSHIP OF STATUTORY MATERNITY PAY WITH BENEFITS AND OTHER PAYMENTS, ETC.

The general principal

1. Except as may be prescribed, a day which falls within the maternity pay period shall not be treated for the purposes of this Act as a day of unemployment or of incapacity for work for the purpose of determining whether it forms part of a period of interruption of employment.

Invalidity

2.—(1) Regulations may provide that in prescribed circumstances a day which falls within the maternity pay period shall be treated as a day of incapacity for work for the purpose of determining entitlement to an invalidity pension.

(2) Regulations may provide that an amount equal to a woman's statutory maternity pay for a period shall be deducted from invalidity benefit in respect of the same period and a woman shall be entitled to invalidity benefit only if there is a balance after the deduction and, if there is such a balance, at a weekly rate equal to it.

Contractual remuneration

3.—(1) Subject to sub-paragraphs (2) and (3) below, any entitlement to statutory maternity pay shall not affect any right of a woman in relation to remuneration under any contract of service ("contractual remuneration").

(2) Subject to sub-paragraph (3) below—
(a) any contractual remuneration paid to a woman by an employer of hers in respect of a week in the maternity pay period shall go towards discharging any liability of that employer to pay statutory maternity pay to her in respect of that week; and
(b) any statutory maternity pay paid by an employer to a woman who is an employee of his in respect of a week in the maternity pay period shall go towards discharging any liability of that employer to pay contractual remuneration to her in respect of that week.

(3) Regulations may make provision as to payments which are, and those which are not, to be treated as contractual remuneration for the purposes of sub-paragraphs (1) and (2) above.

GENERAL NOTE
This Schedule consolidates SS(N.I.)O 1986, Sched. 4, paras. 11–12, and deals with the inter-relationship between statutory maternity pay and other benefits. See General Note to s.164.

TABLE OF DERIVATIONS

Note:

1. The following abbreviations are used in this Table:—

1975	=	The Social Security (Northern Ireland) Act 1975 (c. 15)
1975OC	=	The Industrial Injuries and Diseases (Northern Ireland Old Cases) Act 1975 (c. 17)
1975P	=	The Social Security Pensions (Northern Ireland) Order 1975 (N.I. 15)
1975CB	=	The Child Benefit (Northern Ireland) Order 1975 (N.I. 16)
1976	=	The Social Security and Family Allowances (Northern Ireland) Order 1976 (N.I. 9)
1976IR	=	The Industrial Relations (Northern Ireland) Order 1976 (N.I. 16)
1977	=	The Social Security (Miscellaneous Provisions) (Northern Ireland) Order 1977 (N.I. 11)
1977A	=	The Social Security (Miscellaneous Provisions) Act 1977 (c. 5)
1977SB	=	The Supplementary Benefits (Northern Ireland) Order 1977 (N.I. 27)
1979	=	The Social Security (Northern Ireland) Order 1979 (N.I. 5)
1980	=	The Social Security (Northern Ireland) Order 1980 (N.I. 8)
1980(2)	=	The Social Security (No. 2) (Northern Ireland) Order 1980 (N.I. 13)
1980A	=	The Social Security Act 1980 (c. 30)
1981C	=	The Social Security (Contributions) (Northern Ireland) Order 1981 (N.I. 9)
1981	=	The Social Security (Northern Ireland) Order 1981 (N.I. 25)
1981MC	=	The Magistrates' Courts (Northern Ireland) Order 1981 (N.I. 26)
1982	=	The Social Security (Northern Ireland) Order 1982 (N.I. 16)
1982A	=	The Social Security and Housing Benefits Act 1982 (c. 24)
1982SR	=	The Social Security (Contributions, Re-rating) Order (Northern Ireland) 1982 (SR 1982 No. 413)
1983	=	The Social Security Adjudications (Northern Ireland) Order 1983 (N.I. 17)
1984	=	The Health and Social Security (Northern Ireland) Order 1984 (N.I. 8)
1984F	=	The Fines and Penalties (Northern Ireland) Order 1984 (N.I. 3)
1985	=	The Social Security (Northern Ireland) Order 1985 (N.I. 16)
1985SR	=	The Social Security (Contributions and Credits) (Transitional and Consequential Provisions) Regulations (Northern Ireland) 1985 (SR 1985 No. 260)
1986	=	The Social Security (Northern Ireland) Order 1986 (N.I. 18)
1986A	=	The Social Security Act 1986 (c. 50)
1987	=	The Social Fund (Maternity and Funeral Expenses) (Northern Ireland) Order 1987 (N.I. 8)
1988	=	The Social Security (Northern Ireland) Order 1988 (N.I. 2)
1988E	=	The Employment and Training (Amendment) (Northern Ireland) Order 1988 (N.I. 10)
ICTA 1988	=	The Income and Corporation Taxes Act 1988 (c. 1)
1989	=	The Social Security (Northern Ireland) Order 1989 (N.I. 13)
1990	=	The Social Security (Northern Ireland) Order 1990 (N.I. 15)
1991C	=	The Social Security (Contributions) (Northern Ireland) Order 1991 (N.I. 22)
1991D	=	The Disability Living Allowance and Disability Working Allowance (Northern Ireland) Order 1991 (N.I. 17)
1991R	=	The Social Security (Contributions) (Re-rating) (No. 2) Order (Northern Ireland) 1991 (SR 1991 No. 542)
1991RF	=	The Redundancy Fund (Abolition) (Northern Ireland) Order 1991 (N.I. 2)
1991SP	=	The Statutory Sick Pay (Northern Ireland) Order 1991 (N.I. 9)
1992CP	=	The Social Security (Consequential Provisions) Act 1992 (c. 6)
1992U	=	The Social Security Benefits Uprating Order (Northern Ireland) 1992 (SR 1992 No. 18)
M (followed by a number)	=	The paragraph in the Memorandum under the Consolidation of Enactments (Procedure) Act 1949

2. The Table does not contain any entries in respect of Article 2(3) of the Social Security Pensions (Northern Ireland) Order 1975 (NI 15) under which, with certain exceptions, that Order and the Social Security (Northern Ireland) Act 1975 (c. 15) have effect as if the provisions of the Order were contained in the Social Security (Northern Ireland) Act 1975. The effect is that the general provisions of the Social Security (Northern Ireland) Act 1975 apply to the provisions of that Order.

3. The Table does not show the effect of transfer of functions orders.

Provision	Derivation
1(1)	1975 s.1(1); Industrial Relations (No. 2) (NI) Order 1976 (NI 28) art. 20(2); 1986 Sch. 10; 1989 Sch. 9; 1990 art. 18(1), (2); 1991 RF Sch. 2
(2)	1975 s.1(2); 1991C art. 3(2)
(3)	1975 s.1(3)
(4)	1975 s.1(4); 1991C art. 4(1)
(5)	1975 s.1(4A); 1990 art. 18(2); 1991SP art. 3(4)
(6)	1975 s.1(6); 1991C art. 3(3)
2	1975 s.2
3	1975 s.3(1), (2), (3)
4(1)	1975 s.3(1A); 1982 arts. 25, 30(1); 1986 Sch. 4 para. 10
(2), (3)	1975 s.3(1B), (1C); 1982 art. 30(1)
(4)	1975 s.3(1D); 1989 Sch. 8 para. 1
(5)	1975 s.3(4); 1982 Sch. 4 para. 4
5(1)	1975 s.4(1); 1975P art. 3(1), Sch. 5 para. 18(a); 1985 art. 9(1), Sch. 5 para. 7
(2), (3)	1975P art. 3(2), (3); 1986 art. 75(4)
6(1)	1975 s.4(2); 1976 art. 3(1); 1982 Sch. 5
(2)	1975P art. 6(1); 1984 Sch. 5 para. 4
(3)	1975 s.4(3); 1989 Sch. 7 para. 1(1)
(4)	1975 s.4(2)
(5)	1975 s.4(7); 1979 art. 11(2); 1985 art. 10
(6)	1986 art. 75(3)
7	1975 s.4(4), (5)
8(1)–(3)	1975 s.4(6), (6A), (6B); 1989 art. 3(1)
(4)	1986 art. 75(3)
9(1)–(3)	1975 s.4(6C)–(6E); 1985 art. 9(2); 1989 Sch. 7 para. 1(2); SR 1991 No. 73 art. 2; 1991R art. 2
(4)	1975 s.4(6C), (6E); 1985 art. 9(2)
(5)	1986 art. 75(3)
10	1975 s.4A; 1991C art. 3(5)
11(1)	1975 s.7(1); 1976 art. 3(1); 1984 art. 11(1); 1991R art. 3(a)
(2)	1975P art. 6(2)
(3)	1975 s.7(4)
(4)	1975 s.7(5); 1991R art. 3(b)
(5)	1975 s.7(6)
12	1975 s.7A; 1984 art. 11(2); 1985SR reg. 4(2); 1989 Sch. 7 para. 2, Sch. 9
13(1)	1975 s.8(1); 1976 art. 3(1); 1984 art. 12(1)(a); 1991R art. 4
(2)	1975 s.8(2); 1975P Sch. 6
(3)	1975 s.8(2)(a); 1975P Sch. 6
(4)	1975 s.8(2A); 1984 art. 12(1)(b), (3)
(5)–(7)	1975 s.8(2B)–(2D); 1984 art. 12(3); 1985SR reg. 4(3); 1989 Sch. 7 para. 3
14(1)	1975P art. 7(1); 1986 Sch. 8 para. 4
(2)	1975P art. 7(3)
(3)	1975P art. 7(2)
(4)	1975P art. 7(2); 1977 art. 3(6)
15(1), (2)	1975 s.9(1); 1989 Sch. 7 para. 4(a), (b)
(3)	1975 s.9(2); 1982SR art. 5(a); 1991R art. 5
(4)	ICTA 1988 Sch. 29 para. 14
(5)	1975 s.9(1); 1989 Sch. 7 para. 4(c)
16	1975 s.9(3)
17(1)	1975 s.9(4)
(2)	1975 s.9(5); 1975P Sch. 6
(3)–(6)	1975 s.9(6)
18	1975 s.10; 1982SR art. 5(a); 1991R art. 5
19(1)–(3)	1975 s.11

Provision	Derivation
19(4)–(6)	1975P art. 5(2)–(4); 1986 Sch. 8 para. 3
20	1975 s.12; 1975P Sch. 5 para. 19; 1980 art. 6(1)(i); 1984 Sch. 3 para. 1; 1986 art. 41, Sch. 9 para. 39, Sch. 10; 1989 Sch. 7 para. 5
21(1), (2)	1975 s.13(1); 1980 art. 6(1)(ii); 1986 Sch. 9 para. 40, Sch. 10
(3)	1975 s.13(6)
(4)	1975 s.13(8); 1986 Sch. 9 para. 46(b)
(5)	1975 s.13(6); 1986 Sch. 8 para. 1(6)
(6)	1975 s.13(7)
22(1)	1975 s.13(2); 1986 Sch. 8 para. 1(1)
(2)	1975 s.13(2); 1975P Sch. 5 para. 20(a); 1980(2) Sch.; 1986 Sch. 9 para. 46(a)
(3)	1975 s.13(5); 1986 Sch. 8 para. 1(4)(c); 1989 Sch. 7 para. 6
(4)	1975 s.13(3); 1975P Sch. 5 para. 20(b); 1986 Sch. 8 para. 1(2)
(5)	1975 s.13(4); 1980(2) Sch.; 1986 Sch. 8 para. 1(3)
(6)	1975 s.13(5AA); 1989 art. 6(3)
(7)	1977 art. 18(25)
23(1)	1975 s.13(5); 1979 Sch. 3 para. 4; 1986 Sch. 8 para. 1(4)(a); 1988 Sch. 2 para. 1(1)(a)
(2)	1975 s.13(5ZA); 1988 Sch. 2 para. 1(1)(b)
(3)	1975 s.13(5); 1989 art. 6(2)
(4)	1975 s.13(5A); 1985 Sch. 5 para. 1(b); M1, M12
24(1)	1975 s.13(5B); 1986 Sch. 8 para. 1(5)
(2)	1975 s.13(5C); 1989 art. 6(4)
25(1)	1975 s.14(1)
(2)	1975 s.14(2); 1989 Sch. 1 para. 4(1)
(3)	1975 s.14(3)
(4)	1975 s.14(4); 1975P art. 20(1); 1982 Sch. 4 para. 5
(5), (6)	1975 s.14(6); 1975P Sch. 5 para. 21(b); 1979 Sch. 3 para. 5; 1986 Sch. 9 para. 53; 1989 Sch. 9
(7)	1975 s.14(8)
26(1)	1975 s.18(1)
(2)–(4)	1975 s.18(2)–(2B); 1989 art. 13
(5)	1975 s.18(3)
(6)	1975 s.18(4); 1986 art. 44(1); 1989 Sch. 7 para. 7
27(1), (2)	1975 s.19(1), (1A); 1986 art. 45(1)
(3)	1975 s.19(2)
28(1)	1975 s.20(1); 1986 art. 44(2)(a); Unemployment Benefit (Disqualification Period) Order (NI) 1988 (SR 1988 No. 83) art. 2; 1988E arts. 5(2), 6(a); 1989 art. 14(1)
(2)	1975 s.20(1A); 1986 art. 44(3)(a); 1989 Sch. 9
(3)	1975 s.20(3)
(4)	1975 s.20(3A); 1985 art. 12
(5)	1975 s.20(4); 1989 art. 14(3)
(6)	1975 s.20(5); 1988E art. 5(3)
29	1975 s.20A; 1989 art. 14(4)
30(1)	1980(2) art. 5(1); 1988 art. 8; 1989 art. 11(1)
(2)	1980(2) art. 5(1A); 1982 Sch. 4 para. 19
(3)	1980(2) art. 5(2); 1989 art. 11(1)
(4)	1980(2) art. 5(3)
31(1)	1975 s.14(1)
(2)	1975 s.14(2); 1989 Sch. 1 para. 4(1)
(3)	1975 s.14(2A); 1982 art. 32(3)
(4)	1975 s.14(3)
(5)	1975 s.14(4); 1975P art. 20; 1982 Sch. 4 para. 5
(6)–(7)	1975 s.14(6); 1975P Sch. 5 para. 21(b); 1979 Sch. 3 para. 5; 1986 Sch. 9 para. 53; 1989 Sch. 9
(8)	1975 s.14(8)
32(1), (2)	1975 s.20(2), (3)
(3)	1975 s.20(5)(c)
33(1)	1975 s.15(1); 1989 Sch. 1 para. 5(1)
(2)	1975 s.15(2); 1989 Sch. 1 para. 5(2)

Provision	Derivation
33(3)	1975 s.15(3); 1975P art. 16, Sch. 5 para. 22(b); 1990 art. 6(1)
(4), (5)	1975 s.15(4); 1975P Sch. 5 para. 22(c); 1979 Sch. 1 para. 1, Sch. 3 para. 6; 1986 Sch. 9 para. 53
(6)	1975 s.15(5)
(7), (8)	1975 s.15(5A), (5B); 1991D art. 11(1)
(9)	1975 s.15(6); 1982 Sch. 4 para. 6
(10), (11)	1975 s.15A(1), (2); 1985 art. 18(3)
34(1), (2)	1975 s.16(1); 1985 art. 11(1)(a)
(3)	1975 s.16(2); 1979 Sch. 1 para. 10
(4)–(6)	1975 s.16(2B)–(2D); 1985 art. 11(1)(b); 1986 art. 19(1)(b)
(7)	1975 s.16(3); 1985 art. 11(1)(c)
35(1)–(3)	1975 s.22(1)–(3); 1986 Sch. 4 para. 13
(4)	1975 s.22(4A); 1988 Sch. 4 para. 2(b)
(5)–(7)	1975 s.22(5)–(7); 1986 Sch. 4 para. 13
36(1), (2)	1975 s.24(1), (2); 1986 art. 37(1)
(3)	1975 s.24(3); 1989 Sch. 7 para. 8
37(1)	1975 s.25(1); 1975P Sch. 5 para. 23; 1975CB Sch. 4 para. 10(a); Human Fertilisation and Embryology Act 1990 (c. 37) Sch. 4 para. 3
(2)	1975 s.25(2); 1975CB Sch. 4 para. 10(b)
(3), (4)	1975 s.25(3), (4); 1989 Sch. 8 para. 4(1)
38(1)	1975 s.26(1); 1975P Sch. 5 para. 24; 1986 art. 37(3)
(2), (3)	1975 s.26(3), (4); 1989 Sch. 8 para. 4(2)
(4)	1989 art. 8(1)
39(1)	1975P art. 15(1), (3)
(2)	1975P art. 15(2)
(3)	1986 art. 20(1)(c)
(4), (5)	1975 s.26(2); 1986 art. 37(3)(b)
(6)	1989 art. 8(1)
40(1)	1975P art. 17(1); 1986 Sch. 9 para. 45(a)
(2)	1975P art. 17(1A); 1989 Sch. 7 para. 17
(3)	1975P art. 17(2); 1986 Sch. 9 para. 45(b)
(4)	1975P art. 17(3)
(5)	1975P art. 17(4); 1986 Sch. 9 para. 45(c); 1990 art. 6(2)
(6)	1977 art. 13(6)
(7)	1975P art. 17(5); 1977 art. 5(4); 1989 Sch. 1 para. 10(1)
(8)	1975P art. 17(6)
41(1)	1975P art. 18(1); 1979 Sch. 1 para. 18
(2), (3)	1975P art. 18(2), (3)
(4), (5)	1975P art. 18(4); 1990 art. 6(3)
(6)	1986 art. 20(1)(d)
(7)	1975P art. 18(5); 1977 art. 5(4); 1989 Sch. 1 para. 10(2)
(8)	1975P art. 18(6)
42	1975P art. 18A; 1991D art. 11(3)
43(1)	1975 s.27(6)
(2)	1977 art. 5(1); 1979 Sch. 1 para. 8
(3)–(5)	1975P art. 27
44(1)	1975 s.28(1); 1975P Sch. 5 para. 25; 1989 Sch. 8 para. 4(3)
(2)	1975 s.28(1A); 1989 Sch. 8 para. 4(4)
(3), (4)	1975P art. 8(1); 1992U art. 4(2)
(5)	1975P art. 8(4); 1979 Sch. 3 para. 16
(6)	1975P art. 8(5); 1986 Sch. 8 para. 5(1)
(7)	1975P art. 8(6)
(8)	Transitional
45(1)	1975P art. 8(2); 1986 art. 19(2)
(2), (3)	1975P art. 8(2A); 1986 art. 19(3)
(4), (5)	1975P art. 8(2B); 1986 art. 19(3)
(6), (7)	1975P arts. 8(3), 70A; 1979 art. 14; 1986 art. 19(4)
(8)	Drafting
46(1)	1986 art. 19(6)
(2)	1986 art. 19(5)

Provision	Derivation
47(1)	1975 s.28(7); 1980(2) art. 3(3); 1985 art. 11(2)(a), (b)
(2)–(4)	1975 s.28(7A)–(7C); 1985 art. 11(2)(c); 1986 art. 19(1)(b)
(5)	1975 s.28(8)
(6)	1980(2) art. 3(4)
48(1)	1975P art. 22(1); 1979 Sch. 1 para. 5
(2)	1979 Sch. 1 para. 20
(3)	1975P art. 22(2)
49(1)	1975 s.29(1)
(2), (3)	1975 s.29(2), (3); 1989 art. 9(3)(a)
(4)	1975 s.29(4)
(5)	1975 s.29(5); 1989 art. 9(3)(b)
(6)	1975 s.29(6)
(7), (8)	1975 s.29(9), (9A); 1989 Sch. 8 para. 4(5)
50(1)	1975 s.29(7); 1975P Sch. 5 para. 26
(2)	1975 s.29(8); 1985 art. 11(3)
(3), (4)	1975P art. 9
(5)	1986 art. 20(1)(a)
51(1)	1975P art. 10(1); 1979 Sch. 1 paras. 4, 14
(2)	1975P art. 10(2)
(3)	1986 art. 20(1)(b)
(4)	1975P art. 10(3); 1989 Sch. 1 para. 9(2)
52(1)–(3)	1975P art. 11(1)–(3); 1986 art. 19(1)
(4)	1979 Sch. 1 para. 15
53(1), (2)	1975P art. 12; 1986 art. 19(1)(a)
(3)	1979 Sch. 1 para. 16
54(1), (2)	1975 s.30(3); 1989 Sch. 9
(3)	1975 s.30(4); 1975P Sch. 5 para. 27
(4)	1975 s.30(5); 1989 Sch. 1 para. 2(2)
55	1975P art. 14; 1989 art. 9(4)
56(1), (2)	1975 s.31; 1975CB Sch. 4 para. 11; 1977 art. 18(2)
(3), (4)	1975 s.43(1); 1975CB Sch. 4 para. 16(a)
(5)	1975 s.43(2); 1975CB Sch. 4 para. 16(b); 1977 art. 18(3)
(6)	1986 art. 41
57(1)	1975 s.17(1); 1980(2) art. 3(1); 1989 art. 12(2)
(2)	1975 s.22(4); 1986 Sch. 4 para. 13; 1988 Sch. 4 para. 2(a)
(3)	1975 s.17(2); 1989 art. 12(3); M2
(4)	1975 s.17(2A); 1988 Sch. 4 para. 1
(5)	1975 s.17(2B); 1989 art. 12(4)
(6), (7)	1975 s.17(2C), (2D); 1989 Sch. 8 para. 3
(8)	1975 s.17(3)
(9), (10)	1975 s.17(4), (5); 1980(2) art. 3(4); 1981 art. 6
58(1)	1989 Sch. 8 para. 2(1)
(2)	1989 Sch. 8 para. 2(2); 1990 Sch. 6 para. 19(2)
(3)	1989 Sch. 8 para. 2(3)
(4)	1989 Sch. 8 para. 2(6); 1990 Sch. 6 para. 19(3)
(5)	1989 Sch. 8 para. 2(7)
59(1), (2)	1975 s.20(2), (3)
(3)	1975 s.20(5)(c)
60(1)	1975 s.33(1), (2)
(2), (3)	1986 Sch. 3 para. 10; 1988 Sch. 1 para. 5
(4)–(6)	1975 s.33(3); 1975P Sch. 5 para. 28; 1990 Sch. 6 para. 1(1)
(7)	1975 s.33(4); 1975P art. 21(5); 1986 art. 19(1)
(8)	1986 Sch. 3 para. 10; 1988 Sch. 1 para. 5
61(1)	1977 art. 7(1); 1986 art. 19(1)(a); 1990 Sch. 6 para. 1(3)
(2)	1977 art. 7(2); 1986 art. 19(1)(a); 1990 Sch. 6 para. 1(4)
62	1975P art. 26
63	1975 s.34; 1975P Sch. 5 para. 29; 1984 Sch. 2 para. 2; 1990 art. 4(3); 1991D art. 3(1), Sch. 4
64	1975 s.35(1); 1988 art. 3; 1991D art. 4(1)
65(1)	1975 s.35(2); 1979 art. 3(2); 1989 Sch. 8 para. 5(2)
(2)	1975 s.35(2A); 1979 art. 3(3)

Provision	*Derivation*
65(3)	1975 s.35(3); 1991D Sch. 2 para. 2(2)
(4)	1975 s.35(4); 1989 Sch. 8 para. 5(3)(a); 1991D Sch. 2 para. 2(3)
(5)	1975 s.35(4A); 1980 Sch. 1 para. 8; 1989 Sch. 8 para. 5(4); 1991D Sch. 2 para. 2(3)
(6)	1975 s.35(4); 1979 art. 3(5); 1989 Sch. 8 para. 5(3)(b); 1990 art. 3(2); 1991D Sch. 4
66	1975 s.35(2B), (2C); 1990 art. 3(1); 1991D Sch. 2 para. 2(1)
67(1)	1975 s.35(5A); 1979 art. 3(6)
(2)	1975 s.35(6)
68(1)–(4)	1975 s.36(1)–(4); 1984 art. 5(1)
(5)	1975 s.36(4A); 1985 Sch. 4 para. 2
(6), (7)	1975 s.36(5), (6); 1984 art. 5(1)
(8), (9)	1975 s.36(6A), (6B); 1989 Sch. 8 para. 6
(10)	1975 s.36(6C); 1991D art. 11(2)
(11)	1975 s.36(7); 1984 art. 5(1); 1989 Sch. 8 para. 2(5); 1990 Sch. 6 para. 19(4)
(12)	1989 Sch. 8 para. 2(4)
(13)	1975 s.36(8); 1984 art. 5(1); 1989 Sch. 8 para. 2(6) (part), (7)
69	1975 s.36A; 1990 art. 4(1)
70(1)	1975 s.37(1)
(2)	1975 s.37(2); 1991D Sch. 2 para. 3
(3)–(5)	1975 s.37(3)–(5)
(6)	1975 s.37(6)
(7)–(9)	1975 s.37(7)–(9)
(10)	1975 s.37(6)
71	1975 s.37ZA; 1991D art. 3(2)
72	1975 s.37ZB; 1991D art. 3(2)
73	1975 s.37ZC; 1991D art. 3(2)
74(1)	1977 art. 10(1); 1991D Sch. 2 para. 7
(2)	1977 art. 10(3)
75	1975 s.37ZD; 1991D art. 3(2)
76	1975 s.37ZE; 1991D art. 3(2)
77(1)	1975 s.38(1); 1975CB Sch. 4 para. 13(a)
(2), (3)	1975 s.38(2), (3)
(4), (5)	1975 s.43(1); 1975CB Sch. 4 para. 16(a)
(6)	1975 s.43(2); 1975CB Sch. 4 para. 16(b); 1977 art. 18(3)
(7)	1975 s.38(1)
(8)	1975 s.38(4)
(9)	1975 s.38(5); 1975CB Sch. 4 para. 13(c)
(10)	1975 s.38(6); 1986 art. 46(a)
(11)	1975 s.38(7); 1986 art. 46(b)
78(1), (2)	1975 s.39(1)(a), (b)
(3), (4)	1975 s.39(1)(c); 1979 Sch. 1 para. 2; 1986 art. 19(1)(b)
(5)	1975 s.39(2)
(6)	1975 s.39(2A); 1985 art. 14(1)(b)
(7), (8)	1975 s.39(3), (3A); 1989 Sch. 8 para. 4(6)
(9)	1975 s.39(4)
79	1975 s.40
80(1)	1975 s.41(1); 1975CB Sch. 4 para. 14(a)
(2)	1975 s.41(2); 1984 Sch. 3 para. 2(a)
(3)	1975 s.41(2A); 1984 Sch. 3 para. 2(c)
(4)	1975 s.41(2B); 1984 Sch. 3 para. 2(c); 1992U art. 11
(5), (6)	1975 s.41(4), (5); 1975CB Sch. 4 para. 14(b), (c)
(7)	1975 s.41(2D); 1984 Sch. 3 para. 2(c)
81(1), (2)	1975 s.43(1); 1975CB Sch. 4 para. 16
(3)	1975 s.43(2); 1975CB Sch. 4 para. 16(b); 1977 art. 18(3)
82(1)	1975 s.44(1); 1975CB Sch. 4 para. 17(a); 1980 Sch. 1 para. 5(2); 1988 Sch. 4 para. 3(a)
(2)	1975 s.44(2); 1975CB Sch. 4 para. 17(a); 1980 Sch. 1 para. 5(2)
(3)	1975 s.44(3)(a); 1988 Sch. 4 para. 3(b)
(4)	1975 s.44(3)(c); 1975CB Sch. 4 para. 17(b); 1980 Sch. 1 para. 4

Provision	Derivation
82(5)	1975 s.44(4)
83(1)	1975 s.45(1)
(2)	1975 s.45(2); 1975CB Sch. 4 para. 18; 1988 Sch. 4 para. 4(a)
(3)	1975 s.45(2A); 1985 art. 15(1)
84(1)	1975 s.45A(1); 1984 art. 6; 1985 art. 15(2)(a)
(2)	1975 s.45A(2); 1985 art. 15(2)(b); 1988 Sch. 4 para. 5(a)
(3)	1975 s.45A(3); 1985 art. 15(2)(b)
85(1)	1975 s.46(1)
(2)	1975 s.46(2); 1975CB Sch. 4 para. 19; 1980 Sch. 1 para. 4(b)
(3)	1975 s.46(3)
(4)	1975 s.46(4); 1985 art. 15(3)
86(1)	1975 s.47(1); 1975CB Sch. 4 para. 20; 1980 Sch. 1 para. 5(2); 1989 Sch. 8 para. 7(1)
(2)	1975 s.47(1A); 1985 art. 15(4)(b)
87(1)	1975 s.47A; 1980 Sch. 1 para. 5; 1990 Sch. 6 para. 1(2)
(2)	1975 s.47A; 1990 Sch. 6 para. 1(2)
88	1975 s.48(1)
89	1975 s.47B; 1984 art. 8(a); 1989 art. 11(3)
90	1975 s.49; 1984 Sch. 2 para. 2
91	1975 s.49A; 1986 art. 45(2)
92	1975 s.84A; 1989 Sch. 8 para. 7(2)
93	1991D art. 11(5)
94(1)	1975 s.50(1); 1986 Sch. 3 para. 2
(2)	1975 s.50(1A); 1988 Sch. 4 para. 8
(3)	1975 s.50(3)
(4)	1975 s.50(4); 1982 Sch. 4 para. 8(2)
(5)	1975 s.50(5)
(6)	1975 s.50(6); 1982 Sch. 4 para. 8(3)
(7)	1986 Sch. 10
95(1)–(3)	1975 s.51
(4), (5)	1977 art. 13(3)
96	1975 s.148
97	1975 s.147
98–101	1975 ss.52–55
102(1), (2)	1975 s.50A(1), (2); 1982 art. 32(4)
(3)	1975 s.50A(3); 1982 art. 32(4); 1989 Sch. 1 para. 8(1)
103(1)	1975 s.57(1); 1986 Sch. 3 para. 3(1)
(2)–(4)	1975 s.57(1A)–(1C); 1986 Sch. 3 para. 3(2)
(5)	1975 s.57(3)
(6)	1975 s.57(4); 1982 art. 32(2); 1989 Sch. 7 para. 11
(7), (8)	1975 s.57(6); 1986 Sch. 3 para. 3(4)
104(1), (2)	1975 s.61(1), (2)
(3), (4)	1975 s.61(3), (4); 1986 Sch. 3 para. 6
105	1975 s.63
106	Drafting
107	1975 s.91; 1982 Sch. 4 para. 11, Sch. 5; M4
108(1)–(4)	1975 s.76(1)–(4)
(5)	1975 s.76(4A); 1990 Sch. 6 para. 2(1)
(6)	1975 s.76(5)
109(1), (2)	1975 s.77(1), (2); 1990 art. 5(7), Sch. 6 para. 2(2)
(3)	1975 s.77(3)
(4)–(6)	1975 s.77(4); 1986 Sch. 3 para. 13
(7)	1975 s.77(5); 1986 Sch. 3 para. 13
110	1975 s.78
111	Drafting
112(1), (2)	1977 art. 14(1); 1977SB Sch. 7; 1986 Sch. 10
(3)	1977 art. 14(2); 1986 Sch. 9 para. 49, Sch. 10.
113(1), (2)	1975 s.82(5), (6)
(3)	1975 s.83; 1985 Sch. 5 para. 3
114(1), (2)	1975 s.84(1), (2)
(3)	1975 s.84(4); 1985 art. 15(6)

Provision	Derivation
114(4)	1975 s.84(5); art. 15(8); 1986 Sch. 3 paras. 4, 15
115(1), (2)	1975 s.122(1), (2)
(3)	1975 s.122(2)
(4)	Drafting
116	1975 s.123
117–119	1975 ss.124–126
120	1975 s.152
121	1975 Sch. 17; 1975P Sch. 5 para. 44; 1975CB Sch. 4 para. 37; 1977 art. 18(1); 1980 Sch. 1 para. 7; 1984 Sch. 2 para. 9; 1985 Sch. 5 para. 6; 1986 Sch. 10; 1989 arts. 3(3), 11(2), 14(5), Sch. 1 para. 3(11); 1990 Sch. 6 para. 9; 1991D art. 11(4); drafting
122(1), (2)	1986 art. 21(1), (2); 1991 D art. 8(2), (3)
(3)	1986 art. 32(4)
123(1)	1986 art. 21(3); 1988 art. 6(1); 1989 art. 15(1)
(2)	1986 art. 21(4N); 1988 art. 6(2)
(3)	1986 art. 21(4)
(4)	1986 art. 22(1); 1988 Sch. 4 para. 16(1)
(5), (6)	1986 art. 22(1A), (1B); 1988 Sch. 4 para. 16(2)
124(1)–(4)	1986 art. 21(4A)–(4D); 1988 art. 6(2)
(5)	1986 art. 21(4N); 1988 art. 6(2)
125(1)–(4)	1986 art. 24(1)–(4)
(5)	1986 art. 24(5); ICTA 1988 Sch. 29 para. 32
(6)	1986 art. 24(5A); 1988 Sch. 4 para. 17(1)
(7)	1986 art. 24(6); 1990 Sch. 6 para. 12(2); 1992U art. 15
(8)	1986 art. 24(7); 1990 Sch. 6 para. 12(3)
126	1986 art. 24A; 1988 Sch. 4 para. 18; 1989 Sch. 8 para. 15
127(1)	1986 art. 21(5), (5A); 1988 art. 5(1); 1991D art. 10(1)
(2)	1986 art. 22(2), (3)
(3)	1986 art. 21(6); 1989 Sch. 8 para. 14
(4)	1986 art. 21(10); 1991D art. 10(2)
(5)	1986 art. 22(6)(a)
(6)	1986 art. 79(3)
128(1)	1986 art. 21(6A), (6D); 1991D art. 8(4)
(2), (3)	1986 art. 21(6B), (6C); 1991D art. 8(4)
(4)	1986 art. 21(6E); 1991D art. 8(4)
(5)	1986 art. 22(3A), (3B); 1991D art. 8(8)
(6)	1986 art. 21(6F); 1991D art. 8(4)
(7)	1986 art. 28B(4); 1991D art. 9(1)
(8)	1986 art. 22(6); 1991D art. 8(9)
(9)	1986 art. 79(3); 1991D Sch. 3 para. 6
129(1), (2)	1986 art. 21(7), (8)
(3)	1986 art. 22(4), (5)
(4)	1986 art. 22(6)(b)
130(1)	1986 art. 23(6)
(2)	1986 art. 21(9)
(3)	1986 art. 22(7)
131(1), (2)	1986 art. 23(1), (2)
(3), (4)	1986 art. 23(2A), (2B); 1990 art. 11
(5), (6)	1986 art. 23(3), (4)
132(1)	1986 art. 23(5)
(2), (3)	1986 art. 23(7), (8)
(4)	1986 art. 23(9)
133(1)	1986 arts. 2(2), 21(11), 29(1)(b); 1991D art. 8(6); drafting
(2)	1986 art. 21(12); 1989 art. 15(2); 1991D art. 8(7)
134(1)	1986 art. 33(2); 1987 art. 3
(2)	1986 art. 33(2A); 1988 Sch. 3 para. 1
(3)	1986 art. 34(1A); 1988 Sch. 3 para. 8
(4)	1986 art. 2(2)
135(1)–(3)	1986 art. 34(2)–(4)
(4)	1986 art. 34(4A); 1988 Sch. 3 para. 9

Provision	Derivation
135(5)	1986 art. 34(11)
136(1)	1986 art. 34(9); 1988 Sch. 3 para. 10
(2)	1986 art. 34(10)
(3)	1986 art. 34(10ZA); 1990 art. 12(3)
(4)	1986 art. 34(10A); 1988 Sch. 3 para. 11; 1990 art. 12(4)
(5)	1986 art. 33(11); 1988 Sch. 3 para. 6
137	1975CB art. 3(1)
138(1)	1975CB art. 4(1); 1986 art. 71(1)(a); 1988 art. 6(3)
(2), (3)	1975CB art. 4(1A), (1B); 1986 art. 71(1)(b)
(4), (5)	1975CB art. 4(2), (3)
139	1975CB art. 5
140(1), (2)	1975CB art. 6(1); 1988 art. 6(4)
(3)	1975CB art. 6(2)
141(1)–(4)	1975CB art. 7(1)–(4)
(5)	1975CB art. 24(1)(a)
142	1975CB art. 15
143(1)	1975CB art. 2(2)
(2)–(4)	1975CB art. 2(3)–(5)
(5)	1975CB art. 11
(6)	1975CB art. 2(6)
144	1986 Sch. 6 para. 2
145	1986 Sch. 6 para. 3
146(1)	1986 Sch. 6 para. 1(1)
(2)	1986 art. 2(2), Sch. 6 para. 1(2); ICTA 1988 Sch. 29 para. 32; 1991D Sch. 2 para. 12
(3)	1986 Sch. 6 para. 1(2)
(4)	1986 Sch. 6 para. 1(3)
147(1), (2)	1982 art. 3(1), (2)
(3)	1982 art. 25A(1); 1984 Sch. 5 para. 8
(4), (5)	1982 art. 3(3), (4)
(6)	1982 art. 3(5); 1986 art. 69
148(1), (2)	1982 art. 4(1), (2)
(3)	1982 art. 4(3); Statutory Sick Pay (General) (Amendment) Regulations (NI) 1986 (SR 1986 No. 83) reg. 2(1)
(4)	1982 art. 4(3A); 1985 art. 18(4)
(5), (6)	1982 art. 4(4), (5)
149(1)–(4)	1982 art. 5(1)–(4)
(5)	1982 art. 5(4A); 1985 art. 18(5)
(6), (7)	1982 art. 5(5), (6)
(8), (9)	1982 art. 5(6A), (6B); 1985 Sch. 4 para. 4
(10), (11)	1982 art. 5(7), (8)
(12)	1982 art. 5(9); 1986 Sch. 9 para. 50
150(1)	1982 art. 6(1)
(2)	1982 art. 6(2); 1984 Sch. 5 para. 7
(3), (4)	1982 art. 6(3), (4)
151(1)–(3)	1982 art. 7(1)–(3)
(4)	1982 art. 7(4); 1985 art. 18(1)
(5)	1982 art. 7(5)
152	1982 art. 8
153(1)	1982 art. 9(1); Statutory Sick Pay (Rate of Payment) Order (NI) 1992 (SR 1992 No. 27) art. 2
(2)	1982 art. 9(1A); 1986 art. 68(1); 1990 Sch. 6 para. 11(1)
(3)	1982 art. 9(2)
154(1)	1982 art. 11(1); 1991SP art. 3(1)
(2)	1982 art. 11(1B); 1991SP art. 4(1)
(3)	1982 art. 11(1D); 1991SP art. 4(1)
(4)	1982 art. 11(2); 1985 art. 19(1)(b); 1991SP art. 4(2)
(5)	1982 art. 11(3)(b), (c); 1991SP art. 3(3)
(6)	1982 art. 11(6)
(7)	1991SP art. 4(5)

Provision	Derivation
155	1982 art. 11(1C); 1991SP art. 4(1)
156	Drafting
157	1982 art. 29(1)–(3); 1989 Sch. 7 para. 20
158	1982 art. 24; M9
159(1)	1982 art. 28(1); 1985 Sch. 4 para. 6
(2)	1982 art. 28(2); 1985 Sch. 4 para. 7
(3)–(5)	1982 art. 28(3)–(5)
(6)	1982 art. 28(5A); Health and Personal Social Services (NI) Order 1991 (NI 1) Sch. 5 Part II
(7)	1982 art. 28(6)
160(1)–(6)	1986 art. 47(1)–(6)
(7)	1982 art. 25A(1); 1984 Sch. 5 para. 8; 1986 art. 47(6)
(8)	1986 art. 47(7)
(9)	1986 art. 47(8); 1988 Sch. 4 para. 12(1)
(10)	1986 art. 47(9); 1988 Sch. 4 para. 12(2)
161	1986 art. 48; 1989 Sch. 7 para. 22
162(1)	1986 art. 49(1)
(2)	1986 art. 49(2); 1988 Sch. 4 para. 13
(3)–(8)	1986 art. 49(3)–(8)
163(1)	1986 Sch. 4 para. 1
(2)	M11
(3)	1986 Sch. 4 para. 2
(4)	1986 Sch. 4 para. 5
164	Drafting
165	1986 art. 79(4)
166	1986 art. 80; M9
167(1), (2)	1986 arts. 2(1), 51(1), (2); 1988 Sch. 5; 1989 Sch. 9
(3)	1986 art. 51(2A); Health and Personal Social Services (NI) Order 1991 (NI 1) Sch. 5 Part II
(4)–(6)	1986 art. 51(3)–(5)
168	1982 arts. 28(7), 35(1)(b), (d), (2)(a), (b); 1986 art. 2(4)
169	1975 Sch. 17
170	Drafting
171(1)	1975 Sch. 17; 1986 Sch. 5 para. 17
(2)	1975 s.155(1); Statutory Rules (NI) Order 1979 (NI 12) Sch. 4 para. 16; 1988 art. 15A; 1990 Sch. 6 para. 6(9)
(3)	1975 s.155(2); 1977A Sch. 2
(4)	1975 s.155(3); 1977A Sch. 2; 1989 Sch. 8 para. 9
(5)	1975 s.155(3A); 1975CB art. 24(5A); 1986 art. 63(1), (2)
(6)	1986 art. 81(2)
(7)	1975 s.155(5); 1986 Sch. 10; 1991RF Sch. 2
(8)	1975 s.155(6)
(9)	1975 s.155(7); 1977A Sch. 2
(10)	1975 s.155(8); 1982 art. 29(4); 1986 Sch. 9 para. 70; 1989 Sch. 7 para. 20
(11)	1975 s.155(4A); 1992CP Sch. 2 para. 11
(12)	1975 s.157(4); 1977A Sch. 2
172(1)	1975 s.156(1)
(2)	1975 s.156(2); 1975P Sch. 6; 1979 art. 5(2); 1981C art. 6(1); 1986 arts. 44(3)(b), 63(3), Sch. 9 para. 41, Sch. 10; 1989 Sch. 9; 1991RF Sch. 2; M3
(3)	1975 s.156(3); 1990 Sch. 6 para. 6(1)
(4)	1975 s.156(4)
(5)	1975 s.156(5)
(6)	1990 Sch. 6 para. 6(12), (17)
(7)	1990 Sch. 6 para. 6(13)
(8)	1975 s.156(6)
(9)	1975 s.155A; 1992CP Sch. 2 para. 12
(10)	1990 Sch. 6 para. 6(14), (17)
(11)	1990 Sch. 6 para. 6(15)
(12)	1975 s.156(4); 1990 Sch. 6 para. 6(12); drafting
173(1)	Short title, etc.

Provision	Derivation
173(2)	Commencement
(3), (4)	1975 s.158(2), (2A); 1992CP Sch. 2 para. 12
Sch. 1	
para. 1(1)	1975 Sch. 1 para. 1(1); 1977 art. 3(4)
(2)	1975 Sch. 1 para. 1(1A); 1980 Sch. 1 para. 15; 1985 Sch. 5 para. 5(a)
(3), (4)	1975 Sch. 1 para. 1(1B), (1C); 1985 Sch. 5 para. 5(b)
(5)	1986 art. 75(3)
(6)	1975 Sch. 1 para. 1(1D); 1985 Sch. 5 para. 5(b)
(7), (8)	1975 Sch. 1 para. 1(2), (3)
para. 2	1975 Sch. 1 para. 2
para. 3	1975 Sch. 1 para. 3
para. 4	1975 Sch. 1 para. 4; 1977 art. 3(5)
para. 5	1975 Sch. 1 para. 4A; 1991C art. 4(2)
para. 6(1)	1975 Sch. 1 para. 5(1); 1991C art. 4(3)(a)
(2)–(4)	1975 Sch. 1 para. 5(1A)–(1C); 1990 art. 19(3); 1991C art. 4(3)(b)
(5)	1982 art. 11(4); 1986 Sch. 4 para. 3
(6)	1982 art. 11(5); 1986 Sch. 4 para. 4
(7)	1975 Sch. 1 para. 5(2)
(8)	1975 Sch. 1 para. 5(3); 1990 art. 19(4)
para. 7	1975 Sch. 1 para. 5A; 1990 Sch. 5; 1991C art. 4(4)
para. 8	1975 Sch. 1 para. 6; 1975P Sch. 5 para. 41; 1986 Sch. 9 para. 1; 1989 art. 4; 1990 Sch. 6 para. 7; 1991C art. 4(5)
paras. 9, 10	1975 Sch. 1 paras. 7, 8; 1982 art. 30(2)
Sch. 2	
paras. 1–3	1975 Sch. 2 paras. 1–3; ICTA 1988 Sch. 29 para. 32; Finance Act 1988 (c. 39) Sch. 3 para. 31; Capital Allowances Act 1990 (c. 1) Sch. 1 para. 2
paras. 4, 5	1975 Sch. 2 paras. 5, 6; ICTA 1988 Sch. 29 para. 32
para. 6	1975 Sch. 2 para. 7; ICTA 1988 Sch. 29 para. 32; Social Security Act 1990 (c. 27) s.17(8), (9)
paras. 7, 8	1975 Sch. 2 paras. 8, 9
para. 9	1975 Sch. 2 para. 4; ICTA 1988 Sch. 29 para. 32; Finance Act 1988 (c. 39) Sch. 14 Part VIII and Note 6
Sch. 3	
para. 1(1)	1975 Sch. 3 para. 1(1)
(2)	1975 Sch. 3 para. 1(2); 1986 Sch. 8 para. 2(1); 1988 art. 7(2)(a)
(3)	1975 Sch. 3 para. 1(3); 1986 Sch. 8 para. 2(2), (3); 1988 art. 7(2)(b)
(4)	1975 Sch. 3 para. 1(2)(b); 1986 Sch. 8 para. 2(1)
(5)	1975 Sch. 3 para. 1(3)(b); 1986 Sch. 8 para. 2(3)
(6)	1975 Sch. 3 para. 1(4)
para. 2(1)	1975 Sch. 3 para. 1(1)
(2)	1975 Sch. 3 para. 1(2); 1986 Sch. 8 para. 2(1); 1988 art. 7(2)(a)
(3)	1975 Sch. 3 para. 1(3); 1986 Sch. 8 para. 2(2), (3); 1988 art. 7(2)(b)
(4)	1975 Sch. 3 para. 1(2)(b); 1986 Sch. 8 para. 2(1)
(5)	1975 Sch. 3 para. 1(3)(b); 1986 Sch. 8 para. 2(3)
(6)	1975 Sch. 3 para. 1(4)
para. 3	1975 Sch. 3 para. 3; 1986 Sch. 4 para. 14; 1990 Sch. 6 para. 8
para. 4(1)	1975 Sch. 3 para. 4(1); 1986 Sch. 9 para. 42(a)
(2)	1975 Sch. 3 para. 4(1)(b); 1986 Sch. 8 para. 2(4)
(3)	1975 Sch. 3 para. 4(2)
para. 5(1)	1975 Sch. 3 para. 5(1)
(2)	1975 Sch. 3 para. 5(2); 1975P art. 21(2); 1986 Sch. 8 para. 2(5)
(3), (4)	1975 Sch. 3 para. 5(3); 1986 Sch. 8 para. 2(6)
(5), (6)	1975 Sch. 3 para. 5(4), (5)
(7)	1975 Sch. 3 para. 5(6); 1979 Sch. 1 para. 3
(8)	1975 s.27(2)
para. 6	1975 Sch. 3 para. 6
para. 7(1)	1975 Sch. 3 para. 8(1); 1989 Sch. 7 para. 14
(2)	1975 Sch. 3 para. 8(2); 1986 Sch. 9 para. 42(b)
(3), (4)	1975 Sch. 3 para. 8(3); 1979 Sch. 3 para. 10; 1986 Sch. 8 para. 2(7), Sch. 9 para. 42(b)
para. 8	1975 Sch. 3 para. 10

Provision	Derivation
Sch. 3	
para. 9	1975 Sch. 3 para. 13; 1986 Sch. 9 para. 42(c)
Sch. 4	
Part I	
para. 1	1975 Sch. 4 Part I para. 1(a); 1992U Sch. 1
para. 2	1975 Sch. 4 Part I para. 1(b); 1992U Sch. 1
para. 3	1975 Sch. 4 Part I para. 3; 1992U Sch. 1
para. 4	1975 Sch. 4 Part I para. 4; 1992U Sch. 1
para. 5	1975 Sch. 4 Part I para. 9; 1975P Sch. 5 para. 42; 1992U Sch. 1
para. 6	1975 Sch. 4 Part I para. 10; 1992U Sch. 1
Part II	1975 Sch. 4 Part IA; 1986 art. 37(2)
Part III	
para. 1	1975 Sch. 4 Part III para. 1; 1992U Sch. 1
para. 2	1975 Sch. 4 Part III para. 2; 1984 Sch. 2 para. 2; 1992U Sch. 1
para. 3	1975 Sch. 4 Part III para. 2A; 1990 art. 4(2); 1992U Sch. 1
para. 4	1975 Sch. 4 Part III para. 3; 1992U Sch. 1
para. 5	1975 Sch. 4 Part III para. 4; 1992U Sch. 1
para. 6	1975 Sch. 4 Part III para. 5; 1992U Sch. 1
para. 7	1975 Sch. 4 Part III para. 5A; 1985 art. 14(2)
para. 8	1975 Sch. 4 Part III para. 6
Part IV	
col. (1)	1975 Sch. 4 Part IV col. (1); 1984 Sch. 2 para. 2; 1986 Sch. 10
col. (2)	1975 Sch. 4 Part IV col. (2); 1975CB Sch. 4 para. 35(a); 1986 Sch. 10; 1992U Sch. 1
col. (3)	1975 Sch. 4 Part IV col. (4); 1975CB Sch. 4 para. 35(b), (c); 1992U Sch. 1
Part V	
para. 1	1975 Sch. 4 Part V para. 3; 1992U Sch. 1
para. 2	1975 Sch. 4 Part V para. 7; 1992U Sch. 1
para. 3	1975 Sch. 4 Part V para. 8; 1992U Sch. 1
para. 4	1975 Sch. 4 Part V para. 16; 1992U Sch. 1
para. 5	1975 Sch. 4 Part V para. 4; 1986 Sch. 3 paras. 4, 15; 1992 U Sch. 1
para. 6	1975 Sch. 4 Part V para. 5; 1979 Sch. 1 para. 13; 1986 Sch. 3 paras. 4, 15; 1992U Sch. 1
para. 7	1975 Sch. 4 Part V para. 10; 1986 Sch. 3 paras. 4, 15; 1992U Sch. 1
para. 8	1975 Sch. 4 Part V para. 12; 1986 Sch. 3 paras. 4, 15; 1992U Sch. 1
para. 9	1975 Sch. 4 Part V para. 2; 1986 Sch. 3 para. 3(3); 1992U Sch. 1
para. 10	1975 Sch. 4 Part V para. 13; 1986 Sch. 3 para. 8; 1988 Sch. 1 para. 2; 1992U Sch. 1
para. 11	1975 Sch. 4 Part V para. 14; 1986 Sch. 3 para. 11; 1988 Sch. 1 para. 1; 1992U Sch. 1
para. 12	1975 Sch. 4 Part V para. 15; 1986 Sch. 3 para. 8; 1988 Sch. 1 para. 2; 1992U Sch. 1
Sch. 5	
para. 1	1975P Sch. 1 para. 1; 1989 Sch. 1 para. 3(1)
para. 2(1)	1975P Sch. 1 para. 2(1); 1989 Sch. 1 para. 3(2)
(2)	1975P Sch. 1 para. 2(2); 1989 Sch. 1 para. 3(3)
(3)	1975P Sch. 1 para. 2(3); 1977 art. 4(1)(b); 1989 Sch. 1 para. 3(4)
(4)	1975P art. 70A; 1979 art. 14
(5)	1975P Sch. 1 para. 2(4); 1977 art. 4(1)(c); 1980 art. 4(10)
(6)	1975P Sch. 1 para. 2(4A); 1985 art. 11(5)
(7)	1975P Sch. 1 para. 2(5); 1986 Sch. 9 para. 59(a); 1989 Sch. 1 para. 3(5)
(8)	1975P Sch. 1 para. 2(6); 1977 art. 4(1)(d); 1989 Sch. 1 para. 3(6)
para. 3	1975 Sch. 1 para. 3; 1977 art. 4(1)(e); 1989 Sch. 1 para. 3(7)
para. 4(1)	1975P Sch. 1 para. 4(1); 1979 Sch. 3 para. 22; 1986 art. 20(2); 1989 Sch. 1 para. 3(8)
(2)	1975P Sch. 1 para. 4(2); 1979 Sch. 3 para. 22; 1986 art. 20(2); 1989 Sch. 1 para. 3(8)
(3)	1975P Sch. 1 para. 4(2A); 1986 art. 20(2)
(4)	1975P Sch. 1 para. 4(3); 1979 Sch. 1 para. 6; 1986 Sch. 9 para. 59(a)
(5)	1975P Sch. 1 para. 4(4); 1979 Sch. 1 para. 22

Provision	Derivation
Sch. 5	
para. 5(1), (2)	1975P Sch. 1 para. 4A(1); 1979 Sch. 1 para. 7; 1986 art. 20(3)
(3)	1975P Sch. 1 para. 4A(1A); 1986 art. 20(4)
para. 6(1), (2)	1975P Sch. 1 para. 4A(2); 1979 Sch. 1 para. 7; 1986 art. 20(5)
(3)	1975P Sch. 1 para. 4A(2A)(a); 1986 art. 20(6)
(4)	1975P Sch. 1 para. 4A(2A)(b); 1986 art. 20(6)
para. 7(1)	1975P Sch. 1 para. 4A(3); 1979 Sch. 1 para. 7; 1986 Sch. 9 para. 59(b)
(2)	1975P art. 70A; 1979 art. 14
para. 8(1), (2)	1975P Sch. 1 para. 5(1), (2); 1989 Sch. 1 para. 3(9)
(3)	1975P Sch. 1 para. 5(3); 1989 Sch. 1 para. 3(10)
(4)	1975P Sch. 1 para. 5(4)
para. 9	Drafting
Sch. 6	
para. 1	1975 Sch. 8 para. 1; 1984 Sch. 2 para. 8(a)
paras. 2, 3	1975 Sch. 8 paras. 2, 3
para. 4	1975 Sch. 8 para. 4A; 1984 Sch. 2 para. 8(b)
para. 5	1975 Sch. 8 para. 5A; 1984 Sch. 2 para. 8(c)
para. 6(1)	1975 Sch. 8 para. 4(1); 1982 Sch. 4 para. 12
(2)	1975 Sch. 8 para. 4(1) proviso
(3)–(5)	1975 Sch. 8 para. 4(2)–(4); 1989 Sch. 3 para. 13(1)
para. 7	1975 Sch. 8 para. 5; 1989 Sch. 3 para. 13(2)
para. 8	1975 Sch. 8 para. 6
Sch. 7	
para. 1	1986 Sch. 3 para. 4
para. 2	1975 s.58
para. 3(1)	1975 s.59(1); 1985 art. 11(4)(a)
(2)–(4)	1975 s.59(1A)–(1C); 1985 art. 11(4)(b)
(5)–(7)	1975 s.59(2)–(4)
(8)	1975 s.59(4); 1980(2) art. 3(3)
(9)	1980(2) art. 3(4)
(10)	1975 s.59(5)
(11)	Drafting
para. 4(1)	1975 s.64(1); 1975CB Sch. 4 para. 22(a); 1986 Sch. 3 para. 4
(2)	1975 s.64(2)
(3)	1975 s.64(1A); 1984 Sch. 3 para. 3
(4)	1975 s.64(1B); 1984 Sch. 3 para. 3; Social Security (Industrial Injuries) (Dependency) (Permitted Earnings Limits) Order (NI) 1991 (SR 1991 No. 72) art. 2
(5), (6)	1975 s.64(1C), (1D); 1984 Sch. 3 para. 3
para. 5(1)	1975 s.65(1); 1975CB Sch. 4 para. 23(a)
(2)	1975 s.65(2); 1975CB Sch. 4 para. 23(b); 1977 art. 18(3)
para. 6(1)	1975 s.66(1); 1975CB Sch. 4 para. 24; 1980 Sch. 1 paras. 4, 6; 1986 Sch. 3 paras. 4, 15
(2)	1975 s.66(2)
(3)–(6)	1975 s.66(3)–(6); 1985 art. 15(5)
(7)	1975 s.66(7)
para. 7	1975 s.66A; 1984 art. 8(b); 1989 art. 11(3)
para. 8	1975 s.84A; 1989 Sch. 8 para. 7(2)
para. 9(1), (2)	1975 s.57(1), (5); 1986 Sch. 3 para. 3(3)
(3)	1975 s.57(4); 1982 art. 32(2); 1989 Sch. 7 para. 11
para. 10(1)	1986 Sch. 3 para. 7
(2), (3)	1975 s.62
para. 11(1)	1975 s.59A(1), (10B); 1986 Sch. 3 para. 5(1); 1989 Sch. 7 para. 12; 1990 art. 5(1), (4)
(2), (3)	1975 s.59A(1A), (1B), (10B); 1990 art. 5(2), (4)
(4)–(7)	1975 s.59A(2)–(5); 1986 Sch. 3 para. 5(1)
(8)	1975 s.59A(6); 1986 Sch. 3 para. 5(1); 1990 art. 5(3)
(9)	1975 s.59A(7); 1986 Sch. 3 para. 5(1)
(10)	1975 s.59A(8); 1986 Sch. 3 para. 5(1); 1988 Sch. 4 para. 9(a)
(11)	1988 art. 4(2)
(12)	1975 s.59A(9); 1986 Sch. 3 para. 5(1)

Provision	Derivation
Sch. 7	
para. 11(13)	1975 s.59A(10); 1986 Sch. 3 para. 5(1)
(14)	1975 s.59A(10A); 1988 Sch. 4 para. 9(b)
para. 12(1)	1988 art. 4(3)
(2)	1988 art. 4(4)
(3), (4)	1988 art. 4(4A), (4B); 1989 art. 19(5)
(5), (6)	1988 art. 4(5), (6); 1989 art. 19(6)
para. 13(1)	1975 s.59B(1); 1988 art. 4(1); 1989 Sch. 1 para. 8(2)
(2)	1975 s.59B(2); 1988 art. 4(1)
(3)	1975 s.59B(3); 1988 art. 4(1)
(4)	1975 s.59B(5); 1988 art. 4(1); 1989 Sch. 1 para. 8(5)
(5)	1975 s.59B(5A); 1989 art. 19(3)
(6)	1975 s.59B(6); 1988 art. 4(1)
(7)	Drafting
(8), (9)	1975 s.59B(7), (8); 1989 Sch. 1 para. 8(6)
(10)	1975 s.59B(9); 1990 art. 5(6)
(11)	1975 s.59A(10A); 1988 Sch. 4 para. 9(b)
para. 14(1)	1988 Sch. 1 paras. 2, 3
(2)	1975 Sch. 17
para. 15	1975 s.67; 1977 art. 18(4); 1986 Sch. 3 para. 8(a); 1988 Sch. 1 para. 2
para. 16	1975 s.68; 1975CB Sch. 5; 1986 Sch. 3 para. 8(a); 1988 Sch. 1 para. 2
para. 17	1975 s.69; 1986 Sch. 3 para. 11; 1988 Sch. 1 para. 3
para. 18	1975 s.70; 1984 Sch. 3 para. 4; 1986 Sch. 3 para. 8(b); 1988 Sch. 1 para. 2
para. 19	1975 Sch. 9 para. 1; 1986 Sch. 3 para. 8(c); 1988 Sch. 1 para. 2
para. 20	1975 s.75; 1986 Sch. 3 para. 8(b); 1988 Sch. 1 paras. 2, 6(2)(a)
para. 21	1977 art. 8; 1986 Sch. 10; 1988 Sch. 1 para. 6(2)(b)
Sch. 8	
para. 1	1975OC s.1
para. 2	1975OC s.2; 1990 art. 18(7)(a); 1992U art. 6
para. 3	1975OC s.3
para. 4(1)	1975 s.150(1)
(2)	1975 s.150(3)
para. 5(1)	1975 s.150(2); 1975OC s.9(1)
(2)	1975OC s.9(2); 1977 art. 9(1)
(3)	1986 Sch. 3 para. 15
Sch. 9	1975CB Sch. 1; 1980 art. 5(6); Treatment of Offenders (NI) Order 1980 (NI 10) art. 3, Sch. 1 para. 1; 1984 Sch. 2 para. 11
Sch. 10	1975CB Sch. 2
Sch. 11	1982 Sch. 1; 1984 Sch. 2 para. 13(2)
Sch. 12	
para. 1	1982 Sch. 2 para. 1; 1985 art. 18(6)(a)
paras. 2–4	1982 Sch. 2 paras. 2–4
para. 5	1982 Sch. 2 para. 1A; 1985 art. 18(6)(b)
para. 6	1982 Sch. 2 para. 6
Sch. 13	
para. 1	1986 Sch. 4 para. 11; 1988 Sch. 4 para. 15(1)
para. 2	1986 Sch. 4 para. 11A; 1988 Sch. 4 para. 15(2)
para. 3	1986 Sch. 4 para. 12

TABLE OF DESTINATIONS

CONSOLIDATION OF ENACTMENTS (PROCEDURE) ACT 1949
c.33

1949	c.33
M1	s.23(4)
M2	57(3)
M3	172(2)
M4	107
M9	158, 166
M11	163(2)
M12	23(4)

SOCIAL SECURITY (NORTHERN IRELAND) ACT 1975
c.15

1975	c.15
s.1(1)	s.1(1)
(2)	1(2)
(3)	1(3)
(4)	1(4)
(4A)	1(5)
(6)	1(6)
2	2
3(1)	3
(1A)	4(1)
(1B)	4(2), (3)
(1C)	4(2), (3)
(1D)	4(4)
(2)	3
(3)	3
4(1)	5(1)
(2)	6(1), (4)
(3)	6(3)
(4)	7
(5)	7
(6)	8(1), (2), (3)
(6A)	8(1), (2), (3)
(6B)	8(1), (2), (3)
(6C)	9(1), (2), (3), (4)
(6D)	9(1), (2), (3)
(6E)	9(1), (2), (3), (4)
(7)	6(5)
4A	10
7(1)	11(1)
(4)	11(3)
(5)	11(4)
(6)	11(5)
7A	12
8(1)	13(1)
(2)	13(2)
(2)(a)	13(3)
(2A)	13(4)
(2B)	13(5), (6), (7)
(2C)	13(5), (6), (7)
(2D)	13(5), (6), (7)
9(1)	15(1), (2), (5)
(2)	15(3)
(3)	16
(4)	17(1)
(5)	17(2)
(6)	17(3), (4), (5), (6)
10	18

1975	c.15
s.11	s.19(1), (2), (3)
12	20
13(1)	21(1), (2)
(2)	22(1), (2)
(3)	22(4)
(4)	22(5)
(5)	22(3); 23(1), (3)
(5A)	23(4)
(5AA)	22(6)
(5B)	24(1)
(5C)	24(2)
(5ZA)	23(2)
(6)	21(3), (5)
(7)	21(6)
(8)	21(4)
14(1)	25(1); 31(1)
(2)	25(2); 31(2)
(2A)	31(3)
(3)	25(3); 31(4)
(4)	25(4); 31(5)
(6)	25(5), (6); 31(6), (7)
(8)	25(7); 31(8)
15(1)	33(1)
(2)	33(2)
(3)	33(3)
(4)	33(4), (5)
(5)	33(6)
(5A)	33(7), (8)
(5B)	33(7), (8)
(6)	33(9)
15A(1)	33(10), (11)
(2)	33(10), (11)
16(1)	34(1), (2)
(2)	34(3)
(2B)	34(4), (5), (6)
(2C)	34(4), (5), (6)
(2D)	34(4), (5), (6)
(3)	34(7)
17(1)	57(1)
(2)	57(3)
(2A)	57(4)
(2B)	57(5)
(2C)	57(6), (7)
(2D)	57(6), (7)
(3)	57(8)
(4)	57(9), (10)
(5)	57(9), (10)

1975	c.15
s.18(1)	s.26(1)
(2)	26(2), (3), (4)
(2B)	26(2), (3), (4)
(3)	26(5)
(4)	26(6)
19(1)	27(1), (2)
(1A)	27(1), (2)
(2)	27(3)
20(1)	28(1)
20(1A)	28(2)
(2)	32(1), (2); 59(1), (2)
(3)	28(3); 32(1), (2); 59(1), (2)
(3A)	28(4)
(4)	28(5)
(5)	28(6)
(c)	32(3); 59(3)
20A	28(6)
22(1)	35(1), (2), (3)
(2)	35(1), (2), (3)
(3)	35(1), (2), (3)
(4)	57(2)
(4A)	35(4)
(5)	35(5), (6), (7)
(6)	35(5), (6), (7)
(7)	35(5), (6), (7)
24(1)	36(1), (2)
(2)	36(1), (2)
(3)	36(3)
25(1)	37(1)
(2)	37(2)
(3)	37(3), (4)
(4)	37(3), (4)
26(1)	38(1)
(2)	39(4), (5)
(3)	38(2), (3)
(4)	38(2), (3)
27(2)	Sched. 3, para. 5(8)
(6)	43(1)
28(1)	44(1)
(1A)	44(2)
(7)	47(1)

1975	c.15
s.28(7A)	s.47(2), (3), (4)
(7B)	47(2), (3), (4)
(7C)	47(2), (3), (4)
(8)	47(5)
29(1)	49(1)
(2)	49(2), (3)
(3)	49(2), (3)
(4)	49(4)
(5)	49(5)
(6)	49(6)
(7)	50(1)
(8)	50(2)
(9)	49(7), (8)
(9A)	49(7), (8)
30(3)	54(1), (2)
(4)	54(3)
(5)	54(4)
31	56(1), (2)
33(1)	60(1)
(2)	60(1)
(3)	60(4), (5), (6)
(4)	60(7)
34	63
35(1)	64
(2)	65(1)
(2A)	65(2)
(2B)	66
(2C)	66
(3)	65(3)
(4)	65(4), (6)
(4A)	65(5)
(5A)	67(1)
(6)	67(2)
36(1)	68(1), (2), (3), (4)
(2)	68(1), (2), (3), (4)
(3)	68(1), (2), (3), (4)
(4)	68(1), (2), (3), (4)
(4A)	68(5)
(5)	68(6)
(6)	68(6), (7)
(6A)	68(8), (9)
(6B)	68(8), (9)
(6C)	68(10)
(7)	68(11)
(8)	68(13)
36A	69
37(1)	70(1)
(2)	70(2)
(3)	70(3), (4), (5)
(4)	70(3), (4), (5)
(5)	70(3), (4), (5)
(6)	70(6), (10)
(7)	70(7), (8), (9)
(8)	70(7), (8), (9)
(9)	70(7), (8), (9)
37ZA	71
37ZB	72

1975	c.15
37ZC	s.73
37ZD	75
37ZE	76
38(1)	77(1), (7)
38(2)	77(2), (3)
(3)	77(2), (3)
(4)	77(8)
(5)	77(9)
(6)	77(10)
(7)	77(11)
39(1)(a)	78(1), (2)
(1)(b)	78(1), (2)
(1)(c)	78(3), (4)
(2)	78(5)
(2A)	78(6)
(3)	78(7), (8)
(3A)	78(7), (8)
(4)	78(9)
40	79
41(1)	80(1)
(2)	80(2)
(2A)	80(3)
(2B)	80(4)
(2D)	80(7)
(4)	80(5), (6)
(5)	80(5), (6)
43(1)	56(3), (4); 77(4), (5); 81(1), (2)
(2)	56(5); 77(6); 81(3)
44(1)	82(1)
(2)	82(2)
(3)(c)	82(3), (4)
(4)	82(5)
45(1)	83(1)
(2)	83(2)
(2A)	83(3)
45A(1)	84(1)
(2)	84(2)
(3)	84(3)
46(1)	85(1)
(2)	85(2)
(3)	85(3)
(4)	85(4)
47(1)	86(1)
(1A)	86(2)
47A	87(1), (2)
47B	89
48(1)	88
49	90
49A	91
50(1)	94(1)
(1A)	94(2)
(3)	94(3)
(4)	94(4)
(5)	94(5)
(6)	94(6)
50A(1)	102(1), (2)
(2)	102(1), (2)
(3)	102(3)
51	95(1), (2), (3)
52	98; 99; 100; 101
53	98; 99; 100; 101
54	98; 99; 100; 101
55	98; 99; 100; 101

1975	c.15
s.57(1)	s.103(1); Sched. 7, para. 9(1), (2)
(1A)	103(2), (3), (4)
(1B)	103(2), (3), (4)
(1C)	103(2), (3), (4)
(3)	103(5)
(4)	103(6); Sched. 7, para. 9(3)
(5)	Sched. 7, para. 9(1), (2)
(6)	103(7), (8)
58	Sched. 7, para. 2
59(1)	Sched. 7, para. 3(1)
(1A)	Sched 7, para. 3(2), (3), (4)
(1B)	Sched. 7, para. 3(2), (3), (4)
(1C)	Sched. 7, para. 3(2), (3), (4)
(2)	Sched. 7, para. 3(5), (6), (7)
(3)	Sched. 7, para. 3(5), (6), (7)
(4)	Sched. 7, para. 3(5), (6), (7), (8)
(5)	Sched. 7, para. 3(10)
59A(1)	Sched. 7, para. 11(1)
(1A)	Sched. 7, para. 11(2), (3)
(1B)	Sched. 7, para. 11(2), (3)
(2)	Sched. 7, para. 11(4), (5), (6), (7)
(3)	Sched. 7, para. 11(4), (5), (6), (7)
(4)	Sched. 7, para. 11(4), (5), (6), (7)
(5)	Sched. 7, para. 11(4), (5), (6), (7)
(6)	Sched. 7, para. 11(8)
(7)	Sched. 7, para. 11(9)
(8)	Sched. 7, para. 11(10)
(9)	Sched. 7, para. 11(12)
(10)	Sched. 7, para. 11(13)

1975	c.15
s.59A(10A) ...	Sched. 7, para. 11 (14); 13(11)
(10B) ...	Sched. 7, para. 11(1), (2), (3)
59B(1)	Sched. 7, para. 13(1)
(2)	Sched. 7, para. 13(2)
(3)	Sched. 7, para. 13(3)
(5)	Sched. 7, para. 13(4)
(5A)	Sched. 7, para. 13(5)
(6)	Sched. 7, para. 13(6)
(7)	Sched. 7, para. 13(8), (9)
(8)	Sched. 7, para. 13(8), (9)
(9)	Sched. 7, para. 13(10)
61(1).......	104(1), (2)
(2).......	104(1), (2)
(3).......	104(3), (4)
(4).......	104(3), (4)
62	Sched. 7, para. 10(2), (3)
63	105
64(1).......	Sched. 7, para. 4(1)
(1A)......	Sched. 7, para. 4(3)
(1B)......	Sched. 7, para. 4(4)
(1C)......	Sched. 7, para. 4(5), (6)
(1D)......	Sched. 7, para. 4(5), (6)
(2).......	Sched. 7, para. 4(2)
65(1).......	Sched. 7, para. 5(1)
(2).......	Sched. 7, para. 5(2)
66(1).......	Sched. 7, para. 6(1)
(2).......	Sched. 7, para. 6(2)
(3).......	Sched. 7, para. 6(3), (4), (5), (6)
(4).......	Sched. 7, para. 6(3), (4), (5), (6)
(5).......	Sched. 7, para. 6(3), (4), (5), (6)
(6).......	Sched. 7, para. 6(3), (4), (5), (6)
(7).......	Sched. 7, para. 6(7)

1975	c.15
s.66A	Sched. 7, para. 7
67	Sched. 7, para. 15
68	Sched. 7, para. 16
69	Sched. 7, para. 17
70	Sched. 7, para. 18
75	Sched. 7, para. 20
76(1).......	108(1), (2), (3), (4)
(2).......	108(1), (2), (3), (4)
(3).......	108(1), (2), (3), (4)
(4).......	108(1), (2), (3), (4)
(4A)......	108(5)
(5).......	108(6)
77(1).......	109(1), (2)
(2).......	109(1), (2)
(3).......	109(3)
(4).......	109(4), (5), (6)
(5).......	109(7)
78	110
82(5).......	113(1), (2)
(6).......	113(1), (2)
83	113(3)
84(1).......	114(1), (2)
(2).......	114(1), (2)
(4).......	114(3)
(5).......	114(4)
84A	92; Sched. 7, para. 8
91	107
122(1)......	115(1), (2)
(2)......	115(1), (2), (3)
123	116
124	117; 118; 119
125	117; 118; 119
126	117; 118; 119
147	97
148	96
150(1).......	Sched. 8, para. 4(1)
(2)......	Sched. 8, para. 5(1)
(3)......	Sched. 8, para. 4(2)
152	120
155(1).......	171(2)
(2)......	171(3)
(3)......	171(4)
(3A)....	171(5)
(4A)....	171(11)
(5)......	171(7)
(6)......	171(8)
(7)......	171(9)
(8)......	171(10)
155A	172(9)
156(1)......	172(1)
(2)......	172(2)
(3)......	172(3)
(4)......	172(4), (12)
(5)......	172(5)

1975	c.15
s.156(6)......	s.172(8)
157(4)......	171(12)
158(2)......	173(3), (4)
(2A).....	173(3), (4)
Sched. 1, para. 1(1) ...	Sched. 1, para. 1(1)
(1A) .	Sched. 1, para. 1(2)
(1B) .	Sched. 1, para. 1(3), (4)
(1C) .	Sched. 1, para. 1(3), (4)
(1D) .	Sched. 1, para. 1(6)
(2) ...	Sched. 1, para. 1(7), (8)
(3) ...	Sched. 1, para. 1(7), (8)
2	Sched. 1, para. 2
3	Sched. 1, para. 3; Sched. 5, para. 3
4	Sched. 1, para. 4
4A	Sched. 1, para. 5
5(1) ..	Sched. 1, para. 6(1)
(1A) .	Sched. 1, para. 6(2), (3), (4)
(1B) .	Sched. 1 para. 6(2), (3), (4)
(1C) ..	Sched. 1, para. 6(2), (3), (4)
(2) ...	Sched. 1, para. 6(7)
(3) ...	Sched. 1, para. 6(8)
5A	Sched. 1, para. 7
6	Sched. 1, para. 8
7	Sched. 1, paras. 9; 10
8	Sched. 1, paras. 9; 10
Sched. 2, para. 1	Sched. 2, paras 1; 2; 3
2	Sched. 2, paras. 1; 2; 3
3	Sched. 2, paras. 1; 2; 3
4	Sched. 2, para. 9
5	Sched. 2, paras. 4; 5
6	Sched. 2, paras. 4; 5

1975	c.15
Sched. 2—*cont.*	
para. 7	Sched. 2, para. 6
8	Sched. 2, paras. 7; 8
9	Sched. 2, paras. 7; 8
Sched. 3,	
para. 1(1) . . .	Sched. 3, paras. 1(1); 2(1)
(2) . . .	Sched. 3, paras. 1(2); 2(2)
(b)	Sched. 3, paras. 1(4); 2(4)
(3) . . .	Sched. 3, paras. 1(3); 2(3)
(b)	Sched. 3, paras. 1(5); 2(5)
(4) . . .	Sched. 3, paras. 1(6); 2(6)
3	Sched. 3, para. 3
4(1) . . .	Sched. 3, para. 4(1)
(b)	Sched. 3, para. 4(2)
(2) . . .	Sched. 3, para. 4(3)
5(1) . . .	Sched. 3, para. 5(1)
(2) . . .	Sched. 5(2)
(3) . . .	Sched. 3, para. 5(3), (4)
(4) . . .	Sched. 3, para. 5(5), (6)
(5) . . .	Sched. 3, para. 5(5), (6)
(6) . . .	Sched. 3, para. 5(7)
8(1) . . .	Sched. 3, para. 7(1)
(2) . . .	Sched. 3, para. 7(2)
(3) . . .	Sched. 3, para. 7(3), (4)
10	Sched. 3, para. 8
13	Sched. 3, para. 9
Sched. 4,	
Part I,	
para. 1(a) . . .	Sched. 4, Part I, para. 1

1975	c.15
Sched. 4—*cont.*	
Part I—*cont.*	
para. 1(b) . . .	Sched. 4, Part I para. 2
3	Sched. 4, Part I para. 3
4	Sched. 4, Part I para. 4
9	Sched. 4, Part I para. 5
10	Sched. 4, Part I para. 6
Part IA	Sched. 4, Part II
Part III,	
para. 1	Sched. 4, Part III, para. 1
2	Sched. 4, Part III, para. 2
2A	Sched. 4, Part III, para. 3
3	Sched. 4, Part III, para. 4
4	Sched. 4, Part III, para. 5
5	Sched. 4, Part III, para. 6
5A	Sched. 4, Part III, para. 7
6	Sched. 4, Part III, para. 8
Part IV,	
col. (1)	Sched. 4, Part IV, col. (1)
col. (2)	Sched. 4 Part IV, col. (2)
col. (4)	Sched. 4, Part IV, col.(3)
Part V,	
para. 2	Sched. 4, Part V, para. 9
3	Sched. 4, Part V, para. 1
4	Sched. 4, Part V, para. 5

1975	c.15
Sched. 4—*cont.*	
Part V—*cont.*	
para. 5	Sched. 4, Part V, para. 6
7	Sched. 4, Part V, para. 2
8	Sched. 4, Part V, para. 3
10	Sched. 4, Part V, para. 7
12	Sched. 4, Part V, para. 8
13	Sched. 4, Part V, para. 10
14	Sched. 4, Part V, para. 11
15	Sched. 4, Part V, para. 12
16	Sched. 4, Part V, para. 4
Sched. 8	
para. 1	Sched. 6, para. 1
2	Sched. 6, paras. 2; 3
3	Sched. 6, paras. 2; 3
4(1) . . .	Sched. 6, para. 6(1)
4(1) proviso	Sched. 6, para. 6(2)
(2) . . .	Sched. 6, para. 6(3), (4), (5)
(3) . . .	Sched. 6, para. 6(3), (4), (5)
(4) . . .	Sched. 6, para. 6(3), (4), (5)
4A	Sched. 6, para. 4
5	Sched. 6, para. 7
5A	Sched. 6, para. 5
6	Sched. 8
Sched. 9,	
para. 1	Sched. 7, para. 19
Sched. 17	121; 169; 171(1); Sched. 7, para. 14(2)

SOCIAL SECURITY PENSIONS (NORTHERN IRELAND) ORDER 1975
N.I. 15

1975	N.I. 15
art. 3(1)	s.5(1)
(2)	5(2), (3)
(3)	5(2), (3)
5(2)	19(4), (5), (6)
(3)	19(4), (5), (6)
(4)	19(4), (5), (6)
6(1)	6(2)
(2)	11(2)
7(1)	14(1)
(2)	14(3), (4)
(3)	14(2)
8(1)	44(3), (4)
(2)	45(1)
(2A)	45(2), (3)
(2B)	45(4), (5)
(3)	45(6), (7)
(4)	44(5)
(5)	44(6)
(6)	44(7)
9	50(3), (4)
10(1)	51(1)
(2)	51(2)
(3)	51(4)
11(1)	52(1), (2), (3)
(2)	52(1), (2), (3)
(3)	52(1), (2), (3)
12	53(1), (2)
14	55
15(1)	39(1)
(2)	39(2)
(3)	39(1)
16	33(3)
17(1)	40(1)
(1A)	40(2)
(2)	40(3)
(3)	40(4)
(4)	40(5)
(5)	40(7)
(6)	40(8)
18(1)	41(1)
(2)	41(2), (3)

1975	N.I. 15
art. 18(3)	s.41(2), (3)
(4)	41(4), (5)
(5)	41(7)
(6)	41(8)
18A	42
20	31(5)
(1)	25(4)
21(2)	Sched. 3, para. 5(2)
(5)	60(7)
22(1)	48(1)
(2)	48(3)
26	62
27	43(3), (4), (5)
70A	45(6), (7); Sched. 5, paras. 2(4); 7(2)
Sched. 1,	
para. 1	Sched. 5, para. 1
2(1) . . .	Sched. 5, para. 2(1)
(2) . . .	Sched. 5, para. 2(2)
(3) . . .	Sched. 5, para. 2(3)
(4) . . .	Sched. 5, para. 2(5)
(4A) .	Sched. 5, para. 2(6)
(5) . . .	Sched. 5, para. 2(7)
(6) . . .	Sched. 5, para. 2(8)
4(1) . . .	Sched. 5, para. 4(1)
(2) . . .	Sched. 5, para. 4(2)
(2A) .	Sched. 5, para. 4(3)
(3) . . .	Sched. 5, para. 4(4)
(4) . . .	Sched. 5, para. 4(5)

1975	N.I. 15
Sched. 1—cont.	
para. 4A(1) .	Sched. 5, para. 5(1), (2), (3)
(2) .	Sched. 5, para. 6(1), (2)
(2A)(a)	Sched. 5, para. 6(3)
(b)	Sched. 5, para. 6(4)
(3) .	Sched. 5, para. 7(1)
5(1) . . .	Sched. 5, para. 8(1), (2)
(2) . . .	Sched. 5, para. 8(1), (2)
(3) . . .	Sched. 5, para. 8(3)
(4) . . .	Sched. 5, para. 8(4)
Sched. 5,	
para. 18(a) . .	5(1)
19	20
20(a) . .	22(2)
(b) . .	22(4)
21(b) . .	25(5), (6); 31(6), (7)
22(b) . .	33(3)
(c) . .	33(4), (5)
23	37(1)
24	38(1)
25	44(1)
26	50(1)
27	54(3)
28	60(4), (5), (6)
29	63
41	Sched. 1, para. 8
42	Sched. 4, Part I, para. 5
44	121
Sched. 6	13(2), (3); 17(2); 172(2)

CHILD BENEFIT (NORTHERN IRELAND) ORDER 1975
N.I. 16

1975	N.I. 16
art. 2(2)	s.143(1)
(3)	143(2), (3), (4)
(4)	143(2), (3), (4)
(5)	143(2), (3), (4)
(6)	143(6)
3(1)	137
4(1)	138(1)
(1A)	138(2), (3)
(1B)	138(2), (3)
(2)	138(4), (5)
(3)	138(4), (5)
5	139
6(1)	140(1), (2)
(2)	140(3)
7(1)	141(1), (2), (3), (4)
(2)	141(1), (2), (3), (4)
(3)	141(1), (2), (3), (4)

1975	N.I. 16
art. 7(4)	s.141(1), (2), (3), (4)
11	143(5)
15	142
24(1)(a)	141(5)
(5A)	171(5)
Sched. 1	Sched. 9
Sched. 2	Sched. 10
Sched. 4,	
para. 10(a)	37(1)
(b)	37(2)
11	56(1), (2)
13(a)	77(1)
(c)	77(9)
14(a)	80(1)
(b)	80(5), (6)
(c)	80(5), (6)
16	81(1), (2)
(a)	56(3), (4); 77(4), (5)
(b)	56(5); 77(6); 81(3)
17(a)	82(1), (2)
17(b)	82(4)

1975	N.I. 16
Sched. 4—cont.	
para. 18	83(2)
19	85(2)
20	86(1)
22(a)	Sched. 7, para. 4(1)
23(a)	Sched. 7, para. 5(1)
(b)	Sched. 7, para. 5(2)
24	Sched. 7, para. 6(1)
35(a)	Sched. 4, Part IV, col. (2)
(b)	Sched. 4, Part IV, col. (3)
(c)	Sched. 4, Part IV, col. (3)
37	121
Sched. 5	Sched. 7, para. 16

INDUSTRIAL INJURIES AND DISEASES (NORTHERN IRELAND OLD CASES) ACT 1975
c. 17

1975	c.17
s.1	Sched. 8, para. 1
2	Sched. 8, para. 2
3	Sched. 8, para. 3
9(1)	Sched. 8, para. 5(1)
(2)	Sched. 8, para. 5(2)

SOCIAL SECURITY AND FAMILY ALLOWANCES (NORTHERN IRELAND) ORDER 1976
N.I. 9

1976	N.I. 9
art. 3(1)	s.6(1); 11(1); 13(1)
Sched. 3, para. 6	Sched. 3, para. 6

INDUSTRIAL RELATIONS (NO. 2) (N.I.) ORDER 1976
N.I. 28

1976	N.I. 28
art. 20(2)	s.1(1)

SOCIAL SECURITY (MISCELLANEOUS PROVISIONS) ACT 1977
c. 5

1977	c.5
Sched. 2	s.171(3), (4), (9), (12)

TABLE OF DESTINATIONS

SOCIAL SECURITY (MISCELLANEOUS PROVISIONS) (NORTHERN IRELAND) ORDER 1977
N.I. 11

1977	N.I. 11
art. 3(4)	Sched. 1, para. 1(1)
(5)	Sched. 1, para. 4
(6)	14(4)
4(1)(b)	Sched. 5, para. 2(3)
(c)	Sched. 5, para. 2(5)
(d)	Sched. 5, para. 2(8)
(e)	Sched. 5, para. 3

1977	N.I. 11
art. 5(1)	s.43(2)
(4)	40(7)
(4)	41(7)
7(1)	61(1)
(2)	61(2)
8	Sched. 7, para. 21
9(1)	Sched. 8, para. 5(2)
10(1)	74(1)
(3)	74(2)
13(3)	95(4), (5)

1977	N.I. 11
art. 13(6)	s.40(6)
14(1)	112(1), (2)
(2)	112(3)
18(1)	121
(2)	56(1), (2)
(3)	56(5); 77(6); 81(3); Sched. 7, para. 5(2)
(4)	Sched. 7, para. 15
(25)	22(7)

SUPPLEMENTARY BENEFITS (NORTHERN IRELAND) ORDER 1977
N.I. 27

1977	N.I. 27
Sched. 7	s.112(1), (2)

SOCIAL SECURITY (NORTHERN IRELAND) ORDER 1979
N.I. 5

1979	N.I. 5
art. 3(2)	s.65(1)
(3)	65(2)
(5)	65(6)
(6)	67(1)
5(2)	172(2)
11(2)	6(5)
14	45(6), (7); Sched. 5, paras. 2(4); 7(2)
Sched. 1,	
para. 1	33(4), (5)
2	78(3), (4)
3	Sched. 3, para. 5(7)
4	51(1)

1979	N.I. 5
Sched. 1—cont.	
para. 5	s.48(1)
6	Sched. 5, para. 4(4)
7	Sched. 5, paras. 5(1), (2); 6(1), (2); 7(1)
8	43(2)
10	34(3)
13	Sched. 4, Part V, para. 6
14	51(1)
15	52(4)
16	53(3)

1979	N.I. 5
Sched. 1—cont.	
para. 18	s.41(1)
20	48(2)
22	Sched. 5, para. 4(5)
Sched. 3,	
para. 4	23(1)
5	25(5), (6); 31(6), (7)
6	33(4), (5)
10	Sched. 3, para. 7(3), (4)
16	44(5)
22	Sched. 5, para 4(1), (2)

STATUTORY RULES (NORTHERN IRELAND) ORDER 1979
N.I. 12

1979	N.I. 12
Sched. 4, para. 16	s.171(2)

SOCIAL SECURITY (NORTHERN IRELAND) ORDER 1980
N.I. 8

1980	N.I. 8
art. 4(10)	Sched. 5, para. 2(5)
5(6)	Sched. 9
6(1)(i)	20
(ii)	21(1), (2)

1980	N.I. 8
Sched. 1,	
para. 4	82(4); Sched. 7, para. 6(1)
(b)	85(2)
5	87(1)
5(2)	82(1), (2); 86(1)

1980	N.I. 8
Sched. 1—cont.	
para. 6	Sched. 7, para. 6(1)
7	121
8	65(5)
15	Sched. 1, para. 1(2)

TREATMENT OF OFFENDERS (N.I.) ORDER 1980
N.I. 10

1980	N.I. 10
art. 3	Sched. 9
Sched. 1,	
para. 1	Sched. 9

SOCIAL SECURITY (NO. 2) (NORTHERN IRELAND) ORDER 1980
N.I. 13

1980	N.I. 13
art. 3(1)	s.57(1)
(3)	47(1); Sched. 7,
	para. 3(8)
(4)	47(6); 57(9),
	(10);
	Sched. 7,
	para. 3(9)
5(1)	s.30(1)
(1A)	30(2)
(2)	30(3)
(3)	30(4)
Sched	22(2), (5)

SOCIAL SECURITY (CONTRIBUTIONS) (NORTHERN IRELAND) ORDER 1981
N.I. 9

1981	N.I. 9
art. 6(1)	s.172(2)

SOCIAL SECURITY (NORTHERN IRELAND) ORDER 1982
N.I. 16

1982	N.I. 16	1982	N.I. 16	1982	N.I. 16
art. 3(1)	s.147(1), (2)	art. 7(4)	s.151(4)	art. 30(1)	s.4(1), (2), (3)
(2)	147(1), (2)	(5)	151(5)	(2)	Sched. 1,
(3)	147(4), (5)	8	152		paras. 9; 10
(4)	147(4), (5)	9(1)	153(1)	32(2)	103(6);
(5)	147(6)	(1A)	153(2)		Sched. 7,
4(1)	148(1), (2)	(2)	153(3)		para. 9(3)
(2)	148(1), (2)	11(1)	154(1)	(3)	31(3)
(3)	148(3)	(1B)	154(2)	(4)	102(1), (2),
(3A)	148(4)	(1C) . . .	155		(3)
(4)	148(5), (6)	(1D) . . .	154(3)	35(1)(b) . . .	168
(5)	148(5), (6)	(2)	154(4)	(d) . . .	168
5(1)	149(1), (2),	(3)(b) . . .	154(5)	(2)(a) . . .	168
	(3), (4)	(c) . . .	154(5)	(b) . . .	168
(2)	149(1), (2),	(4)	Sched. 1,	Sched. 1	Sched. 11
	(3), (4)		para. 6(5)	Sched. 2,	
(3)	149(1), (2),	(5)	Sched. 1,	para. 1	Sched. 12
	(3), (4)		para. 6(6)		para. 1
(4)	149(1), (2),	(6)	154(6)	1A	Sched. 12
	(3), (4)	24	158		para. 5
(4A)	149(5)	25	4(1)	2	Sched. 12
(5)	149(6), (7)	25A(1) . . .	147(3); 160		paras. 2; 3; 4
(6)	149(6), (7)		(7)	3	Sched. 12
(6A)	149(8), (9)	28(1)	159(1)		paras. 2; 3; 4
(6B)	149(8), (9)	(2)	159(2)	4	Sched. 12
(7)	149(10), (11)	(3)	159(3), (4),		paras. 2; 3; 4
(8)	149(10), (11)		(5)	6	Sched. 12
(9)	149(12)	(4)	159(3), (4),		para. 6
6	57(9), (10)		(5)	Sched. 4	
(1)	150(1); 172	(5)	159(3), (4),	para. 5	25(4); 31(5)
	(2)		(5)	6	33(a)
(2)	150(2)	(5A) . . .	159(6)	8(2) . . .	94(4)
(3)	150(3), (4)	(6)	159(7)	(3) . . .	94(6)
(4)	150(3), (4)	(7)	168	11	107
7(1)	151(1), (2)	29(1)	157	12	Sched. 6
(2)	151(1), (2),	(2)	157		para. 6(1)
	(3)	(3)	157	19	30(2)
(3)	151(1), (2),	(4)	171(10)	Sched. 5	6(1); 107
	(3)				

SOCIAL SECURITY (CONTRIBUTIONS, RE-RATING) ORDER (NORTHERN IRELAND) 1982
S.R. 1982 No. 413

art. 5(a) . . . . . . s.15(3); 18

HEALTH AND SOCIAL SECURITY (NORTHERN IRELAND) ORDER 1984
N.I. 8

1984	N.I. 8
art. 5(1)	s.68(1), (2),
	(3), (4), (6),
	(7), (11), (13)
6.	84(1)
8(a)	89
(b)	Sched.7,
	para. 7
11(1)	11(1)
(2)	12
12(1)(a). . .	13(1)
(b). . .	13(4)
(3)	13(4), (5),
	(6), (7)

1984	N.I. 8
Sched. 2,	
para. 2	s.63; 90;
	Sched. 4
	Part III,
	para. 2;
	Part IV, col.
	(1)
8(a) . . .	Sched. 6,
	para. 1
(b) . . .	Sched. 6,
	para. 4
(c) . . .	Sched. 6,
	para. 5
9	121
11	Sched. 9
13(2) . .	Sched. 11

1984	N.I. 8
Sched. 3,	
para. 1	s.20
2(a). . .	80(2)
(c) . . .	80(3), (4),
	(7)
3	Sched. 7,
	para. 4(3),
	(4), (5), (6)
4	Sched. 7,
	para. 18
Sched. 5,	
para. 4	6(2)
7	150(2)
8	147(3); 160
	(7)

SOCIAL SECURITY (NORTHERN IRELAND) ORDER 1985
N.I. 16

1985	N.I. 16
art. 9(1)	s.5(1)
9(2)	9(1), (2),
	(3), (4)
10.	6(5)
11(1)(a). . .	34(1), (2)
(b). . .	34(4), (5),
	(6)
(c). . .	34(7)
(2)(a). . .	47(1)
(b). . .	47(1)
(c). . .	47(2), (3),
	(4)
(3)	50(2)
(4)(a). . .	Sched. 7,
	para. 3(1)
(b). . .	Sched. 7,
	para. 3(2),
	(3), (4)
(5)	Sched. 5,
	para. 2(6)

1985	N.I. 16
art. 12.	s.28(4)
14(1)(b). . .	78(6)
(2)	Sched. 4,
	Part III,
	para. 7
15(1)	83(3)
(2)(a). . .	84(1)
(b). . .	84(2), (3)
(3)	85(4)
(4)(b). . .	86(2)
(5)	Sched. 7,
	para. 6(3),
	(4), (5), (6)
(6)	114(3)
(8)	114(4)
18(1)	151(4)
(3)	33(10), (11)
(4)	148(4)
(5)	149(5)

1985	N.I. 16
art. 18(6)(a). . .	Sched. 12,
	para. 1
(b). . .	Sched. 12,
	para. 5
19(1)(b). . .	154(4)
Sched. 4,	
para. 2	68(5)
4	149(8), (9)
6	159(1)
7	159(2)
Sched. 5,	
para. 1(b). . .	23(4)
3	113(3)
5(a). . .	Sched. 1,
	para. 1(2)
(b). . .	Sched. 1,
	para. 1(3),
	(4), (6)
6	121
7	5(1)

SOCIAL SECURITY (CONTRIBUTIONS AND CREDITS) (TRANSITIONAL AND CONSEQUENTIAL PROVISIONS)
REGULATIONS (NORTHERN IRELAND) 1985
S.R. 1985 No. 260

1985	S.R. 260
reg. 4(2).	s.12
(3).	13(5), (6), (7)

1986	N.I. 18
art. 2(1)	s.167(1), (2)
(2)	133(1); 134
	(4); 146(2)
(4)	168
19(1)	52(1), (2),
	(3); 60(7)
(a)	53(1), (2),
	61(1), (2)
(b)	34(4), (5),
	(6); 47(2), (3),
	(4); 78(3), (4)
(2)	45(1)
(3)	45(2), (3),
	(4), (5)
(4)	45(6), (7)
(5)	46(2)
(6)	46(1)
20(1)(a)	50(5)
(b)	51(3)
(c)	39(3)
(d)	41(6)
(2)	Sched. 5,
	para. 4(1),
	(2), (3)
(3)	Sched. 5,
	para. 5(1)
(4)	Sched. 5,
	para. 5(3)
(5)	Sched. 5,
	para. 6(1),
	(2)
(6)	Sched. 5,
	para. 6(3),
	(4)
(8)	Sched. 5,
	para. 5(2)
21(1)	122(1), (2)
(2)	122(1), (2)
(3)	123(1)
(4)	123(3)
(4A)	124(1), (2),
	(3), (4)
(4B)	124(1), (2),
	(3), (4)
(4C)	124(1), (2),
	(3), (4)
(4D)	124(1), (2),
	(3), (4)
(4N)	123(2), (5)
(5)	127(1)
(5A)	127(1)
(6)	127(3)
(a)	127(5)
(6A)	128(1)
(6B)	128(2), (3)
(6C)	128(2), (3)
(6D)	128(1)
(6E)	128(4)
(6F)	128(6)
(7)	129(1), (2)
(8)	129(1), (2)
(9)	130(2)
(10)	127(4)
(11)	133(1)
(12)	133(2)
22(1)	123(4)
(1A)	123(5), (6)

1986	N.I. 18
art. 22(1B)	s.123(5), (6)
(2)	127(2)
(3)	127(2)
(3A)	128(5)
(3B)	128(5)
(4)	129(3)
(5)	129(3)
(6)	128(8)
(b)	129(4)
(7)	130(3)
23(1)	131(1), (2)
(2)	131(1), (2)
(2A)	131(3), (4)
(2B)	131(3), (4)
(3)	131(5), (6)
(4)	131(5), (6)
(5)	132(1)
(6)	130(1)
(7)	132(2), (3)
(8)	132(2), (3)
(9)	132(4)
24(1)	125(1), (2),
	(3), (4)
(2)	125(1), (2),
	(3), (4)
(3)	125(1), (2),
	(3), (4)
(4)	125(1), (2),
	(3), (4)
(5)	125(5)
(5A)	125(6)
(6)	125(7)
(7)	125(8)
24A	126
24B(4)	128(7)
29(1)(b)	133(1)
32(4)	122(3)
33(2)	134(1)
(2A)	134(2)
(11)	136(5)
34(1A)	134(3)
(2)	135(1), (2),
	(3)
(3)	135(1), (2),
	(3)
(4)	135(1), (2),
	(3)
(4A)	135(4)
(9)	136(1)
(10)	136(2)
(10A)	136(4)
(10ZA)	136(3)
(11)	135(5)
37(1)	36(1), (2)
(2)	Sched. 4,
	Part II
(3)	38(1)
(b)	39(4), (5)
41	20; 56(6)
44(1)	26(6)
(2)(a)	28(1)
(3)(a)	28(2)
(b)	172(2)
45(2)	91
46(a)	77(10)
(b)	77(11)

1986	N.I. 18
art. 47(1)	s.160(1), (2),
	(3), (4), (5),
	(6)
(2)	160(1), (2),
	(3), (4), (5),
	(6)
(3)	160(1), (2),
	(3), (4), (5),
	(6)
(4)	160(1), (2),
	(3), (4), (5),
	(6)
(5)	160(1), (2),
	(3), (4), (5),
	(6)
(6)	160(1), (2),
	(3), (4), (5),
	(6), (7)
(7)	160(8)
(8)	160(9)
(9)	160(10)
48	161
49(1)	162(1)
(2)	162(2)
(3)	162(3), (4),
	(5), (6), (7),
	(8)
(4)	162(3), (4),
	(5), (6), (7),
	(8)
(5)	162(3), (4),
	(5), (6), (7),
	(8)
(6)	162(3), (4),
	(5), (6), (7),
	(8)
(7)	162(3), (4),
	(5), (6), (7),
	(8)
(8)	162(3), (4),
	(5), (6), (7),
	(8)
51(1)	167(1), (2)
(2)	167(1), (2)
(2A)	167(3)
(3)	167(4), (5),
	(6)
(4)	167(4), (5),
	(6)
(5)	167(4), (5),
	(6)
63(1)	171(5)
(2)	171(5)
(3)	172(2)
68(1)	153(2)
69	147(6)
71(1)(a)	138(1)
(b)	138(2), (3)
75(3)	6(6); 8(4);
	9(5);
	Sched. 1,
	para. 1(5)
(4)	5(2), (3)
79(3)	127(6); 128
	(9)
(4)	165
80	166
81(2)	171(6)

1986	N.I. 18
Sched. 3,	
para. 2	s.94(1)
3(1) . . .	103(1)
(3) . . .	Sched. 4, Part V, para. 9(1), (2)
(4) . . .	103(7), (8)
4	114(4); Sched. 4, Part V, paras. 5; 6; 7; 8 Sched. 7, paras. 1; 4(1); 6(1)
5(1) . . .	Sched. 7, para. 11(1), (4), (5), (6), (7), (8), (9), (10), (12), (13)
6	104(3), (4)
7	Sched. 7, para. 10(1)
8	Sched. 4, Part V, paras. 10; 12
(a) . . .	Sched. 7, paras. 15; 16
(b) . . .	Sched. 7, paras. 18; 20
(c) . . .	Sched. 7, para. 19
10	60(2), (3), (8)
11	Sched. 4, Part V, para. 11 Sched. 7, para. 17
13	109(4), (5), (6), (7)
15	114(4); Sched. 4, Part V, paras. 5; 6; 7; 8 Sched. 7, para. 6(1) Sched. 8, para. 5(3)

1986	N.I. 18
Sched. 4,	
para. 1	s.163(1)
2	163(3)
3	Sched. 1, para. 6(5)
4	Sched. 1, para. 6(6)
5	163(4)
10	4(1)
11	Sched. 13, para. 1
11A . . .	Sched. 13, para. 2
12	Sched. 13, para. 3
13	35(1), (2), (3), (5), (6), (7); 57(2)
14	Sched. 3, para. 3
Sched. 5,	
para. 17	171(1)
Sched. 6,	
para. 1(1) . . .	146(1)
(2) . . .	146(2), (3)
(3) . . .	146(4)
2	144
3	145
Sched. 8,	
para. 1(1) . . .	22(1)
(2) . . .	22(4)
(3) . . .	22(5)
(4)(a)	23(1)
(c)	22(3)
(5) . . .	24(1)
(6) . . .	21(5)
2(1) . . .	Sched. 3, paras. 1(2), (4); 2(2), (4)
(2) . . .	Sched. 3, paras. 1(3); 2(3)
(3) . . .	Sched. 3, paras. 1(3), (5); 2(3), (5)
(4) . . .	Sched. 3, para. 4(2)
(5) . . .	Sched. 3, para. 5(2)

1986	N.I. 18
Sched. 8—cont.	
para. 2(6) . . .	Sched. 3, para. 5(3), (4)
(7) . . .	Sched. 3, para. 7(3), (4)
3	19(4), (5), (6)
4	14(1)
5(1) . . .	44(6)
Sched. 9,	
para. 1	Sched. 1, para. 8
39	20
40	21(1), (2)
41	172(2)
42(a) . .	Sched. 3, para. 4(1)
(b) . .	Sched. 3, para. 7(2), (3), (4)
(c) . .	Sched. 3, para. 9
45(a) . .	40(1)
(b) . .	40(3)
(c) . .	40(5)
46(a) . .	22(2)
(b) . .	21(4)
49	112(3)
50	149(12)
53	25(5), (6); 31(6), (7); 33(4), (5)
59(a) . .	Sched. 5, paras. 2(7); 4(4)
(b) . .	Sched. 5, para. 7(1)
70	171(10)
Sched. 10	1(1); 20; 21(1), (2); 94(7); 112(1), (2), (3); 121; 171(7); 172(2) Sched. 4, Part IV, cols. (1), (2) Sched. 7, para. 21

STATUTORY SICK PAY (GENERAL) (AMENDMENT) REGULATIONS (N.I.) 1986
S.R. 1986 No. 83

1986	S.R. 83
reg. 2(1)	s.148(3)

SOCIAL FUND (MATERNITY AND FUNERAL EXPENSES) (NORTHERN IRELAND) ORDER 1987
N.I. 8

1987	N.I. 8
art. 3	s.134(1)

SOCIAL SECURITY (NORTHERN IRELAND) ORDER 1988
N.I. 2

1988	N.I. 2
art. 3	s.64
4(1)	Sched. 7, para. 13(1), (2), (3), (4), (6)
(2)	Sched. 7, para. 11(11)
(3)	Sched. 7, para. 12(1)
(4)	Sched. 7, para. 12(2)
(4A)	Sched. 7, para. 12(3), (4)
(4B)	Sched. 7, para. 12(3), (4)
(5)	Sched. 7, para. 12(5), (6)
(6)	Sched. 7, para. 12(5), (6)
5(1)	127(1)
6(1)	123(1)
(2)	123(2); 124(1), (2), (3), (4), (5)
(3)	138(1)
(4)	140(1), (2)

1988	N.I. 2
art. 7(2)(a)	Sched. 3, paras. 1(2); 2(2)
(b)	Sched. 3, paras. 1(3); 2(3)
8	30(1)
15A	171(2)
Sched. 1,	
para. 1	Sched. 4, Part V, para. 11
2	Sched. 4, Part V, paras. 10; 12; Sched. 7, paras. 14(1); 15; 16; 18; 19; 20
3	Sched. 7, paras. 14(1); 17
5	60(2), (3), (8)
6(2)(a)	Sched. 7, para. 20
(b)	Sched. 7, para. 21
Sched. 2,	
para. 1(1)(a)	23(1)
(b)	23(2)

1988	N.I. 2
Sched. 3,	
para. 1	s.134(2)
6	136(5)
8	134(3)
9	135(4)
10	136(1)
11	136(4)
Sched. 4,	
para. 1	57(4)
2(a)	57(2)
(b)	35(4)
3(a)	82(1)
(b)	82(3)
4(a)	83(2)
5(a)	84(2)
8	94(2)
9(a)	Sched. 7, para. 11(10)
(b)	Sched. 7, paras. 11(14); 13(11)
12(c)	160(9)
(2)	160(10)
13	162(2)
15(1)	Sched. 13, para. 1
(2)	Sched. 13, para. 2
16(1)	123(4)
(2)	123(5), (6)
17(1)	125(6)
18	126
Sched. 5	167(1), (2)

EMPLOYMENT AND TRAINING (AMENDMENT) (NORTHERN IRELAND) ORDER 1988
N.I. 10

1988	N.I. 10
art. 5(2)	s.28(1)
(3)	28(6)
6(a)	28(1)

INCOME AND CORPORATION TAXES ACT 1988
c.1

1988	c.1
Sched. 29,	
para. 14	s.15(4)
32	125(5); 146(2); Sched. 2, paras. 1; 2; 3; 4; 5; 6; 9

FINANCE ACT 1988
c.39

1988	c. 39
Sched. 3,	
para. 31	Sched. 2, paras. 1; 2; 3
Sched. 14,	
Part VIII and	
Note 6	Sched. 22, para. 9

UNEMPLOYMENT BENEFIT (DISQUALIFICATION PERIOD) ORDER (N.I.) 1988
S.R. 1988 No. 83

1988	S.R. 83
art. 2	s.28(1)

SOCIAL SECURITY (NORTHERN IRELAND) ORDER 1989
N.I. 13

1989	N.I. 13
art. 3(1)	s.8(1), (2), (3)
(3)	121
4	Sched. 1,
	para. 8
6(2)	23(3)
(3)	22(6)
(4)	24(2)
8(1)	38(4); 39(6)
9(3)(a)	49(2), (3)
(b)	49(5)
(4)	55
11(1)	30(1), (3)
(2)	121
(3)	89;
	Sched. 7,
	para. 7
12(2)	57(1)
(3)	57(3)
(4)	57(5)
13	26(2), (3),
	(4)
14(1)	28(1)
(3)	28(5)
(4)	28(6)
(5)	121
15(1)	123(1)
(2)	133(2)
19(3)	Sched. 7,
	para. 13(5)
(5)	Sched. 7,
	para. 12(3),
	(4)
(6)	Sched. 7,
	para. 12(5),
	(6)
Sched. 1,	
para. 2(2) . . .	54(4)
3(1) . . .	Sched. 5,
	para. 1
(2) . . .	Sched. 5,
	para. 2(1)
(3) . . .	Sched. 5,
	para. 2(2)
(4) . . .	Sched. 5,
	para. 2(3)
(5) . . .	Sched. 5,
	para. 2(7)

1989	N.I. 13
Sched. 1—*cont.*	
para. 3(6) . . .	Sched. 5,
	para. 2(8)
(7) . . .	Sched. 5,
	para. 3
(8) . . .	Sched. 5,
	para. 4(1),
	(2)
(9) . . .	Sched. 5,
	para. 8(1),
	(2)
(10) . .	Sched. 5,
	para. 8(3)
(11) . .	121
4(1) . . .	25(2); 31(2)
5(1) . . .	33(1)
(2) . . .	33(2)
8(1) . . .	102(3)
(2) . . .	Sched. 7,
	para. 13(1)
(5) . . .	Sched. 7,
	para. 13(4)
(6) . . .	Sched. 7,
	para. 13(8),
	(9)
9(2) . . .	51(4)
10(1) . .	40(7)
(2) . .	41(7)
Sched. 3,	
para. 13(1) . .	Sched. 6,
	para. 6(3),
	(4), (5)
(2) . .	Sched. 6,
	para. 7
Sched. 7,	
para. 1(1) . . .	6(3)
(2) . . .	9(1), (2), (3)
2	12
3	13(5), (6),
	(7)
4(a) . . .	15(1), (2)
(b) . . .	15(1), (2)
(c) . . .	15(5)
5	20
6	22(3)
7	26(6)
8	36(3)

1989	N.I. 13
Sched. 7—*cont.*	
para. 11	s.103(6),
	Sched. 7,
	para. 9(3)
12	Sched. 7,
	para. 11(1)
14	Sched. 3,
	para. 7(1)
17	40(2)
20	157; 171(10)
22	161
Sched. 8,	
para. 1	4(4)
2(1) . . .	58(1)
(2) . . .	58(2)
(3) . . .	58(3)
(4) . . .	68(12)
(5) . . .	68(11)
(6) . . .	58(4); 68(13)
(7) . . .	58(5); 68(13)
3	57(6), (7)
4(1) . . .	37(3), (4)
(2) . . .	38(2), (3)
(3) . . .	44(1)
(4) . . .	44(2)
(5) . . .	49(7), (8)
(6) . . .	78(7), (8)
5(2) . . .	65(1)
(3)(a)	65(4)
(b)	65(6)
(4) . . .	65(5)
6	68(8), (9)
7(1) . . .	86(1)
(2) . . .	92;
	Sched. 7,
	para. 8
9	171(4)
14	127(3)
15	126
Sched. 9	1(1); 12;
	25(5), (6);
	28(2); 31(6),
	(7); 54(1), (2);
	167(1), (2); 172
	(2)

SOCIAL SECURITY (NORTHERN IRELAND) ORDER 1990
N.I. 15

1990	N.I. 15
art. 3(1)	s.66
(2)	65(6)
4(1)	69
(2)	Sched. 4, Part III, para. 3
(3)	63
5(1)	Sched. 7, para. 11(1)
(2)	Sched. 7, para. 11(2), (3)
(3)	Sched. 7, para. 11(8)
(4)	Sched. 7, para. 11(1), (2), (3)
(6)	Sched. 7, para. 13(10)
(7)	109(1), (2)
6(1)	33(3)

1990	N.I. 15
art. 6(2)	s.40(5)
(3)	41(4), (5)
11	131(3), (4)
12(3)	136(3)
(4)	136(4)
18(1)	1(1)
(2)	1(1)(5)
(7)(a)	Sched. 8, para. 2
19(3)	Sched. 1, para. 6(2), (3), (4)
(4)	Sched. 1, para. 6(8)
Sched. 5	Sched. 1, para. 7
Sched. 6, para. 1(1)	60(4), (5), (6)
(2)	87(1), (2)
(3)	61(1)
(4)	61(2)

1990	N.I. 15
Sched. 6—cont.	
para. 2(1)	s.108(5)
(2)	109(1), (2)
6(1)	172(3)
(9)	171(2)
(12)	172(6), (12)
(13)	172(7)
(14)	172(10)
(15)	172(11)
(17)	172(6), (10)
7	Sched. 1, para. 8
8	Sched. 3, para. 3
9	121
11(1)	153(2)
12(2)	125(7)
(3)	125(8)
19(2)	58(2)
(3)	58(4)
(4)	68(11)

CAPITAL ALLOWANCES ACT 1990
c.1

1990	c.1
Sched. 1, para. 2	Sched. 2, paras. 1; 2; 3

SOCIAL SECURITY ACT 1990
c.27

1990	c.27
s.17(8)	Sched. 2, para. 6
(9)	Sched. 2, para. 6

HUMAN FERTILISATION AND EMBRYOLOGY ACT 1990
c. 37

1990	c.37
Sched. 4, para. 3	s.37(1)

SOCIAL SECURITY (CONTRIBUTIONS) (NORTHERN IRELAND) ORDER 1991
N.I. 22

1991	N.I. 22
art. 3(2)	s.1(2)
(3)	1(6)
(5)	10
4(1)	1(4)
(2)	Sched. 1, para. 5
(3)(a)	Sched. 1, para. 6(1)
(b)	Sched. 1, para. 6(2), (3), (4)
(4)	Sched. 1, para. 7
(5)	Sched. 1, para. 8

DISABILITY LIVING ALLOWANCE AND DISABILITY WORKING ALLOWANCE
(NORTHERN IRELAND) ORDER 1991
N.I. 17

1991	N.I. 17	1991	N.I. 17	1991	N.I. 17
art. 3(1)	s.63	art. 8(8)	s.128(5)	Sched. 2,	
(2)	71; 72; 73;	(9)	128(8)	para. 2(1)	s.66
	75; 76	9(1)	128(7)	(2)	65(3)
4(1)	64	10(1)	127(1)	(3)	65(4), (5)
8(2)	122(1), (2)	(2)	127(4)	3	70(2)
(3)	122(1), (2)	11(1)	33(7), (8)	7	74(1)
(4)	128(1), (2),	(2)	68(10)	12	146(2)
	(3), (4), (6)	(3)	42	Sched. 3,	
(6)	133(1)	(4)	121	para. 6	128(9)
(7)	133(2)	(5)	93	Sched. 4	63; 65(6)

SOCIAL SECURITY (CONTRIBUTIONS) (RE-RATING) (NO. 2) ORDER (NORTHERN IRELAND) 1991
S.R. 1991 No. 542

1991	S.R. 542
art. 2	s.9(1), (2), (3)
3(a)	11(1)
(b)	11(4)
4	13(1)
5	15(3); 18

REDUNDANCY FUND (ABOLITION) (NORTHERN IRELAND) ORDER 1991
N.I. 2

1991	N.I. 2
Sched. 2	s.1(1); 171(7);
	172(2)

STATUTORY SICK PAY (NORTHERN IRELAND) ORDER 1991
N.I. 9

1991	N.I. 9
art. 3(1)	s.154(1)
(3)	154(5)
(4)	1(5)
4(1)	154(2), (3);
	155
(2)	154(4)
(5)	154(7)

HEALTH AND PERSONAL SOCIAL SERVICES (N.I.) ORDER 1991
N.I. 1

1991	N.I. 1
Sched. 5,	
Part II	s.159(6); 167
	(3)

SOCIAL SECURITY (INDUSTRIAL INJURIES) (DEPENDENCY) (PERMITTED EARNINGS LIMIT)
ORDER (N.I.) 1991
S.R. 1991 No. 72

1991	S.R. 72
art. 2	Sched. 7,
	para. 4(4)

SOCIAL SECURITY (CONSEQUENTIAL PROVISIONS) ACT 1992
C. 6

1991	c.6
Sched. 2,	
para. 11	s.171(11)
12	172(9); 173
	(3), (4)

TABLE OF DESTINATIONS

SOCIAL SECURITY BENEFITS UP-RATING ORDER (NORTHERN IRELAND) 1992
S.R. 1992 No. 18

1992	S.R. 18
art. 4(2)	s.44(3), (4)
6	Sched. 8, para. 2
11	80(4)
15	125(7)
Sched. 1	Sched. 4, Part I, paras. 1; 2; 3; 4; 5; 6; Part III, paras. 1; 2; 3; 4; 5; 6 Part IV, cols. (2), (3) Part V, paras. 1; 2; 3; 4; 5; 6; 7; 8; 9; 10; 11; 12

STATUTORY SICK PAY (RATE OF PAYMENT) ORDER (N.I.) 1992
S.R. 1992 No. 27

1992	S.R. 27
art. 2	s.153(1)

INDEX

References are to sections and Schedules

ABBREVIATIONS, TABLE OF, pages 178–80
AIRMEN, 117
ATTENDANCE ALLOWANCE,
  entitlement provisions, 64
  exclusion by regulation, 67
  period of, 65
  rate of, 65(3)
  terminally ill, for, 66
  See also DISABLEMENT PENSION

BENEFITS,
  See CONTRIBUTORY BENEFITS *and* individual
    benefits

CHILD BENEFIT,
  "child", meaning of, 138
  entitlement provisions, 137
  exclusions from entitlement, 140, Sched. 9
  interpretation, 143
  "person responsible", meaning of, 139
  persons outside Northern Ireland, 142
  priority between persons entitled, 140,
    Sched. 10
  rate of, 141
CHILD'S SPECIAL ALLOWANCE, 56
  contribution conditions, Sched. 3, Pt. I,
    para. 6
  rate of, Sched. 4, Pt. I
CHRISTMAS BONUS FOR PENSIONERS,
  entitlement provisions, 144
  interpretation, 146
COMMENCEMENT, 173(4)
CONSOLIDATED ENACTMENTS, 173(3)
CONSTANT ATTENDANCE ALLOWANCE, 104,
  Sched. 6, para. 8
CONTRIBUTIONS,
  benefits dependent on, 21
  Class 1, 5–9
    earnings limit, 5
    liability for, 6
    primary contributions, calculation of, 8
    secondary contributions,
      calculation of, 9
    secondary contributors, 7
  Class 2,
    late paid, 12
    liability for, 11
  Class 3,
    elections, 13, 19(5)
    restrictions on right to pay, 14
  Class 4, 15–18
    amount, 15(4), Sched. 2
    deferment, 17

CONTRIBUTIONS—*cont.*
  Class 4—*cont.*
    destination of, 16
    exceptions, 17
    liability for, 15
    recoverable under Income Tax Acts, 15
    recoverable under regulations, 18
  Class 1A, 10
  earners, categories of, 2
  liability, regulations for, 19
  married women, 19(4)
  more than one employer, 1(4), Sched. 1
  partial satisfaction for certain pensioners
    and widowed mothers, 60
  system outlined, 1
CONTRIBUTORY BENEFITS,
  contribution conditions, 21, Sched. 3
  descriptions of, 20
  earnings factors, 21–3
  See also individual benefits
COUNCILLORS,
  incapacity for work, and, 58
CROWN EMPLOYMENT, 116, 157, 165

DEPENDANTS, INCREASES FOR,
  adults,
    entitlement provisions, 82
    limited to one, 88
    pensioner (husband), 84, Sched. 4, Pt.
      IV
    pensioner (wife), 83, Sched. 4, Pt. IV
    rate, 82(2), Sched. 4, Pt. IV
  children,
    entitlement provisions, 80
    not living with beneficiary, 81
    rate, 80(5), Sched. 4, Pt. IV
    restrictions on increase, 81
  earnings to include pension payments, 89
  fluctuating earnings, 92
  invalid care allowance, 90
  invalidity pensioner, woman residing with
    husband, 86
  maintenance provisions, 114
  rates, Sched. 4, Pt. IV
  retirement pensioners,
    care of children, 85
    husband residing with wife, 83
    limited to one adult dependant, 88
    reduced contributions, attributable to,
      87
    wife residing with husband, 84
  severe disablement allowance, 90
  termination of employment after entitle-
    ment to disability working allowance,
    93
  trade disputes, effect on entitlement, 91

DERIVATIONS, TABLE OF, pages 180–200
DISABILITY LIVING ALLOWANCE,
  care component, 72
  entitlement provisions, 71
  mobility component, 73
    invalid carriages, 74
  persons aged over 65, 75
  supplementary provisions, 76
DISABILITY WORKING ALLOWANCE,
  dependency increase on termination of
    employment after entitlement to, 93
  entitlement provisions, 128
  invalidity pension after entitlement to, 42
DISABLEMENT GRATUITY, 106(b), Sched. 7, Pt.
  II
DISABLEMENT PENSION,
  assessment of disability, 103(5), Sched. 6
  constant attendance, increase for, 104
  exceptionally severe disablement, increase
    for, 105
  hospital treatment, increase during, 106(c),
    Sched. 7, Pt. III
  industrial accident, entitlement as result of,
    103
  successive accidents, 107
DISQUALIFICATION FROM BENEFITS, 113
DIVORCED WOMEN,
  child's special allowance, 56

EARNERS,
  categories of, 2
EARNINGS,
  defined, 3
  employment protection entitlement, 112
  factors, 21–3
    calculation of, 24
  fluctuating, effect of increases, 92
  payments treated as, 4
  record of, 24
EMPLOYMENT PROTECTION ENTITLEMENT, 112
EXTENT, 173(5)–(6)

FAMILY CREDIT,
  entitlement provisions, 127

GRADUATED RETIREMENT BENEFIT, 62
GUARDIAN'S ALLOWANCE,
  entitlement provisions, 77
  rate, 77(7), Sched. 4, Pt. III, para. 5

HER MAJESTY'S FORCES, 116
HOUSING BENEFIT,
  entitlement provisions, 129

IMPRISONMENT, 113
INCOME-RELATED BENEFITS,
  applicable amount, 131
  categories, 122
  exclusion from, 130
  income and capital, 132
  interpretation, 133
  See also individual benefits
INCOME SUPPORT,
  entitlement provisions, 123
  return to work, effect of, 126
  severe hardship cases, 124
  trade disputes, 125
INCREASES,
  for dependants. See DEPENDANTS, INCREASES
    FOR
  disablement pension. See DISABLEMENT
    PENSION
INDUSTRIAL DEATH BENEFIT, 106(f), Sched. 7,
  Pt. VI
INDUSTRIAL DISEASES,
  benefits payable, 108
    entitlement provisions, 109
  respiratory, 110
  workmen's compensation cases, 111,
    Sched. 8
INDUSTRIAL INJURIES BENEFIT,
  breach of regulations, earner acting
    in, 98
  components of, 94(2), Sched. 7
  disablement pension in respect of accident,
    103
  diseases, for. See INDUSTRIAL DISEASES
  emergency, accident while meeting, 100
  employer's transport, earner travelling in,
    99
  entitlement provisions, 94
  interpretation, 121
  misconduct by another causing accident,
    101
  rate of, Sched. 4, Pt. V
  relevant employments, 95
    employers, prescribed persons as, 96
    illegal employments, accidents in course
      of, 97
  sickness benefit in respect of injury, 102
  successive accidents, 107
  unemployability supplement, 106(a),
    Sched. 7
INTERPRETATION,
  age, 169
  child benefit, 143
  Christmas bonus for pensioners, 146
  income-related benefits, 133
  industrial injury benefit, 121
  statutory maternity pay, 167
  statutory provisions, 170
  statutory sick pay, 159
  territorial waters, 168
INVALID CARE ALLOWANCE,
  entitlement provisions, 70
  increase for dependants, 90
  rate, 70(9), Sched. 4, Pt. III, para. 4

INVALIDITY ALLOWANCE,
  entitlement provisions, 34
  rate of, Pt. I, Sched. 4
INVALIDITY BENEFIT,
  councillor, work as disregarded, 58
  days for which payable, 57
  disqualifications, 59
INVALIDITY PENSION,
  disability working allowance, after entitle-
    ment to, 42
  entitlement provisions, 33
  increase of woman's, 86
  widowers, for, 41
  widows, for, 40

MARRIAGES,
  treatment of certain, 120
MARRIED WOMEN,
  regulations as to, 118
MATERNITY ALLOWANCE, 35
  contribution conditions, Sched. 3, Pt. I,
    para. 3
MATERNITY PAY. See STATUTORY MATERNITY
  PAY

NON-CONTRIBUTORY BENEFITS,
  description of, 63
NORTHERN IRELAND,
  absence from, 112
  persons outside, 119, 142, 158

REDUCED EARNINGS ALLOWANCE, 106(d),
  Sched. 7, Pt. IV
REMUNERATION,
  earnings, treated as, 4
  See also EARNINGS
RETIREMENT ALLOWANCE, 106(e), Sched. 7, Pt.
  V
RETIREMENT PENSIONS,
  age addition, 79, Sched. 4, Pt. III, para. 8
  Category A,
    additional pension, 45
      modifying factors, 46
    entitlement provisions, 44
    former spouse's contributions, use of, 48
    invalidity, increase for, 47
    surviving spouses, provision for, 52
  Category A and B, entitlement to both, 52,
    54
  Category B,
    surviving spouses, provision for, 52
    widowers, for, 51
    women, for,
      entitlement provisions, 49
      rate of, 50, Sched. 4, Pt. I
  Category C, 78, Sched. 4, Pt. III, para. 6
  Category D, 78, Sched. 4, Pt. III, para. 7
  children, persons with care of,
    increase for, 85, Sched. 4, Pt. IV

RETIREMENT PENSIONS—cont.
  Christmas bonus. See CHRISTMAS BONUS FOR
    PENSIONERS
  deferred entitlement, 55
    increase, Sched. 5
  dependants, increase for, 83, 84
  graduated retirement benefit, 62
  husband and wife, 54
  increase excluded for failure to satisfy con-
    tribution condition, 61
  married women, special provision for, 53
  more than one, entitlement to, 43
  payments causing reduction of unemploy-
    ment benefit, 30

SECONDARY CONTRIBUTIONS (CLASS 1),
  calculation of, 9
SECONDARY CONTRIBUTORS, 7
SEVERE DISABLEMENT ALLOWANCE,
  age related addition, 69, Sched. 4, Pt. III,
    para. 3
  assessment of disability, 68(6), Sched. 6
  entitlement provisions, 68
  increase for dependants, 90
  rate, 68(7), Sched. 4, Pt. III, para. 2
SHORT TITLE, 173(1)
SICKNESS BENEFIT,
  contribution conditions, Sched. 3, Pt. I,
    para. 2
  councillor, work as disregarded, 58
  days for which payable, 57
  disqualifications, 32
  entitlement provisions, 31
  industrial injury, in respect of, 102
  rate of, Sched. 4, Pt. I
  See also STATUTORY SICK PAY
SOCIAL FUND,
  awards by officers, 135
  determination principles, 136
  payments out of, 134
STATUTORY MATERNITY PAY,
  Crown employment, 165
  entitlement provisions, 160
  interpretation, 167
  period, 161
  rates of payment, 162
  recovery of, 163
  relationship with other benefits and pay-
    ments, 164, Sched. 13
  special classes, 166
STATUTORY SICK PAY,
  airmen, 158
  Crown employment, 157
  entitlement provisions, 147
  interpretation, 159
  limitations on entitlement, 151
  mariners, 158
  period of entitlement, 149, Sched. 11
  period of incapacity, 148
  persons outside Northern Ireland, 158
  qualifying days, 150
  rate of payment, 153
  recovery by employers, 154
    small employers' relief, 154(2), 155

STATUTORY SICK PAY—*cont.*
relationship with other benefits and payments, 156, Sched. 12
special classes, 158
SUBORDINATE LEGISLATION, 171
control of, 172
SUSPENSION OF BENEFITS, 112

TRADE DISPUTES,
income support, and, 125
increase for dependants, and, 91
unemployment benefit, and, 27

UNEMPLOYABILITY SUPPLEMENT, 106, Sched. 7, Pt. I
UNEMPLOYMENT BENEFIT,
abatement of, 30
conditions to be satisfied, 25
contribution conditions, Sched. 3, Pt. I, para. 1
days for which payable, 57
disqualifications, 28
exemptions from, 29
duration of, 26
pension payments causing reduction of benefit, 30

UNEMPLOYMENT BENEFIT—*cont.*
rate of, Sched. 4, Pt. I
trade disputes, interruption of employment by, 27

WIDOWED MOTHER'S ALLOWANCE,
contribution conditions, Sched. 3, Pt. I, para. 5
entitlement provisions, 36
increase excluded for failure to satisfy contribution condition, 61
partial satisfaction of contributions, 60
rate of, 39
WIDOWER'S INVALIDITY PENSION, 41
WIDOWS,
invalidity pension, 40
payment, 36
contribution conditions, Sched. 3, Pt. I, para. 4
rate of, Sched. 4, Pt. II
pension,
entitlement provisions, 38
rate of, 39
regulations as to, 118
WORKMEN'S COMPENSATION, 111, Sched. 8

SOCIAL SECURITY ADMINISTRATION (NORTHERN IRELAND) ACT 1992*

(1992 c. 8)

ARRANGEMENT OF SECTIONS

PART I

CLAIMS FOR AND PAYMENTS AND GENERAL ADMINISTRATION OF BENEFIT

Necessity of claim

SECT.
1. Entitlement to benefit dependent on claim.
2. Retrospective effect of provisions making entitlement to benefit dependent on claim.

Widowhood benefit

3. Late claims for widowhood benefit where death is difficult to establish.
4. Treatment of payments of benefit to certain widows.

Claims and repayments regulations

5. Regulations about claims for and payments of benefit.

Industrial injuries benefit

6. Notification of accidents, etc.
7. Medical examination and treatment of claimants.
8. Obligations of claimants.

Disability working allowance

9. Initial claims and repeat claims.

The social fund

10. Necessity of application for certain payments.

Child benefit

11. Necessity of application for child benefit.

Statutory sick pay

12. Duties of employees etc. in relation to statutory sick pay.

Statutory maternity pay

13. Duties of women etc. in relation to statutory maternity pay.

Emergency payments

14. Emergency payments by Health and Social Services Boards and other bodies.

PART II

ADJUDICATION

Adjudication by the Department

15. Questions for the Department.
16. Appeal on question of law.
17. Review of decisions.

Adjudication by adjudication officers

18. Claims and questions to be submitted to adjudication officer.

---

* Annotations by Laura Lundy, LL.B., Ray Geary, LL.B., LL.M., both Lecturers in Law, Queen's University of Belfast, and John Mesher, B.A., B.C.L., LL.M., Barrister, Reader in Law and Simmons & Simmons Research Fellow in Pensions Law, University of Sheffield.

19. Decision of adjudication officer.

Appeals from adjudication officers—general

20. Appeal to social security appeal tribunal.
21. Appeal from social security appeal tribunal to Commissioner.
22. Appeal from Commissioners on point of law.

Reviews—general

23. Review of decisions.
24. Procedure for reviews.
25. Reviews under s.23—supplementary.
26. Appeals following reviews or refusals to review.
27. Review after claimant appeals.

Attendance allowance, disability living allowance and disability working allowance

28. Reviews of decisions of adjudication officers.
29. Further reviews.
30. Reviews of decisions as to attendance allowance, disability living allowance or disability working allowance—supplementary.
31. Appeals following reviews.
32. Appeal from social security appeal tribunals or disability appeal tribunals to Commissioners and appeals from Commissioners.
33. Reviews of decisions on appeal.

Questions first arising on appeal

34. Questions first arising on appeal.

Reference of special questions

35. Reference of special questions.

Adjudication officers and the Chief Adjudication Officer

36. Adjudication officers.
37. The Chief Adjudication Officer.

Social security appeal tribunals

38. Panels for appointment to social security appeal tribunals.
39. Constitution of social security appeal tribunals.

Disability appeal tribunals

40. Panels for appointment to disability appeal tribunals.
41. Constitution of disability appeal tribunals.

Adjudication in relation to industrial injuries and disablement benefit

42. Declaration that accident is an industrial accident.
43. Disablement questions.
44. Medical appeals and reference.
45. Review of medical decisions.
46. Appeal etc. on question of law to Commissioner.

Adjudicating medical practitioners and medical appeal tribunals

47. Adjudicating medical practitioners.
48. Constitution of medical appeal tribunals.

The President and chairmen of tribunals

49. The President of social security appeal tribunals, medical appeal tribunals and disability appeal tribunals and chairmen.

Social Security Commissioners

50. Appointment of Commissioners.

References to medical practitioners, the Disability Living Allowance Advisory Board etc.

51. Power of adjudicating authorities to refer matters to experts.
52. Claims relating to attendance allowance, disability living allowance and disability working allowance.
53. Medical examination etc. in relation to appeals to disability appeal tribunals.

Determination of questions of special difficulty

54. Assessors.
55. Tribunal of 2 or 3 Commissioners.

Regulations

56. Regulations as to determination of questions and matters arising out of, or pending, reviews and appeals.
57. Procedure.
58. Finality of decisions.
59. Regulations about supplementary matters relating to determinations.

Industrial diseases

60. Adjudication as to industrial diseases.

Housing benefit

61. Adjudication.

Social fund officers and inspectors and the social fund Commissioner

62. Social fund officers.
63. The social fund Commissioner and inspectors.
64. Reviews.

Christmas bonus

65. Determination of questions.

Restrictions on entitlement to benefit following erroneous decision

66. Restrictions on entitlement to benefit in certain cases of error.
67. Determination of questions on review following erroneous decisions.

Correction of errors

68. Regulations as to correction of errors.

PART III

OVERPAYMENTS AND ADJUSTMENTS OF BENEFIT

Misrepresentation etc.

69. Overpayments—general.
70. Special provision as to recovery of income support.

Adjustments of benefits

71. Overlapping benefits—general.
72. Income support and other payments.

Housing benefit

73. Overpayments of housing benefit.

Social fund awards

74. Recovery of social fund awards.

Great Britain payments

75. Recovery of Great Britain payments.

Adjustment of child benefit

76. Child benefit—overlap with benefits under legislation of other member States.

PART IV

RECOVERY FROM COMPENSATION PAYMENTS

77. Interpretation of Part IV.

Recovery from damages, etc. of sums equivalent to benefit

78. Recovery of sums equivalent to benefit from compensation payments in respect of accidents, injuries and diseases.

Payments, deductions and certificates

79. Time for making payment to Department.
80. The certificate of total benefit.
81. Exemption from deduction in cases involving small payments.
82. Multiple compensation payments.
83. Collaboration between compensators.
84. Structured settlements.
85. Insolvency.
86. Protection of legal aid charges.
87. Overpaid benefits.
88. Death.
89. Payments into court.

Administration and adjudication

90. Provision of information.
91. Applications for certificates of total benefit.
92. Liability of compensator unenforceable if certificate not issued within time limit.
93. Review of certificates of total benefit.
94. Appeals.
95. Recovery in consequence of an appeal.
96. Recovery of relevant payment in cases of default.

Miscellaneous

97. Foreign compensators: duties of intended recipient.
98. Interest on damages: reductions in respect of relevant payments.
99. The Crown.

PART V

INCOME SUPPORT AND THE DUTY TO MAINTAIN

100. Failure to maintain—general.
101. Recovery of expenditure on benefit from person liable for maintenance.
102. Recovery of expenditure on income support: additional amounts and transfer of orders.
103. Reduction of expenditure on income support: certain maintenance orders to be enforceable by the Department.

PART VI

ENFORCEMENT

Inspection

104. Appointment and powers of inspectors.
105. Delay, obstruction etc. of inspector.
106. False representations for obtaining benefit etc.
107. Breach of regulations.
108. Offences relating to contributions.
109. Offences by bodies corporate.

Legal proceedings

110. Legal proceedings.

111. Questions arising in proceedings.

Unpaid contributions etc.

112. Evidence of non-payment.
113. Recovery of unpaid contributions on prosecution.
114. Proof of previous offences.
115. Unpaid contributions—supplementary.

PART VII

PROVISION OF INFORMATION

Inland Revenue

116. Disclosure of information by Inland Revenue.

Persons employed or formerly employed in social security administration or adjudication

117. Unauthorised disclosure of information relating to particular persons.

Notification of deaths

118. Regulations as to notification of deaths.

Personal representatives—income support and supplementary benefit

119. Personal representatives to give information about the estate of a deceased person who was in receipt of income support or supplementary benefit.

Housing benefit

120. Information for purposes of housing benefit.

Statutory sick pay and other benefits

121. Disclosure by the Department for purpose of determination of period of entitlement to statutory sick pay.
122. Duties of employers—statutory sick pay and claims for other benefits.

Statutory maternity pay and other benefits

123. Disclosure by the Department for purpose of determination of period of entitlement to statutory maternity pay.
124. Duties of employers—statutory maternity pay and claims for other benefits.

Maintenance proceedings

125. Furnishing of addresses for maintenance proceedings, etc.

PART VIII

ARRANGEMENTS FOR HOUSING BENEFIT

Housing benefit

126. Arrangements for housing benefit.
127. Housing benefit finance.
128. Claims etc.

PART IX

ALTERATION OF CONTRIBUTIONS AND BENEFITS

Alteration of contributions, etc.

129. Amendments following alterations in Great Britain.
130. Revaluation of earnings factors.
131. Statutory sick pay—power to alter limit for small employers' relief.

Review and alteration of benefits

132. Annual up-rating of benefits.
133. Rectification of mistakes in up-rating orders.
134. Social security benefits in respect of children.

PART X

COMPUTATION OF BENEFITS

135. Effect of alteration of rates of benefit under Parts II to V of Contributions and Benefits Act.
136. Computation of Category A retirement pension with increase under s.52(3) of Contributions and Benefits Act.
137. Effect of alteration of rates of child benefit.
138. Treatment of excess benefit as paid on account of child benefit.
139. Effect of alteration in the component rates of income support.
140. Implementation of increases in income support due to attainment of particular ages.

PART XI

FINANCE

141. National Insurance Fund.
142. Destination of contributions.
143. General financial arrangements.
144. Destination of repayments, etc.
145. Adjustments between National Insurance Fund and Consolidated Fund.
146. The social fund.
147. Allocations from social fund.
148. Adjustments between social fund and other sources of finance.

PART XII

ADVISORY BODIES AND THE DUTY TO CONSULT

Consultation with the Social Security Advisory Committee

149. Functions of Social Security Advisory Committee in relation to legislation and regulations.
150. Cases in which consultation with Committee is not required.
151. Committee's report on regulations and Department's duties.

The Disability Living Allowance Advisory Board

152. The Disability Living Allowance Advisory Board.

PART XIII

SOCIAL SECURITY SYSTEMS OUTSIDE NORTHERN IRELAND

Co-ordination

153. Co-ordination with Great Britain.

Reciprocity

154. Reciprocal arrangements with Great Britain—income-related benefits and child benefit.
155. Reciprocal agreements with countries outside the United Kingdom.

PART XIV

MISCELLANEOUS

Travelling expenses

156. Payment of travelling expenses by Department.

Offences

157. Impersonation of officers.
158. Illegal possession of documents.

Industrial injuries and diseases

159. Research on industrial injuries, etc.
160. Control of pneumoconiosis.

Workmen's compensation, etc.

161. Administration of workmen's compensation etc.

Supplementary benefit etc.

162. Application of provisions of Act to supplementary benefit, etc.

Miscellaneous

163. Certain benefit to be inalienable.
164. Exemption from stamp duty.

PART XV

GENERAL

Subordinate legislation

165. Regulations and orders—general.
166. Assembly, etc. control of orders and regulations.

Supplementary

167. Interpretation.
168. Short title, commencement and extent.

SCHEDULES:
Schedule 1—Claims for benefit made or treated as made before 1st October 1990.
Schedule 2—Commissioners, tribunals, etc.—supplementary provisions.
Schedule 3—Regulations as to procedure.
Schedule 4—Persons employed in social security administration or adjudication.
   Part I—The specified persons.
   Part II—Construction of references to government departments etc.
Schedule 5—Regulations not requiring prior submission to Social Security Advisory Committee.
Schedule 6—Old Cases payments administration.
Schedule 7—Supplementary benefits, etc.

An Act to consolidate for Northern Ireland certain enactments relating to the administration of social security and related matters, with corrections and minor improvements under the Consolidation of Enactments (Procedure) Act 1949. [13th February 1992]

PARLIAMENTARY DEBATES
Hansard, H.L. Vol. 533, col. 864; Vol. 534, col. 1489; Vol. 535, cols. 347, 348.
[*N.B.*: Unless otherwise stated (*i.e.* stated to be decisions of the Northern Ireland Commissioners), references to commissioners' decisions are to decisions of the Great Britain Commissioners. These are frequently cited in the Northern Ireland Tribunals and are considered to be highly persuasive but not binding].

ABBREVIATIONS

AO	:	Adjudication Officer
DAT	:	Disability Appeal Tribunal
MAT	:	Medical Appeal Tribunal
SSAC	:	Social Security Adjudication Committee
SSAT	:	Social Security Appeal Tribunal
UBO	:	Unemployment Benefit Office
Bonner *et al.*	:	Bonner, Hooker and White, Non-Means Tested Benefits: the Legislation (Sweet & Maxwell)

Findlay and Ward:	Findlay and Ward, CPAG's Housing Benefit and Community Charge Benefit Legislation (Child Poverty Action Group)
Mesher	: Mesher, CPAG's Income-Related Benefits: the Legislation (Sweet & Maxwell)
Rowland	: Rowland, Medical and Disability Appeal Tribunals: the Legislation (Sweet & Maxwell)

PART I

CLAIMS FOR AND PAYMENTS AND GENERAL ADMINISTRATION OF BENEFIT

Necessity of claim

Entitlement to benefit dependent on claim

1.—(1) Except in such cases as may be prescribed, and subject to the following provisions of this section and to section 3 below, no person shall be entitled to any benefit unless, in addition to any other conditions relating to that benefit being satisfied—

(a) he makes a claim for it in the manner, and within the time, prescribed in relation to that benefit by regulations under this Part of this Act; or

(b) he is treated by virtue of such regulations as making a claim for it.

(2) Where under subsection (1) above a person is required to make a claim or to be treated as making a claim for a benefit in order to be entitled to it—

(a) if the benefit is a widow's payment, she shall not be entitled to it in respect of a death occurring more than 12 months before the date on which the claim is made or treated as made; and

(b) if the benefit is any other benefit except disablement benefit or reduced earnings allowance, the person shall not be entitled to it in respect of any period more than 12 months before that date,

except as provided by section 3 below.

(3) Where a person purports to make a claim on behalf of another—

(a) for an attendance allowance by virtue of section 66(1) of the Contributions and Benefits Act; or

(b) for a disability living allowance by virtue of section 72(5) or 73(12) of that Act,

that other shall be regarded for the purposes of this section as making the claim, notwithstanding that it is made without his knowledge or authority.

(4) In this section and section 2 below "benefit" means—

(a) benefit as defined in section 121 of the Contributions and Benefits Act; and

(b) any income-related benefit.

(5) This section (which corresponds to section 154A of the 1975 Act, as it had effect immediately before this Act came into force) applies to claims made on or after 1st October 1990 or treated by virtue of regulations under that section or this section as having been made on or after that date.

(6) Schedule 1 to this Act shall have effect in relation to other claims.

DEFINITIONS

"the 1975 Act": s.167.
"claim": *ibid.*
"the Contributions and Benefits Act": *ibid.*
"disablement benefit": *ibid.*
"income-related benefit": *ibid.*
"prescribe": *ibid.*

GENERAL NOTE

Subs. (1)

The general rule is that there cannot be entitlement to benefit unless a claim is made for it. This section applies to income-related benefits, *i.e.* including income support, family credit and disability working allowance, but excluding payments from the social fund (subs. (4)). "Benefit", as defined in s.121 of the Contributions and Benefits Act, does not include income-related benefits. This section applies to claims made on or after October 1, 1990. Schedule 1 deals with earlier claims. The introduction of the predecessor of s.1 was precipitated by the decision of the House of Lords in *Insurance Officer* v. *McCaffrey* [1984] 1 W.L.R. 1353 that (subject to an express provision to the contrary) a person was entitled to benefit if he met the conditions of entitlement even though he had not made a claim for that benefit. Claiming went to payability, not entitlement. This was contrary to the long-standing assumption of the DHSS and was corrected with effect from September 2, 1985. Section 3, which is excluded from the operation of s.1, deals with late claims for widow's benefits where the death of the spouse is difficult to establish.

Subs. (2)

This provision imposes an overall limit of 12 months on the entitlement to benefit before the date of claim. Not all benefits are caught by subs. (1) and there is a further exclusion in para. (b). Regulation 19 of and Sched. 4 to the Social Security Claims and Payments Regulations (Northern Ireland) 1987 (S.I. 1987 No. 465) impose the ordinary time limits for claiming and allow many of those limits to be extended where the claimant proves good cause for the delay. In the case of income support, family credit, disability working allowance and social fund maternity and funeral payments, where there is such an extension the claim is then treated as made on the first day of the period to which the claim is allowed to relate (reg. 6(2)(c)). Although the drafting is not at all clear, the reference in subs. (2) to the 12-month limit period from the date on which the claim is made or is treated as made seems to make the limit start from the date fixed by reg. 6(2)(c). However, reg. 19(4) prevents an extension for good cause in the benefits covered by reg. 6(2)(c) leading to entitlement earlier than 12 months before the actual date of claim. However, the restriction seems to stem from that regulation and not from s.1(2), or the earlier forms set out in Sched. 1.

Retrospective effect of provisions making entitlement to benefit dependent on claim

2.—(1) This section applies where a claim for benefit is made or treated as made at any time on or after 2nd September 1985 (the date on which section 154A of the 1975 Act (general provision as to necessity of claim for entitlement to benefit), as originally enacted, came into force) in respect of a period the whole or any part of which falls on or after that date.

(2) Where this section applies, any question arising as to—

(a) whether the claimant is or was at any time (whether before, on or after 2nd September 1985) entitled to the benefit in question, or to any other benefit on which his entitlement to that benefit depends; or

(b) in a case where the claimant's entitlement to the benefit depends on the entitlement of another person to a benefit, whether that other person is or was so entitled,

shall be determined as if the relevant claim enactment and any regulations made under or referred to in that enactment had also been in force, with any necessary modifications, at all times relevant for the purpose of determining the entitlement of the claimant, and, where applicable, of the other person, to the benefit or benefits in question (including the entitlement of any person to any benefit on which that entitlement depends, and so on).

(3) In this section "the relevant claim enactment" means section 1 above as it has effect in relation to the claim referred to in subsection (1) above.

(4) In any case where—

(a) a claim for benefit was made or treated as made (whether before, on or after 2nd September 1985, and whether by the same claimant as the claim referred to in subsection (1) above or not), and benefit was awarded on that claim, in respect of a period falling wholly or partly before that date; but

(b) that award would not have been made had the current requirements applied in relation to claims for benefit, whenever made, in respect of periods before that date; and

(c) entitlement to the benefit claimed as mentioned in subsection (1) above depends on whether the claimant or some other person was previously entitled or treated as entitled to that or some other benefit,

then, in determining whether the conditions of entitlement to the benefit so claimed are satisfied, the person to whom benefit was awarded as mentioned in paragraphs (a) and (b) above shall be taken to have been entitled to the benefit so awarded, notwithstanding anything in subsection (2) above.

(5) In subsection (4) above "the current requirements" means—

(a) the relevant claim enactment, and any regulations made under or referred to in that enactment, or referred to in it, as in force at the time of the claim referred to in subsection (1) above, with any necessary modifications; and

(b) subsection (1) (with the omission of the words following "at any time") and subsections (2) and (3) above.

DEFINITIONS
"the 1975 Act": s.167.
"benefit": s.1(4).
"claim": s.167.
"claimant": *ibid.*

GENERAL NOTE
There are a number of benefits regarding which entitlement can depend on whether a person was entitled to a benefit at some earlier date (*e.g.* on reaching pensionable age). While the predecessor of s.1 clearly governed such questions from September 2, 1985 onwards, it was arguable that in relation to earlier dates the *McCaffrey* principle (see note to s.1(1) above) had to be applied. *CS 49/1989* decided that this argument was correct. The predecessor of s.2 was inserted by the Social Security (Northern Ireland) Order 1990 (S.I. 1990 No. 1511 (N.I. 15)) to reverse the effect of that decision and to do so retrospectively back to September 2, 1985. The form of s.2 is complex and the retrospective effects are difficult to work out. It applies only to claims made or treated as made on or after September 2, 1985 (subs. (1)). Thus very late appeals or very long good causes for late claim might not be affected. Then on any such claim, if a question of entitlement at any other date arises (including dates before September 2, 1985), that question is to be decided according to the principle of s.1 as it was in force at the relevant time (subs. (2)). The only exception to this is that if for any period benefit has been awarded following a claim, that beneficiary is to be treated as entitled to that benefit even though under the current requirements he would not be (subs. (4)).

Widowhood benefit

Late claims for widowhood benefit where death is difficult to establish

3.—(1) This section applies where a woman's husband has died, or may be presumed to have died, and the circumstances are such that—

(a) more than 12 months have elapsed since the date of death (whether he died, or is presumed to have died, before or after the coming into force of this section);

(b) either—

(i) the husband's body has not been discovered or identified or, if it has been discovered and identified, the woman does not know that fact; or

(ii) less than 12 months have elapsed since she first knew of the discovery and identification of the body; and

(c) no claim for any of the widowhood benefits, that is to say—

(i) widow's benefit,

(ii) an invalidity pension under Article 17 of the Pensions Order, or

(iii) a Category A retirement pension by virtue of paragraph (5) of that Article,

was made or treated as made in respect of the death by the woman before 14th August 1990 (the date of the coming into operation of Article 8 of the Social Security (Northern Ireland) Order 1990, which inserted in the 1975 Act section 154C, the provision of that Act corresponding to this section).

(2) Where this section applies, notwithstanding that any time prescribed for making a claim for a widowhood benefit in respect of the death has elapsed, then—

(a) in any case falling within paragraph (b)(i) of subsection (1) above where it has been determined—

> (i) under subsection (1)(b) of section 18 below on a claim made by the woman; or

> (ii) under subsection (4) of that section on the submission of a question by her,

that the husband has died or is presumed to have died; or

(b) in any case falling within paragraph (b)(ii) of subsection (1) above where the identification was made not more than 12 months before the woman first knew of the discovery and identification of the body,

such a claim may be made or treated as made at any time before the expiration of the period of 12 months beginning with the date on which that determination was made or, as the case may be, the date on which she first knew of the discovery and identification.

(3) If, in a case where a claim for a widowhood benefit is made or treated as made by virtue of this section, the claimant would, apart from subsection (2) of section 1 above, be entitled to—

(a) a widow's payment in respect of the husband's death more than 12 months before the date on which the claim is made or treated as made; or

(b) any other widowhood benefit in respect of his death for a period more than 12 months before that date,

then, notwithstanding anything in that section, she shall be entitled to that payment or, as the case may be, to that other benefit (together with any increase under section 80(5) of the Contributions and Benefits Act).

GENERAL NOTE

The predecessor of this section was part of the Social Security (Northern Ireland) Order 1990 (S.I. 1990 No. 1511 (N.I. 15)). It applies to benefits to which widows are entitled on their late husband's contributions, where the claim is made after July 12, 1990. If there is a delay in discovering or identifying the husband's body or the widow to rely on the presumption of death, s.3 can operate to allow entitlement to be backdated beyond the normal 12 months under s.1. If the husband's body has not to the knowledge (actual, not reasonably to be expected) of the widow been discovered and identified and his death or presumption of death has been determined in an AO's decision (subss. (1)(b)(i) and (2)(a)) a claim may be made within 12 months of that determination. Then there can be entitlement back to the date or presumed date of death, even though that goes back more than 12 months before the date of claim (subs. (3)). Where the widow does know of the discovery and identification of her husband's body, she may claim within 12 months of acquiring that knowledge (subss. (1)(b)(ii) and (2)), with the same element of backdating (subs. (3)). However, if more than 12 months elapsed between the actual identification and the widow's coming to know of it, she cannot rely on s.3 (subs. (2)(b)) if she has not already done so under subs. (1)(b)(i).

Treatment of payments of benefit to certain widows

4. In any case where—

(a) a claim for a widow's pension or a widowed mother's allowance is made, or treated as made, before 14th August 1990 (the date of the coming into operation of paragraph 16(2) of Schedule 6 to the Social Security (Northern Ireland) Order 1990); and

(b) the Department has made a payment to or for the claimant on the ground that, if the claim had been received immediately after that date, she would have been entitled to that pension or allowance, or entitled to it at a higher rate, for the period in respect of which the payment is made,

the payment so made shall be treated as a payment of that pension or allowance; and, if and to the extent that an award of the pension or allowance, or an award at a higher rate, is made for the period in respect of which the payment was made, the payment shall be treated as made in accordance with that award.

Claims and payments regulations

Regulations about claims for and payments of benefit

5.—(1) Regulations may provide—

(a) for requiring a claim for a benefit to which this section applies to be made by such person, in such manner and within such time as may be prescribed;

(b) for treating such a claim made in such circumstances as may be prescribed as having been made at such date earlier or later than that at which it is made as may be prescribed;

(c) for permitting such a claim to be made, or treated as if made, for a period wholly or partly after the date on which it is made;

(d) for permitting an award on such a claim to be made for such a period subject to the condition that the claimant satisfies the requirements for entitlement when benefit becomes payable under the award;

(e) for a review of any such award if those requirements are found not to have been satisfied;

(f) for the disallowance on any ground of a person's claim for a benefit to which this section applies to be treated as a disallowance of any further claim by that person for that benefit until the grounds of the original disallowance have ceased to exist;

(g) for enabling one person to act for another in relation to a claim for a benefit to which this section applies and for enabling such a claim to be made and proceeded with in the name of a person who has died;

(h) for requiring any information or evidence needed for the determination of such a claim or of any question arising in connection with such a claim to be furnished by such person as may be prescribed in accordance with the regulations;

(i) for a claim for any one benefit to which this section applies to be treated, either in the alternative or in addition, as a claim for any other such benefit that may be prescribed;

(j) for the person to whom, time when and manner in which a benefit to which this section applies is to be paid and for the information and evidence to be furnished in connection with the payment of such a benefit;

(k) for notice to be given of any change of circumstances affecting the continuance of entitlement to such a benefit or payment of such a benefit;

(l) for the day on which entitlement to such a benefit is to begin or end;

(m) for calculating the amounts of such a benefit according to a prescribed scale or otherwise adjusting them so as to avoid fractional amounts or facilitate computation;

(n) for extinguishing the right to payment of such a benefit if payment is not obtained within such period, not being less than 12 months, as may be prescribed from the date on which the right is treated under the regulations as having arisen;

(o) for suspending payment, in whole or in part, where it appears to the Department that a question arises whether—

(i) the conditions for entitlement are or were fulfilled;

(ii) an award ought to be revised;

(iii) an appeal ought to be brought against an award;

(p) for withholding payments of a benefit to which this section applies in prescribed circumstances and for subsequently making withheld payments in prescribed circumstances;

(q) for the circumstances and manner in which payments of such a benefit may be made to another person on behalf of the beneficiary for any purpose, which may be to discharge, in whole or in part, an obligation of the beneficiary or any other person;

(r) for the payment or distribution of such a benefit to or among persons claiming to be entitled on the death of any person and for dispensing with strict proof of their title;

(s) for the making of a payment on account of such a benefit—

(i) where no claim has been made and it is impracticable for one to be made immediately;

(ii) where a claim has been made and it is impracticable for the claim or an appeal, reference, review or application relating to it to be immediately determined;

(iii) where an award has been made but it is impracticable to pay the whole immediately.

(2) This section applies to the following benefits—

(a) benefit as defined in section 121 of the Contributions and Benefits Act;

(b) income support;

(c) family credit;

(d) disability working allowance;

(e) housing benefit;

(f) any social fund payments such as are mentioned in section 134(1)(a) or (2) of the Contributions and Benefits Act;

(g) child benefit; and

(h) Christmas bonus.

(3) Subsection (1)(o) above shall have effect in relation to housing benefit as if the reference to the Department were a reference to the authority paying the benefit.

(4) Subsection (1)(g), (j), (m), (q) and (r) above shall have effect as if statutory sick pay and statutory maternity pay were benefits to which this section applies.

DEFINITIONS
"the Contributions and Benefits Act": s.167.
"prescribed": *ibid.*

GENERAL NOTE
See the Social Security (Claims and Payments) Regulations (Northern Ireland) 1987 (S.I. 1987 No. 465). See also the equivalent Great Britain Regulations, the Social Security (Claims and Payments) Regulations 1987 (S.I. 1987 No. 1968) and the commentary in the current editions of Bonner *et al.*, Mesher and Rowland.

Industrial injuries benefit

Notification of accidents, etc.

6. Regulations may provide—

(a) for requiring the prescribed notice of an accident in respect of which industrial injuries benefit may be payable to be given within the prescribed time by the employed earner to the earner's employer or other prescribed person;

(b) for requiring employers—

(i) to make reports, to such person and in such form and within such time as may be prescribed, of accidents in respect of which industrial injuries benefit may be payable;

(ii) to furnish to the prescribed person any information required for the determination of claims, or of questions arising in connection with claims or awards;

(iii) to take such other steps as may be prescribed to facilitate the giving notice of accidents, the making of claims and the determination of claims and of questions so arising.

DEFINITIONS
"industrial injuries benefits": s.167.
"prescribe": *ibid*.

GENERAL NOTE
See regs. 24 and 25 of the Social Security (Claims and Payments) Regulations (Northern Ireland) 1977 (S.I. 1977 No. 351). See also the equivalent Great Britain Regulations, regs. 24 and 25 of the Social Security (Claims and Payments) Regulations 1979 (S.I. 1979 No. 628) and commentary in the current edition of Bonner *et al*.

Medical examination and treatment of claimants

7.—(1) Regulations may provide for requiring claimants for disablement pension—
   (a) to submit themselves from time to time to medical examination for the purpose of determining the effect of the relevant accident, or the treatment appropriate to the relevant injury or loss of faculty;
   (b) to submit themselves from time to time to appropriate medical treatment for the injury or loss of faculty.
   (2) Regulations under subsection (1) above requiring persons to submit themselves to medical examination or treatment may—
   (a) require those persons to attend at such places and at such times as may be required; and
   (b) with the consent of the Department of Finance and Personnel provide for the payment by the Department to those persons of travelling and other allowances (including compensation for loss of remunerative time).

DEFINITIONS
"disablement benefit": s.167.
"prescribe": *ibid*.

GENERAL NOTE
See reg. 26 of the Social Security (Claims and Payments) Regulations (Northern Ireland) 1977 (S.I. 1977 No. 351). See also the equivalent Great Britain regulation, reg. 26 of the Social Security (Claims and Payments) Regulations 1979 (S.I. 1979 No. 628) and commentary in the current edition of Bonner *et al*.

Obligations of claimants

8.—(1) Subject to subsection (3) below, regulations may provide for disqualifying a claimant for the receipt of industrial injuries benefit—
   (a) for failure without good cause to comply with any requirement of regulations to which this subsection applies (including in the case of a claim for industrial death benefit, a failure on the part of some other person to give the prescribed notice of the relevant accident);
   (b) for wilful obstruction of, or other misconduct in connection with, any examination or treatment to which he is required under regulations to which this subsection applies to submit himself, or in proceedings under this Act for the determination of his right to benefit or to its receipt,
or for suspending proceedings on the claim or payment of benefit as the case may be, in the case of any such failure, obstruction or misconduct.
   (2) The regulations to which subsection (1) above applies are—
   (a) any regulations made by virtue of section 5(1)(h), (j) or (k) above, so far as relating to industrial injuries benefit; and
   (b) regulations made by virtue of section 6 or 7 above.
   (3) Regulations under subsection (1) above providing for disqualification for the receipt of benefit for any of the following matters, that is to say—
   (a) for failure to comply with the requirements of regulations under section 7(1) or (2) above;

    (b) for obstruction of, or misconduct in connection with, medical examination or treatment,

shall not be made so as to disentitle a claimant to benefit for a period exceeding 6 weeks on any disqualification.

DEFINITIONS

"industrial injuries benefits": s.167.

GENERAL NOTE

See reg. 38 of the Social Security (General Benefit) Regulations (Northern Ireland) 1984 (S.I. 1984 No. 92). See also the equivalent Great Britain Regulation, *i.e.* reg. 40 of the Social Security (General Benefit) Regulations 1982 (S.I. 1982 No. 1408), in the current edition of Bonner *et al.*

Disability working allowance

Initial claims and repeat claims

9.—(1) In this section—

"initial claim" means a claim for a disability working allowance made by a person—

    (a) to whom it has not previously been payable; or

    (b) to whom it has not been payable during the period of 2 years immediately preceding the date on which the claim is made or is treated as made; and

"repeat claim" means any other claim for a disability working allowance.

(2) On an initial claim a declaration by the claimant that he has a physical or mental disability which puts him at a disadvantage in getting a job is conclusive, except in such circumstances as may be prescribed, that for the purposes of section 128(1)(b) of the Contributions and Benefits Act he has such a disability (in accordance with regulations under section 128(3) of that Act).

(3) If—

    (a) a repeat claim is made or treated as made not later than the end of the period of 8 weeks commencing with the last day of the claimant's previous award; and

    (b) on the claim which resulted in that award he qualified under section 128(2) of the Contributions and Benefits Act by virtue—

        (i) of paragraph (a) of that subsection; or

        (ii) of there being payable to him a benefit under an enactment having effect in Great Britain and corresponding to a benefit mentioned in that paragraph,

he shall be treated on the repeat claim as if he still so qualified.

DEFINITIONS

"the Contributions and Benefits Act": s.167.

GENERAL NOTE

Section 9 supplies some special rules under which some parts of the qualifications for disability working allowance are deemed to be satisfied.

Subs. (1)

An initial claim is one made by a person who has never been entitled to disability working allowance or whose last week of entitlement was more than two years before the date of claim. Any other claim is a repeat claim.

Subs. (2)

On an initial claim a claimant's declaration, on the elaborate self-assessment claim form, that he has a disability that puts him at a disadvantage in getting a job is conclusive. This general rule does not apply if the claim itself contains indications to the contrary or the AO has before him evidence pointing to the contrary (Disability Working Allowance (General) Regulations (Northern Ireland) 1991 (S.I. 1992 No. 78), reg. 4).

Subs. (3)

See the Contributions and Benefits Act, s.128(2)(a) and (4), and the Disability Working Allowance (General) Regulations 1991 (S.I. 1991 No. 2887), reg. 7. When such an award expires and the repeat claim is made within eight weeks, the claimant is deemed to satisfy the requirement. Thus if a claimant initially qualifies on this ground and continues to satisfy the other conditions of entitlement, awards may continue indefinitely.

The social fund

Necessity of application for certain payments

10.—(1) A social fund payment such as is mentioned in section 134(1)(b) of the Contributions and Benefits Act may be awarded to a person only if an application for such a payment has been made by him or on his behalf in such form and manner as may be prescribed.

(2) The Department may by regulations—

(a) make provision with respect to the time at which an application for such a social fund payment is to be treated as made;

(b) prescribe conditions that must be satisfied before any determination in connection with such an application may be made or any award of such a payment may be paid;

(c) prescribe circumstances in which such an award becomes extinguished.

DEFINITIONS

"the Contributions and Benefits Act": s.167.

"prescribe": *ibid*.

GENERAL NOTE

Subs. (1)

This provision applies to the "ordinary" social fund, not to funeral or maternity payments or cold weather payments. See the Social Fund (Applications) Regulations (Northern Ireland) 1988 (S.I. 1988 No. 130). See also the equivalent Great Britain Regulations, the Social Fund (Applications) Regulations 1988 (S.I. 1988 No. 524), with commentary in the current edition of Mesher.

Subs. (2)

See the Social Fund (Miscellaneous Provisions) Regulations (Northern Ireland) 1990 (S.I. 1990 No. 327).

Child benefit

Necessity of application for child benefit

11.—(1) Subject to the provisions of this Act, no person shall be entitled to child benefit unless he claims it in the manner, and within the time, prescribed in relation to child benefit by regulations under section 5 above.

(2) Except where regulations otherwise provide, no person shall be entitled to child benefit for any week on a claim made by him after that week if child benefit in respect of the same child has already been paid for that week to another person, whether or not that other person was entitled to it.

DEFINITIONS

"prescribe": s.167.

GENERAL NOTE

Subs. (1)

See the Social Security (Claims and Payments) Regulations (Northern Ireland) 1987 (S.I. 1987 No. 465), especially reg. 19(6).

Subs. (2)

Payment of child benefit in respect of a child to one person, even if that person is not entitled to payment, generally bars payment to anyone else. See reg. 13A of the Child Benefit (General) Regulations (Northern Ireland) 1976 (S.I. 1976 No. 226).

Statutory sick pay

Duties of employees etc. in relation to statutory sick pay

12.—(1) Any employee who claims to be entitled to statutory sick pay from his employer shall, if so required by his employer, provide such information as may reasonably be required for the purpose of determining the duration of the period of entitlement in question or whether a period of entitlement exists as between them.

(2) The Department may by regulations direct—

(a) that medical information required under subsection (1) above shall, in such cases as may be prescribed, be provided in a prescribed form;

(b) that an employee shall not be required under subsection (1) above to provide medical information in respect of such days as may be prescribed in a period of incapacity for work.

(3) Where an employee asks an employer of his to provide him with a written statement, in respect of a period before the request is made, of one or more of the following—

(a) the days within that period which the employer regards as days in respect of which he is liable to pay statutory sick pay to that employee;

(b) the reasons why the employer does not so regard the other days in that period;

(c) the employer's opinion as to the amount of statutory sick pay to which the employee is entitled in respect of each of those days,

the employer shall, to the extent to which the request was reasonable, comply with it within a reasonable time.

DEFINITIONS
  "prescribe": s.167.

GENERAL NOTE

Subss. (1) and (2)

There is a general obligation on the employee to provide information to the employer to enable a claim for statutory sick pay to be determined. See reg. 7 of the Statutory Sick Pay (General) Regulations (Northern Ireland) 1982 (S.I. 1982 No. 263) and the Statutory Sick Pay (Medical Evidence) Regulations (Northern Ireland) 1985 (S.I. 1985 No. 321).

Subs. (3)

See regs. 15 and 15A of the Statutory Sick Pay (General) Regulations (Northern Ireland) 1982 (S.I. 1982 No. 263).

Statutory maternity pay

Duties of women etc. in relation to statutory maternity pay

13.—(1) A woman shall provide the person who is liable to pay her statutory maternity pay—

(a) with evidence as to her pregnancy and the expected date of confinement in such form and at such time as may be prescribed; and

(b) where she commences work after her confinement but within the maternity pay period, with such additional information as may be prescribed.

(2) Where a woman asks an employer or former employer of hers to provide her with a written statement, in respect of a period before the request is made, of one or more of the following—

    (a) the weeks within that period which he regards as weeks in respect of
       which he is liable to pay statutory maternity pay to the woman;
    (b) the reasons why he does not so regard the other weeks in that period;
       and
    (c) his opinion as to the amount of statutory maternity pay to which the
       woman is entitled in respect of each of the weeks in respect of which
       he regards himself as liable to make a payment,
the employer or former employer shall, to the extent to which the request
was reasonable, comply with it within a reasonable time.

DEFINITIONS
  "prescribe": s.167.

GENERAL NOTE

Subs. (1)
  See regs. 22 and 24 of the Statutory Maternity Pay (General) Regulations (Northern Ireland)
1987 (S.I. 1987 No. 30).

Subs. (2)
  The duty on the employer under subs. (3) to supply the woman with information about the
reasons for decisions on entitlement or non-entitlement to statutory maternity pay supplements
the duties in reg. 25A of the General Regulations, which apply when the woman wishes to claim
another benefit.

Emergency payments

Emergency payments by Health and Social Services Boards and other bodies

    14.—(1) The Department may make arrangements—
    (a) with a Board; or
    (b) with any other body,
for the making on behalf of the Department by members of the staff of any
Board or body of payments on account of benefits to which section 5 above
applies in circumstances corresponding to those in which the Department
itself has the power to make such payments under subsection (1)(s) of that
section; and a Board shall have power to enter into any such arrangements.
    (2) A payment under any such arrangements shall be treated for the
purposes of any statutory provision as if it had been made by the
Department.
    (3) The Department shall repay a Board or other body such amount as the
Department determines to be the reasonable administrative expenses
incurred by the Board or body in making payments in accordance with
arrangements under this section.
    (4) In this section "Board" means a Health and Social Services Board.

PART II

ADJUDICATION

Adjudication by the Department

Questions for the Department

    15.—(1) Subject to this Part of this Act, any of the following questions
shall be determined by the Department—
    (a) a question whether a person is an earner and, if he is, as to the
       category of earners in which he is to be included;
    (b) subject to subsection (2) below, a question whether the contribution
       conditions for any benefit are satisfied, or otherwise relating to a
       person's contributions or his earnings factor;
    (c) a question whether a Class 1A contribution is payable or otherwise
       relating to a Class 1A contribution;

(d) a question whether a person is or was employed in employed earner's employment for the purposes of Part V of the Contributions and Benefits Act;

(e) a question as to whether a person was, within the meaning of regulations, precluded from regular employment by responsibilities at home;

(f) any question as to which surpluses are to be taken into account under section 45(1) of the Contributions and Benefits Act;

(g) any question arising under any provision of Part XI of the Contributions and Benefits Act or this Act, or under any provision of regulations under that Part, as to—

(i) whether a person is, or was, an employee or employer of another;

(ii) whether an employer is entitled to make any deduction from his contributions payments in accordance with regulations under section 154 of the Contributions and Benefits Act;

(iii) whether a payment falls to be made to an employer in accordance with the regulations;

(iv) the amount that falls to be so deducted or paid;

(v) the amount of an employer's contributions payments for any period for the purposes of regulations under section 154(3) of the Contributions and Benefits Act; or

(vi) whether two or more employers or two or more contracts of service are, by virtue of regulations made under section 159(5) of that Act, to be treated as one; and

(h) any question arising under any provision of Part XII of that Act or this Act, or under any provision of regulations under that Part, as to—

(i) whether a person is, or was, an employee or employer of another;

(ii) whether an employer is entitled to make any deduction from his contributions payments in accordance with regulations under section 163 of the Contributions and Benefits Act;

(iii) whether a payment falls to be made to an employer in accordance with the regulations;

(iv) the amount that falls to be so deducted or paid; or

(v) whether two or more employers or two or more contracts of service are, by virtue of regulations made under section 167(2) of that Act, to be treated as one,

and any question arising under regulations made by virtue of paragraph (c), (d) or (f) of section 160(9) of that Act.

(2) Subsection (1)(b) above includes any question arising—

(a) under section 17(1) of the Contributions and Benefits Act as to whether by regulations under that subsection a person is excepted from liability for Class 4 contributions, or his liability is deferred; or

(b) under regulations made by virtue of section 17(3) or (4) or 18 of that Act;

but not any other question relating to Class 4 contributions, nor any question within section 18(1)(c) below.

(3) Regulations may make provision restricting the persons who may apply to the Department for the determination of any such question as is mentioned in subsection (1) above.

(4) The Department may, if it thinks fit, before determining any such question as is mentioned in subsection (1) above, appoint a person to hold an inquiry into the question, or any matters arising in connection with it, and to report on the question, or on those matters, to the Department.

DEFINITIONS
"the Contributions and Benefits Act": s.167.
"the Department": *ibid.*

GENERAL NOTE
This section defines questions which are to be decided by the Department and not by the adjudicating authorities (*i.e.* AO, tribunal and Social Security Commissioner). In Great Britain these questions are determined by the Secretary of State. The questions are mainly to do with the type of contributions which a person is required to pay and whether the contribution conditions for benefits are satisfied. There may well be surrounding issues, such as the identification of the relevant year in which the contribution test must be satisfied (see *R(G) 1/82*), which are for the adjudicating authorities to determine. But, in relation to subs. (1)(b), the core question of whether a claimant has made sufficient contributions for entitlement remains with the Department (*Scrivner* v. *Chief Adjudication Officer, The Times*, November 7, 1989). In that case, the question was whether contributions paid in Belgium could count for entitlement to British unemployment benefit. The Court of Appeal disapproved of the suggestion that *R(G) 1/82* meant that all issues of law were for the adjudicating authorities, with only the provision of the figures being left to the Secretary of State. Many decisions under s.15 are taken by locally based Benefits Agency staff authorised to act on behalf of the Department, but there is also a central unit which deals mainly with difficult questions of the categorisation of earners. The inquiry procedure provided by subs. (4) is also used mainly for such questions. For a detailed description of the history and use of the equivalent powers of the Secretary of State in Great Britain, and a powerful critique of the present arrangements, see Partington, *The Secretary of State's Powers in Social Security Adjudication* (1991).

Appeal on question of law

16.—(1) A question of law arising in connection with the determination by the Department of any such question as is mentioned in section 15(1) above may, if the Department thinks fit, be referred for decision to the Court of Appeal.

(2) If the Department determines in accordance with subsection (1) above to refer any question of law to the court, it shall give notice in writing of its intention to do so—

    (a) in a case where the question arises on an application made to the Department, to the applicant; and

    (b) in any case to such persons as appear to it to be concerned with the question.

(3) Any person aggrieved by the decision of the Department on any question of law within subsection (1) above which is not referred in accordance with that subsection may appeal from that decision to the court.

(4) The Department shall be entitled to appear and be heard on any such reference or appeal.

(5) Rules of court may include provision for regulating references and appeals to the court under this section.

(6) Notwithstanding anything in any Act, the decision of the court on a reference or appeal under this section shall be final.

DEFINITIONS
"the Department": s.167.

GENERAL NOTE
Where the Department has made a formal determination under s.15, there is a right of appeal to the Court of Appeal. The Department may also refer questions of law to the court. Insufficient cases proceed to the courts for the judges nominated to hear such appeals to develop any expertise in the complexities of social security contributions.

Review of decisions

17.—(1) Subject to subsection (2) below, the Department may review any decision given by it on any such question as is mentioned in section 15(1) above, if—

    (a) new facts have been brought to its notice; or

    (b) it is satisfied that the decision—

(i) was given in ignorance of some material fact;
(ii) was based on a mistake as to some material fact; or
(iii) was erroneous in point of law.

(2) A decision shall not be reviewed while an appeal under section 16 above is pending against the decision of the Department on a question of law arising in connection with it, or before the time for so appealing has expired.

(3) On a review any question of law may be referred under subsection (1) of section 16 above or, where it is not so referred, may be the subject of an appeal under subsection (3) of that section, and the other provisions of that section shall apply accordingly.

DEFINITIONS
"the Department": s.167.

GENERAL NOTE
The Department has wide powers to review a decision given under s.15. The fact that it is a ground of review that the decision was erroneous in point of law was seized on by the English Court of Appeal in *Chief Adjudication Officer* v. *Foster* [1991] 3 W.L.R. 473 as a reason for not allowing the Social Security Commissioners (or tribunals or AOs) to determine whether regulations had been validly made. It was said that if the Commissioners could do this in determining whether a tribunal's decision was erroneous in point of law, it would mean that the Secretary of State (or the Department in Northern Ireland) could determine whether he had acted lawfully in making regulations, which would be absurd. It is far from clear that such a consequence would follow. See the notes to s.21 below.

Adjudication by adjudication officers

Claims and questions to be submitted to adjudication officer

18.—(1) Subject to section 52 below, there shall be submitted forthwith to an adjudication officer for determination in accordance with this Part of this Act—

(a) any claim for a benefit to which this section applies;
(b) subject to subsection (2) below, any question arising in connection with a claim for, or award of, such a benefit; and
(c) any question whether, if he had otherwise had a right to it, a person would be disqualified—

(i) by reason of section 28(1) of the Contributions and Benefits Act, for receiving unemployment benefit;
(ii) by reason of any regulations under section 32(1) of that Act, for receiving sickness benefit; or
(iii) by reason of any regulations under section 59(1) of that Act, for receiving invalidity benefit.

(2) Subsection (1) above does not apply to any question which falls to be determined otherwise than by an adjudication officer.

(3) Any question as to, or in connection with, entitlement to statutory sick pay or statutory maternity pay may be submitted to an adjudication officer—

(a) by the Department; or
(b) subject to and in accordance with regulations, by the employee concerned,

for determination in accordance with this Part of this Act.

(4) If—

(a) a person submits a question relating to the age, marriage or death of any person; and
(b) it appears to the adjudication officer that the question may arise if the person who has submitted it to him submits a claim to a benefit to which this section applies,

the adjudication officer may determine the question.

(5) Different aspects of the same claim or question may be submitted to different adjudication officers; and for that purpose this section and the other provisions of this Part of this Act with respect to the determination of claims and questions shall apply with any necessary modifications.

(6) This section applies to the following benefits—

(a) benefit as defined in section 121 of the Contributions and Benefits Act;

(b) income support;

(c) family credit;

(d) disability working allowance;

(e) any social fund payment such as is mentioned in section 134(1)(a) or (2) of the Contributions and Benefits Act;

(f) child benefit;

(g) statutory sick pay; and

(h) statutory maternity pay.

DEFINITIONS
"the Contributions and Benefits Act": s.167.
"the Department": *ibid.*

GENERAL NOTE

Subs. (1)
See subss. (3), (4) and (6) for the benefits to which this section applies. Subsection (2) merely confirms that questions to be determined by the Department under s.18 do not go to the AO.
In *R.* v. *Secretary of State for Social Services*, ex p. *Child Poverty Action Group* [1990] 2 Q.B. 540, the English Court of Appeal decided that the duty to submit a claim "forthwith" did not arise until the DSS (now the Benefits Agency) was in possession of the basic information necessary to determine the claim. However, once that information was there, any need for verification did not justify delay in submitting the claim to the AO. It would then be for the AO to make enquiries, if he considered that verification was necessary. In *R(SB) 29/84* a Tribunal of Commissioners (by a majority) held that the question whether payment had actually been made following an award (*i.e.* what should happen following an allegedly lost Giro) was not a "question relating to supplementary benefit" (Supplementary Benefits Act 1976, s.2(1)), and therefore was not a matter for an AO or SSAT. Any remedy was to be pursued through the courts. *R(IS) 7/91* holds, after an exhaustive review of the legislation, that the result is the same under the predecessor of subs. (1)(b). The question whether the Secretary of State (and consequently the Department in Northern Ireland) has implemented an award of benefit is not a question in connection with an award of benefit.

Subs. (6)
Under para. (e) s.18 applies to funeral and maternity payments and cold-weather payments from the social fund.

Decision of adjudication officer

19.—(1) An adjudication officer to whom a claim or question is submitted under section 18 above (other than a claim which under section 28(12) or (13) or 33(7) below falls to be treated as an application for a review) shall take it into consideration and, so far as practicable, dispose of it, in accordance with this section, and with procedure regulations under section 57 below, within 14 days of its submission to him.

(2) Subject to subsection (3) and section 35 below, the adjudication officer may decide a claim or question himself or refer it to a social security appeal tribunal.

(3) The adjudication officer must decide a claim for or question relating to an attendance allowance, a disability living allowance or a disability working allowance himself.

(4) Where an adjudication officer refers a question as to, or in connection with, entitlement to statutory sick pay or statutory maternity pay to a social security appeal tribunal, the employee and employer concerned shall each be given notice in writing of the reference.

(5) In any other case notice in writing of the reference shall be given to the claimant.

(6) Where—

(a) a case has been referred to a social security appeal tribunal ("the tribunal"); and

(b) the claimant makes a further claim which raises the same or similar questions; and

(c) that further claim is referred to the tribunal by the adjudication officer,

then the tribunal may proceed to determine the further claim whether or not notice has been given under subsection (4) or (5) above.

GENERAL NOTE

Subs. (1)

The general rule is that the AO should make a decision within 14 days, once the claim or question is submitted to him under s.18.

It appears that the need to obtain verification of information may make it not practicable to reach a decision within 14 days. Although the obligation of a claimant under reg. 7 of the Social Security (Claims and Payments) Regulations (Northern Ireland) 1987 (S.I. 1987 No. 465) to provide such evidence, information, etc., as is required by the Department (mentioned in *R(SB) 29/83* as relevant to practicability) is now presumably relevant to s.19, the rest of the decision probably holds. After a reasonable length of time, even if further information is not forthcoming, the AO must make a decision on the evidence available to him. Then, if the decision is adverse, the claimant has something to appeal against and the adequacy of the information before the AO can be dealt with by the SSAT. Note that there is no longer a power for the Department to deem a claim to have been withdrawn if the information required under reg. 7 is not produced.

It has been held that an AO does not "discharge responsibilities of a judicial nature" (Glidewell L.J. in *Jones* v. *Department of Employment* [1988] 1 All E.R. 725, 733), but clearly the AO's administrative decisions must be reached in a judicial manner. The investigatory functions most recently emphasised in the CPAG case do not extend to a duty to investigate the claimant's entire financial situation on a review (*Duggan* v. *Chief Adjudication Officer, The Times*, December 19, 1988; *R(SB) 13/89*). The English Court of Appeal in *Chief Adjudication Officer* v. *Foster* [1991] 3 W.L.R. 473 has decided that the AO (as well as social security appeal tribunals and Social Security Commissioners) must reach decisions on the basis that all regulations are validly made. Only the High Court or the Court of Appeal has the jurisdiction to declare regulations *ultra vires*. While this is true, the proposition that an adjudicating authority must apply a provision which is not validly part of the law of the jurisdiction is very dubious and is to be challenged in the appeal to the House of Lords which will be heard in October 1992. The Court of Appeal in *Foster* does not refer to earlier cases in which the Court of Appeal has raised no objection to the Social Security Commissioners dealing with the validity of regulations (*Bhatia* v. *Birmingham*, appendix to *R(S) 8/83*, and *Kilburn* v. *Chief Adjudication Officer*, appendix to *R(SB) 9/87*). An AO cannot be bound by any assurance given by an employee of the DHSS or the Benefits Agency about a claimant's entitlement, but must come to a proper decision on the law applicable to the case. Even if a claimant had relied on a statement from or on behalf of an AO, this requirement to carry out the statutory duty prevents an estoppel arising (*R(SB) 14/88, R(SB) 14/89* and Woolf L.J. refusing leave to appeal in *R(SB) 4/91*). The claims excluded from the operation of subs. (1) by the words in brackets are certain claims for disability living allowance or disability working allowance. Under ss.28(12) and 33(7), if an award of either of those benefits has been made for a period, a further claim made within that period is treated as an application to review the existing award. Under s.28(13), where an AO's decision is not to award one of those benefits or attendance allowance, any further claim made during the period prescribed for applying for a review of that decision on any ground (*i.e.* three months: Social Security (Adjudication) Regulations (Northern Ireland) 1987 (S.I. 1987 No. 82), reg. 26A) is treated as an application for review.

Subs. (2)

The AO no longer has express power to decide questions in any particular way. The power to make references to the SSAT is used mainly where there is a conflict of evidence which the AO feels unable to resolve. The most common situation is where the accounts of a claimant of unemployment benefit and his ex-employer about the reasons why employment was ended conflict. The question of whether a disqualification was for misconduct or whether the claimant left voluntarily without just cause may then be referred to the SSAT. Another use is where a further claim is made following on from a period which is to be dealt with by the SSAT in determining an appeal (see subs. (6)). The effect of subs. (3) is that such references cannot be made in disability working allowance cases. Section 35 is concerned with the reference of special questions.

Subs. (3)
In these cases the AO must determine the claim or question himself, and so cannot refer a matter to a SSAT or DAT. This is no doubt because the process of appeal for these benefits must start with a review by another AO before there can be an appeal to the SSAT or DAT.

Subss. (4) and (5)
Subsections (4) and (5) do not prescribe any particular period in advance of the hearing for the written notice of a reference to be given. A Tribunal of Commissioners in *R(S) 5/86* decided that whatever is a reasonable time in the circumstances is the test. The same decision holds that the requirement that the reference is to be in writing cannot be waived by the claimant. Note the exception introduced by subs. (6), which has been in operation since April 1990.

Subs. (6)
Once a case has been properly referred to a SSAT under subs. (2), a further claim raising similar questions may be referred to the SSAT for decision without notice in writing being given to the claimant. It is obviously desirable that notice that the SSAT is to be asked to deal with the further claim should be given to the claimant if possible.

Appeals from adjudication officers—general

Appeal to social security appeal tribunal

20.—(1) Subject to subsection (3) below, where the adjudication officer has decided a claim or question other than a claim or question relating to an attendance allowance, a disability living allowance or a disability working allowance—
 (a) if it relates to statutory sick pay or statutory maternity pay, the employee and employer concerned shall each have a right to appeal to a social security appeal tribunal; and
 (b) in any other case the claimant shall have a right to do so.
 (2) A person with a right of appeal under this section shall be given such notice of a decision falling within subsection (1) above and of that right as may be prescribed.
 (3) No appeal lies under this section where—
 (a) in connection with the decision of the adjudication officer there has arisen any question which under or by virtue of this Act falls to be determined otherwise than by an adjudication officer; and
 (b) the question has been determined; and
 (c) the adjudication officer certifies that the decision on that question is the sole ground of his decision.
 (4) Regulations may make provision as to the manner in which, and the time within which, appeals are to be brought.
 (5) Where an adjudication officer has determined that any amount, other than an amount—
 (a) of an attendance allowance;
 (b) of a disability living allowance;
 (c) of a disability working allowance;
 (d) of statutory sick pay; or
 (e) of statutory maternity pay,
is recoverable under or by virtue of section 69 or 72 below, any person from whom he has determined that it is recoverable shall have the same right of appeal to a social security appeal tribunal as a claimant.
 (6) In any case where—
 (a) an adjudication officer has decided any claim or question under Part V of the Contributions and Benefits Act; and
 (b) the right to benefit under that Part of that Act of any person other

than the claimant is or may be, under Part VI of Schedule 7 to that
　　Act, affected by that decision,
that other person shall have the like right of appeal to a social security appeal
tribunal as the claimant.

(7) Subsection (2) above shall apply to a person with a right of appeal
under subsection (5) or (6) above as it applies to a claimant.

GENERAL NOTE

Subs. (1)
　　There is a general right of appeal to a SSAT for a claimant against any decision of an AO on
any claim or question.
　　Note that under subs. (5) for most benefits a person from whom an overpayment has been
determined to be recoverable has the same right of appeal as a claimant.
　　Subsection (1) does not cover attendance allowance, disability living allowance and disability
working allowance, where the appeal on most questions is to a DAT. See ss.28–31.

Subs. (2)
　　See the Social Security (Adjudication) Regulations (Northern Ireland) 1987 (S.I. 1987 No.
82). See also the equivalent Great Britain Regulations, particularly regs. 20 and 63 of the Social
Security (Adjudication) Regulations 1986 (S.I. 1986 No. 2218), in the current editions of
Bonner *et al.* and Mesher.

Subs. (3)
　　There can be no valid appeal to the SSAT where the AO certifies that the sole ground of his
decision was the determination of a question which is for another authority (*e.g.* the Department) to determine.

Subs. (4)
　　See reg. 3 of and Sched. 2 to the Adjudication Regulations. See also the Great Britain
equivalents in the current editions of Bonner *et al.* and Mesher.

Subs. (5)
　　A person from whom it is determined that an overpayment of most benefits is recoverable has
a right to appeal against the AO's decision to that effect. This applies to overpayments under
s.69 (misrepresentation or failure to disclose) and s.72 (duplication of income support and other
payments). A person falling within subs. (5) must be given notice of the decision and the right of
appeal (subss. (7) and (2)).
　　The benefits listed in paras. (a)–(e) are excluded from the operation of subs. (5). See s.30(9)
for rights of appeal against decisions on the recoverability of attendance allowance, disability
living allowance and disability working allowance.

Subs. (6)
　　Part V of the Contributions and Benefits Act concerns industrial injuries benefits. Part VI of
Sched. 7 concerns industrial death benefit, which can only be awarded in respect of deaths
before April 11, 1988. Subsection (6) preserves a right of appeal for the surviving spouse in
relation to decisions about the deceased's entitlement to industrial injuries benefit. Outside
that situation, an appeal abates on the death of the claimant, but is revived by appointment of a
personal representative of the estate or of an appointee under the Social Security (Claims and
Payments) Regulations (Northern Ireland) 1987 (S.I. 1987 No. 465) (*R(SB) 8/88* and *R(SB)
5/90*).

Appeal from social security appeal tribunal to Commissioner

21.—(1) Subject to the provisions of this section, an appeal lies to a
Commissioner from any decision of a social security appeal tribunal under
section 20 above on the ground that the decision of the tribunal was erroneous in point of law.

(2) In the case of statutory sick pay or statutory maternity pay an appeal
lies under this section at the instance of any of the following—
　　(a) an adjudication officer;
　　(b) the employee concerned;
　　(c) the employer concerned;

    (d) a trade union, where—
        (i) the employee is a member of the union at the time of the appeal and was so immediately before the question at issue arose; or
        (ii) the question at issue is a question as to or in connection with entitlement of a deceased person who was at the time of his death a member of the union;
    (e) an association of employers of which the employer is a member at the time of the appeal and was so immediately before the question at issue arose.

(3) In any other case an appeal lies under this section at the instance of any of the following—
    (a) an adjudication officer;
    (b) the claimant;
    (c) in any of the cases mentioned in subsection (5) below, a trade union; and
    (d) a person from whom it is determined that any amount is recoverable under section 69 or 72 below.

(4) In a case relating to industrial injuries benefit an appeal lies under this section at the instance of a person whose right to benefit is, or may be, under Part VI of Schedule 7 to the Contributions and Benefits Act, affected by the decision appealed against, as well as at the instance of any person or body such as is mentioned in subsection (3) above.

(5) The following are the cases in which an appeal lies at the instance of a trade union—
    (a) where the claimant is a member of the union at the time of the appeal and was so immediately before the question at issue arose;
    (b) where that question in any way relates to a deceased person who was a member of the union at the time of his death;
    (c) where the case relates to industrial injuries benefit and the claimant or, in relation to industrial death benefit, the deceased, was a member of the union at the time of the relevant accident.

(6) Subsections (2), (3) and (5) above, as they apply to a trade union, apply also to any other association which exists to promote the interests and welfare of its members.

(7) Where the Commissioner holds that the decision was erroneous in point of law, he shall set it aside and—
    (a) he shall have power—
        (i) to give the decision which he considers the tribunal should have given, if he can do so without making fresh or further findings of fact; or
        (ii) if he considers it expedient, to make such findings and to give such decision as he considers appropriate in the light of them; and
    (b) in any other case he shall refer the case to a tribunal with directions for its determination.

(8) Subject to any direction of the Commissioner, the tribunal on a reference under subsection (7)(b) above shall consist of persons who were not members of the tribunal which gave the erroneous decision.

(9) No appeal lies under this section without the leave—
    (a) of the person who was the chairman of the tribunal when the decision was given or, in a prescribed case, the leave of some other chairman; or
    (b) subject to and in accordance with regulations, of a Commissioner.

(10) Regulations may make provision as to the manner in which, and the time within which, appeals are to be brought and applications made for leave to appeal.

DEFINITIONS
  "Commissioner": s.167.
  "prescribed": *ibid.*

GENERAL NOTE

Subs. (1)

There may only be an appeal from a decision under s.20 to the Commissioner on the ground that the SSAT made an error of law. See s.32 for attendance allowance, disability living allowance and disability working allowance cases. Note also the requirement under subs. (10) for leave to appeal to be given by the SSAT chairman (or a substitute) or a Commissioner. There are a number of other parts of the Commissioners' jurisdiction where appeal is on a point of law only and the well-established tests have been taken over here. In *R(SB) 6/81* the most accurate and concise summary is said to be that set out in *R(A) 1/72*. This holds that a decision would be wrong in law if:

(i) it contained a false proposition of law on its face;
(ii) it was supported by no evidence; or
(iii) the facts found were such that no person acting judicially and properly instructed as to the relevant law could have come to the determination in question. *CSB 29/81* refers to *R(I) 14/75*, which sets out the three heads quoted above and adds:
(iv) breach of the requirements of natural justice; and
(v) failure to state adequate reasons.

The formula of five headings is adopted in *R(SB) 11/83* (although by reference to decisions of the courts rather than the Commissioners) and is now clearly accepted. The result of the Court of Appeal's decision in the *Foster* case (see notes to s.19(1)) is that it is not an error of law under head (i) for a SSAT to apply a regulation which has not been validly made, but which has not been declared to be *ultra vires* in judicial review proceedings. In determining whether there is an error of law under head (iii) it is necessary to look at all the evidence presented to the tribunal, not only that recorded in the findings of fact or the chairman's notes of evidence. It is only if a decision cannot be supported looking at the totality of the evidence presented that an error of law is committed (*CSB 15/82, R(SB) 16/82, R(S) 1/88*). If an item of evidence was not before the SSAT, it cannot in itself be an error of law not to have considered it. The Great Britain Commissioners have held that they are not restricted to looking at the formal SSAT documents but may consider any reliable account of what evidence was presented (*CSB 34/81, R(SB) 10/82, R(SB) 18/83*). However, the approach to such accounts is somewhat cautious. The Commissioner in *R(SB) 10/82* suggested an over-elaborate procedure for the production of an account agreed between the parties to be referred to the SSAT chairman. That approach is rejected in *R(M)1/89*. The Tribunal of Commissioners there holds that it is a matter for the Commissioner's discretion what evidence about the proceedings to admit.

Subss. (2)–(6)

These provisions define the parties who may make an appeal from a SSAT in various kinds of cases and deal with trade unions and other organisations.

Subs. (7)

This important provision on the powers of the Commissioner seems oddly placed in the middle of s.21. Paragraph (a)(i) confirms the power of the Commissioner to give the decision the SSAT should have given where no further findings of fact are necessary. Paragraph (a)(ii) gives the power (new in 1987) for the Commissioner, when he considers it expedient, to make fresh or further findings of fact and then to give a decision in the light of those findings. The power has been used by Commissioners in a large number of appeals, including *R(SB) 11/88* and *CSB 176/1987*. In the first decision, the Commissioner held that the power existed from April 6, 1987 and that it did not matter that the SSAT decision was before that date. In the second, the Commissioner called for quite a lot of new evidence, although there was no real dispute over the facts. A Commissioner is more likely to send factual disputes back to a SSAT, although practice varies. The power is most often used where the SSAT has failed to make express findings on matters which are not in dispute or on which the result of the existing evidence is clear. There may be some difficulty if a Commissioner is making a decision partly on his own assessment of evidence and partly on the SSAT's assessment of evidence which the Commissioner has not directly heard or seen. If para. (a) does not apply, then under para. (b) the case must be referred to a SSAT with directions. These have normally included a direction that no members of the original SSAT should be on the new one, as is now expressly required by subs. (8) unless the Commissioner directs otherwise.

Subs. (9)

A party who wishes to appeal from a SSAT decision must get leave either from the chairman of the SSAT (or a substitute under reg. 26(4) of the Social Security (Adjudication) Regulations (Northern Ireland) 1987) (S.I. 1987 No. 465) or a Commissioner. Regulation 26 deals with the procedure for applying for leave to the chairman, and the time limit is three months (Adjudication Regulations, Sched. 2, para. 5). If the chairman refuses leave, a party has 42 days to apply to a Commissioner for leave (Social Security Commissioners Procedure Regulations (Northern Ireland) 1987 (S.I. 1992 No. 112), reg. 3). A Commissioner may deal with late applications if, for special reasons, he thinks fit (reg. 3(2) and (5)). A mere assertion of a mistake of law is not enough for leave to be granted. There must be some material in the case indicating that there is a sensible argument in support (*R(SB) 1/81*). There is, in the nature of things, not much further guidance given to chairmen about whether to give leave or not. The most helpful statement is in para. 30 of *R(S) 4/82*. The Commissioner stresses that the chairman's discretion is unfettered provided that it is exercised in a judicial manner, but says that chairmen should bear in mind that the object of requiring leave to be given is to restrict appeals to those which are neither hopeless nor frivolous and raise a serious issue. If the conduct of the tribunal's proceedings is seriously in question, leave should be given, but if the allegations are general, with no supporting detail, leave should be refused. The party always has another chance by applying to the Commissioner for leave. It is suggested that if the grounds put forward by the claimant or the AO do not contain any allegations of error of law (either expressly or by obvious implication) then the SSAT chairman should refuse leave to appeal. In particular, if the complaint is that the SSAT should have made a different decision on the facts, or that there is some new or different evidence which was not put to the SSAT (*R(S) 1/88* and Northern Ireland Commissioner's (unreported) Decision No. *C15/87* (Supp. B.)), that is not good enough. It is suggested that normally the chairman should not give leave simply because, on looking beyond the application, he considers that there might be some error of law in the SSAT's decision, such as inadequate findings of fact or reasons. That is something which is better dealt with by a Commissioner if the claimant or the AO makes a further application for leave to appeal.

If the Commissioner refuses leave to appeal, that is not a decision within the meaning of s.22 below and so cannot be appealed to the Court of Appeal (*Bland* v. *Chief Supplementary Benefits Officer* [1983] 1 All E.R. 537, *R(SB) 12/83*). There is no right of appeal from a refusal of leave by a chairman. The only right of appeal is from a decision of a SSAT.

Subs. (10)
See the Social Security (Adjudication) Regulations (Northern Ireland) 1987 (S.I. 1987 No. 82), regs. 3 and 26 and Sched. 2. See also the equivalent Great Britain Regulations, regs. 3 and 26 of and Sched. 2 to the Social Security (Adjudication) Regulations 1986 (S.I. 1986 No. 2218) (in Bonner *et al.* and Mesher), and the Social Security Commissioners (Procedure) Regulations (Northern Ireland) 1987 (S.I. 1987 No. 112).

Appeal from Commissioners on point of law

22.—(1) Subject to subsections (2) and (3) below, an appeal on a question of law shall lie to the appropriate court from any decision of a Commissioner.

(2) No appeal under this section shall lie from a decision except—

(a) with the leave of the Commissioner who gave the decision or, in a prescribed case, with the leave of a Commissioner selected in accordance with regulations; or

(b) if he refuses leave, with the leave of the appropriate court.

(3) An application for leave under this section in respect of a Commissioner's decision may only be made by—

(a) a person who, before the proceedings before the Commissioner were begun, was entitled to appeal to the Commissioner from the decision to which the Commissioner's decision relates;

(b) any other person who was a party to the proceedings in which the first decision mentioned in paragraph (a) above was given;

(c) the Department, in a case where it is not entitled to apply for leave by virtue of paragraph (a) or (b) above;

(d) any other person who is authorised by regulations to apply for leave; and regulations may make provision with respect to the manner in which and the time within which applications must be made to a Commissioner for leave under this section and with respect to the procedure for dealing with such applications.

(4) On an application to a Commissioner for leave under this section it shall be the duty of the Commissioner to specify as the appropriate court—

    (a) the Court of Appeal in Northern Ireland if it appears to him that the relevant place is in Northern Ireland;

    (b) the Court of Appeal if it appears to him that the relevant place is in England or Wales; and

    (c) the Court of Session if it appears to him that the relevant place is in Scotland,

except that if it appears to him, having regard to the circumstances of the case and in particular to the convenience of the persons who may be parties to the proposed appeal, that he should specify a different court mentioned in paragraphs (a) to (c) above as the appropriate court, it shall be his duty to specify that court as the appropriate court.

(5) In this section—

    "the appropriate court", except in subsection (4) above, means the court specified in pursuance of that subsection;

    "the relevant place", in relation to an application for leave to appeal from a decision of a Commissioner, means the premises where the authority whose decision was the subject of the Commissioner's decision usually exercises its functions.

(6) The powers to make regulations conferred by this section shall be exercisable by the Lord Chancellor.

DEFINITIONS
  "the Commissioner": s.167.
  "prescribed": *ibid.*

GENERAL NOTE
  This section provides for an appeal on a point of law to the Northern Ireland Court of Appeal, Court of Session in Scotland or Court of Appeal in England, as appropriate, from a decision of a Commissioner, with the leave of a Commissioner or the court. See the Social Security Commissioners (Procedure) Regulations (Northern Ireland) 1987 (S.I. 1987 No. 112) for the procedure applicable in Northern Ireland. A decision of a Commissioner to grant or refuse leave to appeal to the Commissioner is not a "decision" from which an appeal may lie under this section (*Bland* v. *Chief Supplementary Benefit Officer* [1983] 1 All E.R. 537). Decisions of the Northern Ireland Court of Appeal are binding on the Northern Ireland Commissioners, Tribunals and AOs. Their status in Great Britain is more complex. The Northern Ireland Court of Appeal is sitting in a separate jurisdiction, therefore in theory its decisions should not be binding in Great Britain. However, in *R(SB) 1/90* it was stated that, where there is parity between the two systems of social security, decisions of the Northern Ireland Court of Appeal are binding on Great Britain Commissioners and vice versa.

Reviews—general

Review of decisions

  23.—(1) Subject to the following provisions of this section, any decision under this Act of an adjudication officer, a social security appeal tribunal or a Commissioner (other than a decision relating to an attendance allowance, a disability living allowance or a disability working allowance) may be reviewed at any time by an adjudication officer or, on a reference by an adjudication officer, by a social security appeal tribunal, if—

    (a) the officer or tribunal is satisfied that the decision was given in ignorance of, or was based on a mistake as to, some material fact;

    (b) there has been any relevant change of circumstances since the decision was given;

    (c) it is anticipated that a relevant change of circumstances will so occur;

    (d) the decision was based on a decision of a question which under or by virtue of this Act falls to be determined otherwise than by an adjudication officer, and the decision of that question is revised; or

(e) the decision falls to be reviewed under section 57(4) or (5) of the Contributions and Benefits Act.

(2) Any decision of an adjudication officer (other than a decision relating to an attendance allowance, a disability living allowance or a disability working allowance) may be reviewed, upon the ground that it was erroneous in point of law, by an adjudication officer or, on a reference from an adjudication officer, by a social security appeal tribunal.

(3) Regulations may provide that a decision may not be reviewed on the ground mentioned in subsection (1)(a) above unless the officer or tribunal is satisfied as mentioned in that paragraph by fresh evidence.

(4) In its application to family credit, subsection (1)(b) and (c) above shall have effect subject to section 127(3) of the Contributions and Benefits Act (change of circumstances not to affect award or rate during specified period).

(5) Where a decision is reviewed on the ground mentioned in subsection (1)(c) above, the decision given on the review—

(a) shall take effect on the day prescribed for that purpose by reference to the date on which the relevant change of circumstances is expected to occur; and

(b) shall be reviewed again if the relevant change of circumstances either does not occur or occurs otherwise than on that date.

DEFINITIONS
"Commissioner": s.167.
"the Contributions and Benefits Act": *ibid.*
"prescribed": *ibid.*

GENERAL NOTE
Section 23 does not apply to attendance allowance, disability living allowance or disability working allowance. See ss.28–33 for reviews and appeals in those benefits.

Subs. (1)
Any decision to which s.23 applies may be reviewed by an AO on one of the five grounds set out in paras. (a)–(e). Where, as is normally the case for many benefits, an award is for an indefinite period (Social Security (Claims and Payments) Regulations (Northern Ireland) 1987 (S.I. 1987 No. 465), reg. 17(1)), any alteration to that award must be by way of review and revision. The principle flows from the fundamental rule in s.58 of the Administration Act that a decision on a claim, for whatever period covered by the decision, is final, subject to the processes of appeal or review (see *CSSB 544/1989* and the Common Appendix to the group of decisions including *CSSB 281/1989*).

There are a number of potential exceptions to this general principle. The first is under reg. 17(4) of the Social Security (Claims and Payments) Regulations (Northern Ireland) 1987 (S.I. 1987 No. 465), which is being used as the basis for submissions that awards made for days after the date of claim may be terminated whenever the claimant ceases to satisfy the conditions of entitlement. See the current edition of Mesher for the argument that the Great Britain reg. 17(4) may be *ultra vires* in so far as it has this effect. The second potential exception is that ss.135, 137, and 140 below provide for most alterations in rates of benefit and some prescribed figures to take effect automatically without the need for a decision by an AO. Where some kind of transitional addition to income support is in payment, review by an AO under reg. 69(3A) of the Social Security (Adjudication) Regulations (Northern Ireland) 1987 (S.I. 1987 No. 82) is necessary. Some powers of review in income support cases are given directly by reg. 69(4), and reg. 69(2) sets out circumstances in which review under s.23(1) is not to take place. However, outside these circumstances s.23(1) provides the general rule.

The significance of this is that it is clearly established (see, *e.g. CSB 376/1983* applying *R(I) 1/71* and *CI 11/77*) that the onus lies on the person wanting the review to establish both facts justifying the review and the correctness of the subsequent revised decision. Thus if, as in *CSB 376/1983*, the AO withdraws benefit on a change of circumstances when there is insufficient information to work out benefit, he has to justify the decision on the balance of probabilities. He cannot simply rely on the claimant not having proved his right to benefit. The same approach is taken in *CIS 1/1988* and *CIS 125/1989*. If it is the claimant requesting the review (*e.g.* by raising the question whether a previous decision denying benefit should be revised:

R(SB) 9/84), then the onus is on him. Although s.24(1) mentions an application in writing to the AO, a request for review may be oral or even implied (*CSB 336/1987*).

A number of recent Commissioner's decisions have illuminated the general area of review through a detailed examination of review in supplementary benefit cases (see the individual decisions noted in the 1991 Supplement to Mesher). The most general point is that in principle it is for the party seeking a review to identify the decision which he wishes to have reviewed. Only once that is done can any potential grounds for review be properly identified. However, if, as was often the case, the claimant was not properly notified of the exact terms of an AO's decision (see Social Security (Adjudication) Regulations (Northern Ireland) 1987 (S.I. 1987 No. 82), reg. 63), due allowances must be made (*CSSB 470/1989*). If what is being put forward is a change of circumstances after the date of the decision, it will not be so important to establish the grounds of the original decision. Secondly, doubt is cast on the proposition in *R(A) 2/90* that once one ground of review of a determination is established the whole determination is open to reconsideration (*CSSB 238/1989*). Even if this were right about an attendance allowance decision, the Commissioner holds that it does not apply to supplementary benefit decisions. Supplementary benefit awards (and, it would seem by analogy, income support awards) are made up of a continuing award co-existing with a series of review adjustments to particular elements of the award (*CSSB 238/189* and the Common Appendix to the group of decisions including *CSSB 281/1989*). Thus where there are grounds for review of one element this does not in itself allow review of any other elements. And if one element is revised on review, that does not affect the existence of the underlying continuing award or the other elements of it. Previous decisions appearing to suggest that a decision on review completely supersedes the decision reviewed are shown to be limited to decisions which are different in nature and are indivisible, such as decisions that an overpayment is recoverable (*CSB 64/1986* and *R(SB) 15/87*) or attendance allowance cases where the review is in effect the first stage of an appeal (*R(A) 5/89*). See also *R(SB) 1/82* and *R(P) 1/82*.

Perhaps the most controversial and difficult part of these decisions is the proposition that a request for review must be directed at the last operative decision dealing with the element of which review is sought (Common Appendix to group of decisions including *CSSB 281/1989*, as explained and expanded in *CSSB 238/1989* and *CSSB 544/1989*). If there has been a series of review decisions on that element, the chain must be traced backwards, at each decision asking whether grounds for review of the immediately preceding decision exist. However, the basis for this proposition has not yet been clearly established, and its application could cause considerable problems for claimants and for the DHSS. For instance, if an old award is discovered to have been based on a misrepresentation of a material fact, must the AO trace a chain of review back to the relevant decision in order to carry out the review and revision which is a necessary basis of a decision on recoverability of the overpayment under s.69?

Paras. (a)–(c)

The Social Security Commissioners have drawn a distinction between material facts and conclusions of fact (*e.g.* that a person is incapable of work, or is cohabiting). In *R(I) 3/75* (applied in *R(S) 4/86*) it is held that review is not allowed if the AO is simply satisfied that a mistaken inference was drawn from the evidence. He must go further and prove "that the inference might not have been drawn, or that a different inference might have been drawn, if the determining authority had not been ignorant of some specific fact of which it could have been aware, or had not been mistaken as to some specific fact which it took into consideration." This principle was also applied in *R(A) 2/81*. The Court of Appeal in England in *Saker* v. *Secretary of State for Social Services*, *The Times*, January 16, 1988 (*R(I) 2/88*) has expressly decided that for a fact to be material it is not necessary that knowledge of it would have altered the decision. It is enough that the fact is one that would have called for serious consideration by the authority which made the decision and might well have affected its decision. In *CA 90/1987*, the Commissioner applied this approach to the question of when a change of circumstances is relevant. This throws doubt on decisions such as *R(I) 56/54* and *R(A) 4/81*, where it is said that the change of circumstances must make the original decision cease to be correct. This test may be too stringent, given the authority of *Saker*, but a reported decision would clarify this important area. It is accepted that merely obtaining a different medical opinion is not a change of circumstances, although it may be evidence of an underlying change (*R(S) 6/78, R(S) 4/86*). A change in the law may amount to a change of circumstances (*R(A) 4/81*). It is not clear quite how subs. (2)'s allowing review where a decision was erroneous in law affects the principles noted above. If a wrong inference is drawn from correct primary facts because the wrong legal test is applied, that is clearly an error of law. If no person properly directing himself as to the law could have drawn that inference from those primary facts, then that will be an error of law (*cf. R(A) 1/72, R(I) 14/75*). But if the AO simply changes his mind about an "inference of fact" there has been no error of law.

Para. (d)

This paragraph applies where the benefit decision was based on a decision made by someone other than the AO, typically the Department. If that other decision is revised, the benefit decision is to be reviewed and revised in line with it.

Para. (e)

These provisions of the Contributions and Benefits (Northern Ireland) Act deal with availability and actively seeking work in unemployment benefit.

Regulations 65–71 of the Social Security (Adjudication) Regulations (Northern Ireland) 1987 (S.I. 1987 No. 82) prevent any revision on review in most cases from making benefit payable or increasing the amount of benefit payable before certain dates. The precise rule varies according to the benefit concerned. The test is usually of so many weeks before the date of the request for review. However, these provisions are now subject to reg. 64A, which has replaced the controversial reg. 72, allowing the limit to be lifted in deserving cases.

Subs. (2)

Note that only AO decisions may be reviewed on the ground of error of law, not decisions of SSATs or the Commissioners. Otherwise the provisions on appeals would be undermined. See notes to s.21 for "error of law". Review on this ground is subject to the restrictions of regs. 65–69 and 70 of the Adjudication Regulations (Northern Ireland) 1987, with the exemptions in reg. 64A.

Subs. (3)

No regulations have yet been made prescribing circumstances in which fresh evidence is required to trigger review.

Subs. (4)

Awards of family credit, which are normally made for a fixed period of 26 weeks, may not be reviewed on the ground of an actual or anticipated change of circumstances.

Subs. (5)

There are special rules where there is review in advance of an anticipated change of circumstances under subs. (1)(c). The decision on review takes effect on the date identified by para. 7 of Sched. 7 to the Claims and Payments Regulations. There must be a further review if the change does not happen at all, or happens on a different date.

Procedure for reviews

24.—(1) A question may be raised with a view to a review under section 23 above by means of an application in writing to an adjudication officer, stating the grounds of the application.

(2) On receipt of any such application, the adjudication officer shall proceed to deal with or refer any question arising on it in accordance with sections 19 to 21 above.

(3) Regulations may provide for enabling, or requiring, in prescribed circumstances, a review under section 23 above notwithstanding that no application for a review has been made under subsection (1) above.

GENERAL NOTE

Subs. (1)

Although this provides a useful procedure, it is not compulsory (*CSB 336/1987*). On general principle, review should occur at any time if the AO is satisfied that the conditions are met, wherever the evidence comes from. However, doubt was cast on this conclusion by the introduction of the predecessor of subs. (3) in 1987, after the time relevant to *CSB 336/1987*. In the Common Appendix to the group of decisions including *CSSB 281/1989*, the Commissioner suggests that the duty is on the Secretary of State (Department in Northern Ireland) to submit in writing to the AO any requests for review received, in whatever form, from claimants.

Subs. (3)

This power is only doubtfully necessary (see notes to subs. (1)). No regulations have yet been made.

Reviews under s.23—supplementary

25.—(1) Regulations—

(a) may prescribe what are, or are not, relevant changes of circumstances for the purposes of section 23 above; and

(b) may make provision restricting the payment of any benefit, or any increase of benefit, to which a person would, but for this subsection, be entitled by reason of a review in respect of any period before or after the review (whether that period falls wholly or partly before or after the making of the regulations).

(2) Regulations under subsection (1)(b) above shall not restrict the payment to or for a woman of so much of—

(a) any widow's benefit, any invalidity pension under section 40 of the Contributions and Benefits Act or any Category A or Category B retirement pension; or

(b) any increase of such a benefit or pension,

as falls to be paid by reason of a review which takes place by virtue of section 23(1)(a) or (b) above in consequence of a claim for a widowhood benefit, within the meaning of section 3 above, which is made or treated as made by virtue of that section.

DEFINITIONS
"prescribe": s.167.

GENERAL NOTE

Subs. (1)
No regulations have yet been made under para. (a) prescribing what counts as a change of circumstances. On para. (b) see regs. 65–71 of the Social Security (Adjudication) Regulations (Northern Ireland) 1987 (S.I. 1987 No. 82). See also the equivalent Great Britain Regulations, the Social Security (Adjudication) Regulations 1986 (S.I. 1986 No. 2218), and additional commentary in the current editions of Bonner *et al.* and Mesher.

Subs. (2)
There is a special rule removing the limits on backdating of increases on review of other benefits where a claim for widowhood benefits is made under s.3.

Appeals following reviews or refusals to review

26. A decision given on a review under section 23 above, and a refusal to review a decision under that section, shall be subject to appeal in like manner as an original decision, and sections 19 to 21 above shall, with the necessary modifications, apply in relation to a decision given on such a review as they apply to the original decision of a question.

GENERAL NOTE
The ordinary rights to appeal arise from a revised decision given on review or a refusal to review. This can be a useful way of getting round the time limits on appealing from an AO's decision. A request to review the decision will, if it does not produce all that the claimant wants, generate a fresh right of appeal.

Review after claimant appeals

27. Where a claimant has appealed against a decision of an adjudication officer and the decision is reviewed by an adjudication officer under section 23 above—

(a) if the adjudication officer considers that the decision which he has made on the review is the same as the decision that would have been made on the appeal had every ground of the claimant's appeal succeeded, the appeal shall lapse; but

(b) in any other case, the review shall be of no effect and the appeal shall proceed accordingly.

GENERAL NOTE

The predecessor of this provision made an important change in the relationship between review and appeals. Previously, it was established, at least in relation to some types of decision, that if a decision was reviewed it ceased to exist, being replaced by the decision made on review (*R(SB) 1/82, R(SB) 15/87*). The effect was that any appeal already lodged against the original decision would "lapse", because there was nothing left for the appeal to bite on (*R(A) 5/89*, which contains an authoritative review of all the earlier decisions). It is now clear from *CSSB 238/1989* that this only applies to decisions which are in their nature indivisible, like decisions that an overpayment is recoverable (*R(SB) 15/87*) or attendance allowance decisions reviewed in what is effectively the first stage of the appeal process (*R(A) 5/89*). In other cases, a review of one element of a decision leaves the rest of it intact (*R(P) 1/82*). Commissioners had in any event been able to get round the inconvenient effects of this principle in some circumstances, as by treating the appeal as against the revised decision although no notice of appeal had been given (*R(SB) 15/87*). The suggestion in *R(SB) 1/82* that if an appeal had been lodged a decision should not be reviewed unless the revised decision gave the claimant everything that could have been obtained in the appeal was only patchily applied.

Now, for reviews after April 5, 1990, if there is an appeal pending from an AO decision, a review is only of effect if the AO considers that the revised decision is the same as would have been made if every ground of the claimant's appeal had succeeded. In this case, but no other, the appeal lapses. This in effect turns on the AO's opinion, but, as a matter of general principle, if the claimant disputes that the revised decision is the same as if every ground of the appeal had succeeded, the issue ought to go to the SSAT in the original appeal, although the amendment to reg. 24(1) of the Social Security (Adjudication) Regulations (Northern Ireland) 1987 (S.I. 1987 No. 82) suggests otherwise.

Note that the grounds set out in the claimant's appeal are the crucial elements, not further arguments which might be raised against the AO's decision (see reg. 3(5) of the Adjudication Regulations (Northern Ireland) 1987).

Note also that s.27 only applies to reviews of AO decisions, not to reviews of SSAT or Commissioners' decisions.

Attendance allowance, disability living allowance and disability working allowance

Reviews of decisions of adjudication officers

28.—(1) On an application under this section made within the prescribed period, a decision of an adjudication officer under section 19 above which relates to an attendance allowance, a disability living allowance or a disability working allowance may be reviewed on any ground subject, in the case of a disability working allowance, to section 128(6) of the Contributions and Benefits Act.

(2) On an application under this section made after the end of the prescribed period, a decision of an adjudication officer under section 19 above which relates to an attendance allowance or a disability living allowance may be reviewed if—

(a) the adjudication officer is satisfied that the decision was given in ignorance of, or was based on a mistake as to, some material fact;

(b) there has been any relevant change of circumstances since the decision was given;

(c) it is anticipated that a relevant change of circumstances will so occur;

(d) the decision was erroneous in point of law; or

(e) the decision was to make an award for a period wholly or partly after the date on which the claim was made or treated as made but subject to a condition being fulfilled and that condition has not been fulfilled,

but regulations may provide that a decision may not be reviewed on the ground mentioned in paragraph (a) above unless the officer is satisfied as mentioned in that paragraph by fresh evidence.

(3) Regulations may prescribe what are, or are not, relevant changes of circumstances for the purposes of subsection (2)(b) and (c) above.

(4) On an application under this section made after the end of the prescribed period, a decision of an adjudication officer under section 19

above that a person is or was at any time terminally ill for the purposes of section 66(1), 72(5) or 73(12) of the Contributions and Benefits Act may be reviewed if there has been a change of medical opinion with respect to his condition or his reasonable expectation of life.

(5) On an application under this section made after the end of the prescribed period, a decision of an adjudication officer under section 19 above which relates to a disability working allowance may be reviewed if—

(a) the adjudication officer is satisfied that the decision was given in ignorance of, or was based on a mistake as to, some material fact;

(b) subject to section 128(6) of the Contributions and Benefits Act, there has been any prescribed change of circumstances since the decision was given;

(c) the decision was erroneous in point of law; or

(d) the decision was to make an award for a period wholly or partly after the date on which the claim was made or treated as made but subject to a condition being fulfilled and that condition has not been fulfilled,

but regulations may provide that a decision may not be reviewed on the ground mentioned in paragraph (a) above unless the officer is satisfied as mentioned in that paragraph by fresh evidence.

(6) The claimant shall be given such notification as may be prescribed of a decision which may be reviewed under this section and of his right to a review under subsection (1) above.

(7) A question may be raised with a view to a review under this section by means of an application made in writing to an adjudication officer stating the grounds of the application and supplying such information and evidence as may be prescribed.

(8) Regulations—

(a) may provide for enabling or requiring, in prescribed circumstances, a review under this section notwithstanding that no application under subsection (7) above has been made; and

(b) if they do so provide, shall specify under which provision of this section a review carried out by virtue of any such regulations falls.

(9) Reviews under this section shall be carried out by adjudication officers.

(10) Different aspects of any question which arises on such a review may be dealt with by different adjudication officers; and for this purpose this section and the other provisions of this Part of this Act which relate to reviews under this section shall apply with any necessary modifications.

(11) If a review is under subsection (1) above, the officer who took the decision under review shall not deal with any question which arises on the review.

(12) Except in prescribed circumstances, where a claim for a disability living allowance in respect of a person already awarded such an allowance by an adjudication officer is made or treated as made during the period for which he has been awarded the allowance, it shall be treated as an application for a review under this section.

(13) Where—

(a) a claim for an attendance allowance, a disability living allowance or a disability working allowance in respect of a person has been refused; and

(b) a further claim for the same allowance is made in respect of him within the period prescribed under subsection (1) above,

the further claim shall be treated as an application for a review under that subsection.

<small>DEFINITIONS</small>
"the Contributions and Benefits Act": s.167.
"prescribe": *ibid.*

GENERAL NOTE

Section 28 deals with two types of review in attendance allowance, disability living allowance and disability working allowance cases. The first, under subs. (1), is review as the first stage of appeal against the initial AO's decision. The second, under subss. (2) or (5), is the "ordinary" review, on similar grounds to those provided in s.23(1).

Subs. (1)

There is no provision in the legislation for an appeal from the initial decision of an AO under s.19 on an attendance allowance, disability living allowance or disability working allowance claim. Therefore, a claimant dissatisfied with the initial decision must apply for a review under this provision. The application must be made within the prescribed period, *i.e.* three months from the date on which notice of the AO's decision was given (Social Security (Adjudication) Regulations (Northern Ireland) 1987 (S.I. 1987 No. 82), reg. 26A. See also the Great Britain equivalent, Social Security (Adjudication) Regulations 1986 (S.I. 1986 No. 2218), reg. 26A, and additional commentary in the current editions of Mesher and Rowland). It seems that because review can only be considered "on an application under this section", the claimant must make an application and it must, under subs. (7), be made in writing to an AO. Although the words of subs. (7) are merely permissive, the words of subs. (1) seem to produce a different result from those of s.24(1). This is unfortunate, because review on specified grounds under subss. (2) or (5) is not available until after the end of the prescribed period unless there has already been a review under subs. (1). If, for instance, an AO notices just after an initial decision has been issued to the claimant that there has been an error of law, it appears that the decision cannot be reviewed unless the AO invites the claimant to apply for a review. Possibly an application could be made to the AO by a person acting on behalf of the Department.

Once an application has been made, review may be on any ground. This obviously covers mistake or ignorance of material facts as at the date of the decision or an error of law. But it can also cover a difference of opinion as to what conclusion to draw from the material facts and changes of circumstances after the date of the decision. However, there are a number of limitations. First, if the AO had made an award of disability working allowance, there can be no review on the basis of a change of circumstances (Contributions and Benefits (Northern Ireland) Act, s.128(6)). Second, if the AO's initial decision was not to make an award, any revised decision on review under subs. (1) cannot take effect before the date of the application for review (Social Security (Adjudication) Regulations (Northern Ireland) 1987 (S.I. 1987 No. 82), regs. 65(4C) and 70B(1)). This rule seems completely wrong if review is the first stage of the appeal process and it reveals that the decision has been mistaken from the outset, but it is clearly set out in the regulations.

If, after a decision refusing an award, a claimant makes a new claim during the prescribed period, it is to be treated as an application for review under subs. (1) (subs. (13)). The review is to be carried out by a different AO from the AO who made the initial decision (subss. (9) and (11)). The claimant has a right of appeal to a tribunal under s.33(1).

Subs. (2)

Subsection (2) applies to attendance allowance and disability living allowance. See the notes to subs. (1) for the argument that the opening words of this subsection mean that an application in writing to the AO is necessary before review can be considered. The argument that an application can be made on behalf of the Department is much stronger here, otherwise there would be no way of reviewing an award wrongly made to a claimant. Normally an application under subs. (2) has to be made after the end of the prescribed period of three months from the date on which notice of the AO's initial decision was given (Social Security (Adjudication) Regulations (Northern Ireland) 1987 (S.I. 1987 No. 82), reg. 26A(1)), but if there has been a decision on review under subs. (1), whether favourable or unfavourable to the claimant, then an application under subs. (2) can be made at any time to review that decision (s.29(1)).

See the notes to s.23(1)(a)–(c) and (2) for review under paras. (a)–(d). No regulations have been made requiring fresh evidence to be produced for para. (a), but see reg. 65(4A) of the Adjudication Regulations (Northern Ireland) 1987.

Paragraph (e) is roughly equivalent to reg. 17(4) of the Social Security (Claims and Payments) Regulations (Northern Ireland) 1987 (S.I. 1987 No. 465), which appears to apply a condition to awards of benefit including attendance allowance and disability living allowance.

If a person is dissatisfied with a refusal to review or a decision on review, then there must be an application for a further review under the conditions of subs. (1) before there can be an appeal to a tribunal (s.29(2)).

Subs. (3)

No regulations prescribing what counts or does not count as relevant changes of circumstances have yet been made.

Subs. (4)

Attendance allowance and the care component of disability living allowance can be awarded on the ground of terminal illness. Such awards are made for life. Subsection (4) allows review of such awards where there is a change of medical opinion about the claimant's condition or how long he is expected to live. Normally a change of medical opinion, as opposed to a change in the underlying facts, is not a change of circumstances (*R(S) 4/86*).

Subs. (5)

This provision applies to disability working allowance. See the notes to subs. (2) for the need for an application in writing. See the notes to s.25(1)(a) and (b) and (2) for review under paras. (a), (b) and (c). Section 128(6) of the Contributions and Benefits (Northern Ireland) Act prevents review of an award of disability working allowance, or of the level of benefit, on the ground of change of circumstances. No regulations have been made requiring fresh evidence to be produced for para. (a), but see reg. 70B(2) of the Adjudication Regulations.

Paragraph (d) is roughly equivalent to reg. 17(4) of the Social Security (Claims and Payments) Regulations (Northern Ireland) 1987 (S.I. 1987 No. 465), which appears to apply a condition to awards of benefit including disability working allowance. If a person is dissatisfied with a refusal to review or a decision on review, then there must be an application for a further review under the conditions of subs. (1) before there can be an appeal to a tribunal (s.29(2)).

Subs. (6)

Separate provision needs to be made for requiring notice of initial attendance allowance, disability living allowance and disability working allowance decisions and the right to apply for review under subs. (1) because of the exclusion in s.20(1).

Subs. (7)

This subsection says only that review "may" be started by an application in writing to an AO, but the wording of subss. (1), (2) and (5) seems to require there to be such an application. In the ordinary case the application will be made by the claimant, but if circumstances showing that a ground for review has arisen come to the DHSS's attention a person acting on behalf of the Department should make an application to the AO. Otherwise, there is no way of reviewing a decision based on a misrepresentation or failure to disclose material facts by the claimant. The principle should hold where the review would be in favour of the claimant. No regulations have been made specifying any particular information or evidence to be supplied with the application.

Subs. (8)

No regulations have been made under subs. (8).

Subss. (9)–(11)

Applications for review must be decided initially by an AO. There is no power for the AO to refer a question to a tribunal (s.19(3)). Where the review is under subs. (1) the AO who carries out the review must be a different person from the AO who made the initial decision.

Subs. (12)

If a person has an award of disability living allowance and makes another claim for the allowance during the period of the award, the claim is to be treated as an application for review. A common situation will be where a person has an award of one component of the allowance and makes a claim for the other component. See s.30(2)–(4) for the issues which arise on such a review.

Subs. (13)

If an AO's decision is to refuse the claim and another claim is made within the prescribed period (three months from the date of notice of the AO's decision: Social Security (Adjudication) Regulations (Northern Ireland) 1987 (S.I. 1987 No. 82), reg. 26A(1)), the claim is to be treated as an application for review under subs. (1). The first claim is then to be treated as having been made on the date of the second claim (Social Security (Claims and Payments) Regulations (Northern Ireland) 1987 (S.I. 1987 No. 465), reg. 6). In any case, any award made on the review could only take effect from that date (Adjudication Regulations (Northern Ireland) 1987, regs. 65(4A) and 70B(1)).

Further reviews

29.—(1) Subsections (2), (4) and (5) of section 28 above shall apply to a decision on a review under subsection (1) of that section as they apply to a decision of an adjudication officer under section 19 above but as if the words "made after the end of the prescribed period" were omitted from each subsection.

(2) Subsections (1), (2), (4) and (5) of section 28 above shall apply—

(a) to a decision on a review under subsection (2), (4) or (5) of that section; and

(b) to a refusal to review a decision under subsection (2), (4) or (5) of that section,

as they apply to a decision of an adjudication officer under section 19 above.

(3) The claimant shall be given such notification as may be prescribed—

(a) of a decision on a review under section 28 above;

(b) if the review was under section 28(1), of his right of appeal under section 31 below; and

(c) if it was under section 28(2), (4) or (5), of his right to a further review under section 28(1).

DEFINITIONS
"prescribed": s.167.

GENERAL NOTE

Subs. (1)
A decision on a review under s.28(1) may be reviewed as if it were an initial decision by an AO, but with no need to wait the prescribed three months.

Subs. (2)
If a person wishes to challenge a refusal to review under s.28(2), (4) or (5), there must first be an application for further review under s.28(1) before there can be an appeal to a tribunal.

Subs. (3)
Notice must be given to the claimant of all decisions on review under s.28 (which must include a refusal to review under s.28(5)) and of the appropriate rights of appeal or further review (Social Security (Adjudication) Regulations (Northern Ireland) 1987 (S.I. 1987 No. 82), reg. 20(1)). Separate provision is necessary because of the exclusion in s.20(1).

Reviews of decisions as to attendance allowance, disability living allowance or disability working allowance—supplementary

30.—(1) An award of an attendance allowance, a disability living allowance or a disability working allowance on a review under section 28 above replaces any award which was the subject of the review.

(2) Where a person who has been awarded a disability living allowance consisting of one component applies or is treated as applying for a review under section 28 above and alleges that he is also entitled to the other component, the adjudication officer need not consider the question of his entitlement to the component which he has already been awarded or the rate of that component.

(3) Where a person who has been awarded a disability living allowance consisting of both components applies or is treated as applying for a review under section 28 above and alleges that he is entitled to one component at a rate higher than that at which it has been awarded, the adjudication officer need not consider the question of his entitlement to the other component or the rate of that component.

(4) Where a person has been awarded a component for life, on a review under section 28 above the adjudication officer shall not consider the question of his entitlement to that component or the rate of that component or the period for which it has been awarded unless—

(a) the person awarded the component expressly applies for the consideration of that question; or

(b) information is available to the adjudication officer which gives him reasonable grounds for believing that entitlement to the component, or entitlement to it at the rate awarded or for that period, ought not to continue.

(5) No decision which relates to an attendance allowance or a disability living allowance shall be reviewed under section 28 above on the ground that the person is or was at any time terminally ill, within the meaning of section 66(2) of the Contributions and Benefits Act, unless an application for review is made expressly on that ground either—

(a) by the person himself; or

(b) by any other person purporting to act on his behalf, whether or not that other person is acting with his knowledge or authority;

and a decision may be so reviewed on such an application, notwithstanding that no claim under section 66(1), 72(5) or 73(12) of that Act has been made.

(6) Where a decision is reviewed under section 28 above on the ground that it is anticipated that a change of circumstances will occur, the decision given on review—

(a) shall take effect on the day prescribed for that purpose by reference to the date on which the change of circumstances is expected to occur; and

(b) shall be reviewed again if the change of circumstances either does not occur or occurs otherwise than on that date.

(7) Where a claimant has appealed against a decision of an adjudication officer under section 31 below and the decision is reviewed again under section 28(2), (4) or (5) above by an adjudication officer, then—

(a) if the adjudication officer considers that the decision which he has made on the review is the same as the decision that would have been made on the appeal had every ground of the appeal succeeded, then the appeal shall lapse; but

(b) in any other case, the review shall be of no effect and the appeal shall proceed accordingly.

(8) Regulations may make provision restricting the payment of any benefit, or any increase of benefit, to which a person would, but for this subsection, be entitled by reason of a review in respect of any period before or after the review (whether that period falls wholly or partly before or after the making of the regulations).

(9) Where an adjudication officer has determined that any amount paid by way of an attendance allowance, a disability living allowance or a disability working allowance is recoverable under or by virtue of section 69 below, any person from whom he has determined that it is recoverable shall have the same right of review under section 28 above as a claimant.

(10) This Act and the Contributions and Benefits Act shall have effect in relation to a review by virtue of subsection (9) above as if any reference to the claimant were a reference to the person from whom the adjudication officer has determined that the amount in question is recoverable.

DEFINITIONS
"the Contributions and Benefits Act": s.167.
"prescribed": *ibid.*

GENERAL NOTE

Subs. (1)
See reg. 65(4C) of the Social Security (Adjudication) Regulations (Northern Ireland) 1987 (S.I. 1987 No. 82) for the date from which a replacement award of attendance allowance or disability living allowance on review can take effect. See reg. 70B(1) for disability working allowance.

Subs. (2)
Where a person who has an award of one component of disability living allowance applies for

the other component (either by way of application for review or a purported fresh claim (see s.28(12)) the AO need not consider entitlement to the component which has already been awarded. However, the AO may consider that entitlement, subject to the restrictions in the case of life awards applied by subs. (4) below.

Subs. (3)

Subsection (3) applies a similar rule to that of subs. (2) to a case where a person has been awarded both components and applies for one of those components to be increased.

Subs. (4)

Where a person has been awarded a component of disability allowance for life, that award cannot be reviewed under s.28 unless either he specifically applies for review of that component (thus modifying subss. (2) and (3) above) or the AO has reasonable grounds for believing that entitlement to the particular level of component ought not to continue. This second condition is obviously necessary in order to allow review of awards in the case of unexpected improvement or mistaken initial decisions, where review will be initiated by the AO, but it can also apply where the review is initiated by the claimant.

Subs. (5)

Claims for attendance allowance or disability living allowance on the ground of terminal illness must be made expressly by reference to that ground (Contributions and Benefits (Northern Ireland) Act, ss.66(2) and 72(5)). This provision applies similar rules where there is an application to increase an existing award on that ground.

Subs. (6)

See s.28(2)(c).

Subs. (7)

See notes to s.27.

Subs. (8)

See regs. 65(4A) and 70B(2) of the Social Security (Adjudication) Regulations (Northern Ireland) 1987 (S.I. 1987 No. 82).

Subss. (9) and (10)

Where an AO has decided that an overpayment of attendance allowance, disability living allowance or disability working allowance has been made and is recoverable under s.69, the review and appeal process is the same as for an initial claim.

Appeals following reviews

31.—(1) Where an adjudication officer has given a decision on a review under section 28(1) above, the claimant or such other person as may be prescribed may appeal—

(a) in prescribed cases, to a disability appeal tribunal; and

(b) in any other case, to a social security appeal tribunal.

(2) Regulations may make provision as to the manner in which, and the time within which, appeals are to be brought.

(3) An award on an appeal under this section replaces any award which was the subject of the appeal.

(4) Where a person who has been awarded a disability living allowance consisting of one component alleges on an appeal that he is also entitled to the other component, the tribunal need not consider the question of his entitlement to the component which he has already been awarded or the rate of that component.

(5) Where a person who has been awarded a disability living allowance consisting of both components alleges on an appeal that he is entitled to one component at a rate higher than that at which it has been awarded, the tribunal need not consider the question of his entitlement to the other component or the rate of that component.

(6) The tribunal shall not consider—

(a) a person's entitlement to a component which has been awarded for life;

(b) the rate of a component so awarded; or
(c) the period for which a component has been so awarded,
unless—
(i) the appeal expressly raises that question; or
(ii) information is available to the tribunal which gives it reasonable grounds for believing that entitlement to the component, or entitlement to it at the rate awarded or for that period, ought not to continue.

DEFINITIONS
"prescribed": s.167.

GENERAL NOTE

Subs. (1)
Where there has been a review under s.28(1) following an initial decision on attendance allowance, disability living allowance or disability working allowance by an AO, the claimant may appeal to a tribunal. The effect of paras. (a) and (b) seems to be that if appeal to a disability appeal tribunal (DAT) is possible, that is where the appeal must go. It is only where appeal to the DAT is not possible that the appeal goes to the SSAT. Regulation 26C(1) of the Social Security (Adjudication) Regulations (Northern Ireland) 1987 (S.I. 1987 No. 82) prescribes that the claimant may appeal to the DAT where either a disability question or both a disability question and any other question relating to attendance allowance, disability living allowance or disability working allowance arises. Regulation 26C(2) defines what are disability questions. Broadly they are the medical issues arising on entitlement. Thus a SSAT may never consider a disability question, since if such a question first arises in the course of an appeal properly made to a SSAT, the SSAT cannot deal with it (s.34(2)). However, a DAT has to consider all the conditions of entitlement to an allowance if a disability question arises along with other matters.

Subs. (2)
See Sched. 2 to the Adjudication Regulations (Northern Ireland) 1987.

Subs. (3)
This provision confirms that an award of attendance allowance, disability living allowance or disability working allowance by a tribunal on appeal replaces any award made by the AO.

Subss. (4)–(6)
See the notes to s.30(2)–(4).

Appeal from social security appeal tribunals or disability appeal tribunals to Commissioners and appeals from Commissioners

32.—(1) Subject to the provisions of this section, an appeal lies to a Commissioner from any decision of a social security appeal tribunal or disability appeal tribunal under section 31 above on the ground that the decision of the tribunal was erroneous in point of law.

(2) An appeal lies under this section at the instance of any of the following—
(a) an adjudication officer;
(b) the claimant;
(c) a trade union—
　(i) where the claimant is a member of the union at the time of the appeal and was so immediately before the question at issue arose;
　(ii) where that question in any way relates to a deceased person who was a member of the union at the time of his death; and
(d) a person from whom it is determined that any amount is recoverable under section 69 below.

(3) Subsection (2) above, as it applies to a trade union, applies also to any other association which exists to promote the interests and welfare of its members.

(4) Subsections (7) to (10) of section 21 above have effect for the purposes of this section as they have effect for the purposes of that section.

(5) Section 22 above applies to a decision of a Commissioner under this section as it applies to a decision of a Commissioner under section 21 above.

DEFINITIONS
  "Commissioner": s.167.

GENERAL NOTE

Subs. (1)
  See notes to s.21(1).

Subss. (2) and (3)
  See notes to s.21(3), (5) and (6).

Subs. (4)
  See notes to s.21(7)–(10).

Subs. (5)
  See notes to s.22. Subsection (5) is probably redundant as s.22 was finally drafted.

Reviews of decisions on appeal

33.—(1) Any decision under this Act of a social security appeal tribunal, a disability appeal tribunal or a Commissioner which relates to an attendance allowance or a disability living allowance may be reviewed at any time by an adjudication officer if—
  (a) he is satisfied that the decision was given in ignorance of, or was based on a mistake as to, some material fact;
  (b) there has been any relevant change of circumstances since the decision was given;
  (c) it is anticipated that a relevant change of circumstances will so occur;
  (d) the decision was that a person is or was at any time terminally ill for the purposes of section 66(1), 72(5) or 73(12) of the Contributions and Benefits Act and there has been a change of medical opinion with respect to his condition or his reasonable expectation of life; or
  (e) the decision was to make an award for a period wholly or partly after the date on which the claim was made or treated as made but subject to a condition being fulfilled and that condition has not been fulfilled,
but regulations may provide that a decision may not be reviewed on the ground mentioned in paragraph (a) above unless the officer is satisfied as mentioned in that paragraph by fresh evidence.

(2) Regulations may prescribe what are, or are not, relevant changes of circumstances for the purposes of subsection (1)(b) and (c) above.

(3) Any decision under this Act of a social security appeal tribunal, a disability appeal tribunal or a Commissioner which relates to a disability working allowance may be reviewed at any time by an adjudication officer if—
  (a) he is satisfied that the decision was given in ignorance of, or was based on a mistake as to, some material fact;
  (b) subject to section 128(6) of the Contributions and Benefits Act, there has been any prescribed change of circumstances since the decision was given; or
  (c) the decision was to make an award for a period wholly or partly after the date on which the claim was made or treated as made but subject to a condition being fulfilled and that condition has not been fulfilled,
but regulations may provide that a decision may not be reviewed on the ground mentioned in paragraph (a) above unless the officer is satisfied as mentioned in that paragraph by fresh evidence.

(4) A question may be raised with a view to a review under this section by means of an application made in writing to an adjudication officer, stating the grounds of the application and supplying such information and evidence as may be prescribed.

(5) Regulations may provide for enabling or requiring, in prescribed circumstances, a review under this section notwithstanding that no application for a review has been made under subsection (4) above.

(6) Reviews under this section shall be carried out by adjudication officers.

(7) Except in prescribed circumstances, where a claim for a disability living allowance in respect of a person already awarded such an allowance on an appeal is made or treated as made during the period for which he has been awarded the allowance, it shall be treated as an application for a review under this section.

(8) Subsections (1), (2), (4) and (5) of section 28 above shall apply—

(a) to a decision on a review under this section; and

(b) to a refusal to review a decision such as is mentioned in subsection (1) above,

as they apply to a decision of an adjudication officer under section 19 above.

(9) The person whose claim was the subject of the appeal the decision on which has been reviewed under this section shall be given such notification as may be prescribed—

(a) of the decision on the review; and

(b) of his right to a further review under section 28(1) above.

(10) Regulations may make provision restricting the payment of any benefit, or any increase of benefit, to what a person would, but for this subsection, be entitled by reason of a review in respect of any period before or after the review (whether that period falls wholly or partly before or after the making of the regulations).

(11) Where a decision is reviewed on the ground mentioned in subsection (1)(c) above, the decision given on the review—

(a) shall take effect on the day prescribed for that purpose by reference to the date on which the relevant change of circumstances is expected to occur; and

(b) shall be reviewed again if the relevant change of circumstances either does not occur or occurs otherwise than on that date.

(12) Sections 28(10) and 30(1) to (5) above shall apply in relation to a review under this section as they apply to a review under section 28 above.

DEFINITIONS

"Commissioner": s.167.
"the Contributions and Benefits Act": *ibid.*
"prescribed": *ibid.*

GENERAL NOTE

Subs. (1)

Subsection (1) applies to attendance allowance and disability living allowance. See the notes to s.28(2). A decision of a SSAT, a DAT or a Commissioner cannot be reviewed as being erroneous in point of law, otherwise the appeal process would be subverted. Note that review under subs. (1) does not have to be "on an application made under this section". Therefore it seems that an application under subs. (4) is just one way of raising the question of review and that an AO can carry out a review without an application having been made.

Subs. (2)

No regulations have yet been made under this provision.

Subs. (3)

Subsection (3) applies to disability working allowance. See the notes to subs. (1) above, with the substitution of s.28(5). To make sense, the reference in para. (b) should be to s.128(6) of the Contributions and Benefits (Northern Ireland) Act, not s.128(7).

Subss. (4) and (5)
See notes to s.24(1) and (3). No regulations have been made under this subsection prescribing any information to be provided.

Subs. (7)
See s.28(12)

Subs. (8)
If the claimant is dissatisfied with the decision on a review under this section he must apply for a further review under s.30(1) before he can appeal to a tribunal.

Subs. (9)
See reg. 20(1) of the Adjudication Regulations.

Subs. (10)
See notes to s.28(8).

Questions first arising on appeal

Questions first arising on appeal

34.—(1) Where a question which but for this section would fall to be determined by an adjudication officer first arises in the course of an appeal to a social security appeal tribunal, a disability appeal tribunal or a Commissioner, the tribunal, subject to subsection (2) below, or the Commissioner may, if they or he think fit, proceed to determine the question notwithstanding that it has not been considered by an adjudication officer.

(2) A social security appeal tribunal may not determine a question by virtue of subsection (1) above if an appeal in relation to such a question would have lain to a disability appeal tribunal.

DEFINITIONS
"Commissioner": s.167.

GENERAL NOTE

Subs. (1)
A provision in similar terms to this has existed for some time for benefits which fell directly under the Social Security (Northern Ireland) Act 1975. There was an extension to the non-discretionary social fund, supplementary benefit and family income supplement in April 1987. Now s.34 applies generally. What is its effect? It might at first sight appear to allow a SSAT, DAT or Commissioner to go outside the purview of the appeal and decide any question about entitlement raised by the claimant. The Commissioner in *R(I) 4/75* says that the "useful" provision should be liberally construed. However, s.34 applies only to questions which arise in the course of an appeal. This does not mean in the course of the hearing of the appeal (*CS 101/1986*). The question must be connected with whatever question is properly before the tribunal or the Commissioner in the appeal. Similarly, it is confirmed in *CS 104/1987* that s.34 can only be invoked where the question first arises in the course of an appeal. Thus if an AO has decided a question, from which decision no appeal has been made, the tribunal cannot deal with that question under s.34 as it does not first arise in the course of the appeal. The suggestion in *CS 101/1986* that the section could be used where a question might have been referred to the SSAT, but was not, might then be restricted to cases where the AO has not made a decision on that question. In addition, there are two controls. First, the tribunal or the Commissioner has a discretion to decide the new question. It may consider the argument that when the only appeal from the tribunal is on the ground of error of law, the claimant may be deprived of a stage in the appeal process if the tribunal, rather than the AO, makes an initial decision. Second, the principles of natural justice would require that a tribunal or Commissioner should not make a decision on a new point if all parties have not had a fair opportunity of dealing with it (*R(F) 1/72*).

Subs. (2)
If a SSAT is hearing an appeal on attendance allowance, disability living allowance or disability working allowance and a disability question arises for the first time, then the SSAT

cannot deal with that question. If there is such a disability question (with or without some other point in dispute) when an appeal is made, the whole appeal goes to the DAT (s.31(1) and Social Security (Adjudication) Regulations (Northern Ireland) 1987 (S.I. 1987 No. 82), reg. 26C). It appears, however, that if an appeal has properly gone to the SSAT before the disability question first arises, then the SSAT should continue to deal with the questions raised in the original appeal. By definition, the disability question must have been decided by the AO under s.28(1) in the claimant's favour, otherwise the appeal would already be before the DAT. If something comes to light in the SSAT appeal which casts doubt on that, but the SSAT determines all the other questions in the claimant's favour, there is a difficult question on the SSAT's proper course of action. Should it make an award of benefit, and leave the AO to review that award under s.33(3), or simply determine the questions before it and leave the AO to review the disability question? On balance, the first alternative seems more in line with the scheme of the legislation.

Reference of special questions

Reference of special questions

35.—(1) Subject to subsection (2) below—
  (a) if on consideration of any claim or question an adjudication officer is of opinion that there arises any question which under or by virtue of this Act falls to be determined otherwise than by an adjudication officer, he shall refer the question for such determination; and
  (b) if on consideration of any claim or question a social security appeal tribunal or Commissioner is of opinion that any such question arises, the tribunal or Commissioner shall direct it to be referred by an adjudication officer for such determination.
  (2) The person or tribunal making or directing the reference shall then deal with any other question as if the referred question had not arisen.
  (3) The adjudication officer, tribunal or Commissioner may—
  (a) postpone the reference of, or dealing with, any question until other questions have been determined;
  (b) in cases where the determination of any question disposes of a claim or any part of it, make an award or decide that an award cannot be made, as to the claim or that part of it, without referring or dealing with, or before the determination of, any other question.

DEFINITIONS
  "Commissioner": s.167.
  "the Department": *ibid.*

GENERAL NOTE
  If an AO, a SSAT or a Commissioner considers that a question arises which has to be decided by someone else (*e.g.* the Department under s.15) then that question must be referred to the other person.

Adjudication officers and the Chief Adjudication Officer

Adjudication officers

36.—(1) Adjudication officers shall be appointed by the Department, subject to the consent of the Department of Finance and Personnel as to number, and may include officers of the Department of Social Security appointed with the concurrence of the Secretary of State.
  (2) An adjudication officer may be appointed to perform all the functions of adjudication officers under any enactment or such functions of such officers as may be specified in his instrument of appointment.

DEFINITIONS
  "the Department": s.167.

GENERAL NOTE

Subs. (1)
The Department is not obliged to appoint enough AOs to dispose of all claims submitted to them within 14 days under s.19(1) (*R.* v. *Secretary of State for Social Services*, ex p. *Child Poverty Action Group* [1990] 2 Q.B. 540).

Subs. (2)
The current instrument of appointment was signed by the Department of Health and Social Services on December 19, 1986 and is reproduced as Appendix 1 to Pt. 01 of the Adjudication Officer's Guide for Northern Ireland. It directs that all persons appointed shall carry out all the functions of AOs, unless specifically designated to exercise only specified functions. In practice, most AOs will deal with only a limited number of benefits but will formally have the power to carry out any AO function.
See reg. 64 of the Social Security (Adjudication) Regulations (Northern Ireland) 1987 (S.I. 1987 No. 82) for the consequences of the limited practical range of expertise of individual AOs.

The Chief Adjudication Officer

37.—(1) The Department shall appoint for Northern Ireland a Chief Adjudication Officer.

(2) It shall be the duty of the Chief Adjudication Officer to advise adjudication officers on the performance of their functions under this or any other enactment.

(3) The Chief Adjudication Officer shall keep under review the operation of the system of adjudication officers and matters connected with the operation of that system.

(4) The Chief Adjudication Officer shall report annually in writing to the Department on the standards of adjudication and the Department shall publish his report.

GENERAL NOTE
The Northern Ireland Chief Adjudication Officer combines the functions of the former Chief Insurance Officer and the Chief Supplementary Benefit Officer, but his advisory duties were only given statutory expression for the first time in 1984. The duty to report publicly on standards of adjudication was also new. The Northern Ireland CAO's first report was published for the period 1984–85. The most recent report (1989–90) contains some interesting material on the relationship of the adjudication system with the Benefits Agency.

Social security appeal tribunals

Panels for appointment to social security appeal tribunals

38.—(1) The President shall constitute for the whole of Northern Ireland to act for such areas as he thinks fit and to be composed of such persons as he thinks fit to appoint, panels of persons to act as members of social security appeal tribunals.

(2) The panel for an area shall be composed of persons appearing to the President to have knowledge or experience of conditions in the area and to be representative of persons living or working in the area.

(3) Before appointing members of a panel, the President shall take into consideration any recommendations from such organisations or persons as he considers appropriate.

(4) The members of the panels shall hold office for such period as the President may direct, but the President may at any time terminate the appointment of any member of a panel.

DEFINITIONS
"President": s.167.

GENERAL NOTE
One of the responsibilities of the President of social security appeal tribunals, etc., is to

appoint a panel of persons to act as members of a SSAT. The test for appointment under subs. (2) is a dual one. The member must have knowledge or experience of conditions in the area to which the appointment applies and be representative of persons living or working in the area. The first part seems to be a watered-down version of the old supplementary benefit appeal tribunal test for "Department's" members, omitting the requirement of knowledge or experience of the problems of people living on low incomes. This requirement was presumably thought inappropriate to the wider jurisdiction of the SSAT, but it is a pity that it should be lost altogether.

It is far from clear what the "representative" test requires. The intention apparently is that the range of organisations consulted about membership under subs. (3) should be widened out from Trade Councils, Chambers of Commerce, etc., to include groups representing the disabled, one-parent families, etc. This is laudable in an attempt to secure a balanced panel, although of course it does not secure any specific balance on an individual tribunal. In theory the member does not have to be nominated by an organisation. However, in practice in Northern Ireland members still come from one of these groups: (i) employers' organisations; (ii) employees' associations; (iii) voluntary organisations. Efforts are then made to ensure a balance on individual tribunals.

Constitution of social security appeal tribunals

39.—(1) A social security appeal tribunal shall consist of a chairman and two other persons.

(2) The members other than the chairman shall be drawn from the appropriate panel constituted under section 38 above.

(3) The President shall nominate the chairman.

(4) The President may nominate as chairman—

(a) himself;

(b) one of the full-time chairmen appointed under section 49(1)(b) below; or

(c) a person drawn from the panel appointed by the Lord Chancellor under section 49(1)(c) below.

(5) If practicable, at least one of the members of the appeal tribunal hearing a case shall be of the same sex as the claimant.

(6) Schedule 2 to this Act shall have effect for supplementing this section.

DEFINITIONS
"President": s.167.

GENERAL NOTE

Subs. (1)
For the appointment of chairmen see subss. (3)–(5). For the appointment of the other members, see subs. (2). For an overriding condition on the composition of each particular tribunal hearing an appeal, see subs. (6).

Subs. (2)
The old division between the Trades Council members and the Department's members on supplementary benefit appeal tribunals and between employers' and employees' representatives on national insurance local tribunals has gone. There is no longer any guarantee of having a member from any particular background on any individual tribunal. Members need no longer be summoned in turn to sit on tribunals. See s.38 for appointment to the panel of members.

Subs. (4)
The panel referred to in para. (c) is of the ordinary part-time chairmen of SSATs, appointed by the Lord Chancellor. Since 1984 chairmen have had to have professional legal qualifications. However, even prior to 1984 all but two of the chairpersons in Northern Ireland were legally qualified. The fact that legal qualifications became mandatory was probably inevitable in view of the excessive legalisation of the supplementary benefit system. What remains controversial is the requirement of professional legal qualifications (which, to put it kindly, do not guarantee any knowledge of, or interest in, social security law), rather than some other evidence of legal skills (*e.g.* a law degree).

Subs. (5)
This provision causes difficulty while just under 25 per cent. of members are women

(although 13 out of the 34 chairpersons are women). The President's policy on appointments is to attempt to redress this imbalance. The Commissioner in *R(SB) 2/88* holds that practicability imposes quite a strict requirement. The provision is mandatory, and if the SSAT does not have a member of the same sex as the claimant it must be shown that it was not practicable to do otherwise. This cannot be presumed. The chairman should ask the clerk about the circumstances, and endorse the record of decision (AT3) accordingly. If non-practicability cannot be proved the SSAT's decision will be in error of law even though the claimant consents to the hearing continuing. If it is not practicable to have a member of the same sex as the claimant it might be appropriate to offer the claimant an adjournment.

Disability appeal tribunals

Panels for appointment to disability appeal tribunals

40.—(1) The President shall constitute for the whole of Northern Ireland, to act for such areas as he thinks fit and be composed of such persons as he thinks fit to appoint, panels of persons to act as members of disability appeal tribunals.

(2) There shall be two panels for each area.

(3) One panel shall be composed of medical practitioners.

(4) The other shall be composed of persons who are experienced in dealing with the needs of disabled persons—

(a) in a professional or voluntary capacity; or

(b) because they are themselves disabled,

but may not include medical practitioners.

(5) In considering the appointment of members of the panels the President shall have regard to the desirability of appointing disabled persons.

(6) Before appointing members of a panel, the President shall take into consideration any recommendations from such organisations or persons as he considers appropriate.

(7) The members of the panels shall hold office for such periods as the President may direct, but the President may at any time terminate the appointment of any member of a panel.

DEFINITIONS
  "President": s.167.

GENERAL NOTE
  See s.38 for the general pattern. The distinctive feature of disability appeal tribunals is that the members other than the chairman must come respectively from the two panels set up under s.40. One panel is of medical practitioners. In practice, these are general practitioners, rather than those of consultant status who sit on medical appeal tribunals. The second panel is of people experienced in dealing with the needs of disabled persons, because of either personal disability or professional or voluntary experience. Because of the issues dealt with by DATs and the move away from medical testing, such people are considered to be particularly qualified to assess the needs of disabled people. There is no guarantee that the member of the DAT deciding a particular claimant's appeal will have any experience of the claimant's particular needs.

Constitution of disability appeal tribunals

41.—(1) A disability appeal tribunal shall consist of a chairman and two other persons.

(2) Of the members of a tribunal other than the chairman, one shall be drawn from the panel mentioned in subsection (3) of section 40 above.

(3) The other shall be drawn from the panel mentioned in subsection (4) of that section.

(4) The President shall nominate the chairman.

(5) The President may nominate as chairman—

(a) himself;

(b) one of the full-time chairmen appointed under section 49(1)(b) below; or

(c) a person drawn from the panel appointed by the Lord Chancellor under section 49(1)(c) below.

(6) In summoning members of a panel to serve on a tribunal, the clerk to the tribunal shall have regard to the desirability of at least one of the members of the tribunal being a disabled person.

(7) If practicable, at least one of the members of the tribunal shall be of the same sex as the claimant.

(8) Schedule 2 to this Act shall have effect for supplementing this section.

DEFINITIONS
"President": s.167.

GENERAL NOTE
See s.39. One member must be drawn from each of the two panels set up under s.40. Subsection (6) requires the clerk to consider the desirability of one of the members of the disability appeal tribunal being disabled. The chairman and the medical practitioner member can count for this purpose, and there is no definition of disability. The requirement cannot be more extensive or carers would rarely be able to sit as members.

Declaration that accident is an industrial accident

42.—(1) Where, in connection with any claim for industrial injuries benefit, it is determined that the relevant accident was or was not an industrial accident, an express declaration of that fact shall be made and recorded and (subject to subsection (3) below) a claimant shall be entitled to have the question whether the relevant accident was an industrial accident determined notwithstanding that his claim is disallowed on other grounds.

(2) Subject to subsection (3) below and to section 58 below, any person suffering personal injury by accident shall be entitled, if he claims the accident was an industrial accident, to have that question determined, and a declaration made and recorded accordingly, notwithstanding that no claim for benefit has been made in connection with which the question arises; and this Part of this Act applies for that purpose as if the question had arisen in connection with a claim for benefit.

(3) The adjudication officer, social security appeal tribunal or Commissioner (as the case may be) may refuse to determine the question whether an accident was an industrial accident if satisfied that it is unlikely to be necessary to determine the question for the purposes of any claim for benefit; but any such refusal of an adjudication officer or social security appeal tribunal shall be subject to appeal to a social security appeal tribunal or Commissioner, as the case may be.

(4) Subject to the provisions of this Part of this Act as to appeal and review, any declaration under this section that an accident was or was not an industrial accident shall be conclusive for the purposes of any claim for industrial injuries benefit in respect of that accident.

(5) Where subsection (4) above applies—
(a) in relation to a death occurring before 11th April 1988; or
(b) for the purposes of section 60(2) of the Contributions and Benefits Act,
it shall have effect as if at the end there were added the words "whether or not the claimant is the person at whose instance the declaration was made".

(6) For the purposes of this section (but subject to section 58(3) below), an accident whereby a person suffers personal injury shall be deemed, in relation to him, to be an industrial accident if—
(a) it arises out of and in the course of his employment;
(b) that employment is employed earner's employment for the purposes of Part V of the Contributions and Benefits Act;
(c) payment of benefit is not under section 94(5) of that Act precluded because the accident happened while he was outside Northern Ireland.

(7) A decision under this section shall be final except that sections 23 to 27 above apply to a decision under this section that an accident was or was not an industrial accident as they apply to a decision under sections 19 to 21 above if, but only if, the adjudication officer or social security appeal tribunal, as the case may be, is satisfied that the decision under this section was given in consequence of any wilful non-disclosure or misrepresentation of a material fact.

DEFINITIONS
   "Commissioner": s.167.
   "the Contributions and Benefits Act": *ibid.*
   "industrial injuries benefit": *ibid.*

GENERAL NOTE
   A declaration that a person has suffered an industrial accident may be obtained even though no current award of benefit is made, or even claimed, provided that it might be relevant to some future claim.

Disablement questions

43.—(1) In relation to industrial injuries benefit and severe disablement allowance, the "disablement questions" are the questions—
   (a) in relation to industrial injuries benefit, whether the relevant accident has resulted in a loss of faculty;
   (b) in relation to both benefits, at what degree the extent of disablement resulting from a loss of faculty is to be assessed, and what period is to be taken into account by the assessment;
but questions relating to the aggregation of percentages of disablement resulting from different accidents are not disablement questions (and accordingly fall to be determined by an adjudication officer).
   (2) Subject to and in accordance with regulations, the disablement questions shall be referred to and determined—
   (a) by an adjudicating medical practitioner;
   (b) by two or more adjudicating medical practitioners;
   (c) by a medical appeal tribunal; or
   (d) in such cases relating to severe disablement allowance as may be prescribed, by an adjudication officer.
   (3) Where—
   (a) the case of a claimant for disablement benefit has been referred by the adjudication officer to one or more adjudicating medical practitioners for determination of the disablement questions; and
   (b) on that or any subsequent reference, the extent of the disablement is provisionally assessed,
the case shall again be referred under this section, to one or more adjudicating medical practitioners as regulations may provide for the purposes of such subsequent references, not later than the end of the period taken into account by the provisional assessment.
   (4) Where, in the case of a claimant for disablement benefit, the extent of any disablement of his resulting from an aggregable accident (that is to say, an accident other than the one which is the basis of the claim in question) has been assessed in accordance with paragraph 6(3) of Schedule 6 to the Contributions and Benefits Act at less than 14 per cent., then—
   (a) the adjudication officer may refer the disablement questions relating to the aggregable accident to one or more adjudicating medical practitioners for fresh determination; and
   (b) on any such reference—
      (i) those questions shall be determined as at the first day of the common period; and
      (ii) the period to be taken into account shall be the period beginning with that day.

(5) In subsection (4) above "the first day of the common period" means whichever is the later of—

(a) the first day of the period taken into account by the assessment of the extent of the claimant's disablement resulting from the accident which is the basis of the claim in question;

(b) the first day of the period taken into account by the assessment of the extent of his disablement resulting from the aggregable accident.

(6) In the following provisions of this Act "adjudicating medical practitioner" means, in relation to any case, one such practitioner, unless regulations applicable to cases of that description provide for references to more than one.

DEFINITIONS
"industrial injuries benefit": s.167.

GENERAL NOTE
"Disablement questions" are subject to a special route for adjudication. The initial determination is normally by one or two adjudicating medical practitioners, with an appeal to a medical appeal tribunal. See Section D of Pt. III of the Social Security (Adjudication) Regulations (Northern Ireland) 1987 (S.I. 1987 No. 465). "Disablement questions" are whether there is a loss of faculty in an industrial injuries benefits case, and at what percentage the resulting disablement should be assessed, and the percentage of disablement in severe disablement allowance cases.

See also the detailed discussion on the equivalent Great Britain legislation in the current edition of Rowland.

Medical appeals and references

44.—(1) This section has effect where the case of a claimant for disablement benefit or severe disablement allowance has been referred by the adjudication officer to an adjudicating medical practitioner for determination of the disablement questions.

(2) Subject to subsection (3) below, if the claimant is dissatisfied with the decision of the adjudicating medical practitioner, he may appeal in the prescribed manner and within the prescribed time, and the case shall be referred to a medical appeal tribunal.

(3) If—

(a) the Department notifies the adjudication officer within the prescribed time that it is of the opinion that any decision of the adjudicating medical practitioner ought to be considered by a medical appeal tribunal; or

(b) the adjudication officer is of the opinion that any such decision ought to be so considered,

the adjudication officer shall refer the case to a medical appeal tribunal for their consideration, and the tribunal may confirm, reverse or vary the decision in whole or in part as on an appeal.

GENERAL NOTE
Section 44 provides for a right of appeal by a claimant from a decision of adjudicating medical practitioners to a medical appeal tribunal. The adjudication officer may refer such a decision to a MAT under the conditions in subs. (3).

Review of medical decisions

45.—(1) Any decision under this Act of an adjudicating medical practitioner or a medical appeal tribunal may be reviewed at any time by an adjudicating medical practitioner if satisfied that the decision was given in ignorance of a material fact or was based on a mistake as to a material fact.

(2) Any decision under this Act of an adjudicating medical practitioner may be reviewed at any time by such a practitioner if he is satisfied that the decision was erroneous in point of law.

(3) Regulations may provide that a decision may not be reviewed under subsection (1) above unless the adjudicating medical practitioner is satisfied as mentioned in that subsection by fresh evidence.

(4) Any assessment of the extent of the disablement resulting from the relevant loss of faculty may also be reviewed by an adjudicating medical practitioner if he is satisfied that since the making of the assessment there has been an unforeseen aggravation of the results of the relevant injury.

(5) Where in connection with a claim for disablement benefit made after 20th October 1953 it is decided that the relevant accident has not resulted in a loss of faculty, the decision—

   (a) may be reviewed under subsection (4) above as if it were an assessment of the extent of disablement resulting from a relevant loss of faculty; but

   (b) subject to any further decision on appeal or review, shall be treated as deciding the question whether the relevant accident had so resulted both for the time about which the decision was given and for any subsequent time.

(6) For the purposes of subsection (5) above, a final assessment of the extent of the disablement resulting from a loss of faculty made for a period limited by reference to a definite date shall be treated as deciding that at that date the relevant accident had not resulted in a loss of faculty.

(7) An assessment made, confirmed or varied by a medical appeal tribunal shall not be reviewed under subsection (4) above without the leave of a medical appeal tribunal, and (notwithstanding the provisions of Part V of the Contributions and Benefits Act) on a review under that subsection the period to be taken into account by any revised assessment shall only include a period before the date of the application for the review if and in so far as regulations so provide.

(8) Subject to the foregoing provisions of this section, an adjudicating medical practitioner may deal with a case on a review in any manner in which he could deal with it on an original reference to him, and in particular may in any case relating to disablement benefit make a provisional assessment notwithstanding that the assessment under review was final.

(9) Section 44 above applies to an application for a review under this section and to a decision of an adjudicating medical practitioner in connection with such an application as it applies to an original claim for disablement benefit or severe disablement allowance, as the case may be, and to a decision of an adjudicating medical practitioner in connection with such a claim.

(10) In subsection (6) above the reference to a final assessment does not include an assessment made for the purpose of section 12(1)(a) or (b) of the National Insurance (Industrial Injuries) Act (Northern Ireland) 1946 as originally enacted and having the effect that benefit is not payable.

DEFINITIONS
   "the Contributions and Benefits Act": s.167.

GENERAL NOTE

Subs. (1)
   Decisions of an adjudicating medical practitioner or a MAT may be reviewed on the ground of ignorance of or mistake as to a material fact (see notes to s.23(1)). No regulations have yet been made under subs. (3).

Subs. (2)
   Decisions of adjudicating medical practitioners, but not MATs, can be reviewed for error of law.

Subs. (4)
   This is an important provision in the scheme of industrial injuries benefits. An assessment of

disablement (including by virtue of subss. (5) and (6) decisions that there is no loss of faculty) is to be reviewed if there has been unforeseen aggravation of the results of the industrial injury or disease since the assessment was made. Thus an assessment can be varied upwards if the outcome turns out to be worse than was originally thought or the disablement continues for longer than was originally thought. Any revised assessment can only take effect from a date three months before the date of the application for review (subs. (7) and Social Security (Adjudication) Regulations (Northern Ireland) 1987 (S.I. 1987 No. 465), reg. 68).

Subs. (7)
An assessment made by a MAT cannot be reviewed under subs. (4) unless leave has been given by a MAT. On the date from which a revised assessment can take effect, see the note to subs. (4).
See also Rowland for further discussion.

Appeal etc. on question of law to Commissioner

46.—(1) Subject to this section, an appeal lies to a Commissioner from any decision of a medical appeal tribunal (if given after 6th April 1987) on the ground that the decision is erroneous in point of law, at the instance of—
  (a) an adjudication officer;
  (b) the claimant;
  (c) a trade union of which the claimant was a member at the time of the relevant accident or, in a case relating to severe disablement allowance, at the prescribed time; or
  (d) the Department.
  (2) Subsection (1) above, as it applies to a trade union, applies also to any other association which exists to promote the interests and welfare of its members.
  (3) No appeal lies under subsection (1) above without the leave—
  (a) of the person who was the chairman of the medical appeal tribunal when the decision was given or, in a prescribed case, the leave of some other chairman of a medical appeal tribunal; or
  (b) subject to and in accordance with regulations, of a Commissioner, and regulations may make provision as to the manner in which, and the time within which, appeals are to be brought and applications made for leave to appeal.
  (4) On any such appeal, the question of law arising for the decision of the Commissioner and the facts on which it arises shall be submitted for his consideration in the prescribed manner.
  (5) Where the Commissioner holds that the decision was erroneous in point of law he shall set it aside and refer the case to a medical appeal tribunal with directions for its determination.
  (6) Subject to any direction of the Commissioner, the tribunal on a reference under subsection (5) above shall consist of persons who were not members of the tribunal which gave the erroneous decision.

DEFINITIONS
  "claimant": s.167.
  "Commissioner": *ibid*.

GENERAL NOTE
  An appeal lies from a decision of a medical appeal tribunal to the Social Security Commissioner on the ground that the decision was erroneous in point of law. Leave must be given by the MAT chairman or by the Commissioner. If the Commissioner decides that the decision was erroneous in point of law the case must be referred to a new MAT (subss. (5) and (6)).
  See also the detailed discussion on the Great Britain equivalents in the current edition of Rowland.

Adjudicating medical practitioners and medical appeal tribunals

Adjudicating medical practitioners

47.—(1) Adjudicating medical practitioners shall be appointed by the Department.

(2) The Department may make arrangements whereby any adjudicating medical practitioners for the purposes of the Great Britain Administration Act shall be adjudicating medical practitioners for the purposes of this Act.

(3) Subject to subsections (1) and (2) above, the appointment of adjudicating medical practitioners shall be determined by regulations.

Constitution of medical appeal tribunals

48.—(1) A medical appeal tribunal shall consist of a chairman and two other persons.

(2) The members other than the chairman shall be medical practitioners appointed by the President after consultation with such academic medical bodies as appear to him to be appropriate.

(3) The President shall nominate the chairman.

(4) The President may nominate as chairman—

(a) himself;

(b) one of the full-time chairmen appointed under section 49(1)(b) below; or

(c) a person drawn from the panel appointed by the Lord Chancellor under section 49(1)(c) below.

(5) The Department may make arrangements whereby a medical appeal tribunal for the purposes of the Great Britain Administration Act shall be a medical appeal tribunal for the purposes of this Act.

(6) Subject to subsections (1) to (4) above, the constitution of medical appeal tribunals shall be determined by regulations.

(7) Schedule 2 to this Act shall have effect for supplementing this section.

DEFINITIONS
"President": s.167.

GENERAL NOTE
See the notes to s.39. The medical practitioners appointed as members are of consultant status. There is no longer any extra qualification for MAT chairmen over those for SSAT and DAT chairmen.

The President and chairmen of tribunals

The President of social security appeal tribunals, medical appeal tribunals and disability appeal tribunals and chairmen

49.—(1) The Lord Chancellor may appoint for Northern Ireland—

(a) a President of social security appeal tribunals, medical appeal tribunals and disability appeal tribunals;

(b) full-time chairmen of such tribunals; and

(c) a panel of persons who may be appointed part-time chairmen of such tribunals.

(2) A person is qualified to be appointed President if he is a barrister or solicitor of at least 10 years' standing.

(3) A person is qualified to be appointed a full-time chairman if he is a barrister or solicitor of at least 7 years' standing.

(4) A person is qualified to be appointed to the panel referred to in subsection (1)(c) above if he is a barrister or solicitor of at least 5 years' standing.

(5) Schedule 2 to this Act shall have effect for supplementing this section.

GENERAL NOTE
One of the major innovations in the reform of tribunals in 1984 was the appointment of a President who took over the appointment of social security appeal tribunal and medical appeal tribunal members and clerks, as well as the training of chairmen and members. The President in Northern Ireland since 1984 has been Mr C.G. MacLynn.

In effect, the administration of SSATs and MATs has been removed from the DHSS into the hands of an entirely independent agency. The reality of this independence has largely been secured, but still depends on the resources allowed to the Department of Finance and Personnel. Disability Appeal Tribunals have now been added to the President's remit.

The Lord Chancellor also has the power to appoint full-time chairmen. Owing to the size of the jurisdiction there is only one full-time chairman and 33 part-time chairmen. The tendency towards part-time chairmen is welcome, given that it retains the connections of the chairmen with the local community.

Social Security Commissioners

Appointment of Commissioners

50.—(1) Her Majesty may from time to time appoint for Northern Ireland, from among persons who are barristers or solicitors of at least 10 years' standing—
  (a) a Chief Social Security Commissioner; and
  (b) such number of other Social Security Commissioners,
as Her Majesty thinks fit.

(2) If the Lord Chancellor considers that, in order to facilitate the disposal of the business of Social Security Commissioners, he should make an appointment in pursuance of this subsection, he may appoint—
  (a) a member of the bar of Northern Ireland or solicitor of the Supreme Court of Northern Ireland of at least 10 years' standing;
  (b) a person who has a 10 year general qualification within the meaning of section 71 of the Courts and Legal Services Act 1990; or
  (c) an advocate or solicitor in Scotland of at least 10 years' standing,
to be a Social Security Commissioner (but to be known as a deputy Commissioner) for such period or on such occasions as the Lord Chancellor thinks fit.

(3) Schedule 2 to this Act shall have effect for supplementing this section.

References to medical practitioners, the Disability Living Allowance Advisory Board etc.

Power of adjudicating authorities to refer matters to experts

51.—(1) An authority to which this section applies may refer any question of special difficulty arising for decision by the authority to one or more experts for examination and report.

(2) The authorities to which this section applies are—
  (a) an adjudication officer;
  (b) an adjudicating medical practitioner, or two or more such practitioners acting together;
  (c) a specially qualified adjudicating medical practitioner appointed by virtue of section 60 below, or two or more such practitioners acting together;
  (d) a social security appeal tribunal;
  (e) a disability appeal tribunal;
  (f) a medical appeal tribunal;
  (g) a Commissioner;
  (h) the Department.

(3) Regulations may prescribe cases in which a Commissioner shall not exercise the power conferred by subsection (1) above.

(4) In this section "expert" means a person appearing to the authority to have knowledge or experience which would be relevant in determining the question of special difficulty.

DEFINITIONS
   "Commissioner": s.167.
   "prescribed": *ibid*.

GENERAL NOTE
   This general power may be useful to SSATs in exceptional circumstances, perhaps being more relevant to AOs or MATs and DATs. The question must be of special difficulty and needs to be carefully specified. The power should not be used to get the tribunal off the hook of coming to a decision on conflicting evidence.

Claims relating to attendance allowance, disability living allowance and disability working allowance

52.—(1) Before a claim for an attendance allowance, a disability living allowance or a disability working allowance or any question relating to such an allowance is submitted to an adjudication officer under section 18 above the Department may refer the person in respect of whom the claim is made or the question is raised to a medical practitioner for such examination and report as appears to the Department to be necessary—

   (a) for the purpose of providing the adjudication officer with information for use in determining the claim or question; or

   (b) for the purpose of general monitoring of claims for attendance allowances, disability living allowances and disability working allowances.

(2) An adjudication officer may refer—

   (a) a person in respect of whom such a claim is made or such a question is raised;

   (b) a person who has applied or is treated as having applied for a review under section 28 or 33 above,

to a medical practitioner for such examination and report as appears to the adjudication officer to be needed to enable him to reach a decision on the claim or question or the matter under review.

(3) The Department may direct adjudication officers to refer for advice to a medical practitioner who is an officer of the Department any case falling within a specified class of cases relating to attendance allowance or disability living allowance, and an adjudication officer may refer for advice any case relating to attendance allowance or disability living allowance to such a medical practitioner without such a direction.

(4) An adjudication officer may refer for advice any case relating to disability working allowance to such a medical practitioner.

(5) A medical practitioner who is an officer of the Department and to whom a case or question relating to an attendance allowance or a disability living allowance is referred under section 51 above or subsection (3) above may refer the case or question to the Disability Living Allowance Advisory Board for advice.

(6) Such a medical practitioner may obtain information about such a case or question from another medical practitioner.

(7) A medical practitioner who is an officer of the Department and to whom a question relating to disability working allowance is referred under section 51 above may obtain information about it from another medical practitioner.

(8) Where—

   (a) the Department has exercised the power conferred on it by subsection (1) above or an adjudication officer has exercised the power conferred on him by subsection (2) above; and

(b) the medical practitioner requests the person referred to him to attend for or submit himself to medical examination; but

(c) he fails without good cause to do so,

the adjudication officer shall decide the claim or question or matter under review against him.

GENERAL NOTE
   The powers contained in this section will in disability working allowance cases mainly be used in relation to the disability question under s.128(1)(b) of the Contributions and Benefits Act. They are more likely to be used in attendance allowance and disability living allowance cases. Although the philosophy of the scheme in force from April 1992 is of self-assessment, there will be cases where what is put on the claim form is inconsistent or improbable or where a claimant is appealing against an adverse decision and medical examination is necessary. A random sample of all claims will be referred for medical examination, mainly for monitoring purposes.

Medical examination etc. in relation to appeals to disability appeal tribunals

53.—(1) Where an appeal has been brought under section 31 above, a person who may be nominated as chairman of a disability appeal tribunal may, if prescribed conditions are satisfied, refer the claimant to a medical practitioner for such examination and report as appears to him to be necessary for the purpose of providing a disability appeal tribunal with information for use in determining the appeal.

(2) At a hearing before a disability appeal tribunal, except in prescribed circumstances, the tribunal—

(a) may not carry out a physical examination of the claimant; and

(b) may not require the claimant to undergo any physical test for the purpose of determining whether he satisfies the condition mentioned in section 73(1)(a) of the Contributions and Benefits Act.

GENERAL NOTE

Subs. (1)
   A chairman of a DAT may refer a claimant for medical examination and report. In contrast, the power in s.51 can only be exercised by the DAT as a whole and there must be a question of special difficulty. The prescribed conditions, in reg. 26F of the Social Security (Adjudication) Regulations (Northern Ireland) 1987 (S.I. 1987 No. 82), are that the chairman is satisfied that the appeal cannot be properly determined unless the claimant is examined by a medical practitioner who provides the DAT with information for use in determining the appeal. The need for such a power arises because subs. (2) prevents a DAT from itself physically examining a claimant. The intention is that the power in subs. (1) should be used only in unusual cases, in line with the philosophy of self-assessment. However, there is no express reference to this philosophy in the legislation and it remains to be seen how far DATs feel able to discharge their judicial functions without the benefit of reports of medical examinations.

Subs. (2)
   A DAT may not carry out a physical examination of the claimant or require him to undergo a physical test to determine whether he is unable or virtually unable to walk by reason of physical disablement. No regulations have as yet prescribed any exceptions.
   These limitations appear to be in reaction to the unpopularity of medical examinations and of the "walking tests" carried out by medical boards and medical appeal tribunals for mobility allowance purposes. Now, medical examinations by DATs are prohibited. If such an examination is necessary the powers in s.51 or subs. (1) must be used. Walking tests, for the mobility component of disability living allowance, are not prohibited, but may not be required. A claimant may therefore volunteer to undergo a walking test, but difficulties can be foreseen if DATs attempt to offer the claimant a choice of doing so or not. It will be almost impossible to avoid an impression that some pressure is being put on the claimant to agree. The result is to leave DATs in acute difficulties in mobility component appeals, for self-assessment of walking ability is inherently unreliable.

Determination of questions of special difficulty

Assessors

54.—(1) Where it appears to an authority to which this section applies that a matter before the authority involves a question of fact of special difficulty, then, unless regulations otherwise provide, the authority may direct that in dealing with that matter they shall have the assistance of one or more assessors.

(2) The authorities to which this section applies are—

(a) two or more adjudicating medical practitioners acting together;

(b) two or more specially qualified adjudicating medical practitioners, appointed by virtue of section 60 below, acting together;

(c) a social security appeal tribunal;

(d) a disability appeal tribunal;

(e) a medical appeal tribunal;

(f) a Commissioner;

(g) the Department.

GENERAL NOTE

Presumably the principles laid down in *R(I) 14/51* in relation to earlier legislation will continue to apply. The assessor's rôle is to assist the authority to understand the factual issues and to evaluate the evidence. He does not himself give evidence and so cannot be questioned by the parties to the proceedings. His advice should be summarised and the parties given the opportunity to comment on it.

Tribunal of 2 or 3 Commissioners

55.—(1) If it appears to the Chief Social Security Commissioner (or, in the case of his inability to act, to such other of the Commissioners as he may have nominated to act for the purpose) that an appeal falling to be heard by one of the Commissioners involves a question of law of special difficulty, he may direct that the appeal be dealt with, not by that Commissioner alone, but by a Tribunal consisting of any 2 or 3 of the Commissioners.

(2) If the decision of the Tribunal is not unanimous, the decision of the majority, or, in the case of a Tribunal consisting of 2 Commissioners, the decision of the presiding member, shall be the decision of the Tribunal.

GENERAL NOTE

Under the legislation in force before April 1984 there was no express power for the Chief Commissioner to convene a Tribunal of Commissioners in supplementary benefit or family income supplement cases. The power was found by implication (*R(FIS) 1/82*). It is often invoked where individual Commissioners have reached conflicting decisions.

In Northern Ireland a tribunal of commissioners may consist of either two or three commissioners, whilst in Great Britain it must consist of three. The reason for this is essentially practical: in Northern Ireland there are currently only two commissioners. In the event of a disagreement between the two commissioners on the tribunal, subs. (2) applies.

Individual Commissioners are bound to follow a decision of a Tribunal of Commissioners, unless there are compelling reasons to the contrary (*R(I) 12/75* and *CM 44/1991*). A Tribunal of Commissioners may depart from a previous Tribunal decision if satisfied that it was wrong (*R(U) 4/88*). A tribunal or an AO must follow a Tribunal's decision, whether reported or unreported, in preference to a decision of an individual Commissioner. Possibly, if the individual Commissioner finds compelling reasons for departing from an unreported Tribunal decision, a tribunal would be entitled to follow the individual Commissioner's decision.

Decisions of the Great Britain Commissioners are frequently cited in Northern Ireland tribunals and are considered to be highly persuasive but not binding. The reverse is also true. See, however, *R(I) 14/63*, where a Great Britain Commissioner followed a Northern Ireland Commissioner's decision in preference to a conflicting decision of another Great Britain Commissioner.

Regulations

Regulations as to determination of questions and matters arising out of, or pending, reviews and appeals

56.—(1) Subject to the provisions of this Act, provision may be made by regulations for the determination—

(a) by the Department; or

(b) by a person or tribunal appointed or constituted in accordance with the regulations,

of any question arising under or in connection with the Contributions and Benefits Act or the former legislation, including a claim for benefit.

(2) In this section "the former legislation" means the National Insurance Acts (Northern Ireland) 1965 to 1974 and the National Insurance (Industrial Injuries) Acts (Northern Ireland) 1965 to 1974 and the 1975 Act and Part III of the 1986 Order.

(3) Regulations under subsection (1) above may modify, add to or exclude any provisions of this Part of this Act, so far as relating to any questions to which the regulations relate.

(4) It is hereby declared for the avoidance of doubt that the power to make regulations under subsection (1) above includes power to make regulations for the determination of any question arising as to the total or partial recoupment of unemployment benefit in pursuance of regulations under Article 72(1) of the Industrial Relations (Northern Ireland) Order 1976 (including any decision as to the amount of benefit).

(5) Regulations under subsection (1) above may provide for the review by the Department of decisions on questions determined by it.

(6) The Lord Chancellor may by regulations provide—

(a) for officers authorised by him to determine any question which is determinable by a Commissioner and which does not involve the determination of any appeal, application for leave to appeal or reference;

(b) for the procedure to be followed by any such officer in determining any such question;

(c) for the manner in which determinations of such questions by such officers may be called in question.

(7) A determination which would have the effect of preventing an appeal, applications for leave to appeal or reference being determined by a Commissioner is not a determination of the appeal, application or reference for the purposes of subsection (6) above.

(8) Regulations under subsection (1) above may provide—

(a) for the reference to the Court of Appeal for decision of any question of law arising in connection with the determination of a question by the Department; and

(b) for appeals to that court from the decision of the Department on any such question of law;

and subsections (5) and (6) of section 16 above shall apply to a reference or appeal under this subsection as they apply to a reference or appeal under subsections (1) to (3) of that section.

DEFINITIONS
  "the 1975 Act": s.167.
  "the 1986 Order": *ibid.*
  "the Contributions and Benefits Act": *ibid.*

Procedure

57.—(1) Regulations (in this section referred to as "procedure regulations") may make any such provision as is specified in Schedule 3 to this Act.

(2) Procedure regulations may deal differently with claims and questions relating to—

(a) benefit under Parts II to IV of the Contributions and Benefits Act;

(b) industrial injuries benefit;

(c) each of the other benefits to which section 18 above applies.

(3) At any inquiry held by virtue of procedure regulations the witnesses shall, if the person holding the inquiry thinks fit, be examined on oath; and the person holding the inquiry shall have power to administer oaths for that purpose.

(4) In proceedings for the determination of a question mentioned in section 15(1)(c) above (including proceedings on an inquiry), there shall be available to a witness (other than the person who is liable, or alleged to be liable, to pay the Class 1A contribution in question) any privilege against self-incrimination or incrimination of a spouse which is available to a witness in legal proceedings.

(5) It is hereby declared—

(a) that the power to prescribe procedure includes power to make provision as to the representation of one person, at any hearing of a case, by another person whether having professional qualifications or not; and

(b) that the power to provide for the manner in which questions arising for determination by the Department are to be raised includes power to make provision with respect to the formulation of any such questions, whether arising on a reference under section 111 below or otherwise.

(6) Except so far as it may be applied by procedure regulations, the Arbitration Act (Northern Ireland) 1937 shall not apply to any proceedings under this Part of this Act.

DEFINITIONS

"the Contributions and Benefits Act": s.167.

"industrial injuries benefit": *ibid.*

GENERAL NOTE

See Sched. 3 and the Social Security (Adjudication) Regulations (Northern Ireland) 1987 (S.I. 1987 No. 465). See also the Great Britain equivalents, Social Security (Adjudication) Regulations 1986 (S.I. 1986 No. 2218), and the commentary in the current editions of Bonner *et al.*, Mesher and Rowland.

Finality of decisions

58.—(1) Subject to the provisions of this Part of this Act, the decision of any claim or question in accordance with the foregoing provisions of this Part of this Act shall be final; and subject to the provisions of any regulations under section 56 above, the decision of any claim or question in accordance with those regulations shall be final.

(2) Subsection (1) above shall not make any finding of fact or other determination embodied in or necessary to a decision, or on which it is based, conclusive for the purpose of any further decision.

(3) A decision (given under subsection (2) of section 42 above or otherwise) that an accident was an industrial accident is to be taken as determining only that paragraphs (a), (b) and (c) of subsection (5) of that section are satisfied in relation to the accident, and neither any such decision nor the reference to an adjudicating medical practitioner or a medical appeal tribunal under section 43 above of the disablement questions in connection with any claim to or award of disablement benefit is to be taken as importing a decision as to the origin of any injury or disability suffered by the claimant, whether or not there is an event identifiable as an accident apart from any injury that may have been received; but—

(a) a decision that on a particular occasion when there was no such event a person had an industrial accident by reason of an injury shall be treated as a decision that, if the injury was suffered by accident on that occasion, the accident was an industrial accident; and

(b) a decision that an accident was an industrial accident may be given, and a declaration to that effect be made and recorded in accordance with section 42 above, without its having been found that personal injury resulted from the accident (saving always the discretion under subsection (3) of that section to refuse to determine the question if it is unlikely to be necessary for the purposes of a claim for benefit).

(4) Notwithstanding anything in subsection (2) or (3) above (but subject to the provisions of this Part of this Act as to appeal and review), where for purposes of disablement pension or disablement gratuity in respect of an accident it has been found by an adjudicating medical practitioner or a medical appeal tribunal, on the determination or last determination of the disablement questions, that an injury resulted in whole or in part from the accident, then for purposes of industrial death benefit in respect of that accident the finding shall be conclusive that the injury did so result.

(5) Subsections (2) to (4) above shall apply as regards the effect to be given in any proceedings to any decision, or to a reference under section 43 above, whether the decision was given or reference made or the proceedings were commenced before or after the passing of the National Insurance Act 1972 (section 5 of which originally contained the provisions contained in this section), except that it shall not affect the determination of any appeal under section 46 above from a decision of a medical appeal tribunal given before the passing of that Act, nor affect any proceedings consequent on such an appeal from a decision so given; and accordingly—

(a) any decision given before the passing of that Act that a claimant was not entitled to industrial death benefit may be reviewed in accordance with this Part of this Act to give effect to subsection (4) above; and

(b) the references in subsections (2) and (3) above to provisions of this Act, and the reference in this subsection to section 43 above shall (so far as necessary) include the corresponding provisions of previous Acts.

GENERAL NOTE

Jones v. *Department of Employment* [1988] 1 All E.R. 725 decided that an AO cannot be sued for negligently making a decision, partly because of the effect of s.58. Although decisions are final, under subs. (2) findings of fact or other determinations are not conclusive for further decision. It used to be the case that decisions of the insurance officer on certain questions were conclusive for supplementary benefit purposes. This issue is now covered by reg. 64 of the Social Security (Adjudication) Regulations (Northern Ireland) 1987 (S.I. 1987 No. 82). The issue is only really a live one before a tribunal, and here it is clear from reg. 64 that, although an AO must first make a decision on a relevant question, the SSAT can deal with both income support and the national insurance or child benefit question together.

Subsection (2) also confirms that on a fresh claim, issues of fact and law are for decision afresh. For instance, if an income support claim is rejected on the ground that a claimant has notional capital under the deprivation rule, a claim a month or a week later cannot be rejected simply by reference to the earlier decision.

Regulations about supplementary matters relating to determinations

59.—(1) Regulations may make provision as respects matters arising—

(a) pending the determination under this Act (whether in the first instance or on an appeal or reference, and whether originally or on review)—

(i) of any claim for benefit to which this section applies;

(ii) of any question affecting any person's right to such benefit or its receipt; or

(iii) of any person's liability for contributions under Part I of the Contributions and Benefits Act; or

(b) out of the revision on appeal or review of any decision under this Act on any such claim or question.

(2) Without prejudice to the generality of subsection (1) above, regulations under that subsection may include provision as to the date from which any decision on a review is to have effect or to be deemed to have had effect.

(3) Regulations under subsection (1) above as it applies to child benefit may include provision as to the date from which child benefit is to be payable to a person in respect of a child in a case where, before the benefit was awarded to that person, child benefit in respect of the child was awarded to another person.

(4) This section applies to the following benefits—

(a) benefit as defined in section 121 of the Contributions and Benefits Act;

(b) child benefit;

(c) statutory sick pay;

(d) statutory maternity pay;

(e) income support;

(f) family credit;

(g) disability working allowance; and

(h) any social fund payments such as are mentioned in section 134(1)(a) or (2) of the Contributions and Benefits Act.

DEFINITIONS

"the Contributions and Benefits Act": s.167.

GENERAL NOTE

See the Social Security (Adjudication) Regulations (Northern Ireland) 1987 (S.I. 1987 No. 82) and the Social Security (Claims and Payments) Regulations (Northern Ireland) 1987 (S.I. 1987 No. 465). See also the equivalent Great Britain regulations, *i.e.* the Social Security (Adjudication) Regulations 1986 (S.I. 1986 No. 2218), and the Social Security (Claims and Payments) Regulations 1987 (S.I. 1987 No. 1968), and the current editions of Bonner *et al.*, Mesher and Rowland.

Industrial diseases

Adjudication as to industrial diseases

60.—(1) Regulations shall provide for applying, in relation—

(a) to claims for benefit under sections 108 to 110 of the Contributions and Benefits Act; and

(b) to questions arising in connection with such claims or with awards of such benefit,

the provisions of this Part of this Act subject to any prescribed additions or modifications.

(2) Regulations for those purposes may in particular provide—

(a) for the appointment of specially qualified adjudicating medical practitioners and the appointment of medical officers for the purposes of the regulations (which shall be taken to include, in the case of specially qualified adjudicating medical practitioners, the purposes for which adjudicating medical practitioners are appointed and medical appeal tribunals are established); and

(b) for the payment by the prescribed persons of fees of the prescribed amount in connection with any medical examination by specially qualified adjudicating medical practitioners or any such officer and their return in any prescribed cases, and (so far as not required to be returned) their payment into the National Insurance Fund and recovery as sums due to that Fund.

GENERAL NOTE
See Section A of Pt. IV of the Social Security (Adjudication) Regulations (Northern Ireland) 1987 (S.I. 1987 No. 82). See also the equivalent Great Britain Regulations, *i.e.* Section A of Pt. IV of the Social Security (Adjudication) Regulations 1986 (S.I. 1986 No. 2218), and commentary in the current edition of Rowland.

Housing benefit

Adjudication

61.—(1) Regulations shall require a person who has claimed housing benefit to be notified of the determination of the claim.

(2) Any such notification shall be given in such form as may be prescribed.

(3) Regulations shall make provision for reviews of determinations relating to housing benefit.

GENERAL NOTE
See regs. 77, 78 and 79 of the Housing Benefit (General) Regulations (Northern Ireland) 1987 (S.I. 1987 No. 461).

Social fund officers and inspectors and the social fund Commissioner

Social fund officers

62.—(1) The Department shall appoint officers, to be known as "social fund officers", for the purpose of performing functions in relation to payments out of the social fund such as are mentioned in section 134(1)(b) of the Contributions and Benefits Act.

(2) A social fund officer may be appointed to perform all the functions of social fund officers or such functions of such officers as may be specified in his instrument of appointment.

(3) The Department may nominate for an area a social fund officer who shall issue general guidance to the other social fund officers in the area about such matters relating to the social fund as the Department may specify.

DEFINITIONS
"the Contributions and Benefits Act": s.167.

GENERAL NOTE

Subs. (3)
See s.136(5) of the Contributions and Benefits (Northern Ireland) Act and s.64(9) below for the status of guidance issued by area social fund officers.

The social fund Commissioner and inspectors

63.—(1) There shall continue to be an officer known as "the social fund Commissioner" (in this section referred to as "the Commissioner").

(2) The Commissioner shall be appointed by the Department.

(3) The Commissioner—

(a) shall appoint such social fund inspectors; and

(b) may appoint such officers and staff for himself and for social fund inspectors,

as he thinks fit, but with the consent of the Department and the Department of Finance and Personnel as to numbers.

(4) Appointments under subsection (3) above shall be made from persons made available to the Commissioner by the Department.

(5) It shall be the duty of the Commissioner—

(a) to monitor the quality of decisions of social fund inspectors and give

them such advice and assistance as he thinks fit to improve the
standard of their decisions;

(b) to arrange such training of social fund inspectors as he considers
appropriate; and

(c) to carry out such other functions in connection with the work of social
fund inspectors as the Department may direct.

(6) The Commissioner shall report annually in writing to the Department
on the standards of reviews by social fund inspectors and the Department
shall publish his report.

GENERAL NOTE

One of the functions of the Social Fund Commissioner is to appoint social fund inspectors,
who deal with applications for review from social fund officers under s.64(3), and to oversee
their operation. The Annual Reports of the Social Fund Commissioner contain much interesting material. Inspectors have been recruited from outside and inside the DHSS and have
established an independence of operation.

Reviews

64.—(1) A social fund officer—

(a) shall review a determination made under the Contributions and
Benefits Act by himself or some other social fund officer, if an
application for a review is made within such time and in such form and
manner as may be prescribed by or on behalf of the person who
applied for the payment to which the determination relates; and

(b) may review such a determination in such other circumstances as he
thinks fit;

and may exercise on a review any power exercisable by an officer under Part
VIII of the Contributions and Benefits Act.

(2) The power to review a determination conferred on a social fund officer
by subsection (1) above includes power to review a determination made by a
social fund officer on a previous review.

(3) On an application made by or on behalf of the person to whom a
determination relates within such time and in such form and manner as may
be prescribed a determination of a social fund officer which has been
reviewed shall be further reviewed by a social fund inspector.

(4) On a review a social fund inspector shall have the following powers—

(a) power to confirm the determination made by the social fund officer;

(b) power to make any determination which a social fund officer could
have made;

(c) power to refer the matter to a social fund officer for determination.

(5) A social fund inspector may review a determination under subsection
(3) above made by himself or some other social fund inspector.

(6) In determining a question on a review a social fund officer or social
fund inspector shall have regard, subject to subsection (7) below, to all the
circumstances of the case and, in particular, to the matters specified in
section 136(1)(a) to (e) of the Contributions and Benefits Act.

(7) An officer or inspector shall determine any questions on a review in
accordance with any general directions issued by the Department under
section 136(2) of the Contributions and Benefits Act and any general directions issued by the Department with regard to reviews and in determining
any such question shall take account of any general guidance issued by the
Department under that subsection or with regard to reviews.

(8) Directions under this section may specify—

(a) the circumstances in which a determination is to be reviewed; and

(b) the manner in which a review is to be conducted.

(9) In reviewing a question under this section a social fund officer shall
take account (subject to any directions or guidance issued by the Depart-

ment under this section) of any guidance issued by the social fund officer nominated for his area under section 62(3) above.

(10) A social fund inspector reviewing a determination shall be under the same duties in relation to such guidance as the social fund officer or inspector who made the determination.

DEFINITIONS
"the Contributions and Benefits Act": s.167.
"the Department": *ibid.*

GENERAL NOTE

Subss. (1) and (3)
See the Social Fund (Application for Review) Regulations (Northern Ireland) 1988 (S.I. 1988 No. 20). Subsection (1) establishes the review of an initial SFO decision by another SFO as the first stage of challenge by a claimant.
Subsection (3) establishes the further stage of review by a social fund inspector.

Subs. (4)
A social fund inspector (see s.63) may confirm the SFO's decision, give any decision which the SFO could have made, or refer the matter back to a SFO. However, a social fund inspector is as bound by the factors listed in s.136(1)(a)–(e) of the Contributions and Benefits Act and by directions and guidance from the Department or the area SFO as the SFO (subss. (6), (7), (9) and (10)). There is an additional duty to follow the directions specified in subs. (8).

Subs. (7) and (8)
See directions 31–42 of the Department's directions to SFOs and the directions to SFIs, together with the notes to those directions, in the current edition of Mesher.

Christmas bonus

Determination of questions

65.—(1) A determination by the competent authority that a person is entitled or not entitled to payment of a qualifying benefit in respect of a period which includes a day in the relevant week shall be conclusive for the purposes of section 144 of the Contributions and Benefits Act; and in this subsection "competent authority" means, in relation to a payment of any description of a qualifying benefit, an authority that ordinarily determines whether a person is entitled to such a payment.

(2) Any question arising under that section other than one determined or falling to be determined under subsection (1) above shall be determined by the Department whose decision shall, except as provided by subsection (3) below, be final.

(3) The Department may reverse a decision under subsection (2) above on new facts being brought to its notice or if it is satisfied that the decision was given in ignorance of, or was based on a mistake as to, some material fact.

(4) Expressions used in this section to which a meaning is assigned by section 146 of the Contributions and Benefits Act have that meaning in this section.

Restrictions on entitlement to benefit following erroneous decision

Restrictions on entitlement to benefit in certain cases of error

66.—(1) This section applies where—
(a) on the determination, whenever made, of a Commissioner or the court (the "relevant determination"), a decision made by an adjudicating authority is or was found to have been erroneous in point of law; and
(b) after both—
     (i) 14th August 1990 (the date of the coming into operation of

section 154D of the 1975 Act, the provision of that Act corresponding to this section); and

(ii) the date of the relevant determination,

a claim which falls, or which would apart from this section fall, to be
decided in accordance with the relevant determination is made or
treated under section 5(1)(i) above as made by any person for any
benefit.

(2) Where this section applies, any question which arises on, or on the
review of a decision which is referable to, the claim mentioned in subsection
(1)(b) above and which relates to the entitlement of the claimant or any
other person to any benefit—

(a) in respect of a period before the relevant date; or

(b) in the case of a widow's payment, in respect of a death occurring
before that date,

shall be determined as if the decision referred to in subsection (1)(a) above
had been found by the Commissioner or court in question not to have been
erroneous in point of law.

(3) In determining whether a person is entitled to benefit in a case
where—

(a) his entitlement depends on his having been entitled to the same or
some other benefit before attaining a particular age; and

(b) he attained that age—

(i) before both the date of the relevant determination and the
date of the claim referred to in subsection (1)(b) above, but

(ii) not before the earliest day in respect of which benefit could,
apart from this section, have been awarded on that claim,

subsection (2) above shall be disregarded for the purpose only of determining the question whether he was entitled as mentioned in paragraph (a)
above.

(4) In this section—

"adjudicating authority" means—

(a) an adjudication officer or, where the original decision was
given on a reference under section 19(2) or 23(1) above, a social
security appeal tribunal, a disability appeal tribunal or a medical
appeal tribunal;

(b) any of the following former bodies or officers, that is to say,
the National Assistance Board for Northern Ireland, the Supplementary Benefits Commission for Northern Ireland, the Attendance Allowance Board for Northern Ireland, a benefit officer,
an insurance officer or a supplement officer; or

(c) any of the officers who, or tribunals or other bodies which, in
Great Britain correspond to those mentioned in paragraph (a) or
(b) above;

"benefit" means—

(a) benefit as defined in section 121 of the Contributions and
Benefits Act;

(b) any income-related benefit;

"the court" means the High Court, the Court of Appeal, the Court of
Session, the High Court or Court of Appeal in England and Wales,
the House of Lords or the Court of Justice of the European
Community;

"the relevant date" means whichever is the latest of—

(a) the date of the relevant determination;

(b) the date which falls 12 months before the date on which the
claim referred to in subsection (1)(b) above is made or treated
under section 5(1)(i) above as made; and

(c) the earliest date in respect of which the claimant would, apart
from this section, be entitled on that claim to the benefit in
question.

(5) For the purposes of this section—
(a) any reference in this section to entitlement to benefit includes a reference to entitlement—
(i) to any increase in the rate of a benefit; or
(ii) to a benefit, or increase of benefit, at a particular rate; and
(b) any reference to a decision which is "referable to" a claim is a reference to—
(i) a decision on the claim,
(ii) a decision on a review of the decision on the claim, or
(iii) a decision on a subsequent review of the decision on the review,
and so on.
(6) The date of the relevant determination shall, in prescribed cases, be determined for the purposes of this section in accordance with any regulations made for that purpose.

DEFINITIONS
"the 1975 Act": s.167.
"Commissioner": *ibid.*
"the Contributions and Benefits Act": *ibid.*
"income-related benefit": *ibid.*

GENERAL NOTE
See the notes to s.67 below for the general background and effect of ss.66 and 67, and for discussion of the definitions in s.66(4).
Section 66 can only apply when a claim is actually made after the date of some Commissioner's or court's decision which finds the DHSS view of the law to be wrong. Then, in so far as the claim can be treated as for a period before the date of claim and the claimant would otherwise be entitled to benefit, entitlement for any period before the "relevant date" is to be determined as if the decision had gone the other way (subs. (2)). The "relevant date" is either the date of the decision or 12 months before the actual date of claim, if later (subs. (4), paras. (a) and (b) of the definition). Paragraph (c) of the definition merely seems to confirm what would be the case anyway.
There is a small exception in subs. (3), where payment of the particular benefit at the date in question is not in issue, but merely the establishment of an entitlement to the benefit at a particular age.

Determination of questions on review following erroneous decisions

67.—(1) Subsection (2) below applies in any case where—
(a) on the determination, whenever made, of a Commissioner or the court (the "relevant determination"), a decision made by an adjudicating authority is or was found to have been erroneous in point of law; and
(b) in consequence of that determination, any other decision—
(i) which was made before the date of that determination; and
(ii) which is referable to a claim made or treated as made by any person for any benefit,
falls (or would, apart from subsection (2) below, fall) to be revised on a review carried out under section 23(5) above after 14th August 1990 (the date of the coming into force of section 104(7) to (10) of the 1975 Act, the provision of that Act corresponding to this section) or on a review under section 28 above on the ground that the decision under review was erroneous in point of law.
(2) Where this subsection applies, any question arising on the review referred to in subsection (1)(b) above, or on any subsequent review of a decision which is referable to the same claim, as to any person's entitlement to, or right to payment of, any benefit—
(a) in respect of any period before the date of the relevant determination; or
(b) in the case of a widow's payment, in respect of a death occurring before that date,

shall be determined as if the decision referred to in subsection (1)(a) above had been found by the Commissioner or court in question not to have been erroneous in point of law.

(3) In determining whether a person is entitled to benefit in a case where his entitlement depends on his having been entitled to the same or some other benefit before attaining a particular age, subsection (2) above shall be disregarded for the purpose only of determining the question whether he was so entitled before attaining that age.

(4) For the purposes of this section—

(a) "adjudicating authority" and "the court" have the same meaning as they have in section 66 above;

(b) any reference to—

(i) a person's entitlement to benefit; or

(ii) a decision which is referable to a claim,

shall be construed in accordance with subsection (5) of that section; and

(c) the date of the relevant determination shall, in prescribed cases, be determined in accordance with any regulations made under subsection (6) of that section.

DEFINITIONS

"the 1975 Act": s.167.

"Commissioner": *ibid.*

GENERAL NOTE

The predecessor of s.67 formed a package with the predecessor of s.66 on claims when they were introduced in 1990. The aim is that where an established interpretation of the law is overturned by a decision of a Social Security Commissioner or a higher court, effect can only be given to the new interpretation for other claimants on review or a fresh claim with effect from the date of that decision (the decision is referred to below as the J decision and the date as the J Day).

Background

The general rule on claims for benefit is that there can be no entitlement for a period more than 12 months before the actual date of claim, however good the cause for delay in claiming (s.1(2) above; Social Security (Northern Ireland) Act 1975, s.154A(2)). This limit does not apply to disablement benefit or reduced earnings allowance. Thus if a possible entitlement is revealed by the J decision and the person has not previously claimed, that limit applies.

If the person has already had a decision on a claim and applies for a review of that decision based on the new interpretation, again there is a general limit of 12 months before the date of the request for review (Social Security (Adjudication) Regulations (Northern Ireland) 1987 (S.I. 1987 No. 82), regs. 65 and 69–71). However, there was until August 31, 1991 an exemption from this limit under reg. 72(1) of the Adjudication Regulations where, among other things, the decision to be reviewed was erroneous by reason of a mistake made by an AO. Acting on a mistaken view of the law could obviously come within reg. 72(1) (*R(SB) 10/91* and *CIS 11/1991*), so that a revision on review triggered by the J decision could go back to the date of the original decision. Alarm about this effect led to the insertion of reg. 72(2) from September 1, 1987, which provided that reg. 72 should not apply where review was on the ground that the original decision was erroneous in law by reason of the J decision. The result was that in such cases the normal 12-month limit applied. The argument that the original decision was not erroneous by reason of the J decision, but was simply revealed to have been erroneous all along was rejected in *R(SB) 11/89.*

In an investigation by the Parliamentary Commissioner for Administration (the Ombudsman) into the decision of the Secretary of State about how extensively to trawl back for past entitlements following a Commissioner's decision on the offsetting of payments of occupational pension against dependency additions to invalidity benefit, the Ombudsman raised the effect of reg. 72(2) of the Great Britain Social Security (Adjudication) Regulations 1986 (S.I. 1986 No. 2218) (*Case No. C191/88*, Fourth Report of the PCA for 1989–90). He was concerned that the longer the delay in identifying a claimant's case as requiring review the more benefit was lost, because of the absolute time limit recently reintroduced. He was not convinced that this effect was brought to Ministers' attention. In the course of responding to that point the DSS said that it would introduce a common start date for entitlement on review in such cases, but gave no indication of what sort of date would be chosen. The new provisions introduced by the Social Security Act 1990 (Social Security (Northern Ireland) Order 1990 (S.I. 1990 No. 1511 (N.I. 15))) were said to be in fulfilment of this undertaking. See *Hansard*, H.L. Vol. 519, cols. 684–6 (Lord Henley).

Regulation 72 of the Adjudication Regulations has been replaced with effect from August 31, 1991 by reg. 64A, which also allows the 12-month limit on review to be lifted, but uses a more restricted approach to errors of law. See also the notes to the equivalent Great Britain Regulation, *i.e.* reg. 64A of the Social Security (Adjudication) Regulations 1986 (S.I. 1986 No. 2218), in the current edition of Mesher.

The new provisions came into force on July 13, 1990. Because, as discussed below, there has been a significant change in the legislation in this Act, in force from July 1, 1992, it is necessary carefully to separate the legal position before July 1, 1992 from the position after that date. The current provisions on review (s.67) and claims (s.66) apply where "on a determination, whenever made, of a Commissioner or the court, a decision made by an adjudicating authority is or was found to have been erroneous in point of law" (subs. (1)(a)). Note that appeals from initial decisions (including reviews and refusals to review) which are not affected by the new rules are not within the scope of either section at all. An "adjudicating authority" was originally defined to cover an AO or any of his legislative predecessors, a social security appeal tribunal, a medical appeal tribunal, the Attendance Allowance Board, the Supplementary Benefits Commission or the National Assistance Board. The disability appeal tribunal was added in April 1991. However, the form of words in the 1992 Act (s.66(4)) has introduced a significant change. Tribunals are only included where the original decision was given on a reference by the AO to a SSAT under s.19(2) or 23(1). There was no condition of this kind in the pre-July 1992 legislation. The change is not covered by a Law Commission recommendation (see the Report on the consolidation of certain enactments relating to Social Security: Law Com. No. 203). Therefore, it must have been considered to come within the corrections and minor improvements which can properly be authorised by s.2 of the Consolidation of Enactments (Procedure) Act 1949. The Joint Committee on Consolidation Bills (H.L. Paper 23-I, H.C. Paper 141-I, Session 1991–2) gave their opinion that this was so (although they also considered that the Great Britain Administration Act and the Contributions and Benefits Act (and thus presumably their Northern Ireland equivalents) represented "pure consolidation" of the existing law), so that presumably the new form has to be accepted. See below for some of the resulting problems.

"The court" includes everything above the Commissioner (s.66(4)). If any decision made before J Day falls to be revised on review carried out on or after July 13, 1990 "in consequence of that determination" (s.67(1)(b)), entitlement before J Day is to be determined as if the adjudicating authority's decision had been found not to be erroneous in point of law (s.67(2)). If a new claim is made after J Day, entitlement before that date is to be decided on the same assumption (s.66(2)). These provisions do not seem to achieve the intended aim, and give rise to a number of problems.

The problems

The aim of the provisions is clear: a common start-date for revising other claimants' entitlements when an appeal overturns the previously accepted DHSS interpretation of the law. The main political argument against their introduction was that the start date was placed unacceptably and unfairly late at J Day. While reg. 72(2) of the Social Security (Adjudication) Regulations (Northern Ireland) 1987 (S.I. 1987 No. 82) still existed there was only a common start-date when the review took place within 12 months of J Day. For reviews which take place after reg. 64A has taken over, the 12-month limit will only be lifted if the J decision shows that the previous interpretation involved errors of law of particular kinds (see reg. 64A(3)). However, the form of the new provisions both before and after July 1, 1992 raises more fundamental problems.

The argument on the pre-July 1992 form of the provisions is as follows. For the new rules to apply, a Commissioner or higher court must have found an adjudicating authority's decision to be erroneous in point of law. Thus, if a SSAT adopts the AO's view of the law and the Commissioner holds the SSAT to have made an error of law, the new rules apply. But if a SSAT differs from the AO and the Commissioner holds that the SSAT has not made an error of law, the condition in the predecessor of ss.66(1)(a) and 67(1)(a) is not met. The Commissioner's jurisdiction is only to determine whether the SSAT has made an error of law. Although the reasons for his determination may include an indication that the AO's decision was erroneous in point of law, this is not something which is "found" "on the determination". The words "erroneous in point of law" are precisely those used in describing the Commissioner's powers on an appeal from a SSAT (see s.21(7)). A similar point can be made if the AO's view is accepted by the SSAT and the Commissioner, but the Court of Appeal finds the Commissioner to have been in error of law. The Commissioner is not within the definition of "adjudicating authority". The Court of Appeal will not have "found" an adjudicating authority's decision to be erroneous in point of law and the new rules do not apply. On this view, there might seem to be no point in the inclusion of the AO in the definition of "adjudicating authority", for there is no way in which a Commissioner or court within the normal appeal structure can "find" an AO's decision to be erroneous in point of law. However, an AO's decision may be taken directly to a court in an application for judicial review. Under the Court of Appeal's decision in *Chief Adjudication Officer* v. *Foster* [1991] 3 W.L.R. 473; [1991] 3 All E.R. 846, this is the only way in which an argument that a regulation is *ultra vires* can be raised. It is therefore arguable that if the Divisional Court or some other court decides that a regulation relied on by an AO is *ultra vires*, this involves finding that the AO's decision was erroneous in point of law. If this general argument is correct, the pre-July 1992 rules were applied capriciously, depending on the precise history of the appeal before the J decision. This view was not shared by the DSS (DHSS in Northern Ireland) and there has not yet been any authoritative ruling on it. The contrary view is that "found" does not have any technical meaning, so that if a Commissioner or a court takes a different view of the law from that taken by an AO, this amounts to finding the decision made by the AO to be erroneous in point of law. However, there remains considerable scope for argument that the new rules do not apply in the circumstances identified above. It may be that the change in the legislation from July 1, 1992 was an attempt to "clarify" the law, but what is clear is that it cannot affect the proper interpretation of the legislation as it stood before July 1, 1992. The form of the definition of "adjudicating authority" in force with effect from July 1, 1992 (s.66(4), applied in s.67(4)(a)) adds even further difficulties. It appears to exclude SSATs, DATs and MATs except where the original decision was given on a reference under ss.19(2) or 23(2). Under these provisions, an AO need not make a decision on a claim or an application for review, but may refer the claim or application to a SSAT for decision. The SSAT then makes the original decision on the claim or review. Thus a SSAT deciding an appeal is not an adjudicating authority. In the case of DATs or MATs the original decision cannot have been given on a reference under either of those provisions, which only apply to SSATs. Since the condition seems to govern SSATs, DATs and MATs, this has the effect of excluding DATs and MATs from the definition entirely. If tribunals are excluded from the definition except in the case where the SSAT makes an original decision on a reference, the argument put forward above about the pre-July 1992 law would mean that no Commissioner or court decision which put forward a different interpretation of the law from that adopted by an AO in an original decision could "find" a decision of an adjudicating authority erroneous in point of law, whether it upheld the view of an SSAT or not. This would give ss.66 and 67 such a very narrow application that it must bolster the counter-argument. This is that a Commissioner's decision on appeal from a SSAT which takes a different view of the law to that taken by the AO does "find" the AO's decision to be erroneous in point of law and does therefore come within the scope of ss.66 and 67. But the counter-argument still has to overcome formidable obstacles in the form of the actual words of ss.66(1)(a) and 67(1)(a).

It is highly unsatisfactory that the law should remain in such confusion. If the argument made above about the pre-July 1992 law is right, and this Act has succeeded in changing the law, then this consolidating Act goes well beyond the correction or minor improvement which is allowable. If that argument on the pre-July 1992 law is right and this Act has not made a fundamental change, it has limited the operation of ss.66 and 67 in a most obscure way. If the argument about the pre-July 1992 law is wrong, so that this Act change is merely clarificatory, it is clarification in an exceptionally underhand and oblique way.

There are some other difficulties on issues where there has been no change on July 1, 1992. If the new rules apply, the decision of the relevant adjudicating authority is to be assumed not to have been erroneous in point of law. What if the AO decides according to the accepted DSS (DHSS) interpretation, the SSAT reaches the same result but for peculiar and different reasons and the Commissioner decides that a third approach is correct? It appears to be the SSAT decision which must be assumed not to be erroneous in law, thus incorporating its reasons rather than the DSS (DHSS) interpretation. Similarly, if the SSAT decision is erroneous in several respects, only one of which is the matter which would trigger the review, it appears that all the errors must be assumed not to be errors.

This is linked with the problem of identifying which of a series of decisions ought to count as the J decision. The question is when it is a consequence of one decision that decisions on other claimants' claims should be revised on review as erroneous in point of law. AOs commonly do not carry out such reviews if a single Commissioner's decision goes against the DHSS view, especially if an appeal is being taken to the Court of Appeal. If the Court of Appeal then confirms the Commissioner's decision, the J Day ought to be the date of the Commissioner's decision. But if there are a series of equally authoritative decisions, which one establishes the J Day? It ought to be the earliest one. If the decision which therefore is to be reviewed and revised as erroneous in point of law was made after this J Day, the review based on the effect of the J decision is free of the new rules. The condition in subs. (1)(b)(i) is not met.

Finally, the new provisions are almost certainly ineffective in relation to rulings on the effect of European Community law by the European Court of Justice (see the definition of "court" in s.66(4)) and by U.K. courts. For the U.K. legislature to remove a person's entitlement based on such a ruling would be a breach of the obligation in E.C. law to provide an adequate remedy (see *Von Colson* [1984] E.C.R. 1891).

Correction of errors

Regulations as to correction of errors

68.—(1) Regulations may make provision with respect to—

(a) the correction of accidental errors in any decision or record of a decision given with respect to a claim or question arising under or in connection with any relevant enactment by a body or person authorised to decide the claim or question; and

(b) the setting aside of any such decision in a case where it appears just to set the decision aside on the ground that—

(i) a document relating to the proceedings in which the decision was given was not sent to, or was not received at an appropriate time by, a party to the proceedings or a party's representative or was not received at an appropriate time by the body or person who gave the decision; or

(ii) a party to the proceedings or a party's representative was not present at a hearing related to the proceedings.

(2) Nothing in subsection (1) above shall be construed as derogating from any power to correct errors or set aside decisions which is exercisable apart from regulations made by virtue of that subsection.

(3) In this section "relevant enactment" means any enactment contained in—

(a) the National Insurance Measures (Northern Ireland) 1966 to 1974;

(b) the National Insurance (Industrial Injuries) Measures (Northern Ireland) 1966 to 1974;

(c) the Workmen's Compensation (Supplementation) Measures (Northern Ireland) 1966 to 1974;

(d) the Social Security Act 1973;

(e) the Social Security (Northern Ireland) Acts 1975 to 1991;

(f) the Old Cases Act;

(g) the Child Benefit (Northern Ireland) Order 1975;

(h) the Family Income Supplements Act (Northern Ireland) 1971;

(i) the Supplementary Benefits (Northern Ireland) Order 1977;

(j) the Contributions and Benefits Act;

(k) this Act.

DEFINITIONS
"the Contributions and Benefits Act": s.167.
"the Old Cases Act": *ibid.*

GENERAL NOTE
See regs. 10–12 of the Social Security (Adjudication) Regulations (Northern Ireland) 1987 (S.I. 1987 No. 82). See also the equivalent Great Britain Regulations, *i.e.* regs. 10–12 of the Social Security (Adjudication) Regulations 1986 (S.I. 1986 No. 2218), and the commentary in the current editions of Bonner *et al.*, Mesher and Rowland. The form of subs. (1)(b), which reproduces the earlier legislation, throws doubt on the validity of reg. 11(1)(c).

PART III

OVERPAYMENTS AND ADJUSTMENTS OF BENEFIT

Misrepresentation etc.

Overpayments—general

69.—(1) Where it is determined that, whether fraudulently or otherwise, any person has misrepresented, or failed to disclose, any material fact and in consequence of the misrepresentation or failure—

    (a) a payment has been made in respect of a benefit to which this section applies; or

    (b) any sum recoverable by or on behalf of the Department in connection with any such payment has not been recovered,

the Department shall be entitled to recover the amount of any payment which the Department would not have made or any sum which the Department would have received but for the misrepresentation or failure to disclose.

    (2) Where any such determination as is referred to in subsection (1) above is made on an appeal or review, there shall also be determined in the course of the appeal or review the question whether any, and if so what, amount is recoverable under that subsection by the Department.

    (3) An amount recoverable under subsection (1) above is in all cases recoverable from the person who misrepresented the fact or failed to disclose it.

    (4) In relation to cases where payments of a benefit to which this section applies have been credited to a bank account or other account under arrangements made with the agreement of the beneficiary or a person acting for him, circumstances may be prescribed in which the Department is to be entitled to recover any amount paid in excess of entitlement; but any such regulations shall not apply in relation to any payment unless before he agreed to the arrangements such notice of the effect of the regulations as may be prescribed was given in such manner as may be prescribed to the beneficiary or to a person acting for him.

    (5) Except where regulations otherwise provide, an amount shall not be recoverable under subsection (1) above or regulations under subsection (4) above unless—

    (a) the determination in pursuance of which it was paid has been reversed or varied on an appeal or revised on a review; and

    (b) it has been determined on the appeal or review that the amount is so recoverable.

    (6) Regulations may provide—

    (a) that amounts recoverable under subsection (1) above or regulations under subsection (4) above shall be calculated or estimated in such manner and on such basis as may be prescribed;

    (b) for treating any amount paid to any person under an award which it is subsequently determined was not payable—

        (i) as properly paid; or

        (ii) as paid on account of a payment which it is determined should be or should have been made,

    and for reducing or withholding any arrears payable by virtue of the subsequent determination;

    (c) for treating any amount paid to one person in respect of another as properly paid for any period for which it is not payable in cases where in consequence of a subsequent determination—

        (i) the other person is himself entitled to a payment for that period; or

        (ii) a third person is entitled in priority to the payee to a payment for that period in respect of the other person,

    and for reducing or withholding any arrears payable for that period by virtue of the subsequent determination.

    (7) Circumstances may be prescribed in which a payment on account by virtue of section 5(1)(s) above may be recovered to the extent that it exceeds entitlement.

    (8) Where any amount paid is recoverable under—

    (a) subsection (1) above;

(b) regulations under subsection (4) or (7) above; or

(c) section 72 below,

it may, without prejudice to any other method of recovery, be recovered by deduction from prescribed benefits.

(9) Where any amount paid in respect of a married or unmarried couple is recoverable as mentioned in subsection (8) above, it may, without prejudice to any other method of recovery, be recovered, in such circumstances as may be prescribed, by deduction from prescribed benefits payable to either of them.

(10) Any amount recoverable under the provisions mentioned in subsection (8) above shall, if the county court so orders, be enforceable as if it were payable under an order of that court.

(11) This section applies to the following benefits—

(a) benefit as defined in section 121 of the Contributions and Benefits Act;

(b) subject to section 70 below, income support;

(c) family credit;

(d) disability working allowance;

(e) any social fund payments such as are mentioned in section 134(1)(a) or (2) of the Contributions and Benefits Act; and

(f) child benefit.

DEFINITIONS

"the Contributions and Benefits Act": s.167.

"married couple": Contributions and Benefits Act, s.133.

"prescribed": s.167.

"unmarried couple": Contributions and Benefits Act, s.133.

GENERAL NOTE

The predecessor of s.69 was intended to produce a common rule on overpayments across all social security benefits. Since the new rule was based on the old supplementary benefit rule (Supplementary Benefits (Northern Ireland) Order 1977 (S.I. 1977 No. 2156), art. 25), many of the existing principles developed in Commissioners' decisions will continue to be relevant. The currently authoritative view, following the decision of the English Court of Appeal in *Secretary of State for Social Security* v. *Tunnicliffe* [1991] 2 All E.R. 712, is that s.53 of the Social Security Act 1986 (art. 54 of the Social Security (Northern Ireland) Order 1986) (now replaced by ss.71 and 69 respectively) applies to determinations of overpayments as part of reviews carried out on or after April 6, 1987, when the section came into force. Section 69 applies to the benefits specified in subs. (11) and, by virtue of para. 5 of Sched. 7, to benefits under the National Assistance Act (Northern Ireland) 1948, the Supplementary Benefits Act (Northern Ireland) 1966, the Supplementary Benefits (Northern Ireland) Order 1977 (S.I. 1977 No. 2156) and the Family Income Supplements Act (Northern Ireland) 1971, among others. It does not matter how far back the overpayments occurred, provided that they were made under one of these pieces of legislation. The time limits of the Limitation Acts (Northern Ireland) 1958 to 1982 do not start to run until there has been a determination under s.69 or one of its predecessors giving the Secretary of State the right of recovery (*R(SB) 5/91* and *R(A) 2/86*).

Subs. (1)

This expresses the general rule on recovery of overpayments. There is no provision for the recovery of administrative costs, and if payments are made which go beyond what has been awarded by an AO, recovery is a matter for the civil law (see *CSB 830/1985* on the old s.20). Before considering the main elements of the rule, note the important condition imposed by subss. (2) and (5) that an overpayment determination can only be made in the course of a review of the decision awarding benefit (or an appeal from that decision). A SSAT must be satisfied that a valid review and revision has taken place before considering the rest of s.69. This is often overlooked, which causes great difficulties. See the notes to subs. (5) for further details. For the right of recovery to exist, a person must have misrepresented or failed to disclose a material fact. Then it must be shown that a payment of benefit, or non-recovery, was a consequence of the misrepresentation or failure to disclose. Finally, the amount recoverable must be determined. *R(SB) 2/92* decided that the words "whether fraudulently or otherwise" do not impose any further condition of there having been some kind of dishonesty. This decision was upheld by the Court of Appeal in England in *Page* v. *Chief Adjudication Officer* (*The Times*, July 4,

1991, and appendix to *R(SB) 2/92)*. The Court of Appeal held that the plain meaning of the words is "whether fraudulently or not". It was clearly established under the old s.20 that the burden of proof of all issues lay on the AO (*R(SB) 34/83*). The same will apply to s.69. It was also established that if an initial decision is based on a failure to disclose (or misrepresentation), it is open to a SSAT to base its decision on misrepresentation (or failure to disclose), provided that the claimant has had a fair opportunity of dealing with that new point (*R(SB) 40/84*).

Material fact

Section 69 only applies where there has been a misrepresentation of, or a failure to disclose, a material fact. There is often a concentration on the circumstances of a failure to disclose or a misrepresentation and the significance of whether something is a material fact or not is forgotten. There are three main limitations imposed.

First, matters of law are not covered. It is established for purposes of review that a mistake of law is not a mistake of material fact (*R(G) 18/52*). Entitlement to benefit is a conclusion of law based on findings of fact. Therefore, a representation by a claimant that he is entitled to benefit is not a representation of fact unless it involves, either expressly or by implication, some representation of fact, *e.g.* that circumstances have not changed. Signing the declaration on a benefit order that the claimant is entitled to benefit cannot in itself found a recovery under s.69. Even if a claimant knows that he is not entitled to benefit and has been asked to return the order book, there is no misrepresentation of material fact when the claimant signs a standard declaration that he is entitled to the payment. Often there will be no misrepresentation of material fact in the second part of that declaration, that the claimant has correctly reported any facts which could affect the amount of the payment, for that will be why the order book is to be returned.

These points seem to have been overlooked in *CIS 359/1990*, where the Commissioner criticised as unfair the requirement on the claimant to declare his entitlement, on penalty of being guilty of misrepresentation if he gets it wrong. The unfairness is lessened if such a misrepresentation of law does not found recovery under s.69. It may found recovery under some other legal principles, but not through the mechanism of s.69. Unfortunately, in an unstarred decision, *CSB 249/1989*, the Commissioner upheld recoverability under the old art. 54, based on a misrepresentation of entitlement; but there the point argued was that the misrepresentation was not made to the Secretary of State. The fundamental issue was not raised, and it is open to SSATs to draw a distinction between matters of material fact and law. Second, in the context of the powers to review contained in s.25(1), the Commissioners have drawn a distinction between material facts and conclusions of fact, or inferences from primary fact (*R(I) 3/75*, *R(A) 2/81* and *R(S) 4/86*, discussed in the note to s.23). The same principle should apply here, so that only misrepresentations or failures to disclose primary facts can found recovery under s.69. So a representation that the claimant was incapable of work would not be enough in itself, unless it contained by necessary implication a representation that the claimant's underlying condition had not changed. The third requirement is that the fact in issue is a material fact. In the context of review, the Court of Appeal in England in *Saker* v. *Secretary of State for Social Services, The Times*, January 16, 1988 (*R(I) 2/88*) decided that for a fact to be material it is not necessary that knowledge of it would have altered the decision. It is enough that the fact is one which would have called for serious consideration by the authority which made the decision and which might well have affected the decision. No doubt the same interpretation should be given to "material fact" here, as was effectively done in *CSB 1006/1985*, but since it is only benefit which would not have been paid but for the misrepresentation or failure to disclose which can be recovered under s.69, it is necessary that knowledge of the material fact would have altered the decision awarding benefit. In *R(SB) 2/91* a student was alleged to have failed to disclose that his course was full-time. The Commissioner held that since a student's own opinion of whether the course was full-time was irrelevant (the objective classification of the course being the issue), disclosure was not reasonably to be expected. Although the Commissioner does not expressly say that the student's opinion was not a material fact, the points he makes about the relevant information having to be gathered from the institution at which the claimant was studying lead inevitably to that conclusion. There is, however, an extra complication in s.69 cases. When considering review, only facts material to the question of entitlement are relevant. Under s.69 it may be that facts relevant to the payment of benefit are also important to the review. So if a claimant wrongly declares that he has correctly reported any fact which could affect the amount of his payment, this does not seem to be a misrepresentation of a material fact in the review sense; but if the test under s.69 is whether the fact is material to payment of benefit, then there will have been a misrepresentation of a material fact. It has not yet been explicitly determined which approach is correct, although several of the decisions mentioned below under *Misrepresentation* proceed on the assumption that the second approach is correct.

Misrepresentation

The meaning of misrepresentation is fairly clear. It requires an actual statement to have been made which is untrue (*CSB 1006/1985*). The statement of material fact may be oral or written, or in some circumstances may arise from conduct, *e.g.* cashing a Giro-cheque. But in this last case there must be some positive conduct from which a statement can be implied, rather than a failure to act. An example where this principle worked in the claimant's favour is *R(SB) 18/85*. The claimant had signed a statement of his resources which omitted his Army pension, but he had produced his pension book to the AO who had filled in the form. The Commissioner held that the circumstances surrounding the completion of a form must be looked at in deciding what was written. If the claimant had qualified the written form by saying that the Army pension should be taken into account, the writing could only be taken into account subject to that qualification. The same result would follow if he had indicated by his actions (*e.g.* producing the pension book) that the pension should be taken into account.

Even where there is a straightforward written statement its precise terms must be considered. In *CSB 1006/1985* the declaration on the B1 form (since changed) signed by the claimant was "as far as I know the information on this form is true and complete". Although a capital resource was omitted from the form, there was no misrepresentation because the claimant honestly believed that the resource was not available to him. In *CSB 790/1988* the claimant had signed this declaration on a benefit order: "I declare that I have read and understand all the instructions in this order book, that I have correctly reported any fact which could affect the amount of my payment and that I am entitled to the above sum". The Commissioner, somewhat surprisingly, concluded that this was only a representation of what the claimant believed she had to disclose on the basis of the instructions given to her. In view of the plain words of the declaration, the decision to the contrary in *CIS 359/1990* must be right. The Commissioner held that it is an unqualified representation that the factual position is as the claimant has reported it. By contrast, in *R(SB) 9/85* the claimant regularly signed declarations that his circumstances had not changed although (unknown to him) his wife's earnings had gone up. The Commissioner said that the claimant should have added something like "not to my knowledge" to his declaration. It is not known what would happen if a claimant tried writing something like this on an order book or crossing out some of the declaration. In the unreported decision of a Northern Ireland Commissioner (*No. 1/91 (ICA)*), the claimant, when applying for sickness benefit, had been asked whether she had been getting or claiming any other social security benefits. She had replied "No". She had in fact put in a claim for Invalid Care Allowance, the success of which was dependent on the outcome of a case going to the European Court of Justice. The Commissioner found that it was not disputed that she had answered the question incorrectly, therefore it was not open to the tribunal to decide that there had not been a misrepresentation.

R(SB) 9/85 illustrates that a wholly innocent misrepresentation may trigger recovery. The section applies whether the person acts "fraudulently or otherwise" (see *Page* v. *Chief Adjudication Officer*, above). In *R(SB) 9/85* the rule that the absence of knowledge of the facts which make the statement untrue is irrelevant is justified on the ground that misrepresentation is based on positive and deliberate action. Similarly, the reasonableness of any belief that a fact was not material is irrelevant (*R(SB) 18/85*). In *R(SB) 3/90* it is suggested that a future case might have to determine whether mental incapacity could prevent there being a misrepresentation at all. On the facts, where the claimant was at the crucial time recovering from a nervous breakdown and treatment including ECT and drugs, there was a misrepresentation, but it was wholly innocent. Possibly, a person would have not to realise the nature of what he was doing to be said not to have made a misrepresentation at all.

Failure to disclose

A failure to disclose is a much more troublesome concept, and there is a good deal of confusing case-law. An essential background is that reg. 32 of the Social Security (Claims and Payments) Regulations (Northern Ireland) 1987 (S.I. 1987 No. 465) (see also the commentary on Great Britain equivalent, reg. 32, *i.e.* Social Security (Claims and Payments) Regulations 1987 (S.I. 1987 No. 1968), in the current editions of Bonner *et al.* and Mesher) imposes a duty on claimants entitled to benefit to notify the Secretary of State in writing of any change of circumstance specified in the notice of determination or order book or any other change which the person might reasonably be expected to know might affect the right to benefit. However, there is not a straightforward link with s.69. For example, recovery may be pursued against any person who fails to disclose or misrepresents a material fact (see, *e.g. R(SB) 21/82* (spouse) and *R(SB) 28/83* (receiver of a mentally infirm person's estate)). Such persons may not be covered by reg. 32. Secondly, the right of recovery only arises under the conditions of s.69. If an order book required a claimant to notify the Secretary of State of a fact which was not material, a failure to do so would not trigger s.69. See above for what amounts to a material fact. Although reg. 32 requires notification in writing, it has long been settled that an oral disclosure is as effective as one in writing for the purposes of s.69 (*CSB 688/1982* and *R(SB) 40/84*). What does disclosure mean? In *R(SB)15/87* a Tribunal of Commissioners held, adopting an opinion in an Australian case, that it is a statement of a fact so as to reveal that which, so far as the discloser knows, was previously unknown to the person to whom the statement is made. This is in line with the ordinary everyday meaning of "disclose". Once disclosure has been made to a particular person there can be no question of there being an obligation to repeat that disclosure to the same person. The question of to whom disclosure is to be made is considered below. The Act uses the words "fails to disclose", not "does not disclose". Therefore it is necessary to consider what amounts to such a failure. In *CSB 53/1981* (a decision of a Tribunal of Commissioners, but not reported) the statement of Diplock J. in *R.* v. *Medical Appeal Tribunal (North Midland Region)*, ex p. *Hubble* [1958] 2 Q.B. 228, 242, was applied to the old s.20. "Non-disclosure" in the context of the subsection, where it is coupled with misrepresentation, means a failure to disclose a fact known to the person who does not disclose it. It is innocent if the person failing to disclose the fact does not appreciate its materiality, fraudulent if he does. In *CSB 53/1981*, the claimant had either overlooked or failed to appreciate the relevance of 1,000 premium bonds, so was innocent, but had still failed to disclose. This approach gives the impression that if a fact is material and is known to the person, no other factors are relevant. It is certainly the case that knowledge of the fact is an essential requirement. Where the person is the owner of an asset and has once known of its existence, he will normally be fixed with that knowledge even if he later forgets about it (*R(SB) 21/82*, para. 20(4)). However, in some cases a person may not be mentally capable of knowing that he continues to possess the asset. This was so in *R(SB) 28/83*, where the Commissioner said that it must be shown that the person either knew or with reasonable diligence ought to have known that he possessed the assets. In *R(SB) 40/84* there was a possibility that, in view of her advanced age, the claimant had never known that her superannuation had been increased.

Similar arguments can be applied, for instance, to the addition of interest to building society accounts. Knowledge of this process can normally be assumed if a person knows of the account, but, depending on the medical evidence, may not exist in some circumstances. If the person from whom recovery is sought is not the owner of the asset, it seems that there is less room for assumptions and that knowledge of its existence must be proved (*R(SB) 21/82*, para. 20(4)). Some doubt is expressed in para. 22(2) whether constructive knowledge (*i.e.* what a person ought to know) is enough, but it probably is, since no dishonesty or fraud has to be shown (*Page* v. *Chief Adjudication Officer*, *R(SB) 2/92*). Once it is proved that the person has sufficient knowledge of a material fact, there must still be something which amounts to a "failure". In para. 4(2) of *R(SB) 21/82* the Commissioner said that this "necessarily imports the concept of some breach of obligation, moral or legal—*i.e.* the non-disclosure must have occurred in circumstances in which, at lowest, disclosure by the person in question was reasonably to be expected". This statement has been accepted in many decisions, including *R(SB) 28/83*, *R(SB) 54/83* and *R(SB) 15/87*, but does not provide a simple solution to problems when it is also clear that an innocent failure to disclose can trigger the right to recover. In *CSB 1006/1985* it was suggested that the statement does not apply at all where non-disclosure by the claimant himself of an asset of his own is being considered. This is probably going too far, but it is necessary to attempt to spell out some limitations. First, the test is an objective one. It must depend on what a reasonable person in the position of the person from whom recovery is sought, with that person's knowledge, would have done. Thus, in general, the fact that, as in *CSB 1006/1985*, the claimant did not consider that an asset was relevant, would be irrelevant. A reasonable person would not take that view. But if, say, a DHSS official had expressly assured the claimant that an undoubtedly material fact did not need to be disclosed, this surely would create a situation in which disclosure was not reasonably to be expected. This would be in line with the result of *R(SB) 3/81*, where a course of conduct which had evolved over several years between the DSS and the claimant concerning the handing over of P60s was held to have affected the claimant's obligation. A slight extension is shown in *CSB 727/1987*, where it was held that the terms of a DSS form and the answers given by the claimant are relevant to whether a later disclosure is reasonably to be expected. The claim for supplementary benefit was made soon after the birth of the claimant's child. On the claim form she said that she was owed "family allowance" and had applied for child benefit and one-parent benefit. Supplementary benefit was awarded without any deduction for child benefit or one-parent benefit. The claimant's child benefit and one-parent benefit order book were sent to her on December 17, 1984. She did not notify the local supplementary benefit office until February 24, 1986 and in the meantime supplementary benefit was paid without taking account of the income from child benefit and one-parent benefit. Most SSATs would have regarded this as an open-and-shut case of failure to disclose, but the Commissioner held that in these circumstances disclosure was not reasonably to be expected. The claimant had given detailed answers about her claims and made it clear that she regarded child benefit and one-parent benefit as due to her. She might then expect not to have to report their actual receipt. Although her supplementary benefit did not go down, she might well have thought that such benefits did not affect the amount of supplementary benefit. The questions on the claim form could easily have led her to think that her answers were all the information the DSS required unless they expressly asked for more. Nor did the instructions in the supplementary benefit order book alter the situation, since they concerned reporting income or benefit not already reported to the Issuing Office. The claimant could justifiably think that she had already reported the benefits. The decision must depend on its particular facts, and some of the Commissioner's assumptions might not have held up under close examination of the claimant's actual knowledge, but it does indicate the necessity to consider what is reasonably to be expected in a broad context. The general principle has been applied in a number of unreported decisions.

In *CSB 677/1986* a supplementary benefit claimant was also in receipt of sickness benefit, both being administered in the same local office. He received a notification from the local office that he had progressed from sickness benefit to invalidity benefit (paid at a higher rate). The claimant did not inform the supplementary benefit section, but the Commissioner held that he could not reasonably be expected to inform the office which had informed him, especially if the notes in his order book turned out to refer simply to the "issuing office". In *CSB 1246/1986* it was held that there was no obligation to disclose the annual up-rating of unemployment benefit, since this was public knowledge. *CSB 790/1988* takes the same line as *CSB 677/1986* on whether, when an order book instructs a claimant to report changes to "the issuing office", a claimant would reasonably expect to have to report to one part of an integrated local office receipt of benefit from another part. Precise proof of what instructions were included in the order book actually issued to the claimant was crucial in *CP 20/1990*. An increase of benefit for the claimant's wife was improperly awarded, then excluded from payment by an administrative procedure, but allegedly actually paid to the claimant. The Commissioner said that in an ordinary case where proper awards are made, a photocopy of the Departmental record of the award and the issue of order books, together with a specimen of the order books current at the time, will suffice to show the instructions given in the book about disclosure. But here it could not be assumed that the appropriate order book with the appropriate instructions had been issued. More recently, in *R(SB) 2/91* the Commissioner held that a claimant could not reasonably be expected to disclose a matter which was irrelevant to the question on which entitlement depended. However, it is expecting too much for a claimant to assess whether a matter is relevant or not, and this case would have been better dealt with on the basis that what was not disclosed was not a material fact (see above). *CSB 510/1987* decided that advice from the claimant's solicitor and barrister that she did not need to tell the Department about an increase in her children's maintenance payments would mean that disclosure was not reasonably expected. If one is concerned with disclosure by the claimant of someone else's asset (*e.g.* in *R(SB) 54/83*, the fact that the claimant's wife was working), the *R(SB) 21/82* test may be useful in marginal cases. Its most direct application will be, as in *R(SB) 21/82* itself, in deciding whether some person other than the claimant is under an obligation to disclose. *R(SB) 28/83* is a further example. Since the receiver of the mentally infirm claimant knew of his assets and knew or ought to have known that he was receiving supplementary benefit, he came under an obligation to disclose.

The next issue is to whom must disclosure be made. The leading decision is now *R(SB) 15/87*. Since the concern under the old s.20 (art. 25 of the Supplementary Benefits (Northern Ireland) Order 1977 in Northern Ireland) was with breaches of the obligation to disclose which had the consequence that the Secretary of State incurred expenditure, it was held that the obligation was to disclose to a member or members of staff of an office of the Department handling the transaction giving rise to the expenditure. Although the wording of s.69 is somewhat different, it is thought that the obligation would be similar, relating to the office handling the claim giving rise to the payment of benefit alleged to have been overpaid. The Tribunal rejected the argument that disclosure to any member of the staff of the Department or to anyone in the "integrated office" in which the claimant was claiming would do. It was accepted that the claimant cannot be expected to identify the precise person dealing with his claim, but the Tribunal was then rather vague about how the obligation is to be fulfilled. It said it is best fulfilled by disclosure to the local office, either on a claim form or by making sufficient reference to the claim for the information to be referred to the proper person. If this is done, then there can be no further duty to disclose that matter. In the case of a claimant who is required to be available for work and thus has to deliver his claim form to the unemployment benefit office (UBO), disclosure on a claim form delivered there fulfils the duty.

The Tribunal also accepted the decision in *R(SB) 54/83* that if an officer in another office accepts information in circumstances which make it reasonable for the claimant to think that the information will be passed on to the proper local office the duty is fulfilled. It held that it is only in this kind of situation that there is a continuing duty of disclosure, as suggested in para. 18 of *R(SB) 54/83*. If the claimant should subsequently have realised that the information had not reached the proper person then a further obligation to disclose to the proper person would arise. The Tribunal expressly left open the question whether the claimant must actually know that the information has not got through. Although the decision in *R(SB) 15/87* clears up a number of points, it does still leave some uncertainties. The major one is in what circumstances disclosure to the UBO might fulfil the claimant's obligation. There is one unreported decision of a Northern Ireland Commissioner on this issue. In *Decision No. C6/88 (Supp. Ben.)* the Commissioner stated that the proper test was whether the circumstances were such that it could reasonably have been expected that the information would be transmitted from the UBO to the supplementary benefit section of the Department.

However, it was suggested in *R(SB) 54/83* that in the case of a claimant who is required to declare his availability for work at, and is paid through, the UBO, the UBO is the agent of the supplementary benefit office, so that notice to the UBO would be imputed to the supplementary benefit office (and now the office dealing with income support). The Commissioner did not have to decide the point, but the issue was exhaustively discussed by a Tribunal of Commissioners in *R(SB) 36/84* and *CSB 397/1983*. There is an identical appendix in both decisions setting out in detail the arrangements between the DHSS and the Department of Employment (DE), who administer UBOs. The preliminary conclusion was that, having regard to the past 40 years' arrangements, in particular those under which payment to claimants required to register or be available for work is made on the instructions of the UBO, there is an agency relationship. The decisions were not directly to do with recovery of overpayments, but the result in this context would be as suggested in *R(SB) 54/83*, regardless of the fact that the two Departments are otherwise independent.

Some earlier decisions like *CSB 14/82* must now be rejected as being based on mistaken assumptions about the independence of Departments (although it is clear that the principle can only apply in the special case of claimants paid through the UBO). However, the point has been treated as one of fact for each SSAT, rather than a matter on which a definite legal answer has been given (*R(SB) 10/85*). The Tribunal of Commissioners in *R(SB) 15/87* certainly did not expressly reject the agency argument. Some doubt is raised because the Tribunal mentioned several ways of fulfilling the duty of disclosure, including delivering a claim form to the UBO, without mentioning the general agency argument. There is an obscure passage (para. 30) on causation (see below) which refers to para. 6549 of the S Manual. This does not seem to be relevant, but para. 6548 said that claimants who were required to be available were required to declare their earnings at the UBO. This reinforces the agency argument, but the context in the Tribunal's decision is of a situation where the claimant is said to have failed to disclose. Until there is clarification, the approach of *R(SB) 36/84* should be followed until expressly disapproved. In *R(SB) 2/91* it was accepted by the representative of the Chief Adjudication Officer that the DE were the agents of the DSS for the purposes of the payment of supplementary benefit, so that information given to the UBO constituted information given to the supplementary benefit section of the DSS. This view was approved by the Commissioner. The weight of the decisions is clearly that the DE now acts as the agent of the DHSS where income support is paid through the UBO, so that in those cases disclosure to the UBO is disclosure to the office dealing with the claim.

In *CSB 699/1986* the Commissioner considered the circumstances in which, once disclosure has been made, there is no further obligation to disclose "the same matter". He suggested that the "same matter" is not restricted to one-off events, but could extend to a continuing state of affairs, such as the receipt of another benefit. But a transition from sickness to invalidity benefit would be a different matter. Similarly, disclosure on the claim form on a previous claim for the same benefit does not lift the duty to disclose on a fresh claim (*R(SB) 3/90*). *R(SB) 15/87* also deals with the question of by whom disclosure can be made in order to fulfil the claimant's obligation. One daughter, for whom the claimant had received benefit as a dependant, had made a claim in her own right for supplementary benefit at the same office. In respect of another child who started a YTS course, the child benefit book had been surrendered to the contributory benefits section of the same office by the claimant's wife. The Tribunal held that neither of these actions was sufficient disclosure. Disclosure can be made by a third party on behalf of the claimant, but if this is done in the course of a separate transaction, the information must be given to the relevant benefit office and the claimant must know that it has been done and reasonably believe that it is unnecessary for him to take any action himself. *CSB 347/1983* (approved in *R(SB) 10/85*) held that while an AO might discharge his initial burden of proof by showing that there is no official record of a change of circumstances, thus leaving it for the claimant to prove on a balance of probabilities that he had made a disclosure, this only applies if a proper foundation is laid by evidence (not mere assertion) as to the instructions for recording information and how these are in practice carried out. The distinction between evidence and assertion was strongly supported in *CSB 1195/1984*. The claimant said that she had told two visiting officers that she was receiving unemployment benefit, but there was no official record of such a statement. The Commissioner stressed that what the claimant says about her own acts is evidence, while what a presenting officer says is not evidence unless backed up by personal knowledge of the facts. He says that the new SSAT should call the two visiting officers to give evidence. If they failed to appear without adequate excuse, the weight of the assertions alleged to have been made by them would be reduced to little or nothing. In *CSB 615/1985* it was stressed that there is no rule that only documentary evidence is admissible or that oral evidence requires corroboration.

Causation
    It must be shown by the AO that any overpayment resulted from the misrepresentation or failure to disclose. In *R(SB) 3/81* the SBAT simply failed to look at the issue. In *R(SB) 21/82* the Commissioner held that the right to recovery arises "only on a clearly stipulated causal basis". In that case the claimant's wife had made declarations in 1969 and 1971, but made no more until after the claimant's death in 1979. It was not clear how far any overpayment of benefit was in consequence of those earlier declarations when there were many intervening declarations by the claimant. It is clear that if a claimant has disclosed a material fact to the relevant office in relation to the relevant claim there can be no recovery of subsequent benefit based on a failure to disclose that fact. This was decided in *CSB 688/1982* and *CSB 347/1983*, and confirmed in *R(SB) 15/87*. On principle, it would seem that proper disclosure would rob a subsequent misrepresentation of any causative effect. This appeared to be the result in *CSB 688/1982*, where the claimant orally disclosed to an AO that he had a mine-worker's pension. The AO omitted this from the statement, which the claimant then signed as a true and complete statement of his circumstances. The Commissioner held that the disclosure was fatal to the right of recovery. Although this had been put only on the ground of failure to disclose, the Commissioner felt able to make the decision that the overpayment was not recoverable. Since there had obviously been a misrepresentation, it looked as though the Commissioner must have considered that it could have no legal effect. However, in the very similar case of *R(SB) 18/85* the same Commissioner concentrated on the misrepresentation (see above) and makes no mention of the causation issue. It may be that, since the appeal had to be sent back to the SBAT for proper findings of fact, the decision should be regarded as neutral on the causation issue. The better view is that disclosure does rob a subsequent misrepresentation of causative effect, but the point is not authoritatively decided. In *R(SB) 3/90* the basic principle that, if a misrepresentation induces a person to act, it is irrelevant that the person had a means of verifying the information was applied. But during the currency of one claim the principle of *R(SB) 15/87* would undermine that approach where the means of verification stems from the claimant's disclosure. The most controversial issue here is the effect of the breakdown of procedures within the DHSS for notifying the income support office that a person has been awarded some other benefit (see, *e.g.* Income Support Manual, paras. 3.1207–1212 for the child benefit procedure). The argument is that even though a claimant may have failed to disclose receipt of the other benefit, the operative cause of the overpayment is the failure of the administrative procedure to get notice of entitlement to the other benefit from the other section concerned to the income support office. This argument has been rejected in a number of Commissioner's decisions, most recently in *CSB 64/1986* and *R(SB) 3/90*. The question asked there was, would the Secretary of State have avoided the relevant expenditure if the claimant had not failed to disclose the relevant material fact? If the answer is "yes", then the failure is the cause of the expenditure. The DSS procedure is in that sense a back-up one. The validity of this approach is confirmed by the Court of Appeal in England in *Duggan* v. *Chief Adjudication Officer*, *The Times*, December 18, 1988 (*R(SB) 13/89*). The claimant had failed to disclose his wife's unemployment benefit, but argued that on a review the AO should have investigated the full financial situation. It was held that if one cause of the overpayment was the failure to disclose, the overpayment is recoverable. The new wording in s.69, describing the amount recoverable as any payment which the Secretary of State would not have made but for the misrepresentation or failure to disclose, reinforces this conclusion. However, it is vital to note that the principles just set out only apply when the other section of the DHSS fails to inform the income support section. It is different if the information is received, but the income support section fails to act on it. The Tribunal of Commissioners in *R(SB) 15/87* recognised that if the DSS procedure works it may break the causal link between the claimant's failure and the overpayment. This is now explicitly dealt with in *CIS 159/1990*, where the Child Benefit Centre informed the local office dealing with the income support claim of the issue of an order book with an increased amount of child benefit, plus some arrears. The claimant did not report the arrival of the order book. The Commissioner held that the overpayment was not in consequence of the failure to disclose, because the local office already knew of the material fact. Note that if income support is paid while a claimant is waiting for a decision on entitlement for another benefit and arrears of the other benefit are paid for this period, any excess income support cannot be recovered under this section, since it does not result from a failure to disclose. But s.72 and the Social Security (Payments on Account, Overpayments and Recovery) Regulations (Northern Ireland) 1987 (S.I. 1987 No. 122) (see also the commentary on the equivalent Great Britain Regulations, *i.e.* the Social Security (Payments on Account,

Overpayments and Recovery) Regulations 1988 (S.I. 1988 No. 664), in the current editions of Bonner *et al.* and Mesher) will operate to allow the excess to be deducted from the arrears of the other benefit or recovered from the recipient.

Amount of overpayment
   The calculation of the amount to be recovered has given considerable problems in the past. Subsection (6)(a) below allows regulations to be made on this issue. Regulations 13 and 14 of the Payments Regulations are relevant.
   The starting point is the amount of benefit which would not have been paid but for the overpayment or failure to disclose. This is in line with the approach set out in *R(SB) 20/84* and *R(SB) 10/85* of looking at what the revised decision would be when the full facts are known. Normally there is no difficulty in determining the amount of benefit which was actually paid, but there may be exceptional cases, like *CP 20/1990*, where evidence of the amounts of payment, rather than a second-hand description, is required. A controversial question under the pre-April 1987 law was how far it was possible to take account of underpayments of benefit against the overpayment. Regulation 13(b) of the Payments Regulations provides that from the gross amount of the overpayment is to be deducted any additional amount of benefit which should have been awarded on the basis of the claim as originally presented or with the addition of the facts misrepresented or not disclosed. This allows a somewhat more extensive set-off than under the old law (for which, see *R(SB) 20/84*, *R(SB) 10/85* and *R(SB) 11/86*). *CSIS 49/1990* confirms that the reg. 13(b) deduction is not limited to the period after the beginning of the overpayment, but can go back to the date of claim. But the examination of the additional amount which would have been payable must be based on the claim as originally presented, or with the addition of the material facts misrepresented or not disclosed. Thus, if, for instance, evidence suggesting that a premium should have been allowed is produced for the first time once an overpayment has been determined by an AO, the amount of that premium is not to be offset against the gross amount of the overpayment (confirming the result of *CSB 615/1985*). In that case, any arrears must be obtained through the ordinary process of review under s.23, and subject to the 12-month limit imposed by reg. 69 of the Social Security (Adjudication) Regulations (Northern Ireland) 1987 (S.I. 1987 No. 82). If the award of benefit has been reviewed, *e.g.* to include a premium, but the arrears have not yet been paid when the overpayment is determined, there can be an offset under regs. 5(2), Case 1, and 14(a) of the Payments Regulations. Any other offset under reg. 5 is to be deducted, but no other deduction for underpayments is to be made. Another problem now dealt with by regulations arises when the misrepresentation or failure to disclose is of capital resources. If it emerged that a claimant who had been in receipt of income support or family credit for a few years had throughout had capital of £1 over the limit, it would be most unfair to require repayment of the whole amount of benefit. If the capital had been properly taken into account, so that benefit was not initially awarded, the capital would have immediately been reduced below the limit in order to provide for living expenses. The Commissioners applied the "diminishing capital" principle (*CSB 53/1981*, *CSBO* v. *Leary*, appendix to *R(SB) 6/85*, *R(SB) 15/85*). The position is now governed by reg. 14 of the Payments Regulations. This provides for the reduction of the figure of capital resources at quarterly intervals from the beginning of the overpayment period by the amount overpaid in income support or family credit in the previous quarter. No other reduction of the actual amount of capital resources is allowed (reg. 15(2)). Under the Commissioners' approach, the notional reduction had to be made week by week. It will be considerably easier to make the calculation at 13-week intervals, but the tendency will be for higher amounts of overpayments to be produced. It is for the AO to prove the existence and amount of capital taken into account in calculating an overpayment (*R(SB) 21/82*). Here, sums had suddenly appeared in building society accounts and there was no evidence where they had come from. The Commissioner commended the adoption of a lower figure of overpayment rather than a higher one based on the assumption that the capital assets had been possessed before any evidence existed about them.
   The Commissioner in *R(SB) 34/83* agreed strongly on the burden of proof, but pointed out that if the person concerned was alive and failed to give any proper explanation of the origin of such sums, adverse inferences could be drawn against him, enabling the AO to discharge his burden of proof. He went on to hold that the estate of a deceased person should be in the same position. Therefore, a heavy responsibility devolved on the executor to make every reasonable enquiry as to the origin of the money. But if after such efforts there was no evidence where the money came from the burden of proof would not have been discharged. It is essential that on an appeal a SSAT should clearly state the amount which is recoverable, and state how that amount is calculated (*R(SB) 9/85*). If the SSAT cannot make the calculation at the time of their initial decision they can refer the matter back to the AO for recalculation on the basis determined by the SSAT, but only if the decision expressly allows the matter to be referred back to the SSAT if agreement cannot be reached on the recalculation (*R(SB) 11/86*, *R(SB) 15/87*).

One reason why SSATs must be careful to specify the amount recoverable is that often differing amounts are calculated by the AO after his initial decision. If this is done there is, at least before April 1990, no bar to this operating as a review and revision of the initial decision. The initial decision, being on a single indivisible question, will thus be replaced and any appeal lodged against it will lapse. However, appeals in these circumstances are commonly continued as though they have not lapsed.

In *CSB 64/1986*, where the claimant's representative insisted that the appeal was against the initial decision, the Commissioner held that the SSAT's decision was given without authority, as the appeal had lapsed. In *R(SB) 15/87*, the appeal was treated as against the revised decision, although no notice of appeal against that decision had been given. The Tribunal of Commissioners held that in this case the failure to comply with the procedural requirements did not make the SSAT's proceedings a nullity. There had been substantial compliance with the requirements, there was no public interest in strict compliance and the claimant would be prejudiced if the procedural failure was not ignored, since the time for appealing against the revised decision had expired.

The predecessor of s.27 of this Act provided from April 1990 that once an appeal has been lodged, a review is to be of no effect unless it gives the claimant everything that the claimant could possibly obtain in the appeal.

Subs. (2)
See notes to subs. (5).

Subs. (3)
This provision confirms that amounts are recoverable from the person who made the misrepresentation or failed to make disclosure. Presumably the principle that after the person's death the overpayment is recoverable from his estate (*Secretary of State for Social Services* v. *Solly* [1974] 3 All E.R. 922, *R(SB) 21/82, R(SB) 28/83*) is not affected. Note that the time limit of the Limitation Acts (Northern Ireland) 1958–1982 does not begin to run until there is a determination of an overpayment by an AO which gives the Secretary of State the right of recovery (*R(SB) 5/91, R(A) 2/86*).

Subs. (4)
This provision applies where benefit is directly credited to an account. See reg. 21 of the Social Security (Claims and Payments) Regulations (Northern Ireland) 1987 (S.I. 1987 No. 465) and reg. 11 of the Social Security (Payments on Account, Overpayments and Recovery) Regulations (Northern Ireland) 1988 (S.I. 1988 No. 142) ("the Payments Regulations").

Subs. (5)
The general rule here is taken over from that for contributory benefits, that recovery of an overpayment should follow a revision on review of the decision awarding benefit or its variation on appeal. The result is that if the conditions for review are not met, then even though the initial decision was incorrect, no overpayment can be recovered. However, regulations may provide otherwise and have done so.

Regulation 12 of the Payments Regulations provides that subs. (5) shall not apply where the fact and circumstances of the misrepresentation or non-disclosure do not provide a basis for reviewing and revising the initial decision. This formulation is rather obscure, but it seems to mean that if the conditions for review and revision do not exist, there can still be a determination that an overpayment is recoverable. But if those conditions do exist, then the determination of the recoverable overpayment must be made as part of the review decision or not at all (see also subs. (2)). This has now been decided in *R(SB) 7/91*. A number of decisions have held that (outside the exception in reg. 12 of the Payments Regulations) it is an essential pre-condition of an overpayment determination that there should be proof of a valid revision of entitlement on review. See *CSSB 105/1989*, followed in *CIS 179/1990* and *CIS 360/1990*, and *R(SB) 7/91*. The principle was accepted in *CSSB 316/1989*, where the Commissioner also dealt with the requirement of subs. (5) that the overpayment determination must be made "on the appeal or review". He said "[the] earliest possible correction of a continuing award which has been found to be incorrect is obviously desirable and I accept that an effective decision for the purposes of section 53(1), (1A) and (4) can be made notwithstanding that grounds of review and revisal of the award for the past and the future, which must of course be appropriate, are established at a date prior to the making of the decision establishing the detail of the overpayment".

There remains some uncertainty about what a SSAT should do if faced with an overpayment decision when there has not been a valid revision of entitlement on review.

In *CSSB 105/1989, CSSB 316/1989* and *CSSB 540/1989*, the Commissioner suggested that the SSAT should simply determine that no valid AO's decision on the overpayment has been made.

In *R(SB) 7/91*, the Commissioner holds that if the AO made no review decision, the SSAT should determine that the AO's overpayment decision is of no force or effect. However, this seems to leave the possibility of an AO reviewing the defective AO's decision for error of law under s.23(2) of this Act (suggested in *CSSB 105/1989*) or of the AO starting the overpayment procedure all over again by a valid revision of entitlement on review. A SSAT's decision in this form does not decide that an overpayment can never be recovered. It secures that the proper process must be applied. But the final result may be the same and the claimant has to appeal yet again to challenge it. It may therefore be asked why the SSAT should not follow the general principle put forward in *CSSB 540/1989* that on appeal a SSAT can correct a defective review decision. In *CSB 1272/1989* the Commissioner, in an effort to avoid the expense and delay of starting the whole process again, suggests that where in overpayments cases the AO has omitted to carry out a review, the SSAT should make good the omission using its power under s.34 of this Act (1975 Act, s.102) to determine questions first arising in the course of the appeal. This approach seems rather dubious, since the review question seems to be part and parcel of the overpayment question already before the AO and the SSAT, and not one which first arises in the course of the appeal. In addition, none of the decisions mentioned earlier are cited in *CSB 1272/1989*. The current position thus remains unresolved until some authoritative decision emerges from the Commissioners. At the moment the weight of authority would seem to be in favour of a SSAT determining that no valid overpayment decision has been made. There is in any case a difficulty in "correcting" an AO's decision where no review decision at all has been made. There may however be exceptional circumstances, for instance where a SSAT is clear that an overpayment would not be recoverable under s.69, where a SSAT should deal with the review issue (*cf. CSB 274/1990*).

Subs. (6)
The Social Security (Payments on Account, Overpayments and Recovery) Regulations (Northern Ireland) 1988 (S.I. 1988 No. 142) have been made under these powers.

Subs. (7)
See Pt. II of the Social Security (Payments on Account, Overpayments and Recovery) Regulations (Northern Ireland) 1988 (S.I. 1988 No. 142).

Subs. (8)
The benefits from which deductions may be made are prescribed by reg. 15 of the Social Security (Payments on Account, Overpayments and Recovery) Regulations (Northern Ireland) 1988 (S.I. 1988 No. 142). They include most social security benefits. Limits to the weekly amounts which may be deducted from income support and family credit are set by reg. 16. Regulation 20(2) of the Social Security (Payments on Account, Overpayments and Recovery) Regulations (Northern Ireland) 1987 (S.I. 1987 No. 122) provides that subs. (8) also applies to amounts recoverable under any enactment repealed by the Social Security (Northern Ireland) Order 1986 or regulation revoked by the 1987 Regulations. The Divisional Court in England in *R.* v. *Secretary of State for Social Services*, ex p. *Britnell (Alan)*, *The Times*, January 27, 1989, decided that reg. 20(2) did not offend the rule of construction against retrospection. Its effect was merely to provide an additional method of recovery where there was no dispute that a liability to repay existed. In the English Court of Appeal (*The Times*, February 16, 1990), the point on retrospection was not argued and reg. 20(2) was found to have been validly made under s.89(1) of the 1986 Act.

Subs. (9)
See reg. 17 of the Social Security (Payments on Account, Overpayments and Recovery) Regulations (Northern Ireland) 1988 (S.I. 1988 No. 142).

Special provision as to recovery of income support

70.—(1) Where—
(a) a direction under section 124(1) of the Contributions and Benefits Act is revoked; and
(b) it is determined by an adjudication officer that, whether fraudulently or otherwise, any person has misrepresented, or failed to disclose, any material fact and in consequence of the misrepresentation or failure a payment of income support has been made during the relevant period to the person to whom the direction related,
an adjudication officer may determine that the Department shall be entitled to recover the amount of the payment.
(2) In subsection (1) above "the relevant period" means—
(a) if the revocation is under subsection (3) of section 124 of the Contributions and Benefits Act, the period beginning with the date of the

change of circumstances and ending with the date of the revocation; and

(b) if the revocation is under subsection (4) of that section, the period during which the direction was enforced.

(3) Where a direction under section 124(1) of the Contributions and Benefits Act is revoked, the Department may certify whether there has been misrepresentation of a material fact or failure to disclose a material fact.

(4) If the Department certifies that there has been such misrepresentation or failure to disclose, it may also certify—

(a) who made the misrepresentation or failed to make the disclosure; and

(b) whether or not a payment of income support has been made in consequence of the misrepresentation or failure.

(5) If the Department certifies that a payment has been made, it may certify the period during which income support would not have been paid but for the misrepresentation or failure to disclose.

(6) A certificate under this section shall be conclusive for the purposes of this section as to any matter certified.

(7) Section 69(3) and (6) to (11) above apply to income support recoverable under subsection (1) above as they apply to income support recoverable under section 69(1) above.

(8) The other provisions of section 69 above do not apply to income support recoverable under subsection (1) above.

DEFINITIONS
"the Contributions and Benefits Act": s.167.
"the Department": *ibid.*

GENERAL NOTE
Section 124(1) of the Contributions and Benefits (Northern Ireland) Act enables the Department to direct that a person under the age of 18 is to qualify for income support in order to avoid severe hardship. The direction may be revoked under s.124(3) on the ground of change of circumstances or under s.124(4) on the ground that a mistake or ignorance of material fact led to the determination that severe hardship would result if income support were not to be paid. A special provision is needed for recovery in cases of misrepresentation or failure to disclose because the revocation of the direction is not a review which can found action under s.69. Although the determination is made by the AO under subs. (1), the Department's certificate is conclusive on almost every issue (subss. (3)–(6)). The provisions of s.69 about the mechanics of recovery apply.

Adjustments of benefits

Overlapping benefits—general

71.—(1) Regulations may provide for adjusting benefit as defined in section 121 of the Contributions and Benefits Act which is payable to or in respect of any person, or the conditions for its receipt, where—

(a) there is payable in his case any such pension, allowance or benefit as is described in subsection (2) below; or

(b) the person is, or is treated under the regulations as, undergoing medical or other treatment as an in-patient in a hospital or similar institution.

(2) Subsection (1)(a) above applies to any pension, allowance or benefit payable out of public funds (including any other benefit as so defined, whether it is of the same or a different description) which is payable to or in respect of—

(a) the person referred to in subsection (1);

(b) that person's wife or husband;

(c) any child or adult dependant of that person; or

(d) the wife or husband of any adult dependant of that person.

(3) Where but for regulations made by virtue of subsection (1)(a) above two persons would both be entitled to an increase of benefit in respect of a third person, regulations may make provision as to their priority.

(4) Regulations may provide for adjusting benefit payable to or in respect of any person where there is payable in his case any such benefit as is described in subsection (5) below.

(5) Subsection (4) above applies to any benefit payable under the legislation of any member State other than the United Kingdom which is payable to or in respect of—

(a) the person referred to in that subsection;
(b) that person's wife or husband;
(c) any child or adult dependant of that person; or
(d) the wife or husband of any adult dependant of that person.

DEFINITIONS
"the Contributions and Benefits Act": s.167.

GENERAL NOTE
See the Social Security (Overlapping Benefits) Regulations (Northern Ireland) 1979 (S.I. 1979 No. 242). See also the equivalent Great Britain Regulations, the Social Security (Overlapping Benefits) Regulations 1979 (S.I. 1979 No. 597), and the commentary in the current edition of Bonner *et al.*

Income support and other payments

72.—(1) Where—

(a) a payment by way of prescribed income is made after the date which is the prescribed date in relation to the payment; and
(b) it is determined that an amount which has been paid by way of income support would not have been paid if the payment had been made on the prescribed date,

the Department shall be entitled to recover that amount from the person to whom it was paid.

(2) Where—

(a) a prescribed payment which apart from this subsection falls to be made from public funds in the United Kingdom or under the law of any other member State is not made on or before the date which is the prescribed date in relation to the payment; and
(b) it is determined that an amount ("the relevant amount") has been paid by way of income support that would not have been paid if the payment mentioned in paragraph (a) above had been made on the prescribed date,

then—

(i) in the case of a payment from public funds in the United Kingdom, the authority responsible for making it may abate it by the relevant amount; and
(ii) in the case of any other payment, the Department shall be entitled to receive the relevant amount out of the payment.

(3) Where—

(a) a person (in this subsection referred to as A) is entitled to any prescribed benefit for any period in respect of another person (in this subsection referred to as B); and
(b) either—

(i) B has received income support for that period; or
(ii) B was, during that period, a member of the same family as some person other than A who received income support for that period; and

(c) the amount of the income support has been determined on the basis that A has not made payments for the maintenance of B at a rate equal to or exceeding the amount of the prescribed benefit,

the amount of the prescribed benefit may, at the discretion of the authority administering it, be abated by the amount by which the amounts paid by way of income support exceed what it is determined that they would have been had A, at the time the amount of the income support was determined, been making payments for the maintenance of B at a rate equal to the amount of the prescribed benefit.

(4) Where an amount could have been recovered by abatement by virtue of subsection (2) or (3) above but has not been so recovered, the Department may recover it otherwise than by way of abatement—

   (a) in the case of an amount which could have been recovered by virtue of subsection (2) above, from the person to whom it was paid; and

   (b) in the case of an amount which could have been recovered by virtue of subsection (3) above, from the person to whom the prescribed benefit in question was paid.

(5) Where a payment is made in a currency other than sterling, its value in sterling shall be determined for the purposes of this section in accordance with regulations.

DEFINITIONS

   "prescribed": s.167.
   "the Department": *ibid.*

GENERAL NOTE

   Most of this section was formerly, in substance, art. 25 of the Supplementary Benefits (Northern Ireland) Order 1977 (S.I. 1977 No. 2156 (N.I. 27)). There are changes in form from the old art. 25, but the overall aim is the same, to prevent a claimant from getting a double payment when other sources of income are not paid on time. This is an important provision, which is often overlooked.

Subs. (1)

   Prescribed income is defined in reg. 7(1) of the Social Security (Payments on Account, Overpayments and Recovery) Regulations (Northern Ireland) 1988 (S.I. 1988 No. 142) ("the Payments Regulations") as any income which is to be taken into account under Pt. V of the Income Support (General) Regulations (Northern Ireland) 1987 (S.I. 1987 No. 459). The prescribed date under reg. 7(2) is, in general, the first day of the period to which that income relates. If, as a result of that income being paid after the prescribed date, more income support is paid than would have been paid if the income had been paid on the prescribed date, the excess may be recovered. Note that the right to recover is absolute and does not depend on lack of care on the claimant's part, or on the effect of this section having been pointed out. An example would be where a claimant has not been paid part-time earnings when they were due and as a result has been paid income support on the basis of having no earnings. Once the arrears of wages are received, the excess benefit would be recoverable. Late payment of most social security benefits is covered in subss. (2) and (4), but can also come within subs. (1). For instance, if a claim is made for child benefit and while a decision is awaited income support is paid without any deduction for the amount of the expected child benefit, then if arrears of child benefit are eventually paid in full (*i.e.* the abatement procedure of subs. (2) does not work) the "excess" income support for the period covered by the arrears is recoverable under subss. (1) or (4).

Subs. (2)

   Prescribed payments are listed in reg. 8(1) of the Social Security (Payments on Account, Overpayments and Recovery) Regulations (Northern Ireland) 1988 (S.I. 1988 No. 142) and include most social security benefits, training allowances and social security benefits from other EEC countries. As under subs. (1), a claimant is not to keep excess income support resulting from late payment of one of the prescribed payments. However, the primary mechanism here where the payment is due from public funds in the U.K. is for the arrears due to be abated (*i.e.* reduced) by the amount of the excess income support (subs. (2)(a) and (i)). Note that the abatement may be applied to benefits due to another member of the claimant's family (*e.g.* retirement pension due to the wife of the income support claimant in *CSB 383/1988*). If this mechanism breaks down and the arrears are paid in full, then under subss. (1) or (4) the Department can recover the excess from the income support recipient.

   In the case of other payments (which will normally be benefits due from other E.C. countries), recovery is the primary mechanism (subs. (2)(ii)). If the payment is routed through the DSS (DHSS in Northern Ireland), as was the case for the arrears of a German invalidity pension in *R(IS) 3/91*, a deduction can be made before the arrears are paid over to the claimant. Although reg. 8(1)(g) of the Payments Regulations makes a reference to E.C. Regulation 1408/71, the s.72 procedure is not limited to benefits obtained by virtue of the Regulation. Once again, the operation of the provision is automatic. Any undertaking by the claimant to repay seems superfluous. However, the Department might choose not to enforce its right to recovery.

Under s.69(8)(c), amounts may be recovered by deduction from most benefits.

Subs. (3)

Prescribed benefits are listed in reg. 9 of the Payments Regulations. They are benefits, like child benefit, which can be claimed if a person (A) is contributing to the support of another person (B) at least the rate of the benefit. If income support has been paid for B on the basis that this contribution was not paid, the prescribed benefit may be abated by the amount of the excess income support. If the abatement mechanism breaks down, the Department may recover the excess under subs. (4).

Under s.69(8)(c), amounts may be recovered by deduction from most benefits.

Subs. (4)

See notes to subss. (2) and (3).

Subs. (5)

R(SB) 28/85 had revealed problems in valuing a payment of arrears in a foreign currency which might cover quite a long period during which exchange rates varied. This provision authorises regulations to be made to deal with the conversion. See reg. 10 of the Social Security (Payments on Account, Overpayments and Recovery) Regulations (Northern Ireland) 1988 (S.I. 1988 No. 142), which appears to require the actual net amount received to be taken into account, reversing the effect of *R(SB) 28/85*.

Housing benefit

Overpayments of housing benefit

73.—(1) Except where regulations otherwise provide, any amount of housing benefit paid in excess of entitlement may be recovered by the Department, the Department of the Environment or by the Housing Executive in such manner as may be prescribed.

(2) Regulations may require the Department of the Environment or the Housing Executive to recover such an amount in such circumstances as may be prescribed.

(3) An amount recoverable under this section is in all cases recoverable from the person to whom it was paid; but, in such circumstances as may be prescribed, it may also be recovered from such other person as may be prescribed.

(4) Any amount recoverable under this section may, without prejudice to any other method of recovery, be recovered by deduction from prescribed benefits.

GENERAL NOTE

See the Housing Benefit (General) Regulations (Northern Ireland) 1987 (S.I. 1987 No. 461). See also the equivalent Great Britain Regulations, the Housing Benefit (General) Regulations 1987 (S.I. 1987 No. 1971), and commentary in the current edition of Findlay and Ward.

Social fund awards

Recovery of social fund awards

74.—(1) A social fund award which is repayable shall be recoverable by the Department.

(2) Without prejudice to any other method of recovery, the Department may recover an award by deduction from prescribed benefits.

(3) The Department may recover an award—

(a) from the person to or for the benefit of whom it was made;

(b) where that person is a member of a married or unmarried couple, from the other member of the couple;

(c) from a person who is liable to maintain the person by or on behalf of whom the application for the award was made or any person in relation to whose needs the award was made.

(4) Payments to meet funeral expenses may in all cases be recovered, as if they were funeral expenses, out of the estate of the deceased, and (subject to section 69 above) by no other means.

(5) In this section—

"married couple" means a man and woman who are married to each other and are members of the same household;

"unmarried couple" means a man and woman who are not married to each other but are living together as husband and wife otherwise than in prescribed circumstances within the meaning of section 133 of the Contributions and Benefits Act.

(6) For the purposes of this section—

(a) a man shall be liable to maintain his wife and any children of whom he is the father;

(b) a woman shall be liable to maintain her husband and any children of whom she is the mother;

(c) a person shall be liable to maintain another person throughout any period in respect of which the first-mentioned person has, on or after 24th June 1980 (the date of the making of the Social Security (Northern Ireland) Order 1980) and either alone or jointly with a further person, given an undertaking in writing in pursuance of immigration rules within the meaning of the Immigration Act 1971 to be responsible for the maintenance and accommodation of the other person; and

(d) "child" includes a person who has attained the age of 16 but not the age of 19 and in respect of whom either parent, or some person acting in the place of either parent, is receiving income support.

(7) In subsection (6) above—

(a) the reference to children of whom the man is the father includes a reference to children of whom he has been adjudged to be the father;

(b) the reference to children of whom the woman is the mother includes a reference to her illegitimate children.

(8) A document bearing a certificate which—

(a) is signed by a person authorised in that behalf by the Secretary of State; and

(b) states that the document apart from the certificate is, or is a copy of, such an undertaking as is mentioned in subsection (6)(c) above,

shall be conclusive of the undertaking in question for the purposes of this section and section 101 below; and a certificate purporting to be so signed shall be deemed to be so signed until the contrary is proved.

DEFINITIONS
"prescribed": s.167.

GENERAL NOTE

Subss. (1)–(3)
These provisions give the framework for recovery of social fund loans. See the Social Fund (Recovery by Deductions from Benefits) Regulations (Northern Ireland) 1988 (S.I. 1988 No. 21). See also the equivalent Great Britain Regulations, the Social Fund (Recovery by Deductions from Benefits) Regulations 1988 (S.I. 1988 No. 35), and commentary in the current edition of Mesher.

Subs. (4)
Subsection (4) contains an important provision for the recovery of any social fund payment for funeral expenses out of the estate of the deceased. Regulation 7 of the Social Fund (Maternity and Funeral Expenses) (General) Regulations (Northern Ireland) 1987 (S.I. 1987 No. 150) lists sums to be deducted in calculating the amount of a funeral payment. These include assets of the deceased which are available before probate or letters of administration have been granted. The old Supplementary Benefit (Single Payments) Regulations required the deduction of the value of the deceased's estate, but since it might take some time for the estate to become available, the provision in subs. (4) is preferable. The funeral payment

is to be recovered as if it were funeral expenses. Funeral expenses are a first charge on the estate, in priority to anything else (see *R(SB) 18/84*, paras. 8 and 10). *CIS 616/1990* decides that the right to recover is given to the Department. The AO (and the SSAT) has no rôle in subs. (4).

The only other method of recovery is under s.69, which applies generally where there has been misrepresentation or a failure to disclose and depends on a review of entitlement by an AO, followed by a determination of an overpayment.

Subss. (6)–(9)
See the notes to s.100.

Great Britain payments

Recovery of Great Britain payments

75. Without prejudice to any other method of recovery—
(a) amounts recoverable under any statutory provision having effect in Great Britain and corresponding to a statutory provision mentioned in section 69(8) above shall be recoverable by deduction from benefits prescribed under that subsection;
(b) amounts recoverable under any statutory provision having effect in Great Britain and corresponding to section 73 above shall be recoverable by deduction from benefits prescribed under subsection (4) of that section; and
(c) amounts recoverable under Part III of the Great Britain Administration Act shall be recoverable by deduction from benefits prescribed under subsection (2) of section 74 above and subsection (3) of that section shall have effect in relation to such awards as it has effect in relation to awards out of the social fund under this Act.

DEFINITIONS
"prescribed": s.167.

Adjustment of child benefit

Child benefit—overlap with benefits under legislation of other member States

76. Regulations may provide for adjusting child benefit payable in respect of any child in respect of whom any benefit is payable under the legislation of any member State other than the United Kingdom.

PART IV

RECOVERY FROM COMPENSATION PAYMENTS

Interpretation of Part IV

77.—(1) In this Part of this Act—
"benefit" means any benefit under the Contributions and Benefits Act except child benefit and, subject to regulations under subsection (2) below, the "relevant benefits" are such of those benefits as may be prescribed for the purposes of this Part of this Act;
"certificate of deduction" means a certificate given by the compensator specifying the amount which he has deducted and paid to the Department in pursuance of section 78 below;
"certificate of total benefit" means a certificate given by the Department in accordance with this Part of this Act;
"compensation payment" means any payment falling to be made (whether voluntarily, or in pursuance of a court order or an agreement, or otherwise)—
(a) to or in respect of the victim in consequence of the accident, injury or disease in question, and

(b) either—
　(i) by or on behalf of a person who is, or is alleged to be, liable to any extent in respect of that accident, injury or disease; or
　(ii) in pursuance of a compensation scheme for motor accidents,

but does not include benefit or an exempt payment or so much of any payment as is referable to costs incurred by any person;

"compensation scheme for motor accidents" means any scheme or arrangement under which funds are available for the payment of compensation in respect of motor accidents caused, or alleged to have been caused, by uninsured or unidentified persons;

"compensator", "victim" and "intended recipient" shall be construed in accordance with section 78(1) below;

"payment" means payment in money or money's worth, and cognate expressions shall be construed accordingly;

"the recoupment provisions" means this Part and section 101 of the Great Britain Administration Act;

"relevant deduction" means the deduction required to be made from the compensation payment in question by virtue of the recoupment provisions;

"relevant payment" means the payment required to be made to the Department by virtue of the recoupment provisions;

"relevant period" means—
　(a) in the case of a disease, the period of 5 years beginning with the date on which the victim first claims a relevant benefit in consequence of the disease; or
　(b) in any other case, the period of 5 years immediately following the day on which the accident or injury in question occurred;

but where before the end of that period the compensator makes a compensation payment in final discharge of any claim made by or in respect of the victim and arising out of the accident, injury or disease, the relevant period shall end on the date on which that payment is made;

"total benefit" means the gross amount referred to in section 78(1)(a) below.

(2) If statutory sick pay is prescribed as a relevant benefit, the amount of that benefit for the purposes of this Part of this Act shall be a reduced amount determined in accordance with regulations by reference to the percentage from time to time specified in section 154(1)(a) of the Contributions and Benefits Act (percentage of statutory sick pay recoverable by employers by deduction from contributions).

(3) For the purposes of this Part of this Act the following are the "exempt payments"—
(a) any small payment, as defined in section 81 below;
(b) any payment made to or for the victim under Article 3 of the Criminal Justice (Northern Ireland) Order 1980;
(c) any payment to the extent that it is made—
　(i) in consequence of an action under the Fatal Accidents (Northern Ireland) Order 1977; or
　(ii) in circumstances where, had an action been brought, it would have been brought under that Order;
(d) without prejudice to section 6(4) of the Vaccine Damage Payments Act 1979 (which provides for the deduction of any such payment in the assessment of any award of damages), any payment made under that Act to or in respect of the victim;
(e) any award of compensation made to or in respect of the victim by the Secretary of State under Article 3 or 10 of the Criminal Injuries (Compensation) (Northern Ireland) Order 1988;

(f) any payment made in the exercise of a discretion out of property held subject to a trust in a case where no more than 50 per cent. by value of the capital contributed to the trust was directly or indirectly provided by persons who are, or are alleged to be, liable in respect of—

    (i) the accident, injury or disease suffered by the victim in question; or

    (ii) the same or any connected accident, injury or disease suffered by another;

(g) any payment made out of property held for the purposes of any prescribed trust (whether the payment also falls within paragraph (f) above or not);

(h) any payment made to the victim by an insurance company within the meaning of the Insurance Companies Act 1982 under the terms of any contract of insurance entered into between the victim and the company before—

    (i) the date on which the victim first claims a relevant benefit in consequence of the disease in question; or

    (ii) the occurrence of the accident or injury in question;

(i) any redundancy payment falling to be taken into account in the assessment of damages in respect of an accident, injury or disease.

(4) Regulations may provide that any prescribed payment shall be an exempt payment for the purposes of this Part of this Act.

(5) Except as provided by any other statutory provision, in the assessment of damages in respect of an accident, injury or disease the amount of any relevant benefits paid or likely to be paid shall be disregarded.

(6) If, after making the relevant deduction from the compensation payment, there would be no balance remaining for payment to the intended recipient, any reference in this Part to the making of the compensation payment shall be construed in accordance with regulations.

(7) This Part of this Act shall apply in relation to any compensation payment made after 3rd September 1990 (the date of the coming into operation of Article 24 of the Social Security (Northern Ireland) Order 1989 which, with Schedule 4 to that Order, made provision corresponding to that made by this Part) to the extent that it is made in respect of—

(a) an accident or injury occurring on or after 1st January 1989; or

(b) a disease, if the victim's first claim for a relevant benefit in consequence of the disease is made on or after that date.

DEFINITIONS
"the Contributions and Benefits Act": s.167.
"prescribed": *ibid.*

GENERAL NOTE
    See the annotations in Current Law Statutes to s.22 of and Sched. 4 to the Social Security Act 1989 for the general structure of the system of recovery from compensation payments and to Sched. 1 to the Social Security Act 1990 for some significant amendments. These are equivalent to the following Northern Ireland provisions: art. 24 of and Sched. 4 to the Social Security (Northern Ireland) Order 1989 (S.I. 1989 No. 1342 (N.I. 13)) and Sched. 1 to the Social Security (Northern Ireland) Order 1990 (S.I. 1990 No. 1511 (N.I. 15)).

Recovery from damages, etc. of sums equivalent to benefit

Recovery of sums equivalent to benefit from compensation payments in respect of accidents, injuries and diseases

    78.—(1) A person ("the compensator") making a compensation payment, whether on behalf of himself or another, in consequence of an accident, injury or disease suffered by any other person ("the victim") shall not do so until the Department has furnished him with a certificate of total benefit and shall then—

(a) deduct from the payment an amount, determined in accordance with the certificate of total benefit, equal to the gross amount of any relevant benefits paid or likely to be paid to or for the victim during the relevant period in respect of that accident, injury or disease;

(b) pay to the Department an amount equal to that which is required to be so deducted; and

(c) furnish the person to whom the compensation payment is or, apart from this section, would have been made ("the intended recipient") with a certificate of deduction.

(2) Any right of the intended recipient to receive the compensation payment in question shall be regarded as satisfied to the extent of the amount certified in the certificate of deduction.

DEFINITIONS
　"certificate of deduction": s.77.
　"certificate of total benefit": *ibid.*
　"compensation payment": *ibid.*

GENERAL NOTE
　See the note to s.77.

Payments, deductions and certificates

Time for making payment to Department

79. The compensator's liability to make the relevant payment arises immediately before the making of the compensation payment, and he shall make the relevant payment before the end of the period of 14 days following the day on which the liability arises.

DEFINITIONS
　"compensation payment": s.77.
　"compensator": *ibid.*
　"relevant payment": *ibid.*

GENERAL NOTE
　See note to s.77.

The certificate of total benefit

80.—(1) It shall be for the compensator to apply to the Department for the certificate of total benefit and he may, subject to subsection (5) below, from time to time apply for fresh certificates.

(2) The certificate of total benefit shall specify—

(a) the amount which has been, or is likely to be, paid on or before a specified date by way of any relevant benefit which is capable of forming part of the total benefit;

(b) where applicable—

(i) the rate of any relevant benefit which is, has been, or is likely to be paid after the date so specified and which would be capable of forming part of the total benefit; and

(ii) the intervals at which any such benefit is paid and the period for which it is likely to be paid;

(c) the amounts (if any) which, by virtue of the recoupment provisions, are to be treated as increasing the total benefit; and

(d) the aggregate amount of any relevant payments made on or before a specified date (reduced by so much of that amount as has been paid by the Department to the intended recipient before that date in consequence of the recoupment provisions).

(3) On issuing a certificate of total benefit, the Department shall be taken to have certified the total benefit as at every date for which it is possible to

calculate an amount that would, on the basis of the information so provided, be the total benefit as at that date, on the assumption that payments of benefit are made on the days on which they first become payable.

(4) The Department may estimate, in such manner as it thinks fit, any of the amounts, rates or periods specified in the certificate of total benefit.

(5) A certificate of total benefit shall remain in force until such date as may be specified in the certificate for that purpose and no application for a fresh certificate shall be made before that date.

(6) Where a certificate ceases to be in force, the Department may issue a fresh certificate, whether or not an application has been made to it for such a certificate.

(7) The compensator shall not make the compensation payment at any time when there is no certificate of total benefit in force in respect of the victim, unless his liability to make the relevant deduction and the relevant payment has ceased to be enforceable by virtue of section 92 below.

DEFINITIONS
"certificate of total benefit": s.77.
"compensator": *ibid.*
"intended recipient": *ibid.*
"relevant benefit": *ibid.*
"relevant deduction": *ibid.*
"relevant payment": *ibid.*
"total benefit": *ibid.*
"victim": *ibid.*

GENERAL NOTE
See the note to s.81.

Exemption from deduction in cases involving small payments

81.—(1) Regulations may make provision exempting persons from liability to make the relevant deduction or the relevant payment in prescribed cases where the amount of the compensation payment in question, or the aggregate amount of two or more connected compensation payments, does not exceed the prescribed sum.

(2) Regulations may make provision for cases where an amount has been deducted and paid to the Department which, by virtue of regulations under subsection (1) above, ought not to have been so deducted and paid, and any such regulations may, in particular, provide for the Department to pay that amount to the intended recipient or the compensator or to pay a prescribed part of it to each of them.

(3) The reference in section 77(3)(a) above to a "small payment" is a reference to a payment from which by virtue of this section no relevant deduction falls to be made.

(4) For the purposes of this section—
(a) two or more compensation payments are "connected" if each is made to or in respect of the same victim and in respect of the same accident, injury or disease; and
(b) any reference to a compensation payment is a reference to a payment which would be such a payment apart from section 77(3)(a) above.

DEFINITIONS
"compensation payment": s.77.
"intended recipient": *ibid.*
"prescribed": s.167.
"relevant deduction": s.77.
"relevant payment": *ibid.*

GENERAL NOTE
See note to s.77.

Multiple compensation payments

82.—(1) This section applies where—
(a) a compensation payment (an "earlier payment") has been made to or in respect of the victim; and
(b) subsequently another such payment (a "later payment") falls to be made to or in respect of the same victim in respect of the same accident, injury or disease (whether by the same or another compensator).

(2) In determining the amount of the relevant deduction and payment required to be made in connection with the later payment, the amount referred to in section 78(1)(a) above shall be reduced by the amount of any relevant payment made in connection with the earlier payment, or, if more than one, the aggregate of those relevant payments.

(3) In relation to the later payment, the compensator shall take the amount of the reduction required by subsection (2) above to be such as may be specified under section 80(2)(d) above in the certificate of total benefit issued to him in connection with that later payment.

(4) In any case where—
(a) the relevant payment made in connection with an earlier payment is not reflected in the certificate of total benefit in force in relation to a later payment, and
(b) in consequence, the aggregate of the relevant payments made in relation to the later payment and every earlier payment exceeds what it would have been had that relevant payment been so reflected,
the Department shall pay the intended recipient an amount equal to the excess.

(5) In determining any rights and liabilities in respect of contribution or indemnity, relevant payments shall be treated as damages paid to or for the intended recipient in respect of the accident, injury or disease in question.

DEFINITIONS
"certificate of total benefit": s.77.
"compensation payment": *ibid.*
"compensator": *ibid.*
"intended recipient": *ibid.*
"relevant deduction": *ibid.*
"relevant payment": *ibid.*
"victim": *ibid.*

GENERAL NOTE
See note to s.77.

Collaboration between compensators

83.—(1) This section applies where compensation payments in respect of the same accident, injury or disease fall (or apart from the recoupment provisions would fall) to be made to or in respect of the same victim by two or more compensators.

(2) Where this section applies, any two or more of those compensators may give the Department notice that they are collaborators in respect of compensation payments in respect of that victim and that accident, injury or disease.

(3) Where such a notice is given and any of the collaborators makes a relevant payment in connection with such a compensation payment, each of the other collaborators shall be treated as if the aggregate amount of relevant payments specified in his certificate of total benefit, as in force at the time of that relevant payment, or in a fresh certificate which does not purport to reflect the payment, were increased by the amount of that payment.

DEFINITIONS
"certificate of total benefit": s.77.
"compensation payment": *ibid.*
"compensator": *ibid.*
"relevant payment": *ibid.*
"victim": *ibid.*

GENERAL NOTE
See note to s.77.

Structured settlements

84.—(1) This section applies where—
(a) in final settlement of a person's claim, an agreement is entered into—
    (i) for the making of periodical payments (whether of an income or capital nature) to or in respect of the victim; or
    (ii) for the making of such payments and one or more lump sum payments; and
(b) apart from this section, those payments would fall to be regarded for the purposes of the recoupment provisions as compensation payments.

(2) Where this section applies, the recoupment provisions (other than this section) shall have effect on the following assumptions, that is to say—
(a) the relevant period in the case of the compensator in question shall be taken to end (if it has not previously done so) on the day of settlement;
(b) the compensator in question shall be taken—
    (i) to have been liable to make on that day a single compensation payment of the amount referred to in section 78(1)(a) above (reduced or increased in accordance with such of the recoupment provisions as would have applied in the case of a payment on that day); and
    (ii) to have made from that single payment a relevant deduction of an amount equal to it; and
(c) the payments under the agreement referred to in subsection (1) above shall be taken to be exempt payments.

(3) The intended recipient shall not by virtue of anything in this section become entitled to be paid any sum, whether by the compensator or the Department, and if on a review or appeal under section 93 or 95 below it appears that the amount paid by a compensator in pursuance of this section was either greater or less than it ought to have been, then—
(a) any excess shall be repaid to the compensator instead of to the intended recipient; but
(b) any deficiency shall be paid to the Department by the intended recipient.

(4) Where any further compensation payment falls to be made to or in respect of the victim otherwise than under the agreement in question, subsection (2)(a) above shall be disregarded for the purpose of determining the end of the relevant period in relation to that further payment.

(5) In any case where—
(a) the person making the periodical payments ("the secondary party") does so in pursuance of arrangements entered into with another (as in a case where an insurance company purchases an annuity for the victim from another such company), and
(b) apart from those arrangements, that other ("the primary party") would have been regarded as the compensator,
then for the purposes of the recoupment provisions, the primary party shall be regarded as the compensator and the secondary party shall not be so regarded.

(6) In determining for the purposes of this section whether any periodical payments would fall to be regarded as compensation payments, section 77(3)(a) above shall be disregarded.

(7) In this section "the day of settlement" means—

(a) if the agreement referred to in subsection (1) above is approved by a court, the day on which that approval is given; and

(b) in any other case, the day on which the agreement is entered into.

DEFINITIONS
"compensation payment": s.77.
"compensator": *ibid.*
"intended recipient": *ibid.*
"relevant deduction": *ibid.*
"relevant period": *ibid.*
"victim": *ibid.*

GENERAL NOTE
See note to s.77.

Insolvency

85. Where the intended recipient has been adjudged bankrupt, nothing in the Insolvency (Northern Ireland) Order 1989 shall affect the operation of the recoupment provisions.

DEFINITIONS
"compensation payment": s.77.
"intended recipient": *ibid.*
"relevant deduction": *ibid.*

GENERAL NOTE
See note to s.77.

Protection of legal aid charges

86.—(1) In any case where—

(a) the compensation payment is subject to any charge under the Legal Aid, Advice and Assistance (Northern Ireland) Order 1981, and

(b) after the making of the relevant deduction, the balance of the compensation payment is insufficient to satisfy that charge,

the Department shall make such a payment as will secure that the deficiency is made good to the extent of the relevant payment.

(2) Where the Department makes a payment under this section, then for the purposes of section 80 above, the amount of the payment shall be treated as increasing the total benefit.

DEFINITIONS
"compensation payment": s.77.
"relevant deduction": *ibid.*
"relevant payment": *ibid.*
"total benefit": *ibid.*

GENERAL NOTE
See note to s.77.

Overpaid benefits

87. In any case where—

(a) during the relevant period, there has, in respect of the accident, injury or disease, been paid to or for the victim any relevant benefit to which he was not entitled ("the overpaid benefit"), and

(b) the amount of the relevant payment is such that, after taking account of the rest of the total benefit, there remains an amount which represents the whole or any part of the overpaid benefit,

then, notwithstanding anything in section 69 above or any regulations under that section or Article 54 of the 1986 Order, the receipt by the Department of the relevant payment shall be treated as the recovery of the whole or, as the case may be, that part of the overpaid benefit.

DEFINITIONS
"the 1986 Act": s.167.
"relevant payment": s.77.
"relevant period": *ibid.*
"total benefit": *ibid.*

GENERAL NOTE
See note to s.77.

Death

88. In the case of any compensation payment the whole or part of which is made—

(a) in consequence of an action under the Fatal Accidents (Northern Ireland) Order 1977, or

(b) in circumstances where, had an action been brought, it would have been brought under that Order,

regulations may make provision for estimating or calculating the portion of the payment which is to be regarded as so made for the purposes of section 77(3)(c) above.

DEFINITIONS
"compensation payment": s.77.

GENERAL NOTE
See note to s.77.

Payments into court

89.—(1) Nothing in the recoupment provisions requires a court to make any relevant deduction from, or payment out of, money in court.

(2) Where a party to an action makes a payment into court which, had it been paid directly to the other party, would have constituted a compensation payment, the making of that payment shall be regarded for the purposes of the recoupment provisions as the making of a compensation payment, but the compensator—

(a) may either—

(i) withhold from the payment into court an amount equal to the relevant deduction; or

(ii) make such a payment into court before the certificate of total benefit has been issued to him; and

(b) shall not become liable to make the relevant payment, or to furnish a certificate of deduction, until he has been notified that the whole or any part of the payment into court has been paid out of court to or for the other party.

(3) Where a person making a payment into court withholds an amount in accordance with subsection (2)(a)(i) above—

(a) he shall, at the time when he makes that payment, furnish the court with a certificate of the amount so withheld; and

(b) the amount paid into court shall be regarded as increased by the amount so certified,

but no person shall be entitled by virtue of this subsection to the payment out of court of any amount which has not in fact been paid into court.

(4) Where a payment into court is made as mentioned in subsection (2)(a)(ii) above, the compensator—

(a) shall apply for the certificate of total benefit no later than the day on which the payment into court is made; and

(b) shall become liable to make the relevant payment as mentioned in subsection (2)(b) above, notwithstanding that the relevant deduction has not been made.

(5) Where any such payment into court as is mentioned in subsection (2) above is accepted by the other party to the action within the initial period, then, as respects the compensator in question, the relevant period shall be taken to have ended on the day on which the payment into court (or, if there were two or more such payments, the last of them) was made; but where the payment into court is not so accepted, then—

(a) the relevant period as respects that compensator shall end on the day on which he is notified that the payment has been paid out of court to or for that other party; and

(b) in determining the amount of the relevant payment, that compensator shall be treated as if his payment into court had been made on that day.

(6) In subsection (5) above "the initial period" means the period of 21 days following the making of the payment into court (or, if there were two or more such payments, the last of them), but rules of court may make provision varying the length of that period.

(7) Where a payment into court is paid out wholly to or for the party who made the payment (otherwise than to or for the other party to the action) the making of the payment into court shall cease to be regarded as the making of a compensation payment.

(8) Rules of court may make provision regulating or prescribing the practice and procedure to be followed in relation to such payments into court as are mentioned in subsection (2) above.

DEFINITIONS
"certificate of total benefit": s.77.
"certificate of deduction": *ibid.*
"compensation payment": *ibid.*
"compensator": *ibid.*
"relevant deduction": *ibid.*
"relevant payment": *ibid.*
"relevant period": *ibid.*

GENERAL NOTE
See note to s.77.

Administration and adjudication

Provision of information

90.—(1) Any person who is, or is alleged to be, liable in respect of an accident, injury or disease, or any person acting on his behalf, shall furnish the Department with the prescribed information relating to any person seeking compensation, or in respect of whom compensation is sought, in respect of that accident, injury or disease.

(2) Any person who claims a relevant benefit or who has been in receipt of such a benefit or, if he has died, the personal representatives of such a person, shall furnish the Department with the prescribed information relating to any accident, injury or disease suffered by that person.

(3) A person who makes any payment (whether a compensation payment or not) on behalf of himself or another—

(a) in consequence of any accident, injury or disease suffered, or any damage to property sustained, by any other person, or

    (b) which is referable to any costs incurred by any such other person by
       reason of such an accident, injury, disease or damage,
shall, if the Department so requests him in writing, furnish the Department
with such particulars relating to the size and composition of the payment as
may be specified in the request.

    (4) Any person—
    (a) who is the employer of a person who suffers or has suffered an
       accident, injury or disease, or
    (b) who has been the employer of such a person at any time during the
       relevant period,
shall furnish the Department with the prescribed information relating to the
payment of statutory sick pay in respect of that person.

    (5) In subsection (4) above "employer" has the same meaning as it has in
Part XI of the Contributions and Benefits Act.

    (6) Any person furnishing information under this section shall do so in the
prescribed manner, at the prescribed place and within the prescribed time.

DEFINITIONS
  "compensation payment": s.77.
  "payment": *ibid.*
  "prescribed": s.167.
  "relevant benefit": s.77.

GENERAL NOTE
  See note to s.77.

Applications for certificates of total benefit

    91.—(1) If at any time before he makes the compensation payment in
question the compensator requests the Department to furnish him with a
certificate of total benefit relating to the victim in question—
    (a) the Department shall comply with that request before the end of the
       period of 4 weeks, or such other number of weeks as may be pre-
       scribed, following the day on which the request is, or is deemed in
       accordance with regulations to be, received, and
    (b) any certificate so furnished shall, in particular, specify for the pur-
       poses of section 80(2)(a) above a date not earlier than the date of the
       request.

    (2) Where the Department furnishes any person with a certificate of total
benefit, it shall also provide the information contained in that certificate to
the person who appears to it to be the victim in relation to the compensation
payment in question.

    (3) The victim may apply to the Department for particulars of the manner
in which any amount, rate or period specified in a certificate of total benefit
has been determined.

DEFINITIONS
  "certificate of total benefit": s.77.
  "compensation payment": *ibid.*
  "compensator": *ibid.*
  "prescribed": s.167.
  "victim": s.77.

GENERAL NOTE
  See note to s.77.

Liability of compensator unenforceable if certificate not issued within time limit

    92.—(1) The liability of the compensator to make the relevant deduction
and payment relating to the first compensation payment after the default
date shall not be enforceable if—

(a) he has made a request under section 91(1) above which—

    (i) accurately states the prescribed particulars relating to the victim and the accident, injury or disease in question; and

    (ii) specifies the name and address of the person to whom the certificate is to be sent;

(b) he has in his possession a written acknowledgment, sent to him in accordance with regulations, of the receipt of the request; and

(c) the Department does not, within the time limit referred to in section 91(1) above, send the certificate to the person specified in the request as the person to whom the certificate is to be sent, at the address so specified;

and accordingly, where those liabilities cease to be enforceable, nothing in the recoupment provisions shall prevent the compensator from making that compensation payment.

(2) In any case where—

(a) the liability to make the relevant deduction and payment becomes unenforceable by virtue of this section, but

(b) the compensator nevertheless makes that deduction and payment,

he shall be treated for all purposes as if the liability had remained enforceable.

(3) Where the compensator, in reliance on this section, does not make the relevant deduction and payment, then—

(a) he shall within 14 days of the default date give the Department notice of that fact together with such other particulars as may be prescribed; and

(b) in determining the amount of the relevant deduction and payment to be made in connection with any subsequent compensation payment made by the same or any other compensator, the amount which, apart from this section, would have fallen to be deducted and paid by him shall continue to form part of the total benefit and shall not be treated as if it had been paid.

(4) If, in the opinion of the Department, circumstances have arisen which adversely affect normal methods of communication—

(a) the Department may by order provide that no liability shall become unenforceable by virtue of this section during a specified period not exceeding three months; and

(b) the Department may continue any such order in force for further periods not exceeding three months at a time.

(5) In this section "the default date" means the date on which the time limit mentioned in subsection (1)(c) above expires.

DEFINITIONS

    "compensation payment": s.77.
    "compensator": *ibid.*
    "prescribed": s.167.
    "relevant deduction": s.77.
    "relevant payment": *ibid.*
    "total benefit": *ibid.*
    "victim": *ibid.*

GENERAL NOTE

    See note to s.77.

Review of certificates of total benefit

    93.—(1) The Department may review any certificate of total benefit if the Department is satisfied that it was issued in ignorance of, or was based on a mistake as to, some material fact or that a mistake (whether in computation or otherwise) has occurred in its preparation.

    (2) On any such review the Department may either—

(a) confirm the certificate, or

(b) issue a fresh certificate containing such variations as the Department considers appropriate,

but the Department shall not so vary the certificate as to increase the total benefit.

(3) In any case where—

(a) one or more relevant payments have been made, and

(b) in consequence of a review under this section, it appears that the aggregate amount so paid exceeds the amount that ought to have been paid,

the Department shall pay the intended recipient an amount equal to the excess.

DEFINITIONS
"certificate of total benefit": s.77.
"intended recipient": *ibid.*
"relevant payment": *ibid.*
"total benefit": *ibid.*

GENERAL NOTE
See note to s.77.

Appeals

94.—(1) An appeal shall lie in accordance with this section against any certificate of total benefit at the instance of the compensator, the victim or the intended recipient, on the ground—

(a) that any amount, rate or period specified in the certificate is incorrect, or

(b) that benefit paid or payable otherwise than in consequence of the accident, injury or disease in question has been brought into account.

(2) No appeal shall be brought under this section until—

(a) the claim giving rise to the compensation payment has been finally disposed of; and

(b) the relevant payment, or where more than one such payment may fall to be made, the final relevant payment, has been made.

(3) Notwithstanding subsection (2) above, where—

(a) an award of damages ("provisional damages") has been made under paragraph 10(2)(a) of Schedule 6 to the Administration of Justice Act 1982; and

(b) the relevant payment or, where more than one such payment falls to be made, the final relevant payment in relation to the provisional damages so awarded has been made,

an appeal may be brought under this section against any certificate of total benefit by reference to which the amount of that relevant payment, or any of those relevant payments, was made.

(4) Regulations may make provision—

(a) as to the manner in which, and the time within which, appeals under this section are to be brought, and

(b) for the purpose of enabling any such appeal to be treated as an application for review under section 93 above,

and regulations under paragraph (b) above may, in particular, provide that the circumstances in which such a review may be carried out shall not be restricted to those specified in section 93 above.

(5) If any of the medical questions arises for determination on an appeal under this section, the Department shall refer that question to a medical appeal tribunal, whose determination shall be binding, for the purposes of the appeal, on any social security appeal tribunal to whom a question is referred under subsection (7) below.

(6) A medical appeal tribunal, in determining any of the medical questions, shall take into account any decision of any court relating to the same, or any similar, issue arising in connection with the accident, injury or disease in question.

(7) If any question concerning any amount, rate or period specified in the certificate of total benefit arises for determination on an appeal under this section, the Department shall refer that question to a social security appeal tribunal, but where any medical questions arising on the appeal have been referred to a medical appeal tribunal—

(a) the Department shall not refer any question to the social security appeal tribunal until the Department has received the determination of the medical appeal tribunal on the questions referred to them; and

(b) the Department shall notify the social security appeal tribunal of the determinations of the medical appeal tribunal.

(8) On a reference under subsection (7) above a social security appeal tribunal may either—

(a) confirm the amounts, rates and periods specified in the certificate of total benefit; or

(b) specify any increases, reductions or other variations which are to be made on the issue of the fresh certificate under subsection (9) below.

(9) When the Department has received the determinations of the tribunals on the questions referred to them under subsections (5) and (7) above, it shall in accordance with those determinations either—

(a) confirm the certificate against which the appeal was brought, or

(b) issue a fresh certificate.

(10) Regulations may make provision with respect to the procedure for the reference under this section of questions to medical appeal tribunals or social security appeal tribunals.

(11) An appeal shall lie to a Commissioner at the instance of the Department, the compensator, the victim or the intended recipient from a decision of a medical appeal tribunal or a social security appeal tribunal under this section on the ground that the decision was erroneous in point of law; and for the purposes of appeals under this subsection—

(a) section 21(7) to (10) above shall apply in relation to an appeal from the decision of a social security appeal tribunal; and

(b) section 46(3) above shall apply in relation to an appeal from the decision of a medical appeal tribunal.

(12) In this section "the medical questions" means—

(a) any question whether, as the result of a particular occurrence, the victim suffered an injury, sickness or disease;

(b) any question as to the period for which the victim suffered any injury, sickness or disease.

DEFINITIONS
    "benefit": s.77.
    "certificate of total benefit": *ibid.*
    "compensation payment": *ibid.*
    "compensator": *ibid.*
    "intended recipient": *ibid.*
    "relevant payment": *ibid.*
    "victim": *ibid.*

GENERAL NOTE
    See note to s.77.

Recovery in consequence of an appeal

95.—(1) Where it appears, in consequence of an appeal under section 94 above, that the aggregate amount of the relevant payment or payments actually made exceeds the amount that ought to have been paid, the Department shall pay the intended recipient an amount equal to that excess.

(2) Where it appears, in consequence of such an appeal, that the aggregate amount of the relevant payment or payments actually made is less than the amount that ought to have been paid, the intended recipient shall pay the Department an amount equal to the deficiency.

(3) Without prejudice to any other method of enforcement, an amount payable under subsection (2) above may be recovered by deduction from any benefits which are prescribed benefits for the purposes of section 69 above.

DEFINITIONS
"benefit": s.77.
"intended recipient": *ibid.*
"prescribed": s.167.
"relevant payment": s.77.

GENERAL NOTE
See note to s.77.

Recovery of relevant payment in cases of default

96.—(1) This section applies in any case where the compensator has made a compensation payment but—
  (a) has not requested a certificate of total benefit in respect of the victim, or
  (b) if he has done so, has not made the relevant payment within the time limit imposed by section 79 above.
(2) Where this section applies, the Department may—
  (a) if no certificate of total benefit has been issued to the compensator, issue to him such a certificate and a demand for the relevant payment to be made forthwith, or
  (b) if a certificate of total benefit has been issued to the compensator, issue to him a copy of that certificate and such a demand,
and the amount so certified shall, to the extent that it does not exceed the amount of the compensation payment, be recoverable by the Department from the compensator.

(3) Any amount recoverable under this section shall, if the county court so orders, be enforceable as if it were payable under an order of that court.
(4) A document bearing a certificate which—
  (a) is signed by a person authorised in that behalf by the Department, and
  (b) states that the document, apart from the certificate, is a record of the amount recoverable under this section,
shall be conclusive evidence that that amount is so recoverable; and a certificate purporting to be signed as aforesaid shall be deemed to be so signed unless the contrary is proved.

(5) Where this section applies in relation to two or more connected compensators, the Department may proceed against them as if they were jointly and severally liable for an amount equal to the difference between—
  (a) the total benefit determined in accordance with the latest connected certificate of total benefit issued to any of them, and
  (b) the aggregate amount of any connected relevant payments previously made.

(6) Nothing in subsection (5) above authorises the recovery from any person of an amount in excess of the compensation payment by virtue of which this section applies to him (or, if there are two or more such payments which are connected, the aggregate amount of those payments).

(7) In subsections (5) and (6) above, "connected" means relating to the same victim and the same accident, injury or disease.

DEFINITIONS
  "certificate of total benefit": s.81.
  "compensation payment": *ibid.*
  "compensator": *ibid.*
  "relevant payment": *ibid.*
  "victim": *ibid.*

GENERAL NOTE
  See note to s.77.

Miscellaneous

Foreign compensators: duties of intended recipient

97.—(1) Where, immediately before the making of the compensation payment, the compensator is not resident and does not have a place of business in Northern Ireland, any deduction, payment or other thing which would, apart from this section, fall to be made or done under the recoupment provisions by the compensator shall instead be made or done by the intended recipient and references to the compensator shall be construed accordingly.

(2) The Department may by regulations make such provision as it considers expedient for the purpose of modifying the recoupment provisions in their application in such a case.

DEFINITIONS
  "compensation payment": s.77.
  "compensator": *ibid.*
  "intended recipient": *ibid.*

GENERAL NOTE
  See note to s.77.

Interest on damages: reductions in respect of relevant payments

98. In assessing the amount of interest payable in respect of an award of damages, the amount of the award shall be treated as reduced by a sum equal to the amount of the relevant payment (if any) required to be made in connection with the payment of the damages and, if both special and general damages are awarded, any such reductions shall be treated as made first against the special damages and then, as respects any remaining balance, against the general damages.

DEFINITIONS
  "relevant payment": s.77.

GENERAL NOTE
  See note to s.77.

The Crown

99. This Part of this Act applies in relation to the making of a compensation payment by the Crown as it applies in relation to the making of a compensation payment by any other compensator.

PART V

INCOME SUPPORT AND THE DUTY TO MAINTAIN

Failure to maintain—general

100.—(1) If—

(a) any person persistently refuses or neglects to maintain himself or any person whom he is liable to maintain; and

(b) in consequence of his refusal or neglect income support is paid to or in respect of him or such a person,

he shall be guilty of an offence and liable on summary conviction to imprisonment for a term not exceeding 3 months or to a fine of an amount not exceeding level 4 on the standard scale or to both.

(2) For the purposes of subsection (1) above a person shall not be taken to refuse or neglect to maintain himself or any other person by reason only of anything done or omitted in furtherance of a trade dispute.

(3) Subsections (6) to (8) of section 74 above shall have effect for the purposes of this Part of this Act as they have effect for the purposes of that section.

GENERAL NOTE

Subs. (1)

The criminal offence created by subs. (1) of refusing or neglecting to maintain oneself is at first sight rather extraordinary, but it is only committed if as a consequence income support is paid. Prosecution is very much a last resort after the ordinary sanctions against voluntary unemployment have been used. In 1984/5 there were none in Great Britain (NACRO, Enforcement of the Law Relating to Social Security, para. 8.6). Prosecution of those who refuse or neglect to maintain others is more common.

Liability to maintain

Under subs. (3), liability to maintain another person for the purposes of Pt. V is tested according to s.74(6)–(8). Both men and women are liable to maintain their spouses and children. The definition of child goes beyond the usual meaning in s.133 of the Contributions and Benefits (Northern Ireland) Act of a person under 16 to include those under 19 who count as a dependant in someone else's income support entitlement (s.74(6)(d)). The effect is that in determining whether a person is the father or mother of a child it is irrelevant whether the person was married to the other parent at the time of the birth or not. If a married couple divorce, their liability to maintain each other ceases for the purposes of Pt. V, but the obligation to maintain their children remains. This, then, is the remnant of the old family means-test that used to extend much wider until the Poor Law was finally "abolished" by the National Assistance Act (Northern Ireland) 1948. For the enforcement of this liability, see ss.101–103, and, for a criminal offence, subs. (1).

Section 74(6)(c) was new in 1980. In *R.* v. *West London Supplementary Benefits Appeal Tribunal,* ex p. *Clarke* [1975] 1 W.L.R. 1396, SB7, the court had held that the sponsor of an immigrant was under no obligation to maintain the immigrant for supplementary benefit purposes. This position is now reversed, and s.74(8) provides for conclusive certificates of an undertaking to maintain to be produced. The liability to maintain is enforced under s.101. The SBC policy struck down in *Clarke* had deemed the immigrant to be receiving the support from his sponsor even where it was not forthcoming. This is not now the case. It is only a resource when actually received.

Recovery of expenditure on benefit from person liable for maintenance

101.—(1) Subject to the following provisions of this section, if income support is claimed by or in respect of a person whom another person is liable to maintain or paid to or in respect of such a person, the Department may make a complaint under Part VIII of the Magistrates' Courts (Northern Ireland) Order 1981 against the liable person for an order under this section.

(2) Except in a case falling within subsection (3) below, this section does not apply where the person who is liable to be maintained is an illegitimate child of the liable person.

(3) A case falls within this subsection if—

(a) the liable person is someone other than the child's father; or

(b) the liable person is liable because he is a person such as is mentioned in section 74(6)(c) above.

(4) On the hearing of a complaint under this section the court shall have regard to all the circumstances and, in particular, to the income of the liable

person, and may order him to pay such sum, weekly or otherwise, as it may consider appropriate, except that in a case falling within section 74(6)(c) above that sum shall not include any amount which is not attributable to income support (whether paid before or after the making of the order).

(5) In determining whether to order any payments to be made in respect of income support for any period before the complaint was made, or the amount of any such payments, the court shall disregard any amount by which the liable person's income exceeds the income which was his during that period.

(6) Any payments ordered to be made under this section shall be made—
  (a) to the Department in so far as they are attributable to any income support (whether paid before or after the making of the order);
  (b) to the person claiming income support or (if different) the dependant; or
  (c) to such other person as appears to the court expedient in the interests of the dependant.

(7) Any proceedings for an order under this section shall be included among the proceedings which are domestic proceedings within the meaning of the Magistrates' Courts (Northern Ireland) Order 1981; and Article 88 of that Order (definition of "domestic proceedings") shall have effect accordingly.

DEFINITIONS
  "child": ss.101(3) and 74(6)(d).

GENERAL NOTE
  This section gives the DHSS an independent right to enforce the liability to maintain in s.74(6), which now covers both spouses and children, by an order in the magistrates' court, provided that income support has been claimed or paid for the person sought to be maintained. Note that from April 1993 the Child Support (Northern Ireland) Order 1991 (S.I. 1991 No. 2628 (N.I. 23)) will introduce an entirely new system of determining and enforcing liability to maintain children, through the Child Support Agency.

Spouses
  The usual procedure for Northern Ireland was last described in detail in Chapter 13 of the Supplementary Benefits Handbook for Northern Ireland (1985 ed.) and will presumably continue to apply, since it is repeated in essence in the DHSS Guide to Income Support, although there have recently been some administrative changes. The most common situation is where a breakdown of marriage leads to separation or divorce and the woman claims income support. The same procedures can apply if it is the man who claims benefit. If there has already been a divorce then there is no liability to maintain between the ex-spouses, although there still is for children, and the amount of any court order for maintenance will be relevant to the calculation of income. If there has merely been a separation then the wife is entitled to benefit as a single person, but there will be an investigation of the circumstances to ensure that the separation is genuine. If the husband is already paying maintenance under a court order or the wife has taken proceedings herself which are reasonably advanced, no approach to the husband will be made by the DHSS. Otherwise, the wife will be asked for information about the whereabouts of the liable relative (although producing the information cannot be made a condition of receiving benefit) and he will be contacted as soon as possible. The husband is asked to pay as much as he can, if possible enough to remove the need for income support to be paid to the wife and any children.

  In deciding what level of payment is acceptable on a voluntary basis the DHSS used a formula, which was first revealed in the Report of the Finer Committee on One-Parent Families (Cm. 5629, paras. 4.188–4.189) and is most recently described in para. 13.10 of the Handbook. The supplementary benefit scale rates for the man and any partner or children living with him were taken, plus full rent or mortgage payments (including capital), plus rates. To this was added a margin of £5 or a quarter of the new family's net income (the £5 appeared in the Finer Report, but is obviously out of date and is not mentioned in the Handbook). The excess over this figure was regarded as available to be used for maintenance, but the Handbook emphasised that the excess was to be used only as a basis for discussion and that payment of a lesser amount might be agreed, if there were special expenses. Thus if the man himself were receiving supplementary benefit he would not be expected to pay anything. It is assumed that a similar approach, substituting income support applicable amounts, plus net housing costs (after deducting any housing benefit or income support for such costs), will be applied now. If the husband is unwilling to make a payment voluntarily, although the DHSS believe that he has sufficient income, then legal proceedings may be considered.

The first step will be to see if the wife will take action. The official policy is that the wife will merely be advised on the advantages of taking proceedings herself (that she may get enough maintenance to lift her off benefit and that an order for maintenance will continue if she ceases to be entitled to income support, as by working full-time). The first advantage is likely to be real in only a small minority of cases and the force of the second has been reduced by the introduction of the procedure in s.102(3)–(10). The choice should be left entirely to the woman, although staff have recently been instructed to stress the advantages of encouraging the husband's responsibilities in the maintenance arrangements, especially if children are involved. A wife may of course take proceedings herself even though the DHSS have accepted voluntary payments from the husband. The courts have refused to adopt the "liable relative formula" in private proceedings by wives or ex-wives (*Shallow* v. *Shallow* [1979] Fam. 1) and will only have regard to the man's subsistence level. By this they mean the ordinary scale rates of benefit plus housing costs. A more realistic approach may have been presaged by *Allen* v. *Allen* [1986] 2 F.L.R. 265, where the Court of Appeal in England used the long-term scale rate (now disappeared) as a yardstick. In *Delaney* v. *Delaney* [1990] 2 F.L.R. 457, the Court of Appeal in England accepted the principle that where the man had insufficient resources after taking account of his reasonable commitments to a new family properly to maintain his former wife and family, a maintenance order should not financially cripple him where the wife is entitled to social security benefits. But no calculation of the man's income support level was made. If the wife does not take proceedings, then the DHSS may. The court is to have regard to all the circumstances, in particular the husband's resources, and may order him to pay whatever sum is appropriate (subs. (4)). Presumably, the same principles will govern the amount of an order as in a private application.

There are some new provisions in s.102(1) in cases where the order includes amounts for children, but it is not at all clear how these interact with the general test of appropriateness under subs. (4). The wife's adultery or desertion or other conduct is only a factor to be taken into account, not a bar to any order. Nor is the existence of a separation agreement under which the wife agrees not to claim maintenance a bar (*National Assistance Board* v. *Parkes* [1955] 2 Q.B. 506). Although *Hulley* v. *Thompson* [1981] 1 W.L.R. 159 concerned only the liability to maintain children, because there had been a divorce, it showed that not even a consent order under which the man transferred the matrimonial home to his ex-wife and she agreed to receive no maintenance for herself or the children barred the statutory liability to maintain the children. However, it seems that the existence of the order could be taken into account in deciding what amount it is appropriate for the man to pay. Proceedings by the DHSS are relatively rare.

Unmarried and divorced parents

The position of an unmarried mother is in many ways the same as that of a divorced wife. She is entitled to income support as a single person. Payments from the father of her child only affect her benefit when they are actually received. Equally a father who has care of children may receive payments from the mother.

The procedure to be adopted by the DHSS in the case of a woman was described in detail in the Supplementary Benefits Handbook for Northern Ireland (1985 ed.), paras. 13.13–13.19 and will presumably continue under income support. The woman will be approached after the birth of the child if it is clear that it is not being offered for adoption and benefit is likely to be paid for some time. If she is already receiving maintenance for her child or her own proceedings are reasonably far advanced, information will only be requested about amounts for the calculation of resources. Otherwise, information about the father will be requested, although the Handbook emphasised that it should be made clear that her benefit will continue if she does not give the information. "Provided that the mother has no objection to an approach being made" (para. 13.16), the alleged father will be contacted. If he is willing to meet the full amount of benefit for the child or pay what the DHSS considers reasonable (using the "liable relative formula"—see above) payments will be accepted on a voluntary basis. If the man denies paternity or refuses to make payments, then proceedings will be discussed. No pressure should be put on the mother to take her own proceedings, but the advantages of her doing so will now be stressed. If the DHSS take their own action, she will be asked for information about her relationship with the alleged father and what evidence she can produce to support the allegation of paternity. Once again it is stressed that she does not have to provide such information, although the "normal expectation" is that she will. The policy is thus that no pressure at all should be put on the woman, as was admittedly the case in the past. But everything will depend on how the policy is actually operated, when the appearance of pressure in an emotionally fraught situation may be very subtle. The White Paper *Children Come First* (Cm. 1264) made a controversial proposal to reduce a lone parent's benefit if she declines to take maintenance proceedings or to provide information to the DHSS (para. 5.33), which has been incorporated in the Child Support (Northern Ireland) Order 1991 (S.I. 1991 No. 2628 (N.I. 23)). The provision will come into operation in April 1993.

See the discussion above under *Spouses* for the court's approach to the level of an order to be made, and s.102(1) for some other factors.

The DHSS's right to an order is independent of that of the mother (*National Assistance Board* v. *Mitchell* [1956] 1 Q.B. 56, *National Assistance Board* v. *Tugby* [1957] 1 Q.B. 507). It does not matter even that the mother's own action has been dismissed for insufficient evidence (*Clapham* v. *National Assistance Board* [1961] 2 Q.B. 77). See also *Hulley* v. *Thompson* [1981] 1 W.L.R. 159, under *Spouses* above.

Recovery of expenditure on income support: additional amounts and transfer of orders

102.—(1) In any case where—
(a) the claim for income support referred to in section 101(1) above is or was made by the parent of one or more children in respect of both himself and those children; and
(b) the other parent is liable to maintain those children but, by virtue of not being the claimant's husband or wife, is not liable to maintain the claimant,

the sum which the court may order that other parent to pay under subsection (4) of that section may include an amount, determined in accordance with regulations, in respect of any income support paid to or for the claimant by virtue of such provisions as may be prescribed.

(2) Where the sum which a court orders a person to pay under section 101 above includes by virtue of subsection (1) above an amount (in this section referred to as a "personal allowance element") in respect of income support by virtue of paragraph 1(2) of Schedule 2 to the Income Support (General) Regulations (Northern Ireland) 1987 (personal allowance for lone parent) the order shall separately identify the amount of the personal allowance element.

(3) In any case where—
(a) there is in force an order under subsection (4) of section 101 above made against a person ("the liable parent") who is the parent of one or more children, in respect of the other parent or the children; and
(b) payments under the order fall to be made to the Department by virtue of subsection (6)(a) of that section; and
(c) that other parent ("the dependent parent") ceases to claim income support,

the Department may, by giving notice in writing to the court which made the order and to the liable parent and the dependent parent, transfer to the dependent parent the right to receive the payments under the order, exclusive of any personal allowance element, and to exercise the relevant rights in relation to the order, except so far as relating to that element.

(4) Notice under subsection (3) above shall not be given (and if purportedly given, shall be of no effect) at a time when there is in force a maintenance order made against the liable parent—
(a) in favour of the dependent parent or one or more of the children; or
(b) in favour of some other person for the benefit of the dependent parent or one or more of the children;

and if such a maintenance order is made at any time after notice under that subsection has been given, the order under section 101(4) above shall cease to have effect.

(5) Except as provided by subsections (7) and (8) below, where the Department gives notice under subsection (3) above, it shall cease to be entitled—

(a) to receive any payment under the order in respect of any personal allowance element; or

(b) to exercise the relevant rights, so far as relating to any such element, notwithstanding that the dependent parent does not become entitled to receive any payment in respect of that element or to exercise the relevant rights so far as so relating.

(6) If, in a case where the Department gives notice under subsection (3) above, a payment under the order is or has been made to the Department wholly or partly in respect of the whole or any part of the period beginning with the day on which the transfer takes effect and ending with the day on which the notice under subsection (3) above is given to the liable parent, the Department shall—

(a) repay to or for the liable parent so much of the payment as is referable to any personal allowance element in respect of that period or, as the case may be, the part of it in question; and

(b) pay to or for the dependent parent so much of any remaining balance of the payment as is referable to that period or part;

and a payment under paragraph (b) above shall be taken to discharge, to that extent, the liability of the liable parent to the dependent parent under the order in respect of that period or part.

(7) If, in a case where the Department has given notice under subsection (3) above, the dependent parent makes a further claim for income support, then—

(a) the Department may, by giving a further notice in writing to the court which made the order and to the liable parent and the dependent parent, transfer back from the dependent parent to the Department the right to receive the payments and to exercise the relevant rights; and

(b) that transfer shall revive the Department's right to receive payment under the order in respect of any personal allowance element and to exercise the relevant rights so far as relating to any such element.

(8) A transfer under subsection (3) or (7) above does not transfer or otherwise affect the right of any person—

(a) to receive a payment which fell due to him at a time before the transfer took effect; or

(b) to exercise the relevant rights in relation to any such payment;

and, where notice is given under subsection (3), subsection (5) above does not deprive the Department of its right to receive such a payment in respect of any personal allowance element or to exercise the relevant rights in relation to such a payment.

(9) For the purposes of this section—

(a) a transfer under subsection (3) above takes effect on the day on which the dependent parent ceases to be in receipt of income support in consequence of the cessation referred to in paragraph (c) of that subsection, and

(b) a transfer under subsection (7) above takes effect on—

(i) the first day in respect of which the dependent parent receives income support after the transfer under subsection (3) above took effect, or

(ii) such later day as may be specified for the purpose in the notice under subsection (7),

irrespective of the day on which notice under the subsection in question is given.

(10) In this section—

"child" means a person under the age of 16, notwithstanding section 74(6)(d) above;

"court" shall be construed in accordance with section 101 above;

"maintenance order" means an order for the making of periodical payments or the payment of a lump sum under any statutory provision prescribed for the purposes of this subsection;

"the relevant rights", in relation to an order under section 101(4) above, means the right to bring any proceedings, take any steps or do any other thing under or in relation to the order which the Department could have brought, taken or done apart from any transfer under this section.

GENERAL NOTE

The predecessors of this section and s. 103 formed one of the central strategic objectives of the Social Security Act 1990 and Social Security (Northern Ireland) Order 1990 (S.I. 1990 No. 1511 (N.I. 15)) (*Hansard*, H.C. Vol. 170, col. 1137 (Tony Newton); *Hansard*, H.L. Vol. 518, col. 234 (Lord Henley)), but were only introduced at the Report stage in the Commons. They therefore received relatively little Parliamentary discussion due to the operation of the guillotine. The Government has carried out a general review of the maintenance system, based on a survey of work in U.K. courts and DSS offices and study of overseas systems, and has produced radical proposals in *Children Come First* (Cm. 1264). These proposals have been embodied in the Child Support Act 1991 in Great Britain and the Child Support (Northern Ireland) Order 1991 (S.I. 1991 No. 2628 (N.I. 23)) in Northern Ireland. Both pieces of legislation are due to come into operation in April 1993. Action had already been taken to tighten up the assessment of an absent parent's ability to pay maintenance for his family on income support. The new provisions are regarded as desirable in the short term to improve the effectiveness of the present system, pending more radical reform (*Hansard*, H.C. Vol. 170, col. 566). Section 102 contains two elements. The first relates to the situation where a lone parent is receiving income support, but the absent parent of the child(ren) is not liable to maintain the parent under s.74(6) because the parents are not or are no longer married. Where the DHSS seeks its own order against the absent parent, courts are empowered to take into account income support relating to the lone parent in calculating the amount to be paid for the child(ren) and the DHSS may of course take this into account in negotiating voluntary agreements. The second is to allow a DHSS order to be transferred to the lone parent when that person comes off income support, rather than the lone parent having to obtain a separate private maintenance order.

Subss. (1) and (2)

These provisions comprise the first element identified above. They apply when both of conditions (a) and (b) in subs. (1) are satisfied. Under para. (a), s.101 gives the DHSS power to obtain an order against a person who is liable to maintain a claimant of income support or a person included in the family for claiming purposes. Section 74(6) defines liability to maintain for this purpose. There is a liability to maintain a spouse and any children. Under s.74(6)(d), "child" includes a person aged 16 to 18 (inclusive) who is still a member of the claimant's family for income support purposes (*e.g.* because he is still in full-time education). However, s.102(10) provides that for the purposes of s.102 "child" is restricted to a person under the age of 16. Thus, lone-parent claimants whose children are all over 15 will fall outside this provision. Under para. (b) the absent parent must not be married to the lone parent, so that the obligation to maintain under s.74(6) is only in respect of the child(ren). If both these conditions are met, a court may include whatever amount the regulations determine in respect of the income support paid for the lone parent. The Income Support (Liable Relatives) Regulations (Northern Ireland) 1990 (S.I. 1990 No. 375) specify in general the children's personal allowances, family premium, lone-parent premium, disabled-child premium and the carer premium in respect of care for a child. The intention was said to be that the regulation-making power "will be used to specify that once having looked at the allowances and premiums that are paid because there are children, the court should also have regard to the income support personal allowance paid for the mother" (*Hansard*, H.C. Vol. 170, col. 567). The Liable Relatives Regulations provide that if the liable parent has the means to pay, in addition to the amounts already specified, a court order may include some or all of the dependent parent's personal allowance. It is said that in a private maintenance order for children the court can take account of the parent's care costs and that social security law is thus being brought into line with family law. However, there is nothing as specific as s.102 in family law. The existing power of the court on orders sought by the DHSS is already wide and it is not clear how much real difference the new powers will make.

Under s.101(4) the court may order payment of such sum as it may consider appropriate. The assumption seems to be that not only could the personal allowance for a child under 16 be considered under this provision, but also the family premium (paid to all claimants with a child or young person (16–18) in the family) and the additional lone-parent premium. If such amounts can be considered under the existing law (and they might be considered to reflect the care costs of the lone parent) there seems no reason why the court could not also consider some part of the parent's personal allowance if that was considered "appropriate".

However, s.102(1) and the Liable Relatives Regulations make the position clear, which should be an advantage. It is notable that the court retains a discretion as to what amounts to consider and that the overriding factor under s.101(4) is what is appropriate. Under para. 1 of Sched. 2 to the Income Support (General) Regulations (Northern Ireland) 1987 (S.I. 1987 No. 459) the personal allowance for a lone parent aged under 18 or over 24 is the same as for a single person with no dependants. There is only a difference (currently £8.85 p.w.) for those aged 18 to 24. Subsection (2) provides that if the lone parent's personal allowance under Sched. 2 is covered by the order, this element must be separately identified. This has no bearing on subs. (1), but is relevant to the procedure set up by subss. (3)–(9).

Subss. (3)–(10)

These provisions contain the important procedure allowing the transfer of a DHSS order to the lone parent on coming off income support. The conditions for transfer under subs. (3) are that in such a case (remembering that "child" is defined to cover only those under 16 (subs. (10)) the Department gives notice to the court which made the order and to both the parents. Then the right to enforce or apply for variation of the order (apart from any personal allowance element identified under subs. (2)) is transferred to the lone parent (known as "the dependent parent"). Thus, the personal allowance element, which is of no net benefit to the lone parent while she is on income support, is removed at the point when its value would actually be felt by the lone parent. The DHSS can no longer enforce the personal allowance element of the order (subs. (5)). Under subs. (9)(a) the transfer takes effect on the day on which the dependent parent ceases to receive income support in consequence of ceasing to claim. This is a peculiar way of putting things. If the dependent parent's circumstances change (*e.g.* her capital goes over the cut-off limit or she starts full-time work) her entitlement to income support may be terminated on review by the AO under s.23. She may well then choose not to claim income support again, as it would be a useless exercise. The dependent parent could with some strain be said to cease to claim income support and so to satisfy subs. (3)(c), but the cessation of receipt of income support is not in consequence of the cessation of claiming but of the review and revision by the AO. Subsection (3) is not to apply if a private maintenance order (see subs. (10) for definition) is in existence, and if the dependent parent obtains one after a transfer the right to enforce the DHSS order disappears (subs. (4)). If, after a transfer, the dependent parent makes another claim for income support (presumably only while still having children under 16), the Department may by giving notice to all parties retransfer to the DHSS the right to enforce the order and revive the personal allowance element on the dependent parent becoming entitled to income support (subss. (7) and (9)(b)). Presumably, the revival of the personal allowance element depends on the conditions of subss. (1) and (2) being met at the date of revival.

Reduction of expenditure on income support: certain maintenance orders to be enforceable by the Department

103.—(1) This section applies where—

(a) a person ("the claimant") who is the parent of one or more children is in receipt of income support either in respect of those children or in respect of both himself and those children; and

(b) there is in force a maintenance order made against the other parent ("the liable person")—

      (i) in favour of the claimant or one or more of the children, or

      (ii) in favour of some other person for the benefit of the claimant or one or more of the children;

and in this section "the primary recipient" means the person in whose favour that maintenance order was made.

(2) If, in a case where this section applies, the liable person fails to comply with any of the terms of the maintenance order—

(a) the Department may bring any proceedings or take any other steps to enforce the order that could have been brought or taken by or on behalf of the primary recipient; and

(b) any court before which proceedings are brought by the Department by virtue of paragraph (a) above shall have the same powers in connection with those proceedings as it would have had if they had been brought by the primary recipient.

(3) The Department's powers under this section are exercisable at the Department's discretion and whether or not the primary recipient or any other person consents to their exercise; but any sums recovered by virtue of this section shall be payable to or for the primary recipient, as if the proceedings or steps in question had been brought or taken by him or on his behalf.

(4) The powers conferred on the Department by subsection (2)(a) above include power—

(a) to apply for the registration of the maintenance order under—
    (i) section 17 of the Maintenance Orders Act 1950;
    (ii) section 11 of the Maintenance and Affiliation Orders Act (Northern Ireland) 1966; or
    (iii) the Civil Jurisdiction and Judgments Act 1982; and
(b) to make an application under section 2 of the Maintenance Orders (Reciprocal Enforcement) Act 1972 (application for enforcement in reciprocating country).

(5) Where this section applies, the prescribed person shall in prescribed circumstances give the Department notice of any application—

(a) to alter, vary, suspend, discharge, revoke, revive or enforce the maintenance order in question; or
(b) to remit arrears under that maintenance order;

and the Department shall be entitled to appear and be heard on the application.

(6) Where, by virtue of this section, the Department commences any proceedings to enforce a maintenance order, the Department shall, in relation to those proceedings, be treated for the purposes of any statutory provision relating to maintenance orders as if it were a person entitled to payment under the maintenance order in question (but shall not thereby become entitled to any such payment).

(7) Where, in any proceedings under this section, the court makes an order for the whole or any part of the arrears due under the maintenance order in question to be paid as a lump sum, the Department shall inform the Incorporated Law Society of Northern Ireland of the amount of that lump sum if the Department knows—

(a) that the primary recipient received legal aid under Part II of the Legal Aid, Advice and Assistance (Northern Ireland) Order 1981 in connection with the proceedings in which the maintenance order was made, and
(b) that a sum remains unpaid on account of the contribution required of the primary recipient under Article 12 of that Order in respect of those proceedings.

(8) In this section "maintenance order" has the same meaning as it has in section 102 above, but does not include any such order for the payment of a lump sum.

DEFINITIONS
"the Department": s.167.

GENERAL NOTE
Section 103 enables the DHSS to enforce certain private maintenance orders in favour of lone-parent claimants of income support. Only lone parents are covered by subs. (1)(a), and not mere separated or divorced spouses, but the maintenance order may be in favour either of the parent or the child(ren) or both. The Department may at their discretion and without the consent of the lone parent take steps (including those specified in subs. (5)) to enforce the order as if they were the person entitled to payment under the order (subss. (2), (3) and (6)). But any sums recovered are payable to the primary recipient under the order (subss. (3) and (6)). Under subs. (5) regulations may specify who has to inform the DHSS of applications to vary, suspend, etc., the private order or to remit arrears. Regulation 3 of the Income Support (Liable Relatives) Regulations (Northern Ireland) 1990 (S.I. 1990 No. 375) specifies various court officials. The Department is given the right to be heard on any such application, but has no

power to make such an application, *e.g.* to increase the amount of an order. This is because subs. (2) only operates when there is a failure to comply with the terms (*i.e.* the existing terms) of the order.

Subsection (7) requires the Department to inform the Incorporated Law Society of Northern Ireland when a lump sum of arrears is to be paid when the Law Society of Northern Ireland might be able to recover a contribution out of the lump sum. Overall s.103 is a powerful weapon for the DHSS to enforce the payment of maintenance orders. If the lone parent has her own order, which is not being paid, income support will make up the shortfall. There is thus no great incentive for the lone parent to go through all the hassle of enforcement, and there may be other circumstances making her reluctant to take action. The DHSS will have no such inhibitions.

The Secretary of State for Social Security predicted that the amount of maintenance recovered by the DSS in respect of lone parents on income support would rise to about £260 million in 1990–91, having gone up from £155 million in 1988–89 to £180 million in 1989–90 (*Hansard*, H.C. Vol. 170, col. 570). The predicted increase was based partly on the provisions now contained in ss.102 and 103 and partly on giving greater priority and resources to such work, with changes in the administrative guidance. These changes are to point up the need to stress to lone parents on benefits the advantages of reflecting the absent parent's proper responsibilities in the maintenance arrangements from the outset and also to indicate that the "normal expectation" should be that a lone parent will co-operate in establishing where responsibility lies. It is, however, recognised that there may be circumstances in which lone parents will not wish to name the father of a child. The White Paper *Children Come First* proposes reductions in the lone parent's benefit if she declines without good cause to take maintenance proceedings. Now see the Child Support (Northern Ireland) Order 1991 (S.I. 1991 No. 2628 N.I. 23)), due to come into operation in April 1993.

PART VI

ENFORCEMENT

Inspection

Appointment and powers of inspectors

104.—(1) For the purposes of the legislation to which this section applies the Department may appoint such inspectors, and pay to them such salaries or remuneration, as it may determine with the consent of the Department of Finance and Personnel.

(2) An inspector appointed under this section shall, for the purposes of the execution of that legislation, have the following powers—

(a) to enter at all reasonable times any premises liable to inspection under this section;

(b) to make such examination and inquiry as may be necessary—

(i) for ascertaining whether the provisions of the legislation are being, or have been, complied with in any such premises; or

(ii) for investigating the circumstances in which any accident, injury or disease which has given or may give rise to a claim for industrial injuries benefit, or for any benefit which is a relevant benefit, occurred or may have occurred, or was or may have been received or contracted;

(c) to examine, either alone or in the presence of any other person, as he thinks fit, in relation to any matters under the legislation on which he may reasonably require information, every person whom he finds in any such premises or whom he has reasonable cause to believe to be or to have been a person liable to pay—

(i) contributions under Part I of the Contributions and Benefits Act;

(ii) a state scheme premium; or

(iii) a compensation payment or a relevant payment,

and to require every such person to be so examined;

(d) to exercise such other powers as may be necessary for carrying the legislation into effect.

(3) The premises liable to inspection under this section are any where an inspector has reasonable grounds for supposing that—

   (a) any persons are employed;

   (b) there is being carried on any agency or other business for the introduction or supply to persons requiring them of persons available to do
work or to perform services;

   (c) a personal or occupational pension scheme is being administered; or

   (d) any person—

      (i) who is the compensator in relation to any such accident, injury
or disease as is referred to in subsection (2)(b)(ii) above; or

      (ii) on whose behalf any such compensator has or may have
made, or may make, a compensation payment,

   carries on business or is to be found,

but do not include any private dwelling-house not used by, or by permission
of, the occupier for the purposes of a trade or business.

(4) Every inspector shall be furnished with a certificate of his appointment, and on applying for admission to any premises for the purpose of the
legislation shall, if so required, produce the certificate.

(5) Where any premises are liable to be inspected by an inspector or
officer appointed or employed by, or are under the control of, some other
government department, the Department may make arrangements with
that department for any of the powers or duties of inspectors under this
section to be carried out by an inspector or officer employed by that
department.

(6) In accordance with this section, persons shall furnish to an inspector all
such information, and produce for his inspection all such documents, as he
may reasonably require for the purpose of ascertaining—

   (a) whether—

      (i) any contribution under Part I of the Contributions and Bene-
fits Act;

      (ii) any state scheme premium; or

      (iii) any compensation payment or relevant payment,

   is or has been payable, or has been duly paid, by or in respect of any
person; or

   (b) whether benefit is or was payable to or in respect of any person.

(7) The following persons are under the duty imposed by subsection (6)
above—

   (a) the occupier of any premises liable to inspection under this section;

   (b) any person who is or has been an employer or an employee within the
meaning of any provision of the Contributions and Benefits Act;

   (c) any person carrying on an agency or other business for the introduction or supply to persons requiring them of persons available to do
work or to perform services;

   (d) any person who is or has at any time been a trustee or manager of a
personal or occupational pension scheme;

   (e) any person who is or has been liable—

      (i) to pay contributions or state scheme premiums; or

      (ii) to make any compensation payment or relevant payment;

   (f) the servants or agents of any such person as is specified in any of the
preceding paragraphs,

but no one shall be required under this section to answer any questions or to
give evidence tending to incriminate himself or, in the case of a person who is
married, his or her spouse.

(8) This section applies to the following legislation—

   (a) the Social Security Act 1973;

   (b) the Contributions and Benefits Act;

   (c) this Act;

   (d) the Pensions Order; and

(e) Part II of the 1986 Order.

(9) In this section "relevant benefit" and "relevant payment" mean a relevant benefit and relevant payment within the meaning of Part IV of this Act.

DEFINITIONS
"the 1986 Order": s.167.
"the Contributions and Benefits Act": *ibid.*
"industrial injuries benefit": *ibid.*
"occupational pension scheme": *ibid.*
"the Pensions Act": *ibid.*
"personal pension scheme": *ibid.*

Delay, obstruction etc. of inspector

105.—(1) If a person—
  (a) wilfully delays or obstructs an inspector in the exercise of any power under this Act; or
  (b) refuses or neglects to answer any question or to furnish any information or to produce any document when required to do so under this Act,
he shall be guilty of an offence and liable on summary conviction to a fine not exceeding level 3 on the standard scale.

(2) Where a person is convicted of an offence under subsection (1)(b) above and the refusal or neglect is continued by him after this conviction, he shall be guilty of a further offence and liable on summary conviction to a fine not exceeding £40 for each day on which it is continued.

False representations for obtaining benefit etc.

106.—(1) If a person for the purpose of obtaining any benefit or other payment under the legislation to which section 104 above applies, whether for himself or some other person, or for any other purpose connected with that legislation—
  (a) makes a statement or representation which he knows to be false; or
  (b) produces or furnishes, or knowingly causes or knowingly allows to be produced or furnished, any document or information which he knows to be false in a material particular,
he shall be guilty of an offence.

(2) A person guilty of an offence under subsection (1) above shall be liable on summary conviction to a fine not exceeding level 5 on the standard scale, or to imprisonment for a term not exceeding 3 months, or to both.

Breach of regulations

107. Regulations and schemes under any of the legislation to which section 104 above applies may provide for contravention of, or failure to comply with, any provision contained in regulations made under that legislation to be an offence under that legislation and for the recovery, on summary conviction of any such offence, of penalties not exceeding—
  (a) for any one offence, level 3 on the standard scale; or
  (b) for an offence of continuing any such contravention or failure after conviction, £40 for each day on which it is so continued.

Offences relating to contributions

108.—(1) If a person fails to pay, at or within the time prescribed for the purpose, any contribution which he is liable under Part I of the Contributions and Benefits Act to pay, he shall be guilty of an offence and liable on summary conviction to a fine not exceeding level 3 on the standard scale.

(2) If a person fails to pay at or within the time prescribed for the purpose any sums which he is required by regulations made by virtue of paragraph 6

of Schedule 1 to the Contributions and Benefits Act to pay, he shall be liable to be proceeded against and punished under subsection (1) above without proof of his failure so to pay any particular contribution.

(3) Subsection (1) above does not apply to Class 4 contributions recoverable by the Inland Revenue.

(4) If a person—

(a) buys, sell or offers for sale, takes or gives in exchange, or pawns or takes in pawn a contribution card or a used contribution stamp; or

(b) affixes a used contribution stamp to a contribution card,

he shall be guilty of an offence and liable on summary conviction to a fine not exceeding level 5 on the standard scale or to imprisonment for a term not exceeding 3 months, or to both.

(5) In any proceedings under subsection (4) above with respect to used stamps a stamp shall be deemed to have been used if it has been affixed to a contribution card or cancelled or defaced in any way whatsoever and whether or not it has actually been used for the payment of a contribution.

(6) In this Act "contribution card" means any card issued under regulations for the purpose of payment of contributions by affixing stamps to it.

DEFINITIONS
  "the Contributions and Benefits Act": s.167.
  "prescribed": *ibid*.

Offences by bodies corporate

109. Section 20(2) and (3) of the Interpretation Act (Northern Ireland) 1954 (offences by bodies corporate) shall apply to this Act as if it were an enactment within the meaning of section 1(b) of that Act.

Legal proceedings

Legal proceedings

110.—(1) Any person authorised by the Department, the Department of the Environment or the Housing Executive in that behalf may conduct any proceedings under this Act before a magistrates' court, although not a barrister or solicitor.

(2) Notwithstanding anything in any statutory provision—

(a) proceedings for an offence under this Act other than an offence relating to housing benefit may be begun at any time within the period of 3 months from the date on which evidence, sufficient in the opinion of the Department to justify a prosecution for the offence, comes to its knowledge or within a period of 12 months from the commission of the offence, whichever period last expires; and

(b) proceedings for an offence under this Act relating to housing benefit may be begun at any time within the period of 3 months from the date on which evidence, sufficient in the opinion of the Department of the Environment or the Housing Executive to justify a prosecution for the offence, comes to its knowledge or within a period of 12 months from the commission of the offence, whichever period last expires.

(3) For the purposes of subsection (2) above—

(a) a certificate purporting to be signed by or on behalf of the Head or a secretary, under secretary or assistant secretary of the Department or of the Department of the Environment as to the date on which such evidence as is mentioned in paragraph (a) or (b) of that subsection came to its knowledge shall be conclusive evidence of that date; and

(b) a certificate purporting to be signed by a member of the Housing Executive or by an officer of the Executive authorised by it to act for the purposes of this section as to the date on which such evidence as is mentioned in paragraph (b) of that subsection came to the Executive's knowledge shall be conclusive evidence of that date.

(4) Any proceedings in respect of any act or omission of an adjudication officer which, apart from this subsection, would fall to be brought against a person appointed by virtue of section 36(1) above who is resident in Great Britain, other than proceedings for an offence, may instead be brought against the Chief Adjudication Officer; and, for the purposes of any proceedings so brought, the acts or omission of the adjudication officer shall be treated as the acts or omissions of the Chief Adjudication Officer.

(5) Subject to subsection (6) below, in proceedings for an offence under this Act, the wife or husband of the accused is competent to give evidence, whether for or against the accused.

(6) The wife or husband is not compellable either to give evidence or, in giving evidence, to disclose any communication made to her or him by the accused during the marriage.

Questions arising in proceedings

111.—(1) Where in any proceedings—
(a) for an offence under this Act;
(b) involving any question as to the payment of contributions (other than a Class 4 contribution recoverable by the Inland Revenue); or
(c) for the recovery of any sums due to the Department or the National Insurance Fund,

any such question arises as is mentioned in section 15(1) above, the decision of the Department shall be conclusive for the purposes of the proceedings.

(2) If—
(a) a decision of any such question is necessary for the determination of proceedings; and
(b) the decision of the Department has not been obtained or a question has been raised with a view to a review of the decision obtained,

the question shall be referred to the Department for determination or review in accordance (subject to any necessary modifications) with Part II of this Act.

(3) Subsection (1) above does not apply if—
(a) an appeal under section 16 above is pending;
(b) the time for appealing has not expired; or
(c) a question has been raised with a view to a review of the Department's decision under section 17 above,

and the court dealing with the case shall adjourn the proceedings until such time as a final decision on the question has been obtained.

Unpaid contributions etc.

Evidence of non-payment

112.—(1) Subsection (2) below applies with respect to any period during which, under regulations made by virtue of paragraph 5(1) of Schedule 1 to the Contributions and Benefits Act (deduction with PAYE), contributions fall to be paid in like manner as income tax.

(2) A certificate of a collector of taxes that any amount by way of contributions which a person is liable to pay to that collector for any period has not been paid—
(a) to him; or
(b) to the best of his knowledge and belief, to any other person to whom it might lawfully be paid,

shall until the contrary is proved be sufficient evidence in any proceedings before any court that the sum mentioned in the certificate is unpaid and due.

(3) A document purporting to be such a certificate shall be deemed to be such a certificate until the contrary is proved.

(4) A statutory declaration by an officer of the Department or of the Secretary of State that the searches specified in the declaration for a particular contribution card or for a record of the payment of a particular contribution have been made, and that the card in question or a record of the payment of the contribution in question has not been found, is admissible in any proceedings for an offence as evidence of the facts stated in the declaration.

(5) Nothing in subsection (4) above makes a statutory declaration admissible as evidence in proceedings for an offence except in a case where, and to the extent to which, oral evidence to the like effect would have been admissible in those proceedings.

(6) Nothing in subsections (4) and (5) above makes a statutory declaration admissible as evidence in proceedings for an offence—

(a) unless a copy of it has, not less than 7 days before the hearing or trial, been served on the person charged with the offence in any manner in which a summons in a summary prosecution may be served; or

(b) if that person, not later than 3 days before the hearing or trial or within such further time as the court may in special circumstances allow, gives notice to the prosecutor requiring the attendance at the trial of the person by whom the declaration was made.

DEFINITIONS
  "contribution card": s.167.
  "the Contributions and Benefits Act": *ibid.*

Recovery of unpaid contributions on prosecution

113.—(1) Where—

(a) a person has been convicted of an offence under section 108(1) above of failing to pay a contribution at or within the time prescribed for the purpose; and

(b) the contribution remains unpaid at the date of the conviction,

he shall be liable to pay to the Department a sum equal to the amount which he failed to pay.

(2) Where—

(a) a person is convicted of an offence—

(i) under section 108(3)(b) above;

(ii) under section 13 of the Stamp Duties Management Act 1891 as applied by regulations made under paragraph 8(3) of Schedule 1 to the Contributions and Benefits Act; or

(iii) of contravening or failing to comply with regulations; and

(b) the evidence on which he is convicted shows that he, for the purposes of paying any contribution which he was liable or entitled to pay, has affixed to any contribution card any used contribution stamp; and

(c) the contribution (not being a Class 3 contribution) in respect of which the stamp was affixed remains unpaid at the date of the conviction,

he shall be liable to pay to the Department a sum equal to the amount of the contribution.

DEFINITIONS
  "the Contributions and Benefits Act": s.167.

Proof of previous offences

114.—(1) Subject to and in accordance with subsections (2) to (5) below, where a person is convicted of an offence mentioned in section 113(1) or (2)(a) above, evidence may be given of any previous failure by him to pay contributions within the time prescribed for the purpose; and in those subsections "the conviction" and "the offence" mean respectively the conviction referred to in this subsection and the offence of which the person is convicted.

(2) Such evidence may be given only if notice of intention to give it is served with the summons or warrant on which the person appeared before the court which convicted him.

(3) If the offence is one of failure to pay a Class 1 contribution, evidence may be given of failure on his part to pay (whether or not in respect of the same person) such contributions or any Class 1A contributions or state scheme premiums on the date of the offence, or during the 2 years preceding that date.

(4) If the offence is one of failure to pay a Class 1A contribution, evidence may be given of failure on his part to pay (whether or not in respect of the same person or the same car) such contributions, or any Class 1 contributions or state scheme premiums, on the date of the offence, or during the 2 years preceding that date.

(5) If the offence—

(a) is one of failure to pay Class 2 contributions; or

(b) is one of those mentioned in section 113(2)(a) above,

evidence may be given of his failure to pay such contributions during those 2 years.

(6) On proof of any matter of which evidence may be given under subsection (3), (4) or (5) above, the person convicted shall be liable to pay to the Department a sum equal to the total of all amounts which he is so proved to have failed to pay and which remain unpaid at the date of the conviction.

Unpaid contributions—supplementary

115.—(1) Where a person charged with an offence mentioned in section 113(1) or (2)(a) above is convicted of that offence in his absence under Article 24(2) of the Magistrates' Courts (Northern Ireland) Order 1981 then if—

(a) it is proved to the satisfaction of the court, on oath or in the manner prescribed by magistrates' courts rules under Part IV of that Order, that notice under section 114(2) above has been duly served specifying the other contributions in respect of which the complainant intends to give evidence; and

(b) the clerk of petty sessions has received a statement in writing purporting to be made by the accused or by a solicitor acting on his behalf to the effect that if the accused is convicted in his absence of the offence charged he desires to admit failing to pay the other contributions so specified or any of them,

section 114 above shall have effect as if the evidence had been given and the failure so admitted had been proved, and the court shall proceed accordingly.

(2) Where a person is convicted of an offence mentioned in section 113(1) or (2)(a) above and an order is made under the Probation Act (Northern Ireland) 1950 placing the offender on probation or discharging him absolutely or conditionally, sections 113 and 114 above, and subsection (1) above, shall apply as if it were a conviction for all purposes.

(3) Any sum which a person is liable to pay under section 113 or 114 above or under subsection (1) above shall be recoverable from him as a penalty.

(4) Sums recovered by the Department under the provisions mentioned in subsection (1) above, so far as representing contributions of any class, are to be treated for all purposes of the Contributions and Benefits Act and this Act (including in particular the application of section 142 below) as contributions of that class received by the Department.

(5) Without prejudice to subsection (5) above, in so far as such sums represent primary Class 1 or Class 2 contributions, they are to be treated as contributions paid in respect of the person in respect of whom they were originally payable; and enactments relating to earnings factors shall apply accordingly.

PART VII

PROVISION OF INFORMATION

Inland Revenue

Disclosure of information by Inland Revenue

116.—(1) No obligation as to secrecy imposed by statute or otherwise on a person employed in relation to the Inland Revenue shall prevent information obtained or held in connection with the assessment or collection of income tax from being disclosed—

(a) to the Department;

(b) to the Secretary of State; or

(c) to an officer of either of them authorised to receive such information in connection with the operation of the Contributions and Benefits Act or this Act or of any enactment applying in Great Britain corresponding to either of them.

(2) In relation to persons who are carrying on or have carried on a trade, profession or vocation income from which is chargeable to tax under Case I or II of Schedule D, disclosure under subsection (1) above relating to that trade, profession or vocation shall be limited to information about the commencement or cessation of, and employed earners engaged in, the trade, profession or vocation, but sufficient information may also be given to identify the persons concerned.

(3) Subsection (1) above extends only to disclosure by or under the authority of the Commissioners of Inland Revenue; and information which is subject to disclosure to any person by virtue of that subsection shall not be further disclosed to any person except where the further disclosure is made—

(a) to a person to whom disclosure could by virtue of that subsection have been made by or under the authority of the Commissioners of Inland Revenue;

(b) for the purposes of proceedings (civil or criminal) in connection with the operation of the Contributions and Benefits Act or this Act or of any enactment applying in Great Britain corresponding to either of them; or

(c) for any purposes of sections 15 to 60 above and any corresponding provisions applying in Great Britain.

DEFINITIONS
"the Contributions and Benefits Act": s.167.

Persons employed or formerly employed in social security administration or adjudication

Unauthorised disclosure of information relating to particular persons

117.—(1) A person who is or has been employed in social security administration or adjudication is guilty of an offence if he discloses without lawful authority any information which he acquired in the course of his employment and which relates to a particular person.

(2) A person who is or has been employed in the audit of expenditure or the investigation of complaints is guilty of an offence if he discloses without lawful authority any information—

  (a) which he acquired in the course of his employment;
  (b) which is, or is derived from, information acquired or held by or for the purposes of any of the government departments or other bodies or persons referred to in Part I of Schedule 4 to this Act or in any corresponding enactment having effect in Great Britain; and
  (c) which relates to a particular person.
  (3) It is not an offence under this section—
  (a) to disclose information in the form of a summary or collection of information so framed as not to enable information relating to any particular person to be ascertained from it; or
  (b) to disclose information which has previously been disclosed to the public with lawful authority.
  (4) It is a defence for a person charged with an offence under this section to prove that at the time of the alleged offence—
  (a) he believed that he was making the disclosure in question with lawful authority and had no reasonable cause to believe otherwise; or
  (b) he believed that the information in question had previously been disclosed to the public with lawful authority and had no reasonable cause to believe otherwise.
  (5) A person guilty of an offence under this section shall be liable—
  (a) on conviction on indictment, to imprisonment for a term not exceeding two years or to a fine or to both; or
  (b) on summary conviction, to imprisonment for a term not exceeding six months or a fine not exceeding the statutory maximum or both.
  (6) For the purposes of this section, the persons who are "employed in social security administration or adjudication" are—
  (a) any person specified in Part I of Schedule 4 to this Act or in any corresponding enactment having effect in Great Britain;
  (b) any other person who carries out the administrative work of any of the government departments or other bodies or persons referred to in that Part of that Schedule or that corresponding enactment; and
  (c) any person who provides, or is employed in the provision of, services to any of those departments, persons or bodies;
and "employment", in relation to any such person, shall be construed accordingly.
  (7) For the purposes of subsections (2) and (6) above, any reference in Part I of Schedule 4 to this Act or in any corresponding enactment having effect in Great Britain to a government department shall be construed in accordance with Part II of that Schedule or any corresponding enactment having effect in Great Britain, and for this purpose "government department" shall be taken to include—
  (a) the Commissioners of Inland Revenue; and
  (b) the Scottish Courts Administration.
  (8) For the purposes of this section, the persons who are "employed in the audit of expenditure or the investigation of complaints" are—
  (a) the Comptroller and Auditor General for Northern Ireland;
  (b) the Northern Ireland Parliamentary Commissioner for Administration;
  (c) the Northern Ireland Commissioner for Complaints;
  (d) the Comptroller and Audit General;
  (e) the Parliamentary Commissioner for Administration;
  (f) any member of the staff of the Northern Ireland Audit Officer or the National Audit Office;
  (g) any other person who carries out the administrative work of either of those Offices, or who provides, or is employed in the provision of, services to either of them;
  (h) the Health Service Commissioner for England, Wales or Scotland; and

(i) any officer of any of the Commissioners referred to in paragraph (b), (c), (e) or (h) above;

and "employment", in relation to any such person, shall be construed accordingly.

(9) For the purposes of this section a disclosure is to be regarded as made with lawful authority if, and only if, it is made—

  (a) in accordance with his official duty—
      (i) by a civil servant; or
      (ii) by a person employed in the audit of expenditure or the investigation of complaints, who does not fall within subsection (8)(g) above;

  (b) by any other person either—
      (i) for the purposes of the function in the exercise of which he holds the information and without contravening any restriction duly imposed by the person responsible; or
      (ii) to, or in accordance with an authorisation duly given by, the person responsible;

  (c) in accordance with any statutory provision or order of a court;

  (d) for the purpose of instituting, or otherwise for the purposes of, any proceedings before a court or before any tribunal or other body or person referred to in Part I of Schedule 4 to this Act or in any corresponding enactment having effect in Great Britain; or

  (e) with the consent of the appropriate person;

and in this subsection "the person responsible" means the Department, the Lord Chancellor or any person authorised by the Department or the Lord Chancellor for the purposes of this subsection and includes a reference to "the person responsible" within the meaning of any corresponding enactment having effect in Great Britain.

(10) For the purposes of subsection (9)(e) above, "the appropriate person" means the person to whom the information in question relates, except that if the affairs of that person are being dealt with—

  (a) under a power of attorney;

  (b) by a controller appointed under Article 101 of the Mental Health (Northern Ireland) Order 1986 or by a receiver appointed under section 99 of the Mental Health Act 1983;

  (c) by a Scottish mental health custodian, that is to say—
      (i) a curator bonis, tutor or judicial factor; or
      (ii) the managers of a hospital acting on behalf of that person under section 94 of the Mental Health (Scotland) Act 1984; or

  (d) by a mental health appointee, that is to say—
      (i) a person directed or authorised as mentioned in sub-paragraph (a) of rule 38(1) of Order 109 of the Rules of the Supreme Court (Northern Ireland) 1980 or sub-paragraph (a) of rule 41(1) of the Court of Protection Rules 1984; or
      (ii) a controller ad interim appointed under sub-paragraph (b) of the said rule 38(1) or any receiver ad interim appointed under sub-paragraph (b) of the said rule 41(1),

the appropriate person is the attorney, controller, receiver, custodian or appointee, as the case may be, or, in a case falling within paragraph (a) above, the person to whom the information relates.

Notification of deaths

Regulations as to notification of deaths

118.—(1) Regulations may provide that it shall be the duty of the Registrar General or any registrar to furnish the Department, for the purpose of its functions under the Contributions and Benefits Act and this Act and the functions of the Secretary of State under any enactment applying in Great

Britain corresponding to either of them, with the prescribed particulars of such deaths as may be prescribed.

(2) The regulations may make provision as to the manner in which and times at which the particulars are to be furnished.

(3) In subsection (1) "Registrar General" and "registrar" have the meanings assigned to them in the Births and Deaths Registration (Northern Ireland) Order 1976.

DEFINITIONS
"the Contributions and Benefits Act": s.167.
"prescribed": *ibid.*

Personal representatives—income support and supplementary benefit

Personal representatives to give information about the estate of a deceased person who was in receipt of income support or supplementary benefit

119.—(1) The personal representatives of a person who was in receipt of income support or supplementary benefit at any time before his death shall provide the Department with such imformation as it may require relating to the assets and liabilities of that person's estate.

(2) If the personal representatives fail to supply any information within 28 days of being required to do so under subsection (1) above, then—

(a) the county court may, on the application of the Department, make an order directing them to supply that information within such time as may be specified in the order, and

(b) any such order may provide that all costs of and incidental to the application shall be borne personally by any of the personal representatives.

GENERAL NOTE
Under s.69(3) an overpayment which would have been recoverable from a person is recoverable from that person's estate (*Department for Social Services* v. *Solly* [1974] 3 All E.R. 922). This section provides a specific obligation for the estate to provide information about the assets in it. However, s.119 only applies to the estates of income support or supplementary benefit claimants. It does not apply to family credit, disability working allowance, housing benefit or community charge benefit claimants, all of which can be overpaid by concealing capital. Nor does it apply to anyone other than a recipient of income support or supplementary benefit. Sometimes a person other than a recipient may become liable to recovery by making a misrepresentation or failing to disclose a material fact (*R(SB) 21/82* and *R(SB) 28/83*).

Housing benefit

Information for purposes of housing benefit

120.—(1) The Department may supply to the Housing Executive such information of a prescribed description obtained by reason of the exercise of any of the Department's functions under the Contributions and Benefits Act or this Act as the Executive may require in connection with any of the Executive's functions relating to housing benefit.

(2) The Housing Executive shall supply to the Department such information of a prescribed description obtained by reason of the exercise of the Executive's functions relating to housing benefit as the Department may require in connection with any of its functions under the Contributions and Benefits Act or this Act.

(3) It shall also be the duty of the Housing Executive to supply the Department, in the prescribed manner and within the prescribed time—

(a) with such information as the Department may require concerning the Executive's performance of any of the Executive's functions relating to housing benefit; and

(b) with such information as the Department may require to enable it—

(i) to prepare estimates of likely future amounts of housing benefit expenditure; and

(ii) to decide questions relating to the development of housing benefit policy.

DEFINITIONS
"the Contributions and Benefits Act": s.191.
"prescribed": *ibid.*

Statutory sick pay and other benefits

Disclosure by the Department for purpose of determination of period of entitlement to statutory sick pay

121. Where the Department consider that it is reasonable for information held by the Department to be disclosed to an employer, for the purpose of enabling that employer to determine the duration of a period of entitlement under Part XI of the Contributions and Benefits Act in respect of an employee, or whether such a period exists, the Department may disclose the information to that employer.

DEFINITIONS
"the Contributions and Benefits Act": s.191.

Duties of employers—statutory sick pay and claims for other benefits

122.—(1) Regulations may make provision requiring an employer, in a case falling within subsection (3) below to furnish information in connection with the making, by a person who is, or has been, an employee of that employer, of a claim for—

(a) sickness benefit;

(b) a maternity allowance;

(c) an invalidity pension under section 33, 40 or 41 of the Contributions and Benefits Act;

(d) industrial injuries benefit; or

(e) a severe disablement allowance.

(2) Regulations under this section shall prescribe—

(a) the kind of information to be furnished in accordance with the regulations;

(b) the person to whom information of the prescribed kind is to be furnished; and

(c) the manner in which, and period within which, it is to be furnished.

(3) The cases are—

(a) where, by virtue of paragraph 2 of Schedule 11 to the Contributions and Benefits Act or of regulations made under paragraph 1 of that Schedule, a period of entitlement does not arise in relation to a period of incapacity for work;

(b) where a period of entitlement has come to an end but the period of incapacity for work which was running immediately before the period of entitlement came to an end continues; and

(c) where a period of entitlement has not come to an end but, on the assumption that—

(i) the period of incapacity for work in question continues to run for a prescribed period; and

(ii) there is no material change in circumstances,

the period of entitlement will have ended on or before the end of the prescribed period.

(4) Regulations—

(a) may require employers to maintain such records in connection with statutory sick pay as may be prescribed;

(b) may provide for—
    (i) any person claiming to be entitled to statutory sick pay; or
    (ii) any other person who is a party to proceedings arising under Part XI of the Contributions and Benefits Act,
to furnish to the Department, within a prescribed period, any information required for the determination of any question arising in connection therewith; and

(c) may require employers who have made payments of statutory sick pay to furnish to the Department such documents and information, at such times, as may be prescribed.

DEFINITIONS
    "the Contributions and Benefits Act": s.191.
    "industrial injuries benefit": *ibid.*

GENERAL NOTE
    See regs. 13–15 of the Statutory Sick Pay (General) Regulations (Northern Ireland) 1982 (S.I. 1982 No. 263). See also the equivalent Great Britain Regulations, the Statutory Sick Pay (General) Regulations 1982 (S.I. 1982 No. 894), and the commentary in the current edition of Bonner *et al.*

Statutory maternity pay and other benefits

Disclosure by the Department for purpose of determination of period of entitlement to statutory maternity pay

123. Where the Department considers that it is reasonable for information held by the Department to be disclosed to a person liable to make payments of statutory maternity pay for the purpose of enabling that person to determine—
    (a) whether a maternity pay period exists in relation to a woman who is or has been an employee of his; and
    (b) if it does, the date of its commencement and the weeks in it in respect of which he may be liable to pay statutory maternity pay,
the Department may disclose the information to that person.

Duties of employers—statutory maternity pay and claims for other benefits

124.—(1) Regulations may make provision requiring an employer in prescribed circumstances to furnish information in connection with the making of a claim by a woman who is or has been his employee for—
    (a) a maternity allowance;
    (b) sickness benefit;
    (c) an invalidity pension under section 33, 40 or 41 of the Contributions and Benefits Act; or
    (d) a severe disablement allowance.
(2) Regulations under this section shall prescribe—
    (a) the kind of information to be furnished in accordance with the regulations;
    (b) the person to whom information of the prescribed kind is to be furnished; and
    (c) the manner in which, and period within which, it is to be furnished.
(3) Regulations—
    (a) may require employers to maintain such records in connection with statutory maternity pay as may be prescribed;
    (b) may provide for—
        (i) any woman claiming to be entitled to statutory maternity pay; or
        (ii) any other person who is a party to proceedings arising under Part XII of the Contributions and Benefits Act,

to furnish to the Department, within a prescribed period, any information required for the determination of any question arising in connection therewith; and

(c) may require persons who have made payments of statutory maternity pay to furnish to the Department such documents and information, at such times, as may be prescribed.

DEFINITIONS
"the Contributions and Benefits Act": s.167.

GENERAL NOTE
See regs. 25–26 of the Statutory Maternity Pay (General) Regulations (Northern Ireland) 1987 (S.I. 1987 No. 30). See also the equivalent Great Britain Regulations, the Statutory Maternity Pay (General) Regulations 1986 (S.I. 1986 No. 1960), and commentary in the current edition of Bonner *et al.*

Maintenance proceedings

Furnishing of addresses for maintenance proceedings, etc.

125.—(1) The Department may incur expenses for the purpose of furnishing the address at which a man or woman is recorded by it as residing, where the address is required for the purpose of taking or carrying on legal proceedings to obtain or enforce an order for the making by the man or woman of payments—

(a) for the maintenance of the man's wife or former wife, or the woman's husband or former husband; or

(b) for the maintenance or education of any person as being the son or daughter of the man or his wife or former wife, or of the woman or her husband or former husband.

(2) In subsection (1)(b) above "son or daughter" includes an illegitimate son or daughter.

PART VIII

ARRANGEMENTS FOR HOUSING BENEFIT

Housing benefit

Arrangements for housing benefit

126.—(1) Housing benefit provided by virtue of a scheme under section 122 of the Contributions and Benefits Act (in this Act referred to as "the housing benefit scheme")—

(a) is to be in the form of a rate rebate, if it is in respect of payments by way of rates;

(b) is to be in the form of a rent rebate, if it is in respect of payments, other than payments by way of rates, to be made to the Housing Executive; and

(c) is in any other case to be in the form of a rent allowance.

(2) The rebates and allowances referred to in subsection (1) above may take any of the following forms, that is to say—

(a) a payment or payments by the Housing Executive or the Department of the Environment, as the case may be, to the person entitled to the benefit; and

(b) a reduction in the amount of any payments which that person is liable to make to the Housing Executive or the Department of the Environment, as the case may be, by way of rent or rates; or

(c) such a payment or payments and such a reduction;

and in any statutory provision (whenever passed or made) "pay", in relation to housing benefit, includes discharge in any of those forms.

(3) Housing benefit shall be administered by—

(a) the Housing Executive in so far as it relates to persons who are tenants of the Executive, private tenants or tenants of registered housing associations;

(b) the Department of the Environment in so far as it relates to persons who own and occupy their dwellings.

(4) Regulations may provide that in prescribed cases a payment made by a person entitled to a rent allowance shall be treated for the purposes of subsection (1)(a) above as being, to such extent as may be prescribed, a payment by way of rates.

(5) Circumstances may be prescribed in which a rate rebate may be treated as if it fell to be paid as a rent allowance.

(6) In this section—

"private tenants" means tenants under any tenancy except—

(a) a tenancy under which the estate of the landlord belongs to—

(i) the Housing Executive; or

(ii) a registered housing association;

(b) a tenancy the purpose of which is to confer on the tenant the right to occupy a dwelling-house for a holiday;

"registered housing association" means a housing association registered in the register maintained under Part VII of the Housing (Northern Ireland) Order 1981.

DEFINITIONS

"the Contributions and Benefits Act": s.167.
"dwelling": *ibid.*
"Housing Executive": *ibid.*
"prescribed": *ibid.*

Housing benefit finance

127.—(1) The Department shall in respect of each financial year pay to the Housing Executive a grant towards the expenditure incurred or to be incurred by the Executive in that year under this Part (including, if the Department so determines, an amount towards the cost of administering housing benefit).

(2) The amount of the grant under subsection (1) above which is to be paid to the Housing Executive shall be such as the Department may, with the approval of the Department of Finance and Personnel, determine.

(3) A grant under subsection (1) above shall be payable by the Department at such time and in such manner as the Department may think fit.

DEFINITIONS

"the Housing Executive": s.167.

Claims etc.

128.—(1) Unless the Department otherwise determines, a grant under section 127 above shall not be payable until the Housing Executive has made a claim for it in such form as the Department may determine.

(2) The Department may withhold from the Housing Executive so much of any grant under section 127 above as it thinks fit until either—

(a) the Executive has supplied it with prescribed particulars relating to its claim for a grant and complied with prescribed conditions as to records, certificates, audit or otherwise; or

(b) the Department is satisfied that there is a good reason for the Executive's failure to supply those particulars or comply with those conditions.

(3) If the Housing Executive fails to make a claim for a grant within such period as the Department considers reasonable, the Department may withhold from the Executive such part of the grant as it thinks fit for so long as it thinks fit.

(4) Where the amount of the grant paid to the Housing Executive for any year is found to be incorrect, the amount payable to it for any subsequent year may be adjusted for the purpose of rectifying that mistake in whole or in part.

DEFINITIONS
"prescribed": s.191.

PART IX

ALTERATION OF CONTRIBUTIONS AND BENEFITS

Alteration of contributions, etc.

Amendments following alterations in Great Britain

129. Whenever the Secretary of State makes an order under section 141, 143, 145 or 146 of the Great Britain Administration Act (alteration of contributions), the Department may make a corresponding order for Northern Ireland.

DEFINITIONS
"the Great Britain Administration Act": s.167.
"the Department": *ibid.*

Revaluation of earnings factors

130. Whenever the Secretary of State makes an order under section 148 of the Great Britain Administration Act directing that earnings factors for any tax year be increased by any percentage (in order to restore their value in relation to the general level of earnings so far as they are relevant to the calculation of the additional pension in the rate of any long-term benefit, the calculation of any guaranteed minimum pension or any other calculation required under Part III of the Social Security Pensions Act 1975), the Department may make an order for Northern Ireland directing that corresponding earnings factors for the same year be increased by a corresponding percentage.

DEFINITIONS
"the Great Britain Administration Act": s.167.
"the Department": *ibid.*

Statutory sick pay—power to alter limit for small employers' relief

131. Whenever the Secretary of State makes regulations prescribing an amount which an employer's contributions payments must not exceed if he is to be a small employer for the purposes of section 154 of the Great Britain Contributions and Benefits Act, and Department shall make corresponding regulations for Northern Ireland.

DEFINITIONS
"the Great Britain Contributions and Benefits Act": s.167.
"the Department": *ibid.*

Review and alteration of benefits

Annual up-rating of benefits

132.—(1) Whenever the Secretary of State makes an order under section

150 of the Great Britain Administration Act the Department may make a corresponding order for Northern Ireland.

(2) An increase in a sum such as is specified in subsection (3)(b) below shall form part of the Category A or Category B retirement pension of the person to whom it is paid and an increase in a sum such as is specified in subsection (3)(a) below shall be added to and form part of that pension but shall not form part of the sum increased.

(3) The sums referred to in subsection (2) above are those which are—

(a) payable by virtue of Article 37(6) of the Pensions Order to a person who is entitled to a Category A or Category B retirement pension (including any sum payable by virtue of Article 38(3) of that Order); or

(b) payable to such a person as part of his Category A or Category B retirement pension by virtue of—

(i) an order made under this section corresponding to an order made under section 150 of the Great Britain Administration Act by virtue of paragraph (e)(ii) of subsection (1) of that section;

(ii) an order made under section 120 of the 1975 Act corresponding to an order made under section 126A of the Social Security Act 1975; or

(iii) an order made under Article 64 of the 1986 Order corresponding to an order made under section 63(1)(d) of the Social Security Act 1986.

(4) Where any increment under Article 37(6) of the Pensions Order—

(a) is increased in any tax year by an order under Article 39A of that Order; and

(b) in that tax year also falls to be increased by an order under this section,

the increase under this section shall be the amount that would have been specified in the order, but for this subsection, less the amount of the increase under Article 39A of the Pensions Order.

(5) Where sums are payable to a person by virtue of Article 37(6) of the Pensions Order (including such sums payable by virtue of Article 38(3) of that Order) during a period ending with the date on which he became entitled to a Category A or Category B retirement pension, then, for the purpose of determining the amount of his Category A or Category B retirement pension, orders made under this section during that period shall be deemed to have come into force (consecutively in the order in which they were made) on the date on which he became entitled to that pension.

(6) The reference in subsection (1) above to an order made under section 150 of the Great Britain Administration Act includes a reference to an order made in exercise of the powers conferred by regulations made under subsection (11) of that section.

DEFINITIONS
    "the Great Britain Administration Act": s.167.
    "the Department": *ibid.*
    "the Pensions Order": *ibid.*

GENERAL NOTE
    Section 150 of the Great Britain Social Security (Administration) Act 1992 provides for the annual up-rating of levels of benefit, having regard to movements in prices, rather than earnings. The benefits specified in subs. (3) must be up-rated in line with any increase in prices (subs. (2)(a)). Other benefits, excluding child benefit (on which see s.153 of the Great Britain Administration Act) need only be increased if the Secretary of State considers it appropriate (subs. (2)(b)).

Rectification of mistakes in up-rating orders

133. Whenever the Secretary of State makes an order under section 152 of the Great Britain Administration Act, the Department may make a corresponding order for Northern Ireland.

Social security benefits in respect of children

134.—(1) Regulations may, with effect from any day on or after that on which there is an increase in the rate or any of the rates of child benefit, reduce any sum specified in any of the provisions mentioned in subsection (2) below to such extent as the Department thinks appropriate having regard to that increase.

(2) The provisions referred to in subsection (1) above are the following provisions of Schedule 4 to the Contributions and Benefits Act—

(a) paragraph 6 of Part I (child's special allowance);

(b) paragraph 5 of Part III (guardian's allowance);

(c) column (2) of Part IV (increase for child dependants);

(d) paragraph 7 of Part V (increase of weekly rate of disablement pension in respect of child dependants);

(e) paragraph 12 of Part V (allowance in respect of deceased's children).

DEFINITIONS
"the Contributions and Benefits Act": s.167.

PART X

COMPUTATION OF BENEFITS

Effect of alteration of rates of benefit under Parts II to V of Contributions and Benefits Act

135.—(1) This section has effect where the rate of any benefit to which this section applies is altered—

(a) by a statutory provision made subsequent to this Act;

(b) by an order under section 132 or 133 above; or

(c) in consequence of any such statutory provision or order altering any maximum rate of benefit;

and in this section "the commencing date" means the date fixed for payment of benefit at an altered rate to commence.

(2) This section applies to benefit under Part II, III, IV or V of the Contributions and Benefits Act.

(3) Subject to such exceptions or conditions as may be prescribed, where—

(a) the weekly rate of a benefit to which this section applies is altered to a fixed amount higher or lower than the previous amount; and

(b) before the commencing date an award of that benefit has been made (whether before or after the making of the relevant statutory provision),

except as respects any period falling before the commencing date, the benefit shall become payable at the altered rate without any claim being made for it in the case of an increase in the rate of benefit or any review of the award in the case of a decrease, and the award shall have effect accordingly.

(4) Where—

(a) the weekly rate of a benefit to which this section applies is altered; and

(b) before the commencing date (but after that date is fixed) an award is made of the benefit,

the award either may provide for the benefit to be paid as from the commencing date at the altered rate or may be expressed in terms of the rate appropriate at the date of the award.

(5) Where in consequence of the making of a statutory provision altering the rate of disablement pension, regulations are made varying the scale of disablement gratuities, the regulations may provide that the scale as varied

shall apply only in cases where the period taken into account by the assessment of the extent of the disablement in respect of which the gratuity is awarded begins or began after such day as may be prescribed.

(6) Subject to such exceptions or conditions as may be prescribed, where—

(a) for any purpose of any statutory provision the weekly rate at which a person contributes to the cost of providing for a child, or to the maintenance of an adult dependant, is to be calculated for a period beginning on or after the commencing date for an increase in the weekly rate of benefit; but

(b) account is to be taken of amounts referable to the period before the commencing date,

those amounts shall be treated as increased in proportion to the increase in the weekly rate of benefit.

DEFINITIONS
   "the Consequential Provisions Act": s.167.
   "the Contributions and Benefits Act": *ibid.*
   "the Pensions Order": *ibid.*

GENERAL NOTE
   Section 135 provides for up-rated amounts of benefit under Pts. II–V of the Contributions and Benefits (Northern Ireland) Act to take effect automatically without the need for any claim or review.

Computation of Category A retirement pension with increase under s.52(3) of Contributions and Benefits Act

136. Where a person is entitled to a Category A retirement pension with an increase under section 52(3) of the Contributions and Benefits Act in the additional pension and the circumstances are such that—

(a) the deceased spouse to whose contributions that increase is referable died during that part of the tax year which precedes the date on which the order under section 132 above comes into force ("the initial up-rating order"); and

(b) the deceased spouse's final relevant year for the purposes of section 44 of the Contributions and Benefits Act is the tax year immediately preceding that in which the death occurred,

then, in determining the amount of the additional pension which falls to be increased by the initial up-rating order, so much of that pension as is attributable to the increase under section 52(3) of the Contributions and Benefits Act shall be disregarded.

DEFINITIONS
   "the Contributions and Benefits Act": s.167.
   "tax year": *ibid.*

Effect of alteration of rates of child benefit

137.—(1) Subsections (3) and (4) of section 135 above shall have effect where there is an increase in the rate or any of the rates of child benefit as they have effect in relation to the rate of benefit to which that section applies.

(2) Where in connection with child benefit—

(a) any question arises in respect of a period after the date fixed for the commencement of payment of child benefit at an increased rate—

(i) as to the weekly rate at which a person is contributing to the cost of providing for a child; or

(ii) as to the expenditure that a person is incurring in respect of a child; and

(b) in determining that question account falls to be taken of contributions made or expenditure incurred for a period before that date,

the contributions made or expenditure incurred before that date shall be treated as increased in proportion to the increase in the rate of benefit.

DEFINITIONS
  "the Great Britain Administration Act": s.167.

GENERAL NOTE
  The amount of payment of child benefit increases automatically on an up-rating under s.153 of the Great Britain Administration Act.

Treatment of excess benefit as paid on account of child benefit

138.—(1) In any case where—
  (a) any benefit as defined in section 121 of the Contributions and Benefits Act or any increase of such benefit ("the relevant benefit or increase") has been paid to a person for a period in respect of a child; and
  (b) subsequently child benefit for that period in respect of the child becomes payable at a rate which is such that, had the relevant benefit or increase been awarded after the child benefit became payable, the rate of the relevant benefit or increase would have been reduced,

then, except in so far as regulations otherwise provide, the excess shall be treated as paid on account of child benefit for that period in respect of the child.

  (2) In subsection (1) above "the excess" means so much of the relevant benefit or increase as is equal to the difference between—
  (a) the amount of it which was paid for the period referred to in that subsection; and
  (b) the amount of it which would have been paid for that period if it had been paid at the reduced rate referred to in paragraph (b) of that subsection.

DEFINITIONS
  "the Contributions and Benefits Act": s.167.

Effect of alteration in the component rates of income support

139.—(1) Subject to such exceptions and conditions as may be prescribed, where—
  (a) an award of income support is in force in favour of any person ("the recipient"); and
  (b) there is an alteration in any of the relevant amounts, that is to say—
        (i) any of the component rates of income support;
        (ii) any of the other sums specified in regulations under Part VII of the Contributions and Benefits Act; or
        (iii) the recipient's benefit income; and
  (c) the alteration affects the computation of the amount of income support to which the recipient is entitled,

then subsection (2) or (3) below (as the case may be) shall have effect.

  (2) Where, in consequence of the alteration in question, the recipient becomes entitled to an increased or reduced amount of income support ("the new amount"), then, as from the commencing date, the amount of income support payable to or for the recipient under the award shall be the new amount, without any further decision of an adjudication officer, and the award shall have effect accordingly.

  (3) Where, notwithstanding the alteration in question, the recipient continues on and after the commencing date to be entitled to the same amount of income support as before, the award shall continue in force accordingly.

(4) In any case where—

(a) there is an alteration in any of the relevant amounts; and

(b) before the commencing date (but after that date is fixed) an award of income support is made in favour of a person,

the award either may provide for income support to be paid as from the commencing date, in which case the amount shall be determined by reference to the relevant amounts which will be in force on that date, or may provide for an amount determined by reference to the amounts in force at the date of the award.

(5) In this section—

"alteration" means—

(a) in relation to—

(i) the component rates of income support; or

(ii) any other sums specified in regulations under Part VII of the Contributions and Benefits Act,

their alteration by or under any statutory provision whether or not contained in that Part; and

(b) in relation to a person's benefit income, the alteration of any of the applicable sums—

(i) by any statutory provision; or

(ii) by an order under section 132 or 133 above,

to the extent that any such alteration affects the amount of his benefit income;

"applicable sums" means sums to which an order made under section 132 above corresponding to an order made under section 150 of the Great Britain Administration Act by virtue of subsection (1) of that section may apply;

"benefit income", in relation to any person, means so much of his income as consists of—

(a) benefit under the Contributions and Benefits Act, other than income support; or

(b) a war disablement pension or war widow's pension;

"the commencing date", in relation to an alteration, means the date on which the alteration comes into force in the case of the person in question;

"component rate", in relation to income support, means the amount of—

(a) the sum referred to in section 125(5)(b)(i) and (ii) of the Contributions and Benefits Act; or

(b) any of the sums specified in regulations under section 131(1) of that Act;

"relevant amounts" has the meaning given by subsection (1)(b) above.

DEFINITIONS

"the Contributions and Benefits Act": s.167.

GENERAL NOTE

The general rule under s.139 is that if there is an alteration in the prescribed figures for income support personal allowances, premiums, the relevant sum (*i.e.* assumed "strike pay" in trade dispute cases), or any social security benefits which count as income for income support purposes (subs. (1) and (5)), then any consequent change in the amount of income support which is payable takes effect automatically without the need for a decision by an AO (subs. (2)). Thus no right of appeal arises against the change in the amount, although the claimant can always request a review of the decision awarding benefit, as altered under s.139. The former power to review an award of income support in such circumstances has been removed by the amendment to reg. 69(3) of the Social Security (Adjudication) Regulations (Northern Ireland) 1987 (S.I. 1987 No. 82), except where some kind of transitional addition is in payment. In this latter case, there must be a review under reg. 69(3A) to give effect to the change. See the current edition of Mesher for commentary on the equivalent Great Britain Regulations, reg. 69 of the Social Security (Adjudication) Regulations 1986 (S.I. 1986 No. 2218).

Implementation of increases in income support due to attainment of particular ages

140.—(1) This section applies where—

(a) an award of income support is in force in favour of a person ("the recipient"); and

(b) there is a component which becomes applicable, or applicable at a particular rate, in his case if he or some other person attains a particular age.

(2) If, in a case where this section applies, the recipient or other person attains the particular age referred to in paragraph (b) of subsection (1) above and, in consequence,—

(a) the component in question becomes applicable, or applicable at a particular rate, in the recipient's case (whether or not some other component ceases, for the same reason, to be applicable, or applicable at a particular rate, in his case); and

(b) after taking account of any such cessation, the recipient becomes entitled to an increased amount of income support,

then, except as provided by subsection (3) below, as from the day on which he becomes so entitled, the amount of income support payable to or for him under the award shall be that increased amount, without any further decision of an adjudication officer, and the award shall have effect accordingly.

(3) Subsection (2) above does not apply in any case where, in consequence of the recipient or other person attaining the age in question, some question arises in relation to the recipient's entitlement to any benefit under the Contributions and Benefits Act, other than—

(a) the question whether the component concerned, or any other component, becomes or ceases to be applicable, or applicable at a particular rate, in his case; and

(b) the question whether, in consequence, the amount of his income support falls to be varied.

(4) In this section "component", in relation to a person and his income support, means any of the sums specified in regulations under section 131(1) of the Contributions and Benefits Act.

DEFINITIONS
"the Contributions and Benefits Act": s.167.

GENERAL NOTE
Section 140 extends the process begun by s.139 of taking routine adjustments in the amount of income support out of the ordinary mechanism of review by an AO under s.23.

PART XI

FINANCE

National Insurance Fund

141.—(1) The National Insurance Fund shall continue to be maintained under the control and management of the Department.

(2) Accounts of the National Insurance Fund shall be prepared in such form, and in such manner and at such times, as the Department of Finance and Personnel may direct, and the Comptroller and Auditor General for Northern Ireland shall examine and certify every such account and shall lay copies of it, together with his report on it, before the Assembly.

(3) Any money in the National Insurance Fund may from time to time be paid over to the Department of Finance and Personnel and be invested by that Department in any such manner for the time being specified in Part II of Schedule 1 to the Trustee Investments Act 1961 as the Treasury may specify by an order of which a draft has been laid before Parliament.

(4) The Department of Finance and Personnel shall certify a statement of the securities in which money forming part of the National Insurance Fund is for the time being invested and that statement so certified shall be included with the accounts of that Fund laid before the Assembly under subsection (2) above.

Destination of contributions

142.—(1) Contributions received by the Department under Part I of the Contributions and Benefits Act shall be paid by it into the National Insurance Fund after deducting from contributions of any class, the appropriate health service allocation in the case of contributions of that class.

(2) The contributions referred to in subsection (1) above include those paid over to the Department by the Secretary of State under section 16(5) of the Great Britain Contributions and Benefits Act and by the Inland Revenue under paragraph 6(8) of Schedule 1 to the Contributions and Benefits Act.

(3) The additions paid under section 1(5) of the Contributions and Benefits Act shall be paid, in accordance with any directions given by the Department of Finance and Personnel, into the National Insurance Fund.

(4) The sums paid to the Department by the Secretary of State under section 16(5) of the Great Britain Contributions and Benefits Act and by the Inland Revenue under paragraphs 6(8)(b) and 7 of Schedule 1 to the Contributions and Benefits Act in respect of interest and penalties recovered by them in connection with contributions of any class shall be paid, in accordance with any directions given by the Department of Finance and Personnel, into the National Insurance Fund.

(5) In subsection (1) above "the appropriate health service allocation" means—

(a) in the case of primary Class 1 contributions, 1.05 per cent. of the amount estimated to be that of the earnings in respect of which those contributions were paid at the main primary percentage rate;

(b) in the case of secondary Class 1 contributions, 0.9 per cent. of the amount estimated to be that of the earnings in respect of which those contributions were paid;

(c) in the case of Class 1A contributions, 0.9 per cent. of the amount estimated to be the aggregate of the cash equivalents of the benefits of the cars and car fuel used in calculating those contributions;

(d) in the case of Class 2 contributions, 15.5 per cent. of the amount estimated to be the total of those contributions;

(e) in the case of Class 3 contributions, 15.5 per cent. of the amount estimated to be the total of those contributions; and

(f) in the case of Class 4 contributions, 1.15 per cent. of the amount estimated to be that of the earnings in respect of which those contributions were paid.

(6) In subsection (5) above "estimated" means estimated by the Department in any manner which the Department considers to be appropriate and which the Department of Finance and Personnel has approved.

(7) The Department may by order amend any of paragraphs (a) to (e) of subsection (5) above in relation to any tax year, by substituting for the percentage for the time being specified in that paragraph a different percentage.

(8) No order under subsection (7) above shall substitute a figure which represents an increase or decrease in the appropriate health service allocation of more than—

(a) 0.1 per cent. of the relevant earnings, in the case of paragraph (a) or (b);

(b) 0.1 per cent. of the relevant aggregate, in the case of paragraph (c);

(c) 4 per cent. of the relevant contributions, in the case of paragraph (d) or (e); or

(d) 0.2 per cent. of the relevant earnings, in the case of paragraph (f).

(9) From the health service allocation in respect of contributions of any class there shall be deducted such amount as the Department may estimate to be the portion of the total expenses incurred by it or any other government department in collecting contributions of that class which is fairly attributable to that allocation, and the remainder shall, in the hands of the Department, be taken as paid towards the cost of the health service in Northern Ireland.

(10) Any amounts deducted in accordance with subsection (9) above shall be paid by the Department into the Consolidated Fund.

(11) Any estimate by the Department for the purposes of subsection (9) above shall be made in accordance with any directions given by the Department of Finance and Personnel.

(12) The Department may make regulations modifying this section, in such manner as it thinks appropriate, in relation to the contributions of persons referred to in the following provisions of the Contributions and Benefits Act—

(a) section 116(2) (H.M. Forces);

(b) section 117(1) (mariners, airmen, etc.),

and in relation to any contributions which are reduced under section 6(5) of that Act.

DEFINITIONS

"the Contributions and Benefits Act": s.167.

General financial arrangements

143.—(1) There shall be paid out of the National Insurance Fund—

(a) benefit under Part II of the Contributions and Benefits Act;

(b) guardian's allowance;

(c) Christmas bonus if the relevant qualifying benefit is payable out of that Fund;

(d) any sum falling to be paid by or on behalf of the Department under regulations relating to statutory sick pay or statutory maternity pay;

(e) any expenses of the Department in making payments under section 81, 93 or 95 above to the extent that it estimates that those payments relate to sums paid into the National Insurance Fund.

(2) There shall be paid out of money appropriated by Measure—

(a) any administrative expenses of the Department or any other government department in carrying into effect the Contributions and Benefits Act or this Act;

(b) benefit under Part III of that Act, other than guardian's allowance;

(c) benefit under Part V of that Act;

(d) any expenses of the Department in making payments under sections 81, 93 or 95 above to the extent that it estimates that those payments relate to sums paid into the Consolidated Fund;

except in so far as they may be required by any enactment to be paid or borne in some other way.

(3) The administrative expenses referred to in subsection (2)(a) above include those in connection with any inquiry undertaken on behalf of the Department with a view to obtaining statistics relating to the operation of Parts I to VI and XI of the Contributions and Benefits Act.

(4) Any sums required by a secondary Class 1 contributor for the purpose of paying any secondary Class 1 contributions which are payable by him in respect of an earner in consequence of the earner's employment in an office of which the emoluments are payable out of the Consolidated Fund shall be paid out of that Fund.

(5) Any expenditure in respect of the payment of interest or repayment supplements under or by virtue of paragraph 6 of Schedule 1 to the Contributions and Benefits Act or paragraph 6 of Schedule 2 to that Act shall be defrayed out of the National Insurance Fund in accordance with any directions given by the Department of Finance and Personnel.

DEFINITIONS
"Christmas bonus": s.167.
"the Contributions and Benefits Act": *ibid*.

Destination of repayments, etc.

144.—(1) Subject to the following provisions of this section, so far as it relates to payments out of money appropriated by Measure, any sum recovered by the Department under or by virtue of this Act shall be paid into the Consolidated Fund.

(2) So far as any such sum relates to a payment out of the National Insurance Fund, it shall be paid into that Fund.

(3) So far as any such sum relates to a payment out of the social fund, it shall be paid into that fund.

(4) Sums repaid by virtue of paragraph 1(3)(e) of Schedule 6 to this Act as it has effect for the purposes of regulations under paragraph 2 of Schedule 8 to the Contributions and Benefits Act shall be paid into the Consolidated Fund.

(5) There shall be paid into the National Insurance Fund—
(a) fees so payable under regulations made by virtue of section 60(2)(b) above;
(b) sums recovered by the Department under regulations made by virtue of paragraph 2 or 4 of Schedule 8 to the Contributions and Benefits Act making provision corresponding to that made by or by virtue of section 69 above.

(6) Any sums paid to the Department in pursuance of section 78 above shall be paid—
(a) into the Consolidated Fund to the extent that it estimates that those sums relate to payments out of money appropriated by Measure; and
(b) into the National Insurance Fund to the extent that it estimates that they relate to payments out of that Fund.

DEFINITIONS
"the Contributions and Benefits Act": s.167.

Adjustments between National Insurance Fund and Consolidated Fund

145.—(1) There shall be made out of the National Insurance Fund into the Consolidated Fund or out of money appropriated by Measure into the National Insurance Fund such payments by way of adjustment as the Department determines (in accordance with any directions given by the Department of Finance and Personnel) to be appropriate in consequence of the operation of any statutory provision relating to—
(a) family credit;
(b) disability working allowance;
(c) statutory sick pay;
(d) statutory maternity pay; or
(e) the repayment or offsetting of benefit as defined in section 121 of the Contributions and Benefits Act or other payments.

(2) Where any such payments as are specified in subsection (3) below fall to be made by ways of adjustment, then, subject to subsection (4) below,—
(a) the amount of the payments to be made shall be taken to be such, and
(b) payments on account of them shall be made at such times and in such manner,

as may be determined by the Department in accordance with any directions given by the Department of Finance and Personnel.

(3) The payments mentioned in subsection (2) above are the following, that is to say—

(a) any such payments falling to be made by way of adjustment under subsection (1)(a) to (d) above;

(b) any such payments falling to be made by way of adjustment in consequence of the operation of any enactment or regulations relating to child benefit—

(i) out of the National Insurance Fund into the Consolidated Fund, or

(ii) into the National Insurance Fund out of money appropriated by Measure; and

(c) any such payments falling to be made by way of adjustment in circumstances other than those mentioned in subsection (1) or paragraph (b) above—

(i) out of the National Insurance Fund either to the Department or another government department or into the Consolidated Fund; or

(ii) into the National Insurance Fund out of money appropriated by Measure.

(4) In relation to payments falling within paragraph (a) or (c) of subsection (3) above, subsection (2) above only applies in such cases or classes of case as may be specified by the Department by order.

(5) There shall be paid out of the National Insurance Fund into the Consolidated Fund, at such times and in such manner as the Department of Finance and Personnel may direct, such sums as the Department may estimate (in accordance with any directions given by the Department of Finance and Personnel) to be the amount of the administrative expenses incurred as mentioned in section 143(2)(a) above, excluding—

(a) expenses attributable to the carrying into effect of provisions of the Contributions and Benefits Act or this Act relating to the benefits which by virtue of section 143(2) above are payable out [of] money appropriated by Measure; and

(b) any other category of expenses which the Department of Finance and Personnel may direct, or any enactment may require, to be excluded from the Department's estimate under this subsection;

but none of the administrative expenses of the Christmas bonus shall be excluded from that estimate by virtue of paragraph (a) or (b) above.

Definitions
"Christmas bonus": s.167.
"the Contributions and Benefits Act": *ibid.*

The social fund

146.—(1) The fund known as the social fund shall continue in being by that name.

(2) The social fund shall continue to be maintained under the control and management of the Department and payments out of it shall be made by the Department.

(3) The Department shall make payments into the social fund of such amounts, at such times and in such manner as the Department may with the approval of the Department of Finance and Personnel determine.

(4) Accounts of the social fund shall be prepared in such form, and in such manner and at such times, as the Department of Finance and Personnel may direct, and the Comptroller and Auditor General for Northern Ireland shall examine and certify every such account and shall lay copies of it, together with his report, before the Assembly.

(5) The Department shall prepare an annual report on the social fund.

(6) A copy of every such report shall be laid before the Assembly.

Allocations from social fund

147.—(1) The Department shall allocate amounts for payments from the social fund such as are mentioned in section 134(1)(b) of the Contributions and Benefits Act.

(2) The Department may specify the amounts either as sums of money or by reference to money falling into the social fund on the repayment or partial repayment of loans, or partly in the former and partly in the latter manner.

(3) Allocations—

(a) may be for payments by a particular social fund officer or group of social fund officers;

(b) may be of different amounts for different purposes;

(c) may be made at such time or times as the Department considers appropriate; and

(d) may be in addition to any other allocation to the same officer or group of officers or for the same purpose.

(4) The Department may at any time re-allocate amounts previously allocated, and subsections (2) and (3) above shall have effect in relation to a re-allocation as they have effect in relation to an allocation.

(5) The Department may give general directions to social fund officers or groups of social fund officers, or to any class of social fund officers, with respect to the control and management by social fund officers or groups of social fund officers of the amounts allocated to them under this section.

DEFINITIONS

"the Contributions and Benefits Act": s.167.

"the Department": *ibid.*

GENERAL NOTE

See the social fund directions in the current edition of Mesher. The existence of a fixed budget for each office of the Benefits Agency for the purposes of loans and grants respectively is the most distinctive feature of the social fund. The amount allocated each year is entirely within the discretion of the Department.

Adjustments between social fund and other sources of finance

148.—(1) There shall be made—

(a) out of the social fund into the Consolidated Fund or the National Insurance Fund;

(b) into the social fund out of money appropriated by Measure or the National Insurance Fund,

such payments by way of adjustment as the Department determines (in accordance with any directions of the Department of Finance and Personnel) to be appropriate in consequence of any statutory provision relating to the repayment or offsetting of a benefit under the Contributions and Benefits Act.

(2) Where in any other circumstances payments fall to be made by way of adjustment—

(a) out of the social fund into the Consolidated Fund or the National Insurance Fund; or

(b) into the social fund out of money appropriated by Measure or the National Insurance Fund,

then, in such cases or classes of case as may be specified by the Department by order, the amount of the payments to be made shall be taken to be such, and payments on account of it shall be made at such times and in such manner, as may be determined by the Department in accordance with any direction given by the Department of Finance and Personnel.

PART XII

ADVISORY BODIES AND THE DUTY TO CONSULT

Consultation with the Social Security Advisory Committee

Functions of Social Security Advisory Committee in relation to legislation and regulations

149.—(1) The Department may from time to time refer to the Social Security Advisory Committee for consideration and advice such questions relating to the operation of any of the relevant enactments as the Department thinks fit (including questions as to the advisability of amending any of them).

(2) Subject—

(a) to subsection (3) below; and

(b) to section 150 below,

where the Department proposes to make regulations under any of the relevant enactments, it shall refer the proposals, in the form of draft regulations or otherwise, to the Social Security Advisory Committee.

(3) Subsection (2) above does not apply to the regulations specified in Schedule 5 to this Act.

(4) The Department shall furnish the Social Security Advisory Committee with such information as the Committee may reasonably require for the proper discharge of its functions.

(5) In this section "the relevant enactments" means—

(a) the provisions of the Contributions and Benefits Act and this Act, except as they apply to industrial injuries benefit and Old Cases payments; and

(b) the provisions of Part II of Schedule 3 to the Consequential Provisions Act, except as they apply to industrial injuries benefit; and

(c) Article 52A(10), Part VA and Articles 691 and 70ZA of the Social Security Pensions (Northern Ireland) Orders 1975.

GENERAL NOTE

The Department is obliged under ss.150–151 to consult the Social Security Advisory Committee on proposals to make certain regulations. The SSAC in appropriate cases carries out a public consultation exercise (although often inadequately publicised). Its recommendations are sometimes trenchant and have resulted in wholesale changes in proposed regulations. The SSAC also keeps under review the general area of social security policy within its remit and publishes annual reports and occasional papers. These contain much valuable material. The SSAC's independence of view is firmly established, but the weight of its influence is hard to assess.

Cases in which consultation with Committee is not required

150.—(1) Nothing in any statutory provision shall require any proposals in respect of regulations to be referred to the Committee if—

(a) it appears to the Department that by reason of the urgency of the matter it is inexpedient so to refer them; or

(b) the Committee has agreed that they shall not be referred.

(2) Where by virtue only of subsection (1)(a) above the Department makes regulations without proposals in respect of them having been

referred, then, unless the Committee agrees that this subsection shall not apply, the Department shall refer the regulations as soon as practicable after making them.

(3) Where the Department has referred proposals to the Committee, the Department may make the proposed regulations before the Committee has made its report only if after the reference it appears to the Department that by reason of the urgency of the matter it is expedient to do so.

(4) Where by virtue of this section regulations are made before a report of the Committee has been made, the Committee shall consider them and make a report to the Department containing such recommendations with regard to the regulations as the Committee thinks appropriate; and a copy of any report made to the Department on the regulations shall be laid by it before the Assembly together, if the report contains recommendations, with a statement—

  (a) of the extent (if any) to which the Department proposes to give effect to the recommendations; and

  (b) in so far as it does not propose to give effect to them, of its reasons why not.

(5) Except to the extent that this subsection is excluded by a statutory provision passed or made after 5th November 1986, nothing in any statutory provision shall require the reference to the Committee of any regulations contained in either—

  (a) a statutory rule made before the end of the period of 6 months beginning with the coming into operation of the statutory provision under which those regulations are made; or

  (b) a statutory rule—

    (i) which states that it contains only regulations made by virtue of, or consequential upon, a specified statutory provision; and

    (ii) which is made before the end of the period of 6 months beginning with the coming into operation of that specified statutory provision.

(6) In this section and in section 151 below—

  "the Committee" means the Social Security Advisory Committee;

  "regulations" means regulations under any statutory provision, whenever passed or made.

Committee's report on regulations and Department's duties

151.—(1) The Committee shall consider any proposals referred to it by the Department under section 149 above and shall make to the Department a report containing such recommendations with regard to the subject-matter of the proposals as the Committee thinks appropriate.

(2) If, after receiving a report of the Committee, the Department lays before the Assembly any regulations which comprise the whole or any part of the subject-matter of the proposals referred to the Committee, the Department shall lay with the regulations a copy of the Committee's report and a statement showing—

  (a) the extent (if any) to which the Department has, in framing the regulations, given effect to the Committee's recommendations; and

  (b) in so far as effect has not been given to them, the Department's reasons why not.

(3) Section 41(3) of the Interpretation Act (Northern Ireland) 1954 (procedure for laying documents before the Assembly) shall apply in relation to any document which by virtue of subsection (2) above is required to be laid before the Assembly as if it were a statutory document within the meaning of that Act.

(4) In relation to regulations required or authorised to be made by the Department in conjunction with the Department of Finance and Personnel,

any reference in this section or section 150 above to the Department shall be construed as a reference to the Department and the Department of Finance and Personnel.

The Disability Living Allowance Advisory Board

The Disability Living Allowance Advisory Board

152.—(1) The Disability Living Allowance Advisory Board for Northern Ireland (in this section referred to as "the Board") constituted under Article 5(1) of the Disability Living Allowance and Disability Working Allowance (Northern Ireland) Order 1991 shall continue in being by that name.

(2) Regulations shall confer on the Board such functions relating to disability living allowance or attendance allowance as the Department thinks fit and shall make provision for—
   (a) the Board's constitution;
   (b) the qualifications of its members;
   (c) the method of their appointment;
   (d) the term of office and other terms of appointment of its members;
   (e) their removal.
(3) Regulations may also make provision—
   (a) enabling the Board to appoint persons as advisers to it on matters on which in its opinion they are specially qualified;
   (b) for the appointment of officers and servants of the Board;
   (c) enabling the Board to act notwithstanding any vacancy among its members;
   (d) enabling the Board to make rules for regulating its procedure (including its quorum).
(4) The expenses of the Board to such an amount as may be approved by the Department of Finance and Personnel shall be paid by the Department.
(5) There may be paid as part of the expenses of the Board—
   (a) to all or any of the members of the Board, such salaries or other remuneration and travelling and other allowances;
   (b) to advisers to the Board, such fees; and
   (c) to such other persons as may be specified in regulations such travelling and other allowances (including compensation for loss of remunerative time),
as the Department may with the consent of the Department of Finance and Personnel determine.

(6) The Department may furnish the Board with such information as it considers that the Board may need to enable it to discharge its functions.

PART XIII

SOCIAL SECURITY SYSTEMS OUTSIDE NORTHERN IRELAND

Co-ordination

Co-ordination with Great Britain

153.—(1) The Department may with the consent of the Department of Finance and Personnel make arrangements with the Secretary of State ("the joint arrangements") for co-ordinating the operation of the legislation to which this section applies with a view to securing that, to the extent allowed for in the arrangements, it provides a single system of social security for the United Kingdom.

(2) The responsibility of the Joint Authority shall include that of giving effect to the joint arrangements, with power—
   (a) to make any necessary financial adjustments between the Northern

Ireland National Insurance Fund and the National Insurance Fund; and

(b) to discharge such other functions as may be provided under the joint arrangements.

(3) The Department may make regulations for giving effect to the joint arrangements; and any such regulations may for the purposes of the arrangements provide—

(a) for adapting legislation (including subordinate legislation) for the time being in force in Northern Ireland so as to secure its reciprocal operations with Great Britain;

(b) without prejudice to paragraph (a) above, for securing that acts, omissions and events having any effect for the purposes of the enactments in force in Great Britain have a corresponding effect in relation to Northern Ireland (but not so as to confer any double benefit); and

(c) for determining, in cases where rights accrue both in relation to Northern Ireland and in relation to Great Britain, which of those rights shall be available to the person concerned.

(4) This section applies—

(a) to the Contributions and Benefits Act and this Act; and

(b) to the Great Britain Contributions and Benefits Act and the Great Britain Administration Act,

except in relation to the following benefits—

(i) income support;
(ii) family credit;
(iii) disability working allowance;
(iv) housing benefit;
(v) child benefit;
(vi) Christmas bonus;
(vii) statutory sick pay;
(viii) statutory maternity pay.

(5) Nothing in this Act prejudices the making of any arrangements by the Department under section 11 of the Northern Ireland Constitution Act 1973 for the exercise and performance by or by officers of a department of the Government of the United Kingdom on behalf of the Department of any of the powers and duties of the Department under this Act.

DEFINITIONS
"Christmas bonus": s.167.
"the Contributions and Benefits Act": *ibid.*

Reciprocity

Reciprocal arrangements with Great Britain—income relating benefits and child benefit

154.—(1) The Department may with the consent of the Department of Finance and Personnel make reciprocal arrangements with the authority administering any scheme in force in Great Britain and appearing to the Department to correspond substantially with a scheme contained in the Contributions and Benefits Act and this Act concerning any of the benefits to which this section applies for co-ordinating the operation of those schemes, and such arrangements may include provision for making any necessary financial adjustments.

(2) This section applies to the following benefits—

(a) income support;
(b) family credit;
(c) disability working allowance;
(d) housing benefit; or
(e) child benefit.

(3) Regulations may make provision for giving effect to any such arrangements; and such regulations may in particular provide—

   (a) for modifying any provisions of this Act or the Contributions and Benefits Act or any regulations made under such a provision;

   (b) without prejudice to paragraph (a) above, for securing that acts, omissions and events having any effect for the purposes of the scheme in force in Great Britain shall have a corresponding effect for the purposes of this Act and the Contributions and Benefits Act (but not so as to confer any double benefit);

   (c) for determining, in cases where rights accrue both under that scheme and under this Act and the Contributions and Benefits Act, which of those rights shall be available to the person concerned.

DEFINITIONS
   "the Contributions and Benefits Act": s.167.

Reciprocal agreements with countries outside the United Kingdom

155.—(1) For the purpose of giving effect—

   (a) to any agreement with the government of a country outside the United Kingdom providing for reciprocity in matters relating to payments for purposes similar or comparable to the purposes of legislation to which this section applies, or

   (b) to any such agreement as it would be if it were altered in accordance with proposals to alter it which, in consequence of any change in the law of Northern Ireland, the government of the United Kingdom has made to the other government in question,

the Secretary of State may by order make provision for modifying or adapting such legislation in its application to cases affected by the agreement or proposed alterations.

(2) An order made by virtue of subsection (1) above may, instead of or in addition to making specific modifications or adaptations, provide generally that legislation to which this section applies shall be modified to such extent as may be required to give effect to the provisions contained in the agreement or, as the case may be, alterations in question.

(3) The modifications which may be made by virtue of subsection (1) above include provisions—

   (a) for securing that acts, omissions and events having any effect for the purposes of the law of the country in respect of which the agreement is made have a corresponding effect for the purposes of this Act and the Contributions and Benefits Act (but not so as to confer a right to double benefit);

   (b) for determining in cases where rights accrue both under such legislation and under the law of that country, which of those rights is to be available to the person concerned;

   (c) for making any necessary financial adjustments.

(4) This section applies—

   (a) to the Contributions and Benefits Act; and

   (b) to this Act,

except in relation to the following benefits—

   (i) payments out of the social fund;

   (ii) Christmas bonus;

   (iii) statutory sick pay; and

   (iv) statutory maternity pay.

(5) The power conferred by subsection (1) above shall also be exercisable in relation to regulations made under the Contributions and Benefits Act or this Act and concerning—

   (a) income support;

   (b) family credit;

(c) disability working allowance;
(d) housing benefit; or
(e) child benefit.

DEFINITIONS
"Christmas bonus": s.167.
"the Contributions and Benefits Act": *ibid*.

PART XIV

MISCELLANEOUS

Travelling expenses

Payment of travelling expenses by Department

156. The Department may pay such travelling expenses as, with the consent of the Department of Finance and Personnel, the Department may determine—
(a) to persons required by the Department to attend any interview in connection with the operation of the Contributions and Benefits Act or this Act;
(b) to persons attending social security offices of the Department in connection with the operation—
(i) of the Contributions and Benefits Act or this Act; or
(ii) of any prescribed statutory provision.

DEFINITIONS
"the Contributions and Benefits Act": s.167.
"prescribed": *ibid*.

Offences

Impersonation of officers

157. If any person, with intent to deceive, falsely represents himself to be a person authorised by the Department to act in any capacity (whether under this Act or otherwise) he shall be guilty of an offence and liable on summary conviction to a fine not exceeding level 4 on the standard scale.

Illegal possession of documents

158.—(1) If any person—
(a) as a pledge or a security for a debt; or
(b) with a view to obtaining payment from the person entitled to it of a debt due either to himself or to any other person,
receives, detains or has in his possession any document issued by or on behalf of the Department in connection with any benefit, pension or allowance (whether payable under the Contributions and Benefits Act or otherwise) he shall be guilty of an offence.

(2) If any such person has such a document in his possession without lawful authority or excuse (the proof whereof shall lie on him) he shall be guilty of an offence.

(3) A person guilty of an offence under this section shall be liable on summary conviction to imprisonment for a term not exceeding 3 months or to a fine not exceeding level 4 on the standard scale or to both.

DEFINITIONS
"the Contributions and Benefits Act": s.167.

Industrial injuries and diseases

Research on industrial injuries, etc.

159.—(1) The Department may promote research into the causes and incidence of accidents arising out of and in the course of employment, or injuries and diseases which—
  (a) are due to the nature of employment; or
  (b) it is contemplated might be prescribed for the purposes of sections 108 to 110 of the Contributions and Benefits Act,
either by itself employing persons to conduct such research or by contributing to the expenses of, or otherwise assisting, other persons engaged in such research.
  (2) The Department may pay to persons so employed by it such salaries or remuneration, and such travelling and other allowances, as it may determine with the consent of the Department of Finance and Personnel.

DEFINITIONS
  "the Contributions and Benefits Act": s.167.

Control of pneumoconiosis

160.—(1) As respects pneumoconiosis, regulations may provide—
  (a) for requiring persons to be medically examined before, or within a prescribed period after, becoming employed in any occupation in relation to which pneumoconiosis is prescribed, and to be medically examined periodically while so employed, and to furnish information required for the purposes of any such examination.
  (b) for suspending from employment in any such occupation, and in such other occupations as may be prescribed, persons found on such an examination—
      (i) to be suffering from pneumoconiosis or tuberculosis, or
      (ii) to be unsuitable for such employment, having regard to the risk of pneumoconiosis and such other matters affecting their susceptibility to pneumoconiosis as may be prescribed;
  (c) for the disqualification for the receipt of benefit as defined in section 121 of the Contributions and Benefits Act in respect of pneumoconiosis of any person who fails without good cause to submit himself to any such examination or to furnish information required by the regulations or who engages in any employment from which he has been suspended as mentioned in paragraph (b) above;
  (d) for requiring employers—
      (i) to provide facilities for such examinations,
      (ii) not to employ in any occupation a person who has been suspended as mentioned in paragraph (b) above from employment in that occupation or who has failed without good cause to submit himself to such an examination,
      (iii) to give to such officer as may be prescribed the prescribed notice of the commencement of any prescribed industry or process;
  (e) for the recovery on summary conviction of monetary penalties in respect of any contravention of or failure to comply with any such requirement as is mentioned in paragraph (d) above, but those penalties shall not exceed £5 for every day on which the contravention or failure occurs or continues;
  (f) for such matters as appear to the Department to be incidental to or consequential on provisions included in the regulations by virtue of paragraphs (a) to (d) above or section 110(1) of the Contributions and Benefits Act.

DEFINITIONS
"the Contributions and Benefits Act": s.167.

GENERAL NOTE
See Pt. V of the Social Security (Industrial Injuries) (Prescribed Diseases) Regulations (Northern Ireland) 1986 (S.I. 1986 No. 179).

Workmen's compensation, etc.

Administration of workmen's compensation etc.

161.—(1) Schedule 6 to this Act shall have effect in relation to regulations under paragraphs 2 and 4 of Schedule 8 to the Contributions and Benefits Act.

(2) Regulations may provide for applying in relation to payments under Part II of that Schedule 8 the provisions of this Act relating to the making of claims and the determination of claims and questions in so far as those provisions apply in relation to—

(a) an unemployability supplement;

(b) an increase of a disablement pension in respect of a child or adult dependant; or

(c) an increase of a disablement pension in respect of the need for constant attendance or exceptionally severe disablement,

(as the case may be) subject to any additions or modifications.

DEFINITIONS
"the Contributions and Benefits Act": s.167.

Supplementary benefit etc.

Application of provisions of Act to supplementary benefit, etc.

162. Schedule 7 to this Act shall have effect for the purposes of making provision in relation to the benefits there mentioned.

Miscellaneous

Certain benefit to be inalienable

163.—(1) Subject to the provisions of this Act, every assignment of, or charge on—

(a) benefit as defined in section 121 of the Contributions and Benefits Act;

(b) any income-related benefit; or

(c) child benefit,

and every agreement to assign or charge such benefit shall be void; and, on the bankruptcy of a beneficiary, such benefit shall not pass to any trustee or other person acting on behalf of his creditors.

(2) In calculating for the purposes of Article 30, 73(5)(b), 99(6)(b) or 107 of the Judgments Enforcement (Northern Ireland) Order 1981 or Article 101(5)(b) of the Magistrates' Courts (Northern Ireland) Order 1981 the means of any beneficiary, no account shall be taken of any increase of disablement benefit in respect of a child, or of industrial death benefit.

DEFINITIONS
"the Contributions and Benefits Act": s.167.
"income-related benefit": *ibid.*

Exemption from stamp duty

164.—(1) Stamp duty shall not be chargeable on any document to which this subsection applies.

(2) Subsection (1) above applies to any document authorised by virtue—

(a) of Parts I to VI of the Contributions and Benefits Act; or

(b) of any provision of this Act so far as it operates in relation to matters to which those parts relate,

or otherwise required in order to give effect to those Parts or to any such provision so far as it so operates or in connection with any description of business thereunder.

(3) Stamp duty shall not be chargeable upon such documents used in connection with business under paragraphs 2 and 3 of Schedule 8 to the Contributions and Benefits Act and paragraph 1 of Schedule 6 to this Act as may be specified in regulations made under paragraph 2 of Schedule 8 to that Act.

DEFINITIONS
"the Contributions and Benefits Act": s.167.

PART XV

GENERAL

Subordinate legislation

Regulations and orders—general

165.—(1) Subject to subsection (2) below and to any specific provision of this Act, regulations and orders under this Act shall be made by the Department.

(2) Regulations with respect to proceedings before the Commissioners (whether for the determination of any matter or for leave to appeal to or from the Commissioners) shall be made by the Lord Chancellor.

(3) Any power conferred by this Act to make regulations or orders is exercisable by statutory rule for the purposes of the Statutory Rules (Northern Ireland) Order 1979.

(4) Except in the case of regulations under section 22 or 152 above and in so far as this Act otherwise provides, any power conferred by this Act to make regulations or an order may be exercised—

(a) either in relation to all cases to which the power extends, or in relation to those cases subject to specified exceptions, or in relation to any specified cases or classes of case;

(b) so as to make, as respects the cases in relation to which it is exercised—

(i) the full provision to which the power extends or any less provision (whether by way of exception or otherwise);

(ii) the same provision for all cases in relation to which the power is exercised, or different provision for different cases or different classes of case or different provision as respects the same case or class of case for different purposes of this Act;

(iii) any such provision either unconditionally or subject to any specified condition;

and where such a power is expressed to be exercisable for alternative purposes it may be exercised in relation to the same case for any or all of those purposes; and powers to make regulations or an order for the purposes of any one provision of this Act are without prejudice to powers to make regulations or an order for the purposes of any other provision.

(5) Without prejudice to any specific provision of this Act, any power conferred by this Act to make regulations or an order (other than the power conferred by section 22), includes power to make thereby such incidental, supplementary, consequential or transitional provision as appears to the authority making the regulations or order to be expedient for the purposes of the regulations or order.

(6) Without prejudice to any specific provision of this Act, a power conferred by any provision of this Act, except sections 12, 24, 122 and 152, to make regulations or an order includes power to provide for a person to exercise a discretion in dealing with any matter.

(7) Any power conferred by Part VIII of this Act to make regulations relating to housing benefit shall include power to make different provision for different areas.

(8) Regulations under Part VIII of this Act relating to housing benefit administered by the Department of the Environment under section 126(3) (b) above shall not be made without the consent of that Department.

(9) Any power to make—

(a) regulations prescribing relevant benefits for the purposes of Part IV of this Act;

(b) regulations under section 81 or 152(5)(c) above;

(c) an order under section 142(7), 145(4) or 148(2) above,

shall be exercisable with the consent of the Department of Finance and Personnel.

(10) Any power of the Department under any provision of this Act, except sections 76, 134, 152 and 154, to make any regulations or an order, where the power is not expressed to be exercisable with the consent of the Department of Finance and Personnel, shall if that Department so directs be exercisable only in conjunction with it.

(11) A power under any of sections 153 to 155 above to make regulations, or to make provision by an order for modifications or adaptations of the Contributions and Benefits Act or this Act shall be exercisable in relation to any enactment passed or made after this Act which is directed to be construed as one with them, except in so far as any such enactment relates to a benefit in relation to which the power is not exercisable; but this subsection applies only so far as a contrary intention is not expressed in the enactment, and is without prejudice to the generality of any such direction.

(12) Any reference in this section or section 166 below to an order or regulations under this Act includes a reference to an order or regulations made under any provision of an enactment passed or made after this Act which is directed to be construed as one with this Act; but this subsection applies only so far as a contrary intention is not expressed in the enactment, and is without prejudice to the generality of any such direction.

Assembly, etc. control of orders and regulations

166.—(1) The regulations and orders to which this subsection applies shall be laid before the Assembly after being made and shall take effect on such date as may be specified in the regulations or order, but shall (without prejudice to the validity of anything done thereunder or to the making of new regulations or a new order) cease to have effect upon the expiration of a period of six months from that date unless at some time before the expiration of that period the regulations have, or the order has, been approved by a resolution of the Assembly.

(2) Subsection (1) above applies—

(a) to any regulations made by the Department under section 97(2), 131 or 134 above; and

(b) to any order made by the Department under section 129, 132, 133 or 142 above.

(3) Subsection (1) above does not apply to regulations which, in so far as they are made under the powers conferred by subsection (2)(a) above, only replace provisions of previous regulations with new provisions to the same effect.

(4) Subject to subsection (8) below, all regulations and orders made under this Act by the Department, other than regulations or orders to which subsection (1) above applies, shall be subject to negative resolution.

(5) Subject to subsection (10) below, all regulations made under this Act by the Lord Chancellor shall be subject to annulment in pursuance of a resolution of either House of Parliament in like manner as a statutory instrument, and section 5 of the Statutory Instruments Act 1946 shall apply accordingly.

(6) Section 41(3) of the Interpretation Act (Northern Ireland) 1954 (laying statutory instruments or statutory documents before the Assembly) shall apply in relation to any instrument or document which by virtue of any provision of this Act is required to be laid before the Assembly as if it were a statutory instrument or statutory document within the meaning of that Act.

(7) This subsection applies to any regulations or order made under this Act which—

 (a) but for subsection (8) below, would be subject to negative resolution, and

 (b) are or is contained in a statutory rule which includes any regulations or order subject to the confirmatory procedure.

(8) Any regulations or order to which subsection (7) above applies shall not be subject to negative resolution, but shall be subject to the confirmatory procedure.

(9) This subsection applies to any regulations or order made under this Act which—

 (a) but for subsection (10) below, would be subject to annulment in pursuance of a resolution of either House of Parliament, and

 (b) are, or is, contained in an instrument which is subject to any requirement that a draft of the instrument be laid before and approved by a resolution of each House of Parliament.

(10) Any regulations or order to which subsection (9) above applies shall not be subject as mentioned in paragraph (a) of that subsection, but shall be subject to the procedure described in paragraph (b) of that subsection.

(11) During the interim period (as defined by section 1(4) of the Northern Ireland Act 1974), subsections (1) and (4) above have effect subject to paragraph 3 of Schedule 1 to that Act.

(12) In this section—

 "the confirmatory procedure" means the procedure described in subsection (1) above;

 "subject to negative resolution" has the meaning assigned by section 41(6) of the Interpretation Act (Northern Ireland) 1954 (but as if the regulations or orders in question were statutory instruments within the meaning of that Act).

GENERAL NOTE

   Section 166 defines which regulations under the Act are subject to the affirmative resolution procedure before the Assembly and which to the negative resolution procedure. The Northern Ireland Assembly has been dissolved since 1986. Legislation which is subject to the Assembly's confirmatory procedure is now subject to negative resolution at Westminster. This applies to the Regulations and Orders listed in subs. (2). Legislation which is subject to negative resolution by the Assembly is simply laid before Westminster. This applies to all Regulations and Orders made under the Act, other than those listed in subs. (2).

Supplementary

Interpretation

   167.—(1) In this Act, unless the context otherwise requires—

   "the Assembly" means the Northern Ireland Assembly;

   "the 1975 Act" means the Social Security (Northern Ireland) Act 1975;

   "benefit" means benefit under the Contributions and Benefits Act;

   "Christmas bonus" means a payment under Part X of the Contributions and Benefits Act;

"claimant" (in relation to contributions under Part I and to benefit under Parts II to IV of the Contributions and Benefits Act) means—

(a) a person whose right to be expected from liability to pay, or to have his liability deferred for, or to be credited with, a contribution, is in question;

(b) a person who has claimed benefit;

and includes, in relation to an award or decision, a beneficiary under the award or affected by the decision;

"claim" is to be construed in accordance with "claimant";

"claimant" (in relation to industrial injuries benefit) means a person who has claimed such a benefit and includes—

(a) an applicant for a declaration under section 42 above that an accident was or was not an industrial accident; and

(b) in relation to an award or decision, a beneficiary under the award or affected by the decision;

"Commissioner" means the Chief Social Security Commissioner or any other Social Security Commissioner and includes a Tribunal of 2 or 3 Commissioners constituted under section 55 above;

"compensation payment" has the meaning assigned by section 77 above;

"compensator" has the meaning assigned by section 78 above;

"the Consequential Provisions Act" means the Social Security (Consequential Provisions) (Northern Ireland) Act 1992;

"Consolidated Fund" means the Consolidated Fund of Northern Ireland;

"contribution card" has the meaning assigned to it by section 108(6) above;

"the Contributions and Benefits Act" means the Social Security Contributions and Benefits (Northern Ireland) Act 1992;

"the Department" means the Department of Health and Social Services for Northern Ireland;

"the Department of the Environment" means the Department of the Environment for Northern Ireland;

"the Department of Finance and Personnel" means the Department of Finance and Personnel in Northern Ireland;

"disablement benefit" is to be construed in accordance with section 94(2)(a) of the Contributions and Benefits Act;

"the disablement questions" is to be construed in accordance with section 43 above;

"dwelling" means any residential accommodation, whether or not consisting of the whole or part of a building and whether or not comprising separate and self-contained premises;

"the Great Britain Administration Act" means the Social Security Administration Act 1992;

"the Great Britain Contributions and Benefit Act" means the Social Security Contributions and Benefits Act 1992;

"the Housing Executive" means the Northern Ireland Housing Executive;

"income-related benefit" means—

(a) income support;

(b) family credit;

(c) disability working allowance; and

(d) housing benefit;

"industrial injuries benefit" means benefit under Part V of the Contributions and Benefits Act, other than under Schedule 8;

"invalidity benefit" has the meaning assigned to it by section 20(1)(c) of that Act;

"Joint Authority" means the Head of the Department and the Secretary of State;

"medical examination" includes bacteriological and radiographical tests and similar investigations, and "medically examined" has a corresponding meaning;

"medical practitioner" means—

(a) a registered medical practitioner; or

(b) a person outside the United Kingdom who is not a registered medical practitioner, but has qualifications corresponding (in the Department's opinion) to those of a registered medical practitioner;

"medical treatment" means medical, surgical or rehabilitative treatment (including any course of diet or other regimen), and references to a person receiving or submitting himself to medical treatment are to be construed accordingly;

"National Insurance Fund" means the Northern Ireland National Insurance Fund;

"occupational pension scheme" has the same meaning as in Article 2(2) of the Pensions Order;

"the Old Cases Act" means the Industrial Injuries and Diseases (Northern Ireland Old Cases) Act 1975;

"Old Cases payments" means payments under Part I of Schedule 8 to the Contributions and Benefits Act;

"the 1986 Order" means the Social Security (Northern Ireland) Order 1986;

"the Pensions Order" means the Social Security Pensions (Northern Ireland) Order 1975;

"personal pension scheme" has the meaning assigned to it by Article 2(2) of the 1986 Order;

"prescribe" means prescribe by regulations;

"President" means the President of social security appeal tribunals, medical appeal tribunals and disability appeal tribunals;

"regulations" means regulations made by the Department or the Lord Chancellor under this Act;

"statutory provision" has the meaning assigned to it by section 1(f) of the Interpretation Act (Northern Ireland) 1954;

"tax year" means the 12 months beginning with April 6 in any year;

"widow's benefit" has the meaning assigned to it by section 20(1)(e) of the Contributions and Benefits Act.

(2) For the purposes of Part III of the Northern Ireland Constitution Act 1973 (validity of Measures of the Northern Ireland Assembly, including Orders in Council under the Northern Ireland Act 1974), provisions of this Act which re-enact provisions of a Measure of the Assembly or such an Order are to be treated as provisions of such a Measure or Order.

Short title, commencement and extent

168.—(1) This Act may be cited as the Social Security Administration (Northern Ireland) Act 1992.

(2) This Act is to be read, where appropriate, with the Contributions and Benefits Act and the Consequential Provisions Act.

(3) The enactments consolidated by this Act are repealed, in consequence of the consolidation, by the Consequential Provisions Act.

(4) Except as provided in Schedule 4 to the Consequential Provisions Act, this Act shall come into force on 1st July 1992.

(5) Subject to subsection (4) below, this Act extends to Northern Ireland only.

(6) Section 22 above and this section also extend to Great Britain.

DEFINITIONS
  "the Consequential Provisions Act": s.167.
  "the Contributions and Benefits Act": *ibid.*

SCHEDULES

Section 1(6)   SCHEDULE 1

CLAIMS FOR BENEFIT MADE OR TREATED AS MADE BEFORE 1ST OCTOBER 1990

Claims made or treated as made on or after 2nd September 1985 and before 19th November 1986

1. Section 1 above shall have effect in relation to a claim made or treated as made on or after 2nd September 1985 and before 19th November 1986 as if the following subsections were substituted for subsections (1) to (3)—
    "(1) Except in such cases as may be prescribed, no person shall be entitled to any benefit unless, in addition to any other conditions relating to that benefit being satisfied—
      (a) he makes a claim for it—
          (i) in the prescribed manner; and
          (ii) subject to subsection (2) below, within the prescribed time; or
      (b) by virtue of a provision of Chapter VI of Part II of the 1975 Act or of regulations made under such a provision, he would have been treated as making a claim for it.
    (2) Regulations shall provide for extending, subject to any prescribed conditions, the time within which a claim may be made in cases where it is not made within the prescribed time but good cause is shown for the delay.
    (3) Notwithstanding any regulations made under this section, no person shall be entitled to any benefit (except disablement benefit or industrial death benefit) in respect of any period more than 12 months before the date on which the claim is made.".

Claims made or treated as made on or after 19th November 1986 and before 6th April 1987

2. Section 1 above shall have effect in relation to a claim made or treated as made on or after 19th November 1986 and before 6th April 1987 as if the subsections set out in paragraph 1 above were substituted for subsections (1) to (3) but with the insertion in subsection (3) of the words ", reduced earnings allowance" after the words "disablement benefit".

Claims made or treated as made on or after 6th April 1987 and before 23rd August 1989

3. Section 1 above shall have effect in relation to a claim made or treated as made on or after 6th April 1987 and before 23rd August 1989, as if—
  (a) the following subsection were substituted for subsection (1)—
    "(1) Except in such cases as may be prescribed, no person shall be entitled to any benefit being satisfied—
      (a) he makes a claim for it in the prescribed manner and within the prescribed time; or
      (b) by virtue of regulations made under Article 52 of the 1986 Order he would have been treated as making a claim for it."; and
  (b) there were omitted—
      (i) from subsection (2), the words "except as provided by section 3 below"; and
      (ii) subsection (3).

Claims made or treated as made on or after 23rd August 1989 and before 14th August 1990

4. Section 1 above shall have effect in relation to a claim made or treated as made on or after 23rd August 1989 and before 14th August 1990 as if there were omitted—
  (a) from subsection (1), the words "and subject to the following provisions of this section and to section 3 below";
  (b) from subsection (2), the words "except as provided by section 3 below"; and
  (c) subsection (3).

Claims made or treated as made on or after 14th August 1990 and before 1st October 1990

5. Section 1 above shall have effect in relation to a claim made or treated as made on or after 14th August 1990 and before 1st October 1990 as if there were omitted—
  (a) from subsection (1), the words "the following provisions of this section and to"; and
  (b) subsection (3).

DEFINITIONS
  "disablement benefit": s.167.
  "prescribe": *ibid*.

GENERAL NOTE
  See notes to s.1.

Sections 39, 41 and 48 to 50   SCHEDULE 2

COMMISSIONERS, TRIBUNALS, ETC.—SUPPLEMENTARY PROVISIONS

Tenure of offices

1.—(1) Subject to the following provisions of this paragraph, the President and full-time chairmen of social security appeal tribunals, medical appeal tribunals and disability appeal tribunals shall hold and vacate office in accordance with the terms of their appointment.

(2) Commissioners, the President and the full-time chairmen shall vacate their offices at the end of the completed year of service in which they attain the age of 72.

(3) Where the Lord Chancellor considers it desirable in the public interest to retain a Commissioner, the President or a full-time chairman in office after the time at which he would be required by sub-paragraph (2) above to vacate it, the Lord Chancellor may from time to time authorise his continuance in office until any date not later than that on which he attains the age of 75.

(4) A Commissioner, the President and a full-time chairman may be removed from office by the Lord Chancellor on the ground of misbehaviour or incapacity.

(5) Neither the President nor any full time chairman shall either directly or indirectly practise as a barrister or solicitor or as an agent for a solicitor.

(6) Nothing in sub-paragraph (2) or (3) above or in paragraphs 6 to 7A of Schedule 10 to the 1975 Act (which relate to pensions for Commissioners) shall apply to a person by virtue of his appointment in pursuance of section 50(2) above.

2. Part-time chairmen of such tribunals shall hold and vacate office in accordance with the terms of their appointment.

Remuneration etc. for President and chairmen

3. The Department may pay, or makes such payments towards the provision of, such remuneration, pensions, allowances or gratuities to or in respect of the President and full-time chairmen as, with the consent of the Department of Finance and Personnel, it may determine.

Officers and staff

4. The President may appoint such officers and staff as he thinks fit—
(a) for himself;
(b) for the full-time chairmen;
(c) for social security appeal tribunals;
(d) for disability appeal tribunals; and
(e) for medical appeal tribunals,
with the consent of the Department and the Department of Finance and Personnel as to numbers and as to remuneration and other terms and conditions of service.

Clerks to social security appeal tribunals and disability appeal tribunals

5.—(1) The President shall assign a clerk to service the social security appeal tribunal for each area and the disability tribunal for each area.

(2) The duty of summoning members of a panel to serve on such a tribunal shall be performed by the clerk to the tribunal.

Miscellaneous administrative duties of President

6. It shall be the duty of the President—
(a) to arrange—
    (i) such meetings of chairmen and members of social security appeal tribunals, chairmen and members of disability appeal tribunals and chairmen and members of medical appeal tribunals;
    (ii) such training for such chairmen and members,
  as he considers appropriate; and
(b) to secure that such works of reference relating to social security law as he considers

appropriate are available for the use of chairmen and members of social security appeal tribunals, disability appeal tribunals and medical appeal tribunals.

Remuneration etc.

7. The Lord Chancellor shall pay to a Commissioner such salary or other remuneration, and such expenses incurred in connection with the work of a Commissioner or any tribunal presided over by a Commissioner, as may be determined by the Treasury.

8.—(1) The Department may pay—

  (a) to any person specified in sub-paragraph (2) below, such remuneration and such travelling and other allowances;

  (b) to any person specified in sub-paragraph (3) below, such travelling and other allowances;

  (c) subject to sub-paragraph (4) below, such other expenses in connection with the work of
any person, tribunal or inquiry appointed or constituted under any provision of this Act,

as the Department with the consent of the Department of Finance and Personnel may determine.

(2) The persons mentioned in sub-paragraph (1)(a) above are—

  (a) any person (other than a Commissioner) appointed under this Act to determine questions or as a member of, or assessor to, a social security appeal tribunal, a disability appeal tribunal or a medical appeal tribunal; and

  (b) a medical officer appointed under regulations under section 60 above.

(3) The persons mentioned in sub-paragraph (1)(b) are—

  (a) any person required to attend at any proceedings or inquiry under this Act; and

  (b) any person required under this Act (whether for the purposes of this Act or otherwise) to attend for or to submit themselves to medical or other examination or treatment.

(4) Expenses are not payable under sub-paragraph (1)(c) above in connection with the work—

  (a) of a tribunal presided over by a Commissioner; or

  (b) of a social fund officer, a social fund inspector or the social fund Commissioner.

(5) In this paragraph references to travelling and other allowances include references to compensation for loss of remunerative time but such compensation shall not be paid to any person in respect of any time during which he is in receipt of remuneration under this paragraph.

Certificates of decisions

9. A document bearing a certificate which—

  (a) is signed by a person authorised in that behalf by the Department; and

  (b) states that the document, apart from the certificate, is a record of a decision—

      (i) of a Commissioner;

      (ii) of a social security appeal tribunal;

      (iii) of a disability appeal tribunal; or

      (iv) of an adjudication officer,

shall be conclusive evidence of the decision; and a certificate purporting to be so signed shall be deemed to be so signed unless the contrary is proved.

DEFINITIONS

  "Commissioner": s.167.

  "President": *ibid.*

GENERAL NOTE

Para. 4

Of the President's detailed powers and duties, the duty to assign the clerk to SSATs and DATs (but, oddly, not to MATs) under para. 4 is particularly important. The fact that supplementary benefit appeal tribunal clerks were in the past DHSS employees had long been a source of criticism, although their role had become less prominent as SBATs themselves became stronger. Clerks now work from the President's office as part of his own staff and the independence of this system is now clearly established.

Para. 6

The President's powers to arrange training and to provide materials are unlimited, but he is constrained by the budget allocated to him for these purposes.

SCHEDULE 3

REGULATIONS AS TO PROCEDURE

Interpretation

1. In this Schedule "competent tribunal" means—
(a) a Commissioner;
(b) a social security appeal tribunal;
(c) a disability appeal tribunal;
(d) a medical appeal tribunal;
(e) an adjudicating medical practitioner.

Provision which may be made

2. Provision prescribing the procedure to be followed in connection with the consideration and determination of claims and questions by the Department, an adjudication officer or a competent tribunal, or in connection with the withdrawal of a claim.

3. Provision as to the striking out of proceedings for want of prosecution.

4. Provision as to the form which is to be used for any document, the evidence which is to be required and the circumstances in which any official record or certificate is to be sufficient or conclusive evidence.

5. Provision as to the time to be allowed—
(a) for producing any evidence; or
(b) for making an appeal.

6. Provision as to the manner in which, and the time within which, a question may be raised with a view to its decision by the Department under Part II of this Act or with a view to the review of a decision under that Part.

7. Provision for summoning persons to attend and give evidence or produce documents and for authorising the administration of oaths to witnesses.

8. Provision for authorising a competent tribunal consisting of two or more members to proceed with any case, with the consent of the claimant, in the absence of any member.

9. Provision for giving the chairman of a competent tribunal consisting of two or more members a second or casting vote where the numbers of members present is an even number.

10. Provision empowering the chairman of a social security appeal tribunal, a disability appeal tribunal or a medical appeal tribunal to give directions for the disposal of any purported appeal which he is satisfied that the tribunal does not have jurisdiction to entertain.

11. Provision for the non-disclosure to a person of the particulars of any medical advice or medical evidence given or submitted for the purposes of a determination.

12. Provision for requiring or authorising the Department to hold, or to appoint a person to hold, an inquiry in connection with the consideration of any question by the Department.

GENERAL NOTE
See the Social Security (Adjudication) Regulations (Northern Ireland) 1987 (S.I. 1987 No. 82), with commentary on the equivalent Great Britain Regulations, the Social Security (Adjudication) Regulations 1986 (S.I. 1986 No. 2218), in the current editions of Bonner *et al.*, Mesher and Rowland.

Section 117   SCHEDULE 4

PERSONS EMPLOYED IN SOCIAL SECURITY ADMINISTRATION OR ADJUDICATION

PART I

THE SPECIFIED PERSONS

Government departments

A civil servant in—
(a) the Department;
(b) the Department of Social Security;
(c) the Northern Ireland Court Service.

Other public departments and offices

A member or officer of the Commissioners of Inland Revenue.

Adjudication officers

The Chief Adjudication Officer.
An adjudication officer.

Adjudicating bodies

The clerk to, or other officer or members of the staff or, any of the following bodies—
(a) a social security appeal tribunal;
(b) a disability appeal tribunal;
(c) a medical appeal tribunal;
(d) a vaccine damage tribunal;
(e) a Pensions Appeal Tribunal constituted under the Pensions Appeal Tribunals Act 1943.

The Disability Living Allowance Advisory Board for Northern Ireland

A member of the Disability Living Allowance Advisory Board for Northern Ireland.
An officer or servant of that Board.

The Occupational Pensions Board

The chairman or deputy chairman of the Occupational Pensions Board.
A member of that Board.
A member of the staff of that Board.

The social fund

The social fund Commissioner.
A social fund officer.
A social fund inspector.
A member of any staff employed in connection with the social fund.

Former statutory bodies

An officer or other member of the staff of—
(a) the former Supplementary Benefits Commission for Northern Ireland;
(b) the former National Assistance Board for Northern Ireland;
(c) the former Attendance Allowance Board for Northern Ireland.
A benefit officer.
An insurance officer.
A supplement officer.

PART II

CONSTRUCTION OF REFERENCES TO GOVERNMENT DEPARTMENTS ETC.

1.—(1) The reference in Part I of this Schedule to the Department is a reference to the Department only to the extent that it carries out functions relating to social security or occupational or personal pension schemes.
(2) The reference in Part I of this Schedule to the Department includes a reference to the Department when styled—
(a) the Ministry of Health and Social Services for Northern Ireland, or
(b) the Ministry of Labour and National Insurance for Northern Ireland,
and to any former government department, but only (in each case) to the extent mentioned in sub-paragraph (1) above.
2. The reference in Part I of this Schedule to the Department of Social Security shall be construed subject to paragraph 1 of Part II of Schedule 3 to the Great Britain Administration Act.
3. The reference in Part I of this Schedule to the Northern Ireland Court Service is a reference to that Service only to the extent that the functions carried out relate to functions of the Chief, or any other, Social Security Commissioner.
4. The reference in Part I of this Schedule to the Commissioners of Inland Revenue is a reference to those Commissioners only to the extent that the functions carried out by them or any officer of theirs relate to—
(a) any of the following aspects of social security—
(i) National Insurance contributions;
(ii) statutory sick pay;
(iii) statutory maternity pay; or
(b) the tax treatment of occupational or personal pension schemes.

SCHEDULE 5

REGULATIONS NOT REQUIRING PRIOR SUBMISSION TO SOCIAL SECURITY ADVISORY COMMITTEE

Disability living allowance

1. Regulations under section 72(3) or 73(10) of the Contributions and Benefits Act.

Industrial injuries

2. Regulations relating only to industrial injuries benefit.

Up-rating, etc.

3. Regulations which state that they contain only provisions in consequence of an order under section 129 or 132 of this Act.

Earnings limits

4. Regulations under section 5 of the Contributions and Benefits Act or regulations which state that they contain only regulations to make provision consequential on regulations under that section.

Married women and widows—reduced rate contributions

5. Regulations under section 19(4)(a) of the Contributions and Benefits Act.

Child benefit

6. Regulations prescribing the rate or any of the rates of child benefit.
7. Regulations varying social security benefits following an increase of the rate or any of the rates of child benefit.

Statutory maternity pay and statutory sick pay

8. Regulations under section 154 or 163 of the Contributions and Benefits Act.

Consolidation, etc.

9. Regulations made for the purpose only of consolidating other regulations revoked by them.
10. Regulations making only provision corresponding to provision contained in regulations made by the Secretary of State or the Lord Chancellor in relation to Great Britain.

DEFINITIONS
"the Contributions and Benefits Act": s.167.

SCHEDULE 6

OLD CASES PAYMENTS ADMINISTRATION

Provisions ancillary to paragraph 2 of Schedule 8 to Contributions and Benefits Act

1.—(1) The provisions of this paragraph shall have effect with respect to regulations under paragraph 2 of Schedule 8 to the Contributions and Benefits Act and any such regulations are hereafter in this paragraph referred to as "the regulations".
(2) The regulations shall in particular make provision—
(a) for enabling claims for or in respect of allowances to be made to the Department in such manner as the regulations may provide;
(b) for the determination by the Department of questions arising on or in connection with any such claims or on or in connection with the regulations and for conferring a right of appeal from any decision of the Department on any such question to a Commissioner;
(c) for the review of such decisions in such circumstances and in such manner as the regulations may provide.
(3) Without prejudice to the generality of sub-paragraph (2) above, the regulations may make provision—

(a) for enabling any class or description of such questions as are mentioned in sub-paragraph (2)(b) above to be determined as if they had arisen under Parts II to VI of the Contributions and Benefits Act;

(b) as to the procedure to be followed in connection with the consideration and determination of claims and questions by the Department and the Commissioner;

(c) for applying, with or without modifications, section 163(1) and (2) above, or for making provision corresponding to those subsections;

(d) for requiring persons claiming or receiving allowances to furnish information and evidence and to undergo medical or other examination;

(e) for requiring the repayment to the Department in whole or in part of payments under paragraph 2 of Schedule 8 to the Contributions and Benefits Act subsequently found not to have been due, for the deduction of any sums so required to be repaid from payments under paragraph 2 of that Schedule or by way of industrial injuries benefit, and for the deduction of payments under that paragraph of any sums which may by virtue of any provisions of this Act be recovered by deduction from any payment by way of such benefit.

(4) Subject to any provisions of the regulations for reviewing decisions, the decision in accordance with the regulations of any question arising under the regulations shall be final for the purposes of Schedule 8 to the Contributions and Benefits Act.

(5) Regulations varying earlier regulations may do so in such a way as to make allowances payable, or payable at an increased rate, under the earlier regulations in respect of periods before the making of the later regulations.

(6) The Department may make such payments in connection with the administration of the regulations (including payments on account of travelling expenses or loss of remunerative time or both to persons required to undergo medical or other examination or to attend any hearing for the purpose of determining questions arising under the regulations) as it may, with the consent of the Department of Finance and Personnel, determine.

(7) Notwithstanding anything in this Act or the Contributions and Benefits Act, the regulations shall not require a person to submit himself to medical treatment.

Adjustment of benefit in certain cases

2.—(1) Regulations under paragraph 2 of Schedule 8 to the Contributions and Benefits Act may include provisions for adjusting the rate of, or extinguishing any right to, an allowance under that paragraph in a case where the same person is, or would otherwise be, entitled separately in respect of two or more injuries or diseases to an allowance under that paragraph.

(2) Where, immediately before 10th May 1966, a person was receiving payments by way of one or more allowances under the Workmen's Compensation (Supplementation) Act (Northern Ireland) 1951 or the Workmen's Compensation (Supplementation) Act (Northern Ireland) 1956 of a greater amount or aggregate amount than, but for the provisions of this sub-paragraph, he would have been entitled to receive after the commencement of the Old Cases Act by way of allowances under section 2 of that Act, he shall continue to be entitled to that greater amount or aggregate amount for any period after the commencement of that Act for which he would have so continued if the Workmen's Compensation (Supplementation) Act (Northern Ireland) 1966 and the Old Cases Act had not been passed.

Overpayments

3. Regulations under paragraph 2 of Schedule 8 to the Contributions and Benefits Act may make provision in relation to allowances under that Schedule corresponding to the provision made by section 69 above in relation to the benefits to which it applies.

DEFINITIONS
"the Contributions and Benefits Act": s.167.
"the Old Cases Act": *ibid.*

Section 162 SCHEDULE 7

SUPPLEMENTARY BENEFITS, ETC.

Claims and payments

1.—(1) Section 5 above shall have effect in relation to the benefits specified in sub-paragraph (2) below as it has effect in relation to the benefits to which it applies by virtue of subsection (2).

(2) The benefits mentioned in sub-paragraph (1) above are benefits under—

(a) the former National Insurance Acts;

(b) the former Industrial Injuries Act;
(c) the National Assistance Act (Northern Ireland) 1948;
(d) the Supplementary Benefits &c. Act (Northern Ireland) 1966;
(e) the Supplementary Benefits (Northern Ireland) Order 1977;
(f) the Family Income Supplements Act (Northern Ireland) 1971.
(3) In sub-paragraph (2) above—
"the former National Insurance Acts" means the National Insurance Act (Northern Ireland) 1946 and the National Insurance Act (Northern Ireland) 1966; and
"the former Industrial Injuries Acts" means the Industrial Injuries Act (Northern Ireland) 1946 and the Industrial Injuries Act (Northern Ireland) 1966.

Adjudication

2.—(1) Sections 18 to 27, 34 to 41 and 49 to 59 above shall have effect for the purposes of the benefits specified in paragraph 2(2) above as they have effect for the purposes of benefit within the meaning of section 121 of the Contributions and Benefits Act other than attendance allowance, disability living allowance and disability working allowance.

(2) Procedure regulations made under section 57 above by virtue of sub-paragraph (1) above may make different provision in relation to each of the benefits specified in paragraph 1(2) above.

Overpayments etc.

3.—(1) Section 69 above shall have effect in relation to the benefits mentioned in paragraph 2(2) above as it has effect in relation to the benefits to which it applies by virtue of subsection (11).

(2) Section 72 above shall have effect in relation to supplementary benefit as it has effect in relation to income support.

(3) The reference to housing benefit in section 73 above includes a reference to housing benefits under the Housing Benefits (Northern Ireland) Order 1983.

Inspection

4. Section 104 above shall have effect as if it also applied to—
(a) the Supplementary Benefits (Northern Ireland) Order 1977,
(b) the Family Income Supplements Act (Northern Ireland) 1971.

Legal proceedings

5. Section 110 above shall have effect as if any reference to this Act in that section included—
(a) the National Assistance Act (Northern Ireland) 1948;
(b) the Supplementary Benefits &c. Act (Northern Ireland) 1966;
(c) the Supplementary Benefits (Northern Ireland) Order 1977;
(d) the Family Income Supplements Act (Northern Ireland) 1971.

DEFINITIONS
"the Contributions and Benefits Act": s.167.

TABLE OF DERIVATIONS

Note:
1. Abbreviations used in this Table are the same as those used in the Table of Derivations for the Social Security Contributions and Benefits (Northern Ireland) Bill. They are set out at the beginning of that Table.
2. The Table does not acknowledge the general changes made by Articles 3 and 4 of the Social Security Adjudications (Northern Ireland) Order 1983. Those Articles transferred adjudication functions to adjudication officers, social security appeal tribunals and adjudicating medical practitioners.
3. The Table does not contain any entries in respect of Article 2(3) of the Social Security Pensions (Northern Ireland) Order 1975 (NI 15) under which, with certain exceptions, that Order and the Social Security (Northern Ireland) Act 1975 (c. 15) have effect as if the provisions of the Order were contained in the Social Security (Northern Ireland) Act 1975. The effect is that the general provisions of the Social Security (Northern Ireland) Act 1975 apply to the provisions of the Social Security Pensions (Northern Ireland) Order 1975.
4. The Table does not contain any entries for Transfer of Function Orders.

Provision	Derivation
1(1), (2)	1975 s.154A(1), (2); 1986 Sch. 9 para. 56; 1989 Sch. 8 para. 8; 1990 art. 8(1)
(3)	1975 s.154A(3); 1990 art. 3(6); 1991 D Sch. 1 para. 19
(4)	1975 s.154A(1); 1986 Sch. 9 paras. 32(b), 56; 1990 art. 7(4)
(5), (6)	Drafting
2	1975 s.154B; 1990 art. 7(1)
3	1975 s.154C; 1990 art. 8(2)
4	1990 Sch. 6 para. 16(2)
5(1)	1986 art. 52(1)
(2)	1986 art. 52(2); 1988 Sch. 3 para. 13, Sch. 5; 1991D Sch. 3 para. 2
(3), (4)	1986 art. 52(3), (4)
6	1975 s.88; 1986 Sch. 10
7	1975 s.89; 1982 Sch. 5
8	1975 s.90; 1982 Sch. 5; 1985 Sch. 6; 1986 Sch. 9 para. 55, Sch. 10
9	1986 art. 28B(1)–(3); 1991D art. 9(1)
10(1)	1986 art. 34(1); 1988 Sch. 3 para. 7, Sch. 5
(2)	1986 art. 34(13); 1990 art. 12(5)
11(1)	1975 CB art. 8(1); 1989 Sch. 7 para. 19
(2)	1975 CB art. 8(3)
12(1)	1982 art. 19(2)
(2)	1982 art. 19(2A); 1985 art. 20
(3)	1982 art. 19(3)
13	1986 Sch. 4 paras. 6, 7
14	1988 art. 9
15(1)(a), (b)	1975 s.93(1)(a), (b)
(c)	1975 s.93(1)(bb); 1991C art. 5(1)
(d)	1975 s.93(1)(d)
(e)	1975 s.93(1)(e); 1977 art. 18(5)
(f)	1975P art. 70(1)(a); M5
(g)(i)–(iv)	1986 Sch. 5 Part II para. (b)(i)–(iv); M5
(v)	1986 Sch. 5 Part II para. (b)(vi); 1991SP art. 4(3); M5
(vi)	1986 Sch. 5 Part II para. (b)(v); M5
(h)	1986 Sch. 5 Part II para. (c); M5
(2), (3)	1975 s.93(2), (2A); 1989 Sch. 3 para. 1(1)
(4)	1975 s.93(3); M6
16	1975 s.94; M5
17(1)	1975 s.96(1); 1986 Sch. 5 para. 2; M6
(2), (3)	1975 s.96(2); 1980 Sch. 1 para. 9
18(1), (2)	1975 s.98(1), (2); 1986 Sch. 5 para. 3; 1991D Sch. 1 para. 2
(3)	1975 s.98(1); 1986 art. 53(3), (7)(a); 1991D Sch. 2 para. 11(a)
(4)	1975 s.98(2A); 1986 Sch. 5 para. 3
(5)	1975 s.98(3)
(6)	1975 s.98(1); 1986 art. 53(3)(a), (3A), (6); 1988 Sch. 3 para. 13; 1991D Sch. 2 para. 11, Sch. 3 para. 3(1)
19(1), (2)	1975 s.99(1), (2); 1986 Sch. 5 para. 4; 1991D Sch. 1 para. 3(1), (2)
(3)	1975 s.99(2A); 1986 art. 53(3A); 1991D Sch. 1 para. 3(3), Sch. 3 para. 3(1), (2)
(4), (5)	1975 s.99(3); 1986 art. 53(7)(b)
(6)	1975 s.99(4); 1989 Sch. 3 para. 2
20(1)	1975 s.100(1); 1986 art. 53(3A), (7)(c)(i); 1991D Sch. 1 para. 4(a), Sch. 3 para. 3(1)
(2)	1975 s.100(2); 1986 art. 53(7)(c)(ii), Sch. 5 para. 5(b); 1991D Sch. 1 para. 4(b)
(3)	1975 s.100(3); 1986 Sch. 5 para. 5(c); 1989 Sch. 3 para. 5
(4)	1975 s.100(4); 1986 Sch. 5 para. 5(d)
(5)	1975 s.100(6); 1986 art. 53(7)(c)(iii), Sch. 5 para. 5(e); 1991D Sch. 1 para. 4(c)
(6), (7)	1975 s.100(7), (8); 1990 Sch. 6 para. 4(1)
21(1)	1975 s.101(1); 1986 Sch. 5 para. 6(1)
(2)	1975 s.101(2); 1986 art. 53(3), (7)(d)
(3)	1975 s.101(2); 1986 art. 53(3), Sch. 5 para. 6(2)
(4)	1975 s.101(2)(bb); 1990 Sch. 6 para. 4(2)

Provision	Derivation
21(5)	1975 s.101(3); 1986 Sch. 10; 1990 Sch. 6 para. 4(3)
(6)	1975 s.101(4)
(7)–(10)	1975 s.101(5)–(5B); 1986 Sch. 5 para. 6(3); 1989 Sch. 3 para. 6
22(1)–(5)	1980A s.14(1)–(5)
(6)	1980A s.14(8)(a); 1986A Sch. 9 para. 11(c)(i)
23(1)	1975 s.104(1); 1986 art. 53(3), (3A), Sch. 5 para. 9(a); 1988 Sch. 3 para. 13, Sch. 4 para. 11; 1989 art. 12(5), Sch. 3 para. 11(1); 1991D Sch. 1 para. 8(a), Sch. 3 para. 3(1)
(2)	1975 s.104(1A); 1983 Sch. 1 para. 2; 1986 art. 53(3A), Sch. 10; 1991D Sch. 1 para. 8(b), Sch. 3 para. 3(1)
(3)	1975 s.104(1); 1986 Sch. 5 para. 9(a)
(4)	1986 art. 53(8); M10
(5)	1975 s.104(1ZA); 1989 Sch. 3 para. 11(2)
24(1), (2)	1975 s.104(2), (3)
(3)	1975 s.104(3A); 1986 Sch. 5 para. 9(c)
25(1)	1975 s.104(5); 1986 Sch. 5 para. 9(d); 1989 Sch. 3 para. 11(3), (4)
(2)	1975 s.104(6); 1990 art. 8(3)
26	1975 s.104(4)
27	1975 s.104(3B); 1989 Sch. 3 para. 7
28(1)	1975 s.100A(1); 1986 art. 53(3A), (10); 1991D Sch. 1 para. 5, Sch. 3 para. 3(1), (3)
(2)–(4)	1975 s.100A(2)–(4); 1991D Sch. 1 para. 5
(5)	1975 s.100A(2); 1986 art. 53(3A), (9)(a), (b), (10); 1991D Sch. 1 para. 5, Sch. 3, para. 3(1), (3)
(6)–(11)	1975 s.100A(5)–(10); 1986 art. 53(3A); 1991D Sch. 1 para. 5, Sch. 3 para. 3(1)
(12)	1975 s.100A(11); 1991D Sch. 1 para. 5
(13)	1975 s.100A(12); 1986 art. 53(3A); 1991D Sch. 1 para. 5, Sch. 3 para. 3(1)
29	1975 s.100B; 1986 art. 53(3A); 1991D Sch. 1 para. 5, Sch. 3 para. 3(1)
30(1)	1975 s.100C(1); 1986 art. 53(3A); 1991D Sch. 1 para. 5, Sch. 3 para. 3(1)
(2)–(5)	1975 s.100C(2)–(5); 1991D Sch. 1 para 5
(6), (7)	1975 s.100C(6), (7); 1986 art. 53(3A); 1991D Sch. 1 para. 5, Sch. 3 para. 3(1)
(8)	1975 s.100C(8)(a), 104(5)(b); 1986 art. 53(3A), Sch. 5 para. 9(d); 1991D Sch. 1 para. 5, Sch. 3 para. 3(1)
(9), (10)	1975 s.100C(9), (10); 1986 art. 53(3A); 1991D Sch. 1 para. 5, Sch. 3 para. 3(1)
31	1975 s.100D(1)–(6); 1986 art. 53(3A); 1991D Sch. 1 para. 5, Sch. 3 para. 3(1)
32(1)–(4)	1975 s.101; 1986 art. 53(3A), Sch. 5 para. 6; 1991D Sch. 1 para. 6, Sch. 3 para. 3(1)
(5)	1980A s.14(1)–(4), (8)(b)
33(1), (2)	1975 s.104A(1), (2); 1991D Sch. 1 para. 9
(3)	1975 s.104A(1); 1986 art. 53(3A), (9)(a), (b), (10); 1991D Sch. 1 para. 9, Sch. 3 para. 3(1), (3)
(4)	1975 s.104A(3); 1986 art. 53(3A); 1991D Sch. 1 para. 9, Sch. 3 para. 3(1)
(5)	1975 ss.104(3A), 104A(9)(b); 1986 art. 53(3A), (9)(c), Sch. 5 para. 9(c); 1991D Sch. 1 para. 9, Sch. 3 para. 3(1), (3)
(6)–(9)	1975 s.104A(4)–(7); 1986 art. 53(3A); 1991D Sch. 1 para. 9, Sch. 3 para. 3(1)
(10)	1975 ss.104(5)(b), 104A(9)(c); 1986 art. 53(3A), (9)(c); 1991D Sch. 1 para. 9, Sch. 3 para. 3(1), (3)
(11)	1975 ss.104(1ZA), 104A(9)(a); 1991D Sch. 1 para. 9
(12)	1975 s.104A(8); 1986 art. 53(3A); 1991D Sch. 1 para. 9, Sch. 3 para. 3(1)
34(1)	1975 s.102(1), (2); 1986 Sch. 5 para. 7; 1991D Sch. 1 para. 7(1)
(2)	1975 s.102(3); 1991D Sch. 1 para. 7(2)
35	1975 s.103; 1986 Sch. 5 para. 8; 1989 Sch. 3 para. 15
36	1975 s.97(1), (1A); 1983 Sch. 1 para. 1; 1990 Sch. 6 para. 3(1)
37	1975 s.97(1B)–(1E); 1983 Sch. 1 para. 1
38(1)	1975 Sch. 10 para. 1(1); 1983 Sch. 1 para. 5
(2), (3)	1975 Sch. 10 para. 1(2), (2A); 1984 art. 10(b)
(4)	1975 Sch. 10 para. 1(6); 1983 Sch. 1 para. 5

Provision	Derivation
39(1), (2)	1975 s.97(2), (2A); 1983 Sch. 1 para. 1; 1984 art. 10(a)
(3), (4)	1975 s.97(2C)–(2D); 1983 Sch. 1 para. 1
(5)	1975 Sch. 10 para. 1(8); 1983 Sch. 1 para. 5
(6)	Drafting
40	1975 Sch. 10 para. 1(2), (2A), Sch. 10A paras. 3–8; 1984 art. 10(b); 1991D Sch. 1 para. 16
41(1)–(3)	1975 Sch. 10A paras. 1, 9, 10; 1983 Sch. 1 para. 1; 1991D Sch. 1 para. 16
(4), (5)	1975 s.97(2C), (2D), Sch. 10A para. 2; 1984 art. 10(a); 1991D Sch. 1 para. 16
(6), (7)	1975 Sch. 10A paras. 12, 13; 1991D Sch. 1 para. 16
(8)	Drafting
42	1975 s.107; 1986 Sch. 5 para. 11, Sch. 10; 1988 Sch. 1 para. 6
43(1), (2)	1975 s.108(1), (2); 1983 Sch. 2 para. 1(1); 1984 Sch. 2 paras. 4, 5; 1986 Sch. 3 para. 14(a); 1989 Sch. 3 para. 12(1)
(3)–(6)	1975 s.108(4)–(5); 1983 Sch. 2 para. 1(3); 1989 Sch. 3 para. 12(2)
44	1975 s.109; 1983 Sch. 2 para. 2, Sch. 3; 1984 Sch. 2 para. 6; 1986 Sch. 5 para. 12
45(1)–(9)	1975 s.110; 1979 Sch. 3 para. 7; 1983 Sch. 2 para. 3; 1984 Sch. 2 para. 7; 1986 Sch. 5 para. 13, Sch. 10
(10)	Social Security (Consequential Provisions) Act 1975 (c. 18) Sch. 3 paras. 20, 31
46(1)–(4)	1975 s.112A(1)–(5); 1986A Sch. 9 para. 1; 1989 Sch. 9
(5), (6)	1975 s.112A(5A), (5B); 1989 Sch. 3 para. 9(2)
47(1), (2)	1975 Sch. 12 para. 1; 1983 Sch. 2 para. 7(a)
(3)	1975 Sch. 12 para. 3; 1983 Sch. 2 para. 7(b)
48(1)–(4)	1975 Sch. 12 para. 2(1)–(4); 1983 Sch. 1 para. 6; 1986 Sch. 5 para. 15
(5)	1975 Sch. 12 para. 2(6); 1983 Sch. 1 para. 6
(6)	1975 Sch. 12 para. 3; 1983 Sch. 2 para 7(b)
(7)	Drafting
49(1)–(3)	1975 s.97(2D)(a), Sch. 10 para. 1A(1)–(3); 1983 Sch. 1 paras. 1, 5; 1991D Sch. 1 para. 15
(4)	1975 s.97(2E), Sch. 10A para. 2, Sch. 12 para. 2(5); 1983 Sch. 1 paras. 1, 6; 1991D Sch. 1 para. 16
(5)	Drafting
50(1)	1975 s.97(3); 1979 s.9(2)
(2)	1980A s.13(5); Courts and Legal Services Act 1990 (c. 41) Sch. 10 para. 46
(3)	Drafting
51	1975 s.115A; 1989 Sch. 3 para. 3(1); 1991D Sch. 1 para. 11, Sch. 4
52(1), (2)	1975 s.115C(1), (2); 1986 art. 53(3A); 1991D Sch. 1 para. 13, Sch. 3, para. 3(1)
(3)	1975 s.115C(3); 1991D Sch. 1, para. 13
(4)	1975 s.115C(3); 1986 art. 53(3A), (9)(d); 1991D Sch. 1 para. 13, Sch. 3 para. 3(1), (3)
(5)	1975 s.115C(4); 1986 art. 53(3A), (9)(b); 1991D Sch. 1 para. 13, Sch. 3 para. 3(1)
(6)	1975 s.115C(5); 1991D Sch. 1 para. 13
(7)	1975 s.115C(5); 1986 art. 53(3A), (9)(e); 1991D Sch. 1 para. 13, Sch. 3 para. 3(1), (3)
(8)	1975 s.115C(6); 1986 art. 53(3A); 1991D Sch. 1 para. 13, Sch. 3 para. 3(1)
53	1975 s.115D; 1986 art. 53(3A)(c); 1991D Sch. 1 para. 13, Sch. 3 para. 3(1)
54	1975 s.115B; 1989 Sch. 3 para. 3(1); 1991D Sch. 1 para. 12, Sch. 4
55	1975 s.116; 1980A s.12
56(1), (2)	1975 s.114(1); 1986 art. 53(3)(b), (3A), (6); 1988 Sch. 3 para. 13; 1991D Sch. 3 para. 3(1)
(3)	1975 s.114(2)
(4)	1976IR art. 72(3)
(5)–(7)	1975 s.114(2A)–(2C); 1986 Sch. 5 para. 14
(8)	1975 s.114(5)
57(1), (2)	1975 s.115(1)–(3); 1986 art. 53(3)(c), (3A), (4), (6); 1988 Sch. 3 para. 13; 1991D Sch. 3 para. 3(1)
(3)	1975 s.115(4)
(4)	1975 s.115(4A); 1991C art. 5(2)

Provision	Derivation
57(5), (6)	1975 s.115(5); 1989 Sch. 3 para. 1(2)
58(1)	1975 s.117(1); 1983 Sch. 1 para. 4; 1986 art. 53(3), (3A), (6); 1991D Sch. 3 para. 3(1)
(2)	1975 s.117(2); 1986 art. 53(3), (3A), (6); 1991D SCh. 3 para. 3(1)
(3)	1975 s.117(3); 1983 Sch. 2 para. 6
(4)	1975 s.117(4); 1988 Sch. 1 para. 6
(5)	1975 s.117(5)
59(1), (2)	1975 s.119(3), (4)(a)
(3)	1977 art. 13(5)
(4)	1986 art. 53(3)(e), (3A), (6); 1988 Sch. 3 para. 13; 1991D Sch. 3 para. 3(1)
60	1975 s.113(1), (2)(a), (b); 1983 Sch. 2 para. 4
61	1986 art. 30(1)–(3)
62(1), (2)	1986 art. 33(8), (9); 1988 Sch. 5
(3)	1986 art. 33(10); 1988 Sch. 3 para. 6; 1990 art. 12(2)
63	1986 art. 36
64(1)–(8)	1986 art. 35; 1988 Sch. 5
(9), (10)	1986 art. 33(11), (12); 1988 Sch. 3 para. 6
65	1986 Sch. 6 para. 4
66(1)–(3)	1975 s.154D(1)–(3); 1990 Sch. 6 para. 5(2)
(4)	1975 s.154D(4); 1986 Sch. 9 para. 32; 1990 Sch. 6 para. 5(2), (3); 1991D Sch. 2 para. 4
(5), (6)	1975 s.154D(5), (6); 1990 Sch. 6 para. 5(2)
67	1975 s.104(7)–(10); 1986 art. 53(3); 1990 Sch. 6 para. 5(1); 1991D Sch. 2 para. 11, Sch. 3 para. 3(1)
68	National Insurance Measure (NI) 1974 (c. 4) s.5(1), (4)
69(1)	1986 art. 54(1)
(2)	1986 art. 54(1A); 1989 Sch. 3 para. 14(1)
(3)–(10)	1986 art. 54(2)–(9); 1989 Sch. 3 para. 14(2)
(11)	1986 art. 54(10); 1988 Sch. 3 para. 13, Sch. 4 para. 23(1), Sch. 5; 1991D Sch. 3 para. 4
70(1), (2)	1986 art. 21(4E), (4H); 1988 art. 6(2)
(3)–(6)	1986 art. 21(4J)–(4M); 1988 art. 6(2)
(7), (8)	1986 arts. 21(4F), (4G), 54(10A); 1988 art. 6(2), Sch. 4 para. 23(2)
71	1975 s.85; 1975CB Sch. 4 para. 29, Sch. 5; 1979 art 12
72	1986 art 28
73	1986 art. 30(4)–(7)
74(1)–(3)	1986 art. 34(5)–(7)
(4)	1986 art. 33(4); 1988 Sch. 5
(5)	1986 art. 34(12)
(6)–(8)	1986 arts. 27(3)–(5), 34(8); 1989 art. 7(2), (3), Sch. 9; 1990 art. 10(2)
75	1986 arts. 30(8), 54(7A); 1988 Sch. 4 paras. 19, 21
76	1975CB art. 6A; 1979 art. 12(2)
77(1)	1989 art. 24(3), Sch. 4 para. 1(1); 1990 Sch. 1 para. 1(1)–(3); 1991SP art. 3(5)
(2)	1989 art. 24(3A); 1991SP art. 3(5)
(3)–(5)	1989 art. 24(4)–(6)
(6)	1989 Sch. 4 para. 1(2)
(7)	1989 art. 24(8)
78	1989 art. 24(1), (2)
79	1989 Sch. 4 para. 2
80	1989 Sch. 4 para. 3
81	1989 Sch. 4 para. 4
82	1989 Sch. 4 para. 5
83	1989 Sch. 4 para. 6
84	1989 Sch. 4 para. 7
85	1989 Sch. 4 para. 8
86	1989 Sch. 4 para. 9
87	1989 Sch. 4 para. 10
88	1989 Sch. 4 para. 11
89	1989 Sch. 4 para. 12; 1990 Sch. 1 para. 2
90	1989 Sch. 4 para. 13; 1990 Sch. 1 para. 1(4)

Provision	Derivation
91	1989 Sch. 4 para. 14
92	1989 Sch. 4 para. 15
93	1989 Sch. 4 para. 16
94	1989 Sch. 4 para. 17; 1990 Sch. 1 paras. 3, 4
95	1989 Sch. 4 para. 18
96	1989 Sch. 4 para. 19
97	1989 Sch. 4 para. 21
98	1989 Sch. 4 para. 23; 1990 Sch. 1 para. 5
99	1989 art. 28
100	1986 art. 27; 1989 art. 7(2), (3); 1990 art. 10(2)
101	1986 art. 25
102	1986 art. 25A; 1990 art. 10(1)
103	1986 art. 25B; 1990 art. 10(1)
104(1)–(8)	1986 art. 59(1)–(7); 1989 Sch. 4 para. 20(1)–(6)
(9)	1986 art. 59(10); 1989 Sch. 4 para. 20(3), (7)
105	1986 art. 59(8), (9)
106	1986 art. 56
107	1986 art. 55
108(1)	1975 s.137(1); 1975P Sch. 5 para. 36; 1984F arts. 5(2), 6(1), (3)
(2)	1975 s.1(4), Sch. 1 para. 5(2)
(3)	1975 s.137(2)
(4)	1975 s.137(3); 1981 Sch. para. 3(a); 1986 Sch. 10
(5), (6)	1975 s.137(4)
109	1986 art. 58
110(1)–(3)	1986 art. 57(1)–(3)
(4)	1986 art. 57(3A); 1990 Sch. 6 para. 3(2)
(5), (6)	1986 art. 57(4), (5)
111	1975 s.139; 1986 art. 53(5); M6
112	1975 s.140
113	1975 s.141
114(1), (2)	1975 s.142(1), (2); 1975P Sch. 5 para. 39; 1986 Sch. 10
(3)	1975 s.142(3); 1991C art. 4(6)(a)
(4)	1975 s.142(3A); 1991C art. 4(6)(b)
(5)	1975 s.142(4)
(6)	1975 s.142(5); 1991C art. 4(6)(c)
115(1)	1975 s.143(7); Criminal Justice (NI) Order 1980 (NI 6) Sch. 1 para. 72; 1981 MC Sch. 6 para. 35
(2)–(6)	1975 s.143(1), (3), (4), (5); 1990 Sch. 7
116	1986 art. 60; 1989 art. 22
117	1989 art. 21; 1990 Sch. 6 para. 17
118	1986 art. 61
119	1986 art. 28A; 1989 Sch. 8 para. 16
120	1986 art. 32(1)–(3)
121	1982 art. 19(1)
122(1)–(3)	1982 art. 20; 1984 Sch. 2 para. 13(1)
(4)	1982 arts. 11(3)(a), 19(4)
123	1986 Sch. 4 para. 9
124(1), (2)	1986 Sch. 4 para. 8A; 1989 Sch. 8 para. 17
(3)	1986 Sch. 4 para. 8
125	1975 s.151; Adoption (NI) Order 1987 (NI 22) Sch. 5
126(1)	1986 art. 29(1)
(2)	1986 art 29(1); 1989 art. 16(1)
(3)–(6)	1986 art. 29(2)–(5)
127(1), (2)	1986 art. 31(1), (2)
(3)	1986 art. 31(4); 1989 art. 17
128	1986 art. 31(5)–(8); 1989 art. 17
129	1975 s.120; 1979 Sch. 3 para. 9; 1985 art. 9(5)
130	1975P art. 23; 1985 Sch. 3 para. 1
131	1982 art. 11(1E); 1991SP art. 4(1)
132	1986 art. 64
133	1975 art. 64A; 1989 art. 19(1)
134(1), (2)	1975CB art. 19(1), (2)(a)–(e)

Provision	Derivation
135	1986 art. 65; 1989 art. 19(2)(a)
136	1975P art. 11(3A); 1989 Sch. 8 para. 10
137(1)	1975CB art. 7(5), Sch. 3 paras. 1, 2; 1986 Sch. 9 para. 62
(2)	1975CB Sch. 3 para. 3
138	1977 art 13(4)
139	1986 art. 65A; 1989 art. 20
140	1986 art. 65B; 1990 Sch. 6 para. 13
141	1975 s.127(1)–(4); Finance Act 1980 (c. 48) Sch. 19 para. 5(4)
142(1), (2)	1975 s.128(1), (2); 1991R Sch. 2
(3)	1975 s.128(2A); 1990 art. 18(3)
(4)	1975 s.128(2B); 1990 art. 19(1)
(5)	1975 ss.128(4); 1981 art. 5(2)(b), (c), (3); 1982 art. 5(2); 1985 Sch. 5 para. 4; Social Security (Consolidated Fund of Northern Ireland Supplements to, and Allocation of, Contributions) (Re-rating) Order (NI) 1987 (SR 1987 No. 25) art. 3(2); 1989 art. 3(2); Social Security (Contributions and Allocation of Contributions) (Re-rating) Order (NI) 1989 (SR 1989 No. 89) art. 6(2); 1991RF Sch. 2; 1991C art. 6(a)
(6)	1975 s.128(4); 1985 Sch. 5 para. 4
(7), (8)	1975 s.128(4A), (4B); 1981C art. 5(3)
(9)–(11)	1975 s.128(5)
(12)	1975 s.128(6); 1979 art. 11(3)
143(1)(a), (b)	1975 ss.1(5), 129(1), (2); 1975P Sch. 5 para. 32; 1986 Sch. 10; 1990 art. 18(4); 1991D Sch. 1 para. 18
(c)	1986 art. 82(1)(c)
(d)	1982 art. 11(7); 1985 art. 19(1)(d); 1986 art 82(1)(c)
(e)	1989 art. 29(3)(b)
(2)	1975 s.129(2), (3); 1984 Sch. 2 para. 2; 1989 art. 29(3); 1990 art. 18(4); 1991D Sch. 1 para. 18
(3)	1975 s.129(4)
(4)	1977 art. 3(2)
(5)	1975 s.129(7); 1990 art. 19(2)
144(1)–(3)	1986 art. 82(3)–(5)
(4)	1975OC s.4(3)(e); 1990 art. 18(7)(b)
(5)	1975 s.113(2)(b); 1983 Sch. 2 para. 4(b); 1986 art. 82(6)
(6)	1989 art. 29(2)
145(1)	1975 s.127(5); 1986 art. 82(7); 1991D Sch. 3 para. 7
(2)–(4)	1975 s.127(6); 1975CB art. 25; 1986 art. 82(8)
(5)	1975 s.129(5); 1975P art. 73(1); 1977 art. 20; 1980 art. 14; 1982 art. 37; 1986 art 82(2); 1988 art. 15; 1989 art. 29(1); 1990 arts. 18(5), 20(2)
146(1)	1986 art. 33(1)
(2)–(4)	1986 art. 33(5)–(7)
(5), (6)	1986 art. 3(7A), (7B); 1988 Sch. 3, para. 3
147(1)–(4)	1986 art. 33(8A)–(8D); 1988 Sch. 3 para. 5
(5)	1986 art. 33(8E); 1990 art. 12(1)
148	1986 art. 82(9), (10)
149	1980A ss.9(3), 10; 1986 Sch. 9 para. 64; 1991SP art. 5(1)(b)
150(1)–(4)	1986 art. 62(1)–(4)
(5)	1986 art 62(5); 1989 Sch. 8 para. 11(2)
(6)	1986 art. 62(6); 1989 Sch. 8 para. 11(2)
151	1980A s.10(3), (6), (8), (9)
152	1991D art. 5(1)–(6)
153	1975 s.133; Social Security Pensions Act 1975 (c. 60) Sch. 4 para. 69; 1986 art. 66(1)
154	1975CB art. 16; 1986 art. 66(4); 1991D Sch. 3 para. 5
155(1)	1975 s.134(1); 1975CB art. 17(1); 1977A s.20(3); 1977 art. 16; 1986 art. 66(2), Sch. 10
(2)	1975 s.134(1A); 1975CB art. 17(1A); 1981 art. 7(1), (2)
(3)	1975 s.134(2); 1975CB art. 17(2)
(4)	1975 s.134(1); 1975CB art. 17(1); 1986 art. 66(4); 1991D Sch. 3 para. 5
(5)	1975CB art. 17(3); 1986 art. 66(4); 1991D Sch. 3 para. 6
(6)	1975CB arts. 16(3), 17(3)
156	1986 art. 78

Provision	Derivation
157	1977SB art. 28; 1984F arts. 4, 6(1), (3)
158	1977SB art. 29; 1984F arts. 4, 6(1), (3)
159	1975 s.145
160	1975 s.146
161(1)	Drafting
(2)	1975 s.150(3)(c)
162	Drafting
163(1)	1975 s.87(1); 1975CB art. 14; 1986 Sch. 9 para. 32(a)
(3)	1975 s.87(3); Judgments Enforcement (Northern Ireland Consequential Amendments) Order 1981 (SI 1981/234) art. 5; 1981 MC Sch. 6 para. 34
164(1), (2)	1975 s.153
(3)	1975OC s.7
165(1)	1975 Sch. 17; 1986 Sch. 5 para. 17
(2)	1975 Sch. 17; 1986 Sch. 5 para. 17
(3)	1975 s.155(1); 1986 art. 81(1); 1989 art. 30(1); 1991D art. 13(2)
(4)	1975 s.155(2); 1982 art. 36(1); 1986 art. 81(1); 1989 art. 30(1); 1991D art. 13(2)
(5)	1975 ss.13(2)(c), 155(3); 1975CB art. 24(5); 1982 art. 36(1); 1986 art. 81(1); 1989 art. 30(1), Sch. 8 para. 9(1); M8
(6)	1975 s.155(3A); 1975CB art. 24(5A); 1986 arts. 63(1), (2), 81(1); 1989 art. 30(1); 1991D art. 13(2)
(7)	1986 art. 81(2)
(8)	1986 art 81(5)
(9)	1975 s.127(6); 1986 art. 81(6); 1989 art. 30(5)
(10)	1975 s.155(5); 1982 art. 36(1); 1986 art. 81(7)
(11)	1975 s.155(7); 1975CB arts. 16(3), 17(3); 1977A Sch. 2; 1986 art. 66(4); 1991D Sch. 3 para. 5
(12)	1975 s.157(4); 1977A Sch. 2
166(1)	1975 s.156(1)
(2)	1975 s.156(2); 1975CB art. 24(2); 1982 art. 11(1F); 1986 art. 81(3)(c); 1989 art. 30(2)(h); 1991SP art. 4(1)
(3)	1975 s.156(3)(c); 1975CB art. 24(3); 1990 Sch. 6 para. 6(1)
(4)	1975 s.156(4); 1975OC s.4(9); 1975CB art. 24(4); 1977 arts. 9(2), 19(3); 1982 art. 36(2); 1986 art. 81(4); 1988 art. 15A(2); 1989 art. 30(3); 1990 Sch. 6 para. 6(4), (6), (8), (11)
(5)	1975 s.156(5A); 1989 Sch. 3 para. 16; 1990 Sch. 6 para. 6(16)
(6)	s.156(5)
(7)	1990 Sch. 6 para. 6(12), (17)
(8)	1990 Sch. 6 para. 6(13)
(9)	1990 Sch. 6 para. 6(14), (17)
(10)	1990 Sch. 6 para. 6(15)
(11)	1975 s.156(6)
(12)	1975 s.156(4); 1980A s.14(8); 1986A Sch. 9 para. 11(c); 1990 Sch. 6 para. 6(12)(a)
167	1975 Sch. 17
168	Short title, etc.
Sch. 1	
para. 1	1975 s.154A; 1985 art. 17
para. 2	1975 s.154A; 1985 art. 17; 1986 Sch. 9 para 57; Social Security (1986 Order) (Commencement No. 1) Order (NI) 1986 (SR 1986 No. 339)
para. 3	1975 s.154A; 1986 Sch. 9 para. 56; Social Security (1986 Order) (Commencement No. 3) Order (NI) 1987 (SR 1987 No. 21)
para. 4	1975 s.154A; 1986 Sch. 9 para. 56; 1989 arts. 1(2), (3), Sch. 8 para. 8(1)
para. 5	1975 s.154A; 1986 Sch. 9 para. 56; 1989 Sch. 8 para. 8(1); 1990 arts. 1(3), (4), 8(1)
Sch. 2	
para. 1(1)	1975 Sch. 10 para. 1A(4); 1983 Sch. 1 para. 5
(2)	1975 Sch. 10 paras. 1A(5), 5; 1980A s.13(1); 1983 Sch. 1 para. 5
(3)–(5)	1975 Sch. 10 para. 1A(6)–(8); 1980A s.13(2); 1983 Sch. 1 para. 5
(6)	1980A s.13(5)(a); Judicial Pensions Act 1981 (c. 20) Sch. 3 para. 10
para. 2	1975 Sch. 10 para. 2(1); Sch. 10A para. 11; 1991D Sch. 1 para. 16

Provision	Derivation
Sch. 2	
para. 3	1975 Sch. 10 para. 1A(9); 1983 Sch. 1 para. 5
para. 4	1975 Sch. 10 para. 1A(10), Sch. 10A para. 11; Sch. 12 para. 5A; 1983 Sch. 1 paras. 5, 7; 1991D Sch. 1 para. 16
para. 5	1975 Sch. 10 paras. 1B, 1C, Sch. 10A para. 11; 1983 Sch. 1 para. 5; 1991D Sch. 1 para. 16
para. 6	1975 Sch. 10 para. 1D, Sch. 10A para. 11, Sch. 12 para. 9; 1983 Sch. 1 para. 5; 1991D Sch. 1 para. 16
para. 7	1975 Sch. 10 para. 4; 1986A Sch. 9 para. 10(1)(a), (b)
para. 8	1975 s.113(3), Sch. 10 para. 3, Sch. 10A para. 11, Sch. 12 paras. 4–7; 1983 Sch. 2 para. 7(b); 1991D Sch. 1 para. 16
para. 9	1980 art. 12; 1991D Sch. 2 para. 9
Sch. 3	
para. 1	1975 s.115(2); 1983 Sch. 1 para. 3, Sch. 2 para. 5; 1991D Sch. 1 para. 10
para. 2	1975 Sch. 13 para. 1; 1989 Sch. 3 para. 4
para. 3	1975 Sch. 13 para. 1A; 1986 Sch. 5 para. 16(a)
paras. 4–9	1975 Sch. 13 paras. 2–7
para. 10	1975 Sch. 13 para. 7A; 1989 Sch. 3 para. 10; 1991D Sch. 1 para. 17
para. 11	1975 Sch. 13 para. 10; 1986 Sch. 5 para. 16(b); 1991D Sch. 2 para. 13
para. 12	1975 Sch. 13 para. 11
Sch. 4	1989 Sch. 2; 1990 Sch. 5 para. 17(4); 1991D Sch. 2 para. 13
Sch. 5	
para. 1	1980A Sch. 3 para. 12(4); 1991D Sch. 2 para. 8(b); Disability Living Allowance and Disability Working Allowance Act 1991 (c. 21) Sch. 2 para. 10
para. 2	1980A Sch. 3 para. 12(1)
para. 3	1980A Sch. 3 para. 12(2); 1982A s.42(2); 1986A Sch. 10 para. 99
para. 4	1980A Sch. 3 para. 13(1)
para. 5	1980A Sch. 3 para. 13(1A); 1986A Sch. 10 para. 106; 1986 Sch. 9 para. 73
paras. 6, 7	1980A Sch. 3 para. 14
para. 8	1980A Sch. 3 paras. 15A, 15AA; 1982 Sch. 4 para. 18(3); 1982A Sch. 4 para. 33(3); 1989 Sch. 8 para. 11(3); Social Security Act 1989 (c. 24) Sch. 8 para. 12(6)
paras. 9, 10	1980A Sch. 3 paras. 20, 21; 1986A Sch. 9 para. 13
Sch. 6	
para. 1	1975OC s.4
para. 2	1975OC s.5
para. 3	1986 art. 54(11)
Sch. 7	
para. 1	1986 Sch. 7 paras. 1, 3
para. 2	1986 Sch. 7 para. 4; 1991D Sch. 2 para. 11(b)
para. 3	1986 Sch. 7 para. 5
para. 4	1986 Sch. 7 para. 7
para. 5	1986 Sch. 7 para. 6

TABLE OF DESTINATIONS

CONSOLIDATION OF ENACTMENTS (PROCEDURE) ACT 1949
c.33

1949	c.33
M5	s.15(1)(f)(g) (i)–(vi)(h), 16
M6	15(4), 17(1), 111
M8	165(5)
M10	23(4)

NATIONAL INSURANCE MEASURE (N.I.) 1974
c.4

1974	c.4
s.5(1)	s.68
(4)	68

SOCIAL SECURITY (NORTHERN IRELAND) ACT 1975
c.15

1975	c.15
s.1(4)	s.108(2)
(5)	143(1)(a)(b)
13(2)(c)	165(5)
85	71
87(1)	163(1)
(3)	163(3)
88	6
89	7
90	8
93(1)(a)	15(1)(a)(b)
(b)	15(1)(a)(b)
(bb)	15(1)(c)
(d)	15(1)(d)
(e)	15(1)(e)
(2)	15(2), (3)
(2A)	15(2), (3)
(3)	15(4)
94	16
96(1)	17(1)
96(2)	17(2), (3)
97(1)	36
(1A)	36
(1B)	37
(1C)	37
(1D)	37
(1E)	37
(2)	39(1), (2)
(2A)	39(1), (2)
(2C)	39(3), (4), 41(4), (5)
(2D)	39(3), (4), 41(4), (5)
(2D)(a)	49(1)–(3)
(2E)	49(4)
(3)	50(1)
98(1)	18(1), (2), (3), (6)
(2)	18(1), (2)
(2A)	18(4)
(3)	18(5)
99(1)	19(1), (2)
(2)	19(1), (2)
(2A)	19(3)
(3)	19(4), (5)
100(1)	20(1)
(2)	20(2)

1975	c.15
s.100(3)	s.20(3)
(4)	20(4)
(6)	20(5)
(7)	20(6), (7)
(8)	20(6), (7)
100A(1)	28(1)
(2)	28(2)–(5)
(3)	28(2)–(4)
(4)	28(2)–(4)
(5)	28(6)–(11)
(6)	28(6)–(11)
(7)	28(6)–(11)
(8)	28(6)–(11)
(9)	28(6)–(11)
(10)	28(6)–(11)
(11)	28(12)
(12)	28(13)
100B	29
100C(1)	30(1)
(2)	30(2)–(5)
(3)	30(2)–(5)
(4)	30(2)–(5)
(5)	30(2)–(5)
(6)	30(6), (7)
(7)	30(6), (7)
(8)(a)	30(8)
(9)	30(9), (10)
(10)	30(9), (10)
100D(1)	31
(2)	31
(3)	31
(4)	31
(5)	31
(6)	31
101	32(1)–(4)
(1)	21(2)
(2)	21(2), (3)
(bb)	21(4)
(3)	21(5)
(4)	21(6)
(5)	21(7)–(10)
(5B)	21(7)–(10)
102(1)	34(1)
(2)	34(1)
(3)	34(2)
103	35

1975	c.15
s.104(1)	s.23(1), (3)
(1A)	23(2)
(1ZA)	23(4); 33(11)
(2)	24(1), (2)
(3)	24(1), (2)
(3A)	24(3); 33(5)
(3B)	27
(4)	26
(5)	25(1)
(b)	30(8), (10)
(6)	25(2)
(7)	67
(8)	67
(9)	67
(10)	67
104A(1)	33(1), (2), (3)
(2)	33(1), (2)
(3)	33(4)
(4)	33(6)–(9)
(5)	33(6)–(9)
(6)	33(6)–(9)
(7)	33(6)–(9)
(8)	33(12)
(9)(a)	33(11)
(b)	33(5)
(c)	33(10)
107	42
108(1)	43(1), (2)
(2)	43(1), (2)
(4)	43(3)–(6)
(5)	43(3)–(6)
109	44
110	45(1)–(9)
112A(1)	46(1)–(4)
(2)	46(1)–(4)
(3)	46(1)–(4)
(4)	46(1)–(4)
(5)	46(1)–(4)
(5A)	46(5), (6)
(5B)	46(5), (6)
113(1)	60
(2)(a)	60
(b)	60, 144(5)
(3)	Sched. 2, para. 8
s.114(1)	56(1), (2)

1975	c.15
s.114(2)	s.56(3)
(2A)	56(5)–(7)
(2B)	56(5)–(7)
(2C)	56(5)–(7)
(5)	56(8)
115(1)	57(1), (2)
(2)	57(1), (2); Sched. 3, para. 1
(3)	57(1), (2)
(4)	57(3)
(4A)	57(4)
(5)	57(5), (6)
115A	51
115B	54
115C(1)	52(1), (2)
(2)	52(1), (2)
(3)	52(3), (4)
(4)	52(5)
(5)	52(6), (7)
(6)	52(8)
115D	53
116	55
117(1)	58(1)
(2)	58(2)
(3)	58(3)
(4)	58(4)
(5)	58(5)
119(3)	59(1), (2)
(4)(a)	59(1), (2)
120	129
127(1)	141
(2)	141
(3)	141
(4)	141
(5)	145(1)
(6)	145(2)–(4); 165(9)
128(1)	142(1), (2)
(2)	142(1), (2)
(2A)	142(3)
(2B)	142(4)
(4)	142(5), (6)
(4A)	142(7), (8)
(4B)	142(7), (8)
(5)	142(9)–(11)
(6)	142(12)
129(1)	143(1)(a)(b)
(2)	143(1)(a)(b), (2)
(3)	143(2)
(4)	143(3)
(5)	145(5)
(7)	143(5)
133	153
134(1)	155(1), (4)
(1A)	155(2)
(2)	155(3)
137(1)	108(1)
(2)	108(3)
(3)	108(4)
(4)	108(5), (6)
139	111
140	112
141	113
142(1)	114(1), (2)
(2)	114(1), (2)
(3)	114(3)
(3A)	114(4)
(4)	114(5)
(5)	114(6)

1975	c.15
s.143(1)	s.115(2)–(6)
(3)	115(2)–(6)
(4)	115(2)–(6)
(5)	115(2)–(6)
(7)	115(1)
145	159
146	160
150(3)(c)	161(2)
151	125
153	164(1), (2)
154A	Sched. 1, paras. 1, 2, 3, 4, 5
(1)	1(1), (2), (4)
(2)	1(1), (2)
(3)	1(3)
154B	2
154C	3
154D(1)	66(1)–(3)
(2)	66(1)–(3)
(3)	66(1)–(3)
(4)	66(4)
(5)	66(5), (6)
(6)	66(5), (6)
155(1)	165(3)
(2)	165(4)
(3)	165(5)
(3A)	165(6)
(5)	165(10)
(7)	165(11)
156(1)	166(1)
(2)	166(2)
(3)(c)	166(3)
(4)	166(4), (12)
(5)	166(6)
(5A)	166(5)
(6)	166(11)
157(4)	165(12)
Sched. 1, para. 5(2)	108(2)
Sched. 10, para. 1(1)	38(1)
(2)	38(2), (3), 40
(2A)	38(2), (3), 40
(6)	38(4)
(8)	39(5)
para. 1A(1)	49(1)–(3)
(2)	49(1)–(3)
(3)	49(1)–(3)
(4)	Sched. 2, para. 1(1)
(5)	Sched. 2, para. 1(2)
(6)	Sched. 2, para. 1(3)–(5)
(7)	Sched. 2, para. 1(3)–(5)
(8)	Sched. 2, para. 1(3)–(5)
(9)	Sched. 2, para. 3
(10)	Sched. 2, para. 4
1B	Sched. 2, para. 5
1C	Sched. 2, para. 5

1975	c.15
Sched. 10—*cont.*	
para. 1D	Sched. 2, para. 6
2(1)	Sched. 2, para. 2
3	Sched. 2, para. 8
4	Sched. 2, para. 7
Sched. 10A, para. 1	41(1)–(3)
2	41(4), (5), 49(4)
3	40
4	40
5	40
6	40
7	40
8	40
9	41(1)–(3)
10	41(1)–(3)
11	Sched. 2, paras. 2, 4, 5, 6, 8
12	41(6), (7)
13	41(6), (7)
Sched. 12, para. 1	47(1), (2)
2(1)	48(1)–(4)
(2)	48(1)–(4)
(3)	48(1)–(4)
(4)	48(1)–(4)
(5)	49(4)
(6)	48(5)
3	47(3), 48(6)
4	Sched. 2, para. 8
5	Sched. 2, para. 8
5A	Sched. 2, para. 4
6	Sched. 2, para. 8
7	Sched. 2, para. 8
9	Sched. 2, para. 6
Sched. 13, para. 1	Sched. 3, para. 2
1A	Sched. 3, para. 3
2	Sched. 3, paras. 4–9
3	Sched. 3, paras. 4–9
4	Sched. 3, paras. 4–9
5	Sched. 9, paras. 4–9
6	Sched. 9, paras. 4–9
7	Sched. 9, paras. 4–9
7A	Sched. 3, para. 10
10	Sched. 3, para. 11
11	Sched. 3, para. 12
Sched. 17	165(1), (2), 167

INDUSTRIAL INJURIES AND DISEASES (NORTHERN IRELAND OLD CASES) ACT 1975
c.17

1975	c.17
s.4	Sched. 6, para. 1
(3)(e)	144(4)
(9)	166(4)
5	Sched. 6, para. 2
7	164(3)

SOCIAL SECURITY PENSIONS (NORTHERN IRELAND) ORDER 1975
N.I. 15

1975	N.I. 15
art. 11(3A)	s.136
23	130
64A	133
70(1)(a)	15(1)(f)
73(1)	145(5)
Sched. 5,	
para. 32	143(1)(a)(b)
36	108(1)
39	114(1), (2)

CHILD BENEFIT (NORTHERN IRELAND) ORDER 1975
N.I. 6

1975	N.I. 6
art. 6A	s.76
7(5)	137(1)
8(1)	11(1)
(3)	11(2)
14	163(1)
16	154
(3)	155(6), 165 (11)
17(1)	155(1), (4)
17(1A)	155(2)
(2)	155(3)

1975	N.I. 6
art. 17(3)	s.155(5), (6), 165(11)
19(1)	134(1), (2)
(2)(a)	134(1), (2)
(b)	134(1), (2)
(c)	134(1), (2)
(d)	134(1), (2)
(e)	134(1), (2)
24(2)	166(2)
(3)	166(3)

1975	N.I. 6
art. 24(4)	s.166(4)
(5)	165(5)
(5A)	165(6)
25	145(2)–(4)
Sched. 3,	
para. 1	137(1)
2	137(1)
3	137(2)
Sched. 4,	
para. 29	71
Sched. 5	71

SOCIAL SECURITY (CONSEQUENTIAL PROVISIONS) ACT 1975
c.18

1975	c.18
Sched. 3,	
para. 20	s.45(10)
31	45(10)

SOCIAL SECURITY PENSIONS ACT 1975
c.60

1975	c.60
Sched. 4,	
para. 69	s.153

INDUSTRIAL RELATIONS (NORTHERN IRELAND) ORDER 1976
N.I. 16

1976	N.I. 16
art. 72(3)	s.56(4)

SOCIAL SECURITY (MISCELLANEOUS PROVISIONS) (NORTHERN IRELAND) ORDER 1977
N.I. 11

1977	N.I. 11
art. 3(2)	s.143(4)
9(2)	166(4)
13(4)	138
(5)	59(3)
16........	155(1)
18(5)	15(1)(e)
19(3)	166(4)
20........	145(5)

SOCIAL SECURITY (MISCELLANEOUS PROVISIONS) ACT 1977
c.5

1977	c.5
s.20(3)........	s.155(1)
Sched. 2	165(11), (12)

SUPPLEMENTARY BENEFITS (NORTHERN IRELAND) ORDER 1977
N.I. 27

1977	N.I. 27
art. 28........	s.157
29........	158

SOCIAL SECURITY (NORTHERN IRELAND) ORDER 1979
N.I. 5

1979	N.I. 15
art. 9(2)	s.50(1)
11(3)	142(12)
12........	71
(2)	76
Sched. 3,	
para. 7	45(1)–(9)
9	129

CRIMINAL JUSTICE (N.I.) ORDER 1980
N.I. 6

1980	N.I. 6
Sched. 1,	
para. 72	s.115(1)

FINANCE ACT 1980
c.48

1980	c.48
Sched. 19,	
para. 5(4) ...	s.141

SOCIAL SECURITY (NORTHERN IRELAND) ORDER 1980
N.I. 8

1980	N.I. 8
art. 12........	Sched. 2,
	para. 9
14........	s.145(5)
Sched. 1,	
para. 9	17(2), (3)

SOCIAL SECURITY ACT 1980
c.30

1980	c.30
s.9(3)	s.149
10	149
(3)	151
(6)	151
(8)	151
(9)	151
12	55
13(1)	Sched. 2, para. 1(2)
(2)	Sched. 2, para. 1(3)–(5)
(5)	50(2)
(a)	Sched. 2, para. 1(6)
14(1)	22(1)–(5), 32(5)

1980	c.30
s.14(2)	s.22(1)–(5), 32(5)
(3)	22(1)–(5), 32(5)
(4)	22(1)–(5), 32(5)
(5)	22(1)–(5)
(8)	166(12)
(a)	22(6)
(b)	32(5)
Sched. 3, para. 12(1)	Sched. 5, para. 2
(2)	Sched. 5, para. 3
(4)	Sched. 5, para. 1

1980	c.30
Sched. 3—cont.	
para.13(1)	Sched. 5, para. 4
(1A)	Sched. 5, para. 5
14	Sched. 5, paras. 6, 7
15A	Sched. 5, para. 8
15AA	Sched. 5, para. 8
20	Sched. 5, paras. 9, 10
21	Sched. 5, paras. 9, 10

SOCIAL SECURITY (CONTRIBUTIONS) (NORTHERN IRELAND) ORDER 1981
N.I. 9

1981	N.I. 9
art. 5(3)	s.142(7), (8)

SOCIAL SECURITY (NORTHERN IRELAND) ORDER 1981
N.I. 25

1981	N.I. 25
art. 5(2)(b)	s.142(5)
(c)	142(5)
(3)	142(5)
7(1)	155(2)
(2)	155(2)
Sched., para. 3(a)	108(4)

MAGISTRATES' COURTS (NORTHERN IRELAND) ORDER 1981
N.I. 26

1981	N.I. 26
Sched. 6, para. 34	s.163(3)
35	115(1)

JUDGMENTS ENFORCEMENT (NORTHERN IRELAND CONSEQUENTIAL AMENDMENTS) ORDER 1981
S.I. 1981 No. 234

1981	S.I. 234
art. 5	s.163(3)

JUDICIAL PENSIONS ACT 1981
c.20

1981	c.20
Sched. 3, para.10	Sched. 2, para. 1(6)

SOCIAL SECURITY (NORTHERN IRELAND) ORDER 1982
N.I. 16

1982	N.I. 16
art. 5(2)	s.142(5)
11(1E)	131
(1F)	166(2)
(3)(a)	122(4)
(7)	143(1)(d)
19(1)	121

1982	N.I. 16
art. 19(2)	s.11(2)
(2A)	12(2)
(3)	12(3)
(4)	122(4)
20	122(1)–(3)
36(1)	165(4), (5), (10)

1982	N.I. 16
art. 36(2)	s.166(4)
37	145(5)
Sched. 4,	
para. 18(3)	Sched. 5, para. 8
Sched. 5	7, 8

SOCIAL SECURITY AND HOUSING BENEFITS ACT 1982
c.24

1982	c.24
s.42(2)	Sched. 5, para. 3
Sched. 4,	
para. 33(3)	Sched. 5, para. 8

SOCIAL SECURITY ADJUDICATIONS (NORTHERN IRELAND) ORDER 1983
N.I. 17

1983	N.I. 17
Sched. 1,	
para. 1	s.36, 37, 39(1)–(4), 41(1)–(3), 49(1)–(4)
2	23(2)
3	Sched. 3, para. 1
4	58(1)
5	38(1), (4), 39(5), 49(1)–(3); Sched. 2, paras. 1(1)–(5), 3, 4, 5, 6

1983	N.I. 17
Sched. 1—cont.	
para. 6	s.48(1)–(5), 49(4)
7	Sched. 2, para. 4
Sched. 2,	
para. 1(1)	43(1), (2)
(3)	43(3)–(6)
2	44
3	45(1)–(9)
4	60
(b)	144(5)

1983	N.I. 17
Sched. 2—cont.	
para. 5	Sched. 3, para. 1
6	58(3)
7(a)	47(1), (2)
(b)	47(3), 48(6), Sched. 2, para. 8
Sched. 3	44

HEALTH AND SOCIAL SECURITY (NORTHERN IRELAND) ORDER 1984
N.I. 8

1984	N.I. 8
art. 10(a)	s.39(1), (2), 41(4), (5)
(b)	38(2), (3), 40
Sched. 2,	
para. 2	143(2)
4	43(1), (2)
5	43(1), (2)
6	44
7	45(1)–(9)
13(1)	122(1)–(3)

FINES AND PENALTIES (NORTHERN IRELAND) ORDER 1984
N.I. 3

1984	N.I. 3
art. 4	s.157, 158
5(2)	108(1)
6(1)	108(1), 157, 158
(3)	108(1), 157, 158

SOCIAL SECURITY (NORTHERN IRELAND) ORDER 1985
N.I. 16

1985	N.I. 16
art. 9(5)	s.129
17	Sched. 1,
	paras. 1, 2
19(1)(d)	143(1)(d)
20	12(2)
Sched. 3,	
para. 1	130
Sched. 5,	
para. 4	142(5), (6)
Sched. 6	8

SOCIAL SECURITY (NORTHERN IRELAND) ORDER 1986
N.I. 18

1986	N.I. 18
art. 3(7A)	s.146(5), (6)
(7B)	146(5), (6)
21(4E)	70(1), (2)
(4F)	70(7), (8)
(4G)	70(7), (8)
(4H)	70(1), (2)
(4J)	70(3)–(6)
(4K)	70(3)–(6)
(4L)	70(3)–(6)
(4M)	70(3)–(6)
25	101
25A	102
25B	103
27	100
(3)	74(6)–(8)
(4)	74(6)–(8)
(5)	76(6)–(8)
28	72
28A	119
28B(1)	9
(2)	9
(3)	9
29(1)	126(1)
(1A)	126(2)
(2)	126(3)–(6)
(3)	126(3)–(6)
(4)	126(3)–(6)
(5)	126(3)–(6)
30(1)	61
(2)	61
(3)	61
(4)	73
(5)	73
(6)	73
(7)	73
(8)	75
31(1)	127(1), (2)
(2)	127(1), (2)
(4)	127(3)
(5)	128
(6)	128
(7)	128
(8)	128
32(1)	120
(2)	120
(3)	120
33(1)	146(1)
(4)	74(4)
(5)	146(2)–(4)
(6)	146(2)–(4)
(7)	146(2)–(4)
(8)	62(1), (2)
(8A)	147(1)–(4)

1986	N.I. 18
art. 33(8B)	s.147(1)–(4)
(8C)	147(1)–(4)
(8D)	147(1)–(4)
(8E)	147(5)
(9)	62(1), (2)
(10)	62(3)
(11)	64(9), (10)
(12)	64(9), (10)
34(1)	10(1)
(5)	74(1)–(3)
(6)	74(1)–(3)
(7)	74(1)–(3)
(8)	76(6)–(8)
(12)	74(5)
(13)	10(2)
35	64(1)–(8)
36	63
52(1)	5(1)
(2)	5(2)
(3)	5(3), (4)
(4)	5(3), (4)
53(3)	18(3), 21(2),
	(3), 23(1),
	58(1), (2), 67
(a)	18(6)
(b)	56(1), (2)
(c)	57(1), (2)
(e)	59(4)
(3A)	18(6), 19(3),
	20(1), 23(1),
	(2), 28(1),
	(5)–(11), (13),
	29, 30(1),
	(6)–(10), 31,
	32(1)–(4),
	33(3)–(10),
	(12), 52(1),
	(2), (4), (5),
	(7), (8), 56(1),
	(2), 57(1), (2),
	58(1), (2),
	59(4)
(c)	53
(4)	57(1), (2)
(5)	111
(6)	18(6), 56(1),
	(2), 57(1), (2),
	58(1), (2),
	59(4)
(7)(a)	18(3)
(b)	19(4), (5)
(c)(i)	20(1)

1986	N.I. 18
art. 53(7)(c)(ii)	s.20(2)
(iii)	20(5)
(d)	21(2)
(8)	23(4)
(9)(a)	28(5), 33(3)
(9)(b)	28(5), 33(3),
	52(5)
(c)	33(5), (10)
(d)	52(4)
(e)	52(7)
(10)	28(1), (5),
	33(3)
54(1)	69(1)
(1A)	69(2)
(2)	69(3)–(10)
(3)	69(3)–(10)
(4)	69(3)–(10)
(5)	69(3)–(10)
(6)	69(3)–(10)
(7)	69(3)–(10)
(7A)	75
(8)	69(3)–(10)
(9)	69(3)–(10)
(10)	69(11)
(10A)	70(7), (8)
(11)	Sched. 6,
	para. 3
55	106, 107
56	106
57(1)	110(1)–(3)
(2)	110(1)–(3)
(3)	110(1)–(3)
(3A)	110(4)
(4)	110(5), (6)
(5)	110(5), (6)
58	109
59(1)	104(1)–(8)
(2)	104(1)–(8)
(3)	104(1)–(8)
(4)	104(1)–(8)
(5)	104(1)–(8)
(6)	104(1)–(8)
(7)	104(1)–(8)
(8)	105
(9)	105
(10)	104(9)
60	116
61	118
62(1)	150(1)–(4)
(2)	150(1)–(4)
(3)	150(1)–(4)
(4)	150(1)–(4)
(5)	150(5)

1986	N.I. 18
art. 62(6)	s.150(6)
63(1)	165(6)
(2)	165(6)
64........	132
65........	135
65A	139
65B	140
66(1)	153
(2)	155(1)
(4)	154, 155(4), (5), 165(11)
78........	156
81(1)	165(3)–(6)
(2)	165(7)
(3)(c)...	166(2)
(4)	166(4)
(5)	165(8)
(6)	165(9)
(7)	165(10)
82(1)(c)...	143(1)(c)(d)
(2)	145(5)
(3)	144(1)–(3)
(4)	144(1)–(3)
(5)	144(1)–(3)
(6)	144(5)
(7)	145(1)
(8)	145(2)–(4)
(9)	148
(10)	148
99(4)	19(6)
Sched. 3,	
para. 14(a)..	43(1), (2)
Sched. 4,	
para. 6	13
7	13
8	124(3)
8A....	124(1), (2)
9	123

1986	N.I. 18
Sched. 5,	
para. 2	s.17(1)
3	18(1), (2), (4)
4	19(1), (2)
5(b)...	20(2)
(c)...	20(3)
(d)...	20(4)
(e)...	20(5)
6	32(1)–(4)
(1)...	21(1)
(2)...	21(3)
(3)...	21(7)–(10)
7	34(1)
8	35
9(a)...	23(1), (3)
(c)...	24(3), 33(5)
(d)...	25(1), 30(8)
11	42
12	44
13	45(1)–(9)
14	56(5)–(7)
15	48(1)–(4)
16(a)..	Sched. 3, para. 3
(b)..	Sched. 3, para. 11
17	165(1), (2)
Pt. II,	
para. (b)(i)	15(1)(g)(i)–(iv)
(ii)	15(1)(g)(i)–(iv)
(iii)	15(1)(g)(i)–(iv)
(iv)	15(1)(g)(i)–(iv)
(v)	15(1)(g)(vi)

1986	N.I. 18
Sched. 5—cont.	
para. (b)(vi)	s.15(1)(g)(v)
(c)	15(1)(h)
Sched. 6,	
para. 4	65
Sched. 7,	
para. 1	Sched. 7, para. 1
3	Sched. 7, para. 1
4	Sched. 7, para. 2
5	Sched. 7, para. 3
6	Sched. 7, para. 5
7	Sched. 7, para. 4
Sched. 9,	
para. 32	66(4)
32(a)..	163(1)
(b)..	1(4)
55	8
56	1(1), (2), (4); Sched. 1, paras. 3,4,5
57	Sched. 1, para. 2
62	137(1)
64	149
73	Sched. 5, para. 5
Sched. 10	6, 8, 21(5), 23(2),42, 45(1)–(9), 108(4), 114(1), (2), 143(1)(a) (b), 155(1)

SOCIAL SECURITY ACT 1986
c.50

1986	c.50
Sched. 9,	
para. 1	s.46(1)–(4)
para. 10(1)(a)	Sched. 2, para. 7
(b)	Sched. 2, para. 7
11(c)..	166(12)
(i)	22(6)
13	Sched. 5, paras. 9, 10
99	Sched. 5, para. 3
106 ...	Sched. 5, para. 5

ADOPTION (N.I.) ORDER 1987
N.I. 22

1987	N.I. 22
Sched. 5	s.125

SOCIAL SECURITY (CONSOLIDATED FUND OF NORTHERN IRELAND SUPPLEMENTS TO, AND ALLOCATION OF, CONTRIBUTIONS) (RE-RATING) ORDER (N.I.) 1987
S.R. 1987 No. 25

1987	S.R. 25
art. 3(2)	s.142(5)

SOCIAL SECURITY (NORTHERN IRELAND) ORDER 1988
N.I. 2

1988	**N.I. 2**
art. 6(2)	s.70(1)–(8)
9.........	14
15........	145(5)
15A(2)....	166(4)
Sched. 1,	
para. 6	42, 58(4)

1988	**N.I. 2**
Sched. 3,	
para. 3	s.146(5), (6)
5	147(1)–(4)
6	62(3), 64(9), (10)
7	10(1)
13	5(2), 18(6), 23(1), 56(1), (2), 57(1), (2), 59(4), 69(11)

1988	**N.I. 2**
Sched. 4,	
para. 11	s.23(1)
19	75
21	75
23(1)..	69(11)
(2)..	70(7), (8)
Sched. 5	5(2), 10(1), 62(1), (2), 64(1)–(8), 69(11), 74(4)

SOCIAL SECURITY (NORTHERN IRELAND) ORDER 1989
N.I. 13

1989	**N.I. 13**
art. 1(2)	Sched. 1, para. 4
(3)	Sched. 1, para. 4
3(2)	142(5)
7(2)	74(6)–(8), 100
(3)	74(6)–(8), 100
12(5)	23(1)
16(1)	126(2)
17........	127(3), 128
19(1)	133
(2)(a)...	135
20........	139
21........	117
22........	116
24(1)	78
(2)	78
(3)	77(1)
(3A)..	77(2)
(4)	77(3)–(5)
(5)	77(3)–(5)
(6)	77(3)–(5)
(8)	77(7)
28........	99
29(1)	145(5)
(2)	144(6)
(3)	143(2)
(b)...	143(1)(e)
30(1)	165(3)–(6)
(2)(h)...	166(2)
(3)	166(4)
(5)	165(9)
Sched. 2	Sched. 4

1989	**N.I. 13**
Sched. 3,	
para. 1(1)...	s.5(2), (3)
(2)...	57(5), (6)
2	19(6)
3(1)...	51, 54
4	Sched. 3, para. 2
5	20(3)
6	21(7)–(10)
7	27
9(2)...	46(5), (6)
10	Sched. 3, para. 10
11(1)..	23(1)
(2)..	23(4)
(3)..	25(1)
(4)..	25(1)
12(1)..	43(1), (2)
(2)..	43(3)–(6)
14(1)..	69(2)
(2)..	69(3)–(10)
15	35
16	166(5)
Sched. 4,	
para. 1(1)...	77(1)
(2)...	77(6)
2	79
3	80
4	81
5	82
6	83
7	84
8	85
9	86
10	87

1989	**N.I. 13**
Sched. 4—*cont.*	
para. 11	s.88
12	89
13	90
14	91
15	92
16	93
17	94
18	95
19	96
20(1)..	104(1)–(8)
(2)..	104(1)–(8)
(3)..	104(1)–(9)
(4)..	104(1)–(8)
(5)..	104(1)–(8)
(6)..	104(1)–(8)
(7)..	104(9)
21	97
23	98
Sched. 7,	
para. 19	11(1)
Sched. 8,	
para. 8	1(1), (2)
(1)...	Sched. 1, paras. 4, 5
9(1)...	165(5)
10	136
11(2)..	150(5), (6)
(3)..	Sched. 5, para. 8
16	119
17	124(1), (2)
Sched. 9	46(1)–(4), 74(6)–(8)

SOCIAL SECURITY ACT 1989
c.24

1989	**c.24**
Sched. 8,	
para. 12(6)..	Sched. 5, para. 8

SOCIAL SECURITY (CONTRIBUTIONS) (RE-RATING) ORDER (N.I.) 1989
S.R. 1989 No. 89

1989	**S.R. 89**
art. 6(2)	s.142(5)

TABLE OF DESTINATIONS

COURTS AND LEGAL SERVICES ACT 1990
C.41

1990		c.41
Sched. 10,		
para. 46	....	s.50(2)

SOCIAL SECURITY (NORTHERN IRELAND) ORDER 1990
N.I. 15

1990	N.I. 15	1990	N.I. 15	1990	N.I. 15
art. 1(3)	Sched. 1, para. 5	art. 18(5)	s.145(5)	Sched. 6—*cont.*	
(4)	Sched. 1, para. 5	(7)(b)..	144(4)	para. 4(3)...	s.21(5)
3(6)	s.1(3)	19(1)	142(4)	5(1)...	67
7(1)	2	(2)	143(5)	(2)...	66(1)–(6)
(4)	1(4)	20(2)	145(5)	(3)...	66(4)
8(1)	1(1), (2); Sched. 1, para. 5	Sched. 1, para. 1(1)...	77(1)	6(1)...	166(3)
(2)	3	(2)...	77(1)	(4)...	166(4)
(3)	25(2)	(3)...	77(1)	(6)...	166(4)
10(1)	102, 103	(4)...	90	(8)...	166(4)
(2)	74(6)–(8), 100	2	89	(11)..	166(4)
12(1)	147(5)	3	94	(12)..	166(7)
(2)	62(3)	4	94	(a)	166(12)
(5)	10(2)	5	98	(13)..	166(8)
18(3)	142(3)	Sched. 5, para. 17(4)..	Sched. 4	(14)..	166(9)
(4)	143(1)(a)(b), (2)	Sched. 6, para. 3(1)...	36	(15)..	166(10)
		(2)...	110(4)	(16)..	166(5)
		4(1)...	20(6), (7)	(17)..	166(7), (9)
		(2)...	21(4)	13	140
				16(2)..	4
				17	117
				Sched. 7	115(2)–(6)

DISABILITY LIVING ALLOWANCE AND DISABILITY WORKING ALLOWANCE ACT 1991
C.21

1991		c.21
Sched. 2,		
para. 10	....Sched. 5,	para. 1

SOCIAL SECURITY (CONTRIBUTIONS) (NORTHERN IRELAND) ORDER 1991
N.I. 22

1991		N.I. 22
art. 4(6)(a)	....	s.114(3)
(b).	...	114(4)
(c).	...	114(6)
5(1)	......	15(1)(c)
(2)	......	57(4)
6(a)	......	142(5)

DISABILITY LIVING ALLOWANCE AND DISABILITY WORKING ALLOWANCE (NORTHERN IRELAND) ORDER
1991 N.I. 17

1991	N.I. 17	1991	N.I. 17	1991	N.I. 17
art. 5(1)	s.152	Sched. 1—*cont.*		Sched. 1—*cont.*	
(2)	152	para. 5	s.28(1)–(13), 29, 30(1)–(10), 31	para. 15	s.49(1)–(3)
(3)	152	6	32(1)–(4)	16	40, 41(1)–(7), 49(4); Sched. 2, paras. 2, 4, 5, 6, 8
(4)	152	7(1)...	34(1)		
(5)	152	(2)...	34(2)		
(6)	152	8(a)...	23(1)		
9(1)	9	(b)...	23(2)	17	Sched. 3, para. 10
13(2)	165(3), (4), (6)	9	33(1)–(12)	18	143(1)(a)(b), (2)
Sched. 1,		10	Sched. 3, para. 1	19	1(3)
para. 2	18(1), (2)	11	51	Sched. 2,	
3(2)...	19(1), (2)	12	54	para. 4	66(4)
4(a)...	20(1)	13	52(1)–(8), 53	8(b)...	Sched. 5, para. 1
(b)...	20(2)				
(c)...	20(5)				

TABLE OF DESTINATIONS

1991	N.I. 17
Sched. 2—*cont.*	
para. 9	Sched. 2, para. 9
11	18(6), 67
(a)	18(3)
(b)	Sched. 7, para. 2
13	Sched. 3, para. 11; Sched. 4
Sched. 3,	
para. 2	5(2)

1991	N.I. 17
Sched. 3—*cont.*	
para. 3(1)	18(6), 19(1)–(3), 20(1), 23(1), 28(1), (5)–(13), 29, 30(1), (6)–(10), 31, 32(1)–(4), 33(3)–(10), (12), 52(1), (2), (4), (5), (7), (8), 53, 56(1), (2), 57(1), (2), 58(1), (2), 59, 67

1991	N.I. 17
Sched. 3—*cont.*	
para. 3(2)	19(3)
(3)	19(3), 28(1), (5), 33(3), (5), (10), 52(4), (7)
4	69(11)
5	154, 155(4), 165(11)
6	155(5)
7	145(1)
Sched. 4	51, 54

SOCIAL SECURITY (CONTRIBUTIONS) (RE-RATING) (NO. 2) ORDER (NORTHERN IRELAND) 1991
S.R. 1991 No. 542

1991	S.R. 542
Sched. 2	s.142(1), (2)

REDUNDANCY FUND (ABOLITION) (NORTHERN IRELAND) ORDER 1991
N.I. 2

1991	N.I. 2
Sched. 2	s.142(5)

STATUTORY SICK PAY (NORTHERN IRELAND) ORDER 1991
N.I. 9

1991	N.I. 9
art. 3(5)	s.77(1), (2)
4(1)	131, 166(2)
(3)	15(1)(g)(v)
5(1)(b)	149

INDEX

References are to section numbers

ADJUDICATING MEDICAL PRACTITIONERS,
  appointment, 47
  references to, 44
  review of decisions, 45
ADJUDICATION, 15–68
  adjudication officers, by, 18–19
    claims to be submitted, 18
    decisions of, 19
    questions to be submitted, 18
  appeals,
    Commissioner, from, 22
    Commissioner, to, 21
    on question of law, 16
    questions first arising on, 34
    review of decisions on, 33
    reviews, following, 31
    social security appeal tribunal, from, 21
    social security appeal tribunal, to, 20
  Christmas bonus, 65
  compensation payments, *see also* COMPEN-
    SATION PAYMENTS, 90–96
  disablement benefit, *see* DISABLEMENT
    BENEFIT
  erroneous decisions,
    correction of errors, 68
    questions on review following, 67
    restrictions on entitlement following, 66
  experts, references to, 51
  finality of decisions, 58
  housing benefit, 61
  industrial diseases, 60
  industrial injury, 42
  procedure, 57
  questions for department, 15
  regulations, 56, 59
  review of decisions, 17, 23
    adjudication officers, of, 28
    appeal, on, 33
    appeals following, 26, 31
    awards, effect of, 30
    claimant appeals, after, 27
    procedure for, 24, 29
    "relevant changes", 25
  social fund, 64
  special questions, 35
ADJUDICATION OFFICERS,
  appointment, 36
  Chief Adjudication Officer, 37
ADJUSTMENT OF BENEFITS, *see* OVERPAYMENTS
ALTERATION OF BENEFITS,
  annual up-rating, 132
    rectification of mistakes in, 133
  child benefit, 134, 137
  effect of, 135
  income support, 139
    attainment of particular age, 140

ALTERATION OF CONTRIBUTIONS,
  orders, 129, 131
  revaluation of earnings factors, 130
APPEALS, *see* ADJUDICATION
ASSESSORS, 54
ATTENDANCE ALLOWANCE,
  claims for another, 1(3)
  medical reports, 52
  reviews of decisions, 28, 30

BENEFIT,
  definition, 1(4)
  inalienability of certain, 163

CERTIFICATES OF TOTAL BENEFIT,
  appeals against, 94
  recovery in consequence of, 95
  applications for, 91
  content and effect of, 80
  default, recovery of payment where, 96
  late delivery, effect of, 92
  reviews of, 93
CHILD BENEFIT,
  adjustment of, 76
  alteration of rates, 134, 137
  claims, 11
  excess benefit, treatment of, 138
CHRISTMAS BONUS, 65
CLAIMS, 1–14
  for another, 1(3)
  date of making, 1(5)
  entitlement dependent on, 1
  form of, 1(1), 5
  housing benefit, 128
  initial, 7
  necessity of, 1
  old cases, 1(6), Sched. 1
  regulations, 5
  repeat, 7
  retrospective provisions, 2
COMMENCEMENT, 168(4)
COMMISSIONERS, *see* SOCIAL SECURITY
  COMMISSIONERS
COMPENSATION PAYMENTS,
  adjudication, 90–96
  administration, 90–96
  appeals,
    recovery in consequence of, 95
  certificates of total benefit, *see* CERTIFI-
    CATES OF TOTAL BENEFIT
  collaboration between compensators, 83
  Crown, by, 99

COMPENSATION PAYMENTS—*cont.*
  death, for, 77(3)(c), 88
  exemption for small payments, 81
  foreign compensators, 97
  information, provision of, 90
  insolvency of recipient, 85
  interest on damages, 98
  legal aid charges, subject to, 86
  multiple, 82
  overpaid benefits, and, 87
  payments into court, 89
  recovery from, 75–6
  structured settlements, 84
  time for payment, 79
COMPUTATION OF BENEFITS, 135–40
  alteration of rates, effect of, 135
    child benefit, 137–8
    income support, 139–40
  Category A retirement pension, 136
CONSULTATION WITH ADVISORY BODIES,
  Disability Living Allowance Advisory
    Board, 152
  Social Security Advisory Committee,
    149–51
CONTRIBUTIONS,
  alteration of, 129–31
  unpaid, *see* ENFORCEMENT

DEATHS,
  compensation for, 77(3)(c), 88
  difficult to establish, 3
  notification of, 118
DISABILITY APPEAL TRIBUNALS,
  appeals from, 32
  chairmen, 49
  constitution, 41
  medical reports, 53
  panels, appointment of, 40
DISABILITY LIVING ALLOWANCE,
  claims for another, 1(3)
  medical reports, 52
  reviews of decisions, 28, 30
DISABILITY LIVING ALLOWANCE ADVISORY
  BOARD, 152
DISABILITY WORKING ALLOWANCE,
  claims, 9
  medical reports, 52
  reviews of decisions, 28, 30
DISABLEMENT BENEFIT,
  adjudication, 42
  date of claim, 1(2)(b)
  medical appeals and references, 44
    appeals from, 46
    review of, 45
  questions, 43
DUTY TO MAINTAIN,
  failure to maintain, offence of, 100
  recovery of income support,
    from liable person, 101
    from other parent, 102

EMERGENCY PAYMENTS, 14

EMPLOYEES IN ADMINISTRATION OR ADJUDICA-
  TION, Sched. 4
EMPLOYERS,
  duties,
    statutory maternity benefit, 124
    statutory sick pay, 122
  small, 131
ENFORCEMENT, 104–9
  breach of regulations, 107
  false representations, 106
  inspectors,
    appointment and powers, 104
    delay or obstruction of, 105
  legal proceedings, 110
    questions arising in, 111
  offences relating to contributions, 108
  unpaid contributions, 112
    evidential matters, 115
    previous offences, 114
    recovery of on prosecution, 113
EXPERTS, REFERENCES TO, 51
EXTENT, 168(5)–(6)

FAILURE TO MAINTAIN,
  offence of, *see also* DUTY TO MAINTAIN, 100
FALSE REPRESENTATIONS, 106
FINANCE,
  adjustments between National Insurance
    Fund and Consolidated Fund, 145
  contributions, destination of, 142
  general arrangements, 143
  housing benefit, 127
  National Insurance Fund, 141–2
  repayments, destination of, 144
  social fund, 146–8
FOREIGN SOCIAL SECURITY SYSTEMS,
  reciprocity with, 155

GREAT BRITAIN'S SOCIAL SECURITY SYSTEM,
  co-ordination with, 153
  payments, 75
  reciprocity with, 154

HOUSING BENEFIT,
  adjudication, 61
  arrangements for, 126
  claims, 128
  finance, 127
  information as to, 120
  overpayment, 73

ILLEGAL POSSESSION OF DOCUMENTS, 158
IMPERSONATION OF OFFICERS, 157
INALIENABILITY OF CERTAIN BENEFITS, 163
INCOME SUPPORT,
  adjustment of benefits, 72
  alteration of benefits, 139
    attainment of particular age, 140
  duty to maintain, and, *see* DUTY TO
    MAINTAIN

INCOME SUPPORT—*cont.*
  maintenance order against liable person, 103
  personal allowance element, 102(2)
  personal representatives,
    duty to provide information, 119
  recovery of, 70
  transfer of orders, 102
INDUSTRIAL ACCIDENTS,
  notification of, 6
  research into, 159
INDUSTRIAL DISEASES, 60, 160
INDUSTRIAL INJURIES BENEFIT,
  medical examinations, 7
  notification of accidents, 6
  obligations of claimants, 8
  treatment, 7
  See also DISABLEMENT BENEFIT
INFORMATION,
  benefits, as to, 122
  compensation payments, for, 90
  deaths, as to, 118
  estates of deceased persons, as to, 119
  housing benefit, as to, 120
  Inland Revenue, disclosure by, 116
  maintenance proceedings, as to, 125
  personal representatives' duty as to, 119
  statutory sick pay, as to, 121
  statutory maternity benefit, as to, 123
  unauthorised disclosure, 117, Sched. 4
INLAND REVENUE,
  disclosure of information by, 116
INSPECTORS,
  appointment and powers, 104
  delay or obstruction of, 104
  social fund, 63
INTERPRETATION, 167

JOINT AUTHORITY, 153

LEGAL AID CHARGES,
  compensation payments subject to, 86

MAINTAIN, *see* DUTY TO MAINTAIN
MATERNITY BENEFIT, STATUTORY,
  duties of women, 13
  employers' duties, 124
  information as to, 123
MEDICAL APPEAL TRIBUNALS,
  appeals from, 46
  chairmen, 49
  constitution, 48
  references to, 44
  review of decisions, 45
MEDICAL PRACTITIONERS, *see* ADJUDICATING
  MEDICAL PRACTITIONERS

NATIONAL INSURANCE FUND, 141–8

OFFENCES,
  contributions, relating to, 108–9, 113–15
  failure to maintain, 100
  illegal possession of documents, 158
  impersonation of officers, 157
  unauthorised disclosure, 117
OLD CASES PAYMENTS ADMINISTRATION, 1(6),
  Sched. 6
OVERPAYMENTS,
  adjustment of benefits, 71–2
  child benefit, 76
  compensation payments, and, 87
  general, 69
  Great Britain payments, 75
  housing benefit, 73
  income support, recovery of, 70
  overlapping benefits, 71
  social fund awards, recovery of, 74

PAYMENTS,
  regulations, 5
PAYMENTS INTO COURT, 89
PNEUMOCONIOSIS,
  control of, 160

RECIPROCITY OF SYSTEMS,
  countries outside UK, 155
  Great Britain, 154
RECOVERY,
  from compensation payments, 75
  from damages, 78
REDUCED EARNINGS ALLOWANCE,
  date of claim, 1(2)(b)
REGULATIONS AND ORDERS,
  claims and benefits, 5
  control of, 166
  general, 165
RETIREMENT PENSION, CATEGORY A,
  computation, 136
RETROSPECTIVE PROVISIONS, 2
REVIEWS, *see* ADJUDICATION

SHORT TITLE, 168(1)
SICK PAY, STATUTORY,
  employees' duties, 12
  employers' duties, 122
  information as to, 121
  small employers' contributions, 131
SOCIAL FUND,
  adjustments with other funds, 148
  allocations from, 147
  claims, 10
  Commissioner, 63
  finances of, 146
  inspectors, 63
  officers, 62
    reviews by, 64
  recovery of awards, 74
SOCIAL SECURITY ADVISORY COMMITTEE,
  consultation not required, where, 150
  functions of, 149
  reports and recommendations, 151

SOCIAL SECURITY APPEAL TRIBUNALS,
    appeals from, to Commissioner, 21, 32
    appeals to, 20
    chairmen, 49
    constitution, 39
    panels, appointment to, 38
SOCIAL SECURITY COMMISSIONERS,
    appeals from, on point of law, 22
    appeals to, 21, 32
    appointment, 50
    supplementary provisions, Sched. 2
    Tribunals of 2 or 3, 55
STAMP DUTY EXEMPTION, 164
STRUCTURED SETTLEMENTS, see also COMPENSA-
    TION PAYMENTS, 84
SUBORDINATE LEGISLATION, 165–6
SUPPLEMENTARY BENEFIT, 162, Sched. 7

TRAVELLING EXPENSES, 156
TRIBUNALS,
    procedure, Sched. 3
    See also INDIVIDUAL TRIBUNALS

UNPAID CONTRIBUTIONS, see ENFORCEMENT

WIDOWHOOD BENEFIT,
    date of claim, 1(2)(a)
    death difficult to establish, 3
    late claims, 3
    payments on claims before August 14,
        1990, treatment of, 4
WORKMEN'S COMPENSATION,
    administration, 161

SOCIAL SECURITY (CONSEQUENTIAL PROVISIONS) (NORTHERN IRELAND) ACT 1992

(1992 c. 9)

ARRANGEMENT OF SECTIONS

SECT.
1. Meaning of "the consolidating Acts".
2. Continuity of the law.
3. Repeals.
4. Consequential amendments.
5. Transitional provisions and savings.
6. Transitory modifications.
7. Short title, commencement and extent.

SCHEDULES:
Schedule 1—Repeals.
Schedule 2—Consequential amendments.
Schedule 3—Transitional provisions and savings (including some transitional provisions retained from previous Acts and Orders).
Part I—General and miscellaneous.
Part II—Specific transitional provisions and savings (including some derived from previous Acts and Orders).
Schedule 4—Transitory Modifications.
Part I—Provisions not yet in force.
Part II—Transition from mobility allowance to disability living allowance.

An Act to make provision for repeals, consequential amendments, transitional and transitory matters and savings in connection with the consolidation of enactments in the Social Security Contributions and Benefits (Northern Ireland) Act 1992 and the Social Security Administration (Northern Ireland) Act 1992 with corrections and minor improvements under the Consolidation of Enactments (Procedure) Act 1949.

[13th February 1992]

PARLIAMENTARY DEBATES
Hansard, H.L. Vol. 533, col. 864; Vol. 534, col. 1497; Vol. 535, col. 348.

INTRODUCTION
This Act provides for the consolidation of the law relating to social security for Northern Ireland containing all repeals and consequential amendments in order for the main Acts (the Social Security Contributions and Benefits (Northern Ireland) Act 1992 and the Social Security Administration (Northern Ireland) Act 1992) to be effectively utilised.

Meaning of "the consolidating Acts"

1. In this Act—
"the consolidating Acts" means the Social Security Contributions and Benefits (Northern Ireland) Act 1992 ("the Contributions and Benefits Act"), the Social Security Administration (Northern Ireland) Act 1992 ("the Administration Act") and, so far as it reproduces the effect of the repealed enactments, this Act; and
"the repealed enactments" means the enactments repealed by this Act.

Continuity of the law

2.—(1) The substitution of the consolidating Acts for the repealed enactments does not affect the continuity of the law.

(2) Anything done or having effect as if done under or for the purposes of a provision of the repealed enactments has effect, if it could have been done

under or for the purposes of the corresponding provision of the consolidating Acts, as if done under or for the purposes of that provision.

(3) Any reference, whether express or implied, in the consolidating Acts or any other enactment, instrument or document to a provision of the consolidating Acts shall, so far as the context permits, be construed as including, in relation to the times, circumstances and purposes in relation to which the corresponding provision of the repealed enactments has effect, a reference to that corresponding provision.

(4) Any reference, whether express or implied, in any enactment, instrument or document to a provision of the repealed enactments shall be construed, so far as is required for continuing its effect, as including a reference to the corresponding provision of the consolidating Acts.

Repeals

3.—(1) The enactments mentioned in Schedule 1 to this Act are repealed to the extent specified in the third column of that Schedule (being repeals consequential on the consolidating Acts).

(2) The repeals have effect subject to any relevant savings in Schedule 3 to this Act.

Consequential amendments

4. The enactments mentioned in Schedule 2 to this Act shall have effect with the amendments there specified (being amendments consequential on the consolidating Acts).

Transitional provisions and savings

5.—(1) The transitional provisions and savings in Schedule 3 to this Act shall have effect.

(2) Nothing in that Schedule affects the general operation of section 16 of the Interpretation Act 1978 (general savings implied on repeal) or of the previous provisions of this Act.

Transitory modifications

6. The transitory modifications in Schedule 4 to this Act shall have effect.

Short title, commencement and extent

7.—(1) This Act may be cited as the Social Security (Consequential Provisions) (Northern Ireland) Act 1992.

(2) This Act shall come into force on 1st July 1992, immediately after the Social Security (Consequential Provisions) Act 1992.

(3) Except as provided by subsections (4) to (6) below, this Act extends to Northern Ireland only.

(4) Section 2 above and this section extend to the whole of the United Kingdom.

(5) Where any enactment repealed or amended by this Act extends to any part of the United Kingdom, the repeal or amendment extends to that part.

(6) Section 4 above extends to the Isle of Man so far as it relates to paragraph 21 of Schedule 2 to this Act.

SCHEDULES

SCHEDULE 1

REPEALS

Chapter or Number	Short title	Extent of repeal
1974 c. 4 (N.I.).	The National Insurance Measure (Northern Ireland) 1974.	Section 5(1), (3) and (4).
1975 c. 15.	The Social Security (Northern Ireland) Act 1975.	The whole Act, except sections 97(4) and 158 and paragraphs 5(2), 6, 7 and 7A of Schedule 10.
1975 c. 17.	The Industrial Injuries and Diseases (Northern Ireland Old Cases) Act 1975.	The whole Act.
1975 c. 18.	The Social Security (Consequential Provisions) Act 1975.	In Schedule 2, paragraphs 73, 74, 77, 80, 87, 108, 110 and 112. In Schedule 3, in paragraph 31 the words "17, 18, 20".
1975 c. 25.	The Northern Ireland Assembly Disqualification Act 1975.	In Part II of Schedule 1 the entry beginning "A Medical Board".
1975 c. 60.	The Social Security Pensions Act 1975.	In Schedule 4, paragraphs 68 to 70 and 71(a) and (b).
S.I. 1975/1503 (N.I. 15).	The Social Security Pensions (Northern Ireland) Order 1975.	In Article 2(3), in sub-paragraph (a) the words "Part II and" and in sub-paragraph (b) the words "(except Article 24)". Part II. Articles 8 to 12. Articles 14 to 18A. Articles 20 to 23. Articles 26 and 27. Article 52A(13). Article 70(1)(a). In Article 70A, the words "8(3)," and "of, and paragraphs 2(3) and 4A of Schedule 1". Article 74(3). Schedule 1. In Schedule 5, paragraphs 17 to 28, 33, 36 to 42 and 44.
S.I. 1975/1504 (N.I. 16).	The Child Benefit (Northern Ireland) Order 1975.	The whole Order.
S.I. 1976/427 (N.I. 9).	The Social Security and Family Allowances (Northern Ireland) Order 1976.	The whole Order.
S.I. 1976/1043 (N.I. 16).	The Industrial Relations (Northern Ireland) Order 1976.	Article 72(3).
1977 c. 5.	The Social Security (Miscellaneous Provisions) Act 1977.	Section 20(3) and (4).
S.I. 1977/610 (N.I. 11).	The Social Security (Miscellaneous Provisions) (Northern Ireland) Order 1977.	Article 1(5). In Article 2(2) the definitions of "the 1966 Act", "the Old Cases Act" and "the principal Act". Article 2(3). Article 3.

Chapter or Number	Short title	Extent of repeal
		Article 4(1).
		Articles 5 to 7.
		Articles 9 and 10.
		Articles 13 and 14.
		Article 16.
		Article 18(1) to (5), (16), (17) and (25).
		In Article 19(3), the words from the beginning to "principal Act".
S.I. 1977/2156 (N.I. 27).	The Supplementary Benefits (Northern Ireland) Order 1977.	Articles 28 and 29. In Schedule 6, paragraph 19.
1978 c. 23.	The Judicature (Northern Ireland) Act 1978.	In Schedule 5, in Part II, the amendment to the Social Security (Northern Ireland) Act 1975.
1979 c. 18.	The Social Security Act 1979.	Section 9(2).
S.I. 1979/396 (N.I. 5).	The Social Security (Northern Ireland) Order 1979.	Article 1(3) and (5). In Article 2(2) the definitions of "the principal Act" and "the Order of 1977". Article 3. Articles 5 and 6. Articles 11 to 13. Article 15. Schedule 1. In Schedule 3, paragraphs 3 to 7, 9 to 11, in paragraph 15 the words "8(3) and" and paragraphs 16, 22, 23 and 28 to 30.
S.I. 1979/1573 (N.I. 12).	The Statutory Rules (Northern Ireland) Order 1979.	In Schedule 4, paragraphs 16 and 17.
1980 c. 30.	The Social Security Act 1980.	Section 9(3) and (4). Section 10. Sections 13 and 14. In Schedule 3, Part II.
S.I. 1980/870 (N.I. 8).	The Social Security (Northern Ireland) Order 1980.	In Article 2(2) the definitions of "the principal Act" and "the Supplementary Benefits Commission". Article 3. In Article 4, paragraphs (1) and (10). Article 5(2), (5), (6) and (7). Article 6(1). Article 7(2) to (4). Articles 9 and 10. Articles 12 to 14. Article 15(2). Schedule 1. In Schedule 2, Part II. In Schedule 3, paragraph 8.
S.I. 1980/1087 (N.I. 13).	The Social Security (No. 2) (Northern Ireland) Order 1980.	The whole Order.
S.I. 1981/230 (N.I. 9).	The Social Security (Contributions) (Northern Ireland) Order 1981.	The whole Order.
S.I. 1981/1118 (N.I. 25).	The Social Security (Northern Ireland) Order 1981.	The whole Order.

Chapter or Number	Short title	Extent of repeal
S.I. 1981/1675 (N.I. 26).	The Magistrates' Courts (Northern Ireland) Order 1981.	In Schedule 6, paragraphs 34, 35 and 135.
S.I. 1982/158 (N.I. 4).	The Social Security (Contributions) (Northern Ireland) Order 1982.	The whole Order.
S.I. 1982/1082 (N.I. 14).	The Forfeiture (Northern Ireland) Order 1982.	In Article 6(5), the entry relating to the Child Benefit (Northern Ireland) Order 1975.
S.I. 1982/1084 (N.I. 16).	The Social Security (Northern Ireland) Order 1982.	Articles 3 to 9. Article 11. Articles 19 and 20. Articles 24, 25 and 25A. Articles 28 to 30. Article 32(1) to (4). Article 35. In Article 36(2) the words "those to which section 156(1) of the principal Act applies and". Schedule 1. In Schedule 2, paragraphs 1 to 4. In Schedule 4, paragraphs 3 to 6, 8, 12, 17, 18, 19 and 21.
S.I. 1983/1524 (N.I. 17).	The Social Security Adjudications (Northern Ireland) Order 1983.	The whole Order, except Articles 1, 2, 3(3)(a) and 4(3)(a).
S.I. 1984/1158 (N.I. 8).	The Health and Social Security (Northern Ireland) Order 1984.	Articles 5 to 8. Articles 10 to 12. Schedules 2 and 3. In Schedule 5, paragraphs 1, 2, 4 and 7 to 9.
S.I. 1985/1209 (N.I. 16).	The Social Security (Northern Ireland) Order 1985.	Articles 9 to 15. Article 18. Article 20. Article 23. In Schedule 3, paragraph 1. In Schedule 4, paragraphs 2 and 4 to 7. In Schedule 5, paragraphs 3 to 8 and 31.
1986 c. 50.	The Social Security Act 1986.	In Schedule 9, paragraphs 1, 3(1)(c) and (2)(a) to (g) and (j), 11 and 12.
S.I. 1986/1888 (N.I. 18).	The Social Security (Northern Ireland) Order 1986.	In Article 2(2), the definition of "applicable amount", paragraphs (c) and (d) of the definition of "the benefit Acts", the definitions of "dwelling", "housing benefit scheme", "income-related benefit", "long-term benefit", "primary Class 1 contributions", "secondary Class 1 contributions", "qualifying benefit", "rate rebate", "rent rebate", "rent allowance", "rates", "trade dispute", "war disablement pension" and "war widow's pension". Articles 19 to 25B. Articles 27 to 37. Article 38(1). Article 39. Articles 41 to 52. Article 53(3) to (10). Article 54. Article 56.

Chapter or Number	Short title	Extent of repeal
		In Article 57, in paragraph (1) the words from "or the Department" to "Executive", in paragraph (2)(a), the words "other than an offence relating to housing benefit", paragraph (2)(b) and the word "and" immediately preceding it, in paragraph (3)(a) the words "or of the Department of the Environment", paragraph (3)(b) and the word "and" immediately preceding it and paragraph (3A). Article 59. Articles 62 to 70. Article 71(1). Articles 74 and 75. Article 79(3) and (4). In Article 80(1), the words "and VI". Article 81(2). Article 81(5) and (6). In Article 82, paragraph (1)(c) and (d), paragraph (2), in paragraph (3) the words "and (5)", paragraph (5), in paragraph (6) the words from "and sums" to the end and paragraphs (7) to (10). Schedule 3, except paragraph 17. Schedule 4. In Schedule 5, paragraphs 1 to 17 and in Part II, paragraphs (b) and (c). Schedules 6 and 7. In Schedule 8, paragraphs 1 to 5. In Schedule 9, paragraphs 1, 27(b), 28 to 30, 32, 36(2), 37 to 46, 49 to 51, 53 to 57, 59, 60, 62, 64, 65, 67 to 74 and 76(a).
S.I. 1987/464 (N.I. 8).	The Social Fund (Maternity and Funeral Expenses) (Northern Ireland) Order 1987.	The whole Order.
1988 c. 1.	The Income and Corporation Taxes Act 1988.	In Schedule 29, paragraph 14 and in paragraph 32, the entries relating to the Social Security (Northern Ireland) Act 1975 and the Social Security (Northern Ireland) Order 1986.
1988 c. 39.	The Finance Act 1988.	In Schedule 3, paragraph 31.
S.I. 1988/594 (N.I. 2).	The Social Security (Northern Ireland) Order 1988.	In Article 1(4) the words from "Article 3" to "that Order". Articles 3 to 9. Articles 11 and 12. In Article 15A(2) the words "those to which section 156(1) of the principal Act applies and". Article 16(1). Schedule 1. In Schedule 2, paragraph 1(1). Schedules 3 and 4.
S.I. 1988/1087 (N.I. 10).	The Employment and Training (Amendment) (Northern Ireland) Order 1988.	Articles 5 and 6.

Chapter or Number	Short title	Extent of repeal
S.I. 1989/1342 (N.I. 13).	The Social Security (Northern Ireland) Order 1989.	In Article 2(2), the definitions of "the Old Cases Act" and "the 1982 Order". Articles 3 to 5. Article 6(1) to (4). Article 7. Article 8(1). Article 9(1) to (5). Articles 11 to 21. Article 23. Article 24(1) to (6) and (8). Article 28. In Article 29(1) the words "3 to 6" and "11 to 14 and 24". Article 29(2) and (3). In Article 30, paragraph (2), in paragraph (3) the words from "those to" to "applies and" and paragraph (5). In Schedule 1, paragraphs 1 to 10. Schedules 2 and 3. In Schedule 4, paragraphs 1 to 21 and 23. Schedule 7, except paragraph 18. In Schedule 8, paragraphs 1 to 8, 9(1), 10, 11 and 13 to 18.
1990 c. 1.	The Capital Allowances Act 1990.	In Schedule 1, paragraph 2.
1990 c. 27.	The Social Security Act 1990.	Section 17(8) and (9). In Schedule 1, paragraph 5(4).
1990 c. 37.	The Human Fertilisation and Embryology Act 1990.	In Schedule 4, paragraph 3.
S.I. 1990/1511 (N.I. 15).	The Social Security (Northern Ireland) Order 1990.	In Article 2(2), the definitions of "the 1982 Order", "the 1986 Order", "the 1989 Order", and "the Old Cases Act". Articles 3 to 7. Article 8(1) to (3). Articles 10 to 12. Articles 18 and 19. In Schedule 1, paragraphs 1 to 5. Schedule 5. In Schedule 6, paragraphs 1, 2(1) and (2), 3 to 5, 6(1) to (5), (7), (8), (10), (16) and in (17) the words from "section 5" to "that section, and" and paragraphs 7 to 15, 16(2), 17 and 19.
S.I. 1991/194 (N.I. 1).	The Health and Personal Social Services (Northern Ireland) Order 1991.	In Part II of Schedule 5, the amendments to the Social Security (Northern Ireland) Order 1982 and the Social Security (Northern Ireland) Order 1986.
S.I. 1991/765 (N.I. 9).	The Statutory Sick Pay (Northern Ireland) Order 1991.	Articles 3 and 4. Article 5(1)(a) and (b) and (3) to (5).
S.I. 1991/1712 (N.I. 17).	The Disability Living Allowance and Disability Working Allowance (Northern Ireland) Order 1991.	Article 3. Article 4(1). Article 5. Article 6(1). Articles 7 and 8. Article 9(1). Articles 10 and 11. Articles 13 and 14. Schedule 1. In Schedule 2, paragraphs 2 to 4, 6 to 9 and 11 to 13. In Schedule 3, Part I.

Chapter or Number	Short title	Extent of repeal
S.I. 1991/2294 (N.I. 22).	The Social Security (Contributions) (Northern Ireland) Order 1991.	The whole Order.
1992 c. 6.	The Social Security (Consequential Provisions) Act 1992.	In Schedule 2, paragraphs 12 to 14.

Section 4   SCHEDULE 2

CONSEQUENTIAL AMENDMENTS

Law Reform (Miscellaneous Provisions) Act (Northern Ireland) 1948 (c. 23 (N.I.))

1. In section 3 of the Law Reform (Miscellaneous Provisions) Act (Northern Ireland) 1948—
(a) in subsection (1)(a), for the words "Article 24 of the Social Security (Northern Ireland) Order 1989" there shall be substituted the words "section 77 of the Social Security Administration (Northern Ireland) Act 1992"; and
(b) in subsection (1A), for the words "paragraph 4(1) of Schedule 4 to the Social Security (Northern Ireland) Order 1989" there shall be substituted the words "section 81(1) of the Social Security Administration (Northern Ireland) Act 1992".

Employment and Training Act (Northern Ireland) 1950 (c. 29 (N.I.))

2.—(1) In section 5(3) of the Employment and Training Act (Northern Ireland) 1950 for the words "paragraph 1 of Schedule 3 to the Social Security (Northern Ireland) Act 1975" there shall be substituted the words "paragraph 1 or 2 of Schedule 3 to the Social Security Contributions and Benefits (Northern Ireland) Act 1992".

(2) In section 5(4) of that Act for the words "the Social Security (Northern Ireland) Act 1975" there shall be substituted the words "the Social Security Contributions and Benefits (Northern Ireland) Act 1992".

Judicial Pensions Act (Northern Ireland) 1951 (c. 20 (N.I.))

3.—(1) In sections 3, 16 and 20 of the Judicial Pensions Act (Northern Ireland) 1951 for the words "National Insurance" there shall be substituted the words "Social Security".

(2) In section 22(1) of that Act for the definition of "National Insurance Commissioner" there shall be substituted the following definition—
" "Social Security Commissioner" means a Social Security Commissioner appointed under section 50(1) of the Social Security Administration (Northern Ireland) Act 1992;".

Registration of Births, Deaths and Marriages (Fees, etc.) Act (Northern Ireland) 1955 (c. 29 (N.I.))

4. In the Second Schedule to the Registration of Births, Deaths and Marriages (Fees, etc.) Act (Northern Ireland) 1955 for the entry relating to the Child Benefit (Northern Ireland) Order 1975 there shall be substituted the following entries—
"The Social Security Contributions and Benefits (Northern Ireland) Act 1992.
The Social Security Administration (Northern Ireland) Act 1992.".

Contracts of Employment and Redundancy Payments Act (Northern Ireland) 1965 (c. 19 (N.I.))

5.—(1) In section 27(4B) and (6) of the Contracts of Employment and Redundancy Payments Act (Northern Ireland) 1965 after "1975" there shall be inserted the words "or the Social Security Contributions and Benefits (Northern Ireland) Act 1992".

(2) In section 55(1) of that Act for the words "the Social Security (Northern Ireland) Act 1975" there shall be substituted the words "the Social Security Contributions and Benefits (Northern Ireland) Act 1992".

Maintenance and Affiliation Orders Act (Northern Ireland) 1966 (c. 35 (N.I.))

6. In section 10(2)(e) of the Maintenance and Affiliation Orders Act (Northern Ireland) 1966 for the words "Article 25 of the Social Security (Northern Ireland) Order 1986" there shall be substituted the words "section 101 of the Social Security Administration (Northern Ireland) Act 1992".

Children and Young Persons Act (Northern Ireland) 1968 (c. 34 (N.I.))

7. In section 20(2)(a) of the Children and Young Persons Act (Northern Ireland) 1968 for the words "the Social Security (Northern Ireland) Order 1986" there shall be substituted the words "Part VII of the Social Security Contributions and Benefits (Northern Ireland) Act 1992".

Social Services (Parity) Act (Northern Ireland) 1971 (c. 21 (N.I.))

8.—(1) In section 2 of the Social Services (Parity) Act (Northern Ireland) 1971 for the words "section 129(5) of the Social Security (Northern Ireland) Act 1975" there shall be substituted the words "section 145(5) of the Social Security Administration (Northern Ireland) Act 1992".

(2) In Schedule 1 to that Act for the entries relating to the Social Security Act 1975 and the Industrial Injuries and Diseases (Old Cases) Act 1975 there shall be substituted the following entries—
"The Social Security Contributions and Benefits Act 1992.
The Social Security Administration Act 1992.".

Health and Personal Social Services (Northern Ireland) Order 1972 (S.I. 1972 No. 1265 (N.I. 14))

9. In Article 2(2) of the Health and Personal Social Services (Northern Ireland) Order 1972 for the definition of "trade dispute" there shall be substituted the following definition—
" "trade dispute" has the same meaning as in section 27 of the Social Security Contributions and Benefits (Northern Ireland) Act 1992;".

Social Security (Northern Ireland) Act 1975 (c. 15)

10.—(1) In Schedule 10 to the Social Security (Northern Ireland) Act 1975 at the end of paragraph 5 there shall be added the following sub-paragraph—
"(3) This paragraph and paragraphs 6, 7 and 7A shall have effect as if contained in the Social Security Administration (Northern Ireland) Act 1992.".

(2) In paragraph 6(1) of that Schedule for head (a) there shall be substituted the following head—
"(a) if he retires pursuant to paragraph 1 of Schedule 2 to the Social Security Administration (Northern Ireland) Act 1992;".

Social Security (Consequential Provisions) Act 1975 (c. 18)

11. In section 2(3)(b) of the Social Security (Consequential Provisions) Act 1975 for the words "sections 155 and 156(4) to (6) of the Social Security (Northern Ireland) Act 1975" there shall be substituted the words "sections 165 and 166(4), (6) and (11) of the Social Security Administration (Northern Ireland) Act 1992".

House of Commons Disqualification Act 1975 (c. 24)

12. In Schedule 1 to the House of Commons Disqualification Act 1975—
(a) in Part I, for the entry beginning "Chief or other Social Security Commissioner for Northern Ireland" there shall be substituted the following entry—
"Chief or other Social Security Commissioner for Northern Ireland (not including a deputy Commissioner).";
(b) in Part III, in the entry beginning "Adjudicating medical practitioner" for the words "Part III of the Social Security (Northern Ireland) Act 1975" there shall be substituted the words "Part II of the Social Security Administration (Northern Ireland) Act 1992";
(c) in Part III, in the entry beginning "Member of a Medical Appeal Tribunal for Northern Ireland" for the words "paragraph 2(2) of Schedule 12 to the Social Security (Northern Ireland) Act 1975" there shall be substituted the words "section 48(2) of the Social Security Administration (Northern Ireland) Act 1992";
(d) in Part III, for the entry beginning "Member of the panel of chairmen for Social Security Appeal Tribunals for Northern Ireland" there shall be substituted the following entry—
"Member of the panel of chairmen for Social Security Appeal Tribunals, Medical Appeal Tribunals and Disability Appeal Tribunals for Northern Ireland appointed under section 49(1)(c) of the Social Security Administration (Northern Ireland) Act 1992.".

Northern Ireland Assembly Disqualification Act 1975 (c. 25)

13. In Schedule 1 to the Northern Ireland Assembly Disqualification Act 1975—

(a) in Part I, for the entry "Chief or other National Insurance Commissioner for Northern Ireland" there shall be substituted the following entry—

"Chief or other Social Security Commissioner for Northern Ireland (not including a deputy Commissioner)";

(b) in Part II, in the entry beginning "A Medical Appeal Tribunal" for the words "Part III of the Social Security (Northern Ireland) Act 1975" there shall be substituted the words "Part II of the Social Security Administration (Northern Ireland) Act 1992";

(c) in Part II, the entry beginning "A Medical Board" shall cease to have effect;

(d) in Part III, at the appropriate place in alphabetical order, there shall be inserted the following entry—

"Adjudicating medical practitioner or specially qualified adjudicating medical practitioner appointed under or by virtue of Part II of the Social Security Administration (Northern Ireland) Act 1992";

(e) in Part III for the entry beginning "A full-time Chairman of Social Security Appeal Tribunals" there shall be substituted the following entry—

"Full-time Chairman of Social Security Appeal Tribunals, Medical Appeal Tribunals and Disability Appeal Tribunals for Northern Ireland.";

(f) in Part III for the entry beginning "the President of Social Security Appeal Tribunals" there shall be substituted the following entry—

"President of Social Security Appeal Tribunals, Medical Appeal Tribunals and Disability Appeal Tribunals for Northern Ireland.".

Social Security Pensions (Northern Ireland) Order 1975 (S.I. 1975 No. 1503 (N.I. 15))

14.—(1) The Social Security Pensions (Northern Ireland) Order 1975 shall be amended as follows.

(2) In Article 2(2)—

(a) the following definition shall be inserted before the definition of "average salary benefits"—

" "the Administration Act" means the Social Security Administration (Northern Ireland) Act 1992;"; and

(b) the following definition shall be inserted after that definition—

" "the Contributions and Benefits Act" means the Social Security Contributions and Benefits (Northern Ireland) Act 1992;".

(3) In Article 2(3) for the words "Article 31" there shall be substituted the words "Articles 31 to 31C".

(4) In Article 28(1)(a) for the words "the principal Act" there shall be substituted the words "the Contributions and Benefits Act".

(5) In Article 28 after paragraph (1) there shall be inserted the following paragraph—

"(1A) This Part shall also have effect, where an occupational pension scheme so provides or falls to be treated as so providing, for the purpose of making provision in relation—

(a) to invalidity allowance under section 34 of the Contributions and Benefits Act;

(b) to increases of Category A retirement pensions for invalidity under section 47 of that Act; and

(c) to increases of unemployability supplement under paragraph 3 of Schedule 7 to that Act.".

(6) In Article 29(5) for the words "Article 5" there shall be substituted the words "section 19(4) of the Contributions and Benefits Act".

(7) In Article 31(1)(a) for the words "Article 18" there shall be substituted the words "section 41 of the Contributions and Benefits Act".

(8) In Article 31(2) and (2A) for the words "sections 16(2B), 28(7A) and 59(1A) of the principal Act" there shall be substituted the words "Articles 31A, 31B and 31C".

(9) In Article 31(3) after the words "this Article" there shall be inserted the words "and in Articles 31A, 31B and 31C".

(10) After Article 31 there shall be inserted the following Articles—

"*Contracting-out and invalidity allowance*

31A.—(1) Where for any period—

(a) a person is entitled to one or more guaranteed minimum pensions; and

(b) he is also entitled to an invalidity pension under section 33 of the Contributions and Benefits Act; and

(c) the weekly rate of his invalidity pension includes an additional pension such as is mentioned in section 44(3)(b) of that Act, for that period section 34 of that Act shall have effect as if the following subsection were substituted for subsection (5)—

> "(5) In this section "the relevant amount" means an amount equal to the aggregate of—
>> (a) an amount equal to the additional pension; and
>> (b) an amount equal to the weekly rate or aggregate weekly rates of the guaranteed minimum pension or pensions,
>
> reduced by the amount of any reduction in the weekly rate of the invalidity pension made by virtue of Article 31 of the Pensions Order.".

(2) Where for any period—
  (a) a person is entitled to one or more guaranteed minimum pensions; and
  (b) he is also entitled to an invalidity pension under section 33 of the Contributions and Benefits Act; and
  (c) the weekly rate of his invalidity pension does not include an additional pension such as is mentioned in section 44(3)(b) of that Act,

for that period the relevant amount shall be deducted from the appropriate weekly rate of invalidity allowance and he shall be entitled to invalidity allowance only if there is a balance after the deduction and, if there is such a balance, at a weekly rate equal to it.

(3) In paragraph (2) "the relevant amount" means an amount equal to the weekly rate or aggregate weekly rates of the guaranteed minimum pension or pensions reduced by the amount of any reduction in the weekly rate of the invalidity pension made by virtue of Article 31.

(4) Where paragraph (2) applies, section 34(7) of the Contributions and Benefits Act shall have effect as if for the words "subsection (4) above" there were substituted the words "Article 31A(2) of the Pensions Order".

Contracting-out and increases of Category A retirement pension for invalidity

31B.—(1) Where for any period—
  (a) a person is entitled to one or more guaranteed minimum pensions; and
  (b) he is also entitled to a Category A retirement pension under section 44 of the Contributions and Benefits Act; and
  (c) the weekly rate of his pension includes an additional pension such as is mentioned in section 44(3)(b) of that Act,

for that period section 47 of that Act shall have effect as if the following subsection were substituted for subsection (3)—

> "(3) In subsection (2) above "the relevant amount" means an amount equal to the aggregate of—
>> (a) an amount equal to the additional pension; and
>> (b) an amount equal to the weekly rate or aggregate weekly rates of the guaranteed minimum pension or pensions,
>
> reduced by the amount of any reduction in the weekly rate of the Category A retirement pension made by virtue of Article 31 of the Pensions Order.".

(2) Where for any period—
  (a) a person is entitled to one or more guaranteed minimum pensions; and
  (b) he is also entitled to a Category A retirement pension under section 44 of the Contributions and Benefits Act; and
  (c) the weekly rate of his Category A retirement pension does not include an additional pension such as is mentioned in section 44(3)(b) of that Act,

for that period the relevant amount shall be deducted from the amount that would otherwise be the increase under section 47(1) of that Act and the pensioner shall be entitled to an increase under that subsection only if there is a balance remaining after that deduction and, if there is such a balance, of an amount equal to it.

(3) In paragraph (2) "the relevant amount" means an amount equal to the weekly rate or aggregate weekly rates of the guaranteed minimum pension or pensions reduced by the amount of any reduction in the weekly rate of the Category A retirement pension made by virtue of Article 31.

Contracting-out and increases of unemployability supplement

31C.—(1) Where for any period—
  (a) a person is entitled to one or more guaranteed minimum pensions; and
  (b) he is also entitled—
     (i) to an invalidity pension under section 33 of the Contributions and Benefits Act;

(ii) to a Category A retirement pension under section 44 of that Act; or

(iii) to a Category B retirement pension under section 49 of that Act; and

(c) the weekly rate of the pension includes an additional pension such as is mentioned in section 44(3)(b) of that Act,

for that period paragraph 3 of Schedule 7 to that Act shall have effect as if the following sub-paragraph were substituted for sub-paragraph (3)—

"(3) In this paragraph "the relevant amount" means an amount equal to the aggregate of—

(a) an amount equal to the additional pension; and

(b) an amount equal to the weekly rate or aggregate weekly rates of the guaranteed minimum pension or pensions,

reduced by the amount of any reduction in the weekly rate of the pension made by virtue of Article 31 of the Pensions Order.".

(2) Where for any period—

(a) a person is entitled to one or more guaranteed minimum pensions; and

(b) he is also entitled to any of the pensions under the Contributions and Benefits Act mentioned in paragraph (1)(b); and

(c) the weekly rate of the pension does not include an additional pension such as is mentioned in section 43(3)(b) of that Act,

for that period the relevant amount shall be deducted from the amount that would otherwise be the increase under that paragraph and the beneficiary shall be entitled to an increase only if there is a balance after that deduction and, if there is such a balance, only to an amount equal to it.

(3) In paragraph (2) "the relevant amount" means an amount equal to the weekly rate or aggregate weekly rates of the guaranteed minimum pension or pensions.".

(11) In Article 35(1A) for the words "Article 5" there shall be substituted the words "section 19(4) of the Contributions and Benefits Act".

(12) In Article 37(2ZA) for the words "Article 5" there shall be substituted the words "section 19(4) of the Contributions and Benefits Act".

(13) In Article 37(5) and (7) for the words "Article 23" there shall be substituted the words "section 130 of the Administration Act".

(14) In Article 38(6) for the words "section 27(6) of the principal Act" there shall be substituted the words "section 43(1) of the Contributions and Benefits Act".

(15) In Article 39A(2) for the words from "sections" to "Article 31(1)" there shall be substituted the words "Articles 31(1), 31A(1) and (2), 31B(1) and (2) and 31C(1) and (2)" and for the words "subsections and that paragraph" there shall be substituted the word "paragraphs".

(16) In Articles 43C(4A), 46(6)(a) and 47(3)(a) for the words "Article 23" there shall be substituted the words "section 130 of the Administration Act".

(17) In Article 52A(10) for the words "section 4(3) of the principal Act" there shall be substituted the words "section 6(3) of the Contributions and Benefits Act".

(18) In Article 53D(1) for the words "sections 16(2B), 28(7A) and 59(1A) of the principal Act and Article 31(1)" there shall be substituted the words "Articles 31(1), 31A, 31B and 31C".

(19) In Article 69(1) for the words "Article 64 of Social Security (Northern Ireland) Order 1986" there shall be substituted the words "section 132 of the Administration Act".

(20) In Article 70—

(a) in paragraph (1) for the words "section 93(1) of the principal Act" there shall be substituted the words "section 15(1) of the Administration Act";

(b) in paragraph (3) for the words "section 93(1) nor section 98(1) of the principal Act" there shall be substituted the words "section 15(1) nor section 18(1) of the Administration Act".

(21) After Article 70ZA there shall be inserted the following Articles—

"Offences relating to state scheme premiums

70ZB. If a person fails to pay, at or within the time prescribed for the purpose, any state scheme premium which is payable by him, he shall be guilty of an offence and liable on summary conviction to a fine not exceeding level 3 on the standard scale.

Questions arising in proceedings

70ZC.—(1) Where in any proceedings—

(a) for an offence under this Order; or

(b) involving any question as to payment of a state scheme premium, any such question arises as is mentioned in Article 70(1), the decision of the Department shall be conclusive for the purposes of the proceedings.

(2) If—
    (a) a decision of any such question is necessary for the determination of proceedings; and
    (b) the decision of the Department has not been obtained or a question has been raised with a view to a review of the decision obtained,

the question shall be referred to the Department for determination or review in accordance (subject to any necessary modifications) with sections 15 to 17 of the Administration Act.

(3) Paragraph (1) does not apply if—
    (a) an appeal under section 16 of that Act is pending; or
    (b) the time for appealing has not expired; or
    (c) a question has been raised with a view to a review of the Department's decision under section 17 of that Act,

and the court dealing with the case shall adjourn the proceedings until such time as a final decision on the question has been obtained.

Recovery of unpaid state scheme premiums on prosecution

70ZD. Where—
    (a) a person has been convicted of an offence under Article 70ZB of failing to pay a state scheme premium at or within the time prescribed for the purpose; and
    (b) the premium remains unpaid at the date of the conviction,

he shall be liable to pay to the Department a sum equal to the amount which he failed to pay.

Proof of previous offences

70ZE.—(1) Subject to paragraph (2), where a person is convicted of an offence mentioned in Article 70ZD, evidence may be given of any previous failure by him to pay state scheme premiums within the time prescribed for the purpose; and in that Article "the conviction" and "the offence" mean respectively the conviction referred to in this paragraph and the offence of which the person is convicted.

(2) Such evidence may be given only if notice of intention to give it is served with the summons or warrant on which the person appeared before the court which convicted him.

Unpaid premiums—supplementary

70ZF.—(1) Where a person charged with an offence to which Article 70ZD applies is convicted of that offence in his absence under Article 24(2) of the Magistrates' Courts (Northern Ireland) Order 1981, then if—
    (a) it is proved to the satisfaction of the court, on oath or by affidavit or in the manner prescribed by magistrates' courts rules, that notice under Article 70ZE(2) has been duly served specifying the other premiums in respect of which the complainant intends to give evidence; and
    (b) the clerk of petty sessions has received a statement in writing purporting to be made by the accused or by a solicitor acting on his behalf to the effect that if the accused is convicted in his absence of the offence charged he desires to admit failing to pay the other premiums so specified or any of them,

Article 70ZE shall have effect as if the evidence had been given and the failure so admitted had been proved, and the court shall proceed accordingly.

(2) Where—
    (a) a person is convicted of an offence to which Article 70ZD applies; and
    (b) an order is made under the Probation Act (Northern Ireland) 1950 placing the offender on probation or discharging him absolutely or conditionally,

Articles 70ZD and 70ZE and paragraph (1) shall apply as if it were a conviction for all purposes.

(3) Any sum which a person is liable to pay under Articles 70ZD and 70ZE and paragraph (1) shall be recoverable from him as a penalty.

(4) State scheme premiums recovered by the Department under those provisions are to be treated for all purposes as premiums paid to the Department in respect of the person in respect of whom they were originally payable.".

(22) In Article 71 for paragraphs (1) to (3) there shall be substituted the following paragraphs—

"(1) Regulations prescribing actuarial tables for the purposes of Articles 46(7), 46ZA(14), 46A(3) and 47(4) shall be laid before the Assembly after being made and shall take effect on such date as may be specified in the regulations, but shall (without prejudice to the validity of anything done thereunder or to the making of new regulations) cease to have effect upon the expiration of a period of six months from that date unless at some time before the expiration of that period the regulations have been approved by a resolution of the Assembly.

(2) All regulations and orders made by the Department under this Order other than—

    (a) regulations to which paragraph (1) applies; and

    (b) any order which under any provision of this Order is required to be laid before the Assembly after being made,

shall be subject to negative resolution.

(3) Orders made by the appropriate authority under Article 61 shall be subject to negative resolution.".

(23) After Article 71 there shall be inserted the following Articles—

"Consultation with Social Security Advisory Committee about regulations

71A.—(1) Subject to paragraph (2) and to section 150 of the Administration Act, where the Department proposes to make regulations under Article 52A(10), Part VA, Article 69J or Article 70ZA it shall refer the proposals, in the form of draft regulations or otherwise, to the Social Security Advisory Committee ("the Committee").

(2) Paragraph (1) does not apply to the regulations specified in Schedule 5 to the Administration Act.

(3) The Committee shall consider any proposals referred to it by the Department under paragraph (1) and shall make to the Department a report containing such recommendations with regard to the subject-matter of the proposals as the Committee thinks appropriate.

(4) If after receiving a report of the Committee the Department lays before the Assembly any regulations which comprise the whole or any part of the subject-matter of the proposals referred to the Committee, the Department shall lay with the regulations a copy of the Committee's report and a statement showing—

    (a) the extent (if any) to which the Department has, in framing the regulations, given effect to the Committee's recommendations; and

    (b) in so far as effect has not been given to them, the Department's reasons why not.

Regulations and orders (general provisions)

71B.—(1) Except in so far as this Order otherwise provides, any power conferred by this Order to make regulations or an order may be exercised—

    (a) either in relation to all cases to which the power extends, or in relation to those cases subject to specified exceptions, or in relation to any specified cases or classes of case;

    (b) so as to make, as respects the cases in relation to which it is exercised—

        (i) the full provision to which the power extends or any less provision (whether by way of exception or otherwise);

        (ii) the same provision for all cases in relation to which the power is exercised, or different provision for different cases or different classes of case or different provision as respects the same case or class of case for different purposes of this Order;

        (iii) any such provision either unconditionally or subject to any specified condition;

and where such a power is expressed to be exercisable for alternative purposes it may be exercised in relation to the same case for any or all of those purposes; and powers to make regulations or an order for the purposes of any one provision of this Order are without prejudice to powers to make regulations or an order for the purposes of any other provision.

(2) Without prejudice to any specific provision in this Order, a power conferred by this Order to make regulations or an order includes power to make such incidental, supplementary, consequential or transitional provision as appears to the authority making the regulations or order to be expedient for the purposes of the regulations or order.

(3) Without prejudice to any specific provision in this Order, a power conferred by this Order to make regulations or an order includes power to provide for a person to exercise a discretion in dealing with any matter.

(4) A power conferred by this Order on the Department to make any regulations or order, where the power is not expressed to be exercisable with the consent of the

Department of Finance and Personnel, shall if the Department of Finance and Personnel so directs be exercisable only in conjunction with it.".

(24) In Article 73(1) for the words "Subsection (5) of section 129 of the principal Act" there shall be substituted the words "Section 145(5) of the Administration Act" and for the words "subsection (3)(a) of that section" there shall be substituted the words "section 143(2)(a) of that Act".

(25) In paragraph 8(a)(i) of Schedule 1A for the words from "under" to the end there shall be substituted the words "under section 132 of the Administration Act; or".

(26) In paragraph 6(3)(c) of Schedule 2 for the words "the principal Act" there shall be substituted the words "the Contributions and Benefits Act".

Births and Deaths Registration (Northern Ireland) Order 1976 (S.I. 1976 No. 1041 (N.I. 14))

15. In Schedule 1 to the Births and Deaths Registration (Northern Ireland) Order 1976 for the entry relating to the Child Benefit (Northern Ireland) Order 1975 there shall be substituted the following entries—
"The Social Security Contributions and Benefits (Northern Ireland) Act 1992.
The Social Security Administration (Northern Ireland) Act 1992.".

Industrial Relations (Northern Ireland) Order 1976 (S.I. 1976 No. 1043 (N.I. 16))

16.—(1) The Industrial Relations (Northern Ireland) Order 1976 shall be amended as follows.

(2) In Article 43(4) for "1986" there shall be substituted "1986 or Part XII of the Social Security Contributions and Benefits (Northern Ireland) Act 1992".

(3) In Article 72(2) for sub-paragraph (a) there shall be substituted the following sub-paragraph—
"(a) confer powers and impose duties on industrial tribunals and on adjudication officers and other persons;".

(4) In Article 72(4) for the words "the Social Security (Northern Ireland) Order 1986" there shall be substituted the words "Part III or V of the Social Security Administration (Northern Ireland) Act 1992".

(5) In Article 72(7) for the words "the Social Security (Northern Ireland) Act 1975" there shall be substituted the words "the Social Security Contributions and Benefits (Northern Ireland) Act 1992".

Social Security (Miscellaneous Provisions) (Northern Ireland) Order 1977 (S.I. 1977 No. 610 (N.I. 11))

17.—(1) In Article 17(1)(a) of the Social Security (Miscellaneous Provisions) (Northern Ireland) Order 1977 after the words "Pensions Order" there shall be inserted the words "or section 130 of the Social Security Administration (Northern Ireland) Act 1992".

(2) In Article 17 of that Order for paragraph (3) there shall be substituted the following paragraph—
"(3) In this Article—
"earner" and "earnings" are to be construed in accordance with sections 3, 4 and 112 of the Social Security Contributions and Benefits (Northern Ireland) Act 1992;
"earnings factors" is to be construed in accordance with sections 22 and 23 of that Act;
"tax year" has the meaning assigned to it by section 121(1) of that Act,
and expressions used in Part IV of the Pensions Order have the same meanings as in that Part.".

(3) In Article 19 of that Order for paragraphs (1) and (2) there shall be substituted the following paragraphs—
"(1) Section 165(4), (5) and (10) of the Social Security Administration (Northern Ireland) Act 1992 shall have effect as if references to that Act included references to this Order.

(2) A power under any of sections 116 to 119 of the Social Security Contributions and Benefits (Northern Ireland) Act 1992 or sections 153 to 155 of the Social Security Administration (Northern Ireland) Act 1992 to make provision by regulations or order for modifications or adaptations of those Acts shall be exercisable in relation to any provision in this Order.".

(4) In Article 20 of that Order for the words "Subsection (5) of section 129 of the principal Act" there shall be substituted the words "Section 145(5) of the Social Security Administration (Northern Ireland) Act 1992" and for the words "subsection (3)(a) of that section" there shall be substituted the words "section 143(2)(a) of that Act".

Agricultural Wages (Regulation) (Northern Ireland) Order 1977 (S.I. 1977 No. 2151 (N.I. 22))

18. In Article 5(2)(e) of the Agricultural Wages (Regulation) (Northern Ireland) Order 1977 for the words from "Social Security (Northern Ireland) Act 1975" to the end there shall be substituted the words "Social Security Contributions and Benefits (Northern Ireland) Act 1992".

Rent (Northern Ireland) Order 1978 (S.I. 1978 No. 1050 (N.I. 20))

19. The following Article shall be inserted after Article 25 of the Rent (Northern Ireland) Order 1978—

"*Amounts attributable to services*

25A. In order to assist the Executive to give effect to the housing benefit scheme under Part VII of the Social Security Contributions and Benefits (Northern Ireland) Act 1992, where a rent is registered under this Part, there shall be noted on the register the amount (if any) of the registered rent which, in the opinion of the rent officer or rent assessment committee, is fairly attributable to the provision of services, except any amount which is negligible in the opinion of the officer or, as the case may be, the committee.".

Capital Gains Tax Act 1979 (c. 14)

20. In sub-paragraph (2) of paragraph 5 of Schedule 1 to the Capital Gains Tax Act 1979—
   (a) for the words "section 35 of the Social Security (Northern Ireland) Act 1975" there shall be substituted the words "section 64 of the Social Security Contributions and Benefits (Northern Ireland) Act 1992"; and
   (b) for the words "section 37ZA of the Social Security (Northern Ireland) Act 1975" there shall be substituted the words "section 71 of the Social Security Contributions and Benefits (Northern Ireland) Act 1992".

Vaccine Damage Payments Act 1979 (c. 17)

21. In section 1(4) of the Vaccine Damage Payments Act 1979 for the words "section 57 of the Social Security (Northern Ireland) Act 1975" there shall be substituted the words "section 103 of the Social Security Contributions and Benefits (Northern Ireland) Act 1992".

Pneumoconiosis etc. (Workers' Compensation) (Northern Ireland) Order 1979 (S.I. 1979 No. 925 (N.I. 9))

22.—(1) In Article 2(2) of the Pneumoconiosis, etc. (Workers' Compensation) (Northern Ireland) Order 1979 after the words "section 76 of the Social Security (Northern Ireland) Act 1975" wherever they occur there shall be inserted the words "or section 108 of the Social Security Contributions and Benefits (Northern Ireland) Act 1992".
(2) In Article 2(3) of that Order for the words "(Northern Ireland) Act 1975" there shall be substituted the words "Contributions and Benefits (Northern Ireland) Act 1992 or the Social Security Administration (Northern Ireland) Act 1992" and for the words "that Act" there shall be substituted the words "either of those Acts".
(3) In Article 8 of that Order—
   (a) for the words "Section 94 of the Social Security (Northern Ireland) Act 1975" there shall be substituted the words "Section 16 of the Social Security Administration (Northern Ireland) Act 1992";
   (b) for the words "section 93(1)" and "section 94" there shall be substituted the words "section 15(1)" and "section 16" respectively.

Road Traffic (Northern Ireland) Order 1981 (S.I. 1981 No. 154 (N.I. 1))

23. In Article 129C(2)(a) of the Road Traffic (Northern Ireland) Order 1981—
   (a) in head (i) for the words "section 35 of the Social Security (Northern Ireland) Act 1975" there shall be substituted the words "section 64 of the Social Security Contributions and Benefits (Northern Ireland) Act 1992";
   (b) in head (iA) for "37ZA" there shall be substituted "71";
   (c) in head (iii) for "57" there shall be substituted "103" and for "61(1)" there shall be substituted "104(1)".

Legal Aid, Advice and Assistance (Northern Ireland) Order 1981 (S.I. 1981 No. 228 (N.I. 8))

24. In Part I of Schedule 1 to the Legal Aid, Advice and Assistance (Northern Ireland) Order

1981 in paragraph 3(g) for the words "Article 25 of the Social Security (Northern Ireland) Order 1986" there shall be substituted the words "section 101 of the Social Security Administration (Northern Ireland) Act 1992".

Magistrates' Courts (Northern Ireland) Order 1981 (S.I. 1981 No. 1675 (N.I. 26))

25. In Articles 88 and 98(11) of the Magistrates' Courts (Northern Ireland) Order 1981 for the words "or Article 25 of the Social Security (Northern Ireland) Order 1986" there shall be substituted the words "or section 101 of the Social Security Administration (Northern Ireland) Act 1992".

Forfeiture (Northern Ireland) Order 1982 (S.I. 1982 No. 1082 (N.I. 14))

26.—(1) In Article 6(2) of the Forfeiture (Northern Ireland) Order 1982 for the words "section 115 of the Social Security (Northern Ireland) Act 1975" there shall be substituted the words "section 57 of the Social Security Administration (Northern Ireland) Act 1992".

(2) In Article 6(4) of that Order for the words "Section 155(2) to (3A) of the Social Security (Northern Ireland) Act 1975" there shall be substituted the words "Section 171(3) to (5) of the Social Security Contributions and Benefits (Northern Ireland) Act 1992".

(3) In Article 6(5) of that Order for the words "(Northern Ireland) Act 1975" there shall be substituted the words "Administration (Northern Ireland) Act 1991" and the following entry shall be added after the entry relating to the Social Security (Northern Ireland) Acts 1975 to 1992—

"The Social Security Contributions and Benefits (Northern Ireland) Act 1992,".

Social Security (Northern Ireland) Order 1982 (S.I. 1982 No. 1084 (N.I. 16))

27. In Article 36(1) of the Social Security (Northern Ireland) Order 1982 for the words from the beginning to "principal Act" there shall be substituted the words "Section 165(4), (5) and (10) of the Social Security Administration (Northern Ireland) Act 1992".

Value Added Tax Act 1983 (c. 55)

28. In the seventh note to Group 14 of Schedule 5 to the Value Added Tax Act 1983 for the words "section 37ZA of the Social Security (Northern Ireland) Act 1975" there shall be substituted the words "section 71 of the Social Security Contributions and Benefits (Northern Ireland) Act 1992".

Inheritance Tax Act 1984 (c. 51)

29.—(1) In paragraph (b) of sections 74(4) and 89(4) of the Inheritance Tax Act 1984 for the words "section 35 of the Social Security (Northern Ireland) Act 1975" there shall be substituted the words "section 64 of the Social Security Contributions and Benefits (Northern Ireland) Act 1992".

(2) In paragraph (c) of those subsections for the words "section 37ZA of the Social Security (Northern Ireland) Act 1975" there shall be substituted the words "section 71 of the Social Security Contributions and Benefits (Northern Ireland) Act 1992".

Industrial Training (Northern Ireland) Order 1984 (S.I. 1984 No. 1159 (N.I. 9))

30.—(1) In Article 32 of the Industrial Training (Northern Ireland) Order 1984—
  (a) in paragraph (1) for the words "Chapter IV of Part II of the Social Security (Northern Ireland) Act 1975" there shall be substituted the words "Part V of the Social Security Contributions and Benefits (Northern Ireland) Act 1992" and for the words "sections 52 to 54" there shall be substituted the words "sections 98 to 100";
  (b) in paragraph (2) for the words "section 52" there shall be substituted the words "section 98";
  (c) in paragraph (3) for the words "section 53" there shall be substituted the words "section 99";
  (d) in paragraph (4) for the words "section 54" there shall be substituted the words "section 100".

(2) In Article 33(1) of that Order for the words "Part II of the Social Security (Northern Ireland) Act 1975" there shall be substituted the words "the Social Security Contributions and Benefits (Northern Ireland) Act 1992" and for the words "Chapter IV of that Part" there shall be substituted the words "Part V of that Act".

Social Security (Northern Ireland) Order 1985 (S.I. 1985 No. 1209 (N.I. 16))

31.—(1) In Article 1(9) of the Social Security (Northern Ireland) Order 1985 for the words

"Subsections (2) and (3) of section 155 of the principal Act" there shall be substituted the words "Subsections (4) and (5) of section 165 of the Social Security Administration (Northern Ireland) Act 1992".

(2) At the end of paragraph (1) of Article 7 of that Order there shall be added the words "or

(c) of Part VI of the Social Security Administration (Northern Ireland) Act 1992.".

(3) In Article 7(2) of that Order for the words "Section 155 of the principal Act" there shall be substituted the words "Article 71B of the Pensions Order" and for the words "that Act" there shall be substituted the words "that Order".

Social Security (Northern Ireland) Order 1986 (S.I. 1986 No. 1888 (N.I. 18))

32.—(1) The Social Security (Northern Ireland) Order 1986 shall be amended as follows.

(2) In Article 6(1) for the words from "sections 16(2B)" to "Article 31" there shall be substituted the words "sections 34(4) and 47(2) of the Social Security Contributions and Benefits (Northern Ireland) Act 1992, paragraph 3(2) of Schedule 7 to that Act and Articles 31 to 31C".

(3) In Article 11(5) for the words "Article 18(5) of that Order" there shall be substituted the words "section 41(7) of the Social Security Contributions and Benefits (Northern Ireland) Act 1992".

(4) In Article 18A(1) for the words "Section 134 of the principal Act" there shall be substituted the words "Section 155 of the Social Security Administration (Northern Ireland) Act 1992".

(5) In Article 26(1)(c) for the words "Article 25(3)" there shall be substituted the words "section 101(3) of the Social Security Administration (Northern Ireland) Act 1992".

(6) At the end of Article 26 there shall be added the following paragraph—

"(7) Subsections (6) and (7) of section 74 of the Social Security Administration (Northern Ireland) Act 1992 shall have effect for the purposes of this Article as they have effect for the purposes of that section.".

(7) In Article 53(2) for the words "section 93(1) of the principal Act" there shall be substituted the words "section 15(1) of the Social Security Administration (Northern Ireland) Act 1992.".

(8) In Article 60(3)(c) for the words "Part III of the principal Act including that Part as extended by Article 53(3)" there shall be substituted the words "sections 15 to 60 of the Social Security Administration (Northern Ireland) Act 1992".

(9) In Article 81(1) for the words from the beginning to "principal Act" there shall be substituted the words "Article 71B(1) to (4) of the Pensions Order".

(10) In Article 81 for paragraphs (3) and (4) there shall be substituted the following paragraphs—

"(3) Regulations under Article 7(15)(a), and regulations made by the Department and contained in a statutory rule which includes any such regulations, shall be laid before the Assembly after being made and shall take effect on such date as may be specified in the regulations, but shall (without prejudice to the validity of anything done thereunder or to the making of new regulations) cease to have effect upon the expiration of a period of six months from that date unless at some time before the expiration of that period the regulations have been approved by a resolution of the Assembly.

(4) Regulations and orders made by the Department under this Order, other than those to which paragraph (3) applies and orders under Article 1, shall be subject to negative resolution.".

(11) In Article 81 for paragraph (8) there shall be substituted the following paragraph—

"(8) Sections 171(10) and 172(9) to (11) of the Social Security Contributions and Benefits (Northern Ireland) Act 1992 shall apply to regulations under Article 79(6) as they apply to regulations under section 116(3) of that Act.".

Income and Corporation Taxes Act 1988 (c. 1)

33.—(1) Section 617 of the Income and Corporation Taxes Act 1988 shall be amended as follows.

(2) In subsection (1) for the words "Chapters I to III of Part II of the Social Security (Northern Ireland) Act 1975 or Part III of the Social Security Pensions (Northern Ireland) Order 1975" there shall be substituted the words "or Parts II to IV of the Social Security Contributions and Benefits (Northern Ireland) Act 1992".

(3) In subsection (2)—

(a) in paragraph (a) for the words "the Social Security (Northern Ireland) Order 1986" there shall be substituted the words "Part VII of the Social Security Contributions and Benefits (Northern Ireland) Act 1992"; and

(b) in paragraph (aa) for the words "section 70 of the Social Security (Northern Ireland) Act 1975" there shall be substituted the words "paragraph 18 of Schedule 7 to the Social Security Contributions and Benefits (Northern Ireland) Act 1992".

(4) In subsection (3)(b) for the words "(Northern Ireland) Act 1975" there shall be substituted the words "Contributions and Benefits (Northern Ireland) Act 1992".

(5) In subsection (4) for the words "the Social Security (Northern Ireland) Act 1975" there shall be substituted the words "Part I of the Social Security Contributions and Benefits (Northern Ireland) Act 1992".

(6) In subsection (5) for the words "subsection (2) of section 9 of the Social Security (Northern Ireland) Act 1975" there shall be substituted the words "subsection (3) of section 15 of the Social Security Contributions and Benefits (Northern Ireland) Act 1992".

Wages (Northern Ireland) Order 1988 (S.I. 1988 No. 796 (N.I. 7))

34. In Article 9(1) of the Wages (Northern Ireland) Order 1988—
(a) in paragraph (e) after "1982" there shall be inserted the words "or Part XI of the Social Security Contributions and Benefits (Northern Ireland) Act 1992";
(b) at the end of paragraph (f) there shall be added the words "or Part XII of the Social Security Contributions and Benefits (Northern Ireland) Act 1992".

Social Security (Northern Ireland) Order 1988 (S.I. 1988 No. 594 (N.I. 2))

35.—(1) In Article 13(4)(e) of the Social Security (Northern Ireland) Order 1988 for the words "principal Act" there shall be substituted the words "Social Security Administration (Northern Ireland) Act 1992".

(2) In Article 13(7) of that Order for the words "Section 156(1) of the principal Act" there shall be substituted the words "Section 166(1) of the Social Security Administration (Northern Ireland) Act 1992".

(3) In Article 15 of that Order for the words "Articles 4, 7, 8, 10 and 11" there shall be substituted the words "Article 10".

(4) In Article 15A(1) of that Order for the words "Section 155(1) to (3A) of the principal Act" there shall be substituted the words "Section 171(2) to (5) of the Social Security Contributions and Benefits (Northern Ireland) Act 1992".

(5) In Article 15A(2) of that Order after "1(3)" there shall be inserted "and 13".

Social Security (Northern Ireland) Order 1989 (S.I. 1989 No. 1342 (N.I. 13))

36.—(1) In Article 8(7) of the Social Security (Northern Ireland) Order 1989 for the words "section 104 of the principal Act" there shall be substituted the words "section 23 of the Social Security Administration (Northern Ireland) Act 1992".

(2) In Article 8(9) of that Order—
(a) for the words from the beginning to "principal Act" there shall be substituted the words "Section 26 of the Social Security Administration (Northern Ireland) Act 1992 (appeals from reviews)"; and
(b) for the words "that section" there shall be substituted the words "section 23 of that Act".

(3) In Article 30(1) of that Order for the words "subsections (1) to (3A) of section 155 of the principal Act" there shall be substituted the words "section 171(2) to (5) of the Social Security Contributions and Benefits (Northern Ireland) Act 1992".

Insolvency (Northern Ireland) Order 1989 (S.I. 1989 No. 2405 (N.I. 19))

37. In paragraph 6 of Schedule 4 to the Insolvency (Northern Ireland) Order 1989 for the words "the Social Security Act 1975 or the Social Security (Northern Ireland) Act 1975" there shall be substituted the words "the Social Security Contributions and Benefits Act 1992 or the Social Security Contributions and Benefits (Northern Ireland) Act 1992".

Capital Allowances Act 1990 (c. 1)

38. In the following provisions of the Capital Allowances Act 1990—
(a) section 22(6)(a);
(b) section 36(4)(a),
for the words "Social Security (Northern Ireland) Act 1975" there shall be substituted the words "Social Security Contributions and Benefits (Northern Ireland) Act 1992".

Social Security (Northern Ireland) Order 1990 (S.I. 1990 No. 1511 (N.I. 15))

39.—(1) In Article 20 of the Social Security (Northern Ireland) Order 1990 for the words from "Articles 6" to "and 16" there shall be substituted the words "paragraph 16".

(2) In Article 21(1) of that Order for the words "subsections (1) to (3A) of section 155 of the principal Act" there shall be substituted the words "section 171(2) to (5) of the Social Security Contributions and Benefits (Northern Ireland) Act 1992".

(3) In Schedule 6 to that Order in paragraph 6(12)(b) for the words "section 156(1) of the principal Act" there shall be substituted the words "section 166(1) of the Social Security Administration (Northern Ireland) Act 1992 or section 172(1) of the Social Security Contributions and Benefits (Northern Ireland) Act 1992".

(4) In paragraph 16(3) of that Schedule for the words "section 104 of the principal Act" there shall be substituted the words "section 23 of the Social Security Administration (Northern Ireland) Act 1992".

(5) In paragraph 16(5) of that Schedule for the words "Subsection (4) of section 104 of the principal Act" there shall be substituted the words "Section 26 of the Social Security Administration (Northern Ireland) Act 1992".

Section 5 SCHEDULE 3

TRANSITIONAL PROVISIONS AND SAVINGS (INCLUDING SOME TRANSITIONAL PROVISIONS RETAINED FROM PREVIOUS ACTS AND ORDERS)

PART I

GENERAL AND MISCELLANEOUS

Questions relating to contributions and benefits

1.—(1) A question other than a question arising under any of sections 1 to 3 of the Administration Act—
   (a) whether a person is entitled to benefit in respect of a time before 1st July 1992;
   (b) whether a person is liable to pay contributions in respect of such a time,
and any other question not arising under any of those sections with respect to benefit or contributions in respect of such a time is to be determined, subject to section 66 of the Administration Act, in accordance with provisions in force or deemed to be in force at that time.

(2) Subject to sub-paragraph (1) above, the consolidating Acts apply to matters arising before their commencement as to matters arising after it.

General savings for old savings

2. The repeal by this Act of an enactment previously repealed subject to savings (whether or not in the repealing enactment) does not affect the continued operation of those savings.

Documents referring to repealed enactments

3. Any document made, served or issued after this Act comes into force which contains a reference to any of the repealed enactments shall be construed, except so far as a contrary intention appears, as referring or, as the context may require, including a reference to the corresponding provision of the consolidating Acts.

Provisions relating to the coming into force of other provisions

4. The repeal by this Act of a provision providing for or relating to the coming into force of a provision reproduced in the consolidating Acts does not affect the operation of the first provision, in so far as it remains capable of having effect, in relation to the enactment reproducing the second provision.

Continuing powers to make transitional, etc. regulations

5. Where immediately before 1st July 1992 the Department of Health and Social Services for Northern Ireland (hereafter in this Schedule referred to as "the Department") has power under any provision of the Social Security (Northern Ireland) Acts 1975 to 1991 not reproduced in the consolidating Acts by regulations to make provision or savings in preparation for or in connection with the coming into force of a provision repealed by this Act but reproduced in the consolidating Acts, the power shall be construed as having effect in relation to the provision reproducing the repealed provision.

6. The repeal by this Act of a power by regulations to make provision or savings in preparation for or in connection with the coming into force of a provision reproduced in the

consolidating Acts does not affect the power, in so far as it remains capable of having effect, in relation to the enactment reproducing the second provision.

Provisions contained in enactments by virtue of orders or regulations

7.—(1) Without prejudice to any express provision in the consolidating Acts, where this Act repeals any provision contained in any enactment by virtue of any order or regulations and the provision is reproduced in the consolidating Acts, the Department shall have the like power to make orders or regulations repealing or amending the provision of the consolidating Acts which reproduces the effect of the repealed provision as the Department had in relation to that provision.

(2) Sub-paragraph (1) above applies to a repealed provision which was amended by Schedule 7 to the Social Security (Northern Ireland) Order 1989 as it applies to a provision not so amended.

Amending orders made after passing of Act

8. An order which is made under any of the repealed enactments after the passing of this Act and which amends any of the repealed enactments shall have the effect also of making a corresponding amendment of the consolidating Acts.

PART II

SPECIFIC TRANSITIONAL PROVISIONS AND SAVINGS (INCLUDING SOME DERIVED FROM PREVIOUS ACTS AND ORDERS)

Interpretation

9. In this Part of this Schedule—
"the 1966 Act" means the National Insurance Act (Northern Ireland) 1966;
"the 1973 Act" means the Social Security Act 1973;
"the 1975 Act" means the Social Security (Northern Ireland) Act 1975;
"the former Consequential Provisions Act" means the Social Security (Consequential Provisions) Act 1975; and
"the 1986 Order" means the Social Security (Northern Ireland) Order 1986.

Social Security Pensions (Northern Ireland) Order 1975

10. The repeal by this Act of any provision contained in the 1975 Act or any enactment amending such a provision does not affect the operation of that provision by virtue of Article 2(3) of the Social Security Pensions (Northern Ireland) Order 1975.

Additional pensions

11. The repeal by this Act of Article 19(1) of the 1986 Order (which substituted in any statutory provision a reference to a basic pension for any reference to the basic component of a long-term benefit and a reference to an additional pension for any reference to an additional component of such a benefit) does not affect the construction of any statutory provision amended by that paragraph.

Supersession of National Insurance Acts—provisions derived from Schedule 3 to former Consequential Provisions Act

12. Regulations may provide that, in relation to—
(a) persons who ceased by virtue of paragraph 2 of Schedule 3 to the former Consequential Provisions Act to be insured under the 1966 Act,
(b) persons to or in respect of whom benefit under that Act was, or but for a disqualification or forfeiture would have been, payable immediately before 6th April 1975, and
(c) persons who had a prospective right to, or expectation of, any benefit under that Act immediately before that day,
the Contributions and Benefits Act and the Administration Act (so far as they represent provisions of the 1973 Act) shall have effect subject to such modifications as may be prescribed with a view to securing continuity of the law.

13. Without prejudice to the generality of the powers conferred by paragraph 12 above, regulations under that paragraph may in particular provide for the taking into account, for such purposes and in such manner and subject to such conditions as may be prescribed, of contributions paid or credited or deemed to be, or treated as, paid or credited under the 1966 Act or the National Insurance Act (Northern Ireland) 1946 or any enactment repealed by that Act.

14. Regulations may provide that the Contributions and Benefits Act and the Administration Act (so far as they represent the 1973 Act) and this Part of this Schedule (except this paragraph) shall have effect subject to prescribed modifications in relation to persons who attained the age of 16 before 6th April 1975 and who, immediately before that day, were not insured under the 1966 Act.

15. Notwithstanding any repeal effected by the 1973 Act, provision may be made by regulations for continuing in force, with or without prescribed modifications, such provisions of the 1966 Act or any other enactments specified in the third column of Schedule 28 to the 1973 Act (repeals) as the Department considers appropriate for the purpose of preserving rights to benefit under that Act or those enactments in those cases (if any) in which in its opinion adequate alternative rights to benefit under the Contributions and Benefits Act are not conferred in pursuance of paragraph 12 above, or for temporarily retaining the effect of those provisions for transitional purposes.

16. In the foregoing provisions of this Part of this Schedule, any reference to benefit under the 1966 Act includes a reference to such other benefit, pension or allowance as is mentioned in paragraph 17(2)(b) of Schedule 9 to that Act (pre-1948 beneficiaries).

17.—(1) Any instrument (except regulations, an Order in Council or another order) and any appointment which is in force immediately before 1st July 1992 and was made or has effect as if made under an enactment repealed by the 1973 Act shall, in so far as a corresponding instrument or appointment is capable of being made under any provision of the Contributions and Benefits Act or the Administration Act representing a provision in the 1973 Act, be deemed to be so made except to the extent that regulations otherwise provide.

(2) A reference in any document to an enactment repealed and re-enacted by the 1973 Act with or without modifications shall, in so far as the context permits, be construed as a reference to the Contributions and Benefits Act or, as the case may be, the Administration Act or to the corresponding enactment therein.

Industrial injuries—provision derived from paragraph 12 of Schedule 3 to 1986 Order

18.—(1) The Department may by regulations provide for the payment of prescribed amounts in prescribed circumstances to persons who immediately before the repeal of sections 71 to 73 of the 1975 Act were entitled to any benefit by virtue of any of those sections, but in determining the amount which is to be payable in any case or class of cases the Department may take into account—

(a) the extent to which the weekly rate of industrial death benefit has been modified in that case or class of cases by virtue of section 74 of that Act;

(b) the age of the beneficiary and of any person or persons formerly maintained by the deceased; and

(c) the length of time that entitlement to the benefit would have been likely to continue if those sections had not been repealed.

(2) In this paragraph "prescribed" means specified in or determined in accordance with regulations.

Attendance allowance—provision derived from Article 3 of Social Security (Northern Ireland) Order 1988

19. For the purposes—

(a) of any determination following a claim made before 1st April 1988,

(b) of any review following an application made before that date,

(c) of any review following a decision to conduct a review made before that date,

section 64 of the Contributions and Benefits Act shall have effect as if the following subsection were substituted for subsection (3)—

"(3) A person satisfies the night attendance condition if he is so severely disabled physically or mentally that, at night, he requires from another person either—

(a) prolonged or repeated attention during the night in connection with his bodily functions; or

(b) continual supervision throughout the night in order to avoid substantial danger to himself or others.".

Supplementary benefit and former housing-related benefits—provision derived from Article 18 of Social Security (Northern Ireland) Order 1989

20.—(1) Any expenses of the Department or the Department of the Environment for Northern Ireland in making payments to persons falling within sub-paragraph (2) or (3) below may be paid out of money appropriated by Measure.

(2) A person falls within this sub-paragraph if—
(a) he was entitled to supplementary benefit immediately before 11th April 1988, but
(b) he did not become entitled to income support in respect of the week beginning with that day.

(3) A person falls within this sub-paragraph if he was entitled to any one or more of the former housing-related benefits in respect of a qualifying week but either—
(a) he did not become entitled to housing benefit under Part III of the 1986 Order in respect of the commencement week, or
(b) the amount of any such housing benefit to which he became entitled in respect of that week was less than the amount of the former housing-related benefits to which he had been entitled in respect of the qualifying week.

(4) In this paragraph—
"commencement day" means the day on which the new provisions came into force in the case of the person in question (1st or 4th April 1988, according to the circumstances);
"commencement week", in relation to any person, means the week beginning with the commencement day in his case;
"the former housing-related benefits" means—
(a) rent rebates, rate rebates and rent allowances, within the meaning of the Housing Benefits (Northern Ireland) Order 1983; and
(b) housing benefit supplement;
"the new provisions" means the following provisions of Part III of the 1986 Order, so far as relating to housing benefit, that is to say, Articles 21 to 23, 29 and 30;
"qualifying week", in relation to any person, means any week beginning on or after 21st March 1988 and ending before the commencement day in his case;
"week" means a period of 7 days.

(5) For the purposes of this paragraph—
(a) a person shall be regarded as having been entitled to housing benefit supplement in respect of a week if an amount was applicable in respect of him under regulation 19A of the Supplementary Benefit (Requirements) Regulations (Northern Ireland) 1983 in respect of that week; and
(b) the amount of housing benefit supplement to which he was entitled in respect of that week shall be taken to be an amount equal to the amount so applicable.

Substitution of disability living allowance for attendance allowance and mobility allowance and dissolution of Attendance Allowance Board—provision derived from Article 7 of Disability Living Allowance and Disability Working Allowance (Northern Ireland) Order 1991

21.—(1) The Department may make such regulations as appear to it necessary or expedient in relation to the substitution of disability living allowance for attendance allowance and mobility allowance and the dissolution of the Attendance Allowance Board for Northern Ireland.

(2) Without prejudice to the generality of this paragraph, regulations under this paragraph—
(a) may provide for the termination or cancellation of awards of attendance allowance and awards of mobility allowance;
(b) may direct that a person whose award of either allowance has been terminated or cancelled by virtue of the regulations or who is a child of such a person shall by virtue of the regulations be treated as having been awarded one or more disability living allowances;
(c) may direct that a disability living allowance so treated as having been awarded shall consist of such component as the regulations may specify or, if the regulations so specify, of both components, and as having been awarded either component at such weekly rate and for such period as the regulations may specify;
(d) may provide for the termination in specified circumstances of an award of disability living allowance;
(e) may direct that in specified circumstances a person whose award of disability living allowance has been terminated by virtue of the regulations shall by virtue of the regulations be treated as having been granted a further award of a disability living allowance consisting of such component as the regulations may specify or, if the regulations so specify, of both components, and as having been awarded on the further award either component at such weekly rate and for such period as the regulations may specify;
(f) may provide for the review of awards made by virtue of paragraph (b) or (e) above and for the treatment of claims for disability living allowance in respect of beneficiaries with such awards;

(g) may direct that for specified purposes certificates issued by the Attendance Allowance Board for Northern Ireland shall be treated as evidence of such matters as may be specified in the regulations;

(h) may direct that for specified purposes the replacement of attendance allowance and mobility allowance by disability living allowance shall be disregarded;

(i) may direct that a claim for attendance allowance or mobility allowance shall be treated in specified circumstances and for specified purposes as a claim for disability living allowance or that a claim for disability living allowance shall be treated in specified circumstances and for specified purposes as a claim for attendance allowance or mobility allowance or both;

(j) may direct that in specified circumstances and for specified purposes a claim for a disability living allowance shall be treated as having been made when no such claim was in fact made;

(k) may direct that in specified circumstances a claim for attendance allowance, mobility allowance or disability living allowance shall be treated as not having been made;

(l) may direct that in specified circumstances where a person claims attendance allowance or mobility allowance or both, and also claims disability living allowance, his claims may be treated as a single claim for such allowances for such periods as the regulations may specify;

(m) may direct that cases relating to mobility allowance shall be subject to adjudication in accordance with the provisions of Part II of the Administration Act relating to disability living allowance; and

(n) may direct that, at a time before the Attendance Allowance Board for Northern Ireland is dissolved, in specified circumstances cases relating to attendance allowance shall be subject to adjudication under the system of adjudication for such cases introduced by the Disability Living Allowance and Disability Working Allowance (Northern Ireland) Order 1991.

(3) Regulations under this paragraph may provide that any provision to which this sub-paragraph applies—

(a) shall have effect subject to modifications, additions or amendments; or

(b) shall not have effect.

(4) Sub-paragraph (3) above applies—

(a) to any provision of the 1975 Act which relates to mobility allowance, so far as it so relates;

(b) to any provision of Part VII of the 1986 Order which is relevant to mobility allowance;

(c) to any provision of the Contributions and Benefits Act which relates to disability living allowance or attendance allowance, so far as it so relates; and

(d) to any provision of the Administration Act which is relevant to disability living allowance or attendance allowance.

Regulations—supplementary

22.—(1) Regulations under this Part of this Schedule shall be made by the Department.

(2) Powers under this Part of this Schedule to make regulations are exercisable by statutory rule for the purposes of the Statutory Rules (Northern Ireland) Order 1979.

(3) Any power conferred by this Part of this Schedule to make regulations may be exercised—

(a) either in relation to all cases to which the power extends, or in relation to those cases subject to specified exceptions, or in relation to any specified cases or classes of case;

(b) so as to make, as respects the cases in relation to which it is exercised—

(i) the full provision to which the power extends or any less provision (whether by way of exception or otherwise);

(ii) the same provision for all cases in relation to which the power is exercised, or different provision for different cases or different classes of case or different provision as respects the same case or class of case for different purposes of this Part of this Schedule;

(iii) any such provision either unconditionally or subject to any specified condition.

(4) The powers to make regulations conferred by any provision of this Part of this Schedule other than paragraph 21 above include powers to make thereby such incidental, supplementary, consequential or transitional provision as appears to the Department to be expedient for the purposes of the regulations.

(5) A power conferred by this Part of this Schedule to make regulations includes power to provide for a person to exercise a discretion in dealing with any matter.

(6) If the Department of Finance and Personnel in Northern Ireland so directs, regulations under this Part of this Schedule shall be made only in conjunction with that Department.

(7) Regulations under this Part of this Schedule shall be subject to negative resolution within the meaning of section 41(6) of the Interpretation Act (Northern Ireland) 1954 as if they were statutory instruments within the meaning of that Act.

(8) Sub-paragraphs (12) and (13) of paragraph 6 of Schedule 6 to the Social Security (Northern Ireland) Order 1990 shall apply to regulations under this Part of the Schedule as they apply to regulations under the benefit Acts.

Section 6   SCHEDULE 4

TRANSITORY MODIFICATIONS

PART I

PROVISIONS NOT YET IN FORCE

Introductory

1.—(1) If—
(a) no date has been appointed as the date on which a provision mentioned in column 1 of the following Table is to come into force before 1st July 1992; or
(b) a date has been appointed which is later than 1st July 1992,
then the paragraph of this Schedule mentioned in column 2 of the Table opposite that provision shall have effect until the appointed day.

TABLE

Provision	*Paragraph of this Schedule*
Paragraph 5(1)(b) of Schedule 8 to the Social Security (Northern Ireland) Order 1986.	Paragraph 3.
The repeal in Schedule 10 to the Social Security (Northern Ireland) Order 1986 of section 129(6) of the Social Security (Northern Ireland) Act 1975.	Paragraph 14.
The repeal in Schedule 10 to the Social Security (Northern Ireland) Order 1986 of a reference in paragraph 31 of Schedule 3 to the Social Security (Consequential Provisions) Act 1975.	Paragraph 15.
The repeal in Schedule 10 to the Social Security (Northern Ireland) Order 1986 of the words "Subject to paragraph (5A)," in Article 8(5) of the Social Security Pensions (Northern Ireland) Order 1975.	Paragraph 2.
Article 28 of the Social Security (Northern Ireland) Order 1989.	Paragraph 11.
Paragraph 8(8) of Schedule 1 to the Social Security (Northern Ireland) Order 1989.	Paragraphs 9 and 10.
Article 11 of the Social Security (Northern Ireland) Order 1990.	Paragraph 4.
Article 19(1) of the Social Security (Northern Ireland) Order 1990.	Paragraph 12.
Article 19(2) of the Social Security (Northern Ireland) Order 1990.	Paragraph 13.
Article 19(3) of the Social Security (Northern Ireland) Order 1990.	Paragraph 5.
Article 19(4) of the Social Security (Northern Ireland) Order 1990.	Paragraph 6.
Section 17(8) of the Social Security Act 1990.	Paragraph 7.
Section 17(9) of the Social Security Act 1990.	Paragraph 8.

(2) If—

(a) a date has been appointed as the date on which a provision mentioned in column 1 of the Table in sub-paragraph (1) is to come into force for some purposes of that provision but not for others; and

(b) that date is on or before 1st July 1992,

then the paragraph of this Schedule mentioned in column 2 of the Table opposite that provision shall have effect for those other purposes of that provision (in so far as it is capable of doing so) until the relevant appointed day.

(3) In this paragraph "the appointed day" means—

(a) in the case mentioned in paragraph (a) of sub-paragraph (1) above, such day as may be appointed by an order under this sub-paragraph; and

(b) in the case mentioned in paragraph (b) of that sub-paragraph, the day appointed as the day on which the provision mentioned in column 1 of the Table is to come into force.

(4) An order under sub-paragraph (3) above—

(a) shall, in relation to paragraphs 7 and 8 of this Schedule, be made by the Secretary of State by statutory instrument and, in relation to any other paragraph of this Schedule, shall be made by the Department of Health and Social Services for Northern Ireland by statutory rule for the purposes of the Statutory Rules (Northern Ireland) Order 1979; and

(b) may appoint different days for different provisions or different purposes of the same provision.

The Contributions and Benefits Act

2. At the beginning of subsection (6) of section 44 of the Contributions and Benefits Act there shall be inserted the words "Subject to subsection (7A) below".

3. The following subsection shall be inserted after subsection (7) of that section—

"(7A) The Department may prescribe circumstances in which pensioners' earnings factors for any relevant year may be calculated in such manner as may be prescribed.".

4. In section 131 of that Act subsections (3) and (4) shall be omitted.

5. In paragraph 6 of Schedule 1 to that Act sub-paragraphs (2) to (4) shall be omitted.

6. The following sub-paragraph shall be substituted for paragraph 6(8) of that Schedule—

"(8) The Inland Revenue shall, at such times, and in such manner as the Department of Finance and Personnel may direct, account to the Department for, and pay to it, the sums estimated by the Inland Revenue, in such manner as may be so directed, to have been received by them as contributions in accordance with regulations made by virtue of this paragraph.".

7. The following sub-paragraph shall be substituted for paragraph 6(1) of Schedule 2 to that Act—

"(1) Section 88(1), (4) and (5)(a) and (b) of the Taxes Management Act 1970 (interest on tax recovered to make good loss due to taxpayer's fault) shall apply in relation to any amount due in respect of Class 4 contributions as it applies in relation to income tax; but section 86 of that Act (interest on amounts overdue) shall not apply.".

8. Paragraph 6(2) of that Schedule shall be omitted.

9. The following sub-paragraph shall be inserted after paragraph 11(12) of Schedule 7 to that Act—

"(12A) The reference in sub-paragraph (11) above to a person who has retired from regular employment includes a reference to—

(a) a person who under subsection (3) of section 27 of the 1975 Act was treated for the purposes of that Act as having retired from regular employment; and

(b) a person who under subsection (5) of that section was deemed for those purposes to have retired from it.".

10. At the end of paragraph 12 of Schedule 7 to that Act there shall be inserted—

"(7) The reference in sub-paragraph (1) above to a person who has retired from regular employment includes a reference to—

(a) a person who under subsection (3) of section 27 of the 1975 Act was treated for the purposes of that Act as having retired from regular employment; and

(b) a person who under subsection (5) of that section was deemed for those purposes to have retired from it.".

The Administration Act

11. Section 99 of the Administration Act shall be omitted.

12. In section 142 of that Act subsection (4) shall be omitted.

13. In section 143 of that Act subsection (5) shall be omitted.

14. The following subsection shall be inserted at the end of section 144 of that Act—

"(7) Any sums repaid to the Department in pursuance of section 119(1) of the 1975 Act (which related to the effect of adjudication and was repealed subject to a saving in relation to certain reviews and appeals) shall—

    (a) be paid by it into the Consolidated Fund in so far as they represent benefit which under section 143 above is payable out of money appropriated for the purpose and not out of the National Insurance Fund; and

    (b) otherwise, be paid by it into that Fund.".

This Act

15. In Schedule 3 to this Act—

(a) in the heading before paragraph 18 for the words "provision derived from" there shall be substituted the words "provisions derived from paragraph 18 of Schedule 3 to former Consequential Provisions Act, and"; and

(b) the following paragraph shall be inserted after that heading—

    "17A. In determining a woman's right—

        (a) to a pension or allowance in respect of a deceased person under section 67, 68, 71, 72 or 73 of the 1975 Act; or

        (b) to a pension in respect of a deceased person under paragraph 15 or 16 of Schedule 7 to the Contributions and Benefits Act,

for any period after 25th February 1962, or her right on her re-marriage after that date to a gratuity under section 67 of the 1975 Act, her cohabitation with a man at any time after the deceased's death but before that date shall be disregarded; but a right to benefit arising by virtue of this paragraph shall not, under Schedule 9 to that Act or Schedule 7 to the Contributions and Benefits Act, affect the right of any other persons to benefit awarded before that date.".

Part II

TRANSITION FROM MOBILITY ALLOWANCE TO DISABILITY LIVING ALLOWANCE

16. In the application of subsection (2) of section 128 of the Contributions and Benefits Act to claims made or treated as made before the first day in respect of which disability living allowance is payable paragraph (b) of that subsection shall have effect as if the following sub-paragraph were substituted for sub-paragraph (ii)—

    "(ii) a mobility allowance under section 37A of the 1975 Act;".